DRAMA

CRITICISM

Guide to Gale Literary Criticism Series

For criticism on	Consult these Gale series
Authors now living or who died after December 31, 1999	***CONTEMPORARY LITERARY CRITICISM (CLC)***
Authors who died between 1900 and 1999	***TWENTIETH-CENTURY LITERARY CRITICISM (TCLC)***
Authors who died between 1800 and 1899	***NINETEENTH-CENTURY LITERATURE CRITICISM (NCLC)***
Authors who died between 1400 and 1799	***LITERATURE CRITICISM FROM 1400 TO 1800 (LC)*** ***SHAKESPEAREAN CRITICISM (SC)***
Authors who died before 1400	***CLASSICAL AND MEDIEVAL LITERATURE CRITICISM (CMLC)***
Authors of books for children and young adults	***CHILDREN'S LITERATURE REVIEW (CLR)***
Dramatists	***DRAMA CRITICISM (DC)***
Poets	***POETRY CRITICISM (PC)***
Short story writers	***SHORT STORY CRITICISM (SSC)***
Black writers of the past two hundred years	***BLACK LITERATURE CRITICISM (BLC)***
Hispanic writers of the late nineteenth and twentieth centuries	***HISPANIC LITERATURE CRITICISM (HLC)***
Native North American writers and orators of the eighteenth, nineteenth, and twentieth centuries	***NATIVE NORTH AMERICAN LITERATURE (NNAL)***
Major authors from the Renaissance to the present	***WORLD LITERATURE CRITICISM, 1500 TO THE PRESENT (WLC)***

ISSN 1056-4349

Criticism of the Most Significant and Widely Studied Dramatic Works from All the World's Literatures

VOLUME 11

Lawrence J. Trudeau, Editor

DETROIT • LONDON

STAFF

Lawrence J. Trudeau, *Editor*

Debra A. Wells, *Assistant Editor*

Maria Franklin, *Permissions Manager*
Kimberly F. Smilay, *Permissions Specialist*
Kelly Quin, *Permissions Associate*
Sandy Gore, *Permissions Assistant*

Victoria B. Cariappa, *Research Manager*

Michele P. LaMeau, *Research Specialist*
Julie C. Daniel, Tamara C. Nott, Tracie A. Richardson,
Norma Sawaya, Cheryl L. Warnock,
Research Associates

Mary Beth Trimper, *Production Director*

Patti A. Tippett, *Technical Specialist*
Randy Bassett, *Image Database Supervisor*
Michael Ansari, Robert Duncan, *Scanner Operators*
Pamela Reed, *Photography Coordinator*

Library of Congress Catalog Card Number 92-648805
ISBN 0-7876-3139-6
ISSN 1056-4349

Printed in the United States of America

10 9 8 7 6 5 4 3 2 1

Contents

Special Volume Devoted to

Edward Albee
1928-

Preface

Drama Criticism (DC) is principally intended for beginning students of literature and theater as well as the average playgoer. The series is therefore designed to introduce readers to the most frequently studied playwrights of all time periods and nationalities and to present discerning commentary on dramatic works of enduring interest. Furthermore, *DC* seeks to acquaint the reader with the uses and functions of criticism itself. Selected from a diverse body of commentary, the essays in *DC* offer insights into the authors and their works but do not require that the reader possess a wide background in literary studies. Where appropriate, reviews of important productions of the plays discussed are also included to give students a heightened awareness of drama as a dynamic art form, one that many claim is fully realized only in performance.

DC was created in response to suggestions by the staffs of high school, college, and public libraries. These librarians observed a need for a series that assembles critical commentary on the world's most renowned dramatists in the same manner as Gale's *Short Story Criticism (SSC)* and *Poetry Criticism (PC),* which present material on writers of short fiction and poetry. Although playwrights are covered in such Gale literary criticism series as *Contemporary Literary Criticism (CLC), Twentieth-Century Literary Criticism (TCLC), Nineteenth-Century Literature Criticism (NCLC), Literature Criticism from 1400 to 1800 (LC),* and *Classical and Medieval Literature Criticism (CMLC), Drama Criticism* directs more concentrated attention on individual dramatists than is possible in the broader, survey-oriented entries in these Gale series. Commentary on the works of William Shakespeare may be found in *Shakespearean Criticism (SC).*

Scope of the Series

By collecting and organizing commentary on dramatists, *DC* assists students in their efforts to gain insight into literature, achieve better understanding of the texts, and formulate ideas for papers and assignments. A variety of interpretations and assessments is offered, allowing students to pursue their own interests and promoting awareness that literature is dynamic and responsive to many different opinions.

Each volume of *DC* presents:

- 5-10 entries
- authors and works representing a wide range of nationalities and time periods
- a diversity of viewpoints and critical opinions.

Organization of an Author Entry

Each author entry consists of some or all of the following elements, depending on the scope and complexity of the criticism:

- The **author heading** consists of the playwright's most commonly used name, followed by birth and death dates. If an author consistently wrote under a pseudonym, the pseudonym is listed in the author heading and the real name given in parentheses on the first line of the introduction. Also located at the beginning of the introduction are any name variations under which the dramatist wrote, including transliterated forms of the names of authors whose languages use nonroman alphabets.

- A **portrait** of the author is included when available. Most entries also feature illustrations of people, places, and events pertinent to a study of the playwright and his or her works. When appropriate, photographs of the plays in performance are also presented.

- The **biographical and critical introduction** contains background information that familiarizes the reader with the author and the critical debates surrounding his or her works.

- The list of **principal works** is divided into two sections, each of which is organized chronologically by date of first performance. If this has not been conclusively determined, the composition or publication date is used. The first section of the principal works list contains the author's dramatic pieces. The second section provides information on the author's major works in other genres.

- Whenever available, **author commentary** is provided. This section consists of essays or interviews in which the dramatist discusses his or her own work or the art of playwriting in general.

- Essays offering **overviews and general studies of the dramatist's entire literary career** give the student broad perspectives on the writer's artistic development, themes and concerns that recur in several of his or her works, the author's place in literary history, and other wide-ranging topics.

- **Criticism of individual plays** offers the reader in-depth discussions of a select number of the author's most important works. In some cases, the criticism is divided into two sections, each arranged chronologically. When a significant performance of a play can be identified (typically, the premier of a twentieth-century work), the first section of criticism will feature **production reviews** of this staging. Most entries include sections devoted to **critical commentary** that assesses the literary merit of the selected plays. When necessary, essays are carefully excerpted to focus on the work under consideration; often, however, essays and reviews are reprinted in their entirety.

- As an additional aid to students, the critical essays and excerpts are often prefaced by **explanatory annotations.** These notes provide several types of useful information, including the critic's reputation and approach to literary studies as well as the scope and significance of the criticism that follows.

- A complete **bibliographic citation,** designed to help the interested reader locate the original essay or book, precedes each piece of criticism.

- The **further reading list** at the end of each entry comprises additional studies of the dramatist. It is divided into sections that help students quickly locate the specific information they need.

Other Features

- A **cumulative author index** lists all the authors who have appeared in *DC* and Gale's other Literature Criticism Series, as well as cross-references to related titles published by Gale, including *Contemporary Authors* and *Dictionary of Literary Biography.* A complete listing of the series included appears at the beginning of the index.

- A **cumulative nationality index** lists each author featured in *DC* by nationality, followed by the number of the *DC* volume in which the author appears.

- A **cumulative title index** lists in alphabetical order the individual plays discussed in the criticism contained in *DC.* Each title is followed by the author's name and the corresponding volume and page number(s) where commentary on the work may be located. Translations and variant titles are cross-referenced to the title of the play in its original language so that all references to the work are combined in one listing.

A Note to the Reader

When writing papers, students who quote directly from any volume in *Drama Criticism* may use the following general formats to footnote reprinted criticism. The first example pertains to material drawn from periodicals, the second to materials reprinted from books.

[1]Susan Sontag, ''Going to the Theater, Etc.,'' *Partisan Review* XXXI, No. 3 (Summer 1964), 389-94; excerpted and reprinted in *Drama Criticism,* Vol. 1, ed. Lawrence J. Trudeau (Detroit: Gale Research, 1991), pp. 17-20.

[2]Eugene M. Waith, *The Herculean Hero in Marlowe, Chapman, Shakespeare and Dryden* (Chatto & Windus, 1962); excerpted and reprinted in *Drama Criticism,* Vol. 1, ed. Lawrence J. Trudeau (Detroit: Gale Research, 1991), pp. 237-47.

Suggestions are Welcome

Readers who wish to suggest authors to appear in future volumes of *DC,* or who have other suggestions, are cordially invited to contact the editor.

Acknowledgments

The editors wish to thank the copyright holders of the excerpted criticism included in this volume and the permissions managers of many book and magazine publishing companies for assisting us in securing reproduction rights. We are also grateful to the staffs of the Detroit Public Library, the Library of Congress, the University of Detroit Mercy Library, Wayne State University Purdy/Kresge Library Complex, and the University of Michigan Libraries for making their resources available to us. Following is a list of the copyright holders who have granted us permission to reproduce material in this volume of *DC*. Every effort has been made to trace copyright, but if omissions have been made, please let us know.

COPYRIGHTED MATERIAL IN *DC*, VOLUME 11, WERE REPRODUCED FROM THE FOLLOWING PERIODICALS:

—*CLA Journal,* v. XXVIII, 1984. Copyright, 1984 by The College Language Association. Used by permission of The College Language Association. —*Commonweal,* v. LXXVII, 9 November 1962; v. LXXXI, 22 January 1965. Copyright © 1962, 1965 Commonweal Publishing Co., Inc. Both reproduced by permission of Commonweal Foundation. —*Educational Theatre Journal,* v. XVIII, December 1966; v. XX, March 1968; v. 25, March 1973. © 1966, 1968, 1973 University College Theatre Association of the American Theatre Association. All reproduced by permission. —*English Language Notes,* v. XXXIII, September 1995. © copyrighted 1995, Regents of the University of Colorado. Reproduced by permission. —*English Studies in Canada,* v. VII, Summer 1981. © Association of Canadian University Teachers of English, 1981. Reproduced by permission of the publisher and the author. —*Essays in TheatreÉtudes Théâtrales,* v. 13, May 1995, for "*Tiny Alice: Edward Albee's Mystery Play*'' by Elizabeth Klaver. Reproduced by permission of the author. —*The Hudson Review,* v. XLVII, Autumn 1994. Copyright © 1994 by The Hudson Review, Inc. Reproduced by permission; v. XV, Winter 1962-63, for a review of *Who's Afraid of Virginia Woolf?* by John Simon; v. XIX, Winter 1966-67, for "Theatre Chronicle'' by John Simon. Copyright © 1962, 1967 by The Hudson Review, Inc. Both reproduced by permission of the author. —*Journal of Dramatic Theory and Criticism,* v. XII, Fall 1997, for "Public and Private Thought: The Enthymeme of Death in Albee's *Three Tall Women*'' by August W. Staub. Reproduced by permission of the author. —*Modern Drama,* v. X, December 1967; v. XIII, May 1970; v. XVI, June 1973; v. XVII, June 1974; v. XX, March 1977; v. XXI, September 1978. Copyright © 1967, 1970, 1973, 1974, 1977, 1978, University of Toronto, Graduate Centre for Study of Drama. All reproduced by permission. —*The Nation,* New York, v. 203, 10 October 1966; v. 258, 14 March 1994. © 1966, 1994 The Nation magazine / The Nation Company, Inc. Both reproduced by permission. / v. 195, 27 October 1962; v. 190, 13 February 1960. © 1960, renewed 1988; © 1962, renewed 1990 The Nation magazine / The Nation Company, Inc. Both reproduced by permission. —*The New Leader,* v. LXXVII, 14-28 February 1994. © 1994 by The American Labor Conference on International Affairs, Inc. Reproduced by permission. —*The New Republic,* v. 142, 22 February 1960; v. 147, 3 November 1962; v. 152, 23 January 1965; v. 155, October 1966; v. 172, February 1975; v. 210, 4 April 1994. © 1960, 1962, 1965, 1966, 1975, 1994, The New Republic, Inc. All reproduced by permission of The New Republic. —*New York Magazine,* v. 27, 28 February 1994. Copyright © 1994 PRIMEDIA Magazine Corporation. All rights reserved. Reproduced with the permission of New York Magazine. —*The New York Review of Books*, v. IV, 25 February 1965 for "The Play that Dare Not Speak Its Name'' by Philip Roth. Copyright © 1965 Philip Roth. Reproduced by permission of The Wylie Agency, Inc. —*The New York Times,* 15 January 1960; 15 October 1962; 30 December 1964; 23 September 1966; 27 January 1975; 2 February 1975; 14 February 1994. Copyright © 1960, 1962, 1964, 1966, 1975, 1994 by The New York Times Company. All reproduced by permission. —*The New York Times Magazine,* 25 February 1962. Copyright © 1962 by The New York Times Company. Reproduced by permission. —*The New Yorker,* v. L, 3 February 1975. © 1975 by The New Yorker Magazine, Inc. All rights reserved. Reproduced by permission. / v. XXXV, January 1960 for "And Moreover . . .'' by Donald Malcolm. Copyright © 1960 by Donald Malcolm. Renewed 1988 by The New Yorker Magazine, Inc. All rights reserved. Reproduced with permission of The Wylie Agency. / v. XXXVIII, 20 October 1962 for "Long Night's Journey into Daze'' by John McCarten; v. XL, 9 January 1965 for "Mystical Manipulations'' by John McCarten. © 1962, 1965 by The New Yorker Magazine, Inc. All rights reserved. Both reproduced by permission of the Literary Estate of John McCarten. / v. LXX, 16 May 1994 for "Sons and Mothers'' by John Lahr. Copyright © 1994 by the author. All rights reserved. Reproduced by permission of Georges Borchardt, Inc. for the author. —*Prairie Schooner,* v, XL. Spring 1996. © 1996 by University of Nebraska Press. Reproduced from Prairie Schooner by permission of the University of Nebraska Press. —*The Progressive,* v. 60, August 1996. Copyright © 1996 by The Progressive, Inc. Reproduced by permission of The Progressive, 409 East Main Street, Madison, WI 53703. —*Recherches Anglaises et Amèricaines,* Summer

1972. Reproduced by permission. —*Renascence: A Critical Journal of Letters,* v. XVII, Winter, 1964. © Copyright 1964, Catholic Renascence Society, Inc. —*Renascence: Essays on Values in Literature,* v. XXIII, Spring 1971; v. XXXII, Spring 1980. © copyright, 1971, 1980 Marquette University Press. Both reproduced by permission. —*The Saturday Review,* v. XLVIII, 16 January 1965; v. XLIX, © October 1966; v. 12, © March 1975. © 1965, 1966, 1975 Saturday Review Magazine, © 1979 General Media International, Inc. All reproduced by permission of The Saturday Review. —*Studies in American Drama: 1945-Present,* v. I, 1986. Reproduced by permission. —*Theatre Journal,* v. 46, December 1994. © 1994, University and College Theatre Association of the American Theatre Association. Reproduced by permission of The Johns Hopkins University Press. —*Theatre Survey,* v. 34, November 1993. Reproduced by permission. —*Tulane Drama Review,* v. 9, Summer 1965 for "The Theatre of Edward Albee'' by Lee Baxandall. Copyright © 1965, The Drama Review. Reproduced by permission of the publisher and the author. —*Twentieth Century Literature: A Scholarly and Critical Journal,* v. 16, April 1970; v. 28, Spring 1982. Copyright 1970, 1982, Hofstra University Press. Both reproduced by permission. —*World Literature Today,* v. 69, Autumn 1995. Copyright © 1995 by the University of Oklahoma Press. Reproduced by permission.

COPYRIGHTED MATERIAL IN *DC,* VOLUME 11, WERE REPRODUCED FROM THE FOLLOWING BOOKS:

Adler, Thomas P. *From American Drama, 1940-1960: A Critical History.* Twayne Publishers, 1994. Copyright © 1994 by Twayne Publishers. All rights reserved. Reproduced with the permission of Macmillan Library Reference. —*Albee, Edward.* From an introduction to *Three Tall Women: A Play in Two Acts.* By *Edward Albee.* Dutton, 1994. Copyright © Edward Albee, 1994. All rights reserved. Reproduced by permission of William Morris Agency, Inc. on behalf of the author. In North America and the Philippines by Dutton, a division of Penguin Putnam Inc. —*Amacher, Richard E.* From Edward Albee. Revised Edition. Twayne Publishers, 1982. Copyright © 1982 by G. K. Hall & Company. All rights reserved. Reproduced with the permission of Macmillan Library Reference. —*Anderson, Mary Castiglie* for "Ritual and Initiation in *The Zoo Story,*'' in *Edward Albee: An Interview and Essays.* Edited by Julian N. Wasserman. The University of St. Thomas, 1983. Copyright © 1983 by The University of St. Thomas. All rights reserved. Reproduced by permission of the editor. —*Berkowitz, Gerald M.* From *American Drama of the Twentieth Century.* Longman, 1992. © Longman Group UK Limited 1992. All rights reserved. Reproduced by permission of Pearson Education Limited. —*Bernstein, Samuel J.* From *The Strands Entwinted: A New Direction in American Drama.* Northeastern University Press, 1980. Copyright © Northeastern University 1980. All rights reserved. Reproduced by permission. —*Bigsby, C. W. E. From Confrontation and Commitment: A Study of Contemporary American Drama: 1959-66.* University of Missouri Press, 1967. Copyright © 1967 and 1968 by C. W. E. Bigsby. Reproduced by permission. —*Casper, Leonard* for "*Tiny Alice: The Expense of Joy in the Persistence of Mystery*'' in *Edward Albee: An Interview and Essays.* Edited by Julian N. Wasserman. The University of St. Thomas, 1983. Copyright © 1983 by The University of St. Thomas. All rights reserved. Reproduced by permission of the editor. —*Cohn, Ruby.* From *Dialogue in American Drama.* Indiana University Press, 1971. Copyright © 1971 by Indiana University Press. All rights reserved. Reproduced by permission. —*Debusscher, Gilbert.* From *Edward Albee: Tradition and Renewal.* Center for American Studies, 1967. Reproduced by permission. —*Driver, Tom F.* From "What's the Matter with Edward Albee?'' in *American Drama and Its Critics: A Collection of Critical Essays.* Edited by Alan S. Downer. University of Chicago Press, 1965. © 1965 by The University of Chicago. All rights reserved. Reproduced by permission of the author. —*Esslin, Martin.* From *The Theatre of the Absurd.* Revised Edition. Copyright © 1961, 1968, 1969 by Martin Esslin. All rights reserved. Reproduced by permission of the author. In North America by permission of Doubleday, a division of Random House, Inc. —*Hayman, Ronald.* From *World Dramatists: Edward Albee.* Frederick Ungar Publishing Co., 1971. © 1971 by Ronald Hayman. Reproduced by permission. —*Heldreth, Leonard G.* From "From Reality to Fantasy: Displacement and Death in Albee's Zoo Story,'' in *Contours of the Fantastic: Selected Essays from the Eighth International Conference on the Fantastic in the Arts.* Edited by Michele K. Langford. Greenwood Press, 1987. Copyright © 1990 by Michele K. Langford. All rights reserved. Reproduced by permission of Greenwood Publishing Group, Inc., Westport, CT. —*Hughes, Catharine.* From *American Playwrights: 1945-75.* Pitman Publishing, 1976. © Catharine Hughes 1976. All rights reserved. —*Maslon, Laurence* and Edward Albee. From an interview in *The Playwright's Art: Conversations with Contemporary American Dramatists.* Edited by Jackson R. Bryer. Rutgers University Press, 1995. Copyright © 1995 by Rutgers, The State University. All rights reserved. Reproduced by permission of Rutgers, The State University. —*McCarthy, Gerry.* From *Modern Dramatists: Edward Albee.* St. Martin's Press, 1987. Copyright © Gerry McCarthy, 1987. All rights reserved. Reproduced by permission of Macmillan, London and Basingstoke. In North American by St. Martin's Press, Incorporated. —*Paolucci, Anne.* From *From Tension to Tonic: The Plays of Edward Albee.* Southern Illinois University Press, 1972. Copyright © 1972 by Southern Illinois University Press. All rights reserved. Reproduced by permission of the author. —*Perry, Virginia I.* for "Disturbing Our Sense of Well-Being: The 'Uninvited' in *A Delicate Balance,*'' in *Edward Albee: An Interview and Essays.* Edited by Julian N. Wasserman. The University of St. Thomas, 1983. Copyright © 1983 by The University of St. Thomas. All rights reserved. Reproduced by permission of the editor. —*Porter, Thomas E.* From *Myth and Modern American Drama*. Wayne State University Press, 1969. Copyright ©, 1969 by Wayne State University Press. Ali rights reserved. Reproduced by permission of the publisher and the author. —*Purdon, Liam O.* for "The Limits of Reason: *Seascape* as Psychic Metaphor'' in *Edward Albee: An Interview and Essays*. Edited by Julian N. Wasserman. The University of St. Thomas, 1983. Copyright © 1983 by The University of St. Thomas. All rights reserved. Reproduced by permission of the editor. —*Roudané, Matthew C.* From American Drama Since 1960: A Critical History. Twayne Publishers, 1996. Copyright © 1996 by Twayne Publishers. All rights reserved. Reproduced with the permission of Macmillan Library Reference. —*Roudané, Matthew C.* From *Understanding Edward Albee*. University of South Carolina Press, 1987. Copyright © University of South Carolina 1987. Reproduced by permission. —*Rutenberg, Michael E.* From *Edward Albee: Playwright in Protest*. DBS Publications, Inc., 1969. © Copyright 1969 by Michael E. Rutenberg. All rights reserved. Reproduced by permission of the author. —*Simard, Rodney.* From *Postmodern Drama: Contemporary Playwrights in American and Britain*. University Press of America, 1984. Copyright © 1984 by University Press of America, Inc. Reproduced by permission of the Literary Estate of Rodney Simard. —*Stenz, Anita Maria.* From *Edward Albee: The Poet of Loss*. Mouton Publishers, 1978. © Copyright 1978 Mouton de Gruyter. A Division of Walter de Gruyter & Co. Reproduced by permission. —*Weales, Gerald.* From *The Jumping-Off Place: American Drama in the 1960s*. The Macmillan Company, 1969. Copyright © 1969 by Gerald Weales. All rights reserved. Reproduced by permission of the author.

PHOTOGRAPHS AND ILLUSTRATIONS APPEARING IN *DC,* VOLUME 11, WERE RECEIVED FROM THE FOLLOWING SOURCES:

Edward Albee, photograph. The Library of Congress

Edward Albee, photograph. © Jerry Bauer. Reproduced by permission.

Edward Albee, standing outside of Boston's Colonial Theater where he directed a production of *Who's Afraid of Virginia Woolf?*, photograph. AP/Wide World Photos. Reproduced by permission.

Edward Albee, receiving the Evening Standard Drama Award from Leo Armati, photograph. Corbis/Hulton Deutsch Collection. Reproduced by permission.

From a photograph by Hank Kranzler of a production of Edward Albee's *The Zoo Story*. American Conservatory Theater, San Francisco. Reproduced by permission.

Edward Albee, in front of The Provincetown Playhouse. Corbis-Bettmann. Reproduced by permission.

David Warner in a production of Edward Albee's *Tiny Alice*. © Donald Cooper/Photostage. Reproduced by permission.

David Warner and Irene Worth in a production of Edward Albee's *Tiny Alice*. © Donald Cooper/Photostage. Reproduced by permission.

Irene Worth in a production of Edward Albee's *Tiny Alice*. © Donald Cooper/Photostage. Reproduced by permission.

Hume Cronyn, and Jessica Tandy in a production of Edward Albee's *A Delicate Balance*, photograph. AP/Wide World Photos. Reproduced by permission.

Eileen Atkins, Annette Crosbie, Maggie Smith, James Laurenson, and Sian Thomas in a production of Edward Albee's *A Delicate Balance*. © Donald Cooper/Photostage. Reproduced by permission.

George Grizzard, and Melinda Dillon in a scene from Edward Albee's *Who's Afraid of Virginia Woolf?* AP/Wide World Photos. Reproduced by permission.

George Grizzard, and Uta Hagen in a scene from Edward Albee's *Who's Afraid of Virginia Woolf?* AP/Wide World Photos. Reproduced by permission.

Paul Eddington and Joan Plowright in a production of Edward Albee's *Who's Afraid of Virginia Woolf?* © Donald Cooper/Photostage. Reproduced by permission.

Joan Plowright, Paul Eddington, David Schofield and Mary Maddox in a production of Edward Albee's *Who's Afraid of Virginia Woolf?* © Donald Cooper/Photostage. Reproduced by permission.

Richard Burton, Elizabeth Taylor, George Segal, and Sandy Dennis in a scene from the film adaptation of Edward Albee's *Who's Afraid of Virginia Woolf?* The Kobal Collection. Reproduced by permission.

Anastasia Hille, Maggie Smith, and Frances de la Tour in a production of Edward Albee's *Three Tall Women*. © Donald Cooper/Photostage. Reproduced by permission.

Anastasia Hille, Frances de la Tour, and Maggie Smith in a production of Edward Albee's *Three Tall Women*. © Donald Cooper/Photostage. Reproduced by permission.

Michael Learned, starring in Edward Albee's *Three Tall Women*, photograph. AP/Wide World Photos. Reproduced by permission. xii

List of Playwrights Covered in *DC*

Volume 1
- James Baldwin
- William Wells Brown
- Karel Capek
- Mary Chase
- Alexandre Dumas (*fils*)
- Charles Fuller
- Nikolai Gogol
- Lillian Hellman
- Christopher Marlowe
- Arthur Miller
- Yukio Mishima
- Richard Brinsley Sheridan
- Sophocles
- Thornton Wilder

Volume 2
- Aristophanes
- Albert CamusPedro
- William Congreve
- *Everyman*
- Federico García Lorca
- Lorraine Hansberry
- Henrik Ibsen
- Wole Soyinka
- John Millingon Synge
- John Webster
- August Wilson

Volume 3
- Bertolt Brecht
- Calderón de la Barca
- John Dryden
- Athol Fugard
- Langston Hughes
- Thomas Kyd
- Menander
- Joe Orton
- Jean-Paul Sartre
- Ntozake Shange

Volume 4
- Pierre-Augustin Caron de Beaumarchais
- Aphra Behn
- Alice Childress
- Euripides
- Hugo von Hofmannsthal
- David Henry Hwang
- Ben Jonson
- David Mamet
- Wendy Wasserstein
- Tennessee Williams

Volume 5
- Caryl Churchill
- John Pepper Clark
- Adrienne Kennedy
- Thomas Middleton
- Luigi Pirandello
- Eugène Scribe
- Lucius Annaeus Seneca
- Sam Shepard
- Paul Zindel

Volume 6
- Amiri Baraka
- Francis Beaumont and John Fletcher
- Ed Bullins
- Václav Havel
- Clifford Odets
- Plautus
- Tom Stoppard

Volume 7
- Frank Chin
- Spalding Gray
- John Lyly
- Emily Mann
- Pierre Carlet de Chamblain de Marivaux
- Peter Shaffer
- Terence
- Ivan Turgenev
- Derek Walcott
- Zeami

Volume 8
- Aeschylus
- Jean Anouilh
- Lonne Elder III
- John Ford
- Brian Friel
- Oliver Goldsmith
- Charles Gordone
- Larry Kramer
- Marsha Norman

Volume 9
- Anton Pavlovich Chekhov

Volume 10
- Dario Fo
- Maria Irene Fornes
- Susan Glaspell
- Tony Kushner
- Edmond Rostand
- Victor Séjour
- Luis Valdez

Volume 11
- Edward Albee

Edward Albee
1928-

INTRODUCTION

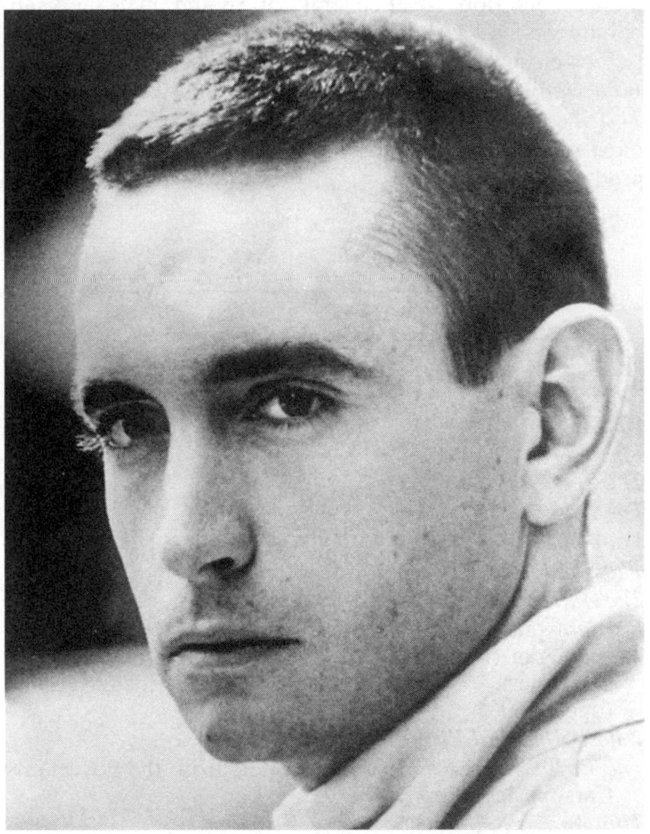

An acclaimed and controversial playwright, Albee is best known for *Who's Afraid of Virginia Woolf?,* his first full-length drama. Although initially characterized either as a realist or an absurdist, Albee combines elements from the American tradition of social criticism—established by such playwrights as Arthur Miller, Tennessee Williams, and Eugene O'Neill—with aspects of the Theater of the Absurd, as practiced by Samuel Beckett and Eugène Ionesco. While Albee's plays often portray alienated individuals who suffer as a result of unjust social, moral, and religious strictures, his works usually offer solutions to conflicts rather than conveying an absurdist sense of inescapable determinism. As Matthew C. Roudané has declared, "Albee's is an affirmative vision of human experience. His vision underscores the importance of confronting one's inner and outer world of O'Neillean 'pipe-dreams,' or illusions. In the midst of a dehumanizing society, Albee's heroes, perhaps irrationally, affirm living." In a career spanning more than thirty years, Albee has received the Pulitzer Prize for Drama three times: for *A Delicate Balance, Seascape,* and *Three Tall Women.*

BIOGRAPHICAL INFORMATION

Albee is the adopted child of Reed and Frances Albee, heirs to the multi-million dollar fortune of American theater manager Edward Franklin Albee I. He began attending the theater and writing poetry at the age of six, wrote a three-act sex farce when he was twelve, and attempted two novels while a teenager. Many critics suggest that the tense family conflicts characteristic of Albee's dramas are derived from his childhood experiences. After attending several private and military schools and enrolling briefly at Trinity College in Connecticut, Albee achieved limited success as an author of poetry and fiction before turning to drama. Although he remained associated with off-Broadway theater until the production of *Who's Afraid of Virginia Woolf?,* he first garnered critical and popular acclaim for his one-act dramas, which prompted comparisons to the works of Williams and Ionesco. In addition to the three Pulitzer prizes, Albee has received several other prestigious honors, including the Tony Award and the New York Drama Critics Circle Award for his dramatic works.

MAJOR WORKS

Albee immediately established himself as a promising young playwright with his first mature play, *The Zoo Story,* which received its American debut on a double bill with a play by Samuel Beckett and which was favorably compared with the elder playwright's work. Albee continued to build his reputation as an innovator in the absurdist manner with such one-act plays as *The Sandbox* and *The American Dream.* Mainstream success came with *Who's Afraid of Virginia Woolf?,* produced on Broadway in 1961. This drama won a number of awards but, in a controversial decision, was denied the Pulitzer Prize. It was made into a film with Richard Burton and Elizabeth Taylor in 1966.

Albee continued to experiment with a variety of forms, subjects, and styles in his succeeding plays; and while several of them failed commercially and elicited scathing reviews for their abstract classicism and dialogue, many scholars have commended his commitment to theatrical experimentation and refusal to pander to commercial pressures. The unorthodox *Tiny Alice,* Albee's follow-up to *Who's Afraid of Virginia Woolf?,* was considered by some critics to be incomprehensible for the manner in which it deviates from realism with respect to setting, characterization, and internal time. Nevertheless, it has, in the years since its first performance, sparked a great deal of critical interest and commentary. While, for its part, *A Delicate Balance* was widely faulted for lacking action and cohesive ideas, it nevertheless garnered approval for its synthesis of dramatic elements and was awarded the Pulitzer Prize. Similarly, Albee's second Pulitzer Prize-winning work, *Seascape,* was regarded by some as pretentious but was commended overall for its lyrical quality and insights into the human condition. After several critical and financial disappointments in the 1980s, including *The Lady from Dubuque* (which closed after only twelve performances) and *The Man Who Had Three Arms,* Albee returned in 1991 with *Three Tall Women,* for which he received his third Pulitzer. His most recent work is *The Play about the Baby,* which was produced in 1998.

PRINCIPAL WORKS

PLAYS

The Zoo Story 1959
The Death of Bessie Smith 1960
Fam and Yam 1960
The Sandbox 1960
The American Dream 1961
Bartleby [adaptor, with James Hinton (libretto) and William Flanagan (music); from the short story "Bartleby, the Scrivener: A Story of Wall-Street" by Herman Melville] (opera) 1961
Who's Afraid of Virginia Woolf? 1962
The Ballad of the Sad Café [adaptor; from the novella by Carson McCullers] 1963
Tiny Alice 1964
A Delicate Balance 1966
Malcolm [adaptor; from the novel by James Purdy] 1966
Everything in the Garden [adaptor; from the drama by Giles Cooper] 1967
**Box* 1968
**Quotations from Chairman Mao Tse-Tung 1968*
All Over 1971
Seascape 1975
Counting the Ways: A Vaudeville 1977
†*Listening: A Chamber Play* 1977
The Lady from Dubuque 1980
Lolita [adaptor; from the novel by Vladimir Nabokov] 1981
The Man Who Had Three Arms 1982
Finding the Sun 1983
Walking 1984
Marriage Play 1987
Three Tall Women 1991
The Lorca Play 1992
Fragments: A Concerto Grosso 1993
The Play about the Baby 1998

*These two works are performed together and referred to as *Box-Mao-Box.*

†This work was first produced as a radio play in 1976.

AUTHOR COMMENTARY

Which Theatre is the Absurd One? (1962)

SOURCE: "Which Theatre is the Absurd One?" in *The New York Times Magazine,* 25 February 1962, pp. 30-1, 64, 66.

[*In the following piece, Albee addresses the label, Theatre of the Absurd, that had been attached to his work. He argues that "The Theatre of the Absurd, in the sense that it is truly the contemporary theatre, facing as it does man's condition as it is, is the Realistic theatre of our time; and that the supposed Realistic theatre—the term used here to mean most of what is done on Broadway—in the sense that it panders to the public need for self-congratulation and reassurance and presents a false picture of ourselves to ourselves is . . . really and truly The Theatre of the Absurd."*]

A theatre person of my acquaintance—a man whose judgment must be respected, though more for the infallibility of his intuition than for his reasoning—remarked just the other week, "The Theatre of the Absurd has had it; it's on its way out; it's through."

Now this, on the surface of it, seems to be a pretty funny attitude to be taking toward a theatre movement which has, only in the past couple of years, been impressing itself on the American public consciousness. Or is it? Must we judge that a theatre of such plays as Samuel Beckett's *Krapp's Last Tape,* Jean Genet's *The Balcony* (both long, long runners off-Broadway) and Eugene Ionesco's *Rhinoceros*—which, albeit in a hoked-up production, had a substantial season on Broadway—has been judged by the theatre public and found wanting?

And shall we have to assume that The Theatre of the Absurd Repertory Company, currently playing at New York's off-Broadway Cherry Lane Theatre—presenting works by Beckett, Ionesco, Genet, Arrabal, Jack Richardson, Kenneth Koch and myself—being the first such collective representation of the movement in the United States, is also a kind of farewell to the movement? For that matter, just what *is* The Theatre of the Absurd?

Well, let me come at it obliquely. When I was told, about a year ago, that I was considered a member in good standing of The Theatre of the Absurd I was deeply offended. I was deeply offended because I had never heard the term before and I immediately assumed that it applied to the theatre uptown—Broadway.

What (I was reasoning to myself) could be more absurd than a theatre in which the esthetic criterion is something like this: A "good" play is one which makes money; a "bad" play (in the sense of "Naughty! Naughty!" I guess) is one which does not; a theatre in which performers have plays rewritten to correspond to the public relations image of themselves; a theatre in which playwrights are encouraged (what a funny word!) to think of themselves as little cogs in a great big wheel; a theatre in which imitation has given way to imitation of imitation; a theatre in which London "hits" are, willy-nilly, in a kind of reverse of chauvinism, greeted in a manner not unlike a colony's obeisance to the Crown; a theatre in which real estate owners and theatre party managements predetermine the success of unknown quantities; a theatre in which everybody scratches and bites for billing as though it meant access to the last bomb shelter on earth; a theatre in which, in a given season, there was not a single performance of a play by Beckett, Brecht, Chekhov, Genet, Ibsen, O'Casey, Pirandello, Shaw, Strindberg—or Shakespeare? What, indeed, I thought, could be more absurd than that? (My conclusions . . . obviously.)

For it emerged that The Theatre of the Absurd, aside from being the title of an excellent book by Martin Esslin on what is loosely called the avant-garde theatre, was a somewhat less than fortunate catch-all phrase to describe the philosophical attitudes and theatre methods of a number of Europe's finest and most adventurous playwrights and their followers.

I was less offended, but still a little dubious. Simply: I don't like labels; they can be facile and can lead to non-think on the part of the public. And unless it is understood that the playwrights of The Theatre of the Absurd represent a group only in the sense that they seem to be doing something of the same thing in vaguely similar ways at approximately the same time—unless this is understood, then the labeling itself will be more absurd than the label.

Playwrights, by nature, are grouchy, withdrawn, envious, greedy, suspicious and, in general, quite nice people—and the majority of them wouldn't be caught dead in a colloquy remotely resembling the following:

> IONESCO: *(At a Left Bank cafe table, spying Beckett and Genet strolling past in animated conversation)* Hey! Sam! Jean!
>
> GENET: Hey, it's Eugene! Sam, it's Eugene!
>
> BECKETT: Well. I'll be damned. Hi there, Eugene boy.
>
> IONESCO: Sit down, kids.
>
> GENET: Sure thing.
>
> IONESCO: *(Rubbing his hands together)* Well, what's new in the Theatre of the Absurd?
>
> BECKETT: Oh, less than a lot of people think. *(They all laugh.)*

Etc. No. Not very likely. Get a playwright alone sometime, get a few drinks in him, and maybe he'll be persuaded to sound off about his "intention" and the like—and hate himself for it the next day. But put a group of playwrights together in a room, and the conversation—if there is any—will, more likely than not, concern itself with sex, restaurants and the movies.

Very briefly, then—and reluctantly, because I am a playwright and would much rather talk about sex, restaurants and the movies—and stumblingly, because I do not pretend to understand it entirely, I will try to define The Theatre of the Absurd. As I get it, The Theatre of the Absurd is an absorption-in-art of certain existentialist and post-existentialist philosophical concepts having to do, in the main, with man's attempts to make sense for himself out of his senseless position in a world which makes no sense—which makes no sense because the moral, religious, political and social structures man has erected to "illusion" himself have collapsed.

Albert Camus put it this way: "A world that can be explained by reasoning, however faulty, is a familiar world. But in a universe that is suddenly deprived of illusions and of light, man feels a stranger. His is an irremediable exile, because he is deprived of memories of a lost homeland as much as he lacks the hope of a promised land to come. This divorce between man and his life, the actor and his setting, truly constitutes the feeling of Absurdity."

And Eugene Ionesco says this: "Absurd is that which is devoid of purpose * * *. Cut off from his religious, metaphysical, and transcendental roots, man is lost; all his actions become senseless, absurd, useless."

And to sum up the movement, Martin Esslin writes, in his book *The Theatre of the Absurd*: "Ultimately, a phenomenon like The Theatre of the Absurd does not reflect despair or a return to dark irrational forces but expresses modern man's endeavor to come to terms with the world in which he lives. It attempts to make him face up to the human condition as it really is, to free him from illusions that are bound to cause constant maladjustment and disappointment * * *. For the dignity of man lies in his ability to face reality in all its senselessness; to accept it freely, without fear, without illusions—and to laugh at it."

Amen.

(And while we're on the subject of Amen, one wearies of the complaint that The Theatre of the Absurd playwrights alone are having at God these days. The notion that God is dead, indifferent, or insane—a notion blasphemous, premature, or academic depending on your persuasion—while surely a tenet of some of the playwrights under discussion, is, it seems to me, of a piece with Mr. Tennessee Williams' description of the Deity, in *The Night of the Iguana,* as "a senile delinquent.")

So much for the attempt to define terms. Now, what of this theatre? What of this theatre in which, for example, a legless old couple live out their lives in twin ashcans, surfacing occasionally for food or conversation (Samuel Beckett's *Endgame*); in which a man is seduced, and rather easily, by a girl with three well-formed and functioning noses (Eugene Ionesco's *Jack, or The Submission*); in which, on the same stage, one group of Negro actors is playing at pretending to be white, and another group of Negro actors is playing at pretending to be Negro (Jean Genet's *The Blacks*)?

What of this theatre? Is it, as it has been accused of being, obscure, sordid, destructive, anti-theatre, perverse and absurd (in the sense of foolish)? Or is it merely, as I have so often heard it put, that, "This sort of stuff is too depressing, too . . . too mixed-up; I go to the theatre to relax and have a good time."

I would submit that it is this latter attitude—that the theatre is a place to relax and have a good time—in conflict with the purpose of The Theatre of the Absurd—which is to make a man face up to the human condition as it really is—that has produced all the brouhaha and the dissent. I would submit that The Theatre of the Absurd, in the sense that it is truly the contemporary theatre, facing as it does man's condition as it is, is the Realistic theatre of our time; and that the supposed Realistic theatre—the term used here to mean most of what is done on Broadway—in the sense that it panders to the public need for self-congratulation and reassurance and presents a false picture of ourselves to ourselves is, with an occasional very lovely exception, really and truly The Theatre of the Absurd.

And I would submit further that the health of a nation, a society, can be determined by the art it demands. We have insisted of television and our movies that they not have anything to do with anything, that they be our never-never land; and if we demand this same function of our live theatre, what will be left of the visual-auditory arts—save the dance (in which nobody talks) and music (to which nobody listens)?

It has been my fortune, the past two or three years, to travel around a good deal, in pursuit of my career—Berlin, London, Buenos Aires, for example; and I have discovered a couple of interesting things. I have discovered that audiences in these and other major cities demand of their commercial theatre—and get—a season of plays in which the froth and junk are the exception and not the rule. To take a case: in Berlin, in 1959, Adamov, Genet, Beckett and Brecht (naturally) were playing the big houses; this past fall, Beckett again, Genet again, Pinter twice, etc. To take another case: in Buenos Aires there are over a hundred experimental theatres.

These plays cannot be put on in Berlin over the head of a protesting or an indifferent audience; these experimental theatres cannot exist in Buenos Aires without subscription. In the end—and it must always come down to this, no matter what other failings a theatre may have—in the end a public will get what it deserves, and no better.

I have also discovered, in my wanderings, that young people throng to what is new and fresh in the theatre. Happily, this holds true in the United States as well. At the various colleges I have gone to to speak I have found an eager, friendly and knowledgeable audience, an audience which is as dismayed by the Broadway scene as any proselytizer for the avant-garde. I have found among young people an audience which is not so preconditioned by pap as to have cut off half of its responses. (It is interesting to note, by the way, that if an off-Broadway play has a substantial run, its audiences will begin young and grow older; as the run goes on, cloth coats give way to furs, walkers and subway riders to taxi-takers. Exactly the opposite is true on Broadway.)

The young, of course, are always questioning values, knocking the status quo about, considering shibboleths to see if they are pronounceable. In time, it is to be regretted, most of them—the kids—will settle down to their own version of the easy, the standard; but in the meanwhile . . . in the meanwhile they are a wonderful, alert, alive, accepting audience.

And I would go so far as to say that it is the responsibility of everyone who pretends any interest at all in the theatre to get up off their six-ninety seats and find out what the theatre is *really* about. For it is a lazy public which produces a slothful and irresponsible theatre.

Now, I would suspect that my theatre-friend with the infallible intuition is probably right when he suggests that The Theatre of the Absurd (or the avant-garde theatre, or whatever you want to call it) as it now stands is on its way out. Or at least is undergoing change. All living organisms undergo constant change. And while it is certain that the nature of this theatre will remain constant, its forms, its methods—its devices, if you will—most necessarily will undergo mutation.

This theatre has no intention of running downhill; and the younger playwrights will make use of the immediate past and mould it to their own needs. (Harold Pinter, for example, could not have written *The Caretaker* had Samuel Beckett not existed, but Pinter is, nonetheless, moving in his own direction.) And it is my guess that the theatre in the United States will always hew more closely to the post-Ibsen/Chekhov tradition than does the theatre in France, let us say. It is our nature as a country, a society. But we will experiment, and we will expect your attention.

For just as it is true that our response to color and form was forever altered once the impressionist painters put their minds to canvas, it is just as true that the playwrights of The Theatre of the Absurd have forever altered our response to the theatre.

And one more point: The avant-garde theatre is fun; it is free-swinging, bold, iconoclastic and often wildly, wildly funny. If you will approach it with childlike innocence—putting your standard responses aside, for they do not apply—if you will approach it on its own terms, I think you will be in for a liberating surprise. I think you may no longer be content with plays that you can't remember half-way down the block. You will not only be doing yourself some good, but you will be having a great time, to boot. And even though it occurs to me that such a fine combination must be sinful, I still recommend it.

Text, Subtext, and Performance (1990)

SOURCE: "Text, Subtext, and Performance: Edward Albee

on Directing *Who's Afraid of Virginia Woolf?,*" by Rakesh Solomon, in *Theatre Survey,* Vol. 34, No. 2, November 1993, pp. 95-110.

[*The following interview was conducted in January 1990, during rehearsals for a production of* Who's Afraid of Virginia Woolf? *that Albee was directing. He here focuses on the play from the dual perspective of playwright and director.*]

"Who's afraid of the Tanks?" proclaimed the headline of the Lithuanian daily, *Lietuvas Rytas,* in its review of Edward Albee's ***Who's Afraid of Virginia Woolf?*** in Vilnius in April 1990, six weeks into the nation's tumultuous declaration of independence that had brought Soviet tanks onto city streets.[1] Seizing the fundamental point of the play—the need to destroy illusion and face reality without fear—Lithuanian audiences saw a distinct analogy with their national situation that demanded they forswear dreams of some painless future solution and confront the reality of Soviet military intervention. Their grasp of the play, despite cultural chasms and the vagaries of simultaneous translation, testified to the clarity of Albee's staging of this classic of the American theatre.

The production originated eight months earlier at the Los Angeles Music Center where Albee directed Glenda Jackson as Martha and John Lithgow as George. This Center Theatre Group/Ahmanson Theatre production, which included Brian Kerwin as Nick and Cynthia Nixon as Honey, played at the Doolittle Theatre from October 5 to December 17, 1989. Because Glenda Jackson's and John Lithgow's film commitments permitted only a limited run, Albee planned the production with first-rate actors as understudies so that they could capably take over as the new cast after the Los Angeles engagement. For this fresh cast of Carol Mayo Jenkins as Martha, Bruce Gray as George, John Ottavino as Nick, and Cynthia Bassham as Honey, Albee also arranged another full fledged four-week period of rehearsals and paid previews, from December 19, 1989, to January 10, 1990, at the Alley Theatre in Houston, where Albee has been an Associate Artist for Direction and Playwriting since 1988. The Music Center's proscenium setting, costume, and lighting designs were also retained: the Alley's resident designers, in consultation with their Los Angeles counterparts, made only minimal modifications for their thrust Large Stage. Following a four-week run at the Alley Theatre, the production proceeded on a short tour of the United States, a three-city engagement in Lithuania, and stints at the Sovremennik Theatre in Moscow and the Maly Theatre in Leningrad.[2]

Albee's comments about his text and production in this discussion are part of an ongoing dialogue that I have had with him for over a decade. Since 1978 I have observed Albee direct professional productions of ten of his own plays in New York and elsewhere—ranging from his first play, ***The Zoo Story,*** to his 1992 American premiere, ***Marriage Play.*** I have also seen Albee stage two of Samuel Beckett's plays, *Ohio Impromptu* and *Krapp's Last Tape,* and I have observed Albee work with his long-time director, Alan Schneider, when the latter staged the Broadway premiere of ***The Lady From Dubuque.*** Typically, I attend every rehearsal for a production—from opening day to final preview—and document and critique each day's work, while carrying on an intermittent conversation with Albee between rehearsal sessions, culminating in one or two extended tape-recorded interviews near opening night. At that time I also tape-record interviews with some actors, scene and lighting designers, and the stage manager. This exchange on ***Who's Afraid of Virginia Woolf?*** was taped at the Alley Theatre on January 6, 1990, concluding my observation of his Los Angeles staging and his Houston rehearsals.

In the following discussion Albee offers insights into the details of his rehearsal process, from his special perspective as both playwright and director. Journalists and scholars have sought and received more interviews from Albee than from most other contemporary American playwrights, both because he continues to provoke interest and because his frequent lecturing, teaching, and directing oblige him to grant interviews. My long professional relationship with Albee and my thorough acquaintance with the particulars of his rehearsals, however, allow me to press, persist, and probe much further. More than most subjects, Albee comes armored against the interviewer's probes: he brings deeply-ingrained, almost reflexive interview habits of defense through deft deflection, shrewd rationalization, the too-simple explanation, or the opaque comment. His caution stems partly from his personality and partly from a distrust of authorial or critical paraphrase as substitute for the essence and experience of a work of art, a trait he shares with many writers in what Nathalie Sarraute terms the "age of suspicion." During our conversations over the years, however, Albee has become progressively less guarded, and I have had to nudge him less. It is still difficult, nonetheless, to elicit from him a candid, blunt, or spontaneous response, especially about matters of subtext, allusion, and interpretation—subjects about which interviewers have found him adroitly evasive or uncooperative.

This conversation on ***Who's Afraid of Virginia Woolf?*** remains distinct from other Albee interviews, moreover, in its sustained attention to a single play and in its concentration on matters of rehearsal and performance. Albee ranges widely from minute details of setting, properties, and timing to broad issues of directorial interpretation. He reveals his rationale for crucial textual revisions made during the Los Angeles and Houston rehearsals and distinguishes between a script's dramaturgic refinement during rehearsal versus updating to suit altered audience expectation. He furnishes subtextual readings, divulges incidental topical references, and considers key problems of characterization, throwing new light on his conceptions of George and Martha. In addition, Albee discusses the appropriate time in rehearsal to address subtext, motivation, and rhythm; the necessity of discrete directorial strategies for different actors; the value of rehearsing durng preview week; and his reasons for shunning demonstration of business and too-detailed scene work.

Albee also explains what impelled him to direct the critically acclaimed 1976 Broadway revival of ***Virginia Woolf?*** with Colleen Dewhurst and Ben Gazzara, and he compares details of his 1976 and 1989-90 stagings with those of Alan Schneider's 1962 premiere production. Moreover, Albee briefly touches upon his philosophy and method as a teacher of playwriting and directing.

Albee's comments about staging ***Who's Afraid of Virginia Woolf?*** and about directing in general must be seen within the context of his extensive directorial experience. He has directed professional productions—revivals or premieres—of nearly all of his original plays. He directed a professional production of his first play, ***The Zoo Story,*** as early as 1961, only two years after its first production.[3] Albee directed the Broadway premieres of ***The American Dream*** (1968),[4] ***Seascape*** (1975),[5] and ***The Man who Had Three Arms*** (1983),[6] besides the revival of ***Who's Afraid of Virginia Woolf?***[7] He also directed the first stage performance of ***Listening*** (1977), the first American performance of ***Counting the Ways*** (1977) at the Hartford Stage Company,[8] and the world premieres of ***Marriage Play*** (1987)[9] and ***Three Tall Women*** (1991)[10] at the English Theatre in Vienna. In addition, Albee co-directed the radio premiere of ***Listening*** (1976), broadcast on National Public Radio and the BBC.[11] Albee has also staged plays by fellow dramatists Lanford Wilson, Sam Shepard and David Mamet, as well as those by Beckett.[12]

Albee's views about rehearsal strategies and the dynamics of performance, moreover, are informed by his long experience in substantially influencing first productions of his plays staged by other directors. The *New York Times* pointed out in 1968 that unlike other playwrights—"new . . . [or] established"—"Edward Albee has managed to take control of virtually all of the pertinent aspects of the production of his own work."[13] Vigorously exercising the prerogative ensured him by the Dramatists' Guild standard contract, Albee from early in his career has been actively involved in most aspects of production, from the choice of director, designers, and cast—including understudies—to the specifics of settings, costumes, properties, and lighting. Alan Schneider recounts in his autobiography, *Entrances: An American Director's Journey,* that halfway through the rehearsals of ***The Zoo Story,*** even though the playwright was receiving his first American production, Albee, together with producer Richard Barr, fired director Milton Katseals and took over the directing, a change not indicated in the program.[14] During the casting of the Broadway production of ***A Delicate Balance*** in 1966, Schneider writes, "My dream of working with Alfred Lunt and Lynn Fontanne vanished" because "Edward was determined to assert his writer's prerogative."[15] Similarly during the Broadway rehearsals of ***The Lady From Dubuque*** that I observed, Albee's preference for a simple set and minimal properties frequently prevailed over Schneider's desire to introduce small set pieces and properties to convey a lived-in feeling or to illustrate information.[16]

Albee's assertions in the following pages thus compel attention because they are grounded in more than three decades of broad practical experience in the American theatre and because they reveal the thinking of an eminent playwright about his most acclaimed work. The way Albee articulates his artistic concerns, moreover, offers a glimpse into his personal sensibility. Above all, without suggesting some naive intentionalism, Albee's views on ***Who's Afraid of Virginia Woolf?*** and its appropriate realization on stage constitute important testimony about his dramaturgical and directorial aesthetic, a testimony invigorated by the immediacy of dialogue.

[Solomon]: *You have spoken of the importance of subtext in the rehearsal process. Did you re-examine the subtext in* Who's Afraid of Virginia Woolf? *prior to your rehearsals in Los Angeles?*

[Albee]: No. I don't prepare that. When I'm doing a play that I've written, I just say it, and the subtext comes to my consciousness. I'm already aware of it.

Did you work on the actors' getting to understand the subtext?

Oh yes, of course, when they don't; but if they're very bright, they do to begin with. Subtext is more important than text even, sometimes. So long as they understand subtext. I'm trying to think of one specific thing with Glenda Jackson in ***Virginia Woolf*** that she didn't understand. Now, I can't remember the very specifics of it. One of the things that I tried to emphasize in the production and finally got Glenda to do—and I'm getting Carol to do here for the most part—is to understand that what they're doing is exorcising a metaphor. Something they both realize is a metaphor, and that it is not the death of a real child. There is a distinction between the death of a metaphor and the death of a real child. And the play for me is more touching and more chilling if it is the death of a metaphor. That's one of the things I'm trying to emphasize in this production. And I think I am getting the through-line of the exorcism of the fantasy-child metaphor a little clearer this time.

Have you seen productions where the intellectual experience is totally absent?

Yes, I have, and I don't like them at all. They're terrible.

Where was the emphasis in the original production that Alan Schneider directed?

I thought it was a little bit toward the emotional. Just a little bit too much.

Compared to your present production?

You see, that production got criticized by a couple of critics . . . I remember Walter Kerr said he couldn't believe that a couple as intelligent as George and Martha could believe that they had a child.[17] They never *did* believe it. So, either he intentionally misunderstood, or the production led him to misunderstand.[18] So that's one of the reasons I started directing this play: to correct that misinterpretation of the nature of the play. Now it may be the play that way—not my way—is a more wrenching emotional experience. I don't know. I tend to think not. I think the mind and the gut together are better involved than one at the expense of the other.

Compared to the 1962 production, have you cut the playing time much more here?

I don't remember what those timings were. I think this may be a little brisker.

Reviews of your 1976 production mentioned how much faster everything seemed.

Seemed. I don't imagine that the difference was more than two or three minutes in each act. But that adds up. This production is just as brisk as the one in 1976.

The 1976 production was much brisker than Alan's 1962 production.

Well, yes. That's true.

And funnier too.

But none of the lines were changed.

Talking of changes . . . you made several changes in your text for this production.

Oh very few. The major change that I made was cutting out the reference to the child in the first scene of the play, which is unnecessary.[19] The other cuts I've made here—what? A word here, two or three words there. That's all. Just for rhythms.[20]

One change does seem to be a big one. Martha's "Truth and illusion, George; you don't know the difference" has become, "Truth and illusion, George; you know the difference." Correspondingly, George's "No; but we must carry on as though we did" has become, "Yes; but we must carry on as though we did not."[21]

Oh well, that's because I wrote it incorrectly to begin with.

How come you didn't notice that earlier?

I don't know. A mind lapse.

Not a change of mind?

No. No, no. No. No, no. It's just that I mis-wrote myself—I didn't put it down correctly.

In your discussion with the actors about it, you kept saying, "That's a very minor matter. That's a very minor matter." Do you really think so?

No, it's a major matter. But what they meant by "major," they wanted to go back to doing it wrong.

Why did you cut George's comment, "What will happen to the tax deduction? Has anyone figured that out yet?" when he speaks of the time when people will make babies in test tubes?[22]

The playwright got better! Logically, couples with children would get tax deductions no matter how their babies were made.

You also deleted the exchange between George and Martha where she suddenly and flagrantly denies Nick and Honey's existence in their living room but then without explanation accepts their presence.[23]

It made Martha too unreasonable.

Did you wish to stress Martha's loquaciousness by substituting "mouth" for "nose" in George's retort, "In my mind, Martha, you are buried in cement, right up to your neck. No . . . right up to your nose . . . that's much quieter."?[24]

Yes, and it makes it clearer and nicer.

Why did you cut one of George's two identical announcements, "Pow!!! You're dead! Pow! You're dead!" when he pulls the trigger of his fake Japanese gun?[25]

Once is enough. Besides, I didn't want the actors to get any ideas!

*Did you think the cuts in Mike Nichol's film version of **Virginia Woolf** were major ones?*

Yes, of course. They took out the whole historical-political argument of the play. They took out the business about science and a number of other things that the play happens to be about.

When directing this 1962 script in 1989-90, did you reconsider things?

No, I don't consciously do that. I've not tried to update this play. I don't think people walked in a different way in the sixties than they do in the eighties. Or even thought in that much of a different way.

In many ways, Nick's values resemble those associated with Yuppies in the eighties.

All good literature is supposed to anticipate the future. True; it does, you know. What I was suggesting was that people who are wise enough to untrick themselves may be better off. I think the least self-deception that people can live with, the better. Well, what does change is audience perception. But you can't go around trying to second guess audience perception, because you distort your work.

Because of changed audience perception, when I taught ***The Zoo Story*** *at the University of California at Santa Cruz, I had to defend Jerry and his viewpoint.*

Well, of course. We're a nation of conformists now. I find that self-deception leads not only to personal trouble but to political malaise and to social irresponsibility. The self-deception that this country has been dealing in for many years now is preferring to be lied to by political leaders, preferring to be conned by short-term values. We may find ourselves in a much greater state of decline than people realize now. Audiences, when they were a little freer with themselves, used to think ***The American Dream*** was very funny. But now you do ***The American Dream*** for a middle-aged audience, and they sit there in silent hostility.

Hostile towards the playwright?

They don't like examining themselves any more. They get very angry about it. Shocking to me.

Why is George so angry at Martha's story about his career—more angry than he is when she mentions the child?

Attrition. Time, time, time, time. It's something—the career—about him being a flop and a failure and not living up to . . . This is something that she—every time she gets a few drinks in her and a little audience—she starts on it. After twenty-three years you get fairly tired of it. You just can't stand it anymore.

Still, I was comparing that anger to the anger that I expected and the anguish I expected when Martha reveals the son to the guests.

Well, George's involvement with the son has never been as emotional as Martha's has. Neither of them literally believes it, but Martha slips into believing it probably because she's a woman. Women and their relation to children, their wombs, and the whole thing. Her involvement with the son is more personal and emotional than George's is.

But George's greater passion about his career throws me off because I thought the emotional focus would remain on the betrayal of the closely-held, private arrangement.

That's interesting. I must look at that. Maybe I'm doing something wrong.

The import of Martha's disclosure seems to get submerged under George's fury.

Mm. I'll look at that. Maybe I have changed my mind about a few things over the years.

In the opening scene when Martha mentions that Honey, the guest they are expecting, has small hips, John Lithgow used to add with some relish, "Oh, God!" It got laughs. It's a small joke, but I'm sure you didn't eliminate it without some reason. Why did you cut that out? Do you think there's a lack of logic?

I think it's a cheap joke. It's a cheap joke. And also it doesn't make any sense. Because George . . .

George says he likes "everything in proportion," and he is not attracted to Honey when she arrives.

Yes. And he does *not* like women without hips. Martha has hips. Martha's ample. It's illogical. John Lithgow and Glenda Jackson liked it. It was a cheap joke, and they liked it. John and Glenda also barked at each other "Woolf! Woolf!" on George's "You'll crack your big teeth."[26] I hated that too. You have to give them little things every once in a while.

You were thinking aloud about how George knows that Martha has been talking about him, when he returns with the liquor from offstage. I think George knows because he comes in on Martha's line about him, "along come George."[27]

If he's heard that coming in, then it's all right. Let's see: "But then George came along . . . along come George," and George reenters. I guess he knows. I guess he knows. I guess it's clear. I believe in being my own devil's advocate from time to time.

If you want to be objective when directing your own work.

Exactly.

After Martha's great howl, "NOOOOOOoooooo," at the finality of George's decision to kill the child, in this production George tells Nick, "She'll be alright now" I think rather quickly.[28]

I gave him a note two days ago not to do that so quickly.

It kept happening.

Yes. I'll remind him. Thank you for reminding me.

Such a quick comment suggests much more premeditation on George's part.

Yes, it does. I should give him that note almost immediately.

I've often wondered about the reference to Crazy Billy, "some little boy about seventy," when George announces the telegram regarding their son's death.[29]

Oh, a friend of mine Bill Flanagan, the composer; he and I worked at Western Union together, and I used to always kid him about how much older he was than me. So, a "little boy about seventy." It's just a private joke.

Another question about a topical reference and possibly subtext. George tells Nick that the abstract painting in their living room was done by "some Greek with a mustache Martha attacked one night."[30]*Is that a reference to the Greek-American artist you know?*

Theodorus Stamos.

Do you own any of his works?

Yes. A couple.

And what was the subtext you suggested to George? During a rehearsal you told him that one evening Martha went to that painter's home and kept . . .

Kept putting the make on him, and then he gave her a painting to get rid of her.

Why did you introduce a picture of Mahatma Gandhi?

Well . . .

Why Gandhi's picture on the living room bookshelf?

It occurred to me that George and Martha are two people who in their growing up in the the 1940s, in their innocent liberalism, admired both Roosevelt and Gandhi very much.

I sense a degree of pacifism in George. Though he doesn't say it, it's probably because of his pacifism that he didn't go to fight in the war. He stayed back and ran the History department.

I don't know why he didn't go. Maybe he was a conscientious objector. It never occurred to me. That's interesting. You do not find Gandhi worthy of admiration?

Oh I do, yes.

Yes. Well, I do too.

Certainly, I was just curious—after all your Oriental jokes!

That Oriental joke is meant to be intentionally in bad taste.[31]

On George's part, of course.

Yes. It's meant to be a parody of the sort of barroom, you know, locker room talk that jocks do together.

How can Honey recite the Latin mass for the dead when she grew up in a fundamentalist home?

I don't understand that. I don't know why. There are depths to that girl that I haven't figured out yet.

All throughout the rehearsals, it seems to me, you gave many more directions to the actor who plays George than to the actor who plays Martha.

Well, George is on stage almost all the time during the entire play. He has many more lines. He also controls the psychological arc of the play. He is in control of the entire arc of the play the entire time. And therefore, I have to be more concerned with making sure that his performance doesn't deviate from my intention, more than I have to be with the other actors. Last night, the notes that I gave him I want to talk to him about again because I didn't do that quite as well as I might have. It's just that more can go wrong. And it has been more tightly controlled. I think the notes I try to give to all of them are fundamental notes as to the nature of characterization. And also I try to give people notes when I see danger signals. When I see they're doing things that I know are going to get them in trouble later in the play. Or distort the character. Now, Bruce Gray [George] is a highly inventive, highly shrewd, and highly skilled actor. And therefore he's more apt to go astray.

And Carol Mayo Jenkins [Martha], in contrast, is . . .

Well, no . . . There is less opportunity for Martha to go astray than there is for George. Let's put it that way.

It must be so since you are saying it, but it is surprising, nonetheless.

Also they're very different kinds of actors. Carol sets performance. We see the gold of the performance. Bruce is constantly shifting his characterization. And now he's gone to the point where I have to bring him back. He's gone too far. he's become baroque and mannered and artificial. And I have to bring him back to truth. And every actor—no two actors work the same way. No two actors work at the same speed. No two actors have the same way of working. So you have to work differently.

Why no rehearsals the last three days [i.e. before one evening technical rehearsal and two evening performances for invited audiences]?

There comes a certain point in rehearsal where if you think the actors know pretty much where you want them to be and what you want them to be doing, you have to let them play the role for a while. And play with the audience. And then after a few days of watching them with the audience, then you can see whether they're going in the right direction or not. You can over-rehearse in theory. I mean, theoretical rehearsal should stop at a certain point, and real rehearsal should start.

What are real rehearsals?

Well . . .

Rehearsals after they've played in front of invited preview audiences?

Yes. That's a different kind of rehearsal.

So you plan to do more work.

I'll do some work next week [with three scheduled previews]. I'll do some work after they open, too.

I haven't noticed you rehearse short scenes in painstaking detail, orchestrating every element. I know you like to give actors general intention notes, and you expect them to come up with the specifics. You used to do that in 1978 when I first saw you; these are more experienced actors by and large, and you can do that more safely. However, sometimes I wonder whether detailed scene work might not benefit this production.

All you tell an actor when you do that, ultimately, is how *you* would do the scene. That doesn't tell them how *they* should do the scene. Then you're asking them to imitate rather than be. That's a last resort. If you can't get it any other way, then you do that. But you've noticed that I *am* very specific, when they miss a beat, or I tell them to wait a beat before they say a line, or accent this word rather than that word. That's very specific stuff.

I understand you give specific notes as well, but I was thinking of sustained moment-to-moment work on selected segments. After the two invited audiences, too, you haven't addressed matters of tempo, speed, and so on.

I didn't find them shifting all that much. I did tell them that the top of three was slow, which it was again. I think they generally know what they're supposed to be doing. Generally.

You've worked with other directors—Alan Schneider, Peter Hall, Franco Zeffirelli—when they've staged your plays. Did you come across closer scene work in their rehearsals?

No, not really.

Not really? Do you have an overall rhythm that you are working for?

I must. I must. Yes, of course. I mean each two minute section has its rhythms. And these rhythms combine to give the whole rhythm of an act, and the three acts give the rhythm of the whole piece.

Do you build towards certain tempos . . .

Most you establish at the very beginning. Now you must remember with these actors here, they sat in from the very first day of rehearsal with Glenda Jackson and John Lithgow. And I spent a lot of time with them the first week discussing character motivation. Everything that I didn't have to discuss here because those actors were there.

Yes, I am aware that they are even borrowing things. Certainly, they're borrowing blocking and even characterization.

Sure. Blocking is fine. Let them borrow that.

Even sometimes rhythms and certain bits of business.

Yes. That's o.k.

So I'm aware that they got a lot of guidance from you in Los Angeles too. But are there some things that you would rather not see here in Houston?

A few of George's mannerisms.

I don't know what his mimicking the child is about.

It's that mimicking I want to remove. It's getting in the way.

While directing were you tempted to include a few asides to the audience?

In this play? No. It's an absolutely naturalistic play. None of my naturalistic plays has direct addresses to the audience. It's only the stylized ones.

I thought there was an aside phase in your career when you introduced asides into earlier texts while directing, as you did with a few plays I saw you stage a few years ago.

In some of my plays, maybe eight or ten of them, people speak to the audience. But those are mostly the stylized plays. It doesn't happen in the naturalistic ones. This is a naturalistic play. All the . . . classical . . . unities and everything. The whole thing.

Why don't you write another one with classical unities and all that?

I have. It's called ***Marriage Play.***

Having directed it in Vienna, will you direct its American premiere as well?

Sure. I'll direct it on Broadway.

Do you have a Broadway producer for ***Marriage Play****?*

Michael Harvey, a young producer who's produced with Richard [Barr] and other people—somebody I've known for twenty-five years because he was very young.

From observing you rehearse ***Who's Afraid of Virginia Woolf?****, I could deduce some of your directorial ideals. When you teach, what kinds of goals and principles of directing do you posit?*

You certainly should have a vision of the way you think the play wants to be performed when you start directing it. Yet at the same time, you must also be ready to shift when you find that the play is somewhat other than you imagined it, or there are other values that you hadn't seen. But you must have an overall vision of the piece. With any production, ninety percent of it is casting. If you cast properly, if you cast correctly—intelligent, gifted actors—our job is so much easier. You don't have to do the line by line thing. Directing, of course, is a lot of knowing how to work with actors. The first two weeks are basically subtext work, so actors really understand why the character behaves the way the character does in a certain section.

What about visual matters? What about rhythm?

Well, there's always a visual thing. You have to stage pictures that you create in your mind. You do have rhythms that you're after. There's tension, release of tension, passive and active moments. And you've got to populate the stage properly in all of those, in all of those times. There's a tie-in between the visual picture and the psychology of the piece, of course, always. Who is moving? Who is standing still? Who's sitting? The tempo of the speeches. The intentions. All of that has to be put together. So it is a combination of music and painting and literature at the same time. You have all three of them.

How do you teach this in your directing class?

I don't teach directing as much as I teach playwriting. I don't *teach* playwriting, either.

There's an apparent contradiction: on many occasions, you have said that you can't teach playwriting, yet you do teach playwriting at universities.

You can't teach. No, you can't. I referee. I point out the way things . . . When I work with playwrights, I try to make sure that they are accomplishing what they want. And then we may discuss possibly whether it's what they should want. I don't try to make them rewrite a play according to the way I think a play should be written. I try to make them write the play so that it really is what they think they've accomplished. With a lot of young playwrights, there's a great difference between what they *think* they've written and what they *have* written. It's not only simple things like that great thirty-second silence that they all request for that important psychological moment, when they need five or four seconds at the most. They just don't think in stage terms. And I try to make them see the play and hear the play on a stage while they write it. That saves an awful lot of time.

In your directing classes, too, I assume you ask students to bring in scenes, and then you referee rather than say . . .

Yeah. Well, I like to look at them working with actors and see if they're working with the actors properly. Also, I like to see if they understand the shape of the play, if they understand the intention. And the why's: "Why did you do it this way?" "Why didn't you do it that way?" And I say, "Try it that way and see how different it is." Then they learn from the experience of doing things in different ways. The one thing I've never been able to accomplish yet in class, and I would love to do it, is to have a young playwright with his new play that he's never seen on stage before and have it rehearsed in two situations separately. One with the author and a young director and a group of actors working without any interference from anybody else. And then me directing the play with professional actors or with another group of actors. And then to do these two scenes one after the other and see the distinction and the difference. It would be instructive for the playwright, and for me, too.

Notes

[1]For further details see Everett Evans, "Alley's 'Virginia Woolf' to play in Soviet Union," *Houston Chronicle* (3 January 1990): Sec. D: 1, and Richard Coe, "Lone Star Over Lithuania," *American Theatre* (September, 1990): 22-27.

[2]Politics caused a last-minute cancellation of the engagement at the Sovremennik Theatre, where artistic director Galina Volchek had herself played Martha in a Russian production of *Who's Afraid of Virginia Woolf?* Coe, 24.

[3]Albee has cited this production on several occasions; for example, see the account of his press conference in Barbara Selvin, "Albee directs Albee," *Village Times* (Stony Brook, NY: 24 August 1978): 7.

[4]Dan Sullivan, "Theater: Albee's 'Bessie Smith' and 'Dream' Revived," *New York Times* (3 October 1968): 55.

[5]Clive Barnes, "Albee's 'Seascape' Is a Major Event," *New York Times* (27 January 1975).

[6]Frank Rich, "Stage: Drama by Albee: 'Man Who Had Three Arms'" *New York Times* (6 April 1983).

[7]Clive Barnes, "Stage: 'Virginia Woolf,'" *New York Times* (2 April 1976): Sec. 2: 1.

[8]Edward Albee, *Counting the Ways and Listening: Two Plays.* (New York: Atheneum, 1977), 4, 56.

[9]"Morning Report . . . Stage," *Los Angeles Times* (14 May 1987): Sec. 6: p. 2.

[10]David Richards, "Edward Albee and the Road Not Taken," *New York Times* (16 June 1991): 14.

[11]Albee, *Counting the Ways,* 56.

[12]Rakesh H. Solomon, "Albee Directs 'Ohio Impromptu' and 'Krapp's Last Tape'" *Beckett Circle* 12. 2 (1991): 1-2; "Notizen," *Theater heute* 26 (November 1985): 67; and John Ottavino, personal interview, 4 January 1990.

[13]Barbara La Fontaine, "Triple Treat on, Off and Off-Off Broadway," *New York Times* (25 February 1968): 42.

[14]Alan Schneider, *Entrances: An American Director's Journey.* (New York: Viking, 1986): 275.

[15]Schneider, *Entrances,* 374.

[16]For more details see my "Crafting Script into Performance: Edward Albee in Rehearsal," *American Drama* 2.2 (Spring 1993): 76-99.

[17]See Walter Kerr, "First Night Report: 'Who's Afraid of Virginia Woolf?'" *New York Herald Tribune* (15 October 1962): 12.

[18]Like Albee, Alan Schneider also chafes at this critical misinterpretation more than twenty years later; unlike Albee, however, Schneider attributes the problem entirely to the reviewer's obtuseness. See Schneider, *Entrances,* 324.

[19]The largest deletion—a page and a quarter in the standard Atheneum edition of the play—contained George's six insistent warnings to Martha not to mention their kid when their guests arrive, and Martha's defiant claim to a right to bring up any subject; *Who's Afraid of Virginia Woolf?* (New York: Atheneum, 1962): 19-20. The second set of excised references consisted of two similar but cryptic exchanges after their guests arrive; *Virginia Woolf?,* 30. The simplicity of Albee's explanation for these deletions belies their inevitable dramaturgic and thematic import.

[20]Although Albee slights these changes, many of them serve to achieve dramatic economy, refine characterization, eliminate ambiguity, or correct faulty logic, as seen in examples below.

[21]*Virginia Woolf?,* 202.

[22]*Virginia Woolf?,* 40.

[23]Martha: "We're alone!" / George: "Uh . . . no, Love . . . we've got guests." / Martha (With a covetous look at Nick): "We sure have." *Virginia Woolf?*, 121.

[24]*Virginia Woolf?*, 64.

[25]*Virginia Woolf?*, 57.

[26]*Virginia Woolf?*, 14.

[27]*Virginia Woolf?*, 80.

[28]*Virginia Woolf?*, 233.

[29]*Virginia Woolf?*, 230.

[30]*Virginia Woolf?*, 21.

[31]According to Albee, public relations people in the Los Angeles production sought unsuccessfully to remove the Oriental references.

Interview with Albee (1991)

SOURCE: An interview with Edward Albee, in *The Playwright's Art: Conversations with Contemporary American Dramatists,* edited by Jackson R. Bryer, Rutgers University Press, 1995, pp. 1-23.

[*The following interview, conducted by Laurence Maslon, was held in the fall of 1991 as part of the "Conversations with Leading American Playwrights" series sponsored by the Smithsonian Institution's Campus on the Mall program. Albee here discusses his approach to play writing and offers his views on the state of American theater.*]

[Laurence Maslon]*: Why are you a playwright?*

[Edward Albee]: Why am I a playwright? Because it's the only thing that I can do halfway decently. If there was anything else I could do, I probably would do it.

Weren't you a poet first?

I attempted poetry, I attempted novels, I wrote short stories and essays—and they were all terrible. I tried to be a composer and that didn't work, I tried to be a painter and that didn't work; I even did sculpture and then there was nothing left, so I started writing plays.

What about being a playwright appeals to you the most?

The fact that I am one, I think. When I started writing plays, I discovered that's what I should have been doing all along. I am a playwright, therefore I write plays; it's not that I write plays and therefore I am a playwright.

How do you feel about the production process? Is it an impediment or is it part of the process?

The great joy is in writing the play, in the creative act itself. Seeing the play produced, if it is produced well, if it is produced honorably and honestly and to the playwright's intention, that's great. But a first-rate play exists completely on the page and is never improved by production; it's only proved by production. All these people who go around saying that a play is just there for actors and directors to turn into a work of art—that's nuts. The creative act, the writing of the play when a playwright sees it and hears it performed on a stage as he writes it, is the best production he'll ever see of a play of his that's any good.

*You once said that **The Sandbox** was the only one of your plays that approached perfection.*

No, I said it was the only one in which I thought I didn't have time to make any mistakes.

Because it was only fifteen minutes long?

Because it was only fifteen minutes long—and I even wrote a shorter one called ***Box.***

Do you think that's more perfect?

Well, I made fewer mistakes in that one since I didn't have as much time.

"There was a time when good plays, plays that were not constructed for the mass market only but plays that were honest with themselves and also honest with the historical continuum of the theatre, there was a time when those plays could run on Broadway, if they didn't get the critical nod. That's no longer true." That statement is certainly true now, but you said it in the summer of 1963.

Well, it's even worse now, isn't it? I just think we should forget about Broadway—ignore it, leave it to the Shubert Organization and the other real estate groups, leave it to the advertising department of the *New York Times* and just ignore it, turn our backs on it completely. The American theatre is in pretty good shape; it exists in the minds of its playwrights, it exists in the majority of its regional theatres, at least those who haven't turned into tryout houses for the Broadway theatres. It exists in the experimental off-Broadway theatres, and it exists in university theatres. Let's just ignore Broadway; it doesn't have anything to do with anything anymore.

To what degree was that quote true in 1963? We usually think of that as some golden time.

We playwrights are supposed to think ahead a little bit and see trends. Even then it was getting clear to me that trouble was about to happen. The star system, the economics of the theatre, the desire of people who were putting on plays to make them as safe and ersatz as film and television: all those forces were beginning to get deeply rooted. The fact that now they have completely taken over the commercial theatre in the United States is sad, but a lot of us saw it coming back in 1963.

When you had your first successes in the sixties, it seemed that America was starting to ask some more questions. Do you think we've lost that edge as theatregoers?

The early sixties were very interesting because off-Broadway had its birth around 1960. We were a society that asked a lot of questions about ourselves then. We've certainly gone away from that. At least for over twenty years now we seem to want our theatre more and more to lie to us: to tell half-truths, to be escapist, to be comforting, to say that "we are fine" rather than hold the mirror up to us as it's supposed to and ask the tough questions. God knows, film and television can't do it in this country anymore. Because of economics, the theatre can, and it's a pity that it's being discouraged from doing that.

Your work confirms the fact that you are a very provocative playwright who likes to prod the audience into using their head. Is that job tougher for you now?

No, I keep right on doing it. It's not tougher for me. Apparently it's tougher for the audience, which indirectly, I suppose, makes it tougher for me, since I like to eat as much as anybody else does. But no, I don't find it any tougher to do. As a matter of fact, I find more of a need to do it.

Since we're in Washington, and since many find the way we fund art in America pretty reprehensible, have we gotten the sort of artistic support that we deserve?

The amount of money that is funded for the education of the public in the arts is ludicrously small, and the attempt on the part of both the know-nothings and the cynics who know better to try to cut that funding is criminal. We have so much waste in our government. There is so damn much pork barrel legislation which transcends the minimal amounts we give to the arts. We would be much better off to support the arts until people couldn't stand it anymore. We should support the arts to such an extent that participation in the arts becomes as natural as breathing.

As an inveterate museumgoer, do you think that theatres should have the kind of accessibility that museums do—with ticket prices that allow more people to attend?

This whole thing about ticket prices is so confusing. The fact that people are willing to spend seven dollars and fifty cents to see appalling movies leads me to conclude that maybe you could charge a little bit more to see a play by Chekhov. I don't know. Maybe people should be willing to pay a little bit more to see a great play than a lousy movie, but God knows there is something wrong with our serious culture in this country when our theatre is more often than not in the possession of the upper middle class which happens to be white. Most of our arts are, as a matter of fact, in possession of that group, and we are a far more diverse society than that. The fact that we have not been able to make our more serious arts broader in scope is deeply troubling to me. That's only partly economic, and it's partly educational as well. It has to do with the double social standard we have in this country.

You've funded different foundations to support artists yourself and are supportive of artists in general. Are there different ways we might go about funding artists in our society from the way we do it?

My foundation doesn't fund artists. It provides a place where painters and sculptors and writers and composers can come and live and work and have some freedom to do their work without financial pressure and also have the opportunity to intermingle with people in the other arts, which they don't normally get the chance to do. In an ideal society we wouldn't need to be funding our creative artists, but the vast majority of the money that goes into the support of the arts in the United States does not go to the support of the creative artist. It goes to things. It goes to buildings; it goes to existing organizations which may or may not be interested in producing the work of living creative artists. I bet no more than 5 percent—and I would say that is maybe a generous figure—of the money that goes to the support of the arts in this country goes to the support of the creative artist individually. I've sat on grant-giving councils all over the place, including the National Endowment and the New York State Council on the Arts, and in both places (although it may have changed in the National Endowment by now) it was assumed that money should be spread around. It should be spread around to institutions, in the Dakotas as well as in more urban areas, on the assumption that, for example, there must be as many first-rate composers of string quartets in Dubuque as there are in New York. I worry when I see millions of dollars of New York State music grant money going not to support worthwhile composers but to support a symphony orchestra somewhere up near, but not in, Buffalo. I'm not sure that we have our priorities correct.

God knows, we should try to make the arts available to all people, but we should not use any kind of federal funding, any grant funding, to lower the standard of the arts, which is quite often what we do, on the assumption that to bring the arts to a large number of people you've got to lower the standard of what is brought to the people. There is a corruption in that that should be avoided. We're talking about such a small amount of money. We're talking about, what, for the National Endowment, $126 million a year, when our deficit this year is going to be $350 billion, and our budget is $2 trillion or some preposterous sum? The amount of extra money that it would cost to do proper funding for the individual creative artist is so tiny, it's almost absurd to have to talk about it.

In the eighties, there was a lot of work and time spent in workshopping plays and developing plays.

That's a term I hate—the verb "to workshop." When did that become a verb, by the way?

Back in the sixties you started Playwrights Sixty-Six, where you worked with up-and-coming playwrights.

We did the first productions of an awful lot of young playwrights including Terrence McNally, Lanford Wilson, Sam Shepard, LeRoi Jones, Adrienne Kennedy, and on and on and on. But one thing we did not do is "workshop." We assumed that these plays were just fine as they were; we liked their rough edges. Most "workshopping" rounds the rough edges of plays so that they can't stick into anybody's mind. It rounds the edges and shaves them down and makes them accessible and acceptable. Plays are meant to be tough and jagged and wrong-headed and angry and all the things that "workshopping" all too often destroys. So we didn't workshop plays. We took angry, tough, imperfect plays, and we put them on the stage, and everybody had a good time.

Have directors become too collaborative in that process, do you think, over the years?

Let's put it this way: as a metaphor or a simile, whichever you like, for a play let us take a string quartet composed by a composer. Let's go back to Beethoven's time, okay? Nobody workshops a string quartet. The first violinist doesn't get together with the second violinist and say, "You know, the composer wrote a C-sharp there; we don't like that, do we? Let's make that into an F." Everybody—directors and actors and producers and dramaturgs and theatre owners and theatre managers—feels that a play is there to be collaborated upon. A play is a work of art, for Christ's sake! You shouldn't do a play that needs to be collaborated upon; you should do a play that you respect and want to do to its total virtue. The idea of directors feeling that they are creative artists rather than interpretive artists, and of actors feeling that they are creative rather than interpretive artists, is so much bullshit. And it's done serious damage to our theatre. We get critics who think that they have the right to be collaborative artists as well—and then we're really fucked up.

Have we lost the ability to trust a playwright?

I don't think we've lost the ability to do it. Somewhere along the line it's become the assumption that the playwright is there to be worked upon instead of letting the playwright work his magic upon other people.

Is that the lack of strong producers who have had commitments to works?

No, it's the fault of strong producers who feel it is their property. Unless you're going to do improvisatory theatre, you can't do it without the playwright. Playwrights, generally speaking, are given a pretty hard time these days. They're not being treated with—I hate the word "respect," but it's a good one. You hear it too infrequently in the arts these days. They are not being given the respect that they deserve.

You were lucky, as you've said in print, that you had a director in your early career, in Alan Schneider, who respected your work.

Alan once said to me that only on two occasions in his professional life (and neither was with a play of mine, I'm happy to say) did he direct a play that he didn't respect. This led him to respect an awful lot of unpopular plays by Beckett, by me, by various other people—but Alan did respect the play. He did not believe that a play should be rewritten during the rehearsal period, did not believe that a play should be rewritten to accommodate the taste of the audience or to accommodate the diminished talents of the actors. If they were diminished talents, he felt that the play was there to be served. Alan did something very, very interesting that taught me a lot both as a playwright and when I became a director as well. Alan would come to me weeks before rehearsal began on a new play of mine with hundreds of questions that he wanted to ask me about my intentions—about the characters, who they were, what their background was. We had several sessions of hundreds of questions each, and it was useful to me because I discovered that I really did know things about my plays and about my characters that I hadn't known because nobody had asked me before. It also indicated to me that he was not going to wing it, that he was going to do what the playwright intended—and that was a very, very good lesson for me.

It's got to be more than mere coincidence that you and Alan Schneider met over a Beckett play.

It is a coincidence that we met over a Beckett play unless you want to assume fate. What are you getting at?

Beckett's been an author you've admired, an author you've been influenced by?

Oh God, yes! Sam Beckett invented twentieth-century drama and made all sorts of amazing things both possible and impossible for the rest of us. Possible because he opened up so many doors and windows for what could be done, and impossible because we all realized we couldn't do it as well as he did. Meeting Alan was nice, but meeting Beckett was much more important.

Do you think that Beckett has been well assimilated, now that Godot *has become a classic?*

I wish you wouldn't say *Godot*. I don't think it's his best play; everybody else does, but I don't. What does "assimilated" mean?

That he's become acknowledged at least by critics and scholars and students to be one of the major playwrights, if not the major playwright, of the twentieth century. Gradually, we've been able to incorporate him and understand him better.

We certainly don't produce him very much, I'll tell you that. I think if you assimilate someone into your culture you give them the respect of producing their work from time to time. I teach down at the University of Houston, and I work quite a lot at the Alley Theatre there, which is a good regional theatre. Last winter I directed a double bill of two of Beckett's plays—*Krapp's Last Tape* and *Ohio Impromptu*—and I discovered in the history of the Alley Theatre it was the second time they had done a production of Beckett's plays, which is astonishing. We were talking about Broadway earlier. You think about the number of playwrights who are not produced in what is meant to be the American theatre in any one given season, the number of playwrights who are not on Broadway this year (well, there aren't any playwrights on Broadway this year), the number of playwrights who regularly do not get produced in our commercial theatres: like Sophocles and Aristophanes and Euripides; and maybe Shakespeare now and again if it's set in Spanish Harlem maybe. Or if the right TV star wants to do it. And Racine, Molière, Beckett, Chekhov, Ibsen, Pirandello—these people are not performed in our commercial theatre. In our theatre consciousness as a theatregoing public, I don't think we've assimilated any of the great playwrights.

But since 1963, when you made the quote that I mentioned earlier, those playwrights are being done. They aren't being done in New York, but they are being done in resident and regional theatres on an ongoing basis. If you take your first statement, which is let's forget about New York anyway, then is it just as well that they are being done around the country?

When I went to Berlin in 1959 for the world premiere of my play ***The Zoo Story,*** I noticed what was being done on the Broadway stages of West Berlin of that time, and it was interesting. It was Brecht, it was Beckett, it was Goethe of course; it was the great playwrights. Maybe that's what prompted those remarks that I made, because I noticed that that wasn't happening in those days on Broadway, from which we took guidance as to what the nature of theatre was. What a bizarre country we are, where our commercial theatre does not concern itself with great art. I'm delighted that those regional theatres that aren't behaving like tryout houses for Broadway are living up to their responsibilities and are doing some of the great plays, balanced nicely with more easily salable stuff usually. I think that's fine. It's the very least they can do, but I don't think that doing the very least they can do is ever enough.

I also have a theory—I've had it for a long time; I've probably been wrong for a long time, but I still have it—that there is nothing innately corrupt about the taste of the American people. It is that they are not given the opportunity of choice, of being able to choose between that which is really good and that which is mediocre. I'm convinced that if not only our Broadway theatres but our regional theatres were secretly funded so that a group of very, very good people (I'd like to be in the group, of course) could decide what plays would be done, and these were the plays that the American audience had access to for a period of ten or fifteen years, I'm convinced that that would probably become the taste of the American theatregoing audience.

I had a long talk with Walter Kerr one night many years ago. He pointed out to me that something really terrible has happened to American taste because back in the Greek days, and in Shakespeare's day, everybody was pouring in to see plays by Sophocles. And I said that there wasn't anything else to do; that's the only entertainment they had; they had to do that. And he said, "Well, what about the Globe Theatre in Shakespeare's day?" And I said that there were three entertainments available to people in Elizabethan England: there were executions, there was bear-baiting, and there was *King Lear.* The people who couldn't get in to the bear-baiting and the executions went to see *King Lear.* Translate bear-baiting and executions into movies and television today. The people who can't get in to the bear-baiting and who can't get in to the executions go to the live theatre.

When you first started writing, you were labeled as part of the group of writers known as the Theatre of the Absurd, but you have an active dislike of labels.

Only when they are inaccurate. When Martin Esslin coined the name Theatre of the Absurd, it was a philosophical concept; but somehow very, very quickly it got translated into being stylistic. So a Theatre of the Absurd play was not a naturalistic play, and that made the whole thing ridiculous. That's when I stared getting fussy about it.

Someone once asked John Gielgud, a man who should know, what style was, and he said, "Style is simply knowing what play you're in."

Exactly. All plays are naturalistic and all plays are highly stylized, because there is no such thing as naturalism except for maybe Paddy Chayevsky and a few other people.

If people walked into a theatre and didn't know it was your play playing there, what would you like them to notice about it to indicate to them that it was your play?

If they knew my work, perhaps there is a sound that my plays make; maybe there is an Albee sound, but I can't find it, I'm not aware of it. Maybe some of my preoccupations and concerns about how we lie to each other—the truths we tell, the evasions—would be prevalent in the play. Beyond that I don't know. I'd like to think that if they're willing to be engaged they'd have an involving time and maybe, possibly, come out changed, conceivably even for the better.

You've often described yourself as the most eclectic playwright who ever wrote. You've tackled all sorts of different kinds of characters and situations. Is there an Albee style? Or does that change from play to play?

I don't know. People tell me to go see a play by this or that new playwright, that it sounds exactly like me; so I go to see it and I don't know what they're talking about. Style is a matter of form and content that codetermine each other. You don't try to take a subject matter that wants to be handled in a fantastic way and stick it in a naturalistic framework. The two relate to each other. There are degrees of stylization in all of my plays. None of them is naturalistic; some of them give the illusion of being more naturalistic than others. There must be a way my characters speak that defines an Albee play to an audience, but I don't know what it is because I don't think about myself in the third person.

Don't actors and directors often make the mistake of erring on the naturalistic side of plays and not enough on the stylized side?

You can't. When you act a play, no matter how stylized a play is (and I've learned this as a director too), all you can act and all you can direct is the moment-to-moment literal naturalistic truth of what is happening to the character at that particular moment. You can't act stylized unless you're a lousy actor. Even if you're in a highly stylized play, you're still acting naturalistically within that play. All of my plays are naturalistic no matter how highly stylized they are, so it's a very tricky matter. You can't act style, in the same way that you can't act metaphor. You can't act meaning; you can only act what is happening.

*Let's talk about **Seascape,** a 1975 play that is set, geographically, on a beach on Long Island, isn't it?*

The beach in ***Seascape?*** No, but I assumed that it has seasons, so it's probably somewhere in the North.

And a middle-aged couple is visited by another middle-aged couple who share some problems with each other, except the second couple are a pair of lizards who come from the sea. That's certainly not a "naturalistic" situation.

Yes, it was absolutely naturalistic. Those weren't metaphorical lizards, those weren't symbolic lizards, those were real lizards, real beach, real humans. It's the old thing with most people and comedies. Most people in comedies don't know that they are being funny. If the actor knows that he's being funny, then the play won't be funny.

*Another thing about **Seascape** that's interesting is that it had an additional act at one point.*

Yes, it did. It was a three-act play at one time. It was about as long as *Parsifal,* not quite as funny but almost as long. I took one act out because, although I had it in at the first rehearsal and I enjoyed it, it was totally unnecessary. The fact that I could remove that entire act overnight like a tooth without any damage to the sense of the play indicated to me that maybe I was being a little bit self-indulgent. So I took it out; but it was staged at some point by some people who got hold of it. Somebody did the whole damn thing in Holland, I believe. The original second act took place at the bottom of the sea. It was nice; I have it somewhere. It made a few problems for the set designer, of course, but he solved them. That was Bill Ritman, who solved them nicely.

You've talked a lot in print about how music has influenced you. How have the fine arts and design influenced you as a writer?

When you write a play, at least when I write a play, when I'm putting it down on paper anyway, and even when I'm thinking about it before I put it down on paper, I see it and I hear it. But I don't see it and hear it in some kind of amorphous general area. I see it and hear it as a performed stage piece, which saves me an awful lot of time in that I don't have to do as many rewrites as other people do, because I see it being performed on the stage. Since I see it and I hear it, I have a fairly comprehensive visual sense of what it should look like and what it should sound like as well as what it should mean. Therefore, I like to work in great detail with the set and lighting and costume designers, not insisting on this or that particularly but having a sense, because I have a sense of the specific environment. I want the set and costume and lighting and sound designers to have that same sense.

Does your interest in modern art influence the way you consciously or unconsciously put a play together or the way you see it visually?

No, I usually try to have a set that is, as Thurber put it, a container for the thing contained. I don't like to sit in the theatre and watch the set. I like sets to be efficient, and I like them not to call any attention to themselves beyond being proper containers for what's happening. As much as I admire twentieth-century art, and while I do like to see it employed both in dance and in opera even far more than it is, sometimes it can get in the way of theatre.

Boris Aronson said the best sets you should notice for two seconds.

About that. There was a time when in every play that Jo Mielziner, who was a very famous set designer, designed the following would happen: the curtain would go up, we'd be in some kind of murk, and lights would very, very slowly start appearing all over the set, and the set would start appearing, and damned if the audience didn't applaud. The set got applauded. Now that's wrong, totally wrong. Aronson's quite right; you should notice the set and then it should go away. Everything should go away in the theatre. You shouldn't be aware of acting, you shouldn't be aware of directing, you shouldn't be aware of playwriting either. You should be aware of the reality of the experience that's happening to you; all of that stuff has got to vanish. If any of it is terribly noticeable to you, then somebody has done his job wrong. And it makes no difference whether it's a naturalistic play or a highly stylized one.

In terms of music, you once said that one day your plays would get to the point where they would have to be conducted.

I write very precisely and carefully. I learned from Chekhov and I learned from Beckett to write very, very carefully and precisely, and I also learned that drama is made up of two things: sound and silence. Each of them has its own very specific duration. Playwrights notate sound and silence, loud and soft, just as precisely as a composer does. There is a profound difference in duration of pause between a semicolon and a period, for example, and a wise playwright knows that, in the same way that a composer knows the difference between durations. I discovered that writing a play is very similar to writing a piece of music. The psychological structure of a play is similar to that of a string quartet. You attempt simultaneity of speech the same way the instruments are playing, although you can't very often do simultaneity because it's easier with instruments. But you are composing in a sense, and I have watched other directors (I was going to say conductors), as well as myself, directing me, directing Beckett; and at a certain point in the rehearsal, the director, off somewhere so no one will see that he has gone quite mad, is standing there not looking anymore, but he is indeed conducting. A play that is written very carefully and very precisely and accurately can be conducted. It is sound and silence; it's a matter of durations, and if you write that carefully you do end up being conducted. When I go back to a play that I've directed (one of mine or Beckett's or anybody's) a week or so later, I don't have to watch the production because I know the actors are going to be standing where they are supposed to be, sitting where they are supposed to be. That's just directing traffic; if you've done that right, then you forget about it. All I have to do is listen and I can tell whether the production is where it should be or whether it's getting sloppy and falling apart and so I go back in and reconduct.

Do you listen to music when you write your plays?

No, I listen to music before I write. I prefer to listen to the music of what my characters are saying when I write. I think everybody should begin the day by listening to a couple of Bach fugues. It sort of gives a sense of order and coherence to the day. Maybe that's a good way to start—after the oatmeal, some Bach. My own musical tastes in what we call serious music go from Obrecht and Gilles right on up to Elliott Carter, so I don't have any problem anywhere there. I have a little problem with some of the second-generation romantic composers like Respighi and people like that.

Can you talk a little bit about your writing process? It sort of goes in two parts for you, doesn't it?

Three. My writing process is in three parts. There is what I assume is going on in my mind creatively without my being aware of it. That must take a fair amount of time because I have never said, with the exception of one play (***The Death of Bessie Smith,*** which I wrote because of my rage at what I believed had happened to her in 1937 in the South), "I must write a play about this or that." I have never been aware of getting an idea for a play; a number of critics would agree with this, but not the way I mean! I become aware that I have been thinking about a play. When I become aware of a play that I have been thinking about, it's already gone a certain distance; it's already quite nicely formed in my head. The characters are already there, the destination is there generally. Generally, the environment of the play is already there when I become consciously aware of it. That's part one.

Part two is, again as Thurber said, let your mind alone: leaving all of that alone, not writing the play down instantly when I'm aware that I have been thinking about it, but letting it develop, mutate, letting it do things, letting it take its own time. I will play tricks to see how well I know the characters that are developing in my head. I will figure out some scene that cannot be in the play, and I will take a walk and improvise dialogue with these characters for a scene that will not be in the play to see how well I know them. I can keep a play in that condition in my head anywhere from four or five months to six or seven years. I always have two or three or four of them sort of floating up there ready to land, in a holding pattern above the airport of my desk. Oh God, I didn't know I was going to say that!

Then comes the time when I decide it is now time to write the play down on paper, to get it out of my head because it's taking up too much space. I haven't the vaguest idea of what the first two, three, four lines of dialogue are going to be; I have no idea of what any of my characters are going to say. That's called writing the play down on paper, where you discover and articulate everything you've been planning. That's the third part of writting, and that for me never takes more than two or three months. I can write a play down in two or three months, but I might have thought of it for, God knows, two or three or four years before I was aware of it. I write one draft, I make pencil corrections, and that's what I go into rehearsal with. I think I do most of my rewrites in my mind before I'm aware of the fact that I'm doing them, so I don't have to do them on the page.

There's an idea for a play that you've mentioned in interviews over the years as being imminent. It's about Attila the Hun.

I still have that play up there; it's still floating around along with a few others. I may get to that. Interesting guy, Attila. Do you know much about him? Very interesting guy. Did you know that Attila the Hun was one of the most educated men in Europe? Did you know that Attila the Hun was raised in the Roman court, as sort of a hostage, and that the Roman emperor's son was raised in Attila's father's camp, so that Attila was one of the most educated men in Europe? Did you know that one of his boyhood friends from when he was living in Rome became Pope Gregory, who was pope when Attila laid siege to Rome? It was the two boyhood friends meeting outside of the walls of Rome, and Pope Gregory somehow persuaded Attila to lift the siege of Rome. That's a good scene to write, let me tell you. Most people don't know these things. It struck me as very interesting that one of the most educated people in Europe would try to destroy civilization. As I watch history, it's not the most novel idea in the world, I suppose, but it certainly is an interesting one. Also, a nice thing about writing that kind of historical play is that there weren't too many journalists around in those days, so there's not too much written and I can make up my facts.

You don't get enough credit for the wonderful parts you write for actors. Do actors as part of the process help you or hinder you?

When I'm writing a character, I don't concern myself with anything except the reality of the character. I would never think about a specific actor for a role, because then I wouldn't write a character; I'd write a role. I don't start thinking about actors until I finish the piece. I try to make the characters as real and as three-dimensional as I possibly can, which maybe, if I succeed, is why actors like to work on them.

Have there been specific moments where actors might have contributed something you hadn't expected that helped you turn a play a certain way or added something to your perspective on a play?

When you write something, you're working both from your conscious and your unconscious mind, and you don't necessarily always know what you have done until somebody points it out to you; so an actor can indeed reveal a facet of a character that I've written, a depth of the character, that I wasn't consciously aware of. But if the actor's done a proper job, the actor is revealing what was there, something merely that I didn't know about. I've evolved a nice rule: If an actor or a director does something to a play of mine which diminishes it, which makes it less interesting than I thought it was, they're wrong, and I will not take any responsibility for it; if, on the other hand, a director or an actor finds something in a character of mine or a play of mine that makes it far more interesting than I have consciously known that it was, I instantly take credit for it. I've never had an occasion where an actor has suggested that things be in the character that were not there and then I've gone ahead and put them in. That's never happened. The actors that I've worked with—and I've worked with some pretty good ones—maybe had their hands full with the characters as written. There have been one or two occasions where I've been unfortunately stuck with a star whose competence was less than tolerable, who tried to simplify a role down to that particular tiny talent that the actor had. Those have been unhappy experiences, but generally the finest actors have been very busy with the characters I've written. They seem happy with them, or if they're not they don't tell me.

You make a distinction in a lot of your interviews between interpretive artists and creative artists. Does directing your own plays help you eliminate the middle man, get closer in contact with what's going on in the play with the actors?

The only reason, I think, that I became a director was to direct my own work with as much accuracy toward what I saw and heard when I wrote the play as I possibly could, on the assumption that that might be useful to somebody, to see what was really going on in the author's mind. The nice thing about directing your own work if you're the playwright is that there are two salaries. That's by far the nicest part. And you have double control over choice of actors, and I like that too. I suspect that when I'm directing a play of mine I'm far more willing to make cuts and changes than I would permit any other director to suggest. Maybe this is because I have greater confidence in myself, and maybe that is because my level of boredom is far lower than most people's.

I think I've probably learned a good deal about playwriting from directing, and probably a good deal about directing from playwriting. The idea put out by the Society of Stage Directors and Choreographers that playwrights should not direct their own work is put out merely because they want to have all the jobs available for the members of their union. It's based on the notion that the playwright shouldn't direct his own work because he understands it. Or perhaps he knows too much about it. Some playwrights can never be objective about their own work and shouldn't direct their own work. Some playwrights shouldn't be allowed in the theatre when their plays are in rehearsal because they will take anybody's suggestion and rewrite and quite often destroy their own work or do serious damage to it. Look what happened with Tennessee Williams and so many of his plays. Elia Kazan changed them. Tennessee always had his commercial success afterwards with Gadge's version, but he would then publish his original version along with it so that he had it both ways.

You once said that one of the reasons you like directing is that when you're not, you watch directors and actors fight over what the subtext is, and when you are, you know what the subtext is because you wrote the subtext.

Yes, but I've also discovered as a director that the author's subtext has nothing to do with the subtext that two different actors will need for the same role. I've directed fifteen or twenty different productions of ***The Zoo Story*** in the past thirty years. For one of the first productions I directed of it, a young actor—now recently dead, alas—named Ben Piazza was playing the role of Jerry. All you have to know to follow this is that in the play the character Jerry has a rather profound relationship with his landlady's dog. On the second day of rehearsal Ben came up to me and said, "When Jerry was growing up, did he have a dog?" This was obviously something Ben the actor needed to use to understand how the character related to his landlady's dog, and I tried to think back to the subtext that I had in my mind when I created the character of Jerry. I couldn't remember, so it occurred to me, let's see, what will be most useful for Ben Piazza to use to create this character? I said, "Oh yeah, Jerry grew up on a chicken farm his father had in New Jersey about fifty-seven miles from New York." I was making all of this up totally. "And there were lots of animals. Not only were there these awful chickens around, there were goats and sheep and two horses and six dogs." And I named the dogs for him, told him what brand they were, and I told him of a couple of the adventures that Jerry had had as a kid with the dogs. Ben nodded, we went back into rehearsal and never discussed it again, and he was a very good Jerry.

Twelve years after that I was directing another very good production of ***The Zoo Story*** somewhere else with totally different actors. This doesn't happen too often, but it happened this time. The actor playing Jerry came up to me the third day of rehearsal and said, "When I was growing up [by "I" he meant Jerry], did I have a dog?" And of course I thought back to what I told Ben Piazza, but then a bell went off and I said, "This actor will work better through deprivation." So I said to him in answer to his question, "No, you weren't allowed to have any pets when you were growing up. You wanted pets very badly, but your father hated dogs. You sneaked a puppy into your room when you were six years old, and your father drowned it." So he nodded, he went back, and we had a very good production of the play. The question is, which is true? Which subtext is true? Both. Because the subtext that each actor needs is the subtext that is valid, that will allow the actor to become the character. I learned as a director that subtext is there not to force but to become the character. If you hired the right actor, an intelligent talented actor, 90 percent of your work is done—if you've written a halfway decent play. I discovered that most problems that actors seem to be having in a scene have less to do with the writing of the scene than they have to do with subtextual choices that have been made.

Who are some of your favorite actors?

I've been very lucky, with the exception of a couple of actors that I would never work with again in my life. I've worked with some extraordinary performers, both English and American, and in foreign languages. Just to mention a few of the ones that I've been lucky enough to work with: John Gielgud, Paul Scofield, Peggy Ashcroft, Colleen Dewhurst, Jessica Tandy and Hume Cronyn, and I'm going to forget a lot of them now. I've worked with some awfully good actors and had a good time working with them. When I first started writing plays and getting involved with actors, I believed what everybody else did: that actors were not necessarily bright or sensitive people. I found that this is quite often true, but the very best are both enormously intelligent and sensitive and deeply caring people. I was very relieved and pleased to find that to be true.

Can you tell us about your most recent play, ***Three Tall Women****?*

Three Tall Women had its world premiere at the English Theatre in Vienna this past June. I directed it. There are four actors in it: three tall women and one fairly tall man. It's in two acts. You need more? I'm very bad about talking about the work. I don't like to tell the stories of plays. All right. In the first act, a ninety-two-year-old woman is in conversation with her fifty-two-year-old sort of nurse-companion and a twenty-six-year-old assistant. The play is basically this old woman rambling variously about her past, about her hates, about her vengefulness, all the things that when you get to ninety-two you seem to get very fond of talking about. She is not senile, but she lives in a past that did not exist quite often. She has a stroke at the end of Act I which silences her.

When Act II begins, the stage is empty except she is there in the bed with an oxygen mask. The fifty-two-year-old woman and the twenty-six-year-old woman come in looking and seeming somewhat different from who they were in the first act, and they stand over the bed of this comatose woman, and then the woman herself comes in and obviously it's a dummy on the bed. We understand fairly quickly that the three women are really the same woman at different ages: at ninety-two, fifty-two, and twenty-six. We learn a great deal more about that woman. We learn a great deal more about how we view life at twenty-six, how we view life from the top of the mountain looking both backward and forward at fifty-two, and how we view ourselves at both twenty-six and fifty-six when we are ninety-two, and how we imagine we are going to be behaving when we are ninety-two when we are both fifty-six and twenty-six. As usual in my plays, not a great deal happens; but all of that happens. The English Theatre in Vienna is very interesting. A lot of the audience speaks far less English than it pretends to, and this includes some of the critics. But the ones who seemed to understand the play were quite fond of it, and those who seemed bewildered were not.

Could you say something about the film version of ***Virginia Woolf****?*

As Beckett says, it was better than a kick in the teeth. When I sold the rights of that play to Warner Brothers, they promised me Bette Davis and James Mason, who were both exactly the right age for it at that time. Bette Davis was fifty-two, and James Mason had always been forty-six, so it was just dandy. Then it was decided that Richard Burton and Elizabeth Taylor were big stars, and so they became Bette Davis and James Mason. I suppose the only problem was that Elizabeth Taylor was thirty-two. She was trying to play a fifty-two-year-old woman, and I don't think she quite convinced me that she was fifty-two. I think they pretended that she was forty-five, which made the nonexistent child no longer on the eve of his twenty-first birthday but younger, which destroyed one of the metaphors of the play for me. Another thing about the film bothered me a little bit, although it's a lot better than a lot of films of plays have been. I wrote the play in color, but for some reason they made the film in black and white. I don't understand that. Maybe that's because black and white is more serious. I don't know. It certainly messed up the video cassette sale, I'll tell you that.

Also, the play is both very serious and very funny. I found the film, maybe because it was not a live experience, very serious but not particularly funny. I also found the film not as claustrophobic as I intended the play to be. The play is meant to be set in one room. I didn't even like them going up to the bedroom or to the kitchen, and when they went out to that ridiculous roadhouse I thought it was doing serious damage to the claustrophobic intention of the play. I imagine that I had been influenced to a certain extent by Jean-Paul Sartre's play *No Exit,* but I also think I probably wrote the play as an answer to another claustrophobic play by Eugene O'Neill called *The Iceman Cometh. The Iceman Cometh* postulates that you have to have pipe dreams or false illusions in order to survive, and I think ***Virginia Woolf*** was written to say, maybe, that you have to have them but you damn well better know that they're false illusions and then survive knowing that you're living with falsity.

I much prefer the film that was made of my play ***A Delicate Balance*** that had Katharine Hepburn, Paul Scofield, and

Kate Reid and a number of other very good people in it, directed by Tony Richardson. I thought that was a somewhat better film. In neither case, however, and this is interesting, was there a screenplay used. I'm told there was a screenplay written for ***Who's Afraid of Virginia Woolf?,*** and indeed it says, "Screenplay by Ernest Lehman," the producer of the film; but as I look at the film (and I've seen it seven or eight times now), as far as I can see he wrote two sentences: "Let's go to the roadhouse," and I believe the other one was something like "Let's come back from the roadhouse." I'm told he paid himself $350,000 for writing the screenplay, so that's $175,000 dollars a sentence, which is pretty good.

I'm told that there was a screenplay that he did write, in which (and I hope this is apocryphal) the nonexistent child had become a seriously retarded child, a real child, and was kept upstairs. Well, so much for historical political metaphor. Anyway, I'm also told that when Burton, Taylor, and Mike Nichols read the screenplay, after their laughter died down they said, "If we have to use this screenplay, we will not make the film," and so they went back and went into rehearsal as if it were a play for a couple of weeks and used my text. They cut about fifteen or twenty minutes out of it; they cut out almost all of the historical political argument, and they unbalanced it slightly, making it more Taylor's film than Burton's film.

The film of ***A Delicate Balance*** was a better film. It was part of that ill-fated American Film Theatre project, where serious films of serious plays were made rather well, as often as not, and then shown without much advertising in places that people could not get to at hours when they would not go. ***A Delicate Balance*** was also rehearsed as a play and was shot in sequence. They shot that movie from the beginning of the play until the end, five days for each act. The only other play of mine that was made into a film I have not seen. That was the film of my adaptation of Carson McCullers's ***The Ballad of the Sad Café.*** I saw some rushes and I saw some shooting of that, and I did not want to see it. I heard it was fairly literal and not very good.

There is a story about ***Virginia Woolf****— that Henry Fonda's agent got the script but didn't tell him about it, and he was furious forever after.*

Yes. This is to say nothing against Uta Hagen and Arthur Hill, who were both superb in their roles, but neither of them was the first choice. Henry Fonda, whom I had seen onstage and whom I respected as a stage actor, was offered the role of George in ***Who's Afraid of Virginia Woolf?*** in the 1962 production. His agent did not show it to him and said, "Mr. Fonda is not interested." Whether he would have taken the role or not, who knows. He said he would have taken the role, but he might not have. I think that was the end of that particular agent for him anyway! We offered the role of Martha originally to Geraldine Page with the agreement both of me and Alan Schneider, who had been hired to direct the play, and Gerry Page was very excited about doing it. But she said in her tiny voice that she would have to talk to Lee Strasburg about it first. She came back a couple of days later with the information that Lee was going to allow her to do the role, and it was okay if Alan Schneider directed it but that he, Lee Strasburg, would have to be at all rehearsals as a sort of éminence grise. And that is why Geraldine Page did not play Martha on Broadway in ***Who's Afraid of Virginia Woolf?***

Do you think it's possible that any of your female characters are actually male homosexuals in disguise? Do you think homosexuality plays a part in much of your work?

Well, let's see, I've got about three plays where there are characters who are gay, so I suppose to that extent that it does. What I've never done is write a male character as a female or write anybody who was gay as straight or straight as gay. There's a difference you may have noticed between men and women, and it would be very very difficult to lie in that particular fashion, and playwriting is not about lying. I don't know how that story about ***Who's Afraid of Virginia Woolf?*** got started that, somewhere along the line, it was written about two male couples. You never know what's going on in the deepest recesses of your mind, so I asked a number of actresses who were playing Martha if they thought they were playing men. I asked Uta Hagen; it had never occurred to her. When I directed it in 1976 with Colleen Dewhurst, I asked her if she thought that she was playing a man, and I asked Ben Gazzara if he thought he was playing a gay man. It had never occurred to either of them. It had never occurred to Elizabeth Taylor that she was playing a man, and it never occurred to me. I don't think all that game playing and role playing are necessary.

There was a disgraceful article written in the *New York Times* by the then drama critic, one of the several they have gotten rid of although they have not gotten rid of all of them that they should have, a man named Stanley Kauffmann. He wrote an insidious and slimy and disgusting article not naming the names of any of the playwrights he was talking about but saying that we all knew, nudge, nudge, did we not, that a number of our most famous American playwrights were homosexuals, and did we not also know, nudge nudge, that they were really writing about males when they were writing their female characters? It was appalling and disgusting and the sort of thing that infiltrates far too much of our criticism. He was talking about Tennessee Williams primarily then, and Tennessee never did that, and I can't think of any self-respecting worthwhile writer who would do that sort of thing. It's beneath contempt to suggest it, and it's beneath contempt to do it. These critics who suggest it ought to grow up or ought to go into another kind of butchery, hog slaughtering perhaps.

You've always had harsh words about critics. What is a good critic?

A good critic is one who likes my work. A bad critic is one who does not. All playwrights feel this way. Some of us are honest enough to admit it.

*It's been said that some of your plays, perhaps most notably **Virginia Woolf** and **Tiny Alice,** reflect your own experience of being adopted. Do you believe that?*

I was adopted and I am real. The child in ***Who's Afraid of Virginia Woolf?*** was metaphorical, so I don't think there's too much relationship there. In ***Tiny Alice,*** I don't think there's any relationship to adoption whatever. The one play where it might be suggested that there is some biographical input in the play is ***The American Dream,*** but even there it is so metaphorical and so highly disguised that I'm not so sure even there. I'm not one of these playwrights who writes about himself very often, maybe because I find my characters much more interesting than I am. And I also find the characters that I can invent are a good deal more interesting than the people that I know. Even in the play ***The American Dream*** the character Grandma, of whom I'm very fond and who's a very, very interesting character, was, I suppose, infinitely more interesting than my maternal grandmother, upon whom it was partially based. I wish she had been as interesting as the character that I wrote, but alas, she was not.

I also think that character is based partially on Beulah Witch. Those of you who are old enough to remember "Kukla, Fran, and Ollie" will remember Burr Tillstrom, whom I knew. Burr would invite me over to his apartment in Chicago for an evening and he would say, "Excuse me, there's somebody who wants to talk to you." And he would disappear into another room, and all of a sudden I would hear this great cackling voice of Beulah Witch say, "Edward, come here!" And I'd go into that room, and there would be a little puppet stage, and Burr would have disappeared behind it, and there would be Beulah, and she and I would sit and have a half-hour conversation. As a matter of fact, I told Burr that ***The American Dream*** should be performed by him and the Kuklapolitan Players, that the play could be done very nicely by all of them. Oliver J. Dragon, of course, could play the American Dream; and Beulah Witch, of course, could play Grandma; and it would have been a nice experience.

I always write about myself in the sense that my characters are limited by my perceptions, though sometimes I think that they can imagine things that I cannot imagine. I'll tell you one thing: they have read things that I haven't, because I can read a book and within six weeks or less completely forget everything about the book. I've started reading books a second time, only realizing three-quarters of the way through that I've read this book before. I forget everything that I read, but twenty years after I've read something and forgotten about it I'm writing a character in a play and the character will quote from something that I cannot remember the experience of having read. I don't write about myself very much. Every character I write is limited by my perceptions but is also basically invented by me from people I've known and from people I've observed plus the particular kind of invention or creativity that we're supposed to do as writers. I've not written many memory plays. I've not written many plays about me or my family.

You once added up the names, didn't you say, of all the writers who influenced you?

Once, back in the middle sixties when I was very interested (much more interested than I am now) in critical evaluations of me and my work, I started noticing that critics, with this particular type of shorthand that passes for critical thought, were saying that Albee's work resembles this one or that one or that one. I was quite pleased by the good list of writers that I'd clearly been influenced by. I made a list of twenty-five contemporary playwrights that I was supposed to have been influenced by. And I looked at a lot of them and I thought, yeah, sure I'd been influenced by them, I would have been a damn fool not to have been. But there were six or seven playwrights on that list that I was supposed to have been influenced by whose work I didn't know. I thought that was going to be the neatest trick of the week, and then I went and read these people's work, and I realized that, of course, I had been influenced by them because we both had been influenced by the same sources.

Everybody, unless he's a self-conscious primitive or a damn fool, is going to be influenced by his predecessors and his betters. It's our responsibility to be; we don't want to reinvent the typewriter. We don't want to be so ignorant that we get a bright idea to write a play about a young man who comes back to the city after having been away since he was a kid and he falls in love with a female mayor of the city who happens to be twenty or twenty-five years older than he and they get married and then he discovers that it's his mother. If we've read *Oedipus Rex* we're not going to do that. But it was interesting to me that there were these playwrights that I was supposed to be influenced by that I hadn't known. Of course I'd been influenced by them because we had been influenced by the same people.

What terrifies you?

Not being asked wonderful questions.

Introduction to *Three Tall Women* (1994)

SOURCE: "Introduction," in *Three Tall Women: A Play in Two Acts,* by Edward Albee, Dutton, 1994, pp. 3-5.

[*In the following remarks prefacing the published version of* Three Tall Women, *the playwright discusses the origin of the play in his experiences with his adoptive mother.*]

People often ask me how long it takes me to write a play, and I tell them "all of my life." I know that's not the answer they're after—what they really want is some sense of the time between the first glimmer of the play in my mind and the writing down, and perhaps the duration of the writing down—but "all of my life" is the truest answer I can give, for it is the only one which is exact, since the thinking about the play and the putting it to paper vary so from play to play.

Few sensible authors are happy discussing the creative process—it is, after all, black magic, and may lose its power if we look that particular gift horse too closely in the mouth, or anywhere else, for that matter; further, since the creative process cannot be taught or learned, but only described, of what use is the discussion? Still, along with "where do your ideas come from?", the question is greatly on the mind of that tiny group of civilians who bother to worry it at all.

With ***Three Tall Women*** I can pinpoint the instant I began writing it, for it coincides with my first awareness of consciousness. I was in a group of four who were on a knoll (I could even now show you the exact spot, the exact knoll) observing the completion of a new house, the scaffolding still on it. There were three adults and tiny me—my adoptive mother, my adoptive father, my nanny (Nanny Church) and, in Nanny Church's arms—what? three-month-old Edward, certainly no older. My memory of the incident is wholly visual—the scaffolding, the people; and while I have no deep affection for it, it *is* my first awareness of being aware, and so I suppose I treasure it.

I have the kind of mind that does not retain much consciously—I experience, absorb, consider, banish into the deeps. Oh, should someone remind me of a significant event, its sights and sounds will come flooding back, but free of emotional baggage—that dealt with at the time of the incident, or catalogued elsewhere. And I know that my present self is shaped by as much self-deception as anyone else's, that my objectivities are guided by the maps I myself have drawn, and that nothing is really ever forgotten, merely filed away as inconvenient or insupportable.

So, when I decided to write what became ***Three Tall Women,*** I was more aware of what I did *not* want to do than exactly what I did want to accomplish. I knew my subject—my adoptive mother, whom I knew from my infancy (that knoll!) until her death over sixty years later, and who, perhaps, knew me as well. Perhaps.

I knew I did not want to write a revenge piece—could not honestly do so, for I felt no need for revenge. We had managed to make each other very unhappy over the years, but I was past all that, though I think she was not. I harbor no ill-will toward her; it is true I did not like her much, could not abide her prejudices, her loathings, her paranoias, but I did admire her pride, her sense of self. As she moved toward ninety, began rapidly failing both physically and mentally, I was touched by the survivor, the figure clinging to the wreckage only partly of her own making, refusing to go under.

No, it was not a revenge piece I was after, and I was not interested in "coming to terms" with my feelings toward her. I knew my feelings, I thought they were pretty much on the mark, and knew that I would not move much beyond the grudging respect I'd slowly developed for her. I was not seeking self-catharsis, in other words.

I realized then that what I wanted to do was write as objective a play as I could about a fictional character who resembled in every way, in every event, someone I had known very, very well. And it was only when I invented, when I translated fact intact into fiction, that I was aware I would be able to be accurate without prejudice, objective without the distortive folly of "interpretation."

I did not cry and gnash my teeth as I put this woman down on paper. I cannot recall suffering either *with* her or because of her as I wrote her. I recall being very interested in what I was doing—fascinated by the horror and sadness I was (re)creating.

Writers have the schizophrenic ability to both participate in their lives and, at the same time, observe themselves participating in their lives. Well . . . some of us have this ability, and I suspect it was this (frightening?) talent that allowed me to write ***Three Tall Women*** without prejudice, if you will.

I know that I "got her out of my system" by writing this play, but then again I get *all* the characters in *all* of my plays out of my system by writing about them.

Finally, when I based the character "Grandma" (***The American Dream, The Sandbox***) on my own (adoptive) maternal grandmother, I noticed that while I liked the lady a lot—we were in alliance against those folk in the middle—the character I created was both funnier and more interesting than the model. Have I done that here? Is the woman I wrote in ***Three Tall Women*** more human, more multifaceted than its source? Very few people who met my adoptive mother in the last twenty years of her life could abide her, while many people who have seen my play find her fascinating. Heavens, what have I done?!

Interview with Albee (1996)

SOURCE: An interview with Edward Albee by Richard Farr, in *The Progressive,* Vol. 60, No. 8, August 1996, pp. 39-41.

[*In this conversation, Albee discusses the social and political content in his plays.*]

Despite wealthy adoptive parents who sent him to exclusive schools like Choate, Valley Forge, and Trinity College, playwright Edward Albee didn't have an easy start. He was expelled from most of the schools, or expelled himself. At eighteen he expelled himself from his parents' home and spent a decade drifting in and out of casual jobs.

He was a messenger for Western Union when, at twenty-nine, he wrote an angry, deeply disturbing one-act play called ***The Zoo Story,*** in which a businessman on a park bench is coerced into stabbing a vagrant.

The play was a sensation, the critics hailed it as the first work of a hugely original talent, and Albee went on to write a series of chilling attacks on the American domestic verities, most notably ***The American Dream*** (1961), ***Who's Afraid of Virginia Woolf?*** (1962), and ***A Delicate Balance*** (1966)—which won Albee his first Pulitzer prize.

Albee said from the start that he hated the commercial values of Broadway, and he was one of the founders of the Off-Broadway movement. Perhaps the critics decided that the very successful Angry Young Man needed a lesson in humility. After 1966 his reputation went into a quarter-century tailspin, as each new offering "failed" to live up to the promise of the early work. Albee continued to produce original drama at the rate of one play per year. Critics responded by dismissing nearly all of it as willfully experimental and obscure, and Albee responded to their criticism by dismissing the most powerful New York critics, by name, as know-nothings.

Albee has always been an experimentalist, and he seems not to have cared that some of his work has not been well received. So there was some irony in the relief critics expressed in 1992, when he won another Pulitzer for ***Three Tall Women.*** "Albee has done it again," was the cry, as if the entire theater community had been waiting thirty years to see if the old dog could jump through the hoop one more time. Albee is a name to reckon with again. ***A Delicate Balance*** has just celebrated its thirtieth birthday on Broadway by winning three Tony awards, including Best Revival.

Albee travels constantly, teaching and lecturing, but in New York he can be found in a cavernous TriBeCa loft, an abandoned cheese warehouse he bought eighteen years ago in the days before cavernous TriBeCa lofts were fashionable. Despite the gray hair, he doesn't look close to his sixty-eight years. We sit on black leather couches in the middle of his extraordinary art collection. A Dogon granary door is propped up just behind the author, a Picasso sketch stands in a frame on a desk, and a Japanese grain-threshing device sits on the floor nearby. An Australian aboriginal war axe lies dangerously on the table between us.

[Farr]: *Your plays don't express very overtly political sentiments. Is that because you don't want to seem to be getting up on a soap-box?*

[Albee]: I do think that all of my plays are socially involved, but sometimes very subtly and very indirectly. Certainly ***The American Dream*** was socially involved. It's about the way we treat old people, the way we destroy our children, the way we don't communicate with each other. ***The Death of Bessie Smith*** was a highly political play. Sometimes it's subtle and sometimes it's fairly obvious.

*It has been suggested that **Who's Afraid of Virginia Woolf?** is "really" about two gay couples.*

If I had wanted to write a play about two gay couples, I would have done it. I've had to close down a number of productions that tried to do that play with four men. It doesn't make any sense; it completely distorts the play. Changing a man into a woman is more than interpretation: It's fucking around with what the playwright intended.

Do you try to exercise strong control over how your plays are produced?

I always tell actors and directors—whether I'm working with them or not—do whatever you like so long as you end up with the play that I wrote. There's more than one way to skin a cat, lots of different interpretations. The only time I really complain is if, either through intention or inattention, the director distorts my play.

Many of your plays are about families, especially about family dysfunction.

This has been going on ever since drama was invented. *Oedipus Rex* is about family and family dysfunction; *King Lear* is about family and family dysfunction. Nothing new about it. If I wrote plays about everyone getting along terribly well, I don't think anyone would want to see them. All serious theater is corrective. You have to show people things that aren't working well, and why they're not working well, in the hope that people will make them work better.

But some playwrights don't focus on the family so much.

Which ones? Brecht maybe. But the atomic family is such a central part of human society. You can't get away from it.

What is your attitude to marriage and the traditional family?

As with all things: When it works, it's fine. When it doesn't, do away with it.

Is the legalization of gay marriage an important issue?

Why do you ask? Look, one day I'll write a play about a dysfunctional gay marriage. OK?

Are you working on a play now?

I have two plays, one that I'm writing now called ***The Play about the Baby***—that's the title of it—which I'm halfway into, and there's another one floating around in my head called *The Goat,* which very much wants to be written down.

Do you write every day?

If writing is thinking about writing then I'm writing all the time. There isn't a day that goes by when I'm not thinking about a new play. But the literal writing down of a play—I seldom do that more than three or four months out of the year. That happens only after the play is fully formed in my mind: I wait until I can't do anything else but write it down. I never make notes because I make the assumption that anything I can't remember doesn't belong there in the first place.

Do you do much rewriting?

I may, in my head, before I write things down. A lot of the writing is in the unconscious. I do very little rewriting once I write a play down on paper, very little.

What's the role of comedy in drama?

I've found that any play which isn't close to laughter in the dark is very tedious. And conversely, even the purest comedy, if it isn't just telling jokes, has got to be tied to reality in some way. I think a play should do one of two things, and ideally both: It should change our perceptions about ourselves and about consciousness, and it should also broaden the possibilities of drama. If it can do both, that's wonderful. But it's certainly got to do one of the two.

Does the artist have a duty not to preach politics in his work?

Most serious drama is trying to change people, trying to change their perceptions of consciousness and themselves and their position as sentient animals. Sometimes it's very overtly political and sometimes very subtly so. The way we vote, the way we function as a society, is determined by our sense of ourselves and our consciousness, and to the extent that you can keep people on the edge, alive, alert, and reexamining their values, then they will deal more responsibly with the particular issues. But didacticism belongs in essays.

Isn't there any good art that's didactic? Dickens? Goya?

In the second half of the twentieth century things get more complex and it's harder to think of examples. David Hare does write didactic plays: *Racing Demon,* for instance, which I have retitled, not unaffectionately, *Raging Didacticism.* When there's too much didacticism going on I start sighing. I say: I know this stuff—dramatize it for me!

You have always opposed the commercial pressures and values associated with Broadway. Do you feel uncomfortable with the success that ***A Delicate Balance*** *is enjoying there now?*

I never feel bad about getting awards; if they're giving out awards, I'd like to have them. But I don't care. They don't matter. The plays that seemed to matter on Broadway this year were very different from what usually wins. None of them originated on Broadway. So maybe something better is happening, though I think it's a little strange.

You have taught at various institutions. Do you make any conscious effort to radicalize your students?

I do, yes. I probably shouldn't because I'll probably get thrown out—we're talking about Texas, where I teach now. I don't give them grades on how radical they've become, but I do talk a lot about their responsibilities. And I do often mention right at the beginning that there isn't a single creative artist whose work I respect who has been anything other than a liberal.

Ezra Pound?

Well . . . there are exceptions.

Have your students changed, politically?

Even back in the "activist" sixties and seventies I would talk to a lot of students and most of them couldn't argue dialectics for more than thirty seconds. They had an emotional involvement and they had a few slogans but they were not informed. Anyway, I teach aspiring writers, almost all of whom are liberal because they realize that anything that is not liberal is not going to respect their freedom of speech, freedom of activity. So quite selfishly, they are liberal, though how they will vote when they make it I have no idea. Some of them will get rich, go to Hollywood, and start voting Republican. Even in a democracy, things like that happen!

In 1961, you said that we were ruled by "artificial values," and you spoke with contempt of the view "that everything in this slipping land of ours is peachy keen." Have we slipped further into "artificial values"?

I think we've slipped a lot further. We have to go back to the fundamental responsibilities of democracy. Democracy is fragile and it must be made to work, which demands an awful lot of effort on everybody's part. I find the real and planned incursions against our civil liberties frightening and dangerous. The so-called religious right of the Republican Party—the Christian right, they call themselves, although in my view they are neither Christian nor right—is after a totalitarian state. But none of these things would be allowed to happen if we had a population a) that bothered to vote; b) that informed itself of the issues; and c) that understood that democracy is a participatory governmental system. We don't live up to our responsibilities to democracy.

Would you describe yourself as a capital-D Democrat?

The first time I ever voted was in a New York City mayoral election. There were three candidates: a Democrat who was perfectly OK but a hack; a Republican who was probably not as terrible as all Republicans are these days; and a candidate for the American Labor Party who everyone said was a Communist. He was actually a leftwing socialist, and he was the only person who a sensible person could have voted for. But the whole question of what is leftwing has shifted so. My God, Nelson Rockefeller would be considered leftwing now. I not only voted for the American Labor Party once, I also voted Republican once—no, twice—to get Javits reelected. But yes, I'm a Democrat, though I'm afraid I'm much more of an unreconstructed New Deal Democrat than most, perhaps because that was when I first had some political consciousness.

People are criticizing Clinton for being too conservative.

Clinton needs a lot of criticism, but don't let's criticize him so much that Dole gets elected. Wait until he gets his second term, if he gets it. Then you'll find a much more liberal President because he won't be up for reelection.

What's it like, in these conservative times, to work on NEA grant committees?

I don't get asked as much as I did. I'm a troublemaker. The pressures that were put on us occasionally to find as many worthwhile sculptors in North Dakota as there were in Brooklyn—well, I'm in favor of populism within rational limits, but. . . . I also served for a while on the New York State Council for the Arts, but I was equally vocal there, and I'm not invited to do those things too much now.

Did you enjoy them?

Yes, I considered it a civic responsibility. You know, in the thirties there was a huge arts program, for the visual arts especially, where a great generation of abstract painters was put to work decorating public buildings. And a lot of writers was put to work in schools. But nobody remembers that. They all think the National Endowment was the first time anyone had thought of using creative artists for the public good. We spend about thirty-eight cents per person per year on support of the arts in this country. In Germany it's five or six bucks. All the howling that's taking place in the fens of ignorant Republicanism attacking these supposedly huge grants is preposterous, it seems to me—sinister and cynical and totally fallacious. This is less money per year than you pay for one pack of cigarettes. If you don't want to educate yourself, you have a responsibility to educate other people, educate your children; this is part of the responsibilities of democratic life.

However, there's a widespread sense that art is really just entertainment for highbrows.

Not only that! Art is dangerous. It's obscene. It's anti-god. And these arguments that the philistines come up with wouldn't work if people were educated to want art.

You helped to create the Off-Broadway movement in the early 1960s, which seems to have been a period when anything was possible in the arts. Why have things gone from there to here?

A combination of fear and greed. I remember a time, I can't give you a date, but all of a sudden college students were informed—I don't know by whom—that what you did was graduate, get a cushy job, and vanish into society. I see it more and more. Mind you, my playwriting students haven't figured it all out yet. They still think that individuality has some virtue; they still think that their responsibility, if they possibly can, is to change the way people think.

So, despite the slough of cultural-conservative despond, you see grounds for optimism?

How old are we, as a country? Two hundred years? I think we'll survive Gingrich and Dole.

What's best in contemporary American theater?

I don't make lists. I always leave somebody good out. We have so many good playwrights in America now, a whole new generation.

Is there any dominant theme or style emerging?

We have great diversity of style. I do find that the more naturalistic a play is, the more popular it tends to be.

Is that a criticism?

Yes.

Why is naturalism a problem artistically?

Theater audiences have been trained towards naturalism. The critics don't like experimental plays generally, and they steer audiences away from them. It's part of the fear of the intellectual in American culture. A big problem in this country.

Do you have an aversion to musicals, in general?

I think it's a bastard art form. The music isn't usually very good. I used to like junk musicals when Rodgers and Hart wrote them, and Cole Porter, but then they didn't have any pretense. The stuff that's on now is supposed to be serious music writing and serious theater, but it's just pretentious, middle-brow junk. I dislike it a lot. The last musical I liked a lot was *Evita,* because it was politically interesting.

I notice that one of the theater reference books lists your religion as Christian. For an Absurdist playwright that seems odd.

That may just be a weird oversimplification of something I said at one time. I'm a great admirer of the revolutionary leftist politics of Jesus Christ, and I am a Christian in the sense that I admire him a great deal. But I don't have any truck with the divinity or with God, or any of that stuff. I just think he's an interesting revolutionary social thinker—and that makes me a Christian, does it not?

Many of your plays seem to be about the maintenance or collapse of illusions. As if the goal is to live life without illusions.

I don't think there's any problem with having false illusions. The problem is with kidding yourself that they're not false. O'Neill said, in that extraordinary play that nobody does, *The Iceman Cometh,* that we have to have pipe dreams. I think ***Virginia Woolf*** was in part a response to that; it's better to live without false illusions, but if you must have them, know that they are false. It's part of the responsibility of the playwright to help us see when they're false.

There seem to be Chekhov-like and Beckett-like elements in your plays. Are you influenced by other playwrights?

I certainly hope so. You learn from people who've come before you and who have done wonderful things. The trick is to take the influences and make them so completely you that nobody realizes that you're doing anything else but your own work.

OVERVIEWS AND GENERAL STUDIES

Tom F. Driver (essay date 1964)

SOURCE: "What's the Matter with Edward Albee?," in *American Drama and Its Critics: A Collection of Critical Essays,* edited by Alan S. Downer, University of Chicago Press, 1965, pp. 240-44.

[*The essay below contains a harshly negative assessment of Albee's work through* **Who's Afraid of Virginia Woolf?** *and asserts that this play enacts "homosexual liaisons."*]

The nation's publicity media, desperately in search of a "gifted young playwright," and unable to practice that asceticism of taste which is the requisite of culture, have praised the mediocre work of Edward Albee as if it were excellence. They have made the author of six bad plays into a man of fame and fortune, which is his good luck. They have also made him into a cultural hero, which is not good for anybody. It is time to disentangle our judgments of his merits from the phenomenon of his popularity.

Four of Edward Albee's six bad plays are too short to fill an evening. Another is a dead adaptation of a famous story. The sixth is the most pretentious American play since ***Mourning Becomes Electra.*** In each of these works there are serious, even damning, faults obvious to anyone not predisposed to overlook them. To get Albee in perspective, we should examine first the faults and then the predisposition of the audience not to see them. As a maker of plots, Albee hardly exists. Both ***The Zoo Story,*** his first play performed in New York and ***Who's Afraid of Virginia Woolf?,*** his most successful, are built upon an unbelievable situation—namely, that a sane, average-type person would be a passive spectator in the presence of behavior obviously headed toward destructive violence. In ***The Zoo Story,*** why does Peter just sit there while Jerry works himself up to suicide? Why doesn't Nick, in ***Who's Afraid?,*** take his young wife and go home when he sees that George and Martha want only to fight the whole night through? In both cases, the answer is either that there is some psychological explanation that has not been written into the play, or that if Peter or Nick did the logical thing and went home the play would be over.

Sometimes it is argued that this objection is out of place. It is held that the passivity of Peter and Nick is allegorical and is supposed to point to our general passivity in the presence of destructive tendencies in modern life. But this is cheap allegory. A situation cannot function well as allegory unless it is a believable situation. Whatever allegorical element is present in the situation of ***The Zoo Story*** and ***Who's Afraid?*** is in conflict with the realistic convention that both plays assume.

Failure to maintain the chosen convention occurs in all the Albee plays, even in ***The American Dream,*** which does not pretend to realism but is more like the "theater of the absurd." It opens in such a manner as to suggest that Albee is imitating Ionesco, or perhaps will parody him. After ten minutes it is no longer clear whether any reference to Ionesco is intended, and it never becomes clear in the rest of the play. On the other hand, no different convention imposes itself. Toward the end of the play the comic mode is destroyed by a long autobiographical speech by the title character, a speech so full of Freudian cliché and self-pity that the only humane response to it is to be embarrassed for the author. No one could have written it who did not regard himself above his art. In the work of amateurs we expect this sort of thing, we forgive it. But we do not praise it, for to do so is to substitute indulgence for criticism.

Who's Afraid? displays another failure to maintain convention. This play is supposedly a realistic depiction of "how life is." I have yet to hear a reasoned defense of it on any other grounds, including that of its director, Alan Schneider (***Tulane Drama Review,*** Spring, 1963). Yet we are shown a married couple who go through life as the "parents" of a twenty-one-year-old "son" who is purely imaginary. The play ends when this "son" is sent to an imaginary "death" by his "father."

To be sure, the message of ***Who's Afraid?*** is clear in spite of this confusion; too clear. In many marriages illusions grow and have to be "exorcised" (this pretentious, crypto-religious word is Albee's), in order to save what is left of the partners. But the device Albee uses to state such a truism is once again from Ionesco. Patched into a realistic play, it turns the whole into a crazy mixture of the obvious and the incredible. This is not, as some have said, a problem in the third act only. The flaw that ruins the third act is already present in the first two, rendering them unbelievable.

Patching and stitching is the mark of Albee's style, if bad habits may be called a style. Scarcely five lines go by without making one feel that something extraneous has been sewn in. The scenes have no rhythm. They give no impression of having developed organically from situations deeply felt or from ideas clearly perceived. Nothing is followed through in the terms initially proposed. There is no obedience to reality outside the playwright's head, nor much evidence of consistency within it.

If Albee's arbitrary manner puts an unnecessary and uninstructive burden upon the audience, it also gives the actors more to do than they can accomplish. The exhaustion that the actors, as well as the audience, say they feel at the end of ***Who's Afraid?*** does not come from having experienced too much but from having pretended to experience it. All acting involves pretense, but there is such a thing as being supported by a role. Albee's roles have to be supported by the actors.

The performances of Uta Hagen and Arthur Hill in ***Who's Afraid?*** are remarkable to see, yet they are pathetic. These two skillful people are forced to manufacture on stage, moment by moment, semblances of character which the script not only does not support but even undercuts. The more brilliantly they perform, the more anguish we feel. But it is anguish for the performers. Arthur Hill manages his tour de force by holding desperately all evening to a few mannerisms, such as his gait, the unbalanced carriage of his shoulders, and his operatic delivery of the lines. Uta Hagen, with more variety, pulls even more tricks out of her professional trunk. In the course of the play's three and a half hours, it is the actors rather than the characters who become hysterical. Faced with the same hurdle in ***The Ballad of the Sad Café,*** Colleen Dewhurst takes a more dignified recourse. Given no intelligible character to enact, she refuses to pretend to act. She poses. Hers is the most beautiful example of non-acting I have ever seen, and I applaud her for it. No slightest hint of emotion escapes to betray the purity of her refusal; she is on strike, declining to do the playwright's work for him.

The falseness of Albee's characters is also due to the fact that they are but surrogates for more authentic ones. The characters who could make psychological sense of ***Who's Afraid?*** are not the two couples on stage but the four homosexuals for whom they are standing in. Granted that George is not very masculine and Martha not feminine, still we are asked to accept them as a heterosexual couple who might love each other. Their mutual sado-masochism renders this request absurd. They maintain their fight with increased pleasure-pain all night long.

I do not deny that heterosexual couples engage in *some* of the same behavior and show *some* of the same psychology. They do. But a play built around such an orgy invites us to ask what part of life it most aptly refers to. The answer is not to marriages but to homosexual liaisons. The play hides from the audience its real subject. This is quite apart from the question whether Albee *knows* what the real subject is. I think he does, but if not his job as a playwright is to find out. And to make his play tell it. We are driven to saying that either Albee does not know what he is saying or else that he is afraid to say what he means.

The significant cultural fact we have to deal with is not the existence of Albee's six bad plays but the phenomenon of their popularity. The public has been sold a bill of goods, but there must be reasons why it is willing to buy. What are these reasons?

Whatever may be said against Albee—and I've only said the half of it—one must also say that his bent is wholly theatrical. All his mistakes are theatrical mistakes. He confuses theatrical conventions, but he does not, except in ***The Ballad of the Sad Café,*** confuse the genre of playwriting with that of film, novel, or television. This is rare in today's theater. I expect this instinct for the theatrical is what people really have in mind when they refer to Albee's talent. "Talent" is the wrong word, for the nature of a talent is to grow, and Albee shows no signs of that. He does show a theatrical instinct.

Although theatricality is an important component in all great drama, it can also characterize some of the worst. That is, it can be used imaginatively or it can be used merely fancifully. Albee's use is the latter. There is evidence that this is a direct cause of his success. The truly imaginative use of theatricality is found today in Samuel Beckett, Eugene Ionesco, and Jean Genêt, none of whom has ever caught on with the large New York theater audience. Critics on the daily papers either misinterpret these playwrights (the *New York Times* told us recently that Genêt's ***The Maids*** is a "social tract") or they find them "obscure." Albee is preferred not because he is better but because he is worse. Since his themes are obvious, even hackneyed, they cannot be obscure. And his reckless inventiveness can pass for complexity without forcing anyone to entertain a complex thought. In short, he provides a theatrical effect conveniently devoid of imaginative substance.

This accounts, I believe, for the so-called "involvement" of the audience at ***Who's Afraid of Virginia Woolf?*** Since the situation and the characters are false, the play provides an occasion for the display of pseudo-emotions: mock anger, mock hatred, mock envy, and finally mock love. These are provided on stage by the actors, with whom the audience enters into complicity. Thus the audience achieves, at no expense to its real emotions, a mock catharsis.

In addition, there is reason to suppose that the very roughness and the gaucheries that mar Albee's plays contribute to his success. Most of the values that operate in our society are drawn from the bourgeois ideal of domestic harmony, necessary for the smooth functioning of the machine. Yet we know that there are subconscious desires fundamentally in conflict with the harmonious ideal. Albee satisfies at once the ideal and the hidden protest against it. In his badly written plays he jabs away at life with blunt instruments. If his jabbing hit the mark, that would be another matter. But it doesn't, no more than does the child in the nursery when he tears up his toys. That is why Albee is the pet of the audience, this little man who looks as if he dreamed of evil but is actually mild as a dove and wants to be loved. In him America has found its very own playwright. He's a dream.

Lee Baxandall (essay date 1965)

SOURCE: "The Theatre of Edward Albee," in *Tulane Drama Review,* Vol. 9, No. 4, Summer 1965, pp. 19-40.

Albee receiving the Evening Standard Drama Award for Best Play of 1964, for *Who's Afraid of Virginia Woolf?*

[In the following essay, Baxandall delineates standard devices, situations, and character types in Albee's plays, in an effort to define the "core of Albee's viewpoint."]

Edward Albee's theatre continues to be controversial. The discussion centers around two questions: one has to do with truth, and the other with dramatic structure. The first runs as follows: is the image of human relations in America which Albee presents justifiable because it is in some sense realistic, or is his an essentially flawed and perverted point of view? The second is: are there valid grounds for the invented child in ***Who's Afraid of Virginia Woolf?*** and the confused events which lead to Julian's death in ***Tiny Alice,*** or is Albee artistically callow and unable to structure a play properly?

The Albee Family America

> Affluence is estranging America from her own ideals. . . . It is pushing her into becoming the policeman standing guard over vested interests.
>
> —Arnold J. Toynbee, *America and the World Revolution*

> The play is an examination of the American Scene, an attack on the substitution of artificial for real values in our society, a condemnation of complacency, cruelty, emasculation and vacuity; it is a stand against the fiction that everything in this slipping land of ours is peachy-keen.
>
> —Edward Albee, Preface to *The American Dream*

What is the structure of Albee's theatre? His characters are definitely interrelated and cohesive from play to play; the heart of his technique is an archetypal family unit, in which the defeats, hopes, dilemmas, and values of our society (as Albee sees it) are tangibly compressed. The device of course is as old as Greek tragedy; only the particularity of *this* family is new. The economy of setting forth a concrete conflict to represent more abstract and even essentially undramatizable situations has always attracted dramatists. (Thus, with a sociologist's insight, C. Wright Mills stressed that public issues erupt as private troubles.) In the family, then, a dramatist can still find the conjuncture of biography and history.

Three generations comprise Albee's archetypal family: *Then,* the epoch of a still-dynamic national ethic and vision;

Now, a phase which breaks down into several tangents of decay; and *Nowhere,* a darkly prophesied future generation. Only two characters are left over from *Then:* Grandma, and a *paterfamilias* or patriarch who is occasionally mentioned but never appears. These establish a polarity based upon the axis of female and male principles. It has been often remarked that Grandma is the sole humane, generous creature in the Albee ménage. She tries to relate to others in a forthright and meaningful fashion, but at her age she no longer commands the requisite social weight. The others, her offspring, do not want Grandma involved in their dubious lives. They ask her to stifle her "pioneer stock" values. Her pleas that she be put to use—"Beg me, or ask me, or entreat me . . . just anything like that"—are not heeded, because she is of a different epoch. She sums up the inheriting generation: "We live in an age of deformity. It's every man for himself around this place."

The *paterfamilias* represents the dynamic principle of the vanishing generation. In ***The Death of Bessie Smith, Who's Afraid of Virginia Woolf?,*** and ***Tiny Alice,*** his function as entrepreneur and primitive accumulator of wealth is described with awe, but he is never seen. He is the Mayor, the capricious tyrant of Memphis, in his time a capable and dynamic figure—"for the Mayor built this hospital"—but incompetent in his senility—"The Mayor is here with his ass in a sling, and the seat of government is now in Room 206." He remains the Mayor from his sick-bed; he continues to wield power, because for his generation to do so is instinctual. Nor do younger persons offer a challenge. The upcoming generation desires nothing better than to serve the Mayor's political machine or to creep to his bedside for small favors. His counterpart in ***Who's Afraid of Virginia Woolf?*** is Martha's father, the College President. George speaks of him (ironically) as "a God, we all know that"; his mansion is nicknamed Parnassus and the whole faculty does obeisance to an infinitely remote and super-powered figure with a "great shock of white hair, and those little beady eyes" like a mouse's—a man who "*is* the college" and "is not going to die." Miss Alice's fortune was accumulated by a departed father. Time and again, it is the Robber Barons vs. the new Organization Men. The elder generation's male was an energetic asocial titan. As reflected in the *paterfamilias* and Grandma, an American ethos is vanishing, an ethos that was purposive and energetic, regardless of whether its humane or ruthless aspects came momentarily to the fore. And whatever else they were, the announced values were real.

The *Now* generation is also dominated by male and female archetypes. Mommy and Daddy of ***The American Dream*** are the most clear-cut representatives of this generation. Looking at them from the standpoint of their elders' values, it is apparent that Mommy provides the transitional figure. She, and not Daddy, takes an interest in practical enterprise; she inherits the male aggressiveness. But although she delights in power, she is glaringly incompetent as the moral steward of her generation. Mean-spirited, immoderate, insincere, and inclined to hysteria, Mommy makes up with wildness what she lacks in confidence. Long relegated to a subordinate family function, Mommy cannot instantly acquire leadership qualities. Yet Daddy has abdicated, for some reason not apparent to her, and someone must govern.

Mommy has several variants, emphasizing one or another aspect of her. Thus the Professional Woman of ***The American Dream,*** Mrs. Barker, provides the grotesque caricature in the Mommy gallery. She makes her way into areas once reserved for men, diminishing as a human being with each triumph. Martha, in ***Who's Afraid of Virginia Woolf?,*** has the essential Mommy traits but her character is more complex; she understands her errant behavior even as she compulsively continues it. Miss Alice, the capricious possessor of great wealth, is a Mommy too, and although she has an ineffectual impulse to "care" about people, she—like the Lawyer, who counsels her in practical affairs—is "saved by dedication" to the cruel values of her culture and can grow "hard and cold" when Julian's life is at stake.

What this "dedication" can imply, taken to an extreme, is shown by the Nurse in ***The Death of Bessie Smith.*** Nurse, though not yet married, is the meanest of the Mommies. Her neurotic and anti-intellectual political attitudes add a sinister dimension to the composite Mommy portrait. Nurse admires Franco, whose opinion, like her father's, "counts for something special." And she is sadistic. Having vehemently refused to put her life on a rational basis, Nurse is prone to hysterical outlets. She could tear the tissue of civilization:

> I am sick of everything in this stupid, fly-ridden *world.* I am sick of the disparity between things as they are, and as they should be! . . . I am sick of talking to people on the phone in this damn stupid hospital. . . . I am sick of the smell of Lysol. . . . I am sick of going to bed and I am sick of waking up. . . . I am tried of the truth . . . I am tired of my skin. . . . I WANT OUT!

This is irrational apocalyptic politics: the voice of the bigot and potential fascist. Why does Albee attribute these tendencies to Mommy, who for him symbolizes contemporary power in America? The first dispute over Albee comes to a head here. Does his representation of Mommy really suggest some important truth? Or is it the distorted revenge of an injured man?

In the first place, Mommy as a political symbol is ambiguous. She represents an emergent force in society, and does anyone doubt that women have strikingly improved their social and economic lot in recent years, that they have gained more professional and managerial positions, hold more property, exercise more real control in the home and community? Is it then surprising that a socially advancing group fails to distinguish itself by urbane reasonableness? In every revolution power has been accrued first and its judicious use learned later. On the other hand, is it not likely that Albee wishes Mommy to represent the political tendency of the nation rather than of simply one sex? We are left uncertain, for, because of his reliance on a family myth and the construction he places on woman's role, Albee's political meaning remains somewhat blurred. Mommy may offer a comment upon power in America. Don't we find in American foreign policy some of the traits attributed to Mommy? Didn't America suddenly rise to world power and responsibility during World War II? Didn't it have to adapt suddenly from an isolationist past? And hasn't there been much comment on the transformation from an "inner-directed" to an "other-directed" personality type in America? If this interpretation is substantially correct, judgments made on Albee's lack of objectivity about *women* need qualification, at the least.

Mommy has taken over the male prerogatives; what is left to Daddy? He has none of his predecessors' traits and the variants of his type are defined by whether they oppose the present passively or with active negation; they have no hope for the future. Daddy trails off toward the *Nowhere* generation; it is often unclear whether he is Mommy's husband or son. Indeed he is best discussed in connection with the *Nowhere* generation, since he and they both behave infantilely. The most passive of the Daddies is in ***The Sandbox*** and ***The American Dream***; he no longer "bumps his uglies" on Mommy or disputes her power, except in quibbles which she enjoys. Whether this Daddy is even employed is uncertain. Surely he is not imaginative. His dreams of becoming a senator, winning a Fulbright scholarship, or leaving Mommy's apartment are ludicrous. George, the history professor in ***Who's Afraid of Virginia Woolf?,*** represents the opposite pole. No less futile practically, he strenuously produces jokes, situations, and other "fun and games"—imaginative avenues away from despair.

Among the younger males the two in ***The American Dream*** show once again, very clearly, the weight Albee gives to this passive-active axis. Only one of the youths actually appears. The other, we learn, was the identical twin of this "American Dream" and died while an infant, just months after Mommy and Daddy adopted him. Both twins are homosexually oriented, making symbolic comment upon an emasculated and narcissistic national vision. Grandma says that the dead twin had been sensitive, resentful, and indomitable, with a wildness which made him unbearable to Mommy—who at last mutilated the boy's genitals. She would have murdered him, had he not cheated her by dying first. The passive twin is, by contrast, welcome in Mommy's home and, it seems, in her bed.

The other Albee males can be located in relation to these poles. In ***The Zoo Story,*** Jerry, with a sensibility so unbridled that he eventually destroys himself, is a counterpart of the twin who died, just as the docile conformist Peter is kin to the "American Dream," the twin who lived. The polarization in ***The Death of Bessie Smith,*** though less focussed, appears in the contrast between an erotically obsessed Intern and an obsequious orderly. In ***Who's Afraid of Virginia Woolf?*** the conformist Nick is a forecast of triumph for the IBM male. In ***Tiny Alice,*** Julian is an imaginative saint with a mission, while the other men passively dissolve into their social roles. This is not so terrible for the butler, whose name, after all, is Butler; Albee suggests that the man's genuine capacities (as society has developed them) do not stand in contradiction to the serving role he plays. The situation of the Cardinal and Lawyer is otherwise. Though they are well educated, their personalities are determined by their social roles and they have no names but their functions. These men have in a sense *chosen* to be types rather than individuals; yet the Cardinal is also provided with a biography which might stand as the classic explanation of why Albee's passive males are that way: his father was a "profiteer," his mother irresponsibly whored around rather than instill him with life values. Even his paternity is in doubt. Thus, lacking tangible origins or values, the Cardinal in craven bafflement "worships the symbol not the substance" and takes the Father proposed by the Church. He will in turn perpetuate symbols over substance. There will, of course, be no offspring.

In the two most recent plays, a female of the third generation also appears. One is Honey, Nick's wife, who has numerous naïve dodges aimed at getting free of responsibility: no child-bearing or growing up for her! She abdicates, as have the more sensitive Albee males. Albee does not say why Honey follows the road of inner emigration, but one may guess that she is appalled by what maturity would require her to be and do. With the example of Mommy before her, she defends her childlike looks and innocence through doses of unwitting hysteria and knowledgeable abortion: *she* will not further this vector of history! Honey's counterpart in ***Tiny Alice*** does not appear, but we hear about her from Julian, who was fascinated by her during his years in the asylum. This woman, like Honey, is infertile and at the same time hysterically focussed on pregnancy. ("A woman who, on very infrequent occasions, believed that she was the Virgin Mary.") She calls upon God in erotic cadences, goes into false pregnancy with the belief that she will deliver the Son of God—and dies from cancer of the womb. Symbolically, this is the fate of all who do not choose, as Julian does, active martyrdom—who instead stay with "the same uproar, the evasions" of sterility.

Thus it ends. Albee's American family undergoes anxiety and terrible barrenness as it staggers into decay. A few fugitives detach themselves and seek solutions in aesthetics. They watch a historical dream wither. What is the core of Albee's viewpoint? The generations move away from practicality toward emasculation; away from the energetic but amoral use of power toward an amoral but inoperative use of power. A frightened populace creating illusory values; a country afraid to articulate its genuine but shoddy rules of conduct; and a handful of males stimulated to imaginative activity of a high order. George's mental purview has little in common with Daddy's sigh, "I just want to get everything over with," and the Intern's lewd unrealized fantasies are nearly as alien to him. George's escape into imagination is the sole solution Albee propounds to the national condition.

Out of the Family into Symbolic Transcendence

> I, thus neglecting worldly ends, all dedicated
> To closeness and the bettering of my mind

> With that which, but by being so retired,
> O'er-prized all popular rate, in my false brother
> Awaked an evil nature; . . .
>
> —Prospero in *The Tempest*

The form of an Albee play derives from some characters' imaginative power to force events, not toward historically viable solutions, but at least into channels which are telling and satisfying symbolically.

The Zoo Story, Albee's first play, uses this artistic strategy in showing the struggle by Jerry—who has cultivated his sensibility and integrity but has paid for it with social failure—to make significant contact with a man called Peter, who is a success and a conformist. Other forms of contact proving impossible, Jerry at last provokes Peter into causing his death by stabbing. This might be nothing but a brute, desperate act, yet it becomes much more because it is instilled with rich overtones of the circumstances which made Jerry abstain from the social order. He has gone out of the family, and he symbolically transcends it by showing Peter why, through the particulars of his death.

Albee's formal cunning can be seen, beneath the colloquial language and precise detail, in his bold and intricate sense of organization. "Plays are constructed rather the way music is," he has said, and a lifetime love of music and friendship with composers has prepared him for building a strong skeleton under the alluring flesh. For example, the associations evoked by the characters' names in ***The Zoo Story*** bring out the polarity of these third-generation males. Peter of course is Greek for rock; he is, as Christ bid, the rock on which the institutions stand. (The existentialists depict persons who live inauthentic existences as being the equivalent of stones, rocks, and trees.) Jerry, like Jeremiah, denounces the false gods of his day. Thus we are prepared, by the names alone, for Jerry's dying whisper to the apostle of conformity, "I came unto you . . . and you have comforted me . . . Dear Peter."

Beyond the force of names is the sheer suggestiveness of sounds. Take the handling of the vocal "O." It becomes, by the play's conclusion, an architectonic element. Early, there is Peter's polite and disinterested "Oh?" as he unresponsively answers the importunate Jerry. It is often used, and is a token of his studied indifference to lives presented to him outside routine channels. Half-way through the play, however, Peter in distress switches to "Oh my; oh my." Jerry tosses back, "Oh your what?" and keeps talking—the "Oh" rises more urgently to Peter's lips. Jerry is stabbed, and Peter howls, "many times, very rapidly," "Oh my God, oh my God, oh my God— . . ." in total incomprehension, to which Jerry replies with"a combination of scornful mimicry and supplication,""Oh . . . my . . . God," and dies. A sound has been imbued with the anguish of the conforming man under stress.

Among the medium-sized units in this play, the fable about the landlady and the obscene dog, for example, is built along the lines of a music-hall sketch. Elsewhere in the Albee plays one can discern arias, duets, and fugues. So much is fairly obvious. The *over-all* symbolic construction of the plays is more complex and deserves close attention, still using ***The Zoo Story*** as our model.

At the start of this section, I quoted Prospero's explanation of how he studied those esoteric subjects for which the world condemned him. The black arts enabled him, in an isolated place away from vested society, to control all events to his hermitic satisfaction. For those Albee characters with extraordinary imaginative powers, matters are similar: in large part they determine the course and outcome of the symbolic actions in which they are willing to participate. Of course, the differences from *The Tempest* are important. The powers granted Albee's figures can be called magical only as a metaphor of efficacy; at the same time, the physical and social sciences have steamrollered personality so that there seems little left to man's initiative which does not play into the game of those forces that crush integrity and sensibility.

It is in this perspective that Albee chooses heroes who use essentially aesthetic means to improve the quality of their lives. Bessie Smith is a working artist; Julian, Jerry, and George build imaginative worlds which provide meaning. Two other characters, Grandma at the conclusion of ***The American Dream*** and Jack, who brings Bessie Smith's corpse into a white hospital though he knows she is already dead, are rather ordinary persons who transcend themselves in situations of extreme indignity. Albee opposes these figures to the world of effete conformity—a world, incidentally, much changed from Shakespeare's, which beckoned to nearly every man with seemingly endless possibilities. An era which produced as heroes Tamburlaine, Faustus, Richard III, Macbeth, Julius Caesar, and Coriolanus, hardly could bring forth from its greatest dramatist a hero who preferred surrogate to practical triumphs; at least not until the end of his career darkened Shakespeare's view. The notable thing about Albee is that, writing late in the epoch which Shakespeare heralded, from the "island" which some think was the model for that in *The Tempest,* he sets out with the premises on which Shakespeare ended, as though there were no others. The resort to fantasy has become *a priori* to practical living. Man is from birth on that deserted isle—with Caliban.

Jerry, George, and Julian are foremost in having exceptional powers of symbolic transcendence. These powers are in life used at various levels of awareness and skill by many persons, even seeming conformists. Passive noncompliance with certain social norms may, when sustained, amount to symbolic negation. More advanced forms are seen in acts of sabotage: pranks, vandalism, riots, the remains of lunches that Detroit auto workers sometimes deposit in a difficult corner of the cars they make. Works of art may provide a lucid, transformed expression of the impulse. Its point is always not only to relieve frustration but also to mock or make manifest some absurdity or indignity inherent in the situation.

Thus Jerry by his death incriminates the good citizen Peter; Jerry has plotted the entire devious development of the action. Probably he had sought and failed to become a writer. In this instance his talents are cunning: "sometimes a person has to go a very long distance out of his way to come back a short distance correctly," and relentless: "don't react, Peter, just listen." He flaunts his superiority over a man whom society has awarded the merit badges; he hopes also, and quite desperately, to find some understanding from him. Should Peter respond, the bitter conclusions drawn in isolation will be disproved and the rebel can live. Yet Jerry has from the start little hope, and Peter does not admit awareness even when faced with Jerry's major effort, the parable of the dog, which brings forth only an indignant "I don't understand!" To admit awareness would force Peter to change values and reject the status he has dearly bought. He lies. And Jerry, weary of the indecisive encounters with the Peters, decides for once upon an indelible communication. "You fight, you miserable bastard," he cries, "fight for that bench; fight for your parakeets; fight for your cats; fight for your two daughters; fight for your wife; fight for your manhood, you pathetic little vegetable (*spits in Peter's face*), You couldn't even get your wife with a male child." Each move is calculated. Jerry knows how to dissolve the aplomb of this antagonist, and it is no difficult matter to induce Peter to seize the knife and hold it thrust out while Jerry, running upon it, dies.

There is symbolic richness in this tableau of death. On the face of it, Jerry is relieved of his unremitting conflict with the Peters. The social process of life-destroying forces in stealthy conquest of life-enhancing forces becomes public and accountable; Peter can no longer deny complicity. "You won't be coming back any more, Peter; you've been dispossessed"—robbed of certitude about his way of life. An audience, should it include Peters, vicariously might be as shaken, as dispossessed. This retribution alone can gratify Jerry. He is so set on broadening Peter's awareness that he urges him to gather his wits and flee before a policeman can come, for it would be futile for the Peters of society to punish Peter; his imagination must do the work. Then Peter may no longer be Peter. This is the primary import of the death.

Jerry's violence and his strategy are like those of American urban juvenile gangs. The gang members feel themselves outcasts; with no other outlets, they turn to destructive but significant acts. Two gangs battling for a turf are struggling for something that, like the park bench, in reality can "belong" to neither. And while they, like Jerry, may dislodge Peter with their knives, the victory is Pyrrhic—that is, symbolic.

From another perspective, Jerry's death is erotic. Jerry withdrew from "normal" sex when he rejected conformist social goals, and it seems mixed up in his mind with the other "normal" activities he despises. Occasional sordid contacts with women and daily encounters with his obscene landlady (another Mommy) reinforce his queasiness. Peter's domesticated heterosexuality is part of what affronts Jerry, and as he throws himself onto the blade in Peter's hand he spears himself on erect sex, terrifying and fascinating because institutional. The irony is that Peter's way of life scarcely has prepared him to perform this duty, and he would not have held the blade out if Jerry had not assaulted the root of his honor: property rights. Jerry is the more capable male; in the real encounter he plays the active partner.

The pattern is of deliberate symbolic adventures which unveil repugnant aspects of society and are symbolically satisfying to the doer. Albee develops this pattern in two ways. The less effective is found in ***The American Dream*** and ***The Death of Bessie Smith.*** In these plays a situation is slowly built up like a mosaic, and the transcendence is sprung suddenly, at the end. Grandma and Jack provide brilliant curtain effects, but this strategy has a bad effect on the total structure. We do not see the characters develop or change (except for the frantic revelations provided by the arrival of Bessie Smith's corpse) and the nature of the final transcendence is obscure.

Who's Afraid of Virginia Woolf? . . .

The scene is a small New England academic community. Martha is the daughter of the college president and her husband, George, is a history professor. One night they return late from a faculty party and begin an orgy of verbal sado-masochism: After tearing at each other's dignity and illusions, they turn on a new faculty couple, Nick and Honey, whom Martha has invited for a nightcap. Martha takes Nick to bed, but he is impotent; meanwhile George has retreated to the disinvolved recesses of his imagination, from which he is able to kill his and Martha's most precious shared illusion, the myth supposed to provide a measure of symbolic transcendence: that they have a son. In this mayhem, George is the catalyst, determining the nature and scope of their "fun and games" and guiding the pivotal story about the child.

What is the context of George's actions? Is it merely a quaint college town? The stage setting of the New York production implicated the entire American educated community. It showed a tasteful home, with fitted, recessed bookshelves, hi-fi, curtains, fireplace, early American period furniture, oak beams, a wrought-iron colonial eagle, an American flag queerly reversed, an impressionist painting over the mantel—the comforts of modern living side by side with rough-hewn tokens of the revolutionary past, but dominating them: an American House of Intellect. George and Martha are what has become of the Washingtons; they quip that they have lived "over the past couple of centuries" in this place. George is a symptomatic American intellectual, the most lucid of all Albee's heroes and the best adjusted to his predicament. He and Julian are the only Albee heroes employed by an institution of society. As a history professor, he has a wider perspective than the average man. He is an insider as well as an outsider, and his situation permits him—far more than Jack, Jerry, the "American Dream," or Grandma—to bare the problems of conformists and malcontents equally.

George's practical failures are his own choice. He was not born incompetent. Martha tells an anecdote about George's refusal to join a sparring match with her father, the college president, during the wartime fitness-program days; Martha took a playful poke at George then, and he went down. He has refused to assume the organization-man etiquette that would qualify him as her father's heir-apparent. "He'd be no good at trustee's dinners, fundraising," Martha notes accurately. "He didn't have any personality, you know what I mean?" What really was objectionable was George's insistence on his right to individuality; given the situation, he had little choice but freely to choose futility.

Like the other Mommies, Martha is an apotheosis of consumerism. With her teeth "like a cocker spaniel," she chews up ice cubes, drinks, George, the young men of the faculty. She describes her dilemma with images from the movies:

> Bette Davis comes home from a hard day at the grocery store . . . she's a housewife; she buys things . . . and she comes home with the groceries . . . and she puts the groceries down, and she says, "What a dump!" . . . she's discontent.

Martha isn't stupid. She is capable of criticizing her own actions, and she can be very affectionate. But she can have no realistic hope of becoming more than a Discontent Housewife while her imagination remains derivative. For although the general situation of "liberated" American women depends on no one woman, it is only through concrete analysis of her own life that any one woman can escape Martha's indefinable frustrations. Again, the imagination is crucial.

Conformist, repressed, neurotic, the wave-of-the-future couple, Nick and Honey, lack the passionate energy that would enable them to control their own fates. Like their lives, their marriage has been "taken for granted." Unfortunately, Nick is bright, a biologist who experiments with chromosomes in the hope of creating human types to order—an intention that troubles humanist George. This expert in the routine of an impersonal science is lost in Martha and George's highly fantasized world. Since Nick and Honey base their lives on unexamined illusions, George is able in no time to reduce their marriage to obscene dust, remarking, "I hate hypocrisy."

George took up talk after he allowed Martha's father to block publication of his first novel. Martha and George are very good indeed in their repartée; like *commedia dell'arte* zanies, they repeatedly enact scenes. George is the more devastatingly inventive, but Martha, once off and running, is the more swinishly effective. She achieves barbarisms that aesthetic George must deftly avoid. Yet George plays the game of withering insult with all his being, for imagination is all he has, while Martha regards the combat as a mere escape-valve for emotions firmly rooted in her consumer mentality. This difference becomes clear in the scene where Martha encourages Nick to "hump the hostess." At first she gives George numerous chances to stop her—any sign of compassion or generosity would do it. Why does George prefer to turn to a book? Given his immense stake in the values of lucidity and imagination, he cannot do otherwise: despite the anguish of the moment, George delights in the image of himself reading while Martha sweats in bed upstairs, for this symbolic revelation of their distinct modes of fleeing the world is too splendid!

After Martha's attempted infidelity, George, who had left the house, re-enters with a bunch of snapdragons which he hurls like spears at Martha and Nick: small phalli of his graceful symbolic revenge. In this one scene, George's commitment to imaginary deeds is completely visible. Martha pleads that the adultery didn't really come off, but George keeps hurling the snapdragons. She cries, "Truth or illusion, George. Doesn't it matter to you?" And George hurls another stalk. The truth for Martha is in the act. For George, intention is the truth.

Thus we come to the question of whether the invented child is an artistic error. Since George (and, to a lesser extent, Martha) is both motivated and gifted enough to sustain that myth, my answer is obvious. Sterile in so many ways, they cannot live with their sterility. With the child, George achieves—if only in fantasy—his crazy wish to perpetuate history "in spite of history" and to keep it under his control a little longer. The fantasy-baby gives Martha someone all her own, to use any way she wants, just as countless women have used their actual children. The motives are not extraordinary, although the resources George brings to the project and his final exorcism of the fantasy are.

At the Masque Theatre in New York, shortly after the play opened, Albee was asked what he thought of O'Neill's message in *The Iceman Cometh* that life-illusions are necessary. He replied that he felt O'Neill had made a very strong case, but that perhaps in the long run it was best for people to try to live with the truth. The tension between truth and illusion is at the heart of Albee's plays. That so many critics condemned the invented child is a comment on the American tendency to respect only the pragmatic and down-to-earth, and to distrust the abstract and intangible. This is the audience's problem, not Albee's—he is entitled to any aesthetic means that work, and this "device" of the child works. However, Albee has been acutely aware of his problems in communicating; his response has been to allow directors, chiefly Alan Schneider, to stress the matter-of-fact possibilities in the scripts, keeping the Broadway customers from confronting the full aesthetic, moral, and intellectual difficulties. But there are side-effects, among them the loss of a perspective in which the more audacious "devices" could be understood.

. . . *Tiny Alice*

Tiny Alice again shows a character's sustained effort to live by imagined values. However, this is the first Albee play in which the form of the symbolic transcendence is *expressed from within.* Everything said and enacted—erotic and ascetic, matter-of-fact and fantastic, incisive and elusive—is Brother Julian's revery.

This is not immediately apparent. The first scene is a struggle over Julian's fate between the forces of humane concern and material temptation; the fight is rigged, as the Cardinal is scarcely more humane than his temptors, Miss Alice and her Lawyer. Offered $100,000,000 a year for twenty years in return for sending Julian—apparently once his lover—to Miss Alice, the Cardinal hardly hesitates. His Church career dominates him even when the pistol is finally raised to kill Julian. As for the Lawyer, the Cardinal is right to describe him as a hyena who tears open at the anus the carrion it finds along the trail of the real predators. (I might add that writers from Freud on have discussed anality as the basis of the capitalist ethos.)

The battle between the Cardinal and the Lawyer is lively but unfair, because whatever its basis in real events it is now occurring in Julian's mind, and is rehearsed only to show cause for Julian's drive toward martyrdom. Critics have generally liked this opening section, but they have failed to grasp the play's development. (***Tiny Alice*** has the logic peculiar to sexual revery; it is compulsive, ambiguous, and obsessive in its events as well as in its language. As Julian tremulously nears the subjective and fantasized heart of his experience, the semblance of rational causation fades. The revery accompanies orgasm or is its sublimated counterpart. We cannot guess this at first. But as the morning sunlight fades into the dark recesses of spirit and the senses the imagery begins to equivocate between gross sensuality and soaring asceticism, and we begin to understand.) Then all light vanishes; the "mouse in the model" on stage—an emblematic Julian—dies. The breath and heartbeat of Julian, or whoever is imagining all this, resound to every corner of the theatre—this is how we hear our own vital organs when relaxing into sleep or, I suppose, death.

In the initial clarity the males included the Lawyer, a hated father-figure who has been Mommy's lover and now schemes to do the dreamer harm, and the Cardinal, who was the beloved but has succumbed to the despicable values of the father-figure. (Enter Mommy as the world's most powerful woman. At first she seems a dreadful hag, but soon she becomes seductive. These exhilarating and terrifying changes correspond to a rising flood of emotion recollected, and not in tranquility. Sexual memories and hallucinations pour forth as the language fragments toward grandiose symbolism or erotic caress. A stable groom with hairtufts on his thumbs; much talk of hair on muscled men's backs; images of penetration by a gladiator's thumbs, by a lion's claws, by the Holy Spirit, all haunt Julian. He recounts the speech of the woman in the asylum who implored the divinity to enter her, a speech climaxed by her verbal "ejaculation" (says Julian), after which all subsided into nothingness. The microcosm of the play's form is in that speech. In turn, a climax to Julian's revery—his ejaculation—comes when the Lawyer fires into the dreamer's abdomen, and the martyr collapses as "blood" spreads over his groin. The other figures, now unimportant, leave. The saint is alone with his pain and ecstasy; his organs throb; the imagining reaches its epiphany.

This is symbolic transcendence with a vengeance. But, although it is grounded in masturbatory fantasy, the play makes powerful statements about the nature of that transcendence and the world which induces some to attempt it. Essentially, ***Tiny Alice*** asserts no values other than those men create. Life is "chance," which men edit into "mystery," the purposes they create for themselves. The Cardinal urges Julian to "accept what you do not understand." "We do not know anything," but a man can develop his "special priesthood" although "an act of faith is required." It is better to "accept" a course leading to saintliness than, like the Cardinal and the Lawyer, to become symbol rather than symbolic transcender. We all are "instruments" whose value, though self-chosen, is conferred from without; it is best to elude the trappings of material power and to answer "How will I know thee, Oh Lord?" with "By my faith!" For, as Julian says, "My faith and my sanity—they are one and the same." All of us are waiting "until the pelvic cancer comes." But to follow one's individual idea of meaningful existence, "not losing God's light, but joining it to my own," is the secret of "how to come out on top, going under." Since "consciousness is pain" and all go under, says Albee, why not at least shape your own path? And he gives us Julian.

We are in the land of a strange metaphysics, communicated through "mental sex play" and with the godhead a woman who becomes, for the pilgrim martyr, anything he requires her to be. Thus Alice is actually "something very small enclosed in something else" (Albee to *Newsweek*). That "else" is at first her institutional wealth. Then, as Julian moves toward saintliness, Alice becomes the Bride of Christ. As he dies, she cradles him in her arms, deliberately in the pose of Michelangelo's Pietà. Julian has created her, first as his nemesis, haunting him with childhood terrors; then, in his triumphant apostate, she becomes Elysium.

Supporting Julian's web of associations is a neo-Platonic "philosophy" of appearance and substance which Albee takes as a metaphor of symbol and substance in social and aesthetic life. Made concrete on stage in the model of the mansion with its mysterious reflection of outside events, this static system intellectualizes and extrudes what is—and should have remained—implicit in Albee's art. Yet it is not hard to see why Albee wished to elaborate it. His plays are allegories saying "this is the *essence* of how it is"; that is the function of his family. The Cardinal provides a good example of what this method does and does not achieve. In the Masque Theatre discussion, Albee talked about Brecht's *Galileo,* which he had seen at the Berliner Ensemble. The scene of the Cardinal-turned-Pope being dressed while the Inquisitor keeps at him for permission to show Galileo the torture instruments had particularly impressed Albee. The meaning of the Brecht scene, however, is in its process: as more and more garments of the Papal authority are placed over his shoulders, and as the footsteps of the faithful continue without cease, the man's consciousness of his obligations to an office and situation becomes overpowering. In contrast, Albee's Cardinal is never capable of choice; allegory rather than process unfolds; the Cardinal merely does what Albee *a priori* deems necessary to his office; and where Brecht had shown a specific opportunity for a knowing man to exercise a social function with more or less rigidity or humanity, Albee builds a metaphysic while denying man freedom within a social role. ***Tiny Alice*** offers one of the purest recent embodiments of the enticing notion that man is born free and enchained by society. No wonder Albee has difficulty showing the dynamics of men within their institutions, and tends to come up with marginal aesthetic "notes," to the damage of his art.

Findings

Albee the satirist is without peer among American playwrights as he crisply negates destructive values through the medium of his family. His ability to affirm values, however, is limited by unconscious acceptance of some attitudes of that very consensus he scorns in other respects, and by the family structure he uses so well for scorn. He also is too close to his heroes, so that when he goes beyond satire his language thickens into solemn rhetoric. At the crucial moments—to return to the problems with which I began this essay—Albee is neither untruthful nor unskillful. But taking the plays in their entirety, what Albee despises provides yeast for his drama; what he hopes is too often chaff.

The basis of Albee's affirmation is stated by George, speaking to Nick: "You disgust me on principle, and you're a smug son of a bitch personally, but I'm trying to give you a survival kit. DO YOU HEAR ME?" Nick replies, "UP YOURS!" and George continues:

> You take the trouble to construct a civilization. . . to . . . to build a society, based on the principles of. . . of principle . . . you endeavor to make communicable sense out of natural order, morality out of the unnatural disorder of man's mind . . . you make government and art, and realize that they are, must be, both the same . . . you bring things to the saddest of all points . . . to the point where there *is* something to lose . . . then all at once, through all the music, through all the sensible sounds of men building, attempting, comes the *Dies Irae.* And what is it? What does the trumpet sound? Up yours. I suppose there's justice to it, after all the years . . . Up yours.

The playwright's grimace and defensive wit fall away; the wicked sybarite is uttering a Liberal's cautions. Government is a form of art and art a means of government. The world goes around because of work, principle, morality.

This world is threatened by the moral vacuity of the Nicks and—what? As George refills Nick's glass he tells us:

> Here we are . . . ice for the lamps of China, Manchuria thrown in. *To Nick.* You better watch those yellow bastards, my love . . . they aren't amused. Why don't you come over to our side, and we'll blow the hell out of 'em. Then we can split up the money between us and be on easy street. What d'ya say?

George, though sarcastic, is quite serious. The West has somehow allowed the Chinese to grow militant as it goes slack, and resistance to the "yellow bastards" is in order. Their threatening independence might be put down if America could recoup purpose and unity, and overseas wealth would pour in as before.

The meaning of the passage is unequivocal, and casts new light on Albee's championing of pioneer attitudes. Apparently he also favors the Liberal principle of building America by exploiting other peoples: Spanish, French, Mexicans, and above all the Negro and the Indian. George's speech bristles with ugly fear in the face of change. Nor is George alone in expressing this hostility to the aspirations of others. The Nurse in ***The Death of Bessie Smith*** also resists such change—again, her speech is not in an ironical context which would "criticize" it, as was her "sick of civilization" speech cited earlier, for example—when she envisions with a shudder a Negro "millenium" and "a great black mob marching down the street, banners in the air." ***Tiny Alice*** has nothing but cliché cynicisms to offer on the topic of radical social change. "Every dictator was once a colonel who vowed to retire, once the revolution was over" and "it is easy to postpone elections." Alice even gives money to some revolutions, along with churches, symphonies, and other reliable institutions. One wonders how the example of the American revolution can have been lost on such "thinking," unless the cause be present-day chauvinism. Yet Albee's terror of other people's rebellious autonomy is of a piece with the American Liberal outlook; now, especially, it blinds one to the agencies of historical affirmation. Thus George:

> When people can't abide things as they are, when they can't abide the present, they do one of two things . . . either they turn to a contemplation of the past, as I have done, or they set about to . . . to alter the future.

His distaste for the latter direction is expressed in a phrase drawn from Martha's sexual conduct: "When you want to change something . . . you BANG! BANG! BANG!"

Left as he is without acceptable doorways to the future, Albee inevitably must end his American family in sterility. This limits his range as a dramatist. "The discord between the present and the past," as Chekhov said, "is first of all felt in the family," yet if one's imagery *ends* there, without exploring the worlds of play, struggle, and work, human potential scarcely can be known. Albee has depicted a hospital, a beach, a Cardinal's residence, yet family relations remain paramount for each. If the plays are to be believed, history will end in the aestheticism of symbolic transcendence. History will continue, of course, and will say something about the limits of Albee's dramatic vision.

Drama is the most socially rooted of the arts, and aestheticism as an affirmation has never been wholly comfortable on stage. Because Albee is so incapable of *historical* affirmations, he identifies too closely with his symbolic transcenders and loses aesthetic distance. These difficulties become audible in George's rhetoric when he is serious: the spark of slang goes and his speech becomes amazingly opaque. This is even more true in ***Tiny Alice,*** since all the characters' language is projected in Julian's mind and can be turned into dry cant. Tired, unfelt commonplaces about the Human Condition abound, ritually uttered substitutes for real human conditions enacted in history.

In ***Tiny Alice*** a final problem also comes to a head, caused by Albee's uncritical presentation of his heroes. Julian's imagination, which creates the action, is too homosexual for general application or comprehension. Most plays "compromise universality" in the other direction; they generalize and fantasize about existence with an implicit heterosexuality just as narrow, and just as blandly disregard the other side of sexuality. However, though a homosexual viewpoint may make some special contribution, it is less generally valid, balanced, and embracing than is the best pondered heterosexual outlook, given a world in which the homosexual still is despised and persecuted. It may be intensively and effectively expressed—Genet's *Our Lady of the Flowers,* as well as ***Tiny Alice,*** shows what remarkable art is thus engendered. But as a rule art gains when a writer pleads neither the homosexual nor the heterosexual vision, but maintains a nice understanding and irony for both. The homosexual vision is not in itself debilitating; what hurts is not to have it set in the broadest perspective.

Arthur K. Oberg (essay date 1966)

SOURCE: "Edward Albee: His Language and Imagination," in *Prairie Schooner,* Vol. XL, No. 1, Spring, 1966, pp. 139-46.

[*The following essay explores Albee's "problems with language," arguing that "Albee's words, seemingly self-generative and unending, become substitutes for real acts."*]

The experience of reading or rereading an Albee play after witnessing its production brings none of the disappointments that follow upon confronting a work of Tennessee Williams or Arthur Miller in print—a discovery of a thinness of text, a suspicion of whatever emotion or power the play managed to evoke on the stage.[1] Albee, in contrast to these dramatists, reads as well as he plays. Yet, criticism of Albee generally has failed to examine the defining quality of that language and its relation to the world and to the characters that Albee chooses to portray. From ***The Zoo Story*** to Tiny Alice we hear "the jazz of a very special hotel,"[2] Albee's unmistakable style. An admission of Albee's debt to Ionesco or Beckett or Coward is only to realize how different Albee's dialogue finally is from anything that the theatre has ever known. Acknowledgement of a debt to O'Neill's confessional *copia* and hacking verbal bitchiness is more helpful, although of a nature that is too general for extended comparison.

Albee's dramatic language is distinguished by its abundance and virtuosity. He has an ear for puns, allusion, and repartee that reveal an inventiveness of the first order. What is heard is a compendium of styles, a style that ranges as wide as the language of any Restoration play. Albee draws upon everything from the high or grand styles of literature down to the vaudeville routines of popular tradition. For the *inclusiveness* of what gets into the dialogue there is an *exclusiveness* of reference, joke, and nuance; not every playgoer shares Albee's metaphysical or literary or sexual play of mind, although if Diana Trilling's appraisal of Who's Afraid of Virginia Woolf? is correct, a large part of an audience's response is aspiration toward this "closed circuit"[3] exclusiveness, an intellectual kinship with the very special persons whom Albee depicts in his plays.

The inclusiveness and exclusiveness of Albee's style are one and the same response to a paralyzed societal situation, specifically American. There is mockery with an elitist vengeance. Albee recognizes the humor and poetry latent in cliché and makes his audience superior to the clichés of advertising, army talk, and Armageddon by inventing a pastiche-made dialogue that topples the idols of the market place.[4] In the world of Albee's plays no one is safe and nothing is sacred. Albee's appropriation of styles as different as baby and Indian and body "talk" becomes an attempt to break down the frozen forms of expression that our public lives variously necessitate. Using metaphor *as cliché* and cliché *as metaphor,* Albee pushes them as far as they will go, exposing established systems and personal arrangements which outworn metaphor thoughtlessly would perpetuate. Albee stands outside the cliché and looks at the disparities indicated—between institution and icon, embodiment and essence, passive and active agent. The dialogue, in the course of indicating and criticizing these divisions, approaches parody that is in danger of turning back upon itself. Cliché, excessively mocked, dwindles from metaphysics and satire into "sophomoric conundrum" and "semantics." Albee, as brilliantly inventive as Salinger in his prose style, risks being betrayed by a creative inclusiveness and exclusiveness that finds expression in his use of cliché. In trying to embrace and transcend all styles, Albee risks concluding by having no style at all.

If there are side roads along which writers would occasionally lead an audience, Albee's language has its own ways of putting us off and of deflecting our attention from what is central. The humor, the repartee, the self-creating inventiveness and *copia* can overwhelm; although Albee's style is consciously and defensively circuitous, we may get lost as the words become ends in themselves. Albee's peculiar metaphysical conceits and logic of *non sequitur* and of illogic may lead an audience away from the matter at hand. The range and the variety of the dialogue reveal a richness that threatens to make the play stop from time to time as the playwright and his characters lingeringly savor the lines or thoughts involved. Inflicted with the burden of consciousness, Albee's protagonists give voice to both an existential and artistic dilemma. As they are caught in the web and the weaving of words, these characters alternate between exposing and hiding what they would say. Who's Afraid of Virginia Woolf? and Tiny Alice, capitalizing upon what were already tendencies in the early plays, veer both toward lyrical incomprehensibility and hinting understatement. When, as in the case of The Ballad of the Sad Cafe, Albee exclusively underwrites, he produces a linguistically flat, boring, and fraudulently suggestive play.

What is unfortunate in any critical consideration of Albee is that certain aspects of his dialogue—the satire, the *copia,* the inventiveness, the showmanship—tend to obscure characteristics of the language which relate to the distinctive strength that the plays elicit in the theatre. The range and the virtuosity of Albee's plays are noticed at the expense of more serious earmarks of the speech. The degree of consciousness that the characters exhibit in formulating their thoughts and in finding and fixing an appropriate language, for example, is intentionally conceived. While comment upon mental and verbal processes from within a play is neither new nor exceptional in the drama, the extent to which Albee's protagonists call attention to the use and mechanism of language merits particular regard. Words are defined, conjugated, declined; from Albee's earliest short plays through Tiny Alice there is repartee in which words and phrases are modified, paraphrased, and corrected. One character refines another's talk, improvising as well at will. Language, a playful and deadly game, forces the Marthas and Georges to indulge in one-upsmanship. They talk for victory and are as conscious of their routines as their guest is made or as Mommy becomes in The American Dream:

> MOMMY: Nonsense. Old people have nothing to say; and if old people *did* have something to say, nobody would listen to them. (*To Grandma*) You see? I can pull that stuff just as easy as you can.
>
> (p. 44)

And in Who's Afraid of Virginia Woolf?:

> NICK (*Snapping it out*): All right . . . what do you want me to say? Do you want me to say it's funny, so you can contradict me and say it's sad? or do you want me to say it's sad so you can turn around and say no, it's funny. You can play that damn little game any way you want to, you know!
>
> (p. 33)

After such knowledge there can be neither forgiveness nor naiveté.

As Albee's characters learn what speech can and cannot do, they realize that the efficacy of language lies in manipulating and controlling themselves, others, and the unknown. What can be named is manageable. The danger, most prominent in Who's Afraid of Virginia Woolf?, is that the rules keep changing and that language, as dialectic, becomes a dangerous game. From Jerry and Peter in ***The Zoo Story*** to Julian and Alice in Tiny Alice there is an awareness of mind and language as subterfuge, of words as concealment and exposé. The movement of several plays toward a stripping down process exemplifies this use of language as confessional instrument or agent. An audience is asked repeatedly to entertain speech as *more than speech.* Language is employed as dialectic and exorcism—in The American Dream Albee uses the metaphysics of cliché to indicate the sterile and outworn lives of Mommy and Daddy; in Who's Afraid of Virginia Woolf? the play moves toward a ritualistic disposing of an imaginary love child by George's recitation of prayers for the dead in Latin. Words, both white and black magic, are wielded as weapon and talisman, and in the dialogues of Albee's plays there are stretches of talk when we hear unmistakable psychoanalytic couch technique. But as language reaches toward therapeutic use there are also reminders and instances of words losing their reference points, terrible moments in which the characters seem to be speaking in different languages. Although language can function as more than speech, there are times when it functions as much less. Words cease to behave as denotative and connotative indices, and the characters work to restore words to old meanings or to raise them to new ones. While an Albee protagonist does not join Beckett's Maddy in his extremity of "struggling with a dead language,"[5] neither does he voice assurance that individual meanings cannot be lost or slip or die.

If we can get beyond the verbal and mental façade of an Albee play to probe what makes ***The Zoo Story*** or The Death of Bessie Smith or Tiny Alice a moving experience, we are struck by a pathos dictated by facts of loneness and loneliness and fear. And it is language to which Albee resorts to fill up the time and the tedium, much like the intent and impression of dialogue in a Beckett play. But something else is involved. Words are employed by Albee's characters as a means of getting through to one another, even when this is possible only by the infinite capacity of words to wound and hurt.[6] Behind the words of Jerry or George we hear all that is painful and pathetic. While language alternates between relentless directness and hinting vagueness (an uncertain *"him"* or "you-know-what," a reference without antecedent) an audience watches as the characters press the limit of their vocabularies. This limit has no end. Dialogue, never adequate, attempts to surround what it would control, seeking victory in its *copia* and in an intensity which is related to this abundance. Against the hacking bitchiness of Albee's dialogue no "survival kit" exists. We are subjected to the kind of afternoon or evening the play provides precisely *because of the pain involved,* a pain that the variety and creativity of the dialogue would desperately hide or at least divert from our notice.

As the rhythms and rapid reversals of Albee's plays establish themselves, language strives not only to function as more than speech but to replace character and action, and to do so entirely. In Albee's world one confronts "special people, special problems" (*Tiny Alice,* p. 135). From Jerry to Julian, Albee is concerned with presenting studies in alienation,[7] characters who are unable to *relate* to the outside world of human relationships. Unable to "relate"—as key a word in Albee as "contact," "rapport," or "syntax"—Albee's protagonists look to language to forge whatever identity and relationship their lives have lacked. The most real thing about Jerry or Grandma or Martha is their words. In the absent Bessie Smith what is most energetic is her song. By turn confessional and obsessive, healing and lethal, their language allows them a confidence and strength that their daily human or even, as in Jerry's case, animal contacts deny or inadequately furnish.

While Albee's characters join a long line of contemporary American and European dramatic protagonists in their painful attempts to "relate," Albee goes on to create the illusion of relationships by a *copia* in language, a "syntax" that masquerades as character and action. This creates as uncomfortable a situation for an audience as that presented in T. S. Eliot's plays where it is *behavior,* partly reflected in speech, that masquerades as action. Albee's words, seemingly self-generative and unending, become substitutes for real acts. As verbal and "mental sex play" (*Tiny Alice,* p. 112), language turns into masturbation, and speeches in Who's Afraid of Virginia Woolf? comment upon this most revealingly:

> GEORGE: But you've moved bag and baggage into your own fantasy world now, and you've started playing variations on your own distortions. . . .
>
> (p. 155)
>
> GEORGE (*Chuckles, takes his drink*): Well, you just hold that thought, Martha . . . hug it close . . . run your hands over it. Me, I'm going to sit down . . . if you'll excuse me . . . I'm going to sit over there and read a book.
>
> (p. 168)

Whatever "contact" Albee's characters manage to establish in the early plays is achieved exclusively *within and by means* of words. In Who's Afraid of Virginia Woolf? and Tiny Alice the verbal veneer more frequently cracks, and Albee is increasingly aware of foreshadowing a world of human relationships *beyond* the dramatic syntax of language. Julian's monologues are anticipated in Martha's speech at the opening of Act III when she admits feelings that language finally can neither replace nor hide:

> I cry all the time too, Daddy. I cry allllll the time; but deep inside, so no one can see me. I cry all the time. And Georgie cries all the time, too. We both cry all the time, and then, what we do, we cry, and we take our tears, and we put 'em in the ice box, in the goddamn ice trays (*Begins to laugh*) until they're all frozen (*Laughs even more*) and then . . . we put them . . . in our . . . drinks.
>
> (pp. 185-86).

George cried in the earlier acts of the play, but under the continual barrage of words this is likely to be forgotten. Unlike a Pirandello play, the overwhelming impression of an Albee play is not one of life and feeling continually asserting itself and breaking out of the confines of art. There is something about an Albee play that in the end is claustrophobic. Whatever contact a character is able to attain *outside of language* occurs too infrequently and is too sketchily imagined. In Who's Afraid of Virginia Woolf? the amount of drinking and hacking bitchiness is too intense to allow an audience to posit any substantially *real* life for Martha and George outside their braying words or after the play. Yet the possibility of such a life is essential if the destruction of the imaginary love child is to be effective beyond its immediate dramatic impact. As for Albee's conception of the wedded state, it seems little more than some third-rate, pulp fiction perception of marriage as hellish argument and being good in bed.

A similar shortcoming in perspective appears in Tiny Alice where physical, heterosexual relations (here seen as epiphany, seduction, and the third and fourth removed reciting and discussion of a D. H. Lawrence poem) take on the feel of mock actions. Albee's problems with language are compounded with and related to those of sex, as we already noted in his confusion of words with orgasm. Unable to conceive of heterosexual relations as anything more than the marriage of a Martha and George or than the relationship of Julian with the physical Alice or with the woman at the asylum, Albee also falls short of establishing "aestheticism as an affirmation" or "symbolic transcendence," achievements which have been remarked in his plays.[8] For there must first be viable, concrete intimations of *real* relationships in order that *transcendent* ideals may be seriously entertained.

Just as the satire and inventiveness of an Albee play are inadequate to explain its power in the theatre, so is Albee's homosexual imagination inadequate to the characters and action of his work. Although the Tyrones are long on their journey into night before the curtain ever rises, there is at least in O'Neill the memory of a time when marriage or the family were more than monstrous conceptions. There is nothing inherently sacred about either family or heterosexual life, but Albee's criticism or attempted transcendence of them loses conviction in the face of his holding only a poor idea of what they *might have been like.* As a result, behind the lunging language of the plays there is more pathos than terror. An hysterical note keeps slipping through the words, and words prove as incomplete as Albee's perspectives. To argue that Albee has made whatever contacts he knows how addresses a consideration that ought never to have been raised. The plays are admittedly dramatic; the texts, impressive; Albee, intellectually honest. But in the end we must return to the plays, an art in which Albee expects language to accomplish too much and in which his confined vision of human relationships begs for alternatives. In The American Dream a hint of the family as other than nightmare might have prevented satire from turning into caricature. In Who's Afraid of Virginia Woolf? some notion of only the *possibility* of a creative marriage—something like that presented in John Updike's short story, "Wife-Wooing"—might have been useful. And in Tiny Alice a clearer idea of the *real* life or "dimension" that Julian rejects might have resulted in less aesthetic confusion and in a more satisfying and major play.

NOTES

[1]The choreographic production of an Elia Kazan has done much to create the impression that the text of a Williams or Miller play is stronger than in truth it is.

[2]Edward Albee, *The Zoo Story*, in *The Zoo Story, The Death of Bessie Smith*, and *The Sandbox* (New York: Coward-McCann, Inc., 1960), p. 30. Other page references given in the text are to the following editions of Albee's plays: *The American Dream* (New York: Coward-McCann, Inc., 1961); *Who's Afraid of Virginia Woolf?* (New York: Atheneum, 1962); *Tiny Alice* (New York: Atheneum, 1965).

[3]Diana Trilling, "The Riddle of Albee's *Who's Afraid of Virginia Woolf?*" *Claremont Essays* (New York: Harcourt, Brace & World, Inc., 1964), p. 219. Diana Trilling borrows this phrase from Mary McCarthy who originally used it of J. D. Salinger's work. An interesting analogy might also be made with Samuel Beckett's "closed set," "closed field" technique and dialectic noted by Hugh Kenner, *Flaubert, Joyce and Beckett: The Stoic Comedians* (Boston: Beacon Press, 1962), pp. 92-93.

[4]For a comparison of Albee's clichés with those of Pinter and Ionesco see Martin Esslin, *The Theatre of the Absurd* (Garden City, N.Y.: Doubleday, 1961), pp. 226-27.

[5]Samuel Beckett, *All That Fall*, in *Krapp's Last Tape and Other Dramatic Pieces* (New York: Grove Press, Inc., 1960), p. 80.

[6]The number of references to speech as weapon and as *all kinds* of weapons in *Who's Afraid of Virginia Woolf?* is significantly large.

[7]For a study of Albee's *social estrangement* in a mechanized America see Peter Wolfe, "The Social Theater of Edward Albee," *Prairie Schooner* XXXIX (Fall 1965), 248-62. For a study of Albee's *aesthetic distancing* see Thomas B. Markus, "*Tiny Alice* and Tragic Catharsis," *ETJ*, XVII (October 1965), 225-33.

[8]Lee Baxandall, "The Theatre of Edward Albee," *TDR*, IX(Summer 1965), pp. 39, 25.

Henry Knepler (essay date 1967)

SOURCE: "Edward Albee: Conflict of Tradition," in *Modern Drama*, Vol. 10, No. 3, December 1967, pp. 274-79.

[*In the essay below, Knepler examines Albee's uneasy mixture of the American dramatic tradition, with its emphasis on rationality, causation, and explanation, with elements of the Theatre of the Absurd, with its stress on senselessness and incomprehension.*]

In The Introduction To His Excellent Collection *American Playwrights on Drama* Horst Frenz remarks, axiomatically, that "O'Neill never founded a school." He is right, of course, if one considers school to refer to the usual stylistic or structural elements of drama. In the Marlovian or Racinian sense O'Neill did not found a school. In the sense in which his work has become engrained in the American dramatic tradition, however, he did. I do not mean the rather facile, negative sense which Professor Frenz refers to in the same sentence: "O'Neill never founded a school, and the constant experimenting and frequent change of style, which are so noticeable in his work, characterize the work of other American dramatists as well." Mere eclecticism of theatrical modes is not the cohering element of a school or a tradition.

Nor has the American drama "sprung full-grown from the imagination of Eugene O'Neill" as it seems to Robert Brustein. Somewhere between these poles lies the meeting ground of O'Neill's talent and the cultural forces through which the drama in America developed into a reasonably coherent literary tradition. That this tradition has a strong affinity for psychological or psychiatric or psycho-analytic modes needs no particularly extended rehearsal. But, again, these modes are not what gives American dramatic literature its particular cohesive quality. The Freudian couch which hovers, Chagall-like, over the American drama, is not of itself a tradition, only a manifestation of it. Rather, the same forces which spread the psycho-analytic interest until it pervaded much of American intellectual life, also underlie the tradition.

Perhaps unawares himself, Arthur Miller characterizes its source: ". . . by force of circumstance I came early and unawares to be fascinated by sheer process itself. How things connected. How the native personality of man was changed by his world, and the harder question, how he in turn could change the world." The key word is repeated in the passage: how. How to build a better mousetrap. How to fix our cities, our youth, our wars, our world, our inner and outer selves. The interest in psycho-analysis is therefore part of a montage made up of, among other things, urban renewal, Dale Carnegie, prohibition, mass education, and what Theodore H. White calls the action-intellectuals. This is said in all seriousness; the American willingness to change things, from cars to countries, is no laughing matter. This leaves man a world in the process of amending itself to which he must make a running adjustment as best he can, his radar spinning away, in David Riesman's analogy, in search of other friendly bleeps in the void.

Eugene O'Neill, transforming personal necessity into brilliant drama, not so much established the tradition as translated it from the larger scene to the stage. In the context of the drama that world view had of course to be made explicit in terms of conflict: this explains not so much the attention as the kind of attention paid to sex and to the family: in the American tradition they do not merely become opponents in a tug of war; the pervasive concern with understanding, explaining and amending them makes them roadstations on the Calvary of change. They are of course also the factors, or reputed to be so, which send American man to the psychiatrist, thereby providing the obverse of the coin: Our fascination with process sends us to the repairshop. And it also gives us the idea that all things can be fixed, if we try hard enough. At this junction of consequence and desire resides the American dream.

In the plays which Edward Albee has written so far the conflict between two traditions, the American and the Absurd, is fierce, because they are intellectually incompatible and because he attempts to use both simultaneously.

The American prescribes that man must attempt to make sense of his environment and, moreover, that someday, somehow, he will. The Absurd, as stated by Martin Esslin (and quoted, with disapproval, by Albee) "attempts to make [man] face up to the human condition as it really is, to free him from illusions that are bound to cause constant maladjustment and disappointment . . . For the dignity of man lies in his ability to face reality in all its senselessness." Albee fights that senselessness with all the brilliance of his characterization, his dialogue and his symbols, while at the same time using the modes and theatrical elements of the Absurd: the disembodied static situation; the hints of other dimensions beyond the real or visible; the allegorical maze; and so on. He uses the means or themes of the Absurd to portray the human condition: isolation; repetition; illusion. But he uses them in the American manner: isolation is very conscious and involuntary; repetition is guiltily self-imposed and recognized; and illusion is hallucinatory, mad, *i.e.,* a clinical matter. And he puts it all in the sexual, familial context of O'Neill, Miller, Williams and Inge. This paper attempts to single out some of the results in Albee's work of the conflict between the two traditions. It does not give an over-all evaluation of his work; it merely tries to describe a sub-surface conflict creating surface dramatic problems which, moreover, Albee seems to be resolving. His latest play, A Delicate Balance, veers rather strongly back to the tradition of O'Neill.

In his two earliest plays, ***The Zoo Story*** and The Death of Bessie Smith, Albee handles the familial, sexual causality directly. As Jerry tells it in ***The Zoo Story*** ". . . good old Mom walked out on good old Pop when I was ten and a half years old; she embarked on an adulterous turn of our southern states . . ." The second scene of Bessie Smith shows the dominance of the Nurse over the would-be invalid father, and their hate for each other, which in turn underlies her domination of her would-be lover, the Intern, and of the Orderly, a Negro, and in turn is vaguely made to underlie not only her racism but all racism. This causal element is of course only one aspect of a series of subtle and complex relationships. The point about this element is, however, that it stands out in both plays and serves, especially in ***The Zoo Story,*** as an almost gratuitous addition to a wealth of other material characterizing Jerry and his position. It stands out, I am inclined to think, as if Albee had felt that, without this bit of Freudian byplay, Jerry or even the Nurse would have been incomplete.

Albee's next play, The American Dream, with its satellite, The Sandbox, need only be compared to Ionesco's *Bald Soprano* and Pinter's *Collection* to show the familial, always heavily sensual, as the burial ground of the human condition. Mommy and Daddy are as desiccated as Mr. and Mrs. Smith in Ionesco's play or the couple in Pinter's, but their condition differs. Mr. and Mrs. Smith show, perhaps, the aimless boredom of middle class existence, the Pinter couple displays the cruelty of replacement and renewal, but Mommy and Daddy are held together by the perdurable hoops of steel made of impotence and guilt, the chief fixings of all couch-based fixes.

In Albee's first full-length play, Who's Afraid of Virginia Woolf, Mommy moves toward reality and becomes Martha, the castrating wife, in a three hour running battle all in the family. In The Ballad of the Sad Cafe, an adaptation of Carson McCullers' novella, Miss Amelia's marriage to Marvin Macy is a necessary part of her Calvary. In Tiny Alice, Miss Alice's marriage to Julian is part of his Calvary—and a very explicit Calvary at that. Mommy and Daddy reappear in A Delicate Balance—softened, more rounded and more realistic, tending toward Inge rather than Ionesco, beset by friends fleeing from a nameless threat, by a daughter back from her third or fourth divorce, and an alcoholic sister as the commentator character. Divorce and alcoholism, like impotence, homosexuality, and loss of religious faith underlie the variations, presented with often great subtlety, of man's isolation without and within himself.

To seal this isolation Albee uses a psychological variant of a device which James O'Neill, Eugene's father, would have remembered well. In nineteenth century drama it was known as the Pathetic Child. With Albee it becomes the would-be child, ranging from the symbolically emasculated young man in The American Dream to the alienated divorcee in A Delicate Balance. The phantom child in Virginia Woolf is the most interesting. Martha and George have invented a child for themselves; it is a secret between them, whose disclosure to visitors leads to George's "killing" him, by means of a fictitious telegram about a car accident at his fictitious college. I was struck by the parallel to Salinger's story "Uncle Wiggly in Connecticut": there, a small girl, alone and alienated from her mother, invents a playmate for herself. When the mother tells a friend about that phantom playmate, the little girl has him killed in a car accident, and calmly invents another. The same air of contamination pervades the story as the play. In Virginia Woolf George and Martha are really children in a statement on arrested development which corresponds to freudian theory. The variations continue: Miss Amelia, in the Sad Cafe, adapts rather than adopts the little hunchback Cousin Lymon as one would a child; she loses him when he runs off with her would-be husband Marvin Macy, to whom she refused to bear a child. The most complicated man-child relationship is in Albee's most equivocal play, Tiny Alice. In different ways the play deals with two children. Brother Julian, the protagonist, in his morning-glory freshness and honesty, is the innocent fallen among the thieves. The other child is part-object of a story he himself tells. An inmate of a mental hospital believes herself to be with child; a medical examination discloses that she has a fatal cancer of the womb. The edifice of symbols surrounding this simple event is a fretwork of mirrors of illusions: the woman believes that she is the Virgin Mary; Julian committed himself to the mental hospital in which she was a patient because of his loss of religious faith which was accompanied by hallucinations. Because of these hallucinations he is not sure if he did or did not have intercourse with the woman. The whole structure of illusion therefore has a medical bent which is also noticeable in other Albee plays. The imaginary child in Virginia Woolf is an indication of his parents' sickness, just as the emasculated and therefore perfect American Dreamboat is of the sickness of society. The Delicate Balance is the one between sanity and insanity, or what we believe these two states to be. The guests who foist themselves upon Agnes and Tobias in that play are driven from their home by an undescribed, hallucinatory experience. Albee, though he may not have intended this, cannot rid his plays of the idea that illusion is sick, or at least a matter of clinical concern. The prevalence of would-be children whether as phantoms, like in Tiny Alice and Virginia Woolf, or as seemingly grown up, like in The American Dream and The Ballad of the Sad Cafe has therefore a double function: isolation and illusion. Except for a few culture heroes like Grandma (The American Dream) and Martha's father (Virginia Woolf) men and women are seen as children and therefore given to illusions. The child-man relationship is not Wordsworthian, however; it is a case of arrested development, of stunted growth or maturity, according to psycho-analytic principles. The trap of human illusion which is sprung for us in *The Caretaker* or *Waiting for Godot* has no such causes, nor could it have.

Repetition, the third major element singled out here, is a central aspect of the Absurd drama. *The Bald Soprano* is a *perpetuum mobile,* ending with the same lines as the opening. *The Balcony* has its variations of a theme in the brothel; repetition is the point in *The Collection*; *The Dumb Waiter* has its hired killers doing just another job; and so on. Repetition serves Albee in the same manner, but it also gets in his way at times. As we watch Who's Afraid of Virginia Woolf, we find that Nick and Honey are not the first victims drawn and quartered on the battleground of Martha and George. The battle is permanent which would make it a condition rather than a process. So Albee contradicts and weakens his impact in several ways: at the end of the play the phantom child has been liquidated, and the ground rules of battle are changed thereby. And Honey, who was afraid of childbirth before, leaves the inferno wanting a child. (She has just one line, one moment, to indicate that, which makes it appear more like the old crime movie where the last sixty seconds show that crime, so lovingly portrayed for eighty-nine minutes, does not pay.)

In Tiny Alice the trouble is exactly the opposite: the uniqueness of the situation, so obviously desired for Julian, is undermined by symbols and conversation until one gets a kind of *déjà vu* effect, as if Miss Alice and her crew were quite used to swatting such flies as Julian. Repetition and illusion are closely linked in Albee's work. There is comfort in repetition and pattern, comfort for children to witness expected and expectable events, comfort for all ages, if we can see that terrifying constant process of change somehow patterned; comfort especially if we remember that the kindly clinician needs to be able to find the pattern in order to cure. That, perhaps, accounts for the occurrence of symbols in circular patterns, often great swaths of interlocking circles. In Virginia Woolf, for example, George tells Nick the story of a prep school friend who advertently-inadvertently killed his parents, later ran his car into a tree, and ended his days in a mental institution. The story reappears as George's own, though we cannot be sure of that, and also as a novel he wrote, which was suppressed by his formidable father-in-law, the President of the College. In the end George reports that the death of the phantom son occurred in the same way as the suicide attempt of the prep school boy.

At times, these great swaths of symbols look most like the creations of a talented, malicious child who wants to provide happy hunting grounds for English teachers. My favorite is the commingling of blood and wine, semen and blood, stringing together a great edifice of sex and faith in Tiny Alice. In the end blood turns back to wine, the bottles of the magnificent wine cellar, poorly tended, are popping the rotting corks; especially of a superb Mouton Rothschild—Blood of the Lamb indeed!

A *New Yorker* cartoon not long ago depicts a group of men and women on folding chairs around a table, on a stage: a first reading of a play. One man is up, talking, his foot on his chair: the director. The caption says: "Now, the first thing we have to get straight is what exactly Aristophanes was trying to say." Albee plays on our culturally conditioned desire to get behind things, to see, in Arthur Miller's phrase, "how things connect." With O'Neill this was legitimate, so to speak, a genuine desire caused by a genuine anguish. With Albee it seems to be a structure consciously made up of rewards and punishments for the audience, which perhaps makes him a Pavlovian rather than a Freudian in the American theatrical tradition. He challenges us deliberately, he dares us to look behind what he says. He does it brilliantly, with a wealth of talent in construction, in dialog, in imagery. Perhaps he is both admired and disliked because his now-you-see-it-now-you-don't view of the human condition gives us the kind of inside dope we currently deserve.

C. W. E. Bigsby (essay date 1967)

SOURCE: "Edward Albee," in *Confrontation and Commitment: A Study of Contemporary American Drama, 1959-66,* University of Missouri Press, 1967, pp. 71-92.

[*In the essay below, Bigsby examines Albee's "insistence on the need to abandon a faith in illusion."*]

American drama in the early sixties has been effectively dominated by one man. In three years Edward Albee took the American theatre by storm. His first play, ***The Zoo Story*** (1959) was greeted by *The Villager* as, 'The finest play, written by an American, that can be seen for love or money' while Who's Afraid of Virginia Woolf? received the New York Drama Critics Circle award for the season 1962-3. Indeed this, his first full-length play, was nominated for a Pulitzer Prize by that Committee's drama jury. The nomination was, however, rejected because, in the words of W. D. Maxwell, a member of the advisory board, 'I thought it was a filthy play'.[1]

Albee, like Gelber, has shown himself to be fully aware of the vision of the European absurdists and indeed he has adopted both their analogical method (***The Zoo Story***) and their style (The American Dream). At the same time, however, again in common with Gelber, he has been struck by the insufficiency of their vision. If Solly, in *The Connection,* represented merely a potential, in Albee's plays that potential is realised and confrontation is accepted as the necessary basis for a life which if absurd in origin need not be so in fact. Albee accepts Camus's suggested progression from absurdity to love and his plays, starting with ***The Zoo Story*** and progressing to Tiny Alice and A Delicate Balance, are directly concerned with that 'momentous enlightment' which leads to a 'real companionship, founded on truth and purged of all falsehood'. Where Gelber has become frozen in stylistic revolt Albee has refined both his method and his thought in formulating a genuine alternative both to illusion and to despair. Indeed in some senses this process of refinement has gone too far so that Tiny Alice is in danger of degenerating into mere esoteric theorising.

Albee's faith is essentially that which Bellow insists upon in *Henderson the Rain King,* which was published in the same year as ***The Zoo Story.*** Indeed it is interesting to note just how closely these two writers' philosophies match one another. To both writers the self is seen as a barrier between the individual and the rest of humanity. Ihab Hassan, in his book *Radical Innocence,* has pointed out that the natural progress of Bellow's heroes is from humiliation to humility[2]—a process which purges this egocentricity while establishing the need for acceptance. This progress is equally true of Albee's protagonists who similarly come to understand that genuine existence lies only through the acceptance of reality and the establishment of a true relationship between individuals. Ironically this is a lesson which both Henderson and Jerry, the protagonist of ***The Zoo Story,*** derive from a contact with animals. In *Henderson the Rain King* it is a lion whose unavoidable qualities teach Henderson the need for acceptance and thus love while in Albee's play the same lesson is taught by a dog.

The Zoo Story describes the life which man has created for himself as a 'solitary free passage' characterised by indifference towards others. The isolation, which is the result of this attitude towards life, is stressed by the image of the zoo which is established in the course of the play as a valid image for man who has come to accept loneliness as the norm of existence. Albee's thesis is that there is a need to make contact, to emerge from these self-imposed cages of convention and false values so that one individual consciousness may impinge on another. This act he defines as love.

The *New York Times* has called ***The Zoo Story***'a harrowing portrait of a young man alienated from the human race'. Yet ironically the play is dedicated to demonstrating that this alienated individual, a man in his late thirties called Jerry, has more sense of the urgent necessity for human contact than does society itself. Jerry has reached a moment of crisis. The purposelessness of his life has begun to evidence itself in his appearance. He is 'not poorly dressed, but carelessly'; his body 'has begun to go fat'. As Albee says, 'His fall from physical grace should not suggest debauchery, he has, to come closest to it, a great weariness' (*Z.S.* p. 11). The origin of this weariness is his growing realisation of the gulf which exists between him and his fellow men. As he admits, 'I don't talk to many people—except to say like: give me a beer, or where's the john, or what time does the feature go on, or keep your hands to yourself, buddy' (*Z.S.* p. 17). Jerry's isolation is complete. Not only does he know nothing of those who share his rooming house—itself in a state of dilapidation which mirrors Jerry's own decline—but he is also effectively cut off from the past. His parents are long dead and the two picture frames which he owns are both empty. But having undergone a sudden enlightenment, a perception of the need for real human contact, he sets out across Central Park to pass on his new-found message. There he meets Peter, the epitome of middle-class complacency.

Peter is 'neither fat nor gaunt, neither handsome nor homely'. He is, in fact, virtually non-existent. His opinions are shaped by *Time* magazine and his values are those of a society to whom status and income rank before communication. He is sitting on his bench in Central Park precisely because here no demands can be made on him. He is remote from other people. If he exists as little more than a stereotype with no individuating characteristics this is essentially how Albee sees him. The world he lives in is essentially that of the American dream. Indeed even his marriage is revealed by Jerry's relentlessly probing questions to be little more than a social contract in which the dominance of the woman has emasculated the man and thus denied the necessity even of sexual contact. In a real sense, therefore, Peter is ultimately as isolated as Jerry had been.

To Albee, rather as to Karl Jaspers, modern society has detached itself from fundamentals and has created a new system of values by which the pursuit of material wealth and technological efficiency have come to replace basic human needs. As Philip Mairet says, paraphrasing Jasper's beliefs, these new values 'console man with the feeling that he is progressing, but make him neglect or deny fundamental forces of his inner life which are then turned into forces of destruction'.[3] Jerry's function in ***The Zoo Story*** is literally to 'save' Peter; to bring him back into a genuine relationship with his fellow man.

Jerry attempts to establish the importance of human contact by explaining the source of his own conversion. He describes a macabre duel which he had fought with a dog. This dog had attacked him each time he had entered his rooming house. Anxious to avoid contact he had tried at first to placate it with food, feeling as he did so rather as if he were offering a sop to Cerberus. When this had failed, he explains to Peter, he had then attempted to kill it. Only when the dog was dying, however, had he suddenly realised that some sort of connection had been possible between the dog and himself—a contact which his action had aborted. It was at this point that Jerry had experienced his 'momentous enlightenment' for he had realised the absolute need for contact between human beings. As he says to Peter, who is clearly disturbed by the story, 'if you can't deal with people, you have to start somewhere, WITH ANIMALS'. (*Z.S.* p. 34.) When Peter refuses to learn the lesson implicit in the parable Jerry goes on explicitly to insist on the validity of animals as an image for humanity, 'I went to the zoo to find out more about the way people exist with animals, and the way animals exist with each other, and with people too. It probably wasn't a fair test. What with everyone separated by bars from everyone else, the animals for the most part from each other, and always the people from the animals. But, if it's a zoo, that's the way it is' (*Z.S.* p. 39-40).

With this insistence on the validity of the zoo as an image for human beings consciously cut off from their kind Jerry comes finally to the conclusion that only through the stimulus of violence will any permanent contact be established. Neither allegory nor direct statement has succeeded in bringing Peter face to face with what Jerry sees as the basic problem of humanity. When his right to possession of the bench is challenged Peter's indignant reply shows that all of Jerry's comments about the evil of human isolation have had no impact. 'I see no reason why I should give up this bench. I sit on this bench almost every Sunday afternoon . . . It's secluded here; there's never anyone sitting here, so I have it all to myself' (*Z.S.* p. 41). Jerry recognises that his defence of the bench has become not only a defence of the solitariness of the human condition but also a justification of the values of a society which, it is implied, distracts man from the real problem of human existence. Jerry's retort expresses Albee's belief that absurdity stems not from the human situation but from man's response to that situation—a response which values the achievement of success above genuine fulfilment. 'You have everything in the world you want; you've told me about your home, and your family, and your own little zoo. You have everything, and now you want this bench. Are these the things men fight for? Tell me, Peter, is this bench, this iron and this wood, is this your honor? Is this the thing in the world you'd fight for? Can you think of anything more absurd?' (*Z.S.* p. 44). Jerry throws Peter a knife and by deliberate insults provokes the violence which ensures that he will not be able to escape the consequences. As Jerry thrusts himself onto the knife one is conscious of the fusion of sexuality and violence which has emerged as a mark of the urge to establish contact. There can be little doubt that contact has at last been established and that Peter will never be able to return to his bench of isolation, 'You won't be coming back here any more, Peter; you've been dispossessed. You've lost your bench' (*Z.S.* pp. 48-9). The message which Jerry had received from the dog in violence he has now passed on to his fellow man also in violence. Like Saul Bellow's Henderson Albee seems to subscribe to the belief that truth comes 'in blows'. Both Jerry and Henderson are shaken out of their private worlds of solitude and illusion by an enlightenment forced on them by an animal. As Henderson admits, '. . . unreality! That has been my scheme for a troubled but eternal life. But now I am blasted away from this practice by the throat of the lion. His voice was like a blow at the back of my head'.[4]

The Zoo Story is thus concerned with stressing the inadequacy of illusion—an illusion which is in essence the American dream. Peter, as we have seen, is a successful man. He has an executive position, a good salary, a family—and he is totally hollow and unaware of the needs of human beings. When Jerry had asked, 'Don't you have any idea, not even the slightest, what other people *need?*' Peter's reply had equated need with physical possessions, 'Well, you don't need this bench. That's for sure' (*Z.S.* p. 45). Peter's failure stems from the fact that he has never dared to confront the reality of his life—the reality which Jerry meticulously and brutally lays bare. The compromise which he has reached with his life has left him effectively emasculated and totally solitary and yet it is not until Jerry forces him to confront this reality that he becomes aware of any insufficiency. Jerry realises that to Peter he is only 'a permanent transient' in 'the greatest city in the world. Amen' (*Z.S.* p. 37) but step by step he brings him to an acceptance of the fact that he has come to accept his pointlessly mundane existence, in the same way that a child uses pornographic playing cards, 'as a substitute for real experience' (*Z.S.* p. 27).

The Zoo Story is concerned, then, with redemption, for Peter is not only brought into a new and more meaningful relationship with reality but is introduced to the need for that genuine human contact which is the antithesis of absurdity. It is clear that Albee would agree with Bellow's Henderson when he says that, 'it's love that makes reality reality'[5] although it is equally clear that this is a humanistic concern for fellow men and not that sexuality which serves merely to emasculate.

While Albee was content, in ***The Zoo Story,*** merely to sketch in the details of an absurd society, in The American Dream, written in the following year but not produced until 1961, he examines the alternative to confrontation. In doing so he borrows directly the techniques of the theatre of the absurd and demonstrates the vacuity of a society which refuses either to accept compassion or the need to embrace reality. While The American Dream is not directly concerned with confrontation it is worth dwelling on it for a moment for in this play Albee clearly identifies his vision of the absurd—a vision which differs fundamentally from the deterministic absurdity of a European drama derived out of Camus. At the same time it is apparent that through this one-act satire Albee is continuing to urge the need for genuine human contact based on a clear perception of the real.

Albee's play is dedicated to revealing the inadequacy of the American Dream—that faith in the inevitability and value of success which Horatio Alger had propounded. It is, as Albee himself has said, 'an examination of the American Scene, an attack on the substitution of artificial for real values in our society, a condemnation of complacency, cruelty, emasculation and vacuity; it is a stand against the fiction that everything in this slipping land of ours is peachy-keen'.[6] The Dream itself is a young man's vision of the future. It is a belief that the here and now is unimportant or that it is merely a step towards the achievement of some ambition which equates wealth with happiness and social acceptance with fulfilment. The future holds out the assurance of success to the young and guarantees a world where everything is 'peachy-keen'. It is a philosophy which must measure worth by utility since achievement is, according to the Dream, evaluated solely by material criteria. By this utilitarian approach, however, people become as liable to obsolescence as do machines. In Albee's play Daddy has fulfilled his social function in marrying Mommy and supplying her with the money which she had coveted while she in turn has completed her function in submitting to his sexual demands. All this lies in the past, however, and all Daddy can do now is to moan plaintively, 'I just want to get everything over with' (*A.D.* p. 70)—a complaint which clearly threatens the substance of the Dream itself. When he does make a concession to the Dream it is in the form of lip-service paid to the validity of ambition. 'All his life, Daddy has wanted to be a United States Senator; but now . . . he's changed his mind, and for the rest of his life he's going to want to be Governor . . . it would be nearer the apartment, you know' (*A.D.* p. 83).

In a functional society the characters are identified by their function. For the most part they are ciphers whose very hollowness is a reflection of the emptiness of the values by which they live. Mommy and Daddy, the endearing terms of family relationships, are identified with casual indifference and expediency on the one hand and emasculated ineffectualness on the other. The only character identified by name is Mrs. Barker and her name is consistently ignored or forgotten. In accepting the standards of society they have lost their individuality and hence their names. Mommy, Daddy, Grandma, the Young Man and Mrs. Barker are the expressionistic realisation of a society in which the humanising aspects of pity, affection and love have given way to a cold, clinical rationalisation which substitutes commercial value for worth and 'cool disinterest' for concern with fellow man.

The traditional foundation and justification of the Dream rests in the home and the family unit. While it is surely between the members of a family that contact can be expected to be initiated Albee shows not only that this initiative is not attempted but that a false scale of values leads to a positive widening of the gap between individuals. Daddy, who is emasculated as a result of an operation, no longer has any physical contact with his wife who has long before shown her disinclination for such contact. The situation is, in fact, reminiscent of that which has pertained in Peter's family life in ***The Zoo Story.***

Marriage is seen by Mommy as no more than a social contract in which she has bought wealth and security with sexuality. It is a commercial transaction. 'We were very poor! But then I married you, Daddy, and now we're very rich . . . I have a right to live off you because I married you, and because I used to let you get on top of me and bump your uglies' (*A.D.* pp. 66-7). If the word 'love' occurs in the dialogue it is in such a context as to emphasise the devaluation of its meaning. Mommy states her 'love' for Grandma but is at the same time planning to have her committed to a home. She brings to her family relationships the criteria of the world of commerce. She seeks above all 'satisfaction'. When her adopted child fails to give her this satisfaction she dismembers it and kills all its senses of compassion, love and affection. The true value of this 'satisfaction' becomes apparent, however, when Mommy greets the Young Man, whom Grandma identifies as the personification of the American Dream, with the toast, 'To satisfaction! Who says you can't get satisfaction?' (*A.D.* p. 126). For although he has an attractive manner and is 'almost insultingly good-looking in a typically American way' (*A.D.* p. 107) it is clear that he is as impotent as Daddy. In fact it transpires that he is the brother of the child whom Mommy had mutilated and that he has suffered injuries corresponding to those inflicted by her. These injuries have left him 'incomplete' and deprived of the emotions which prompt and facilitate human contact. 'I cannot touch another person and feel love . . . I no longer have the capacity to feel anything. I have no emotions . . . I let people touch me . . . I let them draw pleasure from my groin . . . from my presence . . . from the fact of me . . . but, that is all it comes to. As I told you, I am incomplete . . . I can feel nothing . . . I am . . . but this . . . what you see' (*A.D.* p. 115). Thus the faith of this society is placed solely in illusion—in the Dream. The failure to confront reality prevents the establishment of any meaningful relationships. Love becomes impossible and absurdity is accepted as the norm.

The American Dream has been identified by Martin Esslin as an integral part of the theatre of the absurd. While it is true that there are several points of contact between the theatre of the absurd and Albee's work, there does, however, remain one central difference. Esslin derives his definition of the absurd from Camus and Ionesco. Camus says, '. . . in a universe that is suddenly deprived of all illusions and of light, man feels a stranger. His is an irremediable exile, because he is deprived of memories of a lost homeland as much as he lacks the hope of a promised land to come. This divorce between man and his life, the actor and his setting, truly constitutes the feeling of Absurdity'.[7] Absurdity for Camus, therefore, derives directly from the human situation. Albee's expressionistic satire is directed, however, not at the fatuity of life *per se* but rather the nullity to which a false response reduces it. Where Camus suggests that man 'deprived of all illusions . . . feels a stranger' Albee contends, on the contrary, that absurdity lies in a continued adherence to illusion. Ionesco defines the absurd as 'that which is devoid of purpose . . . Cut off from his religious, metaphysical, and transcendental roots, man is lost; all his actions become senseless, absurd, useless'.[8] To Albee a man who is cut off from his religious and transcendental roots still remains a man. Only when he cuts himself off from the reality of his situation does he lose his humanity and become absurd. Albee is not concerned with the absurdity of reality but rather the absurdity of illusion. The target for his satire is the American Dream.

Stylistically The American Dream accepts the European contention that absurdity is most logically portrayed by a non-rational form which reflects and extends the theme. The influence of Beckett and Ionesco is largely restricted to style, however, for Albee insists on a potential for amelioration which would be denied by the European dramatists. His attack on 'the substitution of artificial for real values in our society' assumes the validity of these 'real values' while in the person of Grandma he demonstrates his belief in the viability of dissent. If the inauthenticity of modern life is a mark of man's desire to choose dehumanisation rather than face the true nature of the human condition he implies that this failure of courage is not inevitable. The American Dream, is, however, a slight work which if it successfully adapts Ionesco's style to his own vision (in particular *The Bald Prima Donna* (1950) which similarly ridicules bourgeois society) lacks the sheer intensity and originality of ***The Zoo Story.***

Richard Schechner, the editor of the *Tulane Drama Review,* greeted Albee's next play, Who's Afraid of Virginia Woolf?, as a 'persistent escape into morbid fantasy'. Like W. D. Maxwell he found it a filthy play and indicted it for its 'morbidity and sexual perversity which are there only to titillate an impotent and homosexual theatre and audience'. More perversely he saw in the play 'an ineluctable urge to escape reality and its concomitant responsibilities by crawling back into the womb, or bathroom, or both'.[9] The vigour of this revulsion was shared, however, by other critics who similarly misapprehended Albee's intention in a play which far from endorsing illusion remorselessly peels off protective fantasies in order to reach 'the bone . . . the marrow' (*V.W.* p. 213). Indeed as Alan Schneider, the play's Broadway director, has pointed out, '. . . is Albee not rather dedicated to smashing that rosy view, shocking us with the truth of our present-day behaviour and thought, striving to purge us into *an actual confrontation with reality?'*[10] (my italics).

Who's Afraid of Virginia Woolf? is indeed concerned with the purgation and ultimate destruction of illusion and was in fact at one time to have been called *The Exorcism.* If the play's present title seems at first to be little more than an incomprehensible private joke, however, it is clear that Albee's concern with confrontation does establish something more than a tenuous link between his work and that of Virginia Woolf. For while Mrs Ramsay, in *To The Lighthouse* (1927), had felt that 'To pursue truth with . . . lack of consideration for other people's feelings, to rend the thin veils of civilisation so wantonly, so brutally, was to her . . . an outrage of human decency'[11] on a more fundamental level she had acknowledged the inadequacy of such a reaction for with her mind 'she had always seized the fact that there is no reason, order, justice: but suffering, death, the poor. There was no treachery too base for the world to commit; she knew that. No happiness lasted; she knew that'.[12] This was the very perception which had been granted to Miller's Quentin, while, like Miller, Virginia Woolf urges confrontation as a genuine response to this perception. Mr Ramsay accepts that 'life is difficult; facts uncompromising; and the passage to that fabled land where our brightest hopes are extinguished, our frail barks founder in darkness . . . one that needs, above all, courage, truth, and the power to endure'.[13]

On the purely realistic level the play concerns George, a professor of history at a New England College, and his wife Martha. On returning from a party given by Martha's father, the president of the college, they entertain Nick, a new lecturer in the biology department, and his wife Honey. George and Martha uninhibitedly play out a personal ritual of violence and abuse which seems to stimulate them although it embarrasses their guests. As the liquor flows more freely, however, the guests are included in the games which become more brutally crude and hurtful. Martha breaks some personal taboo by mentioning their son and in the second act, spurred on by her husband's apparent indifference, attempts to commit adultery with Nick; an attempt only frustrated by his drink-induced impotence. In the third act George revenges himself by telling Martha that their son, an illusion accepted by them both as a defence against an impotent reality, has died. When Nick recognises the child as being a compensatory illusion he accepts it as a parallel to his own case. He and Honey leave while George and Martha confide to each other their fear of the reality which they must now learn to face.

In retreat from reality Albee's characters resort to Faustian distractions, passing through the varying degrees of sensuality from drunkenness to sexuality in a play whose second act is aptly entitled Walpurgisnacht. The retreat into illusion which seems to provide an alternative to a harsh existence is not, however, an attractive alternative. For Albee points out that far from facilitating human contact, illusions rather alienate individuals from one another and serve to emphasise their separation. Out of contact with reality they are like the mad—undeveloped. Indeed this immaturity is emphasised by the child-language which recurs throughout the play.

In a story parable which George recounts, a boy accidentally kills his parents. When he loses his mind as a result he is locked up. Finding him unable to face reality 'they jammed a needle in his arm' (*V.W.* p. 96). This is an image of contemporary life as Albee sees it. For if the needle is replaced by liquor the escape of the child becomes valid for the man, '. . . we cry, and we take our tears, and we put'em in the ice box, in the goddam ice trays until they're all frozen and then . . . we put them . . . in our . . . drinks' (*V.W.* p. 186). Where the young boy retreats into the protection of an asylum man retreats into the closed world of illusion. 'Do you know what it is with insane people?' George asks, 'Do you? . . . the quiet ones? . . . They don't change . . . they don't grow old . . . the under-use of everything leaves them . . . quite whole' (*V.W.* p. 97). So the characters in the play itself seem to have arrested their development. In essence they are children. Honey is referred to in Dr. Seuss terms and curls up on the floor like a young child while George and Martha play sad games like 'Vicious children' with a 'manic' manner.

The play is divided into three acts, 'Fun and Games', 'Walpurgisnacht', and 'The Exorcism'—a progression which, like that of ***The Zoo Story,*** leads from humiliation to humility. In the first act Albee begins to probe into the pragmatic values which direct the lives of his four characters and initiates the conflict between Martha and George in which they employ as weapons those fantasies which were to have acted as an asylum. George accuses Martha of having 'moved bag and baggage into your own fantasy world'. She has, he claims 'started playing variation' on these 'distortions' (*V.W.* p. 155). Martha, searching for a weapon with which to hurt her husband, breaks their own code and mentions their son. So the substance of their illusion is used to injure rather than to unify and Martha tells Nick and Honey that 'George's biggest problem . . . about our son, about our great big son, is that deep down in the private-most-pit of his gut, he's not completely sure it's his own kid' (*V.W.* p. 71). The act ends therefore, with George's humiliation.

The second act continues the savage games as George mercilessly lays bare the true nature of his guests' relationship, just as Jerry had penetrated Peter's illusions in Albee's earlier play. With the truth revealed Honey rushes from the room to be sick while Nick retreats into the distraction of drink and sexuality which gives the act its name. This is a retreat familiar enough to George whose whole life since coming to New Carthage has consisted in a similar distraction. He confesses that, 'I'm numbed enough . . . and I don't mean by liquor, though maybe that's been part of the process—a gradual, over-the-years going to sleep of the brain cells' (*V.W.* p. 155). The final physical humiliation which Martha inflicts on him at the end of the act, however, spurs him to wake from this coma. He hurls away the book, which is the symbol of his escapism, as it had been in ***The Zoo Story,*** and determines to force a direct confrontation with reality.

The third act is thus concerned with the ritualistic exorcism of all illusion. While Martha confesses that she has passed her life 'in crummy, totally pointless infidelities' (*V.W.* p. 189) she pleads with George not to continue 'Truth or illusion, George. Doesn't it matter to you . . . at all?' (*V.W.* p. 204). His answer consists in his conscious murder of their fantasy child—a rite watched with growing apprehension by Honey whose own fear of physical reality had resulted in her present sterility, 'NO! . . . I DON'T WANT ANY . . . GO 'WAY . . . I . . . don't . . . want . . . any . . . children. I'm afraid! I don't want to be hurt' (*V.W.* p. 176). George chants the Latin of the burial service as Martha repeats the detailed mythology which they have invented to give substance to their illusion. This act completes the progression from humiliation to humility for all of the characters. Thus the ending, although not definitive, does hold out the hope of 'a real companionship, founded on truth and purged of all falsehood'.

In essence the violent games which George and Martha play are the means whereby they finally attain to this simple acceptance—just as Bellow's protagonists win through to affirmation as a result of humiliation. At first the games clearly act as a substitute for sexual excitement. The mounting fury of their bitterness and invective reaches a shouting crescendo and then relaxes abruptly into tenderness. When George pulls a fake gun on Martha at the climax to one of their fights the symbolism becomes overt and is re-enforced by the conversation between them which follows:

> *George:* You liked that, did you?
>
> *Martha:* Yeah . . . that was pretty good. (*Softer*) C'mon . . . give me a kiss.
>
> (*V.W.* p. 58)

Martha then tries to put George's hand on her breast but he breaks away and aborts the action. Nevertheless their continuing violence does serve to 'get down to the bone . . . the marrow'. If George is not altogether conscious that their games constitute a gradual disintegration of illusion, however, his final act of sacrifice is made with a full understanding of its implications. Indeed there is evidence that, aware of the danger of illusion, he had previously attempted to destroy the fantasy child:

> *Martha:* And George tried.
>
> *George:* How did I try, Martha? How did I try?
>
> *Martha:* How did you . . . what? . . . No! No . . . he grew . . . our son grew . . . up.
>
> (*V.W.* p. 224)

While there is no concrete assurance that a confrontation of reality will permanently restore their fractured relationship the closing tableau is of Martha leaning back on George's arm as he puts his hand on her shoulder. The language of this closing section is drastically simplified and the whole scene provides an audible and visual confirmation of the simple and uncomplicated state to which their relationship has returned,

> *Martha:* . . . You had to?
>
> *George:* Yes.
>
> *Martha:* I don't know.
>
> *George:* It was . . . time.
>
> *Martha:* Was it?
>
> *George:* Yes.
>
> (*V.W.* p. 240)

While before they had disavowed their own failure in attacking others they now admit to their joint responsibility for sterility. Together they accept their inability to have children, '*We* couldn't'—a confession to which Albee adds his own comment in a stage direction, *'a hint of communion in this'* (*V.W.* p. 238). Accepting the Faustian imagery which Albee introduces their final redemption is in essence that which Faust had grasped, 'Those who their lives deplore / Truth yet shall heal'.[14]

If George and Martha are capable of creating a complex mythology rather than face their true situation then so too is the society which they represent. It is Albee's contention that there is as great a need for society to abandon its complete faith in these abstractions—the American Dream, religion and science—as there had been for George and Martha to abandon theirs.

To both Miller and Albee abstractions such as the American Dream are less visions of the future than alternatives to the present. Since this serves to take individuals out of their direct relationship with actuality, which is a factor of the present, it serves also to take them out of any genuine relationship with each other. Alienation thus becomes less an aspect of the human situation than a consequence of an inauthentic response to that situation. The watch-word of this 'success-society' thus becomes 'non-involvement'. Honey does not 'want to know anything' (*V.W.* p. 178) while her husband preserves his 'scientific detachment in the face of . . . life' (*V.W.* p. 100). Attempts at establishing contact are scornfully rejected:

> *George:* (*After a silence*) I've tried to . . . tried to reach you . . . to . . .
>
> *Nick:* (*Contemptuously*) . . . make contact?
>
> *George:* Yes.
>
> *Nick:* (*Still*) . . . communicate?
>
> *George:* Yes. Exactly.
>
> *Nick:* Aw . . . that *is* touching . . . that is . . . downright moving . . . that's what it is. (*With sudden vehemence*) UP YOURS!'
>
> (*V.W.* p. 116)

In the face of this failure in society both Miller and Albee advance the same solution. As an alternative to euphemism and self-delusion Miller urges the necessity to 'take one's life in one's arms' while Albee insists on the need to face 'Virginia Woolf' however harrowing that prospect may be.

Who's Afraid of Virginia Woolf? and *After the Fall* are in essence both modern secular morality plays. The gospel which they teach, as we have seen, is the primacy of human contact based on an acceptance of reality. If Albee sees this as essentially a Christian objective in ***The Zoo Story*** and, indeed, Who's Afraid of Virginia Woolf?, in which a son is sacrificed for redemption, then Miller recognises it as an empirical truth intuitively felt by Holga and painfully and laboriously learnt by Quentin. The religious overtones which abound in all three plays serve to create a myth for this secular religion which is not so far removed from the liberal humanism of Tillich. Where Gelber's Jaybird had congratulated himself on creating 'no heroes, no martyrs, no Christs'[15] Albee creates all three. For deprived of God man is of necessity his own salvation. Following his 'sanctification' of Jerry, in ***The Zoo Story,*** it is not too fanciful, I believe, to note the consistency with which George, the man who is finally responsible for the destruction of illusion, is associated with Christ. The first line of the play, which heralds George's entrance, is 'Jesus' while the act ends with the same apparent identification. Martha leaves George alone on stage with the same contemptuous expletive, 'Jesus'. This identification is repeated in the third act when Nick throws the door open and 'with great rue' shouts out 'Christ' (*V.W.* p. 195). Once again this heralds George's entrance. It is clear, however, that this play lacks the precise parallels which had brought ***The Zoo Story*** to the verge of allegory.

Reduced to its simplest terms New Carthage is a kind of Vanity Fair in which the Worldly Wise distract the pilgrim from his true path. Modern Christian, however, is not urged to forego the pleasures of the American Dream in order to obtain the fruits of his virtue in a later world but rather to enjoy the real consolation of fellow humanity in the alienated world of the present. Failure to accept the need to confront reality is not only to deprive man of dignity but also to leave him adrift in incomprehension, in flight from the world as it really is. This is the modern hell of Albee's morality plays. The salvation of human contact is aborted by the refusal to abandon illusion. All that remains is a frustrating parody of contact in which love begets revulsion, humour begets anger and the aspirations of the two seeking contact are disastrously out of phase. 'George who is good to me, and whom I revile; who understands me, and whom I push off; who can make me laugh, and I choke it back in my throat . . . who tolerates, which is intolerable; who is kind, which is cruel; who understands, which is beyond comprehension . . .' (*V.W.* pp. 190-1).

Strindberg's tortured life gave to his concern with the battle of the sexes almost a manic dynamism which has only really been matched by O'Neill, whose own experience drew him to the Scandinavian's work. It would be an error, however, to see Albee as an extension of this revolt against the natural order. For to him human relationships are out of phase not because of the workings of an ineluctable destiny or because of the arbitrariness of sexual attraction (although, in The Ballad of the Sad Café (1963) he shows he is not blind to this) but because of the demonstrable failure of the individual to establish a genuine relationship between himself and his situation. To Albee, as to Miller, the failure of the man/woman relationship epitomises a more general failure. For it is in this relationship that fruitful contact should be most easily attained. Where O'Neill had been concerned with establishing a compromise between the individual and his situation, and where Beckett presents a vision of that individual overwhelmed by his situation, Albee discovers genuine hope. For he sees in confrontation the first step towards a genuine affirmation, which lies not through 'pipe-dreams' or 'flight' but through a positive acceptance of human limitations.

Albee's success on Broadway with Who's Afraid of Virginia Woolf? presented many critics with a paradox. For while he had formerly been hailed as the leader of the off-Broadway avant-garde his success on Broadway seemed near to sacrilege. Indeed Diana Trilling saw it as proof of his basic conservatism and triviality, although where this leaves Shakespeare is not clear. Yet Albee's play was in truth something of a landmark in American drama. It is the first full-length play to accept the absurdist vision and yet to formulate a response which transcends at once both despair and casual resolution. To the abstract speculation of Pirandello and Genet—who doubt the very existence of an objective reality—he adds a moral dimension while re-instituting the 'humanist heresies' for which Tynan had called. If he abandons the style of the absurdists as demonstrably unsuited to his theme then he still retains the analogical structure of ***The Zoo Story.*** For while he clearly has roots in Strindberg it is equally clear that structurally his plays have more in common with Brecht and Beckett and even the later O'Neill. Like *The Good Woman of Sezuan* (first produced 1943) and *Waiting for Godot* his plays are structured on the metaphor. Albert Camus prefaces his novel *The Plague* (1947) with a quotation from Defoe which is in essence a justification of the analogical form, 'It is as reasonable to represent one kind of imprisonment by another, as it is to represent anything that really exists by that which exists not!'[16] This is a justification which not only Albee but also Durrenmatt and Frisch would endorse, for the extended metaphor is equally the basis for their work. Indeed it is, perhaps, from these writers also that Albee derives his masterful blending of comedy and anguish.

John Gassner has called Who's Afraid of Virginia Woolf? 'essentially naturalistic',[17] and certainly the play has a naturalistic 'texture', that is to say we are not in Willy Loman's insubstantial house. The walls are solid; the setting is 'real'. Yet naturalism implies a concern with surface exactitude which has nothing to do with Albee's method. He himself has described the play's setting as 'womb-like' and while avoiding the simplicities of symbolism (simplicities to which he submits in his next play, Tiny Alice) he is not so much concerned with maintaining a precision of appearance as with seizing an essential reality. Like Brown after him he is concerned with presenting an analogue of the human situation. He himself has called his play realistic, defining the term to mean that drama which faces 'man's condition as it is'. In defining realism in these terms he is clearly also defining what he sees as the role of the dramatist in a society in which the audience is 'so preconditioned by pap as to have cut off half of its responses'. In refusing to pander to a supposed need for 'self-congratulation and reassurance'[18] Albee was not only maintaining his artistic integrity but he was demonstrating that in Who's Afraid of Virginia Woolf?—originally written for off-Broadway production—he had produced a play which could seemingly resolve the paradox of the avant-garde. For where ***The Zoo Story*** played to only moderate audiences in *The Provincetown Playhouse,* Who's Afraid of Virginia Woolf? proclaimed the same message from the stage of the *Billy Rose Theatre* on Broadway and, but for the squeemishness of W. D. Maxwell would have received the Pulitzer Prize it so obviously deserved.

Albee's subsequent plays have served to extend and reenforce his insistence on the need to abandon a faith in illusion which ultimately constitutes little more than moral cowardice. Tiny Alice, which was received somewhat coldly by the critics, represents Albee's rejection of religion as a substitute for confrontation. Like Nigel Dennis, in *Cards of Identity,* he sees belief in an abstraction as merely an excuse for the surrender of responsibility and identity. Its origin lies not in spiritual conviction but in fear; fear of an empty universe in which man must create his own meaning and his own relationships. Where George and Martha had created an imaginary son in Who's Afraid of Virginia Woolf?, the protagonist of Tiny Alice creates what Albee would consider an imaginary son of God. Both inventions are an expression of fear of present reality.

Like T. S. Eliot's *The Cocktail Party* the plot of Tiny Alice is basically concerned with a conspiracy. A group of three people, a lawyer, a butler and their employer, a rich recluse called Alice, are seemingly dedicated to weaning brother Julian, the play's protagonist, away from the church. Julian, a lay-brother, is sent to Alice by his Cardinal in order to arrange the details of a two-billion dollar grant which she is making to the church; a donation which turns out to be the cost of his freedom. In his first interview with her she appears at first as an old woman only to throw off her disguise after a few minutes to reveal herself as an attractive young woman—a contrast between appearance and reality which is an obvious clue to his central theme in a play which he himself has described as 'a morality play about truth and illusion'.[19]

Gradually Alice wins Julian's affection and devotion but it becomes clear that she is merely a surrogate. In embracing her he comes to embrace the concept which she represents; a concept which Albee mistakenly makes concrete in the form of a model castle which dominates the stage during much of the play. This is even referred to as 'Alice' by the conspirators and is an obvious image of the concrete and diminished world which Julian is made to accept vicariously through his marriage to Miss Alice. Julian had been unable to accept fully the God created by man, 'Soft God? The servant? Gingerbread God with the raisin eyes?' (*T.A.* p. 106). In search of a real vision he becomes the ideal subject for the conspirators secular evangelism. Yet he revolts against the limited, 'tiny', world, bereft of comforting abstractions, with which they confront him. Having lived an empty life in which the denial of intimate human contact has been a sworn article of faith he feels that continued belief in God is the only means to self-justification, 'I have . . . have . . . given up everything to gain everything, for the sake of my faith and my peace' (*T.A.* p. 167). When Alice urges him to 'accept what's real' (*T.A.* p. 167) he refuses. Left with no other alternative the conspirators shoot Julian and leave him to discover the truth of their precepts as he faces death.

In ***The Zoo Story*** Albee was prepared to point the way to a secular religion in which man pre-empted the divine function. In Tiny Alice he once again creates a saint for his religion; a saint this time whose message cannot be confused with support for christian mythology. Julian dies finally accepting a diminished universe and accepting a martyrdom which has nothing to do with Christ. He rejects the abstract in favour of the concretely human. Dying in a mock crucifixion he finally confesses his faith in Alice, as opposed to some diffuse and distant God. As R. W. B. Lewis says of the novelist Ignazio Silone's faith, he understands now that 'The first sign of manhood is a shedding of abstractions in an effort to press toward 'an intimate opening on to the reality of others'.[20] This is essentially a description of the process which lies at the heart of Albee's own philosophy. Julian, then, comes finally to accept his error; to accept that the six years which he had spent in an asylum because of a loss of faith were in fact six years of sanity, 'I cannot have so misunderstood my life; I cannot have . . . was I sane *then?* Those *years?* My time in the *asylum?* WAS THAT WHEN I WAS RATIONAL? THEN?' (*T.A.* pp. 168-9). At the end of the play the church is compromised and Julian is finally reconciled to his humanity and to reality. For to Albee belief in an afterlife devalues the present and thus undermines the necessity for human contact in an empty but real world. If he were to formulate the central article of faith for his secular religion it would surely be close to that of Martin Buber as expressed by the Rev. James Richmond, 'Genuine religion means being converted to this life and this world'.[21]

Here, for virtually the first time, therefore, Albee attempts a clearer exposition of his views on the 'consolation' of religion, linking it, seemingly, with a blind faith in science or the American dream as but another inauthentic response to life. Illusion and reality, he suggests have become confused. As the lawyer says, with what Albee rather preciously describes as 'a small smile', 'It is what we believe, therefore what we know. Is that not right? Faith is knowledge?' (*T.A.* p. 165). Clearly a world in which faith and knowledge are accepted as synonymous is inimical to a playwright who insists on the need for a courageous confrontation of reality. As Silone says, 'In no century have words been so perverted from their natural purpose of putting man in touch with man as they are today. To speak and to deceive . . . have become almost synonymous'.[22] It is clear, therefore, why Albee feels that language has to be underpinned by a structure of imagery which facilitates communication on a more fundamental level. It is precisely Albee's failure to master this process in Tiny Alice, however, which detracts from the play's effectiveness. He lacks Chekhov's skill at making the symbol an endemic part of the play. Like Tennessee Williams he seems here to have developed a tendency towards strewing his stage with any number of highly significant objects. The result, however, is less to generate genuine dramatic effect than it is to simulate the appearance of a 42nd Street junk store (dried-up fountain from *Camino Real,* anatomical charts from *Summer and Smoke* and now a phrenological head and model castle from Tiny Alice).

Tiny Alice is not an easy play to understand and in many ways Albee has lost his command of the dramatic medium itself. When asked about its complexities, however, he has replied that, 'the play is not supposed to be terribly easily apprehensible. It's meant to contain things that audiences must take out of the theatre with them and think about.' But perhaps there is more than an element of truth in the answer that he offered to a bewildered John Gielgud shortly before the latter was due to play the part of Julian on Broadway, 'I know you want to know what the play is about, John, but I don't know yet, so I can't say.'[23]

Unfortunately Albee's next play, Malcolm (1966), evidences the same opacity. Based on Purdy's surrealistic novel the play, in the words of the *New Yorker* review, '. . . limped out of the Shubert last week after lingering for seven performances.' The same review found the play 'filled with stilted dialogue, pseudo-profundity, and wearisome vulgarity'[24] while Robert Brustein, writing in *The New Republic,* identified what he saw as a trend in Albee's work whereby his plays 'get more abstract and incoherent until he is finally reduced, as here, to a nervous plucking at broken strings.'[25] Certainly Albee has chosen to adapt a novel whose complexities are, perhaps, not particularly suited to the dramatic medium. Purdy's picaresque indictment of the contemporary world is phrased in the kind of oblique and stylised terms which do not translate well into a form which is so much more demanding of the audience. Nevertheless if he has not entirely succeeded in finding a viable dramatic equivalent for Purdy's unique vision he has continued his commitment to experimentation while producing a play which expands his personal vision of modern society as sketched in The American Dream.

Malcolm is an expression of Albee's sense of alienation from the empty and bizarre world of modern society. It is his vision of a society whose principle gods are money, sex and perjured art and in which everything and everybody is for sale. Malcolm himself is an innocent exposed to and eventually destroyed by the corruption of this society to which, 'Innocence has the appearance of stupidity' (*M.* p. 9). This modern *Billy Budd* sees the destruction of innocence, however, not as a natural corollary of a disciplined society but rather as a by-product of a frenzied hedonism. Malcolm dies of sexual hyperaesthesia—that destructive sexuality which Albee had identified as a substitute for genuine fulfilment in Who's Afraid of Virginia Woolf?

At the beginning of the play Malcolm, like Peter in ***The Zoo Story,*** is seated on a bench—a retreat which is an expression both of his innocence and of his failure of nerve. Where Peter had been 'saved' by Jerry, however, Malcolm never really understands the forces which destroy him. His education, like that of Lemuel Pitkin in Nathaniel West's *A Cool Million,* consists of a series of encounters which gradually destroy him. By degrees he begins to accept the logic of this alien world and to become more remote from a simpler existence which remains for him little more than a vague memory of a genuine familial relationship.

At the end of the play, crucified by a world which understands nothing but exploitation, he returns to another existence; the latest in Albee's lengthening line of saints all of whom have given their lives for a world which steadfastly refuses to understand what they are on about. There is, however, a new note in this play. For although the need for love is stressed by its notable absence from this wretched world, Albee provides us with no one within the play who recognises the significance of this. He has moved, it seems, from sounding the warning bell to sounding the knell of a lost world. For after this Second Coming, a miracle recognised by no one, there lies only the apocalypse—a sobering thought for those who watch Malcolm rise on his golden bench and can only remark, 'he didn't have the stuff . . . that's all' (*M.* p. 138).

Having abused the innocent who had come among them they are left with only an image of him—a painting, itself produced for profit, and now an apt substitute for a purity which can only survive in this ersatz and therefore unthreatening form.

With his latest play, A Delicate Balance (1966), however, Albee takes a step back from the near-despair of Malcolm. Once more he goes about his self-appointed task of dissecting the quiet inhumanity of a fading civilisation. He continues his indictment of a society which has to rely on illusion to survive and which is incapable of realising that the inevitable result of this is a loss of identity and 'the gradual . . . demise of intensity, the private preoccupations, the substitutions'.[26]

A Delicate Balance is set in the affluent suburban home of Agnes and Tobias whose comfortable complacency is only slightly disturbed by the presence of Claire, an alcoholic relation. The action is concerned with the effect on this elderly couple of a visit by their friends, Harry and Edna, who arrive unexpectedly saying that they have experienced 'the terror'. Whatever the nature of the terror the visit serves to upset the delicate balance of middle-class temporising. The characters are made to confront the gulf which has opened up between reality and illusion in their lives and to define their own stance in relation to it. Ultimately, however, the clearest analysis of what Albee calls 'the regulated great gray life' is made by the alcoholic Claire. She expresses what can surely be taken as Albee's own conviction about the America of which he has been so critical, 'We're not a communal nation . . . giving but not sharing, outgoing but not friendly . . . We submerge our truths and have our sunsets on untroubled waters . . . We live with our truths on the grassy bottom, and we examined all . . . the implications like we had a life for nothing else . . . We better develop gills.'[27] As we have seen Albee has already expressed his sense of the urgency of this metamorphosis in Malcolm. A Delicate Balance is merely his latest essay on the need for confrontation.

The relative success of this play on Broadway may be due in part, however, to the fact that the terms in which Albee is here continuing his analysis are more readily available to an audience which found the stylised allegory of Tiny Alice and the surrealistic insights of Malcolm difficult to grasp. It is certainly not a sign that Albee has finally capitulated to the pressures for re-assurance which he has always castigated in the American theatre. Indeed it is clear that without the radical approach of an Albee the American theatre would be in danger of stagnating once again. For if he is capable of grotesque misjudgement, as in Tiny Alice and Malcolm, then he is also capable of the achievement of ***The Zoo Story*** and Who's Afraid of Virginia Woolf?, while his commitment to continued experimentation makes him the chief hope for a developing drama.

Notes

[1]Wendell V. Harris, 'Morality, Absurdity, and Albee', *Southwest Review,* XVIX, iii (Summer, 1964), p. 249.

[2]Ihab Hassan, *Radical Innocence: Studies in the Contemporary American Novel* (New Jersey, 1961), p. 291.

[3]Philip Mairet, 'Introduction', *Existentialism and Humanism,* p. 11.

[4]*Henderson the Rain King,* p. 307.

[5]*Ibid.,* p. 286.

[6]Edward Albee, *The American Dream* and *The Zoo Story* (New York, 1963), pp. 53-4. References to *The American Dream* are abbreviated to '*A.D.*' and corporated into the text.

[7]*The Theatre of the Absurd,* p. xix.

[8]*Ibid.,* p. xix.

[9]Richard Schechner, 'TDR Comment', *Tulane Drama Review,* VII, iii (Spring, 1963), pp. 8-10.

[10]Alan Schneider, 'Why So Afraid?' *Tulane Drama Review,* VII, iii (Spring, 1963), p. 11.

[11]Virginia Woolf, *To The Lighthouse* (London, 1960), p. 54.

[12]*Ibid.,* p. 102.

[13]*Ibid.,* p. 13.

[14]Johann Wolfgang Goethe, *Faust—Part Two,* trans., Philip Wayne (Harmondsworth, 1959), p. 277.

[15]*The Connection,* p. 62.

[16]Albert Camus, *The Plague,* trans., Stuart Gilbert (Harmondsworth, 1962), p. 3.

[17]*Directions in Modern Theatre and Drama,* p. 358.

[18]'Which Theatre is the Absurd One?', pp. 334-5.

[19]Thomas B. Markus, 'Tiny Alice and Tragic Catharsis', *Educational Theatre Journal,* XVII, p. 230.

[20]R. W. B. Lewis, *The Picaresque Saint* (London, 1960), p. 151.

[21]Rev. James Richmond, *Martin Buber* (Nottingham, 1966), p. 13. The text of a lecture delivered at Nottingham University on March 17, 1966.

[22]*The Picaresque Saint,* p. 155.

[23]R. S. Stewart, 'John Gielgud and Edward Albee Talk About the Theatre', *Atlantic Monthly,* 215, iv (April, 1965), pp. 67-8.

Edward Albee

[24]Anon., 'Innocent Astray', *New Yorker,* January 22, 1966, p. 74.

[25]Robert Brustein, 'Albee's Allegory of Innocence', *The New Republic,* January 29, 1966, p. 36.

[26]Edward Albee, *A Delicate Balance* (New York, 1966), p. 82.

[27]*Ibid.,* p. 93.

Martin Esslin (essay date 1969)

SOURCE: "Parallels and Proselytes: Edward Albee," in *The Theatre of the Absurd,* revised edition, Anchor Books, 1969, pp. 226-70.

[*In the following excerpt from the expanded version of his groundbreaking 1961 work, Esslin discusses Albee's plays and declares* The American Dream *"Albee's promising and brilliant first example of an American contribution to the Theatre of the Absurd."*]

The work we have surveyed in this chapter shows that the Theatre of the Absurd has had its impact on writers in France, Italy, Spain, Germany, Switzerland, and Great Britain. The relative absence of dramatists of the Absurd in the United States, however, is puzzling, particularly in view of the fact that certain aspects of American popular art have had a decisive influence on the dramatists of the Absurd in Europe. . . .

But the reason for this dearth of examples of the Theatre of the Absurd in the United States is probably simple enough—the convention of the Absurd springs from a feeling of deep disillusionment, the draining away of the sense of meaning and purpose in life, which has been characteristic of countries like France and Britain in the years after the Second World War. In the United States there has been no corresponding loss of meaning and purpose. The American dream of the good life is still very strong. In the United States the belief in progress that characterized Europe in the nineteenth century has been maintained into the middle of the twentieth. There have been signs, particularly since the shock administered by the Russian successes in the space race, that disillusion and frustration might become a factor in the American scene, but the rise of phenomena like the beat generation has been marginal compared to parallel developments in Europe.

It is certainly significant that such a notable work of the American avant-garde as Robert Hivnor's *Too Many Thumbs,* which has been compared to the fantasies of Ionesco, is in fact an affirmation of a belief in progress and the perfectability of man. It shows a chimpanzee compressing his evolution to the status of man—and far beyond that, to complete spirituality—into a matter of months. The fantasy is there, but certainly no sense of the futility and absurdity of human endeavour.[1]

On the other hand, Edward Albee (born in 1928) comes into the category of the Theatre of the Absurd precisely because his work attacks the very foundations of American optimism. His first play, The Zoo Story (1958), which shared the bill at the Provincetown Playhouse with Beckett's *Krapp's Last Tape,* already showed the forcefulness and bitter irony of his approach. In the realism of its dialogue and in its subject matter—an outsider's inability to establish genuine contact with a dog, let alone any human being—The Zoo Story is closely akin to the world of Harold Pinter. But the effect of this brilliant one-act duologue between Jerry, the outcast, and Peter, the conformist bourgeois, is marred by its melodramatic climax; when Jerry provokes Peter into drawing a knife and then impales himself on it, the plight of the schizophrenic outcast is turned into an act of sentimentality, especially as the victim expires in touching solicitude and fellow-feeling for his involuntary murderer.

But after an excursion into grimly realistic social criticism (the one-act play The Death of Bessie Smith, a re-creation of the end of the blues singer Bessie Smith in Memphis in 1937; she died after a motor accident because hospitals reserved for whites refused to admit her), Albee produced a play that clearly takes up the style and subject-matter of the Theatre of the Absurd and translates it into a genuine American idiom. The American Dream (1959-60; first performed at the York Playhouse, New York, on 24 January 1961) fairly and squarely attacks the ideals of progress, optimism, and faith in the national mission, and pours scorn on the sentimental ideals of family life, togetherness, and physical fitness; the euphemistic language and unwillingness to face the ultimate facts of the human condition that in America, even more than in Europe, represent the essence of bourgeois assumptions and attitudes. The American Dream shows an American family—Mommy, Daddy, Grandma—in search of a replacement for the adopted child that went wrong and died. The missing member of the family arrives in the shape of a gorgeous young man, the embodiment of the American dream, who admits that he consists only of muscles and a healthy exterior, but is dead inside, drained of genuine feeling and the capacity for experience. He will do anything for money—so he will even consent to become a member of the family. The language of The American Dream resembles that of Ionesco in its masterly combination of clichés. But these clichés, in their euphemistic, baby-talk tone, are as characteristically American as Ionesco's are French. The most disagreeable verities are hidden behind the corn-fed cheeriness of advertising jingles and family-magazine unctuousness. There are very revealing contrasts in the way these writers of different nationalities use the clichés of their own countries—the mechanical hardness of Ionesco's French platitudes; the flat, repetitive obtuseness of Pinter's English nonsense dialogue; and the oily glibness and sentimentality of the American cliché in Albee's promising and brilliant first example of an American contribution to the Theatre of the Absurd.

With his first full-length play Who's Afraid of Virginia Woolf? (first performed in New York on 14 October 1962) Albee achieved his breakthrough into the first rank of contemporary American playwrights. On the surface this is a savage marital battle in the tradition of Strindberg and the later O'Neill. George, the unsuccessful academic, his ambitious wife, and the young couple they are entertaining, are realistic characters; their world, that of drink-sodden and frustrated university teachers, is wholly real. But a closer inspection reveals elements which clearly still relate the play to Albee's earlier work and the Theatre of the Absurd. George and Martha (there are echoes there of George and Martha Washington) have an imaginary child which they treat as real, until in the cold dawn of that wild night they decide to 'kill' it by abandoning their joint fantasy. Here the connexion to The American Dream with its horrid dream-child of the ideal all-American boy becomes clear; thus there are elements of dream and allegory in the play (is the dream-child which cannot become real among people torn by ambition and lust something like the American ideal itself?); and there is also a Genet-like ritualistic element in its structure as a sequence of three rites: act I—'Fun and Games'; act II—*'Walpurgisnacht';* act III—'Exorcism'.

With Tiny Alice (1963) Albee broke new ground in a play which clearly tried to evolve a complex image of man's search for truth and certainty in a constantly shifting world, without ever wanting to construct a complete allegory or to offer any solutions to the questions he raised. Hence the indignant reaction of some critics seems to have been based on a profound misunderstanding. The play shows its hero buffeted between the church and the world of cynical wisdom and forced by the church to abandon his vocation for the priesthood to marry a rich woman who made a vast donation dependent on his decision. Yet immediately the marriage is concluded the lady and her staff depart, leaving the hero to a lonely death. The central image of the play is the mysterious model of the great mansion in which the action takes place, that occupies the centre of the stage. Inside this model every room corresponds to one in the real house, and tiny figures can be observed repeating the movements of the people who occupy it. Everything that happens in the macrocosm is exactly repeated in the microcosm of the model. And no doubt inside the model there is another smaller model, which duplicates everything that happens on an even tinier scale, and so on *ad infinitum,* upwards and downwards on the scale of being. It is futile to search for the philosophical meaning of such an image. What it communicates is a mood, a sense of the mystery, the impenetrable complexity of the universe. And that is precisely what a dramatic poet is after.

With A Delicate Balance (1966) Albee returned to a more realistic setting which, however, is also deeply redolent of mystery and nameless fears, while Box and Quotations from Mao-tse Tung (1968) returns to an openly absurdist convention by constructing an intricate pattern of cross-cut monologues, some emerging from tangible people (chairman Mao, a talkative lady), one from an empty box.

NOTE

[1]Less than ten years after that passage was written, the situation is fundamentally changed: under the impact of events like the assassination of President Kennedy, the rise in racial tension and, above all, the war in Vietnam, the self-confidence and naïve optimism of the United States has received a severe jolt. And there has been a veritable flood of plays—and novels—written in the absurdist vein. To do this movement justice would require a study of its own. All that can be done here is to mention the names of some of the outstanding young writers who have emerged in this field: Paul Foster (*Tom Paine*), Megan Terry (*Viet Rock*), Rochelle Owens (*Futz!*), Jean-Claude van Itallie (*America Hurrah*), LeRoi Jones (*Dutchman*), Ed Bullins (*The Electric Nigger*), Israel Horowitz (*This Indian Wants the Bronx*). While these and other plays in a similar style owe a great deal to improvisational techniques, they also quite clearly derive from the dramatists of the Absurd discussed in this book.

Gerald Weales (essay date 1969)

SOURCE: "Edward Albee: Don't Make Waves," in *The Jumping-Off Place: American Drama in the 1960's,* The Macmillan Company, 1969, pp. 24-53.

[*In the following essay, the critic explores the recurring themes of isolation and separation throughout Albee's work.*]

Something tells me it's all
happenin' at the zoo.

—Simon and Garfunkel

Edward Albee is inescapably *the* American playwright of the 1960's. His first play, The Zoo Story, opened in New York, on a double bill with Samuel Beckett's *Krapp's Last Tape,* at the Provincetown Playhouse on January 14, 1960. In his Introduction to Three Plays (1960), Albee tells how his play, which was written in 1958, passed from friend to friend, from country to country, from manuscript to tape to production (in Berlin in 1959) before it made its way back to the United States. "It's one of those things a person has to do," says Jerry; "sometimes a person has to go a very long distance out of his way to come back a short distance correctly."

For Albee, once The Zoo Story had finished its peregrinations, the trip uptown—psychologically and geographically—was a short one. During 1960, there were two other Albee prouctions, largely unheralded—The Sandbox, which has since become a favorite for amateurs, and Fam and Yam, a *bluette,* a joke growing out of his having been ticketed as the latest white hope of the American theater. These were essentially fugitive productions of occasional pieces. In 1961, one of the producers of The Zoo Story, Richard Barr, joined by Clinton Wilder in the producing organization that is always called Theater 196? after whatever the year, offered The American Dream, first on a double bill with William Flanagan's opera Bartleby, for which Albee and James Hinton, Jr., did the libretto,[1] and later, when the opera proved unsuccessful, with an earlier Albee play The Death of Bessie Smith. During the next few years, there were frequent revivals of both Zoo and Dream, often to help out a sagging Barr-Wilder program, as in 1964 (by which time Albee had become a co-producer) when first Dream and later Zoo were sent in as companion pieces to LeRoi Jones's *Dutchman,* after Samuel Beckett's *Play* and Fernando Arrabal's *The Two Executioners,* which opened with Jones's play, were removed from the bill. Albee had become an off-Broadway staple.

By that time, of course, Albee had become something else as well. With Who's Afraid of Virginia Woolf? (1962), he had moved to Broadway and had a smashing commercial success. By a process of escalation, he had passed from promising to established playwright. After Woolf, Albee productions averaged one a year: The Ballad of the Sad Café (1963), Tiny Alice (1964), Malcolm (1966), A Delicate Balance (1966) and Everything in the Garden (1967). None of these were successes in Broadway terms (by *Variety*'s chart of hits and flops), but except for Malcolm, a gauche and imperceptive adaptation of James Purdy's novel of that name, which closed after seven performances, all of them had respectable runs and generated their share of admiration and antagonism from critics and public alike.

Although favorable reviews helped make the Albee reputation, critics have consistently praised with one hand, damned with the other.[2] If Harold Clurman's "Albee on Balance" (*The New York Times,* January 13, 1967) treats Albee as a serious playwright and if Robert Brustein's "A Third Theater" (*The New York Times Magazine,* September 25, 1966) seems to dismiss him as a solemn one, only Broadway serious, the recent collections of their reviews—Clurman's *The Naked Image* and Brustein's *Seasons of Discontent*—indicate that both critics have had the same kind of reservations about Albee from the beginning. Albee, contrariwise, has had reservations of his own. From his pettish Introduction to The American Dream to the press conference he called to chastise the critics for their reactions to Tiny Alice, he has regularly used interviews and the occasional nondramatic pieces he has written to suggest that the critics lack understanding, humility, responsibility.

In spite of (perhaps because of) the continuing quarrel between Albee and his critics—a love-hate relationship in the best Albee tradition—the playwright's reputation has grown tremendously. It was in part the notoriety of Who's Afraid of Virginia Woolf? that turned Albee into a popular figure, and certainly the publicity surrounding the making of the movie version of Woolf helped to keep Albee's name in the popular magazines. Whatever the cause, Albee is now the American playwright whose name has become a touchstone, however ludicrously it is used. Thus, Thomas Meehan, writing an article on "camp" for *The New York Times Magazine* (March 21, 1965), solicits Andy Warhol's opinion of Tiny Alice ("I liked it because it was so empty"), and William H. Honan, interviewing Jonathan Miller for the same publication (January 22, 1967), manages to get Miller to repeat a commonplace criticism of Albee he has used twice before.

All this is simply the chi-chi mask over a serious concern with Albee. According to recent reports of the American Educational Theatre Association, Albee has been jockeying for second place (after Shakespeare) in the list of playwrights most produced on college campuses. In 1963-64, he held second place; in 1964-65, he was nosed out by Ionesco. The attractiveness of short plays to college dramatic groups—as Ionesco's presence suggests—helps explain the volume of Albee productions, but, with The Zoo Story invading text anthologies and Virginia Woolf climbing onto reading lists, it is clear that the interest in Albee in colleges is more than a matter of mechanics. More and more articles on Albee turn up in critical quarterlies—always a gauge of academic fashions—and those that are printed are only the tip of a happily submerged iceberg; Walter Meserve, one of the editors of *Modern Drama,* estimated in 1966 that 80 per cent of the submissions on American drama were about four authors: O'Neill, Williams, Miller, and Albee. The interest abroad is as intense as it is here. This is clear not only from the fact that the plays are translated and performed widely, but in the desire of audiences to talk or to hear about the playwright. Clurman, in that article in the *Times,* reporting on lecture audiences in Tokyo and Tel Aviv, says that there was more curiosity about Albee than any other American playwright. Albee's position, then, is analogous to that of Tennessee Williams in the 1950's. He recognizes this himself. When he wrote Fam and Yam in 1960, he let Yam (the Young American Playwright) bunch Albee with Jack Gelber, Jack Richardson, and Arthur Kopit. In an interview in *Diplomat* (October, 1966) he suggested that playwrights should be hired as critics; it was now Williams and Arthur Miller that he listed with himself.

In "Which Theatre Is the Absurd One?" (*The New York Times Magazine,* February 25, 1962), Albee wrote that "in the end a public will get what it deserves and no better." If he is right, his work may finally condemn or justify the taste of American theater audiences in the 1960's. More than likely, a little of both.

"I consider myself in a way the most eclectic playwright who ever wrote," Albee once told an interviewer (*Transatlantic Review,* Spring, 1963), and then he went on to make an elaborate joke about how he agreed with the critics that twenty-six playwrights—three of whom he had never read—had influenced him. Critics do have a way of getting influence-happy when they write about Albee—particularly Brustein, who persists in calling him an imitator—but they have good reason. There are such strong surface dissimilarities among the Albee plays that it is easier and in some ways more rewarding to think of The Zoo Story in relation to Samuel Beckett and Harold Pinter and A Delicate Balance in terms of T. S. Eliot and Enid Bagnold than it is to compare the two plays, even though both start from the same dramatic situation: the invasion (by Jerry, by Harry and Edna) of private territory (Peter's bench, Tobias's house). Yet, the comparison is obvious once it is made. Each new Albee play seems to be an experiment in form, in style (even if it is someone else's style), and yet there is unity in his work as a whole. This is apparent in the devices and the characters that recur, modified according to context, but it is most obvious in the repetition of theme, in the basic assumptions about the human condition that underlie all his work.

In A Delicate Balance, Tobias and his family live in a mansion in the suburbs of hell, that existential present so dear to contemporary writers, in which life is measured in terms of loss, love by its failure, contact by its absence. In that hell, there are many mansions—one of which is Peter's bench—and all of them are cages in the great zoo story of life. Peter's bench is a kind of sanctuary, both a refuge from and an extension of the stereotypical upper-middle-class existence (tweeds, horn-rimmed glasses, job in publishing, well-furnished apartment, wife, daughters, cats, parakeets) with which Albee has provided him—a place where he can safely not-live and have his nonbeing. This is the way Jerry sees Peter, at least, and—since the type is conventional enough in contemporary theater, from avant-garde satire to Broadway revue—it is safe to assume that the play does, too. Although Albee intends a little satirical fun at Peter's expense (the early needling scenes are very successful), it is clear that the stereotyping of Peter is an image of his condition, not a cause of it. Jerry, who plays "the old pigeonhole bit" so well, is another, a contrasting cliché, and it is the play's business to show that he and Peter differ only in that he does not share Peter's complacency. Just before Jerry attacks in earnest, he presents the play's chief metaphor:

> I went to the zoo to find out more about the way people exist with animals, and the way animals exist with each other, and with people too. It probably wasn't a fair test, what with everyone separated by bars from everyone else, the animals for the most part from each other, and always the people from the animals. But, if it's a zoo, that's the way it is.

"Private wings," says Malcolm in the play that bears his name. "Indeed, that *is* an extension of separate rooms, is it not?" In a further extension of a joke that is no joke, Agnes, in A Delicate Balance, speaks of her "poor parents, in their separate heavens." *Separateness* is the operative word for Albee characters, for, even though his zoo provides suites for two people (Who's Afraid of Virginia Woolf?) or for more (A Delicate Balance), they are furnished with separate cages. "It's sad to know you've gone through it all, or most of it, without . . ." says Edna in one of the fragmented speeches that characterize A Delicate Balance, as though thoughts too were separate, "that the one body you've wrapped your arms around . . . the only skin you've ever known . . . is your own—and that it's dry . . . and not warm." This is a more restrained, a more resigned variation on the Nurse's desperate cry in Bessie Smith, ". . . I am tired of my skin. . . . I WANT OUT!"

Violence is one of the ways of trying to get out. The Nurse is an illustration of this possibility; she is an embryonic version of Martha in Virginia Woolf, with most of the venom, a little of the style, and practically none of the compensating softness of the later character, and she hits out at everyone around her. Yet, she never escapes herself, her cage. The other possibility is love (that, too, a form of penetration), but the Albee plays are full of characters who cannot (Nick in Virginia Woolf) or will not (Tobias, the Nurse) make that connection. The persistent images are of withdrawal, the most graphic being the one in A Delicate Balance, the information that Tobias in fact withdrew and came on Agnes's belly the last time they had sex. Although failed sex is a convenient metaphor for the failure of love, its opposite will not work so well. Connection is not necessarily contact, and it is contact—or rather its absence, those bars that bother Jerry—that preoccupies Albee. He lets Martha and George make fun of the lack-of-communication cliché in Virginia Woolf, but it is that cultural commonplace on which much of Albee's work is built. Jerry's story about his landlady's vicious dog—although he over-explains it—is still Albee's most effective account of an attempt to get through those bars, out of that skin (so effective, in fact, that Tobias uses a variation of it in Balance when he tells about his cat). Accepting the dog's attacks on him as a form of recognition, Jerry tries first to win his affection (with hamburger) and, failing that, to kill him (with poisoned hamburger: it is difficult to differentiate between the tools of love and hate). In the end, he settles for an accommodation, one in which he and the dog ignore each other. His leg remains unbitten, but he feels a sense of loss in the working arrangement: "We neither love nor hurt because we do not try to reach each other."[3]

"Give me *any* person . . ." says Lawyer in Tiny Alice. "He'll take what he gets for . . . what he wishes it to be. AH, it is what I have always wanted, he'll say, looking terror and betrayal straight in the eye. Why not: face the inevitable and call it what you have always wanted." The context is a special one here, a reference to Julian's impending martyrdom to God-Alice, who comes to him in the form or forms he expects. I purposely dropped from the Lawyer's speech the references to "martyr" and"saint" which follow parenthetically after the opening phrase, for as it stands above, the speech might serve as advertising copy for the Albee world in which his characters exist and—very occasionally—struggle. The too-obvious symbol of The American Dream, the muscle-flexing young man who is only a shell, empty of love or feeling, is, in Mommy's words, "a great deal more like it." *Like it,* but not *it.* Appearance is what she wants, for reality, as Grandma's account of the mutilation of the other "bumble" indicates, is dangerous.

The American Dream is a pat example of, to use Lawyer's words again, "How to come out on top, going under." Whether the accommodation is embraced (Dream) or accepted with a sense of loss (Jerry and the dog), it is always there, a way of coping instead of a way of life. It can be disguised in verbal trappings—comic (the games in Virginia Woolf) or serious (the religiosity of Tiny Alice, the conventional labels of A Delicate Balance). In the absence of substance, it can be given busy work; Girard Girard spells everything out in Malcolm: "You will move from the mansion to the chateau, and from the chateau back. You will surround yourself with your young beauties, and hide your liquor where you will. You will . . . go on, my dear." The unhidden liquor in A Delicate Balance (even more in Virginia Woolf, where it serves the dramatic action, as lubricant and as occasional rest) provides an example of such busyness: all the playing at bartending, the weighty deliberation over whether to have anisette or cognac, the concern over the quality of a martini. The rush of words (abuse or elegance) and the press of activity (however meaningless) sustain the Albee characters in a tenuous relationship (a delicate balance) among themselves and in the face of the others, the ones outside, and—beyond that—the nameless terror.

Implicit in my discussion of the separateness of the Albee characters and the bogus forms of community they invent to mask the fact that they are alone is the assumption that this is Albee's view of the human condition. The deliberate refusal to locate the action of his most recent plays (Tiny Alice, Malcolm, A Delicate Balance) strengthens that assumption. In fact, only two of Albee's settings can be found in atlases—Central Park (The Zoo Story) and Memphis (Bessie Smith). Even these, like the undifferentiated Southern town he borrowed from Carson McCullers for The Ballad of the Sad Café and the fictional New England college town of Virginia Woolf, might easily serve as settings for a universal drama. Yet, in much of his work, particularly in the early plays, there is a suggestion, even an insistence, that the problem is a localized one, that the emptiness and loneliness of the characters are somehow the result of a collapse of values in the Western world in general, in the United States in particular. The American Dream, he says in his Preface to the play, is "an attack on the substitution of artificial for real values in our society." Such an attack is implicit in the depiction of Peter in The Zoo Story.

It is in Virginia Woolf that this side of Albee's "truth" is most evident. He is not content that his characters perform an action which carries implications for an audience that far transcend the action itself. He must distribute labels. George may jokingly identify himself, as history professor, with the humanities, and Nick, as biology professor, with science, and turn their meeting into a historical-inevitability parable about the necessary decline of the West, but Albee presumably means it. Calling the town New Carthage and giving

George significant throw-away lines ("When I was sixteen and going to prep school, during the Punic Wars . . .") are cute ways of underlining a ponderous intention. I would not go so far as Diana Trilling (*Esquire,* December, 1963) and suggest that George and Martha are the Washingtons, or Henry Hewes (*The Best Plays of* 1962-1963) that Nick is like Nikita Khrushchev, but Albee is plainly intent on giving his sterility tale an obvious cultural point. Martha's joke when Nick fails to "make it in the sack" is apparently no joke at all: "But that's how it is in a civilized society."

My own tendency is to brush all this grandiose symbol-making under the rug to protect what I admire in Virginia Woolf. If we can believe Albee's remarks in the *Diplomat* interview, however, all this comprises the "play's subtleties"; in faulting the movie version of his play, he says, "the entire political argument was taken out, the argument between history and science."[4] The chasm that confronts the Albee characters may, then, be existential chaos or a materialistic society corrupt enough to make a culture hero out of. . . (whom? to each critic his own horrible example, and there are those would pick Albee himself), or a combination in which the second of these is an image of the first.

There is nothing unusual about this slightly unstable mixture of philosophic assumption and social criticism; it can be found in the work of Tennessee Williams and, from quite a different perspective, that of Eugène Ionesco. The differentiation is useful primarily because it provides us with insight into the shape that Albee gives his material. If the lost and lonely Albee character is an irrevocable fact—philosophically, theologically, psychologically—if all that *angst* is inescapable, then his plays must necessarily be reflections of that condition; any gestures of defiance are doomed to failure. If, however, the Albee character is a product of his societal context and if that context is changeable (not necessarily politically, but by an alteration of modes of behavior between one man and another), then the plays may be instructive fables. He has dismissed American drama of the 1930's as propaganda rather than art, and he has disavowed solutions to anything. Still, in several statements he has suggested that there are solutions—or, at least, alternatives. Surely that possibility is implicit in his description of The American Dream as an "attack." In the *Transatlantic Review* interview, he said that "the responsibility of the writer is to be a sort of demonic social critic—to present the world and people in it as he sees it and say 'Do you like it? If you don't like it change it.'" In the *Atlantic,* he said, "I've always thought . . . that it was one of the responsibilities of playwrights to show people how they are and what their time is like in the hope that perhaps they'll change it."

Albee, then, shares with most American playwrights an idea of the utility of art, the supposition not only that art should convey truth, but that it should do so to some purpose. There is a strong strain of didacticism in all his work, but it is balanced by a certain ambiguity about the nature of the instructive fable. In interviews, he harps on how much of the creative process is subconscious, how little he understands his own work, how a play is to be experienced rather than understood. Insofar as this is not sour grapes pressed to make an aesthetic (his reaction to the reviews of Tiny Alice), it may be his way of recognizing that there is a conflict between his attitude toward man's situation and his suspicion (or hope: certainly *conviction* is too strong a word) that something can, or ought, to be done about it; between his assumption that this is hell we live in and his longing to redecorate it.

Whatever the nature of the chasm on the edge of which the Albee characters teeter so dexterously, to disturb the balance is to invite disaster or—possibly—salvation. If the conflict that I suggest above is a real one, it should be reflected in the plays in which one or more characters are willing to risk disaster. The American Dream and The Sandbox can be passed over here because, except for the sentimental death of Grandma at the end of the latter, they are diagnostic portraits of the Albee world, not actions performed in that setting. The Death of Bessie Smith and The Ballad of the Sad Café are more to the point, but they are also special cases. Although risks are taken (the Intern goes outside to examine Bessie; Amelia takes in Cousin Lymon in Ballad), the plays are less concerned with these acts than they are with the kind of expositional presentation—not particularly satirical in this case—that we get in Dream. Even so, the Intern's risk is meaningless since the woman is already dead; and Amelia's love is necessarily doomed by the doctrine the McCullers novella expounds—that it is difficult to love but almost impossible to be loved—and by the retrospective form the play took when Albee saddled it with a maudlin message-giving narrator. Tiny Alice and Malcolm are two of a kind, particularly if we consider them as corruption-of-innocence plays, although there is also a similarity of sorts between Malcolm's attempt to put a face on his absent father and Julian's attempt to keep from putting a face on his abstracted Father. They are even similar in that Albee, sharing a popular-comedy misconception about what that snake was up to in the Garden, uses sex as his sign of corruption—ludicrously in Alice, snickeringly in Malcolm. Traditionally, one of two things happens in plays in which the innocent face the world: either they become corrupted and learn to live with it (the standard Broadway maturity play) or they die young and escape the corruption (Synge's *Deirdre of the Sorrows* or Maxwell Anderson's *Winterset*). In the Albee plays, both things happen. Julian dies after accepting the world (edited to fit his preconceptions about it) and Malcolm dies, muttering "I've . . . lost so much," and loss, as the plays from The Zoo Story to A Delicate Balance insist, is what you gain in learning to live with it. There are extenuating circumstances for the deaths in these plays (Julian's concept of God is tied in with his desire to be a martyr; Malcolm's death is borrowed from Purdy, although Albee does not seem to understand what Purdy was doing with it in the novel), but these plays, too, are illustrations of the Albee world, and the deaths are more sentimental than central. Everything in the Garden is such an unlikely wedding of Albee and the late Giles Cooper, whose English play was the source of the American adaptation, that it is only superficially characteristic of Albee's work.

It is in The Zoo Story, Who's Afraid of Virginia Woolf? and A Delicate Balance that one finds dramatic actions by which the ambiguity of Albee's attitudes may be tested. In The Zoo Story, so goes the customary reading, Jerry confronts the vegetative Peter, forces him to stand his ground, dies finally on his own knife held in Peter's hand. In that suicidal act, Jerry becomes a scapegoat who gives his own life so that Peter will be knocked out of his complacency and learn to live, or LIVE. Even Albee believes this, or he said he did in answer to a question from Arthur Gelb (*The New York Times,* February 15, 1960): "Though he dies, he passes on an awareness of life to the other character in the play." If this is true, then presumably we are to take seriously—not as a dramatic device, but for its content—Jerry's "you have to make a start somewhere" speech in which he expounds the steps-to-love doctrine, a soggy inheritance from Carson McCullers ("A Tree. A Rock. A Cloud.") and Truman Capote (*The Grass Harp*). That the start should be something a great deal less gentle than the McCullers-Capote inheritance might suggest is not surprising when we consider that violence and death became twisted life symbols during the 1950's (as all the kids said after James Dean's fatal smashup, "Boy, that's living") and, then, turned literary in the 1960's (as in Jack Richardson's *Gallows Humor* and all the motorcycle movies from *The Wild Angels* to *Scorpio Rising*).

The problem with that reading is not that it is awash with adolescent profundity, which might well annoy some of the audience, but that it seems to be working against much that is going on within the play. Although Albee prepares the audience for the killing, it has always seemed gratuitous, a melodramatic flourish. The reason may be that it tries to suggest one thing (salvation) while the logic of the play demands something else. Except for a couple of expositional lapses, Jerry is too well drawn a character—self-pitying and aggressive, self-deluding and forlorn—to become the conventional "hero" (Albee uses that word in the Gelb interview) that the positive ending demands. He may well be so aware of his separation from everyone else that he plans or improvises ("could I have planned all this? No . . . no, I couldn't have. But I think I did") his own murder in a last desperate attempt to make contact, but there is nothing in the play to indicate that he succeeds. At the end, Peter is plainly a man knocked off his balance, but there is no indication that he has fallen into "an awareness of life." In fact, the play we are watching has already been presented in miniature in the dog story, and all Jerry gained from that encounter was"solitary but free passage." "There are some things in it that I don't really understand," Albee told Gelb. One of them may be that the play itself denies the romantic ending.

Virginia Woolf is a more slippery case. Here, too, the play works against the presumably upbeat ending, but Albee may be more aware that this is happening. According to the conventions of Broadway psychology, as reflected, for instance, in a play like William Inge's *The Dark at the Top of the Stairs,* in a moment of crisis two characters come to see themselves clearly. Out of their knowledge a new maturity is born, creating an intimacy that has not existed before and a community that allows them to face their problems (if not solve them) with new courage. This was the prevailing cliché of the serious Broadway play of the 1950's, and it was still viable enough in the 1960's to take over the last act of Lorraine Hansberry's *The Sign in Sidney Brustein's Window* and turn an interesting play into a conventional one. Virginia Woolf uses, or is used by, this cliché.

Although the central device of the play is the quarrel between George and Martha, the plot concerns their nonexistent son. From George's "Just don't start on the bit, that's all," before Nick and Honey enter, the play builds through hints, warnings, revelations until "sonny-Jim[5] is created and then destroyed. Snap, goes the illusion. Out of the ruins, presumably, new strength comes. The last section, which is to be played "very softly, very slowly," finds George offering new tenderness to Martha, assuring her that the time had come for the fantasy to die, forcing her—no longer maliciously—to admit that she is afraid of Virginia Woolf. It is "Time for bed," and there is nothing left for them to do but go together to face the dark at the top of the stairs. As though the rejuvenation were not clear enough from the last scene, there is the confirming testimony in Honey's tearful reiteration "I want a child" and Nick's broken attempt to sympathize, "I'd like to. . . ." Then, too, the last act is called "The Exorcism," a name that had been the working title for the play itself.

As neat as Inge, and yet there is something wrong with it. How can a relationship like that of Martha and George, built so consistently on illusion (the playing of games), be expected to have gained something from a sudden admission of truth? What confirmation is there in Nick and Honey when we remember that she is drunk and hysterical and that he is regularly embarrassed by what he is forced to watch? There are two possibilities beyond the conventional reading suggested above. The last scene between Martha and George may be another one of their games; the death of the child may not be the end of illusion but an indication that the players have to go back to go and start again their painful trip to home. Although there are many indications that George and Martha live a circular existence, going over the same ground again and again, the development of the plot and the tone of the last scene (the use of monosyllables, for instance, instead of their customary rhetoric) seem to deny that the game is still going on. The other possibility is that the truth—as in *The Iceman Cometh*—brings not freedom but death. To believe otherwise is to accept the truth-maturity cliché as readily as one must buy the violence-life analogy to get the positive ending of The Zoo Story. My own suspicion is that everything that feels wrong about the end of Virginia Woolf arises from the fact that, like the stabbing in Zoo, it is a balance-tipping ending that conventional theater says is positive but the Albee material insists is negative.

In A Delicate Balance, the line is clearer. The titular balance is the pattern of aggression and withdrawal, accusation and guilt which Tobias and his family have constructed in order to cope with existence. Agnes suggests that Tobias's "We do what we can" might be "Our motto." When Harry and Edna invade the premises, trying to escape from the nameless fears that have attacked them, they come under the white flag of friendship. Tobias must decide whether or not to let them stay, knowing that the "disease" they carry is contagious and that infection in the household will likely upset the balance. His problem is one in metaphysical semantics, like Julian's in Tiny Alice, although *God* is not the word whose meaning troubles him. "Would you give friend Harry the shirt off your back, as they say?" asks Claire, before the invasion begins. "I *suppose* I would. He *is* my best friend," answers Tobias, and we hear echoes from The American Dream: "She's just a dreadful woman, but she *is* chairman of our woman's club, so naturally I'm terribly fond of her." Dream's satirical fun about the emptiness of conventional language becomes deadly serious in Balance, for Tobias must decide whether the meaning of *friendship* is one with substance or only surface—whether *friendship* is a human relationship implying the possibility of action and risk, or simply a label, like *marriage* or *kinship,* to be fastened to a form of accommodation. As Pearl Bailey sang in *House of Flowers,* "What is a friend for? Should a friend bolt the door?" Tobias (having failed with his cat as Jerry failed with the dog) decides to try doing more than he can; in his long, broken speech in the last act, he displays his fear, indicates that he does not want Harry and Edna around, does not even like them, "BUT BY GOD . . . YOU STAY!!" His attempt fails because Harry and Edna, having decided that they would never risk putting real meaning into *friendship,* depart, leaving a depleted Tobias to rearrange his labels. He will have the help of Agnes, of course, which—on the balance—is a great deal, for she finds the conventional words of goodbye: "well, don't be strangers." Edna, who not many lines before made the "only skin" speech, answers, "Oh, good Lord, how could we be? Our lives are . . . the same." And so they are.

Thematically, A Delicate Balance is Albee's most precise statement. The gesture toward change, which seemed to fit so uncomfortably at the end of The Zoo Story and Virginia Woolf, has been rendered powerless within the action of Balance. Not only are Albee's characters doomed to live in the worst of all possible worlds; it is the only possible world. The impulse to do something about it can end only in failure. Yet, Albee cannot leave it at that. He cannot, like Samuel Beckett, let his characters turn their meaninglessness into ritual which has a way, on stage, of reasserting the meaning of the human being. He almost does so in Virginia Woolf, but his suspicion that games are not enough—a failure really to recognize that games are a form of truth as much as a form of lying—leads to the doubtful exorcism. Although the *angst*-er in Albee cannot let Tobias succeed, the latent reformer cannot help but make him heroic in his lost-cause gesture. He becomes an older, wearier, emptier Jerry, with only the unresisting air to throw himself on at the end.

"Better than nothing!" says Clov in *Endgame.* "Is it possible?" Out of the fastness of his wasteland, and against his better judgment, Albee cannot keep from hoping so.

In my critical and psychological naivety, I assume—as the paragraphs above show—that Albee's plays are really about the accommodations forced on man by his condition and his society. It is impossible, however, to get through a discussion of Albee without facing up to what might be called—on the analogy of the fashionable critical term *subtext*—his subsubject matter. That is the "masochistic-homosexual perfume" that Robert Brustein found hanging so heavily over The Zoo Story. It is a perfume of little importance except insofar as it throws the audience off the scent of the play's real quarry.

A student stopped me on campus a few years ago, hoping I would be able to confirm the story that Who's Afraid of Virginia Woolf? was first performed by four men in a little theater in Montreal. When I expressed my doubt, he went off to call a friend in New York who knew someone who knew the man who had been stage manager . . . although somehow he never got the confirmation he wanted. Except for the circumstantiality of this account (why Montreal?), it was a familiar rumor. Albee, in the *Diplomat* interview, explained that it was a letter to the *Times* that started the whole thing, that from there it passed into print elsewhere, first as rumor, then as fact. "I know the difference between men and women," he said, "and I write both characters." The more sophisticated interpreters simply step over Albee's denials and assume that the play, whoever it was written for, is really about a homosexual marriage. The reasoning here is that homosexual marriages, lacking the sanctions of society, are extremely unstable and that to survive at all they must create fantasy devices to bind the couple together. Hence, the imaginary child—for what other kind of child could come from the union of two men? There is a kind of specious logic in operation here. The flaw in it, however, is the refusal to recognize how much fantasy is a part of any relationship, how two people who are close (husband and wife, lovers of whatever sex, good friends) invent private languages, private rituals, private games which set them off from the others. Jimmy and Alison play at squirrels-and-bears in John Osborne's *Look Back in Anger,* and Sid and Iris play wild-mountain-girl in *The Sign in Sidney Brustein's Window* without either couple being taken as surrogate homosexual unions. My own inclination would be to let Martha and George have their "little bugger," as they call the nonexistent child, without insisting that they have a big one.

I have heard the play praised for the clarity with which it presented a homosexual couple, but, for the most part, such readings are based on a rejection of the possibility that George and Martha may have a representative heterosexual marriage. A similar rejection takes place when the play is dismissed as a kind of homosexual denigration of conventional marriage. Surely the castrating female and the dominated male are such commonplace psychological stereotypes—on and off stage—that their appearance need not be taken as an indication of a perverse attempt to do in all the Darbys and Joans who provide America's divorce statistics. Besides, Martha and George do not really fit those stereotypes. They appear to at the beginning, but as the play goes on it becomes clear that they are really very evenly matched in a battle that has been going on seriously since Strindberg's *The Dance of Death* and comically since *The Taming of the Shrew.* Albee's male wins, as in Shakespeare, but only tentatively, as in Strindberg. Not that Albee is particularly interested in the battle of the sexes as such. He has his own use for it, which is not to attack heterosexuality, but to present one of his many accommodation images: a well-matched pair of antagonists form a balance of sorts.

If a play like Virginia Woolf could call up the homosexual echoes, it is not surprising that Tiny Alice set them roaring. The opening scene between Cardinal and Lawyer is an exercise in bitchiness, primly nasty and insinuating, a marked contrast to the verbal exchanges between Martha and George. It passes from Lawyer's sneering comment on the caged cardinals ("uh, together . . . in conversation, as it were") to a variation on the old joke about the suitability of a boy or a clean old man, to hints of a schoolboy affair between the two men (Lawyer:"I'll have you do your obeisances. As you used to, old friend"), to mutual accusations in which Lawyer becomes an anus-entering hyena and Cardinal a mating bird. The business of the scene is apparently expositional, setting up the donation that will send Julian to Alice, so the tension between the two characters and the implication of their past relationship is gratuitous. So, too, is Lawyer's calling Butler "Darling" and"Dearest." The homosexual overtones in Julian (his attraction to the Welsh stableman, his kissing Miss Alice's hand "as he would kiss a Cardinal's ring," and the sensuality of his martyrdom dream in which the lion seems to mount him and he lingers over the entrance of the gladiator's prongs) might be more legitimate, a suggestion of the ambiguity of celibacy. Still, since he is sacrificed to heterosexuality—in that ludicrous scene in which he buries his head in Miss Alice's crotch, a cunnilingual first for the American stage—there is justice in Philip Roth's celebrated attack on"The Play that Dare Not Speak Its Name" (*New York Review of Books,* February 25, 1965). Roth accused Albee of writing "a homosexual daydream" about the martyrdom of the celibate male and disguising it as a metaphysical drama. Several weeks later (April 8, 1965), a letter to the editor insisted that there was no disguise at all in the play because a "tiny alice" is homosexual jargon for, as the writer so coyly put it, "a masculine derrière." Acting on this information, Bernard F. Dukore added an ingenious footnote to an article in *Drama Survey* (Spring, 1966) in which he considered that Julian, Butler, and Lawyer, all lovers of Miss Alice, might really be lovers of "tiny alice" and the opening doors at the end an anus symbol, but—as he went on to complain—a play that depends on a special argot for its symbolism is lost on a general audience. If "tiny alice" really is a gay word for anus and if Albee is using it consciously, he may be making an inside joke which has some relevance to his presumed serious play. If one of the points of the play is that all concepts of God (from Julian's abstraction to the mouse in the model) are creations of the men who hold them, a sardonic joke about God as a "tiny alice" is possible. Certainly, Albee has made that joke before, casually in Virginia Woolf (where George speaks of "Christ and all those girls") and more seriously in The Zoo Story (where one of the suggestions in Jerry's where-to-begin-to-love speech is "WITH GOD WHO IS A COLORED QUEEN WHO WEARS A KIMONO AND PLUCKS HIS EYEBROWS . . ."). On the other hand, the phrase could turn the play into an audience put-down such as the one described by Clay in *Dutchman,* in which he says that Bessie Smith, whatever the audience thought she was doing, was always saying, "Kiss my black ass."

This kind of speculation, hedged in as it is by *ifs* and *maybes,* is finally pointless. I almost wrote *fruitless,* but I stopped myself, assuming that my use of "inside joke" earlier is contribution enough to a silly game. How cute can a critic get without his tone corrupting his purpose? This question has relevance for the playwright, too. The problem about Tiny Alice is not whether there is a hidden homosexual joke and/or message, but that the obvious homosexual allusions seem to have little relevance to the plot device (the conspiracy to catch Julian), the play's central action (the martyrdom of Julian), or its presumed subject matter (the old illusion-reality problem). Unless Roth is right, the homosexual material is only decoration, different in quantity but not in kind from the additions and emphases that Albee brought to the already campy (old style) surface of Purdy's Malcolm.

The Zoo Story is the only Albee play in which a homosexual reading seems possible and usable in terms of what else the play is doing. It is, after all, the account of a meeting between two men in Central Park ("I'm not the gentleman you were expecting," says Jerry), in which one lets himself be impaled by the other, who has a phallic name. Jerry, dying, says, "I came unto you (*He laughs, so faintly*) and you have comforted me. Dear Peter." Jerry's casual references to the "colored queen" and the police "chasing fairies down from trees" on the other side of the park; his story of his one real love affair with the park superintendent's son, whom Otto Reinert (in *Modern Drama*) identifies with Peter by virtue of Peter's "proprietary claim" to the park bench; the implications in Jerry's "with fury because the pretty little ladies aren't pretty little ladies, with making money with your body which is an act of love and I could prove it"—all contribute to the possibility of this being a homosexual encounter. If it is, then much of the verbal and physical business of the play—Jerry's teasing, his wheedling, his tickling, the wrestling struggle for the bench—can be seen as an elaborate seduction which, since Jerry forces his partner to hold the knife, can only be summed up as getting a rise out of Peter. The dramatic fable can be read this way and still be relevant to the thematic material discussed earlier in this chapter. The problem comes when we consider the end of the play. If it is the positive ending that Albee suggested in the Gelb interview, if Jerry has passed on his "awareness of life," it must be Peter's initiation, and that, as Jerry says earlier, is "jazz of a very special hotel." On the other hand, as John Rechy keeps insisting in his seemingly endless novel, *City of Night,* a homosexual pickup in a park is a particularly workable image for the failure of contact between people.

"You know, I almost think you're serious," says Nick about something other than drama criticism, and George answers, "No, baby . . . *you* almost think you're serious, and it scares the hell out of you."

I feel a little that way about my very plausible reading of The Zoo Story in the section above. For if I am willing to accept the possibility of Peter as phallus, how can I deny all the interpreters who insist on seeing Jerry as Christ and Peter as the rock upon which to build his church? At least, the analogy of the homosexual pickup works comfortably within the action of the play and, less comfortably, with the thematic material. Despite the Biblical echoes ("I came unto you" again), the Christ-Jerry analogue is possible only to the extent that every sacrificial victim is a Christ figure, but that is a tautology which contributes nothing to an understanding of the play. If we see Jerry's suicidal finish as a sacrifice, we learn precious little about his action by nodding wisely and saying: oh, ho, Christ. We might as well say: oh, ho, Sydney Carton. Still, writers will use mythic and historical identifications for their characters (Tennessee Williams in *Orpheus Descending*), and critics will go myth-hunting and trap the slippery beasts. It has now become customary to dive into the underbrush of each new Albee play and bring them back alive.

Albee is partly to blame. He uses obvious symbols such as the muscular young man who is The American Dream and the athletic death figure in The Sandbox. He asks Julian and Miss Alice to form a pietà in Tiny Alice and the dying Julian to spread his arms to "resemble a crucifixion." In some notes prepared for a press conference, later printed in *The Best Plays of 1964-1965,* Albee said of Tiny Alice: "The play is full of symbols and allusions, naturally, but they are to be taken as echoes in a cave, things overheard, not fully understood at first." I take this to mean that they have no functional use in the play, in relation to either character or action, and that at best they provide a texture as allusive words do in some poetry. In a play, as in a poem, an allusion may uncover another realm of possibility (for instance, the ironies that keep emerging in *Peer Gynt*), but it can do so only if it does not wreck itself on the dramatic facts of the play. Take that pietà, for instance. It must either make clear something in the relationship between Julian and Miss Alice that has been implicit all along, or it must seem—as it did on stage—an exercise in literary pretentiousness.

Tiny Alice is the most blatant, but all the Albee plays insist on suggesting that there is more there than meets the eye and ear. This can be seen in the way Albee appears to be playing with the significance-seekers. In Agnes's "We become allegorical, my darling Tobias, as we grow older." In George's "Well, it's an allegory, really—probably—but it can be read as straight, cozy prose." Of course, Albee may mean this, too. In either case, he deserves to have the significant-name game played in his dramatic front yard. So Jerry becomes not only Christ but Jeremiah, and Julian not only Christ but Julian the Apostate. The Washingtons and the Khrushchevs get into Virginia Woolf. When Agnes, commenting on how much Claire has seen, says, "You were not named for nothing," she is presumably making a nasty crack about *claire* as an adjective meaning *bright.*[6] Yet audiences came out of the theater asking questions about St. Clare, St. Agnes, the Apocryphal Tobias, and even Miss Julie.

Albee may be fond of symbols and allusions, echoes and things overheard, but he plainly does not work—as the search for mythic analogies suggests—with dramatic images that come from outside his plays. This does not mean that he is the naturalist he occasionally claims to be, as when he told a *New York Times* interviewer (September 18, 1966) that even Tiny Alice was naturalistic. Even in *Virginia Woolf,* which is certainly the most naturalistic of his plays, the situation is basically unrealistic; the drinking party is a revelatory occasion, not a slice of life in a small New England college. For the most part, his characters have neither setting not profession, and when they are defined by things, the process is either conventionally (Peter's possessions) or unconventionally (the contents of Jerry's room) stereotypical, so obviously so that realism is clearly not intended. Nor do the characters have biographies, at least of the kind one has come to expect from the psychological naturalism of the Broadway stage. Virginia Woolf, harping as it does on the parental hang-ups of its two principals, comes closest to that pattern, but it is never very clear in this play how much of the memory is invention, which of the facts are fantasy. If Virginia Woolf and The Zoo Story are, at most, distant cousins of naturalistic drama, how much more remote are Albee's plainly absurdist plays (The Sandbox, The American Dream), his "mystery" play with its label-bearing characters (Tiny Alice), his drawing-room noncomedy (A Delicate Balance).

A close look at Albee's language provides the clearest indication of the nonrealistic character of his plays. A Delicate Balance is the most obvious example. The lines are consciously stilted, broken by elaborate parenthesis ("It follows, to my mind, that since I speculate I might, some day, or early evening I think more likely—some autumn dusk—go quite mad") or pulled up short by formal negative endings ("Must she not?"; "is it not?")—devices that call for inflections which stop the natural flow of speech. There are lines that are barely comprehensible ("One does not apologize to those for whom one must?"), which cannot be read without great deliberation. The verbal elaboration has particular point in this play since the language itself becomes a reflection of the artificiality of the characters and the setting, a pattern in which form replaces substance. This can best be seen in the play's most intricate digression. "What I find most astonishing," Agnes begins as the play opens, only to interrupt herself with her fantasy on madness. Her thought meanders through Tobias's practical attempt to get the after-dinner drinks, and we are fifteen speeches into the play, past two reappearances of the "astonish" phrase, before her opening sentence finally comes to an end. Seems to end, really, for the phrase recurs just before the final curtain, as Agnes goes her placidly relentless way—"to fill a silence," as the stage direction says—as though the intrusion of Harry and Edna and Tobias's painful attempt to deal with it were an easily forgotten interruption of the steady flow of nonevent.

In the *Atlantic* interview, explaining why he felt that English actors were needed for Tiny Alice, Albee said that he had moved from the "idiomatic" language of Virginia Woolf to something more formal. A Delicate Balance is a further step in elaboration. Yet, the language of the earlier plays, however idiomatic, is plainly artificial. Albee has used three main verbal devices from the beginning: interruption, repetition, and the set speech, the last of which makes use of the first two. The set speeches are almost formal recitations, as the playwright recognizes in The Zoo Story when he lets Jerry give his monologue a title: "THE STORY OF JERRY AND THE DOG!" There are similar speeches in all the plays: Jack's "Hey . . . Bessie" monologue which is the whole of Scene 3 of Bessie Smith; the Young Man's sentimental mutilation speech in The American Dream; George's "bergin" story and Martha's "Abandon-ed" speech in Virginia Woolf; the narrator's speeches in Ballad; Julian's dying soliloquy in Tiny Alice; Madame Girard's Entre-Scene monologue in Malcolm; Jack's direct address to the audience in Garden. Although Albee does not direct the speaker to step into a spotlight—as Tennessee Williams does with comparable speeches in *Sweet Bird of Youth*—he recognizes that these are essentially solo performances even when another character is on stage to gesture or grunt or single-word his way into the uneven but persistent flow of words. Of Tobias's big scene at the end of Balance, Albee says "This next is an aria."[7] In The Zoo Story, Jerry does not use a simple narration; his story is momentarily stopped for generalizing comments ("It always happens when I try to simplify things; people look up. But that's neither hither nor thither") and marked with repeated words ("The dog is black, all black; all black except . . .") and phrases ("I'll kill the dog with kindness, and if that doesn't work . . . I'll just kill him"). The word *laughter* punctuates the "bergin" story the way laughter itself presumably broke the cocktail-lounge murmur of the bar in which the boys were drinking.

It is not the long speeches alone that are built of interruption and repetition; that is the pattern of all the dialogue. On almost any page of Virginia Woolf you can find examples as obvious as this speech of George's: "Back when I was courting Martha—well, don't know if that's exactly the right word for it—but back when I was courting Martha. . . ." Then comes Martha's"Screw, sweetie!" followed by another attempt from George, more successful this time, "At any rate, back when I was courting Martha," and off he goes into an account which involves their going "into a bar . . . you know, a *bar* . . . a whiskey, beer, and bourbon *bar*. . . ." Sometimes the repetitions become echoes that reach from act to act as when Martha's "snap" speech in Act Two is picked up by George in the snapdragon scene in Act Three. From The Zoo Story to Everything in the Garden, then, Albee has consciously manipulated language for effect; even when it sounds most like real speech—as in Virginia Woolf—it is an exercise in idiomatic artificiality.

At their best, these artifices are the chief devices by which Albee presents his dramatic images. Neither naturalist nor allegorist, he works the great middle area where most playwrights operate. He puts an action on stage—an encounter in a park that becomes a suicide-murder, a night-long quarrel that ends in the death of illusion, an invasion that collapses before the defenders can decide whether to surrender or to fight—which presumably has dramatic vitality in its own right and from which a meaning or meanings can emerge. The central situation—the encounter, the relationship implicit in the quarrel, the state of the defenders and the invaders—is defined almost completely in verbal terms. There is business, of course, but it is secondary. Jerry's poking and tickling Peter is only an extension of what he has been doing with words; George's attempt to strangle Martha is a charade not far removed from their word games. When events get more flamboyant—the shooting of Julian, Julia's hysterical scene with the gun—they tend to become ludicrous. The most obvious example in Albee of physical business gone wrong is the wrestling match between Miss Amelia and Marvin Macy in The Ballad of the Sad Café; the fact that it is the dramatic climax of the play does not keep it from looking silly on stage. Ordinarily, Albee does not need to ask his characters to do very much, for what they *say* is dramatic action. "The old pigeonhole bit?" says Jerry in The Zoo Story, and although it is he, not Peter, who does the pigeonholing, the accusation and the mockery in the question is an act of aggression, as good as a shove for throwing Peter off balance.

In the long run, Albee's reputation as a playwright will probably depend less on what he has to say than on the dramatic situations through which he says it. The two Albee plays that seem to have taken the strongest hold on the public imagination (which may be a way of saying they are the two plays I most admire) are The Zoo Story and Virginia Woolf. The reason is that the meeting between Jerry and Peter and the marriage of George and Martha, for all the nuances in the two relationships, are presented concretely in gesture and line; they take shape on the stage with great clarity. Tiny Alice, by contrast, is all amorphousness. It may finally be possible to reduce that play to an intellectual formulation, but the portentousness that hovers over so many lines and so much of the business keeps the characters and the situation from attaining dramatic validity. The Zoo Story is more successful as a play, not because its dramatic situation is more realistic, but because it exists on stage—a self-created dramatic fact.

A Delicate Balance is a much stronger play than Tiny Alice. As the discussion early in this chapter indicates, it is probably Albee's most perfect combination of theme and action, and its central metaphor—the balance—is important not only to the play but to Albee's work as a whole. Yet, compared to Virginia Woolf, it is an incredibly lifeless play. The reason, I think, is that the Martha-George relationship has dramatic substance in a way that the Tobias-Agnes household does not. Too much has been made—particularly by casual reviewers—of the violence, the hate, the anger in the Martha-George marriage. It is just as important that the quarrel be seen in the context of the affection they have for one another and the life—even if it is a long, sad game—which they so obviously share. One of the best inventions in all of Albee is the gun with the parasol in it, for what better way of seeing the relationship of Martha and George than in terms of a murderous weapon that is also a sheltering object; the instrument is a metaphor for the marriage, and its use is a preview of what will happen in the last act.

From the moment the play opens, from Martha's challenge, "What a dump. Hey what's that from?" it is clear that Martha and George play the same games. He may be tired at first, not really in the mood for a session of name-the-movie, or he may be faking indifference because he cannot remember that the "god-damn Bette Davis picture" Martha has in mind is *Beyond the Forest* (1949), but there is companionship in the incipient quarrel that will not disappear as the argument grows more lethal. It can be seen directly in several places. Near the beginning of the play, after a mutual accusation of baldness, they go into a momentary affectionate scene in which his "Hello honey" leads to her request for "a big sloppy kiss." Almost the same phrase, "C'mon . . . give me a kiss," is her compliment for his having been clever enough to introduce the parasol-gun into the game room. Much more important than the grand games to which he gives labels—Humiliate the Host, Get the Guests, Hump the Hostess—are the small games that they play constantly—the play-acting routines, the little-kid bits, the mock-etiquette turns, the verbal games. The whole force of the play depends on their existence as a couple, a relationship made vivid in moments such as the one in Act III when Nick, humiliated at his sexual failure, begins angrily, "I'm nobody's houseboy . . ." and Martha and George shout in unison,"Now!" and then begin to sing, "I'm nobody's houseboy now. . . ." Their closeness is important if we are to recognize that George can be and is cuckolded. This event takes place on stage in Act II when Martha and Nick dance together sensuously and, speaking in time to the music, she tells about George's abortive attempt to be a novelist. It is at this moment that their marriage is violated, that George's anger shows most plainly, that he initiates a game of Get the Guests. "Book dropper! Child mentioner!" accuses George, and we see—perhaps before he does—the connection that forces him to carry "the bit about the kid" to its murderous conclusion. One may come away from Virginia Woolf suspicious of the end of the play and its presumed implications but never in doubt about the dramatic force of either characters or situation.

A Delicate Balance provides a marked contrast. We learn a great deal about the antipathy between Agnes and Claire, the sexual life of Agnes and Tobias, the marriage problems of Julia, the nameless fears of Edna and Harry, but the situation is explained more than it is presented. Some of the language is witty, some of it—particularly Agnes' lines—is quietly bitchy, but speeches do not pass from one character to another, carving out a definition of their relationship; lines fall from the mouths of the characters and shatter on the stage at their feet. Thematically, this is fine, since separateness is what Albee wants to depict, and he is ingenious in the way he lets the artificiality of his language contribute to the general sense of empty facade. Unfortunately, the characters are defined only in terms of their separateness, their significance as exemplary lost ones. Not so indeterminate as Tiny Alice, A Delicate Balance still lacks the kind of concreteness that comes from a dramatic image fully realized on stage. The characters are given a little biography, a few mannerisms, a whisper of depth, but they remain highly articulate stick figures moving through a sequence of nonevents to a foregone conclusion.

Unless Edward Albee is on some unannounced road to Damascus, there is not much doubt about what he will be saying in the plays that lie ahead of him. It is how he chooses to say it that will be important. In the face of his most recent work, in which significance seems to be imposed from the outside instead of meaning rising from within, we have every reason to be afraid, not of, but for Virginia Woolf.

Notes

[1]According to a letter from Albee (October 13, 1966), Hinton, who was writing the libretto, fell ill and Albee finished the work; as he remembers it, he wrote the Prologue, the last scene, and did "considerable revision" on the other three scenes. The title page of the vocal score lists Flanagan with Hinton and Albee as one of the authors of the libretto. The opera, of course, is based on Herman Melville's "Bartleby the Scrivener." My responses are highly suspect since I did not see the opera in production; I read the libretto and listened to at least two of my friends—unfortunately, not at the same time—make piano assaults on the score. I would guess that the most effective scene, musically and dramatically, is Scene 2 in which Mr. Allan (the name given to Melville's nameless lawyer-narrator) goes to his office on Sunday morning and finds Bartleby there; his aria carries him from complacent Sunday-morning ruminations (mostly to slightly doctored lines from Melville) through the confrontation with Bartleby to his attempt to make sense of this clerk who will not do his work and will not go away. Bartleby's one-note "I would prefer not to" echoes in variations all through Allan's confusion in this scene. Less happy moments musically are church bells which chime in the piano part after they have been mentioned in the libretto and the calculated contrast at the end of Scene 3 when beyond the huffing-puffing violence can be heard the soprano of the office boy singing his way back on stage with the ballad-like song that identifies him. For the most part, the libretto is a softening of Melville's story. Since the Bartleby of the story makes a claim on the lawyer which cannot be (or is not) fulfilled, Melville's work has an obvious thematic relevance to Albee's. What is missing in the dramatization is Melville's superb ambiguity; there is not even an attempt in the opera to get the effect that Melville achieves when his narrator, who believes that "the easiest way of life is the best," manages to comfort himself by pigeonholing Bartleby when the clerk is no longer alive and mutely accusing. The "Oh, Bartleby, Oh, humanity" that ends the opera is sentimental although it probably means to be something more exalted. The "Ah, Bartleby! Ah, humanity!" that ends Melville's story is ironic.

Flanagan, to whom Albee dedicated *The Zoo Story,* did the mustic for *The Sandbox, The Ballad of the Sad Café,* and *Malcolm.* Flanagan's music for *The Sandbox* is printed with the play in Margaret Mayorga's *The Best Short Plays, 1959-1960.*

[2]My own reviews, from *The Zoo Story* (*The Reporter,* February 16, 1961) to *Everything in the Garden* (*The Reporter,* December 28, 1967), have suggested with a decreasing amount of flippancy that there is less to Albee than meets the eye. Although my review of *Virginia Woolf* (*Drama Survey,* Fall, 1963) now seems unnecessarily condescending, my general misgivings about Albee as a playwright have not disappeared. What has disappeared, alas, is a letter that Albee sent to *The Reporter* to straighten me out after my review of *The Zoo Story.*

[3]One of the persistent—and, I think, unfortunate—ways of reading Albee is to assume that the animals and the animal imagery which figure in so many of the plays are being used to make some instructive point about man's nature. For instance, John V. Hagopian, in a letter to the *New York Review of Books* (April 8, 1965), insisted that the point of *Tiny Alice* is that "man must embrace his animal nature." It is true that Brother Julian has an abstraction problem in that play, but his acceptance of the world (and all the animals and birds that wander through the lines in *Alice*) is not—as the ambiguity in his death scene indicates—a sure sign of either health or reality. There is a certain amount of sentimentality in such a reading of the play, at least if the "embrace" is taken as positive rather than factual. In Albee's work there is a general equation between man and animal. This can be seen in *The Zoo Story,* not only in Jerry's dog tale and the zoo metaphor, but in the confusion of Peter's children with his cats and parakeets. Perhaps there is something ennobling, an up-the-chain-of-being slogan, in Jerry's comfort to Peter, "you're not really a vegetable; it's all right, you're an animal," but as Mac the Knife would say, "What's the percentage?" Albee's animals reflect the predicament of his men. There are still bars to look through, accommodations to be made.

[4]Perhaps we cannot believe him. In an article on the making of the movie (*McCall's,* June, 1966), Roy Newquist quotes Albee: "They had filmed the *play,* with the exception of five or ten minutes of relatively unimportant material." Although I quote from a number of interviews in this chapter, I am aware that interviews, at best, are doubtful sources of information and opinion. There are the obvious dangers of misquotation and spur-of-the-moment remarks which are untrue (is *The Ballad of the Sad Café* an earlier play than *Virginia Woolf,* as Albee told Thomas Lask in a *Times* interview, October 27, 1963, or are we to believe the dates accompanying the Atheneum editions of his plays?) or only momentarily true (the conflicting opinions about the movie version of *Woolf*). Beyond that, it is clear that Albee, when he is not on his high horse, likes to kid around. I am not thinking of an occasion like the joint interview with John Gielgud (*Atlantic,* April, 1965), where the chummy inside jocularity masks what must have been a major difference of opinion over *Tiny Alice,* but of an interview like the one in *Transatlantic Review,* in which Albee is very solemn and still sounds as though he is putting Digby Diehl on. Or the one in *Diplomat* that got me into this footnote in the first place, for in that one Albee uses what I assume is a running gag, of which Otis L. Guernsey, Jr., never seems aware. In three variations on a single line, he ponders whether or not *Woolf,* Alice,and *Balance* are comedies on the basis of whether or not the characters get what they want or think they want. The joke, of course, is that the line comes from Grandma's curtain speech from *The American Dream*: "So, let's leave things as they are right now . . . while everybody's happy . . . while everybody's got what he wants . . . or everybody's got what he thinks he wants. Good night, dears."

[5]One of the "echoes"—to use Albee's word (*The Best Plays of 1964-1965*) for the unanchored allusions in *Tiny Alice*—must surely be a song that little boys used to sing: "Lulu had a baby, / Named it Sonny Jim, / Threw it in the piss-pot / To see if it could swim."

[6]According to my French distionary, *claire,* as a feminine noun, means "burnt bones or washed ashes used for making cupels." Chew on that.

[7]Albee's one attempt at fiction—the beginning of a novel which *Esquire* (July, 1963) printed as one of a group of works-in-progress, a fragment that was probably written for the occasion—is essentially a long speech like the ones in the plays. *The Substitute Speaker,* a play that Albee has been announcing since 1963, will contain the granddaddy of the solos if it really has in it the forty-minute speech Albee once promised.

Ruby Cohn (essay date 1971)

SOURCE: "The Verbal Murders of Edward Albee," in *Dialogue in American Drama,* Indiana University Press, 1971, pp. 130-69.

[*In the essay below, the critic expresses reservations about the "surface polish" of Albee's dialogue but concludes that he is "the most skillful composer of dialogue that America has produced."*]

Collectively, O'Neill with his realistic idiom, Miller with his varied inflections, and Williams with his functional imagery brought American dialogue to a maturity that was Edward Albee's birthright. Albee-playwright was born at the age of thirty, with perfect command of contemporary colloquial stylized dialogue.

Albee's intensely American yet original idiom is striking if we compare a passage from Albee's first play, The Zoo Story (1959), with the competent translation into German, the language of its first production.

> But good old Mom and good old Pop are dead . . . you know? . . .[1] I'm broken up about it, too . . . I mean really. BUT. That particular vaudeville act is playing the cloud circuit now, so I don't see how I can look at them, all neat and framed. Besides, or, rather, to be pointed about it, good old Mom walked out on good old Pop when I was ten and a half years old; she embarked on an adulterous turn of our southern states . . . a journey of a year's duration . . . and her most constant companion . . . among others, among many others . . . was a Mr. Barleycorn.

> Ja—oh, weh und ach—, Mammi und Pappi sind tot, and ich weiss nicht, ob ich es ertragen könnte, sie dauernd vor mir zu sehen, fein säuberlich eingerahmt. Nebenbei bemerkt, oder vielmehr gar nicht nebenbei: Mammi ist Pappi weggelaufen, als ich zehneinhalb Jahre alt war. Sie hatte sich auf eine ehebrecherische Fahrt durch unsere Südstaaten begeben. Der Ausflug dauerte ein ganzes Jahr. Der beständigste unter ihren Reisegefährten war, wie sich später herausstellte, ein Mister Barleycorn.

The cloud circuit vaudeville act is absent from the German, as are the ironic rhythmic resonances of the repeated "good old." And it is not even clear that the only fidelity of Jerry's mother is to whiskey.

Albee combines this vividly colloquial diction with a seemingly leisurely indirection. In the work of the other three dramatists, dialogue was examined in Aristotelian terms: how did it further the plot? How did it reveal character?

How did it delineate thought (usually interpreted as theme)? These questions are still useful for Albee's plays, and yet the dialogue of The Zoo Story sounds absurdly disjunctive. But under Albee's disjunction lie an eventful plot, coherent characters, and thematic consistency.

The main theme of The Zoo Story is communication. A "permanent transient" tries to communicate with a proper publisher, whom he meets one Sunday on a Central Park bench. One human being tries to communicate with another. Being a highly unorthodox individual, Jerry uses highly unorthodox means of communication—entirely verbal at first. Early in The Zoo Story, Jerry informs Peter: "I took the subway down to the Village so I could walk all the way up Fifth Avenue to the zoo. It's one of those things a person has to do: *sometimes a person has to go a very long distance out of his way to come back a short distance correctly"* (my italics). Jerry's long walk enables him to describe his methodology. Jerry could have gone to New York City's Central Park Zoo by the cross-town bus, but, deliberately indirect, he chose a circuitous route, "a very long distance out of his way to come back a short distance correctly." As Hamlet is "but mad north-north west," Jerry walks "northerly," seeking by indirection to find direction out, seeking by indirection to communicate with Peter. At the verbal climax of the play, Jerry's dog story, he uses the same pointedly clumsy phrase to describe his indirection: "THE STORY OF JERRY AND THE DOG! . . . What I am going to tell you has something to do with how sometimes it's necessary to go a long distance out of the way in order to come back a short distance correctly." When we hear the dog story, we are already familiar with Jerry's "out of the way" dialogue and its two main rhetorical patterns, pointed thrusts and digressive monologues.

The dog story is an analogue for the titular and thematic zoo story, which Jerry does not narrate, though he predicts that it will be in the newspapers and on television. Jerry's dog story is a parable, as Albee's Zoo Story is a parable. In the latter, vagrant confronts conformist on a park bench; in the former, man confronts animal in a dark hallway. Jerry is vagrant and man; conformist Peter replaces the animal as Jerry's friend-enemy. Jerry views Peter as he does the dog—with sadness and suspicion; Jerry tickles Peter as he tempts the dog—into self-revelation; Jerry forces Peter to defend his premises as the dog defends *his* premises; Jerry hopes for understanding from the dog ("I hoped that the dog would . . . understand") and from Peter ("I don't know what I was thinking about; of course you don't understand.") As the dog bit Jerry, Peter stabs Jerry.

However, the dog's hostility to Jerry begins the dog story whereas Peter's hostility to Jerry is only gradually aroused in The Zoo Story. The dog's hostility is at the surface of his animality, but Peter's hostility is calculatedly manipulated by Jerry, whose physical assault on Peter is comprised of five actions—tickling, shoving, punching, slapping, and immolating himself on the knife. But the physical assault has been prepared by Jerry's skillful verbal assault: "I have learned that neither kindness or cruelty by themselves, independent of each other, creates any effect beyond themselves; and I have learned that the two combined, together, at the same time, are the teaching emotion." Jerry combines the two in his education of Peter, with cruelty more immediately evident than kindness.

After Jerry's verbal attack, a terrified Peter screams when Jerry opens his knife: "YOU'RE GOING TO KILL ME!" But Jerry's intention is more subtle. *"Jerry tosses the knife at Peter's feet"* and urges him to pick it up. Once the knife is in Peter's hands, Jerry taunts him into using it. He slaps Peter each time he repeats the word "fight." Since Peter is a defensive animal (when pressed) and not an attacker, Jerry *"impales himself on the knife."* Though Jerry, wounded, screams like a "fatally wounded animal," he dies like a man—talking. In dying, Jerry comes to partial self-recognition through his stream of associations: "Could I have planned all this? No . . . no, I couldn't have. But I think I did." His final broken phrases reflect the disjunctive quality of his behavior.

Jerry's fragmented life and speech contrast with Peter's coherence and order. Peter's effort to light his pipe triggers Jerry's first taunt: "Well, boy; *you're* not going to get lung cancer, are you?" With this thrust, Jerry exposes Peter's caution. At the same time, he introduces death, one of the play's themes, into the dialogue; he will harp on that theme in his account of his parents and aunt, in the dog story, and, finally, in his own death. Only in dying does Jerry shift from cruel to kind words, reassuring Peter that he is "an animal, too." The "too" is significant; Peter and Jerry are both animals, as are the seals, birds, and lions at the zoo; as are the parakeets who make Peter's dinner and the cats who set his table. In his dog story, Jerry says he put *rat* poison into the hamburger bought for a pussy-*cat,* so as to kill the landlady's *dog.* We see no animals on stage, but they recur thematically in the dialogue. Thus, animals become interchangeable. Albee's Zoo Story, the story that is not told, generalizes that men are animals; beneath an illusion of civilization, they live in rooms that resemble zoo-cages. They may use words and knives instead of fangs and claws, but they still can kill.

As Gilbert Debusscher has shown, this aspect of The Zoo Story is reminiscent of Tennessee Williams' *Suddenly Last Summer.* In both plays, too, "the cleverly interrupted monologue moves forward first by jerky and monosyllabic staccatos, then through the largo of long confessional passages, toward an unbearable tension which is resolved in a violent and sensational climax."[2] In both plays, that climax is a kind of mystical ecstasy—erotic, religious, but above all thematic.

By his climactic death, Jerry finally communicates with Peter, teaching him that men are brothers in their animality. However, Jerry does more than reveal Peter's animality to him. Like the Old Testament Jeremiah, whose cruel prophesies were a warning kindness to his people, Albee's Jerry may have educated Peter in his relation to God. Jerry occasionally introduces biblical notes: "So be it." "And it came to pass that . . ." "Amen." Before the dog story, Jerry exclaims: "For God's sake." After poisoning the dog, Jerry promises its owner that he will pray, though he does"not understand how to pray." At the end of the dog story, Jerry recites a list of those with whom he has tried to communicate—a list that begins with animals and ends with God, anagram of dog. In his cruel-kind deviling of Peter, Jerry calls on Jesus, and Peter replies with a "God damn" and a "Great God" almost in the same breath[3]

This undercurrent of religious suggestion is climaxed by the final words of the play. Toward the beginning, Peter reacted to Jerry's unconventional life story with "Oh, my; oh, my." And Jerry sneered: "Oh, your what?" Only after the impalement is Jerry's question answered—by Peter's whispered repetitions: "Oh my God, oh my God, oh my God."—the only words Peter speaks while Jerry dies, thanking Peter in biblical phrases: "I came unto you and you have comforted me." After Jerry's revelation of Peter's animal nature, and Peter's subsequent departure according to Jerry's instructions, we hear "OH MY GOD!" as an off-stage howl—the final proof of Peter's animality, but also of his humanity, since he howls to his God. Jerry, who tells an animal story, closes the play by echoing Peter's "Oh my God" in the difficult combination demanded by the stage direction: *"scornful mimicry and supplication."* That tonal combination is Jerry's last lesson in the pedagogy of cruel kindness. Much of his scornful wit has been mimetic, and yet the wit itself is an inverted plea for love and understanding; the very word "understand" resounds through the play.

Because life is lonely and death inevitable, Jerry seeks communication in a single deed of ambiguous suicide-murder. He stages his own death, and by that staging, he explodes Peter's illusion of civilization, converting him into an apostle who will carry the message of man's caged animality—the zoo story. Jerry's death brings us to a dramatic definition of humanity—born with animal drives but reaching toward the divine. Though this definition is at least as old as Pascal, Albee invests it with contemporary relevance through his highly contemporary idiom.

With gesture and language, Jerry teaches Peter. The relationship of the two men is not simply non-conformist versus conformist, but teacher and student, realist and illusionist, man and fellow-man. Shifting from intimate questions to intimate revelations, Jerry opens a new world to Peter. Even in his dying speech, Jerry does not sentimentalize, and he remains partially mocking as he narrows down to the final spaced syllables: "Oh . . . my . . . God." Homosexual interpretations of The Zoo Story miss its wide resonance, but there *is* love in Jerry's pedagogy—a love rooted in animality and straining toward the divine.

* * *

In The Death of Bessie Smith (1959), Albee changes both structure and texture, but his dialogue continues to combine associational monologues with lethal thrusts. Based on a newspaper story of the death of the Negro blues singer, The Death of Bessie Smith is documentary in origin—a unique phenomenon in Albee's work. But his Bessie Smith is a presence and not a character in his play, whose most sustained character is a voluble young Nurse. Lacking Jerry's pedagogic kindness, the Nurse's dialogue is vitriolic, and yet she is not responsible for the death of Bessie Smith.

In the eight scenes of the play, Albee attempts to counterpoint two story-threads—the trip North of blues-singer Bessie Smith, and the Nurse's sadistic control of a Southern hospital. The Nurse story overshadows that of Bessie Smith, who is known only through the dialogue of her chauffeur-companion, Jack. Albee gives names to the sympathetic Negroes—Jack, Bernie, Bessie Smith—whereas the type-casts the white world—Nurse, Father, Intern, light-skinned Orderly, Second Nurse. Named and unnamed characters are alike in their loquacious inaction. As Paul Witherington has noted, they talk about doing things which they do not do.[4]

The Nurse is the only coherent character in The Death of Bessie Smith, and she coheres through her scornful verbalizations. To her father, she sneers: "I'll tell you what I'll do: now that we have His Honor, the mayor, as a patient . . . when I get down to the hospital . . . If I ever get there on that damn bus . . . I'll pay him a call, and I'll just *ask* him about your 'friendship' with him." The Nurse goads her mulatto orderly: "Tell me, boy . . . is it true, young man, that you are now an inhabitant of no-man's-land, on the one side shunned and disowned by your brothers, and on the other an object of contempt and derision to your betters?"

About half way through the play, Jack's car, with Bessie Smith as passenger, crashes off stage. On stage the Nurse carries on a bored telephone conversation with a second Nurse at another hospital. It is this second Nurse who is indirectly responsible for the death of Bessie Smith, but we do not learn this till the end of the play.

In the two longest of the eight scenes (sixth and last) the cynical but conformist Nurse engages in a thrust-and-parry dialogue with the liberal Intern. At his rare dialectical best, the Intern is as cruel as the Nurse. Though ideologically opposed to her, he desires her—a desire inflamed by her taunts. When his sneer about her chastity evokes her threat to "fix" him, he combines admiration with vengefulness: "I just had a lovely thought . . . that maybe sometime when you are sitting there at your desk opening mail with that stiletto you use for a letter opener, you might slip and tear open your arm . . . then you could come running into the emergency . . . and I could be there when you came running in, blood coming out of you like water out of a faucet . . . and I could take ahold of your arm . . . and just hold it . . . and watch it flow . . . just hold on to you and watch your blood flow . . ." The carefully cadenced pauses augment the cruelty of the words.

The death of Bessie Smith occurs off stage, between the last two scenes of the play. In the brief seventh scene, the Second

Nurse refuses hospital admission to Bessie Smith, injured in an automobile accident: "I DON'T CARE WHO YOU GOT OUT THERE, NIGGER. YOU COOL YOUR HEELS!" Similarly, when Jack brings Bessie Smith to the central hospital in the last scene, the Nurse refuses admission to the singer. As the Intern and Orderly rush out to Bessie in the car, Jack tells the Nurse about the accident, and she recalls the Intern's wish that he might watch while her blood came out "like water from a faucet." But it is Jack who has watched the ebb of the life-blood of Bessie Smith. When the Intern and Orderly re-enter, *"their uniforms are bloodied,"* and Bessie Smith is dead.

In The Death of Bessie Smith nurses do not tend the sick; they converse at hospital admissions desks, refusing care to the injured. "Mercy" is merely an expletive without meaning. The Nurse says that she is sick of things; the word "sick" is on everyone's tongue. But it is Bessie Smith who dies of the sickness in the South. The Nurse speaks of her letter opener in the Intern's ribs, of a noose around his neck, but it is Bessie Smith who dies violently. The Nurse likes Negro blues, but she will not lift a finger to save a Negro blues inger; rather, she mocks dead Bessie Smith, singing until the Intern slaps her. Albee's play indicts the whole sick South for the murder of Bessie Smith; his setting is a Southern hospital in which no one is well, but only Bessie Smith dies. Nevertheless, the singer's story is fragmentary, and we are left with a more vivid impression of the verbal duelling of Nurse and Intern; this is often gratuitous skirmishing in a loosely constructed, morally earnest drama.

* * *

By contrast, satiric caricature is Albee's main technique in The Sandbox (1959) and The American Dream (1960). Both monologues and thrust-and-parry exchanges contain the clichés of middle-class America. The implication is that such clichés lead to the death of Grandma, who represents the vigorous old frontier spirit. In her independence, Grandma resembles Jerry or the Intern, but age has made her crafty, and she has learned to roll with the punches. In both The Sandbox and The American Dream, Mommy delivers these punches verbally, and yet she does not literally kill Grandma.

Of the relationship between the two plays, Albee has written: "For The Sandbox, I extracted several of the characters from The American Dream and placed them in a situation different than, but related to, their predicament in the longer play."[5] The Sandbox is named for the grave of Grandma, the first-generation American, and The American Dream is named for the third-generation American, a grave in himself; in both plays, murderous intention is lodged in the middle generation, especially Mommy. In The Sandbox, Mommy and Daddy deposit Grandma in a child's sandbox, as Hamm deposited his legless parents in ashbins in Beckett's *Endgame.* Half-buried, Grandma finds that she can no longer move, and she accepts her summons by the handsome Young Man, an Angel of Death.

In The American Dream, Ionesco is a strong influence on Albee. Like *The Bald Soprano,* The American Dream thrives on social inanities. Like Ionesco, Albee reduces events to arrivals and departures. As in *The Bald Soprano,* a mock-recognition scene is based on circumstantial evidence—husband and wife in the Ionesco play, and in the Albee play, Mrs. Barker and the American family for whom she barks. Albee also uses such Ionesco techniques as proliferation of objects (Grandma's boxes), pointless anecdotes (mainly Mommy's), meaningless nuances (beige, wheat, and cream), cliché refrains (I don't mind if I do; how fascinating, enthralling, spellbinding, gripping, or engrossing.).

Within this stuffy apartment of Ionesco motifs, Albee places a family in the American grain, with its areas for senior citizens and its focus on money. When Mommy was eight years old, she told Grandma that she was "going to mahwy a wich old man." Sterile, Mommy and Daddy have purchased a baby from the Bye-Bye Adoption Service, that puns on Buy-Buy. Mommy spends much of her life shopping (when she isn't nagging Daddy or Grandma). In The Sandbox, Mommy and Daddy carry Grandma to *death,* but in The American Dream, Mommy nags at Grandma's *life.* She informs a feebly protesting Daddy that he wants to put Grandma in a nursing home, and she threatens Grandma with a man in a van who will cart her away. Mommy treats Grandma like a naughty child; she discusses Grandma's toilet habits, warns her that she will take away her TV, worries about her vocabulary: "I don't know where she gets the words; on the television, maybe."

And Grandma, who is treated like a child, repeats the phrases we learn as American children: "Shut up! None of your damn business." Grandma tells the story of the family child to Mrs. Barker. Since "the bumble of joy" had eyes only for Daddy, Mommy gouged his eyes out; since he called Mommy a dirty name, they cut his tongue out. And because "it began to develop an interest in its you-know-what," they castrated him and cut his hands off at the wrists. Our acquaintance with Mommy has prepared us for Grandma's account of Bringing up Bumble. But more painful than the mutilations are the ailments it subsequently develops, because we can hear in them Mommy's cruel American platitudes: "it didn't have a head on its shoulders, it had no guts, it was spineless, its feet were made of clay." This is Mommy's more insidious castration, nagging the child into a diminutive Daddy, who is "all ears," but who has no guts since he "has tubes now, where he used to have tracts." Daddy's organs are related to housing, on the one hand, and television, on the other—both mass produced in modern America, and both part of the modern American dream life. In The American Dream, like father, like son. Daddy "just want[s] to get everything over with," and his bumble-son does get everything over with, by dying before Mommy can complete her murder of him.

In The American Dream, it is an off-stage bumble that predicts Grandma's death, as an off-stage rumble announces

Grandma's death in The Sandbox. Like the bumble, Grandma escapes Mommy's murderous malice by a kind of suicide. As Jerry turns Peter's reluctant threat into the reality of his death, Grandma turns Mommy's repeated threats into the reality of her disappearance from the family. Mommy is even more conformist than Peter, so that she cannot perform deeds of violence herself. Daddy has been devitalized on an operating table, so that Grandma has to be threatened by a proxy murderer—the man in the van.

When a handsome Young Man arrives, Grandma is alone on stage, and she instantly recognizes the American Dream shaped by Mommy. He shares only appearance and initials with the Angel of Death in The Sandbox, but he has the same meaning. The American Dream is an Angel of Death who is linked to both the mutilated bumble and to Grandma. In a confessional monologue, the Young Man tells Grandma of a twin "torn apart" from him, so that it seemed his heart was "wrenched from his body," draining him of feeling. As his twin brother was mutilated physically, the American Dream is mutilated emotionally.

When Mrs. Barker intrudes upon this confrontation of the numb young modern man with the vigorous old frontier spirit, Grandma introduces him as the man in the van, Mommy's bogey-man. Asking him to carry her boxes, Grandma follows the Young Man out. Boxes and sandbox are coffin and grave; the American Dream leads but to the grave, and Grandma, accepting her fate, goes out in style—escorted by a handsome swain whose gallantry replaces feeling.

Though minatory Mommy later admits that "There is no van man. We . . . we made him up," she readily accepts the American Dream as a replacement for Grandma. Thus, the "comedy" ends happily, though Grandma is dead to Mommy:"Five glasses? Why five? There are only four of us." In spite of Mommy's malice—expressed in the clichés of contemporary America—Grandma and bumble manage to die their own deaths.

In the conversation between a sympathetic Grandma and an ambiguous American Dream, Albee dilutes his satire. In spite of Grandma's pithy frontier comments and her asides on "old people," Grandma docs not openly oppose Mommy. Since the Young Man is first caricatured, then sentimentalized, his long speeches sag. He will "do almost anything for money," and he tries to sell us the sad story of his life. Apparently ignorant of the mutilations to his twin brother, he describes his parallel loss of sensation that has resulted in his inability to love. In spite of Albee's rhythmic skill, this abstract statement of losses is duller than Grandma's pungent summary of the mutilation of his twin, and this dulls the edge of Albee's satire. In spite of the Young Man's warning that his tale "may not be true," the mutual sympathy of Grandma and the American Dream is incongruously maudlin. Albee makes an effort to restore the comic tone by bringing back Mommy and Daddy with their mindless clichés, and the play ends with Grandma's sardonic aside: "everybody's got what he wants . . . or everybody's got what he thinks he wants." The word "satisfaction" has threaded through the play, and the American family finally snuggles into its illusion of satisfaction.

* * *

In Who's Afraid of Virginia Woolf? (1963) such illusion is less satisfactory, and it is expressed in a more varied and vitriolic idiom. As in Albee's earlier and shorter plays, however, murderous dialogue leads obliquely to murder. As the shadow of death lay over the sunny afternoon of The Zoo Story, death lies like a sediment in Martha's gin, Nick's bourbon, Honey's brandy, and mainly George's bergin. George claims that "the favorite sport is musical beds" in New Carthage, but the sport that commands our attention is elaborate word play in a diapason whose dominant note is that of death. And yet this death-dipped gamesmanship—the word "game" is repeated over thirty times—exposes an anatomy of love. Despite the presence of four characters, the play's three acts focus on the relationship of George and Martha, who express their love in a lyricism of witty malice.

Games do not formally begin in Act I, in spite of its title, "Fun and Games." However, the "fun" of stylized questions, exclamations, repetitions, and repartee involves us immediately in the verbal play of George and Martha. During the first few minutes of the drama, Martha calls George cluck, dumbbell, simp, pig, blank, cipher, and zero. George addresses Martha as "dear" and "love," but his offhand accusations relate her to animals—braying, chewing ice cubes like a cocker spaniel, and yowling like a sub-human monster. Through the swift first act, the dialogue rises toward a dissonant duet: Martha chants about George's failures while he tries to drown her voice in the party refrain, "Who's afraid of Virginia Woolf?" Toward the end of Act III, "Exorcism," George and Martha reach "a hint of communion." Despite their exchange of insults, George and Martha are *together* at the end of Acts I and III—the first mercilessly comic and the last mysteriously serious. During the three acts, neither of them can bear the extended absence of the other; each of them praises the other to Nick. Separated between Acts II and III, both George and Martha, independently, think of *A Streetcar Named Desire.* (Martha refers to *The Poker Night,* the original title of Williams' play, and George quotes the Spanish refrain of the Mexican flower-vendor.) However aggressive they sound—both utter the word "No" like a staccato tom-tom—George and Martha are attuned to one another, and they need one another.

George and Martha have cemented their marriage with the fiction of their son. Except for their inventive dialogue, they are outwardly conformist; privately, however, they nourish their love upon this lie. George's playlong preoccupation with death hints that such lies must be killed before they kill.

The distinctive love duet of George and Martha contains Albee's theme of death. Early in Act I, George tells Martha *"murderously"* how much he is looking forward to their guests. Once Nick and Honey are on scene, George shoots Martha with a toy gun, and then remarks that he might really kill her some day. In Act II, Nick and George exchange unprovoked confessions: Nick reveals intimacies about his wife and her father, but George's anecdotes center on death. He tells of a fifteen-year old boy who had accidentally shot his mother; when the boy was learning to drive, with his father as teacher, he swerved to avoid a porcupine, and he crashed into a tree, killing his father. Later in Act II, Martha summarizes George's novel about a boy who accidentally killed both his parents. Martha's father had forbidden George to publish the novel, and George had protested: "No, Sir, this isn't a novel at all . . . this is the truth . . . this really happened . . . TO ME!" George reacts to Martha's mimicry with a threat to kill her, and he grabs her by the throat. Athletic Nick, who resembles the American Dream both in physique and lack of feeling, tears George from Martha, and she accuses her husband softly: "Murderer. Mur . . . der . . . er." But George's stage murder will be performed verbally rather than physically.

While Nick and Martha disappear upstairs, drunk Honey voices her fear of having children, and George needles her: "How you do it? [sic] Hunh? How do you make your secret little murders stud-boy doesn't know about, hunh?" And George proceeds to plan the "secret little murder" of his child of fantasy. In Act III George and Martha declare "total war" on one another, and Martha vows "to play this one to the death." The death happens to a fantasy son, who, by George's account, swerved his car to avoid a porcupine, and crashed into a tree. George's imaginary child and his perhaps imaginary father died in precisely the same way.

Though George fires a toy gun at Martha, then tries to throttle her; though she leaps at him when he kills their child; though Honey shouts: "Violence. Violence." four times, the only stage murder is verbal. Such murder is oblique, and George leads up to it obliquely, with his "flagellation." The idiom that has nurtured their love will serve also to kill the illusion at its heart.

Martha may have downed George with boxing-gloves, but he outpoints her with words. He corrects her misuse of "abstruse" for "abstract," "something" for "somebody," "it" for "him." George insists upon "got" as a correct past participle. He builds balanced periodic sentences, for example his use of triplets in his description of Martha's drinking habits. Martha mocks him as Dylan Thomas, but the very name suggests an appreciation of George's language. Twice, Martha summarizes: "George and Martha: sad, sad, sad." but George and Martha speak the wittiest lines of American drama—economical, euphonic, and perfectly timed for our gaiety rather than sadness.

The sado-masochistic marriage of George and Martha is sustained through their verbal dexterity and their imaginary child, which save them from conventional academic mediocrity. Far from a *deus ex machina,* the child is mentioned before the arrival of Nick and Honey, when George warns Martha not to "start in on the bit about the kid." By that time, they have been sparring in their recurrent pattern, Martha cutting George with his lack of success and George striking at Martha's age, drinking, and promiscuity.

Guests heighten the pitch of the George-Martha exchange, as they move frankly into games. Though George has twice cautioned Martha not to mention their child, he himself is tantalizingly evasive when Nick asks whether they have children. While Martha is upstairs changing, she evidently tells Honey about their son, and that is the change that sets this evening off from similar evenings in the life of George and Martha. Once revealed, their son must die.

But George perceives this only at the end of Act II, and Martha struggles against it. Through two full acts, the couple spars verbally, with Nick as goad. Martha uses the child in Strindbergian fashion, suggesting that George might not be the father of the child. Unlike Strindberg's Captain, however, George is not vulnerable to this blow about their "bean-bag," but he is extremely vulnerable to Martha's taunts about his lack of success. As Martha mouths the phrase: "A great . . . big . . . fat . . . FLOP!" George breaks a bottle and clutches its splintered neck—a gesture that he may have learned from Blanche Dubois in *A Streetcar Named Desire.* But the jagged glass does not prevent Stanley's attack on Blanche, nor does it prevent Martha's attack on George.

Act II introduces some variations in the verbal fencing: George and Nick toward the beginning, Martha and Nick in the middle, and George and Honey at the end. But the bedrock remains George versus Martha. They have a momentary fling in French; they speak of their child in sexually insulting terms. George invents taunts: "Book dropper! Child mentioner!" These taunts summarize the two lies of George's own life—the murder of his father, which is the expression of the end of childhood, and the murder of his son, which may be the expression of the end of marriage. Martha's accusation against George—"Murderer. Mur . . . der . . . er." points both forward and backward in the play.

George charges Martha with "slashing away at everything in sight, scarring up half the world," and she claims that that is the reason he married her. Each insists that the other is sick—a leitmotif of this play as of The Death of Bessie Smith. In the prelude to their declaration of "total war," each marriage partner assaults the other's dominant fantasy:

> MARTHA: . . . before I'm through with you you'll wish you'd died in that automobile, you bastard.
>
> GEORGE: *(Emphasizing with his forefinger)* And you'll wish you'd never mentioned our son!

Each predicts the other's wish to renounce lies, implying an embrace of truth, but predictions are only obliquely fulfilled in Who's Afraid of Virginia Woolf?!

SNAP—sound, word, and gesture—becomes a stage metaphor in the destruction of lies, which may lead to truth. Martha snaps her fingers and informs George: "It's snapped, finally. Not me . . . it. The whole arrangement." She rhymes "snap" with"crap," and uses the word insistently, repetitively, to announce the beginning of their "total war." But George plays more intricate variations on the theme of snapping. His Act III entrance is delayed and mysterious—*"a hand thrusts into the opening a great bunch of snapdragons." "In a hideously cracked falsetto"* he chants: "Flores; flores para los muertos. Flores." In Williams' *Streetcar,* the Spanish words denote the end of the relationship of Blanche and Mitch. Comparably, George seems to announce the end of their relationship, as built upon an illusory son. After Martha lies that Nick is not a houseboy, George *"flourishes the flowers,"* shouting "SNAP WENT THE DRAGONS!!" Then George throws the snapdragons—his flowers for the dead—at Martha, one at a time, stem-first, spear-like, as he echoes her "snaps" at him. St. George slew the dragon; Albee's George slays with hothouse snapdragons and the word "snap."

Before throwing the snapdragons, however, George starts a story about an eccentric moon on a Mediterranean trip, which he claims was a graduation present from his parents. "Was this after you killed them?" asks Nick. *"George and Martha swing around and look at him."* Then George replies ambiguously: "Truth or illusion. Who knows the difference, eh, toots?" Martha charges: "You were never in the Mediterranean . . . truth or illusion . . . either way." Only after Martha tells George that he cannot distinguish between truth and illusion, does he pelt her with the snapdragons. Martha repeats the dichotomy: "Truth or illusion, George. Doesn't it matter to you . . . at all?" This time George doesn't throw anything as he answers her: "SNAP!" And with relish, he sets the scene for snapping their common illusion, in preparation for the possibility of truth.

In his triumphant enactment of the murder, George snaps his fingers for Nick to join the final game, Bringing Up Baby; the ambiguous gerund embraces introduction, education, and vomiting. George himself claims that they have been playing Snap the Dragon, before beginning Peel the Label. Thus, Snap the Dragon becomes Bringing up Baby becomes Peel the Label, as George snaps his fingers for Honey to support his outrageous boast that he ate the death telegram. Death rites are accompanied by snaps, involving all four characters.

The death scene and its aftermath contain the most perfectly cadenced dialogue of a remarkably rhythmed drama. Rhythm abets meaning in George's attack on Martha's illusion. So zealous is he in punishing Martha that it is difficult to believe in the purity of his corrective purpose. George and Martha fire a salvo of mutual sexual accusation. Before breaking the news of the son's death, George joins Martha in a discordant duet, as at the end of Act I. Martha begins a sentimentalized account of the life of their son, while George begins to recite the Requiem Mass. Then Martha shifts to innuendoes against George, and George uses their son as a weapon against her. In harmonious discord, Martha invokes the purity of their son in "the sewer" of their marriage, while George chants the Mass in Latin. As George lingers over his announcement of their son's death, Martha at first reacts with fury but soon wilts like the scattered snapdragons. Suddenly, Nick reveals his illumination about their child, asking: "You couldn't have . . . any?" And George replies: "*We* couldn't."—a sentence that Martha echoes with Albee's scenic direction: *"A hint of communion in this."* It is the broadest hint we have. At the departure of Nick and Honey, the dialogue narrows down to monosyllables; the playlong repetitions of "No" dissolve into a series of affirmatives (with two exceptions, in which George denies the rebirth of illusion). When George hums the title refrain, Martha admits that *she* is afraid of Virginia Woolf—a woman afflicted with a madness that drove her to suicide.[6]

Martha's fear is understandable. Whatever will George and Martha do now that their bean-bag is dead, their illusion exorcized? Since Albee once planned to give the Act III title, "The Exorcism," to the entire play, we know that he attaches importance to it. To exorcise is to drive out evil spirits, and in New Carthage the evil spirits are the illusion of progeny—Honey's imaginary pregnancy and Martha's imaginary son, which terminate in a "Pouf." These imaginary children live against a background of repetitions of the word "baby" in reference to adults.

The illusions of Martha and Honey are both child-connected, but they differ in cause and effect. Honey seems to have forced Nick into a marriage which "cured" her of a psychosomatic pregnancy. During marriage, her "delicacy" is the apparent reason they have no children. Without truth or illusion, they live in a vacuum of surface amenities. But when Martha indulges in an idealized biography of her son (before George kills him), Honey announces abruptly: "I want a child." She repeats this wish just before Martha shifts from the son as ideal biography to the son as weapon against George. Though Honey's conversion is sudden (and scarcely credible), it seems to be sustained.

For George and Martha, the exorcism is less certain, less complete, and far more involving. The marriage of Nick and Honey kills their illusion, but the illusion of George and Martha is born in wedlock, perhaps because they could have no real children and Martha "had wanted a child." Martha's recitation indicates that the conception of the child—intellectual and not biological—may have originated as a game, but the lying game expressed their truest need. The imagery associates their son with classical and Christian divinity—golden fleece and a lamb—but such imagery also links the fathers of the two women, who emerge as calculatingly diabolic. An ambiguous creation through most of the play, son Sunny-Jim is killed on the eve of his maturity—an inverse Oedipal act by which George hopes to rid his domain of sickness.

Uninteresting in themselves, Nick and Honey function as foils and parallels of George and Martha: the syllabic similarity of the names, the parallel fantasies of the women, the similar yet opposing professions of the men, and the cross-couples advancing the plot. Without Nick, Martha's adultery would not have driven George to murder their son; without Honey, George could not have accomplished the murder. Albee's repetitions of "True or False" and "Truth versus Illusion" emphasize truth, but it is problematical whether truth can be sustained in the world of the play, and Albee leaves it problematical, refusing Martha the easy conversion of Honey. Unless the Act III title, "The Exorcism" is ironic, however, George and Martha construct a new relationship on the base of Truth—"Just . . . us?"—though their gifts seem more destructive than constructive. Dawn breaks on Martha's fear, and our lasting impression of the play is not of exorcism but of the exercise of cruel wit.

In Who's Afraid of Virginia Woolf? Albee exhibits rare mastery of American colloquial idiom. Since colloquialism is usually associated with realism, the play has been viewed as realistic psychology. But credible motivation drives psychological dramas, and Albee's motivation is flimsy: Why does George stay up to entertain Martha's guests? Why, for that matter, does she invite them? Why do Honey and Nick submit to being "gotten?" Why do Nick and George exchange confessions? Drinking is only a surface alibi, but the play coheres magnetically only if we accept the *Walpurgisnacht* as a *donnée.* These four people are brought together to dramatize more than themselves.

Of his novel, George says: "Well, it's an allegory, really—probably—but it can be read as straight, cozy prose . . ." No one has called Albee's prose "cozy," but it too has been viewed as"straight" realism, sometimes of "crooked" sexuality.[7] Like George's novel, however, Albee's drama is "an allegory, really—probably." In an interview, Albee himself affirmed: "You must expect the audience's minds to work on both levels, symbolically and realistically."[8]

Albee sets Who's Afraid of Virginia Woolf? in a realistic living-room in a symbolic New Carthage. Carthage (meaning "New City") was founded in the ninth century B.C. by a semi-legendary, deceitful Dido, and it was razed to the ground in 146 A.D. By the fifth century, it had again become a power which St. Augustine called "a cauldron of unholy loves."[9] Albee uses the historical conjunction of sex and power as spice for the American stew he simmers in his cauldron. He himself suggested: "George and Martha may represent the Washingtons and the play may be all about the decline of the West."[10] Nick was named for Nikita Kruschev. In spite of a tongue-in-cheek tone, Albee's hints are borne out by the play.

Albee's unholy lovers are George and Martha, whose names evoke America's first and childless White House couple. As the legendary George Washington could not tell a lie, Albee's George murders in the name of Truth. George describes his fictional son as "Our own little all-American something-or-other." Albee thus suggests that illusion is an American weakness. American drama has been much concerned with illusion, but Albee's America is representative of contemporary Western civilization. George *"With a handsweep take[s] in not only the room, the house, but the whole countryside."* He speaks French, Spanish, and Latin in the play, and he echoes President Kennedy's "I will not give up Berlin." George characterizes the region as "Illyria . . . Penguin Island . . . Gomorrah . . ." Realm of fantasy, realm of social satire, realm of sin—George's condemnatory geography shows an academic foursome in the decline of a romantic mythology, love in the Western World.[11] A humanistic George opposes a mechanized Nick. George can see the handwriting on the wall, and it is the penmanship of Oswald Spengler, whose book George flings at the chimes that become a death knell. On one broad level, then, Who's Afraid of Virginia Woolf? is in the American tradition of dramatized illusion: O'Neill's *Iceman Cometh,* Williams' *Streetcar Named Desire,* and Miller's *Death of a Salesman.*

Albee also reaches out beyond America into an examination of the nature of love, which may be his metaphor for Western civilization. The games of the play—Humiliate the Host, Get the Guests, Hump the Hostess, and Bringing up Baby—suggest a miniature society, and though George mocks his own Napoleonic stance, he *is* preoccupied with history. But his anemic humanist yearnings tend to be submerged in his playlong vitriolic idiom.[12] His views of history are simplistic—the construct-a-civilization speech; his views of science are simpleminded—the mechanical Nick-maker. George wants to defend Western civilization against its sex-oriented, success-oriented assailants—"I will not give up Berlin."—but his defense of life and love is centered in his invective rather than his scrotum. An attacker rather than defender, George is more effective *against* illusory dragons than *for* bastions of civilization. And George's limitations limit the resonance of Albee's play. Despite his keen ear for American idiom, Albee can scarcely bring new social standards to the White House. Martha is finally reduced to her fear, and George to his post-murder "It will be better. . . . It will be . . . maybe." But when has"betterness" emerged from murder, even if the victim is imaginary?

* * *

Albee claimed that Tiny Alice (1965) Is a mystery play in two senses of the word: "That is, it's both a metaphysical mystery and, at the same time, a conventional 'Dial M for Murder'-type mystery."[13] But the play's one murder—the Lawyer's shooting of Julian—takes place before our eyes, without detective story mystery. Instead, the mystery of what is happening on stage dissolves into the larger mystery of what happens in the realm of ultimate reality. Governing both is a conception of mystery as that which is forever hidden from human understanding.

Albee's protagonist is Brother Julian, who claims to be "dedicated to the reality of things, rather than the appearance," but who has to be violently shocked—shot to death—

before he recognizes reality, and even then he tries to convert it into familiar appearance. Using the disjunctive technique of Absurdism and the terminology of Christianity, Albee drapes a veil of unknowing over his mystery. Thus, the play is nowhere in place and time, though the flavor is American and contemporary. The three stage settings are fantastic, and Miss Alice's millions are counted in no currency. Time moves with the fluidity of a dream, and yet it is, as the Lawyer claims: "The great revealer." Except for pointed references to Julian's "six blank years," Albee obscures the *passing* of time; the Lawyer says that Miss Alice's grant is a hundred million a year for twenty years, and after Julian is shot, the Lawyer offers the Cardinal "two billion, kid, twenty years of grace for no work at all." The play may thus last twenty years between the twelve "tick"s in the Lawyer's opening gibberish and Julian's dying question: "IS IT NIGHT . . . OR DAY? Or does it matter?"

Of the five characters, two have names, two are named by their function, and one—Butler—bears the name of his function.[14] Albee has denied that the name Alice stand for Truth and Julian for Apostasy, but he cannot expunge such associations for us. Named or unnamed, however, all characters are locked into a function: Brother Julian into service to his God, the Cardinal into service to his Church, and the castle trio into service to their deity, knowable only as the mouse in the model. Servants of Tiny Alice, they appear to master the rest of the world. Their dialogue suggests that, like the trio in Sartre's *No Exit,* they are bound in an eternal love-hate triangle. Their mission is to deliver victims to Tiny Alice, at once a reduced truth and a small obscene aperture into an aspect of being.[15]

Their victim is Julian, a lay brother, who is a kind of Everyman. As in a medieval Morality, we are involved in the conflict within Everyman's soul, but we are aware too of our world in which that conflict resonates. Rather than Virtue versus Vice, Albee's Julian becomes a battlefield for Truth versus Illusion.

Though Julian is at the center of the play, Albee delays introducing him. Instead, the drama begins with personifications of power à la Jean Genet: Cardinal and Lawyer, sacred and profane, church and state, buddies and enemies, with a long past behind them. We first see Julian at the castle, in conversation with the Butler, whose symbolic function is a stewardship based on his serving of wine, Christian metaphor for blood. Butler also offers Julian water, tea, coffee, before port and champagne—sweet and effervescent forms of wine—and, appropriately, Butler tries to sweeten the ineluctable claims of Tiny Alice upon Julian. Butler guides Julian through the wine-cellar of the castle, and he pours champagne at Julian's wedding, which is his last supper.

As in earlier plays, Albee builds his dialogue with thrust-and-parry exchanges and monologues, but he uses them somewhat differently; the verbal skirmishing often ends in a draw, and the monologues sound explicit but are buried in the central mystery, which is unknowable. As in earlier plays, Albee's thrust-and-parry dialogue leads obliquely to murder. The master verbal fencer of Tiny Alice, the Lawyer, shoots Julian, but Miss Alice is the principal agent of his undoing, and she, as the Lawyer remarks, was "never one with words." Rather, she acts through surprises: the old hag turns into a lovely woman; unprompted, she confesses to Julian her carnal relations with the Butler and the Lawyer; abruptly, she inquires into Julian's sex life; before marrying and abandoning Julian, she alternates a mysterious prayer with an address to "someone in the model." She cradles the wounded Julian, making *"something of a Pietà."* At the end she is cruel and kind; her last words are "Oh, my poor Julian"; yet she leaves him to die alone.

Miss Alice's seduction of Julian is accomplished through deeds rather than words, but Julian himself translates the erotic into a highly verbal mysticism. He defends his loquacity to Miss Alice: "Articulate men often carry set paragraphs." In each of the play's three acts, Julian indulges in a rhapsodic monologue that does not sound like a set paragraph, since its rhythms are jagged. Like the disjunctive monologues of The Zoo Story, the cumulative effect is apocalyptic, but Julian's apocalypse is sexually rooted, *lay* brother that he is (Albee's pun). In Act I, Julian describes a perhaps hallucinatory sexual experience with a woman who occasionally hallucinated as the Blessed Virgin. Not only does Julian speak *of* ejaculation; he speaks *in* ejaculations. Julian's mistress with an illusory pregnancy recalls the illusion-ridden women of Virginia Woolf; as the imaginary child of that play is an evil spirit to be exorcized, the imaginary pregnancy of the hallucinating woman of Tiny Alice proves to be a fatal cancer. And even as Julian confesses to Miss Alice what he believes to be his struggle for the real, she tempts him with her own desirability—very beautiful and very rich.

In Julian's Act II monologue about martyrdom, he shifts his identity—a child, both lion and gladiator, then saint and the hallucinating self of the Act I monologue—all couched in imagery that is sexually suggestive. While Julian describes his eroto-mystical, multi-personal martyrdom, Miss Alice shifts her attitude, first urging Julian to marry her, then spurring him to sacrifice himself to Alice, whom she invokes in the third person.

In Act III, Julian, who left the asylum because he was persuaded that hallucination was inevitable and even desirable, embarks on his final hallucination, which ends in his real death. Abandoned and dying, Julian recollects (or imagines) a wound of his childhood, as Miss Alice in her prayer recollected (or imagined) being hurt in *her* childhood. Alternately a child and the hallucinating woman who called for help, Julian is forced to face himself in death—the prototypical existential confrontation. With phrases of the Thirteenth Psalm, Julian very slowly and desperately dissolves Miss Alice into Tiny Alice into the Christian God. Unable to accept the words of the lucid Lawyer: "There is Alice, Julian. That can be understood. Only the mouse in the model. Just that."—Julian recoils from the hermetic, dust-free vacuum of Tiny Alice, from the unblinking eyes of the phrenological head: "Ah God! Is that the humor? THE ABSTRACT? . . . REAL? THE REST? . . . FALSE." Unable to laugh at such absurd humor, Julian reverts to Christian illusion, to traditional images that protect him from the reality of abstraction, which is death.

Julian calls on deity in the words of Christ on the cross: "ALICE? MY GOD, WHY HAST THOU FORSAKEN ME?" As a "great presence" engulfs him, Julian takes the crucifixion position, injecting his God into Alice: "God, Alice . . . I accept thy will." Albee's play opens on Genet's satiric Balcony, but it closes on the Blackness of Ionesco's dying king; both Julian and Bérenger go down fighting against predatory death, but they both go down. On a throne, or crucified, or whimpering in bed, Everyman is food for Tiny Alice who devours in mystery.

Julian's three experiences pivot on his confusion between illusion and reality: the sexual experience may have been a hallucination; the experience of martyrdom has haunted Julian's imagination, and he dies in an evocation of Christ, the martyr, which may be his last illusion. Rhythms of ecstatic agony and the image of blood link the three experiences, or the three descriptions of experience, which perhaps become experience *through* description.

Between his three monologues as within them, Julian's speech is fragmentary, interrogative, and recapitulatory. In contrast to the sinewy syntax of the Lawyer, Julian's sentence fragments are heavy with gerunds, adjectives, efforts at definition through synonyms. As Jerry's indirection mirrored the theme of The Zoo Story, Julian's phrasal fragmentation mirrors the theme of Tiny Alice, and that fragmentation functions partly as synecdoche.

"In my Father's house are many mansions," said Christ (*John* XIV, 2) and in the mansion of Tiny Alice are many rooms. True to his heredity and calling, Brother Julian praises library, chapel, and wine-cellar—all with religious associations. Alone in the library after his wedding, he recalls the childhood loneliness of an attic closet. But all rooms belong to Tiny Alice, and space does not contain them. When the fire in the model announces a fire in the chapel, Julian asks Miss Alice: "Why, why did it happen that way—in both dimensions?" After his wedding, Julian likens the disappearance of people to "an hour elaps[ing], or a . . . dimension." And shortly after shooting Julian, the Lawyer remarks to his old buddy-enemy, the Cardinal:"We have come quite a . . . dimension, have we not?" In Tiny Alice dimensions are diffused and confused; one does not move, as in the Great Chain of Being, from an animal dimension, to human, to angelic, to divine. Rather, all dimensions are interactive, and point to the whole metaphysical mystery in its more private parts.

Those parts are sexual, but Albee also suggests them through verbal insistence on birds and children—vulnerable both. Bird imagery embraces everyone: the play opens with a nonsense address to birds; the Cardinal has cardinals in his stone-and-iron garden; the Butler speaks of swallows "screeping"; the Lawyer's poem is said to have the grace of a walking crow; Miss Alice is first visible in a *wing* chair, and she later envelops Julian in the "great wings" of her robe; Julian is variously a "bird of pray," a "drab fledgling," and a "little bird pecking away in the library," summarizing his piety, innocence, and sexual vulnerability. At times, too, the characters act like children, or they summon recollections of childhood. Julian is often and explicitly called "little," and in his dying soliloquy, he becomes a little boy calling for his cookie. All these lines suggest the helplessness of birds and children in the world of Tiny Alice, who is at once mouselike, monstrous, and feline.

Like imagery and fragmentation, the tone of Albee's dialogue is complex. Familiar is the stinging salaciousness of the opening scene between the Cardinal and the Lawyer. This functions symbolically, since the Cardinal-Church is the son of a whore, and the Lawyer-State eats offal and carrion. The titillation of these disclosures is counterpointed against the formality of the syntax—first-person plurals, avoidance of contractions, emphasis on prepositional nuance, and self-conscious word-play (the eye of an odor). Only rarely does the Lawyer slip into a vigorous Americanism that underlines his malice: "Oh, come on, your Eminence." "You'll grovel, Buddy. As automatically and naturally as people slobber on that ring of yours." "Everyone diddled everyone else." "We picked up our skirts and lunged for it! IIIIII! Me! Me! Gimme!"

The Lawyer, who evokes Satan for the Cardinal, is the chief instrument of Albee's mutilating dialogue. Not only does he thrust at the Cardinal; he sneers endearments to the Butler, and he woos Miss Alice as "clinically" as he fondles her. At his first meeting with Julian, he belittles the Cardinal and humiliates Julian. After shooting Julian, the Lawyer directs the death-scene, without pity for the dying martyr. The Butler accuses the Lawyer: "You're a cruel person, straight through; it's not cover; you're hard and cold, saved by dedication; just that." And yet, both the Cardinal and the Butler speak of the Lawyer as "good," for he *is* good in his dedication to Tiny Alice.

The cross-relationships of the five characters of Tiny Alice are more complicated than in Virginia Woolf: the Cardinal and the Lawyer loathe each other, Miss Alice detests the Lawyer, and the Lawyer has never liked the Butler. The Cardinal may have had carnal relations with the Lawyer and with Julian; Miss Alice has had the Butler and the Lawyer as lovers; in Julian's presence, the Butler and the Lawyer address each other with words of endearment; the Lawyer and the Butler play at being the Cardinal and the Lawyer, the Butler plays at being Julian the victim, Miss Alice takes the very name of Tiny Alice. Julian is, successively, the Cardinal's secretary, the Butler's protegé, Miss Alice's husband, the Lawyer's victim. And Julian alone seems to be mortal.

As in Albee's earlier plays, violent death leads to a revelation of a deeper layer of reality. Miss Alice tells Julian pointedly: "Accept what's real. I am the illusion." Finally, Miss Alice will be Alice *missing,* as want [desire] of emphasis becomes a lack of emphasis. And yet, the Butler who makes this semantic point, has mocked Julian: "Six years in the loony bin for semantics?" The Lawyer and Butler debate Julian's fate almost as a semantic exercise: Will he be pushed "back to the asylums. Or over . . . to the Truth," which is Tiny Alice.

Julian's wedding day becomes his death day. Earlier, Julian used pious clichés for a business deal: "That God has seen fit to let me be His instrument in this undertaking." Dying, Julian flings the same word at the Lawyer, as an insult: "Instrument." The play reveals the Lawyer as the instrument of absurd reality, which is Tiny Alice. Julian, on the other hand, is first and last the instrument of his own imagination. He is both Everyman and the victim of the "awful humor" of Tiny Alice, precisely because he claims to reject illusion for reality. *That* is his illusion, with which he commits himself to an asylum. And rather than accept the reality of Tiny Alice, he is ready to commit himself again, but is prevented by the Lawyer's fatal shot. The cynical lucid Lawyer has already foretold the pattern of Julian's final behavior, mixing the formal and the colloquial in the same speech: "face the inevitable and call it what you have always wanted. How to come out on top, going under."

Because he bends his imagination to embrace the inevitable, Julian achieves the difficult martyrdom he seeks. On stage, the long dying scene borders on the ridiculous, as Julian's initial resistance to the inevitable *is* ridiculous. But, "going under," he summons the heroic illusion of his culture; not a "Gingerbread God with the raisin eyes," but a human god crucified for man. Julian dies in imitation of Christ, deaf to Tiny monstrous Alice who comes thumping and panting to devour him. The play ends on Alice, truth, reality, after Julian has been crucified in his illusion, but our lasting impression is that of a hero—vulnerable, loquacious, even ridiculous, but nevertheless heroic in the intensity of his imagination.

* * *

Even puzzled audiences have been involved in Julian's plight, which the Butler describes: "Is walking on the edge of an abyss, but is balancing." Albee's next play, A Delicate Balance (1966) is named for that perilous equilibrium. Like Virginia Woolf, the play presents a realistic surface; as in Virginia Woolf, a love relationship in one couple is explored through the impact of another couple. There is enough talking and drinking to convey the impression of a muted, diluted Virginia Woolf. Both plays end at dawn, but the earlier play contains "Exorcism." The later play dramatizes what Albee has called "arthritis of the mind."[16]

Each of the six characters of A Delicate Balance "is walking on the edge of an abyss, but is balancing"; a middle-aged marriage is balancing, too, until a makeshift home in a "well-appointed suburban house" is threatened by both family and friends. In Friday night Act I, terror-driven friends seek refuge in the family home; in Saturday night Act II, the master of the house, Tobias, assures his friends of their welcome, but his daughter Julia reacts hysterically to their presence. In Sunday morning Act III, the friends know that they are not welcome, know that they would not have welcomed, and they leave. The delicate balance of the home is preserved by an "arthritis of the mind."

The play begins and ends, however, on a different delicate balance—that of the mind of Agnes, mistress of the household, wife of Tobias, mother of Julia, sister of Claire. In convoluted Jamesian sentences, she opens and closes the play with doubts about her sanity; at the beginning, she also extends these doubts to an indefinite *you*—"that each of you wonders if each of *you* might not . . ." And as we meet the other members of the family, we can understand the wonder: Claire the chronic drunk, Julia the chronic divorcée, and Tobias who heads the house. Though Agnes starts and finishes the play on her doubts about sanity, each of the acts dramatizes the precarious stability of the other members of the family: first Claire, then Julia, and finally Tobias. In each case, the balance is preserved, a little more delicate for being threatened.

However perilously, the family is bound together by love. In Claire's words to Tobias: "You love Agnes and Agnes loves Julia and Julia loves me and I love you . . . Yes, to the depths of our self-pity and our greed. What else but love?" Agnes, who blames the others for their faults, describes such blame as the "souring side of love" in this drama about the limits of love.

Agnes early characterizes the family to Tobias: "your steady wife, your alcoholic sister-in-law and occasional visits . . . from our melancholy Julia." But her description is only a first approximation: her own steadiness is severely strained, Claire insists that she is not "a alcoholic," and Julia is more hysterical than melancholy. By Act III a harassed Tobias, having suffered his passion, offers a contrasting description of the same family: "And you'll all sit down and watch me carefully; smoke your pipes and stir the cauldron; watch." He thus groups wife, daughter, sister-in-law as three witches, or the three fates "who make all the decisions, really rule the game . . ." And who preside over the term of life until death cuts it short.

As in other Albee plays, death lurks in the dialogue of A Delicate Balance, but death is not actualized in this play. Violence is confined to a single slap, a glass of orange juice poured on the rug, and an ineffectual threat with a gun. In words, however, Claire urges Tobias to shoot them all, first Agnes, then Julia, and herself last. Agnes suggests that Claire kill herself, and Claire in turn asks Agnes: "Why don't you die?" It is this sisterly exchange between Claire and Agnes that inspires Tobias to his digressive monologue, his cat story. Because his cat inexplicably stopped liking him, Tobias first slapped her and then had her killed. Out of the depths of his greed and self-pity, he had her killed.

Like Jerry's dog story, Tobias' cat story is an analogue for the play of which it is part. As Tobias kills the cat, he will effectively kill his friends, Harry and Edna, when he denies them a home. As Claire and Agnes approve his conduct toward the cat, Claire and Julia will approve his conduct toward Harry and Edna. The death of the cat maintains Tobias' delicate emotional balance in spite of his bad conscience, and the departure of Harry and Edna will maintain Tobias' delicate family balance in spite of his bad conscience.

The threat of death is almost personified by Harry and Edna. Julia tries to aim her father's gun at the visitors, and Agnes calls their terror a disease and a plague. In demanding that Tobias make a decision with respect to Harry and Edna, Agnes reminds him of the intimate details of their sexual life after the death of their son, Teddy. She addresses Tobias as "Sir," with a servant's deference to a master. But this master gives no orders, and it is Harry and Edna, conscious of their own mortality, who decide to leave, taking their plague with them.

A Delicate Balance is itself in most delicate balance between the cruel-kindness of its surface and the mysterious depths below, between a dead child and a new dawn, between ways of loving and ways of living. Albee has posed his equilibrium discreetly, without the symbolic histrionics of Tiny Alice, without the corruscating dialogue of Virginia Woolf. At the most general level, the arrival of Harry and Edna raises the question of the limits of love; Tobias says to Harry: "I find my liking you has limits . . . BUT THOSE ARE MY LIMITS! NOT YOURS!" Harry and Edna push each family member to his limits. Before their arrival, Agnes thanks Tobias for a life without mountains or chasms, "a rolling, pleasant land." But the plague can attack rolling, pleasant lands, and it is carried by one's best friends.

In Harry and Edna, Albee creates Janus-symbols, for they are at once Tobias and Agnes, and their friend-enemies. Described in the Players' List as *"very much like Agnes and Tobias,"* Edna and Harry live in the same suburb and belong to the same club. They are godparents to Julia, as Tobias and Agnes are her parents. When Harry serves drinks, Agnes remarks that he is "being Tobias." When Edna scolds Julia, Albee's scenic direction indicates that she *"becomes Agnes."* Just before leaving, Edna speaks in the convoluted formal sentences of Agnes.

Otherwise, however, Harry and Edna do not sound like Tobias and Agnes, and they did not look like them in the original production supervised by Albee. Edna weeps whereas Agnes rarely cries; Edna shows desire whereas Agnes conceals it. As clear-sighted Claire (Albee's pun) points out to Tobias, all he shares with Harry is the memory of a summer infidelity with the same girl. Tobias denies being frightened, while fright ambushes Harry and Edna. Harry admits honestly what Tobias conceals clumsily: "I wouldn't take them in." When Harry and Edna finally depart, Agnes lapses into a rare cliché: "Don't be strangers." to which Edna replies: "Oh, good Lord, how could we be? Our lives are . . . the same." Rather than being *like* Tobias and Agnes, Harry and Edna are the *same* as Tobias and Agnes—minus a family.

Terror drives Harry and Edna from their house because a couple is inadequate bulwark against emptiness; they are free of the blood-ties which protect us from the loneliness of self and the encroachment of living death. Harry and Edna arrive after a family conversation about the bonds of love; their terror has no cause: "WE WERE FRIGHTENED . . . AND THERE WAS NOTHING." They were frightened *because* there was nothing.

In Who's Afraid of Virginia Woolf? George and Martha conceived an imaginary child to sustain their love; in the autumn of their lives Harry and Edna find themselves engulfed by nothing. As Tobias and Agnes would be, were the void not filled with the *repetitive* failings in the family: Agnes and Claire both call Tobias' anisette "sticky"; Agnes says of both Claire and Julia, separately, that either she will come down from her room, or not; Claire and Julia both contrive to apologize accusatively. The game of musical recriminations is what keeps the family love alive, and this is what Harry and Edna need—what they *want,* in the most insistent pun of the play.

In dramatizing the failure of love, which is death, Albee is ascetically sparing of vivid imagery and dazzling dialogue. Though he does not quite indulge in the fallacy of imitative form, he seems to imply that a drama with emptiness at its center, must echo in hollowness. Each time two characters start to thrust and parry verbally, the spark is damped. Each of the characters apologizes at least once, snuffing out verbal fireworks. Damped, too, are the few threads of imagery—the household, childhood, helping, and sinking. So fragile is the sensuous quality of the imagery, that it seems mere verbal repetition. All the characters refer to the house as they all recall a childhood before "Time happen[ed]." Help is usually mentioned in connection with invisible servants, though Agnes says tentatively to Harry and Edna: "If we were any help at all, we . . ."

Rhythm and rhyme emphasize the feelings of fragmentation and displacement. Claire's comic anecdote about the topless bathing-suit is emblematic of her fragmented life. Agnes comments obliquely on the thin surface of all their lives: "It's one of those days when everything's underneath." Claire claims that they all submerge their truths, then turns to Edna: "Do *you* think we can walk on water, Edna? Or do you think we sink?" Edna is *"dry"* as she replies: "We sink." All the drinking in all three acts reveals their ineffectual efforts to develop gills.

Sparing his imagery, Albee plays upon the verb *want* to sustain the delicate balance. Its double meaning, wish and lack, were already suggested in Tiny Alice, and Albee exploits this ambiguity more fully in A Delicate Balance. Claire wishes Agnes to die but doesn't know whether she wants it. Hysterical, Julia shifts from "they [Harry and Edna] want" to "I WANT . . . WHAT IS MINE!" Agnes asks Harry and Edna pointedly: "What do you *really* . . . *want?*" And some minutes later, Edna replies, playing on the same verb: "if all at once we. . .NEED . . . we come where we are wanted, where we know we are expected, not only where we want." Harry insistently questions Tobias: "Do you *want* us here?" And in Tobias' final aria, he shifts from: "I WANT YOU HERE!" to "I DON'T WANT YOU HERE! I DON'T LOVE YOU! BUT BY GOD . . . YOU STAY!"

Love is lack and love is wish in A Delicate Balance, and Albee suggests that the human condition is to be bounded by want—lack and wish. *"The living-room of a large and well-appointed suburban house. Now."* is where we live in contemporary middle-lass America. Not a social America, however, but a metaphysical Kafkaesque America, the leading nation in the decline of the West. The play's American resonances are muted: Republicans and Reno are brief guideposts; Alcoholics Anonymous and tax deductions are possible markers. American slang and imagery are used apologetically:

> CLAIRE: . . . the shirt off your back, as they say.
>
> JULIA: As they say, I haven't the faintest.
>
> AGNES: . . . the fatal mushroom . . . as those dirty boys put it.
>
> TOBIAS: You're copping out . . . as they say.

The "regulated great gray life" is greater, grayer, and more regulated in America, but it reaches out tentacularly over the whole world.

Each of the sisters uses her own distinctive rhythm to state the play's theme.

> AGNES: There *is* a balance to be maintained, after all, though the rest of you teeter, unconcerned, or uncaring, *assuming* you're on level ground . . . by divine right, I gather, though that is hardly so.
>
> CLAIRE: We can't have changes—throws the balance off.

The death of their son, Teddy, has thrown off the balance in the home of Tobias and Agnes, who teetered in a household that gradually took on the balance of a home again. Rather than upset the balance, Claire and Harry both lie to Agnes about the infidelity of Tobias. Rather than upset the balance, the family members play out their identity patterns, with only momentary shifts: Agnes poses as Julia's father, Tobias imitates Julia's hysteria, Claire plays a Tobias who explains to a judge the murder of his family, Julia spouts the opinions of her most recent husband, and Claire may be the nameless upended girl whom Tobias and Harry seduced one "dry and oh, so wet July." Identity itself is in delicate balance in this "regulated great gray life." Edna speaks of and for them all when she summarizes her recognition of the delicacy of all balance, which is life: "It's sad to come to the end of it, isn't it, nearly the end; so much more of it gone by . . . than left, and still not know . . . still not have learned . . . the boundaries, what we may not do . . . not ask, for fear of looking in a mirror."

In generalizing the predicament of his characters into the human condition, Albee relies on biblical associations of "house," as on associations of the names of the two couples, and of the three days between Good Friday and Easter Sunday, when Christ suffered his passion. Harry means torment, and clear-sighted Claire calls him "old Harry," which is a nickname for the devil; in contrast, Agnes is the lamb of God. The two couples, who are the same, range from angelic expressions of love to diabolic noncommitment. The other two names, Tobias and Edna, figure in the Book of Tobit; by angelic intervention Tobias was able to marry Sara, though her first seven bridegrooms died before possessing her; the mother of Sara was Edna. Albee's parallels with the Book of Tobit are obscure; nevertheless, the Book of Tobit is concerned, like A Delicate Balance, with ties of blood and with the burial of the dead. Albee's Tobias is occasionally called Toby or Tobe, and like his biblical eponym, he is faced with the problem of Being.

A number of biblical references to "house" illuminate this family in the "well—appointed suburban house:"

> For I know that thou wilt bring me to death, and to the house appointed for all living.
>
> (*Job* XX, 23)
>
> Thus saith the Lord, Set thine house in order; for thou shalt die and not live.
>
> (*Kings* X, 1; *Isaiah* XXXVIII, 1)
>
> If a house be divided against itself, that house cannot stand.
>
> (*Mark* II, 25)

But biblical prophets and patriarchs were men of great faith whereas Albee's Tobias wants that firm ground, and he quivers in the delicate balance of which his wife is fulcrum. For that is the house he has moulded, under the illusion that it has moulded him.

Like Virginia Woolf, A Delicate Balance ends at dawn, and dawn's meaning is again problematical. In spite of exorcism, Martha continues to fear Virginia Woolf; in spite of the fulcrum, the delicate balance might not last through a morning that Tobias implies is "very late at night." On the stage of A Delicate Balance, moreover, the pale language serves to pale dawn's light. Though Agnes apologizes for being articulate, she and Tobias tend to talk around subjects. Though Claire mocks Tobias: "Snappy phrases every time." she utters the play's few snappy phrases. Written in a minor key, A Delicate Balance lacks the lethal dialogue that has become Albee's trademark, but death nevertheless hangs heavy in the atmosphere.

* * *

In Adapting Giles Cooper's Everything in the Garden, Albee tries a combination of the injurious repartee of Virginia

Woolf and the stilted phrases of A Delicate Balance. Though Albee had earlier adapted two novels—Carson MacCullars' Ballad of the Sad Cafe (1963) and James Purdy's Malcolm (1965)—Everything in the Garden (1967) in his first adaptation of a play, and his dialogue changes are instructive. Most obvious is the transfer from English to American suburbia, with its corresponding idiom. The Madame's name is changed from Mrs. Pimosz—"like primrose, but have no *r's*"—to Mrs. Toothe, whose bite pierces to blood. Jack, the victim who is buried in the garden, is changed to a witty narrator who addresses the audience directly, before and after his death. Both plays—Cooper's and Albee's—too easily indict a comfort literally built on corpses—the "everything" that is buried in the garden, but the dialogue of Albee's indictment shows his habitual rhythms. The wife's reaction to the Madame's offer uses his characteristic pauses:

> COOPER: You must see I can't take money from you like this.
>
> ALBEE: Look, you . . . you can't just . . . *give* me money like this. I can't just. . .take money from you.

Or the husband's curtain line, when he learns the source of his wife's wealth:

> COOPER: Farrow and Leeming! Acton here. I want a case of champagne and two bottles of brandy. Can you deliver them this afternoon?
>
> ALBEE: . . . and . . . and . . . so, so, so, scotch, and . . . bourbon, and . . . (*Full crying now*) . . . and gin, and . . . gin, and . . . gin, and . . . (*the word* gin *takes a long time now, a long, broken word with gasps for breath and the attempt to control the tears*) . . . g-i-i-i-n, and . . . *(Final word, very long broken, a long bowl)* G———i———i———i— ——i———n——— n———n———n. *(Curtain falls slowly as the word continues.)*

Though adaptations permit Albee to exercise his muscular dialogue, their thematic facility is unworthy of him. Like his sketch, Fam and Yam, they are evidence of self-indulgence.

In "two inter-related plays," Box and Quotations from Chairman Mao Tse-Tung, Albee engages in quite different verbal exercises—different from anything he or any other playwright has attempted. For the first time, Albee's murderous thrust-and-parry dialogue vanishes completely, as each of his characters retreats into a solipsistic monologue.[17] Nothing happens on stage; or rather, only the dialogue happens, but the threat of death is implicit in that dialogue.

Box presents us with the titular box that takes up *"almost all of a small stage opening."* While we look at the box, in a constant bright light, we hear the disembodied voice of a woman, which *"should seem to be coming from nearby the spectator."* In the second of the two inter-related plays, Quotations from Chairman Mao Tse-Tung (about eight times the length of Box), an ocean liner appears within the outline of the box; aboard are four characters—Mao, who addresses us from the ship's railing, a stationary Old Woman who also addresses us directly, a Long-Winded Lady in a deck chair who addresses herself to a silent clergyman in his deck chair. The articulate trio is soon joined by brief phrases from the disembodied voice of Box. In the final *Reprise* we see the silhouettes of the four figures of Mao—now silent—as we hear a selection of about half the original Box monologue.

In Virginia Woolf, Albee counterpoints the Requiem Mass against a drunken conversation; in Tiny Alice, he integrates the Thirteenth Psalm into Julian's dying monologue. But in Quotations from Chairman Mao Tse-Tung, Albee makes unparallelled use of quotation—not only selections from Mao's Red Book, but over twenty stanzas of Will Carleton's "Over the Hill to the Poor-House." And since we have already heard the phrases of Box, three of the four voices recite familiar material, all of which functions as background for the only personal story of the play, associationally narrated by the Long-Winded Lady.

Though the voice of Box does not emanate from the box, it uses the cube as its point of departure, and since all we see is a box, verbal associations spring readily for this word—prison, coffin. Albee has already used boxes in The Sandbox and The American Dream, where they are associated with Grandma, the dying frontier spirit. There is a faint echo of this in Box, where a woman's voice reaches us from outside the box, close to us. We are not yet boxed in, but the threat is visually before us throughout the woman's monologue.

The voice belongs to no empiricist, for it moves almost immediately beyond what our senses perceive, to the *possibility* of a rocking chair in the box, to generalizations about crafts, and on to art. Through a lyric threnody of loss, the voice suggests that art is powerless to prevent catastrophe—"seven hundred million babies dead"—and that the very practice of art is a kind of corruption in a time of disaster. And yet, art gives us "the memory of what we have not known," introduces us to experience we cannot otherwise know, as sea sounds can frighten the land-locked. In a world where "nothing belongs," art strives for order.

Mao opens the second play with a fable from Chapter XXI of the Red Book, which glorifies the Chinese masses. Mao then moves on to Communist theory and tactics, growing more and more aggressive in vocabulary, though *"his tone is always reasonable"* and his purpose always pedagogic. Many of the quotations are drawn from Chapter VI of the Red Book, "Imperialism and All Reactionaries are Paper Tigers." In that chapter and in Albee's quotations, the arch-imperialist is the U. S., so that Mao's final words damn America: "People of the world, unite and defeat the U. S. aggressors and all their running dogs." Mao's patiently positive attitude culminates in an injunction to widespread murder.

The Old Woman, who *"might nod in agreement with Mao now and again,"* is not so repetitive in her chant, and Albee stipulates that *"she is reciting a poem,"* even though its subject matter is very close to her. In other words, her poverty is evident in her shabby clothes and the simple food she eats in our presence, but she is not necessarily identical with the persona of Will Carleton's poem. That persona uses limping, heavily accented, rhymed hexameters to complain about the events that sent her "over the hill to the poorhouse." Widowed, she loses five of her six children as, one by one, they go out to live their own lives. After the sixth child marries, she is successively rejected from the homes of each of her children, and finally she is sent to the poorhouse, inspiring her final maudlin prayer: "And God'll judge between us; but I will al'ays pray / That you shall never suffer the half I do today."

Mao has given us a formulaic system, the Old Woman a formulaic lament, but the Long-Winded Lady is entirely original and personal. She starts with an incomprehensible splash, imagining the reaction of "theoretical . . . onwatchers." Associationally, she has a childhood memory of breaking her thumb, then a more recent recollection of a taxi going wild. As she entered with a plate of crullers on the bloody scene (recalling Marie Antoinette and her *brioches* in the face of famine), the Long-Winded Lady comments on the utter inadequacy of any response to disaster. More and more, the theme of death links her disparate associations; uncle, sister, and husband speak of death, and her husband was aware of the perpetual process of dying before he was attacked by the agonizing cancer that killed him. Though his dying is now over, "his *death* stays." And it is with that death that the Long-Winded Lady lives, having no communion with her daughter, and no relationship with anyone else. Finally, toward the end of the play, the Long-Winded Lady describes the opening splash in detail. It is *her* splash, but she describes it without a single "I." She fell off an ocean liner (like the one on which we see her) *splash* into the ocean. Ironically and improbably, however, she did not sink but was rescued. After congratulations came questions: Could anyone have pushed her? Did she throw herself off? Try to kill herself? The Long-Winded Lady closes her monologue and the Mao part of Albee's play with a half-laughing denial: "Good heavens, no; *I* have nothing to die for." It is a brilliant twist of the cliché: "I have nothing to live for." We live—most of us—by natural momentum, but voluntary death demands a dedication beyond the power of the Long-Winded Lady—or most of us.

As the disembodied woman's voice opens the "inter-related plays," so it closes them in a "reprise." But between Box and *Reprise* Albee expunges catastrophe from the Voice's monologue, having suggested disaster in each of the three separate monologues of Mao. *Reprise* retains the Box images of music, birds, order, and an art that hurts. Though the Voice is matter-of-fact, even *"schoolmarmish,"* it is lyrical in the hint that emotion alone invests events with meaning, and yet the emotion of art is unable to act meaningfully upon any event. Pain can merely be contained by order—"Box."

From Chekhov on, we have been familiar with characters who talk past each other rather than engaging one another in dialogue. But in Mao each of the characters is completely unaffected by the other's speech, gives no evidence of hearing the others. And there is no plot connection between the speeches, as there is in Beckett's *Play*. But theme, tone, and contiguity give rise to associations of meaning for us, as the characters speak singly.

Death is the theme that unites the three visible and audible characters—the holy crusade of Mao, the old widow, and the very personal description of dying in the monologue of the long-winded widow. But though death sounds in these monologues, the notes are subtle and discontinuous. Thus, the Old Woman is absent from the following threnodic strain:

> MAO: A revolution is an insurrection, an act of violence by which one class overthrows another.
>
> VOICE, FROM BOX: When art begins to hurt, it's time to look around. Yes it is.
>
> LONG-WINDED LADY: And *I*, he said, *I*—thumping his chest with the flat of his hand, slow, four, five times—*I* . . . am *dying*.

Each of the four voices is distinctive and unique, and yet they may be paired by tone or style. Mao and the Old Woman recite ready-made phrases; the Long-Winded Lady and the Voice speak searchingly, punctuating their discourse with pauses and images. Yet, the Voice is schoolmarmish as Mao is pedagogical; each of them comments on the nature of reality, but their realities are different. By contrast, the persona of the Old Woman and the Long-Winded Lady gradually reveal life stories; both are widows, and both are touched by death. In addition to these pairs, the three women's voices may be grouped by pathos; they sing in a minor key. Masculine Mao, on the other hand, is positive and optimistic, and the masculine clergyman is silent.

Thematically, death binds these four voices, and stylistically repetition is their common technique. Mao emphasizes single words or ideas by reiteration; the Old Woman does not recite Carleton's poem straight through, but chooses certain lines or stanzas to linger over and dwell upon; occasional phrases of the Long-Winded Lady recur—above all "dying"; after the initial performance of Box, all the words of the disembodied voice are repetitions, and the final *Reprise* means repetition. The *Reprise* joins end to beginning in a kind of musical parallel for a box, but since music moves in time, repetition itself becomes thematic through strains of dialogue.

Because the Long-Winded Lady alone has a personal, a *dramatic* monologue, she is at the center of the play. Seeking the counsel of a silent clergyman, she is threatened by the two other figures on this ship of fools—the ruthless system of Mao and the maudlin poverty of the Old Woman. Long-winded, unrooted, she is a middle-aged, middle-class Miss America, that last corrupt and dying outpost of Western civilization. Unlike George and Julian, who also represent the Western tradition in Albee's plays, the Long-Winded

Lady utters no words of optimism or heroism. She can merely offer the stuff of her life to a silent and therefore ineffectual representative of God. Like Joyce's distant artist paring his fingernails, a disembodied voice embraces all experience in the order of art. But the question nags as to whether Albee's particular art is drama.

Edward Albee is the most skillful composer of dialogue that America has produced. His very first play showed thorough mastery of colloquial idiom—syntax, vocabulary, and above all rhythm. With adroit combinations of monologue and witty repartee, Albee dramatizes human situations. He never permits his characters to lapse into discussion, and he rarely inflates them with abstraction. Almost always, he mirrors the meaning of events in the rhythm of his dialogue: Jerry's indirection, George's surgery, Julian's fragmentation, the Long-Winded Lady's long wind. Difficult as marriage is *within* his plays, they contain unusually harmonious marriages of sound to sense.

But suspicion is born of Albee's very brilliance. His plays are too well crafted, his characters too modishly ambiguous, his dialogue too carefully cadenced. This is not to say that he writes perfect plays—whatever that may be—but his surface polish seems to deny subsurface search, much less risk. Again and again, O'Neill stumbled and fell in the darkness of his dramas; even the final achievements lack grace, but their solidity endures. Miller has probed into his own limited experience and into his own limited view of the experience of his time, but his plays sometimes give evidence of reaching to his limits. Williams expresses his guiltiest urges, and though the very naiveté of his guilt restricts the resonance of his plays, he does agonize toward religious resolution. Albee's plays are not devoid of suffering, and in any case one cannot measure the quality of a play by some putative pain of the playwright. Nevertheless, Albee's craftsmanship recalls the meditation of the disembodied voice of Box: "arts which have gone down to craft." And it is particularly ungrateful to turn his own finely modulated words against Albee. But just because his verbal craft *is* so fine, one longs for the clumsy upward groping toward art.

Notes

[1]Albee consistently uses . . . to indicate actors' pauses; in this chapter, therefore, such punctuation is his.

[2]Gilbert Debusscher, *Edward Albee: Tradition and Renewal* (Brussels, 1967), 19-20.

[3]Cf. Rose A. Zimbardo, "Symbolism and Naturalism in Edward Albee's *The Zoo Story*," *Twentieth Century Literature* (April, 1962), 10-17.

[4]Paul Witherington, "Language of Movement in Albee's *The Death of Bessie Smith*," *Twentieth Century Literature* (July, 1967), 84-88.

[5]Preface to Signet edition of *The American Dream*, 9.

[6]*Writers at Work, Third Series* (New York, 1967), 331, gives Albee's account of the origin of his title—soap-writing on the mirror of a Greenwich Village bar—but he nevertheless exploits the resonances of the English novelist's name.

[7]Ibid. for Albee's denial that the play was conceived with four men in mind. Though George calls Nick "toots," "love," and "baby"; though Martha says George is a "floozie," this is irrelevant to the sado-masochistic interdependence of George and Martha.

[8]Ibid., 337.

[9]A comparable *Walpurgisnacht* atmosphere is evoked in Book III of St. Augustine's *Confessions*, which describes his domicile in Carthage from his seventeenth to his nineteenth year. Not only lust, but play-acting and illusion are central to Augustine's experiences in Carthage.

[10]Michael E. Rutenberg, *Edward Albee: Playwright in Protest* (New York, 1969), 232.

[11]Thomas Porter, "Fun and Games in Suburbia," in *Myth in Modern American Drama* (Detroit, 1969), 225-47, presents an excellent critique of the play in this light.

[12]Cf. Lee Baxandall, "The Theatre of Edward Albee," *Tulane Drama Review* (Summer, 1965), 19-40.

[13]*New York Times* (December 27, 1964). Section 2, p. 1.

[14]In the movie *All About Eve*, Marilyn Monroe remarks that it would be funny if the butler were named Butler.

[15]Tiny Alice evidently means "tight anus" in homosexual argot, though Albee has denied having this "arcane information." In any case, *Tiny Alice* does not depend upon knowing the argot, as *Virginia Woolf* does not depend upon knowing St. Augustine's *Confessions*.

[16]Rutenberg, 250.

[17]Rutenberg, 214: "Instead of writing out the speeches one after the other, Albee has said he 'wrote each speech for each character' on a different page."

Rachel Blau Duplessis (essay date 1972)

SOURCE: "In the Bosom of the Family: Evasions in Edward Albee," in *Recherches Anglaises et Américaines*, No. V, Summer,, 1972, pp. 85-96.

[*In the following essay, Duplessis argues that in his plays Albee takes "questions of power, work, failure or success and privatiz[es] them, making social issues appear exclusively as family issues, and solv[es] them as if they were family issues."*]

This is an essay about Edward Albee's family plays, taking Who's Afraid of Virginia Woolf? (1962) as the center of interest, but also treating A Delicate Balance (1966) and, to a lesser extent, The American Dream (1960).[1] Secondarily, it is an essay about the relation of a literary work to its historical context, taking these plays as a test case of a hypothesis about that relationship.

We are used to considering a literary work as a unity. In appreciating or analyzing art, we tend to harmonize it, smoothing arguments that do not fit; taking images, themes or structures as indications of one tendency, rather than of diverse or divisive tendencies; perceiving one ruling idea or world picture. In short, we take hold of a literary work as if it expressed no conflicts or contradictions within it.

However, there are many works which do not fit this critical assumption. There are works in which the endings do not respond to the images, themes and situations which these endings are intended to conclude.[2] There are works in which the author's professed subject violates the traditional conventions, values or artistic decorum to which he/she also adheres.[3] There are works in which the real or embodied ideas and the announced ideology of the author are visibly inconsistent.[4] These examples all suggest that literary works are the site of contradictions or conflicts: discontinuity between the body of a work and its ending, conflict between the subject and accepted aesthetic norms, conflict between the expressed and the covert views of an author. Thus I will postulate that conflict often lies at the heart of the artistic situation and go on to construct a working hypothesis that accounts for it. To formulate the hypothesis, we must ask what are conflicts; how do we identify important ones; how are they resolved; and what do conflicts tell us?

Conflicts within a literary work include 1) fundamental and opposing categories of assumptions built into the world of the work and/or 2) clashes between various formal elements of the work. It is my contention that these fundamental conflicts in literature correspond to a social and historical context in some fashion—directly, or through modifications, distorsions, transformations and omissions.

How does the critic identify *important* conflicts? This is a question about which I can make only an empirical observation. The artist tries to move the conflicts expressed in the work towards some kind of resolution, which may be presented as the ending (but is not necessarily the ending). It follows that at the point at which resolution occurs or is being prepared for, we are most likely to observe the work's *fundamental* contradictions, because it is precisely those which are most in need of resolution, and which it is most satisfying to see resolved.

How, then, are conflicts resolved? I have found two patterns so far. Conflicts can be resolved in a *synthesis* (involving form, incident, character, imagery, etc.), which includes, yet transcends the fundamental and opposing issues. Or, on the other hand, conflicts can be resolved in an *evasion,* a pseudo-synthesis which deliberately and unmistakably avoids the primal quality of the clashes exposed within the work.

Both evasion and synthesis are legitimate ways of handling contradictions. A work is not "bad" if conflicts are evaded, "good" or "successful" if conflicts are synthesized. The question is rather why certain resolutions take shape as they do. To trace this, we must ask why particular conflicts appear in a work by a certain person, at a given historical moment, with a specific set of coordinates (genre, audience, critical reception). A resolution through evasion may be perfectly satisfying to the audience; it may even be what pleases the audience, for perhaps the audience itself would rather avoidthe clash of fundamental issues than see them resolved. Further, evasion may be the only possible resolution, if the social or historical evolution of certain conflicts had not reached the point at which an author could compose a synthesis.

A literary work may reveal contradictions in attitudes and actions in individuals, or within identifiable social groups or reveal clashes between several groups.[5] A literary work may also clarify what historical problems existed, or what were considered problems by contemporaries. It may present contradictions in heightened or flattened form. By a study of conflict, the form, content and social-historical implications of a work are linked in one explanation.

How can we apply this hypothesis to Albee's work? To define the fundamental contradictions in Albee's family plays, we must watch these works at the point of resolution. From such an investigation, we can detach the various contradictions which the ending is designed to resolve.

Two prominent problems resolved by the ending of Virginia Woolf concern the bitch goddess, who is tamed, and the missing child, who is killed. Martha is a brilliantly constructed and dramatically sufficient portrait of the stereotypical emasculating woman. The missing male child is doubly non-existent, for he is imaginary and at the end of the play he is also dead. It is no secret that parent-child and husband-wife relationships (along with the cross-bred combination father/husband and child/wife) figure importantly in Albee's world, although, interestingly, Albee is squeamish about recognizing this.[6] In fact, many relationships in his plays that do not superficially conform to family models can be assimilated to them. Julian is the child to numerous parents—including a destructive sexual mother—in Tiny Alice (1964). These parents are at the mercy of a Larger Parent, the unseen Big Alice. Julian's martyrdom, whatever else it involves, contains the familiar mutilated, destroyed or dead son at its heart. The pattern of weak father, threatening son, and destruction (here by murder/suicide) likewise occurs in The Zoo Story (1958).

Are these family antagonisms the fundamental conflict in Albee? Not, I would say, in themselves, although wife and husband, parent and child clash in dramatic and important ways. To discover the conflict, we must look at the point of resolution to discover what forces the play has unloosed and how the author finally handles them.

Virginia Woolf ends with a now familiar tableau, revealing Martha's essential insecurity and dependence on George, and George's control and dominance of their relationship and her needs. The problems of this prototypical "American" couple to which the tableau is Albee's solution are the failure of the man and the bitchiness of the woman. The problems are constructed in stereotypes (henpecked man, nagging wife) and the solutions are also envisaged in stereotypes. According to the familiar norms Albee proposes for his solution, the man's social function is to engage in productive work, to be a success, and to be emotionally alert and/or sexually potent. The woman's social function is to engage in reproduction and/or non-productive work (both Honey and Martha have distorted these terms, by engaging in non-productive reproduction—not having kids), to help her husband be a success, and to remain a tempting sexual object. The play will accomplish the substitution of these norms for the earlier stereotypes.

The man's world is the world outside the family. The university workplace is rife with rivalries and competition, and the men must succeed in this world, or not at all. In the play there is a running gag about whether Nick is going to take over the Biology or the History Department which effectively expresses the rivalry between the two men and their anxieties about success and failure. Nick also has an opportunistic plan for taking over the whole university, while George is already an established failure ("I am *in* the History Department . . . as opposed to *being* the History Department . . . in the sense of *running* the History Department," p. 38). George engages in intellectual badinage with Nick, deliberately attacking Nick's research. Albee does this more clumsily than it would be done in real life, but he gives a reasonably true picture nonetheless. Starting from Nick's assumed method ("A system whereby chromosomes can be altered," p. 65), George traces the implications of Nick's work. Eventually there will be no more cultural and national differences, and "the sea-hanging rhythm of . . . history will be eliminated" (p. 67). Nick's professional work is an attack on George's professional work, and so George will try to cut him down. George is witty. Nick does not answer. Yet there is never any doubt that George is a failure. But given his wit and intelligence, why is he a failure? Why must we assume that wit and intelligence are associated with failure? What stopped George from "playing the game" of success—for he loves to play other games with Martha? Or, even more crudely, why couldn't George take advantage of his privileged position as the President's son-in-law and step into the President's shoes? No answer is worked out within the play. We are faced with a full-blown and definitive problem, George's failure, for which there is no explanation, and whose source—perhaps in the relation of George's personality to the demands of the workplace—lies entirely outside of the actions of the play.

Albee accounts for George's failure by noting, once, his "high moral sense" which "wouldn't even let him *try* to better himself" (p. 124). For the weight the play puts on George's failure, this is a minimal explanation, which itself hides an unexamined social law: only low and unprincipled people win. More importantly, this "high moral sense" is not entirely ratified by the exhibition of George's malice, bitterness and nastiness in the course of the play.

A second reason Albee offers is more promising. Daddy (the Paterfamilias in Baxandall's terms) prevented George from publishing a novel about a boy who accidentally kills both his parents (a work whose summary is given on pp. 94-97).[7] We must accept that George's major scholarship *as a historian* lies in autobiography: "This isn't a novel at all . . . this is the truth . . . this really happened . . . TO ME!" (Martha's words, dramatizing George's predicament, p. 137). It is striking that the man's major *work* in career terms is about family relations. Nick's major work in biology is also "about" sex and children. This pattern is quite significant; it is repeated in the interchanges between Nick and George. All exchanges (whether sheer monologue by George or dialogue) are arrested by the deliberate change of subject *from* science, technology, the university, genetic regulation, the "wave of the future", *to* sex, women, children and Daddy. This substitution of family questions for other issues raised in the play is an important pattern and will be pursued further here.

Albee's "Mommies" and other of his women surprisingly conform to the stereotyped notions of women's place: that women take care of home and children (imaginary or not) while men take care of the rest of the world. Martha does not try to enter the universe traditionally set apart for men. Rather, she is hostess for her Daddy, courtesan-in-residence for the university, and tries hard to be a mother, telling anecdotes of the imaginary son's imaginary upbringing. Further, despite her situation as a faculty wife, Martha never participates in the "intellectual" discussions that take place between George and Nick. Her realm is caustic remarks, cutting stories and gossip. Similarly, Mommy in The American Dream is an inveterate consumer, endlessly exchanging beige hat for wheat and wheat hat for beige. She holds a malicious, but not inaccurate view of the legal and economic bases of marriage: she is entitled to money from Daddy because Daddy is allowed to fornicate with her. In the same play, Albee's semi-professional woman, Mrs. Barker, plays her role dressed only in her slip; she had been asked to take her clothes off early in the play and willingly conforms to the invitation to be a sex object. Her meager "professional" status as an adoption agency officer is totally undercut, for she does not remember a thing about her clients or her work. Grandma is not exempt either. As a cook, she has prepared uneaten box lunches for her school-age daughter. She is also enough of a trickster to enter a baking contest—and win first prize—under a man's name and with a store-bought cake, but the essential pattern is intact. Mother, courtesan, consumer, sex object, wife, cook, volunteer semi-professional, hostess—these are the dependent social roles Albee's women play. Why then are they accused of emasculating the men?[8]

Because none of his women ever tries to enter the "male" worlds of business, action, productive work and potency, one cannot say they are emasculating because they intrude. However, they do investigate whether the men succeed in their proper sphere. They notice and comment on the men's failure to hold up their half of the bargain, insistently remarking that the Daddies are flops. Thus the women are verbally abusive to the men precisely because the men do not succeed in the same stereotypical terms as the women. So the women fail to conform to the sex role stereotypes only in their refusal to be silent about the failures of their men. But they do not cause these failures.

Failure for Albee's male characters has its source outside the plays. It depends on the men not meeting certain standards of competition and success in the workplace. These assumptions are neither brought into the plays nor made explicit within them. The women's bitchiness and domination have their sources in the men's failure; rather than causing failure, the women simply comment incessantly upon it. What resolution is offered by Albee for these failures?

At the end, the humiliated, weak, unsuccessful man is shown to be stronger than the brutal, emasculating woman. The family problems are solved, not by investigating their real source, which we have seen to lie outside the family, but by further regulating the family relations in a highly normative manner. The man is returned to his position of mastery, dominance and control over a subordinate, dependent woman by exorcising all challengers, upstarts and rivals to the central couple. In this case, George exorcises Martha's Daddy, the missing son, and Nick, who functions as a rival in the workplace and as a substitute son in the Mother's affections.

Up to the time of the play, George had not been able to break the hold that Martha's Daddy has over his daughter. Within the play, he breaks the hold by his superior game-playing abilities; but he wins by making total war on *Martha,* not on Daddy. His success involves a simultaneous parent-child and husband-wife subordination. Martha becomes like a little girl at the end; George emerges as a successful replacement for the Paterfamilias—without touching on any of the issues that made him a failure in the first place.

In addition, to construct this resolution, the male child is killed because he is too tempting to his mother—imaginatively tempting in Virginia Woolf and sexually tempting in American Dream. A powerful mother-son team disrupts the proper order of the family. Thus to return the father to the center, inevitably the child must be broken, as is his mother, but by different means, usually death. In American Dream, the fact that Daddy does not return to power makes the mother-son relationship begin again, cyclically, with a new son. The child may also be regarded as the battlefiled on which the primal couple wages constant war; in any case, by slow death or swift, he is broken. Behind this destruction of the male child lies an assumption about the "proper" order of the family. Albee's implicit definition makes the family a stable couple with an unchallenged head (the dominant male) helped and approved of by the subordinate female. The reasons that lead to the murder or mutilation of the male rival are thus not investigated. Rather, Albee assumes them.

In one of his aspects, Nick is a "son" to George and Martha. He is obliquely referred to as "our own little sonny-Jim" (p. 196). Further, Albee clears the ground for an Oedipal plot by making Honey, nominally a character in the play, spend most of her time off stage on the bathroom floor. The rivalry between George and Nick for Martha can take shape uninterrupted by the superfluous second woman. Nick has indeed threatened to replace George in Martha's bed and in the university, while his work and his attitudes attack George's values. This rivalry, which originates outside the confines of the play, has been transferred entirely from society to family.

In the conclusion, George replaces the Paterfamilias above him, subordinating the wife-child, while successfully fighting a rear-guard action against his own replacement by the son(s) below. This reversal is constructed by Albee's taking questions of power, work, failure or success and privatizing them, making social issues appear exclusively as family issues, and solving them as if they were family issues. Albee shows power entirely in family terms, and often in exclusively sexual terms. In the play's logic, because the President of George's college is Martha's father, relations in the workplace are made over into family relations. Because a younger rival to George is involved as the son in an Oedipal plot, society and the workplace are made over into the family. Albee has evaded discussion of the real source of the men's failure; instead he puts the onus on relationships inside the family and returns to the cliché portrait of the haridan, implying that the men fail *because* their women are emasculating. In fact, investigation of the plays shows that the true position is precisely opposite: the women are emasculating because their men fail.

What then is the fundamental conflict or contradiction in Albee's family plays? A provisional answer can be given now, although we are only part way there. The fundamental conflict is between a) the idea that problems and clashes found in the family actually originate in the family and can be solved in the family and b) the idea that problems and clashes expressed by the family originate *outside* the family and can be solved only by turning to these origins. Albee wants to put forward the first idea; his resolution and the audience's admiration alike are based on it. Yet strong indications of the second idea can be found in his work.

The static family with a man as the unchallenged head is reconstructed by the subordination and destruction of the other family members. But this occurs only on the sufference and with the cooperation of representatives of "problems," which have come into the family from outside and which obligingly leave at the key moment, not really exorcised, not really solved, but simply eased out the front door. In Virginia Woolf, Honey, already an approved-of child-woman, is cured in the same action with Martha and assumes her proper sexual role ("I want a child. I want a baby," p. 223). But Nick represents the problems coming from outside the family, although Albee transposes them by making Nick the "son" of the family. The play's action has not cured these problems. These problems are work, careerism, science, the fall of the west; even—and Albee *is* reasonably serious—the problem of powers politics personified by Nikita Khrushchev ("*Nick* is very much like the gentleman who used to run the Soviet Union": Albee[9]). The problems are a mixed bag of undigested bits, but their very confusion is significant. Something is wrong somewhere—is it the two cultures? or the failure of the "principles of . . . of principle" (p. 117)? of the geo-political threat of the Asian yellow peril (p. 166)? Albee is not clear where the problems lie, what to call them, or how to organize them, but Nick does *represent* them. And there is no dialogue between George and the problems Nick represents. Much of the scenes between them consists of sporty monologues by George. Albee gives Nick no rebuttals.

As a problem from the outside, Nick resembles the friends, Edna and Harry, in A Delicate Balance (1966), who have a vague terror and creep into the play's major family. What is to be done with them? The beginning of the resolution in Delicate Balance, as in Virginia Woolf, requires masculine dominance. At the beginning of the third act, Agnes (the wife) anatomizes the contractual terms on which a man and a woman construct a marriage, by the strictest sexual division of labor.

> She runs the house, for what that's worth; makes sure there's food, and not just anything, and decent linen; looks well; assumes whatever duties are demanded . . . The reins we hold! It's a team of twenty horses, and we sit there, and we watch the road and check the leather . . . if our . . . man is so disposed. But there are things we [women] do not do . . . We don't decide the route . . . We follow. We let our . . . men decide the moral issues . . . Whatever you decide . . . I'll make it work; I'll run it for you . . .
>
> (pp. 136-38)

Agnes' speech is designed to force her husband Tobias to dominate, decide, master his entourage of three child-wives: his real wife, his often-divorced daughter, and his sister-in-law. He must decide something about the invasion by these neighbors who, simply and inexplicably terrified of life, have retreated to the family, putting themselves in a child relationship to parents (who are their contemporaries) and into a sibling relationship with the other dependents of Agnes and Tobias. Albee tries to make their terror take the shape of familiar family patterns.

At the climax of the play, Tobias performs a difficult aria that perfectly expresses the contradictory position of the family in Albee: either as the source of, and cure for problems; or, because not the source of problems, not ultimately their cure. First he states that the family did not ask for this invasion, acknowledging that it was not born inside the family. "I DON'T WANT YOU HERE!" (p. 166). The vague, troubling disease Edna and Harry bring, the "plague," is virtually undefined by the play. But whatever it is, once within the family, the terror is obliged to stay, because in Albee's world it is only in the bosom of the family that the problems can be transformed and solved. "BY CHRIST, YOU'RE GOING TO STAY HERE. YOU'VE GOT THE RIGHT" (pp. 166-67). Why the right? Again, because the family is the place where social problems are transformed to family relationships and resolved by Albee's one characteristic solution: a strong man placed unchallenged as the head, aided by a subordinate—his wife. All social problems are privatized into family problems so they can be solved.

But despite Tobias' pleading to preserve this function of the family, "Stay? Please? Stay?" (p. 167), the problems decide to go home anyway. If on one hand the "delicate balance" of the family has been restored by Tobias' taking—or trying to take—a manly position, on the other hand, it also gets restored—concurrently and necessarily—by letting the problems depart, having them slip away from the family which could not solve them. Because the family cannot solve or resolve the terror of Edna and Harry, it cannot restore a "delicate balance" to society. It is no wonder that Agnes then ends the play (stage direction: "To fill a silence") by attempting a further privatization of solutions. She feels she will lose her mind; she is not sure it hasn't already happened. The individual psyche is frightened by the burdens of history, and the way the psyche resolves troubles, through dreams and nightmares, is proposed as the only solution to its fear. So the family ultimately fails.

According to Albee, the only way problems from the outside are solved is if they can be made over on the model of relationships within the family: Nick as son; Nick and Honey as children (George: "Home to bed, children," p. 238); Edna and Harry as children; the menacing Van Man in American Dream as son (a transformation that occurs off stage); Death as an Oedipal grandson in The Sandbox. Although in Virginia Woolf there is an apparent finality about the solution that implies that the problems entering with Nick have been solved, George does not actually meet the challenge posed by Nick. The problems simply understand and vanish. However cooperative the problems are as they leave, their unmotivated exit is a clear indication that the family cannot and does not solve them. Although the plays overtly state the opposite, in fact not all the problems evoked by the plays can be made over into family relationships.

So the fundamental contradiction in Albee has to do with opposing ideas about the function and centrality of the family. Overtly the plays propose that problems and conflicts seen in the family originate in distortions of family relationships and can be solved by righting these relationships in stereotypical ways. Covertly within the plays the opposing issue is also posed; that problems and conflicts seen in the family originate outside the family (in work, politics and society, all quite vaguely presented by Albee), and that they cannot be solved within the family. The second proposition, shadowing the first and in conflict with it, is present in inarticulated and even immature form, but is nonetheless palpably present.

The resolution turns on two necessarily linked evasions. Order is restored by assimilating all problems to family relationships, and curing them by re-establishing sexual stereotypes and killing (mutilating) the rival; this solution in Virginia Woolf never traces the sources of the man's failure, but rather confuses the cause of the man's failure with its effect—the dominance of the woman. This is the first evasion. Then, problems raised in the play which cannot be assimilated or transformed into family issues simply leave, unsolved and unaccounted for at the end. This is the second evasion, which logically follows from the first.

It remains to establish what relation the contradiction and its resolution in evasions have to larger social issues, and to

American society at the time the plays were written and performed. Certain of the conflicting elements in Albee's family plays can be directly traced to the society. For example, the plays articulate a nervous sense of the existence of undefined or vague problems, such as competition, work and success, and a general challenge to dominance and proper order. But the cure for these problems is privatization, viewing them as family and/or individual issues. So Albee's first cure does not especially differ from that proposed by popularized psychology. Albee's second cure is effected by the unmotivated exit of problems; knowing they cannot be solved, they just go away. This wishful thinking is rather poignant, after all.

This said, the odd clustering of the "problems" Nick represents and the very vagueness of Edna and Harry's terror may provide a clue to the common denominator of the social problems in Albee's family plays. What is the fear—of "nothing," of "the dark" (p. 55), of its being "too late" (p. 169), or "the end" (p. 168)—in Delicate Balance?

The issue posed by the plays is who or what will control the future. Control of the future is implied in everything Nick represents: technology-science, genetic research, world political alignments, the "decline of the west." George stands with his embattled values and combats Nick as the "dry run for the wave of the future" (p. 178). Eventually, Nick leaves, chastened by George's display of mastery over Martha. Presumably, George's setting his house in order according to strict principles of family dominance will enable George to have authority in the outside world. However, it is unclear that this is so. We know that Nick-as-Oedipal-son has been thwarted, but has Nick-as-career-rival really given up? So George's achievement of dominance at home may have to simply substitute for his dominance in the outside world. In any event, it is clear that Albee favors re-establishing traditional order. What remains unclear is what larger effect this restoration will indeed have.

Following this interpretation, we can appreciate the otherwise random political remarks in this play. They all concern attacks on or threats to hegemony. The association of Nick with Nikita Khrushchev; the mention of the "yellow bastards," the alleged decline of the west, the threat of technology to humanism all imply a preoccupation with a fading hegemony. George's question whether the west is declining points up the political trauma of those who considered themselves unquestioned rulers: our position as ruling sex, ruling class or ruling country is not so unchallenged as before, therefore "the west is declining" and civilization, which we embody, is in danger. Although far from logical, this syllogism has always been tempting to a group whose control—inexplicably, to it—is challenged.

At the end of A Delicate Balance, Agnes describes a struggle which she and others of her kind do not even witness, although it is somehow decisive for them.

> Everything becomes . . . too late, finally. You know it's going on . . . up on the hill; you can see the dust, and hear the cries, and the steel . . . but you wait; and time happens. When you *do* go, sword, shield . . . finally . . . there's nothing there . . . save rust; bone; and the wind.
>
> (p. 169)

Something is going wrong. The future is being formed by a battle outside the control of those who felt themselves dominant. And this fact brings terror.

The evasion of problems which the plays construct is what Albee's audience values. Evasion is not the failure of resolution. It is a particular mode of resolution which avoids dealing with the fundamental contradictions exposed within the work. The pseudo-synthesis which resolves the play apparently solves contradictions but does so only by transforming them into other issues for which a solution can be offered. It is a *pseudo*-synthesis because it gives the appearance of solving the original contradictions but does not. In Albee, the evasion is constructed by transforming problems which do not have their origin in the family into family problems. From the "decline of the west" to the failure of the man in the workplace, social problems are evoked in the play, but the establishment of male hegemony in the family fails to solve even the man's problem, much less the larger issues. The significant exit of characters representing these problems shows a further avoidance, concurrent with the first. Therefore Albee does not synthesize the contradiction which he himself sets up. Evasion is his resolution.

Notes

[1]The editions used are: for *Virginia Woolf,* the Jonathan Cape edition; for *Delicate Balance,* the Pocket Books edition; for *American Dream,* the Jonathan Cape edition. All further page references will be to the respective editions and will appear in the text.

[2]Leo Marx, "Mr. Eliot, Mr. Trilling, and *Huckleberry Finn*", in Claude M. Simpson, ed., *Twentieth Century Interpretations of The Adventures of Huckleberry Finn* (Englewood Cliffs, N. J., Prentice-Hall, Inc., 1968), pp. 37-40.

[3]P. J. Keating, *The Working Classes in Victorian Fiction* (London, Routledge and Kegan Paul, 1971), pp. 4-5.

[4]The analytic distinction is from Albert Memmi, "Problèmes de la Sociologie de la Littérature," in George Gurvitch, ed., *Traité de Sociologie* (Paris, Presses Universitaires de France, 1960).

[5]I am generally indebted to Lucien Goldmann, "La sociologie de la littérature: statut et problèmes de méthode," *Marxisme et sciences humaines* (Paris, Gallimard, 1970).

[6]"[Interviewer]: How about the theme of parents who in one way or another are murdering their children, and children, at least symbolically, killing their parents? Albee: That occurs in two plays—*The American Dream* and *Who's Afraid of Virginia Woolf?*—but then again I've written eight plays, so it's hardly a *recurring* theme." Walter Wager, ed., *The Playwrights Speak* (London, Longmans, Green and Co., Ltd., 1969), p. 48.

[7]An excellent study which includes an anatomy of the family in Albee is Lee Baxandall, "The Theater of Edward Albee", in Alvin B. Kernan, ed., *The Modern American Theater* (Englewood Cliffs, N. J., Prentice-Hall, Inc., 1967).

[8]Albee lists emasculation as an important American problem in the Preface to *The American Dream.*

[9]*The Playwrights Speak,* p. 39.

Lawrence Kingsley (essay date 1973)

SOURCE: "Reality and Illusion: Continuity of a Theme in Albee," in *Educational Theatre Journal,* Vol. 25, No. 1, March, 1973, pp. 71-9.

[*In the following essay, Kingsley observes how Albee's "struggle with reality and illusion endures throughout the major part of his career."*]

Albee has had occasion more than once to note the prominence of reality and illusion in his work. Tiny Alice he calls "a perfectly straightforward story, dealt with in terms of reality and illusion, symbol and actuality."[1] The title of Who's Afraid of Virginia Woolf? "means who's afraid of the big *bad* wolf . . . who's afraid of living life without false illusions."[2] The American Dream "is an examination of the American Scene, an attack on the substitution of artificial for real values in our society, a condemnation of complacency, cruelty, emasculation and vacuity; it is a stand against the fiction that everything in this slipping land of ours is peachy-keen."[3]

These three plays then—The American Dream, Who's Afraid of Virginia Woolf?, and Tiny Alice—are preoccupied with the disparity Albee discerns between a fantasy world and the world in which his characters must live. Tiny Alice constitutes the fullest elaboration of this problem, and the preceding plays build toward it in terms of increasing complexity.[4] Though not keyed to quite the same problem, The Zoo Story and A Delicate Balance surround the other three plays in order of composition and relate to them in theme. If we approach Albee from this larger perspective, we observe how his struggle with reality and illusion endures throughout the major part of his career, young though it still is, and leaves a generally coherent body of work inclusive of his best plays.

The genesis of his concern with reality and illusion is the Nietzschean distinction between Apollonian and Dionysiac tragedy. This well-known and many-sided distinction, which Nietzsche likened to the difference between dream and intoxication, arises in Albee from the belief that "there was a time when people believed in deities. And then revolutions came—Industrial, French, Freudian, Marxist. Gods and absolutes vanished. Individuals find this very difficult and uncomfortable. All they have left is fantasy or the examination of the self."[5] Fantasy is the compelling alternative, because when Albee's characters look inward all they find is self-contempt. As Nietzsche said, man is "an incarnation of dissonance" and life, to be borne, needs an absorbing illusion.[6] The Apollonian component in art supplies that illusion, but Nietzsche cautioned that "the image of Apollo must incorporate that thin line which the dream image may not cross, under penalty of becoming pathological, of imposing itself on us as crass reality."[7]

Here is the borderline which Albee's characters fail to heed. Left to their own resources, they construct for themselves a world of illusion which affords escape from their recurring sense of personal inadequacy. Illusion works for a time, but soon brings complications which want redress. Albee therefore introduces illusion only to reassess it, to show how his characters must rid themselves of falsehood and return to the world in which they must live. The Apollonian component must exert itself in conjunction with the Dionysiac, which most primitively is an "ecstatic reality." The Dionysiac impulse "takes no account of the individual and may even destroy him, or else redeem him through a mystical experience of the collective."[8]

Though the Apollonian-Dionysiac duality is infinitely more complex in Nietzsche, it provides the guidelines within which Albee develops his contention that illusion must keep a proper proportion with reality. This is the importance of The Zoo Story: that in it Jerry tries to reorder his life, to break out of the harried existence in which he finds himself, but cannot. The American Dream, which ends inconclusively, then dramatizes an Apollonian dream realm where man has respite from his Dionysiac self-destruction. In Who's Afraid of Virginia Woolf? and in Tiny Alice, Albee moves one step further and purges illusion in the course of the play. In the former this purgation is attained through Bringing Up Baby, during which George "kills off" the fictive child. Purgation in Tiny Alice takes the form of compelling Brother Julian to accept the reality of his situation. A Delicate Balance once again broaches the theme of outer versus inner reality; however, here it is not fantasy which distorts the individual's perception, if by fantasy we understand projection of fiction as reality; rather it is fear which is in question, and Albee verifies the title: he restores balance before the totter proceeds too far, causes loss of self-awareness. The control he exercises may be one reason why that play is less exciting than his earlier work, but it also helps to explain why his characters have gained, in a way, new *rapprochement* with reality, for now they are not permitted to stray very far from the norm of self-candor.

In The Zoo Story Jerry strives for self-candor without attaining it. He announces, "I'm crazy you bastard" (p. 51). To what extent this assertion is true, we cannot say. Is he simply supplying a ready answer for Peter? Or is he taking sadistic pleasure in watching Peter squirm under the revelation of what he knows to be accurate self-description? Whatever the case, he wanders around the city as a *"permanent transient"* (p. 45), trying to rediscover his bearings: "sometimes a person has to go a very long distance out of his way to come back a short distance correctly" (p. 25). Jerry was psychologically dislocated in youth when his father walked into a bus, and his mother ran off with another man. His family problems, as the usual explanation runs, are offered as the source of his inadequacies in love, here manifested as proneness to homosexuality and inability to love the same person more than once. This deviation in love parallels his peregrinations about the city and, in a larger sense, tendency toward schizophrenia.

Throughout the play Jerry tries to bridge the gap between himself and external reality. One way is to insist that Peter understand his problems. A second comes to light in the story of the dog, with which Jerry finally "made contact" (p. 41) after abortively trying to poison it. Considering himself as yet unready for the more difficult task of dealing with human beings, he prepares himself for that next step by establishing rapport between himself and common objects: "A person has to have some way of dealing with SOMETHING. If not with people . . . with a bed, with a cockroach, with a mirror . . ." (p. 42). He is groping for a hold on reality on a one-to-one basis: himself and any object before him.

This quest for greater self-integration, greater amalgamation with the world around him, is partially successful. He cannot change, but at least he knows what is happening to him; he can see his life in a certain perspective, and himself as the agent of the drama he is enacting. He knows that he has decided to walk north from the zoo until he meets someone, that he will provoke a fight, and will be killed. Hence, he tells Peter at the beginning of the play that he can review the event about to occur on the evening news.

In this one-act play there is none of the complexity later involved when Albee challenges one's awareness of reality on subtler counts. We are presented simply with a study of Jerry's attempt to expound his private world to Peter—a world where the encounter with the landlady's dog takes on metaphysical dimension, where God is "A COLORED QUEEN WHO WEARS A KIMONO AND PLUCKS HIS EYEBROWS" (p. 42), where the contest for the park bench is a fight for one's manhood. Say what he will, Jerry fails to communicate; Peter remains passive until the last moment and even then responds to Jerry only in self-defense. Jerry's estrangement is ended merely by death.

Whereas Jerry knows the distinction between fantasy and "real experience" (p. 32), illusions generated in The American Dream are not only unresolved, but unadmitted when the play concludes. The play stops just where Grandma says it does: "let's leave things as they are right now . . . while everybody's happy . . . while everybody's got what he wants . . . or everybody's got what he thinks he wants" (p. 93). Mommy and Daddy have their Young Man; the Young Man has a new home; Mrs. Barker has the adoption fee, and Grandma has release from the home that mistreats her. The only trouble is that their values are built on sand—to take the cue from The Sandbox, an earlier draft of the play. Mrs. Barker accepts a fee for delivering the Young Man who comes there by accident. Muscle-bound and handsome, he would seem a perfect son for Mommy and Daddy, since they are unwilling to go through the rigors of raising an infant and want him, as it were, prefabricated, made to certain specifications. However, he is unable to love his foster parents: "I no longer have the capacity to feel anything. I have no emotions." To that degree, he represents an inverse image of Jerry, who at least tries to respond to the world around him. The American Dream, in contrast, accepts "the syntax around me, for while I know I cannot relate . . . I know I must be related *to*" (p. 78).

Mommy and Daddy also accept the world as it is presented to them. Mommy defers to Mrs. Barker's judgment on the beige-colored hat. Mrs. Barker, we recall, insists that Mommy's hat is wheat-colored instead of beige. Mommy knows that the choice of words is a quibble; but because Mrs. Barker is the chairman of her woman's club, having authority over her, she accepts the better-advised opinion. Daddy similarly yields to false values. He is eager to hear how "masculine and decisive" he is in concurring with Mommy's decision to have Grandma carted away:

> DADDY: Was I firm about it?
>
> MOMMY: Oh, so firm; so firm.
>
> DADDY: And was I decisive?
>
> MOMMY: SO decisive! Oh, I shivered.
>
> DADDY: And masculine? Was I really masculine?
>
> MOMMY: Oh, Daddy, you were so masculine; I shivered and fainted.
>
> (pp. 30-31)

Not even Grandma is immune from pretense. She is the year's winner in a baking contest with a store-bought, day-old cake. From the moment we first see her, she temporizes, seeking to escape with her boxes before the "van people" (p. 29) arrive. Thus, she speaks to the Dream boy about going "into my act, now" (p. 79). Much of her vituperation is part of this act, to speak as old women are supposed to talk. This calculated indulgence of pretense removes her, it seems, from the fault to which the rest of the family fall victim: not realizing the implications or even the fact of their pretense.

Because the play ends abruptly, when Grandma steps forth as interlocutor and calls a halt to the action, sand-castle illusions are allowed to stand. They are not in Who's Afraid of Virginia Woolf?. Here Albee again explores the meaning of a child in a sterile marriage, a problem for which he has a natural feeling, being himself an adopted child. Because they cannot have a child, George and Martha are contemptuous of each other. Martha is fifty-two, stuck in a small college town, unloved by her father, and fond of alcohol. Her father, the president of the college, had hoped that George would follow in his footsteps, but George has never amounted to much even in the History Department. By inventing the existence of a child, George and Martha escape mutual recrimination and provide themselves with the single solace in their marriage. Martha maintains that

> the one thing I've tried to carry pure and unscathed through the sewer of this marriage; through the sick nights, and the pathetic, stupid days, through the deci-

> sion and the laughter . . . through one failure after another, one failure compounding another failure, each attempt more sickening, more numbing than the one before; the one thing, the one *person* I have tried to protect, to raise above the mire of this vile, crushing marriage; the one light in all this hopeless . . . *dark*ness . . . our SON.
>
> (III, p. 227)

Over the years the need for such an outlet has blurred the line between reality and illusion and brought George and Martha to take the easiest way out. "I'm numbed enough," George says, "and I don't mean by liquor, though maybe that's been part of the process—a gradual, over-the-years going to sleep of the brain cells . . . I bring everything down to reflex response" (II, p. 155). Reflexively, George succumbs to the idea of the child; similarly, as Martha states, her son's birth was easy, "once it had been . . . accepted, relaxed into" (III, p. 217). What has happened, plainly, is that George and Martha have evaded the ugliness of their marriage by taking refuge in illusion. Martha points out: "Truth and illusion, George; you don't know the difference." And George replies: "No; but we must carry on as though we did" (III, p. 202). In this way they construct a whole mythology around the child which they treat as fact. He was born on a September night, not unlike the present night, twenty-one years ago from the next day. His parents remember his childhood habits and experiences, how home life was agonizing for him, and carry the story forward to the present, when he is supposed to be away at college. By the end of the play the lad has compiled a sizable personal history.

Each parent delineates this history so as to undercut the other. For example, George says the boy resisted Martha's attempts to turn him into "a weapon" (III, p. 225) against his father. Martha, on the other hand, thinks her son "could not tolerate the shabby failure his father had become" and so asked her "if it—possibly wasn't true, as he had heard, from some cruel boys, maybe, that he was not our child" (III, p. 225). Each parent in this exchange calls what the other says lies. They are able to return from their fantasy world when it suits their convenience.[9]

George is less addicted to illusion than Martha and seems, by and large, merely to be indulging her in her *Walpurgisnacht* or "witch's sabbath," as Albee labels the second act after the famous sequence in Goethe's *Faust.* George accuses her: "you've moved bag and baggage into your own fantasy world now, and you've started playing variations on your own distortions . . ." (II, p. 155). At the same time he accepts his own responsibility: "the one thing in this whole sinking world that I am sure of is my partnership, my chromosomological partnership in the . . . creation of our . . . blond-eyed, blue-haired . . . son" (I, p. 72). George claims he has been trying to clean up this mess for years. His method of doing so is to arrange"The Exorcism," as the last act is called, whereby he simply announces that their son is dead.

With the three-part structure of "Fun and Games," "Walpurgisnacht," and "The Exorcism," Who's Afraid of Virginia Woolf? represents marked advancement over Albee's previous treatment of illusion. Here illusion is not just conjured up, as in The American Dream, and left to the acerbity of its ironic statement for deflation; rather, it is studied for all the mileage of its comic worth in "Walpurgisnacht," and then conceptually purged in the final act. This compulsion to purge illusion sustains Albee in Tiny Alice.

Tiny Alice, however, represents his concern with reality and illusion in a phase where Albee has the experience of his earlier drama for study and can twist and turn the tensions which he has already created. Lack of critical agreement about Tiny Alice arises from a failure to see this pattern of reality and illusion as it develops from his previous work. Reality now exists on different planes and becomes relative: what is illusory may partake of reality within a limited range. Characters joke about reality and take advantage of whoever is denied their perspective. Rather than pursue these issues, critics by and large attempt to find unified allegory, when there is none, or confine themselves to matter-of-fact summary and isolated insight.[10] The confusion that results has unjustly been foisted upon Albee. From the first he has been beleaguered by accusations that the play is intentionally opaque; shortly after it opened he even held a press conference in the interest of dismissing them. "Maybe I meant it [Tiny alice]," he says, "to be something a little different from confusing—provocative, perhaps, rather than confusing."[11] That statement should be underscored, as well as Albee's assertion in the preface that "the play is quite clear."

It may be helpful to summarize what happens literally. Alice, who is compared to the legendary Croesus, the world's richest man, has decided to give the Church an annual hundred million dollars for the next twenty years. By no means does her generosity derive from need to make her peace with God. "Her soul is in excellent repair," Lawyer says, "If it were not, I doubt she'd be making the gesture." She is motivated simply by the Christian notion that God's field must not lie fallow, that it is wrong for money to be idle: "It is, as I said, that she is overburdened with wealth . . . and it is . . . wasted . . . lying about" (I, p. 15); in her wine cellar "bottles have burst, are bursting, corks rotting" from not being used: "Some great years, popping, dribbling away, going to vinegar under our feet" (II, p. 80).

To transact the grant, Alice sends Lawyer to Cardinal. It turns out that the two are old school acquaintances and have always hated each other. They flaid each other in some of Albee's most brilliant dialogue, which serves the further purpose of introducing Julian. In this opening exchange Cardinal betrays his interest in meeting the alluring Alice; trying to feign indifference to her, as would befit his clerical pose, Cardinal is forced to send his secretary to collect the money. Julian is a lay brother and *ingénue.* Partly because of his vow of celibacy, Alice is challenged to seduce and later marry him; but, moreover, she acts at Lawyer's instigation. Lawyer exercises a certain power over her, as we see at the beginning of the second act, and he can humiliate

Cardinal if Alice wins Julian away from the Church. He goes to the extent of making Cardinal conspire in the lay brother's downfall, holding it as one of the conditions of the grant that Cardinal perform the marriage ceremony. Having turned over the money in one lump sum—two billion dollars—Alice, Lawyer, and Butler, another one of her lovers, cast off Julian and change residences.

Julian cannot realize that there are two different Alices and that he marries only one of them. There is Miss Alice who abandons him, and there is Tiny Alice whom he loves vicariously through the former. Only Miss Alice exists in real life, but Julian confuses her with her double, the doll house miniature whence the play's title is taken. Tiny Alice appeals to Julian as offering all the wealth, taste, and sexual gratification he could never enjoy in the Church. However, the Alice with whom Julian has to reckon, Miss Alice, is venial and changeable in affection: she can fulfill his dream only on a temporary basis. Since he, on the other hand, thinks he has bargained for a permanent relationship—marriage no less—Miss Alice becomes a counterfeit of the woman he tries to love: "have done with forgery, Julian," Miss Alice implores, "accept what's real. I am the . . . illusion" (III, p. 167). At the same time what is real to him, as he becomes blinded to all except love, shrinks to the model, the miniature image which is unchanging. Cleaving to his ideal, Tiny Alice becomes the only reality Julian is willing to acknowledge. To show how fully Julian feels her presence at the end, the doll symbolically comes to life: Tiny Alice shadows the stage, and we hear her heartbeat.

Albee makes quite a toy of the model. Assuming Julian's point of view, he would have us believe that the model is not a replica of the castle, but the other way around. In it is another model, and in that yet another, *ad infinitum.* Although Miss Alice says that there are little people running around inside the model, she is jesting. The game of receding mirrors, whereby reality is reflected on ever-smaller levels, is to be taken seriously only when applied to Julian, as when he discovers the fire in the chapel first in the model. This incident of the fire is not explained at the time and is certain to mystify the audience. But perhaps that is Albee's wish—to tease us just enough that we are led to question the nature of reality in this play, and therefore put on the alert for answers that come later, which otherwise we might miss.

The purpose of the model is to give a concrete diagram of a similar abstracting process at work in each character. Just as the model is patterned after some ultimate reality, each character represents something larger than himself. Tiny Alice is abstracted from Miss Alice as only one part of her. Lawyer is an emissary of Miss Alice, Julian of Cardinal, and Cardinal of the Church. Beyond that, Lawyer, according to Butler, is "acting like the man you wish you were" (II, p. 100), and Cardinal "has to wear a face" (II, p. 102), hiding behind ecclesiastical pomp. During Act Two, Scene One, Butler plays Lawyer, and Lawyer interprets Cardinal. What happens in these instances is that reality separates from replica. To mistake replica for reality, as Julian does, is to live in illusion.

Unlike Lawyer, Julian cannot learn "never to confuse the representative of a . . . thing with the thing itself" (I, p. 39). Instead, Julian invests it with an untrue reality. He imputes to Miss Alice an ideal of purity which longer exposure to her soon undercuts. This error in perception may be one to which all divines are subject, for Cardinal is also said to worship "the symbol and not the substance" (II, p. 105). Since God is ineffable, an old argument goes, all we can know are His manifestations. Although Cardinal repeats Julian's mistake, he survives where the lay brother fails because he is worldly enough not to confuse business with Church. But Julian attempts to retain his faith and thinks it is part of God's plan for him to marry Alice. He cannot see that in reality he turns away from the Church and establishes Tiny Alice as his new deity. Not knowing that the two deities, old and new, are incompatible, he worships the new in the language of the old. Hence the infusion of Christian imagery in the death scene, where Julian positions himself in a crucifixion and calls: "Alice? ALICE? MY GOD, WHY HAST THOU FORSAKEN ME?" (III, p. 189).

Julian's Christian role must not be over-emphasized. To a degree, he stands for the Paschal Lamb: he has been sacrificed by the Church for Alice's dowry—"the greatest marriage settlement in history" (III, p. 146). But if he is Christ, he is Christ married to Tiny Alice and condemned to serve as priest at her shrine, the model beside which he dies. Until the moment of his death, he refuses to accept this priesthood; death is required to make it insistent upon him that he has meanwhile been living in illusion.

After Tiny Alice Albee wrote A Delicate Balance. Each of its two contrasting couples, Agnes and Tobias, Edna and Harry, confuse what they fear with what will come to pass; they assume the worst and act on the basis of their expectations. Their response is thus in excess of the circumstances calling it forth, or in other words based upon a warped sense of reality. Comedy is the natural result, as characters seem to react too violently. In this respect the two couples are intended to parallel one another. Agnes says, "we see ourselves repeated by those we bring into it all, either by mirror or rejection, honor or fault" (II, p. 82); and Edna concludes, "Our lives are . . . the same" (III, p. 166).

In the same problem that rocks the Blooms' marriage in Joyce's *Ulysses,* Agnes and Tobias have lost a son whose death is so fixed in their minds that they are afraid to risk another pregnancy. As a consequence they sleep alone, Tobias sequestered upstairs where he practices masturbation. Edna and Harry are similarly impelled to irrational action, though theirs is much more comic. As they sit around their house, a nameless terror descends upon them. They do not know why they are frightened, only that they suddenly want to be with friends. The ensuing visit shows the vacuity of these people, their tendency toward unsupported fiction, but, more importantly, hints at the metaphysical condition of modern man: in an age of anxiety, as Auden calls it, we are aware of impending doom, but never know what form it will take, whether that of the bomb, or reversion to an id mentality, where our darkest fears, without warning, become the reality in which we live.

Once sheltered in their friends' house, Edna and Harry are thrown into conflict with Julia over the possession of her bedroom. This situation gives rise to speculation about who belongs there in the first place and by what right. Tobias attempts to render an answer in his long climatic speech. Harry and Edna, he reasons, are intruders. Their forty-year friendship may have grown to love, but even it has limits. He does not want the intruders, but they must stay, because he is duty-bound to be hospitable. The balancing of these contradictions is Tobias' contribution to the "balancing act" (II, p. 83) of Agnes, and as counterpoise to her, yet another balance.

Agnes, helpmeet that she is, tries to offset the problems in her marriage by maintaining an outward show of calmness: "There *is* a balance to be maintained, after all, though the rest of you teeter, unconcerned, or uncaring, *assuming* you're on level ground . . . though that is hardly so" (II, pp. 81-82). What she tries to steady is pretense of normal life in a family whose members submerge their truths, as her sister Claire says, and have their sunsets on troubled water. The water has been troubled since Teddy's death, which creates an"unreal time" (II, p. 101) for Agnes. She doubts that she loves or is loved, or"that Teddy had ever lived at all" (II, p. 102). Tobias is "racked with guilt" (III, p. 139), and ever since their marriage has been fraught with pain. The long-term effect on her by the time the play opens, is to threaten her with madness. But here too she maintains a delicate balance.

The borderline between reality and illusion is much more firmly drawn in this play than in Albee's earlier work. The child that George and Martha made up really exists this time. Despite what she may think, Agnes is never in any danger of going mad; Claire may be addicted to drinking, but she knows that she is and places no great reliance on the Alcoholics Anonymous as the solution to her problems. Characters still labor under a distorted apprehension of reality, but no longer is their distortion caused by formulating private fictions. Whereas illusion before had to be purged, now there is no formal exorcism; the intruders leave of their own accord, and, purely for want of a bedroom in the crowded house, Tobias ends his siege of sterility. On these counts A Delicate Balance may be thought to find a proximity with reality missing in Albee's earlier work.

The disjunction between reality and illusion has been a continuing theme in Albee, despite his belief that "I don't pay much attention to how plays relate thematically to each other."[12] In each play examined the theme of reality and illusion is, willy-nilly, articulated by the play as a whole, yet diffused throughout the work in individual details which parallel the major conflict: Honey's hysterical pregnancy, Julian's experience in the asylum, or the way Jerry's landlady relives what never happened are examples. The major conflict typically involves characters reluctant to face the self in its pettiness and lack of fulfillment; dodging personal problems, they retreat to an Apollonian realm of illusion, from which a Dionysiac annihilation must return them. Albee is reported to have rejected the argument which O'Neill develops in *The Iceman Cometh* that life-illusions are necessary. After viewing a performance of the play, he said that O'Neill had made a strong case for illusion, but that truth is better to live with.[13]

The need to correct different modes of self-evasion determines not only the burden of each play, but Albee's overall development as a playwright. The Apollonian paradise felicitated in The American Dream is demolished in Who's Afraid of Virginia Woolf? and in Tiny Alice, with The Zoo Story acting as prologue to the search for meaningful reality and A Delicate Balance as epilogue in which that reality is, in some measure, found.

Notes

[1]Quoted in Louis Calta's report of Albee's press conference, *New York Times,* March 23, 1965, p. 33.

[2]Stated in an interview with William Flanagan, "Edward Albee: The Art of the Theatre," *Paris Review,* 39 (1966), p. 103.

[3]Preface to *The American Dream* (New York, 1961), p. 8. This and the following editions are cited only by act and page reference hereafter: *The Zoo Story, The Death of Bessie Smith, The Sandbox* (New York, 1960); *Who's Afraid of Virginia Woolf?* (New York, 1962); *Tiny Alice* (New York, 1965); *A Delicate Balance* (New York, 1966).

[4]His adaptations do not belong to this discussion, for Albee is a relatively faithful adapter, and there is little point in reflecting on him what is already fully developed in his source. In the interest of condensation, I have similarly excluded *The Death of Bessie Smith.* The dreaming nurse there—"sick of the disparity between things as they are, and as they should be" (p. 124)—is less Albee's quarry than is racism.

[5]Quoted in T. B. Morgan, "Angry Playwright in Soft Spell," *Life,* May 26, 1967, p. 93.

[6]*The Birth of Tragedy,* trans. Francis Golffing (New York, 1956), p. 145.

[7]*Ibid.,* p. 21.

[8]*Ibid.,* p. 24.

[9]This is the way I read the play. Michael E. Rutenberg includes "Two Interviews with Edward Albee" as an appendix to *Edward Albee: Playwright in Protest* (1969; rpt. New York, 1970), in which Albee says that George and Martha "are always totally aware that they are dealing with a myth and not reality" (p. 235). In the opinion of Daniel McDonald, "Truth and Illusion in *Who's Afraid of Virginia Woolf?,*" *Renascence,* 17 (Winter 1964), 63-69, each of the four characters is constantly forming new illusions. Ruth Meyer, "Language: Truth and Illusion in *Who's Afraid of Virginia Woolf?,*" *ETJ,* 20 (March 1968), p. 69, believes that there is "no clear cut distinction between truth and illusion in the play."

[10]See, for example, Rutenberg, pp. 111-126; Richard E. Amacher, *Edward Albee* (New York, 1969), pp. 130-153; Mary Elizabeth Campbell, "The Statement of Edward Albee's *Tiny Alice,*" *Papers on Language & Literature,* 4 (Winter 1968), 85-99; C. W. E. Bigsby, "Curiouser and Curiouser: Edward Albee and the Great God Reality," *Modern Drama,* 10 (Dec. 1967), 258-266; William F. Lucey. "Albee's *Tiny Alice:* Truth and Appearance," *Renascence,* 21 (Winter 1969), 76-80, 110.

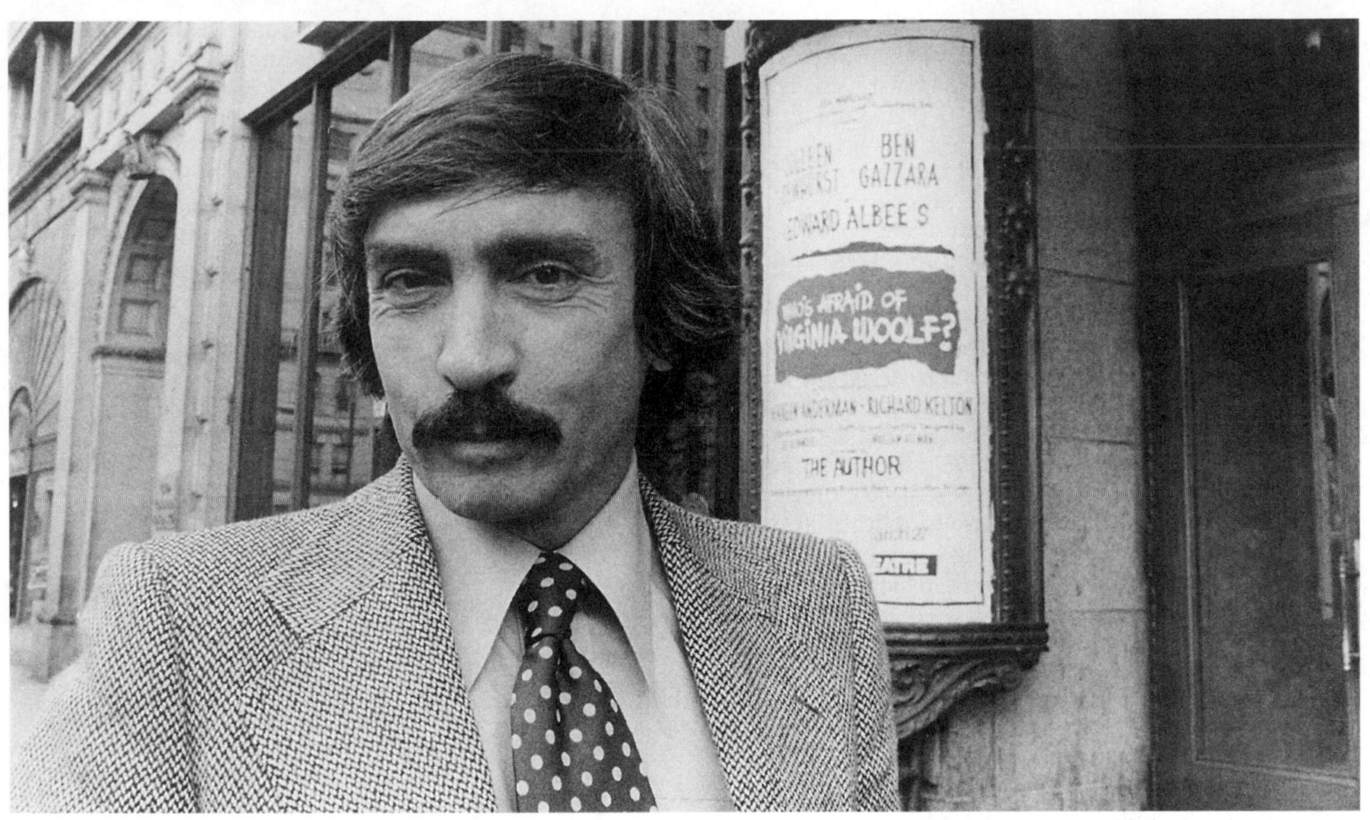

Albee outside the Colonial Theatre in Boston, where he directed a 1976 production of *Who's Afraid of Virginia Woolf?*

[11]R. S. Stewart, "John Gielgud and Edward Albee Talk about the Theatre," *Atlantic,* 215 (April 1965), p. 68.

[12]*Ibid.,* p. 64.

[13]Quoted in Lee Baxandall, "The Theatre of Albee," rpt. in *The Modern American Theatre,* ed Alvin B. Kernan (Englewood Cliffs, N.J., 1967), p. 92.

Nelvin Vos (essay date 1973)

SOURCE: "The Process of Dying in the Plays of Edward Albee," in *Educational Theatre Journal,* Vol. 25, No. 1, March, 1973, pp. 80-85.

[*In the essay below Vos examines Albee's treatment of death in his plays.*]

In Edward Albee's play of 1967, Everything in the Garden, one of the major characters comments:

> You should have been in London in the war. You would have learned about death . . . and violence . . . All those nights in the shelters, with the death going on. Death and dying. Always take the former if you can.

Albee has not been following this advice in his own dramaturgy, for his plays, culminating in his most recent contribution, All Over, have centered largely on the process of dying. The settings, characters, and actions of his plays are haunted by death, both natural and violent. Indeed, as Ruby Cohn has commented, "the shadow of death darkens all Albee's plays."[1] In the presence of "the death going on," the real self is made visible, for illusions are unmasked at this moment. Human freedom may become aware of its limitations, and therefore self-knowledge may be achieved. To confront death therefore becomes frequently the encounter with terror and sometimes the arrival at rest and peace.

I

"Is he dead?" asks the wife as All Over begins. We are in the presence of death, but we never see the dying husband who is behind the hospital screen. Therefore we must concentrate on those who have come to wait out the ritual of his dying: his wife, his mistress, his son and daughter, his best friend, a doctor, and a nurse. The New York production with its cold spotlights and brilliant metallic furniture accurately conveyed the atmosphere of a high black vault, for both the characters onstage and the audience are participating in a deathwatch.

But the various characters, just as we in the audience, view the ritual of the deathwatch in different ways. The Best Friend relies on tradition:

> It *is* more or less required that you *be* . . . I think: here. Family. Isn't it one of our customs? that if a man has not outlived his wife and children—will not outlive them . . . they gather?

The daughter in her cynicism comments that the mass media has brought out a small crowd: "the kind of crowd you'd get for a horse with sunstroke, if it were summer. . . . They're lounging, nothing better to do, and if it weren't night and a weekend, I doubt they'd linger." In reply, the Nurse focusses, as the entire play does, on the process of dying: "That's the final test of fame, isn't it, the degree of it: which is newsworthy, the act of dying itself, or merely the death." With the Kennedys and with King, she continues, the public was cheated, and possessed a kind of anger at having missed the dying. Only in Pope John's dying could one"share," for in those "two weeks of the vilest agony," the confrontation with death became a meaningful experience for the public. In the encounter with death within this play, the Mistress and particularly the Wife become more aware of their own limitations. The Mistress asks tentatively at the beginning of the play, "This is . . . ritual, is it not?" and later asserts: "You can't suffer with a man because he'd dead; his dying, yes. The only horror in participating is . . . well, another time." The suffering horror is revealed in the Wife's confession at the end: "All we've done . . . is think about ourselves." She realizes that she is unwilling to sacrifice:

> Selfless love? I don't think so; we love to *be* loved, and when it's taken away . . . then why *not* rage . . . or pule. All we've *done* is think about ourselves. Ultimately.

Each of the characters is dead to every other; the failure of love is a form of dying, as Albee declared in a *New York Times* interview:

> . . . I write plays about how people waste their lives. The people in this play [All Over] have not *lived* their lives; that's what they're screaming and crying about.[2]

Indeed, the expected last line of the play, "All over," encapsulates the drama: the husband has died, the news of his passing will be broadcast all over, and most of all, for the characters and the audience the ritual of participation in dying has concluded.

II

Albee's plays have frequently concentrated their action in a ritual of deathwatch with a priest, actual or incognito, as officiant. In All Over, the Doctor rather self-consciously comments: "I'm rather like a priest: you have me for the limits, for birth and dying, *and* for the minor cuts and scratches in between."

The earlier play, The Sandbox, in its brief action portrays an embryonic and more satirical version of All Over. The sandbox is Grandma's grave, Mommy and Daddy hire a musician to contribute to the rite, and the Young Man in his calisthenics and in his comforting words to dying Grandma assumes the role of a benediction-giving priest. Grandma is vivacious even while dying, but the inauthentic existence of Mommy and Daddy has not been touched at all. They have been playing funeral; they have not actually participated in the ritualistic process of dying. Only spectators, they leave with the same indifference and blindness with which they arrived.

After Jack's murder by his friends in Everything in the Garden, Albee's stage directions indicate *"This is a wake and the ladies have sorrow on their faces."* Only Jenny is disturbed by the cold-blooded murder which was committed to keep the truth quiet; the others remain detached. By the end of the drama, Jenny too is objectively insisting that the garden in which Jack has been buried should be "well planted and taken care of; kept up. I think it should look like all the others. Don't you think so?" The corruption of values has made their existence a living lie.

In two of Albee's plays, Who's Afraid of Virginia Woolf? and Tiny Alice, a character playing the role of a priest is central to the core of the drama. George's intonation of a Requiem Mass indicates a ritualistic burial of the illusory son. The sacrifice of the child as a scapegoat ("the poor lamb," says Martha) to exorcise the evil spirit of illusion is the last game George initiates: "We're going to play this one to the death." Martha at first refuses to participate in the burial ritual; however, she engages in a confession simultaneous with George's Latin phrases: "I have tried, oh God I have tried. . . ." Nick and Honey are primarily passive spectators to this event, but later Honey does come forth with a Latin response to George's litany, and Nick comments:"Jesus Christ, I think I understand this." Out of this process of dying, purgation and purification emerge. The sacrificial death of the son brings atonement and reconciliation at dawn on a Sunday morning.

Julian in Tiny Alice is actually a lay brother, but he had always wanted to be a priest, and within the drama he performs the roles both of officiant and sacrifice. Albee suggested to John Gielgud, who played the title role in the New York production, that Julian is "the innocent coming into this rather extraordinary assemblage of people."[3] He would have become a priest, but he could not reconcile his idea of God with the god men create in their own image. The Butler accurately tells Julian: "You are of the cloth but have not taken it"; Julian is not yet ready to die to the world. His religious struggle is now put to the test when he is brought to the castle of Miss Alice.[4] His "special priesthood," as his cardinal pointed out to him, is with Alice, the unseen abstract being, and he is to be sacrificed to her. Although he had always hungered for such a vocation ("I have . . . dreamed of sacrifice," and later,"oh, martyrdom. To be that. To be able . . . to be that"), he cannot accept it when it is offered to him. He is torn, as Albee explained in his speech at the Billy Rose Theatre following the opening of the play, "between the selflessness of service and the conspicuous splendor of martyrdom."[5] In his hesitation, the Lawyer mortally wounds Julian with a pistol. When all exit, the audience is left alone to participate in Julian's dying on his wedding day:

> I have never dreamed of it, never imagined what it would be like. I have—oh, yes—dwelt (*Laughs at the word*) . . . dwelt . . . on the *fact* of it, the . . . principle, but I have not imagined dying. Death . . . yes. Not being, but not the act of . . . dying?

To dream of sacrifice may be consoling, but to imagine dying is to face the possibility of nothingness. As he dies, throwing out his arms to receive Alice, his form is in the position of a crucifixion. In his final self-delusion, Julian creates and believes in what he knows does not exist. He has sacrificed himself to a god created by man in his own image. He has died for nothing.

III

To give one's life for another, the action of sacrificial love, has certainly been one of the major motifs in Albee's dramatizations of the process of dying. In The Zoo Story, Peter's murder of Jerry finds its source in Peter's earlier indifference and coldness towards others. Jerry, however, has staged his own act of dying; it is an action of passion; his suicide is transformed into an act of martyrdom. At the cost of his own life, Jerry causes Peter to become aware of man's universal animality ("You're an animal, too") in order to rescue Peter's humanity. Peter is awakened from his spiritual deadness, and Jerry has arrived at the place he desired amid his restlessness: "You have comforted me. Dear Peter." Although both are, as Julian was in Tiny Alice, in a God-forsaken plight at the end ("Oh my God!"), both have gone "a long distance out of the way in order to come back a short distance correctly"; they have arrived at a perception of what it means to face death.

But the opposite of sacrificial love has also intrigued Albee. Not to be willing to give one's self to another implies an indifference and hate which leads to murder. Ironically, the murder in Everything in the Garden is committed by the very women who earlier were very willing to give themselves to another in prostitution. In The Death of Bessie Smith, the neglect of hospital employees, according to Albee's interpretation, contributed to the death of the singer. The Nurse tells Bessie's chauffeur, "YOU WAIT! You just sit down and wait!," and meanwhile Bessie bleeds to death. All of these ordinary people are caught in their own predicaments, and the failure of love (whether the love of the Nurse for her father, the Intern, and the Orderly, or the love of one's neighbor) leads to death.

The relationship of the failure of love and the terror of death is the core of A Delicate Balance. Harry and Edna, coming for shelter and comfort to their neighbors, Tobias and Agnes, insist that fear has overwhelmed them:

> HARRY: It was like being lost: very young again, with the dark, and lost. There was no . . . thing . . . to be . . . frightened of, but . . .
>
> EDNA: WE WERE FRIGHTENED . . . AND THERE WAS NOTHING.

The terror to be faced is the darkness of death, nothingness itself. The household of Agnes and Tobias does not respond to this plea; the inhabitants, as someone has suggested, are "Bad Samaritans." Indeed, in playful conversational interchange, which nevertheless has meaningful nuances, Claire suggests that Tobias kill his wife, Agnes recommends that Claire kill herself, and Claire later flippantly asks, "Why don't you die?" When the distraught daughter of Agnes and Tobias enters the room with a pistol, she is putting into action the deep hatred verging on murder present in the entire household. Clear-sighted Claire's perceptivity, as usual, is accurate:

> "Love" is not the problem. You love Agnes and Agnes loves Julia and Julia loves me and I love you. We all love each other; yes we do. We love each other. . . . Yes; to the depths of our self-pity and our greed. What else but love?

As she cynically remarks later, "I tell ya, there are so many martyrdoms here." But no one lives or dies for another; instead the play conveys the death of marital love (the daughter's past four marriages, the disintegrating marriages of Agnes and Tobias and of Harry and Edna), the death of family love, and the death of friendship. Agnes' response to Tobias' story of the cat he had killed represents the larger action of the play: "Well, what else could you have done? There was nothing to be done; there was no . . . meeting between you." Death has conquered love in this drama.

IV

Not only in the relationship of neighbors, but more especially in the relationship of parents and children, Albee portrays the lack of love which leads to death. Mommy and Daddy place Grandma in the sandbox as if she were an animal. In The American Dream, Mommy and Daddy not only continue their cold indifference to Grandma, but they have emasculated their son. When his twin arrives as the American Dream, Grandma, who possesses the enduring and pioneer convictions of an authentic American Dream, leaves. Questioned about Grandma's leaving, Albee replied that her dying is really a departure "from a form of life that is a great deal more dead than anything else. I guess I meant her specifically to die, but not in the sense that we understand die; to move out of the death within life situation that everybody else in that play was in."[6] Amid the sterility of the household with its worship of materialistic values, Grandma's authentic existence—symbolized by her omniscience—contrasts sharply with the life-lie of the rest of the family.

The death of a son and its influence on the parents' love of one another figures prominently in two of Albee's plays. In A Delicate Balance, Agnes comments about their son's death: "It was an unreal time: I thought Tobias was out of love with me—or, rather, was tired of it, when Teddy died, as if that had been the string." The result of this alienation between the couple is described by Agnes as "Such . . . silent . . . sad, disgusted . . . love."

Although, as Ruby Cohn has indicated, "death lies like a sediment in Martha's gin, Nick's bourbon, Honey's brandy, and mainly George's 'bergin'"[7] in Who's Afraid of Virginia Woolf?, the lacerating dialogue and figurative acts of murder lead to a renewal of love. As Martha recalls the time she knocked down George in a wrestling match, George's sudden appearance with a short-barreled shotgun which opens into a colorful Chinese parasol indicates his murderous intent. "You? . . . Kill me? . . . That's a laugh," comments Martha to which George replies, "Well, now, I might . . . some day." Later, George while grabbing Martha's throat shouts, "I'LL KILL YOU!" to which Martha responds, "Murderer. Mur . . . der . . . er." George's destruction of the fantasy of the son does kill part of Martha and part of himself; it has been their joint creation. Suicide, premeditated homicide, and martyrdom are all intermingled in this mercy killing. The child born of the mind for secret pleasure is killed by an act of the will for public suffering, and the birthday upon which he assumes manhood becomes his death day. As told by George, the cause of the son's death occurred in the identical manner in which he earlier had recounted the accident of killing his father: "He was . . . killed . . . late in the afternoon . . . on a country road, with his learner's permit in his pocket, he swerved, to avoid a porcupine, and drove straight into a . . . large tree." George as son and as father therefore is himself dying in this act of self-sacrificial love. By symbolically eating the telegram containing the news of the son's death, George is perhaps performing a eucharistic sacramental act.[8] Later, one of Martha's stage directions reads *"a hint of communion in this."* All this appears to fulfill George's prophecy that ". . . it's going to make your performance tonight look like an Easter pageant." Out of this cauldron of suffering, the son's death leads to the resurrection of those present. The sacrifice, in the word's etymology, has once more, if only for a moment, "made holy" the relationship of marital love.

In the ritual of death therefore, whether as a participant in the dying of another or in encounter with death itself, one is attempting, as Northrop Frye suggests, "to recapture a lost rapport with the natural cycle."[9] One could add that the ritual of death in Albee's plays also attempts to recapture a lost rapport with other men, both family and neighbors, intimates and strangers.

V

Existential philosophy has reminded us that in the encounter with death, man faces the mystery of Being and Nothingness. Death brings man to the threshold of authentic existence; death is all over, universal as well as conclusive. In such a spirit, Tolstoy in his old age could say to Gorky: "If a man has learned to think, no matter what he may think about, he is always thinking of his own death."[10] So, too, Albee at age forty-three could say in a *New York Times* interview: "I had an awareness of death when I was 15, but I turned 36 or 37 before I became aware that *I,* Edward Albee, was going to die. The realization did not fill me with dread. I simply became aware of the fact that this is the only time around for me."[11] These two quotations play counterpoint to a conversation in All Over:

> THE WIFE: How *old* were you when you became aware of death?
>
> THE BEST FRIEND: Well . . . what it meant, you mean. The age we all become philosophers—fifteen?
>
> THE WIFE: No, no, when you were aware of it for yourself, when you knew you were at the top of the roller-coaster ride, when you knew half of it was probably over and you were on your *way* to it.

To become aware that dying is a process which involves one's self is to gain self-knowledge.

Sharing this theme, but not the tone, with the continental absurdist playwrights, Albee's plays center on the action of a wake/funeral as does Genet's *The Blacks,* on the haunting presence of the absent one as does *Waiting for Godot,* on the suicide-martyrdom of Ionesco's *The Chairs* and *The Lesson,* and on the birthday as death day in Pinter's *The Birthday Party.* And most of all, in his latest play, Albee has transformed Ionesco's portrayal of the encounter with death in *The Killer* and particularly the process of dying in *Exit the King* into an American setting with little of the surrealism which marks most of the absurd plays. What direction Albee will next take in his journey toward death remains to be seen in his future plays.

NOTES

[1]*Edward Albee,* University of Minnesota Pamphlets on American Writers, No. 77 (Minneapolis, 1969), p. 44.

[2]*The New York Times,* April 18, 1971.

[3]"John Gielgud and Edward Albee Talk about the Theater," *The Atlantic Monthly,* April 1965, p. 68.

[4]For a discussion of *Tiny Alice* as a morality play in which Julian is tempted by the World (the Butler), the Flesh (Miss Alice), and the Devil (the Lawyer), see Mary Elizabeth Campbell, "The Tempters in Albee's *Tiny Alice,*" *Modern Drama,* XIII (May, 1970), 22-33.

[5]Cited in *The Playwrights Speak,* ed. Walter Wager (New York, 1967), p. 34.

[6]Cited in Michael E. Rutenberg, *Edward Albee: Playwright in Protest* (New York, 1969), p. 74.

[7]Cohn, p. 17.

[8]For an interpretation of *Who's Afraid of Virginia Woolf?* which develops the play's mythic relationships to Easter, see Rictor Norton, "Folklore and Myth in *Who's Afraid of Virginia Woolf?" Renascence,* 23 (1971), 159-167.

[9]*Fables of Identity: Studies in Poetic Mythology* (New York, 1963), p. 15.

[10]Cited in William Barrett, *Irrational Man* (Garden City, 1958) p. 145.

[11]*The New York Times,* April 18, 1971.

Catharine Hughes (essay date 1976)

SOURCE: "Edward Albee," in *American Playwrights: 1945-75,* Pitman Publishing, 1976, pp. 52-63.

[*In the essay that follows, Hughes presents a largely negative appraisal of Albee's works.*]

Almost from the moment of his first New York production, The Zoo Story (1960), Edward Albee has been regarded as the most 'promising' American playwright since the Williams-Miller generation. With Who's Afraid of Virginia Woolf? (1962), the hopes and hosannas increased. Since, there has been mainly disappointment, a series of plays that fell short of effectiveness interspersed with adaptations of other writers' works. Was Albee, then, yet another flash-in-the-pan, a one-play playwright destined to the same fate as Inge, Anderson and all too many others? It would be easy to concur. Yet Albee (born in 1928) is still in his forties. His two most recent plays, All Over (1971) and Seascape (1975), while not successful on the level of Virginia Woolf, are among his most ambitious.

The Zoo Story takes place in Central Park. It is summer; it is the present and Peter is smoking a pipe, peacefully reading a book, when he is approached by Jerry. He is exactly what he appears to be: a young publishing executive (salary $18,000); one wife, two daughters, two cats, two parakeets and an apartment in Manhattan's East Seventies. He has, in short, all the prerequisites for a character in the Sloan Wilson grey-flannel-suit novels of the period.

Albee sets his theme early: Jerry tells Peter, 'I don't talk to many people—except to say like: give me a beer, or where's the john, or what time does the feature go on . . . You know—things like that. . . . But every once in a while I like to talk to somebody, really talk.'

Who does *talk* to many people? Peter is bewildered by the seeming lack of communication; yet communication, for him, exists only in the realm of the inconsequential. Repeated attempts by Jerry leave him only indifferent, visibly resentful that his afternoon's relaxation has been interrupted by this somewhat unkempt young man. He is unwilling to become involved on any level save the most superficial. With something as important as an argument over who has proprietary rights to the park bench, everything is clear, is on the surface, safe. In trivia there is no necessity for involvement: it is detached from such dangerous areas as the human heart.

The Zoo Story marks the beginning of what has been, to a large extent, Albee's continuing theme. In it, Jerry and Peter 'make contact' only in the play's melodramatic conclusion. Before that, there is the story of Jerry and the dog: for Jerry it is an all-important encounter, one in which he is able to see not only his own tragedy, but the tragedy of an entire generation; for Peter only a somewhat disturbing diversion, one to which he can close his mind. The dog, obviously intended as some form of universal symbol, yet touchingly believable, each day meets Jerry in the hall, then attacks him. One day, Jerry tells Peter, he reached his decision: 'First, I'll kill the dog with kindness, and if that doesn't work . . . I'll just kill him.' After an unsuccessful attempt to poison the animal, Jerry discovers that 'I had tried to love, and I had tried to kill, and both had been unsuccessful by themselves. . . . I hoped that the dog would understand'. 'Don't you see?' he asks Peter, 'a person has to have some way of dealing with SOMETHING. If not with people . . . SOMETHING.' And, after a long series of 'things', he concludes: '. . . with God who, I'm told, turned his back on the whole thing some time ago . . . with . . . someday, with people. People.'

Peter is seemingly uncomprehending throughout Jerry's entire long soliloquy. He reacts at the *proper* moments, of course: wincing at the proposed killing of the dog, but scoffing at the idea of 'contact' between Jerry and the dog. One really is not surprised at his 'I don't understand', for it has become obvious that Jerry expects too much when he seeks someone either to share or comprehend his own experience. Words alone cannot convey it. Peter and, by extension, most of modern man, is incapable perhaps, but more frequently unwilling, just as Jerry and the dog were ultimately unwilling: 'We regard each other with a mixture of sadness and suspicion', Jerry says, 'and then we feign indifference. We walk past each other safely; we have an understanding. . . . The dog and I have attained a compromise; more of a bargain, really. We neither love nor hurt because *we do not try* to reach each other.'

'I DON'T WANT TO HEAR ANY MORE', Peter shouts. Indeed, he does not. For Jerry has come far too close to reaching him; has touched on a problem not merely his own, but that of every man. And so the return to trivia; to the parakeets and, eventually, to the bench dispute and the play's violent ending, wherein Jerry, forcing Peter into an open 'fight', asks him: 'Don't you have any idea, not even the slightest, what other people *need?*' His conclusion, excessively melodramatic though it is, is effectively reached when Jerry, having finally aroused Peter, forces a knife upon him, then impales himself on it.

In The American Dream (1961), Albee's *leit motif* assumes the form of comedy. Incisively satiric, bitingly ironic, the opening exchange between Mommy and Daddy—which occupies several minutes—is over so important, so earth-shaking, a point as the colour of Mommy's new hat; whether it is wheat-coloured or beige. It is the only level on which Mommy and Daddy attempt conversation; a conversation as empty, as meaningless, as the symbolic empty gilt picture frame that hangs over their sofa. It is not merely funny—perhaps not really funny at all. It is the tragedy of two human beings, the daily occupants of each other's world, who really exist without each other, yet attempt to love what they do not know. Albee has written that the names of the two characters are terms of 'empty affection and point up the pre-senility and vacuity of their characters'. It is this vacuity—and the vacuity of 'the American dream'—that absorbs him.

When a Mrs Barker comes into their home—she knows not exactly why, nor do they—she becomes part of Albee's world. A 'professional woman', she is involved in so many Good Works that she cannot keep them separated. Which of her committees, which of her Responsible Citizens Activities, has brought her there? She is the typical socialite, pursuing her works of 'charity' on alternate Mondays, Wednesdays and Fridays. And for what reason; for any motivation beyond filling in time? This is never verbally posed or answered, and perhaps it is just as well. Albee probably comes closest to it when he has Mommy inquire, 'Are you sure you're comfortable? Won't you take off your dress?' 'I don't mind if I do', Mrs Barker replies. One then wonders, amid the empty picture frames and the 'empty' boxes, whether, in the world of Albee's American Dream, anything is what it appears to be. The handsome young man who next comes to the apartment looking for work obviously is not. He describes himself: 'I no longer have the capacity to feel anything. I have no emotion; I have been drained; torn asunder . . . disemboweled. I have, now, only my person . . . my body . . . my face. . . . As I told you; I am incomplete. I can feel nothing. And so . . . here I am . . . as you see me. I am but this . . . what you see. And it will always be thus.'

Is this, then, the American Dream? Possessor of great surface values, yet empty inside, something sought after, yet, when found, unworthy of the seeking? Albee's Young Man, virile, handsome, seemingly the personification of the American ideal, yet a hollow man; illusory, a goal—a dream—which Albee seems to view as, not so much beyond attaining, but as not worth having once achieved. For the surface—the glitter, the chrome, whatever—is not the reality. Whatever else is said, however disarmingly or fantastically some of it is couched, there is always the American Dream—and it is always not exactly what it has appeared.

If there is any one thing that dominates both The American Dream and The Zoo Story, it is probably this: in a society seeking only the personal comfort, the status and the convenience of the material moment, human involvement, human sensitivities, must be ignored. Peter on the park bench denies Jerry's need; the Young Man's identical twin was once cruelly repudiated, spiritually and physically dismembered by 'Mommy' and 'Daddy'. All wish to inhabit their own private world; all wish, most of all, to avoid reaching that point at which they might begin to know, to experience, some share of another's agony.

In Who's Afraid of Virginia Woolf?, Albee brings that agony scorchingly to the surface. Nearly three and a half hours long, the play is a prolix indictment of contemporary society's frequent inability to distinguish illusion from reality, surface from essence. But it is more than that. The love-hate relationship of the middle-aged faculty couple, George and Martha, as it is hurled out in the presence of a younger couple, is a cascading torrent of expletives, vulgarity and imposed 'shock' effects (at least for its time). For all this—and its frequent transparency—Virginia Woolf is almost unquestionably the major theatrical experience provided by an American writer of Albee's generation. It shakes and excoriates, accuses and excuses, with an abandon and consistency seldom seen on recent American stages.

The 'Fun and Games' of Act 1 begin at 2 a.m. Nick and his young wife, Honey, have joined George and Martha for that they think will be a nightcap. What it turns into is an evening from which neither couple can emerge unchanged. In their liquor-sodden discontent, George and Martha cast aside the conventional banality of much modern conversation. Having long since discovered that to love is also to hurt, they carry their realization to its ultimate form. Martha is the daughter of the college president; George is the supposed faculty failure, the man for whom the bright future once envisioned has turned to the ashes of frustration. As they attack each other on this and other questions from the past, a present emerges. It is in this present that Virginia Woolf oversteps itself in its reliance upon a plot thread finally too flimsy to sustain the surface brilliance of its first two acts.

George and Martha have a son—or so they tell Nick and Honey. He is essential to their relationship, imperative to their need to rail each other for their respective failures with him. Yet, George warns her, 'Just don't start the bit, the bit about the kid'. In a sense, he is an echo of the Young Man in The American Dream. Frequent allusions to him provide much of the forward momentum in an otherwise largely plotless drama. When, in 'The Exorcism' of Act 3, it finally becomes apparent that he is, after all, illusory, the imaginary creature of their childless marriage, the play suffers from what borders on a *reductio ad absurdum.* In tying together the pieces, Albee has—as have so many before him—imposed a conclusion which is fundamentally artificial. It is more than merely artificial; it is melodrama tagged on to something inherently literal, tinsel as the appendage of realism. For George, in his revenge on Martha, his desire to win this 'game' they play, decides to 'kill' their imaginary son. Over this death of illusion he reads, in Latin, the prayers for the dead. Martha cries out that he cannot do it; cannot make this decision alone, but she pleads in vain. 'It will be better', George tells her. The illusions by and for which we live are fragile, Albee suggests, waiting only for the word by which they topple. That the word is not more frequently spoken is a testimony only to our civilized pretence, our power of self-deception. Were we to cut through them to a kind of ultimate and impossible honesty, foundations would alter, a world would be changed. Or, as George reminds Honey: 'When people can't abide things as they are, when they can't abide the present, they do one of two things . . . either they turn to a contemplation of the past as I have done, or they set about to . . . alter the future. And when you want to change something . . . you BANG! BANG! BANG! BANG! BANG!'

In the flagellation and self-flagellation, the anguish and peculiar kind of love of George and Martha, Albee unleashes a verbal avalanche. Repetitive and excessive, it is frequently also moving and startlingly evocative. There remain, however, moments in which Albee's self-indulgence causes one to pause. The achievement of Virginia Woolf was a distinctly relative one. In saying, as one critic did, that it towered 'over the common run of contemporary plays', how much really had been said?

'Truth and illusion. Who knows the difference, eh, toots?' George demands of young Nick. 'Truth and illusion, George;

you don't know the difference', Martha insists to George. 'No,' he responds, 'but we must carry on as though we did.' So they do, in their shared final agony over the 'death' of the child they could not have, the child George insists they had to 'kill'.

With Tiny Alice (1964) Albee continued to be controversial, but added an element of pretentiousness and calculated obscurantism, a pseudo-*Cocktail Party* atmosphere, that resulted in a deservedly brief Broadway run.

A lawyer who once attended school with the Cardinal, where they were ardent antagonists, arrives representing a client who wants to give $100,000,000 to the Church 'now' and 'the same amount each year for the next twenty'. She is 'overburdened with wealth'. It is one of several 'bequests—arrangements' she (Miss Alice) is making at the moment: to Protestants, to Jews, to Catholics, to hospitals, to universities, to orchestras, to 'revolutions here and there'.

Brother Julian, the Cardinal's secretary, is to be sent to take care of the 'odds and ends'. He is, the Cardinal says, 'an old friend of ours', a lay brother.

In Miss Alice's mansion is a 'huge doll's house model of the building of which the present room is a part. It is as tall as a man'. It is exact, 'even with tiny candlesticks on the tables'. So exact that there is a model within the model.

Miss Alice's lawyer has a dossier on Brother Julian, but it has six 'blank' years, years when he was in his thirties, and he declines to fill them in. When the lawyer is gone, however, he admits to Butler, the butler, that 'I lost my faith. In God', and that he had put himself in a mental home.

When Julian first meets Miss Alice, she has a face that is 'that of a withered crone, her hair grey and white and matted; she is bent; she moves with two canes'. But he had been told that she was a *young* woman. Hers, however, is a disguise, a game. She tells Julian that Butler was once her lover, that the lawyer now is.

The bemused, utterly confused, Julian acknowledges: 'I imagined so many things, or . . . did so many things I thought I had imagined. The uncertainty . . . you know?' Miss Alice has what is perhaps the only feasible reply: 'Are you sure you're not describing what passes for sanity?'

Miss Alice decides he should perhaps 'move in' and thus be available to answer her questions.

As often happens, however, deliberate obscurantism becomes tedious. As Alice and the lawyer argue, the model catches fire. The chapel. But the actual chapel is on fire. When they succeed in extinguishing the fire in the house the one in the model goes out as well.

When Julian comes to stay in the house, he realizes he is being tested. Why? 'And why am I being tempted? By luxury, by ease, by . . . by content . . . by things I do not dare to discuss.' In time, he reveals his desire for martyrdom, is self-entranced when Alice suggests, 'Marry me'.

And marry they do, after further deliberate obscurantism. Then there occurs what is described as 'the ceremony of Alice', in which the 'great benefit to the Church' resulting from their marriage is alluded to. He is then told that he has married 'her', the Tiny Alice in the model. 'You are hers.' He insists he will return to the asylum, wondering whether *that* was when he was 'rational'.

Instead, the lawyer shoots him and, as they leave Julian goes through a long, long, *long* monologue in which he seems to equate Alice and God, the God who has apparently deserted him, but whose will he accepts.

Although Albee has claimed that the critics are to blame for imposing on Tiny Alice things he never intended, he is mistaken. It is a bad, and a pretentious play.

A Delicate Balance (1966), which received the Pulitzer Prize that many think should earlier have gone to Virginia Woolf, offers a marked and welcome change of pace. Like much of Pinter and the theatre of the absurd, of which Albee was at least marginally a member, it suggests a hidden, unnamed element of menace, disaster lurking just outside the door, perhaps just up the stairs.

Agnes and Tobias are a well-off couple in their fifties. Her sister, Claire, whom she has railed at earlier in the evening, returns to the living room in the play's opening scene to say: 'I apologize that my nature is such to bring out in you the full force of your brutality.' Tobias suggests that she attend meetings of Alcoholics Anonymous, but she responds with the glib sense of irony that characterizes her behaviour throughout the play: 'They were alcoholics, and I was not. . . . I was just a drunk. . . . They couldn't help it; I could, and wouldn't. . . . They were sick and I was merely . . . willful.'

Shortly thereafter, Harry and Edna, their best friends, appear quite unexpectedly. Why have they come? It seems they had been sitting at home and suddenly they 'got frightened'. There was seemingly nothing to cause it, says Harry, 'but we were very scared', and could not remain there, so they have come to visit Agnes and Tobias, who put them up in their daughter Julia's room.

Julia returns home the next day, yet another marriage—her fourth—on the rocks. Harry and Edna have remained upstairs all day. They appear briefly, with their coats, but it is only to announce they are going home to pick up their things and will return. When they do, they are clearly 'moving in'.

'Edna and Harry have come to us', Agnes tells Claire and Julia, 'dear friends, our very best, though there's a judgment to be made about that, I think—have come to us and brought the plague. Now, poor Tobias has sat up all night and wrestled with the moral problem', the problem of whether they shall be permitted to remain. When Harry comes downstairs, he asks Tobias 'Do you want us here?' but only moments later, he volunteers that, in Tobias's position, he would not let *them* stay. Tobias, however, insists they've 'cast [their] lot together, boy, we're friends'. He cannot keep up the facade, however; he wants them to leave and finally must acknowledge it, though still insisting they remain.

Edna, however, knows that it is all over. 'It's sad to come to the end of it', she says, 'nearly the end; so much more of it gone by . . . than left, and still not know—still not have learned . . . the boundaries, what we may not do . . . not ask for fear of looking in a mirror. . . . It's sad to know you've gone through it all, or most of it, without . . . that . . . the only skin you've ever known . . . is your own—and that it's dry . . . and not warm.' And so they leave. Agnes, Claire and Tobias are left to themselves and, Agnes reflects,'we'll all forget . . . quite soon'.

Every man, perhaps, is an island, with in the end only his own resources to draw upon, whether those resources include something known as the spiritual, a god, God—or nothing. Yet, he cannot avoid the process of life, with all it entails, or of death, even the small deaths that take place every day. It is the plague, the 'disease', that pursues him. In A Delicate Balance, an at times very funny, at others quite poignant, play, Albee alludes to all of this and makes it far more palpably believable than it was to be in either of his more recent works.

All Over (1971) is what is sometimes referred to as a 'difficult' play. A great man is dying. He is not otherwise identified; a politician perhaps; an artist or a financier. In the event, he is a celebrity. As the press and television crews lurk downstairs awaiting his death, others, too, maintain their vigil: The Wife, The Daughter, The Mistress, The Doctor, The Son, The Best Friend, The Nurse. Albee does not further identify them.

Albee is at his best when his characters are at their bitchiest. The Wife and The Mistress possess a degree of rapport. Both after all—the wife of fifty years and the mistress of twenty—love the man who is dying, bicker though they do over whether he should be cremated or buried, food for flames or food for worms. The children, middle-aged children, sulk about, failures and haters. Hated, too. Especially The Daughter, who periodically erupts in a vitriol, scorn and bitterness reminiscent of Virginia Woolf. The Best Friend and lawyer reflects—on his wife, on his former relations with the dying man's wife, on the things a deathwatch recalls—while the eighty-six-year-old Doctor and The Nurse occasionally leave their places beside the screened-off bed upstage to venture their own observations and memories.

Initially, they all speak in formalized cadences and heightened language, a dialogue that is both non-realistic and precise: 'This is what I have come to love you so little for: that you love yourself so little.' 'He said he thought not.' 'While I merely your wife of fifty years.' . . . 'Baleful as I suppose my gaze must have been to him.' Since this was Albee's twelfth play and he has written some of the most vibrant dialogue in the American theatre, it seems safe to assume the artificiality is intentional. It is not what Albee does best, and he does not do it well in All Over, though the language fortunately becomes somewhat more lifelike, if not really alive, as the play wears on.

The Wife talks of 'the little girl I was when he came to me' and The Mistress of her 'status' and her first love affair during a long-ago summer. The Daughter, who is incapable of love, lacerates her mother for her failure to do so; The Son, an emotional eunuch, finally becomes emotional when he details not some memory of his father's kindness or lack of it, but the unchanged contents of his bathroom.

So they continue through the play's two acts, haranguing each other, exhibiting their rancour and their venom, their sarcasm and their spleen. They seek themselves, but not within themselves. Virtually everything that emerges emerges in terms of their attempts to define themselves in relation to the dying man. It does not really work. We know no more of him when the play ends than we did in its first few moments and only marginally more of them.

'All we've *done* is think about ourselves. Ultimately', The Wife says as the play approaches its conclusion. There has been a great deal of talk and a great deal of surface emotion has been expended. There have been some completely riveting moments, but The Wife, The Mistress and all the rest are attempting to bring to life characters who are essentially the puppets of a playwright's vision, figures who move about speaking arias that refuse to sing, lines that refuse to resound in the vacuum of a deathwatch that ultimately has as little to say about living as about dying.

Seascape (1975) has been described, by the author, among others, as the 'life' part of a life/death play that began with All Over. Regrettably, life is one of the things it most obviously lacks.

A middle-aged couple by the names of Nancy and Charlie have been spending some time by the sea. 'Can't we just stay here forever?' she asks, for she loves the water as Charlie once did. As a boy, he wanted to live under the sea, wanted to be 'fishlike'. He used to go 'way down, and try to stay'. He would go in, 'take two stones, look up one final time at the sky . . . relax . . . begin to go down. . . . And one stops being an intruder, finally—just one more object come to the bottom, or living thing, part of the undulation and the silence. It was very good.'

Charlie hasn't, however, done it since he was seventeen and it has been 'too long' for him to go back again, as Nancy urges. He would rather 'remember'. He would rather do nothing. And that is precisely what they do for approximately thirty-five minutes of the first act: nothing but review their lives tediously and acrimoniously, though this acrimony has none of the acerbic bite and bitchy humour of Virginia Woolf and certainly none of the interest.

Just when tedium threatens to become numbness, two lizard-like creatures emerge from the sea. They are Sarah and Leslie and they too are apparently middle-aged (though telling a middle-aged lizard from a young lizard is clearly beyond my competence). At first, the two couples are afraid of each other, then gradually they begin to develop points of contact, are in turn aggressive, responsive, patronizing, curious. Charlie tells Nancy that what is happening is not real, that they are in fact dead from the liver paste they had at lunch. 'We ate the liver paste and we died.'

The two couples experience both harmony and conflict, things shared and things unknown to the other. What is one to make, for instance, of Nancy having had only three children, and taken care of them for twenty or more years, when Sarah has had seven hundred and abandoned them?

Albee, however, is more concerned with similarities than with differences. 'In the course of the play', he has commented in an interview, 'the evolutionary pattern is speeded up billions of revolutions.' Thus, it slowly evolves that Sarah and Leslie are, or have the potential to be, every bit as bigoted, every bit as middle-class in their values and behaviour, as Nancy and Charlie. They, however, aren't put off by blacks or 'foreigners', but by fish: 'There's too many of them; they're all over the place . . . moving in, taking over where you live . . . and they're stupid!'

Why had they come up from the sea, these two green-scaled creatures, who, at least, still enjoyed an innocence, a sense of wonder, long gone from the couple they have come upon? '*We* had changed', Sarah reveals, 'all of a sudden, everything . . . down there . . . was terribly . . . interesting, I suppose; but what did it have to do with *us* anymore?' So they came up from what Charlie refers to as the 'primordial soup, the glop'. What has been going on, he tells them, is 'called flux. And it's always going on; right now, to all of us.' And maybe, he admits, he envies them, 'down *there,* free from it all; down there with the beasts'.

Envy or no, Charlie causes Sarah to cry at the thought that Leslie will one day die, go away forever. It is an alien concept and Leslie attempts to choke him, for Sarah has never cried before.

'It's . . . rather dangerous . . . up here', Leslie concedes.'Everywhere', returns Charlie. So they decide they will go back down again. It goes almost without saying, however, that they will not, cannot; the process must go on.'You'll have to come back', advises Nancy, 'sooner or later. You don't have any choice.' And Sarah and Leslie recognize the truth of what she says, which prompts their anxiety. Nancy tells them she and Charlie could 'help'. At the curtain, Leslie has acceded: 'All right. Begin.'

As a course in very elementary Darwinism, Seascape just might have some value; as a play, it is pretentious, simplistic, verbose and banal. Albee prides himself on being a 'literary' writer, but is it literary or pretentious when Nancy advises: 'Charlie has decided that the wonders do not occur; that what we have not known does not exist; that what we cannot fathom cannot be; that the miracles, if you will, are bedtime stories; he has taken the leap offaith, from agnostic to atheist; the world is flat; the sun and the planets revolve about it, and don't row out too far or you'll fall off'?

As in All Over, the writing is presumed (by the author) to be poetic and resonant, profound, when in reality it is devoid of life and artificial, the producer of inertia. In Seascape, it would seem only to confirm what has become more and more evident with the passing years: that it is to such plays as Tiny Alice, Malcolm, All Over and Seascape, not the earlier, more vital and vibrant—even more profound—Zoo Story and Virginia Woolf, that one must look for the 'real Edward Albee'. It is a sad discovery to make.

Lucina P. Gabbard (essay date 1982)

SOURCE: "Edward Albee's Triptych on Abandonment," in *Twentieth Century Literature: A Scholarly and Critical Journal,* Vol. 28, No. 1, Spring, 1982, pp. 14-33.

[*In the essay below, Gabbard explores the theme of abandonment in* The Zoo Story, The Death of Bessie Smith, *and* The Sandbox, *maintaining that each is a "unique picture of abandonment . . . all hinged together by the shared and related themes of ambivalence, escape into fantasy, and preoccupation with death."*]

Edward Albee's earliest plays—The Zoo Story, The Death of Bessie Smith,and The Sandbox—ring with rage at society's disregard for its outcasts. An adopted child himself, Albee wrote these plays in the late fifties when he was temporarily estranged from his legal parents and, thereby, transferred from wealth to near-poverty. Considering this personal closeness to the theme of abandonment, it is not surprising that his first plays express a serious concern for life's expendable ones. This concern struck a chord with the youth of the sixties who vented their own rage by fighting for Civil Rights and protesting the Viet Nam War. In the sixties Albee's one-acts were among the most frequently performed plays on American college campuses. Jerry became the prototype of American youth, unheard by the government and abandoned to the war in Viet Nam. Bessie Smith became the symbol of the disadvantaged Blacks for whom students marched in the South. Grandma was a rallying point for youthful disenchantment with the middle-aged establishment who had rejected old folk along with young adults.

Beneath these sociological realities, however, the plays comprise a deeper unity and a more universal experience based on the psychoanalytic concepts of separation anxiety and abandonment depression. Psychiatrists James Masterson and Donald Rinsley have described a major effect of these neuroses as a feeling that life offers only two alternatives: "either to feel bad and abandoned . . . or to feel good . . . at the cost of denial of reality and self-destructive acting out."[1] Each of Albee's first three plays illustrates this choice; the central figures choose fantasy and death as escapes from the hostility and despair of rejection. Indeed, the three plays form a triptych, each panel a unique picture of abandonment and all hinged together by the shared and related themes of ambivalence, escape into fantasy, and preoccupation with death.[2]

The Zoo Story, as its title indicates, is built on stories; and these stories, which Jerry tells to Peter, set up the psychoanalytic patterns common to all three plays. In this first play the central conflict is between Jerry, the abandoned one who seeks understanding and acceptance, and Peter, the indifferent father-figure who desires privacy and freedom from intrusion. The play reveals that Jerry has been reenacting this same conflict all his life, continuously locked into the role of outcast, locked out of love and belonging. He was only ten years old when his mother deserted him and his father for a spin with adultery and alcohol. A year later, both she and his father died within two weeks. Jerry was passed on to a dour aunt who forsook him on high school graduation day by dropping dead on their apartment stairs.[3] Jerry is currently languishing in loneliness at a cheap rooming house where a hostile dog tries to forbid him entrance. He calls himself a "permanent transient" (*ZS,* p. 37), forever denied a home of his own. Jerry's sense of abandonment extends to heaven itself; he has tried to relate to God just as he has tried to deal with people, animals, a bed, a cockroach, a mirror, pornographic playing cards, and the "pretty little ladies" (*ZS,* p. 35). However, his search for the Divine is locked into the same pattern that controls all Jerry's efforts at contact. By his megalomaniac tendencies he identifies with Jesus, the son, and casts God in the role of the indifferent parent. Jerry is the anguished son drying on the cross of pain calling out, "My God, my God, why hast Thou forsaken me?" (Matt. 27-47).

The image of Jerry's abandonment is intensified by his position in the deep center of a honeycomb of outcasts. Mother gave up the ghost alone in an Alabama dump after which father solitarily drowned his despair in an alcoholic binge ended by a collision with a city bus. The rooming house is a cluster of castaways: "the colored queen," the Puerto Rican family, the unseen tenant in the front room, and the crying woman (*ZS,* p. 33). The landlady too is isolated with her gin, her unsatisfied desire, and her infected, misused dog. In Jerry's mind, the rooming house with miserable ones confined in every cubicle is like a zoo where animals are caged behind bars. The rooming house, the zoo, society itself—each is a prison where offenders are deprived of their natural habitats and sentenced to permanent exclusion. The inmates are too lost in their own needs to answer anyone else's call. Thus, their abandonment deepens.

In their entrapment these people suffer from a combination of separation anxiety and abandonment depression. The two states can be differentiated: separation anxiety is the fear of losing the loved one or his love, while abandonment depression is the despondent aftermath of realizing this loss. Characteristically, however, the anxiety and the depression intermingle, holding the individual psyche in their double grip and blending their manifestations into indistinguishability. Jerry, for example, in his search for acceptance continually expresses his anxiety to Peter: "You're not angry?" (*ZS,* p. 26) and "You're not thinking of going are you?" (*ZS,* p. 29). Finally, as he dies, Jerry admits the full measure of his concern: "Oh, Peter, I was so afraid I'd drive you away. You don't know how afraid I was you'd go away and leave me" (*ZS,* p. 48). This fear of being left alone has spurred Jerry's constant search for contact, his effort to find a way to deal with something—"If not with people . . . SOMETHING" (*ZS,* p. 34). But he has never been able to maintain a loving relationship. His empty picture frames are an effective symbol of the roots of his depressed and anxious state.

Catalyst to Jerry's anguish is hostility, his defense against loss of love. His hostility and his feelings of rejection create a spiraling action, one intensifying the other.[4] Thus, Jerry's yearning for contact is foredoomed to failure by the hostile behavior that comes in its wake. He invariably insults and offends those whose love and attention he seeks. His speech about "the teaching emotion" echoes this pattern of response:

> I have learned that neither kindness nor cruelty by themselves, independent of each other, creates any effect beyond themselves: and I have learned that the two combined, together, at the same time, are the teaching emotion. And what is gained is loss.
>
> (*ZS,* p. 36)

Jerry's words suggest an interrelationship between mother and child explained by Masterson and Rinsley. The insecure mother, threatened by her child's attempts at individuation, withdraws her emotional support and affection. Only when the child regresses to infantile behavior does she reward him again. "The twin themes (reward and withdrawal) of this interaction are subsequently introjected by the child," becoming "the leitmotif of his psychic structure. . . ."[5] In Jerry's parlance, reward equals kindness and withdrawal equals cruelty.

Clearly, Jerry learned this equation in childhood, and his conduct both with the dog and with Peter can be construed as a paradigm of his ambivalent relationship with his parents. In the story about the dog, Jerry explains that he was so offended by the dog's snarling attacks that he decided to "kill the dog with kindness." If that failed to win acceptance, Jerry would "just kill him [the dog]" (*ZS,* p. 31). For kindness, Jerry offered hamburgers. The dog gobbled them up and, after a momentary smile, attacked again. Jerry counterattacked by kneading rat poison into the hamburgers. When the dog became "deathly ill" (*ZS,* p. 30), Jerry discovered that he loved the dog and wanted to be loved by him. After the dog's recovery, however, every confrontation was a stand-off.

Jerry's behavior with Peter follows the same pattern. Jerry has become so offended by society's rejection that he decides, while at the zoo, to make a kind, friendly overture to whomever he meets on his walk: "I would tell you things . . . and the things I would tell you . . . Well, here we are. You see?" (*ZS*, p. 48). When Jerry speaks these words, he lies dying; and he is flooded with love—as he was when the dog lay dying. Consequently, Jerry leaves unspoken the hateful side of his zoo plan: if the person does not give Jerry understanding and acceptance, Jerry will kill himself. Jerry throws hamburgers at Peter in the form of conversational gambits designed to make contact, friendship. Peter responds reluctantly; he even listens. In other words, he smiles momentarily. Then Peter withdraws by refusing to understand, and Jerry's murderous impulse is aroused. He counterattacks. He shoves Peter off the bench and forces him to pick up the knife onto which Jerry runs. The act of violence completed, Jerry becomes loving again. He thanks Peter for his comfort and, protectively, hurries him off.

As models for Jerry's relationship with his parents, these incidents reveal the ambivalent alternation of love and anger, the recurring swing between the longing for closeness and the wish to kill. The repeated compromise is the retreat into feigned indifference where there is neither love nor hurt. Writing about early ego integration, Dr. Otto Kernberg describes a similar pattern as one of the "phases of the syndrome of maternal deprivation in infants":

> The stage of initial search behavior and rage after abandonment by mother may represent the activation of the "all bad" self- and object-image, the absence of the "good mother" being equivalent to the activation of the "bad mother." The later phase of resignation, indifference, and final disappearance of the capacity for attachment may reflect the eventual deterioration of the good self-object image and the subsequent weakening of attachment behavior.[6]

Kernberg explains that only the mother's tolerance of the infant's anger can strengthen his image of the good self and the good object and "decrease his fear of his own aggressive tendencies." Moreover, projection sometimes complicates this picture. The infant attributes his own rage to his mother and sets up "a vicious circle of misinterpreting mother's behavior" in terms of "paranoid distortions of her." Consequently, the bad self- and object-image is reinforced.[7]

Projecting this all bad mother-image is especially apparent in Jerry's description of the landlady as "a fat, ugly, mean, stupid, unwashed, misanthropic, cheap, drunken bag of garbage" (*ZS*, p. 27). By pushing Peter off the bench, Jerry forces his father-image to assume the murderous rage that so terrifies Jerry within himself. Even God is not immune from Jerry's defensive projections. Rose Zimbardo has pointed out that "the Story of Jerry and the Dog" is a Christian parable by which Jerry reveals "to Peter the nature of the human condition."[8] On a more personal level, Jerry describes his own private condition, his projection of inner hostility onto everyone, including God, who "turned his back on the whole thing some time ago" (*ZS*, p. 35). Jerry's anger is also evident in his devaluation of people into animals. Jerry, for example, relates Peter's wife and daughters to their cats and parakeets; he associates the alienated people of his world with animals in the zoo.

Jerry's complex relationships with people and the dog are dominated by these combined defenses—projection, dehumanization, and splitting (separating the good self and object from the bad self and object). The dog, for instance, represents part-images of both Jerry's mother and his father.[9] Thus, the dog and the landlady are split images of mother, and the dog and Peter are split images of the father. The dog is the withdrawing, hostile mother who attacks Jerry when he needs supplies or attention.[10] Significantly, the attacks come as Jerry tries to reenter the rooming house after having left autonomously. The landlady is the immature mother who, out of her own need, rewards her child's clinging, regressive behavior. The landlady "presses her disgusting body up against" Jerry, making him "the object of her sweaty lust" (*ZS*, p. 28). Jerry perceives the landlady and the dog as one when he refers to them as "the gatekeepers of my dwelling" (*ZS*, pp. 27-28). On the other hand, the dog is the attacking father whose identity is fused with the image of bad mother. Father attacks when too many demands are made upon him; and Jerry exhibits the megalomaniac, demanding behavior typical of rejected children. Peter is the mildly friendly father—passive and unwilling to acknowledge Jerry's needs, too indifferent to supply the closeness Jerry longs for. The story of Jerry and the dog, therefore, is an externalization of parts of both Jerry's parental relationships. The story of Jerry and the landlady and the action between Jerry and Peter represent the other halves of these relationships.

Similarly, splitting and fusion underlie Jerry's messianic view of himself and his association of God with the other roomers. Part of the time, Jerry idealizes himself as the caring, searching, mistreated one. When he asks, "*was* trying to feed the dog an act of love?" (*ZS*, p. 36), the implied answer is—yes. On the other side of the coin, Jerry's narcissism allows him to be demanding, manipulative, and self-righteous.[11] He fuses God with the fellow roomers who are abandoned by the world and withdrawn from it into self-absorption. God is "A COLORED QUEEN WHO WEARS A KIMONO AND PLUCKS HIS EYEBROWS"; he is "A WOMAN WHO CRIES WITH DETERMINATION BEHIND HER CLOSED DOOR" (*ZS*, p. 35). Capital letters blare out this message, which transforms God into a pitiful freak and a self-pitying outcast—neither of whom shows any interest in Jerry or the world.

When efforts to devalue, control, and exploit have failed, Jerry exhibits a pronounced propensity for escape from reality into illusion. The most significant case is the occurrence at the zoo. Jerry is consistently vague about what happened at the zoo—ostensibly as a suspense-building technique to maintain Peter's interest. He uses the broad pronoun *it* as he declares that Peter will read about *it* in the papers or see *it* on television. Early in his encounter with Peter, he speaks as if he had consciously planned a course of action at the zoo, but he seems confused about the reality of his plan: ". . . could I have planned all this? No . . . no, I couldn't have. But I think I did" (*ZS,* p. 48). Jerry's confusion is over the difference between fantasy and reality. He inadvertently discloses his frequent fantasizing in discussing the pornographic playing cards with Peter; he says when a person gets older he uses "real experience as a substitute for . . . fantasy" (*ZS,* p. 27). Evidently, while at the zoo Jerry indulged his favorite pastime: he wove a fantasy. When events spontaneously unfold exactly as he imagined them, he is surprised. Undoubtedly, Jerry has spun this same fantasy many times, but never before has it become real experience. In their psychological study of suicide, Schneidman, Faberow, and Litman explain the origin of self-destructive acts in fantasy:

> Suicide acts, as a general rule, are not sudden, unpredictable, impulsive, momentary, or random acts. In most cases, the suicide plan has been developed gradually and rehearsed in fantasy and preliminary action. In nearly every case of suicide there is evidence of crisis, conflict, ambivalence, mixed motivations, and multiple determinants.[12]

The same authors add that the most serious suicide cases "seem to be living out a memory-fantasy of being abandoned and left to die."[13]

This then is what happened at the zoo: Jerry rehearsed once more his plan to kill himself if he could not gain the acceptance he so badly needed. What better way to show his symbolic parents the effect of their behavior. By his suicide he could punish them for abandoning him; they would be sorry when they saw his dying face on television. In fantasy Jerry has gone "a long distance out of the way in order to come back a short distance correctly" (*ZS,* p. 30). Jerry has finally substituted real experience for this long-rehearsed fantasy, but he has confused his revenge-victim. He has laid the guilt on a mere image of his father, a random acquaintance—Peter. Finally, Jerry brings his fantasy to full fruition by urging Peter to flee, thereby enabling himself to die abandoned and alone.

Such self-destructiveness is only one of the manifestations of Jerry's continuing preoccupation with death. Another is his empty picture frames, which keep alive his awareness of the demise of his parents. Peter's pipe-smoking suggests a fatal illness—lung cancer (*ZS,* p. 13). Even Peter's daughters' birds prompt a macabre response in Jerry; he thinks it a shame they are not diseased so "the cats could eat them and die" (*ZS,* p. 18). He openly confesses his murderous plan for the landlady's dog.

Hanging over all these smaller concerns with death is the suicide plan. Like a black storm cloud, it envelops the atmosphere of the play, making it close and threatening. Jerry keeps his plan alive by his constant references to the zoo and the face Peter will see. In hindsight, these references appear to outgrow mere suspensefulness and become ominous. As Jerry smiles and relaxes into his final speech and Peter stands stunned and transfixed, the answer to what happened at the zoo crashes into clarity—Jerry planned to kill himself. The purpose of his entire plan of action was death, the alternative to a loveless life.

By the development of these four basic themes—abandonment, ambivalence, escape into fantasy, preoccupation with death—The Zoo Story presents Albee's vision of suffering humanity crying for help. The problem is capsuled in the title image; the world is a zoo, not a forest. Locked out of their compatibility with nature and community, men become imprisoned within hostile selves. They feel isolated, alienated, and alone. Their despair centers on anger, and they must separate themselves from one another to prevent their mutual destruction by hate and violence. Therefore, their sense of abandonment deepens until the only answer to the call for help seems to lie in self-destruction.

In The Death of Bessie Smith the locale shifts from New York to Memphis, Tennessee, where oneness is missing in the whole racial structure. The bigoted White nurse and the "Uncle Tom" Black intern make explicit the play's social protest; however, white and black are also color representations of the "all good" and "all bad" dichotomy peculiar to the sufferer from separation anxiety. This disunity is also inherent in the play's divided form; its one act is broken into eight scenes. Color and fragmentation are further emphasized in the setting. The Death of Bessie Smith is played in fragmentary scenery against a sky drop that changes color to fit the events on stage. The play, moreover, entwines two separate groups of characters—Jack and Bessie versus Nurse, Intern, and Orderly.

The sociological conflict in this play matches that of The Zoo Story. The first play pits the established upper class against the rooming house outcasts; this one opposes the White establishment with the Black outcasts. On the individual level, however, the plays have reverse patterns. The weak father-figure is in the foreground of The Zoo Story whereas the hostile mother-figure, Nurse, takes the forefront in The Death of Bessie Smith. Jerry, the chief figure of abandonment, dominates the stage in The Zoo Story, while Bessie remains an unseen character in The Death of Bessie Smith. Even the scenic images are reversed. The Zoo Story is played outdoors in the park where Jerry meets his death. The entry hall of the rooming house where Jerry met rejection is merely part of the exposition. The Death of Bessie Smith is played indoors at the admissions desk where Bessie is rejected, while her outdoor death is made known through an announcement by Intern.

Both plays feature the abandonment theme, but The Zoo Story centers on the outcasts, Jerry and his counterparts in the rooming house. The Death of Bessie Smith shows that separation anxiety and abandonment depression are experienced by the establishment as well. A sense of entrapment in loneliness and frustration pervades the whole drama and is communicated by the background music that swells and fades with the rhythm of the play. The very essence of the

"Blues" is musical melancholy, and Bessie Smith's popularity was born of this plaintive call to inner sadness. As her voice sings out its forlorn message, her physical absence is transformed into omnipresence; and her mournful spirit hovers over the play. This omnipresence is intensified at the outset by the "hot blue" sky that silhouettes the darkened set,[14] symbolizing the repressive gloom that envelops the play.

The opening scene introduces the homelessness of Jack, who is "travelin'" to that "big Place"—"North" (*TP*, p. 27). He is traveling with Bessie, in a last-ditch effort to revive her career. But Bessie is paralyzed by abandonment depression. She has faded from sight in the last four or five years, victim of her own efforts to escape the world in drink. At Nurse's house, the Father growls his anger at being left alone. He refuses to cooperate in his own abandonment by driving Nurse to work, but he defends against everyday loss by ordering Nurse to "Go on! Go!" (*TP*, p. 36). At the hospital, the Orderly has "Uncle Tom'd . . . [himself] right out of the bosom of . . . [his] family." He lives in"no-man's land," shunned by his peers and derided by his betters (*TP*, p. 47). Intern lives in dissatisfaction, tormented by the "sense of urgency" and "dislike of waste" that ulcerates his own stagnation. His voice is quiet and intense as he speaks his anguish at being separated from his perception of a more satisfying life: "I am *stranded* . . . here . . ." (*TP*, p. 59). Nurse speaks for both herself and her waning culture as she questions Orderly's awareness of the "way things are":

> Haven't you been appraised of the way things *are?* . . . Our knights are gone forth into sunsets . . . behind the wheels of Cord cars . . . the acres have diminished and the paint is flaking . . . that there is a great . . . abandonment?
>
> (*TP*, p. 70)

She feels imprisoned in the world's sickness, and she longs to be out of it; but she fights her need for others by ordering them about.

The end of the play is a montage of abandoned figures. Jack in his shock is abandoned by the entire staff, who offer him neither understanding nor comfort. Intern is not only frustrated by his inability to be helpful to an already dead Bessie Smith, but he is totally vulnerable to Nurse's hysterical dictum: "You are finished. You have had your last patient here . . . Off you go, boy!" (*TP*, p. 80). He returns the rejection by a slap across her face and backs away. Orderly, as the nervous witness, verbally abandons his Black race by echoing the indignation of White segregationism: "I never heard of such a thing . . . bringing a dead woman here like that . . ." (*ibid.*). Behind his words, the music swells; and Bessie's doleful "Blues" prompt the mental image of her abandoned body, bleeding its life away "like water from a faucet" (*TP*, p. 76).

Inseparably intertwined with this abandonment is the ambivalence, manifested by searingly discordant relationships. Nurse battles with Father, who exhibits resentment at her leaving him each day; yet he also reveals a wish to cling to her as he pouts about her patients getting more attention than he (*TP*, p. 35). All of Nurse's relationships—with Father, with Orderly, and with Intern—are characterized by devaluation and manipulative efforts. She calls Orderly a "genuine little asslicker" (*TP*, p. 46) and sends him out for her cigarettes. She spurns Intern's proposal of marriage, insisting that Orderly can better afford "realistically, economically" to marry her (*TP*, p. 56). She and Intern attack and counterattack with ferocity born of an extreme sensitivity to criticism that undercuts their false self-images.[15] Intern calls her a "cloistered maiden" with a "collection of anatomical jokes for all occasions" (*TP*, p. 53). She responds by calling him a "lance-high, love-smit knight" whose real interest is "a convenient and uncomplicated bedding down" (*TP*, p. 55). Thus, they project a sexual promiscuity and coarseness which is the substitute for their inability to experience tender feelings for one another.

The splitting and projection of these characters is highlighted by the color imagery—black opposed to white. The traditional associations, however, are reversed. The Whites are the bad characters. For example, a nurse is usually an angel of mercy robed in the purity of a white uniform; but Nurse is the archetypal black witch—hostile, vengeful, and aggressive. The great white doctor, as Nurse characterizes Intern, is not only impotent to save lives, he is destructive in his love relationship with Nurse. Even his supposed liberalism is exposed as false. Orderly is included among the bad people by another color reversal; he is a "white nigger." The Whites are bad chiefly because they reject the good Blacks, and the Blacks are good primarily because they are rejected. Secondarily, they are good because their destructiveness is turned inward: they harm themselves, unpremeditatedly, whereas the Whites harm others willfully.

Within this split of the bad Whites versus the good Blacks, identity diffusion is a complex construct of shifting antagonists and counterparts. Jack and Bessie, for instance, are counterparts to Nurse and Father, for within both pairs there is a parent-child relationship. Nurse and Father interchange these roles; he is the biological father, but she is the breadwinner. They alternately punish one another by withdrawing love and support. Jack, however, is a consistent parent-figure and caretaker to Bessie. He takes all the responsibility: he makes the plans, calls the "son-of-a-bitch in New York" (*TP*, p. 37), and gets Bessie moving. He is protective and even affectionate; he calls her "Honey" and "Baby." And indeed, she is his baby. She spends the day asleep in bed; she leaves the entire conduct of her affairs to Jack. He is truly "cartin' her around."

On the other hand, Nurse and Bessie are counterparts, bad and good mother-figures. Nurse is the hostile present one, and Bessie is the benign absent one. In this sense, Bessie bears a resemblance to Jerry's mother in The Zoo Story, who died of alcoholism in the South. Nurse, with her unsatisfied lust and guardianship of the building, is reminiscent of Jerry's landlady. Within The Death of Bessie Smith, many clues link Nurse and Bessie as opposite sides of one coin. Nurse fills her house, her ears, and her spirit with the sound of Bessie's music. Bessie's career has dwindled to little more than a famous name, like Nurse's cultural heritage. As Bessie is tended by Jack, Nurse is tended by Orderly, who fetches her cigarettes, and Intern, who brings coffee and chauffeurs her home. Nurse even insists to Intern that she sings—as Bessie does: "I sing, too, boy . . . I sing real good" (*TP,* p. 80). Bessie bleeds to death when her arm is wrenched off as a result of Jack's careless drunken driving. Intern envisions a similar death for Nurse: the stiletto she uses for a letter-opener slips and tears open her arm; then Intern holds it while the blood flows like water running from a faucet (*TP,* p. 67).

Intern, Orderly, and Jack are the split father-figures. Intern is the lustful aspect, Orderly the subservient aspect, and Jack the protective aspect; but all are ineffectual. The Father and the Mayor, in this system, are necessarily grandfather-figures—authoritative and self-centeredly unconcerned. This construct of male figures blends a collection of antithetical qualities—authority and servitude, sexuality and impotence, protectiveness and unconcern—all fluctuating to match the changing emotions of the aggressive-regressive female constructs. The pattern of ambivalence is appropriate to the alternating independence and regression of the child caught in the throes of anxiety over separation and loss. It is also the wellspring of the family discord that recurs in Albee's plays.

The unhappy people in The Death of Bessie Smith indulge in a variety of fantasies and escape mechanisms to deny their sordid realities. Bessie has chosen alcohol, which allows her to drink away her nights and sleep away her days. Jack too escapes in drink, but he still dreams of wealth and fame as Bessie's entrepreneur. Unfortunately, the "bird" Jack carts around is too "soused" to fly. In fact, all the characters in this play express their fantasies in terms of "moving" imagery. Jack and Bessie are "drivin' north" to New York (*TP,* p. 38). Orderly does not intend to stay in Memphis "carrying crap pans"; he sees himself "going beyond that" (*TP,* p. 42). Nurse says he bleaches his hands, face, and neck every night so that he can step across the color line. Intern fancies himself in Spain. He is intense as he tells Nurse his desire: "If I could bandage the arm of one person . . . if I could be over there right this minute" (*TP,* p. 59). Nurse has some vague nostalgia for the lost grandeur of the Southern past, where a white knight would have courted her. She bitterly demands fulfillment of this doomed dream from Intern: "You will be my gallant . . . You will court me, boy, and you will do it *right!*" (*TP,* p. 63). She escapes from the disappointment of this lost illusion by wishing to be gone from the hospital. Her uniform "scratches"; she is tired of her skin; "I WANT OUT!" she cries (*TP,* p. 71). The Father's fantasy of moving covers less distance; nevertheless, it elevates him to a sense of importance. He goes down to the Democratic Club, where he smokes expensive cigars, talks big, and pretends to be close friends with the mayor. All these illusions of movement and action are as ironic as Jack's bird image, for all these dreamers are steeped in apathy, trapped in feelings of helplessness and hopelessness.

The individual apathy blends with the sick society in a dying world. In fact, death imagery dominates the play. As the rooming house and the zoo represented The Zoo Story's imprisoning world, the hospital represents The Death of Bessie Smith's decaying world. The mayor himself is in the hospital "flat on his belly" (*TP,* p. 40). Father has headaches and takes pills, and Nurse calls him "a poor cripple" (*TP,* p. 33). Orderly's inner sickness is symbolized by his bleaching out. Intern's sexual desire is wasting into sterility. His proposals of marriage make Nurse sick. She is, moreover, "sick of everything in this hot, stupid, fly-ridden world" (*TP,* p. 70). Jack's sickness has been alcoholism, and forevermore it will be guilt—for Bessie's death.

This imagery of sickness and death intertwines with the color imagery. As the ambivalence theme opposes the colors white and black, the death imagery moves from pale sickness in white hospital rooms, to fiery images of lynchings and mutilation, and to the darkness of the grave. The day itself is dying; the "great sunset blazes" (*TP,* p. 80) at the end of the play. The racist culture is scorched; "the pillars of the houses are blistered and flaking" (*TP,* p. 57). Intern perceives the whole world burning in the setting sun:

> The west is burning . . . fire has enveloped fully half of the continent . . . the . . . fingers of the flame stretch upward to the stars . . . and there is a monstrous burning circumference hanging on the edge of the world.
>
> (*TP,* p. 51)

Over "half a million people" have been killed by gunfire in Spain (*TP,* p. 59). Love itself, the source of all life, is being consumed in its own flames: Intern's "body burns" as his "heart yearns" (*TP,* p. 52). Nurse, "chained to . . . [her] desk of pain," perceives him as a "monstrous burning intern hanging on the edge of . . . [her] circumference" (*TP,* p. 51).

Burnings blend into images of lynchings as Intern drolly reminds Nurse that it is permissible to burn orderlies at will (*TP,* p. 57). When his jokes have turned to insults and her laughter to fury, she advises him to keep her threats "burning in the back of . . . [his] brain" because—she says with wild laughter—his "neck is in the noose" (*TP,* p. 63). Earlier she has envisioned Father with a shotgun across his lap waiting to shoot birds. Nurse conceals her racist fear in ridicule of Orderly as she speaks of "the great black mob marching down the street' with Orderly's "bleached-out, snowy-white face in the middle of the pack" (*TP,* p. 46). She laughingly completes the image moments later with, "You white niggers kill me" (*TP,* p. 47).

The hospital includes a cluster of mutilation images. The mayor has "his ass in a sling" as a result of surgery for his hemorrhoids. A man two rooms down walked into the hospital "with his hands over his gut to keep his insides from spilling out" (*TP,* p. 40). Castration images have been perversely projected onto the emasculating females. Intern conjures up the picture of Nurse tearing open her arm (a phallic symbol) with the stiletto-like letter-opener, and Jack describes the matching image of Bessie's right arm torn off at the shoulder.

Finally, death imagery is the focal point of the play's title, The Death of Bessie Smith. Bessie was already dead when Jack brought her to Nurse's all-white hospital. Nurse and Orderly reject and abandon her corpse, but they do not kill her. Intern even attempts to save her. The accident that killed her was the result of carelessness—Bessie's and Jack's. They had both been drinking. Jack had no idea of his driving speed. He and Bessie had been "riding along . . . laughing" and Bessie had heedlessly allowed her arm to hang out the window (*TP,* p. 76). Bessie's bloody, violent death was caused basically by her alcoholism—a sickness often called slow suicide. Bessie was not only dead before arrival at the hospital, she was dead before the accident. She had killed her career and her spirit several years earlier by drinking instead of meeting her commitments. It was a dead weight Jack was carting to New York. Bessie's spirit had been stifled and started on its suicidal course by the oppressive racist culture that spawned her. She was the unfortunate infant of a disturbed community who rewarded her for her dependent, servile behavior and punished her for all attempts at self-assertion and individuation. Bessie was smothered into self-destructiveness by a sick society.

The Death of Bessie Smith presents a society founded on hostility, epitomized in the murderous mind of Nurse. The play shows that hostility within ripples out into larger and larger spheres, souring and tainting everything in its wake. Nurse's anger encompasses everyone around her—White and Black. She is contemptuous of her co-workers, the patients, her parents, the town authorities, even the national leaders. And, ironically, she is the unhappiest one of all. But Albee's vision is not one-sided; he shows the source of Nurse's hostility in the selfish, demanding spirit of her intended nurturers, the absence and unavailability of her intended protectors. Anger is portrayed as the result of a reciprocal withdrawal from fear of the loss of love. The only alternative to aggression against others is the path Bessie took, self-destruction.

Thus, The Death of Bessie Smith is a group picture of lovelessness and self-concern. The final moments of the play reveal the malaise to be hopeless because no one even suspects his own blame, and no one breaks out of himself. Orderly draws over himself the self-protective cloak of "Uncle Tomism" and abandons his suffering Black brother, Jack. Intern steeps himself in self-pity and indignation that his pseudo-heroic effort to save Bessie, motivated primarily by spite for Nurse, was spoiled by Bessie's premature demise. Nurse's fury has recoiled into frozen wrath. Only Jack has any sense of his own guilt. But stunned and comfortless, he is already reaching for the balm of rationalization. And Bessie is past all self-revelation. Bessie is dead!

The Sandbox concerns itself with Grandma's abandonment in death. Unlike Jerry and Bessie, however, Grandma does not die violently. Her death is slow and, at the end, peaceful. Albee wrote this play in memory of his grandmother, who died in 1959 at the age of eighty-three, and in it he blends the rejection of the young and of the old by placing Grandma in a sandbox to die. The setting communicates the centrality of the title symbol; the sandbox, an elevated, raked enclosure, occupies center stage. Only two chairs, side by side, share the remaining space. The circumstances of Grandma's death emphasize the play's comment on society's neglect of both children and the aged. Thus, The Sandbox adds new texture to the trio of plays on abandonment. The Zoo Story deals with class opposition, The Death of Bessie Smith with racial opposition, and The Sandbox deals with opposition between the generations. Appropriately, the three plays move inward from a community of strangers in a New York rooming house and park, to a smaller company of co-workers in a Memphis hospital, to the basic family unit. The characters no longer represent parent-figures; they are aggressive Mommy and passive Daddy, sharing the focus with Grandma, the aged, abandoned child. The Young Man is a lifeguard watching over Grandma from behind her sandbox. In this play, the sandbox is the entrance hall of life, the hospital dying room, and the grave. It is located on a sandy beach near the sea, whose waters symbolize both birth and death. The focus on the life cycle is intensified by the sky drop behind "which alters from brightest day to deepest night" (*TP,* p. 9). As the action of the play proceeds, the symbolism deepens. Mommy and Daddy, seated opposite the sandbox, perform two rituals simultaneously: baby-sitting and death-watching.

The theme of abandonment begins graphically as Grandma is carried in by the armpits, drawn up rigid, and dumped unceremoniously into the sandbox. The look of "puzzlement and fear" (*TP,* p. 11) on her face expresses her anxiety; her sounds of protest, "Ahhhhhh! Graaaaa!" *(ibid.)* emphasize her dual role of infant and old woman. As The Zoo Story's central conflict is between Jerry's desire for understanding and Peter's desire for freedom from intrusion, The Sandbox pits Grandma's need for the final comfort of the dying against Mommy's wish to be free of the inconvenience. Mommy's commands—to Grandma, "Be quiet," and to Daddy, "Don't look at her" (*TP,* p. 13)—express the wish for riddance. Like Jerry, Grandma tells the story of her life of rejection. She begins with the here-and-now of her eighty-six years: "Honestly! What a way to treat an old woman! Drag her out of the house . . . stick her in a car . . . bring her out here from the city . . . dump her in a pile of sand . . . and leave her here to set" *(ibid.)*. Then, she flashes back to her widowhood at thirty, when she was left to raise Mommy "all by . . . [her] lonesome" (*TP,* p. 14). After Mommy married rich Daddy, they moved Grandma out of her natural habitat, the farm, into their big town house where they treated her like a dog: they "fixed a nice place for me under the stove . . . gave me an army blanket . . . and my own dish . . ." (*TP,* p. 15-16). Mommy verifies Grandma's story of rejection by her actions. As the lights dim to indicate night, Mommy "Shhh's" Daddy in a wordless demonstration of the pattern of neglect perpetrated on infants and aging parents, put out to play in the daytime, put to bed at night—in both cases, out of the way.

Ultimately, Grandma plays dead so that Mommy and Daddy are free to complete her abandonment. They grasp the opportunity to depart, feigning mourning and leaving Grandma to the final ministrations of the hired help—the Young Man. He and Grandma are counterparts in this portrait of abandonment. She, representing infancy and old age, is excluded from the inner circle of the family. He, representing adult youth, is excluded from the inner circle of his chosen profession—acting in the movies. The studios have not even given him a name, and he is forced to earn his living by hiring out as a lifeguard. Nevertheless, the unclaimed youth and the deserted matriarch share a desolate moment of tenderness in the final moments of Grandma's abandonment.

The sweet smiles of Grandma and the Young Man and their expressions of endearment at the end of the play are the only manifestations of love in The Sandbox. All else is the other side of ambivalence. Even the names Mommy and Daddy are, by Albee's directions, significant of the "empty affection" and "vacuity" of the characters (*TP,* p. 8). Mommy depersonalizes Daddy by dismissing his complaints and mocking his lack of authority with rhetorical queries like, "What do you think, Daddy?" (*TP,* p. 9). His docile obedience to her every command is the symptom of his repressed anger. Mommy accentuates her contempt for Daddy by her flirtatious behavior toward the Young Man. Daddy's question, "Shall we talk to each other?" reveals their alienation; and Mommy's response, ". . . if you can think of anything to *say,*" measures its depth.

Both Mommy and Daddy show total disregard for Grandma. Daddy's concern is only for himself as he whines about the heat and the cold. He dismisses all responsibility for Grandma with the reminder that she is Mommy's mother, not his (*TP,* p. 10). Mommy's only words to her dying mother are reprimands. Only when she thinks death has finally taken Grandma does she express a pretense of grief calculated to gain solicitude for herself: "—poor Grandma . . . I can't bear it!" (*TP,* p. 17). However, she quickly finds solace in her pride at having done things well, by which she means having spent enough money to bury Grandma in style.

Grandma's behavior, presented as it is in terms of the baby in the sandbox, is similar to the acute distress of the abandoned child.[16] Grandma bangs her toy shovel against her pail and yells, "Haaaaaa! Ah-haaaaaa!" (*TP,* p. 12). When Mommy does not respond with loving attention, Grandma throws a shovelful of sand at her and screams at Daddy (*TP,* p. 13). Also like an abandoned child, who ultimately gives up angry response for sociability with his nurses,[17] Grandma turns her attention away from Mommy to the audience and the Young Man. She addresses them both with smiles and acceptance. And, significantly, she willingly acquiesces to death, shoveling furiously to bury herself, then assuming the corpse-like pose of folded hands over her prostrate body. Grandma's behavior could be alternately described as split into the good self and the bad self. The bad self she offers to Mommy and Daddy; the good self she gives to the Young Man. He, in turn, as her counterpart in abandonment, represents the emptiness and self-worthlessness that comes with rejection. He perceives himself as "the kiss of death." Grandma, however, perceives his other aspect, his ideal self; and she accepts his kiss as an act of affection. She returns it and ignites a brief spark of divine love.

Thus, Grandma departs willingly from the two-faced environment on the beach, a world dominated by Mommy's and Daddy's counterfeit love and grief. This hypocrisy is the keynote of the confusion of reality and fantasy in The Sandbox, and Albee emphasizes it by use of the play/life metaphor. The audience is made aware that Mommy and Daddy are staging a performance by the presence of the Musician and by the characters' references to themselves as actors and role players. The metaphor also brings out in relief two prominent traits of people with histories of mental deprivation. Kernberg describes these as "a great need to be loved and admired by others" (true of actors) and "an emotional life" that is "shallow"[18] (true of role players).

The entire action of the play is cast in the form of a stage illusion. Mommy signals its start by the words, "Let's get on with it" (*TP,* p. 10) while summoning the Musician onto the stage. He places his music on his stand; she orders him to begin; he nods to the Young Man; and then Mommy and Daddy go through all the ritual motions of providing playtime for baby and funeral time for Grandma. Everything occurs on cue. When the lights dim, Grandma asks for "nice and soft" music for "this part" (*TP,* p. 16). At the sound of an "off-stage rumble," Mommy begins to weep, for that is the cue that Grandma's time has come (*TP,* p. 17). Grandma starts burying herself in an obliging effort to die at the moment designated in Mommy's scenario. When she does not quite succeed, she calls out to the electrician: "Don't put the lights up yet . . . I'm not ready" (*TP,* p. 18). But the lights rise anyhow—on cue, and Mommy recites to Daddy that their long night of suffering is over and they must now "face the future" (*ibid.*). Grandma plays dead, giving them their next cue. The Young Man steps in and insists on playing his part: "I . . . I have a line here," he says (*TP,* p. 19). Then he delivers his speech: "I am the Angel of Death. I am . . . uh . . . I am come for you" (*TP,* p. 20). After his kiss, she compliments his performance. The curtains close on the final tableau, and Mommy's show is over. The entire family has performed dual roles. Unloving Mommy and Daddy have also portrayed the falsely bereaved daughter and son-in-law. Grandma has been ignored both as infant and as aged parent. The Young Man has played several roles—would-be actor, lifeguard, and the Angel of Death who flaps his wings, claims a life, and metamorphoses the sandbox into a coffin.

As the Angel of Death, the Young Man also concretizes the theme of preoccupation with death. Hovering over the sandbox, he recalls the Beckettian image of man born astride a grave. Within the setting of Albee's play both the sea and the box blend birth and death, and the sand suggests the aridity and the sterility that infects the characters. Only Grandma shows any genuine feeling, but at the outset even she has lost the suppleness of a body warmed by love. She is already "quite rigid" (*TP,* p. 11) as they carry her in. Mommy and Daddy emit an inner deadness which they can only try to conceal by pretended emotions. Daddy's passivity reflects his loss of the power to think and act. He can only ask "What do we do now?" (*TP,* p. 13). Mommy's answer to Daddy is her deadly refrain: "We wait. We . . . sit . . . and we wait . . . that's what we do" (*TP,* p. 12). Again the image is Beckettian; but Albee's "Godot" is on stage, flapping his wings and waiting for the cue to assume his role.

The Young Man, seeking an identity to fill his empty self, easily accommodates the role of Angel of Death because of his self-loathing, born of the absence of love. He is the manifestation of the inner deadness that Mommy and Daddy breed; he is their symbolic child. Finally, Grandma exhibits the will to self-destruction by her cooperation with death. She lets the Young Man ease her into eternity with his gentleness. It is a poignant moment of union and rebirth, for she gives the Young Man a taste of affectionate approval that nudges his buried soul: "Oh . . ." he says "blushing." In death Grandma stirs the blood of life within the Young Man.

The final effect justifies Albee's satisfaction with this play: "I'm terribly fond of The Sandbox. I think it's an absolutely beautiful, lovely, perfect play."[19] Indeed, it does make its statement with poetic simplicity. Its unfolding events oppose an extravagance of fakery with a speck of authenticity, an excess of hostility with a crumb of benevolence, a lifetime of rejection with a moment of love; and the power of the diminutive transmutes emptiness and anguish into peace.

Thus, the triptych is complete. Each of the three panels pictures abandonment, each with the same secondary themes springing out of the same sociological and psychoanalytic roots. Yet, on the surface each panel is a different painting—different central figure, different setting, different colors, different imagery, different symbols. Likewise, each play ends with the death of the abandoned one; but in each case the tone is unique. Jerry dies alone, calling out to God in scornful supplication. Bessie bleeds to death, unattended but silent and unconscious. Grandma accepts death knowingly and peacefully during an exchange of affection that whispers of rebirth.

Notes

[1]James F. Masterson and Donald B. Rinsley, "The Borderline Syndrome: The Role of the Mother in the Genesis and Psychic Structure of the Borderline Personality," *International Journal of Psychoanalysis,* 36 (1975), 171. This article, like most of those cited in this paper, was written about the Borderline Syndrome, a malaise rooted in maternal deprivation and featuring separation anxiety and abandonment depression. Since the meaning and relevance of the terms separation anxiety and abandonment depression seem more self-evident, they have been used throughout this study in place of Borderline Syndrome. The choice of terms also includes the implication that people can suffer from these neuroses without necessarily being classified as clinical cases.

[2]Actually these four related themes are basic to all of Albee's original plays, but individual ones shift their emphasis from one theme to another. Thus, these first three plays create a special grouping by their primary focus on the abandonment theme.

[3]Edward Albee, *The American Dream and The Zoo Story* (New York: New American Library, 1961), p. 35. Subsequent references to *The Zoo Story* will be to this edition and will be cited parenthetically in the text as *ZS.*

[4]See John Bowlby, "Separation Anxiety," *International Journal of Psychoanalysis,* 61 (1960), 20. Bowlby describes the increase of both anxiety and hostility as they interact within the infant.

[5]Masterson and Rinsley, "The Borderline Syndrome," p. 165.

[6]Otto Kernberg, "Early Ego Integration and Object Relations," *Annals of New York Academy of Science,* 193 (1972), 240-41.

[7]*Ibid.,* p. 241.

[8]Rose A. Zimbardo, "Symbolism and Naturalism in Edward Albee's *The Zoo Story,*" in *Edward Albee: A Collection of Critical Essays,* ed. C. W. E. Bigsby (Englewood Cliffs, N.J.: Prentice-Hall, 1975), p. 51.

[9]See Otto Kernberg, "Borderline Personality Organization," *Journal of American Psychoanalytic Association,* 15 (1967), 679. Kernberg describes this kind of fusion: "Hatred of mother extends to hatred of both parents who are later experienced as a 'united group' by the child. . . ."

[10]Doctors Norman Litowitz and Kenneth M. Newman also describe various levels of identification among Jerry, the dog, the landlady, and Peter in "Borderline Personality and the Theatre of the Absurd," *Archives of General Psychiatry,* 16 (Mar. 1967), 279.

[11]See Kernberg, "Borderline Personality Organization," p. 676. Kernberg states that identification with primitive "all good" self- and object-images is accompanied by "deep feelings of having the right to exploit and to be gratified."

[12]Edwin S. Schneidman, Norman L. Faberow, and Robert E. Litman, *The Psychology of Suicide* (New York: Science House, 1970), p. 297.

[13]*Ibid.,* p. 300.

[14]Edward Albee, *Two Plays: The Sandbox and The Death of Bessie Smith* (New York: New American Library, 1960), p. 17. Subsequent references to these two plays will be to this edition and will be cited parenthetically in the text as *TP.*

[15]See Peter Hartocollis, "Affects in Borderline Disorders," in *Borderline Personality Disorders,* ed. Peter Hartocollis (New York: International Universities Press, 1977), p. 504. Hartocollis mentions such sensitivity as typical of Borderline Personalities.

[16]Bowlby, "Separation Anxiety," p. 2.

[17]*Ibid.*

[18]Kernberg, "Borderline Personality Organization," p. 655.

[19]William Flanagan, "Edward Albee" (an interview), in *Writers at Work,* 3rd series (New York: Viking Press, 1967), p. 346.

Mary Susan Yates (essay date 1984)

SOURCE: "Changing Perspectives: The Vanishing 'Character' in Albee's Plays," in *CLA Journal,* Vol. XXVIII, No. 2, 1984, pp. 210-29.

[In the following essay, Yates charges that over the course of Albee's career his characters have grown increasingly abstract, eventually becoming "mere vehicles for the expression of. . . ideas."]

As an American dramatist, Edward Albee moves from the philosophical position that reform can be affected by creating an awareness of social problems to the conclusion that man's condition is irremediable. In between these two stages of his career, Albee concentrates on psychological problems which result from restrictive social situations. As Albee moves closer philosophically to the absurdists, form follows content and the characters in his plays undergo a gradual process of dehumanization.

From the early plays to the middle plays, Albee shifts his emphasis from the idea that society is a force for good or evil to the idea that individuals are psychologically motivated by this force. To portray these ideas, realistic characters present social problems through discussions and arguments. Other, more emotionally complex, characters reveal their personal conflicts through monologues and stories. The social-problem plays include The Zoo Story (1959), The American Dream (1959-60), and The Sandbox (1959), while Who's Afraid of Virginia Woolf? (1962) and A Delicate Balance (1966) are more concerned with psychological problems.

Later Albee's perspective changes drastically and the situation itself assumes control of the action; the character is portrayed as victim. As a personality, the character literally vanishes from the stage because in these more recent plays, Albee has either characters who do not speak at all or a disembodied voice which replaces the characters. In effect his works lose their dramatic quality. Plays from this category include Box and Quotations from Mao Tse-Tung (1968) and Counting the Ways and Listening: Two Plays (1977).

Characters in Albee's Social-Problem Plays

Albee's first play, The Zoo Story,[1] is an almost totally realistic play written in the spirit of an Ibsen social drama. Like Ibsen, Albee views society as a force in building relationships, and gaining control of this force becomes the focus of Jerry's efforts throughout the play. Although Albee simplifies the problem of class structures by having only two characters in Zoo Story, Jerry's question about "the dividing line between upper-middle-middle class and lower-upper-middle class" (p. 23) indicates an awareness on Albee's part of the issue's complexity. For Albee, like Ibsen, the solution lies in revolutionizing a society which fosters empty alliances and which sets up obstacles to meaningful relationships.

Albee stresses the disparity between Jerry's and Peter's economic situations by having Jerry describe himself as a "permanent transient" (p. 45) whose home is in a "sickening rooming house on the West Side of New York City" (p. 45) while Peter is identified as a publishing executive who lives in an apartment in the East Seventies. Furthermore, their dialogue reveals that Peter is a "happily" married man with two daughters, two cats, and two parakeets. In contrast, Jerry has no family ties, nor does he have a girl friend. He tells Peter, "I've never been able to have sex with, or, how is it put . . . make love to anybody more than once" (p. 30).

However, as Jerry points out, Peter's relationship with his wife and family is no more emotionally satisfying than Jerry's contact with prostitutes. Like Ibsen, Albee develops the characters of Jerry and Peter by emphasizing the importance of the past in their present situation. Also like Ibsen, Albee stresses that the barriers which divide all classes are artificial.

The problem of class leads to problems with communication, and since Jerry feels he cannot speak directly to Peter about his needs, he relates a parable. The story of Jerry and the dog gives insight into Jerry's character and serves to emphasize the play's theme. Briefly, the story tells how Jerry deals with the malevolence of his landlady's dog. First, he plans to "kill the dog with kindness, and if that doesn't work . . . just kill him" (p. 37). As Peter follows the story with distaste, Jerry pleads with him for understanding: "You must believe me; it is important. We have to know the effect of our actions" (p. 40). However, Peter does not understand; words are inadequate without the crisis which Jerry provokes. Peter's social consciousness, like that of the audience whom Albee is trying to reform, can only be shocked into awareness.

The anagnorisis for both Peter and the audience comes when Jerry forces him to defend his territorial rights and to commit murder.

> PETER: (*Does not move, but begins to weep*) Oh my God, oh my God.
>
> JERRY: (*Most faintly, now; he is very near death*) You won't be coming back here any more, Peter; you've been dispossessed. You've lost your bench, but you've defended your honor. And Peter, I'll tell you something now; you're not really a vegetable; it's all right, you're an animal. You're an animal, too.

Peter learns that he and Jerry are as close as brothers and he becomes a psychologically motivated character capable of making the changes (within society) that Albee recommends.

Albee develops the personalities in his first plays by parallels and contrasts in their relationships. Although the degree of realism varies from play to play, the development of "character" in the traditional sense of the term is subordinate to the emphasis on a character's role within the family structure and within the larger context of society. Even early in his career, Albee subordinated character to theme.

Following Zoo Story one year later with The American Dream,[2] Albee flattened out his characterizations for the purpose of illustrating the consequences of failed human relationships. With the exception of Grandma, these characters have no personalities: any identities they might have had have been submerged by the social roles they play. However, unlike Jerry and Peter's association, which is dominated by love and brutality, the relationships among Mommy, Daddy, Grandma, and the beautiful young man are characterized by sterility.

In her full-length study of Albee, Anne Paolucci says, "They [his characters] are not, properly speaking, individuals but rather states of mind or conscience, or guilt and sin and apathy and regret and indifference—often in opposition to one another."[3] She adds that the people in Albee's plays are "not so much embodiments of a dominant trait as fluid states, dissolving masks, a series of psychological x-rays."[4] Paolucci fails, however, to note Albee's levels of characterization. Grandma is much more realistic than Mommy, Daddy, and the beautiful young man. As a character, Grandma's function is to interpret the consequences of Mommy and Daddy's empty relationship although, unlike the traditional "pointer" character, she remains at all times the center of the play's conflict.

The theme of The American Dream operates on two levels. First is the failure within the family to achieve real contact and closeness, as symbolized by Mommy and Daddy's sterility—their inability to have a child or even to rear one. Then, as the title suggests, there is the wider social reference: the pursuit of the American way of life eliminates concern for both the old and the young by perpetuating the myth that material goods are an adequate substitution for love.

Mommy and Daddy have no self-awareness and gain none throughout the play. Mommy's tirade on the hat for which she demands satisfaction is indicative of the level to which their relationship has fallen. What appears to be a pointless and childish discussion on whether a hat is beige, wheat, or cream-colored is actually a commentary on Mommy and Daddy's values. They have no fixed standards except materialistic ones. Their values are as relative as the color of the hat, which changes according to the amount of artificial light it receives.

The old and the young are squeezed out of the family structure as a result of Mommy and Daddy's middle-class American values. Grandma, who finally runs away, is constantly threatened by Mommy with the Van People while the beautiful young man is separated from his twin brother and robbed of his ability to relate to other people. The implication is that this lack of feeling is responsible for the death of Grandma, an event which Albee reserves for The Sandbox.[5]

In The Sandbox, Mommy and Daddy bury Grandma in a child's sandbox and piously observe her death in a parody of the death watch. They do not mourn, and, in fact, Grandma is not yet dead when Mommy exits by saying, "It pays to do things well" (p. 156). The audience is never allowed to forget that this entire drama has been carefully orchestrated by Mommy.

As a character, Grandma represents the old American pioneer spirit and provides a sense of the past which has led to her death. She is also the character used by Albee to interpret the action for an audience which might be confused by players who provide their own stage directions. In an aside to the audience, Grandma says:

> I had to raise . . . that over there all by my lonesome; and what's next to her there . . . that's what she married. Rich? I tell you . . . money, money, money. They took me off the farm . . . which was real decent of them . . . and they moved me into the big town house with them . . . gave me an army blanket . . . and my own dish . . . my very own dish! So what have I to complain about? Nothing, of course. I'm not complaining.
>
> (p. 152)

Somehow the values of independence, ingenuity, and industriousness, which made it possible for Grandma to raise Mommy, have been lost.

At least some of Albee's early characters are psychologically motivated individuals who also function symbolically. In The Zoo Story, The American Dream, and The Sandbox, Jerry, Peter, and Grandma are believable people portrayed by Albee with compassion and insight; they are his spokesmen for reform. All three have been victimized by society, but they are not defeated. On the other hand, Mommy, Daddy, and the young man are almost "cartoon characters,"[6] as Anita Maria Stenz has described them, due to the fact that they symbolize the emptiness of the American dream. Albee maintains his sense of character in these three plays by assigning moral responsibility although he introduces flat characters in The American Dream and in The Sandbox to show what happens when social positions and roles become more important than the people who fill them.

Characters in Albee's Psychological Problem Plays

In the plays following The Sandbox and The American Dream, Albee's attention is directed to psychological problems of a more personal nature. Environmental influences are still important in Albee's middle plays, but in them he carefully sets up valid cause-and-effect relationships as reasons for aberrant social behavior. To paraphrase Agnes in A Delicate Balance,[7] Albee at the height of his career, beginning with Who's Afraid of Virginia Woolf?[8] and ending with A Delicate Balance, is not so much concerned with what choices are available as with what choices are made (Act III, p. 142). He becomes more concerned with motivations and he internalizes his characters to reflect this interest.

This section will be an examination of the main characters in both Who's Afraid of Virginia Woolf? and A Delicate Balance, for both plays illustrate Albee's ability to handle social and psychological concerns simultaneously while portraying consistent, fully developed characters. George and Martha, Nick and Honey, and Agnes and Tobias are distinct identities, yet they are Everybody Else. These three couples are examples of very emotionally complex characters who explore the sources of their conflicts and deal with their illusions through arguments, discussions, monologues, and stories.

One method of understanding the paradox of universals represented by the particular is to compare George and Martha with their counterparts in The American Dream. Mommy and Daddy are very flat characters who passively accept the consequences of their decisions. As universal types, they illustrate the debilitating effects of social positions and roles. On the other hand, George and Martha are very creative, three-dimensional characters whose efforts to come to grips with their existence result in the birth and death of their only "son." Furthermore, we know nothing of Mommy and Daddy's background other than the fact that social conditioning has motivated them to accept their roles. Of George and Martha, we know everything although their past is a mixture of fact and fantasy confused by their difficulty in separating the two. Like Mommy, Martha is another "braying" bitch (Who's Afraid of Virginia Woolf? Act I, p. 1031) while George is another emasculated husband like Daddy. But in Who's Afraid of Virginia Woolf? we are given insight into why they have these traits. As Anita Maria Stenz has noted, we have the story of "a Mommy who tried in vain to solve the problems of her existence in marriage and of a Daddy who found society's definition of success wanting."[9]

In the later play Albee does not suggest sweeping reforms in the social structure but the improvement of the quality of individual relationships. He implies through George and Martha that the answer to social problems lies in an honest and painful reassessment of human relationships. Unlike Mommy and Daddy, George and Martha both gain insight into the consequences of their illusions and learn to accept themselves and each other without preconceived ideas about social roles. Like many of Albee's characters, George and Martha have difficulty communicating, so they play very painful games to strip each other of pretense. Before "The Exorcism," Martha tells George, "Truth and illusion, George; you don't know the difference." He replies, "No; but we must carry on as though we did" (Who's Afraid of Virginia Woolf? Act III, p. 1093). After "The Exorcism," bereft of their illusions, George and Martha face the dawn and the task of rebuilding their relationship:

> GEORGE (*puts his hand gently on her shoulder; she puts her head back and he sings to her, very softly*): Who's afraid of Virginia Woolf, Virginia Woolf, Virginia Woolf,
>
> MARTHA: I . . . am . . . George . . .
>
> (Act III, p. 1106)

At the end of the play, George and Martha have no more defense mechanisms.

As in the older realism of Ibsen, the present crisis which George and Martha face is explained by the past. Through stories and dialogue, the two protagonists give their versions of why all their disappointments and disillusions have erupted this particular evening. However, in contrast to Ibsen's realism, their viewpoints represent not only the differing perspectives of a man and woman but also a curious mixture of fact and fantasy which both George and Martha have difficulty separating. In an Afterword on the play, Otto Reinert and Peter Arnott note that "when George 'kills' his and Martha's child, he destroys an illusion that has been a reality of their life together." Both characters rationalize their failures and distort the truth.

> Mommy died early, see, and I sort of grew up with Daddy. (*Pause—thinks*) . . . I went away to school, and stuff, but I more or less grew up with him. Jesus, I admired that guy! I worshipped him . . . I absolutely worshipped him. I still do. And he was pretty fond of me, too . . . you know? We had a real . . . rapport going . . . a real rapport.
>
> (Act I, p. 1054)

Martha's attitude toward her father is that of a child anxiously awaiting parental approval. Later, she decides to marry into the college and supply her father with a successor since she herself can not take over the presidency. Every action Martha takes is calculated to please her benevolent "Daddy."

George destroys Martha's illusion of her father by calling him "a great white mouse" (Act I, p. 1053) with white hair and red beady eyes. George also destroys the myth of Martha's relationship with her father: "She has as well a tiny problem with spiritous liquors—like she can't get enough . . . and on top of all that, poor weighed-down girl, PLUS a father who really doesn't give a damn whether she lives or dies, who couldn't care less *what* happens to his only daughter . . ." (Act III, p. 1120). In actuality, Martha's relationship with her father has made it impossible for George and Martha to have a real marriage.

George also has his illusions and childish stories of wish fulfillment. Like many children, George has hated his parents and wished at times to kill them. Forced to repress the anger, George felt guilty as a child, but as an adult he deals with his hostility creatively. George writes a book about a son who killed his parents and then pretended it was an accident. When Martha's father forbids him to publish his manuscript, George replies, "No, Sir, this isn't a novel at all . . . this is the truth . . . this really happened . . . TO ME!" (Act II, p. 1072). Just as George destroyed her illusions, Martha cruelly exposes George's fantasy to Nick and Honey. Ironically, through this book George had hoped to achieve the professional status Martha blames him for lacking. The unraveling of truth from illusion gives the play its modern psychological perspective.

To a certain extent, George's role in relation to Martha is similar to Jerry's relationship with Peter in Zoo Story. The audience never knows what provokes Jerry, but Martha's public humiliation of George finally gives him the impetus to hurt her enough to destroy the illusions fostered by them both. Max Halperen accurately explains that "In killing the child, so enmeshed in the lives of the 'parents,' George effectively kills the old George and Martha. . . . The illusory father dies, as well as the illusory mother. It is now possible for George and Martha to be reborn into the reality that is this, not the after life, a life that has never been possessed by either of them."[10]

Through George and Martha's example, the younger generation is revitalized. Honey, who has refused to have children, is led to the point of confessing "I want a child" (Act III, p. 1100), while Nick is treated to a look at the destructive force of unbridled ambition. In response to "The Exorcism," Nick says, "Jesus Christ, I think I understand this" (Act III, p. 1104). Albee implies that like George and Martha, Nick and Honey will reevaluate their relationship and reestablish it on a more honest, adult basis. Instead of viewing each other as a means to an end, each can now regard the other as an individual. The play transcends the personal problems of two sick marriages and makes a very positive social comment on life in America. George, Martha, Nick, and Honey have all learned that the pursuit of materialism and social position leads only to dissatisfaction. In Who's Afraid of Virginia Woolf? Albee says that the American dream is dead, but that the American family structure is very much alive.

In an interview at Pan American University, April 22, 1980, Albee was asked why he showed so much hatred or disappointment in the family. He replied:

> There are several ways for families to hang together. One is to ask no questions, another is to ask all questions. When you ask no questions, you hang together until you just disintegrate and aren't aware of why the disintegration is taking place and if you ask all questions, you may possibly recreate a family structure but with firmer bonding.[11]

His observation is applicable to both Who's Afraid of Virginia Woolf? and A Delicate Balance. In the former, George and Martha strengthen their relationship by airing grievances and disappointment which have occurred over a period of approximately twenty-one years. In the latter, Agnes struggles to maintain the delicate balance between sustaining her family and keeping her own sanity. She seeks only to "keep this family in shape" (Act II, Scene 2, p. 80). A Delicate Balance is a quieter, more pessimistic statement on the family structure than Who's Afraid of Virginia Woolf? In mood it has more in common with The American Dream. As a result, although Agnes and Tobias are fuller, more realistic versions of Mommy and Daddy, they are still flat and lifeless.

This time Albee's American family is made up of an older couple facing retirement, an alcoholic sister-in-law, and, at times, their daughter Julia, who is thirty-six years old. Each character has his or her private grief, which accounts for the repressed tension within the family. They wonder aloud about the solutions to their problems and, at times, seem to address the audience rather than each other with their grievances. What their friend Edna says about herself and Harry is true of Agnes and Tobias' family also: ". . . that the only body you've wrapped your arms around . . . the only skin you've ever known . . . is your own—and that it's dry . . . and not warm" (Act III, p. 164). They are all isolated characters who come together only when threatened with the invasion of Harry and Edna.

Tobias is a retired businessman who has had a successful career in the city. Having fulfilled his financial obligations to his family, he has retired to the suburbs to enjoy the good life. However, as a father and a husband, Tobias has failed and he feels guilty about his inadequacies. His daughter Julia cannot establish a mature relationship with a man because she has never felt secure in her relationship with her father. They have never been able to communicate, and Tobias still does not feel comfortable talking to Julia. He announces to no one in particular, "If I thought I might break through to her, and say, 'Julia . . .' but then what would I say? 'Julia . . .' Then Nothing" (Act I, p. 33). He describes the relationship between himself and his daughter by telling a story about a cat he once had. The cat had been his for about fifteen years when suddenly it stopped liking him. The same thing happened between himself and Julia when Julia reached adolescence.

Like Jerry in the story of Jerry and the dog, Tobias tried to reach the cat with first kindness and then cruelty. He felt betrayed and resentful when the cat did not respond, so he took her to the vet and had her killed. Now he is wracked with guilt that he did not go on and accept the cat's indifference. Tobias feels that he has somehow destroyed Julia, and he is resentful because he does not see where he has failed. As a husband, Tobias failed to support Agnes emotionally when their son died. He cheated on his wife that same summer and refused to father another child or even express his sense of loss. He knew that his wife was sexually unfulfilled, so he "coped" with his inadequacies by withdrawing to a separate bedroom.

Agnes is a very different character from Albee's mommy figures. She has allowed Tobias to make the important decisions of their lives while she has ordered her life around his. In contemplating their life together, Agnes says that a woman "assumes whatever duties are demanded—if she is in love, or loves; and plans . . . The reins we hold! It's a team of twenty horses, and we sit there, and we watch the road and check the leather . . . if our . . . man is so disposed" (Act III, p. 131). As usual, the rhetorical quality of Agnes' speech emphasizes that she has difficulty expressing her particular desires, so she speaks in terms of universals.

Agnes and Tobias do not really communicate until Agnes feels that she is being threatened in her own home by their best friends, who arrive and announce that they are staying. She is aware of the instability in her own family and fears the terror that Harry and Edna have brought with them. Gently and with tact, she brings Tobias to the understanding that he cannot make up for his failures as a husband and a father by being a true friend. At this point, Agnes and Tobias are actually talking to each other, rather than in general, although the quiet, intense quality of their discussion indicates that they are still not saying what they really think.

Furthermore, Agnes brings Tobias to the point that he can be honest when Harry finally asks whether or not he and Edna are really wanted. Tobias' answer is a passionate response.

> (Soft) You've put nearly forty years in it, baby; so have I, and if it's nothing, I don't give a damn, you've got the right to be here, you've earned it.
>
> (Loud) and by god you're going to take it! do you hear me? you bring your terror and you come in here and you live with us! i don't want you here! i don't love you! but by god . . . you stay!
>
> (Act III, p. 162).

When the play ends with the departure of Harry and Edna, Tobias and Agnes welcome the restoration of order in their household. Agnes stands with her arm around her husband in a gesture of support. Tobias recognizes that at this stage in life, he can afford no more guilt: all he can say to his family is "I'm sorry. I apologize" (Act III, p. 170) and let the past go. Earlier in the play, Tobias has said that if there is no love, at least "there can be silence, even having" (Act I, p. 33). As Agnes tells him, he has only two choices: to be content with simply having his wife's company, his alcoholic sister-in-law, and occasional visits from Julia, or to reestablish his relationship with these three women on a more honest and loving basis.

A Delicate Balance is an interesting play in terms of an overall view of Albee's career. The play contains bits and pieces of the others, but it marks a major change in both style and philosophy. In A Delicate Balance, Albee indicates that he doubts modern man's ability to form personal relationships which help alleviate the stress of restrictive social situations. Because of this philosophical viewpoint, Albee's characters are isolated from each other and somewhat overwhelmed by the circumstances of the play. To paraphrase Jerry in The Zoo Story, Agnes, Tobias, Harry, Edna, Julia, and Claire can neither hurt nor love each other. For example, when Tobias finally unburdens himself by confessing that he does not really want his best friends to move in, Edna very calmly replies, "Harry, will you bring our bags down? Maybe Tobias will help you. Will you ask him?" (Act III, p. 163). There are fewer arguments in this play and more monologues and stories than in those previously discussed. The whole play has a rather detached quality which Albee further develops in his later plays—specifically, in Box and Quotations from Chairman Mao Tse-Tung and in Counting the Ways and Listening, In spite of the fact that in 1966 A Delicate Balance won the Pulitzer Prize, which had been denied Who's Afraid of Virginia Woolf? there is justification in Walter Kerr's criticism that the play is more like an essay than an experience.[12]

The ending of A Delicate Balance is not unlike the conclusion of Who's Afraid of Virginia Woolf? Both plays present the same choices and focus on the motivations of the characters involved. However, in the latter, George and Martha tear down their barriers to communication through "fun and games" (title of Act I) and slash away at each other until they are finally purged of illusions. In contrast, Tobias and Agnes reveal their estrangement through calm, philosophical monologues directed more at the audience than at each other. Their speeches lack the wit and the sharpness of George and Martha's night-long brawl and, as a result, Tobias and Agnes are rather flat characters when compared with George and Martha.

The Introspective Plays

In Box, Quotations from Mao Tse-tung, [13] Counting the Ways, and Listening,[14] form follows content, as in Albee's earlier drama. In Box, Albee has no characters onstage and uses, instead, a disembodied voice to express his philosophy. In Quotations, he has four characters, three who speak in disconnected monologues and one silent character. In Counting The Ways, Albee has a man and woman, identified only as "He" and "She," who step in and out of the play as they discuss their relationship with each other and with the audience. In Listening, there are three characters—the Man, the Woman, and the catatonic Girl—and another disembodied voice that counts to divide the play's scenes. The characters in Listening are symbolic in that they represent universal man by the fact that they have no particular personality traits or individual experiences which give them life. Because Albee is focusing on "the condition of 'man'" [15] at this stage in his career, he structures the later plays around his characters' recollections of universal experiences—disillusionment, isolation, and death. The characters are portrayed as victims who recount their experiences in an effort to establish some cause-and-effect relationship between their past and their present isolation. They can establish no logical sequence of events, and hence they become "non-characters." They are merely vehicles for the expression of Albee's ideas and, in some instances, extreme abstractions. These characters seldom address each other, sometimes do not speak at all, and occasionally do not appear onstage. In these later plays, Albee loses his sense of character. He has no plays but only the essays which Kerr earlier accused him of writing.

In his experiment with "the application of musical form to dramatic structure," Albee uses Box as a "parenthesis"[16] around Quotations from Mao Tse-tung. There are no characters in Box but only a Voice which "should seem to be coming from near by the spectator," according to the stage directions (p. 127). Onstage is a box which is "solid, perfect joints . . . good work," as it is described by the Voice (p. 128). Because the play is a meditation on the box, the members of the audience become the "characters" in the play. That the speaker expects some kind of response is evident by her manner of address. To the audience, she says, "If only they had *told* us! Clearly! When it was clear that we were not only corrupt" (p. 129). Again, she includes the audience in her meditation: "Well, we can exist with anything; without" (p. 131). The response to the dialogue takes place within the minds of the spectators if they are receptive to the "play."

In the play which both introduces and concludes Mao, Albee is making two statements. First, all arts are degenerating. In Albee's words, "Many arts: all craft now . . . and going further" (p. 128). Second, "art hurts" because "it reminds us of loss"—of the order of the past (p. 130). There is no play as such because the kind of art symbolized by the box is no longer possible. The present is disordered as represented by the fact that seven hundred million babies die of starvation in one place while milk is spilled at another location.

Quotations from Mao Tse-tung is an effort on Albee's part to write more personal variations on the theme of order. Three of the characters recall their pasts in an effort to establish some reason for the disorder of their present lives. However, none of the characters address the others although at times their monologues almost seem to be responses to each other. The following excerpt is an example of the introspective technique which Albee develops in his later plays:

> CHAIRMAN MAO: . . . On a blank sheet of paper free from any mark, the freshest and most beautiful characters can be written, the freshest and most beautiful pictures can be painted.
>
> LONG-WINDED LADY: And so high!
>
> OLD WOMAN: Over the hill to the poor-house.
>
> (pp. 139-40)

All three speeches make some reference to height. The audience is aware of the connection, but the players seem to be totally isolated and unaware of each other's presence. Albee assumes that the audience will relate to one or more of the characters and also meditate on the theme of order, but the actual effect of Mao is that the audience is isolated from the characters.

The minister who represents organized religion is an extreme example of this isolation. He does not speak in the play, and as a silent character, he represents the ineffectiveness of the church in modern life. The minister never responds to the Long-Winded Lady who attempts to communicate with him. According to the stage directions, "He must try to pay close attention to the Long-Winded Lady, though—nod, shake his head, cluck, put an arm tentatively out, etc. . . . He must never make the audience feel he is looking at them or is aware of them" (p. 136). Albee intends for the audience to understand that the minister cannot speak.

In Mao, the Long-Winded Lady turns to the silent minister in her search for identity, but the other characters turn to the audience with their monologues. The members of the audience, in effect, become silent characters for the players onstage who are making their pleas for understanding. Albee does not really expect any kind of response in terms of action from the audience. He is very pessimistic in these later plays and increasingly hostile toward the general public in his later interviews.

Isolation as a theme is explored in both Counting the Ways (1976) and Listening (1975). Counting the Ways is a discussion by two "universal" characters—He and She—of that sense of aloneness which Albee believes exists in every marriage. "Scene Fourteen" is representative of the entire play. The audience is told that the couple's king-size bed has mysteriously divided and become two single beds. He wants to discuss the situation, but She at first refuses.

> SHE (*Smiles a small, superior smile*): Then, we are at an impasse. (*Fr. pronunciation*)
>
> HE: No, we are not; we will discuss it.
>
> SHE (*Didactic*): If I will not, and only you will, that is not a discussion.
>
> HE (*He, too*): Silence is a reply.
>
> SHE (*Snorts*): Of sorts. For some I suppose. Martyrs in the desert? Old people at the post office.
>
> (Scene 14, pp. 28-29)

In Listening, two of the characters—the Girl and the Woman—have no sense of the past and no basis for communication. Although the Man, who was once the Woman's lover, tries to get her to recall their past relationship, she disdains his attention and refuses to be pained by the memory.

> THE MAN: I knew which flowers you preferred; you told me all about your father's whip, and all about the day you were strong enough to take it from him, and how you beat him for an hour. . . .
>
> THE WOMAN (*Curiously unconcerned*): No, I never told you any of that; it was someone else.
>
> THE MAN: Do you *still* not shave beneath your arms?
>
> THE WOMAN (*After a pause*): Who *are* you?
>
> (p. 122)

Even though they have been lovers, the Man and the Woman are still strangers.

The catatonic Girl represents the voice of the dramatist. She is Albee's spokesman for the only "message" he has to offer in these later plays: "You don't listen . . . Pay attention, rather, is what you don't do" (p. 73). The Girl cuts her wrists at the end of the play because no one is listening or paying attention to her and because she learns from the Man and Woman's conversation that the empty fountain was once full. She can no longer bear to live because what she sees hurts too much.

Albee apparently can no longer bear to write about "the condition of 'man'"[17] because he finds the situation too painful. In Box, the Voice says, "When art begins to hurt . . . when art begins to hurt, it's time to look around" (p. 129).

Albee's last plays "hurt" because they are so abstract and pessimistic that the audience is alienated. As a dramatist, Albee becomes so concerned with relating his opinions in these last plays that his characters become merely vehicles for the expression of these ideas. They become symbolic characters as Albee seeks to communicate the meaninglessness of American life. As a result, Albee loses his sense of character and his sense of the dramatic.

Notes

[1]Edward Albee, *The Zoo Story,* in *Three Plays* (New York: Coward-McCann, 1960), pp. 11-62. All references to the play are made to this edition.

[2]Edward Albee, *The American Dream* (New York: Coward-McCann, 1960), pp. 11-93. All references to the play are made to this edition.

[3]Anne Paolucci, "The Existential Burden," in *Tension to Tonic: The Plays of Edward Albee* (Edwardsville: Southern Illinois Univ. Press, 1972), p. 26.

[4]Paolucci, p. 35.

[5]Edward Albee, *The Sandbox,* in *Three Plays* (New York: Coward-McCann, 1960), pp. 143-58. All references to the play are made to this editon.

[6]Anita Maria Stenz, *Edward Albee: The Poet of Loss* (New York: Mouton Publishers, 1978), pp. 32-33.

[7]Edward Albee, *A Delicate Balance* (New York: Atheneum, 1967), pp. 1-170. All references to the play are made to this edition.

[8]Edward Albee, *Who's Afraid of Virginia Woolf?* in *Twenty-Three Plays,* ed. Otto Reinert (Boston: Little, Brown & Co., 1978), pp. 1030-1105. All references to the play are made to this edition.

[9]Stenz, p. 38.

[10]Max Halperen, "What Happens to Who's Afraid . . ." in *Modern American Drama: Essays in Criticism,* ed. William E. Taylor (DeLand: Everett/Edwards, 1968), pp. 140-41.

[11]"Edward Albee: An Interview," in *Edward Albee: Planned Wilderness,* Living Author Series, No. 3, ed. Patricia De La Fuente (Edinburg, Texas: Pan American University, 1980), pp. 6-7.

[12]Michael Rutenberg, *Playright in Protest* (New York: DBS Publications, 1969), pp. 140-41.

[13]Edward Albee, *Tiny Alice, Box,* and *Quotations from Chairman Mao Tse-tung* (Harmondsworth, England: Penguin, 1971). All quotations from the plays listed in the title are from this edition.

[14]Edward Albee, *Counting the Ways* and *Listening* (New York: Atheneum, 1977). All quotations from the plays listed in the title are from this edition.

[15]Albee, Introduction, *Box* and *Quotations from Chairman Mao Tse-tung,* p. 124.

[16]Ibid., p. 123.

[17]Ibid., p. 124.

Rodney Simard (essay date 1984)

SOURCE: "Harold Pinter & Edward Albee: The First Postmoderns," in *Postmodern Drama: Contemporary Playwrights in American and Britain,* University Press of America, 1984, pp. 25-47.

[*In the excerpt below, Simard explores Albee's technique of undercutting "conventional expectations by dividing his emphasis between external and internal reality." The critic further argues that Albee's "realistic framework, the family, serves as the point of departure for his own type of subjective reality, an examination of his characters' psyches."*]

Albee was early heralded in America as the brilliant young playwright and the inheritor and savior of the native dramatic tradition. Like Pinter in Britain, Albee was the first American dramatist to look beyond national boundaries and offer an infusion of Continental experimentalism to a drama that was dominated by the social realism of Miller and the psychological realism of Williams, although neither of these playwrights had produced a major work for some time. And also like Pinter, Albee looked to the European absurdists for his methods, which he turned to an examination of particularly American concerns, recognizing the limits of absurdism but also the value in its expansion of dramatic possibility.

Tom F. Driver observes that "the story of American theater is that of an attempt, not entirely successful, to create an indigenous art for a mass audience that is highly materialistic and is experiencing an astonishingly rapid growth in material power and technical knowledge," adding that the American sensibility has little awareness of man's being born to catastrophe, and that interiority in drama has traditionally been expressed in therapeutic, neo-Freudian terms, seldom, if ever, in terms of Chekhovian tragicomedy.[1] American drama had indeed made significant advances since O'Neill, and in a relatively short period, but one must not fail to note the parallel development with Britain, which had also been fairly static in terms of development since the burst of originality in Shaw. American drama dates from O'Neill, for both America and Britain share the same dramatic heritage before his emergence. Perhaps the lack of a distinctly native tradition in contrast to the British tradition, which stretches back beyond Shakespeare, is the reason why many modern dramatic critics have so frequently deplored the condition of native drama, but by the late 1950s, everyone was willing to herald the emergence of originality. Unlike Pinter, who emerged during the burst of activity of New Wave drama, Albee was alone in his attempts and seemed to be the figure America had been awaiting to revitalize moribund Broadway.

Catapulted into fame and immediately subjected to rigorous scrutiny, Albee has always been simultaneously lauded and reviled, and he continues to suffer from extremes in evaluations of his works. While in the early 1960s, the usually astute Driver could dismiss Albee as "the author of six bad plays,"[2] Tennessee Williams could also say that he "is the only great playwright we've had in America."[3] The inheritor of a realistic Anglo-American tradition, Albee rejected that tradition and looked to Europe, especially to Ionesco and Beckett, and became the first American postmodern dramatist, like Pinter inspiring a new generation of writers whose experimentation has largely escaped the attacks Albee experienced while working in seeming isolation. Rejecting "our one-dimensional dramatic tradition, his search for a new dramatic language is part of a deep-rooted instinct to find adequate expression for the existential dilemma at the heart of the modern experience," asserts Anne Paolucci.[4]

In 1962, while observing that the Theater of the Absurd is either on its way out or undergoing a fundamental change, Albee was able to "submit that The Theatre of the Absurd, in the sense that is is truly the contemporary theater, facing as it does man's condition as it is, is the Realistic theater of our time. . . ."[5] And Paolucci notes that,

> The theater of the absurd has struggled to find ways of redefining these essentials, Juxtaposing internal *landscape* and external events, facts and fantasy, reshaping language to suit the splintered action, using everything that the stage offers to do so. But the kind of protagonist that emerges within this new medium is forever threatening to dissolve into a voice, a mind, a consciousness, a strange creature without identity or personality.[6]

Albee, like Pinter, avoids the traps of enclosure and reduction to essence evident in Beckett's work, attempting like the Englishman to achieve a plurality of vision and to avoid creating existential artifacts. Paralleling the course of Pinter's experimentalism, Albee's work continues to explore the means to expand the limits of dramatic reality with each new play, building on the concepts and methods asserted in each succeeding work. Much like Pinter's, his technique is to undercut conventional expectations by dividing his emphasis between external and internal reality. He terms his method "selective reality,"[7] which is a combination of the concept of plastic theater as evidenced in Williams' *The Glass Menagerie,* a memory play which breaks down the time continuum and portrays a subjective, impressionistic reality, and the metaphorical allusiveness of the Beckett canon. His characters and situations are both specific and general, functioning on one level of reality within the context of the drama as well as suggesting multi-leveled layers of universal significance. His national inheritance is evident in his specific social criticism, an established American convention since the 1920s, and while he criticizes institutions, they are not necessarily specifically American, although they tend to be more specific than the menace, or threat to individuality, evident in Pinter's work.

Often using the family as a microcosm of society, he examines the nature of human bonds in a situation where the present is contingent on both past and future. His realistic framework, the family, serves as the point of departure for his own type of subjective reality, an examination of his characters' psyches, dramatized in as late a play as All Over/ Albee's method, as a brief overview of his canon will suggest, is to uncover and reveal the unconscious of his characters, making internal reality his mode and the interplay of personalities and values his dramatic action. His producer, Richard Barr, has noted that "Edward was the first playwright to say that people invent their own illusions to give themselves a reality. And his characters are aware of it- . . . . The awareness was what was new."[8]

Albee's subject matter is the conventional system of false values, empty language, and sterile emotion that are the means by which modern individuals, not simply Americans, "illusion" themselves from reality. External reality is not the true reality of modern existence but lies beneath the surface in the individual mind, riddled with its own subjective set of illusions and anxieties. His work is social criticism only insofar as modern individuals are social creatures. He examines people not in the isolation of the room/womb as Pinter does, but in their familial environment, which Albee sees as a cage which separates them from all other people who inhabit their own individual cages. He attacks language as a masking illusion, composed of clichéd conventions which obscure meaning rather than conveying it. In his early plays particularly, such as The American Dream and The Sandbox, where the influence of Ionesco is strongest, the trite speeches of his characters demonstrate their lack of feeling and their inhumanity, the danger and horror of the ordinary, as they avoid communication with those people seemingly closest to them, an effect underscored by their familial situation.

All of Albee's characters experience a glimpse into the void of meaninglessness, but only those who surrender to it become the human wreckage many critics find to be the hallmark of his drama. Even one of the bleakest of his plays, Who's Afraid of Virginia Woolf? offers the possibility of redemption at the end. If George and Martha, like all his characters, can confront the reality of the emptiness of their lives and throw off their insulating illusion, such as their personal myth of the nonexistent child, then they may have the hope of constructing a subjective validity of existence. Only when stripped of illusion can humanity hope for redemption and salvation, an elevation invariably offered in terms of establishing meaning and assigning value to another person in an honest and aware relationship. While Pinter dramatizes choice on a metaphoric level, examining characters as they construct a method for dealing with life, Albee suggests that self-value is ultimately reflected in one's relationships with others. One must discard lies and evaluate self for what it is, then subjectively construct a set of values that recognize that, while essentially isolated, people give meaning to themselves only by choosing to value other people and by finding strength in others in order to confront the void. While Albee does not deny that the existential reality of life is isolation and a subjective perception of reality, he goes one step further than Pinter by suggesting that people must be social creatures and must establish realistic means for dealing with others. Love and commitment are his chief weapons against meaninglessness.

Like Pinter, Albee's range of experimentation is wide and he continues to produce works that further develop certain basic premises. His first play, The Zoo Story (1959), examines the isolation of modern life and argues for the need and difficulty of meaningful, as opposed to empty, human communication. Humans are no better than animals if they refuse to recognize the presence of their cage and then break out of it and touch another human being. Realistically grounded, the play uses standard absurdist techniques to heighten reality and to suggest its internal quality, for while it hinges dramatically on the murder/suicide of Jerry, the resolution is in Peter's psyche, as he, like the reader, struggles to make sense of what he has experienced. The Death of Bessie Smith (1960) is more clearly rooted in external reality and explores the social cages created by gender, race, profession, and psychology, pointing out the disparity between things as they are and things as they should be.

Following this venture into psychological realism, he produced The Sandbox(1960) and The American Dream (1961), two absurdist plays that are variations on a theme and are paradigmatic of the early Albee. Evidencing the strong influence of both Ionesco and Beckett, these episodic works are constructed of linking situations and employ conventional, cliche-ridden language. While the three generations of family members function allegorically to point out the emptiness of modern life as well as to direct several important social attacks, their primary function is to underscore the isolation and lack of communication in relationships externally structured on love but internally founded on lies and sterility. Time past (Grandma) is discarded by the mechanized and inhuman present (the solipsistic Mommy and emasculated Daddy), whose heir is the empty and materialistic young man (the American Dream), the personification of anesthetized external beauty who will do anything for money. He is the future of the modern individual who refuses to place value on internal qualities.

These allegorized metaphors of modern humanity give way to the more realistic and specific characters of his first full-length play, Who's Afraid of Virginia Woolf? (1962). A dramatization of the empty ritual by which people insulate themselves from an awareness of themselves, the play exposes the internal horror beneath the surface of ordinary social interaction as the characters flail about in the void of meaninglessness without attempting to face the reality of their lives and construct a sense of subjective worth and direction. Enclosed in their room, George and Martha savage each other in an attempt to externalize the blame for the emptiness of their lives, which are based on multiple illusions, such as the imaginary child and George's ascension to the presidency of the college. Only at the end of the play when they have brutally stripped each other of these illusions does the possibility exist of facing reality. At the close of Act III, "The Exorcism," Martha admits her fear of Virginia Woolf, the fear of madness in denying reality, as she and George retire to rest for the new day, literally and metaphorically the new beginning of their lives together. While quite specifically about two people in a specific situation, wielding words as weapons to cloak reality, the play is also open to metaphoric interpretations reminiscent of Beckett's work. The roots of American idealism are suggested by their names, the disparity between public existence (Nick and Honey) and private reality (George and Martha) is contrasted, and one can read the play as a conflict between failed history (George) and the new methods of science (Nick). Thus, this play, as is characteristic of all of Albee's plays, functions in a specific way, exploring the layers of subjective reality, as well as in a general way, providing metaphors for many of the conflicts of modern existence.

Albee's next effort was at sustained religious allegory, Tiny Alice (1964), and is a not altogether successful attempt at presenting subjective, existential reality in symbolic terms. His restrained A Delicate Balance (1966) is perhaps Albee's finest exploration of existential terror in its attempts to probe his basic philosophic preoccupations within a realistic framework. Like Beckett and Pinter, he takes this idea to further dramatic extremes in his brace of experimental works, Box and Quotations from Chairman Mao Tse-tung (1968). These theatrical attempts at allegorical minimalism are lyrical intertwinings of interior monologues which attempt to present objective and subjective reality simultaneously.

However, Albee returned to his more characteristic realistic mode with his next works, All Over (1971) and Seascape (1975), which were originally planned as companion pieces under the collective title of Life and Death. The former is a modern morality play, at once naturalistic and symbolic, which eschews exposition and explores the veiling nature of memory and the subjectivity of time. Clearly Pinteresque in technique, it remains characteristic of Albee in its final insistence on human values and the abandonment of illusion for personal salvation. The latter play defies external reality by presenting two lizards as human prototypes in its attempt to dramatize a collapse of time, confronting modern humanity with what it once was. By suggesting that individuals must assume a stance of negative capability and confront the unknowns of life boldly, Albee once again affirms the power of emotion in the renewed, realistic bond between Charlie and Nancy, his existential everymen.

The following year, Albee again returned to Beckettian (and Pinteresque) experimentation with Listening, an exploration of the subjectivity of perception. His allegorized—yet specific—Man and Woman are portraits in isolation and the inability to communicate as they drift in the haze of memory, detached from time, exploring the impossibility of verification of self. Counting the Ways (1977) continues this exploration into minimalism and subjectivity, as He and She maintain their own delicate balance, threatened with non-existence. Affirming love at the conclusion, it charts the impossibility of knowing or communicating anything, especially redemptive emotion. Reality for these characters is completely subjective as they attempt to break through their cages of isolation; they realize the impossibility of empirical knowledge yet the necessity of affirmation as She responds to his "Do you love me?" with "I think I do."[9] Albee's recent play, The Lady from Dubuque (1979), is a return to the realistic mode. It presents a social group of characters who are nonetheless isolated from each other despite the elaborate network of connections they have imposed on their lives. Personified psychological states, they represent individual reactions to nothingness. Again, he underscores the subjectivity of reality by insisting that no matter what social bonds we construct to illusion ourselves, we are essentially alone. Contemporary people can find sustenance in love and the courage to face the unknown, but their reactions and values are intensely personal.

John von Szeliski states that "in Edward Albee's A Delicate Balance we have the most significant representation of the essence, and the effective treatment, of a world view of the 1960s or the 1970s."[10] Awarded a Pulitzer Prize (which many people maintain was a consolation for losing it with Who's Afraid), this play is perhaps the best example of the polarity in Albee criticism, but many of the attacks on the play may be surprise reactions to the uncharacteristic understatement of the work. It is an examination of free-floating anxiety, the "Terror," to which all human beings are susceptible, manifested here as a failure of love and a fear of isolation. The balance of the title is the delicate line which separates reality from illusion, which the typical Albee couple, Agnes and Tobias, try to walk. In Pinteresque fashion, they inhabit their room, insulated from reality, and face threats from all sides; they are poised between extremes in their own family, for Claire represents escape in self-withdrawal and Julia is escape in flight. Faced with varieties of isolation, from cynicism to romance within their own family structure, they have to confront the Terror brought into their home by intruders, their best friends, Edna and Harry.

The power of the drama arises from its shift from the external to the internal, from objective to subjective reality, and the conclusion is much like that of Who's Afraid: battle weary, scarred, and exhausted, Agnes and Tobias, like George and Martha, have undergone an ordeal and are indeed drained, but they lack the cushioning illusion they held at the beginning of the play which separated them from self-awareness and from each other. Agnes' closing line, "Come now; we can begin the day" (170), holds the promise of a new beginning, a brutal facing of reality highly reminiscent of the sunrise in Ibsen's *Ghosts.* While apparently less than they once were, the characters have achieved a new potentiality simply by losing what they once had: the illusions that made them withdraw into the room in isolation from each other and the world. Having glimpsed the void, their fear is generalized as a fear of meaninglessness or nothingness, but it has specific applications as well. Their lives are obviously not what they had been trying to believe they were, for the concept of family and the ritual of communication are empty, merely gestures to maintain the illusion of emotion and meaning where none actually exist. So not only do they fear an abstract philosophical concept, they fear the emptiness and isolation of their collective and individual lives as well.

As in Pinter's work, the menace in this play is an abstraction, but Albee goes further by giving it very specific applications as well. While the nature of action in Pinter is relatively unimportant, since he stresses the importance of the decision process itself, Albee maintains that action is vital while suggesting the nature of the action: people must strip themselves of illusion, bond themselves to one another, and emerge from their rooms to face the daylight of shared reality. Subjective reality is every individual's terrain and the realm of personal consciousness, but it is isolating. Fragmented subjective realities must be bound together to form a collective, for people cannot retreat from the society of which they are a part, even if the unit is as small as a marriage or a family. Like Pinter, studying the response to external demands, Albee presents the fear by fiat; nothingness is an existential reality. His concern is with how his characters deal with abstractions, with the choices they make. Action in the face of contingency is the primary postmodern dramatic subject.

As in Beckett and Pinter, Albee's plays generally begin in recognizable, external reality and shift to specific explorations of inner realities within the characters. His method of selective reality within a traditional framework allows him to expand the limits of conventional realism by dramatizing characters in the process of self-exploration, stripping away the layers of illusion to reach the emptiness of their lives, the naked masks of Pirandello. But Albee is not content with a dramatization of choice and his characters are not stalemated abstractions, such as Reader in *Ohio Impromptu* or even Disson in *Tea Party.* They are recognizable, individualized characters who reach their lower depths and stand stripped of false notions of self, attaining a universality by their nakedness. Albee's drama is a celebration of the possibility of ascent, of the possibility of redefining self and emerging from isolation to make contact with others. His optimism lies in his belief in redemptive emotion, a positive valuation of one's self and one's fellow human beings. Albee may be cynical about the difficulty involved in the struggle for self-awareness, but his drama concludes with possibility. The thunder in the drama holds a tentative promise of rain in the existential wasteland of postmodern existence.

In summary, both Pinter and Albee represent a distinct break with the Beckettian tradition, itself a fusion of realism and experimentalism. Their plays stand at the crossroads of twentieth-century drama, and various attempts have been made to place them technically and historically, the most important theories being dissonance, compressionism, and contextualism. While each of these views has its merits, both playwrights must be viewed as unique transition figures, the first of the postmoderns, for whom no specific categories are immediately applicable.

In the Beckettian tradition of minimalism and the movement toward essence, some plays by Pinter and Albee, such as *Landscape* and Box, have been viewed by Robert Mayberry as comprising a theater of dissonance or discord, "the disassociation of the visual and the verbal media"; similar in form to the interplay between objective and subjective reality which characterizes all these plays, this particular theory asserts that "Beckett relocated the central conflict traditionally found in a struggle between characters to the more abstract level of conflicting media," placing the dramatic actions of the plays within the minds of the readers.[11] Both Pinter and Albee have returned to conventional forms that adhere to a basic realistic tradition after their experiments in theatricality, yet they preserve the effect of dissonance. Within a recognizable mode of external reality, their plays probe the consciousnesses of individual characters, exposing at once the social framework of their lives as well as their interiority. The juxtaposition of the specific and the general, the subjective and the objective, the particular and the universal, the interior and the exterior, the imagistic and the metaphoric, creates both the plurality of form and response, defying probability for possibility to engage readers to the limits of their own awareness. These dramas expand from the specificity of the text to the consciousness of the characters to the perception of the reader. Meaning in these plays spirals inward to the point where it is given substance only in response to the dramatic action. Readers are at once alienated from a form which seems familiar on the surface but thwarts their expectations while they are actively engaged in the resolution of the action and the assignment of value. The subjectivity of reality, therefore, embraces reader/audience perception, and the postmodern form is one which simultaneously alienates and engages.

Noting that absurdism denies the "weapons" of traditional drama, Laurence Kitchin observes that the mode "attacks us below the threshold of consciousness, mainly by visual devices and by language in a state of fragmentation, in short, by a kind of intellectual clowning." Dismissing absurdism as a fruitless experiment in form, Kitchin goes on to maintain that the two basic forms of postmodern drama are the epic and compressionism, the latter being plays "in which the characters are insulated from society in such a way as to encourage the maximum conflict of attitudes."[12] While such a term aptly describes the works of Pinter and Albee, it tends to suggest the theatricalism of the late Beckett canon more than the existential realism of the postmoderns. Maintaining that realism, not theatricalism, is the essential mode of modern drama, John Gassner argues for a contextual view of drama that results in the "coexistence of realism and nonrealistic stylization turned into an active and secure partnership in the interests of essential realism." He observes that,

> In one way or another, modern drama has again and again manifested an instinct for organization, as against disorganization; a feeling for crescendo, as against *decrescendo, stasis,* and *circularity;* a regard for language, as against a disregard for it in favor of silent mimesis or mime; and, in general, a marked esthetic orientation, as against a sense of disintegration and chaos.[13]

The tension between these impulses is precisely the difference in direction between Beckett and his successors, Pinter and Albee. They reject his dissolution into essence and insist on a dramatic portrayal of existence, and their works are contextual in a similar sense to which the term was originally applied to poetry, relying on tensions of context rather than direction, probing and displaying vertical depth rather than horizontal movement.

As Marvin Rosenberg observes, the modern impulse is to hold time at bay, to circumscribe the present and to isolate a non-narrative felt life. He points out that this impulse can follow two paths, toward the "pure," a theatrical embodiment of a mental state, where the character becomes a transparent image rather than an intermediate symbol (as in *Godot*), or becomes a condition of living (as in the late Beckett); or it can follow traditional development, wherein character is extended in dimension (as in *Death of a Salesman*). As Rosenberg maintains, contextual drama seeks to represent the psyche which rebels against pattern,[14] but as Bert O. States points out, Rosenberg's concept of contextual form is actually a description of effect. He maintains that the plays of the "New drama" "do not imitate actions, they imitate the mind; or, in clearer terms, these plays do not have plots, they have psychology."[15] The positions of both scholars are extremes, for postmodern drama, as established by Pinter and Albee, seeks to dramatize consciousness detached from time, and the action or plot is the interplay of individually apprehended consciousnesses and subjective evaluations of reality. Reality is what the individual character (and reader) apprehends it to be, and the dramatic action is often the disparity between one view and another or between perceived and external reality. What appears to be a realistic drama staged in terms of external reality is found to be actually unfolding on the level of the subconscious, and it is on this level that it has its effect on the reader. The external framework acts as a touchstone to measure the depth of the playwright's probing into subjective perception. By the continual interplay between external and internal reality, readers are able to chart the depth and progress of their own involvement in the play. The readers' positions and responsibilities are to integrate the two (or more) levels of reality and draw their own subjective conclusions. Thus, in the most Brechtian manner are the readers involved in the work, and they must apprehend the totality of the dramatic experience to interpret it, for the form is decidedly not discursive in the traditional sense. Even the language is unreliable, for text often serves only to point to a more important subtext, which underscores the essential literary condition of postmodern drama, for form and content are inseparable, and while performance adds another dimension to the individual play, direct interpretation of the text alone discloses the theatrical and dramatic intentions of the playwright.

Pinter and Albee effectively point the direction for the unification of the late modern interior view of the human condition with traditional realism in an effective, integrated form. Their adaptation of experimental techniques, especially those advocated by Beckett and the other absurdists, to conventional form has allowed an expansion of possibility for the exploration of a paradoxically reduced postmodern concern, the existential reality of human existence. The individual applications of these concepts by a new generation of dramatists signal the establishment of a distinctly postmodern dramatic literary aesthetic.

NOTES

[1]*Romantic Quest and Modern Query* (New York: Delacorte, 1970), pp. 285, 321-22.

[2]"What's the Matter with Edward Albee?" in *The Modern American Theater,* ed. Alvin B. Kernan (Englewood Cliffs, NJ: Prentice-Hall, 1967), p. 99.

[3]Quoted in Richard E. Amacher, *Edward Albee* (New York: Twayne, 1969), p. 170.

[4]*From Tension to Tonic: The Plays of Edward Albee* (Carbondale: Southern Illinois Univ. Press, 1972), pp. 10, 5.

[5]Quoted in John Gassner, *Directions in Modern Theatre and Drama* (New York: Holt, Rinehart and Winston, 1966), p. 334.

[6]Paolucci, p. 10.

[7]Quoted in Amacher, p. 34.

[8]Quoted in David Richards, "Edward Albee: Who's Afraid of the Critics?" *Clarion-Ledger* (Jackson, MS), 18 Feb. 1982, Sec. C, p. 8.

[9]Edward Albee, *Counting the Ways,* in *The Plays* (New York: Atheneum, 1982), III, 51; subsequent references to the various plays in this four volume edition will appear as page numbers in parentheses in the text.

[10]*Tragedy and Fear* (Chapel Hill: Univ. of North Carolina Press, 1971), p. 23.

[11]"A Theatre of Discord: Some Plays of Beckett, Albee, and Pinter," *Kansas Quarterly,* 12 (1980), 7.

[12]*Drama in the Sixties* (London: Faber and Faber, 1966), pp. 30, 21, 46; see also his "Compressionism: The Drama of the Trapped," *New Hungarian Quarterly,* 18 (1965), 188-90.

[13]Gassner, pp. 354, 358; italics in the original.

[14]"A Metaphor for Dramatic Form," in Gassner, pp. 342-50.

[15]"The Case for Plot in Modern Drama," *Hudson Review,* 20 (Spring 1967), 52-53.

Gerald M. Berkowitz (essay date 1992)

SOURCE: "1960-1975: The Post-Broadway Era" and "1975-1990: A National Theatre," in *American Drama of the Twentieth Century,* Longman, 1992, pp. 121-65, 166-208.

[*In the following excerpts, Berkowitz surveys Albee's career through the 1980s, juding his later works embarrassing failures.*]

EDWARD ALBEE: THE OFF-BROADWAY PLAYS

Of the many writers whose plays appeared in the first flourish of new Off-Broadway drama—from, say, 1958 to 1965—some proved less interesting than novelty made them seem at first, some turned out to have only one play in them, some left the theatre for other callings. Among those who did produce one or more works of lasting interest, either for their inherent merits or as representatives of the time, only a very few were able or inclined to graduate from the fringe to the mainstream theatre. Most notable among these was Edward Albee, whose move to Broadway helped establish him as the dominant serious American dramatist of the 1960s.

Albee's first produced play, The Zoo Story (Berlin, 1959; New York, 1960), is essentially an extended monologue by a young New Yorker so alienated that any contact with another being, however one-sided or incomplete, is a relief:

> A person has to have some way of dealing with SOMETHING. If not with people . . . if not with people . . . SOMETHING. With a bed, with a cockroach, with a mirror . . . no, that's too hard, that's one of the last steps. With a cockroach, with a . . . with a . . . with a carpet, a roll of toilet paper . . . no, not that, either . . . that's a mirror, too; always check bleeding. You see how hard it is to find things? [. . .] with . . . some day, with people.
>
> [All but bracketed ellipses Albee's]

He chooses a conventional man he meets in the park to be his first attempt at human contact, but is unable to move his listener sufficiently by merely telling his story. Desperate for reassurance of his existence and his ability to affect another, he starts a knife fight and impales himself on his opponent's blade, dying with thanks for this ultimate proof: 'I came unto you and you have comforted me.'

The effect of this eloquent but tragically alienated character on the American theatre was of the same sort, if not the same magnitude, as the effect of John Osborne's Jimmy Porter on the British theatre. This was a new voice which had not been heard before in the drama but which was instantly recognizable as authentic, representing the experience of a hitherto ignored or unnoticed portion of the population. On the basis of a one-act play Albee was hailed as an important new writer and looked to for new insights into contemporary American life, an assignment he soon implicitly accepted.

After two brief and minor works, The Sandbox (1960), in which a dying woman meets a friendly Angel of Death, and Fam and Yam (1960), about the disconcerting effect of a young playwright (evidently Albee) on an older one (evidently Inge), Albee turned to an analysis of American racism in The Death of Bessie Smith (Berlin, 1960; New York, 1961), based on the traditional story that blues singer Bessie Smith died because she was refused admission to a white hospital after an automobile crash. Albee's central character is the admitting nurse at the hospital to which Bessie's driver brought her after being turned away elsewhere, and the bulk of the play precedes the arrival of the body. In the Nurse's bitter interactions with other characters, Albee shows how the emptiness of her life has produced a frustration and resentment for which racism is merely a convenient outlet. The climax of the play is not Bessie's death, but the Nurse's explosion a moment before it:

> I am *sick.* I am sick of everything in this hot, stupid, fly-ridden *world.* I am sick of the disparity between things

> as they are, and as they should be! [. . .] I am sick of going to bed and I am sick of waking up. . . . I am tired . . . I am tired of the truth . . . and I am tired of lying about the truth . . . I am tired of my skin . . . I WANT OUT!
>
> [All but bracketed ellipses Albee's]

This kind of pain must be avenged on somebody, and blacks are as convenient a scapegoat as any.

The American Dream (1961) is a darkly comic piece that combines echoes of Ionesco's *Bald Soprano* (in such toying with language as the extended discussion about whether a hat is wheat or beige coloured, and in the cartoonishly exaggerated characters) with a chilling condemnation of American values. On one level, then, the play is in the tradition of Arthur Miller's *Death of a Salesman,* using a domestic story, however unrealistically presented, to comment on the society outside the living room. But, where Miller condemned the American Dream for being impossible to achieve, Albee caustically depicts its dehumanizing success. Presenting what is implicitly a typical American family—selfish and catty Mommy, emasculated and almost invisible Daddy and wise-cracking Grandma—Albee satirizes and condemns a hollowness in American values that is not the result of inadequacy but of deliberate choice. Themselves almost totally inhuman, having withdrawn into a self-absorption from which they stir themselves only with great difficulty—it takes Daddy several pages to gather up the energy and determination to answer the doorbell—Mommy and Daddy *want* to be empty. Their comical abuse of language is not the result of linguistic incompetence, but a concerted effort to free themselves from the human obligations implied by communication. Grandma explains what happened to the child they once adopted in terms that explicitly identify misused words with acts of inhumanity:

> GRANDMA: One night, it cried its heart out. . . . Then it turned out it only had eyes for its Daddy.
>
> MRS BARKER: For its Daddy! Why, any self-respecting woman would have gouged those eyes right out of its head.
>
> GRANDMA: Well, she did. . . . But *then,* it began to develop an interest in its you-know-what.
>
> MRS BARKER: In its you-know-what! Well! I hope they cut its hands off at the wrists!
>
> GRANDMA: Well, yes, they did that eventually. But first, they cut off its you-know-what. . . . And then, as it got bigger, they found out all sorts of things about it, like: it didn't have a head on its shoulders, it had no guts, it was spineless, its feet were made of clay. . . .

The Young Man who appears at the end of the play is the twin of the unsatisfactory baby, who has been sympathetically affected by his brother's mutilation:

> Once . . . it was as if all at once my heart . . . became numb . . . almost as though I . . . almost as though . . . just like that . . . it had been wrenched from my body . . . and from that time I have been unable to love. Once . . . I was asleep at the time . . . I awoke, and my eyes were burning. And since that time I have been unable to see anything, *anything,* with pity, with affection . . . with anything but . . . cool disinterest [. . .] there are more losses, but it all comes down to this: I no longer have the capacity to feel anything.
>
> [All but bracketed ellipses Albee's]

Grandma recognizes immediately that this Young Man will satisfy Mommy and Daddy as his brother never did, because he is the American Dream. Mommy and Daddy did not mutilate their child to punish it, but to turn it into this; and the baby's only failure was in dying before it achieved the perfection of its brother. Mid-century America is characterized by an emptiness of spirit that requires emptiness around it, says Albee. A culture with waning values is not backsliding from what it really wants to be; it is actively striving for its complete loss of values, and will celebrate beautiful deadness as the achievement of all its desires. The artistic and commercial success of The American Dream prompted Albee's move to Broadway, where he became the predominant representative of the new generation of playwrights in the mainstream theatre; his Broadway plays will be discussed later in this chapter.

. . . . .

EDWARD ALBEE: THE BROADWAY PLAYS

Who's Afraid of Virginia Woolf? (1962), Albee's first Broadway production, is without question his best play, ranking just behind the very best of O'Neill, Williams and Miller in the American repertoire. It is the picture of a seemingly hellish marriage whose positive and supportive aspects we only gradually appreciate, as we understand how frightened and alienated the characters are, in an America similar to that of The Zoo Story and The American Dream. George and Martha (the names suggest an archetypal American couple) subject each other and another couple to a long liquor-filled night of humiliation and exposure, culminating in the revelation that their adult son is a fantasy they have maintained for twenty-one years to comfort themselves in the face of life's disappointments. Chastened by this exposure to a desperation far beyond their shallow experience, the other couple leave George and Martha to face the future without one of their most depended-on emotional crutches. The play has nothing to do with Virginia Woolf; its title, a parody of a song from a Disney cartoon, 'Who's Afraid of the Big Bad Wolf,' begins as a characterizing device, identifying George and Martha as intellectual and verbal games-players, and later comes to symbolize the unnamed fears and insecurities of modern life.

Albee has three purposes in the play: to show that George and Martha's experience of life, like Jerry's in The Zoo Story, is dominated by an insecurity and alienation that make the task of coping with day-to-day disappointments overwhelming; to argue that their commitment to survival, even if the only means is degrading or abhorrent behaviour, is heroic; and, slightly peripherally, to expose the cause of this painful experience as a dehumanizing force in the American culture, similar to that revealed in The American Dream, and identified in this play with the second couple, Nick and Honey. The emphasis on depicting and celebrating characters who find daily life overwhelming puts Albee squarely in the tradition of Tennessee Williams, a debt Albee acknowledges in the play with brief allusions to *A Streetcar Named Desire.*

Throughout the play George and Martha let slip veiled or open admissions of their sense of weakness and failure, as in Martha's third-act confession of her need for him:

> George who is good to me, and whom I revile; . . . who can hold me, at night, so that it's warm, and whom I will bite so there's blood; who keeps learning the games we play as quickly as I can change the rules; who can make me happy and I do not wish to be happy, and yes I do wish to be happy . . . who has made the hideous, the hurting, the insulting mistake of loving me . . . who tolerates, which is intolerable; who is kind, which is cruel; who understands, which is beyond comprehension.

Torn between fear of their inadequacy and refusal to avoid the struggle for existence, they live lives defined by pain. George offers as a self-description the declension 'Good, better, best, bested', and Martha admits to the portrait of her father, 'I cry all the time too, Daddy. I cry allllll the time; but deep inside, so no one can see me.'

Like many of Williams's characters and like Jerry in The Zoo Story, George and Martha seem less bizarre when we interpret their behaviour as reactions to a world that offers them no support. Their games are attempts to cope with the pain, either as distraction—Martha calls them 'the refuge we take when the unreality of the world weighs too heavy on our tiny heads'—or as a way of keeping themselves in shape for the battle: George assures Nick, 'Martha and I are merely . . . exercising . . . that's all . . . we're merely walking what's left of our wits' [Ellipses Albee's]. A particularly skilful blow is likely to be met by congratulations or mutual celebration, and they refuse to let each other relax and coast: when George scores points off the completely outmatched Nick and Honey, Martha's reaction is contempt for his 'pigmy hunting;' and when George decides on the final battle over destroying the fantasy son, he insists that Martha be at full strength to fight him.

If George and Martha must use every tool at their disposal to help them fight the dehumanizing forces pitted against them, then the loss of any tool must seriously endanger their struggle. The imaginary son compensated for their sterility, helped to hold them together and gave them a constant in their lives, but he has become a weapon they use against each other, and therefore must be sacrificed. After the initial trauma Martha accepts this judgement, and the play ends with them facing an uncertain future with a bravery that consists of admitting their fear but not turning back.

Albee forces us to recognize this immersion in life as heroic, particularly in contrast to the bland, evasive and ultimately cowardly Nick and Honey, who consciously avoid the challenges of living. Nick keeps what emotions he has under control, tries not to get involved in unpleasantness, and admits there is no passion in his marriage or in his pursuit of Martha. Honey drinks until she passes out, decides not to remember unpleasant things, and takes secret precautions to avoid having children. They do not even have real identities: 'Nick' is the name used in the stage directions, but it is never spoken in the play; and 'Honey' is merely his perfunctory endearment for her. Such lifelessness is not merely evasion of responsibility; Albee sees it as a cause of the central couple's pain. The main reason for setting the play in a university is the ease with which the two men can be characterized by their specialities. In Act One George defines the contrast in an extended mockery of Nick's genetic research:

> It's very simple, Martha, this young man is working on a system whereby chromosomes can be altered.[. . .] We will have a race of men . . . test-tube-bred . . . incubator- born . . . superb and sublime.[. . .] *But!* Everyone will tend to be rather the same.[. . .] I suspect we will not have much music, much painting.[. . .] There will be a certain . . . loss of liberty. [. . .] Cultures and races will eventually vanish . . . the ants will take over the world.
>
> [Unbracketed ellipses Albee's]

George's academic discipline symbolizes his commitment to life: 'And I, naturally, am rather opposed to this. History, which is my field [. . .] will lose its glorious variety and unpredictability.[. . .] the surprise, the multiplexity, the sea-changing rhythm of . . . history, will be eliminated. There will be order and constancy . . . and I am unalterably opposed to it.' The force that causes life to be painful and difficult for those committed to living it is the irresponsibility of those who attempt to find security by rejecting their humanity.

One important quality of Who's Afraid of Virginia Woolf? to which this analysis has not done justice is its passion. George and Martha experience and express extreme and uncensored emotions, and the play celebrates those passions, good and bad, as part of the couple's commitment to the challenge of living. Oddly, that passionate quality, which had also driven The Zoo Story, begins to disappear in Albee's later plays, displaced by a dry intellectuality that dooms some to failure and deprives even the most successful of the theatrical power of the early plays. Tiny Alice (1964) is the story of a religious man faced with what he has wanted all his life, the opportunity to sacrifice himself to an impossibility that can only be accepted through faith. But Albee presents this adventure as a series of gratuitously mystifying puzzles and paradoxes, more an intellectual construct than a living drama. The mystery Julian is asked to worship is not God but Alice, an essence who may be nothing more than a mouse in a dollhouse, and who is represented by a woman named Alice who seduces him and then orders his death. The play ends with Julian's long dying monologue, in which he either rambles incoherently or accepts Alice as his God:

> How long wilt thou forget me, O Lord? Forever? How long wilt thou hide thy face from me? [. . .] Oh, Alice, why hast *thou* forsaken me? [. . .] Alice? . . . God? SOMEONE? Come to Julian as he . . . ebbs. [. . . Is that the humor? THE ABSTRACT? . . . REAL? THE REST? . . . FALSE? It is what I have wanted, have insisted on. Have nagged . . . for. [. . .] COME, BRIDE! COME, GOD! [. . .] I accept thee, Alice, for thou art come to me. God, Alice . . . I accept thy will.
>
> [Unbracketed ellipses Albee's]

What makes Tiny Alice difficult is Albee's conviction that what cannot be understood through any means other than faith must be kept outside the audience's understanding; he simply fails to make the story clear much of the time. Meanwhile, the general air of mystification is maintained through secondary puzzles and red herrings, and through the general refusal of any of the secondary characters to act in recognizably human ways. Given its ambitions, it may be remarkable that Tiny Alice is as nearly comprehensible as it is, but it certainly tests the outer limits of a theatre audience's ability to grasp abstract ideas.

A Delicate Balance (1966) returns to some of the same concerns as Who's Afraid of Virginia Woolf?, though in a considerably subdued manner. When friends unexpectedly demand refuge with Tobias and Agnes, their presence disrupts the tenuous stability of the household, inspiring alcoholic sister Claire to ever more outrageous conduct, and driving daughter Julia to territorial hysteria. But it is their departure, when they decide they are imposing, that finally panics Tobias, who cannot bear the discovery that even the closest friendship has limits.

The title thus refers to the fragility of both social constructs and individual psychology. Agnes opens the play by entertaining herself with the prospect of going mad, but Julia's leap from childish petulance to the murderous defence of her turf, and Claire's from mildly anti-social to aggressively bizarre behaviour, show how thin the line of sanity is. Even more disturbingly, the carefully maintained balance of peace and civility in the household, the preservation of the illusion of normality, is shown to be very easily disrupted. The first half of A Delicate Balance has some parallels to the opening of Eugene O'Neill's *The Iceman Cometh,* in that an apparently diseased social milieu becomes somewhat more attractive in retrospect when a disrupting influence produces something much worse.

But more central than that, and tying this play to Virginia Woolf, is the recognition that social constructs, family rituals and even aberrant behaviour are defence mechanisms against an unnameable existential fear. Claire's drinking, Julia's regularly scheduled returns to her childhood, Agnes's reduction of every unpleasant thought to the level of abstract intellectual speculation, and Tobias's constant placating and smoothing-over of awkward moments are all ways of protecting themselves from what Agnes calls a plague of communicable terror. As Claire reminds Tobias, whole lives can be built on the fantasy of order: 'We have our friends and guests for patterns, don't we?—known quantities. The drunks stay drunk; the Catholics go to Mass, the bounders bound. We can't have changes—throws the balance off. . . . Just think, Tobias, what would happen if the patterns changed: you wouldn't know where you stood.' For everyone there is the unbearable reality that an entire life must be constructed to blot out. For Tobias it is the possibility that no commitment is absolute and there is no promise one human can make to another that has no bounds. So, at the end of the play, when Harry and Edna decide that they have indeed imposed, their attempt to spare their friend the terror they carry actually brings it on.

The abstractly intellectual quality of Albee's later plays is seen in its purest form in Box and Quotations from Chairman Mao Tse-Tung (1968), an interrelated double bill sometimes called Box-Mao-Box because the first play is repeated at the end of the second. In Box we see only a hollow cube, while the recorded voice of a woman muses on its philosophical and moral implications. In Mao Mao Tse-Tung lectures on the class struggle, a Long-Winded Lady describes her fall overboard from an ocean liner, and an Old Woman recites a Robert Service-like poem about being rejected by her children in her old age. About midway through, the voice from Box joins the rotation of monologues, speaking a line or two from that play; at the end, the live actors are silent while the voice finishes her reprise.

The theme of both plays is cultural decay; the voice moves from an admiration of the workmanship of the box to a recognition that all standards are declining, and that we have gone beyond noticing the loss. The three monologues of the inner play demonstrate this decline through Mao's dependence on empty rhetoric, the Lady's self-centredness and the Old Woman's bathetic verse. But Box-Mao-Box is as much an intellectual exercise as a dramatic statement, a Beckett-like experiment in how little can be put on a stage and still have a play, and an attempt to structure the interlocking monologues musically. With Tiny Alice before it and All Over after, it represents Albee's furthest swing of the pendulum away from the passionate psychological realism of his early plays.

All Over (1971) is set in a more recognizable reality than Box-Mao-Box, but it is no less desiccated and lifeless. Its dramatic situation is in fact a deathwatch: an important man is dying, and his Wife, Mistress, Son, Daughter and Best Friend (who are given no other names) wait out his final moments. They show very little emotion; the few brief lapses, generally by the Son and Daughter, are treated as distasteful self-indulgences. Only at the very end does the Wife allow herself an open expression of grief—not for her husband's death, but for her lifetime of unhappiness. Like Honey in Virginia Woolf and Agnes in A Delicate Balance these characters distance themselves from experience to save themselves from the pain of having it. The difference is that Albee seems to approve, and to offer such deliberately chosen lifelessness as an acceptable model. That this seems to contradict everything his earlier plays stood for is a minor difficulty—authors have the right to change their minds. But a play full of characters repressing all emotions and keeping all interactions at a safe distance runs the risk of being as anaesthetized as they are; and the biggest problem with All Over is that it is dull.

In contrast to the dry plays that preceded it, Seascape (1975) is a charming and happy fable, using an entertaining bit of fantasy to make a positive if not particularly original statement. Nancy and Charlie, a middle-aged couple relaxing on a beach, encounter Sarah and Leslie, two human-size lizard-like amphibians who have chosen this moment to evolve out of the sea. After some comic shock on both sides, the newcomers prove to be very much like the humans, with middle-class amphibian values and parallel tensions in their marriage. But the introduction to life on shore involves discovering some painful new sensations, such as human emotions, and the lizards waver in their decision to evolve. Nancy and Charlie beg them not to go back into the sea, and the play ends with the human's promise to help their new friends through their great adventure.

Sarah and Leslie are delightful characters, and their little breakthroughs—learning to shake hands, marvelling at Nancy's breasts, experiencing sorrow for the first time—almost steal the show. But the fact that they do not appear until the end of Act One is a clue that the play is actually about Nancy and Charlie, the lizards' evolutionary leap a metaphor for the humans' uncertainty about what to do now that the main business of their lives seems completed. Charlie's commitment to helping the newcomers find their way is also his recognition that, for humans as well as lizards, the end of one stage in life is the cue to evolve into the next. Seascape is a small play, and one might even feel that Albee wasted a particularly clever invention on a fairly clichéd message. But it makes its small point effectively, and with a liveliness and lightness of touch that had been missing from Albee's plays for over a decade.

. . . . .

Edward Albee and Other Dramatists of the 1960s

Edward Albee's rate of production, like Arthur Miller's, slowed in the 1970s and 1980s, in his case through an admitted frustration with a theatre and audience that seemed unable to appreciate his work; his last commercial success was A Delicate Balance in 1966. The general trend of cold intellectuality and lack of dramatic vitality in his plays that was noticed in the last chapter continued to the point almost of self-parody, as Albee seemed more and more like an author talking to himself in a private vocabulary. Listening (British radio, 1976; Hartford, 1977) presents three people in the decaying garden of a mental hospital, two staff members and a patient who make fragmented and unsuccessful attempts to penetrate each other's self-absorption. The Man begs The Woman to acknowledge that they were once lovers; The Woman goes through the rituals necessary to break through The Girl's catatonic withdrawal; and The Girl, in her occasional lucid moments, must constantly interrupt the others' conversations to be heard. In the end The Girl slits her wrists and, although The Man is frightened, The Woman seemingly approves and allows her to die.

As early as The American Dream and The Death of Bessie Smith Albee had made the Miller-like judgement that self-absorption was immoral and could be murderous. But just as All Over seemed to be celebrating the emotionless, life-avoiding characters he had condemned in his earlier plays, so Listening seems to accept behaviour he had previously rejected. The play offers no particular sympathy to The Man, who seems most interested in making human contact with the others, and it makes no real criticism of their self-absorption. When The Man finally explodes and cries to The Woman, '*Reveal* yourself!' she replies, 'There is no revelation *in* me'; and a moment later her only response to The Girl's suicide attempt is an aesthetic approval: 'Done beautifully.' In The Zoo Story Albee presented the inability to communicate with others as tragic, and in such plays as Virginia Woolf and A Delicate Balance he stressed the human need for integration and involvement with others. But in Listening he seems to be postulating, without emotion, a view of human existence as so empty and without external value that self-referential detachment is an appropriate behaviour.

Oddly, a companion piece, Counting the Ways (London, 1976; Hartford, 1977), seems to take the opposite position, celebrating romantic love with a benign and comic awareness of its foibles and imperfections. Beginning when She asks He, 'Do you love me?' it is a series of sketches and blackouts presenting situations in which love may be called into question: in the midst of unsuccessful sex, after an argument, at a time of grief, while consulting flower petals, etc. Nothing really unpleasant is discovered, so the last scene, in which He finally asks if She loves him and She replies, 'I don't *know.* I *think* I do' is a reassuring joke, suggesting the occasion for another round of considerations, not a negative. Albee labels the play 'A Vaudeville', and it functions as an occasionally thoughtful but never threatening light entertainment.

The Lady from Dubuque (1980) is Albee's most ambitious and significant play of the period, ultimately a failure of execution rather than of conception. A stranger appears in the home of a dying woman and claims to be her mother, here to help her through the process of dying. (The title refers to a comment made in the 1920s about the sophisticated magazine *The New Yorker,* that it was not edited for the archetypal mid-westerner; Albee seems to use it to identify Elizabeth as the ultimate Other.) Whether she is meant to be the angel of death or just a guide along the way, the play has echoes of both Thornton Wilder's *Our Town* and Tennessee Williams's *The Milk Train Doesn't Stop Here Anymore* in the idea that dying is a weaning away from life that requires some assistance. But one of the problems of the play is that this process is never really dramatized; Jo's departure seems quick and easy, and is seen entirely from the outside, while her husband's feeling of desertion and exclusion is most strongly dramatized, even though the play keeps declaring it to be irrelevant: 'What does Sam know? Sam only knows what *Sam* needs. . . . And what about what Jo needs? What does what Sam needs have to do with that?'

There are other structural flaws to the play. Since the supernatural visitor does not appear until the very end of the first act, there is no clear focus to the first half, and the audience must spend Act Two recalling and reinterpreting earlier events while keeping up with the new action. Meanwhile, Elizabeth is so pointlessly and cruelly coy about her identity and mission through much of the second act that the audience is likely to turn against her before her role as comforter and guide is finally made clear, and thus to sympathize with Sam's outrage more than the play desires. The potential power of The Lady from Dubuque lies in its insight that death is a process the dying must be guided through, even at the cost of excluding the living. The failure of The Lady from Dubuque lies in the basic error, far too representative of Albee's later work, of presenting this as an intellectual concept rather than as the play's dramatic and emotional core.

The Man Who Had Three Arms (Chicago, 1982) is a failure of another sort: like some of Tennessee Williams's late plays, it seems to reflect an author unable to separate himself from his own creation. The play takes the form of a lecture by the title character, whose physical abnormality made him a celebrity until the third arm withered and the public lost interest in him; he is reduced now to being the substitute speaker on a minor lecture circuit, telling his story and venting his anger at the fickleness and cruelty of the world. (An Albee play titled *The Substitute Speaker* was repeatedly announced as in progress during the 1960s.) There are some small indications that Albee intended the play as a study in the harmful effects of celebrity on the celebrated, so that Himself's petulance, self-pity and lashing-out would be seen as signs of his spiritual decay. The problem is that Himself's story, of instant elevation to stardom on the basis of his curiosity value and just as instant rejection when he no longer continued to amuse, is very close to Albee's own experience; and Albee was never reticent about expressing his resentment towards the critics and audiences that forsook him after his early triumphs. In the absence of any effective distancing of the play's voice from its central character's, it must inevitably be experienced as Albee's own uncensored demand that the world apologize. Albee's few short plays since 1982 have been kept away from the commercial theatre and neither published nor revived after their brief runs, so, like Williams's late self-pitying works, The Man Who Had Three Arms makes an embarrassing coda to a career that began with such accomplishments.

Thomas P. Adler (essay date 1994)

SOURCE: "From the Margins: Edward Albee and the Avant-Garde," in *American Drama, 1940-1960: A Critical History,* Twayne Publishers, 1994, pp. 201-14.

[*In the excerpt below, Adler contends that Albee's early short plays "serve as a culmination or summing up of many of the central emphases of post-World War II American drama."*]

A compelling case can be made that the birthsites of modern American drama during the 1915-16 season were one of the nation's earliest "regional" theaters and an off-Broadway playhouse, when short works by Susan Glaspell, such as the protofeminist play "Trifles," and by Eugene O'Neill, such as the sea plays like "Bound East for Cardiff," were first produced at the Wharf Theater on Cape Cod and later at the Provincetown on Macdougal Street in New York. An equally compelling argument can be made that the birthsites of contemporary American drama during the 1959-60 season were again off-Broadway and out in the regions, with premiers in New York but away from Times Square of the first theatrical works by Edward Albee, Jack Gelber, and Jack Richardson and of plays in Cambridge, Massachusetts, by Arthur Kopit. Both groups of artists, separated by nearly a half-century, wrote against the Broadway establishment of their times and for audiences desiring something more than commercial pap. As Stuart Little remarks at the beginning of his historical survey entitled *Off Broadway: The Prophetic Theater,* "Off-Broadway is a state of mind, a set of production conditions, a way of looking at theater at every point at odds with Broadway's patterns."[1]

Kopit, whose *Oh Dad, Poor Dad, Mama's Hung You in the Closet and I'm Feeling So Sad* (for marquees large enough to accommodate it, the subtitle is: "A Pseudoclassical Farce in the Bastard French Tradition") finally reached off-Broadway in 1962, explains that these dramatists were committed to reinvigorating an American theater so fallen into desuetude that it bore "little more than superficial resemblance to the society and culture surrounding it" and so, unlike theater in most European countries, "lacked necessity" and did not matter.[2] In cultural histories of France, 1959 stands out as something of an annus mirabilis, with three important New Wave directors, Jean-Luc Goddard, Alain Resnais, and Francois Truffaut, all making first films that radically altered the grammar and style of the cinematic medium, *Breathless, Hiroshima, Mon Amour,* and *The 400 Blows.* The 1959-60 theatrical season in America would be hardly less a breath of fresh air, definitively announcing the end of the postwar era with Albee's The Zoo Story Gelber's *The Connection,* and Richardson's *The Prodigal. . . .*

Albee and the Absurd

Like O'Neill a half-century earlier, Albee chose initially to write what he calls "the brief play," and, in fact, he was introduced to New York audiences at the very same theater, the Provincetown Playhouse in Greenwich Village, where O'Neill had been. Nor had there been any dearth of important one-act plays during the 50 intervening years by American writers as various as Clifford Odets (*Waiting for Lefty*), Thornton Wilder ("The Long Christmas Dinner," "Pullman Car Hiawatha," "The Happy Journey to Trenton and Camden"), Tennessee Williams ("27 Wagons Full of Cotton," "Portrait of a Madonna"), and William Inge ("To Bobolink, for Her Spirit," "The Boy in the Basement"). In his landmark study, *The Theatre of the Absurd* (1961), Martin Esslin was the first critic to suggest that Albee, on the basis of his earliest one-act plays, should be grouped together with Samuel Beckett, Eugene Ionesco, Jean Genet, and company. Albee, in fact, refers to Ionesco's writings in his frequently reprinted essay, "Which Theatre is the Absurd One?" (1962). Playing with possible senses of the word "absurd," the dramatist's own answer to the question posed by his title is "the commercial Broadway one," for "what could be more absurd than a theater" that measures aesthetic quality by the amount of money taken in at the box office; that relegates the playwright to a collaborative position; that worships imports from London next to idolatry; and that in some seasons sees "not a single performance of a play by Beckett, Brecht, Chekhov, Genet, Ibsen, O'Casey, Pirandello, Shaw, Strindberg—or Shakespeare?" Albee goes on to propose "that the supposed Realistic theater" that encompasses most of the works produced on Broadway "panders to the public need for self-congratulation and reassurance and presents a false picture of ourselves to ourselves," whereas "The Theatre of the Absurd, in the sense that it is truly the contemporary theater," forces audiences to "face up to the human condition as it really is."[3]

Albee dramatizes the same point in his slight little sketch, Fam and Yam (1960), which is "An Imaginary Interview" between The Famous American Playwright of the post-World War II generation, probably William Inge, and The Young American Playwright of the nascent off-Broadway movement, almost certainly Albee himself. The playlet might be seen as his clarion call for a new American theater as opposed to the ailing and sickly old, which was characterized by "greedy" theater owners, "opportunistic" producers, "slick" directors, "assembly-line" critics, "pin-headed" theater parties, and playwrights who themselves elevated financial over artistic success.

Along with excoriating most commercial Broadway theater in his essay, Albee offers his personal perspective on what constitutes absurdist drama: "As I get it, The Theatre of the Absurd is an absorption-in-art of certain existentialist and post-existentialist philosophical concepts having to do, in the main, with man's attempts to make sense for himself out of his senseless position in a world which makes no sense—which makes no sense because the moral, religious, political and social structures man has erected to 'illusion' himself have collapsed" (147). Albee's works do, indeed, consistently explore the illusions that humankind creates in every area of endeavor to cushion and help make bearable the reality of that existence. In doing so, he recurrently employs many of the theatrical techniques—incomplete exposition; breakdown of causal connections; ambiguous closure; language games—that have come to be associated with one or other of the major Continental absurdist playwrights.

Yet there remain serious questions as to whether Albee in his early short plays does in fact subscribe to the central ideological tenets of the absurd. Brian Way, for instance, has argued convincingly that Albee "retreat[s] from the full implications of the absurd [wherein] the arbitrary, the disconnected, the irrelevant, non-reason, are seen to be the main principle or non-principle of the universe," because he "still believes in the validity of reason—that things can be proved, or that events can be shown to have definite meanings."[4] While Albee might at times embrace absurdism in style, he generally does not (except in his metaphysical drawing-room play, Tiny Alice [1964]) adhere to or advance an uncompromisingly absurdist philosophy. Ideologically, he remains a traditional liberal humanist, assuming much the same philosophical stance and political agenda as Lillian Hellman, Arthur Miller, and Lorraine Hansberry before him, exalting the natural virtues of an enlightened commitment to ideals of conduct guided by reason; a criticism of moral failure within a framework of compassion; and an overriding sense of responsibility to the community of humankind.

This is not to deny, however, Albee's leadership among the theatrical avant-garde, which he describes as "free-swinging, bold, iconoclastic, and often wildly, wildly funny." He continues by promising audiences, "If you will approach it with childlike innocence—putting your standard responses aside, for they do not apply—if you will approach it on its own terms, I think you will be in for a liberating surprise" ("Which Theater?" 150). Albee's fullest statement of his aesthetic goals appears in the introduction to his most experimental drama, Box and Quotations from Chairman Mao Tse-Tung (1968), where he speaks about the dual obligation facing the serious dramatist: "first, to make some statement about the condition of 'man' . . . and, second, to make some statement about the nature of the art form with which he is working. In both instances he must attempt change." Refusing to placate or be satisfied with the status quo entails, in turn, a commitment on the part of the playwright to "try to alter his society [and] to alter the forms within which his precursors have had to work." Nor does he omit his spectators or readers from the equation, for "an audience has an obligation (to itself, to the art form in which it is participating, and even to the playwright) to be willing to experience a work on its own terms." If they are to fulfill his own dicta, Albee's one-act plays, then, will partake in a spirit of anarchy, challenging preconceived ideas, theatrical conventions, and audience expectations.

Albee's One-Act Plays

First premiered in 1959 in West Berlin, before its New York opening on a double bill with Beckett's *Krapp's Last Tape* in January 1960, Albee's The Zoo Story despite its brevity, establishes itself as emblematic of the age that produced it. A parable of alienation and spiritual dislocation in the nuclear age of anxiety, it dramatizes "the way people exist," afraid of aloneness yet equally leery of making contact, "everyone separated by bars from everyone else." The bench on a Sunday afternoon in Central Park, the only object on a minimally dressed stage, becomes symbolic of the space, so close and yet so distant, that separates and imprisons individuals within their own shells; and the park/garden itself intimates a fallen world of discord rather than harmony. Contemporary urban society is filled with outcasts, the marginalized and the disenfranchised. As Jerry catalogues them, in his roominghouse alone there live, among others, "a colored queen" who frequently plucks "his eyebrows . . . with Buddhist concentration"; "a Puerto Rican family" of husband, wife, and uncounted children; a "person in the front room whom [he's] never seen"; and a "woman who cries deliberately behind her closed door."

In a pattern he will repeat over and again in his later works, Albee brings a character from the outside into the playing space to challenge someone already there. On the park bench reading sits Peter, a fortyish, Madison Avenue type textbook editor who lives on the Upper East Side with his nuclear family, consisting of a wife and two of everything else, daughters, cats, parakeets, TVs—but no sons. Ironically, the happily conformist and complacent Peter is perhaps the most unknowingly isolated of all. Fulfilling the image of the perfect organization man in the gray flannel suit, he is so predictable as to be a nonentity, and thus can be described only by what he is not: "neither fat nor gaunt, neither handsome or homely"; through Peter's characterization, Albee removes the veneer from the "peachy-keen" Eisenhower era, revealing the shallowness and disquietude lurking underneath. Most damning of all for someone in the world of books and education who should be a sophisticated reader, Peter seems baffled by the narrative text that the intruder Jerry creates for him.

Jerry, whose handsome good looks have been replaced by "a great weariness," possesses an awareness of loneliness and death-in-life that Peter lacks. Orphaned at a young age (his memory box contains two empty picture frames), he experienced a loving homosexual relationship for a week when he was 15; now, however, Jerry is a "permanent transient" who finds himself unable to have sex with the same person more than once. Forcing the reluctant Peter to be his audience, in one of the wonderful verbal arias for which Albee will become known, he narrates "THE STORY OF JERRY AND THE DOG!" Standing guard for his "ugly, misanthropic" landlady is a dog who, unlike almost everyone else, displays not just indifference to Jerry but open hostility. Disliking such antipathy, Jerry vows to break through and make "contact"; he determines to "kill the dog with kindness, and if that doesn't work . . . just kill him," first by feeding him hamburgers and then, if necessary, by poisoning the meat. The dog survives, but they do reach "an understanding." Moreover, Jerry, having tried to break down the bars between self and other "in this humiliating excuse for a jail," has "learned that neither kindness nor cruelty by themselves, independent of each other, creates any effect beyond themselves; and . . . that the two combined, together, at the same time, are the teaching emotion. And what is gained is love." His epiphany that "we neither love nor hurt because we do not try to reach each other" espouses Albee's belief that the necessity to break out of the shell of self and effect communion with the other can justify hurting that other to bring him or her to awareness. To be creative, love sometimes must be corrosive.

Peter fails to see that Jerry, in narrating the story of himself and the dog, actually tells the drama of himself and Peter as it acts itself out on a Sunday afternoon in Central Park. When Jerry as fabulist proves ineffectual because of the recalcitrance and lack of perception of his listener, he must employ other, increasingly brutal tactics. In answer to Peter's protest "I DON'T UNDERSTAND! . . . I DON'T WANT TO HEAR ANY MORE," Jerry first tickles Peter; when that does not work, in a version of the child's game King of the Mountain, he pushes him off the bench; and when that still fails to create the desired effect, he ultimately forces Peter to pick up a knife and hold it while Jerry impales himself on it and dies. Now, at last, Peter may no longer be "a vegetable" but at least "an animal" whose conscious life will never be the same. Some critics have interpreted Jerry's death as either a suicide that he was unable to effect on his own or a disguised homosexual act, and validity may inhere in both readings. But it seems that Albee, as Rose Zimbardo proposes in her seminal essay,[5] intended viewers of his own "story of Jerry and Peter" to understand Jerry's death as a potentially salvific sacrifice meant to raise Peter from the illusion of well-being and complacency to greater knowledge of what it means to be fully human, a reading that finds support in the biblical pharaseology ("So be it"; "I came unto you") that Albee employs near the startling close of his play.

Commissioned to provide a short dramatic piece for Gian Carlo Menotti's 1959 Festival of the Two Worlds in Spoleto, Italy, Albee decided to take the characters from another brief play on which he was working and place them into a different situation. What resulted was The Sandbox a near perfect little gem of a play, only around 20 minutes in performance, that blends symbolism with surrealism, dedicated to the memory of his much beloved grandmother. The minimalist setting is "a bare stage" against the sea and the sky. Mommy and Daddy, with a Musician in tow who provides flute accompaniment on cue to set the mood, enter carrying Grandma "under her armpits" and rather unceremoniously plop her down in a "child's sandbox" where, somewhat like Winnie in Beckett's *Happy Days* (1962), she proceeds to bury herself. Mommy and Daddy, whom the stage directions denote as presenile and vacuous, are deliberately flat stereotypes: she "imposing" and dominating, he "whining" and submissive, tending to respond with "Whatever you say, Mommy." They sit and, as Mommy says, "We . . . wait." As a number of commentators have remarked, waiting has become, after Beckett's seminal play, one of the central images of post-World War II theater. And Sandbox, as a deathwatch, is a play of waiting. Yet the platitudinous Mommy and Daddy cannot respond with any true feeling, mouthing instead only the ready-made inanities familiar from greeting cards. The ritual exists for them stripped of any meaning, except getting Grandma out of their lives and "fac[ing] the future" with the same lack of awareness with which they have gotten through the past.

Just as nothing "real" exists beneath the outer shell of Mommy and Daddy, so, too, is the "well-built" young actor, not yet given a name or identity by Hollywood, all surface and role. But dressed in a bathing suit and doing calisthenics so that his arms resemble the "fluttering of wings," he plays well and sensitively his role as the Angel of Death. Sandbox achieves its forcefulness and, finally, real poignancy, in the way that Grandma, who experiences "puzzlement" and "fear" and tangentially decries the lack of respect shown aged parents, breaks through the predictable to experience genuine emotion. What at first she thought simply a game or role, playing at dying, becomes the reality of death, come for her and waiting to be accepted. She grows in awareness, in recognition and resignation. Functioning partly as mocking chorus of her children's phony responses as well as partly stage manager who orchestrates her own end provides her with a measure of control and contributes to the dignity and tranquillity of her death. Grandma can finally "go gentle into that good night" at what is for Albee at this point in his career an uncharacteristically tender close to the play.

In his preface to The American Dream (1961), Albee writes explicitly about the intention behind his lengthy one-acter: "The play is an examination of the American Scene, an attack on the substitution of artificial for real values in our society, a condemnation of complacency, cruelty, emasculation and vacuity; it is a stand against the fiction that everything in this slipping land of ours is peachy keen." He comments further about his work's manner: "Is the play offensive? I certainly hope so; it was my intention to offend—as well as amuse and entertain." In its use of flat, cartoonlike characters, banal and repetitious dialogue, and outrageous non sequiturs (Mommy greets a visitor by asking "Won't you take off your dress?" to which Mrs. Barker replies "I don't mind if I do"), American Dream comes closest of all Albee's plays stylistically to the absurdist drama of someone like Eugene Ionesco in *Bald Soprano* (1948), in which no soprano, let alone a bald one, ever appears. As satiric social criticism, Albee's work dramatizes the devaluation of the family—in a pluralistic society traditionally the main source of moral values—brought about through an embrace of material culture, a diminution of affective response, and a restrictive definition of sex roles that diminishes and delimits the individual.

Albee indicates this progressive deterioration in values by contrasting three generations. The wizened yet still wise Grandma hails from feisty "Pioneer stock"; the boxes in which she has packed the things "one accumulates" forge her link with the past. Now treated like a dog and bundled up to await the van man who will cart her off to the nursing home, something she would never have done to her own mother, she predicts that because it lacks a "sense of dignity" modern "civilization's doomed." She terms the present time an "age of deformity." Her daughter and son-in-law, expanded portraits of the Mommy and Daddy from Sandbox who bear the same name, are like a parody of the Strindbergian couple. Mommy, whose more realistically portrayed antecedents in the American theater of the 1950s include the man-hating Ann from Joseph Kramm's *The Shrike* (1953) and the domineering Eliza Gant from Ketti Frings's stage adaptation of *Look Homeward, Angel* (1956), is the archetypal emasculator; she orders Daddy to "Pay attention" and deems Mrs. Barker's husband "adorable" since he is confined to a wheelchair. Marriage was entered into strictly as a business proposition, money to live off of in exchange for sexual favors; Mommy, nevertheless, is more than content that Daddy "has tubes now, where he used to have tracts," though she insults him for being "indecisive" and turned to jelly. Mommy adopts as her motto in all things the great American advertising slogan, "Satisfaction guaranteed or your money back." Unable to have a child of their own, Mommy and Daddy—unlike George and Martha in Albee's later masterpiece, Who's Afraid of Virginia Woolf? (1962), who refuse to blame each other for their sterility—adopt their little "bumble of joy" for use in the war against one another from the Bye-Bye (read "Buy, Buy") Adoption Agency. Finding him not to their liking, they mutilate him.

Now years later, baby arrives resurrected, so to speak, in the form of his twin brother, a "clean-cut, midwest farm boy type, almost insultingly good-looking in a typically American way," whom Grandma immediately dubs "the American Dream." Another actor like the Young Man from Sandbox he is a beautiful hulk on the outside, but spiritually undernourished, without feelings or moral sense within. For when his twin brother, whom he describes as "the rest of [him]self," underwent mutilation, he, too, "suffered losses. . . . A fall from grace . . . a departure of innocence" so that, cold and emotionless, he has "not been able to love anyone." His fall from grace evidences the blighting of the American Eden. Admitting that he will "do almost anything for money," he will stay as substitute son, ready to serve as stud-boy to Mommy.

Grandma finally becomes not only both stage manager/manipulator and detached onstage audience to these proceedings but also a choral commentator, speaking a tongue-in-cheek epilogue that sends the audience home while "everybody's got what he thinks he wants. . . . I mean, for better or worse, this is a comedy, and I don't think we'd better go any further." Her valedictory to this eulogy for the American Dream gone mad relates directly back to Albee's intention to shock his audience into an awareness that, if taken further, what he actually outlines here is closer to "the American tragedy."

The central image of marginalization of the "other," of the silencing of difference in all of Albee's one-act plays comes in The Death of Bessie Smith (1960). The playwright's coup de theater is to have the great blues singer never appear or be heard; her absence becomes in itself a powerful symbolic statement of the invisibility of blacks in white society, except when they can be commodified through their music, as Bessie was, or through their menial service, as the hospital Orderly willingly is. In life, Bessie had been answerable to her white producers and promoters, who lived off her financially and for whom she had to "hustle"; in death—and this forms the background of Albee's play—her body, shattered in a car crash, was shunted off from a segregated white hospital to a black hospital in Clarksdale, Mississippi, in 1937. (In a New York revival late in the 1960s, Albee agreed to the addition of original recordings and photographic slides of Bessie, which he had at first rejected as too emotional a ploy; indeed, the text would seem to invite such multimedia or even cinematic treatment.) Both the racial bigotry of the South, however, and the battles between the sexes are subsumed here under a more general examination of power structures, sometimes achieved solely through language.

The Nurse dominates all the men with whom she comes in contact. She belittles her father, who seems to have schooled her in prejudice, as a "hanger-on" and a "flunky." Reduced to using a cane, he no longer even wields that powerfully, but instead raps it in "a helpless and pathetic flailing." She patronizes the black Orderly for his deferential behavior, calling him "boy" and "ass-licker," sending him to fetch cigarettes and accusing him of bleaching his skin. Like Clay in LeRoi Jones/Amiri Baraka's *Dutchman* (1964), he has become an Uncle Tom, trying to "advance" himself by telling whites what they "want to hear" and buying into their value system. The Nurse both desires and derides the good-looking blond Intern, teasing him yet putting him off, reminding him of his place socially and economically, and abusing him physically. When he refuses her orders not to go outside and treat Bessie, she threatens to ruin his career at the hospital.

Some hazy writing on Albee's part leaves slightly blurry whether or not the Nurse recognizes the aloneness likely to result from her attempt to dominate others and so suffers self-hatred because of it; she professes a distaste for existence ("I am sick of everything in this hot, stupid, fly-ridden world. . . . I am tired of my skin. . . . I WANT OUT!") and is somewhere between laughter and tears as she ineffectually mocks the Intern's humanity. The apocalyptic image of "the great sunset blaz[ing]" that concludes the play hints that the Intern's earlier description of sundown, "The west is burning . . . fire has enveloped fully half the continent," might be read symbolically as pronouncing the decline of the West, consumed by exploitation, subjugation, and victimization of weaker by stronger, minority by majority, outsider by insider. Albee's archetypal Jerry, for example, is as socially, and perhaps sexually, marginalized as Inge's characters, who could only be true to their identity and feelings—that is, their essential humanness—when hidden away in closets or in basements.

Undeniably, some recurrent patterns in Albee's short plays—a character's arriving onstage to challenge the "other" to overcome fear of the unknown and awake to a fuller humanity; power conflicts in gender relationships; criticism of middle-class stasis and moral complacency—look forward to later, more major works by the playwright, such as Who's Afraid of Virginia Woolf? (1962), A Delicate Balance (1966), and Seascape (1975). At the same time, however, the early one-acts serve as a culmination or summing up of many of the central emphases of post-World War II American drama. With their intimations of absurdity they speak, as do the works of Eugene O'Neill, of alienation and dislocation, mourning the estrangement of modern humankind from any source of ultimate meaning. They castigate, as do the plays of Lillian Hellman, Arthur Miller, and Tennessee Williams, an ethos of commodification that reduces culture to money and power and enshrines the material over the immaterial. Albee regrets; as does Miller, the replacement of a once empowering dream of an Eden regained by an enslaving devotion to competition and success. He reveres, as does Williams, the transmutative possibilities of art, the imaginative creation of a narrative/text or role/mask as a grace-filled moment that is potentially educative and salvific. And like Lorraine Hansberry, his art tries to subvert those social structures and benighted attitudes that inhibit human progress and potential.

What Robert Motherwell, the American abstract expressionist painter, wrote about modern abstract art in 1951 as a response to "a feeling of being ill at ease in the universe" over "the collapse of religion, of the old close-knit community and family" provides a fit summation of the thrust of modern American drama from 1940 to 1960 as perfected by Albee and such forbears as O'Neill and Williams: "It is a fundamentally romantic response to modern life—rebellious, individualistic, unconventional, sensitive, irritable."[6] And also, Motherwell might have added, at its best moments, glorious.

NOTES

[1]Stuart Little, *Off-Broadway: The Prophetic Theater* (New York: Coward, McCann and Geoghegan, 1972), 13-14.

[2]Arthur Kopit, "The Vital Matter of Environment," *Theatre Arts,* 45.4 (April 1961): 13.

[3]Edward Albee, "Which Theater Is the Absurd One?" in *American Playwrights on Drama,* ed. Horst Frenz (New York: Hill and Wang, 1965), 169-70; hereafter cited in text as "Which Theater?"

[4]Brian Way, "Albee and the Absurd: *The American Dream* and *The Zoo Story,*" *American Theatre (Stratford-upon-Avon Studies 10),* ed. John Russell Brown and Bernard Harris (London: Edward Arnold, 1967), 189, 191.

[5]Rose Zimbardo, "Symbolism and Naturalism in Edward Albee's 'The Zoo Story,'" *Twentieth Century Literature* 8, no. 1 (April 1962): 10-17.

[6]Robert Motherwell, quoted in Hilton Kramer, review of *The Collected Writings of Robert Motherwell, New York Times Book Review,* 28 February 1993, 24.

Matthew C. Roudané (essay date 1996)

SOURCE: "Rejuvenating the American Stage" in *American Drama since 1960: A Critical History,* Twayne Publishers, 1996, pp. 23-48.

[In this excerpt, Roudané investigates Albee's "affirmative vision of human experience." Although the "world of the Albee play is undeniably saturated with death," he observes, "the internal action, the subtextual dimension of his plays, reveals the playwright's compassion for his fellow human beings and a deep-rooted concern for the social contract."]

No other playwright in the 1960s influenced American drama more than Edward Albee. The beneficiary of his American predecessors, O'Neill, Miller, and Williams especially, he also was receptive to European influences, particularly those of Samuel Beckett, Eugene Ionesco, Peter Handke, Jean Genet, and Harold Pinter. Albee would ultimately prove able to move freely, if somewhat uncomfortably, between the alternative environs of the Off-Off-Broadway theatrical movement to Broadway. While gaining inspiration from his dramatic forebears here and abroad, Albee also looked ahead, encouraging and supporting a number of then-unknown dramatists—Kennedy, Baraka, and Shepard, among others. A playwright more at ease in staging his work in the margins, Albee found himself at the very epicenter of the American dramatic world.

Reed and Frances Albee adopted Edward on 12 March 1928, two weeks after he had been abandoned by his natural parents at birth. They named him after his adoptive grandfather, owner of the largest and most profitable chain of vaudeville theaters in the country. Taken in by a wealthy family with a theatrical background, the young Albee met such writers as Thornton Wilder and W. H. Auden, who were friends of the family. A rebellious youth, Albee resisted formal education. After being expelled from a number of preparatory schools and, after a brief stay, from Trinity College, Albee worked for ten years at a series of odd jobs before composing The Zoo Story (1959), his spectacular first success. Over two dozen plays, three Pulitzer Prizes, and numerous other accolades later, Albee rightly stands side by side with the best American dramatists. He remains one of the major shapers of the American dramatic imagination. Albee's influence was especially felt the 1960s, when he found himself both lionized and attacked by the critics. He suddenly won esteem as the "best" new playwright in whose scripts the American public might find fresh theatrical validation. In a sense, however, he was the best.

Philosophical Issues

Albee draws much of his plays' essential subjects from personal experiences. As he writes in the introduction to Three Tall Women, "So, when I decided to write what became Three Tall Women . . . I knew my subject—my adoptive mother." Three Tall Women—which first opened at Vienna's English Theatre on 14 June 1991 and, after its 30 July 1992 showing at the Rivers Arts Repertory in Woodstock, New York, had its New York City premiere on 27 January 1994 at the Vineyard Theatre—seems to be Albee's most frankly autobiographical work. As in such carlier works as The Zoo Story and The American Dream (1961), Three Tall Women replicates uneasy familial tensions and the playwright's lifelong preoccupation with death. A Beckettian play, Three Tall Women opens in a well-appointed bedroom in which three women—named A, B, and C—reflect on and challenge one another's lives. A is the eldest, whose nearness to death seems more pronounced with her props of a sling and walking cane; B is a middle-aged, acerbic confidante who tends to A; and C is a young attorney, a model of political correctness.

Clearly approaching her own death, A launches into a series of reflections, some bordering on vintage Albee verbal assaults, reflections dealing with death and dying. She points out the inevitability of death—it is "downhill from 16 on for all of us"—but her conception of death extends well beyond the physical. Although A appears to be a mean spirited and bigoted old woman, she also radiates more life than B and C. A recalls a past filled with loss, a sterile marriage, and a son who cannot reciprocate her love. At the end of the first act, A's anguish produces tears and a stroke.

Throughout his career, Albee subverts audience expectation, and Three Tall Women extends this pattern. In act 2 he presents a deathwatch scenario, reminiscent of All Over (1971), in which things change and time passes. A, bedridden, lies under an oxygen mask. B, humpbacked and nasty in the first act, now appears composed and regal, while C, in pink chiffon, has transformed herself into a gracious, elegant debutante.

Albee shifts away from realism to nonrealism, subverting the theatergoers sense of objective reality. The three women are really one woman. A reappears, the figure lying in the bed being a dummy, allowing the play to blend the three narratives of A, B, and C into one woman at three different stages of her life—A at ninety, B at fifty-two, and C at twenty-six. Although the three women share the same life experiences, A and B join forces in their opposition to C and in their rejection of illusions. Deception and betrayal form the greatest illusions, they tell C, forewarning that her life will be filled with disappointment. The young boy of act 1 appears as a young man now, visiting his dying mother for the last time. All of the characters, representative of various phases of a single woman's life, are haunted by sickness, denials, the process of dying, and, ultimately, death. Only A accepts her fate, embraces the reality of her death, affirming that "the happiest moment is coming to the end of it." Three Tall Women, Albee has said, was inspired by the memory of his domineering adoptive mother, with whom he felt little connection. His mother's arid marriage to a wealthy and submissive father, her marital battles with him, and the reluctant son mirror the facts of Albee's upbringing. Although Albee claims that he "did not want to write a revenge piece" and "was not interested in 'coming to terms'" with his feelings toward his mother, he calls the writing of the play "an exorcism." The play is his way of putting in perspective his mother (and father), who provided material comfort but little love; he also implies that the play is a reckoning with his own mortality. More tellingly, Three Tall Women embodies major philosophical issues that have long been synonymous with Albee's work.

Those issues first surfaced in The Zoo Story, The American Dream, and Who's Afraid of Virginia Woolf? (1962). After Jerry astonished audiences by impaling himself on a knife in The Zoo Story and Grandma reported with appalling specificity the spiritual dismemberment of the child in The American Dream, Albee was either lauded or loathed for his dramatization. Verbal challenges, social confrontations, sudden deaths—real and imagined, physical and psychological—permeate his theater. From The Zoo Story through Marriage Play (1987) and Three Tall Women, his plays typically address such issues as betrayal, abandonment, sexual tension, the primacy of communication, loss of personal ambition, and withdrawal into a death-in-life existence—hardly issues squaring with the taste of Broadway for entertainment.

Given the militancy of his scripts and his penchant for filling his stage world with self-devouring characters, many critics pigeonhole Albee as a pessimistic or nihilistic writer. Such labels do not reflect accurately the kind of artist Albee is, however. Albee, like Eudora Welty, is a moral optimist. For Albee's worldview presupposes the talismanic powers of the theater to elicit public awareness and private insight. Within the Albee canon, one can locate an affirmative vision of human experience, a vision that belies Albee's reputation as an anger artist. The world of the Albee play is undeniably saturated with death. But the internal action, the subtextual dimension of his plays, reveals the playwright's compassion for his fellow human beings and a deep-rooted concern for the social contract. What Albee calls a "full, dangerous participation" in human intercourse is a necessary correlative to living authentically. In his plays, essays, and interviews, Albee has long argued that it is only through the hurly-burly process of immersing oneself fully, dangerously, and honestly in daily experience that the individual may sculpt a "better self government."[1] For Albee, the play becomes equipment for living. As the Girl in Listening (1976) recalls, "We do not have to live, you know, unless we wish to; the greatest sin, no matter what they *tell* you, the greatest sin in living is doing it badly—stupidly, as if you weren't really alive." In plays as conceptually different as A Delicate Balance (1966), Finding the Sun (1983), Walking (1984), and Fragments—A Concerto Grosso (1994), Albee implies that one can consciously choose to mix intellect and emotion into a new whole, measured qualitatively, which leads to the heightened awareness for which Living Theatre founders Judith Malina and Julian Beck yearned.

A technically versatile dramatist, Albee demonstrates, often at the cost of commercial if not critical success, a willingness to take aesthetic risks, a deliberate attempt to explore the ontological status of theatricality itself. As he writes in his prefatory remarks to two of his most experimental plays, Box and Quotations from Chairman Mao Tse-Tung (1968), "Since art must move, or wither—the playwright must try to alter the forms with which his precursors have had to work." Each Albee play demonstrates his ongoing effort to reshape dramatic language and contexts.

A Question of Participation

One of the qualities of distinguishing American drama is the importance of audience participation. Albee remains a leader in asking his audiences to become active participants in the stage experience. He rejects the idea of audience as voyeur. Interestingly, the French actor, director, and aesthetician Antonin Artaud, founder of the Theatre of Cruelty, deeply influenced Albee. For Artaud, the dramatic experience should "disturb the senses' repose," should "unleash the repressed unconscious," and should spark "a virtual revolt."[2] Cruelty, for Artaud, is the key alchemical ingredient that generates an apocalyptic revolt within the audience. Although Artaud and Albee would disagree on many theatrical issues, they share a belief in the use of violence. "All drama goes for blood in one way or another," Albee explains. "If drama succeeds the audience is *bloodied,* but in a different way. And sometimes the act of aggression is direct or indirect, but it is always an act of aggression. And this is why I try very hard to involve the audience. . . . I want the audience to participate in the dramatic experience" (Interview). More significantly, Albee believes that if the audience participates in the play, the violence and death, paradoxically, become positive elements. As Albee suggests, "The theater is a live and dangerous experience—and therefore a *life-giving force*" (Interview).

Physical, psychosexual, and spiritual forces: these stand as the elements that so often converge in Albee's characters. This mixture, furthermore, precipitates an elemental anxiety, what the playwright calls in the preface to The American Dream "a personal, private yowl" that "has something to do with the anguish of us all." Accordingly, the power of his plays emanates from their philosophic content as well as from their sheer theatricality, from a language that rejuvenated the American stage.

Albee's experiments with dramatic forms at times place him within a postmodernist movement, but his work harkens back to a romantic tradition as well. Like Miller and Williams, Albee believes in the talismanic powers of the imagination and art to liberate, to create a liberal humanism. Underneath his characters' public bravado lies an ongoing inner drama, a subtext that presents his characters' quests for awareness. The tragic irony and feeling of loss stem from the characters' inability to understand the regenerative power implicit in self-awareness. If from the perspective of the twenty-first century such a belief seems clichéd or even shrill, it nevertheless appealed to most theatergoers and dramatists when Albee emerged as an incendiary force in the American theater in the 1960s and early 1970s.

For Albee, the play becomes the hour of consciousness. In brief, Albee's is an affirmative vision of human experience. His vision underscores the importance of confronting one's inner and outer world of O'Neillean "pipe-dreams," or illusions. In the midst of a dehumanizing society, Albee's heroes, perhaps irrationally, affirm living. If Ionesco's or Beckett's characters seem aware of suffering, they also tend to accept an attitude that precludes any real moral growth. In contrast, Albee's heroes suffer and dwell in an absurd world but realize the opportunity for growth and change. The Albee hero often experiences a coming to consciousness that draws him or her toward "the marrow"—to allude to a key metaphor in Who's Afraid of Virginia Woolf?—the essence, the core of human relationships. In brief, Albee's theater consistently stages the possibility that his heroes, and perhaps the audience, can, through the process of seeing and being seen, become more honest with both their inner and outer worlds. Such honesty, for Albee, is at once a deeply personal and a deeply political force.

To regard Albee's use of verbal dueling and death as proof of some pessimistic vision is to overlook the true source of his theatrical power. As he argues in the introduction to volume 1 of The Plays, he has throughout his career defined "how we lie to ourselves and to each other, how we try to live without the cleansing consciousness of death." To experience the "cleansing" effects of such self-awareness—as Jerry in The Zoo Story, Grandma in The Sandbox (1960), Tobias in A Delicate Balance, the Wife in All Over, Charlie in Seascape (1975), Jo in The Lady from Dubuque (1980), and Jack and Gillian in Marriage Play discover—has long unified Albee's theater.

The Zoo Story is a classic fable of anxiety and identity. First staged in Berlin, Germany, on 28 September 1959 at the Schiller Werkstatt Theater, The Zoo Story embodies many of the qualities that have since come to characterize vintage Albee. The necessity of ritualized confrontation, the primacy of communication, the paradoxical mixture of love and hate, the cleverly abrasive dialogues, the religious and political textures, the tragic force of abandonment and death, and the penalty of consciousness all coalesce in The Zoo Story. The play elevates its two seemingly indeterminate figures, Peter and Jerry, into tragic figures, in the specifics of whose fall Albee sets forth nothing less than the general tragedy of modern existence itself.

Albee generates much tragic tension by yoking opposites together. Peter, the passive listener, lives on the East Side of New York City, and his world seems well-ordered. He represents the businessman, the upper-middle-class family man. Jerry, on the other hand, lives on the West Side of the city in a sordid world. He appears as the fatigued loner, the cosmic waif. Throughout Jerry reflects that "sometimes a person has to go a very long distance out of his way to come back a short distance correctly," a reflection that culminates in a fatal chance meeting between the two characters in New York's Central Park. A random meeting turns into a mortal contest. For Jerry has decided to make "contact" with Peter by shattering his comfortable world. The play revolves around the clash of two worlds whose values and attitudes seem as separate as the men representing them. Hence the verbal jest turns into the physical assault, culminating with Jerry's ritualized suicide/murder.

When he impales himself on the knife held by a terrified Peter, Jerry not only gains the kind of purpose and expiation for which he has been searching but he also shatters Peter's predictable world. Whether judging Jerry as a psychopath living in a "zoo" (New York City), as a Christ figure, or as a shaman, critics generally acknowledge Albee's chief cultural point: to present a Peter who, through "the cleansing consciousness of death" (to use Albee's words), progresses from ignorance to awareness through Jerry's self-sacrifice. Mixing pity, fear, and recognition in the play's ending, Albee transfers the tragic insight Peter gains to the audience. For Albee, communication shatters isolation.

In The Zoo Story and, indeed, in all of his plays, Albee must be seen as a social constructionist. That is, he sees himself as an artist who, through his plays, can destabilize models of communities, expose the inherent weaknesses they harbor, and through catharsis reconstruct a new model of community and citizenship. The Zoo Story, then, is a life-affirming play. Subordinating pessimism to the possibility that the individual can communicate honestly with the self and the other, Albee presents that potential for regeneration, a source of optimism that underlies both his sense of social constructionism and his overtly aggressive text and performance. Jerry experiences a degree of religious fulfillment by giving his life. His death liberates him from an impossible present and also confirms the vitality of the "teaching emotion" he had discovered earlier. Jerry's death gives way, in brief, to nothing less than Peter's rebirth, a recharging of the spirit. Albee even claims that "Peter has become Jerry to a certain extent." Peter and Jerry, like their author, have traveled a long distance out of the way to come back a short distance correctly.

Albee does not limit the recuperative spirit of The Zoo Story to the actors but extends it to the audience. Such a deliberate attempt to diminish the actor/audience barrier—in evidence again three decades later in The Man Who Had Three Arms (1982)—essentializes Albee's dramatic theories. When Jerry dies and an absolved Peter exits, Albee envisions actor and audience as a unified collective, sharing in the emotional intensity of the action. Again, by successfully mixing pity, fear, and recognition in the play's closure, Albee transfers the tragic insight Peter gains to the audience.

This remarkable play, which made its U.S. debut at the Provincetown Playhouse in New York City on 14 July 1960, energized American theater. Its impact, for many, was more pronounced because America's then preeminent dramatists failed to excite the public. In the 1960s Tennessee Williams entered what he called his "stoned age," producing until his death in 1983 plays denuded of theatrical power. Arthur Miller staged two important plays in the 1960s, *After the Fall* (1964) and *The Price* (1968), which, despite their power, did little to lessen the public's detachment.

Albee therefore emerged at the right place at the right time. The dialogue in The Zoo Story, The Death of Bessie Smith, and other plays rekindled an excitement in the American theater not seen since the earlier Miller and Williams and, before them, O'Neill. Further, The Zoo Story was one of the first American plays to sensitize audiences to the vitality of Off-Off-Broadway theater. And while Kenneth H. Brown, with *The Brig* (1963), and Jack Gelber, with *The Connection* (1959), under the tutelage of Beck and Malina, waned as dramatic voices, Albee grew. The American debut of The Zoo Story was a fabulous inspiration to the struggling young Albee. After all, his play was one-half of a twin bill, the other being *Krapp's Last Tape* (1958), written by none other than the world's foremost modern dramatist, Samuel Beckett. Albee's The American Dream only enhanced his reputation.

Versions of the American Family

The American Dream, regarded as America's first significant contribution to the Theater of the Absurd, is a satiric attack on a culture that, for Albee, places its faith in a consumerist, materialist world. A post-Eisenhower America, its unfettered enthusiasm for wealth and security an anodyne for the horrors of two world wars and a depression, prompted Albee to ironize "the myth of the American dream." Satiric in tone, absurdist in technique, American in cadence, The American Dream was Albee's attack on what he saw as American complacency. The play offended many. But for its author, the humorous anger was appropriate. For when he wrote this play, an optimistic nationalism—symbolized by the "right stuff" attitude of the space race, technological prowess, a renewal of faith in science, youth, and capitalism—saturated the American consciousness. The American Adam was now transformed into a postlapsarian figure, his youthful innocence tempered (and corrupted) by a blatantly self-reliant consumerism.

Such a cultural milieu invited Albee to ironize his theater. It also prompted him to experiment with absurdist satire. "The play is an examination of the American Scene," he announces in the preface, "an attack on the substitution of artificial for real values in our society, a condemnation of complacency, cruelty, emasculation and vacuity; it is a stand against the fiction that everything in this slipping land of ours is peachy-keen." Albee stages his attack through language. Receptive to the European absurdists, he uses the absurdist technique of devaluing language, resulting in an often illogical, cliché-ridden repartee that signifies the characters' banality. Like lonesco's *The Bald Soprano* (1950), The American Dream parodies language and definition, substitutes cliché for genuine comprehension, and mocks social convention and audience expectation.

With its domineering Mommy, weak Daddy, rejected Grandma, and banal Young Man (the embodiment of the American Dream), many at the time felt that the play reflected the hypocrisy of much of American life: relationships are subordinated to social categories, and often these categories function as psychological screens behind which the characters lose all sense of original thought. The power of love that Jerry tried to understand in The Zoo Story dissipates in this play. Like Mommy in The Sandbox, Mommy in The American Dream is the badgering, manipulative female, the controller of a defenseless, emasculated Daddy. And Daddy is the patriarch of several Albee male characters who earn Mommy's wrath, in part because his primary social strategy is one of withdrawal, with the path of least resistance he takes prefiguring an ossified spirit.

Grandma is the one source of vitality in the play. She neither participates in nor is entrapped by the absurdism of the dialogue. Dignified though treated with disrespect, clear-sighted though elderly, she represents for the author a singular source of caring, an admittedly sentimental character based on Albee's own adoptive grandmother. She understands and accepts her condition, her eighty-six years of experience revealing her adaptability. An individual living "in the age of deformity," as Albee writes, she emerges as an independent figure who endures familial rejection.

Albee counterbalances Grandma's humanity with Mommy's and Daddy's cruelty. After buying a baby twenty years ago through Mrs. Barker's agency, Mommy and Daddy became deeply disappointed that their boy failed to mature into their version of the American Dream. When the boy refused to conform, they mutilated him. The appearence of the Young Man allows Mommy and Daddy the chance to recover the myth of the new American Dream; he will, of course, "do almost anything for money."

Clearly, Albee satirizes the American family. Perhaps Albee's childhood accounts for part of the unsparing satire. Albee saw in Mommy and Daddy traces of his adoptive parents, whose wealth allowed them, it appears, to substitute material pleasure for love. Perhaps these factors account for the anger of The Zoo Story and The American Dream; only in Three Tall Women, staged some three decades later, has Albee been able to come to terms with his family. Such issues as rejection, abandonment, lovelessness, spiritual withdrawals, and deaths dominate his theater. Perhaps Albee's homosexuality only added to the strained relations between uncaring parents and child. In the plays, it expresses itself in the animosity between the sexes. But Albee and his grandmother loved each other, which probably explains the positive treatment the elderly receive in The Sandbox, The American Dream, and Three Tall Women. In any event, the satire points toward a spiritual fissure that Albee feels deforms the primal family unit.

The American Dream seems somewhat dated today. Audiences have become accustomed to the outrageousness of the absurd. The political and artistic richness of absurdism, while still compelling, has been appropriated by the mass media and public art so much that its shock value has diminished. Dysfunctional families hardly seem unique anymore. Historically, however, the play exerted a notable influence on American theater following its 24 January 1961 premiere at the York Playhouse in New York City, giving inspiration and added significance to Off-Off-Broadway. Although he is not an absurdist playwright, Albee did succeed in using absurdist techniques in a play that inspired a whole generation of dramatists to experiment with the traditional, the predictable. In Who's Afraid of Virginia Woolf? Albee continues to dare, but with a success that exceeds his own expectations.

Challenging Broadway

A volatile confluence of theatrical forces—social, political, historical—conspired to make Who's Afraid of Virginia Woolf?, Albee's Broadway debut, especially timely. "To many people," observes Bigsby, "the American theatre seemed threatened with imminent collapse, while the great dramatists who had sustained the international reputation of American drama for so long were no longer in evidence" [C. W. E. Bigsby, ed. Edward Albee: *A Collection of Critical Essays.* Englewood Cliffs, N.J.: Prentice Hall, 1975, p. 4]. In other words, Broadway had reached a low point by the time Who's Afraid of Virginia Woolf? made its epochal premiere that Saturday evening, 13 October 1962. Albee suddenly found himself "as the man singled out to take on the burden formerly carried on by O'Neill, Miller, and Williams," a position that surely thrilled the young playwright but one with which he never felt fully comfortable (Bigsby 1975, 5). If Albee experienced the pressures of one anointed to redeem Broadway theater, he succeeded with Who's Afraid of Virginia Woolf?, a play that checked, if not halted, Broadway's decline. The play ran before packed houses for 664 performances. Whether in praise or scorn, theatergoers *responded.* The movie version, starring Elizabeth Taylor and Richard Burton, became one of the most lucrative films of 1966 for Warner Brothers and garnered thirteen Oscar nominations that year. Simply stated, the play dominated the theater world in the 1960s and 1970s with successful revivals.

Controversy and Albee go hand in hand. His plays provoke sharply divided critical opinions, which are as mightily opposed as the characters in Who's Afraid of Virginia Woolf? His masterwork only exacerbated the critical battles. The play earned Albee the reputation of being a nihilist, social protester, moralist, allegorist, parodist, dramatic innovator, affirmative existentialist, charlatan, and absurdist. Whether perceived as an account of the decline of Western civilization or as "an elaborate metaphor for what Albee sees as the willing substitution of fantasy for reality, the destructive and dangerous infantilising of the imagination and the moral being by fear," Who's Afraid of Virginia Woolf? revitalized American drama [C. W. E. Bigsby, *A Critical Introduction to Twentieth-Century American Drama.* Vol. 2. Cambridge: Cambridge University Press, 1984, p. 265].

Prior to the appearance of Who's Afraid of Virginia Woolf? critics questioned Albee's status as a major dramatist, despite the fame of The Zoo Story and The American Dream. The Sandbox, Fam and Yam, and The Death of Bessie Smith (all produced in 1960) are important works insofar as they reveal Albee's emerging unity of vision and skill as an acerbic dialogist. But they are hardly major plays. Instead, they bear the growing pains of a new playwright sorting through personal, ideological, and technical concerns. Critics viewed Albee as a promising but untested composer. Was he yet another American playwright with but one or two good plays in his repertoire? Were those who praised him, perhaps in their eagerness to anoint the Next American Playwright, too hasty in their accolades? Would Albee, like his Off-Off-Broadway contemporaries Jack Gelber, Jack Richardson, and Kenneth H. Brown, fade after a promising start? Albee had not fulfilled two requirements, the Broadway reviewers felt, to ascend to "major" dramatist ranking: he had yet to compose a full-length play or to stage a play on Broadway. Albee knew such requirements were superficial, based largely on money and mass popularity rather than substance. He emphatically argued the point the Sunday before Who's Afraid of Virginia Woolf? opened at the Billy Rose:

> Everybody knows that Off Broadway, in one season, puts on more fine plays than Broadway does in any five seasons. Everybody knows that Beckett, Genet and Brecht . . . are more important playwrights than almost anybody writing on Broadway today. . . . I do know that, uptown [on Broadway], "success" is so often equated with cash while, downtown [off Broadway], value does not always have a dollar sign attached. . . . Nonetheless, I am told by some of the cognoscenti that if this play [Virginia Woolf] is a success it will be a more important success than the others, and that if it is a failure the failure will be more disastrous than it could be downtown. It may be so, but I can't quite get it through my head why.[3]

Who's Afraid of Virginia Woolf? changed the reviewers' reservations about Albee and ratified his place in the American literary canon.

Finally, it seemed, a qualitative voice had emerged to help Hellman, Williams, and Miller, whose contributions in the 1960s were less than satisfying, sustain the modern American dramatic heritage established by O'Neill and his contemporaries.

Realism and Theatricalism

Realism and theatricalism, a fusion of the illusion of reality and dramaturgic invention, crystallize in Who's Afraid of Virginia Woolf? Its verbal dueling, Strindbergian sexual politics, and unexpected exorcism within a claustrophobic set generate excitement and outrage. If nothing else, Albee's masterpiece inspires theatergoers to react. "Only a fortnight after its opening at the Billy Rose Theatre it has piled up an astonishing impact," reported one reviewer in the *New York Times.* "You can tell from the steady stream of letters it has precipitated. Elated, argumentative and vitriolic, they have been pouring across my desk and, no doubt, into the offices of my colleagues. Whether they admire or detest the play, theatergoers cannot see it and shrug it off. They burn with an urge to approve or differ. They hail the play's electricity and condemn it as obscene. . . . The public is aroused."[4]

Many theatergoers saw in the play Albee's endgame, a quintessential negative work. Such an assessment, however, fails to capture the spirit of the performance.

Who's Afraid of Virginia Woolf? remains Albee's most affirmative work. Beneath the devastating gamemanship lies the animating principle of love, which unites its players. Near the end George explains to Honey, "When you get down to bone, you haven't got all the way, yet. There's something inside the bone . . . the marrow . . . and that's what you gotta get at." The "marrow" allusion marks a key dramatic moment, for George realizes what needs to be done to save not his marriage but his and Martha's very existence: the son-myth crippling their world must be confronted and purged from their psyche. The"marrow" allusion signifies George's awareness that stripping away the illusion governing their lives is necessary for survival.

The play's ending stages the re-visioning process Albee insists is necessary for his characters' spiritual aliveness. The hatred between George and Martha gives way to rapprochement, rapprochement succumbs to relationship, and relationship leads to love. George and Martha, connoisseurs of verbal dueling, now communicate directly. Once ennobled by their lexical inventiveness, conferring on an illusion the status of objective reality, George and Martha are brought to earth not merely by sacrificing their son but also by sacrificing the very language that defined their moral imagination. The game playing, for now, is over. The ending of Who's Afraid of Virginia Woolf? heralds the first step toward living authentically. For O'Neill illusions help; for Albee they destroy.

Albee's Virginia Woolf-like awareness of and sensitivity to fear informs the exorcism of the play. Whether in praise or scorn, the exorcism bringing the play to a climax has been the source of endless debate. It is also the source of the play's theatrical power. Throughout Albee challenges the audience's sense of logic and what is or is not real. This subversion of audience perception reaches its apogee through the exorcism of the son-myth. But the audience does not comprehend this insight until after the fact. After seeing the play the audience realizes that Albee has worked very carefully to orchestrate what turns out to be the murdering of the son-myth, but until the end of the work, the audience has no clue that the child is anything but real. While seeing the play unwind, live, the audience finds itself caught, like Nick and Honey, in the cross fire. Until Nick's epiphanic moment of comprehension minutes before the play ends—"JESUS CHRIST I THINK I UNDERSTAND THIS!"—Albee manipulates the audience to believe that the son lives. Even in the midst of exorcising the son-myth, the playwright draws upon that very illusion to highlight the intermixture of appearances and realities and to keep the audience's sense of what is verifiable shrouded in mystery.

If the audience harbors some doubt about the existence of "the bit," such misgivings seemingly vanish in act 3. The meticulous recall of the child confirms his very being. Even George concedes the point. George, whose levelheadedness maintains the psychic order of the play, announces before all that "the one thing in this whole sinking world that I am sure of is my partnership, my chromosomological partnership in the . . . creation of our . . . blond-eyed, blue-haired . . . son." All dialogue and nonverbal gestures reinforce the spectator's conviction that the child lives, requiring no great deduction on the audience's part. To think otherwise would be to miss what the characters have been telling the audience and each other for nearly four hours. In essence, Albee sets up his viewers: he prepares them for an even greater emotional shock by emphasizing the presence of the illusion that, through the unexpected reversal and subsequent recognition, will explode before their gaze.

In act 3 Albee explores the interstice generated by the matrix of truth and illusion. The fictive son assumes a most real place within Martha's consciousness during the exorcism. She has a pathological obsession with her child, a fantasy conceived out of her fearful need twenty-one years before to fulfill a void in her marriage and her own existence. Psychically dependent on her fantasy, she crosses a threshold, for her child does not merely occupy her thoughts—he possesses her, like some demon spirit. George recognizes her reaction and, especially in the final act, he sets his sights on one thing: to banish the son-myth that interpenetrates his and Martha's world.

George precipitates a ritualized form of expiation through the exorcism performance. Albee mediates the entire third act with a stylized process of expunging what at one time was an innocuous private game but has now grown to assume horrific proportions. For Albee wishes the audience to associate "the exorcism," the original title of the play, with the mythological history of past rites of cleansing evil demon spirits inhabiting individuals.

Mythologically, an exorcism is a ceremony that attempts to dispel or frighten away evil or demonic forces. In old German lore, St. Walburga, a British missionary, worked in an eighth-century convent that became one of the chief centers of civilization in Germany. She is often associated with *Walpurgisnacht,* the May first festival in which witches reveled in an orgiastic, ritualized Sabbath on Brocken, the tallest peak in the Harz Mountains. Located on the German border, these rugged, craggy mountains were in St. Walburga's day thickly forested. During "Walburga's Night" (the witches' Sabbath), as it is known in Central Europe, witches exorcise demon spirits from villages and villagers in a heightened rite in which they use a cacophony of loud noises, incense, and holy water to achieve purgation. The mysteriousness of all the religious and cultural connotations of the exorcism myth and ritual becomes an invisible force, part of the iconography of Albee's play. Structurally, then, act 3 plays counterpoint to the *Walpurgisnacht* of act 2. By invoking the rite of exorcism, Albee broadens the scope of his domestic drama: the sacredness of the Unknown and the inscrutability of an existential Terror become the mystical screen on which George and Martha enact their fears. In act 3 demon spirits are first confronted, then through "Bringing Up Baby" are externalized, and finally banished by the exorcism itself.

In his influential study of myth and ritual, René Girard theorizes that sacrifice is essential if community order and harmony are to be restored. "Violence is the heart and secret soul of the sacred," Girard writes in *Violence and the Sacred* (1977).[5] Sacred violence in the form of a ritual sacrifice, suggests Girard, ultimately cleanses the community of violence. Girard develops a fascinating account concerning the relatedness of anthropology, classical tragedy, and Freud. His ideas about the roles of violence, sacrifice, and the ways in which these forces influence community and spiritual vitality place the violence and exorcism in act 3 of Who's Afraid of Virginia Woolf? in a positive context. George, by the third act, must come to terms with the sacred violence that he is forced to unleash. Thus, as conductor of the exorcism, George first must discover "some way to really get at" his wife, a point that critics often seem to take as proof of the couple's viciousness and hatred for each other. Such is not the case, however. To orchestrate the exorcism. George begins with an invocation to the inner demons released in *Walpurgisnacht* by enraging Martha to a psychological breaking point. He thereby can bring up the demons for an essentially religious reckoning and escalate the action to "[t]otal war." The viciousness of George's and Martha's arguments is a necessary ingredient, as Girard might suggest, a method of exteriorizing their unconscious fears, and the demons lurking within Martha's psyche.

When Martha reimagines her child, experiencing the height of her pain by spreading her hands in a crucifixion pose, George recites the Mass of the Dead. Here George evolves into a secularized High Priest exorcist. Through these hypnotic scenes, Albee places us within "the marrow" of the play. The illusion shattered by George's latest fiction concerning her son's car accident (the third and final representation of a "Bergin" story), Martha cleanses her soul—"(*A howl which weakens into a moan*): NOOOOOOoooooo"—her purging cry signifying the death of the illusion and the rebirth of some semblance of sanity.

The denouement of the play suggests that the son-myth, for now, has vanished. The *"hint of communion"* informing George and Martha's verbal and nonverbal communication implies the start of a loving armistice, a definitive change in their relationship. The play's closure, with its Joycean affirmative texture, implies more than a reconciliation of man and wife; it further suggests that they can now accept their life, with its cajoling ambiguity and terrifying flux, without illusion. In their resolution, George and Martha, and perhaps Nick and Honey, acknowledge the dread implicit in human existence and affirm the importance of living honestly. The messy inconclusiveness of the play's closure, then, minimizes sentimentality while functioning thematically: Albee provides no promise that the marriage will be redeemed or that the illusion is inexorably shattered. But he does present the very real possibility of a truthful, loving renaissance for his heroes. Their new-tempered union will be measured in terms of their willingness to keep at bay the illusion that at one time was a source of happiness but, on this night in New Carthage, erupted in all its appalling forms. As such, the play stands as Albee's valediction forbidding mourning.

Truth and Illusion

After Who's Afraid of Virginia Woolf? and his adaptation of Carson McCullers's The Ballad of the Sad Café (1963), Albee staged the baffling Tiny Alice, a provocative, if not fully successful, work. Addressing the way in which the truth/illusion matrix influences one's religious convictions, Tiny Alice raises more questions than it answers. Refusing to compromise artistic instinct for box office revenue, Albee's play confused audiences on its 29 December 1964 opening at the Billy Rose Theatre. The play concerns Julian, a lay brother who, on his cardinal's orders, tries to finalize a multimillion dollar donation to the church, to be given by Miss Alice. She is beautiful—and happens to be the wealthiest woman on earth. Julian enters her house, a castle, only to find himself the object of a conspiracy. The Lawyer, Butler, Miss Alice, and even the Cardinal succeed in destroying Julian's faith in God. They convince him that he worships a denatured abstraction of God, not God himself. Julian's quest for meaning and his fear of sexuality and the unknown leave him vulnerable to his antagonists' scheme, which culminates in his marriage to Tiny Alice (not, as he thinks, to Miss Alice), who is yet another abstraction, a false deity who lives in the model of the castle. When Julian protests and threatens to thwart his enemies, he is shot. As he lies bleeding to death, he confronts the truth: that he cannot rely on metaphysical abstractions and that he has been betrayed by his own faith.

Tiny Alice is a dream play. Its obscurity and mystery, its homosexual overtones, and its apparent indictment of the church made for critical jousting (especially since it opened during the Christmas season). Albee's real interest, however, centers not so much on public crimes of business or the church as on private crimes of the heart. He raises broader epistemic issues than in the earlier plays, as seen through Julian's struggles with the ambiguous tensions created through truth and illusion, abstract and concrete knowledge, the relation between sexual ecstasy and religious celebration, and, of course, humankind's idea of God versus the reality of God. Even the model of the castle, an exact replica of the stage set, objectifies the complexity and mystery of the universe in which ambivalences are the norm. Albee stages the ethical dilemmas and contradictions within Julian's subconscious. The final irony in the play concerns Julian's finding "himself again," but only within a universe whose mysteries define the inscrutability of God and the reality of death.

A Delicate Balance, first performed at the Martin Beck Theatre, New York City, on 12 September 1966, signaled Albee's return to critical favor after the bewildering Tiny Alice and his failed adaptation of James Purdy's Malcolm in January 1966. A Delicate Balance, which earned its author his first Pulitzer Prize, is Albee's most blatant staging of the existentialist predicament. The play does not chart cataclysmic changes but rather the subtle shifts in human relationships: from engagement to habit, from commitment to estrangement, from love to indifference. The play stages the way in which, as the character Claire says, "we submerge our truths and have our sunsets on untroubled waters," a pattern by now assuming a thematically preeminent position within Albee's aesthetic. The play's slow-paced action captures well the spiritual inertia that has gradually ossified this family. Consciousness comes too late, it seems, for by the play's ending Agnes and Tobias's awareness reveals a void. Agnes, Tobias, and Claire allow vital lies to take over their lives. Although their friends Harry and Edna come to an awakening, the other characters, on the brink of living honestly, succumb to the illusions that so distort their existences.

The play dramatizes the lives of Agnes and Tobias, a couple nearing their sixties, whose comfortable suburban life seems as well ordered as it is fulfilled. But other people—Claire, Agnes's alcoholic sister who lives with the couple, Julia, the often-divorced daughter, and Harry and Edna, the family's best friends who move in because of their "terror"—upset this complacent home. The unexpected and unwanted intrusions of these people force Agnes and Tobias to reassess the nature of their love, their values, indeed, their very existences. As the play closes, however, Albee ironically suggests that Agnes and Tobias willingly accept the failure of their own individual nerve. The play presents a sense of aloneness in the midst of company, dread in the common, and terror in the real.

The play reaches its climax when Harry and Agnes ignite an awakening in Tobias. Such an awakening, however, does not lead to a definitive change. With Agnes, Tobias realizes their lives have been wasted, and his ravings at the end merely serve as a painful reminder of the wasted opportunities that have long immobilized the family. A positive reading of Agnes's closing speech hints at the possibility of regeneration. Maybe Tobias and Agnes will, like George and Martha before them, live more honestly "when daylight comes again." A bleaker reading of the end, however, seems more in accord with Albee's intentions. Both Agnes and Tobias have the chance to confront the illusions governing their world, Tobias's epiphanic litany at the ending signaling a qualitative shift from an anesthetized stance to a state of aliveness. But they choose, instead, to maintain the delicate balance, which tragically preserves their vital lies.

Relinquishing and Replenishing the Spirit

After some forgettable work—Breakfast at Tiffany's (1966), a musical based on Truman Capote's book, and Everything in the Garden (1968), an adaptation of Giles Cooper's play—Albee staged the inventive companion pieces, Box and Quotations from Chairman Mao Tse-Tung (1968), plays outlining the collapse of language and human contact itself. These two plays, concerned with the collapse of human connection and the absence of a divine grace, forced the audience to work very hard. In essence, Albee invited theatergoers to become active participants in Box and Quotations from Chairman Mao Tse-Tung, which premiered at the Studio Arena Theatre in Buffalo, New York, on 6 March 1968. "You lead a whole life," the Long-Winded Lady reflects near the end, but "no matter what, you say your name . . . and they have . . . never . . . heard of it."

He next staged All Over, a drama whose subject matter revolves around death. Indeed, the reality of death shapes this play, first performed at the Martin Beck Theatre, New York City, on 27 March 1971. Although its working title was simply "Death," All Over reveals the kinds of pressures death exerts on those still living. Albee reconnoiters a psychic terrain of the survivors. The play extends Albee's interest in death seen in Quotations from Chairman Mao Tse-Tung, whose Long-Winded Lady laments, "Death is nothing; there . . . there *is* no death. There is only life and dying."

In terms of plot and action, little happens. The characters congregate around a famous (and never seen) dying man, forming a socially awkward deathwatch. As the play develops, we see that all of the characters have abrogated their essential selves; their petty deceits and minor betrayals have grown into death-in-life patterns of behavior. The play ends with the famous man's death, but clearly Albee implies that life has been "all over" for the living characters for too long.

Elisabeth Kübler-Ross's theories on death and dying influenced Albee while he was composing All Over. Her research on familial and cultural reactions to death, published shortly before All Over appeared, centers on the psychological stresses the living and the dying experience during the various stage of the dying process. Among her complex findings she suggests a simple observation that serves, in dramatic terms, as Albee's point of departure in All Over as well as in The Lady from Dubuque and Three Tall Women: "The dying patient's problems come to an end, but the family's problems go on."[6] Albee's interest lies well beyond the dying man, for what strikes most forcibly are the other characters' "problems" and their responses toward themselves. Their egocentrism clouds judgment; the dying man remains an afterthought.

Within All Over the egocentric preoccupations of the characters so infiltrate their motives and language that humane values fade, becoming distant social forces. A special kind of death replaces any humanistic values: not the physical disintegration of the body but the metaphysical dissolution of the individual spirit. Like Bessie in The Death of Bessie Smith, who never takes the stage, the dying man in All Over remains invisible. Yet, like Bessie Smith, he asserts his presence throughout the play. His dying, ironically, gives definition to the others' lack of aliveness. Albee deliberately hides the famous man behind a screen, the symbolic separator of the dying patient from the living family members. The screen represents, for Albee as for Kübler-Ross, a disturbing cultural distancing response, a way to deny an unwanted otherness. Finally, Albee emphasizes the inactive spirit of the characters by having them perform as if they were partially anesthetized, sleepwalking through their lives. Throughout the play Albee refers to a dream world, the central problem of All Over revolving around the "moral sleep" that so engaged Thoreau and, later, Camus and Bellow. Such a relinquishment of the spirit is, for Albee, unacceptable. The playwright will rethink some of the larger issues embedded in All Over in each of his subsequent plays, especially with the more optimistic work, Seascape.

If the collapse of moral nerve forms a central problem in Albee's work through Box and Quotations from Chairman Mao Tse-Tung, then death informs his work since All Over. Seascape, which opened on 26 January 1975 at the Sam S. Schubert Theatre in New York City and which won Albee his second Pulitzer Prize, represents the dramatist's persistent concern with the problem of what may occur if the human spirit withers. Here Albee is not writing merely about the naturalistic evolution of the human and animal species but about the evolution of human consciousness itself. The sentimental play, a not-always-convincing mixture of fairy tale, myth, and history, is nonetheless one of Albee's more optimistic works.

A companion to All Over, Seascape was first entitled "Life." The design of the play seems simple enough. Nancy and Charlie are vacationing at the beach, relaxing and figuring out what they will do now that their children are grown and their own years seem numbered. When two tall green-scaled sea lizards emerge from the sea, conveniently anthropomorphized, Albee joins two distinct worlds, here represented by the human world and the animal world. Whereas in so many Albee plays the joining of two worlds leads to violence and death, in Seascape the comingling showcases the force of love and sharing. The bringing together of the sea lizards and humans does not produce illusions, but rather leads toward understanding.

During the play, the couples learn about the privileging of engagement and love. Things are not "all over" in this play. Albee, if nothing else, implies that through the sweep and play of evolutionary patterns, humankind has transcended both noble savagery and the instinctive response to nature to become beings whose mentor increasingly is reason. The power of reason, for Albee, is useful, even positive. Still, in Seascape the dominance of the rational faculties poses a real threat. The danger is that, with rationality triumphing over the instinctive, the primordial life-giving passions will dissipate and, for Charlie at least, be irreplaceable by another source of vitality. Unless reason and emotion exist in counterpoise, more ground will be lost in the wonders of evolution than gained. Albee implies that evolved humanity will cease to feel deeply, or, continuing to feel at all, will care for only the wrong things. After all, Albee called this guardedly optimistic play "triste."

Albee continues to produce and direct. Listening, commissioned as a radio play for B.B.C. Radio Three in 1976, and Counting the Ways, staged at the National Theatre in London in 1976, went largely unnoticed in the United States, as did Finding the Sun (1983) and Marriage Play (1987). Not so with his lackluster adaptation of Nabokov's Lolita in 1981, or his The Lady from Dubuque (1980) and The Man Who Had Three Arms (1982), original plays that drew mainly negative responses and quickly closed after feeble showings at the gate. Fragments—A Concerto Grosso (1994) received mixed reviews and closed virtually unnoticed. If the success of Three Tall Women in 1994 marks the return of his mimetic powers, Albee faltered slightly with The Lady from Dubuque and stumbled noticeably with The Man Who Had Three Arms.

The Lady from Dubuque, first performed at the Morosco Theater on 31 January 1980, focuses on vintage Albee themes: death, dying, and failed communication among the living. What makes the play engaging is its examination of how the central couple, Jo and Sam, ultimately respond to Jo's dying. Through Sam and the other characters who are brought into the orbit of Jo's dying, Albee suggests that, although Jo's life is about to cease physically, she radiates more life than do the physically healthy characters. Jo, in brief, is not the only figure who is dying. Her companions, long before this play begins, have succumbed to a debilitating disease that now paralyzes them. Indeed, the spiritual malaise from which they suffer pervades the play, for throughout one finds an array of wasted relationships, wasted love, and wasted lives.

In several of Albee's earlier plays the characters come to realize that they may seize upon some spiritual regeneration. This motif informs The Zoo Story, Who's Afraid of Virginia Woolf?, and Seascape. In The Lady from Dubuque, however, the characters remain incapable of seeking fresh understanding of the public and private self. Fred and Carol, with Edgar and Lucinda, retreat into their familiar habits, unchanged or only embittered by their recent experience. Elizabeth and Oscar, probably messengers of death, perform their duty and, with Jo's death, simply take leave. Sam—unlike Peter in The Zoo Story, George and Martha in Who's Afraid of Virginia Woolf?, or even Charlie in Seascape—learns little about love or acceptance. He sees the help Elizabeth and Oscar give Jo but quickly loses sight of that comfort. He remains a self-centered man. With his guest he remains as dead as the Romulus and Remus figures in the game of Twenty Questions. They have conducted themselves as if they were "the very dead; who hear nothing; who remember nothing; who are nothing," as Elizabeth says near the play's end.

Herein lies the irony of The Lady from Dubuque. As in All Over, death remains a ubiquitous force, encompassing not only Jo's literal death but also including figuratively the death of her friends and husband. The presence of death gives Sam a chance to confront his real self and allows him the opportunity to embrace a well-known Albeean theme: to participate in his life honestly, compassionately, and fully. That Sam and the others do no accept this kind of immersion into their daily encounters, however, confirms the wasted opportunity.

If The Lady from Dubuque outlines wasted opportunities, The Man Who Had Three Arms addresses another form of waste: the collapse of the individual's moral nerve as a result of a public that demands a hero, even though that hero lacks substance. The Man Who Had Three Arms, which opened at the Goodman Theatre in Chicago on 4 October 1982, presents a man savagely divided against himself and his world. Himself, the protagonist fixed behind the podium, emerges as one of Albee's least sympathetic characters, for what strikes the viewer is the character's stance toward the audience. He relentlessly lashes out at the theatergoer. Himself berates the audience in an attempt to come to terms with the incubi haunting his soul: his undeserved fame and subsequent fall from undeserved stardom. After he mysteriously grows a third arm, the media and public instantly elevate the man to celebrity status. When that third arm disappears, however, so goes his fame, money, family, and sense of self-composure.

The shaping idea of the play works as Albee explores the corrupting and transitory effect of stardom on the individual, but his presentation lacks the moral clarity and dramatic focus of some of his earlier works. Albee revised the script extensively and delayed publication for years. Himself does emerge as a more understandable, if not more likable, figure in the version appearing in the Selected Plays of Edward Albee (1987). At the end of this version, Himself, with eyes looking *"more-or-less heavenward,"* yells, "It's [the third arm] coming back, you fuckers! (*Fist upward and clenched*) You'll get yours, you mothers!" Himself thinks that his celebrated third arm is returning, but much to his surprise a foot, not an arm, appears as the final curtain falls. A Pirandellian play that Albee, if not the critics, still enjoys, The Man Who Had Three Arms (and feet?) again indicates that the playwright remains eager to restructure his stage according to the demands of his performance instincts.

If his work since Seascape lacks the theatricality of the earlier plays, he still must be seen as one of the most influential American playwrights since 1960. When he is at his best, Albee produces in certain characters and, ideally, in the audience what Robert Frost calls "a momentary stay against confusion," a still point in the messy business of living that creates the opportunity for existing with some heightened sense of self-responsibility. Heated repartee, sexual tensions, illusions, the collapse of language itself—these are the issues that Albee mines, but not from the position of a nihilist. Rather, he explores these issues because they can trigger in the plays catharsis and, ultimately, some life-affirming experience. To understand the role of death in his theater is to understand the compassion and optimism of his worldview. The plays seem overburdened with death, to be sure, but they are so conceived because the presence of death, once internalized, shapes the quality of human existence for their author.

Albee remains a regenerative figure in recent American drama. If his later works, with the exception of Three Tall Women, do not compare favorably with his earlier compositions, he nonetheless has emerged, with Arthur Miller, as an elder statesman of the American theater. His language, which once so engaged (and enraged) audiences, has become more mannered, abstract, and forced. Many of the later plays, which seem more like unfinished experiments than polished, unified plays, do not sustain the dramaturgic burdens Albee places on them. Some of these plays, many critics feel, simply repeat already outworn themes. Adding to Albee's problematic reputation are the newer voices that have eclipsed his own. Wendy Wasserstein's humor, David Mamet's elided street dialogue, Sam Shepard's mythicized stages, and August Wilson's fables now stir more critical and popular attention. On the other hand, Albee's clever use of language and moral seriousness revolutionized as it rejuvenated American drama. Long a supporter (financially and symbolically) of his fellow artists, Albee pushed American drama from the margins toward the center of cultural discourse. He continues to display an acute sensitivity to other dramatic traditions and remains intent on an experimentalism that requires a restructuring of the contemporary stage. Many feel that Three Tall Women signals a return of his mimetic powers, a recovery of the imaginative processes that were so cogent in the plays through A Delicate Balance. An innovator, he refuses to repeat old formulas or to write "safe" productions that might raise his reputation commercially. For him this bow to popular tastes and commercial expectations would compromise his commitment to produce original theater.

Albee received his third Pulitzer Prize for Three Tall Women in 1994. The only other dramatist to win more Pultizers is O'Neill. After the award Albee said, "If you really thought you were old fashioned, you could get glum about it. But there is not always a great relationship between popularity and excellence. If you know that, you can never be owned by public or critical response. You just have to make the assumption you're doing good work and go on doing it."[7] Albee has been "doing good work" for some four decades. He remains not merely one of the most controversial, helpful, and influential contemporary dramatists but also one of the few Americans responsible for introducing European influences into a uniquely American cadence and context. And he must be credited with revitalizing the American theater with his dazzling language, what Anne Paolucci calls his "verbal pyrotechnics." Albee may rightfully be credited with rejuvenating the American stage.

Notes

[1]Interview with the author, 23 September 1980; hereafter cited in the text as Interview.

[2]Antonin Artaud, *The Theatre and Its Double,* trans. Mary Caroline Richards (New York: Grove, 1958), 41.

[3]Edward Albee, "Wants to Know Why," *New York Times,* 7 October 1962, 1, 3.

[4]Howard Taubman, "Cure for the Blues," *New York Times,* 28 October 1961, 1.

[5]René Girard, *Violence and the Sacred,* trans. Patrick Gregory (Baltimore: Johns Hopkins University Press, 1977), 31.

[6]Elisabeth Kübler-Ross, *On Death and Dying* (New York: Macmillan, 1969), 18.

[7]David Richard, "Critical Winds Shift for Albee, A Master of the Steady Course," *New York Times,* 13 April 1994, B-1.

FURTHER READING

BIBLIOGRAPHIES

Amacher, Richard E. and Margaret Rule. *Edward Albee at Home and Abroad: A Bibliography.* New York: AMS Press, 1973, 95 p.

Features primary and secondary sources from England, Germany, Switzerland, and other countries as well as the United States.

Giantvalley, Scott. *Edward Albee: A Reference Guide.* Boston: G. K. Hall, 1987, 459 p.

Comprehensive annotated collection of sources.

Green, Charles Lee. *Edward Albee: An Annotated Bibliography, 1968-1977.* New York: AMS Press, 1980, 150 p.

Chronological listing of sources designed as a supplement to the work of Amacher and Rule.

Tyce, Richard.*Edward Albee: A Bibliography.* Metuchen, N. J.: The Scarecrow Press, 1986, 212 p.

Includes a chronology of initial productions of Albee's plays, and information on their first publications, as well as a listing of critical studies.

AUTHOR COMMENTARY

Kolin, Philip C., ed. *Conversations with Edward Albee.* Jackson: University Press of Mississippi, 1988, 223 p.

Contains over two dozen interviews from the 1960s to the 1980s.

Samuels, Steven. "Yes is Better Than No." *American Theatre* 11, No. 7 (September 1994): 38.

Interview in which Albee discusses the success of *Three Tall Women.* The text of the play follows.

OVERVIEWS

Bigsby, C. W. E. *Albee.* Edinburgh: Oliver and Boyd, 1969, 120 p.

Includes chapters on Albee's life, early plays, adaptations, *Who's Afraid of Virginia Woolf?, Tiny Alice,* and *A Delicate Balance.*

———, ed. *Edward Albee: A Collection of Critical Essays.* Englewood Cliffs, N. J.: Prentice-Hall, 1975, 180 p.

Reprints more than twenty essays by Gerald Weales, Alan Schneider, Diana Trilling, and others.

Cohn, Ruby. *Edward Albee.* Minneapolis: University of Minnesota Press, 1969, 48 p.

General survey of Albee's life and early career.

Hirsch, Foster. *Who's Afraid of Edward Albee?* Berkeley, Calif.: Creative Arts Book Company, 1978, 142 p.

Discusses Albee's plays in thematic groups and types, such as "Living Room Wars," "Chamber Plays," and "Closet Dramas."

Kolin, Philip C., and J. Madison Davis, eds. *Critical Essays on Edward Albee.* Boston: G. K. Hall, 1986, 218 p.

Collects reviews, essays on Albee's place in world drama, critical studies of the plays, and other materials.

Lewis, Allan. "The Fun and Games of Edward Albee." In *American Plays and Playwrights of the Contemporary Theatre,* pp. 81-98. New York: Crown Publishers, 1970.

Asserts that Albee has "performed the true role of the playwright: to express the human condition metaphorically, to establish new myths, and to reveal the power of the drama to have a direct and immediate impact on the audience."

Mayberry, Bo. *Theatre of Discord: Dissonance in Beckett, Albee, and Pinter.* Rutherford, N. J.: Fairleigh Dickinson University Press, 1989, 90 p.

Focuses on *Box* and *Quotations from Chairman Mao Tse-Tung.*

Nelson, Gerald. "Edward Albee and His Well-Made Plays." *Tri-Quarterly,* No. 5 (1966): 182-88.

Examines Albee's "compulsion to be discursive rather than dramatic," to narrate rather than to present the action in his plays, which, Nelson maintains, has the effect of diminishing the audience's involvement.

Roudané, Matthew C. *Understanding Edward Albee.* Columbia: University of South Carolina Press, 1987, 221 p.

Traces Albee's development as a playwright through *The Man Who Had Three Arms.*

Sterling, Eric. "Albee's Satirization of Societal Sterility in America." *Studies in Contemporary Satire* 15 (1987): 30-9.

Analyzes Albee's satire of the emptiness of American values in *The Zoo Story* and *The American Dream.*

Vos, Nelvin. *Eugène Ionesco and Edward Albee.* William B. Eerdmans, 1968, 48 p.

Examines Albee's work as operating within the tradition of the Theatre of the Absurd.

Witherington, Paul. "Albee's Gothic: The Resonances of Cliché." *Contemporary Drama* IX, No. 1 (Spring 1970): 151-65.

Examines how Albee's use of cliché in his plays demonstrates his "affinity with Gothic writing."

Additional coverage of Albee's life and career is contained in the following sources published by The Gale Group: *Authors in the News,* **Vol. 1;** *Contemporary Authors,* **Vols. 5-8R;** *Contemporary Authors Bibliographical Series,* **Vol. 3;** *Contemporary Authors New Revision Series,* **Vols. 8, 54, 74;** *Concise Dictionary of American Literary Biography, 1941-1968*; *Contemporary Literary Criticism,* **Vols. 1, 2, 3, 5, 9, 11, 13, 25, 53, 86, 113;** *Dictionary of Literary Biography,* **Vol. 7;** *Major 20th-Century Writers*; *World Literature Criticism*; *Discovering Authors*; *Discovering Authors: British Edition*; *Discovering Authors: Canadian Edition*; *Discovering Authors: Modules*—**Dramatists Module and Most-Studied Authors Module;** *Literature Resource Center.*

The Zoo Story

INTRODUCTION

Albee's first play, *The Zoo Story,* is a one-act satire set in New York City. It was first staged on 28 September 1959, in a production directed by Walter Henn at the Schiller Theatre Werkstatt in Berlin. It received its first American performance on 14 January the following year, in a production at New York's Provincetown Playhouse, directed by Milton Katselas. The play centers on Jerry, a young drifter, who encounters Peter, a conservative publishing executive, on a bench in Central Park. Jerry attempts to force conversation on Peter, becoming increasingly more personal and direct in his questioning as the reticent Peter fails to respond. Ultimately, Jerry instigates a physical confrontation with Peter, who defends himself with a knife that the drifter has thrust into his hand. During the scuffle, Jerry purposely impales himself on the blade.

CRITICAL RECEPTION

While many critics have regarded *The Zoo Story* as an absurdist condemnation of the artificiality of American values and the failure of communication, others have described the work as an allegory of Christian redemption in which Jerry martyrs himself to demonstrate the value of meaningful communication. Martin Esslin has cited the play's attack on "the very foundations of American optimism" as evidence for placing Albee in the context of the Theater of the Absurd. On the other hand, Rose Zimabardo has viewed *The Zoo Story* as operating not within an absurd Godless universe, but rather a distinctly Christian one. She has termed the work a "modern Morality play" that employs traditional Christian symbolism to present the theme of "human isolation and salvation through sacrifice." Robert S. Wallace and Mary M. Nilan, among others, have also explored the play's themes of alienation and social polarization, and Robert B. Bennett has examined its religious and spiritual content in support of his contention that *The Zoo Story* is a tragedy and not merely a melodrama.

PRODUCTION REVIEWS

Brooks Atkinson (review date 15 January 1960)

SOURCE: "Theatre: A Double Bill Off Broadway," in *The New York Times,* 15 January 1960, p. 37.

[*The following review of* The Zoo Story *praises it, calling it "consistently interesting and illuminating—odd and pithy" but flawed by a melodramatic ending.*]

After the banalities of Broadway it tones the muscles and freshens the system to examine the squalor of Off Broadway.

Three actors suffice for the two short plays put on at the Provincetown Playhouse last evening. Samuel Beckett's *Krapp's Last Tape* makes do with one actor—Donald Davis from the Crest Theatre in Toronto. Edward Albee's ***The Zoo Story*** needs two—George Maharis and William Daniels.

Both plays are dialogues. Both plays are interesting, and both of them are well acted by intelligent professionals. Nothing of enduring value is said in either play. But each of them captures some part of the dismal mood that infects many writers today.

Krapp's Last Tape takes a wistful look back into the memories of an aging, creaking curmudgeon. All that happens really is that Krapp listens to a tape record of an idyllic day in his youth. But that is all Mr. Beckett needs. For he has a highly original sense of the grotesque comedy of life. Although Krapp looks like a Skid Row veteran he is the relic of an exultant writer; and everything Mr. Beckett says is a grim criticism of life.

Having once studied the sullen method of *Endgame,* Alan Schneider is the perfect director for *Krapp's Last Tape.* The scenery consists of a morose library table and chair, an ugly lamp and a messy array of cartons—disorder incarnate. As Krapp, Mr. Davis has very little to say and do. But he makes every movement significant and every line caustic. The whole portrait is wonderfully alive. If *Krapp's Last Tape* is a joke, the joke is not on Mr. Beckett.

Mr. Albee's ***The Zoo Story*** does not have so much literary distinction. Mr. Beckett has a terrifying sense of the mystery of life. Mr. Albee is more the reporter. There are two characters and two benches in his play set in Central Park. A cultivated, complacent publisher is reading a book. An intense, aggressive young man in shabby dress strikes up a conversation with him.

Or, to be exact, a monologue. For the intruder wants to unburden his mind of his private miseries and resentments, and they pour out of him in a flow of wild, scabrous, psychotic details. Since Mr. Albee is an excellent writer and designer of dialogue and since he apparently knows the city, ***The Zoo Story*** is consistently interesting and illuminating—odd and pithy. It ends melodramatically as if Mr. Albee had lost control of his material. Although the conclusion is theatrical, it lacks the sense of improvisation that characterizes the main body of the play.

Milton Katselas has staged ***The Zoo Story*** admirably; and Mr. Maharis' overwrought yet searching intruder, and Mr. Daniels' perplexed publisher are first-rate pieces of acting.

Although the Provincetown bill is hardly glamorous, it has a point of view. Both Mr. Beckett and Mr. Albee write on the assumption that the human condition is stupid and ludicrous.

Donald Malcolm (review date 23 January 1960)

SOURCE: "And Moreover . . ." in *New Yorker,* Vol. XXXV, No. 49, 23 January 1960, p. 72-76.

[*The following review praises* The Zoo Story*'s "acute observation of two authentic and interesting types."*]

The cheerful news of this week comes from the Provincetown Playhouse, which is presenting an excellent double feature. The first item on the bill is *Krapp's Last Tape,* by Samuel Beckett. It reveals that author in an unwontedly unambiguous and almost chatty frame of mind. His playlet concerns a solitary and unsuccessful old writer named Krapp, whose singular habit it is to make a yearly tape recording of his reflections on the events of the preceding twelve months. This eccentric figure shuffles around his dismal room, eats a banana or two with senile relish, and then plays back a tape he made many years earlier, when he was young. As the playback proceeds, the old man listens with unseemly avidity to his younger self describing a romantic interlude, and then interrupts, with sulphurous comments, his own youthful rhapsodies on the meaning of life and art. Krapp then attempts to record his impressions of the current year, only to find that there is "nothing to say. Not a squeak." That, substantially, is all there is to the production, but its effectiveness is startling. The tape recorder permits Mr. Beckett to present his hero, simultaneously, at two different stages of his career, and so to suggest, with great compression, the whole course of his life, while the interplay of actor and recording produces a remarkable blend of irony and sentiment. The sketch is much indebted for its success to a brilliant cast, which consists of Donald Davis. It would have been accomplishment enough, I should think, merely to keep from looking foolish while spending all that time in listening attitudes, but Mr. Davis manages to make every ripple of expression speak, either comically or touchingly, of the terrible attrition of the years.

The second play is ***The Zoo Story,*** and it was written by a hitherto unknown young playwright named Edward Albee. It deals with the chance encounter of two men at a bench in Central Park. The seated member of the pair, called Peter, is a thoroughly respectable young executive. His accoster, Jerry, seems at first to be just another of those talkative cranks with which this city abounds. His efforts to strike up a conversation are awkward in the extreme; he fidgets around Peter's bench and asks startlingly direct questions: "You married? How many children you got? Any pets?" The information he volunteers about himself is no less personal. He itemizes his few possessions, scrupulously including his deck of pornographic playing cards. He describes his appalling room in a West Side tenement. He relates his attempt to make friends with the landlady's mangy dog, which has persistently tried to bite him. He describes his attempt to poison the dog, which failed but which led to a mutually wary coexistence of man and beast. All this is presented with a keen sense of natural, spoken comedy that does not, I'm afraid, translate readily to paper. But as the lopsided and somewhat menacing conversation proceeds, one also senses the desperate loneliness of Jerry's life in his effort to make friends by sheer enforced intimacy. When Peter, who is sympathetic but understandably nervous, fails to respond to these overtures, Jerry forces that stolid citizen to do battle with him, and so contrives matters that he runs upon his own knife and kills himself, while Peter looks on aghast, murmuring repeatedly, "Oh, my God!" There is a disturbing suggestion, in the final moments of the play, that the author would not be disappointed if one were to relate Jerry and Peter to a pair of celebrated figures from the New Testament, but the hint is sufficiently oblique to be safely ignored by those who like to think that there is more to godhead than a warm heart, an addled brain, and an urgent need to com*mu*nicate, like. The merit of the piece lies in its acute observation of two authentic and interesting types, and one is encouraged to expect many more good things from Mr. Albee. Like its predecessor on the bill, this play owes much to its performers. As Jerry, George Maharis is at once sinister and appealing, and William Daniels, who is obliged to do nearly as much listening as Donald Davis, acquits himself with nearly equal art. Mr. Daniels' expression on being told that "*Time* magazine isn't written for blockheads, ya know" transcends mere grimace to become a species of Higher Criticism.

Henry Hewes (review date 6 February 1960)

SOURCE: "Benchmanship," in *Saturday Review,* Vol. XLIII, No. 6, 6 February 1960, p. 32.

[*In the following review, Hewes calls* The Zoo Story *"an extraordinary first play" and one of the finest achievements of the theatrical season.*]

Last week these columns were devoted mainly to a discussion of Samuel Beckett's rich and poetic playlet, *Krapp's Last Tape.* This play is the first half of a twin bill currently at the Provincetown Playhouse. The second play there, titled ***The Zoo Story,*** is equally exciting, not only because it is compelling theatre, but also because it introduces Edward Albee, a young (circa thirty) playwright of considerable potentiality.

Mr. Albee's play is quite simple in form. A dull, respectable man with that upper-middle-middle expression on his face is reading on a park bench when an obnoxious stranger approaches him with irritating personal questions and remarks. The stranger has a desperate need to make contact with someone, and as a last resort pushes his listener to violence.

The details of these events are made fascinating by the actors George Maharis and William Daniels. To the role of Jerry, the beatnik, Mr. Maharis brings a quietly hypnotic rhythm that comes across as theatrically colorful yet integrated with his own personality. And as Peter, the square, Mr. Daniels provided a genuine humor. He is at his best in the early part of the play where the tone *is* humorous, as Jerry ridicules the clichés he is able to smoke out of Peter's Madison Avenue existence. Of course, this ridicule has itself become a cliché, and if unimaginatively played would seem merely tired and predictable satire. But director Milton Katselas has permitted each actor an awareness of the situation and of what the dialogue means to the one who speaks it. Jerry tends to have this awareness at the precise moment he speaks. And Peter has it a second or two after he has said his line. Even an ordinary interchange (JERRY: "Well, *Time* magazine isn't for blockheads." PETER: "No, I suppose not.") becomes subtly hilarious when given this particular treatment. And it is not just funny, for as he considers each random question, Peter becomes more and more aware of inadequacies not really faced before.

Jerry, on the other hand, seems compelled by an inner, not quite understood drive, an unwillingness to stop short of scraping out the last layer of truth. And even when he is using such colorful language as "But that was the jazz of a very special hotel," it is not done for effect, but rather because that is the best way he knows to express his nostalgia without oversentimentalization. The high point of his performance is reached when he tells "The Story of Jerry and the Dog." In the parable Jerry attempts first kindness and then cruelty to a dog that tries to bite him every time he comes into his boarding house. The result is an eventual compromise in which both Jerry and the dog arrive at a state in which they neither love nor hurt because they no longer try to reach each other. This state—the basis of so many relationships in modern adult society—is what has driven Jerry into his present pilgrimage up Fifth Avenue to the zoo, where he had hoped to find out more about the way people exist with animals, animals with each other, and animals with people. As he tells Peter the story of what he saw at the zoo, Jerry attempts, through cruelty, to provoke some animal feeling in Peter, and though the ending is melodramatic and violent, Jerry—like Christ—succeeds at the cost of his life in arousing the human soul out of its deep modern lethargy to an awareness of its animal self.

The Zoo Story is done so well that we can afford to point out that Mr. Katselas might have made this production even more effective if he had been able to highlight some of the author's points more distinctly and had found a more interesting way of expressing the animal stirring within Peter at the play's melodramatic end. We can also afford to wonder if Mr. Albee's suggestion that Jerry's boarding house is a West Side purgatory in which God is a queen who plucks his eyebrows and goes to the john is not one that needs the fuller development he might give it in a longer play. And doesn't his description of Jerry's deceased mother ("She embarked on an adulterous turn of our Southern states . . . and her most constant companion among others, among many others, was a Mr. Barleycorn") owe something to Tennessee Williams? No matter. Mr. Albee has written an extraordinary first play, which, next to Jack Gelber's *The Connection,* constitutes the finest new achievement in the theatre this season. Thank God for Off-Broadway, and, I guess, thank God for beatniks.

Harold Clurman (review date 13 February 1960)

SOURCE: A review of *The Zoo Story,* in *The Nation,* Vol. 190, No. 7, 13 February 1960, pp. 153-54.

[*The review below asserts that* The Zoo Story ". . . *gives ample evidence of genuine feeling and an intimate knowledge of certain aspects of the contemporary scene."*]

Samuel Beckett's *Krapp's Last Tape* and Edward Albee's ***The Zoo Story*** (Provincetown Playhouse) have this in common: both are studies in loneliness. Beckett's play is a sort of marginal sketch in the body of his more ambitious work; Albee's play is the introduction to what could prove to be an important talent on the American stage. . . .

The Zoo Story is flawed by improbabilities and perhaps needless notes to provoke shock or outrage—comic and horrifying by turn. Yet the play gives ample evidence of genuine feeling and an intimate knowledge of certain aspects of the contemporary scene, especially of our metropolitan area. If there were not some danger of being taken too superficially, I should say that in ***The Zoo Story*** certain tragic and crucial factors which have contributed to produce the "beat" generation have been brilliantly dramatized.

The young man in ***The Zoo Story,*** who intrudes on a respectable and modest citizen sitting on a Central Park bench, is isolated in his poverty, his self-educated ignorance, his lack of background or roots, his total estrangement from society. He has no connection with anybody, but he seeks it—in vain. When he succeeds in approaching an animal or a person, it is always through a barrier of mistrust and in a tension of disgust, fear, despair. When he breaks out of the emotional insulation of his life, it is only by a violent intrusion into the complacent quiet of the mediocre citizen on the park bench; and that unoffending bystander is then forced into effecting the mad young man's suicide. To put it another way: the derelict finally achieves a consummation of connection only through death at the unwitting and horrified hands of society's "average" representative.

This story is conveyed with rude humor—very New York—a kind of squalid eloquence and a keen intuition of the humanity in people who live among us in unnoticed or shunned wretchedness. We come not only to know the pathetic and arresting central figure as well as the astonished stranger he "victimizes," but through them both we also meet the unseen but still vivid characters of a lady janitor, a Negro homosexual neighbor, a dog and other denizens in the vicinity of both the West and East Seventies of Manhattan.

The Zoo Story interested me more than any other new American play thus far this season. I hope its author has the stuff to cope with the various impediments that usually face our promising dramatists.

The play is perfectly cast. George Maharis and William Daniels give admirable performances. Maharis, as the play's interlocutor, is truthful as well as intense. His acting is both economical and gripping. He seems possessed by all the hurts, resentment and compressed hysteria of the bewildered youth we hear so much about, but who is rarely made this real in newspaper reports, editorials, sermons or fictions.

Robert Brustein (review date 22 February 1960)

SOURCE: "Krapp and a Little Claptrap," in *The New Republic,* Vol. 142, No. 8, 22 February 1960, pp. 21-22.

[*In this review, Brustein argues that* "The Zoo Story *embodies the same kind of sexual-religious claptrap we are accustomed to from Allen Ginsburg. . . . Mr. Albee's love-death, like Mr. Ginsburg's poetry, yields more readily to clinical than theological analysis."*]

Krapp's Last Tape is Samuel Beckett's latest, and very possibly his best, dramatic poem about the old age of the world. Still obsessed with the alienation, vacuity, and decay of life upon a planet devoid of God and hope, Beckett is finally able to sound those chords of compassion which have always vibrated quietly in his other work.. . .

Accompanying Beckett's play at the Provincetown is an underground work by Edward Albee called ***The Zoo Story,*** a colloquy between a well-dressed bench sitter and a psychotic hipster who accosts him in the park. Out of this dialogue—or, rather, monologue (for the hipster does the talking while the bench sitter responds with raised eyebrows)—comes a convoluted story about the hipster's inability to connect with human beings. A brief account of his sexual failures with both men and women leads to a longer account of his relationship with animals, particularly his landlady's dog which he tried to poison because this "black monster of a beast" was always making vicious passes at his leg. The murder, despite elaborate preparations, does not come off ("I wanted the dog to live so that I could see what our relationships would come to"); instead, the hipster experiences a kind of pseudo-Zen religious conversion. Realizing that his attempt to kill, along with the dog's effort to bite, was really an expression of love, he begins to see God everywhere: in the Negro queen who lives above him, in his lecherous landlady, even in the pornographic playing cards he keeps in his room. And, undoubtedly to prove his love for the bench sitter, he expropriates his bench, punches him in the ribs, maligns his manhood—goads him, in other words, into holding a knife on which he gratefully impales himself. Having scared the poor bench sitter half out of his wits, the hipster tells him, "Now you know what you see on your TV," frees him from the charge of being a vegetable, commends himself to God, and dies.

I should report immediately that portions of this play are extremely well-written. The bench sitter is less a character than an idea (Mr. Square, straw man of the Beat Generation) so ***The Zoo Story*** lacks a convincing antagonist; but the dialogue, suspense, and sheer narrative flow of the work indicate that Mr. Albee, who is no Broadway sibling, has a powerful dramatic talent. On the other hand, I am deeply depressed by the uses to which this talent has been put. In its implicit assumption that the psychotic, the criminal and the invert are closer to God than anyone else, ***The Zoo Story*** embodies the same kind of sexual-religious claptrap we are accustomed to from Allen Ginsberg. The tendency of Beat writers to invest the French Rebel tradition (de Sade—Rimbaud—Jean Genet) with a pseudo-religious flavor seems to me quite similar to the tendency of Broadway playwrights to identify romantic love with God; and although such ideas may endear these writers to the Luce publications, they signifiy general flabbiness in American feeling and thought. I will not bore you with a discussion of the masochistic-homosexual perfume which hangs so heavily over ***The Zoo Story*** except to say that Mr. Albee's love-death, like Mr. Ginsberg's poetry, yields more readily to clinical than theological analysis. In short, Mr. Albee has successfully avoided Broadway stereotypes only to fall into Beat ideology, and Jack Gelber remains the only new American dramatist steering a clear path between the two.

CRITICAL COMMENTARY

Rose A. Zimbardo (essay date 1962)

SOURCE: "Symbolism and Naturalism in Edward Albee's *The Zoo Story,*" in *Twentieth Century Literature: A Scholarly and Critical Journal,* Vol. 8. No. 1, April, 1962, pp. 10-17.

[*The essay below presents the view that* The Zoo Story *is a "modern morality play" that places Christian symbolism in a context of "naturalistic dialogue, situation and setting."*]

The acclaim, both popular and critical, which has greeted Albee's ***The Zoo Story*** leads one to speculate upon the direction American drama is likely to take in the future. Concern with idea, rather than character or plot, is not new in the American theatre, nor is the use of symbolism for the realization of idea. There is, however, about American plays which employ symbolism—from O'Neill to Williams—a strong suggestion of the gimmick. Because American playwrights have been self-conscious in employing symbols, their symbolism is almost always embarrassingly obvious. It calls attention to itself and exists as a kind of scaffolding which the audience feels the playwright should either have built over or removed. For example, O'Neill's symbolistic drama, which has, of course, shaped all later American drama, directs attention toward the symbol as symbol rather than upon a whole dramatic structure within which symbolism operates. The audience must identify the symbols and their equivalents to work out the play's meaning. Symbol and meaning are, therefore, external to the play's design. *Mourning Becomes Electra* provides an excellent example.

What marks ***The Zoo Story*** as a new development of our drama is the way in which Albee blends symbolism with naturalism to realize his theme. Somewhat startling is the realization that Albee's are traditional Christian symbols which, despite their modern dress, retain their original significance—or, more precisely, express their original significance in modern terms. The relationship between traditional symbol and naturalistic dialogue, situation and setting is, however, never forced, as it so often is in, say, a Williams play. Rather symbolism is part of the very fabric of the play functioning within, as well as enlarging, its surface meaning.

On the simplest level ***The Zoo Story*** is concerned with human isolation. The world is a zoo "with everyone separated by bars from everyone else, the animals for the most part from each other, and always the people from the animals" (49); that is, men are not only separated from each other, but from their own basic animal natures (as Peter, one of "the people" is, until the end of the play, separated from his own animal nature).

The play opens upon Peter, who is seated on a bench in the park. As Albee tells us in his description of the dramatis personae, Peter is "neither fat nor gaunt, neither handsome nor homely." He is, in fact, in no way distinctive. Peter is the modern version, in middle-class stereotype, of Everyman. He reads the "right" books, lives on the "right" side of the park, has the average number of children, and the "right" Madison Avenue job. His is the New Yorker ad life to which most middle-class citizens, consciously or unconsciously, aspire. He blends perfectly into the brightly-packaged emptiness of the modern landscape. The "bars" which separate Peter from his own nature and from other people are the material goods and the prefabricated ideas with which he surrounds himself. He has himself carefully constructed his isolation.

Peter would prefer not to talk with Jerry but is too polite and too afraid of anyone's bad opinion, even Jerry's, to ignore him. Once engaged in conversation, he tries to avoid talking about any subject that has real relevance, anything that has roots penetrating the carefully prepared mask which he presents to the world, and even to himself. When Jerry, trying to establish some real contact with Peter, questions him about his having more children, he withdraws from the conversation, furious that Jerry might have spotted a chink in his armor.

> JERRY: And you're not going to have any more kids, are you?
>
> PETER: (a bit distantly) No. No more. (Then back and irksome) Why did you say that? How would you know that?
>
> JERRY: The way you cross your legs perhaps; something in the voice. Or maybe I'm just guessing. Is it your wife?
>
> PETER: (furious) That's none of your business. Do you understand?
>
> (18)

Peter, who hardly acknowledges his own physicality, is furious and frightened that a stranger should try to expose it.

Although Peter, in spite of himself, becomes interested in Jerry's confessions, he is embarrassed by Jerry's candor. He would much prefer to steer the conversation to the safe, if shallow, waters of conventional small talk. He tries to restrict himself to talk about the weather or books. And the only time during the conversation that he feels comfortable, indeed expansive, is when he launches into a "canned" evaluation of the comparative merits of Marquand and Baudelaire, which Jerry, to his dismay, cuts short and dismisses as pretentious. Jerry disturbs Peter because he cannot easily be fit into any of Peter's neatly labelled pigeonholes.

> PETER: Oh, you live in the Village (this seems to enlighten Peter)
>
> JERRY: No, I don't . . .
>
> PETER: (almost pouting) Oh, I thought you lived in the Village.
>
> JERRY: What were you trying to do? Make sense out of things, bring order? The old pigeonhole bit?
>
> (25)

Peter, then, is self-isolated. His life of things and prejudices protects him from himself and from the world. While it provides no gut-pleasures, neither does it allow for gut-pain. Peter's is a kind of middle-class stoicism. But while genuine stoicism raises a man above pleasure and pain, this middle-class variety protects by anaesthesizing him in the commonplace.

While Peter is one of the "people" who is separated from the animal in himself and others, Jerry is an animal (he knows his own nature) who fights separation from the other animals. In part his isolation is forced upon him. But in large measure it grows out of his need for truth. He is determined to discover the essential nature of the human condition. Therefore, he strips himself of goods, things, obvious relationships. He has a strong box without a lock, picture frames without pictures, and pornographic playing cards that remind him of the difference between love and sexual need. Deprived of the usual family relationships, he refuses either to sentimentalize them or to console himself for what he is with comforting justifications built upon memories of an unhappy childhood.

The same urge for truth that enables Jerry to know himself makes communication between him and the other animals almost impossible, for the truth about human relationships that Jerry recognizes is that men are islands irrevocably cut off from one another. Contact is from time to time made, but always with great pain and difficulty and never with any assurance that it can be sustained. Jerry tells Peter what he has learned about human relations in his tale of Jerry and The Dog.

Being cut off from one another, we fear, and fearing, we hate with an unreasoning hatred any creature who threatens to invade that little area of the world that provides us with security. The dog attacks Jerry only when Jerry tries to enter the house, "whenever I came in; but never when I went out. . . . I could pack up and live in the street for all the dog cared." (37) The dog considers the house his domain just as Peter, later in the play, considers the park bench which he has appropriated his. Both Peter and the dog are willing to fight to the death any invader of their territories.

We cannot buy love or understanding, nor can we establish real contact by any easy means. Jerry bribes the dog with hamburgers but this gains him only the tactical advantage of a few extra minutes to race up the stairs before the dog attacks him.

> Poor bastard, he never learned that the moment he took to smile before he went for me gave me time enough to get out of range. But there he was, malevolence with an erection waiting.
>
> (39)

The dog reflects with deadly accuracy all of the qualities which Jerry finds in the animals of his own species (his parents, for instance, or the landlady): hatred, lust, smiling exploitation, and treachery. Jerry and the dog stand in antithetical relation to one another. They are a pair of armed enemies sizing each other up, waiting to spring or to outmaneuver one another. Theirs is a perfect model of most human relationships, as Jerry sees them. Any superficial attempt at conciliation merely lulls for a moment the enmity which is caused by their isolation and fear.

To establish contact one must reach below the surface to the level of pain and pleasure, to the animal core. "I have learned," Jerry says, "that neither kindness or cruelty, independent of each other creates any effect beyond themselves; and I have learned that the two combined, together, at the same time are the teaching emotion." One must reach into the realm where emotions themselves are not sharply differentiated. But, as Jerry explains, even the flash of understanding that can result from such a contact gives no assurance that the contact can endure for more than an instant. "And what is gained is loss. And what has been the result; the dog and I have attained a compromise: more of a bargain, really. We neither love nor hurt because we do not try to reach each other."

Jerry applies the knowledge he has gained from his contact with the dog in trying to establish contact with Peter. Realizing that Peter cannot be drawn out of his tough shell with talk, that words when they do penetrate Peter's surface, merely cause him to throw up further barriers to contact, Jerry tries to touch Peter beneath this consciously preserved surface. He begins by tickling Peter. Tickling, being a pleasure-pain experience, perfectly implements Jerry's theory that the teaching emotion involves cruelty and kindness combined. It must perforce elicit a primitive, animal response. The effect upon Peter of the tickling is startling and immediate. It enables him, for the first time, to relax his grip upon the shield that his "perfect" life provides.

> PETER: Oh hee, hee, hee. I must go. I . . . hee, hee, hee. After all, stop, stop, hee, hee, hee, after all the parakeets will be getting dinner ready soon. And the cats are setting the table. Stop, stop . . . and we're having . . .
>
> (Jerry stops tickling Peter but the combination of the tickling and his own mad whimsy has Peter laughing almost hysterically. As his laughter continues, then subsides, Jerry watches him with a curious, fixed smile.)

Peter goes on laughing and Jerry reminds him that something has happened at the zoo about which Peter is curious.

> PETER: Ah ha, ha, the what? Oh, yes, the zoo. Well, I had my own zoo there for a moment with . . . hee, hee, the parakeets getting dinner ready. . . . Oh my, I don't know what happened to me.
>
> (48)

The teaching, pleasure-pain emotion has enabled Peter to see clearly for a brief moment the emptiness of his life, a life in which cats, children, wife, and parakeets are interchangeable because they are all merely props whose function it is to disguise nothingness and isolation.

After he has established this first contact, which is comparable to the contact he had achieved with the dog in that its purpose was to enlighten, Jerry goads Peter into a fight. In forcing Peter to fight for the park bench, Jerry is once again challenging Peter's attachment to material things that are in themselves without value to him. Peter responds to the invasion of his "property" with the same ferocity that the dog has shown. Peter is again forced by Jerry to respond at the animal level, like a savage fighting for a bone. Finally, Jerry makes Peter kill him. Peter, we assume, can never again exist on the surface level, can never again avoid contact with himself. And Jerry has at last established a contact that must endure, for Peter will never be able to forget a man he has killed.

It is within the naturalism that we have been discussing that the play's symbolism operates. The symbols are large and are, as I said earlier, traditional Christian symbols. There is Jerry, or Jesus, a thirty-year-old outcast whose purpose is to establish contact "with God who is a colored queen who wears a kimono and plucks his eyebrows, who is a woman who cries with determination behind her closed door . . . with God, who I'm told, turned his back on the whole thing some time ago. . . ." And there is Peter, St. Peter, an average worldling who is stripped by the irresistible Jerry or his material goods and led toward a revelation of truth. So carefully constructed and maintained is the symbolic pattern that it skirts being allegory. What preserves it as symbol is that its function in the naturalistic design of the play is never lost. Let us examine the symbolic pattern more closely and observe its relation to thc pattern of meaning we have discussed.

Jerry, when we meet him, has lived for a short time in a rooming house on the West Side. The inhabitants of the rooming house are a Negro homosexual, a Puerto Rican family, and a woman who cries incessantly. They are, in effect, the outcasts, the doomed, the "least of these." The gate keepers (the word is Jerry's) of the rooming house are a foul woman and a dog, "a black monster of a beast: an oversized head, tiny, tiny ears and eyes. . . . The dog is black, all black except for the bloodshot eyes." (36) The description immediately identifies the dog as Cerebus, the monster, all black with flaming eyes, who guards Hell. The drunken, lewd woman whose affection for the dog is almost maternal adds a further dimension to the allusion for we recognize the pair as Milton's Sin and Death. The symbol is again reinforced and expanded when Jerry throws poisoned meat to the dog in his effort to gain safe passage, for this is an unmistakable allusion to the myth in which Theseus throws drugged honey-cakes to Cerebus to gain entrance to the Underworld. The West Side rooming house, then, is Hell and Jerry's adventures with the dog symbolize the mythical hero's or God's descent into Hell. We see here Albee's method of symbolism. He chooses old symbols, that carry with them a wealth of meaning but that yet do no violence to the naturalistic surface of his play.

To go on to the identification of Jerry as Jesus—when the landlady asks him to pray for her sick dog, Jerry replies, "Madam, I have myself to pray for, the colored queen, the Puerto Rican family, the person whom I have never seen, the women who cries behind the closed door, and the rest of the people in all the rooming houses everywhere." This modernized Messiah first identifies himself with the outcasts and the afflicted and then assumes responsibility for them.

From time to time Albee gives the audience broad clues to his symbolic equivalents so that his meaning cannot be mistaken. For example, when Jerry is revealing to Peter the nature of the human condition by means of the parable of the dog (for that, indeed, is what the Tale of Jerry and the Dog is, a parable), he uses, in broad parody, a Biblical locution, "And it came to pass that the beast was deathly ill." Or again, after Jerry-Jesus has harrowed Hell (that is, gained entrance into the rooming house and assumed responsibility for its inmates) and is ready for the job of salvation, he must come to Peter by a very curious route.

> . . . I took the subway down to the Village so I could walk all the way up Fifth Avenue to the zoo. It's one of those things a person has to do; sometimes a person has to come a very long distance out of his way to come back a short distance correctly.
>
> (25)

The journey downtown and up, at the end of which lies the salvation of a man is, of course, Christ's descent into Hell and Resurrection which are necessary before the Redemption can begin.

Peter refuses Jerry-Jesus' message when it appears in the parable of the dog. He first deliberately resists understanding, then he pretends that he has not understood, and finally he covers his ears to escape the truth that has been revealed to him.

> JERRY: Oh, come on now, Peter, tell me what you think.
>
> PETER (numb): I . . . I don't understand what . . . I don't think I . . . (Now almost tearfully) Why did you tell me all of this?
>
> JERRY: Why not?
>
> PETER: I DON'T UNDERSTAND.
>
> JERRY (Furious, but whispering): That's a lie.
>
> PETER: No, no, it's not.
>
> JERRY (Quietly): I tried to explain to you as I went along. I went slowly; it all has to do with—
>
> PETER: I DON'T WANT TO HEAR ANY MORE.
>
> (44, 45)

Jerry's parable, like the Gospels, is spoken slowly and framed in the simplest terms. But, like the Gospels, it is rejected by Everyman who pretends not to understand, who pleads confusion, and who finally flees from the responsibility that understanding would demand. Jerry's truth cannot be conveyed in words.

In tickling Peter and causing him for a second to lose his grip, to penetrate the falsity of his life, Jerry is, in effect, symbolically stripping Peter of his worldly goods and causing him to "follow" him. Once Peter has, even whimsically, questioned the "happiness" of having the right life, the right family, the right pets, he has taken the first steps toward his salvation. He has taken the first step in a journey that will lead him to the realization of what it is like to be essentially human and to be an outcast. Finally, realizing the futility of trying to reach Peter with words, realizing too the fragility of the vision of truth that has flashed before Peter's mind during the tickling, Jerry dies for Peter. He dies to save Peter's soul from death by spiritual starvation. Peter will be forced by Jerry's death to know himself and to feel kinship with the outcasts for whom Jerry has prayed.

In the dialogue of the death scene Albee again makes his allusions very broad. In the instant before Jerry decides to impale himself upon the knife there is a suggestion of his momentary indecision, followed by acceptance of his fate which he declares in a spoken resolution.

> PETER: I'll give you one last chance to get out of here and leave me alone.
>
> (He holds the knife with a firm hand but far in front of him, not to attack, but to defend.)
>
> JERRY (Sighs heavily): So be it.
>
> (59)

This decision to accept death for man's salvation, with its air of the culmination of a foreordained pattern, is the modernized scene at Gethsemane. Again the somewhat archaic locution strengthens the allusion.

In the death scene itself the allusion is so broad that it becomes ironic. Peter's calling "Oh, my God" operates so well on both symbolistic and naturalistic level that the one level becomes an ironic commentary upon the other. The words are, of course, the very words we feel we would utter were we caught in so horrible a situation, so that they are naturalistically "true" and yet, ironically, on the symbolistic level it *is* God, the God he has slain, whom Peter is addressing.

> PETER: Oh my God, Oh my God, Oh my God.
>
> JERRY (Jerry is dying, but now his expression seems to change. His features relax, and while his voice varies, sometimes wrenched with pain, for the most part, he seems removed from his dying.): Thank you, Peter, I mean that now; thank you very much. I came unto you and you have comforted me, dear Peter.
>
> PETER (Almost fainting): Oh my God.
>
> JERRY: You'd better go now. Somebody might come by and you don't want to be here when anyone comes.
>
> PETER (Does not move, but begins to weep.): Oh my God, Oh my God.
>
> JERRY (His eyes still closed, he shakes his head and speaks: a combination of scornful and mimicry and supplication.): Oh . . . my . . . God.
>
> (62)

The allusion is perfectly sustained and in the mouth of a skillful actor Peter's repetition of the phrase contains infinite variety, expressing varying degrees of awareness. This Crucifixion scene is also underscored by Peter's betrayal when, taking his book and leaving the dying Jerry, he, in effect, denies that "he knows the man."

What Albee was written in ***The Zoo Story*** is a modern Morality play. The theme is the centuries old one of human isolation and salvation through sacrifice. Man in his natural state is alone, a prisoner of Self. If he succumbs to fear he enforces his isolation in denying it. Pretending that he is not alone, he surrounds himself with things and ideas that bolster the barrier between himself and all other creatures. The good man first takes stock of himself. Once he has understood his condition, realized his animality and the limitations imposed upon him by Self, he is driven to prove his kinship with all other things and creatures, "with a bed, with a cockroach, with a mirror. . . ." (The progression that Jerry describes is Platonic.) In proving this kinship he is extending his boundaries, defying Self, proving his humanity, since the kinship of all nature can be recognized only by the animal who has within him a spark of divinity. He finds at last, if he has been completely truthful in his search, that the only way in which he can smash the walls of his isolation and reach his fellow creatures is by an act of love, a sacrifice, so great that it altogether destroys the self that imprisons him, that it kills him. Albee, in recreating this theme, has used a pattern of symbolism that it is an immensely expanded allusion to the story of Christ's sacrifice. But the symbolism is not outside of the story which he has to tell, which is the story of *modern* man and *his* isolation and hope for salvation. He uses the allusion to support his own story. He has chosen traditional Christian symbols, I think, not because they are tricky attention-getters, but because the sacrifice of Christ is perhaps the most effective way that the story has been told in the past.

Ronald Hayman (essay date 1971)

SOURCE: *"The Zoo Story,"* in *World Dramatists: Edward Albee,* Frederick Ungar Publishing Co., 1971, pp. 3-17.

[*The following essay examines* The Zoo Story *and concludes that it "is not a homosexual play, not an Absurd play, and not a religious play, but it is a moral play."*]

Technically, ***The Zoo Story*** was the most audacious play to be successful since *Waiting for Godot.* Though neither Beckett, at forty, nor Albee, at thirty, was making his first attempt at playwriting, in both cases the play was the first of their works to be produced. This probably helped them find the courage to take the risks they did.

> Before I wrote ***The Zoo Story,*** I didn't know how one wrote a play; before I saw rehearsals of ***The Zoo Story,*** I didn't know how a play was rehearsed.

There was no question for Albee of making concessions to the medium, of doubting whether a narrative about off-stage action was too long to be wedged into the dialogue, or whether he had created sufficient theatrical tension to carry him through a passage where a protagonist was doing nothing more than speaking the thoughts in his mind. Albee was a natural playwright whose inherent confidence saved him from balking at formidable technical problems and whose instincts carried him—with a superb appearance of effortlessness—to perfectly viable solutions.

Like Beckett, Albee dispensed almost completely with action in the accepted theatrical sense. ***The Zoo Story*** culminates in an act which is as violent as the climax of any melodrama, but there is scarcely any physical action in the conversation that leads up to it, and whereas the action of *Waiting for Godot* depends on relationships between Vladimir and Estragon, between Pozzo and Lucky, which are already in existence when the play begins, Jerry and Peter in ***The Zoo Story*** start off as strangers. But Albee's dialogue convinces us that within the short time (less than an hour) that the play runs, Jerry inflicts himself on Peter with such uncompromising determination that in spite of all Peter's efforts to fend him off, he gets to know Jerry better than he has ever known his wife or his daughters—and better than he will ever get to know anyone else. In fact Peter will be lonelier than before, because more aware of his aloneness.

The play starts unpromisingly—like so many drama school improvisations—with two men of contrasted types on a park bench. Peter, in his early forties, is obviously an Average Middle-Class Father. He wears a tweed jacket, smokes a pipe, reads a book through horn-rimmed glasses, and does not like conversations with strangers. He is careful, conservative, conventional, where Jerry, slightly younger and carelessly dressed, soon gives the impression of not wanting to hold on to things, of not having much that is worth holding on to. His opening gambit—"I've been to the zoo"—is a curious one, and what immediately makes the conversation theatrically interesting is a slight feeling of danger in the air. Jerry is ironic and capable of using his irony as a weapon, though Peter at first receives only a pinprick.

> JERRY (*watches as Peter, anxious to dismiss him, prepares his pipe*): Well, boy; you're not going to get lung cancer, are you?
>
> PETER (*looks up, a little annoyed, then smiles*): No, sir. Not from this.
>
> JERRY: No, sir. What you'll probably get is cancer of the mouth, and then you'll have to wear one of those things Freud wore after they took one whole side of his jaw away. What do they call those things?
>
> PETER (*uncomfortable*): A prosthesis?
>
> JERRY: The very thing! A prosthesis. You're an educated man, aren't you?

After this Jerry gets the conversation going properly by asking Peter outright whether he minds if they talk. Peter obviously does mind but faced with the direct challenge he does not have the courage to be rude and say he would rather read his book. Then, after slackening the theatrical tension by talking about the weather, Jerry screws it up again. After another reference to the zoo, he adds:

> You'll read about it in the papers tomorrow, if you don't see it on your TV tonight.

Which must mean either that he is mad or that something sensational has happened or is going to happen. Our curiosity is whetted and the conversation can afford to return to the casual chat in which the basic facts about Peter are established. That he has two daughters; that he had wanted a son. And in a reluctant reply to a less casual question, Peter admits that he and his wife are not going to have any more children. Several times the pattern is repeated: a casual sequence of question and answer, a deliberate provocation from Jerry (the pinprick going slightly deeper each time) a protest from Peter, an easy piece of soothing from Jerry, a resumption of the catechism. We learn that Peter has a home on 74th Street, with cats and two parakeets, and that he is an executive in a company which publishes textbooks. He earns around 18,000 dollars a year.

He is at a big disadvantage in the conversation because of his basic insecurity, which Jerry, superficially more self-confident, takes pleasure in exposing. Each time Peter rises to the bait of Jerry's provocation, it is easy for Jerry to make him feel guilty for having become angry or patronizing. The more uncertain Peter is of the extent to which he is being mocked, the more confused he becomes in trying to cope with the situation. Even when Jerry asks an absurd question like "What's the dividing line between upper-middle class and lower-upper-middle class?" or a loaded one like "Who are your favorite writers? Baudelaire and J. P. Marquand?" Peter is trapped by his ingrained habit of politeness. His instinct is always to play safe and he has been conditioned to believe there is always safety in politeness.

A point is soon reached where Jerry, bored with interviewing Peter, starts to use him as an audience.

> JERRY: Do you know what I did before I went to the zoo today? I walked all the way up Fifth Avenue from Washington Square; all the way.
>
> PETER: Oh; you live in the Village! (*This seems to enlighten Peter.*)
>
> JERRY: No, I don't. I took the subway down to the Village so I could walk all the way up Fifth Avenue to the zoo. It's one of those things a person has to do; sometimes a person has to go a very long distance out of his way to come back a short distance correctly.

It is as if Jerry has been going a long distance out of his way in questioning Peter as he has. No meaningful contact could possibly have been established through a tired exchange of the conventional questions and answers of casual conversation. This can provide, at most, the illusion of contact, and Jerry is after the real thing. He is going to have to inflict himself totally on Peter, as now, again going a long distance out of his way, he inflicts the basic facts of his existence.

Ostensibly the motive is to prevent Peter from pigeonholing him as a Greenwich Village type by providing an alternative pigeonhole. He lives in a small room on the rear side of the top floor of a brownstone rooming house on the upper West Side. Jerry talks about the other roomers, whose lives all sound miserable. None of them has any contact with him. There is a black homosexual with rotten teeth who plucks his eyebrows with Buddhist concentration and goes to the john a lot. There is a Puerto Rican family all living together in one of the front rooms, and there is someone else living in the other, whom Jerry has never seen. In the front room on the third floor there is a woman who can be heard crying whenever Jerry passes her door.

Jerry also lists his possessions for Peter—toilet articles, a few clothes, a hotplate, a can opener, a knife, two forks and two spoons, three plates, a cup and saucer, a glass, two empty photograph frames, eight or nine books, a pack of pornographic playing cards, an old typewriter, and a small strongbox of pebbles collected when he was a child.

> Under which . . . weighed down . . . are some letters . . . *"please"* letters . . . "please why don't you do this, and please why do you do that" letters. And *"when"* letters, too. "When will you write? When will you come?"

The assortment is well chosen to give an impression of a lonely, penurious, frustrated life. Peter's questions about the empty photograph frames cue Jerry's explanation about his parents' broken marriage and their deaths, the deaths of his dour aunt, and the brevity of his relationships with women.

> I never see the pretty little ladies more than once, and most of them wouldn't be caught in the same room with a camera.

His longest-lived sexual relationship was when he was fifteen—an eleven-day homosexual affair with a sixteen-year-old Greek, son of a park superintendent.

For a moment it looks as though by telling Peter about himself, Jerry is inviting advice, but he is not.

> PETER: Well, it seems perfectly simple to me. You just haven't . . .
>
> JERRY (*angry. Moves away*): Look! Are you going to tell me to get married and have parakeets?

From Jerry's point of view, and perhaps from Albee's, marriage is no cure for loneliness. The pornographic playing cards are used to make the point that

> When you're a kid you use the cards as a substitute for real experience, and when you're older you use real experience as a substitute for the fantasy.

It is after this that Jerry starts on the long narrative about the landlady and the dog, whom he jointly describes as "the gatekeepers of my dwelling," which makes us think of the rooming house as Hades, though later, if we are thinking in symbolic terms at all, the sexual imagery makes the entrance hall into a symbolic orifice of the body. The landlady is described as "a fat, ugly, mean, stupid, unwashed, misanthropic, cheap, drunken bag of garbage." The dog is black, with an oversized head, tiny ears, bloodshot eyes, a red open sore on one of its forepaws, and an almost permanent erection, which is also red. Both assault Jerry, the woman by pressing her body up against him in a corner, the dog by biting his ankles. The woman Jerry can keep at bay:

> When she presses herself to my body and mumbles about her room and how I should come there, I merely say: but Love; wasn't yesterday enough for you, and the day before? Then she puzzles, she makes slits of her tiny eyes, she sways a little, and then, Peter, and it is at this moment that I think I might be doing some good in that tormented house, a tormented smile begins to form on her unthinkable face, and she giggles and groans as she thinks about yesterday and the day before; as she believes and relives what never happened.

He is giving her a fantasy as a substitute for real experience.

About the dog Jerry talks uninterruptedly for five and a half pages of the script. First he tried to make friends with it by buying hamburgers and giving it the meat from them. But after devouring the meat, the dog still tried to attack him. Still, he went on buying meat for it for five more days and after being attacked five more times, he mixed rat poison into the meat. Though his intention had been to kill the dog, he would have been disappointed if it had died. He wanted to see how his relationship with it would develop.

> I loved the dog now, and I wanted him to love me. I had tried to love, and I had tried to kill and both had been unsuccessful by themselves. I hoped . . . and I don't really know why I expected the dog to understand anything, much less my motivations . . . I hoped that the dog would understand. It's just . . . it's just that . . . (*Jerry is abnormally tense, now.*) . . . it's just that if you can't deal with people, you have to make a start somewhere. WITH ANIMALS! Don't you see? A person has to have some way of dealing with SOMETHING.

But now there is no contact at all. Recovering from the poison, the dog no longer attacks Jerry. Allowed free passage, he feels more solitary than ever.

> I have *gained* solitary free passage, if that much further loss can be said to be gain. I have learned that neither kindness nor cruelty by themselves, independent of each other, creates any effect beyond themselves; and I have learned that the two combined, together, at the same time, are the teaching emotion. And what is gained is loss. And what has been the result: the dog and I have attained a compromise; more of a bargain, really. We neither love nor hurt because we do not try to reach each other. And, *was* trying to feed the dog an act of love? And, perhaps, was the dog's attempt to bite me *not* an act of love? If we can so misunderstand, well then, why have we invented the word love in the first place?

The story of Jerry and the dog has become an analogue of Albee's view of human relationships. It foreshadows ***Who's Afraid of Virginia Woolf?,*** which is very different as a story about human relationships but similar in its recognition that a combination of kindness and cruelty is more instructive than either separately. (The emphasis in it may be on cruelty, but George and Martha both teach each other something during the course of the action; to overlook the love between them is to miss the point of the play.)

Peter, of course, understands that in telling him the story, Jerry is trying to make contact with him, and he therefore pretends not to understand the story.

PETER (*numb*): I . . . I don't understand what . . . I don't think I . . . (*Now, almost tearfully.*) Why did you tell me all of this?

JERRY: Why not?

PETER: I DON'T UNDERSTAND.

JERRY (*furious, but whispering*): That's a lie.

PETER: No. No, it's not.

JERRY (*quietly*): I tried to explain it to you as I went along. I went slowly; it has all to do with . . .

PETER: I DON'T WANT TO HEAR ANY MORE. I don't understand you, or your landlady, or her dog.

Jerry cannot be fended off so easily. Next he tries a physical approach, tickling Peter's ribs, which makes him giggle and joke childishly about his own animals.

I must go. I . . . hee, hee, hee. After all, stop, stop, hee, hee, hee, after all, the parakeets will be getting dinner ready soon. Hee, hee. And the cats are setting the table.

But Jerry detains him by saying he still hasn't heard what happened at the zoo.

I went to the zoo to find out more about the way people exist with animals, and the way animals exist with each other, and with people too. It probably wasn't a fair test, what with everyone separated by bars from everyone else, the animals for the most part from each other, and always the people from the animals. But if it's a zoo, that's the way it is.

In his rooming house, as he describes it, that is exactly the way it is. And that is the way it still is with Peter, despite the momentary contact Jerry has made by tickling him. As in Jerry's relationships with girls, and as in Peter's relationship with his wife, physical contact does not necessarily mean that the individuals are breaking through the bars to each other. But Jerry, who has decided to stop at nothing in his experiment in human contact, now tries to break through by playing an aggressive game of territorial acquisitiveness. The bench that Peter is sitting on is in his territory, and Jerry tries to dispossess him of it. At first when Jerry pokes him on the arm, telling him to move over, Peter complies amiably enough, but soon Jerry is punching him hard on the arm and ordering him off the bench. Jerry acknowledges that he is behaving irrationally ("I'm crazy, you bastard") but he also makes Peter behave crazily, first shouting for the police and then almost crying in his furious possessiveness about the bench.

I've come here for years; I have hours of great pleasure, great satisfaction, right here. And that's important to a man. I'm a responsible person, and I'm a GROWN-UP. This is my bench, and you have no right to take it away from me.

It is at this point that Jerry tells him to fight for it. Peter is sufficiently provoked to be quite willing to fight but, saying that they are not evenly matched, Jerry produces a knife. Terrified, Peter thinks Jerry is going to kill him, but Jerry tosses the knife to him telling him to use it. Peter tries to run away, but Jerry catches him and slaps him.

JERRY (*slaps Peter on each "fight"*): You fight, you miserable bastard; fight for that bench; fight for your parakeets; fight for your cats; fight for your two daughters; fight for your life; fight for your manhood, you pathetic little vegetable. You couldn't even get your wife with a male child.

Infuriated, Peter picks up the knife and backs away, saying he'll give Jerry one last chance to go away and leave him alone. He holds out the knife as if it were a weapon of defense; with a resigned "So be it," Jerry rushes in to impale himself on it. Dying, he thanks Peter.

Oh, Peter, I was so afraid I'd drive you away. (*He laughs as best he can.*) You don't know how afraid I was you'd go away and leave me . . . Peter . . . thank you. I came unto you (*He laughs, so faintly.*) and you have comforted me. Dear Peter.

Contact has been made.

It is a play about contact but it has been much misunderstood. According to Richard Kostelanetz in *On Contemporary Literature,* it is a play about a failed homosexual pass, and the dogs and cats which are mentioned are symbolical.

Dogs are surrogate-males, and cats become females. Thus, when Jerry says he wants companionship with a dog, he symbolically announces his homosexual designs.

The stiff arm holding the knife on which Jerry finally impales himself becomes a symbol of the erect phallus.

The religious interpretation strikes me as equally one-sided. In an article called "Symbolism and Naturalism in Edward Albee's *The Zoo Story*"[1] Ruth Zimbardo argues that Jerry's self-sacrifice is essentially Christian. Dr. C. W. E. Bigsby in his book, *Albee,* follows this interpretation:

Jerry is "crucified" so that Peter and his fellow men may be redeemed. When he accepts the need for sacrifice it is with the biblical expression of acceptance, "So be it."

He even sees significance in the fact that the bench, like the cross, is made of wood and iron. Jerry becomes Jesus, and Peter becomes the Apostle.

The man who had denied Jerry's message, as the biblical Peter had denied Christ, now recognizes him in the triple affirmation which had marked Peter's return to a real relationship with Christ and man. He replies to Jerry's cry of "Peter . . . Peter? Peter" with the exclamation, "Oh my God . . . Oh my God, oh my God."

It is also misleading to interpret ***The Zoo Story*** in terms of Theatre of the Absurd. For Martin Esslin, Albee "comes into the category of the Theatre of the Absurd precisely because his work attacks the very foundations of American optimism,"[2] and he finds that it is "closely akin to the work of Harold Pinter" because of "the realism of its dialogue and its subject matter—an outsider's inability to establish genuine contact with a dog, let alone any human being." I would have said that the resemblance to Pinter (who also uses the animal analogy in writing about the human territorial imperative) is fairly superficial and that if the Theatre of the Absurd is a valid category—which I doubt—Albee's work certainly does not belong to it. Esslin, who coined the phrase, uses the word "absurd" in the same sense as Camus does when speaking in *Le Mythe de Sysiphe* of a divorce between man and his life, between the actor and his setting, and in the same sense as Ionesco in his essay on Kafka.[3]

> Cut off from his religious, metaphysical, and transcendental roots, man is lost; all his actions become senseless, absurd, useless.

But without accepting the Christian interpretation of Jerry's sacrifice, it is easy to see that it should not be dismissed as useless. It is because he does not appreciate the relationship of Jerry's death to the rest of the play that Esslin attacks the ending as melodramatic:

> When Jerry provokes Peter into drawing a knife and then impales himself on it, the plight of the schizophrenic outcast is turned into an act of sentimentality, especially as the victim expires in touching solicitude and fellow-feeling for his involuntary murderer.

It is important not to forget that Jerry is a character in a play. His death, like the death of many tragic heroes in earlier plays, is an illustration of the impossibility of living in accordance with the values that he represents. To make real contact with a fellow human being, he has to take his life in his hands just as Columbus did when he set out on a voyage from which there would have been no return if he had not found what he was looking for. Without killing his hero, Albee would not have been able to make the point that Jerry could not have got through to Peter in any other way, and the important question is not whether the action at the end looks melodramatic—if the actors are good enough it does not—but whether the dialogue that leads up to it has successfully established the encounter between two strangers on a park bench as a valid analogue of human relationships in contemporary society, and whether Peter is acceptable as a personification of contemporary conformism.

In a sense, the Everyman role is divided between the two protagonists. Jerry represents the questing, idealistic side of the personality, the element that used to be called the spirit, while Peter represents the side that wants to settle complacently for the middle-class comforts. In fact Jerry's calculated assault on Peter's lazy desire to be left in peace is a projection of the playwright's calculated assault on the audience's desire not to be disturbed.

In the first published version of the play, in the *Evergreen Review,* No. 12, Jerry's dying speech began:

> You won't be coming back here any more, Peter; you've been dispossessed. You've lost your bench, but you've defended your honor.

These two sentences were subsequently cut, but as Lee Baxandall has pointed out (*Tulane Drama Review,* Vol. 9, No. 4) "an audience, should it include Peters, vicariously might be as shaken, as dispossessed." Jerry's attack on Peter is an attack on a society in which there are scarcely any real relationships. The audience, like Peter, settles for domesticity—a regular salary, children and pets. We never find out what, if anything, Jerry does to earn his living, but he is capable of greater honesty than Peter because he has invested less in the social structure. He is more of a man than Peter, and he is less like the average member of the audience. If his death is necessary, it is because we are being shown—violently—that most of us are most of the time settling for less than half. ***The Zoo Story*** is not a homosexual play, not an Absurd play, and not a religious play, but it is a moral play.

Notes

[1]*Twentieth Century Literature,* Vol. VIII (1962).

[2]*The Theatre of the Absurd,* p. 230.

[3]Eugène Ionesco, "Dans les Armes de la Ville," *Cahiers de la Compagnie Madeleine Renaud-Jean-Louis Barrault,* Paris, No. 20, October, 1957.

Robert S. Wallace (essay date 1973)

SOURCE: "*The Zoo Story:* Albee's Attack on Fiction," in *Modern Drama,* Vol. XVI, No. 1, June, 1973, pp. 49-54.

[*The following essay contends that in* The Zoo Story, *Albee is "attacking the fictions which North American society has developed to escape the alienation and discord which he views as modern urban realities."*]

In a Widely Published Article Entitled "What's the Matter with Edward Albee?" Thomas Driver attacks the basic situation of ***The Zoo Story*** maintaining that Peter's passive acceptance of Jerry's aggressive behavior is illogical and unrealistic. Driver states that no "sane, average-type person would be a passive spectator in the presence of behavior obviously headed towards destructive violence."[1] In the same article Driver makes a similar criticism of ***Who's Afraid of Virginia Woolf?*** arguing the improbability of Nick and Honey's remaining at George and Martha's when the older couple obviously "want only to fight the whole night through."[2] Driver's criticism of both plays misses a fact which is central to their development and to an understanding of Albee's work in general. Peter remains on the park bench for the same reason that Nick and Honey remain at George and Martha's: he is entertained by story-telling, particularly when the story-teller is very obviously his opposite.

Simple in itself, this fact has complex ramifications when one understands Albee's purpose in writing: basically he is attacking the fictions which North American society has developed to escape the alienation and discord which he views as modern urban realities. In his preface to ***The American Dream,*** he states this purpose most succinctly:

> The play is an attack against the fiction that everything in this slipping land of ours is peachy-keen.[3]

The use of "fiction" here is not an arbitrary one. What concerns Albee is the vicarious experiencing of life which prevents the individual's real and meaningful communication with others. Such vicarious experience is most often achieved through stories, either in print or on the stage. Driver asks: "Why doesn't Nick . . . take his young wife and go home?"[4] The answer also applies to the audience: they would rather watch life than experience it.

Albee's attack on fiction as a substitute for life is developed throughout ***The Zoo Story*** in such a way that the audience will come to understand not only Peter's dependence on fiction but its own as well. Albee has acknowledged that it is "one of the responsibilities of playwrights to show people how they are and what their time is like in the hope that perhaps they'll change it."[5] To achieve this end in ***The Zoo Story,*** Albee attempts simultaneously to involve the audience with the stage illusion and to alienate them from it. Regarding the dramatic effect of his plays, Albee has said:

> You can teach at the same time as you are engaging. I think perhaps the entire theory of alienation is a little misunderstood by the majority of the people who use the term. Of course, it is not an attempt to alienate the audience but merely an attempt to keep the audience at a sufficient distance so that two things are happening simultaneously, that the audience is being objective about the experience it is having.[6]

In ***The Zoo Story,*** this simultaneous reaction is developed by deliberately frustrating the audience's expectations and thus creating for them a discomfort which is akin to Peter's. This is appropriate in that Peter serves as audience to Jerry's "Zoo Story" on the stage just as the audience does in the theatre.

The discomfort Peter experiences during ***The Zoo Story*** results from Jerry's truthful description of his life and his attempts to communicate. Such a life is alien to him for he has escaped the loneliness Jerry describes by accepting the illusions of harmony and happiness that his lifestyle supports. After Jerry describes his landlady, Peter says, "It's so . . . unthinkable. I find it hard to believe that people such as that really *are*" (p. 28). Jerry replies, "It's for reading about, isn't it?" (p. 28); later he says "And fact is better left to fiction" (p. 29). This last line is a pithy summation of Jerry's position in the play as well as an ironical comment on Peter's attitude towards reality. The line reiterates Jerry's earlier speech about pornographic playing cards in which he says,

> . . . when you're a kid you use the cards as a substitute for a real experience, and when you're older you use real experience as a substitute for the fantasy.
>
> (p. 27)

Jerry realizes that facts are too often avoided by the use of fiction. His story about his landlady demonstrates his own use of fiction to escape the unpleasant fact of her sexual advances. He explains to Peter how he avoids these advances by convincing her of their contact the day before. The landlady retires giggling "as she believes and relives what never happened" (p. 28). Unfortunately Jerry is unable to employ such fiction to achieve the communication he desperately needs in other relationships. Having lived in "the sickening roominghouses on the West Side of New York" (p. 38), he is aware of the facts about which Peter has only read. When he tries to communicate these facts, however, Peter treats them as fiction, unable to understand or admit situations he has never before had to face. Ironically, Jerry finally communicates with Peter by making another fiction real—the fiction that something happened at the zoo. The something is, of course, Jerry's own death, the real experience substituting for the fantasy in the most painful sense.

The discomfort Peter feels at the conclusion of ***The Zoo Story*** results from his realization that he too is an animal in the zoo which Jerry equates with life. Forced to face his complicity in Jerry's death, he must face the shallowness of his life as well. "Dispossessed" (p. 49) of his bench, he is also dispossessed of his illusions about life. Appropriately, the bench has been his reading-place: neither it nor fiction now remain as sanctuary. For the audience a similar discomfort is effected by the play, developed by different means but aiming at the same ends. Basically, it results from the audience's inability to pick a "winner" or "loser" in the play. Discussing the dramatic effect of ***The Zoo Story,*** Gerald Nelson echoes Albee's comment about audience alienation when he writes,

> A viewer likes the safety of being once removed and yet, at the same time, wants to feel himself imaginatively a part of the action—simultaneously both involved and safe.[7]

Such simultaneous feelings are related to the involvement and objectivity that Albee desires of the audience. Both are achieved in the play by a merging of theatrical conventions and by a shifting of the audience's associations between Peter and Jerry.

Discussing this last point, Nelson suggests that the audience will most probably relate to Peter at the outset of the play, he being the respectable family man who is accosted by an unkempt bohemian. Inherent in Nelson's suggestion is the similarity of Peter's position with that of the audience. Like the audience, Peter desires a vicarious experiencing of life that offers no personal threat. Like the audience, he wants to remain simultaneously involved and safe, a position which he initially feels is possible with Jerry. As the play progresses, however, and Jerry's attacks on Peter become physical as well as verbal, Peter is forced to realize that involvement with Jerry is far from safe; Jerry will not allow him to remain merely a spectator like the audience—he must actively defend himself and the bench which has become a symbol of his world. The audience, of course, comes to realize this as well. Rather than continue to side with Peter, however, the audience will probably relate to Jerry instead, because, as Nelson points out, he is both more interesting than Peter and successful in exposing Peter's superficialities. Peter and the typically middle-class life-style he represents (a wife, two daughters, two parakeets and an apartment on East Seventy-fourth Street) can't compete with Jerry for either dramatic appeal or pathos, Jerry being the *"permanent transient"* (p. 37), who wants to pray for himself, "the colored queen, the Puerto Rican family, the person in the front room whom I've never seen, the woman who cries deliberately behind her closed door, and the rest of the people in all roominghouses, everywhere" (p. 33). This shift in allegiances between characters becomes important when Jerry dies at the end of the play; respectable Peter has become a murderer while bohemian Jerry has become a martyr to the cause of truth, a truth which reveals the violence submerged beneath Peter's ordered existence as well as the desperation inherent in Jerry's chaotic one. The confusion the audience now feels about the characters forces it to examine them in relation to its own values. The fact that neither Jerry nor Peter can be catagorized as villian or hero reflects the moral confusion which Albee feels is characteristic of twentieth century life. The fact that neither character "wins" or "loses" in the play frustrates the audience's desire for a presentation of a "right" and wrong" atitude towards life. Like ***The American Dream, The Zoo Story*** illustrates the fact that appearances are often deceptively fictitious; any initial expectations about the characters are definitely frustrated.

The frustration of expectations is crucial to the objectivity Albee desires of the audience. The set of ***The Zoo Story*** which is simply two park benches and *"foliage, trees, sky"* (p. 11) offers little clue to the dramatic effect desired; such an effect is almost totally dependent upon language. Although the language of ***The Zoo Story*** for the most part progresses naturalistically, it is sometimes exaggerated so that it has a distancing effect. "The language that the two characters engage in is . . . only realistic to the ears of those who are supercilious enough to think they could be so witty."[8] The sarcasm of many of Jerry's remarks, the rapid banter between Jerry and Peter, Jerry's unnaturally long monologues—all work to remind the audience that it is watching an illusion of life by intermittently interrupting the naturalistic flow of the play. Peter, who describes himself as "normally . . . uh . . . reticent" (p. 19) and who says "I don't express myself too well sometimes" (p. 20), prefers superficial dialogue—marked by clichés like "every man wants a son" (p. 16)—to attempts at more penetrating conversation. Jerry's acknowledgement of this often results in the sarcastic mockery which gives the play much of its brittle wit: for example, he uses another cliché—"That's the way the cookie crumbles" (p. 19)—to ridicule Peter's earlier one. Similarly, many of the characters' quick verbal exchanges at the beginning of the play are exaggerated in their pace and ironic significance to the degree that they become games of "one-upmanship." Both the characters acknowledge this themselves after Jerry asks Peter "Who are your favorite writers? Baudelaire and J. P. Marquand?" (p. 21). Jerry's interruption of Peter's empty reply demonstrates his frustration with this particular game at the same time as it forces Peter to recognize his own insincerity: Peter replies "I . . . sorry" (p. 21). The extent to which the audience finds the characters' verbal games, as well as Jerry's subsequent monologues, interruptive will naturally depend on its own sensibility as well as on the actors' performance. Hopefully both will facilitate the simultaneous involvement and objectivity that Albee feels is so important to his play.

The importance of language in the play both to involve and distance the audience is directly related to Albee's attack on fiction. Language is, of course, the chief means of storytelling. That Jerry attempts to communicate with Peter by telling stories is one of the reasons he fails. Although he states his purpose is to *"really talk"* (p. 17), Jerry confronts Peter with lengthy stories of his encounters, stories that hinder rather than help dialogue; the short personal questions he intersperses between these stories have the same effect, which Peter acknowledges when he says, ". . . you don't really carry on a conversation; you just ask questions" (p. 19). More important, however, Jerry's stories work to remind the audience of the stage illusion at the same time as they distance Peter. Thus the stories resemble the monologues of Brechtian Epic Theatre, providing the audience with the objectivity that allows it to criticize "from a social point of view."[9] This is directly in keeping with the "teaching" purpose Albee has acknowledged in his writing. Unlike the audience, however, Peter is unable to learn from Jerry's words. At the end of Jerry's monologue about his landlady's dog, he says, "I . . . I don't understand what . . . I don't think I . . . Why did you tell me this?" (p. 36). His response is maddening to Jerry because it is exactly the opposite of what he desires. What Jerry has failed to realize is that his use of words has added to his isolation rather than alleviated it. Arthur Oberg points out that Jerry is similar to all of Albee's protagonists in his reliance on words: ". . . unable to 'relate' . . . (they) look to language to forge whatever identity and relationships their lives have lacked."[10] "Dialogue, never adequate, attempts to surround what it would control, seeking victory in its *copia* and in an intensity which is related to this abundance."[11]

Jerry's abundance of words in creating his stories has the ironic effect of adding to his isolation from others. It also has the effect of isolating the audience from the play. In both cases, the implication is that words—the chief mode of fiction—are inadequate in communicating real experience. Jerry finally communicates with Peter not through language and stories but through sheer physical contact. The devaluation of words inherent in this fact is one of the reasons that ***The Zoo Story*** is discussed as Theatre of the Absurd. Jerry's abundance of words can be considered an exaggeration or magnification of human folly similar to the over- and under-reactions of the characters in ***The American Dream*** or ***The Sandbox.*** That the play incorporates conventions of Absurd Theatre within a naturalistic framework has prompted critics such as Driver to accuse Albee of confused and self-

Scene from an American Conservatory Theater production of *The Zoo Story,* in which Jerry and Peter begin the struggle that will result in Jerry's death.

conscious writing. The error here lies in the critics' failure to understand the play's attempt to expose the use of fiction as a substitute for real experience. Albee's combining of theatrical techniques deliberately emphasizes the dramatic illusion and forces the audience to realize its own vicarious use of fiction. In ***The Zoo Story,*** the integration of form and content cleverly makes the play a teaching experience.

Notes

1In *The Modern American Theatre,* ed. Alvin B. Kernan, Englewood Cliffs, 1967, p. 81.

2Driver, p. 99.

3*The American Dream and The Zoo Story,* New York, no date, p. 54.

4Driver, p. 99.

5Edward Albee, "John Gielgud and Edward Albee talk About the Theatre," *Atlantic,* 215, April, 1965, p. 65.

6Edward Albee, "An Interview with Edward Albee," in *The American Theatre Today,* ed. Alan S. Driver, New York, 1967, p. 119.

7"Edward Albee and his well-made plays," *Tri-Quarterly,* V, Spring, 1967, p. 185.

8Thomas B. Markus, "Tiny Alice and Tragic Catharsis," *ETJ* 17, March, 1965, p. 226.

9Bertolt Brecht, "Street Scene," in *The Theory of the Modern Stage,* ed. Eric Bentley, Harmondsworth, 1968, p. 91.

10"Edward Albee: His Language and Imagination," *Prairie Schooner,* Spring, 1966, p. 143.

11Oberg, p. 143.

Mary M. Nilan (essay date 1973)

SOURCE: "Albee's *The Zoo Story:* Alienated Man and the Nature of Love," in *Modern Drama,* Vol. XVI, No. 1, June, 1973, pp. 55-59.

[*The essay below examines whether "the central tragedy of* The Zoo Story *reside[s] in the fact that in modern life the very concept of love has been distorted and corrupted and that* both *halves of polarized society are equally incapable of communication."*]

> If we can so misunderstand, well then, why have we invented the word love in the first place.
>
> Jerry in *The Zoo Story*

Edward Albee's ***The Zoo Story*** centers about two themes: the polarization of modern society and the difficulty of human communication. To date, most commentators have viewed Peter, the representative of "those who have," the insiders of modern society, as the chief obstacle to any real communication; whereas Jerry is seen as one filled with compassion for his fellow beings, willing to sacrifice himself to save them. For example, for Rose Zimbardo, Jerry is a Christ-figure in a "modernized scene of Gethsemane" and the theme is one of "human isolation and salvation through sacrifice."[1] Peter she conceives as Everyman who will not reveal his true self for fear of being "known" as a person. Jerry, on the other hand, is seen as desperately desiring to "know," to reach an understanding with another. Charles R. Lyons sees Jerry as attempting two means to establish some contact: "compassion" (with the dog) and "an act of sacrifice" (with Peter).[2] Jerry's sacrifice is compassionate, Lyons maintains, because "it functions to initiate Peter into an acute awareness of his reality."[3] George E. Wellwarth adds another dimension to this portrait of a compassionate, self-sacrificing character when he notes that Jerry represents for him "the person cursed (for in our society it undoubtedly *is* a curse) with an infinite capacity for love" and thus he sees the drama as "about the maddening effect that enforced loneliness of the human condition" has on such a person.[4]

But if Jerry, representative of the alienated, the permanent transient, "the outsider," does indeed have such an "infinite capacity for love," why then do *all* his attempts to achieve communication fail? Does the fault always lie with the other—with all "the pretty little girls," with the dog, as well as with Peter? Or perhaps is Jerry himself, the other half of polarized society, at least equally culpable for the isolated condition, the zoo of cages each man constructs for himself?

Perhaps Jerry's universal predicament is best summarized by Eric Fromm in *The Art of Loving:*

> Man—of all ages and cultures—is confronted with the solution of one and the same question: the question of how to overcome the separateness, how to achieve union, how to transcend one's own individual life and find at-onement.[5]

The "solution" is of course to overcome separateness through "love," but this essentially involves giving, not receiving. Longfellow remarked that love gives itself; it is not bought, bringing to mind the New Testament, which tells us that God so loved the world, He gave His only begotten Son. This giving, in Fromm's words, "implies to make the other person a giver also and they both share in the joy of what they have brought to life."[6] Thus the question arises: if man is impotent, that is, unable to produce love in another or he himself the object of love, may it not be because *he* has not truly given of himself or perhaps has found that he is incapable of such selflessness? On this point it is necessary to analyze closely the pattern of Jerry's attempts to "love," in the sense of establishing an "I/Thou" relationship with another.

Essentially our knowledge of these attempts falls into three categories. First, scattered throughout the play we have a series of facts about his past and present life. Second, in the lengthy sequence of "Jerry and the Dog" we hear of his deeds—since communication with an animal must be established by deeds, not words. Finally, there is the main action of the piece, an essentially verbal confrontation with Peter.

Jerry provides us with some facts about his past life. He has, for example, "two picture frames, both empty," symbolic of course of the emptiness of his own life. But when questioned by Peter, he maintains that there isn't "anyone to put in" the frames. He has apparently given his love to no one. Peter suggests the natural objects of "parents" or a "girlfriend," but Jerry can relate to neither. Abandoned by his mother, he rejects not only her but also his father (who, despondent over his wife's desertaion, had turned to drink) and the aunt who cared for him (but incoveniently died the day of his high-school graduation!). Where is Jerry's compassion for these two? Why does he comment: "I have no feelings about any of it that I care to admit to myself"? Moreover, in his relations with "the pretty little ladies," it is apparently only a purely sexual, never a personal relationship he attempts to achieve: "I've never been able to have sex . . . to make love to anybody more than once." How is his desperate drive to truly "know" another exemplified here? Only once, he tells us, was he able to sustain a relationship for any duration and then only an adolescent homosexual one. Such a relationship tends to suggest the attraction of a "mirror image"; moreover, since the park superintendant's son's "birthday was the same," the two would seem to be symbolic twins. This indicates an egotistical union in which the individuals involved identify themselves with each other, merely enlarging the single individual into two, a relationship which hardly fulfills the ideal selfless character of genuine love.

"The Story of the Dog" provides an opportunity to observe the more recent pattern of Jerry's actions as he attempts to forge a new bond. He offers hamburgers to the starving beast, the "gatekeeper" of his apartment, but what is his motivation: compassion or bribery? Certainly his words reflect no genuine affection: "I decided first I'll kill the dog with kindness and if that doesn't work . . . I'll just kill him." However, the natural instincts of the animal apparently inform him that there is no love involved, that the meat is not a free gift, and thus he does not change his response to the man. Rejected, Jerry turns to violence, poisoning the beast. And then Jerry himself suddenly asks, "*Was* trying to feed the dog an act of love?" The episode seems to have led to a new understanding. Now he ponders: "Perhaps was the dog's attempt to bite me *not* an act of love?" Moreover, Jerry has made an even more startling discovery for only after committing violence he tells Peter: "I loved the dog *now* and wanted him to love me!"

Feeling he has gained insight from this experience, the alienated now attempts a verbal confrontation with the "establishment," personified by Peter. One half of polarized society reaches out to forge a union. At first the confrontation follows, in words, much the same pattern as the sequence with the dog. Because Jerry was, as he tells Peter at the end, "so afraid I'd drive you away . . . you'd go away and leave me," he offers a bribe. If Peter remains he will be told the mysterious "zoo story." Each time Peter starts to retreat, the enticement is repeated:

> JERRY: Don't go. You're not thinking of going, are you?
>
> PETER: Well . . . no, I don't think so.
>
> JERRY: [*as if to a child*] Because after I tell you about the dog, do you know what then? Then . . . then I'll tell you about what happened at the zoo.

As earlier Jerry had demanded that the dog move, abandon his defense of the passageway, so now he repeatedly commands Peter to "move over," to give up his bench: "Get off this bench, Peter, I want it."

So far the sequence with Peter has closely paralleled that of Jerry and the dog. But the pattern is suddenly broken. Jerry impales himself on the outstretched knife held by Peter as that symbol of the social "status quo" strives to defend himself against the violence of "the outsider" who seems to threaten his very existence. Visually of course the picture recalls the sexual act with the outstretched knife serving as a phallic symbol. And for Jerry this apparently is the consummation of a perverse kind of "love."

Jerry had found the dog's attacks, his attempts at "contact," preferable to indifference; thus he forces Peter to overcome the separateness, to make contact. Moreover, from the earlier experience Jerry had learned that the initial violence toward the dog was followed by a certain kind of love for the beast. Jerry now seems deliberately to assume the role of the victim, apparently hoping that Peter, now placed in the murderer's role, will come to feel a sense of oneness with him. Obviously at the end Jerry does give totally of himself but what is the actual motivation behind this "gift"? Does he die to redeem the Peters of this world or to become the object of a relationship which insures he will remain forever in the mind, if not the heart, of another? Is this not the essence of the "zoo story" which the dying Jerry tells Peter:

> I think *this* is what happened at the zoo . . . I think that while I was at the zoo I decided to walk north . . . until I found you. . . . And now you know what you'll see in your TV, and the face I told you about . . . my face, the face you see right now.

Incapable of forging a normal I/Thou relationship, Jerry has turned to the perversion of a murderer/victim bond. For by his very nature man needs to love in order to overcome separateness in union with another, and apparently Jerry can find no other way to fulfill his nature. But he is not just one individual case; he is a universal symbol of the alienated modern man. He is not the only one who desires to be the object of love but seems incapable of giving of himself in the normal sense. There is his landlady who can only make purely physical overtures and must be content with the fantasy of what "happened the day before." There is the colored queen who "plucks his eyebrows," "wears a kimono," and "goes to the john," but for some reason "never has anyone up to his room." There is the lady "who cries with determination behind her closed door." Moreover Jerry finds himself surrounded by material things which are incomplete: empty picture frames; a strong box without a lock; a typewriter that prints nothing but capital letters. Don't all these symbolize and reinforce the incompleteness and unnatural predicament of impotent modern man who can not love?

In *The Testament of Samuel Beckett,* Josephine Jacobsen and William Mueller noted that Beckett uses parodies of love scenes to evoke the most mirthless laughs. And the authors commented:

> . . . we are struck hard by the writhing irony of the affirmation that the world is so deficient in love. . . . Yet we know that love, in one or another of its manifestations is the source of the greatest tragedy as of comedy . . . for in love man feels he comes closest to the divine essence.[7]

Apparently in Albee's eyes this is also a great tragedy of modern man's condition. In ***The American Dream,*** his Young Man tells of an inability to "feel" or to love in the normal sense. Yet, at the same time, he expresses the need to be the object of love:

> I accept the syntax around me, for while I know I cannot relate . . . I know I must be related *to.* I let people love me. . . . I let them draw pleasure . . . from the fact of me . . . but that is all it comes to. . . . I can feel nothing. . . . And it will always be thus.

His condition is reminiscent of Jerry's.

Doesn't the central tragedy of ***The Zoo Story*** reside in the fact that in modern life the very concept of love has been distorted and corrupted and that *both* halves of polarized society are equally incapable of communication? Isn't the distinction between Peter and Jerry that whereas the former wishes to retain the "status quo," remaining detached and "separated from all the animals" in the zoo, the latter is desperately driven to be the object of love but, like the Young Man in ***The American Dream,*** has lost the ability to feel and can not relate? Moreover, ***The Zoo Story*** appears to pose an even more critical problem. Here we see that when alienated man is driven to overcome separateness yet finds himself incapable of doing so, he turns to violence in a last desperate effort to establish some semblance of contact. Albee leaves unanswered the final question: Is such a perversion of love the only method left whereby modern man can bridge the gap, unite with another, communicate?

NOTES

[1]"Symbolism and Naturalism in Edward Albee's *The Zoo Story,*" in *Twentieth Century Literature,* VIII, 1962, pp. 10-17.

[2]See "Two Projections of the Isolation of the Human Soul: Brecht's *Im Dickicht Der Staedte* and Albee's *The Zoo Story,*" in *Drama Survey,* IV, 1965, pp. 121-138.

[3]*Ibid.,* p. 135.

[4]*The Theatre of Protest and Paradox,* New York, 1964, p. 276.

[5]New York, 1956, p. 9.

[6]*Ibid.,* p. 25.

[7]New York, 1964, p. 98.

Robert B. Bennett (essay date 1977)

SOURCE: "Tragic Vision in *The Zoo Story,*" in *Modern Drama,* Vol. XX, No. 1, March 1977, pp. 55-66.

[*The following essay contends that* The Zoo Story *is a tragedy, not a melodrama, as many critics have charged. Bennett observes that, "in the manner of tragedy, this play tests and questions, by the experience it presents, the propositions of religion and philosophy."*]

While the conclusion to ***The Zoo Story*** has met with the approval of some readers and the disapproval of others, the meaning of the protagonist's death has not been disputed. The consensus has been that Albee intends us to understand Jerry's death as a Christ-like sacrifice. Rose Zimbardo and George Wellwarth praise the symbolism. Martin Esslin and Brian Way complain that the play's ending loses absurdist rigor and degenerates into sentimentality.[1] Similarly Lee Baxandall argues that when Albee resorts to aesthetic solutions, which are symbolically instead of historically meaningful, he does not offer a solution viable in drama, "the most socially rooted of the arts."[2]

Apparently unheeded by all these viewpoints are Albee's stage directions. These, it seems to me, are included in order to prevent us and the actor who plays Jerry from either sentimentalizing his death scene or regarding it purely as a Christ-like sacrifice. Albee writes:

> Oh, Peter, I was so afraid I'd drive you away. (*He laughs as best he can*) You don't know how afraid I was you'd go away and leave me. . . . Peter . . . thank you. I came unto you (*He laughs, so faintly*) and you have comforted me. Dear Peter.[3]

The biblical phrasing and the expression of thanks and affection would, by themselves, be sentimental. Laughter, however, is an expression not of compassion, but of psychic distance. Moreover, Jerry's going on to praise Peter for being an animal like the rest of us ("You're an animal, too" [p. 49]) may be laughable and depressing, but it is not melodramatic; and his scornfully mimicking Peter in his dying breath should discourage us from accusing Jerry of emotional over-indulgence. At the same time, however, Jerry clearly wants to believe that a God exists and that love is possible; and he has witnessed what seem to be similar longings in the other persons in his rooming-house. Indeed, Jerry is not a hardened absurdist;[4] and if Albee's stage directions are followed, there will be supplication along with mimicry in his ambivalent last words. Jerry hopes that his death is possibly sacrificial and that he has created by his act an effect beyond itself; but he is not so spiritually entranced as to fail to realize that his Christ-like self-sacrifice for Peter's regeneration—what Baxandall means presumably by his "aestheticism of symbolic transcendence" (p. 98)—may possibly be no more than a glorified front to a suicide. In other words Jerry, and Albee, are as conscious of the frailty of the symbolic solution as Baxandall is.

To regard the dramatic experience of ***The Zoo Story*** as embodying a doctrinally absolute statement underestimates the play's complexity. Albee does not here presume the absurdist's certainty that all is meaningless nor the social protester's certainty that he knows what is wrong and how to correct it.[5] Rather, in the manner of tragedy, this play tests and questions, by the experience it presents, the propositions of religion and philosophy. Through Jerry, Albee asks how we can tell whether spiritual love is a genuine human faculty or an illusion. Jerry hopes that man is a spiritual creature, expects that he is no more than an animal with illusory and frustrated spiritual longings, and fears that man may have lost even his animal instincts as a result of social conditioning. At the time of the play Jerry is consumed by a need to resolve these doubts; and, to borrow Arthur Miller's description of the tragic hero, he "is ready to lay down his life, if need be, to secure . . . his personal dignity."[6]

Jerry's concern about his personal dignity is more cosmic than social, and is centered in the question, "If we can so misunderstand, well then, why have we invented the word love in the first place?" (p. 36) Jerry realizes that if man is incapable of loving, he cannot be blamed for not loving. On this level of perception, Jerry sees Peter as man (*Homo sapiens*) to be understood by comparison with animal and vegetable nature. Jerry does not pigeonhole Peter as the-affluent-New-York-businessman; this label is merely the superficial and illusory identity that he sees standing in the way of Peter's self-knowledge. Whereas Michael Rutenberg sees Jerry as a social critic like Vance Packard,[7] I find him less obviously but more importantly a philosopher like Hamlet. Just as Hamlet questions why the Creator has given us "godlike reason / To fust in us unus'd" (IV.iv.33-39),[8] so Jerry wonders why man possesses the urge for spiritual communion if there is no worldly way to express and fulfill it. If love can only "fust in us unus'd," he seems to say, then man is "a beast, no more."

The dramatic power of tragedy usually depends heavily upon the playwright's giving expression to a full complex of feelings and perceptions within the protagonist toward himself and his world. These will have been generated by an experience that has jarred him from a conventional pattern of existence. In ***The Zoo Story*** the three attitudes of love, hate, and indifference provide the general frames of reference for the conflicting forces within Jerry himself and between Jerry and Peter. Kindness proceeds from spiritual nature; cruelty from animal nature; and indifference from social conditioning which reduces one's personality, Jerry suggests, to the level of a vegetable. Jerry, as author of the incident, tries to shape his actions according to the hypothesis that kindness (love) and cruelty (hate) in combination form the teaching emotion, an emotion which can harmonize the elements of spirit and body in man, and resolve the tensions that divide his amphibian nature. The seeming antithesis between the separate emotions of love and hate dissolves, Jerry has learned, when both are understood to be expressions of passionate commitment that together vie against the inclination toward apathy in the effort to define what man is or what he can become. Although one probably first thinks of the play as a conflict between the loving-hating Jerry and the indifferent Peter, I shall try to show that indifference has not been foreign to Jerry's nature, either in his past or in the present, and that the play is also importantly a conflict of all three attitudes within Jerry himself. As is true of most tragedies, there is no clear resolution in this play's conclusion. Death ends the struggle but does not definitively answer the questions, although the final projection is admittedly bleak.

In order fully to understand ***The Zoo Story*** as tragedy, we must first reassess some of the common assumptions that, if accepted, undermine the play's basic dynamics and reduce the play from a dramatic experience to a philosophical lesson. Frequently Jerry is spoken of as a symbol "meaning" something instead of a human being who is doing and feeling something. "The old pigeonhole bit" of calling Jerry a Christ figure or "a universal symbol of alienated modern man"[9] automatically sets a critical distance between us and Jerry, and makes genuine sympathy for him impossible. We have already seen the inadequacy of a strict reading of Jerry as Christ-like. This is an image to which he consciously aspires but not one that he uncritically accepts as achieved or even as valid. The symbol, thus, remains subordinate to and less than the experience. Those who suggest that Jerry is "alienated modern man" incapable of love not only limit the play's vision but seriously misrepresent it. While their argument rightly observes that Jerry in the past has not been able to love "the little ladies" or his lonely compeers in the rooming-house, it must assume, in order to sustain its point, that Jerry, contrary to his claim, has learned nothing from his experience with the dog, and that he shows no love in his relationship with Peter. It must interpret Jerry's sharing with Peter his most personal feelings, thoughts, and experiences as insincere or as yielding to an irresistible impulse rather than, in the way Albee's stage directions urge, as an honest and difficult giving of himself. In general, studies have discussed Jerry as if his nature were frozen, not vital and developing. Jerry's comment, "every once in a while I like to talk to somebody, really *talk*" (p. 17), has encouraged critical inferences such as, "Jerry, weary of the indecisive encounters with the Peters . . ." (Baxandall, "Theater of Edward Albee," p. 88), which see his present action as part of an habitual effort to make contact. But Jerry's own account of his past indicates that what he is doing with Peter is as new to him as it is to Peter. When Jerry describes the colored queen who leaves his door open and the woman who cries behind her closed door, we realize that he observed and did not respond to their passive invitations for a relief from loneliness. Similarly Jerry never saw the prostitutes more than once. Jerry's intense assault on Peter is in striking contrast to his former aloofness. The intervening event between his past and present that causes this change is his collective encounter with the landlady and the dog. This is an experience of tragic awakening which shapes his vision of man and possesses his spirit.

Jerry differs from Peter and from us not in his complex human nature but in his particular tragic experience; and his plight sets in bold relief a universal human problem. Two experiences, his lifelong poverty and the recent rooming-house episode, separate Jerry from Peter. Jerry's poverty has made him more aware than Peter of a spiritual side to his nature that needs fulfillment. Preoccupation with the paraphernalia of society, says *The Zoo Story* (in a manner that reminds us of *Everyman*), encourages man to ignore the existential loneliness of his human condition and, hence, stifles his initiative to seek spiritual fulfillment. The traditional tragic situation in which alienation from society brings suffering and spiritual awareness is present here in the colored queen, the weeping woman, and the little ladies, as well as in Jerry. It is because these characters manifest in their actions an intense spiritual longing, a sensitivity not evident in Peter, that Jerry holds the existence of God and love possible ("with making money with your body which is an act of love . . . WITH GOD WHO IS A COLORED QUEEN . . . WHO IS A WOMAN WHO CRIES WITH DETERMINATION BEHIND HER CLOSED DOOR" [p. 35]). But whereas poverty has simply stimulated an awareness of spiritual privation, the encounter with the landlady and the dog has gone farther by jolting Jerry with the suggestion that the fault for his loneliness lies not with God, the stars, or society, but with himself. The actions of his two assailants not only force Jerry to recognize his own resistance to involvement, but also suggest to him a possible method for overcoming such resistance in others. The landlady made advances of love to Jerry, so far as her level of being could approach it, and Jerry responded with the same wish to be rid of her that Peter has toward him. The dog made advances that Jerry describes as antipathy and, on reflection, possibly love; and it received a similar resistance from Jerry. Jerry fed and poisoned the dog to get it to leave him *alone.* Critics impose a conventional symbolism on the dog's behavior, ignoring Jerry's unconventional perception; and they miss the point of the encounter. Rutenberg writes:

> The symbolism, unmistakably, is that the dog represents that vicious aspect of society which attacks whenever Jerry tries to gain entrance. The dog never attacks when Jerry leaves the premises, only when he enters. Later in the play Peter "will respond to the invasion of his 'property' with the same ferocity the dog has shown," clearly illustrating this animalistic reaction to an invasion of one's private thoughts.
>
> (*Edward Albee,* p. 31)

Perhaps the dog was protecting his domain (which is an animal trait people possess, not a feature of society which dogs have picked up), but Jerry believes and tries to explain to Peter that the dog's attempt to bite him was probably an act of love. The parallels between the dog and Peter that Rutenberg, quoting Zimbardo, draws are misleading (*Edward Albee,* p. 13). The dog attacks Jerry of its own initiative. Peter, left to his own initiative, would have walked home. His defense of the bench comes only after Jerry's calculated efforts to provoke at least an animal response in Peter. There is nothing in the play's final action which relates to an invasion of Peter's private thoughts, about which Jerry has ceased to concern himself since Peter's reaction to Jerry's long monologue. The parallels that do exist are between the dog's attack on Jerry and Jerry's assault on Peter, and between Jerry's attempts to keep the dog away and Peter's efforts to avoid involvement with Jerry. For Rutenberg's symbolic formula to work, Peter would have to knock Jerry off the bench the moment Jerry sits down. Albee's point is that Jerry has worked Peter out of his social mold as a vegetable into an animal state that is at least Peter's own self. The importance to Jerry of the assaults of the landlady and the dog is that together they have had effects outside of themselves. They have aroused in Jerry strong feelings, a violent antipathy toward the landlady and a love for the dog, curiously counterbalancing the feelings they have shown him. They have possessed Jerry with an idea of communication that he must test. And apparently they have dispossessed him of the rooming-house, just as he will dispossess Peter of the bench. Quickly, as if embarrassed to admit it, Jerry tells Peter toward the end of his narrative, "I have not returned" (p. 35). Their invasion of Jerry's private space has made it impossible for him to remain spiritually isolated, aware only of his own loneliness and his own needs.

Yet, however illuminating Jerry's experience with the dog has been, it has concluded unsatisfactorily. After claiming they made contact, Jerry says in apparent contradiction, "We had made many attempts at contact, and we had failed" (p. 35). Ironically, what seems to have happened is that their actions have resulted not in a meeting of minds but in a transference of attitudes. The dog has received Jerry's message in the feeding and poisoning and now leaves him alone, and Jerry, believing now that the dog attacked him out of affection, loves the animal! Jerry has socially conditioned the dog to indifference at the same time that the dog has engendered in him a compelling desire for establishing a relationship. The change, of course, is not the one Jerry ultimately hoped for: ". . . I loved the dog now, and I wanted him to love me. . . . I don't really know why I expected the dog to understand anything, much less my motivations . . . I hoped that the dog would understand" (p. 34). Jerry seems to sustain his hope for a spiritual communion by concluding he expected too much of the dog, limited as it is by its animal nature. If his longing can ever be fulfilled, it must be through communion with a person.

Jerry brings from his rooming-house experience more than a pain-pleasure teaching technique. Having his own indifference toward others revealed to him, he has learned a compassionate explanation for others' indifference toward him that allows at least a part of him to feel affection and sympathy for Peter. Indifference, which gives the impression of irresponsible neglect, complacency, selfishness, and presumptuous superiority, may actually be the embarrassed response of one who wants but does not know how to share feelings with others. Jerry's description of his final relationship with the dog is suggestive of a much broader human situation: "We regard each other with a mixture of sadness and suspicion, and then we *feign* indifference" (p. 35, my italics). Jerry realizes that the family man Peter, who spends his free time alone on a park bench, is as lonely as he is, though suffering less because he is more lost.[10] Jerry approaches Peter, then, as an enlightened brother and not, as Wellwarth (p. 323) and Nilan (p. 59) claim, as a polar opposite.

Neither hope nor despair totally governs Jerry at the opening of the play. The new and driving hope generated by the rooming-house incident counters but by no means eliminates his "great weariness," his old and ingrained fear of involvement and responsibility. Jerry's hope is evident in his passionate displays of love and hate for Peter; his indifference, in his mocking and patronizing manner. The former attitude seeks to establish a kinship while the latter longs simply for death. On the surface it looks as if death has been Jerry's primary objective; his early prophecy of what Peter would see on TV and his retrospective "could I have planned all this? . . . I think I did" (p. 48) encourage this assumption. It is more accurate, though, to see Jerry at the start expecting and half hoping to die but hoping more to establish a relationship on spiritual rather than physical terms. Jerry's anger and disappointment when Peter fails to respond with loving understanding to his confessional narrative are directly proportional to the degree to which his passionate hope has overweighed his detached expectation; and Albee's stage directions indicate that the conclusion of Jerry's story and the period immediately following are the moments of greatest emotional intensity in the play.

To this point I have tried to demonstrate Jerry's basic and complex humanity, and the conditions and experiences that have raised him to a special level of sensitivity and awareness. There remains, though, in claiming for Jerry a tragic status, the need to admire his encounter with Peter as a skillful and honest attempt to resolve the basic tensions within himself and, by extension, within man. For if his effort is either facile or fundamentally misguided, or if his feelings are maudlin and excessive, his state is less than tragic.

An answer to critics' complaints that Jerry does not carry on a real conversation with Peter provides us with a means for examining Jerry's effort in specific terms.[11] For in Peter, Albee has effectively dramatized his belief that "the sentences people make half the time bear absolutely no resemblance to what people think."[12] Peter, at his present level of sensitivity, is not able to "really talk." And Jerry knows that he cannot genuinely communicate with Peter until he has shown him that "normal conversation" is typically a rhetorical exercise designed to avoid self-expression. In order to establish real contact with Peter, therefore, Jerry himself must "go a very long distance out of his way to come back a short distance correctly." His verbal assault is the pedagogical tool by which he hopes to make Peter aware of the enslaving formula of polite conversation. With this awareness, he hopes, will come a willingness from Peter to say what he feels and thus to establish a spiritual union in which conversation will become a sharing of selves. Up through the story of the dog, Jerry moves the conversation toward greater and greater directness. When, however, Peter proves himself incapable of responding openly to Jerry's narrative, Jerry removes himself from an intensely spiritual to a less demanding physical level of confrontation. By doing this, Jerry brings Peter finally to a level where he can unite feeling and words in his angry cry, "You're a bum . . . that's what you are" (p. 43). It is Peter's most honestly felt statement in the play, however inadequate it may be as a description of Jerry. Jerry resorts to the rhetorical more than the denotative power of language to excite emotion and stimulate thought in Peter. The nature and effect of Jerry's rhetorical approach have been largely ignored or poorly understood. Zimbardo says that "words, when they do penetrate Peter's surface, merely cause him to throw up further barriers to contact" ("Symbolism," p. 13). It is true that Peter resists the total commitment Jerry demands of him, which implicitly is to give up all his external tokens of identity, his occupation, family, and material wealth; but it is equally true that without his verbal stripping, Jerry could never have brought Peter to the level of animal commitment that he achieves at the end. Peter's almost cordial reaction to Jerry's tickling would have been unthinkable without the prior establishment of a personal bond. Robert Wallace, arguing against Tom Driver's position that the plot is implausible because any normal person would not have put up with Jerry, says the reason Peter stays is that he has been captivated by Jerry as storyteller and is interested in finding out what happened at the zoo.[13] While the mystery surrounding the zoo is an enticement for staying, Jerry, before the narrative of the dog, is not for the most part telling a story nor is he desperately holding out the incident at the zoo as a lure to Peter. If Albee had made the story about the zoo the only thing holding Peter, I would agree with Driver's complaint of implausibility.

It is, however, through a skillful verbal application of the teaching principle, kindness and cruelty combined, that Jerry keeps Peter listening to him. First coercing and then cajoling, insulting then flattering, Jerry keeps Peter constantly off balance emotionally while he probes into Peter's personal life. The process gradually strips away Peter's formal defenses and establishes a bond of intimacy through shared information that makes Peter even forget at points that he is talking with a complete stranger. Jerry's approach is effective theater because it is spontaneous and improvisational; Jerry takes whatever details he can grasp about Peter and, combining the pain-pleasure formula with a fine psychological reading of his pupil, he works his effect. Consider, for example, the following sequence. Jerry, after some undirected small talk, watches Peter light his pipe and comments, "Well, boy; you're not going to get lung cancer, are you?" (p. 13) Peter, although initially annoyed by the personal and physical implications of the comment, is on reflection pleased by Jerry's apparent respect for pipe smokers. The pipe is an identity symbol for Peter. But Jerry deflates the impression and strips away the status symbol immediately by suggesting the physical reality, the likelihood of cancer of the mouth. Yet before Peter can let his irritation and discomfort motivate him to leave, Jerry plays once again to his ego by eliciting from Peter the term *prosthesis* and praising him for being an educated man and, with a cynicism that escapes Peter, a reader of *Time*. Jerry follows essentially the same pattern in probing Peter about his family, pets, occupation, and income. As the process develops, Peter is held less by Jerry's superficial—and calculated—flattery than by the pleasure of sharing personal concerns with another, although the initial rendering of facts and feelings each time is painful.

Once Jerry has involved himself with Peter, he can and must proceed to the more difficult task of involving Peter with him. He must subject himself to the pain-pleasure experience. It is painful for Jerry to tell Peter the embarrassing and degrading personal details of his life;[14] and his occasionally cavalier tone, a feigned indifference, helps him to endure the process. Equally intimidating to Jerry is his knowledge that in trusting himself to Peter's understanding he runs the risk, should Peter fail him, of facing an even deeper isolation. We see Jerry's anxiety reflected in his shift from an immobile stance while he quizzes Peter to a pacing about as he tells about his life. Jerry during this period ceases to mock Peter so insistently, and the pretended affection and calculated scorn of the earlier part of the play yield now to more genuine sympathy and at points to more genuine anger as Jerry comes to expect greater sensitivity from Peter. As Jerry frees Peter from the tyranny of a code of polite behavior, the desired likelihood that Peter will act according to his own wishes increases; whereas earlier Jerry would manipulate Peter against his wishes through a hollow rhetorical trick ("Do you mind if we talk?"), now he holds him more through an exercise of Peter's own will. Admittedly Jerry still lures Peter as if he were a child with the promise of the story about the zoo, but there is an adult directness in his challenge, "You don't *have* to listen. Nobody is holding you here; remember that. Keep that in your mind" (p. 29); and Jerry commences the narrative which culminates his attempts at establishing a spiritual kinship only when he can feel that Peter's continued presence is due to willing involvement and not to customary politeness.

Throughout the entire process of educating Peter, Jerry has to keep control over himself as well; and it is with an heroic effort that he prevents his own conflicting thoughts and emotions from spoiling his systematic approach. In probing Peter for the banal details of his conventional existence, Jerry is in danger of being so uninterested in the information that he will not summon enough energy to pursue his assault. Once, when Peter inquires about what he is to see on TV, Jerry glides into a revery on his anticipated death from which he is barely able to emerge and continue his probe of Peter's life. When Jerry begins to tell Peter his history, the danger shifts to his having too little distance from himself to take Peter's perception of his life sympathetically into account. Jerry becomes surprisingly angry at Peter's kindly intended gauche presumptions: "Oh, I thought you lived in the village" (p. 21), and "Well, it seems perfectly simple to me" (p. 25). Jerry's sharp retort to the latter of these remarks so alienates Peter that Jerry, frightened by Peter's anger, has quickly to apologize in order to prevent him from walking away.

Jerry's account and interpretation of his encounter with the dog climaxes his attempt to make spiritual contact with Peter, that is, to achieve a meeting of the minds, sympathy, and love. He knows that if the story succeeds in removing all the remaining barriers of ignorance and insensitivity that still separate Peter from him, he will no longer need to manipulate Peter, who will then be spiritually free, and he will also have resolved his own emotional conflicts. During his climactic personal monologue, Jerry rarely protects himself with an air of cynical indifference. Here, except in the stylizing and partially ironic scriptural phraseology with which he frames the account, Jerry entrusts to Peter a confession and a vision essentially untouched by euphemistic or distancing language. As Jerry brings his long monologue to a close, we see a playing out of the pain-pleasure principle on its most abstract, spiritual level, objectified physically in Jerry's passing from intense exhaustion to exhilaration. Albee's stage directions reveal to us the course of Jerry's feelings and involvement:

> Jerry *is abnormally tense now . . . Much faster now, and like a conspirator . . .* Jerry *sighs the next word* [People] *heavily. . . Here* Jerry *seems to fall into almost grotesque fatigue . . . then* Jerry *wearily finishes* [and at the end of the story] Jerry *moves to* Peter's *bench and sits down beside him. . . .* Jerry *is suddenly cheerful.*
>
> (pp. 34-36)

Jerry's sitting down, sharing the bench with Peter, is clearly a physical manifestation of a spiritual union he hopes now exists.

Jerry has excited Peter, stunned him, and moved him to tears; but by placing himself totally at Peter's mercy at the same time, Jerry has demanded more than Peter, even in his emotionally and intellectually hightened state, can provide. Peter is frightened because he has not comprehended with his whole being Jerry's metaphysics of possession. "Ownership" to Jerry means spiritual kinship, not legal or physical possession. Jerry is initially furious at Peter's refusal to admit that he understands Jerry's message, and Peter's shaken state indicates that he does in fact understand a great deal. Baxandall ("Theater of Edward Albee," p. 88) and Zimbardo ("Symbolism," p. 15) are partly right in contending that Peter lies. But if Jerry's vision of a spiritual union as the highest bliss were valid, then Peter would embrace it if he really understood it. The fact that he resists proves that he understands only what will be lost, not what will be gained. Jerry retreats to his great weariness after Peter, still in panic, cries, "I don't understand you, or your landlady, or *her* dog" (p. 37, my italics). That Peter would still perceive the dog as belonging to the landlady in whose physical possession it remains leaves Jerry with the feeling not only that Peter has not understood his vision ("*Her* dog! I thought it was my . . ."), but that the vision itself is probably an illusion ("No, No, you're right") and that man's conception of himself as a spiritual being is a presumption or wish without foundation in experience.

Jerry's spiritual commitment really ends here, for from this moment he ceases to aspire toward realizing a spiritual nature in Peter and seeks only to verify his earlier projection, spoken quizzically, that Peter is "an animal man" (p. 18). Jerry's tickling and hitting are simply a reduction from spiritual to physical terms of his kindness-and-cruelty mode of instruction. Free will is no longer an urgent concern to Jerry since he seeks only to prove Peter an animal; and with little emotional strain he manipulates Peter to his desired catastrophe.

When Jerry thanks Peter for comforting him, we cannot know, nor need we think that Jerry knows, to what degree each of the various impulses inside him—his suicidal weariness, his wish to be remembered, and his selfless desire to save Peter from a death-in-life existence—contributes to whatever satisfaction he finds in dying in this manner. But we do know that Jerry has chosen no easy way to die. In tragic defiance of the existential loneliness that seems to be humanity's lot, Jerry has marshalled heroic resources of courage, energy, manipulative cleverness, and sensitivity in an effort to realize an idea of kinship. The play's tragic affirmation emerges more from the powers Jerry manifests in his quest than from the result he obtains.

The play's story is bizarre, but so are most tragedies. Its mode is tragic realism, not social realism. The incident provides Albee a context for exploring the limits of human aspiration and potential for love. Jerry is an extremest in ideals, like most tragic heroes, and he does not place a modest demand upon Peter or himself; he seeks a total commitment. Realism is sufficiently present for us to identify with the characters, but it properly is a dramatic tool, not an end in itself. ***The Zoo Story*** aims to excite feelings in us, as we experience the play sympathetically, that we seldom, if ever, exercise because we are not confronted with situations of such intensity in our own lives. These feelings, moreover, accompany and gain their legitimacy from the enlightening vision of human nature worked out in experiential terms. The play is modest in scope, but it possesses a resonance and power that one finds only in tragedy.

Notes

[1]Zimbardo, "Symbolism and Naturalism in Edward Albee's *The Zoo Story," Twentieth Century Literature* 8 (April 1962), 15; Wellwarth, *The Theater of Protest and Paradox,* 2nd ed. (New York, 1971), p. 322; Esslin, *The Theatre of the Absurd,* 2nd ed. (Garden City, New York, 1969), p. 267; Way, "Albee and the Absurd," in *American Theatre,* ed. J.R. Brown and Bernard Harris (New York, 1967), p. 204.

[2]"The Theater of Edward Albee," in *The Modern American Theater,* ed. Alvin Kernan (Englewood Cliffs, New Jersey, 1967), p. 98.

[3]Edward Albee, *The American Dream* and *The Zoo Story* (New York, 1959), p. 48. All page references are from this edition.

[4]Spokesmen for *The Zoo Story* as absurdist theater include Esslin, *Theatre of the Absurd,* p. 267; Charles R. Lyons, "Two Projections of the Isolation of the Human Soul: Brecht and Albee," *Drama Survey* 4 (Summer 1965), 121. Way sees the play as a confusion of absurdist and social protest drama ("Albee and the Absurd," p. 204). Spokesmen against the absurdist designation include Michael Rutenberg, *Edward Albee: Playwright in Protest* (New York, 1969), p. 11; and Thomas B. Morgan, "Angry Playwright in a Soft Spell," *Life,* 26 May 1967, p. 97.

[5]The majority of critics, including Rutenberg, Baxandall, and Morgan, read *The Zoo Story* as a social tract.

[6]From "Tragedy and the Common Man," *New York Times,* 27 Feb. 1949, II, pp. 1, 3; rpt. in *Death of a Salesman: Text and Criticism,* ed. Gerald Weales (New York, 1967), pp. 143-47.

[7]*Edward Albee,* pp. 16 and 20.

[8]*The Riverside Shakespeare* (Boston, 1974), p. 1172.

[9]Mary M. Nilan, "Albee's *The Zoo Story:* Alienated Man and the Nature of Love," *Modern Drama* 16 (1973), 58.

[10]Cf. Arthur Miller's comparison of Biff and Hap Loman, *Death of a Salesman,* p. 19.

[11]Robert Wallace, "Albee's Attack on Fiction," *Modern Drama* 16 (1973), 53.

[12]Quoted in Melvyn Gussow, "Albee: Odd Man In on Broadway," *Newsweek,* 4 Feb. 1963, p. 50.

[13]Wallace, "Albee's Attack on Fiction," p. 49; Driver, "What's the Matter with Edward Albee?" in *The Modern American Theater, op. cit.,* p. 99.

[14]I differ with Rutenberg's position, which seems to be widely held, that Jerry is "in [a] fervor to spill out his own lonely feelings" (*Edward Albee,* p. 19).

Richard E. Amacher (essay date 1982)

SOURCE: "Ancient Tragedy and Modern Absurdity," in *Edward Albee: Revised Edition,* Twayne Publishers, 1982, pp. 29-42.

[*In the essay below, Amacher conducts a broad survey of the construction of* The Zoo Story *and observes that the play "stands up well as a tragedy in the Greek manner: its plot hangs together well in terms of its cause-effect sequence of episodes or main parts, and it contains a reversal and more than one discovery."*]

Classical Plot in Central Park

The Zoo Story[1] has a rather simple and easily comprehensible structure of three main parts that are climactically ordered. In the first part we are introduced to Jerry and Peter and to their differences with respect to person, background, economic status, marital status, literary taste, philosophy, desire for communication, the way they talk, and so on. The second part deals with the story of Jerry and the dog, and the third is the zoo story—what happened at the zoo.

The action of the entire drama is played against the background of *"foliage, trees, sky"* in Central Park in New York City on a summer Sunday afternoon in the present.[2] There are two park benches, and Peter is seated on one of them, reading a book, his habitual activity for such afternoons. The setting is definitely pinpointed as within visibility of the intersection of Fifth Avenue and Seventy-Fourth Street, on the east side of the park (12-13), within walking distance of Peter's residence between Lexington and Third Avenue on Seventy-Fourth Street (22).

The opposition between the characters of Jerry and Peter—the distinctive effect of part one—consists at least partly in the fact that Jerry lives on the west side of the park. The two men, however, do have one thing in common: they are nearly the same age. Peter, *"a man in his early forties,"* suggests *"a man younger"*; Jerry, in his later thirties, looks older, because of his *"fall from physical grace,"* hinted at by the fact that his *"lightly muscled body has begun to go to fat"* (11). Jerry also has *"a great weariness"* (11), possibly because of his long walk down to Washington Square and back again, which he tells about, but possibly, too, because of the totality of his life-experience—one so different in kind from that of the favored Peter.

The contrast between the two characters, as already indicated, is revealed by the progress of the topics they discuss. The conversation actually begins with Jerry's forcing himself upon Peter's attention by announcing three times, progressively louder, that he has been to the zoo. After Jerry discovers where he is—he had lost his way during his long hike—he moves the talk along by a series of intrusive questions, or they appear so to Peter, who wants to be let alone. But Jerry persists; for, as he explains, he had felt, for at least once, a deep desire to communicate with another human being instead of mouthing such usual remarks as "give me a beer, or where's the john, or what time does the feature go on, or keep your hands to yourself, buddy . . ." (19). "Every once in a while," he says, "I like to talk to somebody, really *talk;* like to get to know somebody, know all about him" (19).

This isolation, a common element of life in large cities, Jerry feels challenged to combat—vigorously, aggressively, and, as it happens, to the death. Thus the theme of the play bears directly on a current social problem and at the same time on the deeply philosophical subjects handled by Ionesco, Beckett, and Genet—the breakdown of language, the attempt to live by illusion, the alienation of the individual from his fellow men, the terrible loneliness of every living human being.

Jerry's questions to Peter elicit such facts about the latter's life as that he thinks he can avoid cancer by smoking a pipe, that he is acquainted with the life of Freud, that he is educated, that he reads *Time* magazine, that he owns two television sets (an extra one for his two daughters), that he wanted a son but that his wife would have no more children, that he doesn't really want cats but that his daughters and wife have brought both cats and parakeets into his household, that he has "an executive position with . . . a small publishing house" handling textbooks, and makes"around eighteen thousand a year" (21), that, though he prides himself on his good taste in literature, he cannot tell Jerry the difference between two such different writers as Baudelaire and J. P. Marquand (24), that he is disappointed to find out that Jerry doesn't live in Greenwich Village, and that he is reticent generally (22) and embarrassed about discussing his sex life (32).

In the course of his cross-examination of Peter, Jerry shows no reluctance whatever about revealing his own private life. The following points come out about him: he is not married, but apparently has had plenty of one-night sex experiences with women and was even, at one stage in his development, a homosexual. He resents Peter's patronizing attitude toward him; he has had an entirely different kind of education—the "school of hard knocks." He is aware of the finicky economic class distinctions that seem to mean so much to some Americans, such distinctions as the difference between the "upper-middle-middle-class" and the "lower-upper-middle class." And he is direct and honest.

He lives on the West Side under circumstances far different from Peter's, in a "laughably small room" on the top floor, between Columbus Avenue and Central Park West. He is observant of his neighbors—the Puerto Rican family that entertains a lot; the woman who cries determinedly all day; the homosexual who plucks his eyebrows "with Buddhist concentration" (26) but who keeps his hands to himself; and the fat, elderly, gin-soaked landlady of whose sweaty lust he (Jerry) is the object (33). He seems strangely affected by the fact that he has never seen and will never get to know a person who lives in a room within a few feet of his own: "And in the other front room, there's somebody living there, but I don't know who it is. I've never seen who it is. Never. Never ever" (26).

In contrast to Peter's "apartment in the East Seventies" and his "one wife, two daughters, two cats and two parakeets," and other possessions, Jerry's personal accessories include such items as can openers, a hot plate, a few clothes, a knife, a fork, "eight or nine books," a "pack of pornographic playing cards," some rocks which he has picked up on the beach, love letters, and, among other things, two empty picture frames (27). Asked about these, he explains the sordid details of his mother's adulterous tour of the Southern states, ending with her death in Alabama, and, shortly afterward, his drunken father's accidentally stepping in front of "a somewhat moving city omnibus" (28). Following this "vaudeville act" (28) had come what he calls "a terribly middle-European joke," the death of his mother's sister "on the afternoon of my high school graduation" (29). (Jerry characterizes her as having done "all things dourly: sleeping, eating, working, praying." [28-29].) Apparently she had reared him from the time he was ten and a half—after his parents' departure. Despite these "hard knocks," Jerry does not feel sorry for himself; he is tough-minded about all aspects of his personal experience.

But Jerry suffers from certain unanswered questions arising from his experience, and these questions the other two parts of the play dramatize for us. At the beginning of part two, "The Story of Jerry and the Dog," Jerry prefaces his remarks by saying: "What I am going to tell you has something to do with how sometimes it's necessary to go a long distance out of the way in order to come back a short distance correctly" (36). The rather profound answer to this enigmatic opening becomes clear only at the end of this story, although the audience already knows at the merely physical level that Jerry has trudged all the way down to Washington Square and back again. Too, the audience is ready for the story because Jerry, in his account of his landlady's sweaty lust and his way of putting her off—by referring to their love of the previous day, "and the day before," so that she actually "believes and relives what never happened"—also has mentioned to Peter that the landlady's companion in these encounters is a "black monster of a dog" (34). This animal forthwith becomes Jerry's antagonist in part two of the play.

Albee presents the animal vividly. The dog is old, misused, and black all over except for its bloodshot eyes and the red, open sore on its right front paw. The dog "almost always has an erection . . . of sorts. [And] that's red, too." But "when he bares his fangs," "there's a gray-yellow-white color" (36). From the first, the dog had unmistakably declared his intention of biting him, as Jerry explains:"I worried about the animal the very first minute I met him. Now, animals don't take to me like Saint Francis had birds hanging off him all the time. What I mean is: animals are indifferent to me . . . like people (*He smiles slightly*) . . . most of the time. But this dog wasn't indifferent. From the very beginning he'd snarl and then go for me, to get one of my legs" (36-37).

Thurber has a somewhat similar dog in his well-known story *The Dog That Bit People,* but his animal bit indiscriminately and ubiquitously. The curious thing about Albee's dog is that he apparently does not bother the other roomers—only Jerry—and only when Jerry comes in, never when he goes out. After over a week of narrow escapes and torn trousers, Jerry decides to "kill the dog with kindness" and, if that doesn't work, to "just kill him" (37).

To his great surprise, neither plan succeeds. First, when he offers the dog "six perfectly good hamburgers with not enough pork in them to make it disgusting," the dog eats them ravenously, "making sounds in his throat like a woman," then tries to eat the paper bag they came in, and finally, after a quiescent moment in which Jerry thinks the dog smiles at him, "BAM" (38), it snarls and charges him again. Second, when he poisons the dog, it becomes deathly ill—so ill, in fact, that the drunken landlady sobers up and asks Jerry to pray for her "puppykins." But both "puppykins" and landlady recover: the former, its health; the latter, her thirst.

After this episode Jerry and the dog have a confrontation—Jerry now "unafraid" and the "beast" looking "better for his scrape with the nevermind" (41). They stare at each other for a long time; and, "during that twenty seconds or two hours that" they look into each other's eyes, they *make contact* (41). Jerry, who now refers to the dog as his *friend,* says: "I loved the dog now, and I wanted him to love me. I had tried to love, and I had tried to kill, and both had been unsuccessful by themselves . . . I hoped that the dog would understand . . . it's just that if you can't deal with people, you have to make a start somewhere. WITH ANIMALS! . . . with . . . some day, with people" (42-43).

This passage brings us close to the theme, as does the one that immediately follows it. The contact made during that moment, it seems, had been only a transient one; for now, as Jerry says, whenever they meet they both regard each other "with a mixture of sadness and suspicion, and then we feign *indifference*" (43; my italics). An "understanding" has been reached: the dog no longer rushes him; he no longer feeds or poisons the dog.

> I have gained solitary free passage, if that much further loss can be said to be gain. I have learned that neither kindness nor cruelty by themselves, independent of each other, creates any effect beyond themselves; and I have learned that the two combined, together, at the same time, are the *teaching emotion* [my italics]. And what is gained is loss. And what has been the result: the dog and I have attained a compromise; more of a bargain really. We neither love nor hurt because we do not try to reach each other. And, *was* trying to feed the dog an act of love? And, perhaps, was the dog's attempt to bite me *not* an act of love? If we can so misunderstand, well then, why have we invented the word love in the first place?
>
> (43-44)

Following this important passage of what Aristotle would call *Thought* (see *Poetics*), Albee has indicated silence for emphasis and has also written into the stage directions that at this point Jerry moves to Peter's bench and sits down beside him for the first time in the play. At the same time the playwright makes Jerry announce, "The Story of Jerry and the Dog: the end," thus unmistakably bringing to an effective and highly dramatic close this important second part of the play.

Although the transition to part three may seem somewhat long, it is nevertheless effective in doing two rather necessary things. First, it brings Jerry and Peter into an intensity of conflict that their differences of background and character had only begun to develop in part one. Second, it provides the motive for Peter's remaining on the scene in spite of this difference in character. An intense and fierce struggle between Jerry and Peter is necessary, for it is ultimately the cause of what happens at the final climactic point of the play—the death of Jerry at Peter's hands. If one character is going to kill another at the end of the play, the author must obviously provide preparation for such an act.

Albee's procedure in handling this preparation shows remarkable skill. He begins by having Jerry ask Peter about selling the story concerning the dog to the *Reader's Digest* in order to "make a couple of hundred bucks for *The Most Unforgettable Character I've Ever Met.*" This fair question is put to Peter since he knows all about how to make money in publishing, but it also points up the great difference between Jerry and Peter. For Peter, Jerry suggests, the only value of the story might be its potential as lucre; for Jerry, however, what happened between him and the dog represents possibly the most exciting and meaningful experience of his entire life—something that has nothing at all to do with money value. So, when Peter says he does not understand why a perfect stranger should spill out his private life to him in such a tale, Jerry remonstrates with a furious whisper, "That's a lie." For he knows that Peter is not only educated (at least superficially) but is also experienced and intelligent enough to understand exactly what he (Jerry) is trying to express. Whatever this is, it has to do with the common humanity between the two men, or between any two men; and since Peter refuses to acknowledge it, it must be acted out and dramatized in a way he will never forget—which is exactly what happens in part three.

Peter's refusal to "understand" and his not wanting to hear any more about Jerry, the landlady, or the dog (45) depress Jerry and solidify the superficial but extreme opposition between the characters. Jerry says at this point, ". . . of course you don't understand. (*In a monotone, wearily*) I don't live in your block; I'm not married to two parakeets, or whatever your setup is. I am a permanent transient, and my home is the sickening roominghouses on the West Side of New York City, which is the greatest city in the world. Amen" (45).

After a little desultory conversation (46), Peter looks at his watch and threatens to leave. To prevent his departure, Jerry tickles him into helplessness, into willingness to listen to the second story—what happened at the zoo. Here Peter begins the process of self-discovery, for he notes with surprise that he cannot quite explain what had happened to him, what had caused him to succumb to the almost hysterical fit of laughing. Even Jerry remarks, "Yes, that was very funny, Peter. I wouldn't have expected it" (49).

After this five-page transition—or interruption of the action—Jerry continues as follows:

> Now I'll let you in on what happened at the zoo; but first, I should tell you why I went to the zoo. I went to the zoo to find out more about the way people exist with animals, and the way animals exist with each other, and with people too. It probably wasn't a fair test, what with everyone separated by bars from everyone else, the animals for the most part from each other, and always the people from the animals. But if it's a zoo, that's the way it is. (*He pokes* PETER *on the arm*): Move over.
>
> (49)

This speech marks the beginning not only of part three but also of a series of moves on Jerry's part to unseat Peter from his bench. At first Peter responds with friendliness and gives him more room; but, as Jerry's requests become progressively less polite and always rougher and more demanding, unreasonably demanding, until he at last wants the whole bench—"my bench," as he calls it—Peter is aroused to fighting fury. Almost in tears, he shouts, "GET AWAY FROM MY BENCH!"

Jerry replies tauntingly, "Why? You have everything in the world you want; you've told me about your home, and your family, and *your own* little zoo. You have everything, and now you want this bench. Are these the things men fight for? Tell me, Peter, is this bench, this iron and this wood, is this your honor? Is this the thing in the world you'd fight for? Can you think of anything more absurd?" (55-56).

Peter refuses to discuss the question of honor with Jerry, who, he says, wouldn't understand it anyway. Jerry continues adding insult to injury: "This is probably the first time in your life you've had anything more trying to face than changing your cat's toilet box. Stupid! Don't you have any idea, not even the slightest, what other people *need?*" (56). When Peter replies that Jerry doesn't *need* this particular bench, Jerry shoots back, "Yes; yes, I do." Peter, *"quivering"* with anger, lets out that he has come there for years, has had "hours of pleasure, great satisfaction, right here . . . This is my bench, and you have no right to take it away from me" (56). And Jerry retorts:"Fight for it, then. Defend yourself; defend your bench." He also insults him further by calling him "a vegetable," a "slightly nearsighted one . . ." (57).

At this crisis the two men are ready for battle. Jerry clicks open a wicked-looking toad-stabber. The Westside jungle has at least conditioned him for this eventuality, and he rises to it *"lazily,"* but nonetheless confidently and fully equipped, quietly ready for combat. Peter, on the other hand, awakes to the reality of the situation with horror and melodramatically cries out, "You are mad! You're stark raving mad! YOU'RE GOING TO KILL ME!" (58). Jerry tosses the knife at Peter's feet, saying "You have the knife and we'll be more evenly matched" (58).

When Peter refuses to accept this challenge, Jerry in turn grows infuriated. He rushes Peter, grabs him by the collar, and says with great intensity, "Now you pick up that knife and you fight me. You fight for your self-respect; you fight for that god-damned bench" (58). But, when Peter only struggles to escape, Jerry begins slapping him in the face. He slaps him each time he says *fight* during the following speech: ". . . fight, you miserable bastard; fight for that bench; fight for your parakeets; fight for your cats, fight for your two daughters; fight for your wife; fight for your manhood, you pathetic little vegetable" (59). Finally, he spits in Peter's face and insults him still again by saying, "You couldn't even get your wife with a male child" (59).

All this is at last too much for Peter. He picks up the knife and backs off a little, breathing heavily. He holds the knife far out in front of him rigidly, frozen into defensiveness; then Jerry, realizing they have reached a point of no return, sighs heavily and with a "So be it!" "*charges* PETER *and impales himself on the knife*" (59).

From this point to the end of the play, Jerry dies. But, before the last breath of life has escaped him, he clarifies the theme of the play in two fairly long speeches. In the second, the less important, he congratulates Peter on the defense of his honor, although at the loss of his bench; for Peter, he says, will never return to it because of what has happened. He also says Peter is not really a *vegetable* but an *animal.* In the first, or more important of the two speeches, he thanks Peter. (Peter is aghast at this gratitude, for he knows he has been the means of Jerry's death—the agent and unwitting executioner, despite Jerry's suicidal act.) "Oh, Peter," he says, "I was so afraid I'd drive you away . . . You don't know how afraid I was you'd go away and leave me" (60). Then he goes on to say,

> And now I'll tell you what happened at the zoo. I think . . . I think this is what happened at the zoo . . . I think, I think that while I was at the zoo I decided that I would walk north . . . *northerly rather* . . . until I found you . . . or somebody . . . and I decided that I would talk to you . . . I would tell you things . . . and things that I would tell you would . . . Well, here we are. You see? Here we *are*. . . . And now I've told you what you wanted to know, haven't I? And now you know all about what happened at the zoo. And now you know what you'll see in your TV, and the face I told you about . . . you remember . . . the face I told you about . . . my face, the face you see right now.
>
> (60 61; first italics are mine)[3]

What happened at the zoo, according to Jerry, had simply been the decision to walk in a northward direction and to try to find some person with whom he could make contact. For he had not really made contact with the dog (in the second part of the play), it will be recalled, although they had come to "an understanding" (43). Jerry expresses this situation this way: "We neither love nor hurt because we do not try to reach each other" (44). Yet Jerry says that, from his experience with the dog, he had learned "the teaching emotion," that combination of kindness and cruelty that formulates, for him at least, life itself (44).

This same formula, this "teaching emotion," plays itself out in the grim ending. When Jerry pierces the defensive armor of Peter, he *makes contact* with him in a way he never had with the dog.[4] And he takes comfort in his success, even though it is achieved at the expense of his life—with cruelty, *fated,* as it were, in the chain of events. For he says: "I came unto you (*He laughs, so faintly*) and you have comforted me. Dear Peter" (61). And he asks: ". . . could I have planned all this? No . . . no, I couldn't have. But I think I did" (60).

Problems and Comments

There are three separate problems in this episode, as I see it, that Albee thrusts deliberately into the attention of the reader or the playgoer. First, there is the problem of the biblical language and what he means to convey by his use of it; second, there is the face on the television screen, alluded to earlier (16, 19); third, certain implications concerning human existence, either particularized or generalized. For it seems to me that Albee is working partly, but only partly, from an Existentialist position.

Earlier in the story of his encounter with the Dog, Jerry had also paraphrased the Bible, *with irony,* saying, "AND IT CAME TO PASS THAT THE BEAST WAS DEATHLY ILL," just after he had fed it the poisoned hamburgers.[5] Two sentences after this quotation he tells of his landlady's maudlin announcement that "God had struck her puppy-dog a surely fatal blow" and her request that he "pray" for its recovery (44). Thus the audience is prepared for the kind of diction we discover at the end of the play.

But what does Albee intend? Or perhaps, more accurately, what do the words suggest? In the New Testament, Peter betrays Christ instead of comforting him.[6] In the play, Peter's comfort of Jerry amounts to his not leaving him. But Jerry's faint laughter (61), as he states his gratitude, shows his insight; for he knows that such comfort as he has managed to draw out of Peter has not been freely given; it has been supplied not only with indifference and reluctance but perhaps also with latent *cruelty* (the other part of the "teaching emotion")—the cold steel of the knife that had brought him death. Therefore, the passage can only be construed as *ironical,* as in the earlier biblical paraphrase.

As for the face on the television screen, Jerry's mention of it early in the play, when he first encounters Peter (16), seems at first glance to be part of his tough-minded attitude toward himself. It is as if he were arguing, against his better judgment, the importance of his private visit to the zoo by placing it in the same category with more public and possibly more newsworthy events—such as appear daily in metropolitan newspapers and on nation-wide television broadcasts. Such an argument shows Jerry's strong individualism and makes him an appealing character, particularly as it is voiced in rebellion against the strong pressures that beset struggling individualists of all kinds in big cities like New York. Albee emphasizes the point by making Peter ask, shortly afterward (19), "What were you saying about the zoo . . . that I'd read about it, or see . . ." Jerry, however, puts him off by saying he will tell him about it soon. At this point in the play, all Jerry wants is conversation—a listener at any price.

At the end of the play, however, where Jerry says, "And now you know what you'll see in your TV, and the face I told you about . . . my face . . ." the earlier prophecy, or preparation, has been fulfilled. Murder, suicide, and accidental death belong to the category of the sensational that makes up so large a part of newspaper and television news; Jerry's death (what Aristotle and the Greeks called "tragic incident" in a tragedy) combines all three—murder, suicide, and accident. How, then, can we explain Jerry's elaborate precautions to see that Peter will not be detected as participant in this event? (He wipes Peter's fingerprints off the knife, reminds him to take his book along with him, and urges him to hurry away. [62]) The answer must surely lie in what Jerry knows about Peter: the kind of person he has discovered him to be. Whatever else he is, Peter is bookish; introspective; and, above all, highly conformist—in short, the kind of person who can never forget this incident, or Jerry. The face, then, that he will see on the television screen will be one that he projects there himself, the face of Jerry, one that will forever come between him and the other sensational events that we so often see on this medium.

Finally, the play exhibits certain characteristics of Existentialism. It impresses us, especially that part of it dealing with Jerry's life, as a struggle for existence—in the jungle of the city. The conflict of values, the attack on the bourgeois code that Jerry continues as long as there is breath in him, is acted out on a park bench and is surely one of the basic situations of human existence that Sartre talks of as constituting dramatizable material.[7] Moreover, Jerry qualifies as an Existentialist hero: he makes his choices freely. His decision to impale himself on the knife Peter is stiffly holding is a deliberate act. "So be it," he says simply; but he nonetheless knows full well exactly what he is doing.[8]

Jerry also represents what another writer refers to as "the strange, inaccessible self [that] . . . remains when a person has lost the whole world but not himself, the very real inner impassioned feel of self, the self beyond the transcendental unity" of Kant which is"unknowable and incommunicable."[9] His death is a deliberate act of protest against the wrongs of the city, the injustice of the system, the bourgeois values that cause *nausea,* the feeling of life being lived in a void, the isolation of man. The play suggests that the price of survival under these conditions may be the murder of our fellow man, even when accomplished accidentally or unwittingly. We have heard this cliché of men's expendability bandied about by militarists in connection with the rationalizing of dropping atomic bombs to end war, but not much with respect to the cannibalism of our socioeconomic system. As Albee presents this human condition, it becomes completely absurd; and he makes this point strongly when at the end he lets Jerry taunt Peter, the survivor, with this little grotesquerie: "Hurry away, your parakeets are making the dinner . . . the cats . . . are setting the table . . ." (62).

That man's condition is not only absurd but also subhuman is perhaps what, in the last analysis, Albee means by the title, *The Zoo Story.* Yet for Jerry, who knows life closely and well, all men are divided into two classes—vegetable and animal; the former comprise those who merely subsist and the latter those who are willing to fight and kill, as animals do, for survival. At first he is unwilling to grant Peter the high praise of admission to the animal class, but ultimately, when dying, he does: "And Peter, I'll tell you something now; you're not really a vegetable . . . you're an animal." But it is significant that no terms—other than vegetable and animal—are used to describe the condition of man.

Jerry is in the midst of a rebellion against this condition, and wants desperately to "make a start somewhere," with animals if not with people; with anything, as he says eloquently in his account of his earlier experience with the dog; or even with a "GOD WHO IS A COLORED QUEEN WHO WEARS A KIMONO AND PLUCKS HIS EYEBROWS, WHO IS A WOMAN WHO CRIES WITH DETERMINATION BEHIND HER CLOSED DOOR . . . with God who, I'm told, turned his back on the whole thing some time ago . . . in this humiliating excuse for a jail . . ." (42-43).

Let us remember here that the Existentialist view of life as a trap is really not so very different from the older Puritan concept of the world as a vale of tears with a possibly more restricted liberty of choice, or freedom of the will, than the Existentialists offer us. If, then, we reject the view of God presented in ***The Zoo Story,*** one to which Jerry is driven in desperation, we should not necessarily conclude that Albee speaks from an atheist, rather than a theist, position. For the stage directions that Albee has written for the last speech of the play, "Oh . . . my . . . God"—in which, with full consistency of character, Jerry continues his derision of Peter right to the end—call for the delivery of these words in a *"combination of scornful mimicry and supplication"* (62).

We also must always remember that, simply because Albee treats Jerry this way in a work of fiction, we cannot really make any very valid conclusions about Albee's own personal religious convictions, which may be entirely different from those of any character in his play. In summary, we must conclude either that the character of Jerry is slightly inconsistent here, because of his earlier representations of an ineffectual or indifferent deity (42-43), or that the peculiar brand of Existentialism offered is nearer to orthdoxy or to the theism of Marcel than to the atheism of Sartre or Camus.[10] It does not necessarily follow, of course, that because Jerry feels that God is indifferent to human suffering, he is bound to assume that God does not exist. However Albee might defend the consistency of his characterization of Jerry by arguing the indifference or the nonexistence of God and the influence of either on Jerry's final statement, the fact remains that the tragic effect is heightened by Albee's inclusion of the word *supplication,* difficult as it is for any actor to express the complex tonal combination of simultaneous mimicry and prayer for which the author calls (62).

Tragedy in the Greek Manner

The Zoo Story stands up well as a tragedy in the Greek manner: its plot hangs together well in terms of its cause-effect sequence of episodes or main parts, and it contains a reversal and more than one discovery. If, in considering the *reversal,* we conceive the plot in terms of Jerry's struggle for existence against forces that threaten his highly individualistic, nonconformist character, as well as his protest against the consequent isolation that a conformist society punishes him with for daring to assert such individualism, then his confrontation with Peter, a representative of that society, becomes a kind of crisis or a climax to his entire life. And when Jerry discovers that he can pierce the barrier of this ever increasing isolation—and at the same time maintain his integrity—only at the cost of his life, and when he consequently rushes on the knife held by Peter, the plot reverses itself.

Until this moment in the plot there has never been any doubt about the ability of Jerry (the nonconformist, the poisoner of the dog, the confident battler willing to even the odds by letting Peter have the knife) to *survive.* On the contrary, he has always given the impression of being able to take care of himself. He has been bothered, deeply bothered, to be sure, by certain problems—his landlady's repulsive love-making, his unhappy neighbors, his episode with the mean dog, his sense of growing alienation—but there has never been any real doubt about survival as such. He has always been able to outrun the dog, to keep homosexuals at bay.

But now there is real doubt; his former good fortune turns to bad fortune. Peter picks up the knife, goaded by Jerry's insults. When Peter takes his stand, no alternative exists for Jerry. Given this situation—the aroused emotions of the combatants, the depth of their conflict, Jerry's past—there is absolutely no other way for him to make contact with the conditioned, calloused Peter (who, I repeat, represents the coldly adamantine exterior which society turns on the nonconformist) than by lunging at the knife. Jerry consequently triumphs over Peter and shows the superiority of his code and his character. He becomes in his death a kind of hero, and the playgoer experiences a genuine catharsis of pity and fear.[11]

Turning now to *discovery* or *recognition,* we immediately observe that we have a double one.[12] We have already considered Jerry's discovery or recognition that there is no other course open for him except suicide. We have seen how Peter becomes, at least momentarily for him, an enemy. And this change from friendliness to hate on Jerry's part is what Aristotle means by *recognition*—"a change from ignorance to knowledge, producing love or hate between the persons destined by the poet for good or bad fortune."[13] For Peter, too, there is a *recognition,* beginning at the point where he thinks Jerry is going to kill him (58). But by a skillful twist Albee surprises the audience (and this is the proper effect the reversal of the plot should have, as long as it follows the law of probability) and makes Peter actually kill Jerry. With the realization of what he has done, Peter changes from his earlier tolerance for Jerry to horror of what Jerry has made him—a murderer. *Horror* is perhaps not the same as Aristotle's "hate," but Albee does speak of love and hate together as the teaching emotion; and such a mixture of love and hate is the emotional state of both protagonist and antagonist as the drama closes. At first, Peter weeps, repeating again and again "Oh my God, oh my God." Then, at Jerry's injunction, he begins to *"stagger away,"* and the last we hear from him is a pitiful offstage howl, "OH MY GOD!" (61-62). Thus the absurdity of survival in the twentieth century is dramatized with peculiarly Grecian effectiveness.

Notes

[1]Used by permission of Coward-McCann, Inc., from *The Zoo Story, The Death of Bessie Smith, The Sandbox: Three Plays* by Edward Albee; © 1960.

[2]Edward Albee, *The Zoo Story, The Death of Bessie Smith, The Sandbox: Three Plays, Introduced by the Author* (New York, 1960), p. 11. Numbers in parentheses throughout this and the next two chapters refer to this volume.

[3]The fact that Jerry here corrects himself with Peter's language seems to show his recognition of the fact that communication has been achieved.

[4]Jerry had actually made contact, *briefly,* with the dog earlier. See p. 41, where he says "during that twenty seconds . . . we made contact." But this rapprochement had lapsed into indifference, in which they neither loved nor hurt each other, nor—what seems worse—any longer tried "to reach each other" (44).

I am indebted personally to Martin Esslin for permission to quote the following interesting note from his *Reflections: Essays on Modern Theatre* (Garden City, N.Y.: Doubleday, 1969), p. 70: In Brecht's short story *Brief über eine Dogge* [Letter about a Bulldog, 1925] "a young man totally alone in the world who lives in San Francisco . . . desperately tries to make friends with a bulldog belonging to a family inhabiting the same tenement. Bur the dog develops a deep aversion to the narrator, and when, during the great San Francisco earthquake, the narrator finds the dog half buried under debris and wants to rescue it, the animal snarls at him, preferring to die rather than to be touched by the narrator." As Esslin points out, "Brecht has here totally anticipated the situation between Jerry and the dog in Albee's *The Zoo Story.*"

[5]I say *with irony* advisedly, because in the Bible the phrase "And it came to pass" usually refers to actions outside human control, whereas here Jerry controls, or rather instigates, the situation, however underhandedly he goes about it.

[6]See Luke 22:54-62. It would be silly, of course, to identify Jerry with Jesus Christ; for, although both come unto Peter, Jerry seems to sense the vast difference between himself and Christ. And this may be the reason he laughs at his own words. For the view that Jerry represents Christ and Peter, St. Peter, see Rose A. Zimbardo, "Symbolism and Naturalism in Edward Albee's 'The Zoo Story'," *Twentieth Century Literature* 8 (April 1962): 14. For an even more fantastic interpretation, equating Jerry with the Ancient Mariner in Coleridge's poem (Peter becomes the wedding guest and the dog, the albatross), see Peter Spielberg, "The Albatross in Albee's Zoo," *College English* 27, no. 7 (April 1966):562-65.

[7]See Sartre's "Forgers of the Myth," tr. Rosamond Gilder in *Theater Arts Anthology.* Reproduced in R. W. Corrigan's *The Modern Theater* (New York: Macmillan, 1964), p. 782.

[8]Although the language may seem a little strange here, Albee prepares us with one earlier "So be it" in the mouth of Jerry (24).

[9]Marjorie Grene, *Dreadful Freedom, A Critique of Existentialism* (Chicago: University of Chicago, 1948), p. 24.

[10]See Gabriel Marcel, *The Philosophy of Existentialism,* 5th paperbound edition (New York: Citadel Press, 1965), pp. 9-46.

[11]See Aristotle's *Poetics,* 13:2, for definitions of *pity* and *fear.*

[12]See Gerald F. Else, *Aristotle's Poetics: The Argument* (Cambridge, Mass.: Harvard University, 1963), pp. 342-55, for an extended discussion of *recognition,* either with or without *reversal.*

[13]Butcher translation, *Poetics,* 11:2.

Mary Castiglie Anderson (essay date 1983)

SOURCE: "Ritual and Initiation in *The Zoo Story,*" in *Edward Albee: An Interview and Essays,* edited by Julian N. Wasserman, The University of St. Thomas, 1983, pp. 93-108.

[The following essay contends that The Zoo Story *"might well be seen as a portrayal of a ritual confrontation with death and alienation in which Jerry acts the role of shaman/guide who directs the uninitiated Peter through the initiatory rite necessary for Peter to achieve his maturity and autonomy."]*

Although variously explained as a sociopolitical tract, a pessimistic analysis of human alienation, a modern Christian allegroy of salvation, and an example of absurdist and nihil-

Albee standing in front of the Provincetown Playhouse in New York City, where *The Zoo Story* had its American premiere in 1960.

ist theater, Albee's ***The Zoo Story*** has managed to absorb these perspectives without exhausting its many levels of meaning with the result that much of the critical controversy which has surrounded the play since its American premier in January 1960 has remained unresolved.[1] However, Albee himself provides what is possibly the best framework for understanding his first play when he speaks of his attempt to depict through his drama the danger of a life lived without "the cleansing consciousness of death."[2] Thus, ***The Zoo Story*** might well be seen as a portrayal of a ritual confrontation with death and alienation in which Jerry acts the role of shaman/guide who directs the uninitiated Peter through the initiatory rite necessary for Peter to achieve his maturity and autonomy.

Such rituals are, of course, associated with the entering into adulthood and the leaving behind of childish ways. Peter's lack of development and, hence, his need for initiation are immediately apparent in several ways. He is, for instance, relatively inarticulate and unassertive. He tells Jerry, "I'm normally . . . reticent" and "I don't express myself too well, sometimes."[3] His responses, when he does give them, tend to be formulaic, showing him to be for the most part a rather unthinking spokesman for the unexamined attitudes of his social class. In his parroting of these values and attitudes, Peter demonstrates the passive acceptance of a child rather than the independence of thought which should characterize an adult. In contrast, the much more linguistically flexible Jerry consistently finds occasion to mock not only Peter's thoughts but the awkwardness and rigidity with which they are expressed. Thus, to Peter's admission of his own feelings of paternal inadequacy because ". . . naturally, every man wants a son" (p. 16), Jerry employs the cliché, "But that's the way the cookie crumbles." Jerry, whom the stage directions describe here as"lightly mocking," has as his purpose not an attack on Peter's virility or ability to "produce" sons, but rather a mocking challenge of Peter's unquestioning ("naturally") belief in the myths of that virility as well as the emotionless and thoughtless manner of its expression. Similarly, the interchange which is generated through Peter's citation of *Time* magazine reveals the great extent to which Peter's thought is derivative. Peter, himself, self-consciously jokes, "I'm in publishing, not writing" (p.

20). Infant-like, in that he has no real language of his own, Peter has no way of articulating his personal feelings and sensibilities, and without that ability, Peter, it may be argued, lacks any real identity or place within his world. What Jerry effects within the play is the initiation of Peter into an adult world of feelings and the responsibilities which are attendant with their expression.

Jerry sums up Peter's character in one line: "You're a very sweet man and you're possessed of a truly enviable innocence" (p. 23). Peter maintains this innocence by remaining almost completely passive to two forces he has subliminally set up as displaced "parent" figures. Because Peter has invested these figures with such enormous power over the course of his life, they have become for him deterministic structures with seemingly independent lives of their own. The first, his wife, presides over the domestic realm; as a maternal symbol whose individual characteristics remain significantly vague, she seems to exert an influence on Peter which corresponds to the maternal paraphernalia he uses to define himself. The second of these "parental" forces, the essentially male defined and controlled social structure, is the patriarchal authority to which Peter remains obedient. One has, of course, already witnessed Peter's adherence to this authority in the form of his "natural" desire for a son.

Because of his adherence to the forms of that authority, much has been said of Peter as the Organization Man.[4] However, the emphasis has usually been placed on his moral blindness and guilt, which critics have seen as represented by the glasses he cleans and puts on at the opening of the play Like most of Albee's symbols, the glasses cannot be limited to a single meaning. Peter is certainly blind to the real world, but he is also an "onlooker" to life in general and to his own life in particular. The price he pays for the protection of his social place (his "cage" according to the metaphor Albee employs) is his identity which, already severely dwarfed, is at the point of being completely obliterated. He is, consequently, in a serious personal crisis; his glasses also imply, therefore, that he is searching for something.

Hints of Peter's dissatisfaction with his own life become apparent as soon as Jerry begins his interrogation/conversation. Within the play, Peter's bench quickly becomes the focal point of the complex web of contradictory desires and fears, intentions and obsessions competing beneath the character's surface rationalizations. When threatened with the loss of the bench late in the play, Peter desperately attempts to articulate the value which the bench has come to have for him: "I sit on this bench almost every Sunday afternoon, in good weather. It's secluded here; there's never anyone sitting here, so I have it all to myself" (p. 41). He cannot, as yet, consciously appreciate that his weekly sojourn in the park is a small but symbolically significant gesture violating the role of group man. This is the one way Peter has devised to detach himself from the larger group.

Once outside the parameters of his socioeconomic class, however, Peter risks isolation (immediately suggested by the image of a man sitting alone at a bench in the middle of a large city) by calling attention to himself (becoming "obtrusive") and being approached by someone outside his usual milieu. Because Peter recoils from these risks, the bench symbolizes *both* his desire for autonomy and the crutch he clings to in his effort to go just so far but no further. Peter has been coming to his bench, as he says, "for years" (p. 45), years in which he has maintained his habit as a compromise between freedom and security. Much later in the play, after he has narrated his experience with the dog, Jerry describes the type of emotional sterility, perhaps even death, which results from this kind of reasonable, decorous compromise. In speaking of his renewed relationship with the dog, Jerry says, "And what has been the result: the dog and I have attained a compromise, more of a bargain, really. We neither love nor hurt because we do not try to reach each other" (p. 36). The commentary applies as well to Peter's lifetime avoidance of pain and risk, an attitude which Jerry challenges by forcing Peter to violate the carefully laid down limits of decorum with which he has circumscribed himself. The action of ***The Zoo Story*** is, consequently, Peter's rite of exorcism: chaotic, disorienting, generally disruptive in nature, meant to sever his dependencies and to return to Peter the individual's control over his own life which is traditionally practiced by adult members of society. In it, Albee provides a model of a process offering the possibility for meaningful existence in the modern world, a process in which pain is not only unavoidable but is, in the end, regenerative.

In his capacity as shaman of this rite, Jerry, significantly orphaned and socially outcast, appears to Peter as the "Other," or double—the embodiment of characteristics Peter has designated as antithetical to himself. The physical differences between the characters immediately and visually define them as polar and complementary. Peter, although "moving into middle age," dresses and acts in such a way as to "suggest a man younger," while Jerry, though actually younger, has fallen from physical grace and has a "great weariness" suggesting age (p. 11). Peter in his innocence and Jerry in his "over-sanity" (Albee's term) both lack completeness; each provides the other with a "missing half." Robert Bennett has pointed out that, though most critics see the pair as polar opposites, "Jerry approaches Peter. . . . as an enlightened brother."[5] Actually, both evaluations are true. As is the case with doubles, the characters are irrevocably linked *and* set apart by means of their antithetical characteristics.

The double in literature tends to emerge in the consciousness of the first self (in this case, Peter) at the moment of crisis for the purpose of effecting some major change.[6] C. G. Jung's terminology for this second self—"the immortal within the mortal man" and "the long expected friend of the soul"[7]—interestingly echoes Jerry's intimation that, on at least some level, his arrival was not completely expected:

> JERRY: Peter, do I annoy you, or confuse you?
>
> PETER: *(lightly)* Well, I must confess that this wasn't the kind of afternoon I'd anticipated.

> JERRY: You mean I wasn't the gentleman you were expecting.
>
> PETER: I wasn't expecting anybody.
>
> JERRY: No, I don't imagine you were. But I'm here, and I'm not leaving.
>
> (pp. 37-38)

Ultimately, the appearance of such doubles presupposes the presence, both in the individual and the society which he represents, of a natural psychic equilibrium which of necessity attempts to reassert itself. Whether consciously or unconsciously summoned, Jerry responds to Peter's subliminal attraction to individually, a-rationality, and rebellion by playing "dark twin" to Peter's "favored son." Since Peter's personal identity is at stake, Jerry is a call for renewal generated by Peter's own psyche. This explains why Peter does not leave, although he is clearly annoyed by Jerry's presence. Peter's summoning of Jerry is also seen in the hints of Jerry's own lack of free will in shaping the events which take place during their encounter.

In his dealings with Peter, Jerry seems to be following a format with an outcome so inevitable that it may be prophesied almost as soon as he encounters Peter: "You'll read about it in the papers tomorrow, if you don't see it on your T.V. tonight" (p. 15). Jerry's plan seems less the product of his own invention than the result of some other-worldly revelation. Although, from the outset, Jerry appears to have an inchoate understanding of the inevitability of his meeting with Peter, it is not until these inevitabilities have played themselves out that he is able to acknowledge his complicity with them: "I think that while I was at the zoo I decided that I would walk north . . . northerly rather . . . until I found you . . . or somebody . . . and I decided that I would talk to you . . . I would tell you things . . . and the things that I would tell you would . . . well, here we are. You see? Here we *are*. But . . . I don't know . . . could I have planned all this? No . . . no, I couldn't have. But I think I did . . . and now you'll know what you'll see in your T.V." (p. 48). None of this is meant to suggest that Jerry is simply a volitionless symbol. On the contrary, as the above speech suggests, he is a fully dimensional character with complex motivations of his own. Yet Albee, at his best, can masterfully create characters who are both surrealistically dreamlike and perfectly realistic. In this play, Peter and Jerry reveal different aspects of one personality *and* represent very real people in a very real situation. Peter's reactions to Jerry both correspond to struggles within himself and are realistic responses to the situation which Jerry creates.

By creating the situation, or argument, over the bench, Jerry forces Peter to acknowledge the existence of his other half, so that what has been a continuous monologue for Jerry at last becomes a clearly polarized debate, the prerequisite for resolution. As the archetypal "stranger," Jerry intrudes on Peter's solitude, his personal affairs and, most importantly, his bench. In doing so, Jerry forces Peter to consider the value which he has invested in his personal symbol. In the face of Jerry's challenge for proprietorship of the bench, Peter's dilemma becomes increasingly difficult. If on the one hand he cedes the bench to Jerry without putting up any sort of struggle, Peter will be renouncing his one claim to personal distinction and succumb completely to his stereotypic role of child-like passivity. On the other hand, confrontation with Jerry will force him to acknowledge both the reality of his own will and the existence of a contradictory reality threatening to his identification with a collective structure. Jerry, priest and playwright, orchestrates the ritual/drama between them in order to externalize Peter's internal conflict and force a choice on Peter's part. Choice implies personal responsibility, which is the hallmark of the initiated adult. For his own part, Jerry, in presiding over the rite through which Peter enters the world of the initiated, goes on to gain an identity or definition of himself. He is shaman or guide in the initiatory rites, and, indeed, Jerry consistently acts as though he were the keeper of mystical secrets which he can only just share with his unenlightened counterpart.

Much of the stage action in ***The Zoo Story*** does bear the mark of ritual. And while there is an implicit connection between all drama and ritual, Albee seems to call special attention to this connection within ***The Zoo Story.*** Jerry's actions when he catalogues his possessions and when he relates the parable of the dog "as if reading from a billboard" (p. 30), ending with an incantation that is a kind of litany and invocation, are explicitly ritualistic. Throughout the play, Jerry also employs Biblical language, combining it with a speech pattern so vernacular that the juxtaposition emphasizes a dichotomy between sacred and profane, the spiritual and the temporal—a dichotomy which Jerry will eventually resolve. The ritualistic quality of the play is also conveyed through its setting—"a place apart" (p. 11)—where, should Peter yell, no one would hear him—and in Albee's suggestion of how Jerry should use space on stage: "The following long speech, it seems to me, should be done with a great deal of action, to achieve a hypnotic effect on Peter, and on the audience, too" (p. 29). Accordingly, Jerry tends to direct his own actions during his long monologue as if following a dance or ritualistic scheme: "I'll start walking around in a little while, and eventually I'll sit down" (p. 19).[8]

The key element of Jerry's ritual, the story of himself and the dog, contains all of the elements that have long been recognized as parts of the mythic quest. The hero, Jerry, must gain admittance to a certain place which has associations with the underworld. He is prevented first by an old crone (his landlady). Once he gets past her by repeating the right formula, he is accosted by a "raging beast" (the dog) which he must either tame or kill. Having undergone these ordeals, he can resume his place in the real or everyday world with the possession of some new knowledge and understanding. Significantly, Jerry defines this as "something to do with how sometimes it's necessary to go a long distance out of the way in order to come back a short distance correctly" (p. 21).

Moreover, the mythic aspects of Jerry's tale are brought into high relief by the fact that the rooming house clearly has symbolic associations with the underworld; it is a place full of obvious outcasts, people somehow "dead" to most of society, as Peter admits: "It's so . . . unthinkable. I find it hard to believe that people such as that really *are*" (p. 28). This underworld is, in turn, connected to the unconscious. Jerry's rooming house in Albee's first play functions much like Miss Alice's house does in ***Tiny Alice***—as a dream-like center of mystery. As with Miss Alice's house, it is a place with many rooms and levels, having four stories. Jerry lives on the top floor, the place closest to consciousness. The rooms are all "laughably small," separate from each other, and "better as you go down, floor by floor" into unknown territory (p. 22). Jerry carefully points out that he does not know "any of the people on the third and second floors" (p. 27). As he says of one of the unknown rooms, "there's somebody lives there, but I don't know who it is. I've never seen who it is. Never, never ever" (p. 22).

Significantly, within primitive rites of initiation, the novice is often led into a house representing a microcosm of society or of human consciousness. The initiate's entrance into such a house is his symbolic installation at the center of the universe. Anthropologist Arnold Van Gennep in *Rites of Passage* defines the first step in this type of initiation as the rite of separation.[9] Typically, the hero must encounter the labyrinth separating him from his former life. The entrance into new life is symbolized as passing through a door, since to cross a threshold is to unite oneself with a new world. Thus, Jerry draws specific attention to his place of confrontation with the dog: "And where better, where better to communicate one single, simple-minded idea than in an *entrance hall?* Where? It would be a START! Where better to *make a beginning* . . . to understand and just possibly be understood" (italics added) (p. 35).

The landlady and her dog are guardians of the threshold, and, as in the traditional quest format, they must be honored and appeased. The former, a displaced sybil-figure, personifies the seductress and the witch. Jerry describes her as a "fat, ugly, mean, stupid, unwashed, misanthropic, cheap, drunken bag of garbage" who comes after him with her "sweaty lust" (p. 28). Usually this figure tries to prevent the seeker's entrance into the place which is the source of knowledge. If the person has the right information—such as the knowledge of the labyrinth design, the right password, or if he makes the right request—he finds his road easily. If not, the woman devours him.[10] Jerry, however, has found the formula to undercut her power: "But I have found a way to keep her off. When she presses herself to my body and mumbles about her room and how I should come there, I merely say: but, Love; wasn't yesterday enough for you, and the day before?" (p. 28).

Yet Jerry, as questing hero, must also find a way to avoid the dog who functions as an avatar of the monstrous landlady when she, herself, is not present. To be sure, the dog is an extension of the landlady; in fact, they look alike: "She had forgotten her bewildered lust, and her eyes were wide open for the first time. They looked like the dog's eyes" (p. 32). Traditionally, dogs have been associated in mythology with the priesthood of Great Mother figures and the "Male votaries of the Great Goddess who prostituted themselves in her name."[11] Like its owner, the dog in ***The Zoo Story*** is bent on devouring Jerry: "this dog wasn't indifferent. From the very beginning he'd snarl and then go for me, to get one of my legs. Not like he was rabid you know; he was sort of a stumbly dog, but he wasn't half-assed either. It was a good stumbly run; but I always got away . . . (*Puzzles*) I still don't know to this day how the other roomers manage it, but you know what I *think:* I think it had to do only with me" (p. 30), and like its owner, it can only be appeased with a symbolic offering. Jerry, as we learn, makes an effort to appease the dog by offering it various pieces of food with pretended good will. In the cases of both the landlady and her pet, the offering is a fiction, pretended sexual encounters and pretended good will, which is designed to act as a symbolic substitute for the sacrifice of Jerry. In each case, the fiction is created in order to prevent the rendering of the desired object which is, literally, Jerry's flesh. Yet such sacrifices or substitutions ultimately prove to be unsatisfactory. Jerry, in his desperation, attempts to do away with the canine sentry who blocks his free entry into the rooming house by placing poison in one of the "offerings" which he makes to the dog which he calls "a descendant of the puppy that guarded the gates of hell or some such resort" (p. 33).

The result of this act is to place Jerry in the next stage of the initiatory process. In the format of primitive rites of initiation, the ordeal for the novice typically has four basic stages which lead to his rebirth as a new, mature individual: separation from his mother and from his counterparts, confrontation with danger and death, hallucination or loss of consciousness with a resultant identification with the external world, and, finally, an inevitable sense of loss upon the return to the world of ordinary consciousness. As we have already seen, Jerry is set apart by both the landlady and her dog and has been locked in a desperate struggle to avoid being consumed or subsumed by his adversaries. The essence of Jerry's struggle has been the preservation of his pre-initiatory identity. However, with the events following the poisoning and recovery of the dog, both Jerry and the dog are transformed by a seeming merging of their separate consciousnesses and the creation of a new knowledge or understanding between them. The possibility of the dog's recovery creates in Jerry the expectation of a transformation: "I wanted the dog to live so that I could see what our new relationship might come to" (p. 33).

That new relationship is shaped by Jerry's loss of self-consciousness and the subsequent momentary communion which he and the dog achieve: "during that twenty seconds or two hours that we looked into each other's faces, we made contact" (p. 34). The transformation is poignant and personal for Jerry, arousing within him a previously unfelt need for a sense of kinship with the external world. In the encounter, the two become each other. That such communion is possible is the essence of Jerry's revelation.

Yet Jerry also learns that, as a sentient being, he is subject to more than biological needs and impulses which are necessary for physical survival. The understanding—his revelation—immediately alienates him from nature by virtue of his rationality, self-reflection, and ability to define his experience. He simultaneously realizes both the separateness of personal enlightenment and the longing for companionship which such a sense of separateness engenders. Such transcendence is, then, not achieved without cost. There is the separation from those who are uninitiated and have therefore not shared the experience. There is the sense of loss of the transcendental when the initiate returns to ordinary, albeit made-over, consciousness. Thus, despite the validity and intensity of their transcendent experience, Jerry and the dog must eventually re-enter the world of time and space and face the inevitable sense of loss which accompanies all such returns. The two are no longer "one," and yet they cannot simply return to their old relationship of two set against each other. They surrender to a new "fiction" in order to define their madeover relationship: "When the dog and I see each other, we both stop where we are. We regard each other with a mixture of sadness and suspicion, and then we feign indifference. We walk past each other safely; we have an understanding. It's very sad, but you have to admit it's an understanding" (p. 35).

While Jerry clearly speaks for Albee in regard to the necessity of such fictions or understandings in the face of the "sadness and suspicion" of return to the non-transcendental, that need has long been recognized as an important after-effect of the experience of initiation. Ortega y Gasset, for instance, writes: "In the vacuum arising after he has left behind animal life, [Man] devotes himself to a series of non-biological occupations which are not imposed by nature but invented by himself. This invented life—invented as a novel or a play is invented—man calls human life, well being. It is not given to man as its fall is given to a stone or the stock of its organic acts—eating, flying, nesting—to an animal. He makes it himself, beginning by inventing it."[12]

It is this vacuum which is the source of man's creative life, and while Jerry has long been seen as Albee's symbol for the modern artist, what has not been fully understood is that the source of Jerry's creative drive is the sense of loss created by his own initiatory experience and related in his tale of himself and the dog. Art, then, is born of both vision and suffering, out of both gain and loss: "I have learned that neither kindness nor cruelty by themselves, independent of each other creates any effect beyond themselves; and I have learned that the two combined together, at the same time, are the teaching emotion. And what is gained is loss" (p. 36).

Jerry's lines suggest that, as long as those impulses are kept rigidly apart, they cannot convey the totality of human experience. This enforced separation, in turn, precludes any movement beyond these emotions to stronger expressions of love and hate. However, society, implicitly equated with the zoo within Albee's play, tends to separate human emotions and impulses into appropriate categories or "cages." In extreme cases, such as that of Peter, the result of such careful isolation of emotions is a lack of identity or completeness of self.

Conflicting emotions, such as the kindness and cruelty of which Jerry spoke, simultaneously function in the full complexity of human motives, and no complete self-understanding is possible unless individuals acknowledge their often simultaneous capacity for good and evil. While Jerry's experience with the dog has brought him a greater knowledge of the facts of his existence, it has also caused him to lose the purity of simple, clearly defined motives in an easily apprehended and described universe. It is the paradoxical complexity of that universe which often leads man to create fictions as a means of survival. In the end, all explanations become mere fictions because of the inadequacy of language in the face of such complexity. This awareness on Jerry's part accounts for his paradoxical use and condemnation of such verbal fictions as well as the extreme self-consciousness of his language.[13]

Jerry goes further in his analysis of the inadequacy of language to express the totality of experience: "And *was* trying to feed the dog an act of love? And, perhaps, was the dog's attempt to bite me *not* an act of love? If we can so misunderstand, well then, why have we invented the word love in the first place?" (p. 36). Words in ***The Zoo Story,*** as this passage indicates, are another example of a "cage" imposed upon reality. Jerry here attempts to find the category, or pigeonhole, that will help him understand and order his experience with the dog. At the same time, however, he resists all categories, which he perceives as limiting and therefore falsifying experience. Any definition, he implies, would exclude some aspect of the whole experience.

The problem of setting limits which surfaces in Jerry's consideration of the delimiting nature of language is also apparent in Jerry's constantly voiced concern with the issue of circumscription, both voluntary and involuntary, as Jerry moves from a consideration of the separation of humans from animals, to that of humans from humans, and ultimately to the individual from awareness of himself. To understand how he perceives these divisions, one must look to the numerous references he makes throughout the play to the separation between animals and humans. He went to the zoo, he says, to see about "the way people exist with animals and animals with each other and with people" (p. 39). Early in the play, he focuses on the separation of Peter's parakeets from their natural predators, the cats. When he finally begins to relate the story about the zoo, he gets as far as the lion keeper entering the lion's cage before he begins to "enter" Peter's "cage" by challenging him for the bench. Jerry's own encounter is with an animal who, at first, responds to him simply as one animal would respond to another in nature; that is, without acknowledging the "understanding" of "one's place" imposed by civilization. Jerry eventually realizes that it was this level of understanding which provided common ground between them. He attempts to rediscover this common ground with Peter as a basis for their communication.

To establish such a common ground with Peter, Jerry resorts to the threat of violence. When he begins to punch and insult Peter, Jerry moves them toward an interchangeability that reinforces their relationship as doubles whose very opposition presupposes their unity. That is, the confrontation Jerry initiates over the bench isolates and focuses the sharp yet arbitrary differences between Peter and Jerry which, when broken down by means of their mutual anger, reveal their essential sameness.[14]

Jerry's expressed need for Peter's bench is an incidental focus for his real need to possess Peter's being, or, in his own words, to "get through to" the other man, to "make contact" (p. 34). Jerry's choice of the bench is obvious since Peter identifies that particular object with himself. Once Peter is threatened with its loss, he articulates the identification by associating it with his adulthood, his manhood, and his sense of responsibility: "I've come here for years; I have hours of great pleasure, great satisfaction, right here. And that's important to a man. I'm a responsible person, and I'm a GROWNUP. This is my bench and you have no right to take it from me" (p. 45).

In challenging Peter's right to the bench, Jerry leads Peter away from the social structures dividing them—structures which make Peter unable to accept the original brotherhood Jerry offers—by provoking him to a level of interaction at which they can share experience, that level outside society which Jerry calls "animal." Their conflict first clearly differentiates them as antagonists and then dissolves the differences by creating for each a reflection of his own antagonism in the other. In the end, the sameness of the mutual violence comes to overshadow the differences which originally gave rise to their violent impulses. Thus, when Jerry rushes to grab Peter by the collar, Albee's stage directions indicate that their faces must almost touch (p. 46).

Within ***The Zoo Story,*** the unity and reciprocity which violence effects finds its most striking expression in the climactic tableau scene (p. 47). There, for all their initial differences, Peter and Jerry unite beyond all definitions, structures, and language—even the line between victim and victimizer becomes blurred, as it was earlier in the case of Jerry and the dog. The moment of their transcendence of these fictions is necessarily one of silence and absence of movement. In that moment, too, the act leading to Jerry's death loses its distinction as either suicide or murder. Jerry's sacrifice/death is, then, necessary: the cultural crisis culminating in the characters' violent interaction over the bench must find an outlet upon which to expend itself; otherwise their distinctions (and, by extension, the social order) cannot be restored.

The lesson inherent in Peter's initiation is, consistent with the motif of the double, just the reverse of Jerry's, since Peter has been all but subsumed by human-defined culture from which he must eventually be severed by reawakening his less reflective impulses. Jerry as much as predicts this early in the play when he tells Peter that he "looks like an animal man" (p. 18). When Peter finally "loses control," he undergoes a series of basic emotions, he becomes "tearful," "beside himself," "hysterical" with laughter, "whining," "enraged." For the first time in the play (and, one might conjecture, for the first time in his adult life), Peter's responses are immediate reactions to real feelings, uninterrupted by the lag of self-conscious deliberation.

The direct alignment of "animal" and "rational" within Peter fulfills the intention of Jerry's ritual. Ritualistic overtones continue in the chant Peter whispers as Jerry is dying. According to the stage directions, Peter repeats "Oh my God, oh my God, oh my God," "many times, very rapidly" before he breaks down in tears and exits, uttering the same words in "a pitiful howl" (p. 49). The cry, echoing Jerry's scream of "an infuriated and fatally wounded animal" when he impales himself on the knife, must certainly be meant to be one of recognition. Albee's drama, unlike many of its contemporaries, is nothing if not cathartic.

There has been a tendency to interpret the ending of ***The Zoo Story*** as Albee's parody of religious feeling. On the contrary, Peter's ritual, in which he sits on a bench reading a book every Sunday "in good weather," is the playwright's example of the ritualistic impulse grown remote from its original roots and compromised by the pervasive influence of materialism. Though still alive, the impulse has, to use Jerry's terminology, "no effect beyond itself."[15] Unlike the modern mentality, the pre-civilized mind, as it is reflected in original initiation ceremonies, views the frightening agents of the rite itself and the often violent symbolic death the initiate must face as regenerative, causing the novice to move from innocence to experience. The initiate is separated from a narcissistic attachment to his mother and, by means of his experience with death, becomes an adult member of his tribe. Albee's play employs a similar structure, and perhaps it is on this basis that it is often misunderstood. However, unlike primitive initiation, Albee's ritual of initiation is not an initiation into society but, instead, into autonomy, into the maturity to resist surrender to absolute systems of belief and external sources of self-definition. Peter's break with the security of the social collective is symbolized by the severance from his bench and by the confrontation he has with death. When Jerry takes out and clicks open an "ugly looking knife," the realization of his mortality and the apparently arbitrary imperatives that exist beyond rationality dawn on Peter: "You *are* mad! You're stark raving mad. YOU'RE GOING TO KILL ME!" (p. 46). Jerry, by his death, incorporates the principle he represents back into society, an idea amplified by his contention that Peter will see Jerry's face on television—the reflector of modern America's experiences and self-images. His death also restores order, not cyclically, but with the crucial difference implied that Peter must restructure his life without his bench from which, as Jerry tells him, he has been "dispossessed" (p. 49).

The message of ***The Zoo Story,*** as of later Albee plays, is that the patterns inherited in life are of necessity untested. Yet, in reaching beyond such patterns, Jerry and Peter come to what Lawyer in ***Tiny Alice*** calls "the edge of the abyss" to face the primal fears of abandonment and loss of identity. Put another way, the characters temporarily escape all limits, dissolve all distinctions, encounter formlessness, and, if the form of their initiation holds true, strike their own bargain with reality and experience. Inherent in the structure of Albee's play is the idea that all patterns are created fictions, fictions which are necessary nonetheless, since they are the only means through which experience can be made comprehensible. Yet, because humans create their fictions, they can both control and change them. Albee holds forth the possibility, through Peter, that the disintegration of an old identity (an identity "borrowed" from identification with external authority) along with the inevitable panic such disintegration encourages may be the means for a new, more consciously formed personality. Such life-shaping structures, his play suggests, must be created rather than inherited by the individual and must continuously be reformed, so as never to be mistaken for the absolute and implacable.

NOTES

[1]See, for instance, Michael E. Rutenberg, *Edward Albee: Playwright in Protest* (New York: Avon Books, 1969), p. 29; Mary M. Nilan, "Albee's *The Zoo Story:* Alienated Man and the Nature of Love, *Modern Drama* 16 (June 1973):58-59; Rose A. Zimbardo, "Symbolism and Naturalism in Edward Albee's *The Zoo Story,*" *Twentieth Century Literature* 8 (April 1962): 15; Gilbert Debusscher, *Edward Albee—Tradition and Renewal,* trans. Anne D. Williams (Brussels: American Studies Center 1967), p. 12; Anne Paulocci, *From Tension to Tonic: The Plays of Edward Albee* (Carbondale: Southern Illinois University Press, 1972), p. 43. For critical analyses focusing on the questions the play poses rather than the solutions it offers, see Ruby Cohn, *Edward Albee* (Minneapolis: University of Minnesota Press, 1969), p. 10; C. W. E. Bigsby, *Albee* (Edinburgh: Oliver and Boyd, 1969), p. 16; Robert Bennett, "Tragic Vision in *The Zoo Story,*" *Modern Drama* 20 (March, 1977):58.

[2]Introduction to Edward Albee, *The Plays,* Volume I (New York: Coward, McCann & Geoghegan, 1981), p. 10.

[3]Edward Albee, *The American Dream* and *The Zoo Story* (New York: Signet, 1963), p. 19 and p. 20. All subsequent page references appear in the text.

[4]Rutenberg, p. 30.

[5]Bennett, p. 60.

[6]For a comprehensive analysis of the double in literature see Carl F. Keppler, *The Literature of the Second Self* (Tucson: University of Arizona Press, 1972).

[7]C. G. Jung, *Four Archetypes: Mother/Rebirth/Spirit/Trickster*, trans. R. F. C. Hull (Princeton: Princeton University Press, Bollingen Series, 1959, 1969), p. 55.

[8]Jerry's directorial role is Albee's subtle use of the alienation effect, meant to remind the audience that the stage frames mimetic, not real, action. Albee, in his characterization of Jerry, strikes a balance between realistic and stylized actions, an aesthetic balance that reflects the theme of balancing opposites.

[9]Anold von Gennep, *The Rites of Passage,* trans. Monika B. Vizedom (Chicago: University of Chicago Press, 1960), pp. 65-115; see also Mircea Eliade, *Birth and Rebirth: The Religious Meanings of Initiation in Human Culture,* trans. Willard R. Trask (New York: Harper and Row, 1958), p. x.

[10]Eliade, p. 62.

[11]Erich Neumann, *The Origins and History of Consciousness,* trans. R. F. C. Hull (Princeton: Princeton University Press, Bollingen Series, 1954), p. 61. There have been various other explanations of mythological animals. Joseph Campbell in *The Hero with a Thousand Faces* writes of how the hero "comes at last to the Lord of the Underworld . . . [who] rushes against him, horribly bellowing; but if the shaman is sufficiently skillful he can soothe the monster back again with promises of luxurious offerings" (p. 100); Joseph Henderson in *The Wisdom of the Serpent* calls the mystic animals "sacred animals possessing secret wisdom the dreamer wishes to learn" and representatives of the experience of "submission to a power greater than the hero himself" (p. 51). C. G. Jung refers to them as "part of the instinctive psyche" which has been lost or separated from consciousness like a "loss of soul" (Jung, p. 73).

[12]Quoted in Tony Tanner, *City of Words: American Fiction,* 1950-1970 (New York: Harper and Row, 1971), p. 29.

[13]Tanner in *City of Words* calls the self-conscious use of language, "foregrounding." In his view this stylistic device permeates most of American literature. His thesis is that American writers particularly have been overwhelmingly concerned with the tension between structure of artifice and reality. Though Tanner does not refer to Albee in his book (which deals only with fiction), his contention that "American writers seem from the first to have felt how tenuous, arbitrary, and even illusory, are the verbal constructs which men call description of reality" applies equally to the playwright. We can see this tension in Jerry's frustration with the inadequacy of definition. See also Robert S. Wallace, "*The Zoo Story:* Albee's Attack on Fiction," *Modern Drama* 16 (June 1973), pp. 49-54; Arthur K. Oberg, "Edward Albee: His Language and Imagination," *Prairie Schooner* 40 (1966): 139-46.

[14]This thesis of the role of violence in ritual and drama is put forth by René Girard, *Violence and the Sacred,* trans. Patrick Gregory (Baltimore: Johns Hopkins University Press, 1977).

[15]Albee's play realizes many of the tenets of Antonin Artaud's "Theatre of Cruelty." Artaud's theory was that theatre would representationally confront modern humans with their most primal impulses in order to annihilate their comforting social forms and reinvolve them in their own lives.

Leonard G. Heldreth (essay date 1987)

SOURCE: "From Reality to Fantasy: Displacement and Death in Albee's *Zoo Story,*" in *Contours of the Fantastic: Selected Essays from the Eighth International Conference on the Fantastic in the Arts,* edited by Michele K. Langford, Greenwood Press, 1987, pp. 19-28.

[*In the essay below, Heldreth asserts that* The Zoo Story *demonstrates how "American society has deteriorated into a vicious fantasy, a zoo in which human animals, some real and some imaginary, scream and fight and die."*]

Both those who regard ***The Zoo Story*** as one of Albee's "more realistic" plays (Woods 224) and those who see it as "part fantasy and part truncated realism" (Dubler 253) tend to focus on the connections with Ibsen and Strindberg.[1] An alternate approach is to see the play as a precursor of the fuller fantasies embodied in ***The American Dream*** and

Who's Afraid of Virginia Woolf? Dubler asserts, "The common denominator of all incidents alluded to and situations enacted in ***The American Dream*** is that they involve private fantasies" (247), and the same evaluation holds true of ***The Zoo Story.*** Because Jerry's fantasies have an air of realism about them—Peter says Jerry described people "vividly"—and because Peter's fantasies are standard ones of the middle class, their illusory quality is less obvious than the fantasies in several of Albee's other plays.[2] Yet Peter's fantasy insulates him from the reality of people such as Jerry, and Jerry's fantasy leads him to death.

This theme of fantasy appears in two short stories that appeared before ***The Zoo Story*** and may have influenced Albee in writing the play. In 1953, Jean Stafford's "In the Zoo" was published in *The New Yorker,* and in 1955, Carson McCullers published "A Tree, a Rock, a Cloud"; ***The Zoo Story*** was produced in Germany in 1958. These stories have striking parallels with many of the elements and some of the ideas of Albee's one-act play. He was probably familiar with McCullers's work, since he later adapted ***The Ballad of the Sad Cafe*** to the stage; he may also have known Stafford's story, since "In the Zoo" received the O. Henry Award, First Prize, in 1955.[3] Noting the similarities between these stories and ***The Zoo Story*** may shed some light on the later work.

The initial scene of "In the Zoo" is virtually identical to the set of the play. In Stafford's story, two middle-aged women, Daisy and her unnamed sister, the narrator, are sitting on a park bench in the Denver Zoo, passing the time until the sister's train arrives. As Jerry throughout the play compares people to animals—the zoo animals, Peter's cats and parakeets, the landlady's dog—so the two women note the similarity between the animals they are watching and people they have known as children, and immediately both are plunged into a reverie on their past. Later in the story, they compare Mr. Murphy's pets to people, and the people in Mrs. Placer's boarding house to animals.

As Jerry tells Peter of his childhood and past experiences, so the narrator of "In the Zoo" relates the story of her childhood and youth. Jerry's mother died when he was between eleven and twelve, and about three weeks later his father was killed by a bus; the parents of the girls died "within a month of each other," when Daisy was ten and the narrator was eight. Jerry moved in with his aunt, who neither drank nor sinned (24), while the girls moved into a boarding house run by Mrs. Placer, who was equally dour and had "old cardboard boxes filled with such things as W.C.T.U. tracts and anti-cigarette literature and newspaper clippings relating to sexual sin in the Christianized islands of the Pacific" (114). Jerry, at the time of the play, lives in a boarding house whose landlady possesses traits of both Mrs. Placer, the girls' guardian, and Mr. Murphy, the drunk Irishman who gives them a dog. Jerry's landlady spies on him (28), while Mrs. Placer has spies all over town and ridicules the girls until "Daisy and I lived in a mesh of lies and evasions, baffled and mean, like rats in a maze" (111). Each afternoon Jerry's landlady drinks a pint of lemon-flavored gin, and Mr. Murphy, the girls' friend, stays drunk most of the time, gradually becoming "enfeebled with gin" (111).

The strongest parallel, however, between the two landladies is their use of fantasy. Jerry's landlady, in her drunken stupor, remembers, with a little urging from him, an affair with Jerry that never took place. Mrs. Placer, ridiculing everything from the girls' boyfriends to their achievements, constantly reshapes the facts brought to her by the girls until they suit her view of the world. The best example of her manipulation of reality is her reaction when Mr. Murphy offers the girls a puppy, a reaction that is first negative as she considers "this murderous, odiferous, drunk, Roman Catholic dog," and then, as the "fantasy spun on, richly and rapidly," (98) she completely reverses herself and sees him as "a pillar of society" (99). Reality is constantly manipulated in the story to fit Mrs. Placer's beliefs. Even her name reflects the children's being placed with her as, according to various critics, Jerry's and Peter's names reflect their parts in the play.

The most obvious connection between the two narratives, however, is the central position occupied in each by the dog.[4] In the story, Caesar, who was originally named Laddie and belonged to the girls, has been taken over by Mrs. Placer and turned into a vicious brute who attacks the milkman, the paperboy, the meter man, and even a salesman, whose wound required stitches. He is lustrous black, sleeps in Mrs. Placer's bedroom, and "gulped down a whole pound of hamburger" (110) that Mr. Murphy had poisoned. The dog in ***The Zoo Story*** is also black, he attacks Jerry when his territory is intruded upon, and he "gobbled" down a hamburger that Jerry had filled with rat poison. The only significant difference between the two dogs is that Caesar dies from the poison and the other dog, after suffering, recovers.

Other details in the story parallel those in the play. Mr. Murphy plays solitaire with cards that anticipate the regular decks in Jerry's box; the fire chief in Stafford's story, like Jerry, visits prostitutes; on the day of Caesar's death, the narrator announces, "Oh, it was hot that day!" (108), while on the critical day of the play, Jerry says, "It's a hot day" (40); and Mrs. Placer's phrase, "I just have to laugh," repeated by the narrator at the end of Stafford's story, anticipates Peter's uncontrollable hysteria when Jerry tickles him.[5]

Less obvious but more important, however, are the motivational parallels in the two stories. Near the end of Stafford's story, the narrator acknowledges, "You may be sure we did not unlearn those years as soon as we put her [Mrs. Placer] out of sight in the cemetery" (113), and the rest of the narrator's behavior in the story, to the concluding hysterical laughter, bears out her statement: the behavior they were forced to follow has imposed a pattern on their young lives and motivates their adult actions. In her concluding comments on the train, she describes the marijuana she thinks she sees in the fields outside the windows and spins an elaborate fantasy about a priest riding with her on the train. Jerry in ***The Zoo Story*** also follows patterns of behavior he learned as he grew up, and these account for much of his motivation.

His philosophy, however, seems taken over almost directly from a character in Carson McCullers's story "A Tree, a Rock, a Cloud," published in 1955, two years after "In the Zoo" and three years before ***The Zoo Story.*** This story also has circumstantial parallels with Albee's play. As Peter is accosted in a public park by Jerry, who tells him his life story, so here a young newsboy stops at a diner, a public place, for a cup of coffee, where he is accosted by an old man who describes how his wife had run away ten years before. The old man sought her in "Tulsa, Atlanta, Mobile, Chicago, Cheehaw, Memphis" (101), just as Jerry's mother had left his father for an adulterous trip through the southern states. Both Jerry and the old man act as teachers; and while Leo, the diner owner, refers to the old man as a "prominent transient" (99), Jerry refers to himself as a *"permanent transient"* (37).

Yet these patterns of similarity are less important than the thematic one, the nature of love. Like Jerry, the old man attempts to impose his view of life upon an unresponsive audience, and he anticipates Jerry's philosophical statement on how one should learn to love. The old man tells the boy that at first he wanted only to find his wife but, as time went on, he forgot what she looked like. He learned to love objects he found in the road, then a goldfish, a street full of people, a bird in the sky, a tree, a rock, a cloud, or the newsboy that he is now addressing. Jerry also believes that he must learn to deal "with a bed, with a cockroach, . . . some day, with people" (34-35). Each character states that the ability to love must be learned in a gradual ascension from simple inanimate objects to human beings. Each main character ends by declaring his love; the old man for the newsboy, and Jerry, in his perverse fantasy, for Peter.

These two stories, together with the embedded narratives in Albee's play, suggest answers to some questions that, within the explicit structure of the play, remain unanswered. The play describes four periods in Jerry's life: his childhood and adolescence, including the death of his family and his first sexual experiences; the recent conflict at his rooming house, known in the play as "The Story of Jerry and the Dog"; his experience at the zoo earlier in the day during which the play takes place; and finally, the central event of the play, his encounter with Peter in the park. Each section is clearly delineated except for the third, the experience at the zoo. The importance of this section, however, is emphasized by the play's title and Jerry's opening line, "I've been to the zoo. . . . I said, I've been to the zoo. MISTER, I'VE BEEN TO THE ZOO!" Throughout the play, Jerry reminds Peter and the audience of this event's significance with lines such as, "Do you want to know what happened at the zoo or not?" (39). This motif sets the audience up for a climatic description, but it is one that never appears in the play. Jerry begins to tell the zoo story, but then abruptly starts the fight with Peter. The four narratives of the play parallel each other so carefully, however, that by examining the other three, together with the short stories described earlier, we can extrapolate and determine what happened at the zoo and why Jerry's ideas of love are so intertwined with death. The four narratives reinforce each other through four major themes: love, death, territorial conflicts, and past conditioning that leads to fantasy.

Jerry presents his narratives quite carefully, and although he begins with the incident at the zoo, he quickly shifts to questions about his location; later he starts again to tell of the zoo but veers away: "let me tell you some other things" (27). The implication is that these "other things" will illuminate the incident at the zoo to the extent that it will not need to be explicitly recounted.

Among these "other things" which Jerry will tell are his first experiences with physical love and death. His most extensive physical relationship, he tells us, occurred when he was fifteen; for eleven days, he had a homosexual relationship with a park superintendent's son (25).[6] Jerry tells nothing about why the relationship ended after eleven days. Did the boy move away? Were they discovered and forbidden to meet again? Or did the superintendent's son, like so many other boys in Albee's plays, die—literally, like the mistreated twin in ***American Dream,*** or figuratively, like the imaginary son or the boy who drank "bergin" in ***Who's Afraid of Virginia Woolf?*** Whatever his fate, he simply disappears from the account.

Such disappearances and deaths were common in Jerry's early life. When he was ten, his mother ran away, and after a year-long absence, she died in Alabama (24). His father brought the body home in late December, and after a two-week drinking binge, his father was killed by a city bus. Jerry moved in with his mother's sister for seven or eight years, and then she died on the afternoon of his high school graduation. With the possible exception of his affair with the Greek boy, every relationship Jerry has experienced has ended in death.

Nor is Jerry's concern with territory, which culminates in his takeover of the park bench, surprising. Homeless, obligated to see his aunt's home first as "her apartment" and then as "my apartment" (24), he now has no turf to call his own. Further, each family member died out of home territory—the mother in Alabama, the father in a city street, and the aunt on the stairs to her apartment. None of the characters die in their own houses or beds. The pattern seems clear, and Jerry learns it: venturing out of one's territory is dangerous and perhaps deadly. This pattern will be repeated when Jerry ventures into the dog's domain at the boarding house and when he tries to take over Peter's bench in the park. Like the girls of "In the Zoo," events in Jerry's childhood are shaping him to react in a predictable way.

After Jerry describes his early life, he assures Peter that despite his youthful homosexual experience, he now loves "the little ladies" (25). Yet, other lines of dialogue indicate

Jerry's continued interest in men. He tells Peter he doesn't talk to many people except in phrases such as "keep your hands to yourself, buddy" (17). He also admits his women "aren't pretty little ladies" (34-35). Does this mean that his women are fat and ugly, probably whores? Their reluctance to be photographed (25) seems to fit such an interpretation; yet he is filled with fury over this fact, and his comment on the deck of pornographic playing cards, that fantasy becomes a substitute for real life, may mean that these little ladies are men whom he sees once and then, in guilt and anger, never sees again. The next phrase in this particular speech, which begins an attempt to show how a man must learn to deal with things, speaks of "making money with your body which is an act of love" (35). Jerry seems to be denying, except for an early experience, his homosexual desires and is having compulsive one-night stands with either prostitutes or men who he pretends to himself are women. He also denies his own prostitution. Despite his comment that people must know the effects of their actions (33), Jerry cannot face himself or his actions: a relationship with a mirror is "too hard, that's one of the last steps. With . . . toilet paper . . . that's a mirror, too; always check bleeding" (34). He cannot accept his own image, his homosexuality, or even his animalistic nature, which manifests itself in the blood on the toilet paper, so he maintains his distance from everyone, including himself.

Jerry cannot avoid his landlady, however, in the next section, the story of Jerry and the dog; she presses her body against him and Jerry resorts to fantasy, perhaps of the type he is even now telling Peter. When the landlady attempts to seduce him, he lies to her about what they had done in her room in earlier meetings and she is satisfied. His use here of fantasy is the reverse of his earlier statement about the pornographic playing cards, which for boys are "a substitute for a real experience," but adults "use real experience as a substitute for the fantasy" (27). His statement criticizes a world that cannot live up to his fantasy expectations and indicates a desire for another relationship as valid as that with the Greek boy. His later sexual relationships seem to be merely experiences through which he can recapture, in fantasy, the ecstasy of this earlier love. The comment about the pornographic playing cards functions as a metaphor for Jerry's entire outlook on life. Unable to face the life he lives, Jerry shapes reality into something more meaningful; he constantly reevaluates the past, turning it into a pattern that he only now perceives. For example, only *after* Jerry has tried to kill the dog and failed does he begin to rationalize, telling Peter that he really wanted the dog to live and that the experience was a learning process. After Peter expresses horror, Jerry acknowledges, in an echo of his statement about the pornographic cards, that such real-life experiences make good fantasies to read about (29).

More significant, however, than the landlady is her dog, and Jerry reminds us that the story of the dog is associated with his visit to the zoo and the park (30). The landlady's large, black dog, all black except for bloodshot eyes and a red sore on its forepaw, "almost always has an erection. . . . That's red, too" (31). The dog with his aggression and his erection is a masculine image who contrasts with cats, a feminine image: the man selling hamburgers asks if the meat is for his pussycat, but Jerry denies pussycats, which earlier he had identified with wives and daughters. Yet the dog, like the little ladies, appears as a dual sexual image, for as he eats the hamburger that Jerry offers, he makes "sounds in his throat like a woman" (31). The dog's color, black with some red, is the color of death.

Jerry's relationship with the dog parallels his attitude toward himself. He remarks to Peter, "*Her* dog? I thought it was my . . . No. No. You're right. It *is* her dog." If this dog, "Malevolence with an erection," is seen as Jerry's sexual drive, *his* dog, then his initial love for it parallels his early love affair, and his attempt to kill the dog is a metaphor for his attempt to destroy his sexuality, an attempt to deny his homosexuality. But he cannot destroy his sexual side, and the dog survives, albeit somewhat weakened: "I had tried to love and I had tried to kill, and both had been unsuccessful by themselves." (34). This failed attempt at destroying the animalistic side of his nature anticipates the successful and final attempt at death in the park.

Jerry's monologue following this story of the dog is virtually a gloss on the old man's "science" of love in the McCullers's story (103-4). When the boy asks the old man, "Have you fallen in love with a woman again?" the old man replies, "I am not quite ready yet." Jerry apparently *is* ready, for after the speech about love, he compliments Peter, says he's not leaving, and begins to tickle Peter.

The territorial concerns in the dog story are fairly obvious. Jerry ventures into what he thinks is neutral territory in the rooming house, but the dog regards the hall as his territory, and the conflict leads to violence and then attempted murder as Jerry fights for the right to reach the stairs to his room.

Jerry has promised Peter to tell next about what happened at the zoo (29), and now he begins. The zoo experience has traumatized Jerry, for in his first conversation with Peter, after commenting on the weather, he returns to his original subject, saying "I've been to the zoo" (15). Jerry carefully orchestrates his account, telling Peter, "I went to the zoo to find out more about the way people exist with animals" (40).

Jerry's motivation reminds us of his attempt to establish contact with the dog, and his account of the zoo recalls many of the earlier themes. The animals and people remind us of the landlady's dog, Peter's parakeets and cats, and all the people enclosed in the boarding house where Jerry lives; the children remind us of Peter's two daughters and no sons and of Jerry's orphaned childhood; the animal stench brings to mind the landlady; the vendors selling balloons and ice cream call to mind the man from whom Jerry bought the hamburger; and the barking seals and screaming birds echo the masculine/feminine dichotomy that runs throughout the play: the seals, barking, are doglike and masculine; the birds, slang for women in England and associated with daughters and disease, are feminine. The last description of the zoo in this section is, "the lion keeper comes into the lion cage . . . to feed one of the lions" (40). Then Jerry begins harassing Peter into the fight that ends the play. But Jerry had earlier stated what happened when a person ventured into territory not his own; his mother died, his father died, his aunt died, and he was attacked by a dog. Thus, when the lion keeper goes into the cage to feed the lion, the pattern of Jerry feeding the dog will be repeated: it will eat the food and then go for him. The lion was evidently successful in its surprise attack on the keeper because Jerry has said, "Wait until you see the expression on his face" (19). It is the attack on the zoo keeper and his face that will be seen on TV that night and read about in the paper the next day. It is also the event that reinforces all of Jerry's earlier beliefs and starts him walking northerly to the park where he suicidally invades Peter's territory.

Each of the directions mentioned in the play has symbolic significance and is associated with a character. Because Peter lives between Lexington and Third Avenue on 74th Street, in the east 70's, he embodies the East, with culture, sophistication, and the other characteristics of the eastern seaboard. Jerry, in contrast, lives in a rooming house "on the upper west side . . . Central Park West; I live on the top floor; rear; west." By associating himself with the West, Jerry links himself with the more masculine western image. Jerry states early in the play, "I don't like the West side of the park that much." When Peter asks, "Why?" Jerry replies, "I don't know" (14). The reason is given obliquely later in the play. Peter threatens to call a policeman, but Jerry says,"They're all over on the west side of the park chasing fairies" (43). Jerry's repression of his homosexuality is disturbed by the blatant displays so obvious in the west side of the park. If he had accepted his sexuality, Jerry would have accepted the west side of the park as his home turf, just as his boarding house is on the upper west side (22), but he has suppressed his feelings so much he no longer knows why he dislikes that side of the park.

South is associated with Jerry's mother, for her journey after abandoning the boy and his father was through the southern states, until her death. North is associated with cold, detachment, frozen bodies and minds, and ultimately death. Jerry emphasizes his mother being a "northern stiff," and he describes how "I've been walking north . . . but not due north." He is moving toward death, but circuitously, just as he slowly leads up to the story of the zoo. As the boy said about the old man in "A Tree, A Rock, A Cloud," "He sure has done a lot of traveling" (105).

Jerry is now in a foreign environment: like his mother, he has gone "a long distance out of the way to come back a short distance correctly." He had made a journey south that morning to the village in order to walk back north, pausing at the zoo, but he has not yet reached the safety of his area of town. His mother's return north as a corpse anticipates his own journey north to death. Out of his home territory, as he tries to take over Peter's bench, Jerry sets the stage for disaster.

The last major section, the conflict in the park, ties together the strands that have been carefully developed. After dropping his account of what happened at the zoo, Jerry begins to tickle Peter in a displaced sexual advance: tickling is traditionally associated with sexuality because of the loss of control and the physical intimacy involved. Peter is nervous because tickling is looked upon with suspicion among adult members of the same sex. The advance is a part of Jerry's efforts to make Peter over into the kind of person he is looking for. Jerry has walked straight from the zoo "until I found you . . . or somebody" (48), but he has also ridiculed Peter for his lack of masculinity. Jerry is looking for a human equivalent of the dog and the lion, but Peter, on first impression, does not fit the image. Jerry has already ridiculed Peter's marriage, the daughters he has instead of sons, and the daughters' birds and cats. Peter's profession as a textbook editor and his decision to have no more children, implying emasculation, have allied him with the cultured, passive, scholarly, feminine point of view. Failing, as he knew he would, in his attempt to reach Peter through intimacy, Jerry now tries to reach him, as he did the dog, through violence.[7] Jerry shapes the reality he has found until it fulfills his death fantasy. Conditioned by experience to believe that love leads to pain and death, that sex is a one-time affair,[8] and that people who venture into alien territory are in grave danger, Jerry sets up Peter to act out a fantasy of love and death; in it he will kill the animalistic self that, symbolically, he failed to destroy when he poisoned the dog.

In the conflict that follows, he goads Peter to a fury in which Peter loses his temper, becomes revitalized, seizes the knife, and holds it in front of him. The phallic image is obvious. Jerry, however, has learned his lesson well: *he* is the outsider intruding into the alien territory; *he* has failed to accommodate himself to society's norms; and *he* is repelled by the sexual and physical sides of his nature that refuse to stay locked in cages. Therefore, *he* must die, and he rushes upon the knife. In the stage directions, Albee specifies for tableau of "Jerry impaled on the knife at the end of Peter's still firm arm" (47). The themes of perverse sexual love, of death, of reality shaped into fantasy, and of the price paid by the outsider are all embodied in this climactic image. Then the two men scream.

Jerry now explains to Peter, "Now you know all about what happened at the zoo . . . the face I told you about . . . my face, the face you see right now" (48). Some critics have interpreted this passage literally—that it is Jerry who will be featured in the TV story, but he is speaking metaphorically. He is in the park, several blocks from the zoo, and Peter's understanding of what happened at the zoo, if he does understand, comes from Jerry's parallel actions. Like the lion keeper, Jerry came into the lion's home area and, even though this lion had to be revitalized, Jerry directed the part and the actions as he felt they must inevitably go. And when he says "my face," he again is speaking metaphorically, indicating that the agony on the lion keeper's face and that on his face are identical, for earlier he had referred to "the expression on his face" (19).

Like the old man in the McCullers's story, Jerry wants to learn to love, but what he has learned about himself and love is unacceptable. Like the girls in the Stafford story who "lived in a mesh of lies and evasions, baffled and mean, like rats in a maze" (111), he is reduced to ritual fantasy. His final action is inevitable because it came from within: "Could I have planned all this? . . . I think I did" (48).

In conclusion, Mrs. Placers's fantasies enabled her, in Stafford's story, to deal with a world she would not accept, one that denied her the status she demanded. Unable to tolerate the rigidity she imposed on their childhoods, the girls also retreated into fantasy, a habit that continued into their adulthoods. Jerry also faced a world that rejected him, and he manipulated reality until it fit his destruction fantasy: he was unable to learn to love; he was unable to accept his own physical nature and his homosexuality; and failing, he chose death. He deliberately set up a pattern of destruction that imitated his mother's one-year destructive trip, for he went south and then came north to death; he orchestrated his own death as carefully as he planned the death of the dog; and he used his death as a method both of revitalizing Peter and symbolically restoring Peter's virility through violent action. But at the end of the play, the audience is left with the vision of the zoo, in which people are alienated from one another in rooms like cages, and in which a sexual caress has been displaced to a knife embedded in the chest. As Albee stated in more detail in ***The Sandbox, The Death of Bessie Smith, The American Dream,*** and ***Who's Afraid of Virginia Woolf?,*** American society has deteriorated into a vicious fantasy, a zoo in which human animals, some real and some imaginary, scream and fight and die.

Notes

[1]William M. Force summarizes, somewhat cynically, the major critical positions on the play.

[2]Dubler notes in Genet's *The Balcony* that "private fantasy is achieved only through the conscientious accumulation of realistic details" (54), details that Jerry generously supplies. In conversation, however, Albee stated to me that Jerry was a "liar."

[3]Albee acknowledged knowing Stafford's work but refused to comment on the connection between either of the stories and his play, a stand consistent with his public discussions of his writings.

[4]Levine cites a parallel between Jerry's dog and a black dog in Thomas Mann's "Tobias Mindernickel," in which the main character stabs the dog to death, as Peter does Jerry. Albee's use of a character named Tobias in *A Delicate Balance* may tie in with the same story.

[5]Albee also uses such uncontrollable laughter for the young man who kills his father in *Virginia Woolf.*

[6]Making the boy "Greek" may be a homosexual pun.

[7]No one has accepted Jerry's statement that Peter was expecting to meet another man in the park. Yet such an assignation, whether Peter was actually married or was lying, would explain his being in the park regularly ("I sit on this bench almost every Sunday afternoon, in good weather. It's secluded here . . ." [41]), his determination to protect his meeting place, and his reason for not leaving earlier, a passive stance that many critics see as unbelievable.

[8]Brown (1969) accurately states, "Sex in Albee very rarely, if ever, is something done out of love; it is a weapon; it is a vile appetite" (49).

Works Cited

Albee, Edward. *"The American Dream" and "The Zoo Story."* New York: New American Library, 1961.

Brown, Daniel R. "Albee's Targets." *Satire Newsletter* (Spring 1969): 46-52.

Dubler, Walter. "O'Neill, Wilder, Albee: The Uses of Fantasy in Modern American Drama." Ph.D. diss., Harvard University, 1964.

Force, William M. "The *What* Story? or Who's Who at Zoo?" *Studies in the Humanities* 1 (1969-70): 47-53.

Irwin, Robert. "The 'Teaching Emotion' in the Ending of *The Zoo Story.*" 6 (1976). 6-8.

Levine, Mordecai H. "Albee's Liebestod." *College Language Association Journal* 10 (March 1967): 252-55.

McCullers, Carson. *Collected Short Stories and the Novel "The Ballad of the Sad Cafe."* Boston: Houghton Mifflin, 1955.

Ramsey, Roger. "Jerry's Northerly Madness." *Notes on Contemporary Literature* 1 (1971): 7-8.

Stafford, Jean. *Bad Characters.* New York: Farrar, Strauss & Giroux, 1964.

Woods, Linda. "Isolation and the Barriers of Language in *The Zoo Story.*" (September 1968): 224-31.

Zindel, Paul, and Loree Yerby. "Interview with Edward Albee." *Wagner Literary Magazine* 3 (1962): 1-10.

FURTHER READING

Atkinson, Brooks. "Village Vagrants."*The New York Times* (31 January 1960): II 1.

Review of *The Zoo Story* that finds the play "original and engrossing" but considers the ending "conventional melodrama."

Matthews, Honor. "The Disappearance of the Image in England and America." In *The Primal Curse: The Myth of Cain and Abel in the Theatre,* pp. 187-205. London: Chatto and Windus, 1967.

Includes a discussion of *The Zoo Story.* Matthews views the story of Jerry and Peter a "twisted" version of the Cain and Abel tale, for in Albee's play "the agressor throws down the knife at his victim's feet, and himself . . . achieves before death a transient fulfillment and peace."

Way, Brian. "Albee and the Absurd: The 'American Dream' and 'The Zoo Story'." In *American Theatre,* ed. John Russell Brown and Bernard Harris, pp. 189-207. London: Edward Arnold, 1967.

Examines the conflict between realism and the Theatre of the Absurd in two of Albee's early works. Way argues that while Albee adopts elements of the Theatre of the Absurd, he fails to achieve that drama's power.

Who's Afraid of Virginia Woolf?

INTRODUCTION

Who's Afraid of Virginia Woolf? premiered on 13 October 1961 at the Billy Rose Theater, New York, in a production directed by Alan Schneider. The play has generated popular and critical notoriety for its controversial depiction of marital strife. It depicts the alternately destructive and conciliatory relationship between George and Martha, a middle-aged history professor and his wife, during a late-night party in their living room with Nick, George's shallow colleague, and Honey, his spouse. As the evening proceeds, George and Martha alternately attack and patronize their guests before Martha seduces Nick with the intent of hurting her husband; George retaliates by announcing the death of their imaginary son, whom the couple had created to sustain their relationship. The conclusion suggests that George and Martha may be able to reappraise their relationship based on the intimacy—which was both feared and sought all evening—that arises from their shared sorrow.

CRITICAL RECEPTION

Although faulted by some commentators as morbid and self-indulgent, *Who's Afraid of Virginia Woolf?* was honored with two Antoinette Perry (Tony) Awards, a New York Drama Critics Circle Award, and other accolades. When Albee failed to receive the Pulitzer Prize because one trustee objected to the play's sexual subject matter, drama advisors John Gassner and John Mason Brown publicly resigned. The play has since been assessed as a classic of American drama for its tight control of form and command of both colloquial and abstruse dialogue. Variously interpreted as a problem play in the tradition of August Strindberg, a campus parody, or a homosexual critique of conventional relationships, *Who's Afraid of Virginia Woolf?* has generated a wide array of critical analyses. Daniel McDonald, Ruth Meyer, and many others have focused on the play's exploration of truth, illusion, and ambiguity. Thomas E. Porter has argued that the play represents a rejection of a number of American myths: "the success myth, the image of American manhood and womanhood, the institution of marriage itself." Contrarily, Rictor Norton has argued that "underlying mythic patterns account for the intense dynamic effect of Albee's drama," and Orley I. Holtan has viewed *Who's Afraid of Virginia Woolf?* specifically as an "allegory for the American historical experience." Other critics have examined the play's language and its depiction of the problematic relationship between love and sex.

PRODUCTION REVIEWS

Howard Taubman (review date 15 October 1962)

SOURCE: A review of *Who's Afraid of Virginia Woolf?*, in *The New York Times,* 15 October 1962, p. 33.

[*In the following review of the debut of* Who's Afraid of Virginia Woolf? *Taubman considers the play impressive but judges the device of the imaginary son improbable. "This part of the story," he states, "does not ring true, and its falsity impairs the credibility of his central characters."*]

Thanks to Edward Albee's furious skill as a writer, Alan Schneider's charged staging and a brilliant performance by a cast of four, ***Who's Afraid of Virginia Woolf?*** is a wry and electric evening in the theater.

You may not be able to swallow Mr. Albee's characters whole, as I cannot. You may feel, as I do, that a pillar of the plot is too flimsy to support the climax. Nevertheless, you are urged to hasten to the Billy Rose Theater, where Mr. Albee's first full-length play opened Saturday night.

For ***Who's Afraid of Virginia Woolf?*** is possessed by raging demons. It is punctuuated by comedy, and its laughter is shot through with savage irony. At its core is a bitter, keening lament over man's incapacity to arrange his environment or private life so as to inhibit his self-destructive compulsions.

Moving onto from off Broadway, Mr. Albee carries along the burning intensity and icy wrath that informed ***The Zoo Story*** and ***The American Dream.*** He has written a full-length play that runs almost three and a half hours and that brims over with howling furies that do not drown out a fierce compassion. After the fumes stirred by his witches' caldron are spent, he lets in, not sunlight and fresh air, but only an agonized prayer.

Although Mr. Albee's vision is grim and sardonic, he is never solemn. With the instincts of a born dramatist and the shrewdness of one whose gifts have been tempered in the theater, he knows how to fill the stage with vitality and excitement.

Sympathize with them or not, you will find the characters in this new play vibrant with dramatic urgency. In their anger and terror they are pitiful as well as corrosive, but they are also wildly and humanly hilarious. Mr. Albee's dialogue is dipped in acid, yet ripples with a relish of the ludicrous. His controlled, allusive style grows in mastery.

In ***Who's Afraid of Virginia Woolf?*** he is concerned with Martha and George, a couple living in mordant, uproarious antagonism. The daughter of the president of the college where he teaches, she cannot forgive his failure to be a success like her father. He cannot abide her brutal bluntness and drive. Married for more than 20 years, they claw each other like jungle beasts.

In the dark hours after a Saturday midnight they entertain a young married pair new to the campus, introducing them to a funny and cruel brand of fun and games. Before the liquor-sodden night is over, there are lacerating self-revelations for all.

On the surface the action seems to be mostly biting talk. Underneath is a witches' revel, and Mr. Albee is justified in calling his second act "Walpurgisnacht." But the means employed to lead to the denouement of the third act, called "The Exorcism," seem spurious.

Mr. Albee would have us believe that for 21 years his older couple have nurtured a fiction that they have a son, that his imaginary existence is a secret that violently binds and sunders them and that George's pronouncing him dead may be a turning point. This part of the story does not ring true, and its falsity impairs the credibility of his central characters.

If the drama falters, the acting of Uta Hagen and Arthur Hill does not. As the vulgar, scornful, desperate Martha, Miss Hagen makes a tormented harridan horrifyingly believable. As the quieter, tortured and diabolical George, Mr. Hill gives a superbly modulated performance built on restraint as a foil to Miss Hagen's explosiveness.

George Grizzard as a young biologist on the make shades from geniality to intensity with shattering rightness. And Melinda Dillon as his mousy, troubled bride is amusing and touching in her vulnerable wistfulness.

Directing like a man accustomed to fusing sardonic humor and seething tension, Mr. Schneider has found a meaningful pace for long—some too long—passages of seemingly idle talk, and has staged vividly the crises of action.

Who's Afraid of Virginla Woolf? (the phrase is sung at odd moments as a bitter joke to the tune of the children's play song, "Mulberry Bush") is a modern variant on the theme of the war between the sexes. Like Strindberg, Mr. Albee treats his women remorselessly, but he is not much gentler with his men. If he grieves for the human predicament, he does not spare those lost in its psychological and emotional mazes.

His new work, flawed though it is, towers over the common run of contemporary plays. It marks a further gain for a young writer becoming a major figure of our stage.

John McCarten (review date 20 October 1962)

SOURCE: "Long Night's Journey into Daze," in *The New Yorker,* Vol. XXXVIII, No. 35, 20 October 1962, pp. 85-6.

[*In the review below, McCarten censures* Who's Afraid of Virginia Woolf? *as a "vulgar mishmash."*]

Edward Albee, the creator of ***Who's Afraid of Virginia Woolf?,*** at the Billy Rose, is a young man who has written some short plays that have become quite popular Off Broadway, and, for that matter, from Berlin to Buenos Aires. Having achieved fame in short sprints, he has now set out to experiment with his talent over a route, so we have with us a three-and-a-half-hour interpretation of what makes a weird quartet connected with a New England college tick. Mr. Albee, it seems to me, has assumed the prerogative of loquacity that must be granted to, say, O'Neill, and has done so without having anything much to talk about. His dialogue is so heavily burdened with elementary epithets that I imagine the running time of ***Who's Afraid of Virginia Woolf?*** could be cut in half just by the elimination of all the "God damn"s, "Jesus Christ"s, and other expressions designed, presumably, to show us that this is really modern stuff. It is Mr. Albee's whimsey to entitle his three acts "Fun and Games," "Walpurgisnacht," and "The Exorcism." In "Fun and Games," an associate professor of history staggers home to his campus digs with his wife after a cocktail party at her father's manse (the old man is president of the college), and is immediately set upon by his spouse for not laughing very hard at *Who's afraid of Virginia Woolf?,* a joke she made up or heard at the gathering. That leads to interminable bickering between the couple, with the conversation boiling down to the cruel facts that he is not an academic world beater and that she, when the opportunity presents itself, is promiscuous and is also inclined toward an incestuous relationship with her father. This colloquy begins at 2 A.M., and in the course of it we learn that the wife has invited a newcomer to the college and his wife over for a drink. When the pair arrives, there ensues a consumption of booze that might have given pause to the late W. C. Fields. (How the actors could absorb all that tea, water, or whatever it was is beyond me.) Through a cloud of double-entendres, fo'c'sle witticisms, and general dishevelment, we learn that the newcomer is a biologist, that his wife is a hysterical alcoholic, and that they are lately come from the Middle West. Since the newcomer has been a college middleweight boxing champion, and has kept in good shape, our heroine suggests that they should waste no time in cuckolding the history professor. In "Walpurgisnacht," or Act II, we have more of the same, including a lot of arguments between the historian and his wife about a mysterious son who is supposed to be just reaching his majority. The professor says that his wife has had a practically incestuous relationship with their son (obviously, Mr. Albee is crazy about incest), and the wife contends that the boy hates his father because the pedagogue is an insipid sort. Now, as it happens, the historian is a great one for making up games, among them a form of Truth or Consequences in which, I guess, he hopes to establish the truth, even though everybody is evasive, or tries to be, upon being grilled. During one of these frolics, he asks his wife whether he has a son or hasn't, and we get around to the answer in "The Exorcism," when day is ready to break. (Mr. Albee, you see, observes the unities, if nothing else.)

In this vulgar mishmash, there are indications here and there that Mr. Albee has a certain dramatic flair, however ill-directed it may be in the present enterprise, and the actors—Uta Hagen as the wife; Arthur Hill, as the put-upon professor; and George Grizzard and Melinda Dillon, as the Middle Western couple—are interesting and often exciting, even when they aren't making much sense.

Henry Hewes (review date 27 October 1962)

SOURCE: "Who's Afraid of Big Bad Broadway?" in *Saturday Review,* Vol. XLV, No. 43, 27 October 1962, p. 29.

[*In the review below, Hewes struggles to name the type of drama* Who's Afraid of Virginia Woolf? *is, noting that it is neither tragedy nor Theatre of the Absurd. "For want of a better term," he concludes, "let's call* Who's Afraid of Virginia Woolf? *a neo-naturalistic horror comedy and enjoy it with the uneasiness its scowling but frequently merry author would like to evoke."*]

Edward Albee's first long play, ***Who's Afraid of Virginia Woolf?,*** begins with deceptive casualness. An Associate Professor of history named George, and his wife, Martha, who is also the daughter of the college's president, return home from a party a little crocked. As this middle-aged pair start to quarrel over trivial matters, and to swill down more liquor than even full professors can afford, they seem more interested in fighting and hurting one another than they are in whatever they find to quarrel about. Soon they are joined by a young biology instructor and his wife, whom Martha has invited to come back to their house for a long nightcap into daylight.

What is the source of the savage events that follow? Is it Martha's disappointment that George is a failure at his profession? Is it some acquired sexual frigidity which causes her to seek gratification in a constant emasculative assault on her husband? Or could it be, as the playwright suggests, a mass progress towards impotence and depersonalization by the declining Western World?

Whatever it is, its symptoms are revealed in four fascinating and cruel games which are only extensions of incidents you might see at a number of modern well-oiled parties. The first of these is "Humiliate the Host," in which we see Martha rip every protective layer of dignity off of George to the point where he goes berserk and tries to kill her.

Game Number Two is "Get the Guests," with George driving a splinter of unpleasant truth into the young wife's illusions about her husband, Nick. Then comes "Hump the Hostess," of necessity a partly offstage charade which suggests that the scientific Nick, who played too many doctor games with little girls as a child, is having potency problems as an adult. And finally there is "Bringing up Baby," or George's exorcism from their lives of the apparently fictitious son he and Martha have privately pretended they have had during their twenty-three year period of adjustment.

At the end George and Martha are left together in a state of peace following the violent but gratifying games that seem to have served them as a sex-substitute. Ironically, he sings her to sleep with the title song.

Mr. Albee's first Broadway effort contains some of the Freudian criticism of modern behavior that ran through his earlier ***The American Dream*** and ***The Death of Bessie Smith.*** And like his play ***The Zoo Story,*** it accepts the necessity for violence as the ultimate means of human contact. But ***Who's Afraid of Virginia Woolf?*** is more recognizably real and self-generating than were its predecessors. We don't need to accept psycho-sexual explanations to believe and to be held by this play's events. Indeed we suspect that George's eloquent plea for vulnerable and mysterious humanity in its death struggle with an all-perfecting scientific synthesis voices Mr. Albee's own rejection of psychological determinism.

Under Alan Schneider's relaxed direction, a cast of four plays the three and a half-hour work so entertainingly that we eagerly anticipate each new grim gambit. Arthur Hill captures the slow-burning desperation of George in a way that would have delighted the late James Thurber. Uta Hagen is uproarious as the loud-mouthed Martha. George Grizzard and Melinda Dillon paint an amusing portrait of younger-generation materialism and vapidity. And throughout the evening William Ritman's womb-like set remains inviting, while preserving a formal mystery.

The best things in the play make us laugh, because of what Mr. Albee describes as their "sense of the ridiculous." If we don't find George and Martha as tragic as Strindberg would have drawn them, it is perhaps because their plight seems more voluntary than enforced. On the other hand, things are hardly exaggerated enough to be called "Theatre of the Absurd," either. For want of a better term, let's call ***Who's Afraid of Virginia Woolf?*** a neo-naturalistic horror comedy and enjoy it with the uneasiness its scowling but frequently merry author would like to evoke.

Harold Clurman (review date 27 October 1962)

SOURCE: A review of *Who's Afraid of Virginia Woolf?,* in *The Nation,* Vol. 195, No. 13, 27 October 1962, pp. 273-74.

[*In this evaluation of the premiere production of* Who's Afraid of Virginia Woolf? *Clurman declares: "What I . . . object to in [Albee's] play is that its disease has become something of a brilliant formula, as slick and automatic as a happy entertainment for the trade."*]

Edward Albee's ***Who's Afraid of Virginia Woolf?*** (Billy Rose Theatre) is packed with talent. It is not only the best play in town now: it may well prove the best of the season.

Its significance extends beyond the moment. In its faults as well as in its merits it deserves our close attention.

It has four characters: two couples. There is hardly a plot, little so called "action," but it moves or rather whirls on its own special axis. At first it seems to be a play about marital relations; as it proceeds one realizes that it aims to encompass much more. The author wants to "tell all," to say everything.

The middle-aged wife, Martha, torments her somewhat younger husband because he has failed to live up to her expectations. Her father, whom she worships, is president of a small college. Her husband might have become the head of the history department and ultimately perhaps her father's heir. But husband George is a nonconformist. He has gone no further than associate professor, which makes him a flop. She demeans him in every possible way. George hits back, and the play is structured on this mutually sadistic basis. The first cause of their conflict is the man's "business" (or career) failure.

Because they are both attracted to what may be vibrant in each of them, theirs is a love-hate dance of death which they enact in typical American fashion by fun and games swamped in a sauce of strong drink. They bubble and fester with poisonous quips.

The first time we meet them they are about to entertain a new biology instructor who, at twenty-eight, has just been introduced to the academic rat race. The new instructor is a rather ordinary fellow with a forever effaced wife. We learn that he married her for her money and because of what turned out to be "hysterical pregnancy." The truth is she is afraid of bearing a child though she wants one. Her husband treats her with conventional regard (a sort of reflexive tenderness) while he contemplates widespread adultery for gratification and advancement in college circles. George scorns his young colleague for being "functional" in his behavior, his ambition, his attitudes.

So it goes: we are in the midst of inanity, jokes and insidious mayhem. Martha rationalizes her cruelty to George on the ground that he masochistically enjoys her beatings.

Everyone is fundamentally impotent, despite persistent "sexualizing." The younger wife is constantly throwing up through gutless fear. Her light-headedness is a flight from reality. The older couple has invented a son because of an unaccountable sterility. They quarrel over the nature of the imaginary son because each of them pictures him as a foil against the other. There is also a hint that as a boy George at different times accidentally killed both his father and mother. Is this so? Illusion is real; "reality" may only be symbolic—either a wish or a specter of anxiety. It does not matter: these people, the author implies, represent our environment; indeed they may even represent Western civilization!

The inferno is made very funny. The audience at any rate laughs long and loud—partly because the writing is sharp with surprise, partly because an element of recognition is involved: in laughter it hides from itself while obliquely acknowledging its resemblance to the couples on the stage. When the play turns earnestly savage or pathetic the audience feels either shattered or embarrassed. Shattered because it can no longer evade the play's expression of the audience's afflictions, sins and guilts; embarrassed because there is something in the play—particularly toward the end—that is unbelievable, soft without cause. At its best, the play is comedy.

Albee is prodigiously shrewd and skillful. His dialogue is superbly virile and pliant; it also *sounds.* It is not "realistic" dialogue but a highly literate and full-bodied distillation of common American speech. Still better, Albee knows how to keep his audience almost continuously interested (despite the play's inordinate length). He can also ring changes on his theme, so that the play rarely seems static. Albee is a master craftsman.

Strangely enough, though there is no question of his sincerity, it is Albee's skill which at this point most troubles me. It is as if his already practiced hand had learned too soon to make an artful package of venom. For the overriding passion of the play is venomous. There is no reason why anger should not be dramatized. I do not object to Albee's being "morbid," for as the conspicuously healthy William James once said, "morbid-mindedness ranges over a wider scale of experience than healthy-mindedness." What I do object to in his play is that its disease has become something of a brilliant formula, as slick and automatic as a happy entertainment for the trade. The right to pessimism has to be earned within the artistic terms one sets up; the pessimism and rage of ***Who's Afraid of Virginia Woolf?*** are immature. Immaturity coupled with a commanding deftness is dangerous.

What justifies this criticism? The characters have no life (or texture) apart from the immediate virulence of their confined action or speech. George is intended to represent the humanist principle in the play. But what does he concretely want? What traits, aside from his cursing the life he leads, does he have? Almost none. Martha and George, we are told, love each other after all. How? That she can't bear being loved is a psychological aside in the play, but how is her love for anything, except for her "father fixation," and some sexual dependence on George, actually embodied? What interests—even petty—do they have or share? Vividly as each personage is drawn, they all nevertheless remain flat—caricatures rather than people. Each stroke of dazzling color is superimposed on another, but no further substance accumulates. We do not actually identify with anyone except editorially. Even the non-naturalistic figures of Beckett's plays have more extension and therefore more stature and meaning. The characters in Albee's ***The Zoo Story*** and ***Bessie Smith*** are more particularized.

If we see Albee, as I do, as an emerging artist, young in the sense of a seriously prolonged career, the play marks an auspicious beginning and, despite its success, not an end. In our depleted theatre it has real importance because Albee desperately wishes to cry out—manifest—his life. The end of his play—which seeks to introduce "hope" by suggesting that if his people should rid themselves of illusion (more exactly, falsity) they might achieve ripeness—is unconvincing in view of what has preceded it. Still, this ending is a gesture, one that indicates Albee's will to break through the agonizing narrowness of the play's compass.

Albee knows all he needs to know about play-making; he has still to learn something other than rejection and more than tearfulness. His play should be seen by everyone interested in our world at home, for as Albee's George says, "I can admire things I don't admire."

The Production—under Alan Schneider's painstaking direction—is excellent, as is the cast. Uta Hagen, with her robust and sensuously potent *élan,* her fierce will to expression and histrionic facility, gives as Martha her most vital performance since her appearance as Blanche in *A Streetcar Named Desire.* She is an actress who should always be before us. George Grizzard is perfect in conveying the normal amusements and jitters of the mediocre man. Melinda Dillon as his debilitated spouse is appallingly as well as hilariously effective, and though I have some difficulty in accepting Arthur Hill, in the role of Martha's husband, as a tortured and malicious personality he does very well with a taxing part.

A final note: though I believe the play to be a minor work within the prospect of Albee's further development, it must for some time occupy a major position in our scene. It will therefore be done many times in different productions in many places, including Europe. Though I do not know how it is to be effected, I feel that a less naturalistic production might be envisaged. ***Who's Afraid of Virginia Woolf?*** verges on a certain expressionism, and a production with a touch of that sort of poetry, something not so furiously insistent on the "honesty" of the materials, might give the play some of the qualities I feel it now lacks; it might alleviate the impression of, in the author's pithy phrase, "an ugly talent."

Robert Brustein (review date 3 November 1962)

"Albee and the Medusa Head," in *The New Republic,* Vol. 147, No. 18, 3 November 1962, pp. 29-30.

[*In the following, Brustein gives an "equivocal" response to* Who's Afraid of Virginia Woolf?, *contending that the play demonstrates that "Albee is a highly accomplished stage magician, but he fails to convince us there is nothing up his sleeve. His thematic content is incompatible with his theatrical content—hi-jinks and high seriousness fail to fuse."*]

Edward Albee's new work embodies both the failings and the virtues of his previous plays. But its positive achievements are substantial, and I am finally beginning to regard

George Grizzard as Nick and Melinda Dillon as Honey in the orginal production of *Who's Afraid of Virginia Woolf?*

this playwright's future with real expectation. Albee's technical dexterity has always been breathtaking—for sheer theatrical skill, no American, not even Williams, can match him—but like Williams, he has been inclined to falsify his native gifts, distorting experience through self-defensive reflecting mirrors. In ***Who's Afraid of Virginia Woolf,*** Albee is still not looking the Gorgon smack in the eye. Still, he has conjured up its outline. And if he tends to focus more on writhing snakes than on the other features of this terrifying monster, then even these quick glances are more penetrating than I have come to expect; and they are always projected in steaming, raging, phantasmagoric theatrical images.

Virginia Woolf is an ambitious play, and it evokes the shades of the most ambitious dramatists. The central conflict—a Strindbergian battle royal between George, a contemplative History professor with an unsuccessful career, and Martha, his bitterly shrewish wife—proceeds through a series of confessions, revelations, and interior journeys which recall the circuitous windings of O'Neill's late plays. Glued together by mutual hatred and mutual recriminations, the couple can connect only through enmity, each exposing the other's failures, inadequacies, vices, and secret illusions in language of savagely ironic scorn. Though the climax of the work is built on such an exposure, however, Albee seems less interested in the real history of his characters than in the way they conceal and protect their reality:

the conflict is also a kind of game, with strict rules, and what they reveal about each other may not be true. This comedy of concealment reminds one of Pirandello, and even more of Jean Genet. For George and Martha—each by turns the aggressor—shift their identities like reptiles shedding skins. And as the evening grows more alcoholic, and the atmosphere more distended and surrealistic, their "total war" becomes a form of ritual play acting, performed upon the shifting sands of truth.

The "setting" for this play-within-a-play is a late night party; the "audience" is composed of a hollow young biology instructor, Nick, and his demure, simpering wife, Honey. A conventionally shallow couple, they are at first innocent bystanders embarrassed by the squabbling of their hosts, then full participants, as George sadistically exposes their guilty secrets. Nick's academic opportunism, Honey's surreptitious abortions. The waspish "fun and games" begin to take the form of ruthlessly aggressive charades. After "Humiliate the Host" and "Get the Guests" comes "Hump the Hostess" as Martha and Nick, in revenge against George, make a feeble attempt to cuckold him in the bedroom. The last episode, "Bringing Up Baby," constitutes George's revenge on Martha—not because she tried to betray him (her infidelities are apparently innumerable), but because she broke one of the rules of the game: she mentioned their "son" to strangers. Forcing Martha to recount the childhood history of this absent youth, George reads the requiem for the dead, climaxing this litany with the announcement that their son has been killed in an auto accident. But the child has never existed. He is merely the essential illusion of the childless Martha, a consoling fiction in her inconsolable reality. The play ends with Honey now determined to have a child, and Martha, submissive and frightened, being comforted by George.

Everyone seems to have boggled at this fictional child; and it is certain that the play collapses at its moment of climax. But the difficulty is not that the author introduces a spurious element into an otherwise truthful play. It is, rather, that he suddenly confronts us with a moment of truth after an evening of stage illusions. Albee's theatrical inventiveness rests mainly on incongruous juxtapositions: when George aims a shotgun at his braying wife, for example, it shoots not bullets but a Japanese parasol. These shock tactics are a surefire comic technique, but they have the effect of alienating the spectator from the action the very moment he begins to accept it. Thus, when George launches a blistering attack on the evils of modern science, Albee undercuts it with a ludicrous non-sequitur: "I will not give up Berlin." And when Martha speaks of her need to escape reality, he has her do so in a broad Irish brogue. George responds to Martha's infidelity by nonchalantly offering her flowers; he tells a harrowing story of matricide and patricide which is proved, first, to be autobiographical, and second, to be false; and when asked about the telegram announcing his son's death, he claims to have eaten it. Truth and illusion may be confused, as one character tells us, but after three and a half hours of prestidigitation, we become reluctant to accept one of these magical tricks as the real thing. In short, Albee is a highly accomplished stage magician, but he fails to convince us there is nothing up his sleeve. His thematic content is incompatible with his theatrical content—hi-jinks and high seriousness fail to fuse.

On the other hand, the author has a fine time showing off his sleight of hand, incidentally, I suspect, conjuring his action into the outlines of a classical myth (the evidence is jumbled, and I may be crazy, but I think I can detect elements of the story of Aphrodite, Ares, and Hephaestus, mixed with pieces from the story of Aphrodite and Adonis). . . .

In spite of all the excellence of play and production, however, I am left with my equivocal response. In his latest play, Edward Albee proves once again that he has wit, cunning, theatricality, toughness, formal control, poetry—in short, all the qualities of a major dramatist but one: that selfless commitment to a truthful vision of life which constitutes the universal basis of all serious art. Possibly out of fear of such commitments, Albee is still coquetting with his own talent, still resisting any real identification with his own material, so that he tends to confuse his themes, shift his attitudes, and subvert his characters. Yet, a genuine insight, merely sketched in his earlier work is now beginning to find fuller expression: that in a time of deadened instinct, people will use any methods, including deadly hatred, in order to find their way to others. This, or something like it, may become the solid foundation of Albee's future writing; but whatever it is, I await what is to come with eagerness. For if Albee can confront the Medusa head without the aid of parlor tricks or mirrors, he may yet turn us all to stone.

Richard Gilman (review date 9 November 1962)

SOURCE: "Here We Go Round the Albee Bush," in *The Commonweal,* Vol. LXXVII, No. 7, 9 November 1962, pp. 175-76.

[*In this review, Gilman charges that in* Who's Afraid of Virginia Woolf? *Albee "wants to say something profound about the human condition, and he ends . . . offering a cliché about illusions."*]

Because *Who's Afraid of the Big Bad Wolf?* is copyrighted, the title of Edward Albee's first full-length play is sung by its characters to the tune of *Here We Go Round the Mulberry Bush,* thereby establishing a pattern for the evening's procedures and the public discussion that this unsettling work has provoked. Nearly everything is a substitution or an imposture: a folk melody when Mr. Albee would clearly have preferred a tinny contemporary one; an enormous three-act play whose conception rattles around in the space; experiment clothed in conventional attire so as to be allowed to live; on our part, the acceptance, as an imaginative breakthrough, of the play's intentions instead of its accomplishment, or its out-of-hand rejection on grounds having more to do with decorum than esthetics.

I accuse Albee of nothing. He is not a confidence-man, and if some people have given him theirs it is because there is nowhere else to put it. He is the American stage's young master *faute de mieux.* He makes us feel alive and of our time, he will not let us get away with our habitual evasions and behavior. He is in fact a transcriber of those evasions and that behavior, everything he has written, culminating in ***Who's Afraid of Virginia Woolf?*** being less a construction of new vision than a series of split-level suburban houses in which we can see ourselves the way the neighbors only speculate. He makes Lillian Hellman seem like the recording secretary of a garden club.

But he also makes a playwright like Ionesco, from whom he used to borrow certain materials, appear more than ever a model of fulness, unity, zest and staying-power. For ***Virginia Woolf,*** though the most interesting play of the season, a work of many compelling virtues, high seriousness and enormous verbal éclat, is an exemplary failure, a fascinating demonstration of the difficulties American playwrights face in trying to cope with all our sundered realities: the split between commerce and art, between tradition and the single voice, between surface and substance and between those aspects of the imagination we identify as form and content.

Hebbel wrote that content presents the task and form the solution. From the moment the curtain goes up on ***Virginia Woolf*** and we hear Albee's central characters—a history professor at a New England college and his wife, the daughter of the school's president—tell one another that "You make me puke," and "I'm six years younger than you, always have been and always will be," and "If you existed, I'd divorce you," we are aware that there is going to be a struggle on a more consuming level than that of personal antagonism. For the ferocity of Albee's domestic scene, the feral quality of his naturalism, isn't going to be satisfied with a conventional theatrical destiny—there is going to be a mighty conflict between a dramatic task and its elusive solution.

The evening grows more and more violent. The love-hate relationship of the couple fills the stage with wounds, glancing blows, destructions of confidence and of attitudinal clichés, revulsions, weaponless and unbearable intimidations, bitter exaltations and hopeless embraces. The wife despises the husband for his lack of *cojones,* his inability to step into her father's shoes; he is revolted by her promiscuity and her intolerable sexual pressure. Another couple arrives, a young All-American biology instructor and his inane, ethereal wife, and they begin to function as audience for and participants in the marital horror story.

There is nothing "absurd," about this play. Albee has largely abandoned the specific parodic elements and dragooned whimsy of ***The Sandbox*** and ***The American Dream*** and the obliquities of ***The Zoo Story*** and has, if anything, returned to ***The Death of Bessie Smith*** for savage inspiration and neurotic prototypes. But he has advanced from that problem play. Here the action is more inward and the rhetoric, apart from a few speeches of improbable and high-pitched lamentation, is straightforward, cocky, brutal, knowing and tremendously *au courant* . . . and very funny.

When the wife, played robustly—too robustly, perhaps—by Uta Hagen, stretches out in a chair after an abortive offstage dalliance with the visiting biologist and huskily announces "I'm the earth mother . . . and you're all flops," we are with Mr. Albee at his insider's best. And when the husband, whom Arthur Hill enacts crisply, but without much force, remarks that "I've been to college like everybody else," we receive confirmation about one source of Albee's appeal. He is the poet of post-Freudian, post-Riesmanian, post-intellectual, wised-up and not-to-be-had, experiential and disenchanted United States of America 1962 Man.

But poets, of course, want to sing, discover new lands of the imagination, be healers. That is Albee's self-imposed "task," and it is his downfall. The pressure in him towards the transcendence of naturalism and psychological notation had previously resulted in the painfully coerced denouement of ***The Zoo Story*** and the descent into incoherence of ***The American Dream.*** In ***Virginia Woolf*** the failure is on a larger scale. He has driven into the body of his scrupulously observed *Walpurgisnacht* (the title of Act II; Act I is called *Fun and Games,* Act III *The Exorcism*) a shaft of fantasy designed to point up our sad psychic aridity and fix the relationship between reality and illusion. Its effect is to break the back of the play.

We had been led to believe that the couple have a son in college, much of their mutual recrimination having concerned his upbringing and present attitude towards them. In Act III we learn—as a *coup de théâtre*—that he is imaginary; unable to have children, they had invented him, keeping him a secret and using his legendary existence as the major bond uniting them in their enmity and need. But when the wife mentions him to the visitors, she breaks their pact and the husband decides to kill him off, announcing his death in an accident and thereby ending the reign of illusion. The play ends with the wife sorrowfully accepting the necessity to live without myths, while whispering that she remains "afraid of Virginia Woolf," afraid, presumably, of life, art and truth.

There is something doubly wrong with this. Structurally, it leaves the play in division from itself, the psychological realism separated by a gulf from the metaphysical data, just as in ***The American Dream*** the parody and fantasy lay gasping out of each other's reach. But more than this there is the question of vision, of dramatic truth and rightness, of the proper means to an end, in short, of a "task" and its solution. What Albee has done is to smuggle in an element alien to his physical procedure, asking it to carry the burden of revelation he cannot distill from his mere observation of behavior. He wants to say something profound about the human condition, and he ends, like O'Neill in *The Iceman Cometh,* offering a cliché about illusions.

The sharpest psychological observation will no longer communicate the kind of truth we need and that Albee, with acute but limited sensibility, keeps trying for. As so many developments in art have demonstrated, the psyche is only

George Grizzard as Nick and Uta Hagen as Martha in the 1962 production of *Who's Afraid of Virginia Woolf?*

one element among others and needs to be *located,* tested against other realities, and not simply described. Naturalism gives us nothing but our reflections. However painful, bold and accurate they are, as in ***Virginia Woolf,*** they are not enough, we are not changed by them, as we are not ultimately changed by this play. The paradox is that human reality can best be apprehended today by indirection, by "inhuman" methods, which means a step beyond the literal, the behavioral, the natural. Our condition is extreme; old measures won't work, but neither will new half-measures, half-dramas such as Albee continues to produce.

John Simon (review date Winter 1962-63)

SOURCE: A review of *Who's Afraid of Virginia Woolf?,* in *The Hudson Review,* Vol. XV, No. 4, Winter 1962-63, pp. 571-73.

[*In the following assessment of* Who's Afraid of Virginia Woolf?, *Simon states: "The Trouble with Mr. Albee's play is that, instead of being motivated by stern impartiality or a fierce muckraking fervor, it seems mostly to be getting nasty little kicks from kicking society in the groin."*]

With ***Who's Afraid of Virginia Woolf?,*** the Broadway season at last comes into possession of a play. By now everyone must know that Edward Albee's drama concerns an all-night drinking session in a New England college. The hosts, a jaded, middle-aged failure of a history professor and his despair-maddened wife, taunt and torment each other and their guests, an *arriviste* of a young biology instructor and his vapid little bride, who retaliate as best they can but end up, in turn, lacerating each other and revealing their own insecurity or hysteria. There is also a plot device about an imaginary son of the elder couple that has to be painfully exorcised from their fantasies by the end of the third act, though one wishes that he could have been exorcised from the author's fantasy before the beginning of the first. The most obvious achievement of the play is that by a generally efficacious mixture of wit, cuttingly or touchingly true dialogue, and often staggering savagery, it gives one's emotional and intellectual apparatus a well-sustained, extensive and meaningful workout.

Mr. Albee's play assumes, artistically speaking, its rightful place in the tradition which Rilke, in a letter to his wife, correctly traced to Baudelaire's "Une Charogne." It was necessary, wrote Rilke, for artistic contemplation to be able to see "even in the horrible and the seemingly wholly repellent, the Existing, which, along with all else that exists, is valid. . . . A single turning away ever, thrusts [the artist] from the state of grace, makes him altogether sinful." Following in the footsteps of O'Neill and Williams, Albee looks unflinchingly at the putrescent cadaver, or near-cadaver, of our collective decency. But, with Albee, there is a catch. There is an old anecdote about a husband who, tied up, has to watch his wife being raped. When the assailant has fled, she unties her husband who promptly slaps her face. When she cries out in protest that she was overpowered, and could not help being raped, the husband retorts, "Yes, but you could have helped enjoying it." The trouble with Mr. Albee's play is that, instead of being motivated by stern impartiality or a fierce muckraking fervor, it seems mostly to be getting nasty little kicks from kicking society in the groin.

What is seriously wrong here is not that the structure of the play resembles too closely that of *Long Day's Journey Into Night,* or that the equivocating little flicker of hope at the end smacks strongly of Tennessee Williams, or that there is a little too much transposing—whether it be Albertine strategy or simply grafting hip talk, beatnikism, and the more fearfully flamboyant aspects of Fire Island on a college community which, however corrupt and sterile, would not boast of a decay that lights up like neon signs. No, the main deficiency here is that, though Albee has splendidly mastered Baudelaire's, or Rilke's, lesson, he has not drawn the corollary conclusion: that for the artist to avert his gaze deliberately from what good persists in the world is equally delinquent and debilitating. Not that Mr. Albee does this continually; but he does it a little too often, and a little too gleefully. I object, not on moral, but on strategic grounds: the playwright is just as apt to miss his mark—the audience—by overshooting as by under-shooting.

Still, Mr. Albee has made a significant and, if I may be allowed a vanishing paradox, beautiful contribution to the Poetry of the Obscene. There are times when his somberly flaming sarcasm reminds us more of the Earl of Rochester than of Baudelaire or Bosch. But even Rochester is not to be dismissed lightly. And when at its best, Albee's furibund fun produces lightnings like the definition of insanity as "Just the refuge we take when the unreality of the world weighs too heavy on our tiny heads" (note the double-edged sword), or like the richly metaphoric evocativeness of a middle-agedly professorial but youthfully cruel wife's exclaiming as she finds all her victims temporarily out of her range "Abandonèd!" How gravely and acutely, with just one accent, learning is ridiculed!

The performances, except for Uta Hagen's tendency to ham, are all imposing; Arthur Hill's history professor is more than that: a major creation in the contemporary American theatre. So, too, is Alan Schneider's magnificent staging which finds patterns of movement and vocal music befitting the author's variety of invention. And not the least salute must go to producers Barr and Wilder, who have demonstrated that for hardly more money than was needed for some of Off-Broadway's more pretentious undertakings, it is possible to bring an important play to Broadway, and, while the handsome profits are being counted, make it count as art.

CRITICAL COMMENTARY

Daniel McDonald (essay date 1964)

SOURCE: "Truth and Illusion in *Who's Afraid of Virginia Woolf?,*" in *Renascence,* Vol. XVII, No. 2, Winter 1964, pp. 63-9.

[*McDonald contends that in* Who's Afraid of Virginia Woolf? *Albee "illustrates how human beings begin with the illusory excellences of youth, see their ideals destroyed by the dark realities of experience, and seek to compensate by creating new illusions."*]

The danger in reading Albee's ***Who's Afraid of Virginia Woolf*** is in becoming too involved with the symbolism. The individual who is largely concerned with Martha's being "the Earth Mother" and her father's being "a God," will miss the point of a fine drama. Essentially, the play is not an allegory about Godot, or Good Deeds, or The American Dream; it is a story of real people and their illusions.

Through the story of a history professor and his wife enduring an all-night party with another university couple, Albee describes reality—i.e., human aspirations and emotions in the human situation—as "aimless . . . wanton . . . pointless." (The ellipsis marks in this paper will invariably be those of Mr. Albee, who uses many of them.) His theme is the necessity of illusion to sustain one in such an environment. By juxtaposing the two couples—the new and the old generation—he illustrates how human beings begin with the illusory excellences of youth, see their ideals destroyed by the dark realities of experience, and seek to compensate by creating new illusions. In such a situation, truth and illusion become confused; one cannot always tell the difference.

* * *

The two couples demonstrate the idealistic promise of youth and its subsequent failure. Nick and Honey have come to the New England college with exactly the same gifts and ambitions that George and Martha had twenty years before.

There exists, for example, the physical and mental keenness of youth. Nick is a varsity athlete who has kept his physique, a scholar who took his Master's degree at nineteen. Honey is organically healthy, and educated enough to respond to Latin prayers. Similarly, George is recalled as "young . . . intelligent . . . and . . . bushy-tailed, and . . . sort of cute," a new history professor,"A.B. . . . M.A. . . . Ph.D. . . . ABMAPHID!" And Martha remembers that she had both physical and intellectual gifts: "I wasn't the albatross."

The characters have moral gifts as well. Despite their present conduct, there are references to an initial moral integrity. George, we are told, is basically good, kind, understanding, and tolerant. Martha, though she abuses him, insists she does it out of a wild sense of justice, because she feels he needs and expects punishment. Even when she plans to cuckold him with Nick, for example, her declared motive is punitive, not sensual: "You come off this kick you're on, or I swear to God I'll do it." Nick's motive is similar; he is long tolerant of George's antagonism before seeking Martha. And toward his wife Honey, he is, as George notes, "solicitous to a point that faileth human understanding." The characters all show some elements of moral concern.

Enjoying such characteristics, they know youth a time of joy and promise. George recalls ordering "bergin and water" in a happy speakeasy: "the grandest day of my . . . youth." A young teacher, he wed a girl with money and influence, the daughter of the college president. Martha was "a Romantic at heart." She rejoiced in her rapport with her father, and she enjoyed her courtship with George, going into bars and ordering exotic drinks. She married him and had great hopes for his future:"He'd take over some day . . . first he'd take over the History Department, and then, when Daddy retired, he'd take over the college . . . you know."

Nick and Honey have the same memories and ambitions. He was an impressive student, a college quarterback, the intercollegiate state middleweight champion. He has a loving wife, one with money, and he is in biology, the coming science. His rise within the college seems an "inevitability." Honey rejoices in her husband's career and in her own youthful enthusiasm. Together they leave the world of youth—as George and Martha did earlier—with impressive gifts of health, innocence, and promise. It is clear that their end will be the same too: the cruelty and frustration that feed on human disillusionment. Like the older couple, Nick and Honey will find their physical and moral gifts, their ideals and hopes, sadly ephemeral.

George and Martha have deteriorated physically. George is now forty-six and looks a decade older. He is graying, balding, and losing his teeth. Martha calls him "Paunchy" and loves to mortify him by comparing him with Nick ("Still at the old middleweight limit, eh?"), and by recalling her own triumph ("Hey, George, tell 'em about the boxing match we had"). George can respond by citing Martha's infirmities: she had big teeth; she cannot have children; she is six years older than he is. But the whole subject is painful to him. He says, "One of the saddest things about men is the way they age."

Though Nick and Honey can rejoice in the momentary vigor of youth, the seeds of their downfall are apparent. Honey is delicate: sometimes, for no reason, she just throws up. She fears having children, and she dreads the thought of death. And Nick, for all his athletic prowess, has glimpses of future weakness. He is alcoholically impotent with Martha. Recommending exercise, he says he does not want to give up his firm body until he has to. And he recognizes the qualified triumph it will be to be chairman of his department, as George predicts, "when you're forty something and look fifty-five."

Like physical health, the intellectual promise of youth fades over the years. George describes "ABMAPHID" as "a wasting disease of the frontal lobes"—and all the characters demonstrate the process. Either they indulge in pointless pedantry: they correct each other's use of the words "chromosomes," "gaggle," "got," "abstract," etc. Or they employ the coarsest profanity: After they have been screaming obscenities at each other, George explains, "Martha and I are merely . . . exercising . . . that's all . . . we're merely walking what's left of our wits."

The moral breakdown of the characters is particularly apparent. During the second act, for example, they involve themselves in a pointless round of cruelties. Stung by George's references to their son, Martha, with Nick's encouragement, mortifies her husband by revealing his part in the death of his parents. George responds by describing in a cruel allegory the courtship, the required marriage, and the hypocrisy of Nick and Honey. Nick counters by embracing Martha and taking her upstairs. And George takes out his wrath on Honey by ridiculing her childlessness. Invariably, such acts derive from a revenge motive. The vicious person is raging back at someone who burst his private dream, his ideal of promise—at someone who cried the truth at him.

For all the characters the truth is ugly. The promise of George's youth has failed. His marriage to the college president's daughter has turned into a screaming farce. His professional life has stalemated. Only an associate professor after twenty-two years of service, he describes his career as "good, better, best, bested." His former ambitions rest with a novel his father-in-law would not let him publish.

George tries to rationalize the situation. He explains that circumstances defeated him, that "there are easier things than to be married to the daughter of the president of that university." The arrangement, he says, necessitated the loss of individuality, integrity, manhood: granting that some men would give their right arm for his situation, he declares that "the sacrifice is usually of a somewhat more private portion of the anatomy."

Everyone sees through this rationalization. Martha's father decided that George "didn't have the *stuff*" to be department chairman; Nick dismisses him as a sneaky ineffectual type; and Martha laughs off his threat to kill her some day: "Fat chance." It is clear that George's hatred of his wife derives, not so much from her being a coarse, violent woman, as from her repeating the sad truth. He is, in fact, an old bog in the History Department—"somebody without the *guts* to make anybody proud of him."

For Martha, the realities are equally unpleasant. She has lost the rapport she once had with her father and the hopes she once had for her husband. And like George she tries to rationalize her situation, to justify the kind of person she has become. She describes her vicious coarseness, her drunken infidelity, as efforts to force George ahead in his career, to mortify him into advancement. She insists she never wanted to be the kind of person she is. After humiliating George before guests, she tells him, "You can stand it! You married me for it." And when she gives up all concern in his career, she says, "I've tried with you, baby . . . really I've tried."

But this explanation satisfies no one, not even Martha. She recognizes what she is. Whatever factors caused the change, the gracious young hostess at her father's parties has become a vulgar middle-aged woman—"spoiled, self-indulgent, willful, dirty-minded, liquor-ridden." Despite her denials, she knows that George's claims are true: she does bray; she does swill it down; she does make up to other men. It is a sad moment of truth when Martha has to say, "I disgust me."

Like the older couple, Nick and Honey are made to see the reality behind their illusions. In one drunken and revealing night, Nick is shown to be both weak and ambitious. Under all his bright talk and acceptable manners there is a core of selfishness. Despite his courtesy to Honey, he does not really consider her. Before others, he tells her she is drinking too much; he tells her to shut up. To George he reveals intimate facts about their premarital sex, her hysterical pregnancy, etc. And when George humiliates Honey by repeating these facts in their ugliest light, Nick is too weak to stop him. The summary after the event is revealing: Nick ignores the effect on his wife, who has gone sick to the bathroom. He condemns the story as damaging—"Damaging! To me!"

His ambition is made of sterner stuff. He jokes about being one of the "wave-of-the-future" biologists and about his plans to use pressure and stratagem to advance at the university. And when George cites the element of truth in the levity ("You almost think you're serious, and it scares the hell out of you"), Nick acts outraged. But he has to admit the fact when, returning from the bedroom with Martha, he tries to deny being a "houseboy." Martha, daughter of the college president, counters—

> Sure you are! You're ambitious, aren't you, boy? You didn't chase me around the kitchen and upstairs out of mad driven passion, did you now? You were thinking just a little bit about your career, weren't you? Well, you can just houseboy your way up the ladder for a while.

Thereafter, when Martha tells him to answer the door, Nick protests, considers, then answers the door. When George commands he go bring his wife from the bathroom ("Fetch, good puppy, go fetch"), he starts to remonstrate, then goes for his wife. Here Nick is illustrating what George noted earlier: that a certain kind of ambition requires the sacrifice of a "private portion of the anatomy."

For Honey, too, the confrontation with truth is disturbing. Her whole life, in fact, is a willful retreat from reality. Fortifying herself with brandy, she refuses to credit weakness in the world, in Nick, in herself. When George and Martha struggle physically and Nick works to separate them, Honey clings to her bottle and sings out "Violence! violence!" When George tries to make her recognize the illicit relationship between Nick and Martha, she says, "I don't want to listen to you." And when he berates her for not wanting children and inquires vulgarly about her contraceptive devices, Honey will not hear him. Her only comment: "I want my husband! I want a drink!"

But, like the rest, Honey is not deceived. All her efforts with brandy and party gaiety do not obscure the fact that her situation is ugly, that her husband is weak, and that she exists as a "mindless echo." When George challenges her, "It's just some things you can't remember . . . hunh?"—Honey admits the truth."Don't remember," she says, "not can't."

* * *

For all the characters, then, the physical and moral vigor, the memory and promise of youth, prove illusory qualities. The truth is bitter, and does prevail. The individuals must, therefore, seek new illusions with which to mask reality.

Both couples seek the consolation of alcohol. George says that Martha is a secret drinker, whose gin bottles he has to sneak out after midnight. And she explains—in a moving passage—that they both drink for the same reason, to respond to the sadness of their lives:

> I cry all the time. And Georgie cries all the time too. We both cry all the time, and then, what we do, we cry, and we take our tears, and we put 'em in the ice box, in the goddam ice trays until they're all frozen and then . . . we put them . . . in our . . . drinks.

Similarly, Nick, taking another bourbon on the rocks, cites a general response to the human condition: "Everybody drinks a lot here in the East. (*Thinks about it.*) Everybody drinks a lot in the middle-west, too."

Nick illustrates another technique used to avoid the emotional ramifications of reality: he assumes a pose of indifference, of scientific dispassion. He tells George that he does not like getting involved in other people's affairs, that he doesn't make judgments regarding behavior like Martha's, and, even, that he had no particular passion for Honey when they were first married. George scores Nick's "scientific detachment" as smug and self-righteous, but uses the same pose in his own marriage. He tells Martha:

> (*Calmly, matter-of-factly*) I'm numbed enough . . . and I don't mean by liquor, though maybe that's been part of

> the process—a gradual over-the-years going to sleep of the brain cells—I'm numbed enough, now, to be able to take you when we're alone. I don't listen to you . . . or when I *do* listen to you, I sift everything, I bring everything down to reflex response, so I don't really *hear* you, which is the only way to manage it.

And Martha's response to their marriage is identical: When George complains of her vulgar behavior at parties, she responds, "I can't even see you . . . I haven't been able to see you for years."

Further, the characters try to escape reality by creating illusions, by telling lies. George says the boy who killed his parents was another, not himself; he claims his father and mother once took him sailing off Majorca. Martha says that Nick was an adequate lover. Honey recalls her false pregnancy as appendicitis and claims she seldom drinks much. Nick, aged thirty, says he is twenty-eight. And Martha and George pretend they have a son, a kind of ideal youth nearing his twenty-first birthday. Though each accuses the other of driving the boy away, they both cherish him as a feature of the good life they once envisioned.

Other avenues of retreat are mentioned. Martha cites death as a relief: "You make all sorts of excuses to yourself . . . *you* know . . . this is life . . . the hell with it . . . maybe tomorrow he'll be dead . . . maybe tomorrow you'll be dead." George envies those insane people who "maintain a . . . a firm-skinned serenity" and do not seem to grow old. And when Nick charges, "You're all crazy; nuts," Martha affects a brogue and generalizes: "Aww, 'tis the refuge we take when the unreality of the world weighs too heavily on our tiny heads."

There is, however, no permanent refuge from truth. The characters find their created illusions no more satisfying than their youthful ones. Drunken euphoria does not last. The pose of indifference fails under emotional pressure. Lies are cruelly shattered. And madness and death are not easy alternatives to choose. George, Martha, Nick, and Honey, after a night of savage tension, know that life is an ugly experience and that there is no place to hide.

At the end of the play, after George has "killed" their imaginary son, Martha asks if they can exist without illusions: "Just . . . us?" And when he sings "Who's afraid of Virginia Woolf," she whispers,"I . . . am . . . George . . . I . . . am . . ."

* * *

The view that *Who's Afraid of Virginia Woolf* concerns the breakdown of youthful illusion is reinforced by the allegorical symbolism of the play. Many elements of the drama can be related to the religious—and often specifically Christian—concept of man's fall from grace.

Martha's father, for example, is called "a God" and is said to live at "Parnassus." He not only built the college: "He *is* the college." Rumored to be "over two hundred years old," he has "a sense of history . . . of continuation." He is "a strong man" who "expects loyalty and devotion out of his . . . staff." Martha responds appropriately, saying, "I worshipped him . . . I absolutely worshipped him. I still do." But George reveals that her father "really doesn't give a damn whether she lives or dies."

Martha calls herself "the Earth Mother" and makes references to an Edenic state where she was a kind of Eve. Now "a hundred and eight . . . years old," according to George, she recalls the blissful years when she was the young hostess at her Daddy's house. She was once corrupted by a "gardener's boy," and later caused George's downfall in a garden: wearing boxing gloves she knocked him flat in a huckleberry bush. The symbolic value of this *fall* is made almost explicit: Martha says, "I think it's colored our whole life. Really I do! It's an excuse anyway. It's what he uses for being bogged down, anyway." George calls her a "Satanic bitch"—and she explains that he made "the insulting mistake of loving me and must be punished for it."

Other allegorical elements might be established. Their son—"this state, this perfection"—could be a reference to Christ, *the* Son. And this son—"poor lamb"—never really existed; he was simply an illusion necessary to sustain existence in New Carthage. George describes their cruel and chaotic existence as "for lack of a better word—Life."

Such allegory does reinforce the theme of the play and should be examined as such. But I repeat my fear that anyone who pursues it too exclusively will miss the point of the drama. The reader who insists on knowing why Honey's father was a "man of God" or what Martha's stepmother's warts mean, will lose sight of the fact that the individuals here are real and their plight is real. The characters find that the world is a violent, unsatisfactory place, that illusion is necessary for man's existence, and that even illusion does little good. Their situation is summarized in Martha's response to George's grand tale of once sailing past Majorca with his parents. "You were never in the Mediterranean," she says, "truth or illusion . . . either way."

Ruth Meyer (essay date 1968)

SOURCE: "Language: Truth and Illusion in *Who's Afraid of Virginia Woolf?*," in *Educational Theatre Journal,* Vol. XX, No. 1, March 1968, pp. 60-9.

[*In this essay on* Who's Afraid of Virginia Woolf?, *Meyer argues that "language is a major device in the play by which the relativity and ambiguity of truth are accomplished."*]

As George tries to determine whether guest Nick is "stud" or "houesboy," Martha pleadingly accuses him of the inability to judge: "Truth or illusion, George; you don't know the difference" (202).[1] And the audience, too, at this point near the end of the play may readily concede that they along with George have lost contact with the neat distinctions be tween truth and illusion. For indeed in Edward Albee's ***Who's Afraid of Virginia Woolf?*** the distinction between truth and illusion is not readily perceived. If one accepts as truth that which the characters say is true and ignores their later contradictions, he can find a fairly clear-cut differene between truth and illusion. Daniel McDonald seems to distinguish between truth and illusion on merely this literal basis. Such over-simplification leads to statements such as "Honey rejoices in her husband's career and in her own youthful enthusiasm."[2] In actuality, the only enthusiasm she exhibits in the play is for "[dancing] like the wind" (126) and drinking brandy. Similarly McDonald's statement that "Martha mortifies her husband by revealing his part in the death of his parents"[3] ignores two basic facts: George claims this happened to a friend of his, and he also attributes circumstances similar to the murder to the death of their imaginary son.

Truth and illusion is indeed a major theme of the play, but on a more complex level than this. A more perceptive evaluation is given by Robert Brustein:

> Albee seems less interested in the real history of his characters than in the way they conceal and protect their reality: the conflict is also a kind of game, with strict rules, and what they reveal about each other may not be true. This comedy of concealment reminds me of Pirandello, and even more of Jean Genet. For George and Martha . . . shift their identities like reptiles shedding skins.[4]

Language is a principal means by which Albee achieves this "comedy of concealment." The dialogue of the characters which both reveals and conceals identity establishes the ambiguity between truth and illusion and in part accounts for the violent disagreement among the critics as to the "message" of the play. For example, George's use of clichés reveals a characteristic of his personality; at the same time, it protects him from any exposure of real identity.

In order to discuss illusion, one should first define and identify truth; to discuss exaggeration, there must first be a norm. "Truth" is generally considered a verifiable fact, "illusion" a false mental image, thus one that is unverifiable. It is from definitions as clear cut as these that difficulties arise, because throughout the play there is a constant interpenetration of truth and illusion; similarly, so many false roles are assumed by the characters during the night's performance that no definite norm can be established. Although language is the principal means of creating the ambiguity, it is not the only means, as seen in the frequent stage directions concerning facial expression and stance.

Throughout the play, situations and experiences are hinted at: Did George actually experience the death of his father and mother as related in his novel, the novel Martha claims he said "really happened"? (137) Does Martha's father actually "not give a damn" for her, as George says? (225) Did George sail past Majorca, or for that matter, did the moon, after going down, "pop . . . back up again"? (199) Has Honey been committing secret abortions, as George hints? (177) Is Nick "stud" or"houseboy," and is liquor the only excuse for his failure to "hump the hostess"? (188,197)

Albee's dexterity in creating ambiguity is perhaps best demonstrated by the scene in which George confronts Honey with her fear of having children. The audience is already aware that Nick married Honey during her false pregnancy; it is also aware that she "[gets] sick . . . occasionally, all by [herself]" (119). Having heard Honey's admission of "I. . . don't . . . want . . . any . . . children. I'm afraid! I don't want to be hurt . . ." George sums up the evidence: "I should have known . . . the whole business . . . the headaches . . . the whining . . . the. . . ." He quickly concludes: "How do you make your secret little murders studboy doesn't know about, hunh? Pills?"(177) Honey has admitted fear of having children; she doesn't"want to be hurt." Through the use of "hurt," ambiguity is already created; does she fear the physical pain of childbirth or the psychological pain, unverifiable but nonetheless very real, involved in being a parent? George's quick conclusion furthers the ambiguity; unfortunately, many critics pounce on George's accusation as the revelation of a truth. Alfred Chester, however, has noted a significant factor in this scene: "So the truth is out at last. But what truth?" Chester continues:

> . . . we realize that, after all, Honey has said nothing, and George's mind has said it all. . . . But somehow George has hit home . . . We begin to realize that the"truth" about Nick and Honey's reproductive dilemma will never be revealed as an objective fact.[5]

Even at the start of the play the focus is on the language of the characters. With the first lines, Albee establishes a device he will use throughout the play. Martha's drunken "Jesus H. Christ" is not only shocking but is also distorted. The "H."—a good old American middle initial, no doubt—is sufficiently unfamiliar to draw attention to itself. Walter Kerr points out that Albee "peppers us with them [Jesus Christ's and God damn's] as a kind of warning rattle, to make sure that our ears will be attentive when he decides really to burn them—with something else."[6] This may be evidenced by the incongruity of George's term "Chastity" (199) applied with knowing inaccuracy to Martha after her attempted adultery with Nick or his "Whatever *love* wants" (19, italics mine) as she badgers him to greet their guests. Calling Martha "Chastity" does not make her chaste; referring to her as "love" does not make her loved. But her adultery attempt *has* been unsuccessful, and there *is* some sort of mutual concern, a rather distorted love, existing between George and Martha. Through the use of a term which in context seems highly inappropriate, Albee focuses on the fine distinction between truth and illusion.

As has already been noted, the ambiguity between truth and illusion is a major concern of the play. The occupation of the characters is significant: college professors and their wives have achieved a level of education that would imply precise and fluent use of language and also an awareness of the use of clichés. Albee exploits both of these factors, principally through George, who early in the play evidences an exaggerated concern for precise diction and later retreats from painful reality by assuming a false role, the falseness of which is indicated mainly by dialogue. Litany-like repetitions support the ambiguity, since a litany is an artificially structured response and may not represent the truth of the moment. The false roles and the litany-like repetitions culminate in the oldest and most universal of rituals—the Mass, but even this in the context of the play furthers rather than resolves the ambiguity.

In the play the characters themselves acknowledge a concern with language. They are aware that certain levels of speech belong to certain groups. As George warns Martha not to start in on the "bit" (about their "child") (18), Martha replies, "The bit? The bit? What kind of language is that?" and then, "You imitating one of your students, for God's sake?" George warns Nick and Honey that "Martha's a devil with language" (21). Martha defends her intellect by clarifying her statement that biology is less "abstruse" than math and taunts George with "Don't you tell me words" (63). As George recovers from their round of Humiliate the Host, he badgers them with "I mean, come on! We must know other games, college-type types like us . . . that can't be the . . . limit of our vocabulary, can it?" (139) By emphasizing the importance of "vocabulary" to "games," George acknowledges the centrality of language to their existence, since much of their existence consists in playing games. At the same time, since their games involve mainly the concealment of the truth about themselves, through the assumption and abandonment of false dialogue and false roles, George's statement comes very near to identifying Albee's technique in creating the ambiguity between truth and illusion.

It thus seems fairly evident that George and Martha are quite aware of the language they use. And there is, particularly on George's part, a willingness to haggle over vocabulary and to search for the accurate word. George argues with Nick over whether a bunch of geese are a "gaggle" or a "gangle" (113), bickers again with him over whether Honey is "slim-hipped" or "frail" (89), points out the inadequacies of "courting" (23) when used to refer to his time spent with Martha prior to their marriage, and uses "Life" because of "lack of a better word" (100). His exaggerated precision in use of language becomes for him the norm, or as near to a norm as we will find amid the slippery truth presented in the play. Nevertheless, he is amused that Nick will admit to being "testy" (99), but resents being told that he is "upset." He knows that "*Got* the ice" is correct, albeit a bit archaic—like Martha (166). His awareness of the stupidity of conventional euphemisms comes to a peak when he tells Martha to show Honey "where we keep the . . . euphemism" (20), a phrase totally lost on Honey's liquor-fogged brain.

Despite the fact that she tells George he doesn't need to "tell her words," Martha is much less precise in her use of them. Almost in a manner reminiscent of Holden Caulfield, she adds an "or something" to her phrases. She says that Nick is "in the math department, or something" (9). As Nick points out the error in her quotation of her father's favorite phrase, she admits, "Well, maybe that *isn't* what he says . . . something like it" (55). Similarly, she accuses Nick that he "Plucked [her] like a goddamn . . . whatever-it-is . . . creeping vine" (185), and then calls, "What are you doing: hiding or something?" (185) Martha "swings wild" (193), as Nick observes; she hits her target, but she frequently takes in the surrounding area as well. She shoots, but frequently with buckshot—the whole area, or something, is riddled with her fire. Never does she evidence George's concern with precision in speech. Her references to Bette Davis, who is married to Joseph Cotton or something, is merely a result of her carelessness with language; her reference to Nick and Honey (prior to their arrival) as "What's their name" is, as she puts it, the result of meeting"fifteen new teachers and their goddamn wives" (63).

The contrast between Martha's disregard for precision and George's meticulous and exaggerated insistence upon the right word seems clear. And yet at times George, too, pretends to slip. As he tells Nick that "since I married . . . uh, What's her name . . . uh, Martha" (32) it is not because of the forgetfulness or confusion which causes Martha to use "What's their name" in reference to Nick and Honey. How better to show detachment and disregard of someone or something than either to forget the name or to get it wrong. As he discusses the proposed scientific advances with Nick, he says,"You're the one's going to make all that trouble . . . making everyone the same, rearranging the chromozones, or whatever it is" (37). Contempt could scarcely be more clearly expressed. When we consider George's occasional disregard for precision in light of his usual even though exaggerated concern for accuracy, we see Albee's device of presenting a masked truth—for example, George's contempt for science. Because the norm is an exaggerated one, and therefore not an unquestionable norm, the ambiguity between truth and illusion remains.

Much of the dialogue of the play consists of clichés, and Albee uses them in a manner that contributes to the truth/illusion situation. Albee, like Ionesco, is a master of the cliché, but while Ionesco demonstrates the inadequacies of language to describe phenomena, Albee demonstrates the adequacy and power of words. The power of words is perhaps best demonstrated by their ability to both reveal and conceal truth, frequently at the same time. In ***Virginia Woolf,*** Albee often reveals a significant facet of his characters through a slanted cliché, one that has been tampered with in order to indicate a special meaning. The effectiveness of this device rises out of the contrast between what one expects to hear and the significantly pointed distortion. But since any cliché by its very nature is seldom considered a particular and applicable truth, even the distortion of one has an air of ambiguity about it. Albee, nonetheless, comes closer to presenting unambiguous truth through the use of clichés than in any other instance in the play.

This use of clichés may be seen in the following incidents. As Martha taunts George at the beginning of the play with

"Georgie-Porgie, put-upon pie" (12), the slanted cliché reveals George's position; he is made the unwilling host for a 2:00 A.M. after-party party. Similarly by switching from "musical chairs" in George's statement to Nick that "Musical beds is the faculty sport" (34), Albee foreshadows the night's activities. A slanted cliché appears again as Martha assures Nick that a "friendly little kiss" won't matter since "It's all in the faculty" (163). And as Martha recalls her life at the opening of Act III, she bemoans the fact that she was "left to her own vices" (185), a fairly appropriate statement considering her action just prior to this.

One other slanted cliché is particularly important to the play, George's accusation that Martha is a "child mentioner" (140). "Child molester" is what an audience would anticipate, and for a flesh-and-blood child it would be the appropriate term. But just as appropriate to an illusion is the word "mentioner," for talking of ideas corresponds to touching objects. Thus the illusion that some critics[7] feel has been sprung at the end of the play has been foreshadowed by Albee's slanted cliché only halfway through the play.

Albee also uses clichés as they are normally used, but attaches great importance to them by showing that, rather than being devoid of meaning because they are usually not a consciously thought out expression, they express, because of their very spontaneous composition, significant meaning. Personalities are revealed by balancing a cliché with a responding literal application of it. As Martha says that George's Dylan Thomas-y quality "gets [her] right where [she] lives," George applies this quite literally and comments on Martha's obsession with sex by responding, "Vulgar girl!" (24) In the same manner, a few moments later Martha, in ridiculing George for not taking advantage of being the son-in-law of the president of the college, says "*some* men would give their right arm for the chance!" (28) Taking the cliché literally again, George corrects her by remarking, "Alas, Martha, in reality it works out that the sacrifice is usually of a somewhat more private portion of the anatomy."

As George and Martha bicker over why Honey got sick—neither of them acknowledges that the brandy she's been downing all night might have something to do with it—Martha nags at George to apologize for making Honey throw up. George rejects his responsibility for this: "I did not make her throw up." As Martha continues her assault, "Well, who do you think did . . . Sexy over there? You think he made his *own* little wife sick?" To which George—"helpfully," Albee directs—concludes, "Well, you make *me* sick" (118). The cliché goes both ways: figuratively, he is "sick" of Martha; literally, Nick might have made Honey physically ill. In a similar situation, George is able to turn Nick's threat of "You're going to regret this [telling the real basis for Nick and Honey's marriage]" to futility by admitting, "Probably. I regret everything" (150). In these instances, by taking literally and giving specific application to a cliché which usually functions in a figurative and general manner, Albee comes closest to presenting unambiguous truth.

Although Martha still considers herself the Earth Mother, ironically since she is beyond menopause, it is George who is the Creative Force in the play. One might call him a director who attempts to set things in motion yet remain detached. In the movie, he openly announces: "I'm running this show." His attempt to assume the role of director is an integral part of the truth/illusion situation, for as he vacillates between detachment and involvement, his statements attain their ambiguity.

He is presented with his audience—the new biology professor and his wife. As the guests wait at the door, George assumes his controlling roll by admonishing Martha not to "start in on the bit [about their "son"]" (18). Obviously he intends to run the show, to direct the conversation. Despite his attempts to remain an outside creator, from time to time he is involuntarily drawn into the action itself.

There are four major painful confrontations for George, all times during which he contributes to the ambiguity between truth and illusion by adopting a false stance. Involved in the false stance is not only language, but gesture and action as well; all function in George's attempt to remain a director, and each interacts and supports the others. The first is the revelation that Martha beat him in a boxing match, a revelation made more painful and more personally degrading by the fact that Nick was "inter-collegiate state middleweight champion." Just prior to this, George has resisted Martha's goading to gush over Nick's having received his masters when he was "twelve-and-ahalf." Albee notes that George is to strike "a pose, his hand over his heart, his head raised, his voice stentorian" and announce: "I am preoccupied with history" (40-50). Under the guise of an actor, using words which in another context would seem normal, not pretentious, he states the truth. But because it is obviously an act, he can admit the truth with no involvement. (Later, p. 178, he admits, sincerely this time, that he has turned to a contemplation of the past.) After being able to admit the truth, he is confronted with Martha's "Hey George, tell 'em about the boxing match *we* had." His only response when caught without the defense of role-playing is to exit "with a sick look on his face" (57). But he is not gone long. He returns, as an actor with a gun. His "Pow!! You're dead! Pow! You're dead!" is again his assumption of a role, because he had been pushed to involvement and disgrace. To understand the Chinese parasol which substitutes for a bullet, we need only to consider his stentorian pose for the admission of his life's focus; the "Pow! You're dead!" is as much of a reality—in his mind and intention—as his preoccupation with history. Both are masked in false dialogue and action. His role as director has been challenged, he is forced to involvement, and he meets this challenge by ostentatiously playing a part. He retreats to the realm of illusion in the face of what is for him a painful truth. But the degree to which this is an illusion is difficult to determine because, as has already been pointed out, the norm is by no means clearly established.

As in the first conflict, Martha is the instigator in the second conflict. During George and Nick's get-acquainted session while Martha and Honey were upstairs, George has told of an experience that happened to one of his friends during their youth. Now Martha brings up the fact that George has written a novel dealing with this experience, one which elicited from her father the judgment: "You publish that goddamn book and you're out . . . on your ass!" (135) George's pained "Desist! Desist!" gets only laughter from Martha and a mocking "De . . . sist!" from Nick. His equally false formal dialogue, "I will not be made mock of!" again gets only a mocking response from Nick. George is pushed to the breaking point as Martha concludes, supposedly quoting George's statement to her father, "No, Sir, this isn't a novel at all . . . this is the truth . . . this really happened . . . to me!" (137) He lunges at Martha, grabbing her by the throat. His threat, "I'll kill you," now is carried out; the Chinese parasol is replaced by grasping hands. In both instances, however, George has first relied on or been pushed to dialogue which is unnatural for him, which both masks and reveals his intention.

Similarly in the third crisis, the one in which Martha challenges George to intervene in her proposed adultery with Nick, George retreats to the most obvious of all detached roles—reading a commentary on the situation. This retreat is preceded by a reliance on making literal application of a cliché, the humor of which allows him to remain a director, a detached person controlling or at least only viewing the antics of the others. Consider the scene near the end of Act II as Martha seeks to *get* George:

> MARTHA: I'm entertaining. I'm entertaining one of the guests. I'm necking with one of the guests.
>
> GEORGE: Oh, that's nice. Which one?
>
> (170)

Grammatically, Martha's speech has left her vulnerable for George's bitter question. It also affords him a chance to be "seemingly relaxed and preoccupied" as the directions indicate. Humor becomes his shield. And later, as he reads:

> MARTHA: Oh, I see what you're up to, you lousy little. . . .
>
> GEORGE: I'm up to page a hundred and . . .

again he finds refuge behind a humorous literal application of her statement. By taking the cliché referring abstractly to anticipated, frequently unorthodox action and applying it literally to the present situation, George does reveal the truth—he is "up to page a hundred and. . . ." But he also creates for himself an escape from the truth of Martha's proposed adultery. As Martha's fury rises, she says:

> MARTHA: Why, you miserable . . . I'll show *you*.
>
> GEORGE: No . . . show him, Martha, he hasn't seen it.

As in the preceding quotation, George protects himself from the threat of Martha's statement. At the same time, he caustically degrades Martha's sexual attractiveness, the very things she is trying so desperately to prove to him and to herself. And George's final deadly, revealing reversal of accusation shows the skill with which George is able to shatter the moral illusion under which the others operate while protecting his own:

> NICK: You're disgusting!
>
> GEORGE: Because *you're* going to hump Martha, *I'm* disgusting?
>
> (172)

As with humor, so the quotation from the book serves as a screen for his emotions. " 'And the west, encumbered by crippling alliances, and burdened with a morality too rigid to accomodate itself to the swing of events, must . . . eventually . . . fall' " (174). This, by the context surrounding it, should be a sort of thesis statement of the play. But who actually has the "crippling appliances," whose morality is"too rigid"? George, because the circumstances of his novel really happened and he cannot ignore or depreciate them? Martha, because she is the president's daughter and is bound to the college, the faculty, and its sports? Or perhaps does it have application only in the literal, the universal—the West? Once again, a "great truth" has been presented—almost. And again, the ambiguity is a direct result of the language. Finishing the quotation, George "gathers all the fury he has been containing within himself . . . he shakes . . . with a cry that is part growl, part howl, he hurls [the book] at the chimes" (174). Once again, false dialogue has masked temporarily his involvement and pain.

The final encounter is one manipulated by George: the death of and Mass for their "son." George begins the action by appearing in the kitchen doorway, snapdragons covering his face; Albee notes that he should speak in a "hideously cracked falsetto": "Flores; flores para los muertos. Flores" (195) (Flowers; flowers for the dead. Flowers), he announces to Martha and Nick. Here is Albee's most complete interposing of dialogue which in another context would not be unusual, but which in this context again both reveals and conceals. As with the reading, so with the foreign language; George can say exactly what he means without being involved. George shifts roles at this point; his face "gleeful," he opens his arms to Nick and says, "Sonny! You've come home for your birthday! At last!" A moment later, "Affecting embarassment" Albee directs, "I . . . I brung ya dese flowers, Mart'a, 'cause I . . . wull, 'cause you'se . . . awwwwww hell. Gee" (196).

George is therefore able, actor that he is, to argue quite convincingly—concrete examples and all—with great logic that the "moon may very well have gone down . . . but it came back up" (199). The argument is no more superficial than any other transactions at this point. From this Martha moves to a taunting jibe about George's parents and the novel; next they focus on whether Nick is a "stud" or"houseboy." The main elements of conflict are thus reinstated in the drama; the stage is ready for the battle—and George again assumes a role to escape the pain, this time the role of a priest.

Albee's "message," if indeed the play gives one, is largely determined by the attitude George assumes in reciting the Mass. Is the murder of the son an act of revenge, as the conclusion of Act II would lead us to believe? Or is it, on the contrary, an act of compassion, the act of an uninvolved director freeing his actors of their illusions? If ***Virginia Woolf*** elicits disagreement from critics concerning dialogue, the motivation for George's action has called forth a stand from nearly everyone writing about the play; an account of their opinions would be little more than a list under "Revenge" and "Compassion." Rather than merely tally up the votes, let us look at two performances of the play.

In the recording[8] of the New York play, George's (Arthur Hill's) voice indicates a determined, almost angry attempt to kill, once and for all time, this cherished illusion. "Requiescat in Pace" sounds as though it were to be followed by the stomp of a foot and perhaps a quick "Damn it!" not altogether unanticipated at this point in the play. There has been no switch from the revenge motive; this is the thing that will "get" Martha; therefore George does it, does it well, does it determinedly, does it almost with glee.

In a presentation of the play by the Repertory Theatre at the University of Nebraska a rather striking difference was apparent. Martha's rendition of the "child's" life was not merely a defense or a justification of his existence; it was a confession: "I have tried, O God, I have tried . . . through one failure after another. . . ." (227) On her knees, in a voice of restrained agony, she becomes the figure of man tormented with sudden awareness of his condition. But to the confession there can be no Absolution. Martha the confessant receives counsel but no pardon. And this it seems is central to understanding the character of George throughout the play. To give Absolution, the Confessor must be consecrated, set apart, uninvolved. This George would like to be, tries to be, but is not.

Creator he is: his novel, though unpublished and scorned by "respectable" New Carthage standards, is the mark in the academic jungle of a creative mind. The past histories (Nick and Honey's marriage and the part played by "Jesus money, Mary money," for example) originate in his mind (143). The actions offstage (Honey's being curled up fetus-like on the bathroom floor, for example) reach us through George's reports (167). Therefore he can function at times as a director. But as we have seen, he does not have the ability to remain separate from his creation; his retreat behind false dialogue does not protect him from the slings and arrows which plague the others. He is not set apart; he is not, therefore, able to give Absolution to Martha. Significantly he can only say, "*We* couldn't [have children]" (238).

It seems, considering the pattern that Albee has established in the play itself, that the presentation of George as a compassionate, but deeply involved person is more consistent with the whole. George's action is no longer one of revenge, nor is it solely one of freeing Martha from illusion, illusion which she may or may not be better off without. He is painfully involved; the altar upon which he celebrates the Mass holds a part of him: "There are very few things in this world that I am sure of . . . but the one thing in this whole stinking world that I am sure of . . . is my partnership, my chromosomological partnership in the . . . creation of our . . . blond eyed, blue haired . . . son" (72). He is director become actor in a play he had hoped to control, an unconsecrated priest playing one more painful game. The interpenetration of truth and illusion is nowhere more vividly presented: he did create the "son," but paradoxically the"son" does not exist.

Just as we cannot separate the discussion of language in the play from the characters, so can we not separate Albee's manipulation of language from the overall meaning of the play. Repeatedly Albee pounces on the word "know," showing how little we really do know of another's experience. Communication is frequently a theme of Albee's works, and ***Virginia Woolf*** is no exception. The fact that there may be a discrepancy between what someone *says* happened and what *did* happen, as well as our inability to appreciate an unexperienced situation, receives attention in the play. Truth for the person merely observing a particular situation may not be truth for the one experiencing it; what is truth for one may seem illusion to the other. Early in Act I George clears up a humorous confusion of pronoun references by reminding Nick that George's wife is Martha. "Yes . . . I know," Nick responds. George counters: "If you were married to Martha you would know what it means. (Pause) But then, if I were married to your wife I would know what that means, too . . . wouldn't I?" (36) This scene is picked up later as Nick reminds George, ". . . your wife is Martha.""Oh, yes . . . I know (with some rue)" (89). Similarly, as Martha sums up the story of her quick marriage to the "lawn mower" with "It was very nice," Nick is quick to agree: "Yes. Yes." Martha's response,"What do you mean, yes, yes? How would you know?" (78) again focuses on the inability of one to know another's experience, and hence to know the"truth."

There is, then, no clear cut distinction between truth and illusion in the play. Although non-existant and known by George and Martha to be non-existant, the "son" is nevertheless a reality in their lives, a reality by which they define their relationship to each other. Similarly George's "murder" of his parents may be real in his mind only, but it, too, is a reality which shapes his life. The same could be said of Honey's hysterical pregnancy or Nick's "potential."

Although we have seen the exorcism of an illusion, there is no truth revealed in its place. Reality, Albee seems to be saying, is a painful interpenetration of verifiable fact and imagination, with the "fact" of the mind often far more real than that of the body.

When Martha accuses George of not knowing the difference between truth and illusion, he admits, "No: but we must carry on as though we did." In this play, set in one room which becomes a world in itself with its own games, its own rules, "All truth," as George admits, "[becomes] relative" (222). And language is a major device in the play by which the relativity and ambiguity of truth are accomplished.

Notes

[1]Edward Albee, *Who's Afraid of Virginia Woolf?* (New York: Pocket Books, Inc., 1962). Subsequent references in the text to the play will be designated *Virginia Woolf* and page number.

[2]Daniel McDonald, "Truth and Illusion in *Who's Afraid of Virginia Woolf?*" *Renascence,* XVII, 64.

[3]*Ibid.,* p. 65.

[4]"Albee and the Medusa Head," *New Republic,* CXLVII (November 3, 1962), 29.

[5]"Edward Albee: Red Herrings and White Whales," *Commentary,* XXXV (April 1963), 299.

[6]"Along Nightmare Alley," *Vogue,* CXVI (April 1, 1963), 119. Certainly not all critics share Mr. Kerr's evaluation of the dialogue. For example, John McCarten, who assesses the play as "vulgar mishmash," writes: "*Who's Afraid of Virginia Woolf?* could be cut in half by the elimination of the 'God-damn's,' 'Jesus Christ's,' and other expressions designed, presumably, to show us that this is really modern stuff." See "Long Night's Journey Into Daze," *The New Yorker,* XXXVIII (October 20, 1962), 85.

[7]Richard Schechner, "Who's Afraid of Edward Albee?" *Tulane Drama Review,* VII (Spring 1963), 8.

[8]Columbia Records No. DOL 287.

Thomas E. Porter (essay date 1969)

SOURCE: "Fun and Games in Suburbia: *Who's Afraid of Virginia Woolf?,*" in *Myth and Modern American Drama,* Wayne State University Press, 1969, pp. 225-47.

[*In the essay below, Porter reads* Who's Afraid of Virginia Woolf? *as a satire in which Albee attacks "the manners and attitudes of society that keep man from communication."*]

The placid citizenry of Grover's Corners [in Thorton Wilder's *Our Town*] and the sophisticated suburbanites of New Carthage in Edward Albee's ***Who's Afraid of Virginia Woolf?*** are light-years apart. Social harmony, closeness to nature and love within the family circle, except as nostalgic ideals, are not apparently operative in a large segment of the affluent American society of the 1960s. Racial strife, brush wars abroad, the rise of the cosmopolis and the decentralization of family life (talk of togetherness is symptomatic) are the facts that fly in the face of these ideals. Awareness of a deep uneasiness is inescapable, and misgivings about "the American way of life" churn below the surface of the group-mind. Given this uneasiness, the ideals that shape and sustain our societal institutions can become conventional defenses against the truth; we can avoid confronting problems by the standard procedure of repeating slogans and affirming faith. Edward Albee lays open the center of this uneasiness by dealing with "our town" of the 1960s—the American family in suburbia. His treatment is a satiric indictment, sometimes savage, of American manners and mores and the cultural assumptions that shape them. Ideals that Wilder exalts as milk and honey in the Promised Land Albee attacks as the leaven of the Pharisees.

The essential problem that is covered over by manners and mores, as Albee sees it, is the break-down of real communion between individuals. "We neither love nor hurt because we do not try to reach each other," says the protagonist of ***The Zoo Story.*** Observing social amenities and accepting a stereotyped role make it possible for people to converse without communicating, to live together while remaining strangers. Because Albee feels strongly the alienation of the individual in the midst of a group-oriented society, his work has an affinity with the continental playwrights of the Absurd; because he feels that social conventions have become defense mechanisms that contribute substantially to this alienation, his method is that of the satirist.

Though the playwright of the Absurd is also satirist, Albee does not belong to the tribe of Beckett, Ionesco and Genet. The satirical spirit holds the foibles of society up to ridicule in order to restore a balance; the Absurdist goes farther:

> Behind the satirical exposure of the absurdity of inauthentic ways of life, the Theatre of the Absurd is facing up to a deeper layer of absurdity—the absurdity of the human condition itself in a world where the decline of religious belief has deprived man of certainties. When it is no longer possible to accept simple and complete systems of values and revelations of divine purpose, life must be faced in its ultimate, stark reality.[1]

Thus, Absurd drama brings modern man face to face with the Void and explores this moment of confrontation dramatically—what grips the mind, what images occur to the visionary, what emotions arise at this moment. This confrontation is the subject matter of Absurd drama and the individual's reaction to it is the form. Albee does not go this far; ***Virginia Woolf*** does not insist on the ultimate meaninglessness of existence and of the struggle to communicate. Whether man *can* communicate or whether communication is ultimately worth-while Albee does not decide; he does attack the manners and attitudes of society that keep man from communication. Once the artificial barriers are down, then we can see whether or not there is a hope of community. Albee uses the satirist's ax to demolish these barriers.

"Satire," says Northrop Frye, "is militant irony: its moral norms are relatively clear, and its assumed standards against which the grotesque and the absurd are measured."[2] At first glance, it would seem that Albee has no "moral norm" against which to measure American society. He attacks its most cherished assumptions—that the marriage bond is a source of communion, that the business failure is a weakling, that fertility is a blessing—without offering any systematic replacements for these attitudes. He is no Swift who can point to reason and experience as a norm when he exposes the fool and lashes the knave; Albee's *reductio ad absurdum* does not balance abuse against a proper use of objective norms of behavior. Nonetheless, he does invoke, implicitly, a "moral norm"—***Virginia Woolf*** demands that the spectator recognize that societal standards can become defenses that the individual uses to avoid the pain of facing reality. The title is a riddle whose answer enunciates this norm. The threat that is "Virginia Woolf" is the world of fantasy that the attitudes of society can support.

The satirical thrust of the play is indicated by the ironic way in which Albee constructs his façade—setting, dialogue, character-types—to represent a recognizable segment of the American scene. George and Martha live in the small New England town of New Carthage. Their "wonderful old house" suggests the renovated middle-class home with tiled bathroom, door-chimes and a portable bar. There is a comfortable supply of liquor on hand. This atmosphere is lifted to a level of sophistication by the intellectual aura of a college milieu, and invested with more than a suggestion of decadence by the name of the town. "New Carthage" is an ironic comment on the usual comparison (itself not altogether favorable) of American and Roman civilizations. *Carthago delenda est;* the "Romans" of New Carthage are in the process of destroying themselves from within. The enemies leveling the town are its occupants.

The situation of the play—a married couple entertaining another couple—resembles that of a Noel Coward drawing-room comedy, a house party in miniature. The two couples drink together and carry on a conversation in what would be Noel Coward fashion were it not for the language. The elements typical of the situation are submerged by the shock of the dialogue which is very atypical—at least for the stage. The language is not the polished, veiled innuendo that might be expected from this social class (or in the drawing-room comedy), nor do the characters thrust and parry with rapier-like repartee. The weapons here are finger-nails. George and Martha, from the beginning of the play, "tear at one another's vitals" like truck-drivers. The opening expletive sets the tone: "Je*sus.*" Host and hostess do not moderate their language for the sake of the guests; Nick's attempt at polite small-talk is cut off quickly by George's sarcasm and Honey is "monkey-nipples" and "angel-tits" to George, a comparative stranger. By having his characters talk like teamsters, Albee satirizes a social institution which allows strangers to talk brightly together without revealing their real feelings. This house party is *different;* it begins on the level that Eliot's *Cocktail Party* reaches painfully by small-talk indirection. In ***Virginia Woolf*** Albee begins one layer down by making explicit the conflicts that standards of politeness conceal.[3] Thus the contrast between the accepted norm and the real situation is implicit while, at the same time, the playwright points to a blight in the relationships among the characters that is more than social. As George points out: "When one gets down to bone, there is always the marrow." The marrow is what Albee is after.

The cultural attitudes that come under fire in ***Virginia Woolf*** cut across the spectrum of American culture: the success myth, the image of American manhood and womanhood, the institution of marriage itself. These attitudes are defined in the games that are played (which we will investigate as such later) by host, hostess and guests. Their relationships involve certain assumptions on which the action of the play makes an ironic comment.

The marital relationship of George and Martha is qualified, in the first instance, by George's failure to advance in his profession. He is "*in* the History department," but he is "*not* the History department." Even marrying the boss's daughter, the classic climax of the Horatio Alger success-story, is no help to him. "Bogged down," he grows old without hope of preferment. The fact that he cannot compete successfully in academia makes it clear that he could not succeed anywhere. He is, under a façade of wry detachment, the antithesis of the go-ahead charmer that the success myth praises. Martha taunts him with his failure and his intellectuality:

> He'd [George'd] be . . . no good . . . at trustees' dinners, fund raising. He didn't have any . . . personality, you know what I mean? Which was disappointing to Daddy, as you can imagine. So, here I am, stuck with this flop. . . .
>
> *George* (Turning around): . . . don't go on, Martha. . . .
>
> *Martha:* . . . this BOG in the History Department. . . .
>
> *George:* . . . don't, Martha, don't. . . .
>
> *Martha:* . . . who's married to the President's daughter, who's expected to *be* somebody, some bookworm, somebody who's so damn . . . contemplative, he can't make anything out of himself, somebody without the *guts* to make anybody proud of him.[4]

Failing at his job, George cannot come up to standard as husband. The conventional image demands that the husband be breadwinner, the dominant figure in the household, a practical man of affairs. He is a flop and Martha cannot respect him. She controls the activities of the household; George does not know that she has invited guests; he does not assert his rights when she sets out to seduce Nick. Nick's appraisal, though more cautions, is the same as Martha's: "You ineffectual sons of bitches . . . You're the worst" (*VW,* p. 111). George does not meet the minimum standards for a husband set by society. Albee has made sure that George cannot hide behind the mask of achievement. When his worth as a person emerges in the action, it will be clear that it is not dependent on his achievement of status either in the business world or at home.

The character of Martha, as counterpart to George, is an unpleasant parody of the independent and aggressive American female. Her vulgarity, which George underscores at every turn, offsets qualities that the stereotype holds up for admiration. She cultivates the appearance of fertility in spite of her age, she exercises independence in satisfying herself by dominating her environment. If she lacks spiritual refinement, if she dominates her husband, this is not the way she wanted it.

> *Martha:* My arm has gotten tired whipping you.

GEORGE (Stares at her in disbelief): You're mad.

MARTHA: For twenty-three years!

GEORGE: You're deluded . . . Martha, you're deluded.

MARTHA: IT'S NOT WHAT I'VE WANTED!

(*VW*, p. 153)

The judgment of society sits lightly on such a woman because she is only reacting to the abdication of responsibility by her husband. Nonetheless, Albee makes the stereotype repulsive, softening it only by the note of frustration that marks Martha's braying.

Nick and Honey function as contrasts to George and Martha. Nick is the dominant male headed for success, bright, young and aggressive without being too crass (at least at the outset) about it. He has a consuming self-interest and a driving ambition which he masks by a cool deference. His sexual attractiveness makes him a foil for Martha and provides the material for "Hump the Hostess." Honey is the defenseless female, the weaker partner. She is slim-hipped and infertile, given to hysterical pregnancies, no match for the figure Martha cuts. Nick and Martha, then, represent in outline two stereotypes in American culture. Each will suffer, in the course of action, a transformation that amounts to an ironic commentary on a "realistic" societal standard of judgment. The games these people play will strip away the masks and expose both bone and marrow.

Though the traditional Western view of the institution of marriage, rooted in Judaeo-Christian values, is not universally accepted in practice, Americans still pay lip-service to an ideal of married stability and communion. The recent flurry of concern about "togetherness" both reflected a sense of loss of values and also paid tribute to the ideal. In ***Virginia Woolf*** marriage is a matter of expediency. It is the occasion for a vivid antagonism, a highway to success and an opportunity for sexual "fun and games." Martha married George because she was infatuated and because she and her father saw in him a successor to the presidential chair. "I actually fell for him. And the match seemed . . . practical, too. You know Daddy was looking for someone to . . . take over when he was ready to . . . retire" (*VW*, p. 82). Nick married Honey because her father was rich and he wanted to avoid a scandal. Now marriage provides Nick and Martha with opportunities for adultery. This is the rule, not the exception, in New Carthage. George remarks that "musical beds is the faculty sport around here" (*VW*, p. 34). This activity is more than just "fun and games"; it is also the way to promotion. "The way to a man's heart is through his wife's belly" (*VW*, p. 113). The "serious" aspects of the marriage commitment are not fidelity and communion but expediency and "the games people play." The playwright accentuates the satirical contrast between the accepted ideal and the George-Martha relationship by making the really serious business of the play go on in the context of "fun and games."

In order to make this contrast vivid, Albee draws on another American attitude. By and large, the American public takes games very seriously. Dedication to bridge, to golf, to following football and baseball teams is part of the cultural heritage; "being a good sport" is a social virtue. This attitude is the more significant since, in a fragmented culture that has no agreed-upon values, the game creates a severely limited world, tightly organized with absolute rules and values. It generates a miniature culture that exists outside the context of satisfaction of immediate wants and appetites.[5] It constitutes a community, a society, that works together voluntarily according to the order prescribed by the rules. In fact, the distinction between game-experience and life-experience does not lie in the playfulness of one and the seriousness of the other, but rather in the absoluteness and disinterestedness of game-values opposed to the relativity and self-interest of life-values. In ***Virginia Woolf*** only the game supplies a value-system that is meaningful. The rules provide a context for an expression of the personality when they are observed and, even more significantly, when they are broken. These people who cannot love can constitute a play-world of vicious games in which they reach one another by hurting.

The antagonistic spirit that informs this game-world is established from the outset of the play. Even on the level of "ordinary" conversation between husband and wife there are small contests of knowledge and wit: what is the name of the Bette Davis movie? who's afraid of Virginia Woolf? and of alcoholic capacity: "Martha, I gave you that prize years ago . . ." (*VW*, p. 16). When the guests arrive, Nick senses this antagonism and tries to stay aloof from it, to play the neutral guest. George immediately sets about alienating him by not allowing small-talk.

NICK (Indicating the abstract painting): Who . . . who did the . . .?

MARTHA: That? Oh, that's by. . . .

GEORGE: . . . some Greek with a mustache Martha attacked one night in . . .

HONEY (To save the situation): Oh, ho, ho, ho, Ho.

NICK: It's got a . . . a . . .

GEORGE: A quiet intensity?

NICK: Well, no . . . a . . .

GEORGE: Oh. (Pause) Well, then, a certain noisy relaxed quality, maybe?

(*VW*, pp. 21-2)

These antagonisms will fluctuate somewhat. George and Nick, left alone while the ladies go upstairs, confide in one another. These confidences involving the past turn out to be less trustworthy than the revelations of the games.

The content of the games allows the partners to strike at each other by revealing the nature of their private lives. George's failure to achieve distinction in the History department and his abortive attempt at novel-writing are the bases for "Humiliate the Host" (*VW*, p. 38). Nick's opportunistic marriage to Honey and her hysterical pregnancy allows George to retaliate in "Get the Guests" (*VW,* pp. 93, 103). Martha's attraction to Nick, her attachment to her successful father and her desire for revenge in the face of George's indifference to her infidelity provide the ingredients for "Hump the Hostess" (*VW,* pp. 9, 15, 53, 55). Martha's revelation to Nick and Honey that she and George have a son is the foundation for "Bringing Up Baby." Each game results in an excursion into the private world of the individual, a probe that is calculated to hurt the antagonist while justifying the actions of the prober. The innocuous party-game is thereby turned into a means of attack and defense; it creates a miniature culture with rules, conventions and a value-system. The rules are subject to change without notice, it is true, but the antagonist can always turn about and create a new game in response to the challenge.

The games move into the area of the private experiences of the past when "Humiliate the Host" moves from a discussion of George's academic failure (a public fact) to his failure as a novelist. This latter sniping makes use of a private fact that George has covertly revealed to Nick, "bergin" as a mispronunciation of "bourbon." It allows the guests a glimpse of George's past. Up to this point he has been able to score points by ridiculing Nick's specialty and Martha's vulgarity, now he feels his identity at stake. He tries to call a halt: "THE GAME IS OVER!" (*VW,* p. 136). Martha refuses to stop and makes it clear that the incidents of the novel are, at least for the purposes of the game, autobiographical.

This breach of confidence establishes a new set of rules which George promulgates for "Get the Guests." "This is my game! You played yours . . . you people. This is my game!" (*VW,* p. 142). He then uses Nick's confidential statements to construct an allegory that slashes to the bone of Nick and Honey's marriage. As George was hurt by Martha's betrayal of him before the guests, so he adroitly adapts her technique to get revenge on the company. In self-defense, he cuts Nick down to size in front of Martha. "Blondie and his frau out of the plain states came." Honey is literally sickened by the recital and flees to the bathroom; George and Martha add up the score in the interval.

> *Martha:* You make me sick.
>
> *George:* It's perfectly all right for you . . . I mean, you can make your own rules . . . you can go around like a hopped-up Arab, slashing away at everything in sight, scarring up half the world if you want to. But somebody else try it . . . no sir!
>
> (*VW,* pp. 151-2)

Martha then accuses George of masochism—"My arm has gotten tired whipping you." George's countercharge is in the same vein: "You're sick." The real antagonists are now squared off—Martha will play the game suggested earlier by George, "Hump the Hostess" (*VW,* p. 139). He accepts the challenge: "You try it and I'll beat you at your own game" (*VW,* p. 158). Martha's "own game" involves changing the rules at whim in order to strike home more surely; it is now a struggle to the finish.

"Hump the Hostess" develops to a stand-off in which the game degenerates from a test of wit and invention, however cruel, to destructive action. Huizinga remarks that "the predominance of the antagonistic principle does lead to decadence in the long run" because the real feelings that are aroused cannot be easily controlled by the rules.[6] While Martha leads Nick on, George sits in the corner reading a book. Among the standard ground-rules for "Hump the Hostess" is a possessive attitude on the part of the husband, based on proprietal rights if nothing else. Instead, George assumes the intellectual's pose of unconcern so that Martha cannot claim a victory. The spectator knows, however, that he has been stung: after Martha goes upstairs with Nick, he "stands still . . . then, quickly, he gathers all the fury he has been containing within himself . . . he shakes . . . he looks at the book in his hand and, with a cry that is part growl, he hurls it at the chimes" (*VW,* p. 174). In the chiming of the doorbell and in his conversation with Honey on child-bearing, he discovers the ultimate weapon with which to "get" Martha: the "murder" of their son. The final game will be "Bringing Up Baby."

George's references to their "son" have contained a note of warning from the beginning of the play. It is clear that "the kid" is a hole-card that George would rather not play.

> *George:* Just don't start in on the bit, that's all.
>
> *Martha:* The bit? The bit? What kind of language is that? What are you talking about?
>
> . . . . .
>
> *George:* Just don't start in on the bit about the kid, that's all.
>
> (*VW,* p. 18)

Martha does "start in" quite early in the games and "Hump the Hostess" tips the balance; George will murder the child. Martha is soothed into telling the story of their son to Nick and Honey who have now been reduced to spectators. The antagonism that characterized the earlier games is heightened by a head-on collision, Martha claiming that she protected and perfected their son, George claiming the opposite. He then delivers the *coup de grâce;* their son is dead. A dazed Honey corroborates the statement; George "ate" the telegram that contained the announcement. Martha is shattered and defenseless:

> *Martha:* You're not going to get away with this.
>
> *George* (With disgust): YOU KNOW THE RULES, MARTHA, FOR CHRIST'S SAKE, YOU KNOW THE RULES!
>
> *Martha:* No!
>
> *Nick* (With the beginning of a knowledge he cannot face): What are you two talking about?
>
> *George:* I can kill him, Martha, if I want to.
>
> *Martha:* HE IS OUR CHILD!
>
> . . . . .

GEORGE: AND I HAVE KILLED HIM!

(*VW*, p. 235)

Martha has broken the rules by talking about the son with outsiders. And so George has exercised his right to "kill" him. Nick (along with the audience) begins to understand that the son is a figment of Martha's (with George in collusion) imagination: "Jesus Christ, I think I understand this." With Honey as clerk, George finishes the party with a prayer: *Requiescat in pace. Amen.* The party is over.

It is clear that the games provide a comment on the masculine and feminine stereotypes outlined above and also on the relative values that American society places on them. Through antagonistic contact, the give-and-take of the game framework, Albee reverses the roles of the contenders. Nick, the virile, practical scientist, and Martha, Earth-goddess and mother, are cut down to size, and their masks destroyed. When Nick fails to give satisfaction in "Hump the Hostess," Martha declares that George is the only man who has ever done so and Nick is relegated to the role of houseboy, which was George's role in the first act: "Get over there and answer the door" (*VW*, p. 19)

MARTHA: You can be houseboy around here for a while. You can start off being houseboy right now.

NICK: Look, lady, I'm no flunky to you.

MARTHA (Cheerfully): Sure you are! You're ambitious, aren't you, boy? You didn't chase me around the kitchen and up the goddamn stairs out of mad, driven passion, did you now? You were thinking a little bit about your career, weren't you? Well, you can just houseboy your way up the ladder for a while.

(*VW*, p. 194)

The image of the sexually dominant and ambitious male loses stature when Nick is forced to accept this role. Martha alone is unscathed up to "Bringing Up Baby"; her image as the Earth-mother who teems with fertility and sex appeal is destroyed by that game. For all practical purposes her final status approximates Honey's; once George has destroyed the baby, Martha is infertile and childlike. The impractical and ineffectual George has established control over the threesome. These idols of American culture are shown to have clay feet.

The social satire that the playwright injects through the games is augmented by the use of ritual details. The subterranean seriousness of the play-world is underscored by a gradual progression from a house-party atmosphere into the atmosphere of ritual. The title of the second act "Walpurgisnacht" suggests a preternatural context that parallels the Witches' Sabbath in Goethe's *Faust.* In that play Mephistopheles describes the scene to his companion:

Just look! You barely see the other end.

A hundred fires in a row, my friend!

They dance, they chat, they cook, they drink, they court.

Now you tell me where there's better sport![7]

As in the Witches' Sabbath, the couples drink, chat, and kiss; Martha and Nick dance as a prelude to the game of "Hump the Hostess." George remarks on the nature of the dance: "It's a familiar dance . . . It's a very old ritual . . . as old as they come" (*VW*, p. 131). This New England house is also the mountaintop where the witches gather—those unholy souls who congregate to observe the May festival.[8]

The Faustian analogue includes another illuminating reference to the games. The celebrants of Walpurgisnacht participate in "half-childish games" and there is posed "many a riddle knottily tied." People crowd about the Devil, says Faust, "where many riddles must be solved," and the Devil, adds Mephistopheles, poses many new ones of his own.[9] The ritual riddle has a significance for the persons who must solve it; it is, in this context, a matter of life-and-death.

From one point of view all the games in ***Virginia Woolf*** are riddles, word-games in that they depend on the exercise of power in knowledge. The riddle is a means of expressing and concealing knowledge; in primitive cultures the secrets of the tribe are often concealed in a riddle. The man who could unknot it acquired the wisdom it contained, and with that wisdom, power.

The riddle is a sacred thing full of secret power, hence a dangerous thing. In its mythological or ritual context it is nearly always what German philologists know as the *Halsrätsel* or "capital riddle," which you either solve or forfeit. The player's life is at stake.[10]

Thus "Who's Afraid of Virginia Woolf?" can be read as a "capital riddle." It seems to require no answer at the outset but gathers significance in repetition. Unless it can be finally solved, the players are in danger of not finding an identity to replace the one they have lost in the games. Other riddling features of the games include the "bergin" narrative which gives the strangers the power of understanding George's past. Martha uses a riddle-form in framing her revelation about his past:

Well, Georgie-boy had lots of big ambitions

In spite of something funny in his past. . . .

Which Georgie-boy turned into a novel

His first attempt and also his last. . . .

Hey! I rhymed! I rhymed!

(*VW*, p. 133)

Martha's insistence on the rhyme calls attention to the riddle-form—a capsulated mystery to be solved. George does not employ rhyme in his story of "Blondie and his frau," but the allegorical style, with its reference to "Childe Roland," achieves a similar effect. Both put their material into a formal pattern that at once reveals and conceals. The lives of the players do depend on the answers to these riddles in that, when the other players solve them, the individual loses identity and can no longer exercise the same kind of control over the situation. George, Nick and Honey are exposed, to some extent, in the first three games; Martha is exposed in "Bringing Up Baby," the climactic riddle-game which adds explicitly ritual actions.

The most notable ritual addition is George's use of the Roman Catholic funeral service as accompaniment to the news of "Baby's" passing. He has built up to this by bringing in snapdragons to the chant *"Flores par los muertos."* The mock solemnity of this chant, with its veiled threat, becomes explicitly antagonistic when George throws the flowers, spear-like, at Martha. But the antagonism goes underground and the ritual solemnity is focused when George begins to recite the requiem. He vouches for the objectivity of his message and the necessity of the death of the son by following the ritual. Though this "news" is part of the game, George is not joking. Baby is dead and cannot be resurrected by any effort on Martha's part. The ritual dimension guarantees the objectivity of this game and its far-reaching effect. What is destroyed here is not only a social stereotype but a conviction about procreation that reaches into the marrow of the human situation.

"Bringing Up Baby" raises a question about the nature of the union between husband and wife. Though all the games demonstrate that social conventions cannot be defenses against life-experience, the illusions attacked in the first three games are fostered by certain conventional American attitudes: that a man must be a success in his profession or trade, that marriage is a romantic adventure based on "true love," that adultery is "fun and games." "Bringing Up Baby" does not quite fit the pattern here. It attacks a convention less ephemeral than these: the notion that the child is (or can be) a real bond of union between husband and wife. While it can be argued that the child is imaginary and so hardly a fair test-case, the fact is that, in ***Virginia Woolf,*** even the couple that has a child is sterile. The child is laid to rest with the ritual solemnity of a funeral service, its relationship to each parent is argued at length, it has as much reality as the experiences that are related about George's parents and Martha's father. Whether or not we like it, what the final game says is clear enough—the child functioned as an actual child of flesh and blood would function in marriage. George and Martha have stayed together "for the sake of the child." Albee is ultimately striking at a radical and accepted attitude toward marriage: the child as bond of union between the partners.

The episode of the "imaginary baby" has been the largest stumbling block for critics who have evaluated the play. They are in general agreement that introduction of the child is inept and incredible, and their judgment ranges from a gentle disagreement with this sequence to a bitter indictment of the entire play.[11] The issue is taken to be the credibility of the child. Certainly, if the play is seen as the tragedy of two incompatible neurotics, the imaginary baby should be thrown out with the bath-water. But the same difficulty regarding credibility can be leveled at the contents of the other games; histories narrated by George and Martha contain details that seem to contribute to an understanding of their present situation, but on reflection it is impossible to sort out fact from fiction. The "bergin" story seems to go far toward explaining George's lack of virility and passiveness in the marital situation. He hated his parents and destroyed them. But uncertainties proliferate as the factual contents of the stories are weighed in the balance. The conclusion of the murder tale that George tells Nick does not fit the facts. "He was put in an asylum. That was thirty years ago. . . . And I'm told for these thirty years he has . . . not . . . uttered . . . one . . . sound" (*VW,* p. 96). On the other hand, Martha talks as if another detail were actually true: "You'd wish you'd died in that automobile, you bastard" (*VW,* p. 154). Finally, there is no certainty at all about the actual events:

> *George:* Once . . . once, when I was sailing past Majorca, drinking on deck with a correspondent who was talking about Roosevelt, the moon went down, thought about it for a little . . . considered it, you know what I mean: . . . and then, POP, came up again. Just like that.
>
> *Martha:* That is not true! That is such a lie!
>
> *George:* You must not call everything a lie, Martha. (To Nick) Must she?
>
> *Nick:* Hell, I don't know when you people are lying, or what.
>
> . . . . .
>
> *Martha:* You were never in the goddamn Mediterranean at all . . . ever. . . .
>
> *George:* I certainly was! My Mommy and Daddy took me there as a college graduation present.
>
> (*VW,* pp. 199-200).

It is not even clear how seriously we are to take Martha's story about the lawn boy, her first husband. When Nick brings him up again, she says: "I'd forgotten him. But when I think about him and me it's almost like being a voyeur" (*VW,* p. 190). George sums up the situation in the prelude to the final game: "Truth and illusion. Who knows the difference, eh, toots?" (*VW,* p. 201). The "truth" of the son's existence lies in the subjective reactions to it. The other games may involve illusions that are "true"; whether or not George actually killed his parents is not at issue. He may have created the experience for fictional purposes, but he treats it as real. Their son must "die" because he is—in some sense—real. Logically, then, it seems that what the critics are objecting to is not a breach of dramatic credibility, but rather the *significance* of the son's presence and demise. "Bringing Up Baby" makes an uncomfortable point; it is no wonder that the critics are restive under its impact.

We have seen, then, that the setting, character-types and the use of situations conspire to produce ironic contrasts between accepted social conventions, cultural stereotypes and the actual relationships between persons. The structure of the play reinforces these contrasts and makes a statement of its own about them.

Northrop Frye points out that "as structure, the central principle of ironic myth is best approached as a parody of romance: the application of romantic mythical forms to a more realistic content which fits them in unexpected ways."[12] The game-motif and what it reveals is the "realistic content" in ***Virginia Woolf***; the structure is "romantic" in that it follows the comic pattern in outline and in detail. The movement of the plot, then, is the familiar one of temporary liaison followed by separation and alienation which heals into a new union at the conclusion of the play. Underneath the snarl and snap of the dialogue and the satiric twists given to the incidents, ***Virginia Woolf*** progresses to a wedding.

The phases of this comic structure are carefully defined in the action. It is important to notice that the incidents that define the structural movement occur outside the context of the games. At the outset, after the opening riddles, George and Martha make it clear that their marriage is not altogether satisfactory:

> *Martha:* I swear . . . if you existed I'd divorce you.. . .
>
> *George:* Well, just stay on your feet, that's all. . . . These people are your guests, you know, and. . . .
>
> *Martha:* I can't even see you . . . I haven't been able to see you for years. . . .
>
> *George:* . . . if you pass out, or throw up, or something. . . .
>
> *Martha:* . . . I mean, you're a blank, a cipher. . . .
>
> (*VW*, p. 17)

Their "communication" is a double monologue, each trying to hurt the other with invective and name-calling. There is vital contact, but this contact does nothing to reassure us about the future of their relationship.

The mutual violations of confidence that follow threaten this antagonistic mode of communication and, at the center of the drama, Martha announces that the order of their world has broken down. Outside of the game-context, she tells her husband:

> You know what's happened, George? You want to know what's *really happened?* (Snaps her fingers) It's snapped, finally. Not me . . . *it.* The whole arrangement. You can go along . . . forever, and everything's manageable. You make all sorts of excuses to yourself. . . *you* know . . . this is life . . . the hell with it . . . maybe tomorrow he'll be dead . . . maybe tomorrow you'll be dead . . . all sorts of excuses. But then, one day, one night, something happens . . . and SNAP! It breaks.
>
> (*VW*, pp. 156-7)

There is no further attempt to explain the "snap"; the pressure on the rapport, tenuous at best, is cumulative and the straw that breaks the camel's back snaps the bond. The point of complete separation is indicated clearly because, apparently, after the snap nothing has changed. The games go on; Martha continues to play, though "Hump the Hostess" is not just a word-game, and George plays by refusing to accept the stereotyped role of outraged husband. "I'll beat you at your own game" (*VW*, p. 158) Thus the break, as described in the dialogue above, seems gratuitous. It functions rather to define the plot-pattern, to call attention to the divisions of structure.

The final movement of the structure, as we have come to expect, is the reconciliation of the principals, the "wedding" or conclusion of the pattern. We are prepared for this reconciliation by Martha's confession to Nick, again outside the games, that George is the man for her. She begins to face her own problems, but without much hope:

> [To Nick] You're all flops. I am the Earth Mother, and you're all flops. (More or less to herself) I disgust me. I pass my life in crummy, totally pointless infidelities . . . (Laughs ruefully) *would*-be infidelities. Hump the Hostess? That's a laugh. A bunch of boozed-up . . . impotent lunk-heads. . . . That's how it is in civilized society. (To herself again) All the gorgeous lunk-heads. Poor babies. (To Nick, now: earnestly) There is only one man in my life who has ever made me happy. Do you know that? One! . . . George; my husband.
>
> . . . . .
>
> George who is out somewhere there in the dark. . . . George who is good to me, and whom I revile; who understands me, and whom I push off; who can make me laugh, and I choke it back in my throat; who can hold me, at night, so that it's warm, and whom I will bite so there's blood; who keeps learning the games we play as quickly as I can change the rules; who can make me happy and I do not wish to be happy, and yes, I do wish to be happy. George and Martha: sad, sad, sad.
>
> (*VW*, pp. 189-91)

Here Martha recognizes her problem—she wishes to be happy and she has no right to be happy. "They" are all flops and she is the Earth Mother, but she is not happy with her dominant role. George made the "hideous mistake" of loving her and "must be punished for it" (*VW*, p. 191). Martha feels that she is not worth loving and she has punished herself for it. But there is no hope for her alone; "Bringing Up Baby" can save her, but only on George's initiative. The reconciliation occurs because George kills their son and, with him, the image of herself that holds Martha captive.

After the games are over and the ritual laid aside, George and Martha are reconciled. They find the answer to the "capital" riddle "Who's Afraid of Virginia Woolf?" in the destruction of Martha's fantasy. She is stripped of her role as Earth Mother, the fertile goddess, powerful and attractive, by George's refusal to "play." The sought-for communion becomes a possibility when Martha accepts their sterility, facing the truth rather than hiding in illusion; the communion which heretofore has been accessible only in the antagonism of the game-context is available in the cold, five-o'clock-in-the-morning world of a mutual need.

> *George* (Long silence): It will be better.
>
> *Martha:* (Long silence): I don't . . . know.
>
> *George:* It will be . . . maybe.
>
> . . . . .
>
> *Martha:* Just . . . us?
>
> *George:* Yes.
>
> (*VW,* pp. 240-1)

Martha is now afraid of Virginia Woolf, of that private world of fantasy built into a public face according to what society expects and demands. Without masks, husband and wife can begin to create a new life, maybe, out of a mutual isolation and a mutual need.

The satiric tone of the play seems to have disappeared in this final scene—two exhausted people alone in the cold light of dawn seem to have little satiric potential left. Albee's use of the comic structure, however, continues to make its own comment. In the drawing-room comedy the "reconciliation" movement would have a bright uplift about it, "true" love triumphing in a sophisticated way. In a broader perspective, this "reconciliation" would involve a kômos, the "unmasking" of bride and bridegroom that reveals their true identity in a nuptial ceremony that celebrates fertility and the birth of a new society. The prototype here remains the wedding of the Earth-goddess and the Eniautos daimon; the resonances of fertility and new life that are explicit in that marriage endure in all the variations of it. In ***Virginia Woolf*** these resonances are established by the playwright to create an ironic contrast with the final situation of George and Martha.

The irony here is observable, first, in the identity of the reconciled parties. Martha, who claimed an Earth-goddess identity until unmasked by "Bringing Up Baby," is a tired and lonely child, dependent on George. George's "unmasking," however, does not involve so obvious a revelation. He never had a chance to disguise himself in an accepted stereotype; his pose as a detached intellectual is as much a weapon for attack as a mask for defense. Behind his egghead pose works the eiron who uses his detachment to destroy the alazontes, the intruders, that are in charge of society.[13] The function as eiron explains the quasi-heroic impression we have of George. His philosophic stance toward the situations he cannot change immediately liberates him for the attack when the time is ripe. Because of it, he is capable of seeing the complexities of data in experience. When he tries to warn Nick about the dangers of social-climbing by adultery, and Nick answers with an obscenity, "Up yours!" George replies:

> You take the trouble to construct a civilization . . . to . . . build a society, based on principles of . . . of principle . . . you endeavor to make communicable sense out of natural order, morality out of the unnatural disorder of man's mind . . . you make government and art, and realize that they are, must be, both the same . . . you bring things to the saddest of all points . . . to the point where there *is* something to lose . . . then all at once, through all the music, through all the sensible sounds of men building, attempting, comes the *Dies Irae.* And what is it? What does the trumpet sound? Up yours. I suppose there's justice to it, after all the years. . . . Up yours.
>
> (*VW,* p. 117)

George's warnings to Nick and to Martha are largely ignored so that he has to attack. This feature of his character reflects a specific eiron that has for its model a traditional figure from romance—the giant-killer.[14]

In the final phase, then, George's character appears "unmasked" as "giant-killing eiron." There has been considerable preparation for this revelation through the course of the play. After Martha's recitation of her one-punch knockout victory over George, he gives the company a turn by popping a parasol from a short-barreled shotgun. "POW! . . . You're dead! Pow! You're dead." He "might kill" the braying Earth-goddess someday (*VW,* pp. 57, 60). After "Get the Guests," Martha compliments George on his "pigmy-hunting." He replies: "Baby, if quarterback there is a pigmy, you've certainly changed your style. What are you after now . . . giants?" (*VW,* p. 151). The "giant-killer" image continues into the last act when he throws the snapdragons at Martha. "Snap went the dragons!" (*VW,* p. 202). This symbolic violence leads up to the slaying of the most significant dragon, the imaginary son. Like the over-matched Davids of the romance, he destroys those enemies of truth who are in charge of the society, the conventional images and attitudes, personified in Nick and Martha, that are obstacles to a communion in spirit and in truth.

Beside the unmaskings, the ironic conclusion of ***Virginia Woolf*** reverses the significance of other comic motifs: the celebration of fertility and the establishment of a new social order. Though Albee uses some of the images that traditionally reinforce the fertility motif, he inverts their meaning. The snapdragons that George picks "in Daddy's greenhouse" by the light of the moon are "flowers for the dead." They do not come from the garden outside, but from the hothouse—force-fed and artificial. Martha sees them as a "wedding bouquet": "Pansies! Rosemary! Violence! My wedding bouquet!" (*VW,* p. 196). The Ophelia overtones here connect the fertility images of flowers, water and the bridal with death. When George hurls the snapdragons at Martha, he echoes her "SNAP!" the breakdown of their tenuous relationship. The cumulative effect of this irony is added to the explicit development of the sterility motif in Honey's character. She is afraid of child-bearing and reverts to the child's role when she is threatened by it—lying in a foetal position "sucking her thumb" on the cool bathroom floor. When Martha's situation is finally equated with Honey's at the unmasking, the symbols of fecundity with which she is surrounded, ironically treated as they are, simply reinforce her sterile condition.

From this perspective the ritual killing of the child also reverses a traditional pattern. Instead of a wedding ceremony there is a funeral; the child, which could be seen as a new creation symbolic of rebirth, is shown to be an illusion, an obstacle to real communion. Martha does see the child as savior, a medium of reconciliation and redemption in a hostile universe.

> And as he grew . . . and as he grew . . . oh! so wise! . . . he walked evenly between us . . . (She spreads her hands) . . . a hand out to each of us for what we could offer by way of support, affection, teaching, even love . . . and these hands, still, to hold us off a bit, for mutual protection, to protect us all from George's . . . weakness . . . and my . . . necessary greater strength . . . to protect himself and *us*.
>
> (*VW*, p. 222)

In Martha's fantasy, this savior-child is "poor lamb" who broke his arm when a cow moo'd back at him—the two sacrificial symbols of Dionysus and Christ are morticed together here by an allusion to James Joyce[15] (*VW*, p. 221). He is also a child of the sun, Apollo, with his rubber-tipped bow and arrow under his bed, and a *lux oriens*:[16] "the one light in all this hopeless *dark*ness . . . OUR SON" (*VW*, p. 227). George sees the baby not as Dionysus or Christ born to inaugurate a new age or to save his people, but as a demon to be exorcized, the product of a Walpurgisnacht orgy. While Martha eulogizes the savior, George asks in ritual Latin that they be allowed to rest in peace when the Lord comes to judge the world by fire. *"Dum veneris judicare saeculum per ignem"* (*VW*, p. 227). The suitable rite is the funeral service and a judgment on the world. There is no savior, neither Dionysus nor Christ, available to the cosmos of New Carthage.

The "new social order" established by this conclusion is "just us," two people alone in their weakness and their need. Martha sends Nick and Honey home; they leave wordlessly, for there is nothing to be said. George shows his concern for Martha in this late, cold and tired world.

> *George:* Do you want anything, Martha?
>
> *Martha* (Still looking away): No . . . nothing.
>
> *George:* All right. (Pause) Time for bed.
>
> *Martha:* Yes.
>
> (*VW*, p. 239).

This mutual concern, for the truth as they see it and for each other with George exercising his role as protector and with Martha accepting him in it, is all the couple has to work with. Tomorrow is another day—"Sunday, all day"—and perhaps, with the evil giants dead and the riddle of ***Virginia Woolf*** solved, things will be better . . . perhaps.

We now perceive that the "convention" that is being attacked finally in ***Virginia Woolf*** is the notion that we can expect salvation from without. The standards of politeness that govern social intercourse serve to conceal a basic antagonism. Once the veneer has been peeled off, like the label on Honey's brandy bottle, and the essential problem of communication is revealed, Albee is able to strike at the radical "illusion," as he sees it, the hope of salvation from some agent outside the individual. History and religious cult do not hold out any such hope; George, quoting Spengler, demolishes progressive optimism: "And the west, encumbered by crippling alliances, and burdened with a morality too rigid to accommodate itself to the swing of events, must . . . eventually . . . fall" (*VW*, p. 174). The only applicable rituals are the "capital-riddle," a witches' sabbath and the requiem Mass. Biology, as typified by Nick, offers only the tyranny of the super-man, a race of smooth, blond men right at the middleweight limit "dedicated to and working for the greater glory of the super-civilization" (*VW*, p. 66). The forces of nature no longer offer ground for hope; entering into the creation of new life does not afford a psychological basis for the union of husband and wife. The creative urge has no magic in it that can unify the procreators. It is simple biology, mechanistic and impersonal. The tendency to deify this urge in the "divine child" is one more convention that keeps man from realizing the truth of his condition.

Whether or not ***Virginia Woolf*** is a fair test of this latter view can be questioned. The critical dissatisfaction with the device of the "imaginary child" seems ultimately to stem from a restiveness about the validity of Albee's treatment. By introducing the ritual details, Albee is trying to universalize a particular case, that is, he moves from satire on *American* attitudes to an ironic comment on values that permeate all Western culture. George and Martha's last name may be "Washington"; we are not so willing to accept "Mankind." We find it hard to believe that the birth of an actual child would have made no difference at all in their relationship. The cultural generalization is much too sweeping. Thus the dissatisfaction with the denouement is more than an objection to the imaginary nature of the baby. The unitive potential of procreation is still an accepted value in our society; it is precisely this value that Albee calls into question in ***Virginia Woolf.***

Uneasiness over this issue of creative potential is increased by the fact that ***Virginia Woolf,*** in the final scene, ceases to be satire. In his one-act plays Albee often reaches into the vitals of American attitudes to strike at what he thinks sham and superficiality. In ***The Zoo Story*** he reveals the complacent businessman to be a vegetable incapable of experiencing any kind of real feeling; in ***The American Dream*** he presents our idealization of physical beauty and sexual power in all its vacuity. The validity of the satire in these plays rests on the exposure of the veneer that disguises fear, ruthlessness, savagery and self-interest without any attempt to solve the problems. There is always an implicit recognition of the depth of the problem. It cannot be solved by any quick panacea. It is the mark of the satirist that he avoids the simple solution: "It is precisely the complexity of data in experience which the satirist insists on and the simple set of standards that he distrusts."[17] The conclusion of ***Virginia Woolf,*** however, advocates a simple standard: no salvation from without, a reliance on "truth" and the resources of the personality. Though Albee sounds the "maybe" of caution with regard to the final situation of George and Martha, he also holds out a "romantic" hope that "it will be better." But the ironist of the first two-and-a-half acts has left his imprint on the play. There seems no reason why the old cycle of games should not begin again.

Though George and Martha do find a new basis for union, their union is isolationist, sterile, dependent on a mutual need. They are left facing the Void. When all the props of manners and mores have been kicked away, there is only the wasteland into which no life-giving streams flow. The note of hope that rings in their mutual concern seems like whistling in the graveyard. In the last analysis being afraid of Virginia Woolf in the world of New Carthage is not much different than simply being afraid.

Notes

[1]Martin Esslin, *The Theatre of the Absurd* (Garden City, N.Y., 1961), p. 292.

[2]*Anatomy of Criticism,* p. 223.

[3]There is a striking parallel to the *Virginia Woolf* situation and an illustration of the "polite" level of concealment in a poem from another era, George Meredith's sonnet sequence "Modern Love." Meredith treats the theme of alienation and infidelity in marriage. Sonnet 17 in the sequence describes a dinner party with husband and wife presiding:

> At dinner she is hostess, I am host.
> Went the feast ever cheerfuller? She keeps
> The Topic over intellectual deeps
> In buoyancy afloat. They see no ghost.
> With sparkling surface-eyes we ply the ball:
> It is in truth a most contagious game:
> HIDING THE SKELETON, shall be its name.
> Such a play as this the devils might appall!

[4]Edward Albee, *Who's Afraid of Virginia Woolf?* (New York, 1965), p. 85. Subsequent citations in the text, abbreviated vw, refer to this edition.

[5]See J. Huizinga, *Homo Ludens* (London, 1949), pp. 7-15.

[6]Ibid., pp. 74-75.

[7]*Faust,* trans. Walter Kaufmann (Garden City, N.Y., 1961), 11. 4056-9.

[8]The Faustian allusion tempts the reader to allegorize. Identifying Faust and Mephistopheles with Nick and George respectively (or vice versa) is a fascinating intellectual exercise, but the parallels do not work out. For instance, when Mephistopheles leads Faust from a larger celebration to a small conclave of minor pleasures, Mephistopheles announces that he will be matchmaker and Faust suitor. Faust dances with a young witch, Mephistopheles dances with the "old" witch (*Faust,* 11. 4123-27). The reference to *Faust* is rather a matter of atmosphere. The trip to Brocken is phantasmagoric, a transition to the world of the grotesque. "The Walpurgisnacht is a dream sequence mirroring an inner state of moral and emotional confusion . . . Spring rites in which the humanist might discern survivals of ancient fertility worship are viewed . . . as a cult of obscenity and bestiality, so that pregnancy and birth—the theme is traditional in the lore of witchcraft, but the emphasis given it would indicate that Faust has at least considered the possibility of Margarete's being with child—represent only ugliness and evil." See Stuart Atkins, *Goethe's Faust* (Cambridge, Mass., 1958), pp. 90-93.

[9]*Faust,* ll. 4039-41.

[10]Huizinga, *Homo Ludens,* p. 108.

[11]The favorable critical extreme is represented by John Gassner ("Broadway in Review," *Educational Theatre Journal,* XV [March, 1963], 77-80) who compares Albee with O'Neill, then states: "Does not the play move to a veritable anticlimax, moreover, when cause and effect are so disproportionate; when we learn at the end that they never had a son to whom something terrible had happened? They have been tearing at each other's vitals for a deprivation that does not prevent some human beings from behaving with decency and consideration toward each other." At the other extreme, Richard Schnechner ("Who's Afraid of Edward Albee?" *Tulane Drama Review,* VII [Spring, 1963], 7-10) writes: "There is no real, hard bed-rock of suffering in *Virginia Woolf*—it is all illusory, depending on a "child" who never was born: a gimmick, a trick, a trap. And there is no solid creative suffering in the writer who meanders through a scene stopping here and there for the sake of a joke or an easy allusion that almost fits." Neither critic considers the satiric nature of the play; *Virginia Woolf* is not a tragedy or a near-tragedy.

[12]*The Anatomy of Criticism,* p. 223.

[13]"The *eiron* is the man who deprecates himself, as opposed to the *alazon.* Such a man makes himself invulnerable, and though Aristotle disapproved of him, there is no question that he is a predestined artist, just as the alazon is one of his predestined victims." See Northrop Frye, *Anatomy of Criticism,* p. 40.

[14]Ibid., pp. 227-28.

[15]"once upon a time and a very good time it was there was a moocow coming down along the road and this moocow that was coming down along the road met a nicens little boy named baby tuckoo. . . ." This "moocow" image is later transmogrified into the image of the "crowned bull," *bous stephanoforos,* that is identified with the hero Stephen Daedalus (*A Portrait of the Artist* [New York, 1964], p. 7). The *bous stephanoforos* leads the procession in a late spring festival of Dionysus (See *Themis,* pp. 153-4). This connection is strengthened by the earlier reference to Martha's paganism: "Martha is the only true pagan on the eastern seaboard" (vw, p. 73). It is confirmed by Martha's claim to the title of "Earth Mother." Dionysus, Zeus-Young Man, is the son of Semele, the Thracian Earth Mother. (See Jane Ellen Harrison, *Mythology* [Boston, 1924], p. 134.) This Dionysian reference is bracketed by Christ imagery. George quotes the sequence of the funeral Mass: "*Et gratia tua illis succurrente, merantur evadere judicium ultionis*—And with the help of your grace, may they be able to escape the vengeful judgment." The boy breaks his arm—"poor lamb." Both Christ and Dionysus were "sons of God," suffered, died and were resurrected. It suffices to say that, in *Virginia Woolf,* the savior-image is firmly attached by these resonances to the child.

[16]In his first appearances in Greek literature, the bow-and-arrow is the equipment of Apollo. In the Homeric hymn he draws near with his shining bended bow. In the first Book of the Iliad he appears as "Fardarting Apollo, and "fierce is the clang of the silver bow." Later he appears as his own counterpart, that is, the Destroyer is also Healer. He is also equated, in Orphic literature, with the sun. "Helios = supreme god = Dionysus = Apollo." (See W.K.C. Guthrie, *Orpheus and Greek Religion* [London, 1952], p. 43.) To this resonance is added that of "fleece": "in the sun his hair . . . became . . . fleece" (*VW,* p. 220). The boy, relates Martha, scooped out a banana to make a boat with green-grape oarsmen and orange-slice shields—a miniature *Argos* in the light of the above reference. The story of the golden fleece combines the motif of sacrifice with that of sterility. A famine in Alus is to be adverted by sacrifice of the King's children who escape on the ram with the golden fleece (J.G. Fraser, *The New Golden Bough,* ed. Theodor H. Gaster [New York, 1964], pp.

Paul Eddington as George and Joan Plowright as Martha in *Who's Afraid of Virginia Woolf?* at the National Theatre, London, 1981.

296-7). Martha's vision of her child makes him savior and hero; he *will* die for his parents, but ironically, according to George's formula.

[17]Frye, *Anatomy of Criticism,* p. 232.

Rictor Norton (essay date 1971)

SOURCE: "Folklore and Myth in *Who's Afraid of Virginia Woolf?,*" in *Renascence,* Vol. XXIII, No. 3, Spring 1971, pp. 159-67.

[*In the following essay, Norton argues that* Who's Afraid of Virginia Woolf? *is unified by "underlying mythic patterns."*]

Most critics have recognized the presence of mythic symbolism in Edward Albee's ***Who's Afraid of Virginia Woolf?,*** but few have done little more than to mention in passing that Martha is a self-confessed Earth Mother, and that George might be a comic Dionysus. Critics have not demonstrated how the mythic folklore levels of the play give coherent meaning and unification to it. The symbolism is usually seen as an absurdist counter to the action on stage rather than as an essential embodiment of that action, and some critics apparently feel, as does Daniel McDonald, that "the danger in reading Albee's ***Who's Afraid of Virginia Woolf*** is becoming too involved with the symbolism. The individual who is largely concerned with [the symbolism] will miss the point of a fine drama. Essentially, the play is not an allegory about Godot, or Good Deeds, or the American Dream; it is a story of real people and their illusions. . . . [Albee's] theme is the necessity of illusion to sustain one in such an environment [of futility]."[1] I hope I have not missed the dramatic values of the play, even though I shall give little attention to them in this study, but I doubt that a consideration solely of the realistic level of the drama will sufficiently enable us to grasp its "point" or theme. I feel that McDonald, by undervaluing the symbolism, has in fact misinterpreted the theme of the drama. That which is illusory on the realistic level is often that which is more "real" on the symbolic level. As I shall show presently, the son's "real" but symbolic rather than actual existence is important in recognizing the positive and affirmative nature of Albee's drama; without any symbolic considerations we might too easily interpret the play only in negative terms. It is true that Albee has not written an absurdist allegory, as he did in ***The American Dream***; but he has gone far beyond this, and has succeeded in uniting myth and realism. To make a primordial ritual appealing to the contemporary audience, he has hinted at basic ritual patterns by the use of jokes, allusions, and illusions.

Who's Afraid of Virginia Woolf? occurs within the framework of the concepts of *Dies Irae,* Easter, and The Birthday; Albee originally planned to entitle it *The Exorcism,* but relegated this as the title of the third act.[2] It is a ritual of purgation and purification, a Dionysian revel in New England, a "tragedy" in the original sense of the term—a "goat song." Martha is the Mother Goddess, in her particular manifestation as the Bitch Goddess, fought over by Nick, the God of the New Year, and George, the God of the Old Year. George allows Nick to possess Martha during an intercalary moment, but reasserts his divinity by devouring his son in the form of a eucharistic telegram, thus being reborn.

The primary level of the play consists of the conflict between Nick's Apollonian faith in the perfection of man by biological means, and George's Dionysian faith in the historical process of birth, life, death, and rebirth. This level is set in a New England college town which allows us to believe in the existence of such people as George and Martha. They are two ultra-sophisticates who make clever jokes, drink a great deal, and take out their frustrations upon each other and their guests. Such New England college towns, such professors, and such professors' wives are not actually "realistic"; but they are convincing because they fit certain traditions and stereotypes.

This setting provides the believability of the clever jokes, abundant drinking, and the mental and physical violence which occur in the play. This primary level justifies "absurd" references to nursery rhymes and ancient ritual, the secondary and tertiary levels of the play. The folklore level—the big bad wolf and the three little pigs—serves as a link between the first and third levels by being as foolish as the college town setting, and by pointing to the myth of the pig goddess Demeter. I shall try to elucidate these last two levels by an analysis of the title, the time and place of the setting, and the characters. My basic critical assumption is that nothing in the play is "absurd," arbitrary, fortuitous, or superfluous, but that everything is symbolically interrelated.

* * *

Critics have regarded the title as merely one more example of Albee's absurdist technique; or, they may go so far as to interpret it as "Who's afraid of the truth, or the stripping away of reality?" This may be partially correct, but as a meaning it does not organically inhere to the title *per se;* it is merely a substitute title. A more meaningful interpretation might be found by giving serious attention to its source in the nursery rhyme:

> Who's afraid of the big bad wolf,
> the big bad wolf,
> the big bad wolf;
> Who's afraid of the big bad wolf,
> So early in the morning?

The folk tale which encloses this song concerns three little pigs who each built a house—one of straw, one of sticks, and one of brick. The two pigs who built their houses of straw and sticks sing this song in mockery of the third little pig who built his house of brick. They think that he is foolish to go to such trouble to protect himself from the big bad wolf, whom they fear not. But, alas, their houses are blown down—"I'll huff, and I'll puff, and I'll blow your house down"—and, in some versions, they are eaten. The third little pig's house survives the onslaught, and the wolf dies when he sneaks in through the chimney and lands in the fireplace or pot of boiling water. Moral: If you do not fear the wolf sufficiently, you shall be destroyed. In the Egyptian, Roman, Gnostic, and Nordic mythologies, the wolf symbolizes the chaotic and destructive potential of the universe. The pigs symbolize different types of humans on their most animalistic level. The one who builds his house—*i. e.,* his repository of wisdom, out of the firmest substance—*i. e.,* the strongest and truest, endures; he who most acknowledges the reality of the wolf's power is the most able to cope with it. Now what has this to do with the play?

I suggest that Honey is the first little pig. That she is a pig is evidenced by George's manner of calling her back to the party: "(*Hog-calls toward the hall*) Sooowwwiiieee! Sooowwwiiieee!" She is "a petite blond girl, rather plain"—that is, rather straw-complexioned, and her frail response to reality is a mere house of straw, one which was blown down: "The wind was . . . the wind was so cold." Martha is the second little pig. Or rather a big pig. Martha is an amalgam of a number of animals, but that she is a pig is evidenced by George's calling her a "Cochon," literally, "pig" or"swine" in French. Her house of sticks, stronger than Honey's straw, is torn away and her inner being is left brutally exposed, enabling her insight into her illusion at the end of the play. George is the third little pig: Martha shouts "You pig!" and he replies "Oink! Oink!" George is fully aware of the wolf's power of destruction, but survives it and uses it to destroy the illusions of the others and to make way for rebirth. Nick is the big bad wolf. He huffs and puffs, and he conceives a "puff" in Honey instead of a baby, and is impotent with Martha. He may be impotent sexually, but he does succeed in destroying Honey's faith in his constancy and Martha's belief that she did not need George. As we shall see later, however, Nick does not succeed in destroying George's house of brick, but is in turn defeated by George.

But this is only one aspect of the title; the other aspect concerns Virginia Woolf, the first successful user of the stream-of-consciousness technique, and in some ways the originator of modern prose fiction. Woolf characteristically favors the individual rather than authority or conformity, emotion rather than system or method, and the mystic's search for "cosmic identification" rather than the existentialist's acceptance of actuality. For her, reality is a harmonious relation with all things, achieved through a Blakean visionary insight. In *To The Lighthouse,* her finest novel, this insight is symbolized by images of the sun, light, brilliance, and illumination. For Mrs. Ramsay, her central character, the lighthouse and its beam of light symbolize the light of truth which reveals reality and integrates one's personality. It is simultaneously pitiless yet beautiful, remorseless yet revelatory.

Unifying the two aspects of the title, we might say that the Wo(o)lf means "that which has the power of destroying illusions and illuminating reality." The last line of the nursery rhyme—"So early in the morning"—unites the sun and light symbolism of Woolf's work, and the fact that the play takes place very early on Sunday morning. Mike Nichols, the director of the movie version of the play, has appropriately seen fit to end the movie with the sun rising above the clasped hands of George and Martha. This sunrise is justified by a reference to the dawn in the play. Martha, by admitting her fear of the Wo(o)lf, in effect now has a vision of ultimate reality. The "blow your house down" aspect of the folktale parallels the *"ventura ira"* (the "wind of wrath") referred to in the *Exorcism,* and points up the exorcistic structure of the play. One must destroy illusion, or exorcise the false demons, to make way for reality, to allow the reality of one's soul to regain control. This reality is hinted at in the Woolf-like light symbolism in the *Exorcism: "Et lucis aeternae beatitudine perfrui"; "Et lux perpetua luceat eis."*

The action of the play occurs from 2 a.m. to sunrise on Sunday. This may be viewed as a literal fact, but it may also be viewed as a symbolic fact. The play occurs between that which is old and will be destroyed—George says, "It's late, you know? Late"—and that which is new and will be reborn. In primitive calendars there always occurs a space of time which is set aside for rites of renewal. This period, termed the "intercalary days" by the anthropologists, is essentially timeless, and connects the temporal world of the community with the eternal world of the gods. The primordiality of the play's time scheme is emphasized by the fact that Martha is not merely "a hundred and eight . . . years old," but has "taken a new tack . . . over the past couple of centuries," and is "archaic." George went "to prep school, during the Punic Wars"; and Martha's father "is over two hundred years old." The timelessness of the play is summed up when Nick asks "You've been here quite a long time, haven't you?" and George answers"Forever."

The renewal or regeneration aspect of the play is evidenced by the references to the *Sacre du Printemps,* "a rhythm Martha understands," and the *Walpurgisnacht* of the second act. The unbreakable link between death or destruction and rebirth is emphasized by references to the Twenty-First Birthday, at which time the child dies and the adult is born; the Easter pageant; and the *Dies Irae* of the *Exorcism,* at which time *"veneris judicare saeculum per ignem,"* and as a result *"lux perpetua luceat eis."*

Although the setting of the play is New Carthage in New England, its "real" setting is a primordial Everywhere; George says, "And this . . . (*With a handsweep taking in not only the room, the house, but the whole countryside*) . . . this is your heart's content—Illyria . . . Penguin Island . . . Gomorrah. . . ." Places such as Parnassus, Carthage, Majorca, the Aegean, China, Manchuria, and Crete are mentioned. Another place, not the least important, is the *Paradisium* in the *Exorcism.* New Carthage is the intermediate between that which went before—old Carthage; and, by its connoted destruction, that which will come after—*Paradisium. Paradisium* is given concrete representation by the dawn at the end of the play. George's belief that "We should live on Crete, or something" might allow us to discuss the symbolism of the Cretan labyrinth. Any labyrinth is basically an illusory Many, a Maze of Errour, surrounding and concealing the One of absolute reality at its center. George and Martha reach this center and confront the Wo(o)lf-Minotaur. Just as Albee does not allow the Wo(o)lf to be killed because its destruction makes way for rebirth, so we may assume that neither will the Minotaur be merely overcome; instead, the Dionysian faith that destruction brings about rebirth will be affirmed.

* * *

Just as the title, the time, and the place of the play point up the positive nature of Albee's theme, so likewise do the characters' mythic qualities and their ritual actions. Martha's Daddy, for example, may be the Head of the University, but he may also be the Ruler of the Universe. He organizes "these goddamn Saturday night orgies," orgies which take place on Saturday, a day sacred to Saturn, and which are related to the fertility rites of the Saturnalia. He lives at Parnassus, and there are rumors that "the old man is not going to die." Martha says, "I worshipped him . . . I absolutely worshipped him. I still do." George resembles Martha's Daddy insofar as both are concerned with Dionysian history; Daddy had a sense of history . . . or . . . continuation," and George is Head of the History Department. George will later take over Daddy's role of Saturn when he, as in Goya's painting, devours his son in the form of a telegram.

On the folklore, rather than mythic, level, Martha's Daddy is "a great big white mouse" with "tiny red eyes." In Chinese symbolism such a mouse is an evil diety of the plague, a reasonable analogy to a university president who entombs his staff in halls covered with creeping ivy.[3] Since Martha will usurp most of the perogatives of the Great Mother, there is no room for another mythic correlative of the Great Mother; therefore her mother is relegated to only the folklore level, and exists only as a relatively insignificant stepmother and a good witch with warts.

Martha's name comes from the Aramic *Martha,* which means simply "lady." During the last part of the play, after Nick discovers what Martha really is, he appropriately refers to her only as "Lady." The two appelations are interchangeable, for Martha is the Archetypal Feminine in her many roles. She is "destructive," "Voluptuous," "wicked," a "monster," a "sub-human monster," a "Monstre!" a "Bête," a "Putain!" and a variety of repulsive or brutish animals and insects. She is "limitless" because she is the Earth Mother: "You're all flops. I am the Earth Mother, and you're all flops. (*More or less to herself*) I disgust me. I pass my life in crummy, totally pointless infidelities . . . (*Laughs ruefully*) *would*-be infidelities." She is "the only true pagan on the eastern seaboard," "paints blue circles around her things," and understands the rhythm of *Sacre du Printemps.* Like all Mother Goddesses, she is a perpetual Virgin although Harlot: "Anyway, so I was revirginized."

Martha rules like Circe over her hogs: "Martha thinks that unless . . . you carry on like a hyena you aren't having any fun." "Hyena" comes from the Greek *hyaina,* a "sow," from *hys,* a "hog." She is also the tri-headed Hecate: "There aren't many more sickening sights than you with a couple of drinks in you and your skirt up over your head, you know . . . your *heads,* I should say." However, Martha is essentially the Mother Goddess in her most negative aspect, that of the Bitch Goddess. George says that she chews her ice cubes "like a cocker spaniel," and that when she was courting him she would "sit outside of my room, on the lawn, at night, and she'd howl and claw at the turf." At one point Nick says to George, "Well now, I'd just better get her off in a corner and mount her like a goddam dog, eh?"—such an act would of course literally make Martha a bitch. This aspect of Martha is summed up when George shouts at her, "YOU SATANIC BITCH!"

Martha is also a dragon. George, who in this context should be called Saint George, plucks a bunch of snapdragons in the moonlight, and hurls them "spear-like" at her, shouting "SNAP WENT THE DRAGONS!!" in his attempt to destroy her. By the end of the play, he has effectually succeeded in destroying her illusions, and has thereby destroyed the dragon, the Circe, the Bitch, the Satanic, the destructive aspects of *Martha,* thus making way for the positive, creative aspects of the Mother Goddess to manifest themselves. Martha's Dianic moon has set, but it will reappear, just as the moon in the play:

> MARTHA (*With finality*): There is no moon; the moon went down.
>
> GEORGE (*With great logic*): That may very well be, Chastity; the moon may very well have gone down . . . but it came back up.
>
> MARTHA: The moon does *not* come back up; when the moon has gone down it stays down.
>
> GEORGE (*Getting a little ugly*): You don't know anything. *If* the moon went down, then it came back up.
>
> MARTHA: bull!
>
> GEORGE: Ignorance! Such . . . ignorance.

Honey is the absolute antithesis of Martha. Since Martha encompasses so much, very little is left over for Honey. She possesses all the passive, unproductive aspects of the chaste Artemis. She is as effectual as a foetus curled up on the bathroom floor, and little more need be said.

Nick's name has several possible meanings. On the folklore level, he is perhaps Olde Nick, the Devil. On the etymological level, his name is a diminutive form of "Nicholas," which means "victory over the people." Several critics implicitly accept this last interpretation by maintaining that Nick's biological evolution will eventually be victorious over George's historical process. I, however, believing that there is definite evidence in the play demonstrating that he will never be victorious, would emphasize that "Nick" is a *diminutive* form of "Nicholas," and would view his name as an ironic comment upon his success. Be this as it may, there is a third, more plausible, interpretation of his name: George caricatures Nick as one who will perform "tiny little slicing operations that will leave just the smallest scar"—or *nick*—"on the underside of the scrotum" in order to produce a race of genetic supermen.

* * *

Nick, who is going to counteract history by means of biological genetics, and who is going to create everyone in his own perfect image, is essentially the false Apollo type as caricatured by Robert Graves in *The White Goddess* and by Blake in the person of Urizen. But Nick will never succeed in his desires because he cannot create; his loins are "solid gold," he produces only a "puff" with his wife, and he is impotent in the bed of the Mother Goddess. Nick, instead of enabling humanity to ascend the evolutionary ladder, will not even be able to hold it at a standstill; he will *descend* this ladder for the following symbolic reason: When Martha asks George to light her cigarette, he says, "No . . . there are limits. I mean man can put up with only so much without he descends a rung or two on the old evolutionary ladder . . . (*Now a quick aside to Nick*) . . . which is up your line . . . (*Then back to Martha*) . . . sinks, Martha, and it's a funny ladder . . . you can't reverse yourself . . . start back up once you're descending." By lighting Martha's cigarette later in the play, Nick begins his fall: "Hey . . . hand me a cigarette . . . lover (*Nick fishes in his pocket*). That's a good boy. (*He gives her one*) Unh . . . thanks. (*He lights it for her*)." Nick in fact descends to being a "houseboy" and a "stud"—a stud who cannot breed. Nick is also "Narcissistic," and the fate of Narcissus is by no means victorious. In one version of the myth, Narcissus simply wastes away beside his own image in the pool; in another version he drowns in this pool. This second version of the myth may be alluded to when George says "We gotta play a game"; Martha quips "Portrait of a man drowning," and George says "(*Affirmatively, but to none of them*) I am not drowning." Nick, the only other man present, may be the one who is drowning.

Nick is the God of the New Year attempting to usurp the rightful place of George—the God of the Old Year—as the mate of the Mother Goddess. Just as Zeus castrated Cronos and took over his rule, so Nick wishes to castrate George. George explains how Nick's race of genetic supermen will be created:

> Millions upon millions of them . . . millions of tiny little slicing operations that will leave just the smallest scar, on the underside of the scrotum but which will assure the sterility of the imperfect . . . of the ugly, the stu-

> pid . . . the . . . unfit. [. . . History] will lose its glorious variety and unpredictability. I, and with me . . . the surprise, the multiplexity, the sea-changing rhythm of . . . history, will be eliminated. There will be order and constancy . . . and I am unalterably opposed to it. [. . . I will not give up things like that. No . . . I won't. I will fight you, young man . . . one hand on my scrotum, to be sure . . . but with my free hand I will battle you to the death.

As George says, he will not allow himself to be castrated by the up-and-coming God of the New Year. Instead, he allows Nick to possess Martha during an intercalary moment, and then reappears to regain his supremacy, his rightful kingship. In primitive ritual the king was annually sacrificed or castrated, and replaced by the new king. However, it is important to bear in mind that this was often only theoretical, for in practice the king might be ritually slain in the form of a tree, an animal, or a human substitute. This surrogate would be allowed to rule for a limited period of time before his deposition; such a rite was the origin of the Feast of Fools and its Lord of Misrule. After the sacrifice of this surrogate, the original king would reappear and proclaim himself reborn. Nick is such a surrogate, and after his brief rule Martha tells him, "There is only one man in my life who has ever . . . made me happy. Do you know that? One! [. . .] George; my husband."

Sometimes, however, the surrogate would be the king's son. George not only allows Nick, as surrogate, to rule and then be deposed; he also sacrifices his illusory son in his stead. After George tells Martha that their son is dead, a scene occurs which indicates George's god-like powers:

> MARTHA: You can*not.* You may not decide these things.
>
> NICK: He hasn't decided anything, lady. It's not his doing. He doesn't have the power . . .
>
> GEORGE: That's right, Martha; I'm not a God. I don't have the power over life and death, do I?
>
> MARTHA: You can't kill him! You can't have him die!

This son, whom George does indeed have the power to kill, is a little Apollo: "He loved the sun! . . . He was tan before and after everyone . . . and in the sun his hair . . . became . . . fleece"; he is called "sunny-Jim," and used to keep "the bow and arrow" under his bed. He is also "the Lamb," and George is "going to make [Martha's] performance tonight look like an Easter pageant," a ritual in which the sacrifice of the Son brings atonement for the living. By symbolically eating the eucharistic telegram containing the news of the death of his son on the day of that divine Son's Birthday, George is reborn, resurrected, and reunited with Martha the Mother Goddess at sunrise on Sunday. On the symbolic level, George and Martha are not really uncreative. The son in every archetypal family is always in a sense superfluous; he has no separate personality, but is a reincarnation of his father. His purpose is to be a renewed manifestation of his father, or to die so that his father may be reborn. George and Martha will no longer live a life of manifold illusions; they will live a life of eternal reality. They will play no more games, for they have reached the Center of the labyrinth. They have been purged by the exorcism. At the end of the play, George tells Martha that it is "time for bed," and that it will be "Sunday tomorrow; all day"—words which echo the *"Requiescat in pace"* and *"Et lux perpetua luceat eis"* in the *Exorcism.*

It may be, if Jungian psychology is correct in its assertion that myth is instinctive rather than traditional, that these underlying mythic patterns account for the intense dynamic effect of Albee's drama. Every time I read the play, or see it performed, or see the movie version, I am almost totally absorbed by it, and experience a wild demonic joy. The violence of the dialogue and action may also account for this response by appealing to a Poëan "innate imp of the perverse," but, as all great drama, Albee's play demonstrates the cathartic principle that destruction and violence are not ends in themselves, but purge both the actors and the spectators, and prepare the way for rebirth.

NOTES

[1]"Truth and Illusion in *Who's Afraid of Virginia Woolf?" Renascence,* XVII (1964), 63.

[2]Allan Lewis, "The Fun and Games of Edward Albee," *ETJ,* XVI (1964), 34

[3]I feel justified in mentioning Chinese symbolism because of its presence elsewhere in the play: the red and yellow Chinese parasol which pops out of George's gun. This is the Chinese *yin-yang* symbol, which signifies the unity of opposites, and supports the "destruction equals rebirth" theme of the play.

Anne Paolucci (essay date 1972)

SOURCE: "Exorcisms: *Who's Afraid of Virginia Woolf?,*" in *From Tension to Tonic: The Plays of Edward Albee,* Southern Illinois University Press, 1972, pp. 45-63.

[*In this excerpt from her full-length study, Paolucci maintains that in* Who's Afraid of Virginia Woolf? *Albee has depicted "the excruciating agony of love as it struggles to preserve the fiction of its purity through a mass of obscenities and the parody of sex."*]

> "Truth and illusion, George; you don't know the difference."
>
> "No; but we must carry on as though we did."
>
> *Who's Afraid of Virginia Woolf*

Who's Afraid of Virginia Woolf? is in many important respects a "first." In addition to being the first of Albee's full-length plays, it is also the first juxtaposition and integration of realism and abstract symbolism in what will remain the dramatic idiom of all the full-length plays. Albee's experimentation in allegory, metaphorical clichés, grotesque parody, hysterical humor, brilliant wit, literary allusion, religious undercurrents, Freudian reversals, irony on irony, here for the first time appear as an organic whole in a mature and completely satisfying dramatic work. It is, in Albee's repertory, what *Long Day's Journey into Night* is in O'Neill's; the aberrations, the horrors, the mysteries are woven into the fabric of a perfectly normal setting so as to create the illusion of total realism, against which the abnormal and the shocking have even greater impact. In this play, for the first time, the "third voice of poetry" comes through loud and strong with no trace of static. The dramatist seems to have settled back silently, to watch while his characters take over the proceedings, very much like those six notorious characters who pestered Pirandello's dramatic imagination.

In ***Who's Afraid of Virginia Woolf?*** the existential dilemma is dramatized with full sympathy in its most painful human immediacy. The weak are redeemed in their helplessness, and the vicious are forgiven in their tortured self-awareness. The domineering figure of Woman is no longer the one-sided aberration of ***The Sandbox*** and ***The American Dream***; it is a haunting portrait of agonized loyalty and destructive love. The submissive Male is raised to the point of tragic heroism in his understanding of the woman who would kill the thing she loves. The action itself is beautifully consistent; it makes no excessive demands, but moves along simply and with utter realism to the edge of a mystery.

Martha and George stumble on the scene with aimless talk about a black wig and a Bette Davis movie featuring Joseph Cotten, and then settle down by the liquor cabinet to wait for the party to begin. That party, one soon discovers, is not just Nick and Honey but all of us. The younger couple mirror our own embarrassment and our public selves; Martha and George, our private anguish. The possibilities for identification are infinite; each moment is a step toward recognition.

It is a peculiarity of Albee's and a trademark of his that the protagonists of his plays are at one and the same time distinctly themselves and just as distinctly Everybody Else. In Martha and George, Nick and Honey, this identity is perfected dramatically, so that the play appears—from one point of view—a psychoanalytic "happening" in which the audience is intimately involved. The strength of such a play lies in this immediate and growing identification of the audience with the protagonists on stage; the difficulties of the characters, though rooted in mystery, are simple enough to grasp in their social implications.

As in the earlier plays, Sex is the dynamo behind the action. But in this case, instead of an oversimplified statement about homosexuality and who is responsible for it, or a brief reminder of how private sexual indulgence turns into prurient lust, or an unsympathetic suggestion of how heterosexual demands within a materialistic society corrupt and destroy the individual, we have for the first time an examination of the various phases through which a sexual relationship passes in its normal, or rather, its inevitable development. Like Shaw, who shocked a good many of his contemporaries, and still shocks a good many of his readers today, by insisting that love and sex don't mix easily in marriage, Albee is here reminding us of the deterioration which even the best-matched couple will suffer in their sexual relationship if love is not properly distinguished from it and nurtured apart from it. There is almost an Augustinian conviction in Albee's insistence on what sex in marriage is *not.*

St. Augustine long ago described the paradox when he noted that the outgoing altruism of love is always destroyed in the act of sex, which by its very nature is a selfish and private affair, even when it corresponds with its selfish and private expression in the other person. It was his view—and the view of the Church from earliest times—that, for a marriage to succeed, the concupiscence of sex had gradually to be transformed into the sacrifice of love. The sacrifice becomes embodied in the child born of sex; in the attention and care the child requires, the selfish and very human demands of the parents are turned into selfless giving. In their offspring, the parents really become one; the children's claims give them the opportunity of rising above themselves, of losing themselves lovingly in the desire they have made flesh. Where this transformation does not take place, sex seeks other outlets, searches for excitement, gratifies the normal desire for self-sacrifice in all kinds of perversions. In ***Tiny Alice*** this theme will be beautifully elaborated in Brother Julian's despairing search for martyrdom—which turns out to be an erotic indulgence. In ***Who's Afraid of Virginia Woolf?*** the theme is examined within the context of a marriage grown stale.

Albee is no Augustinian, and he might even reject Shaw; but what he succeeds in doing is giving their view added authority. He has depicted in this play the excruciating agony of love as it struggles to preserve the fiction of its purity through a mass of obscenities and the parody of sex. The Son-myth is the embodiment of that fiction. It is the frustration around which the action of the play revolves.

Albee plays on the theme a number of ways, one of which is the introduction of a kind of Shakespearean subplot, in the story of the second couple. Honey and Nick have some kind of sex together, but little love and no children. Honey confesses, late in her drunken stupor, that she doesn't want children. Her fear of pregnancy is also a fear of sex, basically, and throws new light on the story of her courtship and marriage. The hysterical pregnancy which "puffed her up" and made Nick marry her has its own complicated explanation, no doubt; but at the time it took place, it served—in part at least—as a guard against sexual abandonment and a way back into conventional and acceptable relationships. Honey's predicament is characteristic of Albee's handling of complicated human motivation. He neither blames nor prescribes a moral "cure." His dramatic instincts keep him from easy labels; not once does he betray his characters into clinical diagnoses of the kind that O'Neill was prone to. Honey is anything but a case history; in her own way she is pathetically attractive and appealing. There is a kind of strength in her not wanting to keep up with the others. Her childlike trust looks ridiculous in that company, but it is incongruous in the same way that the impossible purity of Martha's fictional son is incongruous. When she returns from the "euphemism," after George's vicious Get the Guests, she says simply, "I don't remember anything, and you don't remember anything either." Her despair, though different from Martha's, is just as intense and real to her. Like the fictional son of her hosts, her innocence is already compromised. The *Walpurgisnacht* is her initiation party. Her childish decision not to remember unpleasant things has to be put to the test.

Honey, like Martha, is childless; but the parallel is propped up by contrast. Martha wanted children and hasn't any; Honey doesn't want them and manages to keep from having them—or, rather, she doesn't want to go through the pains of childbirth. At the end she confesses pathetically that she fears the physical labor connected with childbirth and reveals a very different kind of impulse. The two stories move toward the same psychological vacuum. The hysterical pregnancy and the fictional son are conceived in different ways, but they are essentially the same kind of birth. Both are the result of impotence, or rather, of a willful assertion which proves abortive. George fails to measure up to Martha's ambitions for him as the son-in-law of the college president; Nick fails to measure up to Honey's romantic dream. Both women give birth to an unsubstantial hope.

Sex is the name of the game; but around Martha—the embodiment of Mother Earth—everything sexual seems to collapse. Men are all flops, and she herself a fool to be tempted by them:

> I disgust me. I pass my life in crummy, totally pointless infidelities . . . WOULD-be infidelities. Hump the Hostess? That's a laugh. A bunch of boozed-up . . . impotent lunk-heads. Martha makes goo-goo eyes, and the lunk-heads grin, and roll their beautiful, beautiful eyes back, and grin some more, and Martha licks her chops, and the lunk-heads slap over to the bar and pick up a little courage . . . so, FINALLY, they get their courage up . . . but that's all baby! Oh my, there is sometimes some very nice potential, but, oh my! My, my, my. . . .

In spite of appearances and what she says in her verbal skirmishes, George is the only man who has ever satisfied her sexually. Even the suggestion of physical impotence is canceled out in the end, when George proves that the ultimate power of life and death lies with him.

The parallel between the two couples is strengthened by other contrasts. Nick and Honey are just starting out and have something of the hopes and energies that George and Martha had when they first came together; but where George failed, Nick might well succeed. He is willful in a petty way, knows exactly what he wants, and is callous enough to reach out and grab it. His plans are clear and realizable. He is much more practical and less idealistic than George, but lacks George's potential to adjust to what the world calls failure. George's *failure* is incomprehensible to Nick: would anyone, in his right mind, turn down a high administrative post simply to indulge a passion to write the great American novel? The irony is that Nick wants what George had in his grasp and turned down. In this context, Nick's designs seem downright petty, while George's worldly failure takes on heroic colors. For George, money means compromise; for Nick, it is the one sure sign of success. His decision to assume the "responsibilities" of marriage was in large measure determined by the fact that Honey was rich; but already he has failed in his role, unable to share his wife's fears and hopes. He is absolutely callous to her emotional needs, bent on humoring her in order to get what he wants. His relationship with Honey is an excellent barometer of his relationship with the rest of the world. He will very likely get everything he wants; but the world will hold his success against him, for his ambition is utterly transparent. George and Martha have understood this and are contemptuous of him; Honey suspects it but cannot bring herself to face the truth.

These ironic oscillations produce something resembling the oppressive emptiness of the plays of Beckett and Sartre. The inescapable dialectic builds up to the recognition, on the part of each of the protagonists, of what he is not and cannot ever be. Each absorbs as much as he is capable of taking in; the rest of the lesson is there to be heard and carried away in the memory. In their hell, the will continues to assert itself in impotent frustration. The exorcism which finally comes about is a vacuum—stylistically, the play reflects the collapse of the will in a quick staccato of monosyllables which brings the action to its close. The exhaustion of pretense is caught neatly in the tired jingle which earlier in the evening, at Daddy's party, brought down the house. Nothing happens in the play, but reality is changed completely in the gradual discovery and recognition of what is inside us all. Whatever else Martha will hit on to substitute for Junior, it can never be confused again with the real condition of her life. This is not necessarily an advantage; confession craves absolution, but all Martha can hope for (and George) is compassion.

The existential mood is caught by means of ambiguous explanations, unfinished or incomplete stories, emotional climaxes suddenly deflated into absurdity. The scene where George "shoots" Martha is a striking example of the explosion of emotional tension into frivolity. Martha is playing up to Nick, as George watches; when she brings up the story about the boxing match in which she managed to stun George, he leaves the room. Martha goes right on—it's all part of their repertory—and George eventually returns with a shotgun which he raises, aims . . . and shoots. But what bursts out, without a bang, is a Chinese parasol. The tension breaks; there is a moment of hysterical relief—but it is only the prelude to a new emotional buildup.

The parasol is perhaps the neatest symbol of George's impotence in his destructive relationship with Martha. It is given sexual overtones by Martha's exchange with Nick, a few moments later—"You don't need any props, do you baby?" "Unh-unh." "I'll bet not. No fake Jap gun for you, eh?" Nick too will turn out to be another "pointless infidelity," and will be relegated to the humiliating role of "houseboy" at the end. No one can match George, but George cannot altogether satisfy her shifting moods. He understands them and adjusts to them—but at his best he must appear weak. He is her scapegoat, the articulate challenger who keeps Martha on her toes, the constant reminder of her own inadequacies. Martha needs victims, and she can pick them up anywhere; but George is the only one who rises to the occasion each time she lashes out. There is some secret understanding between them; she has ruined him with her excessive demands and her domineering ways; but he has not been crushed. His strength reassures her, even when she forces it against herself. George is her conscience and her accuser. In her soliloquy she admits that all the things he says are true—even to Daddy's red eyes—but she fights him for having said them. In some strange way, their fighting is their only means of real communication. George's obstinacy is the reassurance that he has understood the script and can play it out. Martha accuses him of wanting the flagellation she inflicts, but the statement is only partly true. He wants it because he knows she needs it as an excuse. She herself can't say this, but there is every reason to believe that she has grasped and accepted that conclusion. She comes close to confessing it in the soliloquy.

> I cry all the time too, Daddy. I cry all the time; but deep inside, so no one can see me. I cry all the time. And Georgie cries all the time, too. We both cry all the time, and then, what we do, we cry, and we take our tears, and we put 'em in the ice box, in the goddam ice trays . . . until they're all frozen . . . and then . . . we put them . . . in our . . . drinks.

In this summing up of the vicious cycle which is the aimless habit of their life, Martha turns a commonplace into a poetic image. The futility of all that frustrated energy is beautifully captured in those ice cubes which will go into furnishing new energy for new recriminations and fresh tears.

In his verbal agility and his instinctive grasp of things, George has a Hamlet-like appeal. Somewhere in his soul, his aimless puns have meaning. His verbal fencing with Nick on at least two occasions succeeds in humiliating the younger man, who thinks he *knows.* But *knowing* means being married to Martha and being able to fence in that way. *Knowing* means weaving in and out of irrelevancies and coming back each time to the sore spot; it means indulging in confusion which is not altogether accidental. Even his absentmindedness seems to have a purpose. With a kind of fixation, George keeps coming around to the subject of the History Department and his own abortive role in it. His failure is a challenge hurled at his potential rival. Nick may be more likely to succeed, but he cannot hold his own in the hard-hitting duel of words.

The only worthy challenger is Martha. Both have an uncanny gift for turning obvious disadvantage into victory through wit, ad-libbing where the familiar script seems to repeat itself monotonously and turning the unexpected into an integral part of the dialogue. The game is brilliant and vicious when they indulge in it together; it takes on a sad, pathetic quality when one or the other indulges in it with Nick or Honey. Honey is, on the whole, too naïve to be an effective foil, but Nick is just self-conscious enough to draw blood. And George and Martha are always ready to catch the faintest suggestion of hypocrisy, any hint of weakness that can be turned into a weapon. They enjoy the game as only experts can. If at times others are hurt, it isn't so much that they enjoy inflicting pain but that their nature demands satisfaction. In his insistence on false pragmatic values, in his false dignity, Nick repeatedly invites such cruelty. The verbal parrying is inspired by the recognition of humbug; irony and sarcasm cut into the surface of things and expose the raw nerves of the offender. The urge is the urge to grasp reality.

All this talk serves, paradoxically, to underscore the incommunicability which is the heart of the play. Nick tolerates his wife and uses her—and, presumably, her money—for his own private ends; Honey is too preoccupied with her own puffed-up fears to realize what is going on and face up to the difficulties in her marriage; George and Martha prefer to indulge in private games and public hostility rather than face their shared loneliness. Occasionally, some attempt is made to reach out—as when George warns Nick about the danger of being overconfident and using people callously to get what he wants. To Nick, George is simply a jealous husband, the impotent male wounded in his vanity.

Frustration is the dramatic impulse of the play. The invitation to Nick and Honey is a frenzied attempt at oblivion through a kind of saturnalia; the verbal skirmishes are frustrated attempts at communication; the history of the two couples is the story of frustrated love; the accusations are frustrated attempts at understanding; a frustrated prayer celebrates the end of the nightmare.

The climax of the play is the high point of frustration, where George's anger presents an immediate threat and—miraculously—is turned instead into the inspiration which gives focus and purpose to the aimless action up to that point. Nick and Martha are in the kitchen; and George, in his lonely despair, throws the book he has been reading across the room, hitting the door chimes which are set off by the impact. Honey returns from the bathroom at this moment and George's frustration is turned full blast on her. He lashes out cruelly, trying to enlighten her about the hard realities she chooses to ignore—

> There are a couple of people in there . . . they are in there, in the kitchen . . . Right there, with the onion skins and the coffee grounds . . . sort of . . . sort of a . . . sort of a dry run for the wave of the future.

Honey's desperate retreat into ignorance enfuriates George; he has found her weak spot—"you simpering bitch . . . you don't want CHILDREN?"—and all his accumulated hatred is turned on her. Honey has managed to find a way to avoid pregnancy without Nick's knowing—but Nick is out in the kitchen trying to "hump the hustess" while the host struggles to contain his anger. The moment is explosive. Both Honey and George are aware at that moment of the demonic force which has been let loose and which threatens to destroy them all. It is at this point that Honey, in her childish attempt to distract her enemy, reminds him about the chimes ringing. To George—who must adjust to the change—it is "the sound of bodies" at first; but his feverish imagination is quick to answer the challenge and he shapes the sound into a purposeful plot meant to punish Martha:

> . . . somebody rang . . . it was somebody . . . with . . . I'VE GOT IT! I'VE GOT IT, MARTHA . . . Somebody with a message . . . and the message was . . . our son . . . OUR SON! . . . It was a message . . . the bells rang and it was a message, and it was about . . . our son . . . and the message . . . was . . . and the message was . . . our . . . son . . . is. . DEAD!

With characteristic resiliency, George manages to turn chaos into meaningful reality. Impotence is transformed into creative purpose; the two separate vectors—Honey's desperate demand for reassurance and George's demonic spite—come together at this crucial moment to give new direction to the action. From that moment on, George is in command, a providential agent calling the moves right up to the resolution and fulfillment of his plan.

In resolving to destroy the fiction of the son, George is responding to his own impotent spite; but there is a certain tragic justice in the plan. Martha keeps changing the rules of the game, after all; and although George has gone along up to that point ("learning the games we play as quickly as I can change the rules" as Martha says), she has gone too far, stepping over some invisible line; she has betrayed some tacit agreement. George's plan to punish her is, by her own admission, the fulfillment of her paradoxical impulses: she needs his love but does not deserve it; she hates him for his idealism but acknowledges her weakness in exposing him; in taunting him she is expressing disgust at her own shortcomings; she will not forgive him "for having come to rest; for having seen me and having said: yes; this will do; who has made the hideous, the hurting, the insulting mistake of loving me and must be punished for it." In hatred, as in love, they are indissolubly bound; in punishing Martha, George is also punishing himself. This paradox is the source of their frustration: it gave birth to the Son-myth and will now destroy it.

Martha's fictional son is the child of her will, the symbol of potency and virility, the imaginative embodiment of all the masculine roles idealized and idolized. He is the perfect lover, the perfect son and husband, the successful breadwinner, the creature of all her hopes. George points up the erotic implications of Martha's obsessive interest in the boy:

> He's a nice kid, really, in spite of his home life; I mean, most kids'd grow up neurotic, what with Martha here carrying on the way she does: sleeping 'till four in the P.M., climbing all over the poor bastard, trying to break the bathroom door down to wash him in the tub when he's sixteen, dragging strangers into the house at all hours. . . .

Martha herself suggests a very different picture. With nostalgia she recalls all the vivid details of the child's discovery of the world, the cane headboard he wore through with his little hands, the croup tent and the shining kettle hissing in the one single light of the room "that time he was sick," animal crackers, and the bow and arrow he kept under his bed, her beautiful boy walking "evenly between us . . . to protect us all from George's . . . weakness . . . and my . . . necessary greater strength . . . to protect himself . . . and US." Martha's child is perfection and George the "drowning man" who threatened repeatedly to destroy that perfection. Instinctively, we understand that this exchange marks the moment of destruction—Martha's recollections are the examination of conscience that precedes confession and the entire cycle of purification. George—who has always stopped her from bringing up the subject—this time has actually encouraged her to do so. It is part of his plan.

Martha's moment of grace is short-lived. Having named George in her reminiscences, she turns her full attention to describing his negative influence on the child and the boy's shame at the "shabby failure" his father has become over the years. The quarrel resumes with these accusations and recriminations, rising to a pathetic climax with Martha's claim that the child is "the one thing, the one person I have tried to protect, to raise above the mire of this vile, crushing marriage; the one light in all this hopeless . . . DARKness . . . OUR SON." Against her stark accusations, we hear the funeral service for the dead, intoned in Latin by George; both end at the same moment. There is a brief interruption by Honey, at this point, and then George's triumphant announcement that sunny-Jim is dead.

Martha's account almost convinces us, but there is no sunny-Jim, of course. By the time the exorcism is over even Nick has seen the light. Martha's furious "YOU CANNOT DO THAT! YOU CAN'T DECIDE THAT FOR YOURSELF!" leaves no more room for doubt. George has killed the myth and Martha finally has to accept the fact. But the reasoning behind the fact is a private understanding, a tacit agreement between George and Martha.

> MARTHA (*Great sadness and loss*): You have no right . . . you have no right at all. . . .
>
> GEORGE (*Tenderly*): I have the right, Martha. We never spoke of it; that's all. I could kill him any time I wanted to.
>
> MARTHA: But why? Why?
>
> GEORGE: You broke our rule, baby. You mentioned him . . . you mentioned him to someone else.

The tacit agreement was that the boy remain their private dream, not to be shared with anyone else, not to be corrupted by exposure to an unsympathetic world. Martha's indulgence in confiding to others, her breaking the rules and telling "the bit" about their "son" is the cue that private communication is breaking down. George's decision was not so much punishment as necessity. It had been "an easy birth . . . once it had been . . . accepted, relaxed into"; presumably it will be an easy death, once it is accepted in the same way. Martha must give him up because the myth has taken over and entered into her public life. Private necessity has turned into a public joke. George has tried to protect her from this moment; but when the shared myth turns into a stunted fact, he destroys it. Like an inexorable agent of fate, he guides Martha through the long reminiscences and the subsequent "confession." Having been exposed, the myth must be properly laid to rest.

The "death" scene is one of the most suggestive of the play and, in spite of the presence of Nick and Honey, a private conversation between Martha and George. They speak the same language, but never try to explain the contradictions to the others. Nick and Honey will take away what they can absorb; their reaction—like that of the audience—is the measure of their insight. The scene is sober and naturalistic, in keeping with the "tragic" end of the child. The "eulogy" anticipates the straightforward, transparent language of ***Tiny Alice*** in its sentimental reminiscences, but it is simultaneously an ironic *ritual.*

Albee takes great pains to develop these two distinct voices here, for Martha's "son"—invisible but real—is the most striking paradox of the play. He is the imagination made flesh—or, more precisely, the "word" made flesh, for Martha and George have brought him into the world as talk, as a game between them, in which he arbitrates, comforts, gives strength to his parents. He is clarity, insight, parable. If one were disposed to take on the burden of a polysemous reading, one might trace some interesting religious analogies, such as the "lamb" and the "tree" against which the boy met his death, and the "porcupine" which he tried to avoid, like the crown of thorns in the story of Christ.

One need not labor such analogies, however, to grasp the rich content of the Son-myth. He is Martha's hope, her way of getting psychological relief, her faith that some corner of life remains untouched and pure. Birth came easily, "once it had been accepted"; but his life was not easy, for he bore the burden of his parents' mutual accusations and suffered the agony of their mutual guilt. Innocence and guilt—the divine and human—come together in him. "He walked evenly between us," Martha recalls, "a hand out to each of us for what we could offer by way of support, affection, teaching, even love"; but those same hands held them off, too, "for mutual protection." He ran off periodically, but always returned—just as he was returning that day, the day of his birthday, of his majority. He was expected back; he *did* come back; but in his majority he forced them into a new and unexpected relationship. His death suggests, by way of contrast, a new beginning, a kind of salvation in truth. His sacrifice should be the gift of love.

Such a reading brings to light several hints of a "virgin birth." Martha refers many times to "my" son and George repeatedly tries to correct her; and in one place, at least, she attributes to George a doubt that "deep down in the privatemost pit of his gut, he's not completely sure it's his own kid." George's casual remark to Nick that "Martha doesn't have pregnancies at all" strengthens this suggestion: Martha has no pregnancies, but she has nevertheless miraculously given birth.

In this context, the exorcism at the end of the play is the confession which will restore spiritual health. George, the high priest, has already prophesied what must come.

> We all peel labels, sweeties; and when you get through the skin, all three layers, through the muscle, slosh aside the organs (An aside to NICK) them which is still sloshable—(Back to HONEY) and get down to the bone . . . you know what you do then? . . . When you get down to bone, you haven't got all the way, yet. There's something inside the bone . . . the marrow . . . and that's what you gotta get at . . . The marrow.

In his role of prophetic high priest, George hears Martha's "confession," blessing it with his reading of the service for the dead. And like the priest, who in the sacrifice of the Mass becomes once again the figure of Christ, and who in the mystery of the transubstantiation turns ordinary bread and wine into the body and bread of Christ, George too emerges gradually as celebrant of a mystery.

Whether or not he really is the same person that he describes in his story to Nick—the young boy who ordered "bergin" and who killed his mother and father in two separate tragic accidents within several months of one another—can never be decided with certainty. Nor does the *fact* of such an identity really matter. The story, after all, is George's and the boy in it his creation. Some kind of identity does exist, and Martha herself sets up some curious parallels, reminding her audience that there is "something funny" in George's past, insisting that the story George tells Nick is a true one that "really happened," threatening her husband with "before I'm through with you you'll wish you'd died in that automobile, you bastard." George sets up psychological reverberations of his own in his account of how their "son" died—an account strangely similar to the account in the original story. "He was . . . killed . . . late in the afternoon . . . on a country road, with his learner's permit in his pocket, he swerved to avoid a porcupine, and drove straight into a . . . large tree."

The boy in the "bergin" story and the boy in George's book come into focus in the Son-myth, all of whom are in some way connected with George himself. He is the double image—both father and son—celebrating in his inspired reading of the Latin service his own death and rebirth. The parody of transubstantiation is completed in his claim that he ate the telegram (the only proof of the story he is telling), just as the priest at the elevation eats the consecrated Host in remembrance of Christ's last supper. What seems a disjointed, purposeless narrative takes on a providential aspect even in the manner in which the idea of sunny-Jim's death

Joan Plowright (Martha), Paul Eddington (George), David Schofield (Nick), and Mary Maddox (Honey) in a National Theatre, London, production of *Who's Afraid of Virginia Woolf?*

first came to him. The chimes had rung—as they do to alert the participants of the Mass that the elevation is imminent—and had inspired him. Grace—insight—takes the form of a mystical revelation, a flash of meaning in which the scattered nonsense of the entire evening suddenly falls into place and assumes a purpose.

The Son-myth, like Brother Julian's fantasies in ***Tiny Alice,*** turns out to be a private indulgence of faith where there is nothing to believe. It is faith that must try to create from its own wreck the thing it contemplates. George comes to realize that such faith must be accepted all the way, to the point of exposure. The Son-myth has come of age; which means, simply, that it must reveal itself at last for what it is. The agony of the end is as painful as the labor that brought it into being, but there is no salvation to soothe the loss. Martha must suffer through it, for there is no choice left.

> I don't mind your dirty underthings in public . . . Well, I DO mind, but I've reconciled myself to that . . . but you've moved bag and baggage into your own fantasy world now, and you've started playing variations on your own distortions.

Lucidity and purpose are a gain—if that much further loss can be called "gain." The religious undercurrents and the ironic paradox which is the result of sacrifice are indeed strangely reminiscent of ***The Zoo Story.***

The exorcism culminates in a kind of religious abandonment. Nick—the scientific skeptic without a trace of sympathy—sees in all this simply the frustration of a childless couple. Honey senses something of the mystery and cries out for some small part of the experience. A kind of religious awe pervades the closing minutes of the play; the coming of dawn is the paradoxical symbol of exhaustion and death. The mystery is a dilemma; revelation a trap. The mystical experience is reduced to a pathetic series of monosyllables.

The existential conclusion is at the same time an assertion. Martha and George find each other in the poverty of their self-hatred. Nick and Honey are properly subdued; but in their tragic awareness of the emptiness they have created, Martha and George are redeemed. The Son-myth, like a mystical death, is resurrected in the agony of love.

Orley I. Holtan (essay date 1973)

SOURCE: "*Who's Afraid of Virginia Woolf?* and the Patterns of History," in *Educational Theatre Journal,* Vol. 25, No. 1, March 1973, pp. 47-52.

[*In the following essay, Holtan views* Who's Afraid of Virginia Woolf? *as a "rich and troubling allegory for the American historical experience."*]

Near the end of the second act of ***Who's Afraid of Virginia Woolf?*** George, the professor of history, is left alone onstage while Martha, his wife, and Nick are playing the preliminary rounds of "hump the hostess" in the kitchen. Attempting to control his hurt and anger he reads aloud from a book he has taken from the shelf, "And the West, encumbered by crippling alliances and burdened with a morality too rigid to accommodate itself to the swing of events must—eventually—fall" (II, 174).[1] George is clearly encumbered with a crippling alliance—his marriage to Martha—and does seem to be burdened with a kind of morality that makes it difficult for him to respond in kind to her vicious attacks. At the same time, this observation on the movements of history, read in connection with the events of George's personal history, is a splendid example of how Albee has managed to endow the events of the family drama with a deeper significance, suggestive of larger events and movements. Various critics have noted a number of possible interpretations and levels of meaning in the play.[2] I feel that one of the most profitable ways of looking at ***Who's Afraid of Virginia Woolf?*** is to see it as an allegory for the American historical experience.

Indeed, Albee had previously used the domestic setting in just such an allegorical way, though not so subtly or successfully. ***The American Dream,*** produced off-Broadway in 1961, depicted a symbolic couple, Mommy and Daddy, who had mutilated and emasculated their adopted son when he showed signs of independence and who threaten to send Grandma, with her pioneer toughness and independence, off to a home.[3] In replying to the attacks of certain critics on the play Albee remarked that it was "a stand against the vision that everything in this slipping land of ours is peachy keen."[4] Similarly, in talking about ***Who's Afraid of Virginia Woolf?,*** Albee told Michael Rutenberg that George and Martha were deliberately named after George and Martha Washington and that the imaginary child could represent the uncompleted revolutionary spirit of this country.[5]

My argument is further strengthened by the fact that history figures so prominently in the play. The word or a variant of it runs like a leitmotif through the entire play, being used twenty-eight times in the first act alone. George is a professor of history who does not run the history department, Nick's timetable is history, Martha's father had a sense of history and, in the second act after the "get the guests" sequence, George remarks, "the patterns of history" (p. 148). It would seem appropriate then, before the play is examined at length, briefly to consider the special significance of history in American thought and experience.

One of the principal myths on which this country was founded was the notion that America was a New Eden, a second chance ordained by God or Providence in which man could begin all over again, freed from the accumulated sin and corruption of Western history. Not only could the American become a New Adam and found upon the unspoiled continent an ideal human polity, but this new way of life and new order of society could serve as a shining example to redeem erring Europe from her own sinfulness. America had established a covenant with God or with Nature (the myth had its beginnings with the Puritan settlements and became secularized as time went on) and could remain free of the vicissitudes of history provided she kept the terms of the covenant, retained her simplicity, shunned European complexity and sophistication and avoided the twin temptations of urbanization and industrialization.[6] Unfortunately, such a dream of perfection could not find realization in an imperfect world; the troubles and complexities Americans thought they had left behind began to invade the New World. Yet so strong was the myth that the tendency of American thinkers and historians was to locate the causative factor not in the nature of man nor the impossibility of the dream but in the failure of the new nation to keep the covenant, and to look backward to a golden age in the past before Americans had allowed themselves to be seduced by alien complexities and affectations. Thus the majority of American historians, says David Noble, have been Jeremiahs, decrying America's involvement within the transitory patterns of European history and calling Americans back to their duties and obligations.[7] Having started with such a dream of innocence and perfection, much of the American experience has involved a deeply felt sense of loss and failure.[8]

As one looks at the attitudes of George and Martha one is immediately struck by the fact that the orientation of both characters is to the past and is coupled with an acute sense of failure which, furthermore, has often involved a loss of innocence. When George was first courting Martha, for example, she had liked "real ladylike little drinkies." Now her taste runs to "rubbing alcohol." Over the years she has learned that alcohol "pure and simple" is for the "pure and simple" (I, 24). The adjectives applied to Martha are ironic for whatever she may have been in the days of their courtship she is now obviously neither pure nor simple. The note of past failure is struck even more clearly a few minutes later in a scene between George and Nick:

> NICK: . . . you . . . you've been here quite a long time, haven't you?
>
> GEORGE: What? Oh . . . yes. Ever since I married . . . uh, what's her name . . . uh, Martha. Even before that. Forever. Dashed hopes and good intentions. Good, better, best, bested. How do you like that for a declension, young man? Eh?
>
> (I, 32)

Through this scene, of course, the play remains on a comparatively realistic level. Martha's changed drinking habits and George's sense of failure in his career need not be taken allegorically. In the second act, however, matters become more complex. Shortly after the beginning of the act George tells a long story about a boy who had ordered "bergin" in a speakeasy (an error growing out of innocence and unworldliness). He is described as having been blonde with the face of a cherub and as laughing delightedly at his own error. Yet this "cherub" had killed his mother with a shotgun some time before, "completely accidentally, without even an unconscious motivation" (II, 94), and later, when he learned that he had killed his father also, in an automobile accident, he went mad and has spent the last thirty years in an asylum. George follows the story with an observation about insane people. They don't age in the usual sense; "the underuse of everything leaves them quite whole" (p. 97). Martha later indicates that the story came from George's unpublished novel and that George himself may have been the boy in question. The facts of the case are never clear. They are specifically contradicted in the third act; furthermore, George has obviously not spent the last thirty years in a literal asylum. The issue is clouded even further by the suggestion that even the unpublished novel may be an invention, another of the "games" with which the couple keeps themselves occupied. In the light of the confusion over the "facts" an allegorical interpretation almost forces itself upon us. George, in fact, gives the audience a nudge in that direction when talking about his "second novel"; "it was an allegory really, but it could be read as straight cozy prose" (II, 142).

Allegorically, then, how is the story to be taken? Clearly it is the passage from innocence to guilt and madness. America had begun as a fresh, unspoiled continent, convinced that it was unique in human history in its opportunity to create a perfect society. In cutting itself off from its European tradition and history it had, in effect, killed its "parents." Yet one cannot escape history. Even if one kills one's parents, literally or symbolically, one cannot wipe out the objective fact of their having existed nor destroy the genetic and environmental influences they have given one. Only by retreating into madness can one escape the vicissitudes of history and live completely in one's own world.[9] It is clear that George envies those (the mad) who have remained untouched by life's experience; he would like to escape from reality, from aging, from history but he has been unable to do so. Both George and Martha indicate at various points that "back there," "in the beginning," "when I first came to New Carthage," there might have been a chance for them. That chance was lost and now their "crippling alliance" exacts its toll from both of them.

George's failure to run first the history department and then the college fits well into this line of argument. The college seems to comprise the universe within which the two exist: it surrounds and encompasses them. The outside world rarely enters into the action or dialogue. Martha's father is president of the college and there are allusions, though admittedly subtle ones, to "Daddy's" divinity ("He's a God, we all know that," I, 26; "The old man is not going to die," I, 41; "I worshipped that guy. I absolutely worshipped him," I, 77). Furthermore, Daddy had a sense of dynastic history. It was his idea that George should take over the history department, then eventually step into his place and take over the college. George was to be the heir apparent. Daddy, however, watched for a couple of years and came to the conclusion that George lacked leadership potential, that he was not capable of filling the role. George failed and Martha has never let him forget that failure.

Rutenberg has suggested that the six-year age differential between George and Martha may actually be six centuries (again there are subtle suggestions of this in the script), and that Martha, therefore, represents Mother Church while George stands for the new spirit of Protestantism. While Albee agreed that the interpretation was ingenious, he discounted it.[10] If the play is regarded as an allegory of the American historical experience, however, there is another way in which the six-century age differential can be applied. Europe took the first steps toward her long climb out of the Middle Ages in approximately the eleventh century. This was the century of the Viking discovery of America (1000 A.D.), the Norman Conquest (1066) and the First Crusade (1095). The first settlement in North America (Virginia) was in 1607 and the founding of Plymouth Colony and the Massachusetts Bay Colony occurred in 1620 and 1630 respectively.[11] Thus, there is a difference of not quite six centuries from the dawning of national consciousness in Europe to the colonizing of North America. If we date backward from the ratification of the Constitution in 1787 to the signing of the Magna Carta in 1215, we have five hundred and seventy-two years, again almost six centuries. Thus, George came, bright-eyed and bushy tailed as Martha describes him, into the history department and Martha, six years older, fell for him. Similarly, America, full of promise and hope for the future burst upon the scene of history and Europe did fall for America. The idea of America as a New Eden originated, after all, among Europeans who either looked toward or came to America.[12] As George fell short of Martha's expectations, so perhaps did Albee's America fall short of the expectations of Europe and of Providence. Interestingly enough, George did run the history department for a period of four years during the war, but when everybody came back he lost his position of leadership. In the same way America's position of world leadership went virtually unchallenged during World War II but once the war ended and the recovery of Europe became a fact that leadership began to decline. By the time ***Who's Afraid of Virginia Woolf?*** was produced in 1962, America was trying to exercise her hegemony over increasingly recalcitrant followers.

When all these threads are pulled together one can see that George's marriage and his career can be read as analogues for the American historical experience. America had begun by feeling that she could escape from history, control her own destiny and preserve her innocence, but that fond hope soon met with failure. The American dream—the child which was to be given birth upon the new continent—never really materialized; the paradise on earth was not founded. Instead America was increasingly caught up in the same corruptions, compromises and failures as the rest of the world. That failure may have been all the more painful because America was the victim of her own idealism, unable to escape the realities of history but simultaneously unable to play the game of power politics with the same unscrupulousness as the older nations—"encumbered by crippling alliances and burdened with a morality too rigid to accommodate itself to the swing of events."

Within the contexts of the play there are two possible ways of dealing with this failure. One is to pretend that it never occurred, to create the child out of the imagination and stubbornly to insist, as does Martha, that "everything is fine." The other is to look backward, recognizing that something has gone wrong but rather than trying to rectify it or questioning the validity of the dream itself, merely to mourn its passing and try to place the blame on something or somebody else. It may be that Albee sees these two modes of dealing with the failure of the dream as characteristic of American behaviour.

But if, in Albee's opinion, America's attempt to escape from or to control history has proved to be a failure, other forces in the contemporary world have not learned her lesson. These other forces are represented by the young biologist, Nick. Albee was asked if Nick were named after Nikita Khruschev. He answered yes, in the same way that George and Martha were named after the Washingtons, but went on to assert that that fact was not very significant.[13] Yet an examination of Nick's function in the play reveals a number of connections if not explicitly with Communism at least with the idea that history can be "scientifically" organized and controlled. George accuses Nick of seeking to alter the chromosomes and to sterilize the unfit, thus creating a new super-civilization of scientists and mathematicians, all "smooth, blonde and right at the middleweight limit" (I, 66). In such a world history will have no relevance, diversity will vanish, and a condition of social, intellectual and biological uniformity will be imposed upon the world. Nick makes light of the accusation at first, later is angered by it, but never denies it. In fact, smarting under George's attack he sarcastically avers that he is going to be "the wave of the future." In the second act, with his guard somewhat lowered by George's confidences, he discloses his career plans:

> NICK: . . . What I thought I'd do is . . . I'd sort of insinuate myself generally, play around for a while, find all the weak spots, shore 'em up, but with my own name plate on 'em . . . become sort of a fact, and then turn into a . . . a what?
>
> GEORGE: An inevitability.
>
> NICK: Exactly . . . an inevitability.
>
> (p. 112)

Historical inevitability, a term George later twice applies to Nick, is, of course, one of the catch phrases of communism and it is possible to see the post World War II policy of the Soviet Union as a process of insinuating itself and shoring up weak spots. Furthermore, if we conclude for the sake of the argument that Martha represents a Europe originally enraptured but ultimately disillusioned with America, Nick's wooing of her (and hers of him) coincides once again with the patterns of history. Out of his own bitter experience George tries to warn Nick of the folly of trying to control history but Nick, young, brash, and overconfident merely replies, "up yours!" (p. 116). This interpretation clarifies George's two puzzling speeches, that in which he declares, "I will not give up Berlin" (I, 67)[14] and that about "ice for the lamps of China" (II, 166). This latter line, especially coming as it does on the heels of Nick's wooing of Martha, suggests the presence in the world of the third force, in the face of which the seduction of Europe by the Soviet Union (or vice-versa) may be futile.

Yet in the "get the guests" sequence George manages to damage Nick heavily and later, when Nick gets Martha off to bed, he proves to be impotent. Indeed, Nick has provided George with the very ammunition that the latter uses against him, the revelation of the compromise and subterfuge on which his marriage is based. Honey has trapped him with a false pregnancy and he has used Honey and her father's money as "a pragmatic extension of the big dream" (II, 145); her wealth will help him attain his goals. Pursuing the allegorical interpretation, then, in what sense has the Soviet Union compromised? One fact that comes immediately to mind is her perversion of Marx's understanding of the evolution of communism. The state, in the Soviet Union, has not withered away but has become even stronger than it was in the days of the Czars. Furthermore, Russia has had, to some degree, to adopt some of the methods of Western capitalism which she affects to despise. It is interesting in this context, that both couples are barren. George and Martha have an imaginary child; Honey has had at least one false pregnancy. If the communist revolution was to usher in the land of milk and honey, that dream, too, has been stillborn, as surely as the dream of perfection which was to be brought forth on the American continent has failed to materialize. Nick's impotence might suggest that neither the Soviet Union nor the United States is capable of controlling history. Nick simply does not understand the forces with which he is dealing. Devoted to his own ideology—his own "scientific" understanding of the world—he fails to see that no matter how foolish or feeble George may look he is not yet defeated. Nor does he realize the full implications of his attempted affair with Martha. In courting her in order to further his own ambitions he has got himself into a position from which he cannot easily extricate himself. As a matter of fact, in the third act Nick is put through exactly the same paces as was George in the first. He is ridiculed for his failure, taunted with his lack of knowledge, and ordered to answer the door. Far from being in control of the patterns of history he too has become their victim, as George had warned him he would.

The exorcism of the third act functions also within this context. George first forces Martha to recount the tale of the imaginary son—the birth, the innocent childhood, the attempt to bring him up, with its failures and corruptions, but he will not allow her to stick to the pretence that everything is fine. He forces her to acknowledge the failure, to accept her part of the blame and at last "kills" the son. This act seems to create a sense of peace and the beginnings of communion between them and seems also to have a beneficent effect on Nick and Honey. If, as Albee has suggested, the child is taken to represent the notion inherent in the American dream that the new nation could escape from history and the failings of human nature and create a perfect society, that belief is shown to be an illusion which must be destroyed if the couple and the nation are to face the future realistically.[15] The future is, of course, uncertain; there is no guarantee that once illusion is cast away success and happiness will automatically follow—thus the lingering fear of "Virginia Woolf." However, so long as George and Martha, and symbolically America, persist in living in dreams and in refusing to recognize that there is anything wrong, they cannot hope to survive. The end of the play is therefore ambiguous but perhaps guardedly hopeful.

In order for the illusion to be destroyed, however, a night of carnage and chaos has been required. It is undoubtedly significant that the name of the town in which the college is located is New Carthage, with its echoes of the struggle between two great powers, one destroying the other in the interests of Empire, and then destroyed in its turn.

Many critics may object to an analysis of this type. They may argue that the work of art is meant to have immediate impact in the theatre, primarily on the emotional level. Production of ***Who's Afraid of Virginia Woolf?*** does, I think, fulfill that criterion, but it does something else. Like Ibsen's *The Wild Duck* or *The Master Builder,* for example, it teases the mind of the spectator and will not easily be erased from the consciousness. Albee once remarked that the trouble with most modern plays is that the only thing the spectator is thinking about when he leaves the theatre is where he parked the car.[16] One cannot say that about the spectator of ***Who's Afraid of Virginia Woolf?***. In this play Albee has created a rich and troubling allegory for the American historical experience, the story of a nation that began in boundless optimism and faith in its own power to control the future and that has had to come to grips not only with external challenges but with its own corruption, compromise and failure, that has reached the point where it must cast away its comforting dreams and look reality in the face.

Notes

[1]All citations from the text are are from the Atheneum edition, 1966.

[2]For a variety of interpretations of this play and of Albee's work in general, see Richard E. Amacher, *Edward Albee* (New York, 1969), pp. 82-108; Ruby Cohn, *Edward Albee* (Minneapolis, 1969), pp. 17-26; Thomas E. Porter, *Myth and Modern American Drama* (Detroit, 1969), pp. 225-247; Michael Rutenberg, *Edward Albee, Playwright in Protest* (New York, 1969), pp. 95-115 and Lee Baxandall, "The Theatre of Edward Albee," *Tulane Drama Review* 9 (Summer 1965), pp. 19-40.

[3]The pioneer, agrarian character of Grandma is even clearer in Albee's short play, *The Sandbox,* from which *The American Dream* seems to have been developed.

[4]Preface to *The American Dream* (New York, 1960).

[5]Rutenberg, pp. 230-31.

[6]This theme has been discussed by a number of writers and scholars, most importantly by Perry Miller, *Errand Into the Wilderness* (Cambridge, Mass., 1956), R. W. B. Lewis, *The American Adam* (Chicago, 1955), and David Noble, *Historians Against History* (Minneapolis, 1965).

[7]Noble, p. 4.

[8]Already in the Puritan era Miller notes a deep sense of failure and a tendency in the election sermons of 1663-77 to accuse the colonists of having failed to keep the terms of their covenant (p.2). Noble traces similar accusations of failure through American historiography and imaginative literature.

[9]Noble points out that in Mark Twain's notebooks he has Huck Finn returning after many years in the Indian territory, his last refuge from civilization, as a madman. *The Eternal Adam and the New World Garden* (New York, 1968), p. 62.

[10]Rutenberg, p. 231.

[11]Miller points out that the original settlers of Plymouth Colony came to the New World chiefly to escape persecution. The second wave of colonists, however, came with a clear sense of mission. It is this which he refers to as the "errand into the wilderness." (pp. 5-6).

[12]The impact of the new continent in Europe is discussed in a number of sources but a particularly good treatment is found in Leslie A. Fiedler, *The Return of the Vanishing American* (New York, 1969), especially the first forty-nine pages.

[13]Rutenberg, p. 232.

[14]Like Honey in the play, some of the critics have failed to see "what Berlin has to do with anything." Brustein called the line a "ludicrous non-sequitur." Quoted by Rutenberg, 102.

[15]Even the child has certain symbolic overtones which are interesting in this context. Martha describes it as "a red, bawling child with slippery firm limbs and a full head of black fine, fine hair which later . . . became blonde as the sun" (III, 218). And he kept a bow and arrow under his bed. There may be an allusion here to the original inhabitants of the continent, the "red men" who were swallowed up by the blonde Anglo-saxon tide.

[16]In an article in *The Saturday Evening Post* January 18, 1964. Quoted by Rutenberg, p. 115.

Charlene M. Taylor (essay date 1973)

SOURCE: "Coming of Age in New Carthage: Albee's Grown-up Children," in *Educational Theatre Journal,* Vol. 25, No. 1, March 1973, pp. 53-65.

[*In the essay below, Taylor analyzes Albee's use of language in* Who's Afraid of Virginia Woolf?, *contending: "Through his use of apparently simple naturalistic language which closer examination proves complexly metaphoric and allusive, Albee brings at least George and perhaps all of the characters to a realization that to refuse to recognize, either wilfully or through avoidable ignorance, the complexities of life, to attempt to live in the simpler world of childhood is dangerous and finally unproductive, sterile."*]

I

Almost all of the critics who have written about Albee's ***Who's Afraid of Virginia Woolf*** agree on one point: the play is immensely powerful. Further than this, the critics are less unanimous; the play has been described as realistic, naturalistic, absurdist, or some blend of these three.[1] There is almost as much disagreement about whether it is optimistic or pessimistic and whether George's killing of the phantom child is the supreme example of one-ups-manship or an indication of compassion.[2] A fruitful approach to the play, it seems to me, can be made through a careful analysis of Albee's use of language, especially of his imagery and allusion. Such analysis suggests that Albee takes George and Martha through a kind of rite of passage into full adulthood. Survival of this rite does not make them invincible, but it offers the only chance they have.

Albee's coming-of-age theme can be seen by analyzing the three ways in which the language of the play is remarkable: thematically of least importance, for its so-called naturalistic quality; more importantly, for its use of childish language and its references to children's games; and for some highly significant passages of an almost lyric nature in which Albee makes heavy use of allusion, metaphor, or both. Unfortunately, many critics have assumed that the play is essentially a new example of realism or naturalism; if they discuss Albee's language at all, they consequently focus on the naturalistic aspect of it. Such an assumption, though partially valid, is dangerously limiting. The beginnings of an analysis of Albee's rich and allusive language have been undertaken by Arthur K. Oberg and by Ruth Meyer;[3] but Albee's techniques are more sophisticated than either of these critics suggest and neither one goes on to explore fully the relationship between Albee's language and his theme. Ruth Meyer, for example, notes that the ambiguity of the language is one of the reasons for the disagreement among critics about the interpretation of the play, but suggests that Albee "comes closer to presenting unambiguous truth through the use of clichés than in any other instance in the play."[4] Albee's use of cliché is somewhat more complex than such a statement suggests. He uses not so much ordinary clichés, but rather modified or distorted ones which call attention both to the original and to the implications of his revised version. Martha, trying to seduce Nick, answers his half-objection that George might come back with "Besides, who would object to a friendly little kiss? It's all in the faculty."[5] If we are immediately amused by the apt use of the modified cliché, the implications which it opens are a perversion of the original. The cliché calls to mind the traditional concept of the family as a closely-knit, loyal island of strength, especially in confrontation with non-family. And Martha's modification of "family" to "faculty" reminds one that Daddy, as president of the college, apparently sees himself as a patriarchal figure for whom the college serves as a kind of family business or estate. But Albee has already made us aware of the grossly different reality of George and Martha's family life and of the distance between the concept of "all in the family" and the reality of the faculty. His use of cliché, then, is more complex than the naturalistic, implied comment on the sterility and banality of American society which a more conventional use of cliché's might have presented.

Albee's language has been praised for accuracy of reflection and for virtuosity of styles; but, like the language of Restoration plays with which it has been compared,[6] it is more than a repeating of overheard cocktail party conversation and, like Restoration comic playwrights, Albee uses carefully tailored speech patterns for each character to indicate a great deal more about the characters and their relationships than is ever formally stated. Albee's language is apparently naturalistic in its use of slang, profanity, and interruptions. Yet consider the complex effect of his curious and careful use of the word, "hunh," which appears thirty-eight times during the play. Only once does Albee use the more common spelling, "huh" (III, 192). All three of the characters who use it (Honey does not and Nick, only once), use it not as a vocalized question mark or to mean "isn't that the case, don't you agree with me?" which is its more expected use. Rather, in growing intensity, its unpleasantly nasal quality makes it a taunting sound suggesting that the speaker strongly disagrees with the statement. Compare Martha's one use of "huh" answering Nick's comment that he doesn't think George has a vertebra intact, "You don't huh? You don't think so. Oh, little boy, you got yourself hunched over that microphone of yours . . ." with her phrase five speeches later, "Oh . . . you know so little. And you're going to take over the world, hunh?" (III, 192). The latter, which is typical of Albee's use of the device, helps to suggest that the person spoken to is, in Martha's phrase,"such a cluck" (I, 3) that it is highly unlikely any observation of his could ever be correct; it is, consequently, a highly useful device in antagonizing or excoriating another. Martha uses the word primarily in the first act, and her use steadily decreases during the play; George does not use it at all in the first act but uses it twelve times in the second act (primarily after his own humiliation and as part of his counter-attack) and seven times in the third act. The sound becomes a useful emotional barometer, indicating the intensity and the movement of power.

Albee also occasionally uses the sophisticated techniques of the naturalistic playwrights, such as Chekhov's use of parallel conversations which comment on each other. Albee uses extended parallel speeches once in each act: when George tries to drown out Martha by singing her song "Who's Afraid of Virginia Woolf?" at the end of thc first act (I, 85); when George and Nick discuss their respective marriages without really listening to each other (II, 103-104); and when George recites part of the Burial Service while Martha is finishing the recitation of "Our son" (III, 227). In the last two of these sets the conversations certainly comment on each other; the first set probably functions in the same way though the relationship is less obvious. But if aspects of Albee's language are similar to naturalistic writing, the total effect of his language is more ambitious; as George says of his second novel, "Well, it's an allegory, really—probably—but it can be read as straight, cozy prose . . ." (II, 142). The confusions about theme which are left uncertain if we consider only the naturalism of Albee's language are resolved, however, when we move on to his use of other kinds of language.

II

One of the major ways in which Albee presents the coming-of-age theme is his heavy use of childish language and of references to children's games. At a naturalistic level this might appear to be only the habit of speech of some childless couples, but Albee's use of this device carries symbolic suggestion. He continues his habit of modification in the use of four nursery rhymes: "Georgie Porgie," "Who's Afraid of the Big Bad Wolf?," "Pop Goes the Weasel," and "Here We Go Round the Mulberry Bush." Three of these are used in modified form and the unmodified one is already highly suggestive; all of them have symbolic importance in the coming-of-age theme. When George is sulking before the guests arrive, Martha calls him "Poor Georgie-Porgie, put-upon-pie" (I, 12). If his and his wife's names are used to suggest the founders of the country and thus to make them serve as representatives of American society, George's name is also, here, linked with the protagonist of the nursery rhyme who torments the girls by kissing them, but runs away from the boys; George's behavior, at least through this point in his life, seems to have followed this pattern. Martha constantly accuses him of being a weakling, and his academic career seems to have been shaped by his lack of ability to join with or stand up to other men. He apparently submitted to Daddy's demand that he withdraw the manuscript of his novel (II, 135), and it is interesting that he was left behind to serve as chairman of his department during the war (I, 38). His relations with women are troubled and showed by an apparent need to hurt, as evidenced in the play by his actions toward both Martha and Honey; and if we assume that George is the boy who (accidentally or not) killed his mother, his troubled relationship can be traced further back in his life. Though he feels threatened by Nick (the chromosome quarrel is the most overt example of his hostility), he backs off from a direct confrontation with Nick on several occasions and turns his most direct fire on Honey. That he has damaged Nick's self-esteem by this maneuver is an unexpected bonus for him (II, 149). But George, in the progress of the night, outgrows his little-boy need to torment the girls and may be able to allow the more mature part of his nature—suggested by his hints of real affection for Martha—to have full play.

The importance of one of the images suggested in the second nursery rhyme has been noted by Ruby Cohn in her insistence on the importance of the word "snap": "In the destruction of illusion, which may lead to truth, 'snap' becomes a stage metaphor—sound, word, and gesture."[7] She emphasizes the importance of the single word and links the image with the St. George legend. But "snap" comes from another of Albee's modified nursery rhymes, this time "Pop Goes the Weasel." It, like the other rhymes, helps to suggest the abnormal, childish natures of George and Martha and their consequent need to come of age. The snap sound, of course, comes into prominence even before this scene; in Act II, Martha insisted that the "whole arrangement" snapped (for her) at Daddy's party. But the image of Act II is only destructive. And while Cohn sees the image as insisting on the reduction of stature in modern life, "St. George slew the dragon; Albee's George slays with snapdragons,"[8] the implications of the imagery of this scene are more complex. Into the "Snap go the dragons" refrain, George introduces still another nursery rhyme, "Here we go round the Mulberry Bush" (III, 202-203). This is the only rhyme which appears unmodified, but it is, of course, reminiscent of Eliot's well-known modification of the line "Here we go round the prickly pear" (in "The Hollow Men"). Albee's reversed modification (back to the original) seems to be drawing on the rich and appropriate suggestion of Eliot's poem. George and Martha have been hollow men whose shouting matches are their whispers of communication and whose activity is as sterile and as purposeless as Eliot's hollow men. But through this last battle, if George can act, the maiden may yet be saved and she and George can live "happily ever after." Their creation, embodied concretely in their imaginary son, is only words and only with words can it be killed. The battle is not the less potentially deadly for being fought with words, nor is the dragon less real for being their illusion.

The fourth, and perhaps the most important, of the nursery rhymes is the basis of Albee's title song, "Who's Afraid of the Big, Bad Wolf?". It comes from the Disney version of the three little pigs story, and while the melody of "Here We Go Round the Mulberry Bush" was substituted in the stage version (because of copyright problems), one must consider the suggestions implicit in Albee's choice of this rhyme. In Disney's version of the story, the first two little pigs, who laugh at their brother for his seriousness and his refusal to have fun, come out rather poorly in their confrontations with the wolf; they do, however, escape with their lives (unlike the first two pigs in the most common versions of the nursery tale), and through the efforts of the third little pig, who behaves in a more mature fashion, they are able to turn the tables on their persecutor. Albee's choice of this rhyme, then, would tend to reinforce the theme of the play, that only through giving up the childish quest for fun and games can one hope to survive. Yet Albee's characters are not the simpler three little pigs, but two children who have aged but never become fully adult, and so he substitutes Virginia Woolf for the earlier Big Bad Wolf. Cohn suggests that the substitution represents a fear of madness which can lead to suicide,[9] but while this is one of the suggestions raised by the change, it seems to me that the allusion is richer than a simple reference to the end of Virginia Woolf's life. In her novels, Virginia Woolf is much concerned with the nature of reality and of personality; she seems to suggest, like a good many other modern novelists, that it is impossible to know reality fully or to be able to define another person.[10] Yet she, like George, also suggests that though it is probably impossible to know the difference between truth and illusion, as George says, "we must carry on as though we did" (III, 202). If there is some suggestion of madness associated with Martha (and George does speak of having her committed), the substituted phrase has richer suggestions, implying not only the fear of madness and death, but also the fear of the fully-committed, adult life represented by Woolf's novels. Martha's acknowledgment of her fear of what Virginia Woolf represents at the end of the play is not quite so dark, then, as it would be if one considered only Woolf as a person; Martha is afraid of adult life in its full implications, but in that acknowledgement lies some hope. Martha, throughout the play, sees herself (falsely) as a great earth mother—both supremely maternal and irresistibly feminine. But the reality of her life, as we see it in the play and as she describes it, presents a contrasting picture of Martha as a sterile mother and an incomplete sex symbol. Only if she gives up playing her present role (in which she must dominate George) is there a hope that they may come to full adult life.

III

Albee offers his strongest statement of his coming-of-age theme and his clearest revelation of the intricacies of character in richly suggestive passages which occur in all three acts. In these he frequently depends not simply on the metaphoric impact of the words themselves but also clusters around them allusive backgrounds which open a wider context and increase the richness of the passages.

The first act is dominated by one such cluster of images and allusions. Albee first introduces the motif when George, rather unwarrantedly, attacks Nick as part of a group (or perhaps the moving force in it) who are "making everyone the same, rearranging the chromozones, or whatever it is" (I, 37); several speeches later he comments that "I read somewhere that science fiction is really not fiction at all . . ." and rather quickly veers off into other conversation. Albee has thus suggested his allusion to the most famous account of controlled birth and development, Huxley's *Brave New World;* and, through George's question, "Do you believe that people learn nothing from history? Not that there is nothing to learn, mind you, but that people learn nothing?" (I, 37), has also posed his own question for his audience. Albee begins his major exploration of the motif later in the act when (having found out more about Nick and having been further provoked by Martha's telling Honey about the child) George re-opens the attack on Nick as biologist. Commenting that he finds him terrifying, George claims that Nick is working on a plan to re-order the chromosomic pattern of the sperm cell; one could thus arrange for the survival of desired qualities, could create a race of men "test-tube-bred . . . incubator-born . . . superb and sublime" (I, 65). Such a system, he contends, will have disadvantages: a necessity for sterilization of those considered unfit for breeding and a certain lack of diversity of the new civilization. George suspects that not much will be left of the arts but that there will be a race of scientists and mathematicians who will make an ordered and stable universe. He, of course, is opposed to this and laments that history "will lose its glorious variety and unpredictability. I, and with me the . . . the surprise, the multiplexity, and sea-changing rhythm of . . . history, will be eliminated. There will be order and constancy . . . and I am unalterably opposed to it. I will not give up Berlin!" (I, 67).

The contrived opposition which George has been setting up between himself and Nick has generally been taken as a symbolic confrontation between the humanities and science (with possible overtones of democracy versus totalitarianism). But the Huxley allusion (with its enclosed allusion to Shakespeare's *The Tempest*) opens a somewhat different and a finally more coherent interpretation. In the seventeenth chapter of *Brave New World,* the Savage and Mustapha Mond, the Controller for Western Europe, have probably the central discussion of Huxley's novel. Here the Savage discovers that not only is art, especially literature, simplified and ordered to suit the new morality (Shakespeare is banned as smutty) and in his opinion drained of aesthetic and moral value, but also that science is strictly limited and controlled. The opposition between science and humanities, in Huxley's terms, turns out to be illusory. Mond argues that happiness and ordered stability can only be achieved by abandoning the search for truth and beauty. Implicit in the Savage's demands for a society with God, poetry, real danger, freedom, goodness, and sin is, as they both acknowledge, "the right to be unhappy."[11] At the end of the chapter, Mond is still willing to accept his plastic society and to leave the Savage to his own notions. Albee, in the passage quoted above, is drawing on Huxley's summing up of the two societies.

When Honey protests that she does not understand George's Berlin reference, George amplifies his refusal to give up Berlin by commenting that "There is a saloon in West Berlin where the barstools are five feet high. And the earth . . . the floor . . . is so . . . far . . . below you. I will not give up things like that" (I, 67-68). Thus Berlin initially seems to be a symbol of the freedom to create pleasant but unfunctional things, a concrete, if trivial, embodiment of the sea-changing rhythm; but there is a darker strain in this complex melody. If Berlin has many positive associations for twentieth century man, it is also indissolubly linked with the madness of Hitler and the Third Reich. And Hitler also refused, in the closing days of the war, to give up Berlin.[12] George's use of Berlin as a symbol of the world he supports carries both positive and negative overtones. His world will have—in addition to its five-foot-high barstools—its Hitlers, its possibility of madness, of suicide. George, like the Savage, rejects the comfortable but sterile brave new world pictured by Huxley. Albee here forecasts George's decision to enter the difficult world of adult life—a decision which necessitates the abandonment of relatively comfortable illusion and a commitment to the difficult, continuing search for truth. It is a mistake, then, to limit George and Nick to symbolic representatives of humanities and science, of democracy and totalitarianism;[13] they may be this, but their opposition, like most of the oppositions of the play, turns out to be an illusion. As Huxley points out the unbreakable link between humanities and science, so Albee, by the end of the play, suggests that both George and Nick have accepted the unpleasantness of truth in preference to the sterile world of illusion.

In the second act, "Walpurgisnacht," Albee turns to a rather more penetrating analysis of the present and past of his characters. Here, again, language which seems naturalistic turns out to have metaphoric overtones. One of the primary indications of George's character is contained in his story which ostensibly is about a drinking episode in his youth. Here he describes the boy who killed his mother and was responsible for the death of his father. George says the accident with the father happened when the boy was sixteen; the boy was taken off to an asylum where for thirty years he has not uttered one word (II, 96). Forty-six, is, of course, George's present age. There are other links between George and the unnamed boy. The boy killed his mother with a shotgun (II, 94) and George, in his first symbolic act of violence against Martha, "shoots" her with a "short-barreled shotgun" (I, 57). This action perhaps also serves as the first foreshadowing of his destruction of her role as mother. While Martha frequently refers to herself as Mummy, George neither calls himself nor is referred to by anyone else as Daddy. He affirms his "partnership in the . . . creation of our . . . blond-eyed, blue-haired . . . son," (I, 72) but he seems less concerned with fatherhood than is Martha with her role as mother. In his story, George insists that the boy killed his mother "accidentally, completely accidentally, without even an unconscious motivation, I have no doubt, no doubt at all—" (II, 94). But George still suffers from a sense of guilt about his mother's death, a guilt on which Martha plays (e.g., II, 138); he must resolve this childhood trauma if he is to survive and built a mature, adult relationship with his wife. George's account of the death of the father (killed in an accident caused by the boy's swerving to avoid a porcupine and hitting a large tree) is curious; there is a quality of unreality about it which makes one wonder if this is a factual account. One suspects not; it seems possible, in view of George's strong and continuing reaction to his mother's death, that the story masks a suicide attempt which, ironically, killed the wrong person. Still another link between the boy and George is his description of the fifteen-year-old boy:"blond and he had the face of a cherub" (II, 95); thus the boy seems to resemble not only George and Martha's phantom child but also Nick, whom George will later pretend to mistake for their son (III, 195-6). George ends the first part of the story with the comment that the "bergin" day was "the grandest day of my . . . youth" (II, 95), a point he does not amplify. What seems to be suggested here is that for once George had a feeling of acceptance, of being part of a group. But with the death of his father, George has retired into a shell which he has not left for thirty years. Finally, one must consider George's comments about the contrast between normal aging and that of the quietly insane, that they do not age in the normal way, that "They maintain a . . . a firm-skinned serenity . . . the . . . the under-use of everything leaves them . . . quite whole" (II, 97) as a comment on himself. As George admits later in the act, in the progress of his twenty-three year marriage to Martha, he has simply learned to endure her, to shut her out (II, 155). Their conflicts are surface ones rather than indications of attempts to come together; hiding behind their vicious childish games, George has refused to come to terms with adult relationships, and only Martha's increasing pressure succeeds in forcing him from this protective shell.

Walpurgisnacht, in Teutonic folklore, is a witches' sabbath celebrated with revelry and dancing. Appropriately, Albee has a dance motif at the center of this act: when Honey insists on dancing, George puts on a record—the second movement of Beethoven's Seventh Symphony. Such action is, of course, a means of provoking Martha, but Albee also uses it to expand our knowledge of these two characters. Though most of the Seventh Symphony is quite cheerful—Richard Wagner has called it "the apotheosis of dance"[14]—the second movement has elements of poignancy and tragedy. Selden Rodman and James Kearns, in *The Heart of Beethoven,* speak of the power and depth of this movement. "Who can say . . . what emotion the grave Allegretto of the Seventh projects? Is its sombre yet buoyant march rhythm indicative of sorrow or joy? It includes both, and simultaneously."[15] Such music, then, is entirely appropriate for their almost demonic gathering. When Martha insists on changing the record, George remarks "Martha's going to put on some rhythm she understands . . . Sacre du Printemps, maybe," (II, 129). George here seems to be identifying himself with the rather more cerebral, almost metaphysical music of Beethoven while he identifies Martha with the complex but pagan and sensual ballet music of Stravinsky.

Towards the end of the second act as the demonic revelry grows more and more frantic, Albee's use of apparently naturalistic language becomes more allusive and metaphoric. A close reading of the end of the act makes one realize that George, calling what he recognizes as Martha's bluff (her provocative flirtation with Nick), challenges her to make an adult commitment—either to himself or Nick (II, 169-173). But George, in spite of his manipulation, cares far more for Martha than he admits, a point of which she is well aware even if others are not. This becomes clear after Martha has left the room when George reads aloud from Spengler: "And the west, encumbered by crippling alliances, and burdened with a morality too rigid to accommodate itself to the swing of events, must . . . eventually . . . fall" (II, 174). The quotation is an accurate reflection of George's position; he is burdened with crippling alliances and he has a morality which can no longer accommodate itself to the kind of life he has been leading. But, here again, the language becomes heavily allusive as the action takes on symbolic overtones. With a cry that is *"part growl, part howl,"* George hurls the book at the door chimes which have already sounded twice previously (when Martha bumped into them). As the third chiming of the bell during the Mass signals the approaching moment of transformation, George is about to undergo his own transformation, a change which will bring the chance of salvation for them all. Honey wanders in asking about the "Poe-bells" which have awakened her. In Poe's poem, the first section describes sleigh bells, the second wedding bells, the third alarm bells (for a fire), and the final section the tolling of funeral bells; Albee, then, is forecasting George's decision to kill the child, the symbol of their retreat from reality. Implicit in this decision, though not yet revealed, is George's positive commitment to enter the adult world. Significantly, it is during this section that Albee reveals to George (and to the audience) the truth about Nick and Honey's childless marriage; like George and Martha, but in a more literal way, Honey and Nick are childless because at least one and probably both partners in the marriage have refused to enter the adult world of responsibility. This linking of the two couples helps to expand the tentative optimism of the ending of the play, since Nick and Honey, if they cease acting as children and accept adult roles, can have a real child.

In the last act, "The Exorcism," Albee's language becomes even more suggestive if not symbolic as the thematic motifs of the first act and the explorations of character of the second act are brought together into a full statement of the theme. Martha opens the act in a soliloquy which begins with complaint about her abandonment and loneliness in terms of the immediate situation but which moves swiftly into a metaphoric and allusive exploration of her essential loneliness. That she has not yet thrown off her childish ways is evident by her references to the children's game, "Hide and Go Seek," "I'LL GIVE ALL YOU BASTARDS FIVE TO COME OUT FROM WHERE YOU'RE HIDING!!" (III, 186). She says that, like Daddy, she and George cry all the time, and "we take our tears, and we put 'em in the ice box, in the goddam ice trays (*Begins to laugh*) until they're all frozen (*Laughs even more*) and then . . . we put them . . . in our . . . drinks. (*More laughter, which is something else, too*)" (III, 186). Their unhappiness, instead of being put to creative use, is frozen and used as an ingredient in their unsuccessful search for forgetfulness and comradeship. They drink together, but that is their only communion. She continues (after a *"sobering silence"*) "Up the drain, down the spout, dead, gone and forgotten. . . . Up the spout, not down the spout: *Up* the spout: THE POKER NIGHT. Up the spout . . ." (III, 186). Part of what Albee is suggesting here is the reversal of the sexually-charged dissolution cliché; thus Martha insists on her change to "up" rather than "down." "THE POKER NIGHT," in addition to its sexual connotations, is an allusion to Tennessee Williams' *A Streetcar Named Desire.* In the stage directions for Scene Three (subtitled "The Poker Night"), Williams emphasizes a combination of adult and childhood images.[16] Williams' scene is dominated by the violence between Stanley and Stella which is their expression of love even as Martha and George's more sophisticated violence is an expression of their need and love. Williams ends his scene with Blanche calling for kindness from Mitch; George and Martha also need kindness in their relations with each other, but what is at issue in the play is whether they have the strength, unlike Blanche, to break out of their childish and now nightmarish illusion.

In the almost antiphonal recitation which follows her soliloquy, Martha speaks of her relationship with George and indicates that she has a fuller understanding of herself and of him than might have been suspected. George is the only one, she says, who has ever made her happy (III, 189-190); this statement, as Nick assumes, has immediate sexual implications, but Martha means a good deal more by it. The two of them need each other but she cannot forgive him for having "made the hideous, the hurting, the insulting mistake of loving me" (III, 191). Notwithstanding all her claims of superiority (which she will renew later in the act), she suffers from a strong sense of inferiority; she has never come to terms with herself any more than George has. Thus, the child is a symbol of their full lack of self-acceptance; he is the only means they have of coming together, even if only to quarrel, like children over an imaginary playmate.

Later in the scene Albee includes a direct quotation from Williams when George enters with the snapdragons and begins his final attack with the words, "Flores; flores para los muertos. Flores" (III, 195). In Scene Nine of *Streetcar,* when Blanche's illusionary world is first shattered by Mitch's rejection of her, a blind Mexican vendor woman comes to the door and offers tin flowers to Blanche with these words. Albee uses the allusion here partially as another of the elements foreshadowing the death of the child; but the contrast between the two struggles in illusory worlds, comfortable and safe but finally sterile, also enriches and strengthens the characters of Martha and George.

Having pretended to mistake Nick for their son, George switches to another role; putting on an accent and parodying the inarticulate, bashful suitor, he stammers that he's brought her flowers. Martha's reply, "Pansies! Rosemary! Violence! My wedding bouquet!" (III, 196) is an indirect allusion to Ophelia's bouquets in her mad scene in *Hamlet.* Martha's transformation of violets to violence probably harks back to Honey's cries of "Violence" in Act II (137, 195). Yet if Ophelia's mad use of the flowers indicates her escape into illusion when reality, with its violence, became too painful, Martha's wedding bouquet is a transformation of the idea. Ophelia escapes from violence, Martha to violence, but they are both escapes. Additionally Martha's speech serves as an ironic commentary on her marriage—composed of thoughts, remembrance, and violence.

George and Martha get into an argument about whether the moon was up or down when he picked the flowers and whether, if the moon does go down, it can come back up—an argument which leaves Nick baffled. But closer examination of the passage (see III, 199-201) clarifies the terms of the argument somewhat; they are, in fact, still talking primarily about whether or not Nick "made it in the sack" (III, 202). George insists on his own fidelity and on Martha's; in his answer to her statement that the moon has gone down, "That may very well be, Chastity; the moon may very well have gone down . . . but it came back up" (III, 199), he is arguing that while she might think about being unfaithful, having considered it she would, like the moon, come back up. Once one remembers that Diana, the moon goddess, is also the patron of chastity, one begins to see the terms of their game. The difference between "truth and illusion" and "truth or illusion" (see III, 201-204) provides further insight; their stories are sometimes distorted truth ("truth and illusion"), sometimes complete, but wished for and possible fantasy ("truth or illusion"). When Martha lyingly confirms Nick's statement that he is not a houseboy (III, 202), George accepts the statement and begins his dragonkilling, commenting that it no longer matters to him (III,

204); that is, he is now firmly committed to destroying the illusory basis of their relationship and is ready to proceed to the final game, "Bringing Up Baby."

George goads Martha into the recitation of "Our son" (III, 217-224) and allows her to get well started on the description of the childhood of the boy who kept his rubber-cupped arrows under his bed "for fear, Just that: for fear" (III, 219). The boy is, of course, partially a symbol of their marriage—a marriage in which they are united in their need to stave off their fears about themselves. Their attacks, like the boy's rubber-cupped arrows, are part of the games they play in an effort to mask their fears. As Martha continues, George begins to recite, correctly, the Tract from the service for the burial of the dead. After the story of how the boy broke his arm, George inserts the first line of the hymn usually sung as the coffin is moved out of the church after the burial service, and then goes on to recite the second sentence of the Gradual, which normally precedes the Tract. If the recitation is, in part, another of the atmospheric foreshadowings of the announcement of death, it is also specifically relevant. Here, after Martha's statement that the boy "walked evenly between us . . . (*She spreads her hands*) . . . a hand out to each of us for what we could offer by way of support, affection, teaching, even love . . . and these hands, still, to hold us off a bit, for mutual protection, to protect us all from George's . . . weakness . . . and my . . . necessary greater strength . . . to protect himself . . . and *us*" (III, 221-222), George says (in Latin) "The righteous person shall be in everlasting remembrance; he shall not fear evil tidings." The child, then, is no longer to be the buffer or barrier between them; they will now have to offer support, affection, teaching, even love directly. Later, as Martha protests that she has tried "to protect, to raise above the mire of this vile, crushing marriage; the one light in all this hopeless *darkness* . . . OUR SON," George recites the final prayer for the dead, normally said at the foot of the coffin at the end of the service (III, 227). He is now ready to announce the death of the boy, and his description of their son's death is the description, only slightly modified, of the death of the father of the boy who killed his mother. Their son, then, is not only a symbol of the childishly unresolved guilts and of their lack of acceptance of themselves. He was the phantom playmate of the two "vicious children, with their oh-so-sad games, hopscotching their way through life, etcetera, etcetera" (III, 197); the time has now come to put away childish things and to emerge as mature adults. As Nick and Honey (who have finally come to an understanding of the situation and perhaps to an understanding of themselves) exit, the scene closes on the remaining couple. In their last interchanges, Albee sketches their condition briefly but clearly. George, now completely broken free from his shell-retreat and firmly in control, will not let them lapse back into childhood and Martha's acknowledgment of her fear of Virginia Woolf is both optimistic and subtly threatening; through her acknowledgment, the way is opened for salvation, but the very image which suggests her now acknowledged fear of reality also suggests the terrible dangers which lie ahead.

IV

Looking at the play as a whole and keeping in mind the suggestions presented through Albee's sophisticated use of language, one comes to recognize that exorcism of the crippling ghosts of their pasts, symbolized by the phantom child, is necessary for George and Martha's coming of age and perhaps for their survival. Identifying these ghosts and their effects on the characters, one must recognize that what George and Martha say about their respective pasts is essentially true though not necessarily factual—a device of half-communication with which they are both quite familiar through their game-playing. The full picture of Martha emerges through hints given in speeches which ostensibly present almost the opposite picture. Not having been loved as a child, Martha has come to see herself as unlovable; consequently she must achieve domination as a tacit acknowledgment of her value. Her speeches describing what she sees as her extraordinary rapport with her father, however, reveal fathoms of self-doubt beneath her confident surface: "Mommy died early, see, and I sort of grew up with Daddy. (*Pause—thinks*) . . . I went away to school, and stuff, but I more or less grew up with him. Jesus, I admired that guy! I worshipped him. . . . I absolutely worshipped him. I still do. And he was pretty fond of me, too . . . you know? We had a real . . . rapport going . . . a real rapport" (I, 77). While worship may be one of the attitudes a young child has for its father, through Martha's overstated insistence on her continuing worship of her father, Albee delineates what is basically a one-way relationship. Further, George's comment at the end of the play, that her father "really doesn't give a damn whether she lives or dies, who couldn't care less *what* happens to his only daughter" (III, 225), confirms the suggestions of her speech as well as indicating George's clear-sighted perception of Martha's nature. But in spite of her sense of inferiority, Martha loves George as much as she can permit herself to love any real person. Her description of herself planning to marry the heir-apparent and then falling for George (see I, 81-83) suggests this; even the boxing incident reveals a hidden affection and love for George. For all the fact that she now tells the story to humiliate him, she still insists that her knocking him down was an accident, that George was undoubtedly "off balance" (I, 56).

George's ghosts—his guilt feelings about the deaths of his parents—have already been identified. And if Martha married for love, there are also indications in George's language that he loves her; when George and Nick are talking about their wives, George starts to make a significant distinction between himself and Nick: "Things are simpler with you . . . you marry a woman because she's all blown up . . . while I, in my clumsy, old-fashioned way . . ." (II, 102). Later, speaking of their present relationship, he insists that "Now, on the surface of it . . . it looks to be a kind of knock-about, drag-out affair, on the *surface* of it . . . but somewhere back there, at the beginning of it, right when I first came to New Carthage, back then . . ." (II, 103-104). Further, his reaction in the moments when he thinks that Martha may be unfaithful to him (especially at the end of Act II) seems unusually strong for a man who doesn't care about his wife. Finally, his behavior at the end of the play, especially as indicated in the stage directions, is full of a tenderness that is inexplicable unless he still cares for Martha. In dealing with Albee's multi-faceted characters, one must go beneath the surface of their language if one is to recognize the truth behind their protective masks of illusion. In spite of their attacks on each other (which are really defensive rather than offensive), they are still in love. Their marriage has been strained to the snapping point, and an exorcism of their childhood ghosts is clearly imperative.

Albee constructs the play carefully, slowly increasing the tempo and the intensity. In the first act, "Fun and Games," the conflicts are only slightly enlarged from reality. And even in this act, as has been noted, Albee indicates through the language that the play is, like most of the great naturalistic plays, more than simply a photograph of society. The conflicts between George and Nick and between George and Martha serve as a prelude, an introduction of themes which thunder forth in the more explicit character revelation of the second act. There, as the revelry grows wilder, George's violence towards Martha ceases to be symbolic, as with the toy gun, and becomes actual, in the attempt to throttle her. The need to prove herself attractive drives Martha beyond her flirtation of the first act as she tries increasingly desperate measures to awaken a response from George. Nick, who early in the act had joked about the best way to further his career, finds himself attempting to act out his joke while Honey retreats to the bathroom to curl up in a foetal position. The last act functions as an exorcism of their childish guilts and illusions while it also suggests that George, and perhaps all the characters, take on new knowledge and responsibilities. The truth or illusion game no longer interests George; he recognizes that one must act as though reality could be defined. On the death of the phantom son, the embodiment of their ghosts, they must put the past away and, in the uncertain light of dawn, face reality.

That Albee has been concerned with something more than surface realism, that his plays have been his vision of reality presented symbolically, is evident even in his earlier work. An examination of the language of this play suggests that the real world has always been more complex than any of Albee's characters (except perhaps George) realized, and even he attempted to ignore important distinctions because they complicated his life. Through his use of apparently simple naturalistic language which closer examination proves complexly metaphoric and allusive, Albee brings at least George and perhaps all of the characters to a realization that to refuse to recognize, either wilfully or through avoidable ignorance, the complexities of life, to attempt to live in the simpler world of childhood is dangerous and finally unproductive, sterile. One must, as Eliot suggested in "The Hollow Men" and as Huxley suggested in *Brave New World,* accept the full range of possibilities—both good and evil—if one is to have a chance of succeeding; otherwise one exists in the large bottle of deadness, whether induced by alcohol or soma, but one does not accomplish anything except the creation of a phantom child. New Carthage, with its allusion to its more famous ancestor's history of passionate love, is the appropriate residence of all Albee's characters in this play. Like Aeneas and Augustine, who took up their mature, adult roles only after leaving Carthage, Albee's characters must leave their juvenile residence and move into the adult world. Nick and Honey's coming of age is sketched less fully, but Albee suggests it by her announcement that she wants a child and by his finally beginning to understand what is going on. For George and Martha, Albee demonstrates, the acceptance of themselves as adults is dangerous but necessary for their immediate survival and, insofar as they are the spiritual parents of us all, for the continuation of the race.

NOTES

[1]For a representative sampling of opinion on this point see Anthony C. Hilfer, "George and Martha: Sad, Sad, Sad," in *Seven Contemporary Authors: Essays on Cozzens, Miller, West, Golding, Heller, Albee and Powers,* ed. Thomas B. Whitbread (Austin, 1966), pp. 121-139; Joy Flasch, "Games People Play in *Who's Afraid of Virginia Woolf?*", *Modern Drama,* 10 (1967), 280-288; Michael E. Rutenberg, *Edward Albee: Playwright in Protest* (New York, 1969) pp. 95-115; Henry Knepler, "Edward Albee: Conflict of Tradition," *Modern Drama,* 10 (1967), 274-279; C. W. E. Bigsby, *Albee* (Edinburgh, 1969); and Anne Paolucci, *From Tension to Tonic: The Plays of Edward Albee* (Carbondale, 1972), pp. 45-63.

[2]See Max Halperan, "What Happens in *Who's Afraid of Virginia Woolf?*" in *Modern American Drama: Essays in Criticism,* ed. William Edward Taylor (Deland, Florida, 1968); Gilbert Debusscher, *Edward Albee: Tradition and Renewal* (Brussels, 1967); and Emil Roy, "*Who's Afraid of Virginia Woolf?* and the Tradition," *Bucknell Review,* 13 (1965), 27-36.

[3]Arthur K. Oberg, "Edward Albee: His Language and Imagination," *Prairie Schooner,* 40 (1966), 139-146; Ruth Meyer, "Language: Truth and Illusion in *Who's Afraid of Virginia Woolf?*", *ETJ,* 20 (1968), 60-69.

[4]Meyer, p. 56.

[5]Edward Albee, *Who's Afraid of Virginia Woolf?* (New York, 1966), p. 163. Further references to the play will be made parenthetically in the text.

[6]Oberg, p. 139.

[7]*Edward Albee* (Minneapolis, 1969), p. 121.

[8]*Ibid.,* p. 21.

[9]*Ibid.,* p. 22.

[10]This seems to be especially true in *Jacob's Room* and *Mrs. Dalloway.*

[11](New York, 1932), p. 288. The preliminary material of this discussion occurs in chapter sixteen.

[12]See the account of Hitler's radio speech promising that he "would stay in Berlin and defend it to the end," in William L. Shirer, *The Rise and Fall of the Third Reich* (New York, 1960), p. 1113.

[13]See Roy, p. 35 and Rutenberg, p. 100.

[14]*Richard Wagner's Prose Works,* trans. William Ashton Ellis, (New York, 1966), I, 124.

[15](New York, 1962), p. 80.

[16]"There is a picture of Van Gogh's of a billiard-parlor at night. The kitchen now suggests that sort of lurid nocturnal brilliance, the raw colors of childhood's spectrum." (New York, 1947), p. 46.

Thomas P. Adler (essay date 1973)

SOURCE: "Albee's *Who's Afraid of Virginia Woolf?:* A Long Night's Journey into Day," in *Educational Theatre Journal,* Vol. 25, No. 1, March 1973, pp. 66-70.

Richard Burton (George), Elizabeth Taylor (Martha), George Segal (Nick), and Sandy Dennis (Honey) in the 1966 film adaptation of *Who's Afraid of Virginia Woolf?*

[*In this essay, Adler investigates the role of the younger couple in* Who's Afraid of Virginia Woolf?, *arguing that in the course of the play "George and Martha have bared themselves so that Nick and Honey can be saved, and in the process they themselves are saved."*]

Before the curtain falls on Edward Albee's ***Who's Afraid of Virginia Woolf?,*** Nick and Honey, the young guests of George and Martha at their pre-dawn round of "fun and games," can be seen as undergoing a radical change. Honey, for years "afraid" of pregnancy and childbirth because she "[doesn't] want to be hurt,"[1] now asserts three times, "I want a child" (III, 222-223); while Nick, who earlier rejects George's philosophical and ethical system, now acknowledges (likewise three times), "Jesus Christ, I think I understand this" (III, 236). These responses seem to signal a redirection in the lives of Honey and Nick to which most critics of Albee's drama have paid only scant attention.[2] Furthermore, such a redirection—which is brought about largely through the instrumentality of George and Martha—would not only parallel but would also buoy up the sense of new communion between the older couple at the end of the play.

In the decade which has now passed since the play opened on Broadway, critics have persistently cited the illusion/reality dichotomy as the central thematic motif, although there is certainly no consensus of opinion on the question of which Albee believes is preferable, illusion or reality. Daniel McDonald and Richard Amacher both feel that Albee is championing the role of illusion.[3] If Michael Rutenberg is just as certain that Albee believes "life cannot be lived through illusion, no matter how comforting," Ruby Cohn is not at all sure that Albee would say life can be lived through truth either, "since George's attack on Martha's illusion is so theatrically punitive that his redemptive intention is questionable."[4] Albee's conclusion, however, may be less ambiguous if we no longer insist on the centrality of the illusion/reality theme, thus removing ourselves from any temptation to conclude, along with Richard Gilman, that Albee "wants to say something profound about the human condition, and . . . ends . . . offering a cliché about illusions"[5]—or about truth. Far from ambiguity or cliché, the play's predominantly hopeful conclusion contains a large measure of profundity.

Rictor Norton, in his article isolating the "mythic folklore" elements employed by Albee, has insisted on the "positive and affirmative nature of Albee's drama" since "it is a ritual of purgation and purification"; however, Norton sees as the basis for affirmation the fact that "George and Martha will no longer live a life of manifold illusions."[6] Yet the affirmation has, I suggest, a deeper basis than simply the destruction of the illusionary child. It arises from the audience's recognition that George exorcises the child not only to kill the illusion and live in reality, but to destroy one reality—that in which he has failed to exercise the strength necessary to make the marriage creative even without children—and create a new reality to take its place. George, through mapping out for Nick and Honey the way to redirect their lives, achieves for Martha and himself a radical redirection of their own.

Midway through ***Virginia Woolf,*** George tells Nick, "You disgust me on principle, and you're a smug son of a bitch personally, but I'm trying to give you a survival kit"; he is trying "to reach" Nick, to "make contact," to "communicate" (II, 115-116). George is doing for Nick exactly what Jerry does for Peter in ***The Zoo Story.*** Both George and Jerry realize "that neither kindness nor cruelty by themselves, independent of each other, creates any effect beyond themselves," and that ordinarily "we neither love nor hurt because we do not try to reach each other."[7] Such a belief implies, of course, that if love does fail then one must be willing to hurt the other person in order to reach him. So Jerry "hurts" Peter out of his conformity and unconcern and into an assertion of his humanity by forcing Peter to hold the knife on which Jerry impales himself, just as George "hurts" Nick and Honey because he *must* hurt them to help them survive. Each man recognizes the total inadequacy of the motto Tobias adopts in ***A Delicate Balance***: "We do what we can."[8] Desperate measures are often necessary. Thus, in ***Virginia Woolf*** what at first may seem like vicious games at the guests' expense are actually George's attempts to do what he must to make Honey understand the selfishness and destructiveness of her fears and Nick the sterility of his life on all levels-biological, intellectual, and ethical.

Criticising ***Virginia Woolf*** as if it were purely naturalistic, Richard Dozier has charged Albee with a lack of dramatic integrity in his "reluctance to see [the adultery between Nick and Martha] through." Because Nick is temporarily impotent with Martha, Dozier claims that "Martha's adultery is reduced to a farce."[9] What Dozier has evidently failed to see is the symbolic dimension of Nick's temporary impotence, which Albee uses to suggest the sterility of Nick's entire life. First, his very intellectuality is impotent in that his narrow scientific theories, unenhanced by any humanistic concerns, are destructive rather than creative. Martha herself taunts Nick for being a "lunkhead": "You see everything but the goddamn mind; you see all the little specks and crap, but you don't see what goes on, do you?" (III, 192). And George accuses him of being "a smug and self-righteous scientist" who would substitute inevitability and determinism for history's "glorious variety and unpredictability." Whereas George, as an historian, sees beauty in "the surprise, the multiplicity, the sea-changing rhythm of . . . history," Nick wants to erase this variety; he would rearrange chromosomes and alter genetic composition to produce"a race of men . . . test-tube-bred . . . incubator-born . . . superb and sublime" (I, 65-67)—and all preferably modelled after himself. George regards this as the death knell for civilization, which sounds doubly harsh to his ears now that history has advanced to the point where civilization finally matters.

Second, Nick, in effect, is being rendered biologically impotent by Honey. Nick, the all-American boy so conscious of his masculinity (he is kin to the Young Man in Albee's ***American Dream***), has, at least figuratively, been emasculated by his wife Honey. It is not just that he married her while she was experiencing a false pregnancy and is now "solicitous" of his "mousey" wife "to a point that faileth human understanding" (II, 144). If, as George suspects, Honey has been aborting their children without Nick's knowledge, by "secret little murders stud-boy doesn't know about" (II, 177), then Honey is actually unmanning Nick. In her compassion for Martha and George over the "death" of their child, Honey feels very sharply her own loss as well, so her fears of having a child dissolve, and Nick's potentiality as a progenitor is restored.

Significantly, the only time when George and Martha do not thrust the blame at each other for their own failures is in their inability to have children. Confronted by Nick's query, George replies, and Martha echoes with *"a hint of communion,"* "*We* couldn't" (III, 238). Nick is unable to fully articulate his response: "I'd like to. . . ."; (III, 238). The ellipsis perhaps suggests an unsaid "thank you," for the new creativity in Nick and Honey's marriage is largely the result of George and Martha's sacrifice and concern. Interestingly, George bids the young couple, "Home to bed, children; it's way past your bedtime" (III, 238); in a sense, Nick and Honey have become the older couple's adopted children, taking the position once filled by the now-exorcised illusory child. Nothing could be further from Albee's point than Thomas Porter's assertion that the playwright, by attacking the"notion that the child is (or can be) a real bond of union between husband and wife," is "call[ing] into question. . . the unitive potential of procreation."[10]

If Nick was figuratively emasculated by Honey, it is even more true that George has been subjected to some rearrangement of chromosomes at the hands of Martha.[11] Whereas in ***The American Dream*** there is no question that it is Mommy who is totally responsible for emasculating Daddy, here there is some ambiguity about just where the blame should be placed.[12] There is no disputing that the process of George's emasculation began when Martha, disgusted at his lack of aggressiveness in the boxing match with her father, knocked George down "flat . . . in a huckleberry bush," an event which has"colored [their] whole life," since George has used it as an excuse "for being bogged down, . . . [for] why he hasn't gone anywhere" (I, 56-57). At various times during their rounds of verbal flagellation, Martha calls George "a blank, a cipher," "a zero," "a great . . . big . . . fat . . . FLOP!" without "any . . . personality," "a man drowning" who lacks"the guts" to "rip me to pieces" (I, 17, 84-85; II, 139, 158). She claims that George married her to be humiliated and torn apart, and that she only "wear[s] the pants in this house because somebody's got to" (II, 157). The reason for Martha's dominance is, finally, "George's . . . weakness and my . . . necessary greater strength" (III, 222). George, however, denies these allegations, insisting that she is "deluded"; he is actually disgusted at the constant ridicule she heaps upon him and has "been trying for years to clean up the mess I made" (II, 102). Who is to blame, then, is clearly not as important in Albee's mind as the fact that both George and Martha urgently desire a changed relationship, a marriage rebuilt on a new foundation, for they sense that the opportunity and ability to establish one diminish with the passing of time. As Agnes says in ***Delicate Balance,*** "Everything becomes . . . too late, finally. . . . time happens. When you *do* go, sword, shield . . . finally. . .there's nothing there . . . save rust; bone; and the wind" (III, 169). So George and Martha are, as the stage direction tells us, "*relieved . . . elated*" now that "total war" has come (II, 159); they have arrived, and none too soon, at the point of ultimate hurt in order to reach one another.

Martha not only asserts that her "arm has gotten tired whipping" George (II, p. 153), but is also honestly afraid that she will someday destroy the only "man in my life who has ever . . . made me happy" if a new balance is not achieved soon in their marriage: "Someday . . . hah! some *night* . . . some stupid, liquor-ridden night . . . I will go too far . . . and I'll either break the man's back . . . or push him off for good . . . which is what I deserve" (III, 189, 191). Martha, therefore, emphatically wants George to assert his strength. Whenever George gets the upper hand in one of the games they play, as with the gun that fires the Chinese parasol, she is openly pleased with him:"that was pretty good" (I, 58). But she realizes, at the same time, that the gun is just a substitute, a "prop," and so she goads George on by comparing him unfavorably with Nick, who does not "need any props" because he is "right at the meat of things" (I, 61, 63). However, by the next time that George symbolically asserts his manhood—when he throws the snapdragons "*spear-like*" at Martha—what Martha calls Nick's "dandy potential" (III, 188) has been proven, on that night anyway, simply a sham, whereas George will soon need no symbolic prop as a substitute for actual manly strength.

For George, too, has decided that the time for a reordering of their relationship has come. He will not be made a mock of any longer, since "man can put up with only so much without he descends a rung or two on the old evolutionary ladder" (I, 51) and begins an irreversible process of descent. When you "can't abide the present" as it is, George says there are just two options open: people can either "turn to a contemplation of the past, as I have done, or they can set about to . . . alter the future. And when you want to change something . . . you BANG! BANG! BANG! BANG!" (II, 178). Until now, he has contemplated the past; from now on, he will "alter the future" by asserting *his* "necessary strength." As Forrest Hazzard says, "by exercising firmness and love intelligence [the male principle] must tame matter [the female principle] without abusing it. If this mastery occurs, the two principles fuse into a higher synthesis or enter, so to speak, into a marriage; and from this union flow all the achievements of civilization."[13] George, despite Martha's vehement insistence that "I WILL NOT LET YOU DECIDE THESE THINGS!" (III, 232), exorcises the child. In so doing, he "tames" Martha without "abusing" her and establishes his strength as the foundation and sustenance of their renewed marriage.

George and Martha have bared themselves so that Nick and Honey can be saved, and in the process they themselves are saved. It is early Sunday morning, but it is not at all like the false dawn that presages a return to darkness with which ***Delicate Balance*** ends. In that play, Agnes' "Come now; we can begin the day" (III, 175) is ironic, for she is assuring her family that the condition of balance, of stasis, that had for so long marked their hollow death-in-life existence can be re-established. Agnes and Tobias have seen the emptiness of their lives reflected in the mirror image of Harry and Edna, but they have simply reasserted that emptiness and indifference by their decision to "do what we can" instead of more. Tobias, unlike George and Jerry, will do for others only conditionally, only if they can give something in return—in this case, the assurance that his own life has not been a complete waste, "has not all been empty" (III, 156). If Thomas Porter's judgment that "they are left facing the Void" were applied not to George and Martha but rather to Agnes and Tobias, then it would be more appropriate. Although Porter admits that "George and Martha do find a new basis for union, their union," he insists, "is isolationist, sterile, dependent on a mutual need. . . . The note of hope that rings in their mutual concern seems like a whistling in the graveyard."[14] It is not precisely accurate to see the communion between George and Martha at the end of ***Virginia Woolf,*** however, as founded wholly on "*mutual* need," though it does involve "mutual *concern,*" which is something quite different and, for Albee, quite positive, since he suggests that there is no greater love than not failing another in a moment of need. George, like Jerry but unlike Tobias, actually gives more than he receives, for the real strength that he wins for himself is not so much his self-respect as it is the strength not to fail Martha in her time of fear. He takes hold of her with love, and she, in her fear and weakness, finds assurance in his "necessary greater strength." Yet they only enter upon this new beginning because they first did not fail to satisfy the needs of Honey and Nick, even though this involved suffering for themselves.

Notes

[1]Edward Albee, *Who's Afraid of Virginia Woolf?* (New York, 1962), p. 176. Further references are to this edition and will be cited by act and page number in the text.

[2]R. H. Gardner even claims that "Nick and Honey are incidental" to the play (*The Splintered Stage: The Decline of the American Theater* [New York, 1966], p. 149).

[3]Daniel McDonald, "Truth and Illusion in *Who's Afraid of Virginia Woolf?," Renascence,* 17 (Winter 1964), 63; Richard Amacher, *Edward Albee* (New York, 1969), p. 107.

[4]Michael E. Rutenberg, *Edward Albee: Playwright in Protest* (New York, 1970), p. 107; Ruby Cohn, *Edward Albee* (Minneapolis, 1969), p. 22.

[5]"Here We Go Round the Albee Bush," *The Commonweal,* Nov. 9, 1962, p. 176.

[6]"Folklore and Myth in *Who's Afraid of Virginia Woolf?," Renascence,* 23 (Spring 1971), 159-167.

[7]*The American Dream and The Zoo Story* (New York, 1961), pp. 35-36.

[8]*A Delicate Balance* (New York, 1967), p. 19. Further references are to this edition and will be cited by act and page number in the text.

[9]"Adultery and Disappointment in *Who's Afraid of Virginia Woolf?," Modern Drama,* 11 (Feb, 1969), 432, 436.

[10]*Myth and Modern American Drama* (Detroit, 1969), p. 237.

[11]George, of course, also feels threatened with "intellectual" emasculation by Nick if the younger man's scientific theories should prevail: "I will fight you, my young man . . . one hand on my scrotum, to be sure . . . but with my free hand I will battle you to the death" (I, p. 68). And, contrary to Dozier's opinion that "by the time we reach the third act the talk about chromosomes is all but forgotten" (p. 435), the audience will probably remember the earlier mention of chromosomes, since it is not merely extraneous small talk but is integral to an understanding of the change which George and Martha's relationship undergoes.

[12]There is even greater ambiguity on this question in *A Delicate Balance,* since Albee, like Strindberg, becomes more understanding and sympathetic towards women in his later plays.

[13]"The Major Theme in *Who's Afraid of Virginia Woolf?," The CEA Critic,* 31 (Dec. 1968), 10.

[14]Porter, p. 247.

Denise Dick Herr (essay date 1995)

SOURCE: "The Tophet at Carthage: Setting in *Who's Afraid of Virginia Woolf?*," in *English Language Notes,* Vol. XXXIII, No. 1, September 1995, pp. 63-71.

[*In the following essay, Herr compares New Carthage, the fictional town in which* Who's Afraid of Virginia Woolf? *is set, with the historical city of Carthage, where it is known that child sacrifices were held. "Obviously, ancient Carthage witnessed numerous child sacrifices," she observes; "perhaps it is only appropriate to expect at least one such sacrifice in New Carthage."*]

The action in Edward Albee's drama ***Who's Afraid of Virginia Woolf,*** takes place in a living room in New Carthage, somewhere in New England. Because the characters George and Martha repeatedly mention New Carthage (they do so six times), the audience soon notices it is a strange name—a name relatively foreign to New England—and begins to wonder what symbolic meanings are inherent in the setting.

On the surface, the New Carthage living room of the original set seems to be "perfectly normal,"[1] "grounded in everyday, verifiable reality,"[2] or reassuringly naturalistic;[3] however, Alan Schneider, who helped create the set, states that there is more to it than is noticed at first glance. He says that it "has all kinds of angles and planes that you wouldn't ordinarily have, and strong distortions," and that "we certainly never thought of it as being realistic."[4] Albee joins with his set designer to encourage audiences and critics to see beyond the surface of drama. "If people were a little more aware of what actually is beneath the naturalistic overlay," he says, "they would be surprised to find how early the unnaturalistic base had been set. When you're dealing with a symbol in a realistic play, it is also a realistic fact. You must expect the audience's mind to work on both levels, symbolically and realistically."[5] He also says, "A play, to be at all interesting, has got to move on two or possibly three or four levels."[6] In ***Who's Afraid of Virginia Woolf?,*** New Carthage alludes to its ancient name-sake on at least four levels, all enriching the play.

First there is the allusion to the passionate love story of Dido and Aeneas.[7] Martha, as the daughter of the college president who fell in love with the new history teacher, is somewhat like Dido, the Queen of Carthage who fell in love with the young traveller, Aeneas. Furthermore, the destructive nature of George and Martha's relationship echoes Dido's suicide at Aeneas's departure.

On another level, ancient Carthage is a place mentioned and condemned by St. Augustine.[8] Augustine's announcement in *The Confessions,* "To Carthage I came,"[9] is echoed by George's statement: "When I first came to New Carthage."[10] Augustine continues: "At Carthage, there reigns among scholars a most disgraceful and unruly license."[11] Nick, who thinks he can advance in the college if he can "plow a few pertinent wives" (112), clearly illustrates this attitude. Augustine adds: "There sang all around me in my ears a cauldron of unholy loves."[12] All four of the characters reveal their "unholy loves" in their misplaced values: George has sold out for ambition; Martha is coarse and vulgar; Nick is cruel, weak and ambitious; and Honey is simply an echo.[13] All of them have minimized their lives by "not rebelling against a loveless god."[14]

A third level on which New Carthage parallels its ancient counterpart is the political front. Carthage, with its economic vitality in the sixth and fifth centuries BCE, was a strong force in the western Mediterranean; however, it engaged in a power struggle with Rome over colonies in Sicily and Sardinia and was finally destroyed in the Third Punic War (149-146 BCE). One critic says that the town is "ominously named New Carthage to suggest impending destruction,"[15] while others see that "the name insinuates inevitable doom for whatever place this campus really represents,"[16] or even that "New Carthage is yet another image of fallen civilization, in particular a symbol of failed America" that includes the "dehumanizing values of materialism, pragmatism, and accommodation."[17] George's reading of Spengler's *Decline of the West* leads still another critic to see parallels between ancient and New Carthage: "For Spengler," writes C.W.E. Bigsby, "there was a clear parallel to be drawn between Carthage and modern America. In both, power and money provided the principal axes for behaviour. In his cyclical view of history, both marked . . . the victory of money power over culture. And the consequence was a brutalism and sterile intellectualism."[18]

Ancient Carthage was the scene of a tragic love story, a place condemned by St. Augustine, and a symbol of impending destruction. But most importantly, it is the site of a tophet—a child sacrifice precinct. Activities in the tophet at ancient Carthage parallel the climax of the play when George "kills" his phantom child. Although many critics speak of George's "sacrifice" of his son, only one observes that child sacrifice was required in ancient Carthage, and that George and Martha's son must be sacrificed.[19] Most of the other critics ignore this important parallel.

Carthage is well-known for child sacrifices. Shelby Brown, who has studied inscriptions in the tophet, states, "Carthage provides the best evidence for the nature and practice of this rite [child sacrifice]. . . . The Carthaginians were the most influential, famous representatives of western Phoenician culture, and the sacrificers of the largest number of their own children. The sacrificial cemetery at Carthage is the largest ever found and the one with the longest span."[20]

Knowledge of the tophet at Carthage would have been available to Albee in classical sources. Silius Italicus, a Latin poet writing in the last quarter of the first century CE, reports that the Carthaginians "were accustomed to appease the gods by human sacrifice and to offer up their young children—horrible to tell—upon fiery altars."[21] Diodorus of Sicily, who wrote a history during the mid-first century BCE, records that at one time during the Punic Wars, the citizens of Carthage were in such great distress that between 300 and 500 children were sacrificed in an attempt to achieve victory. He describes the bronze image with extended hands and the fiery pit that were used for the sacrifices.[22] Kleitarchos a third century BCE author, whose work is available to us only in paraphrase by later authors, details the sacrifices:

> . . . the Phoenicians, and especially the Carthaginians, whenever they seek to obtain some great favor, vow one of their children, burning it as a sacrifice to the deity, if they are especially eager to gain success. There stands in their midst a bronze statue of Kronos [the Greek equivalent of Ba'al Hamon, the main god of the Tyrian-Carthaginian pantheon], its hands extended over a bronze brazier, the flames of which engulf the child. When the flames fall upon the body, the limbs contract and the open mouth seems almost to be laughing, until the contracted (body) slips quietly into the brazier.[23]

In his 1862 romantic novel *Salammbô,* Gustave Flaubert combined the mass sacrifice related by Diodorus and the description of Kleitarchos: "The brazen arms were working more quickly. They paused no longer. Every time that a child was placed in them the priests . . . spread out their hands upon him to burden him with the crimes of the people."[24] James Frazer uses these and other classical descriptions in *The Golden Bough,* where he writes of children sliding from the hands of an image into an oven while flutes and timbrels are played in an attempt to drown the screams of the dying.[25]

Archaeological excavations at the tophet, located in Salammbo, a suburb of Tunis, have taken place since the site was discovered in 1921, and excavation results have been available to the public.[26] Archaeologists have discovered that burials laid on bedrock date to approximately 750 BCE,[27] shortly after the alleged founding of the city in 814 BCE. The burials continue for approximately 600 years until 146 BCE when the city was destroyed by the Romans. Numerous burials have been found: Donald Harden, a Phoenician expert, reports that in the tophet, which has not yet been fully excavated, thousands of urns have been found, most containing burned bones of children.[28] One archaeologist who excavated the tophet in the 1970's, estimates an area of 5,000 to 6,000 square meters (minimum) was used for burials during the fourth and third centuries BCE, and that 20,000 urns were buried during those 200 years.[29] Obviously, ancient Carthage witnessed numerous child sacrifices; perhaps it is only appropriate to expect at least one such sacrifice in New Carthage.

The sacrifice of George and Martha's son echoes the sacrifices reported in classical sources and the data discovered on archaeological excavations. According to classical sources, at one point only noble children were sacrificed, but later, children of poorer families were bought for sacrifice, although this was not the approved practice.[30] Inscriptions of stelae marking burial sites support this concept: archaeologists find that in the second and third centuries BCE, a process of democratization occurred and children of more common people, such as doctors, ironcasters, scribes, and teachers could also be legally sacrificed.[31] Thus, the sacrifice of the son of an associate professor of history is most appropriate.

Classical sources always speak of the sacrifice of children—not adults—and analysis of the charred bones from Carthage attest to the fact that most of the sacrifices were of young children, perhaps 75% of them newborn, most of them less than two, and only a few as old as 12.[32] How can this coincide with the fact that George and Martha's imaginary son was sacrificed on the eve of his twenty-first birthday? "Sunny-Jim" is still not legally an adult, and the sharpest images that Martha shares are about a young child—childhood diseases, a bow kept under the bed, the boat made from a banana. In their minds—the only place this phantom child dwells—he is still a child although they gave him "birth" almost 21 years earlier.

The motive for child sacrifice has intrigued scholars for centuries. On the one hand, the inscriptions on most of the stelae mention that the sacrifice was offered because of vows made by the supplicants.[33] "When seeking a certain boon from the deity," according to Carl Graesser, "the worshipper would promise that upon the granting of this boon he would 'repay' his vow by offering a sacrifice, erecting a stele, or some such appropriate act of thanksgiving."[34] This practice is illustrated by the biblical story of Jephthah who vowed that, in return for victory over the Ammonites, he would sacrifice whomever first came from his house to meet him. To his dismay, it was his daughter, and he had to sacrifice her (Judg. 11:30-39). The only vow we find George and Martha have made is for silence regarding their son, and when this vow is broken, George sacrifices his son; however, since this sacrifice is not done in thankfulness to repay a vow, it does not parallel the archaeological findings. On the other hand, sacrifices go beyond just making vows. Sabatino Moscati, a student of ancient Mediterranean cultures, thinks that "offerings seemed to rejuvenate the deity and bind him/her to the sacrificer."[35] If this is true, then, as Shelby Brown suggests, "The victim's death is life insurance (or quality-of-life insurance) for those who remain to reap the benefits."[36] In other words, by an act of sacrifice, either the lives of the individuals offering the sacrifice or the life of the community should improve. Ancient stories clearly illustrate this idea: in the Bible, Mesha, King of Moab, sacrifices his son on the city wall in order to rid his country of Israelite invaders (2 Kings 3); in classical sources, Agamemnon sacrifices Iphigenia to change the winds at Aulis. Like Mesha and Agamemnon, George is seeking a more salubrious life when he sacrifices his child.

It is easy to see how the lives of George and Martha are less than ideal before the sacrifice. Martha nags at George about his lack of social skills and enterprise; George is embarrassed by Martha's coarseness. They play destructive games in front of guests, trying to embarrass and wound each other. Nevertheless, there is a reason to try to remedy the situation: they still share a sort of love. Martha states that George is the only man who has ever made her happy, and Albee comments that they have "had a lot of battles, but they enjoy each other's ability to battle."[37] They indicate that in the past creating their fantasy child bolstered their marriage by unifying them and enabling them to share a common dream. There is still a relationship between them—a rocky one filled with illusions—but one that may be worth saving. However, when Martha speaks of their fantasy child to others, George realizes that the situation needs to be changed because Martha is using their imaginary child "to injure rather than to unify."[38] In fact, at least one reader thinks that George deliberately encourages Martha to mention their son so he can initiate healing by making her face reality.[39] George is clearly seeking to remedy a domestic crisis.

Many critics see that the sacrifice of their son brings "redemption" to George and Martha, the sacrificers:[40] Martha no longer blames only George for their barrenness; they talk quietly instead of fighting, and as they sit together they have a "hint of communion" (238). Indeed, the fact that they converse rather than battle indicates that the relationship may have a new beginning. Albee himself states, "I think once they've brought their marriage down to level ground again and gotten rid of the illusion, they might be able to build a sensible relationship."[41] Others see that the sacrifice has benefitted not only the sacrificers themselves, but also a wider group: the redemption extends both to Nick, who offers his hand to his wife as they leave, and to Honey, who finally wants a child.[42]

In the tophet of ancient Carthage, parents would offer their children to the gods, hoping that the sacrifice would foster a better future for their family and for the community. When George sacrifices his son in the "tophet" of New Carthage, he hopes for—and accomplishes—a similar end.

Notes

[1]Anne Paolucci, *From Tension to Tonic: The Plays of Edward Albee,* Crosscurrents (Carbondale: Southern Illinois UP, 1972) 45.

[2]Matthew C. Roudané, Who's Afraid of Virginia Woolf?: *Necessary Fictions, Terrifying Realities,* Twayne's Masterwork Studies 34 (Boston: Twayne, 1990) 90.

[3]C.W.E. Bigsby, *A Critical Introduction to Twentieth Century American Drama: Volume 2 Tennessee Williams, Arthur Miller, Edward Albee* (Cambridge: Cambridge UP, 1984) 277.

[4]Richard Shechner, "Reality is Not Enough: An Interview with Alan Schneider," *Edward Albee: A Collection of Critical Essays,* ed. C.W.E. Bigsby (Englewood Cliffs, NJ: Prentice, 1975) 72.

[5]William Flanagan, "Edward Albee," *Writers at Work: The Paris Interviews,* 3rd series (New York: Viking, 1967) 337.

[6]Adrienne Clarkson, "The Private World of Edward Albee," *Conversations with Edward Albee,* ed. Philip C. Kolin, Literary Conversations Series (Jackson: UP of Mississippi, 1988) 90.

[7]Richard Amacher, *Edward Albee,* rev. ed. Twaynes's United States Authors Series 141 (Boston: Twayne, 1982) 72; Alison Hopwood, " 'Hey, What's that From?'—Edward Albee *Who's Afraid of Virginia Woolf?, Atlantis: A Woman's Studies Journal* 3 (Spring 1978): 103; Roudané 93; and Charlene Taylor, "Coming of Age in New Carthage: Albee's Grown-Up Children," *Educational Theatre Journal* 25 (Mar. 1973): 53-65.

[8]C.W.E. Bigsby, *Albee,* Writers and Critics (Edinburgh: Oliver and Boyd: 1961) 48; Hopwood 103; Terry Otten, *After Innocence: Visions of the Fall in Modern Literature* (Pittsburgh: U of Pittsburgh P, 1982) 176.

[9]St. Augustine, *The Confessions of St. Augustine,* trans. E.D. Pusey, Everyman's Library 200 (London: Dent, 1907) 3.1.1.

[10]Edward Albee, *Who's Afraid of Virginia Woolf?* (New York: Pocket Books, 1962) 108. Subsequent references to the play will be taken from this edition and noted parenthetically in the text.

T.S. Eliot also uses a similar statement "To Carthage then I came" in "The Wasteland" (307). This line and the themes of sterility and sexuality found both in "The Wasteland" and in *Who's Afraid of Virginia Woolf?* may point to Eliot's influence on Albee's play.

[11]Augustine 5.8.14.

[12]Augustine 3.1.1.

[13]Daniel McDonald, "Truth and Illusion in *Who's Afraid of Virginia Woolf?,*" *Renascence* 17 (Winter 1964): 65-67.

[14]Otten 181.

[15]Gerry McCarthy, *Edward Albee,* Modern Dramatists (New York: St. Martin's, 1987) 61.

[16]Michael E. Rutenberg, *Edward Albee: Playwright in Protest* (New York: DBS Publications, 1969) 100.

[17]Otten 176.

[18]Bigsby, *Critical Introduction* 265.

[19]Leonard G. Heldreth, "The Dead Child as Fantasy in Albee's Plays," *Spectrum of the Fantastic,* ed. Donald Palumbo, Contributions to the Study of Science Fiction and Fantasy 32 (Westport, CT: Greenwood, 1988) 206.

[20]Shelby Brown, *Late Carthaginian Child Sacrifice and Sacrificial Monuments in Their Mediterranean Context,* JSOT/ASOR Monograph Series 3 (Sheffield: U of Sheffield, 1991) 14.

[21]Paul G. Mosca, "Child Sacrifice in Canaanite and Israelite Religion: A Study in *Mulk* and *Molech,*" diss. Harvard U, 1975, 11.

[22]*Diodorus Siculus X,* trans. Russel M. Geer, Loeb Classical Library (London: Hienemann, 1954) 20.14.5-6.

[23]Mosca 22.

[24]Gustave Flaubert, *Salammbô: A Romance of Ancient Carthage,* The Complete Works of Gustave Flaubert, vols. 3 and 4 (New York: Dunne, 1904) 4:110.

[25]James George Frazer, *The Golden Bough: A Study in Magic and Religion,* abridged ed. (New York: Macmillan, 1958) 327.

[26]See Donald B. Harden, "Punic Urns from the Precinct of Tanit at Carthage," *American Journal of Archaeology* 31 (1927): 297-310; Donald B. Harden, "The Pottery from the Precinct of Tanit at Salammbo, Carthage," *Iraq* 4 (1937): 59-89; F. Icard, "Découverte de l'area du sanctuaire de Tanit à Carthage," *Revue tunisienne* 29 (1922): 196-206; F.W. Kelsey, *Excavations at Carthage, 1925: A Preliminary Report* (New York: Macmillan, 1926); and L. Poinssot and R. Lantier, "Un sanctuaire de Tanit à Carthage," *Revue de l'histoire des religions* 87 (1923): 32-68.

[27]Lawrence E. Stager and Samuel R. Wolff, "Child Sacrifice at Carthage—Religious Rite or Population Control?" *Biblical Archaeology Review* 10.1 (1984): 35.

[28]Donald Harden, *The Phoenicians,* Ancient People and Places (London: Thames and Hudson, 1962) 95-101.

[29]Lawrence E. Stager, "The Rite of Child Sacrifice at Carthage," *New Light on Ancient Carthage,* ed. John Griffiths Pedley (Ann Arbor: U of Michigan P, 1980) 3; Stager and Wolff 32.

[30]Diodorus 20.14.4; and Mosca 14.

[31]Stager and Wolff 47.

[32]Harden 95-101; and Mosca 101.

[33]Mosca 102; and Stager and Wolff 44.

[34]Carl Graesser, "Standing Stones in Ancient Palestine," *Biblical Archaeologist* 35 (1972): 42.

[35]Sabatino Moscati, *The World of the Phoenicians,* trans. Alastair Hamilton (New York: Praegar, 1968) 142-43.

[36]Brown 147.

[37]Kathy Sullivan, "Albee at Notre Dame," *Conversations with Edward Albee,* ed. Philip C. Kolin, Literary Conversations Series (Jackson: UP of Mississippi, 1988) 187.

[38]C.W.E. Bigsby, *Confrontation and Commitment: A Study of Contemporary American Drama 1959-66* (n.p.: U of Missouri P, 1967) 8.

[39]Anita Maria Stentz, *Edward Albee: The Poet of Loss,* Studies in American Literature 32 (The Hague: Mouton, 1978) 48-50.

[40]Thomas P. Alder, "*Who's Afraid of Virginia Woolf?:* A Long Night's Journey into Day," *Educational Theatre Journal* 25 (Mar. 1973): 70; Bigsby, *Critical Introduction* 270; Jane F. Bonin, *Major Themes in Prize-Winning American Drama,* (Metuchen, NJ: Scarecrow, 1975) 134; Rictor Norton, "Folklore and Myth in *Who's Afraid of Virginia Woolf?,*" *Renascence* 23 (Spring 1971): 166-67; Otten 190; and Paolucci 63.

[41]Sullivan 187.

[42]Adler 70; Bigsby, *Critical Introduction* 267; and Otten 191.

FURTHER READING

Chester, Alfred. "Edward Albee: Red Herrings & White Whales."*Commentary* 35 (April 1963): 296-301.

Argues that Albee's scheme for *Who's Afraid of Virginia Woolf?* is "all contrivance and that . . . it functions to conceal the fact that the author is really out to . . . get his characters."

Choudhuri, A. D. "*Who's Afraid of Virginia Woolf?*: Death of an Illusion." In *The Face of Illusion in American Drama,* pp. 129-43. New York: Humanities Press, 1979.

Characterizes *Who's Afraid of Virginia Woolf?* as a "drama of domestic life" in which "many of the cherished and comforting illusions have been destroyed to make us wide awake to the power and impact of illusions that lie at the heart of American culture."

Davis, Walter A. "The Academic Festival Overture: *Who's Afraid of Virginia Woolf?*" In *Get the Guests: Psychoanalysis, Modern American Drama, and the Audience,* pp. 209-62. Madison: The University of Wisconsin Press, 1994.

Contends that *Who's Afraid of Virginia Woolf?* enacts the "movement to death, self-fragmentation, and the descent into psychotic anxieties."

Dozier, Richard J. "Adultery and Disappointment in *Who's Afraid of Virginia Woolf?*" *Modern Drama* XI, No. 4 (February 1969): 432-36.

Considers *Who's Afraid of Virginia Woolf?* "an unsatisfactory play, a play of half-heartedly developed ideas, a play that does not live up to its promise."

Flasch, Joy. "Games People Play in *Who's Afraid of Virginia Woolf?*" *Modern Drama* 10, No. 3 (December 1967): 280-88.

Analyzes the psychological "games" the characters in *Who's Afraid of Virginia Woolf?* play on one another.

Harris, Wendell V. "Morality, Absurdity, and Albee."*Southwest Review* XLIX, No. 3 (Summer 1964): 249-56.

Maintains that *Who's Afraid of Virginia Woolf?* is "in its presuppositions and implicit philosophy the most cheering and morally hopeful of Albee's plays."

Hazard, Forrest E. "The Major Theme in *Who's Afraid of Virginia Woolf?*" *The CEA Critic* XXXI, No. 3 (December 1968): 10-11.

Asserts that *Who's Afraid of Virginia Woolf?* is "a modern parable about . . . the delicate relationship that must bind the symbolically masculine and feminine principles of creation together if life is to progress."

Helperen, Max. "What Happens in *Who's Afraid . . .?*" In *Modern American Drama: Essays in Criticism,* ed. William E. Tayor, pp. 129-86. DeLand, Fla.: Everett/Edwards, 1968.

Examines *Who's Afraid of Virginia Woolf?* in the context of "Albee's vision of the world" as expressed throughout his works.

Roudané, Matthew C. Who's Afraid of Virginia Woolf?: *Necessary Fictions, Terrifying Realities.* Boston: Twayne Publishers, 1990, 125 p.

Wide-ranging study of *Who's Afraid of Virginia Woolf?,* covering the play's historical context, critical reception, characters, setting, and other issues.

Roy, Emil. "*Who's Afraid of Virginia Woolf?* and the Tradition." *Bucknell Review* XIII, No. 1 (1965): 27-36.

Assesses the influence of works by Eugene O'Neill and other writers on *Who's Afraid of Virginia Woolf?*

Tiny Alice

INTRODUCTION

Tiny Alice debuted on 29 December 1964 in a production directed by Alan Schneider at the Billy Rose Theatre in New York. The drama addresses the crisis of faith arising from the human tendency to represent the infinite and supreme with symbols that—as human constructs—are necessarily limited and inadequate. The action surrounds Julian, a Catholic lay brother who is sent by the Cardinal to negotiate with Miss Alice, a wealthy recluse who purportedly wishes to bestow an enormous sum on the Roman Catholic Church. Within her mansion, Julian finds, besides Alice herself, her lawyer, her butler, and a huge model of the mansion. He is then confronted by a series of bewildering circumstances and events, including Alice's initial appearance as a decrepit old woman and her subsequent revelation as a young woman disguised; a fire in the model mansion which exactly mirrors a simultaneous conflagration in the actual building; and his marriage to Miss Alice, presided over by the Cardinal. In the end, all the characters but Julian engage in a ritual surrounding the model. When Julian refuses to acknowledge the divinity of the miniature Alice within the model, he is shot by the Lawyer. As he slowly dies, he finally announces: "I accept thee, Alice . . . God, Alice . . . I accept thy will."

CRITICAL RECEPTION

Tiny Alice initially met with critical consternation. John McCarten, for instance, was "bewildered" by the play, and Robert Brustein found it "meaningless" and censured Albee's "sham profundity." Subsequent commentators, while not necessarily judging *Tiny Alice* a complete success, have found a coherence and meaningfulness that the early reviewers had missed. These critics have focused on the play's exploration of the nature of reality and of the limits of human intellect and rationality when grappling with ideas of God and infinity, which by definition, exceed human reason. Leonard Casper has perhaps best summarized these approaches to the play in his observation that "*Tiny Alice* is a dramatization of all that must remain tantalizing beyond the mind's reach: all mysteries whose permanence we deny even as impressions of their permanence accumulate in our experience."

PRODUCTION REVIEWS

Howard Taubman (review date 30 December 1964)

SOURCE: A review of *Tiny Alice,* in *The New York Times,* 30 December 1964, p. 14.

[*In the following review of the premiere of* Tiny Alice *at the Billy Rose Theater, Taubman declares that Albee's writing "abounds in moments touched with pungency and irony," but he admits he was disappointed by the play's ending.*]

The mark of a real writer is his refusal to stand still or repeat himself. In ***Tiny Alice*** Edward Albee has moved into the difficult, mysterious, ever tantalizing realm of faith.

In this new play, which opened last night at the Billy Rose Theater, Mr. Albee has attempted nothing less than a large, modern allegory on a theme that after almost two millenniums is essentially timeless. He is writing about the passion of a Christ-like figure, if not of Christ Himself.

Mr. Albee has not, unless I am mistaken after a first hearing, cast fresh light on this theme. But he has written with the literacy of a man who knows that the word itself can be charged with drama and with a gift for making a scene on a stage reverberate with subtle overtones.

Indeed, his command of sheer theater grows steadily, and it has been richly and imaginatively abetted by Alan Schneider's staging. Even if you find Mr. Albee's subject and treatment too enigmatic, ***Tiny Alice*** provides the kind of exhilirating evening that stretches the mind and sensibilities.

Tiny Alice, for all its cryptic way with plot, characters and settings, does not seem to me all that enigmatic. But Mr. Albee has virtually ordered his critics not to give away his play's surprises, and my aim is to be obedient. I shall not reveal the ending, except to whisper that it comes as no surprise once you have grasped the play's symbolism.

Mr. Albee begins with a scene that shows him at the top of his bent as a dramatist in command of his métier and his subject. In the garden of the Cardinal's impressive residence a lawyer and His Eminence meet again. They had known and loathed each other as schoolfellows. The lawyer, played with fierce, insulting intelligence and pride by William Hutt, duels verbally with the Cardinal, a shrewd figure under rich red robes and his air of silken benevolence, as played by Eric Berry.

Mr. Albee brings these two to life so swiftly, vividly and brilliantly with his relish for snapping, sardonic humor that you expect them to be characters in a realistic drama. But once they get down to business, you amend your expectations.

The lawyer tells the Cardinal that he is the representative of the richest woman in the world. His mission—and his announcement is tinctured with the venom of a serpent rather than the grandeur of mighty philanthropy—is to give the church $100 million a year for the next 20 years. Now you are sure that this is not realism. Not even J. Paul Getty could afford to be that magnanimous. The Ford Foundation, perhaps, but no individual.

The richest woman turns out to be Miss Alice, and she lives in a magisterial castle that has been shipped beam by beam and stone by stone from England and reconstructed somewhere, presumably in America. Mr. Albee does not say, but one imagines that this is where the richest woman in the world would live. Who but an American would take apart, ship and reconstruct so enormous a castle?

What's more, a large, scrupulously exact model of the castle stands on a platform in the vast, high-ceilinged, paneled library, which is the most elegant of William Ritman's three elegant sets. This model is apparently furnished and peopled like the castle itself, and it not only reflects what is going on in the building but also serves as a further symbol of a world within a world.

To negotiate what the lawyer calls "the odds and ends" of the incredible gift, Julian, a lay brother and the Cardinal's secretary, must come to the castle to meet Miss Alice. The lawyer has investigated Julian's history thoroughly but has not been able to account for six years. While Julian will not give away his secret to the lawyer, he does not hesitate to tell it to Butler, who is the butler.

John Gielgud in his black robe and with a simple dignity that does not disguise his wounds and uncertainties makes of Brother Julian a touching figure of humility. John Heffernan as Butler is familiar and impertinent, yet oddly wise and tender. Both roles are difficult to encompass, for they do not grow out of a base of realism, as do those of the lawyer and Cardinal.

The most difficult role of all is that of Miss Alice. For she resembles Kundry in Wagner's *Parsifal*—a woman who is suffering mother and enveloping temptress. The only place where Irene Worth does not carry off her challenging assignment is at her first appearance, where she briefly masquerades as an ancient hag, and here one feels Mr. Albee's notion has not worked out.

In her scenes with Julian, Miss Alice is gentle and teasing, seductive and devouring. In her relations with the lawyer she flares up and cringes, as if indeed she were Kundry and he were her Klingsor, the evil magician in *Parsifal.* Miss Worth ranges over these demanding changes with delicacy of nuance, and Mainbocher has dressed her with equal distinction of nuance.

Mr. Albee knows how to make individual scenes count. He has conceived confrontations that tingle provocatively and images suffused in a muted religious light. His writing abounds in moments touched with pungency and irony. His observations on wealth, established religion, service and martyrdom emerge sharply from the dramatic context.

In the final scenes ***Tiny Alice*** all but drops the mask of allegory. The symbols become virtually the figures they were meant to represent. And the play itself loses the richness of texture it has had in the course of its development. One realizes that Mr. Albee is reduced to illustrating rather than illuminating his theme. If one is disappointed at the end, one does not forget the boldness and wonder of the journey Mr. Albee has dared to undertake.

John McCarten (review date 9 January 1965)

SOURCE: "Mystical Manipulations," in *The New Yorker,* Vol. XL, No. 47, 9 January 1965, p. 84.

[*In the review below, McCarten finds* Tiny Alice *bewildering.*]

In ***Tiny Alice,*** at the Billy Rose, Edward Albee leads us ingeniously into an allegorical maze, but once he has got us in the middle of the thing, his sense of direction seems to fail him, and we find ourselves bewildered. During his guided tour through metaphysical territory previously explored by the likes of T. S. Eliot, Graham Greene, and Friedrich Dürrenmatt, we are favored with all kinds of puns and ponderosities, but enlightenment about the characters we encounter is in very short supply. The drama commences with an acid colloquy between a cardinal and a lawyer who once were schoolmates. The cardinal's mother, the lawyer remarks in passing, was a whore, whereupon the cardinal points out that the lawyer's nickname when they were boys together was Hyena. The lawyer then makes some references to homosexuality among the clergy, and after that the gentlemen take up the details of the business that has brought them together. It seems that one Miss Alice, the richest woman in the world, would like to give the Roman Catholic Church a hundred million dollars a year for the next twenty years, provided that Julian, a lay brother who is secretary to the cardinal, oversees the operation. We move now from the cardinal's garden, where the former schoolmates have conducted their tête-à-tête, into Miss Alice's mansion, which is about the size of the Château Frontenac. Most of the action takes place in an enormous chamber containing a miniature of the establishment, in which everything that happens in Miss Alice's big house is tinily reënacted. Just what this Chinese-box arrangement signifies I do not know. I'm not certain, either, that I can explain the significance of the doings in the mansion—maybe "castle" would be a better word for it—after Brother Julian drops in to make sure that Miss Alice's gift flows smoothly into the coffers of the Church. The lawyer suddenly becomes mysterious, Miss Alice's butler becomes mysterious, Miss Alice becomes mysterious, and so, for that matter, does Brother Julian, who, it develops, once spent six years in an insane asylum after losing his faith in God, and may or may not have had an affair during his incarceration with a woman passing herself off as the Virgin Mary. Eventually, there are indications that Miss Alice and her lawyer and her butler are in a sort of conspiracy to seduce Brother Julian from the bosom of his church, and when Miss Alice eventually persuades him to marry her, it appears that spiritually he is a goner. Maybe he is, maybe he isn't but at the climax of ***Tiny Alice*** he is certainly dead, after being shot and putting on a death scene that Little Eva might envy.

Under the direction of Alan Schneider, John Gielgud, as Brother Julian; Irene Worth, as Miss Alice; William Hutt, as the lawyer; John Heffernan, as the butler; and Eric Berry, as the cardinal, all go about their work with a confidence that is, in the circumstances, highly commendable. The sets are by William Ritman, and they are so impressive as to be almost overpowering.

Henry Hewes (review date 16 January 1965)

SOURCE: "Through the Looking Glass, Darkly," in *Saturday Review,* Vol. XLVIII, No. 3, 16 January 1965, p. 40.

[*In the following mixed review, Hewes asserts that* Tiny Alice *"seems to care less about entertaining us than about expressing the playwright's personal terror."*]

Edward Albee has written the most controversial play of the season. It is titled ***Tiny Alice*** (after the girl on the unreachable side of the looking glass?), and its controversy is increased by the frequent ambiguities that make it difficult even to state the controversy. While we plan to wrestle with the play more fully in the January 30 issue of *SR,* a quick first reaction might define ***Tiny Alice*** as being about a would-be martyr named Julian who is pushed to a strange destiny by several terrestrial agents of God. These include a greedy Cardinal who rationalizes selling a man's soul for the benefit of the Church, and whose hypocrisy serves to push Julian away from the unreality of sham religion. There is the lawyer, a Satanic provocateur who surehandedly and cruelly masterminds the whole transaction. There is Butler, a Mephistophelean super-servant who gives friendly and practical assistance. And there is Miss Alice, a compassionate temptress who leads Julian through what are to him the unpleasant realities of physical sex to a divine and pure marriage with "Tiny Alice," whom she represents.

The action and badinage take place in an enormous house inside which there may be many mansions. Designed with massive impressiveness by William Ritman, it includes a big sealed dollhouse that is an exact replica of the larger house. And we are told that inside the replica is at least one more miniature model of the model, and, of course, "the mouse" who is the play's title character. At one point in the play it is implied that Julian is a Christ figure torn between the protection of an insane asylum where he can live without faith but with hallucinations in the real world whose corruptions and chaos are unbearable, or the better-organized but less fathomable abstraction of the universe represented by the model. They ask Julian in absentia, "Who's God? Soft God? The Servant? Gingerbread God with raisin eyes? . . . There is a true God, there's an abstraction . . . It cannot be understood, you cannot worship it . . . There's Alice, Julian. *That* can be understood. Only the mouse in the model. Just that. The mouse, Julian, believe it. Don't personify the abstraction. Don't limit it. Don't demean it. Only the mouse, the toy. And that does not exist, but is all that can be worshipped." On a psychological level, one might also interpret Tiny Alice as the subconscious secondary self within ourselves. If this is intended, Mr. Albee may be suggesting that a reunion with this self, whether accomplished by sex, psychiatry, or death, is perhaps the only Heaven possible for man.

Whatever meaning may emerge for each of us from Mr. Albee's triple crostic—and we would suppose that Mr. Albee would like it to have many meanings—the bizarre and symbolic nature of its characters make it a most difficult play to perform. Alan Schneider seems to have decided to direct the proceedings in such a way that they will appear credible as "natural behavior," and he has most dextrously seen to it that the play's elusively witty insults and quips are fully realized. Sir John Gielgud offers us a Julian who, unlike the great actor himself, is naïve and afraid of passion.

While this puts him somewhat at a disadvantage, Sir John's magnificent vocal instrument is most helpful to the play's highly literate long speeches. Irene Worth is unevasive in her attempts to underline the lusty wretchedness of a by-now corrupted Virgin Mary and/or Eve figure, who is both mother and seducer of Julian. William Hutt is convincingly nasty as the impersonally lecherous lawyer. John Heffernan gives us a fine mixture of sad compassion and a servant's get-on-with-it impatience as Butler. And Eric Berry makes a poisonous Cardinal, who will, if curses work, die of stomach cancer or a coronary.

Indeed, this parting curse, delivered by the play's most vicious character, underlines the play's mistrust and anger with religion as we know and practice it. As in ***Who's Afraid of Virginia Woolf?*** the playwright is here making a both playful and shocking exploration of truth-seeking man's need to vomit up his illusions, only to arrive at an emptiness that is equally unsatisfactory. In contrast with the former play, ***Tiny Alice*** seems to care less about entertaining us than about expressing the playwright's personal terror. But if one has the patience to bear with it, this strange and overreaching fable can leave us with an unforgettable vision and a new perplexity.

Wilfred Sheed (review date 22 January 1965)

SOURCE: "Mirror, Mirror," in *Commonweal,* Vol. LXXXI, No. 17, 22 January 1965, pp. 543-44.

[*In the review below, Sheed contends that* Tiny Alice *is, at best, "an intriguing grotesque, an elegant mime of a partic-*

ular emotional state, but not the big statement about life and death that Albee's rather windy rhetoric seems to enshroud."]

I believe that Edward Albee has asked reviewers not to discuss the plot of his new play in detail: so out of deference to this Hitchcockian whim, I shall content myself here with a few cryptic reflections, calculated to leave the matter one hundred percent obscure.

There are, as every mid-cult critic knows, two things you can do when you are shook up and shocked to the core by a work of art. You can pretend to be bored, or you can pretend to be amused. "I found Lady Chatterly dull" is the first (or Orville Prescott) reaction; "I found it a scream" is response number two.

I mention this only because I happen to have found myself—between spasms of slightly hysterical interest—alternately bored and amused by whole sections of ***Tiny Alice,*** and feel that this circumstance is suspicious enough to require an explanation.

Tiny Alice is, to begin at the beginning, a symbolic play, in which everything apparently represents something else. When people say that they don't understand a play of this kind, they mean that they haven't been able to match up all the symbols—if this fellow is death, who is that fellow? Since Mr. Albee claims not to know what the play means himself, it is safe to conclude that some of the symbols don't match up with anything, and that the play *has* no meaning, in this sense. It is an impressionistic equation, in which some of the unknowns have fixed values and others can be whatever you like.

Thus, when the author states that no attack on religion is intended by his play, we can reasonably take his word for it. The Church, to be sure, plays an arrestingly venal and cynical part in the action; but the Church could easily mean something else, or nothing at all. The churchmen involved might be representing almost anything—except, possibly, churchmen. Like the psychiatrist in *The Cocktail Party* (a play which ***Alice*** rather outrageously resembles at times), they are never established professionally. Outside of their costumes and titles, they could be F.B.I. men, or diplomats for a second-rate power.

Which means either that Mr. Albee knows less about the Church than anyone who has ever written about it, or that he has gone out of his way not to identify his clerical characters correctly. I incline to the latter view. (Anyone with Mr. Albee's ear who wished to write an anti-clerical play could easily acquaint himself with the episcopal grace-notes, the conversational forms; but he hasn't even bothered.)

Unfortunately for both Albee and Eliot, there is a limit to the liberties you can take with living classes of people. Priests and psychiatrists are not characters in the court of King Tut but are still walking the earth, and they have their own particular pungency, their own private styles of good and evil, wisdom and stupidity. To put them on the stage without reference to this is to court the *fou rire,* the boffo supreme.

Eliot's psychiatrist must have caused a riot in professional circles. So too with Albee's clergymen. One tries to remember that they really represent something else—worldliness, greed, exploitation of belief—but they look an awful lot like priests. (I suppose a German would feel the same way about a Conrad Veidt Nazi-movie.) Disbelief is suspended by a thread over symbolic plays anyway; the metaphors must be accurate on the literal level or they will fail even as metaphors.

Since this probably sounds like nothing so much as sectarian one-upmanship, let me hasten to broaden the point. If ***Tiny Alice*** eviscerates the clergy in the cause of symbolism and expressionism, it does no less for the human race at large. People also have a certain pungency, a certain odor of place and association. Mr. Albee acknowledges this, but only up to a point. Although the characters in his play come from no particular country, and have no lives to speak of outside the theater, they do belong to a class. They go horseback riding. They reek of money.

This would be enough for most purposes. Provided the characters have a recognizable resonance, we don't need detailed information about them. But Albee has filled the vacuum in their personalities with a kind of neutral bitchiness left over from his other plays which defines them as Albee characters but not as human beings.

This is important, because the play has a point to make about human beings: and again the metaphor proves inadequate on the literal level. It is one thing to show that life is meaningless for Albee characters, quite another to show that it is meaningless for real people. It is no trick to tell us that lives like these are empty dreams—they have never looked like anything else. The characters have phony names and no addresses; they lack either position or magnitude. And since they do not seem to share the illusions that the rest of us have—the illusion that words like New Jersey and (your name) and father and child have meaning—these illusions are unaffected by the play.

All of which is to say that too much of ***Tiny Alice*** consists in one more listening-in on Edward Albee's private quarrel: the obsessions are decked-out to look like something else, like universal truths in fact, but they are only Albee truths about Albee people. The result is an intriguing grotesque, an elegant mime of a particular emotional state, but not the big statement about life and death that Albee's rather windy rhetoric seems to enshroud.

In the way of ideas, ***Tiny Alice*** is mystifying only in expression. It has a fairly simple central idea, which is deliberately fuzzed over and shimmered, like an impressionistic painting. (The idea could be described as the infinite refraction quandary: subject sees himself in an endless multiplication of mirrors: which one is he actually in?) This is no criticism. Mr. Albee has warned us not to worry about the ideas as such, just to open ourselves to the impression. It is precisely this that I find weak in too many places, although full of freakish vigor in others.

Of the actors, John Gielgud whimpers uncomprehendingly throughout, seriously weakening the only character who might have human resonance. John Heffernan, who has already done well this season in *The Alchemist,* goes himself one better as a Pinteresque butler. But the real star of the evening is William Ritman, whose sets give the play a majesty which Mr. Albee is never quite able to match.

Robert Brustein (review date 23 January 1965)

SOURCE: "Three Plays and a Protest," in *The New Republic,* Vol. 152, No. 4, 23 January 1965, pp. 32-7.

[*In the following excerpt, Brustein condemns what he feels is the "sham profundity" of* Tiny Alice. *"To approach* Tiny Alice *as a coherent work of art," he insists, "would be a mistake, since, in my opinion, most of it is meaningless—a frozen portent without an animating event."*]

Edward Albee has called his new play a "mystery story," a description which applies as well to its content as to its genre. The work is certainly very mystifying, full of dark hints and riddling allusions, but since it is also clumsy and contrived, and specious in the extreme, the mystery that interested me most was whether the author was kidding his audience or kidding himself. ***Tiny Alice*** may well turn out to be a huge joke on the American culture industry; then again, it may turn out to be a typical product of that industry. The hardest thing to determine about "camp" literature, movies, and painting is the extent of the author's sincerity. A hoax is being perpetrated, no doubt of that, but is this intentional or not? Is the contriver inside or outside his own fraudulent creation? Does Andy Warhol really believe in the artistic validity of his Brillo boxes? ***Tiny Alice*** is a much more ambitious work than the usual variety of "camp," but it shares the same ambiguity of motive. For while some of Albee's obscurity is pure playfulness, designed to con the spectator into looking for non-existent meanings, some is obviously there for the sake of a sham profundity in which the author apparently believes.

My complaint is that Albee has not created profundity, he has only borrowed the appearance of it. In ***Tiny Alice,*** he is once again dealing with impersonation—this time as a metaphor for religious faith—and once again is doing most of the impersonating himself. The central idea of the play—which treats religious ritual as a form of stagecraft and playacting—comes from Jean Genet's *The Balcony*; its initial device—which involves a wealthy woman handing over a fortune in return for the sacrifice of a man's life—comes from Duerrenmatt's *The Visit of the Old Lady*; its symbolism—revolving around mysterious castles, the union of sacred and profane, and the agony of modern Christ figures—is largely taken from Strindberg's *A Dream Play;* and its basic tone—a metaphysical rumble arising out of libations, litanies, and ceremonies created by a shadowy hieratic trio—is directly stolen from T. S. Eliot's *The Cocktail Party.* The play, in short, is virtually a theatrical echo chamber, with reverberations of Graham Greene, Enid Bagnold, and Tennessee Williams being heard as well; but Albee's manipulation of these sources owes more to literature than to life, while his metaphysical enigmas contribute less to thematic perception than to atmospheric fakery.

To approach ***Tiny Alice*** as a coherent work of art, therefore, would be a mistake, since, in my opinion, most of it is meaningless—a frozen portent without an animating event. There are thematic arrows, to be sure, planted throughout the play: allusions to the imperfectability of human knowledge, appearance and reality, the unreachableness of God, but all these ultimately point down dead-end streets, or are bent and twisted by leaden paradoxes. Let me, in consequence, try to discharge my duties to the play simply by outlining the plot.

In return for a hundred million dollars—presented to a waspish Cardinal by a bitchy Lawyer who used to be his schoolfellow—a lay brother in the Roman church named Julian is sent to the home of Alice, the millionairess who donated the money. Alice later turns out to be a priestess in the service of a god (or goddess) named Alice, for whom she is acting as surrogate. She is also identified with the Virgin Mother (the Lawyer has suggestions of Satan), even though she seems to have slept with everybody, including her butler (named Butler), who functions as a kind of hierophant. Alice, Lawyer, and Butler all live in a gigantic castle, which represents the universe. Inside one room is a perfect miniature model of this castle, called "The Wonders of the World," and inside the "Wonders," presumably, is another miniature—and so forth, on the principle of Chinese boxes. The possibility arises that the actual castle is merely a model within an even larger room, which is itself only a miniature, *ad infinitum.* The "Wonders," however, is not only a symbol of the expanding universe, but also an altar, to which the mysterious threesome pray, and inside which the god Alice may reside (thus, "tiny" Alice).

Slowly, it is revealed that this priestly trio is preparing Julian for a ritual sacrifice. He will eventually be forced to reenact the death of Christ, a role for which he qualifies not by virtue of any moral beauty, visionary power, or special sanctity, but rather because of certain pathological attributes. He longs to debase himself, is subject to hallucinations, and enjoys masochistic fantasies of being bloodied by gladiators and eaten by lions. His martyrdom, however, comes in quite a different way. First, he is seduced by Alice; then she marries him; then deserts him; and finally the Lawyer shoots him. Now the Passion begins, accompanied by a hailstorm of religious symbols. Julian, dying, is held, like Jesus in the Pietá, by a blue-cloaked Alice, who begs him to accept the godhead of Alice. Julian refuses at first, and is left in isolation. Then, in what may be one of the longest death scenes on record (it is surely among the dullest), he cries "Alice, oh Alice, why hast thou forsaken me?" and stumbles—arms outstretched in crucifixion—against the "Wonders of the World." Accepting Alice at the last, he expires, his heartbeat and breathing still being amplified over a loudspeaker.

The only thing that might redeem a concept like this from its own pretentiousness is some kind of theatrical adroitness; but I regret to say that Albee's customary ingenuity has deserted him here. The language, first of all, is surprisingly windy, slack, sodden, and repetitive; the jokes are childishly prurient ("The organ is in need of use," says the sexually undernourished Julian upon visiting the chapel); and the usual electricity of an Albee quarrel has degenerated—when it is employed in the opening scene between the Cardinal and the Lawyer—into mere nagging. Furthermore, Albee has not been able to exploit his own devices sufficiently. The miniature castle is a good conceit; but it functions more for obfuscation than for theatrical effect, being used to advantage only once (when it catches fire). And finally, the play vacillates between excessive fruitiness and excessive staginess, whether Julian is being enfolded within the wrapper of the naked Alice (and disappearing somewhere near her genital region), or being gunned down by the Lawyer in a manner reminiscent of Victorian melodrama.

As for the production, it staggers under the ponderousness of the play. John Gielgud is probably one of the few actors in the world capable of disguising the ludicrousness of his role; but he is forced to maintain a pitch of exaltation, bordering on hysteria, throughout the entire evening, and even he cannot prevent his speeches from sounding monotonous. Irene Worth, the most charming of actresses, is warm and womanly as Alice, and John Heffernan has a wry, laconic quality as the butler, but the production, as a whole, does not work, for the director, Alan Schneider, has been unable to find a convincing histrionic equivalent for the portentous style of the writing. Only William Ritman's setting, a massive affair with huge wooden doors and expansive playing areas, is really very satisfying, for it supplies that sense of solidity and substantially that the play so sorely lacks.

CRITICAL COMMENTARY

Philip Roth (essay date 1965)

SOURCE: "The Play that Dare Not Speak Its Name," in *The New York Review of Books,* Vol. IV, No. 2, 25 February 1965, p. 4.

[*In the following review of the published version of* Tiny Alice, *Roth charges that the play is "obviously a sham" that attempts to obscure its "true subject." It is, he contends, "a homosexual daydream in which the celibate male is tempted and seduced by the overpowering female."*]

In ***Who's Afraid of Virginia Woolf?,*** Edward Albee attempted to move beyond the narrowness of his personal interests by having his characters speculate from time to time upon the metaphysical and historical implications of their predicament. In ***Tiny Alice,*** the metaphysics, such as they are, appear to be Albee's deepest concern—and no doubt about it, he wants his concerns to seem deep. But this new play isn't about the problems of faith-and-doubt or appearance-and-reality, any more than ***Virginia Woolf*** was about "the Decline of the West"; mostly, when the characters in ***Tiny Alice*** suffer over epistomology, they are really suffering the consequences of human deceit, subterfuge, and hypocrisy. Albee sees in human nature very much what Maupassant did, only he wants to talk about it like Plato. In this way he not only distorts his observations, but subverts his own powers, for it is not the riddles of philosophy that bring his talent to life, but the ways of cruelty and humiliation. Like ***Virginia Woolf, Tiny Alice*** is about the triumph of a strong woman over a weak man.

The disaster of the play, however—its tediousness, its pretentiousness, its galling sophistication, its gratuitous and easy symbolizing, its ghastly pansy rhetoric and repartee—all of this can be traced to his own unwillingness or inability to put its real subject at the center of the action. An article on the theater page of *The New York Times* indicates that Albee is distressed by the search that has begun for the meaning of the play; the *Times* also reports that he is amused by it, as well. When they expect him to become miserable they don't say; soon, I would think. For despair, not archness, is usually what settles over a writer unable to invent characters and an action and a tone appropriate to his feelings and convictions. Why ***Tiny Alice*** is so unconvincing, so remote, so obviously a sham—so much the kind of play that makes you want to rise from your seat and shout, "Baloney"—is that its surface is an attempt to disguise the subject on the one hand, and to falsify its significance on the other. All that talk about illusion and reality may even be the compulsive chattering of a dramatist who at some level senses that he is trapped in a lie.

What we are supposed to be witnessing is the destruction of a lay brother, sent by the Cardinal to whom he is secretary, to take care of the "odds and ends" arising out of a donation to the Church of two billion dollars. The gift is to be made in hundred-million-dollar installments over a twenty-year period by a Miss Alice; the wealthiest woman in the world, she lives in a castle with her butler and her lawyer, each of whom has been her lover. On a table in the library of the castle stands a huge model of the castle itself; deep within the replica, we are eventually encouraged to believe, resides the goddess Alice, whose earthly emissary, or priestess, or cardinal, is the millionairess, Miss Alice. In the name of, for the sake of, Alice, Miss Alice sets out in her filmy gown to seduce Brother Julian; once that is accomplished, a wedding is arranged, presided over by the Cardinal. At this point Miss Alice promptly deserts Julian—leaving him to Alice, she says; the Cardinal turns his back on what he knows is coming and takes the first hundred million; and the lawyer shoots the bridegroom, who dies with his arms outstretched, moaning at the end, "I accept thee, Alice, for thou art come to me. God, Alice . . . I accept thy will."

None of this means anything because Albee does not make the invention whole or necessary. The play strings together incidents of no moral or intellectual consequence, and where the inconsistencies, oversights, and lapses occur, the playwright justifies them by chalking them up to the illusory nature of human existence. It is as though Shakespeare, having failed to settle in his own mind whether Desdemona did or did not sleep with Cassio—and consequently leaving the matter unsettled in the play—later explains his own failure of imagination by announcing to the press that we can never penetrate reality to get to the truth. The world of ***Tiny Alice*** is mysterious because Albee cannot get it to cohere. To begin with, the donation of two billion dollars to the church is irrelevant to the story of Julian's destruction—what the money will *mean* to the church doesn't enter his mind. In fact, though he is sent to the castle to make arrangements for the gift, not a word is said of the money until the Cardinal appears at the end to pick up the cash, and then we learn that Church lawyers have been working out the essentials of the deal on the side. And why does the Cardinal want the money? Hold on to your hats. Though he dresses like a prince of the Lord, he is really greedy!

Least convincing of all is what should be the most convincing—Tiny Alice Herself, and the replica, or altar, in which her spirit resides. The implications of a Woman-God, her nature, her character, and her design, are never revealed; but is this because they are beyond human comprehension, or beyond the playwright's imagination? Though *his* God is mysterious, certainly the Cardinal could discuss Him with some conviction and intelligence (and ought to, of course, instead of appearing as a pompous operator). Why can't Miss Alice or the lawyer discuss theirs? Why don't they answer the questions that are put to them? There is, after all, a difference between the idea that life is a dream and a predilection to being dreamy about life. But withholding information is Albee's favorite means of mystifying the audience; the trouble comes from confusing a technique of dramaturgy, and a primitive one at that, with an insight into the nature of things.

> *Butler:* This place [the real castle] was in England.
>
> *Miss Alice:* Yes, it was! Every stone, marked and shipped.
>
> *Julian:* Oh, I had thought it was a replica.
>
> *Lawyer:* Oh no; that would have been too simple. Though it is a replica . . . in its way.
>
> *Julian:* Of?
>
> *Lawyer:* (*Points to model*) Of that. (*Julian laughs; the lawyer says*) Ah well.

But instead of getting him off the hook with "Ah well," why doesn't Albee press the lawyer a little? Why doesn't Julian inquire further? For a lay brother who is, as he so piously says, "deeply" interested in the reality of things, how little persistence there is in Julian's curiosity; how like a child he is in the answers he accepts to the most baffling mysteries that surround him. Indeed when Albee begins to see Julian as a man who walks around acting like a small boy in a huge house full of big bad grownups, he is able to put together two or three minutes of dialogue that is at least emotionally true. To the delights and dangers of the Oedipal triangle (boy in skirts, mother in negligee, father with pistol) Albee's imagination instantly quickens; but unfortunately by presenting Julian as a befuddled boy, he only further befuddles the audience about those metaphysical problems that are supposed to be so anguishing to Julian as a man. For instance, when a fire miraculously breaks out in the chapel of the castle and in the chapel of the replica, one would imagine that Julian, with his deep interest in reality, would see the matter further along than he does in this exchange:

> *Julian:* Miss Alice? Why, why did it happen that way—in both dimensions?
>
> *Miss Alice:* (*Her arms out*) Help me.
>
> *Julian:* Will you . . . tell me anything?
>
> *Miss Alice:* I don't know anything.
>
> *Julian:* But you were . . .
>
> *Miss Alice:* I don't *know* anything.
>
> *Julian:* Very well.

That is the last we hear of the fire. But how *did* it happen? And why? I know I am asking questions about the kind of magical moment that qualifies a play for the Howard Taubman Repertory Theater for Sheer Theater, but I would like to know who this Alice is that she can and will cause such miracles of nature. Might not Julian, a lay brother, who has the ear of a Cardinal, rush out to tell him of this strange occurrence? But then the Cardinal exists, really, only as another figure to betray and humiliate poor Julian, the baffled little boy. As a Cardinal, he is of no interest to Albee, who seems to have introduced the Catholic Church into the play so that he can have some of the men dressed up in gowns on the one hand, and indulge his cynicism on the other; he does nothing to bring into collision the recognizable world of the Church and its system of beliefs, with the world that is unfamiliar to both Julian and the audience, the world of Tiny Alice. Such a confrontation would, of course, have made it necessary to invent the mysteries of a Woman-God and the way of life that is a consequence of her existence and her power. But Albee is simply not capable of making this play into a work of philosophical or religious originality, and probably not too interested either. The movement of the play is not towards a confrontation of ideas; it is finally concerned with evoking a single emotion—pity for poor Julian. In the end the playwright likens him to Jesus Christ—and all because he has had to suffer the martyrdom of heterosexual love.

Tiny Alice is a homosexual daydream in which the celibate male is tempted and seduced by the overpowering female, only to be betrayed by the male lover and murdered by the cruel law, or in this instance, cruel lawyer. It has as much to do with Christ's Passion as a little girl's dreaming about being a princess locked in a tower has to do with the fate of Mary Stuart. Unlike Genet, who dramatizes the fact of fantasying in *Our Lady of the Flowers,* Albee would lead us to believe that his fantasy has significance altogether removed from the dread or the desire which inspired it; consequently, the attitudes he takes towards his material are unfailingly inappropriate. His subject is emasculation—as was Strindberg's in *The Father,* a play I mention because its themes, treated openly and directly, and necessarily connected in the action, are the very ones that Albee has so vulgarized and sentimentalized in ***Tiny Alice***: male weakness, female strength, and the limits of human knowledge. How long before a play is produced on Broadway in which the homosexual hero is presented as a homosexual, and not disguised as an *angst*-ridden priest, or an angry Negro, or an aging actress; or worst of all, Everyman?

C. W. E. Bigsby (essay date 1967)

SOURCE: "Curiouser and Curiouser: A Study of Edward Albee's *Tiny Alice,*" in *Modern Drama,* Vol. 10, No. 3, December 1967, pp. 258-66.

[*In the essay below, Bigsby considers* Tiny Alice *Albee's failed effort to "define reality and reject the escapism of intellectual abstraction."*]

When *Tiny Alice* first appeared in New York its reception was something less than ecstatic. The general impression was that Albee had moved over to join that school of the deliberately boring and repulsive then in process of being identified as *Camp.* At best it was thought to be a personal therapy paralleled perhaps by Tennessee Williams' *Camino Real*; at worst it was a confidence trick pulled on the world in general and the drama critics in particular. Certainly Albee's bland assurance in a note to the published version that the play was "less opaque in reading than it would be in any single viewing" was an incredible admission of failure on the part of a dramatist. Nevertheless for all its weaknesses ***Tiny Alice*** does serve to demonstrate Albee's commitment to continuing experimentation. Yet while he consciously abandons the formula which had so nearly won him a Pulitzer Prize it is clear also that thematically speaking ***Tiny Alice*** represents a logical step forward from ***Who's Afraid of Virginia Woolf?*** So that a close examination of the play, while not redeeming its validity on the stage, does reveal Albee's continuing fascination with the theme of reality and illusion, and his concern with refining his own definition of these terms.

If the need to face reality was the main principle which emerged from ***Who's Afraid of Virginia Woolf?*** then Albee had done little to define exactly what he meant by reality in that play. ***Tiny Alice*** remedies this and in fact attempts a definition which is in many ways anti-Platonic. The illusions of ***Who's Afraid of Virginia Woolf?*** had been largely the Faustian distractions of sensuality and sterile scholarship. He had made no attempt, however, to integrate the metaphysical world into this picture nor to assess its validity as a part of the reality to which he urged his characters. ***Tiny Alice*** continues to urge the acceptance of reality as a way to some kind of secular salvation but in doing so Albee clearly rejects the validity of metaphysical abstractions, identifying them as an expression of man's fear of facing the reality of the human condition.

The plot can be stated fairly simply. Miss Alice, a young but apparently eccentric semi-recluse, wishes to leave a large sum of money to the church. She accordingly sends her lawyer to a Cardinal who, on promise of the money, agrees to send a young lay-brother, brother Julian, to Miss Alice to arrange terms. When Julian goes to the castle in which Miss Alice lives it becomes apparent that she, in conjunction with the lawyer and her butler, is part of a conspiracy aimed at seducing him away from the church. A marriage is arranged between Alice and Julian at which the Cardinal officiates. After the marriage, their mission apparently completed, they leave, having first shot Julian when he refuses to accept their version of reality. He dies clinging onto a model of the castle which has dominated the stage throughout most of the play.

The origin of Julian's early acceptance of the metaphysical world as a kind of supra-reality is outlined by Albee by means of quasi-parables. It becomes apparent that the impulse to predicate an abstraction, in his case and by implication in others, derives from the harshness of the facts of the temporal world. Julian describes, for example, the situation of a person finding himself locked inside a closet in an attic. In order to retain sanity that person is forced to predicate the existence of somebody who can eventually open the door and release him. As Julian says, "My faith and my sanity . . . are one and the same."[1] The need to personify the abstraction to which the mind gives existence results in a belief in a god. Similarly in another story/parable Julian describes the moment in his childhood when he had first felt the need for this predication which is clearly seen by Albee as a form of escapism. He had been severely injured in a fall and his calls for help had gone unanswered. Gradually his call changes from a cry for his grandfather to a plea to God, whose non-appearance is accountable and who is the personification of the need to be helped. The abstraction is thus seen as a compensation for the apparent inadequacies of the temporal world and man's fear of loneliness. It provides an apparent escape from the insistent facts of the world. So that if man cannot avoid birth or the aging process it seems to Julian that the invention of an afterlife avoids the relevance of death.

Julian is chosen as a good subject by the conspirators, apparently, because of his genuine regard for reality as opposed to appearance. At one stage in his life he had lost his faith. He had gone to an asylum, not so much to seek for his lost faith as to escape the fact of the loss. His position as lay-brother emphasises his failure to accept even now.

Tiny Alice in fact amounts to Albee's attempt to define reality and reject the escapism of intellectual abstraction. He chooses religion as a specific example of the belief in an abstraction which stems from a fear of immediate reality although, as the lawyer points out, he could have chosen predestination, fate or chance. To convince the audience of the necessity of facing this reality he uses what are close to being Platonic arguments to endorse an anti-Platonic conclusion. The central symbol of a play which presents a morass of symbols, is that of the 'model' castle which dominates most of the scenes in the play. The play is concerned with the 'conversion' of Julian from a belief in abstraction, which would have relieved him of responsibility, to a knowledge of reality as represented by the model. This would seem to be an equivalent of a rise in the Platonic scale in so far as it involves the realisation that what he formerly took for originals are in fact only images or copies. This necessitates his acceptance, in symbolic terms, of the 'model' castle as the 'real' one and the larger version as merely a projection of it. It is significant that Plato's word for the ultimate form was 'paradigm' which was also the word for an architect's model. While Plato's model was seen as an abstraction, however, Albee here turns the tables and literally cuts Plato down to size.

The world of reality is, however, almost by definition, unattractive to those who have lived sufficiently long with illusion. The sort of trauma which faces Julian when he is urged to accept the apparently diminutive 'model' as being reality is comparable to that which faced Plato's man in the cave.[2] Far from seeing reality as a means of perceiving more clearly, it is seen as a restriction on perception and is rejected as such, ". . . they would laugh at him and say that he had gone up only to come back with his sight ruined; it was worth no one's while even to attempt the ascent."[3] While it is clear that Plato's idea of reality differs in kind from Albee's one feels that they would both concur in Plato's statement that the function of knowledge is "to know the truth about reality."[4]

In ***Tiny Alice*** the conspiracy is clearly devoted to the end of convincing Julian that he should accept this apparent diminution of his concept of reality. "Don't personify the abstraction, Julian," the lawyer urges him, "limit it, demean it. Only the mouse, the toy . . . is all that can be worshipped." (*T.A.* p. 107.) The role of the conspirators is clearly the same as that assigned in Plato's Republic to those 'philosophers' who, having glimpsed reality, were bound to descend into the cave with the message. To Plato reality and truth were synonymous. It is hardly surprising, therefore, to find that Alice, who finally becomes identified with the forces of reality, derives her name from the Old German word for 'truth'.

Alice, in fact, is herself identifiable with the model castle. She is a more acceptable form of the reality to which the conspirators must urge Julian. She is a lure, a symbol of the reality to which Julian must marry himself. "Julian, I have tried to be . . . *her*. No; I have tried to be . . . what I thought she might, what might make you happy, what you might use, as a . . . what? . . . We must . . . represent, draw pictures, reduce or enlarge to . . . to what we can understand." (*T.A.* p. 161.) Although she is closely identified with the model—to the extent even that the conspirators speak to it and give it the name of Alice—she is still its servant. She does have an identity outside of her symbolic role, however. She even regrets her function just indeed as had Plato's 'philosophers' whose very unwillingness had been their chief qualification. "I have tried very hard to be careful, to obey, to withhold my . . . nature? I have tried so hard to be good, but I'm . . . such a stranger . . . here." (*T.A.* p. 92.)

In urging the rejection of a non-temporal god it is clear that, as in ***Who's Afraid of Virginia Woolf?*** Albee is suggesting that man is his own god and that the paraphernalia of religion may be as appropriately applied to the finite as to the non-finite world. Clearly the marriage of Julian and Alice is parallel to the marriage with the church at which Julian, only a lay-brother, had balked. It is his inability to accept the general view of "God as older brother, scout leader" (*T.A.* p. 106.) which makes him an ideal subject for, as the conspirators realise, he "Is walking on the edge of an abyss, but is balancing. Can be pushed . . . over, back to the asylums /. . . Or over . . . to the Truth." (*T.A.* p. 106.) If he cannot accept the God of society then they are ready to offer him a 'true' God. The butler insists, "there is *some*thing. There is a *true God*." (*T.A.* p. 107.) It is the lawyer, however, who identifies it, "There is Alice, Julian. That can be understood. Only the mouse in the model. Just that." (*T.A.* p. 107.) When Julian dies he suffers the martyrdom for which he had always longed but it is a martyrdom for the new religion of man—a religion founded on truth and reality. He dies with his back to the model and in a reversal of his former 'conversion' his cry for God now changes to a cry for Alice, "ABSTRACTION! . . . ABSTRACTION! . . . Art coming to me. How long wilt thou forget me, O Lord? . . . I accept thee, Alice, for thou art come to me. God, Alice . . . I accept thy will." (*T.A.* pp. 189-190.) This religion even has its own ritual, although this is founded securely on the mundane but real world. "Bring me my slippers, the sacrimental wine, my cookie." (*T.A.* p. 187.) In the light of this concept of a religion founded on the observable world Julian's earlier experience while in the asylum becomes strongly relevant. He describes an experience which he cannot positively identify as being hallucinatory or real. He describes his sexual relations with a woman who believed herself to be the Virgin Mary and who subsequently claimed herself to be pregnant with the Son of God. This represents, in fact, Albee's attempt to build up a mythology around the secular religion which he had in part formulated in his earlier plays. This concentration on the physical stands also in stark contrast to a religion which is no more than a codification of the abstract need to escape. The woman is indeed not the Virgin Mary of this religion in which impregnation is an act of faith and an intellectual concept. She is rather the Virgin Mary of a new religion in which impregnation is an animal fact of "the taste of blood and rich earth in the mouth, sweet sweaty slipping . . . ejaculation." (*T.A.* p. 62.) This act, in fact, is the summation of the contrast between the two worlds which Albee brings into confrontation. The one is an abstraction, a belief which gives validity to escapism; the other is an acceptance of the physical base of life and the need to build an approach to existence on that base. Even the physical structure of the asylum suggests a material parallel to the "many mansions" of heaven. Here, Julian tells us, there are many "sections-buildings" just as in the castle there are many rooms. Thus despite the fact that he had gone to the asylum to escape it is here that he encounters the first intimations of the falsity of his beliefs.

Julian's death is pointedly a crucifixion, *"His arms are wide, should resemble a crucifixion . . .* JULIAN*dies, head bows, body relaxes some, arms stay wide in crucifixion."* (*T.A.* p. 190.) This crucifixion is enacted, however, against the model castle which has come to be referred to as Alice and which is the epitome of reality and truth. In the moments before his death Julian recognises the inversion of his values which has resulted from his contact with Alice, a conversion which results in his dying for a religion of man rather than for that of an extra-temporal god. In comparing a phrenological head, which Albee has rather pointedly left on stage throughout most of the play, with Alice he realises that his compulsion had always been to make the abstract real and the rest unreal; to see man, in fact, in terms of this head with its eyes focused on some far horizon rather than as a creature of flesh and blood existing in a concrete world:

> Is that the . . . awful humor? Art thou the true arms, when the warm flesh I touched . . . rested against, was . . . nothing? And she . . . was not real? Is thy stare the true look? Unblinking, outward, through, to some horizon? And her eyes . . . warm, accepting, were they . . . not real? Art thou my bride . . . Ah God! Is that the humor? THE ABSTRACT? . . . REAL? THE REST? . . . FALSE? . . . It is what I have wanted, have insisted on. Have nagged . . . for. IS THIS MY PRIESTHOOD, THEN? THIS WORLD?
>
> (*T.A.* pp. 188-189.)

It is significant that once again, as in ***The Zoo Story*** and ***Who's Afraid of Virginia Woolf?,*** violence is presented as the catalyst necessary for this conversion. Like Bellow, Albee seems to believe that truth comes "in blows." Before the lawyer shoots him Julian is still determined to escape, to go back to the asylum which, although it had contained the seeds of his new faith, had been seen by him at the time as a refuge from that faith. When he has been shot, however, his mind reverts to the image of the person shut up in the attic closet and he admits, what he would not have admitted before, that "No one will come." (*T.A.* p. 176.) He arrives at a realisation which one might take as a justification for Albee's obsessive insistence on the necessity of violence, "Consciousness, then, is pain." (*T.A.* p. 181.)

If the symbolic pattern of ***Tiny Alice*** is essentially Platonic the dilemma which that pattern highlights is, as he has shown in his previous plays, a central one to modern society. It is interesting to see, in fact, just how closely Julian matches the archetypal neurotic in retreat from reality as outlined by a pioneer in psychology, Alfred Adler. The very precision of this parallel, in fact, tends to grant to Albee's creation the general application which is clearly his aim. Adler terms escapism'safeguarding through distance.' His description of the neurotic fits Julian's situation precisely. Unable to face the world as it is Julian had retreated into religious faith in early childhood. In an attempt to compensate and obsessed by the fact of death he longs for a martyrdom which will reinstate his superiority. He longs, as he says, to "shout my humility from the roof." (*T.A.* p. 119.) As Adler says in describing the neurotic's situation:

> The neurotic's faulty picture of the world is constantly being so shaken by reality that he feels threatened from many sides. Consequently he narrows down his sphere of activity; he always presents pedantically the same opinions and the same attitudes which he accepted early in his life. Eventually, as a result of the "narrowing down" process, he shows an inferiority complex with all its consequences. Then, in order to escape this inferiority complex and because he finally sees himself threatened by the problem of death, he convulsively constructs a superiority complex.[5]

His references to the past, his concern with death and his choice of religion are all recognised by Adler as symptoms of this desire to "safeguard through distance," "To think about the past is an unobtrusive, and therefore popular, mean of shirking. Also, fear of death or disease. . . . The consolation of religion with the hereafter can have the same effect, by making a person see his actual goal only in the hereafter and the existence on earth as a very superfluous endeavor. . . ."[6]

If Albee is concerned here with describing the dilemma of modern society in retreat from reality the title would seem to suggest that he saw a fellow spirit in Lewis Carroll. While it is clear that Alice's wonderland, as an escape from 'dull reality,' can be seen as a parallel to Julian's wonderland of religion, it would be unwise to press the parallel too closely. For while Carroll's literally 'tiny' Alice is clearly a part of the illusory world Albee's tiny Alice is herself the symbol of reality. If Carroll insists on returning his protagonist to the real world at the end of his books it is not without a nostalgic glance back over his shoulder to his wonderland. There is no such nostalgic glance in Albee. Julian has to relinquish the abstract which is his retreat from reality. In doing so he abandons the robes of the church for the clothes of ordinary life, a change which symbolises his shift of identity. This assumption of identity as a function of commitment to an abstraction is reminiscent of Nigel Dennis's satire on the great abstracts of modern society, *Cards of Identity* (1956). Here too a conspiracy of three effect a change of identity in a man lured to their mansion by the prospect of monetary gain—a change signified here, as in ***Tiny Alice,*** by a physical change of clothes. To Dennis, also, religion is one of those projections whereby man escapes from the immediate reality of his situation and accepts a ready-made identity. It is an escape, moreover, which implies a denial of intellect as it does a denial of reality. In Dennis's ironical words, "God is worshipped as a solid only by backward people; once educated, the mind reaches out for what cannot be grasped, recognises only what cannot be seen: sophistry adores a vacuum,"[7] or, more succinctly as he puts it in his unabashed satire on religion, *The Making of Moo* (1957), "You have nothing to lose but your brains."[8]

In a sense also ***Tiny Alice*** can be seen as Albee's prose version of Eliot's *The Cocktail Party* (1949). In this play Eliot had presented a similar conspiracy of three designed to'save,' in this case, four people. He makes a distinction, however, between a reconciliation to the human condition which leads to a comatose contentment and a true confrontation with the apocalyptic vision. One character alone chooses to confront the stark reality of her situation. Celia, while convinced that man is alone and that "the dreamer is no more real than his dreams," pursues the vision, the ecstacy which she feels to be present behind the projected shadows. She chooses what Julia, one of the conspirators, calls 'transhumanisation.' Such a process brings her into confrontation with solitariness and forces her to relinquish her artificial personality. She ceases to see reality as an extension of her own dreams. She accepts a re-definition of that reality which in turn destroys the escapist nature of her life and leads on to her literal crucifixion. When she makes this decision it is consecrated by the conspirators in a champagne toast, just as is Julian's decision in ***Tiny Alice.*** To confront the apocalyptic vision, to accept the limitation of reality which that involves and yet to pursue a sense of ecstacy is to invite crucifixion but this is presented by both Eliot and Albee as a better conclusion and purpose than the trivia of social posturing. Celia turns her back on a phantasmal world where people are shaped by the roles they play, just as the great abstractions shape Albee's Cardinal and even Genet's Bishop. When Julian faces crucifixion in ***Tiny Alice*** it is with a similar, if tardy, understanding of the true nature of things. He is urged "to accept . . . our ecstacy." (*T.A.* p. 165.) The play concludes with his realisation that reality is not an aspect of a defined role or an extension of individual desires but rather the immediate result of choices made in the context of a concrete world whose only premise and conclusion is ultimate death.

Thus the abstract fear of ***Who's Afraid of Virginia Woolf?*** is here crystallised in Julian's perception of the terrifying loneliness of man. Used to the projections of his own sensibilities he has come to accept a diminution of his concept of reality. As Goetz had said in Sartre's *Lucifer and the Lord* (1951), "God is the loneliness of man . . . If God exists, man is nothing."[9] So too Albee is insisting that man's freedom and identity depend on his ability to discount reliance on an abstraction which is the creation of his own metaphysical solitude. But if Julian dies in the moment of comprehension in doing so he is consecrating a myth. He becomes, like Jerry in ***The Zoo Story,*** a martyr. But Albee's myth lacks the fundamental requirement of simplicity while his sensitive probing of his chosen theme constantly verges on the merely esoteric.

Camino Real is perhaps a useful play to invoke in the context of this study for even Tennessee Williams has come to regard his expressionistic nightmare more as a piece of personal therapy than compelling drama. Perhaps every dramatist has a right to a ***Tiny Alice*** just as a drama professor once told Williams that every artist has a right to paint his nudes. Unfortunately Albee's next play, ***Malcolm,*** evidences much the same opacity. Based on Purdy's surrealistic novel it seemed to Robert Brustein, writing in *The New Republic,* to confirm the tendency of Albee's plays to "get more abstract and incoherent until he is finally reduced, as here, to a nervous plucking at broken strings."[10] Nevertheless it is clear that without the radical approach of an Albee the American theater would be in danger of stagnating once again. For if he is capable of grotesque misjudgement, as in ***Tiny Alice*** and, apparently, in ***Malcolm,*** then he is also capable of the achievement of ***The Zoo Story*** and ***Who's Afraid of Virginia Woolf?*** Neither can ***Tiny Alice*** justifiably be called regressive for it evidences both Albee's continuing concern with stylistic experimentation and his determination to examine every aspect of his chosen theme. So long as Albee remains committed to extending the range of drama itself and so long as he refuses to pander, as he himself puts it, to a supposed need for "self-congratulation and reasurrance"[11] then he is in danger of losing the sympathy of his audiences. But by the same token it is only through the courage of such a dramatist that American drama can ever hope to realize its full potential.

NOTES

[1]Edward Albee, *Tiny Alice* (New York, 1965), p. 45. All further references to this play are abbreviated to *T.A.* and incorporated in the text.

[2]Plato describes the difference between reality and illusion by means of the simile of the cave. At the bottom of a cave, which has an entrance to daylight, men are fastened so that they can only look at a huge screen on the back wall. On this screen the images of men and objects are projected by a fire built in the entrance to the cavern. He posits the difficulty of one of this number when suddenly released and confronted with true reality and the unwillingness of those others to accept the validity of a reality which would seem more diminutive than the images to which they are used.

[3]Plato, *The Republic of Plato,* trans. with introduction and notes F. M. Cornford (London, 1955), pp. 225-226.

[4]*Ibid.,* p. 180.

[5]Alfred Adler, *The Individual Psychology of Alfred Adler,* ed. H. L. Ansbacher and R. R. Ansbacher (London, 1958), p. 277.

[6]*Ibid.,* p. 277.

[7]Nigel Dennis, *Two Plays and a Preface* (London, 1958), p. 7.

[8]*Ibid.,* p. 194.

[9]Jean-Paul Sartre, *Lucifer and the Lord,* trans. Kitty Black (London, 1952), p. 133.

[10]Robert Brustein, "Albee's Allegory of Innocence," *The New Republic,* January 29, 1966, p. 36.

[11]Edward Albee, "Which Theatre is the Absurd One?" in John Gassner, *Directions in Modern Theatre and Drama* (New York, 1965), p. 334.

Gilbert Debusscher (essay date 1967)

SOURCE: "A Dead End or a New Direction?" in *Edward Albee: Tradition and Renewal,* Center for American Studies, 1967, pp. 70-81.

[*In the following excerpt from his full-length study of Albee, Debusscher finds* Tiny Alice *baffling but concedes that the play "may be the first truly modern tragedy, in which man's fatal flaw is nothing other than his humanity."*]

Malcolm with all its obvious shortcomings did not, however, completely compromise Albee's reputation. A year before its disastrous run, those who had hailed the author of ***Who's Afraid of Virginia Woolf?*** as a true successor of Eugene O'Neill had been given new grounds to substantiate their judgment, whereas those who considered him a success-seeker found fresh arguments in his new original play. Already, the fact that ***Who's Afraid of Virginia Woolf?*** had demolished the invisible barrier between New York's two theatrical centers, and the unexpected heights of his commercial success, had rendered him suspect in the eyes of Broadway's intransigent adversaries. His Moscow trip under the aegis of the State Department then confirmed them in this attitude. At the time of ***Tiny Alice***'s premiere, the accusations of commercialism, snobbism, joking for jaded intellectuals, or gigantic obfuscation, emanated primarily from those who had formerly collaborated to establish the young playwright's reputation. ***Tiny Alice*** was surrounded by precautions unusual on Broadway; the author made enigmatic allusions to it in several interviews; Alan Schneider, the producer, refused to allow observers at the rehearsals, which were unusually prolonged. The stars, Sir John Gielgud and Irene Worth, respected the law of absolute silence, while the publicity of course announced "the theatrical event of the year." All of this atmosphere smacked unpleasantly of the commercial methods of the Broadway theatrical industry. It called the author's sincerity further into doubt and was one factor in the reserved critical reception of the play. The other was the confusion of the journalists in the face of this disconcerting work.

It is uncertain whether there is any plot in ***Tiny Alice,*** so I will limit myself to a scene-by-scene resume. The curtain rises on the garden of an episcopal residence. From one wall hangs a cage containing two cardinal birds. A violent conversation takes place between the Lawyer and the Cardinal, who are former schoolmates. The Lawyer accuses the Cardinal of having a prostitute for a mother, to which the prince of the Church replies by recalling that at school they had nicknamed the other "the hyena," an allusion to certain vicious practices. The Lawyer counters immediately with references to the homosexuality of the clergy. Finally, they come to the object of their meeting: the Lawyer is charged with informing the Cardinal that Miss Alice, the richest woman in the world, it would appear, wishes to make a gift to the Church of a hundred million dollars per year for twenty years, on the condition however that the lay Brother Julian, personal secretary to the Cardinal, be in charge of the transaction.

The second scene takes place in the library of Miss Alice's castle. In the center of the room is an enormous model of the castle. Julian is discussing this toy for the rich with Butler, the mysterious domestic, when the Lawyer appears. It emerges from his speech that he has carefully accumulated a dossier on Julian's past but that six years are missing to him. Julian refuses to fill in the gap. The Lawyer then takes him to Miss Alice's apartment. Whereas he expects to find the young woman the Cardinal has told him about, it is to a wrinkled crone, bent with rheumatism and almost deaf, that the Lawyer abandons him. After making fun of him for a moment, the old woman straightens up, pulls off her mask and wig, throws aside her canes and reveals to the dazed Julian a beautiful and seductive Miss Alice. When he has recovered from his surprise, Julian agrees to enlighten his hostess on the subject of the six "empty" years of his past: he had spent the whole time in a mental hospital, his faith in God having left him, and during his seclusion had perhaps (if it was not a hallucination) intimately known a woman who occasionally believed herself to be the Virgin Mary. He cherishes the memory (or hallucination) of a particularly sensual episode by a pool. He seems to recall also that this woman had died of cancer of the womb a month later. When he leaves Miss Alice, the Lawyer reappears to learn the outcome of the interview. His attitude is curiously jealous and threatening.

The first scene of the next act finds Miss Alice and the Lawyer in the library. They are absorbed in a violent dispute in which the man spits out his jealousy while the woman describes the disgust which the naked body of this man, who is her lover, inspires in her. However, she lets herself be caressed by him without responding, under the indifferent eye of Butler who has just entered. The trio ends their little game at the arrival of Julian who has been visiting the wine cellar and the chapel, both in a pitiful state. During a discussion of the needed repairs, and the mysterious history of the real castle and the model, smoke and flames begin to escape from the part of the miniature representing the chapel. The three men rush toward that part of the big house, and Julian returns to announce to Miss Alice that the chapel has narrowly missed being totally destroyed by fire.

The second scene, once more in the library, between Butler and the Lawyer, confirms the increasing jealousy of the latter over the relationship apparently being established between Miss Alice and Brother Julian. The two men decide to go at once to the Cardinal and have him celebrate the peculiar marriage which they have just planned for Alice and Julian. In the third scene of the second act, Julian is alone in Miss Alice's apartment, while she removes her riding costume in the next room. When she appears, she is dressed in a sumptuous black negligee. The conversation lingers for a moment on D. H. Lawrence and the sensuality of rural types, then Julian reproaches himself for the idle and gluttonous life he has led since coming to the castle. He reveals to Miss Alice the conclusion at which he had arrived after his six years of retreat: he wants to lead a life of service without reward. While he describes with passion the ardent desire for martyrdom which had possessed him even as a child, Miss Alice winds herself about him, caresses and embraces him. When he falls clutching her knees, she opens her negligee and encloses him completely against her naked body. The last act in the library sees an acceleration of events. Julian and Miss Alice have been married by the Cardinal, but the former lay brother cannot find his wife. Everyone seems to have disappeared except Butler, who occupies himself with covering the furniture with dustcovers as if before an extended absence. He stops his work and goes out to get the champagne ordered by Julian. Meanwhile, the Cardinal comes on the stage. Julian tells him of his confusion and exaltation at the idea that this marriage ordered by the Cardinal will be accomplished for the greater glory of God. But while blessing his secretary, the prince of the Church lays stress on the role of obscurity, sacrifice, resignation and even death which this union implies. When Julian goes out to look for his bride, the Lawyer comes to announce to the Cardinal that the affair is concluded and officially approved by the lawyers of the Church. He removes a pistol from a drawer and checks its working order, while the Cardinal expresses the hope that he will not have to use it. Julian reappears, more baffled than ever, still unable to find his wife. It is Butler who finally brings her by force to toast her marriage. When everyone has his glass, a ritual ceremony begins, of which the model, the dwelling place of a tiny Alice, seems to be the altar.

All the characters with the exception of Julian are ready to leave. The Lawyer tells him that they wish to leave him to his fulfilment, to his marriage, his wife and his personal mission. In spite of his protestations, each one tries, in vain, to make him accept his fate. When Julian firmly refuses to acknowledge the miniature divinity, the Lawyer shoots him, Miss Alice takes his dying body on her knees and, while Butler finishes covering the furniture, the Lawyer offers the Cardinal the whole two billion dollars—"the total grant"—in a briefcase.

Everyone leaves the library, which is plunged in shadow. Julian is at the point of death; he addresses his God in a long monologue during which, inside the model, a small light moves from the chapel along the corridors toward the library. As the light draws near, heartbeats begin to be heard; they become louder and louder until they are deafening. Julian stands, his back against the model, and announces through the din: "I accept thee, Alice, for thou art come to me—God, Alice . . . I accept thy will." He slowly falls again, dead; the heartbeat is heard three more times, then total silence. The light on Julian dissolves to complete darkness. Only then does the curtain fall.

It is easy to imagine the perplexity of the critics, who had to write a hundred lines in the hour following the premiere for the edification of thousands of readers. Nothing seems more complicated in fact than to determine what had taken place on the stage, and to extract its significance—so much so that the next day their confreres of the weekly press demanded clarification by the author. Far from speaking of the content, Albee contented himself with indicating a way to see the play: not to try to understand, but to submit passively to the theatrical metaphors which he proposed to us, and let them reverberate in us; above all not to tell the story to those who had not seen the play.

From this Hitchcockian recommendation the first conclusion to be drawn is that physical representation in a theater is indispensable for this play; its text cannot be taken as a finished literary product, but rather as a musical score to which only the execution can give real life. Albee's recommendations were well founded. The pure spectacle was so fascinating in spite of its obscure content that one critic concluded his review with these words: "One leaves the theater with the feeling of having seen the most dynamic play of the season—and one wonders why!"[1] The scenes are organized around certain themes which repeat themselves throughout the play without, however, being explained, developed or concluded. It certainly seems that the plot centered on Julian is meant to show how purity is betrayed on all levels of our society: by the Church which, in its cupidity, neglects the individual soul; by ruthless capitalism, by the cynical and impotent proletarian, and finally by woman—image of the seductive mother or the evasive lover. When his faith abandons him, the Pure Man secludes himself voluntarily in an asylum, to emerge six years later ready to serve for no other reward than a martyr's crown. And here lies the treason, for the forces which govern us, the Church, Wealth, Woman, exert themselves to turn him from his objective and to see reality "as it is." When finally he consents, when he gives himself to the woman and the money, they reveal to him that all this is no more reality than the other, that his sacrifice has only served a commercial transaction. What he accepts then in the replica-Alice which he calls God is perhaps the inanity, the uselessness of his death, the huge joke which was his life and his sacrifice, the ultimate void which he experiences. The eternal problem of a man in search of God runs a parallel course. Julian's career is nothing but a series of evasions: his refusal to pronounce final vows and his desire to remain in the service of the Church; his rejection of God as he is presented by men, and his creation of a more personal God; his desire to serve and his doubt about the usefulness of his sacrifice. Some have seen in all this the spasms of modern man alienated from his society, whose God has been slain and not replaced. Modern man loses himself in the metaphysical labyrinth not because he is incapable of finding the way out but because he knows there is no way out.

Another thematic direction of the play is that which develops the opposition between appearance and reality, which tends to show (or to hide) the nature of the illusion and the limits of the real. Julian remains uncertain (as does the audience) of this boundary between the dream and the act; the facts of his past life are perhaps only dreams, hallucinations, but his present life is just as irrational, incomprehensible and mysterious. Where exactly does the proliferation of miniatures within miniatures stop, and which of the multiple reproductions of the library does he take for the real one? More, what is this strange divinity of which Miss Alice seems to be the high priestess? Of what forces is he the toy? In what design of dark destruction does he collaborate in obeying orders? His death takes on the appearance, in many ways, of the heroic sacrifice of a Greek or Shakespearean tragedy, with this difference, that neither gods nor destiny nor tragic flaw determines the ineluctable course of the destruction. Albee seems to suggest that this absurd annihilation is the substance of human destiny, that all existence leads to this ultimate nothingness. ***Tiny Alice*** may be the first truly modern tragedy, in which man's fatal flaw is nothing other than his humanity. Each of these themes which I have suggested exists only in obscure allusions, disconcerting insinuations which leave the reader and the audience frustrated. Each scene, each act, introduces a new element, a false point of departure, a different direction which invariably leads to an impasse. The end is easily recognized: the protagonists leave the stage, Julian dies, the lights are extinguished and the curtain falls. The question, however, is: What exactly has ended? A metaphysical enchantment, a mysterious intrigue, a detective story? A parable of the situation of man before the infinity of the universe, a criticism of the Church and its methods, the incoherent dreams of one deluded? Albee refused any clarification even to the actors, a fact which inspired one of his critics to attribute to him Robert Browning's famous retort: "When I wrote it, only God and Robert Browning knew its meaning—now only Gods knows."

On the subject of his characters, the playwright was scarcely less sparing of information. He has affirmed, however, that Miss Alice is a woman who makes herself out to be Miss Alice who is, in turn, the personification of the abstract "Tiny Alice" who lives in the miniature; she is, then, only an employee whose role is to represent the true Miss Alice through a series of adventures of which he has permitted us to see a sampling. It is evident that Albee wished to apply to this character the technique of the Chinese box, which is found throughout the play and of which the endless castles in miniature inside one another and inside the big castle are the most visible image. We find the same principle from the first scene in the cage with the two cardinal birds, tiny reflection of the two men who are talking; later in the name Butler for the butler, then again in the old woman's mask worn by Miss Alice. Only Julian escapes this game, precisely because it is meant to baffle him.

Albee has declared that Julian is the only flesh-and-blood character. This is doubtless evident in the essentially sexual aspect of his hallucinations. But what is one to think of the evident jealousy of the Lawyer, of the alleged homosexuality of the Cardinal, of the unmistakable sensuality of Miss Alice? Their motivation is no more clarified than their identity by the events, but they pursue their objective with such relentlessness that the suspense never ceases to mount and our astonishment to increase. One may disapprove of this kind of dramaturgy, but one can only with difficulty resist the force given off by these mysterious characters and their unalterable progress toward an unknown end. Structurally, ***Tiny Alice*** is a masterpiece of calculated effect. The curtain rises on an argument whose violence is sustained by a vocabulary as obscene and a rhythm as electric as that of ***Who's Afraid of Virginia Woolf?*** It is clear after several exchanges that the Cardinal and the Lawyer detest one another and take a cruel pleasure in recalling their inglorious days as schoolmates. After this first scene, which could pass for a traditional exposition, begins a new story, that of Julian at the castle. On this are grafted the first mysteries which quicken our interest and increase the tension. Who is Butler? What is this miniature? What does this mysterious language conceal? The third scene answers none of these questions, but replaces them skillfully with others. It opens with a *coup de théâtre,* the masquerade by Miss Alice, and closes on a new question: is there an intimate relationship between her and the Lawyer? Thus, the first act has not brought in preliminary elements of action, it has unveiled the outlines, the possibilities, but no direction has imposed itself. The tension is maintained from beginning to end, and a process emerges which attracts the attention: that of the reduction or the reflection reduced from all that happens on the stage. The second and third acts proceed in exactly the same fashion; the possibilities of relationships between the characters are more and more numerous, sometimes contradictory, never explicit; the unexpected multiplies itself—the double fire in the chapel, the seduction episode on the stage; the action takes the most unexpected turns: Julian marries Miss Alice, she disappears immediately after the ceremony, all the protagonists leave, Julian is killed. The last scene surpasses in intensity all the others and establishes once again a *moment de théâtre* particularly fascinating: the sound of the heartbeats, the moving light in the miniature castle, the hero's death agony. The whole is thus structured by a series of scenes particularly effective in themselves, of moments of "pure theater" which do not achieve their impact through a chain of elements, a gradual construction, an illumination in comparison with other less important events—but through an independent dramatic weight, an intrinsic emotional power. This composition is evidently much more perceptible in the performance than in the reading; it creates in the former this peculiar fascination of which its spectators speak, but also the disappointment of the reader incapable of visualizing the stage and experiencing the full spectacular potential which he senses in the reading.

These shock scenes are reinforced by a particularly calculated language; it takes an exceptional skill with polyvalencies to suggest so many possibilities and succeed in imposing none. If we recognize here the virulence of ***Who's Afraid of Virginia Woolf?*** and a vitality which sweeps everything, including the questions raised by the action, along with it, certain passages on the other hand underline the ritual aspect by their repetitive and incantatory style. The final scene becomes thus the holocaust of an expiatory victim. That Julian paraphrases at this moment the words of Christ accentuates this aspect still more. However, there are in the text lines which seem to suggest that the author was amusing himself with the entertainment he himself had composed: "This is an endless metaphor," "Abstractions *are* upsetting," "Articulate men often carry set paragraphs." One of the play's detractors believes he discerns in all these lines a stratagem by which Albee shows us where the work fails in his own eyes in such a way as to make us forget where it fails in ours. If so, his success in integrating them so perfectly in the dialogue becomes an even greater *tour de force.*

Tiny Alice finds its natural position in an unceasing artistic research to which each play brings an innovation, an original direction, while relating in various aspects to the preceding works. Several dramatic elements were already present for example in ***Who's Afraid of Virginia Woolf?*** The opposition between the real past and the embellished memory was exploited in the episode of George's autobiographical novel. In his case more than in that of Julian, we are hard put to decide where the frontier between facts and invention lies. Likewise, the principle of the game and its interaction with reality, on which is based the experience of Martha and George, is developed in ***Tiny Alice*** to such a degree that reader and spectator alike lose their way. Finally, the tendency to employ the mysterious, the unexplained, the unexpected, already apparent in the plot of the mythical son, is so marked throughout this play that some have wondered if Albee was making fun of his public or of himself. As for the metaphysical aspect, it was present in the first play of his career, ***The Zoo Story,*** but one can also find external models. As usual, we recall the Jean Genet of *The Balcony* for the religious ritual which becomes a dramatic form, but also the T. S. Eliot of *The Cocktail Party* for the metaphysical obscurities rising from the libations, litanies and various ceremonials performed by a hieratic trio. The symbolism of the mysterious castle, the union of the sacred and the profane, the death agony of a modern Christ, bring to mind Strindberg's *Dream,* while one aspect of the plot, a woman who for an enormous sum of money buys the soul and body of a man from Society to destroy them, comes straight from Friedrich Dürrennatt's *The Visit.* Be that as it may, Albee has amalgamated perfectly these multiple "borrowings" and so created a play if not coherent at least highly personal. One might conclude this analysis of the work which was the talk of the 1964-65 theatrical season by the revealing juxtaposition of two comments, one by Albee himself (who returns but with more moderation to one of his favorite positions): "What a critic should tell his reader is how effectively he thinks the play has said whatever it chooses to say"; and the other by one of his critics: "As I closed my notebook, I wondered if Mr. Albee would have been pleased if someone had called ***Tiny Alice*** 'a play that unfolds with great skill, whatever the hell it is choosing to say'."[2]

NOTES

[1]Theophilus Lewis, "Tiny Alice," *America,* 112: 336-337, March 6, 1965.

[2]Henry Hewes, "The *Tiny Alice* Caper," *Saturday Review,* 48: 38-39, 65, January 30, 1965.

Mary Elizabeth Campbell (essay date 1970)

SOURCE: "The Tempters in Albee's *Tiny Alice,*" in *Modern Drama,* Vol. XIII, No. 1, May 1970, pp. 22-33.

[*In this essay, Campbell uncovers similarities between* Tiny Alice *and medieval morality plays, "with their moral and theological basis, their sometimes moving portrayal of man's frailty and susceptibility to temptation, their characters that are either personifications or, occasionally, type figures, [and] their morally serious . . . plots."*]

> JULIAN: Am I . . . am I being temp—tested in some fashion?

While controversy over the meaning and, by corollary, the worth of Edward Albee's ***Tiny Alice***[1] has been considerable, at least on one point critics are pretty much in harmony—the play is non-realistic and is indeed essentially symbolic, allegorical, allusive. If one acts on this assumption and examines in depth the structural lines of the play, the thesis that then reasonably tends to emerge is this: a man in modern Western civilization encounters as many difficulties as ever in being fully human—creature of both flesh and spirit—and nowadays yet other exigent, subtle difficulties besides; for he lives among the material easements and spaciousness that present-day scientific achievements increasingly afford, surrounding him to such a degree that the spiritual aspects of his nature may dwindle unnoticed, the more so if the spiritual guidance on which he relies itself turns renegade, leaving him to the hazard of being finally stripped of the essentials of his humanity, the merest dead soul. To phrase this more specifically, at the primary level the model mansion, importantly highlighted in Miss Alice's library, takes on significance very early and gradually presents itself as a shrine, altar, temple, place of magic, which is sacred to the powerful, wholly unfeeling goddess, Alice; at the same time one becomes aware of its having yet other, insistently notable peculiarities, of the kind most likely to be found in a delicately-formed specimen of modern scientific machinery, such as, for example, a computer center. On the upper level of such a drama, then, the model mansion represents the remarkable world of materialistic advantages and easement wrought by contemporary achievement in the natural sciences, mathematics, and yet other sciences that build on these, and Alice herself is the potent sway that such a world can have over the minds and lives of modern men.

As to the play's operating on more than one level, allegorically, this perception begins coming to the viewer from the first. In Scene 1, the admirably wrought interview between the Cardinal and the Lawyer, these two have an insistent larger-than-life quality about them, requiring a certain *empressement* in the acting, that suggests a significance beyond the literal sense of the encounter. There is no mention of their individual names; on the contrary, at the very opening and again at the curtain, the dialogue and action concerning the two cardinals in their cage—indeed something unusual about birds of that kind actually in a cage fastens the attention on them—impresses on one visually and aurally the idea of "cardinal," and to that degree moves one away from the sense of the Cardinal, the figure, as an individual and toward the sense of him as a functionary, thence possibly a representative, a type figure. The huge amount of the contemplated gift, and at that only one of a number of

David Warner as Julian in a Royal Shakespeare Company staging of *Tiny Alice,* 1970.

such projected gifts, invites the mind toward the non-realistic. The Lawyer's own qualities as shown in that scene—ruthless, cagey, savoring his detestation of his host—leave one well set psychologically, at the very peak of the action, for the infuriated and defeated Cardinal's single-word, hissed malediction: "Satan!" The word is driven home by the Lawyer's pause, by his rejoinder: "Satan? You would believe it . . . if you believed in God," and by his burst of sardonic laughter.

Especially suggestive of the allegorical is the manner of naming the five characters. Besides "The Cardinal" and "The Lawyer" there is "The Butler"—phrasings familiar to us since the time of the old moralities, with the characters named for personifications or types. Early in the play, in the second scene, it is impressed on the viewer that the Butler's surname—his first name goes unmentioned—is Butler, presumably with the intent that one should focus strongly on the importance of his function—the individual man is perhaps type cast? His own bearing and both Miss Alice's and the seldom amiable Lawyer's attitude indicate a figure to whom they attribute special importance and value. Julian and Miss Alice we have without surnames. That Brother Julian is left thus is scarcely striking. But Miss Alice left thus in a realistic modern *milieu*? It could scarcely be. Calling her "Miss Alice" of course draws sharp attention to her close association with the shadowy overlord figure whom she serves. And indeed a turn of phrase in Act III suggests that "Miss Alice" is merely that lady's *nom de guerre.*[2] Indeed it would scarcely be needful to give Miss Alice a name indicating her function—her comportent proclaims it! By the close of her first scene her designs on the celibate Julian are patent, and just as patent is it, as the play goes on, that Julian's being brought over to Alice's camp requires, as a special, late-in-the-day gambit, his physical seduction by Miss Alice.[3]

With regard, then, to the allegorical play ***Tiny Alice,*** the present essay considers three of the five characters—the Butler, Miss Alice, and the Lawyer, and suggests that at the upper level of Albee's allegory these three personify the temptations of the World, the Flesh, and the Devil.

Edward Albee, who in general has been remarkably close-mouthed about the meaning of ***Tiny Alice,*** was considerably more communicative before the play opened. Ten days before the Broadway opening at the end of December, 1964, Albee was quoted as saying in a *New Yorker* interview: "It's a mystery play in both senses. And it's a morality play."[4]

As to its being a mystery play in the modern sense, one need only remark that a good many critics ere now have found it not only the sort of mystery which obliges one not to reveal the *dénouement* to prospective audiences, but considerably more strikingly, one which so excels in mystification as to leave the auditor still struggling with his bewilderment at the last curtain.[5]

As for Albee's regarding ***Tiny Alice*** as a mystery play in the older meaning of the term, strands in ***Tiny Alice*** do indeed echo the intent and certain distinct sections of the medieval guild cycles. The whole of any such extant cycle, resting as it does on Scripture and Scriptural lore, is a rich presentation of the Fall of Man and the Redemption; and two salient elements in these cycles appear to have important kinship with elements in ***Tiny Alice,*** these being (1) Lucifer's (Satan's) proud, impious nature, his rebellion against God and fall from Heaven, his later malevolent functioning, and his persistent hatred of God and man,[6] man, and (2) the three all-inclusive temptations of Christ in the wilderness—the temptations of the flesh, the world, and the devil.[7]

Turning from the kind of dramatic tradition that conceivably lay behind Albee's referring to ***Tiny Alice*** as a medieval mystery play, one may look for a moment at ***Tiny Alice*** considered as a morality play. The medieval moralities, with their moral and theological basis, their sometimes moving portrayal of man's frailty and susceptibility to temptation, their characters that are either personifications or, occasionally, type figures, their morally serious three plots, have considerable relevance to ***Tiny Alice.***

In general, ***Tiny Alice*** rests upon the morality plot motif of "The Struggle of the Vices and the Virtues," though one notes in Act III the rise of another of the morality plots, the one that forms *Everyman,* "The Coming of Death." The Virtues are personified in a single specialized Mankind figure, Julian—specialized in that he has far fewer ethical frailties than most of us mortals. Albee has formed him with marked success, for he is able to stand up to the considerable dramatic competition of his antagonists, and is personally a thoroughly admirable kind of man, courageous and good, sensitive and scrupulous both spiritually and intellectually. Opposed to him are three Vices—the Butler, Miss Alice, and the Lawyer; these last are aided by one too readily lured and buffeted into their service by means of his pride and greed, the Cardinal.[8]

The three personifications of which this essay treats—the Lawyer, Miss Alice, the Butler—Albee reveals during the course of the drama in four different aspects of their existence.

In the first place, each of the three has his own life as a private individual, with an individual's past, present, and sense of the possible lines of his future. Touches of their past are dotted in from time to time, strengthening one's sense of their being figures in the round and deepening the sense of their natures during the time span of the play.[9] Their present as private individuals reveals itself pretty clearly as the play moves along; the most salient fact is that Miss Alice, the mistress of the Lawyer, as she once was of the Butler, shows considerable signs of falling in love with the attractive and gently-bred Julian, to the hazard of the Lawyer's self-control (Act II, Scene 1) and consequently the trio's professional enterprise.

From a second approach, one notes the position and standing which these three maintain in the eyes of the world: Miss Alice is a fantastically wealthy lady of philanthropic tendencies, the Lawyer is her competent, trusted attorney and man of affairs, and the Butler is the quietly-appreciated head of her household staff. This is the way they intended Julian to see them till the trap is sprung in the "ceremony of Alice" in the last act; whatever they hinted beyond this, or accidentally revealed, did not much affect the intended front. This is the way the Cardinal, too, is intended to see them till some point after Act II, Scene 2; in this scene the Lawyer and the Butler practice, Falstaff-Prince Hal fashion, for their projected interview with the Cardinal, which, we gather later, must have apprised him of their full purpose and persuaded him to an active part in it.

The three are enabled to occupy the positions of such wealth, status, and ease in order that they may carry out a special kind of enterprise. From a third approach, then, one views them as the members of this enterprise, a task force of three, expert, professional, engaged during the time of the play upon a single mission—the bringing over of a human being to their superior, Alice. The drift of the play suggests: the more spiritual the human being, the greater the challenge and the conquest. The Lawyer has charge of the over-all operation, figures the lines of the strategy, and makes the crucial decisions; Miss Alice is responsible not only for the opalescent, feminine light she casts over the world opening to Julian, but also for her special, late contribution toward the end of the process of entrapment; the Butler unobtrusively, practically, sees to it that Julian is a Phaeacian guest after Julian's own taste, with a considerable dash of his own comfortable, down-to-earth presence thrown in, and smooths his colleagues' difficulties besides. As in any successful cooperative venture, their efforts often dovetail, overlap, and re-enforce one another. Similar missions have been their professional lot for years, and they look to other such missions to follow. They are Alice's "agents"—her slaves rather, for disobedience is punishable by death, and they seemingly can anticipate no escape save by this route. Still, their chains are golden chains, and they live in luxury and elegance and in freedom from a thousand constrictions of the kind imposed by the rigors of ordinary life or the behests of generally acceptable ethical codes. The audience is exposed to a good part of the evidence on these matters during the first two acts, and to the rest of it in Act III. Not so for Julian, to whom little more than an uneasiness and, especially later, a sense of being alone in an echoing emptiness, gives any warning of the shock awaiting him in the "ceremony of Alice."

The personal and professional lives of this trio, as sketched above, belong to the primary level of the allegory. And at this level their designations as the Lawyer, Miss Alice, and the Butler are indeed appropriate. However, as one moves to the upper level of the allegory—a fourth kind of approach—three other designations for these characters rise to the mind, designations springing both from the basic natures which these characters reveal and from their manner of functioning in their roles as Alice's agents.

To consider now the Lawyer. In the first scene the Lawyer's total action suggests to the alert viewer a sense of something Mephistophelean there. The Cardinal's hissed curse "Satan!" possibly shifts the direction of this perception, for the Lawyer appears then—and thereafter, too—far from the attractive tempter found in Marlowe, Goethe, Gounod's opera, whose sureness of tact in witty companionship and bright adventure helps charm the victim into the snare. Satanic then? Milton's Satan? Scarcely. Rather, this figure is in the tradition that comes down to us in Lucifer-Satan from the Scriptures and Scriptural lore, as in the old moralities, a hating kind of figure, both in Eden and in the wilderness a miracle of skillfully-directed guile. The lawyer seems to have even more kinship with Dante's analysis of the Evil One. Down through the circles of lower Hell, the circles of hatred or malice, goes the Dantean pilgrim, earlier through the circle of hatred evinced in forms of violence, farther down through the circles of hatred evinced in forms of deceit and guile, of which the last form is treachery, calling on violence as well in its performance, till he reaches the epitome of evil, the final coldness, the negation of all love. Albee's Lawyer is conceived pretty much on the lines of the Dantean analysis. In Scene 1 the Lawyer's antipathies and his verbal violence, at once extreme and excruciatingly well calculated, are obvious; his guile is there too, as the audience, like the Cardinal, comes to realize in retrospect in succeeding scenes, for the crushed, still money-hungry Cardinal is left plastic not only to the trio's subsidiary later designs on himself, but also to immediately permitting his modest secretary, the trio's main objective, to enter precincts and negotiations which involve one whose every facet of character the Cardinal has long ago noted and deplored.

The Lawyer's guile, for projects immediate or remote, is evident enough. In Scene 1 his brief "That's all" qualifies in both respects; in the last scene he casually advises the Cardinal that just then he hasn't time to lie to him. In the rest of the play we see him in charge of the whole operation of entrapment. He has a care over the gambits of the other two, plans the timing and the approach for the chancy final bringing round of the Cardinal, takes a preview of the crucial persuading of Julian, conducts with formality, ribaldry, and cool satisfaction the "ceremony of Alice," decides when Julian is no longer likely to be persuaded to abjure and finishes him, gives a final polish to the Cardinal's misery, present and to come, and gathers his team's morale for the next mission.

As for his violence, his verbal violence was evident in Scene 1. This, exacerbated by jealousy of Julian, in Act II, Scene 1, passes into the physical in his brutal manhandling of Miss Alice, as suggested by the lines, in the scene's opening and again at the time of the fire. One notes it in his casual assumption, to Miss Alice, to the Butler, lastly to the Cardinal, that if Julian cannot be brought over, he can readily be done away with.

Whether operating in guile or violence, the Lawyer's essentially hating nature finds its preferred idiom in cruelty. His own main contribution to bringing over Julian consists in goading and belittling him, as if to say that it was the trio's world of wealth and resultant status and Julian's lack of these that enabled them to treat him as they would and obliged Julian to bear all. The Butler notes the Lawyer as naturally cold and unable to feel love; Miss Alice describes him as dead; in Act III his cruelties rising, not as part of his job, but simply from the hate gnawnig at his heart, are amazing.

What it felt like to the Lawyer to be the Lawyer, Miss Alice's penetrating taunts—that "dead"—finally press out of him. "Does it hurt?" the Lawyer echoes Miss Alice. "Everything! Everything in the day and night, eating, resting, walking, rutting, everything! Everything hurts!" . . . Julian, dying, fully aware at last of all the fraud practiced on him, sums up the Lawyer, both nature and function, in one decent, devastating word: "Instrument!"

In the trio's enterprise of bringing Julian over to Alice's camp Miss Alice has the crucial gambit. Her efforts, one observes, would have had but ill-success, however, had Julian not already been unwittingly in a posture acquiescent to the dominance of materialism, for the panoply of her great wealth and his mission under the Cardinal to secure her huge donation bring him to take in stride, outwardly at once and inwardly fairly soon, the news of her unsavory sex life, which she coolly, early, and purposefully summarizes for him. Her task is his seduction. Once brought to the altar, with the marriage contract signed, he is then to be apprised that Miss Alice has been but a proxy for her principal, Alice. The team work of the other two—the one mostly goadingly, the other amiably, divertingly—so distract their unsuspecting victims that the poor fellow, who can in any case neither flee nor repulse and still be faithful to an honorably undertaken task, fails to recognize till too late the shifting in the quality of his own inclinations or Miss Alice's intent. Offering the temptation of the Flesh, within a beauty and ease of setting that presents the temptation of the World, Miss Alice offers not the bait of bread to one who hungered, but of sex to a vigorous man long vowed to celibacy.

Miss Alice first appears in the last scene of Act I. She has genuine charm and warmth and a certain combination of the winsome and the slightly daunting, and she goes at once to work. She opens with a disconcerting little practical joke, comic in its own right, not unnatural in a light-minded, somewhat bored heiress, and finished off with a pleasingly fairy-tale transformation; even so, one is left with an echo of something unpleasant, perhaps sinister. Alternating between sudden little shocks and an atmosphere of sympathetic *rapport,* by the end of the scene she has successfully surrounded Julian with a number of erotic vantage points, from any or all of which she can smoothly move forward. What an interview for a man who has never before kissed a woman's hand! In the climactic last scene of Act II, presumably some weeks later, we see her concluding her project. With her back to the audience, the great wings and draperies of her negligee flow back, then close to enfold the kneeling Julian, and the curtain falls on her long, triumphant cry to "Alice!"

In the first scene of Act II and in Act III, one receives further indications of Miss Alice's nature—not so much as the Temptation of the Flesh as, simply, the Flesh. Cultivated and sophisticated as she is, and intelligently alert in all that pertains to her *métier,* she is pointedly shown to be a non-intellectual.[10] In general one receives also the impression of her susceptibility to pain. In natural consequence of this trait, one is not surprised that, though she responds with mordant cruelty to the Lawyer's willingness to cow and manhandle her, gentleness is the quality she over and over again desires in others and wistfully venerates. It has its part, one may surmise, in her graceful effect of a pietà toward the end of Act III.

Miss Alice's love for Julian is of the flesh only—it is clearly not of the kind that bears it out even to the edge of doom. Albeit reluctantly, she sacrifices him to the trio's business; and as his death approaches, like Beauty seeing Everyman's grave agape, she would take her tap in her lap and be gone: even in the same breath as she tenderly assures Julian she hates to leave him—it is simply that she must, she says—she is quite practically concerned to have the wig brought downstairs that she has forgotten. Julian, slowly realizing the depths and sources of his betrayal—"all disappointments, all treacheries . . . Oh, God"—finally gathers strength to say strongly as Miss Alice bends over him: "*Leave me!*" She pauses a moment, mute, then turns and exits.

All the same, Miss Alice has not quite left us. When one saw her first, in the opening of the third scene of Act I, in her macabre little practical joke, she had the look, voice, and manner of an aged shrew—hoary, bent, crippled, deaf, shrill, menacing—horrifying to Julian, who had been led to expect a much younger woman. Finished with her jest, she tossed aside her shawl and canes, stripped off wig and thin grey mask, returned to her normal voice and carriage. Thus one may feel that the first glimpse of her on stage was a sort of preview of what the flesh is heir to—mutability, withering. The symbol is continued in the last act. As the Lawyer returns with the wig Miss Alice has forgotten, he catches up the polished phrenological head from the library table, sets it beside Julian on the floor, with the wig atop the head. "Do you want company?" he says to Julian. "Do you want a friend?" And he leaves it there, hoary locks, lifeless countenance, to be its own commentary, like a bizarre *memento mori,* on the Flesh's latter end, mutability and death.

Lastly we come to examine the Butler, considered here as one of the three tempters, the temptation of the World. Albee does well to intimate early, by showing the Butler's personal name and the name of his position to be identical, that there is an overlapping, perhaps a unity, of his personality as a private individual and his guise as a member of Miss Alice's household and a member of the shadowy Alice's task force of three. The total effect tends to waft one toward a realization of his position, at the upper level of the allegory, among the three Temptations.

His nature as an individual, whether in Julian's presence or not, is presented consistently throughout the play: he is at home in the world stretching out all about him, understands it and takes its anomalies in easy stride, finds its abundant, ever-emerging gifts enjoyable and flavorsome, and allows the sense of the world that comes flowing in to him to flow out again to the world, including its inhabitants.[11] Thus he smooths the personal animosities of his teammates as he does the practical difficulties of the team's enterprise, and at the same time keeps refreshed Julian's enjoyment of the world of Miss Alice, despite some continual painful hardships connected with his mission, with the Lawyer, and with the sometimes daunting Miss Alice.

The Butler's concept of himself in his second aspect—that is, as the quietly appreciated butler in a great house—is specialized. Harmonious with his other aspects and contributing markedly to the team's chances of success, on the one hand the Butler's sense of his role frees him from any look of being merely subordinate, subservient, out of things—a posture hard for a man like Butler to sustain indefinitely—and on the other hand, it enables him to have an effortless, unassuming *rapport* with the modest Julian, the more readily to enhance, in his capacity as chief of Miss Alice's household, the attractiveness of the Miss Alice world. One can best summarize the Butler's concept of his butler role by saying that it has hovering formidably behind it the ghost of Shaw's ever-memorable Enry Straker.

Julian would ignore or alertly combat any of the grander temptations of the World. After the bludgeoning spiritual and intellectual experiences of his six "blank years" and his perception, slowly, reflectively reached, of God and a spiritual way of life as the ultimate realities, he is unlikely to be swept overboard by the temptations of the World presented in the majestic form found in St. Matthew and St. Luke. For all that, Julian is a cultivated man, gently bred, eager-minded, and courteously out-going; of late years he has been immured in the scrupulous life of an ascetic minor cleric, ever under the rule of his own and others' soul-searching. To such a man, arriving at Miss Alice's in line of duty, the beauty of a way of life, the obvious spaciousness, freedom, leisure, easy elegance, and creature comforts—all that "the world of the moneyed and powerful" could, after so long, spread open to him, would be attractive indeed. With pointed intention, the tempters could make it more than attractive. That they have done so is revealed in the climactic last scene of the second act, for there Julian details to Miss Alice—hesitantly, fully—his realization that this world is mattering more to him than it should, enveloping him, and he pleads to be allowed to finish his mission and be dismissed.

In Act II the Butler makes his own further special effort to the bringing over of Julian to Tiny Alice. The marriage has taken place, but would Julian, finally alerted, prove recalcitrant after the "ceremony of Alice"? And to shore up against this possibility rather than have him die, the Butler brings in beforehand his painfully evocative image of the dark attic closet, then shortly after returns to it, in order to impress his thought: if Julian is indeed fully against sham and is devoted to reality rather than illusion, would he care, really, who it is who rescues him from the black attic closet? On the upper level of the allegory his argument would run. "Since materialistic considerations will in any case ultimately take over a man, is it not better to accept the advantages which that state affords and survive than, declining, struggle futilely and die?" In the upshot Julian takes his stand for the spiritual and ethical values by which he has lived and repudiates the soulless entity Alice. In his slow dying, passing through stages of feeling himself utterly deserted, the pressure of the image and the panic of the Butler's attic closet re-exerts itself, too late for the Butler's intent, for Julian has already recognized the trap that had enmeshed him and the worth of his final repudiation.

Toward the end of the third act, in a series of departures that distantly echoes the exits at the last of *Everyman,* the Butler is the last to leave—the only one to give the blessing of farewell. The Butler's good-bye is far from the Cardinal's whose whole being at the moment was bent toward a status-preserving exit; or Miss Alice's, whose pitying efforts were rather more of an instinctive salving of her own sensibilities than anything else—Julian's dismissal left her to a wordless departure; or the Lawyer's, whose brutally casual "Good-bye" was met by Julian's decently-phrased, one-word malediction. The Butler's sense of the World is kindly, and he regrets to see a kindly man leaving the fair World when he might have stayed. The Butler, kneeling beside Julian, says: "Dear Julian," and kisses his forehead. His kiss, one thinks, has the sincerity of Julian's own quality of sincerity in a kiss, whether to a Cardinal's amethyst or to a lady's offering of hand or self. Still, since the Tiny Alice lacked, for Julian, as for her three agents, the inevitability of final dominion which the three attributed to her, their sacrifice of Julian to her was an uncalled-for act, a betrayal indeed, and the Butler's kiss, for all his well-wishing, suggests the over-thought of a Judas kiss.

Such is the part of the three tempters in Albee's morality play. The spirit of materialism, like old Covetousness on his scaffold-throne in *The Castle of Perseverance,* broods over the scene. The effects of contemporary scientific achievement present to Albee's Alice a much more far-reaching, pervasive, and subtle power than that of her blunter, more recognizable ancestor. In Acts I and II what life in Alice's thrall is like is shown in its delightful externals to Julian, and in its unlovely and corruscating underpinnings to the audience. Both aspects of their lives the three reveal before Julian in Act III as he lies dying—the vitality, charm, luxury, and far horizons of their outer life, and their inner sense as well of weariness, tedium, blankness—a painful moral wasteland. Julian's physical dying only epitomizes what is theirs spiritually already.

Notes

[1]Edward Albee, *Tiny Alice* (New York: Atheneum, 1965); the Broadway opening night performance was on December 29, 1964.

[2]*Tiny Alice,* p. 181.

[3]For a discussion of the allegory and of the thesis of this play, as these seem to me, see my article "The Statement of Edward Albee's *Tiny Alice,*" *Papers on Language & Literature,* IV (Winter, 1968), 85-100.

[4]"Albee Revisited," *The New Yorker,* XL (December 19, 1964), 33. See also another interview given before the opening night, Mel Gussow, "Who's Afraid of Success?" *Newsweek,* LXV (January 4, 1965), 51.

[5]Among the articles which have laid some emphasis on the relationship of the characters of *Tiny Alice* to one another and to the development of the play, one might mention, as having some relevance to the topic of this paper: Philip Roth, "The Play That Dare Not Speak Its Name," *The New York Review of Books,* IV (February 25, 1965), 4; Walter Kerr, "Albee's 'Tiny Alice'—Walter Kerr's Review," review of the opening night performance, *New York Herald Tribune,* December 30, 1964; "Tiny Alice," *Newsweek,* LXV (January 11, 1965), 75 ("demonic trio"); Barry Ulanov, "Tiny Alice," *Catholic World,* CC (March, 1965), 383-384; Henry Hewes, "Through the Looking Glass, Darkly," *Saturday Review,* XLVIII (January 16, 1965), 40; Harold Clurman, "Tiny Alice," *The Nation,* CC (January 18, 1965), 65, col. 1; Gordon Rogoff, "The Trouble with Alice," *The Reporter,* XXXII (January 28, 1965), 53-4. See also two interviews, Henry Hewes, "The Tiny Alice Caper," *Saturday Review,* XLVIII (January 30, 1965), 38-39, 65; R. S. Stewart, "John Gielgud and Edward Albee Talk about the Theatre," *Atlantic Monthly,* CCXV (April, 1965), 61-68. Note Michael E. Rutenberg, *Edward Albee: Playwright in Protest* (New York: DBS Publications, 1969). Ch. 7.

[6]Genesis 3: 1-24. See *The Chester Plays: a Collection of Mysteries Founded upon Spiritual Subjects . . .* ed. Thomas Wright (London: The Shakespeare Society, 1843), "The Fall of Lucifer," pp. 12-19; "The Creation and Fall," pp. 25-37; *York Plays: the Plays Performed by the Crafts or Mysteries of York . . .* ed. Lucy Toulmin Smith (New York: Russell and Russell [1885], 1963), "The Creation, and the Fall of Lucifer," pp. 1-7; "Man's Disobedience and Fall from Eden," pp. 22-28; *Ludus Coventriae,* ed. K. S. Block (Oxford: E. E. T. S., Oxford University Press [1922], 1960), "The Fall of Lucifer," pp. 16-19; "The Days of Creation," "The Fall of Adam," pp. 19-29; *The Towneley Plays,* ed. George England and Alfred W. Pollard (London: E. E. T. S., Kegan Paul, Trench, Trübner, 1897), "The Creation," pp. 3-6, 8-9; the twelve leaves lost from the manuscript at this point would contain presumably the Temptation of Adam and the Expulsion from Eden. Cf. C. F. Tucker Brooke, *The Tudor Drama* (Boston: Houghton Mifflin, 1911), pp. 7-25; E. K. Chambers, *The Medieval Stage* (Oxford: the Clarendon Press, 1903), II, 103-105, 106-148.

[7]Whereas in the Old Testament, in the Garden, Adam and Eve when tempted fell, in the New Testament, in the wilderness, Christ when tempted stood. Whether all temptations are included in the temptation in the Garden of Eden is a point over which the Church Fathers have labored. Whether all temptations are subtended under the three temptations in the wilderness requires no straining. Consider them for a moment, in St. Luke's great climactic order, Milton's preference, of course, in *Paradise*

David Warner as Julian and Irene Worth as Miss Alice in a Royal Shakespeare Company staging of *Tiny Alice.*

Regained: first, the temptation of the Flesh—for one who is hungry, to convert a stone into bread at the devil's behest and out of distrust of Providence; secondly, the temptation of the World—all the kingdoms of the world spread out before Christ, to be his if he would but worship Satan; lastly, the temptation of the devil's own devising—that Christ at the devil's inviting should fling himself down from a pinnacle of the temple, thus, says the devil, showing his faith in God and fulfilling Scriptural promise—a powerful and subtle temptation to pride. (Matthew 4: 1-11; Mark 1: 12, 13: Luke 4: 1-13. Cf. *The Chester Plays,* "The Temptation," pp. 201-208; *York Plays,* "The Temptation of Jesus," pp. 178-184; *Ludus Coventriae,* "The Temptation," pp. 193-200; in *The Towneley Plays* there is a gap from "John the Baptist" to "The Conspiracy." See Elizabeth Marie Pope, *Paradise Regained: the Tradition and the Poem* (Baltimore: the Johns Hopkins Press, 1947), pp. 51-69.

[8]See *The Castle of Perseverance* and *Everyman* and other moralities in *English Mystery Plays, Moralities and Interludes,* ed. Alfred W. Pollard (Oxford: the Clarendon Press [1927], 1961).

[9]In the Lawyer's individual past, for instance, lay the schoolboy destestation between him and the Cardinal, and the kind of schoolboy the Lawyer once was, as revoltingly particularized by the Cardinal—presumably the Lawyer's schoolboy hate rose mainly from the other's having recognized what was detestable in him; in Act III the Lawyer favors the already wretched Cardinal with a sex episode from, one supposes, the Lawyer's childhood; to the Butler the Lawyer recounts with casual distain an English master's long-ago over-witty comment on the Lawyer's adolescent verses. Miss Alice recalls her schoolgirl excitement over D. H. Lawrence; as she eases the wrist the Lawyer has just twisted, she recalls another day when some boy had hurt her wrist; she recollects, sadly enough, her young girl's panic at the thought of her life's passing without her having lived it. The Butler evidently had a past that familiarized him with great houses, though he seems by no means one who has come up through the household ranks; he suggests with something of pleasure a sense of his having been a member of his family, recalling an example of his father's preferences in diction; he touches regretfully, equably on the passing of his relationship with Miss Alice.

[10]The Lawyer's disporting with logic and with speculation on the nature of reality finally drives Miss Alice to refer to his remarks as "sophomoric conundrums." At the time of the fire, as she makes her prayers, alone on stage and facing the model, it becomes evident that, unlike the other two, she has formed no over-all sense whatever of the trio's ever-continuing enterprises, and her effort at thought sounds rather like a young child's.

[11]The Butler desires the flavor of the pleasures of like for himself and for others—he casts, for instance, a casually Rubaiyat light over his image of Julian and Miss Alice's picnicking out in the estate—"Cold chicken, cheese, a Montrachet under an elm." He enjoys observable fact—that Julian can show him something new about ferns in the solarium, that crows mostly walk only when they are sick—and is surprised at himself that he has never "examined" phrenology. He enjoys the turns and twists of casual conversation, invents a word—the barn swallows' "screeping" as evening comes on, recalls his father's eighteenth-century use of "want," recognizes the great Psalm from which Julian's earlier prayers take their phrasing. He offers the world no meanness, and finds no more coming back to him than he can dismiss or tolerate.

Mary Castiglie Anderson (essay date 1980)

SOURCE: "Staging the Unconscious: Edward Albee's *Tiny Alice,*" in *Renascence,* Vol. XXXII, No. 3, Spring 1980, pp. 178-92.

[*In the following essay, Anderson conducts a psychological reading of* Tiny Alice, *viewing Julian's "conscious spirituality" as based on a "subconscious carnality."*]

Near the end of his lengthy monologue about himself and the dog, Jerry, in Edward Albee's ***The Zoo Story,*** unleashes a desperate rambling which springs from his deep need to establish contact with something: "If not with people . . . if not with people . . . SOMETHING. With a bed, with a cockroach, with a mirror. . . ." But here he stops: "no, that's too hard, that's one of the last steps."[1] It is approaching this last step that we find the lay brother, Julian, in ***Tiny Alice,*** Albee's most cryptic play. Julian's odyssey within Miss Alice's house takes him, in fact, *through* the looking glass on a quest for self-discovery, a quest resounding with psychic implication and leading (if we accept the conclusion as epiphany) to a revelation of mythic proportion.

Most critics willing to go beyond Robert Brustein's and George Wellwarth's dismissal of the play as "meaningless" have interpreted its theme as ironic; among them, Anne Paolucci and Ruby Cohn agree on a definition of Alice as "an incomprehensible Nothing" while Lee Baxandall and Leighton M. Ballew see her as simply the manifestation of Julian's need to believe in something, the final irony being that he accepts the man-made symbol of God he so strongly resisted.[2] Harold Clurman pans the play as an ultimately uninteresting effort "to prove the world an intolerably damned place," and only John Gassner is willing to concede that its concern with "the enigmas of life" or "the futility of trying to explain existence rationally" has claimed playwrights' attention from the beginning of literate theatre.[3] Albee himself has said of the ending of ***Tiny Alice***:

> [Julian] is left with pure abstraction—whatever it be called: God or Alice—and in the end, according to your faith, one of two things happens. Either the abstraction personifies itself, is proven real, or the dying man, in the last necessary effort of self-delusion, creates and believes in what he knows does not exist.[4]

The ironic interpretation remains ultimately unsatisfying, however, especially since in all his drama, most critical interpretations notwithstanding, Albee has never shown himself to be either absurdist or nihilist. In ***The Zoo Story,*** he portrays the wasteland of modern society in which the chasm between one human being and another has become so vast that Jerry must sacrifice his life in order to bridge it. But, by so doing, he does, in fact, manage to break through Peter's carefully designed cage of false security and self-preservation. The essence of Jerry's communication with Peter at the moment their lives touch is disturbingly transient and enigmatic. Albee questions the substance of one human being's contact with another, but he never doubts that somehow that contact is possible, and he posits unquestioningly that it is essential.

Who's Afraid of Virginia Woolf? is a purgation rite in which George and Martha strip each other of their defenses, illusions, and fictions. The destruction of their metaphorical son provides at least the potential for their rebirth into a new and more authentic relationship where before none had existed. But again, Albee will not define for us the nature of authenticity nor even suggest whether that authenticity can ever be actualized and sustained between George and Martha. His message is only that in order to *begin* we must face our past, admit our illusions and our vulnerability, and accept our fear.

In ***Seascape*** we find Charlie, who must learn to relinquish the womblike security to which he has retreated (as a child he would descend to a cove at the bottom of the sea where mentally he has remained through his adult life) in order to accept the challenge of assisting a new species, themselves emerging from the sea, to "Begin." In this context, then, it is plausible to give ***Tiny Alice,*** despite its dark and foreboding tone, an apocalyptic reading.

It has been suggested often enough that the play operates on numerous levels, the simplest being an apparent betrayal story of a man offered by his church to a group of demonic characters for the sum of a hundred million dollars a year for twenty years. The man is sent as an emissary to the house of the donor, an eccentric woman named simply Miss Alice, to "clear up odds and ends." While there, this man, a celibate and ascetic, is lured into a strange and mysterious world by the temptations of wealth, luxury, friendship, and finally sexuality. He is offered happiness in the form of marriage to Miss Alice; but once he accepts he is abandoned by her and her cohorts (including his Cardinal who sent him on the bizarre mission), fatally shot, and left to die alone on the altar of Alice, the mysterious goddess whom they all seem to serve, thus becoming their sacrifice to her.

But the play seen on this level leaves many ambiguities, the chief of which is, perhaps, the role of the three tempters: Lawyer, Butler, and Miss Alice. They seem at first sinister agents of an evil force sent to undermine the virtues of Julian. But often they indicate to him that they are helping him, that the process he is undergoing, painful though it is, is for his own benefit. In the last act, for instance, when Julian asks Butler, "Are you my friend?" Butler responds, "I *am;* yes; but you'll probably think not."[5] In the same scene, Julian insists that all his life he has "fought against the symbol" and Miss Alice tells him, "Then you should be happy now" (162), indicating his struggle is over. We must question, too, whether Julian's virtues, sincere though they seem as far as he is aware of them, are in fact genuine. As he begins to reveal himself to Miss Alice, it becomes apparent that his conscious spirituality has been based all along on a subconscious carnality.

* * *

This insistent split demands a more subtle interpretation of the play, one focused on Julian's psychology. The disclosure of Julian's personal unconscious with its powerful, repressed sex drive is prepared for early in ***Tiny Alice*** by the motif of revealing information (as one would reveal repressed motivations). The first scene between Lawyer and Cardinal is filled with persistent references to secret pasts, dossiers, and the manifestation of defamatory information. When, in the following scene, Julian refuses to reveal to Lawyer the details of his years in the asylum, Lawyer hisses prophetically, "You will . . . in time. Won't he, Butler? Time? The great revealer?" (42).

The action of the drama will unveil the layers of Julian's psyche, from the exposure of his repressed sexuality to the disclosure of the Oedipal drive and the father-son conflict. And beyond that we will find yet a deeper layer—so that we might concur with Miss Alice when she exclaims "expansively" at one point, "Oh, my Julian! How many layers! Yes?" (114). That the play undertakes a journey through his mind is made clear from the very first scene in which Julian appears and describes his experiences in the mental home to Butler: "I . . . declined. I . . . shriveled into myself; a glass dome . . . descended, and it seemed I was out of reach, unreachable, finally unreaching, in this . . . paralysis, of sorts" (43). The model house, the home of Alice, a shriveled version of the real house sealed by a glass dome also appears on stage for the first time in this scene. Clearly, it presents itself to us as a symbol of Julian's unconscious.

Butler explicates the theme of self-confrontation when he suggests to Julian that one feels one should see one's self in the model (25). The theory he poses on the care one would take if one had such a "dream toy" made invites psychic correlation: "It would almost be taken for granted—one would think—that if a person or a person's surrogate went to the trouble, *and* expense, of having such a dream toy made, that the person *would* have it sealed, so that there'd be no dust" (26). "Dream toy" becomes a significant word choice here when considered in terms of the subconscious. Julian remarks as he gazes into it, "it seemed so . . . continual" (25); and in response to Butler's comment that the house is enormous he replies,"Endless!" (27). Significantly, in both dimensions, the house has many rooms, as Miss Alice's *non sequitur* points out: "I . . . am a very beautiful woman. . . . And a very rich one. . . . And I live here, in all these rooms" (63). Throughout the play, other references to rooms, divisions, and partitions—the asylum to which Julian committed himself was "deep inland" and had "buildings, or floors of buildings" (58)—bolster the mind imagery. The phrenological head is an obvious symbol.

As I've already suggested, it becomes clear early in the play that Julian's expressed intentions are belied by the unconscious drives which motivate them. The fantasies and hallucinations he divulges betray the libidinous forces threatening his conscious self-concept. In his scenes with Miss Alice, Julian is always the one to initiate an atmosphere of high-tensioned eroticism by relating a past fantasy. (Act II, scene iii is surely the best example of this.)

Julian sublimates his sexual drives into a desire to serve and constructs a persona of himself as martyr, refusing to accept that any self-actualization must be channeled into a role which serves his human needs one way or another. In other words, Julian's image of himself as martyr does not eliminate or even substitute for his other needs; it simply displaces them. This repression accounts for the perverse eroticism which fills the stage each time Julian divulges his fantasies. According to C. G. Jung, the ideal relationship of the unconscious to the conscious is compensatory, with the one balancing the extremes of the other. The more repressed the unconscious tendencies—the more, in Julian's case, the sexual needs are denied—the less displaced and the more primitive, even distorted, these tendencies become. The stronger his desires make themselves felt to Julian as doubts or temptations (since the effects of the unconscious will always present themselves as forces outside the person), the more his conscious attitude takes on an extreme, rigid position to compensate. In turn, the unconscious drives become even more exaggerated and grotesque in a continuously vicious cycle. What might have been the healthy expression of his sexuality has become for Julian violent, distorted, and pathological.

Julian's desire for martyrdom, then, is anything but a healthy expression of his faith. It is, rather, an obsessive, fanatical drive to counteract the threat from his unconscious. He is *obsessed* with martyrdom. We might also see this obsession as an impulse toward self-destruction brought on by the tension between his conflicting desires, as well as an unrealized longing for punishment for his transgressions, unconscious though they be. But Albee is hardly offering us any profound insight when he suggests that religious fanaticism if often based upon sexual repression. If his play sought only to uncover Julian as a fraud at the end, after having uncovered institutional religion as a fraud right from the start, ***Tiny Alice*** would simply be a social statement against all the spiritual trappings, even the most strenuous, with which we surround ourselves. There is certainly that statement made in the play, but it is not the central issue. For one thing, unlike Soeur Jeanne des Anges in John Whiting's *The Devils,* Julian is far too attractive a character. Some critics have suggested that he is, in fact, the most appealing of Albee's protagonists. He is sincerely confused in regard to this area of his life, but in other respects he is open, intelligent, flexible, genuinely simple, and, unlike his Cardinal, without conscious ulterior motives.

And Julian, like George in ***Who's Afraid of Virginia Woolf?*** and Jerry in ***The Zoo Story,*** is an outsider, belonging wholeheartedly neither to the traditional hierarchical church, which uses God for its own gains, nor to the secular world, which has long since substituted money and technology for God. His title, lay brother, typifies his situation: "You are of the cloth but have not taken it" as Butler puts it (28). Because, like Jerry and George, his sensibility precludes his place within traditional structures, Julian is set apart as a modern hero, who, in Jung's words, "has become 'unhistorical' in the deepest sense and has estranged himself from the mass of men who live entirely within the bounds of tradition." We find him isolated and at a crossroads: either he must block out the outside world completely and return to the asylum, or he must discard his personal illusions, accept and understand himself, and acknowledge that, again to quote Jung, he "has come to the very edge of the world, leaving behind him all that has been discarded and outgrown, and . . . he stands before the Nothing out of which All may grow."[6]

Therefore, it is difficult to accept that the main motive of the tempters in ***Tiny Alice*** is to uncover Julian's weaknesses and undermine his good intentions simply to punish him with abandonment and death. If it is necessary for Julian to recognize and discard the fictions he has clung to, as it was for George and Martha to discard their fictional son, we might question whether his possibility for new light and understanding should be any less than theirs. And, if these unconscious motives are uncovered, leaving a more balanced Julian, can we accept that he is betrayed and punished for these unless we accept his own original, distorted definition of his "sins"?

The questions turn on the meaning of Alice and the significance of Julian's acceptance of her. The first part of the play, in which Julian's personal unconscious does become integrated, is only a first or preparatory step, leading to some understanding of even greater, deeper consequence. What this is can be understood in part by viewing ***Tiny Alice*** not in the context of realistic, ironic tragedy, but within the genre of allegorical romance. Several signs in the play point in this direction.

Northrop Frye states that "in romance the characters are still largely dream characters" and that they function as "expressions of emotional attachments, whether of wish-fulfillment or of repugnance."[7] The very first word we hear Julian utter, "Extraordinary," in the light of Frye's definition is very apt. From the moment he enters Miss Alice's house there is a sense that he has entered a dreamlike or extra-ordinary world, where commonsense logic will not apply. The characters who people that world are, by their very names, embodiments of ideas, concepts, or split-off parts of Julian's own psyche, on one level at least. Lawyer, for instance, is the prototype of everything repugnant and reductive, Julian's Shadow or dark side as it were, and critics who accept his commentary as a key to understanding the play are hearing only one bias.

Julian's mission contains the obvious allegorical overtones of the life-cycle quest: the accomplishment of a task to achieve a treasure, represented by the money Miss Alice promises to the church. In traditional mythological format, the hero is sent on a task or journey by a divine superior, a role into which the Cardinal fits nicely (36). Part of his reward is the winning of a bride, whom he takes from the hands of a previous, older lover; the hero, though he must die, is exalted at the end. According to Frye, the quest has three stages: "the stage of the perilous journey and the preliminary minor adventures; the crucial struggle, usually some kind of battle in which either the hero or his foe, or both, must die; and the exaltation of the hero" (187).

From the beginning of Act II, it becomes very clear that little but open hostility exists between Lawyer (the evil ogre) and Miss Alice: lustful pursuit on the part of the one, revulsion and evasion on the part of the other. Lawyer makes such little effort to conceal his tremendous hatred of his successor that Butler can easily observe, "I've noticed, you've let your feelings loose lately; too much: possessiveness, jealousy" (99). Julian himself is fully cognizant of the rivalry, as his accusation to Miss Alice attests: "You have allowed that . . . that *man,* your . . . your lover, to . . . ridicule me. You have *permitted* it. . . . You have allowed him to abuse me, my position, his, the Church; you have tolerated it, and *smiled*" (117).

To quote Frye once again, apropos of Miss Alice:

> This bride-figure is ambiguous: her psychological connection with the mother in an Oedipus fantasy is more insistent than in comedy. She is often to be found in a perilous, forbidden, or tabooed place . . . and she is, of course, often rescued from the unwelcome embraces of another and generally older male, or from giants or bandits or other usurpers.
>
> (193)

The tension between Lawyer and Julian reflects the son-father rivalry for the mother. Miss Alice does, in fact, treat Julian as a favored child, referring to him as "my little Julian" and "little recluse." The three characters' interaction as hero/rescuer, bride, and ogre is structured upon the son, mother, father psychological triad in which the child perceives his father as a rival hurting his mother who must be rescued.

That is one level on which the quest motif operates in ***Tiny Alice.*** On another level, Miss Alice herself is the temptress, and as mother-figure she personifies the most formidable taboo. Julian articulates his instinctive dread of what she represents toward the end of Act II: "WHY AM I BEING TESTED? . . . And why am I being tempted? By luxury, by ease, by . . . content . . . by things I do not care to discuss" (117).

The quest for the treasure is the more generalized version of Julian's specific or personal lifetime preoccupation: the search for the Father, in his terms, God. Within Miss Alice's house his dual purposes converge. He realizes only intuitively at this point that the latter is the search for his Self, a fact implicit in his declaration, "My faith and my sanity . . . they are one and the same" (45).

The motif of the search for the Self brings us, finally, to the last and most elusive level of Albee's play. If the house is the symbol of Julian's unconscious (as well as a female archetype), and Alice lives there, then Alice must be the personification of something within Julian which he must confront. That something can be explored through the Jungian theory of the Anima, the female principle existing inside all men.

The Anima first appears as an image in a man's mind of the nuturing, all-embracing, protecting mother (but it includes other archetypal images as well, such as the virgin, the temptress, the witch, and the spiritual guide). It is not clear from where this image arises for it does not come from the real mother. Jung attributed it to the collective unconscious, present *a priori* in a person's mind; while other psychological studies do not accept this completely, they do concede, in the words of Maud Bodkin, that "where forms are assimilated from the environment upon slight contact only, predisposing factors must exist in mind and brain."[8]

In his infantile or immature state, the man will cling to this first image of the mother, his unconscious desire for what Jung calls "the enveloping, embracing, and devouring element."[9] He projects this desire first onto his real mother and later onto the substitute mother, that is, the wife or lover. Seen in this context, Miss Alice is Julian's projection of part of his Anima or his desire, in Jungian terminology, to be caught, sucked in, enveloped, and devoured. This is easily supported from the play by the numerous images of envelopment, for instance, Miss Alice's quote from D. H. Lawrence's "Love on the Farm":

> And down his mouth comes on my mouth! and down
> His bright dark eyes over me . . .
> . . . his lips meet mine, and a flood
> Of sweet fire sweeps across me, so I drown
> Against him die and find death good!
>
> (112)

In Julian's fantasies of martyrdom he sees himself devoured by a lion and after a graphic description he concludes: "And as the fangs sank in, the great tongue on my cheek and eye, the splitting of the bone, and the *blood* . . . just before the great sound, the coming dark and the silence. I could . . . experience it all. And was . . . *engulfed*" (124). When Julian finally comes to Miss Alice in Act II, scene iii, the stage directions indicate that she opens her gown like great wings unfurling and "Julian utters a sort of dying cry and moves, his arms in front of him, to Miss Alice; when he reaches her, she *enfolds* him in her great wings" (127). And, of course, in the final scene the darkness moves out of the model house, surrounds Julian as a presence and, again to quote Albee's directions, "his eyes, his head move to all areas of the room, noticing his *engulfment*" (189-90). (All emphases, except the first, mine.)

Mother Church, to which Julian's loyalties lie before he relinquishes them to Miss Alice, is also an archetypal Anima—the female counterpart to Christ, the male Animus. We might recollect, too, that Julian's memory of his first sexual experience which "did or did not happen" involved a woman who believed herself to be yet another female archetype: the Virgin Mary, Mother of God.

* * *

When Miss Alice appears in Act I, scene iii as, in Albee's directions, a "withered crone, her hair gray and white and matted," bent and moving with two canes, and speaks "with a cracked and ancient voice," this is more than simply an indication that in this play things will not be as they seem, though it certainly is that. The disguise is also a sign, from the outset, that she is playing a role—the donning of a mask transforms the wearer into an archetypal image—a role with mythic significance. In this case, she is the projection of another aspect of the Anima of Julian's psyche: the Terrible Mother, which appears in archetypal dream imagery as a witch or crone. The duality between the Good Mother and the Terrible Mother is explained best by a quotation from Ruth L. Munroe regarding Jungian theory:

> For the infant the mother is the major image, regardless of the sex of the child, and the mother remains the symbol of bliss, repose, comfort, and total passivity, the source of life. But a duality is apparent in the definition. Life is not passive. The child must go forth into the real world. So while the man retains a nostalgia for the Eternal Mother . . . he must also leave the Mother. The Good Mother of his deepest dreams is also the Terrible Mother . . . within the person's own psyche.[10]

The Terrible Mother is associated with death and the dark side of life a man must accept in order to live actively. Therefore, when Miss Alice appears to Julian first as a crone this is a message to him from his own psyche that, in order to find what he is looking for, he must first leave the safety of his secluded world, the confines of Mother Church. In light of this, the exchange between Julian and Miss Alice after she has removed the mask makes more sense than it otherwise would:

> MISS ALICE: Oh, indulge us, please.
>
> JULIAN: Well, of course, it would be my pleasure . . . but, considering the importance of our meeting . . .
>
> MISS ALICE: Exactly. Considering the importance of our meeting.
>
> JULIAN: A . . . a test for me.
>
> (53)

Julian comes very close to a conscious awareness of the meaning of the Terrible Mother when he describes his meeting with her as a test. He will not arrive at full consciousness of everything that is happening to him, however, until the very end of the play. These events and the people who act within them are simply signals from his unconscious, similar to the symbols of dreams, revealing a great deal of what his conscious self cannot immediately comprehend. The extent to which this is true adds weight to the association frequently made between the title of the play and the wonderland of Lewis Carroll's Alice. It may be to her function as a dream symbol (which is experienced but not always understood) that Miss Alice refers when she says early in the play, "It may be I am . . . noticeable, but almost never identified" (59).

Though Julian is obviously fascinated and enticed by Miss Alice, this alone would not provide sufficient incentive for his renunciation of the safety of Mother Church. Miss Alice must lure him out of that world and into a dynamic participation in life. In her primary role of Temptress, she does this by being to him still another projection of his desire for "the protecting, nourishing, charmed circle of the mother." He succumbs to this illusion when he comes to her uttering "a sort of dying cry" and she enfolds him in her wings (127). This is a point of initiation for Julian, necessitating the loss of innocence (Albee, in an interview appearing in the April 1965 issue of *The Atlantic Monthly,* referred to Julian as an innocent); he undergoes a symbolic death and an entrance into experience resulting in the sacrifice of rigidly idealistic (and, by implication, immature) beliefs. Thus, as the hero, Julian experiences a kind of initial rebirth into a more autonomous individualism, enabling him to continue on his quest to penetrate the mysteries of life and death. A definition from Jung further explicates Miss Alice's role: "the seductress . . . draws him into life with her Maya [Illusion personified as a celestial maiden] and not only into life's reasonable and useful aspects, but into its frightful *paradoxes* and *ambivalence* where good and evil, success and ruin, hope and despair counterbalance one another" (*Aion,* 13).

That Julian has, in fact, progressed in his journey and shed his limiting and self-protecting beliefs is suggested by his words to the Cardinal in the scene following his marriage to Miss Alice:

> But then I judge it is God's doing, this . . . wrenching of my life from one light to another . . . though not losing God's light, joining it with . . . my new. I can't tell you, the . . . radiance, humming, and the witchcraft, I think it must be, the ecstasy of this light, as *God's* exactly; . . . the blessed wonder of service with a renewing, not an ending joy—that joy I thought possible only through martyrdom.
>
> (140)

Julian intuits that his entrance into life has had something to do with witchcraft. Though he is focusing on the bright side (which is real), he senses that there is a dark side as well (also real). His first experience of leaving the mother's womblike safety is abandonment. In fact, at the opening of that same scene we see Julian, the bridegroom, confused and anxious as to why everyone, including his new wife, has left him on his wedding day. One of the first things he says is, "I feel quite *lost,*" and a little later, "There I was . . . one moment married, flooded with white, and . . . then . . . the next, alone. Quite alone . . ." (132). Entering the continuum of life he begins to experience the "frightful paradoxes" Jung speaks of, where light and dark, the Apollonian and the Dionysian, expansion and diminution exist side by side.

Miss Alice seems to be Julian's betrayer by initiating him into that world, but he must take that necessary step toward the goal he has set for himself, a goal he cannot reach without *conscious* acceptance (in the final scene) of everything happening to him so far in his unconscious. His only alternative is complete withdrawal from the world; that is, total surrender to his unconscious, the substitution of hallucination for reality. Lawyer and Butler refer to these two alternatives when they speak of Julian in Act II, scene ii as "walking on the edge of an abyss, but . . . balancing. Can be pushed . . . over, back to the asylums. Or over . . . to the Truth" (106). This Truth will come with the integration of the conscious and the unconscious, with the attainment of the masculine principle to balance the feminine, and with the acceptance of the ambiguities, paradoxes, and limitations which will become recognizable. In this sense, it must be remembered that Miss Alice is the projection of Julian's own Anima seeking this balance. And even when, in Act III, he is lost and abandoned after his marriage, he has not forsaken his quest (138). The pain of "the reality of things" is so great, however, that Julian's ego resists it to the point where he almost opts for insanity:"I . . . cannot . . . accept . . . this. . . . No, no, I will . . . I will go *back!* I will . . . go *back* to it. To . . . to . . . I will go back to the asylum" (169-70).

According to Jung, if the conscious and the unconscious become too split, as in the case of Julian, a tension arises, and the functions of the Anima in a man and the Animus in a woman, "harmless till then, confront the conscious mind in personified form and behave rather like systems split off from the personality, or like part souls" (*Aion,* 20). It must be made very clear, I think, that on one level Lawyer, Miss Alice, and Butler function as full, three-dimensional characters with independent motivations and psychologies. But on another level, they are projections of Julian's mind. It is because of this dual function that their roles and rhetoric become so confusing.

If, in the case of Julian, the Anima can be withdrawn from projections, these projections can be integrated into consciousness. Thus, to a certain extent, the Anima represents a *function* which filters the collective unconscious through to the conscious mind. Alluding to this function, Miss Alice attempts to explain to Julian, "I have tried to be . . . *her.* No; I have tried to be . . . what I thought she might, what might make you happy, what you might use, as a . . . what?" (161), and later, "accept what's real. I am the . . . illusion" (167); and to which Lawyer refers when he says, "We are surrogates; *our* task is done now" (162). As functionaries of Julian's psyche, Lawyer's, Butler's, and Miss Alice's tasks are done as they bring him to the point of consciousness, in which they can no longer be personified for him by projections, and so in a sense must abandon him. As archetypal symbols, however, they function beyond Julian's psyche in the realm of a collective unconscious. Therefore, they remain autonomous even after he has integrated them into his ego ("On . . . and on . . . we go" [99]). Because of this, Lawyer declares, "You have brought us to the end of our service here. We go on; you stay" (161). The indications are that they will continue to act the same roles within other circumstances (177-78).

* * *

Like Sophocles' Oedipus, Julian had been on a search for the truth; like Oedipus who questioned everyone, Julian was sent to Miss Alice's house to take care of "a few questions and answers"; and like Oedipus, Julian had not bargained for the outcome that truth is painful, that it brings with it the recognition of unconscious forces and existential alienation, and that it leads ultimately to self-confrontation. His anger toward, and rejection of, Miss Alice's protective gesture in the last act of ***Tiny Alice*** (183) underscores the dawning of his understanding of autonomy and acceptance of responsibility: "It is what I have wanted, have insisted on. Have nagged . . . for" (188).

Albee has insisted that though "The sound of heartbeats and heavy breathing as the doors open have widely been misinterpreted as being those of an increasingly terrified Julian . . . they are meant to belong to whatever comes through the door."[11] Alice is the abstraction of the Anima which exists in the most sublimated realm of Julian's unconscious—his archetypal or collective unconscious. In recognizing *her,* Julian finds her counterpart, the Animus, or the God for which he has been searching (190); and consequently he comes to possess himself.

The Animus or Logos representing the male aspect of spirit and intellect, and the Anima or Eros representing the female or Earth Mother are, as Jung tells us, godlike because of the great psychic energy they produce:

> Both of them are unconscious powers, "gods" in fact, as the ancient world quite rightly conceived them to be. To call them by this name is to give them that central position in the scale of psychological values which has always been theirs whether consciously acknowledged or not; for their power grows in proportion to the degree that they remain unconscious.
>
> (*Aion.* 21)

In accepting them both, Julian has reached his epiphany which, according to Northrop Frye, is:

> the symbolic presentation of the point at which the undisplaced apocalyptic world and the cyclical world of nature come into alignment. . . . Its most common settings are the mountain-top, the island, the tower, the lighthouse, and the ladder or staircase. Folk tales and mythologies are full of stories of an original connection between heaven or the sun and earth.. . .The movement from one world to the other may be symbolized by the golden fire that descends from the sun . . . and by its human response, the fire kindled on the sacrificial altar.
>
> (203-04)

The setting for Julian is up against the model house, the altar of Alice, but it is interesting that Albee originally intended him to be locked in an attic closet (corresponding more closely to Frye's tower or ladder), an idea he had to forego for the sake of dramatic effect. The movement of the world of Nature (Alice) into the world of the Spirit (God) comes in the form of the light descending through the rooms of the model house into the room Julian occupies (Frye's golden fire descending from the sun). Julian is the human response on the sacrificial altar.

Through a modern rite of initiation Julian comes, at last, to achieve the integration he sought. What the drama depicts, finally, is a birth-rebirth ritual in which he is first outfitted in ritual robes (in his case, a business suit), shot with a pistol (phallic symbol of fertility), and united with the Earth Mother who destroys in order to immortalize. In an impressive feat of dramatic compression, the scene of his death, with heartbeats and ensuing darkness, carries unmistakable overtones of a birth—expulsion from the womb. The modern audience may well remain impervious, however, to the suggestion of spiritual rebirth for Julian since, as Jung argues in his essay "Freud and Jung," our civilization has by and large forgotten the meaning of divine procreation and tends to overlook the possibility that incestuous longings go back past the desire for the temporal father and mother to a primal desire for unity with the spirit and with nature.[12]

Perhaps in this play, in which Albee must surely have been working out of his own unconscious, his contention that the use of the unconscious is twentieth-century theatre's most interesting development comes most fully to bear.[13] The psychological processes dissected here occur simultaneously in the play so that the overall effect contributes to its most fascinating element: the capacity to re-create the atmosphere of the dream. Thus, it is haunting and disturbing despite its resistance to discursive logic.

Like many of Albee's plays, the effect of the ending of ***Tiny Alice*** is one of suspended motion; there is a sense of resolution but it remains intangible. Julian's epiphany is as elusive as the elation Jerry experiences right before his death in ***The Zoo Story***: a bright flash of light before what remains, for us, darkness. Both characters, at their deaths, take the full implication of their visions with them, leaving the audience to ponder, finally, the persistent sense of mystery which remains.

Notes

[1] *"The American Dream" and "The Zoo Story"* (New York: Signet, 1963), p. 34.

[2]Robert Brustein, *Seasons of Discontent* (New York: Simon and Schuster, 1965), p. 308; George Wellwarth, *The Theatre of Protest and Paradox,* 2nd ed. (New York: New York Univ. Press, 1971), p. 332; Anne Paolucci, *From Tension to Tonic: The Plays of Edward Albee* (Carbondale: Southern Illinois Univ. Press, 1972), p. 96; Ruby Cohn, *Currents in Contemporary Drama* (Bloomington: Indiana Univ. Press, 1969), p. 249; Lee Baxandall, "The Theatre of Edward Albee," *Tulane Drama Review,* 9 (Summer 1965), 35; Leighton M. Ballew, "Who's Afraid of *Tiny Alice?*" *Georgia Review,* 20 (1966), 299.

[3]Harold Clurman, *The Naked Image* (New York: Macmillan, 1966), p. 24; John Gassner, *Dramatic Soundings* (New York: Crown, 1968), p. 602.

[4]Quoted in Alice Mandanis, "Symbol and Substance in *Tiny Alice,*" *Modern Drama,* 12 (May 1969), 92.

[5]*Tiny Alice* (New York: Atheneum, 1965), p. 138. All page references are from this edition.

[6]Carl Gustav Jung, "The Spiritual Problem of Modern Man," in *Civilization in Transition,* Vol. X of *The Collected Works,* trans. R. F. C. Hull (New York: Bollingen, 1964), p. 75.

[7]*Anatomy of Criticism: Four Essays* (New York: Atheneum, 1968), p. 206. All page references are from this edition.

[8]*Archetypal Patterns in Poetry* (London: Oxford Univ. Press, 1934), pp. 4-5.

[9]C. G. Jung, "The Syzygy: Anima and Animus," in *Aion: Researches Into the Phenomenology of the Self,* Vol. IX of *The Collected Works,* trans. R. F. C. Hull (New York: Bollingen, 1959), p. 11.

[10]*Schools of Psychoanalytic Thought: An Exposition, Critique, and Attempt at Integration* (New York: Henry Holt, 1955), p. 542.

[11]Quoted in Henry Hewes, "The *Tiny Alice* Caper," *Saturday Review,* 30 Jan. 1965, p. 39.

[12]C. G. Jung, *Modern Man in Search of a Soul,* trans. W. S. Dell and Cary F. Baynes (New York: Harcourt, Brace & World, 1933), p. 123.

[13]Michael E. Rutenberg, *Edward Albee: Playwright in Protest* (New York: Avon, 1969), p. 227.

Leonard Casper (essay date 1983)

SOURCE: "*Tiny Alice:* The Expense of Joy in the Persistence of Mystery," in *Edward Albee: An Interview and Essays,* edited by Julian Wasserman, Joy L. Linsey, and Jerome A Kramer, The University of St. Thomas, 1983, pp. 83-92.

[*In the essay below, Casper proposes that* Tiny Alice *"resists being treated as an allegory because its meaning lies in the persistence, rather than the resolution of mystery," and that it is "a tribute to finite man's terrifying instinct for infinity."*]

When Edward Albee was asked by his publisher to provide a preface for ***Tiny Alice*** which would explain its peculiarities, he at first consented; then recanted, having decided that "the play is quite clear."[1] Further, he declared that even more people shared his view than found his work obscure. Among the latter, however, were those daily reviewers who had the most immediate access to the Geilgud-Worth production in the Billy Rose Theater: Taubman of the *Times,* Kerr of thc *Herald-Tribune,* Watts of the *Daily Post,* and Chapman of the *Daily News.*[2] The bafflement of such otherwise friendly critics perhaps was epitomized best by contradictory reviews which appeared in *Time* early in 1965. The first, on January 8, referred to the play as a "tinny allegory," dependent more on mystification than mystery; more on echolalia than on eloquence; more on pretentious reprise of Nietzschean nihilism than on profound, fresh inquiry. Only one week later, the same source was at least willing, half-facetiously, to take part in the controversial deciphering of ***Tiny Alice*** by suggesting that meaning might lie dormant in such apparent clues as references to a "homosexual nightmare," Julian the Apostate, and cunning old Fury's decision in *Alice's Adventures in Wonderland* to try poor Mouse with intent to condemn him to death for lack of anything better to do that day.

Aside from agit-prop plays, whose ideological direction is extensively detailed, most plays submit to risks of misunderstanding involved in the indirection of their argument. But ***Tiny Alice*** has continued to be considered exceptionally difficult. Even critics who have tried to admire it have shown signs of testiness, undergoing trials originating at times in their own ingenuity. Harold Clurman, one of the earliest, was willing to say that he saw an allegory in which "the pure person in our world is betrayed by all parties," themselves corrupt. "Isolated and bereft of every hope, he must die—murdered." But the result, somehow, reminded him of a Faustian drama written by "a highly endowed college student."[3] Later and more elaborately, Anne Paolucci described ***Tiny Alice*** as "the most impressive of Albee's paradoxical affirmations of negation."[4] To be consistent with this conclusion, she was compelled to treat the play as an intricate allegory: the three agents of Alice, for example, compose a sinister "unholy trinity" concelebrating a parodic ritual of faith; the play is an extended enactment of the smaller scale sexual-spiritual abandon/abandonment experienced by Julian in the asylum. It is a confession of despair: the Invisible Presence is, in fact, an Immense Absence. Ruby Cohn's version of the play was similarly bleak, finding its central struggle in the wilful resistance of Julian's imagination to his pronounced desire for the real. A ceremony is contrived, to wed him to reality: "and even then he tries to rearrange it into familiar appearance." In the moment of death, Julian experiences "the prototypical existential confrontation"[5]—complete isolation; but unable to bear it, invokes Christian allusions/illusions. Presumably, according to Cohn's version, reality = death = abstraction = Tiny Alice = self-negation. In her judgment, a man of true integrity should face this Absurdity with courage, not cower as Julian does, regressing to childhood. Michael Rutenberg's decoding of Albee's allegory perceived a diabolic force bartering a billion ordinary souls for one especially sensitive and worth corrupting, even as the visible conspirators form a chorus half-sympathetic with the victim.[6] Although Rutenberg had to admit the ambiguity of the ending, however interpreted, Julian is lost—to Nothingness; or to an Evil Deity; or to a benevolent but all-devouring God. Positive projections of the ending have been rarer, perhaps because they have been considered too naive by the critical mind. And all have ignored the possibility that any definitive reading is too narrow for Albee.

But suppose ***Tiny Alice*** resists being treated as allegory because its meaning lies in the persistence, rather than the resolution, of mystery. Suppose risk, natural to reconnoitering the previously undiscovered or unexplored, is being offered as itself the supreme reality. Suppose ***Tiny Alice*** is a tribute to finite man's terrifying instinct for infinity. The play has at least two structural elements which provide a degree of stability to dimensions otherwise often in flux: the central presence of Julian and the strategic placement of visions at the climax of each of the three acts. As visions deriving from the virginal Julian, they are, of course, suspect. Two of them are even placed offstage and can therefore readily be dismissed as hallucinations in a disturbed mind. Albee offers no clear persuasion of his own but only suggests how best to submit to the play's passions and impressions: "Brother Julian is in the same position as the audience. He's the innocent. If you see things through his eyes, you won't have any trouble at all.'"[7] Or, perhaps, just the trouble appropriate to flawed and still falling man—trouble not wholly distinguishable from the gift of choice to the half-informed.

When towards the end of Act I Julian reveals to Miss Alice his principal memory of all the six hermitic years spent sealed in an asylum, he cannot declare that it was not something wholly imagined. He had withdrawn so far from external realities that what he relates could have been pure fantasy rather than fabulous consummation. *Was* there an introverted woman who claimed to be the Virgin Mary? *Did* he ejaculate in ecstatic union with her? *Did* she become pregnant with the Son of God as a result? Julian's doctor advises him that some hallucinations are healthy and desirable: clearly *he* knows the difference between mystic insight and self-delusion. He informs Julian flatly that the woman died later of cancer of the womb. Julian, however, remains stricken with wonder.

The strangeness of this tale uncorroborated by onstage enactment, in addition to Julian's own indecisiveness about its nature, authorizes the greatest possible skepticism towards the play's final moments as a prelude to any Ultimate Vision. Are faith and sanity really one, as Julian declares? Or is his final submission, his passionate utterances of faith, a sign of a man now totally mad? Earlier, in Act III, Lawyer has been completely cynical about the consolations of self-delusion: Any man will "take what he gets for . . . what he wishes it to be. AH, it is what I have always wanted, he'll say, looking terror and betrayal right in the eye. Why not face the inevitable and call it what you have always wanted? How to come out on top, going under" (p. 148). According to the testimony of his own recollections, Julian has always associated sexual desire, death and union with God, in incongruous sublimation. Is that not how he sees the culmination of his life, with self-induced grace that eases the agony of the human condition? Is his vision not voided; any thought of his sanctification not sacrilegious? Are such inversions not to be expected in Alice's Wonderland; such nihilism not inevitable in an Absurdist play?

But the sweet simplicity of that conclusion fails to account for the other vision at the end of Act II, which is unquestionably of the flesh, as naked to the eye as any revelation can be and, therefore, far from hallucinatory. It is precisely the very real presence of Miss Alice which makes possible serious consideration of ***Tiny Alice*** as an argument that things visible *may* be evidence of things invisible. The tableau in which Miss Alice offers herself as a transparency through which Alice can be seen might easily serve as illustration for Platonic Ideals or Christian Incarnation.

That so traditional a notion could be entertained by Albee should not be disquieting.[8] From the beginning, his plays have complained about the decline of such "ancient verities" (to use Faulkner's words) as family cohesiveness, community life, and continuity in the history of evolving civilization.[9] The Grandmother figure in the early one-act plays represents all of these ideals—as does George, on a more intellectual plane, in ***Who's Afraid of Virginia Woolf?***. ***Tiny Alice***provides dimensions that infinitely expand the dream/hope that there is more to life than our day-to-day living may signify. One begins to feel less ill at ease with ***Tiny Alice*** the moment one releases Albee from the box of Absurdism/defeatism where his techniques—the linkage of humor and horror, the seeming cross purposes and discontinuities—invited earlier critics to imprison him. For Albee such mannerisms are, simultaneously, metaphors for the dissipation of faith in meaningfulness and untraditional measures for reinvoking, resurrecting, reconstructing traditions at their best.

Albee does distinguish—again, like Faulkner—between dead convention and living tradition, between inflexible institutions and an order of growth congenial with diversity of direction and possibility. Daddy, in ***The Sandbox*** and ***The American Dream,*** is a figure of impotence, his human tracts having been replaced by tubes. Nick, in ***Who's Afraid of Virginia Woolf?,*** seems to epitomize health and youthful promise, but his proposed eugenics, a form of self-propagation, is indistinguishable from Daddy's living death. In ***Tiny Alice,*** the Church, represented by the most venal, most self-inflating aspect of the Cardinal, becomes one more Establishment mechanism for deadening human sensibilities.

Beyond its attempt to revitalize traditions of activated faith, ***Tiny Alice*** more subtly recognizes that the God-ache suffered by man is foremost an outcry to be born free but not abandoned. The play provides a continuous experience, rather than a philosophical discussion, of two profoundly permanent problems: how can man imagine the incommensurate (but we think we do), and how can man separate service from servitude (but we think we must)? Is there a discernible point beyond which the search for self in the other annihilates either that other or one's self? Can self-centeredness be transcended, yet selfhood be fulfilled? If we attempt to think of an unknowable unknown—such as God—do we delude ourselves more by conjuring anthropomorphic images or by approximating an abstraction of perfection? Do we earn an afterlife only by refusing to want one? Such are the dilemmas torturing the mind that aspires to be, become, belong and, especially, to define beyond desire.

Tiny Alice is replete with talk of serving. The Cardinal and Lawyer are, to a large extent, self-serving; so is Miss Alice, inasmuch as she finds a joy beyond pleasure in Julian's company; and even Butler often delights in comforting this unfortunate novice beyond the call of duty. Something of self is retained by all these four agents of causes/missions larger than themselves. Is this their flaw, or even in the worst of them is this some sign of grace, of a superior love that allows them a measure of freedom from complete depersonalization? Does omnipotence require impotence? In the last scenes, do not all these agents act out that love—though with varying degrees of reluctance—in their compassion for Julian? Or does their similarity lie in their failing to rise above self-pity mirrored in another's pain?

The question deepens when applied to Brother Julian himself. Early in the play he tells Butler that he committed himself to an asylum for six years because he was paralyzed by his inability to reconcile his own view of God, as creator and mover, with the popular view of God as a kind of miracle-worker on call. With Miss Alice he manages to be more open and confesses to having been impatient with God and excessively proud of his humility, as a lay brother in the pretended service of the Lord. Even now he wishes not to be forgotten for whatever services he renders; not to be unborn, in death. Miss Alice accuses him of still more ambition—negotiating martyrdom—and he admits that his unrelenting dream has been "To go bloodstained and worthy . . . upward" (p. 124). Immediately afterwards, she leads him from the ecstasy of that memory, to the sacrifice of himself, and to Alice through her own body.

Is this climatic moment of Act II the seduction of his soul or an advanced stage in its salvation? Julian wants his marriage to end in Miss Alice. It is required of him, however, that he not confuse symbol with substance, as the Cardinal regularly does. When Julian persists, despite Miss Alice's assurance that "I am the . . . illusion" (p. 167), he is executed by Lawyer. Julian feels forsaken by God as well as by those departing the scene. Finally, accepting his destiny, provided it is not eternal death, he prays in desperation-:"Then Come and Show Thyself! Bride? God?" (p. 189). Lights move through the model/replica of the mansion; sounds approach, in rhythm with his heartbeat. Total darkness descends.

Has this entire drama been a hallucination in the mind of a recluse become catatonic? Has Julian finally married him-*self?* Or has his role merely served as insane filter, discoloring the reality of the others? Has this, after all, been a downfall into the void? Can one reconcile Albee's candid admission that "There are some things in the play that are not clear to me"[10] with his assertion that if one positions himself in Julian's place, the play is as clear as need be/can be?

To argue that the direct vision of Miss Alice at the end of Act II may validate the reported visions that, respectively, climax the other acts still acknowledges ambiguities enough to satisfy many an alternate version of ***Tiny Alice***'s meaning(s). Remembering Albee's bitter resentment of his abandonment two weeks after birth by his natural parents and his often unhappy childhood with his adoptive parents, one might be inclined to see as pure autobiographical projection this play about a She-God who gives life, only to demand its sacrificial return.[11] Beyond the possibility that all this is personal complaint, problems that are more universal remain. Lawyer remarks in II,2 that God is an abstraction which therefore can neither be understood nor worshipped; whereas Alice, "the mouse in the model" (p. 107), *can* be understood and worshipped, although it does not exist. What does existence mean, here? Does Alice have no permanent reality, no true substance, being only an exotic mask of God? Or is Alice a manifestation, a function of the Godhead, a further stage in man's adventuring towards divinity? Or is Lawyer, in his bitterness/limited knowledge, just distorting the truth? Are Lawyer, Butler and Miss Alice agents of a malignant surrogate God, and are all of them hyenas, scavengers of the dead vitals of men? Are they impure agents in prolonged process of purgation (Butler too still prefers Miss Alice to Alice) of a merciful and loving God or merely "angels of death," imperfect companions to those chosen for possible perfection? Is Alice, like the son in ***Who's Afraid of Virginia Woolf?,*** invented out of desperate human need to be part of, instead of apart from, some lasting meaning? Is Julian, secretly dedicated to his own destruction by denying that God may be gentle, courting death disguised as a demanding deity? Is his attraction to Miss Alice only a brief interlude in his inevitable marriage to darkness?

Or is this a parable of grace, one more fortunate fall? Does Brother Julian lose his celibacy but gain proper priesthood? The name "Alice" derives from the Greek word for truth. Suppose Butler (the working class) once thought he possessed her; so, more recently, did Lawyer (law makers and stewards of justice). But what single system can speak for the whole Truth? The Church (Miss Alice as "missal"?) and, certainly, individual churchmen have their own insufficiencies; there are cobwebs in the chapel. Julian himself is no chaste Adam, as his childhood fantasies prove, and he falls again—not into the flesh, which has been sanctified by the Incarnation, but into a denial that flesh is symbol rather than substance. He becomes a proper man of God, not in retreat (the asylum) but in the world, in communion. Julian has equated faith and sanity, but at last he accepts the mystery, terror and all beyond reason and historic revelation and rituals that become routine. His uncertainty becomes his cause; he makes the desperate but not despairing mystic leap. Is it implied that we are all called to be Marys whose wombs bring God into his world and the delirious world to its destinate groom? All called but few chosen? And of those chosen, even fewer who reach supreme parturition? Or is such speculation itself not pretending to provide the sort of single-system answer which the general explication set out to refute?

If one could appeal to the rest of Albee's work in this dilemma, the probability is that he would align himself with those who see ***Tiny Alice*** as a determined quest for spiritual coordinates, for opportunities to convert chance into choice and so to collaborate with life against one's own loneliness and that of others. In his first four one-act plays, Albee implied that we try to compensate for our incompleteness by neglecting the needs of others, although, ironically, the only human strength lies in mutual aid among the weak. Albee at first wrote angrily because he resisted adding to the alienation and displacement and deprivation which some of his predecessors and peers considered *the* human condition. Those plays, like the violent act of Jerry in ***The Zoo Story,*** were cruel blows intended kindly. The same indignation and hope for reform, though presented with less grotesque humor, persist in ***All Over,*** one of whose attendants at a wake finally recognizes how they have wasted their lives, how corpselike *they* are: "All we've done is think about ourselves." In ***The Lady from Dubuque,*** when the dying woman receives little solace from her husband who is over-concerned with himself, she has to turn to the kindness of strangers.[12]

The surface of such plays to the contrary, Albee has been less death- than dream-haunted: by the dream of a bond beyond bondage, a love that allows privacy but not loneliness. In ***A Delicate Balance*** a plague drives one family into the house of a friend, who then must decide if they have as much right to remain as his own daughter, who wants them out. Tobias the husband delays, reminded of his own terrors by those of his friends, and when they finally leave, he knows that an opportunity to live generously and even expansively has been lost. The bonding of characters in ***Who's Afraid of Virginia Woolf?*** is more successful because not only is their reliance on one another renewed, but, in Nick and Honey's willingness to bear children, their passion for (re)generation is satisfied vicariously. The same sense of compatibility and continuity, the same ready submission to growth, flourishes in ***Seascape*** between different species in the same global enterprise.

Early and late, Albee's plays have sprung from a faith remote from both nihilism at one extreme and romanticism at the other. Like Eugene O'Neill before him, he knows the variety of dimensions in dreaming: they can be destructive or soporifically protective, as well as creative. The will-to-believe, therefore, has to be examined and re-examined scrupulously—man being a cunning, rationalizing animal—but that will-to-believe can be ignored or denounced only at the risk of sinking back into mindlessness.

Because of his constant attention to dreams, ultimately it is less important to argue that Albee leans toward the more positive interpretations of ***Tiny Alice*** than to recognize the implications of the play, itself, as exciting perplex. How it does *not* end is extremely significant. Each member of the audience is compelled to decide (those chronically passive, probably with reluctance) what the next moment after the death/descent of darkness will bring—if indeed there can even be a next moment. ***Tiny Alice*** is a dramatization of all that must remain tantalizingly beyond the mind's reach: all mysteries whose permanence we deny even as impressions of their persistence accumulate in our experience. The play solicits, proclaims, reveres man's active imagination, its thrust through symbols towards its outermost reaches, its visionary onsets.

In the end, ***Tiny Alice***'s mystery is not only unresolved but not even well-defined. Yet, as irresistibly attractive as a black hole with all the blinding consequences of its super density, that mystery is retained. What is knowledge but a holding operation, a beachhead on the immense unknown? A plenitude of possibilities about the nature of the universe and man's miniscule/magisterial parts in it arise from doubt turned back on itself before achieving a dedicated nullity. Can we imagine man's lacking an imagination; can the mind unthink itself?

Tiny Alice is no facile confirmation of faith's efficacy. Even as it celebrates the mind's urgent outreach, the continuous Adamic demand to know the whole truth, it recognizes hazards: the smallness of man adventuring into vastness. The world is full of wonder. A variety of critical responses to his play not only is to be expected by Albee and tolerated; it is, in fact, invited and essential to this theme. Only when the questions end is there reason to worry about the human cause. No phrenological head can accurately map all the compartments of man's intelligence. As a realist of the irrational, Albee knows this—knows that serious literature, like life itself, is a trial embodiment of imagined purpose.

Notes

[1]Edward Albee, "Author's Note" to *Tiny Alice* (New York: Atheneum, 1965). All further page references appear in the text. For the playwright's comments on *Tiny Alice,* see the following: Michael E. Rutenberg, "Two Interviews with Edward Albee," contained in *Edward Albee: Playwright in Protest* (New York: DBS, 1969), pp. 229-60, and Otis L. Guernsey, "Edward Albee Confronts Broadway, 1966," *Diplomat,* October 1966, pp. 60-63.

[2]Reprints of reviews of the 1965 Billy Rose Theater production of *Tiny Alice* are reprinted in Harold Clurman, *The Divine Pastime: Theatre Essays* (New York: Macmillan, 1974), pp. 267-72.

[3]*Nation,* 18 January 1965.

[4]Anne Paolucci, *From Tension to Tonic: The Plays of Edward Albee* (Carbondale: Southern Illinois University Press, 1972).

[5]Ruby Cohn, *Edward Albee* (Minneapolis: The University of Minnesota Press, 1969), p. 28.

[6]Rutenberg, p. 199.

[7]Quoted in *Time,* 15 January 1965, p. 68.

[8]Mordecai H. Levine, "Albee's Liebstod," *College Language Association Journal,* 10 (March 1967), pp. 252-55, has demonstrated Albee's use of such "traditional" religious themes and symbolism in *The Zoo Story.*

[9]For examples of typical critical treatments of these themes, see Daniel Brown, "Albee's Targets," *Satire Newsletter* (Spring 1969): 46-52 as well as C. N. Stavrou, "Albee in Wonderland," *Southwest Review* 60 (Winter 1975): 46-61.

[10]*Time,* 15 January 1965, p. 68.

[11]We are reminded also that Albee's 1963 play was called, in Czechoslovakia, *Who's Afraid of Franz Kafka?*

[12]The mothering lady from Dubuque and her marital companion have typically been interpreted as angels of death. Citing Elisabeth Kübler-Ross, Albee himself prefers to think of them as figures of a reality *summoned* out of a need for compassion and companionship rather than one *sent. New York Times,* 27 January 1980, Section 2, p. 5.

Dennis Grunes (essay date 1986)

SOURCE: "God and Albee: *Tiny Alice,*" in *Studies in American Drama, 1945-Present,* Vol. I, 1986, pp. 61-71.

[*In the following, Grunes investigates Albee's presentation of God in* Tiny Alice, *noting that it is "in God that the mystery of the play resolves itself without ever being definitely 'solved' . . . God being the eternal mystery that admits no rational or jigsaw puzzle solution."*]

More than twenty years have passed since Edward Albee's great ***Tiny Alice*** first confounded audiences. With its publication in 1965 the author declined to cast light on the play's difficult meaning, insisting instead that the text was already quite clear enough. (This, despite his facetious remark to the lead actor during the play's original New York run: "I know you want to know what the play is about, John, but I don't know yet, so I can't say" [Stewart 68].) Certainly no author can be blamed for preferring that his work speak for itself. This is, of course, as it should be. There are times, too, when an author will not admit that his work has failed to communicate its meaning coherently. Indeed, in Albee's case, an ongoing distress at the lack of appreciation of "serious" drama by today's theatregoing public suggests a delicate ego in addition to a clear eye (Krohn and Wasserman 1-5).

However "clear" ***Tiny Alice*** may be in Albee's own eye, the variety of interpretations it has engendered—many of them openly perplexed—attest to the contrary. Mary Elizabeth Campbell, for instance, isolates Albee's core concern in the threat of materialism to man's spiritual progress, while Anita Maria Stenz finds the play "demonstrating how faith, especially when it is confused with a passion for the absolute, can become a substitute for full participation in life" (61). On the other hand, Mary Castiglie Anderson sees in the play the religious martyrdom of an individual as a sublimation of his sexual desires (181)—a view akin to that of Foster Hirsch, who interprets that character's "religious confusion—his ache to serve the Church, his struggle to understand the infinite" as "a mask for his sexual hysteria" (111). Richard E. Amacher, though, finds something else: the author's "opposition to certain Satanic forces and persons that, in the world we inhabit, have attempted to reduce God to something infinitely small and powerless" (131). My own view, however, has more in common with that of Leonard Casper, who finds an unresolvable and inviolable mystery at the heart of the play. This mystery I would call Tiny Alice.

It is this mystery which is mostly neglected in Albee's own otherwise useful summary of the plot, which he gave in his New York City press conference on March 22, 1965:

> A lay brother, a man who would have become a priest except that he could not reconcile his idea of God with the God which men create in their own image, is sent by his superior to tie up loose ends of a business matter between the church and a wealthy woman. The lay brother becomes enmeshed in an environment which, at its core and shifting surface, contains all the elements which have confused and bothered him throughout his life: the relationship between sexual hysteria and religious ecstasy; the conflict between selflessness of service and the conspicuous splendor of martyrdom. The lay brother is brought to the point, finally, of having to accept what he had insisted he wanted . . . union with the abstraction, rather than man-made image of it, its substitution. He is left with pure abstraction—whatever it be called: God, or Alice—and in the end, according to your faith, one of two things happens: either the abstraction personifies itself, is proved real, or the dying man, in the last necessary effort of self-delusion[,] creates and believes in what he knows does not exist.
>
> (qtd. in Amacher 119-20)

It may be that Albee does not fully grasp his own play; or else, in a pained effort to free himself of charges of being a hollow, insubstantial writer, he has overdone his rational explanation, thereby seeming to diminish the authentic mystery which is at its heart and which culminates in the lay brother's final passage from human life to human death, a passage presided over by God, whose infinite darkness—suggestively rendered on stage—incorporates the unfathomable grace that converts death to everlasting life. Too much rationalizing and psychologizing, I fear, tend to move God—not as abstraction or human fabrication, but as God—out of the play. It makes no sense that this was Albee's intent; for the "abstraction" in the mind of Julian, the lay brother, could not possibly "personify itself" except by the grace of God. It is in God that the mystery of the play resolves itself without ever being definitively "solved" (thus the confusion readers and audiences have encountered), God being the eternal mystery that admits no rational or jigsaw puzzle solution.

"In ***Tiny Alice,***" Anne Paolucci writes, "everything is reduced to image and symbol," while at the same time the play's allegory "is a moving and expanding realism built on intuitive associations" (67). This befits a drama whose world is replete with symbolic representations and correspondences over which an enormous mystery holds sway. Thus the play exhibits both reductive and expansive tendencies. Incorporating both is its central symbol, an expressionistic marvel: the house enclosing the model inside which is a smaller model (or models). Any reader or spectator of the play must somehow come to grips with this nearly omnipresent symbol patterned after Chinese boxes, a smaller box inside each. Julian N. Wasserman, for instance, observes:

> The house, it seems, was originally constructed in England and then disassembled and rebuilt in its present location. The house, therefore, is not by definition an "original" but is, rather, a "replica." Although built of the materials of the original, the replica can no more be the original than a word can be identical to the mental image which it signifies. The replica once again presents the playwright's preoccupation with the translation of ideas, persons, and objects. Translation, however, in these terms implies an absolute alteration of the item translated, for it implies a definite and distinct change from one location or state of being to another. In the midst of the replica stands a "model"—the proportionately correct although scaled down symbol which is derivative, though wholly separate from the original. . . . If the model is to be exact, it must contain a model, which,

> in turn, must contain a model. The process must go on *ad infinitum.* The infinite nature of the series of reflective models required to establish the model as an exact duplicate of the replica presents an example of Xeno's paradox concerning the tortoise and the hare. Just as the hare can never in theory overtake the tortoise, so the model can never reach its goal of reduplicating either the replica or the original.
>
> (41-42)

It may be, however, that Wasserman is setting the symbol in too rigid a naturalist mold. It is true that only a single model is seen inside the model; but the full mystery of the thing is suggested teasingly by Butler—and almost as quickly dismissed by Julian:

> BUTLER (A shy smile): You don't suppose that within that tiny model in the model there, there is . . . another room like this, with yet a tinier model within it, and within . . .
>
> JULIAN (Laughs): . . . and within and within and within and . . .? No, I . . . rather doubt it.
>
> (25)

But the possibility of an infinity of models surely does exist; and surely, too, Julian's bemused dismissal reverberates with that other, more obviously compelling "doubt" of his—his religious doubt, his uncertain faith in God. For each of the components of the play's most visible symbol—the house, the model, the tiny model(s)—corresponds to a different dimension of experience, each of which is identified with a different "God": Miss Alice, Alice, Tiny Alice. Commentators generally distinguish between Miss Alice and another Alice, to whom they may or may not refer as "Tiny Alice." Indeed, much of the difficulty in understanding that the play has met—even by those who otherwise refer to the tripartite structure of the house/model/model-inside-the-model—stems from the misconception that there are only two, not three, Alices.

Of the three dimensions, the first, the house, is easiest to identify. With its ordinary objects (chairs, tables, books, and so forth), Miss Alice's mansion—in particular, the mansion library, where most of the drama unfolds—represents the material world which is our home. There our possessions are to be found, as by proxy are we ourselves, at least insofar as the Lawyer's lust, the Cardinal's greed, and Julian's weakness to temptation are all too recognizable human traits. Underlining the materiality of this realm of things (including the flesh) is dust, the stuff of matter. Having prepared the house for the departure of its occupants, Butler is described by Albee as "[r]ubbing something for dust" (170)—a stage direction whose lack of specificity underscores the fact that *all* physical things decompose. Indeed, our own similar eventual fate is intimated when, prior to their leaving, Butler asks Miss Alice: "Will we be coming back . . . when the weather changes?" (176).

On the other hand, the miniature or model inside the house is free of dust. Butler tells Julian, "It is sealed. Tight. There is no dust" (25). But for this and its size, however, the model and the house seem to be identical. But the house is a replica of the model, not vice versa:

> BUTLER: This *place* was . . . in England.
>
> MISS ALICE (As if suddenly remembering): Yes, it was! Every stone, marked and shipped.
>
> JULIAN: Oh; I had thought it was a replica.
>
> LAWYER: Oh no; that would have been too simple. Though it *is* a replica . . . in its way.
>
> JULIAN: Of?
>
> LAWYER (Pointing to the model): Of that.
>
> (83)

Julian takes this for a joke, but Butler refers also to the library they are in—not the one in the model—as the "replica" (84). By extension, then, objects inside the house library are copies of those inside the model library: like the room itself, they find their origins—their original forms—in the model. The model, then, appears to be a projection of the mind of man, where objects originate as images, abstractions, or ideas. Both Anderson and Campbell have made this point, though Anderson specifies a particular individual whose mind the model projects: "Clearly," she writes, "it presents itself to us as a symbol of Julian's unconscious" (180). On the other hand, Campbell regards the model as "man's House of Life, the universe that is his home; narrowed in focus, the concrete place that of all others he calls home, his own being; narrower still, his final stronghold; his mind" (95).

The relationship between material copy and abstract form is made clear with the incidence of the fire. When Julian discovers that the model is on fire (88), Butler deduces from its location in the model chapel that the house chapel must also be ablaze. Butler, Julian, and the Lawyer rush upstairs. Once the fire is extinguished, it is discovered that the flames have also vanished from the model. But what caused the fire in the first place? The origin has been hinted at. Earlier, Miss Alice had shouted at the lustful Lawyer; "I'll give you *fire*works!" (69; Albee's emphasis). May we not surmise, then, that it is in Miss Alice's mind that the "fire" begins, her threat made in the heat of anger eventually igniting the house in a kind of poetic consummation? "We're burning down! Hurry!" she implores the Lawyer (89), as if somehow the fire were especially theirs, he having provoked it, she having *in*voked it. While the others rush upstairs, Miss Alice remains behind to begin the long incantation which alone extinguishes the fire in the model, the one in the house following suit: "Let the fire be put out," she chants; "Let the chapel be saved; let the fire not spread; let us not be consumed" (89).

The model is not the play's sole indication of a mental realm; there is also the "asylum" where Julian was once a patient. For a time, he remarks, he had been without faith, his faith having left him—this the climax of his personal struggle to prove that man's God is a false God:

> I . . . declined. I . . . shriveled into myself: a glass dome . . . descended, and it seemed I was out of reach, unreachable, finally unreaching, in this . . . paralysis, of sorts. I . . . put myself in a mental home.
>
> (43)

Like the model, by its "glass dome" this "mental home"—this other home of the mind—was also sealed. Later, model and asylum are even more closely linked. Butler says that Julian is "walking on the edge of an abyss, but is balancing. Can be pushed . . . over, back to the asylums" (103). But the conspirators' plan is to trick Julian into the *model* where he would marry Alice thinking she is Miss Alice, which, when the truth is revealed, might in turn "push" him back to the asylum. Butler's plural "asylums," then, enforces the connection between model and asylum. Fittingly, during his tenure in the asylum Julian accepted as real whatever he witnessed or experienced, just as he later believes he has married Miss Alice in the house chapel when he has married Alice in the model chapel instead. (Paolucci also relates the model to the asylum when she says that Julian "recognizes in the model the symbol of the confusion in himself; the fascination it exerts is a reminder of his struggle to distinguish hallucination and reality in the days when he had been confined in an asylum" [71].)

In the asylum, we realize, Julian fell prey to the sort of false God he had fought against in the outside objective world. More specifically, he himself was the false God whose worshipper he became there, both his mental and spiritual definitions having become encased in his own ego. The patient with whom he made love, who believed she was the Virgin Mary, subsequently announced she was pregnant with the son of God. Of course, we have no way of knowing whether this is only Julian's own perverse fantasy fulfilling his wish to be God the father. Certainly the illusionary nature of the whole episode is suggested in this curious exchange between Julian and Miss Alice:

> JULIAN: [The doctor] told me, then . . . that the woman has been examined, that she was suffering from cancer of the womb, that it was advanced, had spread. In a month, she died.
>
> MISS ALICE: Did you believe it?
>
> JULIAN (Small smile): That she died?
>
> MISS ALICE: That you spoke with your doctor.
>
> JULIAN (Pause): It had never occurred to me until this moment to doubt it. He has informed me many times.
>
> MISS ALICE: Ah?
>
> JULIAN: I *do see* him . . . in reality. We have become friends, we talk from time to time. Socially.
>
> MISS ALICE: Ah. And it was he who discharged you from . . . your asylum?
>
> JULIAN: I was persuaded, eventually, that perhaps I was . . . overconcerned by hallucination; that some was inevitable, and a portion of that—even desirable.
>
> (63-64)

However teasingly, Miss Alice is suggesting to Julian that the objective world whose "reality" he takes for granted is as riddled by illusion as is the interior world where he acted out his hallucination. "Truth and illusion, Julian," it is as if she were asking him, "don't you know the difference?" Moreover, by following the advice that to maintain some illusions is all to the good Julian has only drifted from one illusionary realm to another. For instance, his delusion in the asylum of being God the father has given way in Miss Alice's house to his quest for martyrdom, that is, the delusion of being God the son, material man as well as God. This yearning of his for martyrdom is conscious:

> Oh, martyrdom [he tells Miss Alice]. To be that. To be able . . . to be that. . . . The . . . death of the saints . . . was always the beginning of their lives. To go bloodstained and worthy . . . upward.
>
> (121)

When finally he succumbs to Miss Alice, his dream begins to be realized.

The objective and the subjective, the physical/material and the mental: these, then, are two of the three dimensions symbolized by the house and the model. But what of the model inside the model, only briefly mentioned? This structure suggests a third dimension, that of the real and eternal as distinct from all mutable matter and the illusions of man. In this realm the fire we have examined would be self-existent; for this is the realm of origination, of a God neither material nor abstract but wholly spiritual. (Albee quite possibly drew part of the sense of his three dimensions from the three natures—generation, being, and space—described by Plato in "Timaeus," where in fact the image of a self-existent fire is evoked.) Moreover, the Platonism upon which the play more generally draws has been noted by several commentators. Before relating the house/model to Platonism, for instance, C. W. E. Bigsby notes that Julian "proves incapable of seeing through the symbol, incapable of realising that in embracing Miss Alice he is not embracing reality but only the seductive and attractive image of that reality, the Platonic shadow" (283-4).

Indeed, a different God, or Alice, inhabits each of the three dimensions. In the house, for instance, Miss Alice reigns. With her great wealth and allure, she is a pagan goddess to be worshipped by materialist and sensualists—or, more accurately, by the materialist or sensualist in each of us. Through the Lawyer the Cardinal sells her for gold to his lay secretary; the Lawyer, Butler, and Julian have all had or are having a love affair with her. As befits such a god, she lives in the mansion tower, and Julian must be brought up to meet her. Interestingly, the word *up* is used eight times in this context (41-44). Once they have met and talked, Miss

Alice asks Julian if she terrifies him. "You *did,*" he replies, "and you are still . . . awesome" (53). She is indeed like a god, and the power she derives from her wealth suggests just what sort of a god she is.

But Miss Alice is only the agent, the fleshly copy, of the Alice in the model. This other Alice in the model is the one that Julian has in mind (pun intended) when he says, "Men create a false God in their own image, it is easier for them!" (44). Egotistically, Julian believes that the God that *he* imagines must be more real than the God that others imagine; but the definition of Alice encompasses both. Alice is the symbol, the abstraction originating in the mind of man, that Miss Alice represents and impersonates, as we may suspect when, for her first meeting with Julian, Miss Alice masquerades as a white-haired, near-deaf hag. "[Y]ou do your part," the Lawyer later warns her (75); and still later, the impersonation is explicitly revealed:

> BUTLER: I think it would be a lovely touch were the Cardinal to marry them, to perform the wedding, to marry Julian to . . .
>
> LAWYER: Alice.
>
> BUTLER: *Miss* Alice.
>
> LAWYER: Alice!
>
> BUTLER: Well, all right; one through the other.
>
> (102)

"Miss Alice . . . I have married you," Julian (as if to certify the fact) says in the house library following the ceremony that has in fact taken place in the model chapel; "No, Julian," she replies; "you have married *her* . . . through me" (157).

Play-acting as Julian, Butler earlier is told by the Lawyer that Alice is, in effect, the false God inside the model, the real one being an unapproachable, incomprehensible abstraction that mortals can neither copy nor invent in their material realm:

> BUTLER: But there is *some*thing. There is a *true* God.
>
> LAWYER: There is an abstraction, Julian, but it cannot be understood. You cannot worship it.
>
> BUTLER: There is more.
>
> LAWYER: There is Alice, Julian. That can be understood. Only the mouse in the model. Just that.
>
> BUTLER: There must be more.
>
> LAWYER: The mouse. Believe it. Don't personify the abstraction, Julian, limit it, demean it. Only the mouse, the toy. And that does not exist . . . but is all that can be worshipped.
>
> (104-105)

The play's worldly participants, then, cannot distinguish between God as abstraction and God as God, that is to say, the God whose reality lies beyond our subjectivities and imaginations. This distinction, it should be noted, some commentators also have difficulty making. "Abstraction, in the context of ***Tiny Alice,***" writes one, for instance, "seems to be the essence of pure reality that lies beyond either physical existence or symbolical representation" (Langdon 60). This equation of abstraction and "pure reality" misses the point. Although the God we humanly worship is necessarily an idea we have devised so that our worship can be enacted, there is yet another God beyond our imagining who ultimately receives this imperfect (because human) worship. Neither a function of our communal mind or of our separate minds, this God cannot be understood by us. In this context Albee's image of the mouse simultaneously suggests a diminution of God—like the terrified mouse in Tennyson's poem "Mariana"—and something more elusively fleeter of foot than whatever gods men can grasp. Shared by both man and God as intermediary, then, the "mouse in the model" leads either upwards or downwards in terms of transcendence, arbitrating between the lowest and highest realms of the house/model/tiny model(s). (William Willeford also relates the model to a transcendental order, but with something rather different in mind.) For although these dimensions are architecturally distinct for man, it is altogether different for God, who renders the entire structure fluid when by his grace he redeems a human soul. This is the self-existent God who, we are meant to infer, resides inside the infinity of progressively tinier models inside the model library. Miss Alice and Alice, of course, are mentioned throughout the play; Tiny Alice is not—except by Albee, in the title. This in itself evokes the silent, unchartable, anonymous presence of the eternal God whose name translates as the Unnameable.

The "silence" of this God, though, can be felt; for it is precisely this silence which participates in the great final scene of Julian's death. Julian has been shot, by the Lawyer. As he expires, a light surrounded by an immense black shadow appears over him. Stage directions read as follows: "Absolute silence for two beats. The lights on Julian fade slowly to black" (184). Surely this is more an indication than it is a direction, for nothing "absolute" can be staged by man; even the word itself evokes the awesome otherness of God. We can only guess at what occurs during those two beats of silence; they indicate a metaphysical mystery that is beyond us. But the visual impression that the playwright has devised intimates the dual possibility of God's grace and human redemption, with Tiny Alice gathering up Julian's soul as his conscious mind closes shop and Alice covers his physical remains. The "black" we see thus resonates in all three symbolic dimensions.

By definition grace is purely a matter of God's prerogative (it is, in fact, His essence); but we mortals are nevertheless inclined to search out what might dispose God toward Julian. If good intentions do not always lead to hell, his vulnerability and real religious confusion may in fact gain him credibility (at least in our eyes) as a candidate for grace. Julian does not want to believe that he has wedded a false God, Alice, through Miss Alice (though it is impossible to determine to what extent, if any, he has unconsciously participated in the deception that the others perpetrate against him). Afterwards, he insists, "I HAVE ACCEPTED GOD," in effect declaring himself, with anguished pride, pure in heart, mind, and spirit. "Then accept his works," the Lawyer answers back, with Miss Alice adding that Julian's sacrificial priesthood—the martyrdom that in his pride he had longed for—is now complete (163). Julian is perplexed, humbled, broken. Rather than stay with Alice he will return to the asylum, a refuge, a kind of mental womb; shot by the Lawyer, he falls in front of the model whose priest he has become (164). By the conclusion of his final monologue (which Albee trimmed for the acting version of the play), he is resigned to accept the only God that seems to have come to him, the one that he already knows is false, illusionary: Alice. "I accept thee, Alice," he says at death's point, "for thou art come to me. God, Alice . . . I accept thy will" (184). Beyond the pale of his earlier prideful lust for martyrdom, he finds neither peace nor glory in death; confused, he cries and trembles. Nor is he able any longer to feel superior to those of his kind who worship a false God. Knowing he has married Alice through her play-God surrogate, he is better able now to gauge the true power of illusion. This knowledge has led him to self-knowledge, namely, an understanding of his own shortcomings and susceptibility to egotism; and with this has come humility. That he is prepared now to embrace a false God against the pride of a lifetime, therefore, shows in his case spiritual advancement.

Dying, Julian pleads: "Alice? . . . God? SOMEONE? Come to Julian as he . . . ebbs" (182). The degree of his turmoil suggests he is not consciously—pridefully—imitating Christ when in his apparent isolation he laments, "MY GOD, WHY HAST THOU FORSAKEN ME?" (183)—Christ's own lament, on the Cross. Having shed all illusions about himself and about those false gods to whom he is as vulnerable as any other mortal, he longs for God to come to him. But God does not seem to respond. Julian can at least "see" Alice; she now manifests his urgent desire for someone—*any*one—to come to him. But Tiny Alice *is* there; she is the light described in the stage direction. In that absolute silence, it is implied, an equally silent Julian accepts Tiny Alice, who, for her part, accepts Julian just as she had accepted Christ who had likewise despaired at being forsaken by God. Julian's body relaxes in its crucifixion (184)—a wonder that is the culmination of the mystery of the play. Shorn of his fantasies of being God and Christ, Julian thus dies like Christ after all. He becomes an inhabitant of eternity, that infinity of tiny models which, depending on your faith, may or may not exist beyond the range of human sight.

WORKS CITED

Albee, Edward. New York City press conference. March 22, 1965.

———. *Tiny Alice.* New York: Pocket Books, 1966.

Amacher, Richard E. *Edward Albee.* Boston: Twayne, 1982.

Anderson, Mary Castiglie. "Staging the Unconscious: Edward Albee's *Tiny Alice.*" *Renascence* 33 (1981): 178-92.

Bigsby, C. W. E. *A Critical Introduction to Twentieth-Century Drama: Williams, Miller, Albee.* Vol. 2. Cambridge: Cambridge University Press, 1984.

Campbell, Mary Elizabeth. "The Statement of Edward Albee's *Tiny Alice.*" *Papers on Language and Literature* 4 (1968): 85-100.

Casper, Leonard. "*Tiny Alice:* "The Expense of Joy in the Persistence of Mystery." In *Edward Albee: An Interview and Essays.* Ed. Julian Wasserman et al. Houston: University of St. Thomas, 1983. 83-92.

Hirsch, Foster. *Who's Afraid of Edward Albee?* Berkeley: Creative Arts Book Company, 1978.

Krohn, Charles S. and Julian N. Wasserman. "An Interview with Edward Albee, March 18, 1981." In *Edward Albee: An Interview and Essays.* 1-27.

Langdon, Harry N. "Ritual Form: One Key to Albee's *Tiny Alice.*" *Theatre Annual* 35 (1980): 57-72.

Paolucci, Anne. *From Tension to Tonic: The Plays of Edward Albee.* Carbondale: Southern Illinois University Press, 1972.

Plato. "Timaeus." In *The Collected Dialogues of Plato.* Ed. Edith Hamilton and Huntington Cairns. New York: Pantheon Books, 1961. 1161-80.

Stenz, Anita Maria. *Edward Albee: The Poet of Loss.* The Hague: Mouton Publishers, 1978.

Stewart, R. S. "John Gielgud and Edward Albee Talk About the Theater." *The Atlantic Monthly* (1965): 61-68.

Wasserman, Julian N. " 'The Pitfalls of Drama: The Idea of Language in the Plays of Edward Albee." In *Edward Albee: An Interview and Essays.* 29-53.

Willeford, William. "The Mouse in the Model." *Modern Drama* 12 (Sept. 1969): 135-45.

Elizabeth Klaver (essay date 1995)

SOURCE: "*Tiny Alice:* Edward Albee's Mystery Play," in *Essays in Theatre / Études Théâtrales,* Vol. 13, No. 2, May 1995, pp. 171-82.

[In the essay below, Klaver argues that Tiny Alice *plays on the inherent instability of language and other forms of signification, leading to both the unresolvable uncertainty within the play and the great number of opposing interpretations of the work.]*

When Edward Albee's play ***Tiny Alice*** was first performed in December 1964, it produced a number of extreme reactions. Audiences were bewildered and angered by the play's ambiguity and, except for the occasional viewer like Peter Wolfe who saw in it a revision of Albee's earlier disparagement of modern woman, critics tended to condemn it. Robert Brustein accused it of a "sham profundity"; Philip Roth called it simply "a sham"; and Lee Baxandall and Arthur K. Oberg castigated it for having an inadequate vision. Curiously, friendly and hostile critics alike were able to agree on one of the play's features, in their terms a mysterious quality, obscure and elusive. To add to its inscrutability John Gielgud, who played Julian, admitted that the play baffled him in many respects (Talk 68), and throughout 1965 Albee himself offered various contradictory explanations. In an interview, he wondered aloud if he had deliberately intended

Irene Worth as Miss Alice in the guise of an old woman in the Royal Shakespeare Company's 1970 production of *Tiny Alice.*

to make the play confusing and provocative (Talk 68). Yet, when called upon to write an explanatory note for the first publication, he called the play "quite clear" (Author's Note).

Evidence that the play is not clear can be seen in the wide variety of interpretations offered by the later critics of ***Tiny Alice,*** interpretations that range from William Lucey's metaphysical reading to the existentialism of Anne Paolucci, Matthew Roudané, and C. N. Stavrou to the ritual and psychological allegories of Harry Langdon, Mary Elizabeth Campbell, and Mary Castiglie Anderson. Nevertheless, as Leonard Casper rightly points out, a variety of critical interpretations should be invited, especially of a play that is concerned with the persistence of mystery rather than its resolution (91, 84).

In fact, the textual and linguistic issues that had appeared in the early plays of the absurdists—Beckett, Ionesco, Genet—were quickly surfacing across the Atlantic in the work of American playwrights such as Albee. By 1964, ***Tiny Alice*** is thoroughly enmeshed in semiotic problematics, looking at its own textual processes in ways suggested by the fictionality of his earlier work, ***The Zoo Story*** and ***Who's Afraid of Virginia Woolf?,*** and anticipatory of the more formal design of later pieces such as ***Box*** and ***Quotations from Chairman Mao Tse-tung.*** Situating itself in an absurdist landscape, ***Tiny Alice*** builds its dramatic world out of ambiguous and arbitrary materials—the shifting sands of varying figural states—and thereby creates uncertainty in the dramatic world which affects the ontological status of the text. Questions of unreadability and interpretation, introduced to drama by his European counterparts, become critically important in Albee's play.

The inability of readers and audiences to feel comfortable with an interpretation of ***Tiny Alice*** arises for the most part out of the play's semiotic and textual self-examination. The play's language is used to help establish a dramatic, fictional construct, positing an alternate world through a discourse of statement, description, and dialogue. Created by the speakers who inhabit it, the play world consistently refers to itself, for language always works from within to generate and maintain the construct (Elam 112). What to do, then, with a play that opens like this:

> LAWYER: Oomm, yoom, yoom, um? Tick-tick-tick-tick-tick. Um? You do-do-do-do-do-um? Tick-tick-tick-tick-tick-tick-tick-um? Do-do-do-do-do-do-do? Aaaaaaww-www! Oomm, yoom, yoom, um?
>
> (1)

While there appears to be a verbal pattern here, the odd English word and recognizable punctuation, this opening speech is basically gibberish, sound virtually bereft of meaning. The text has immediately foregrounded linguistic problematics, cutting itself off from referential transparency and bracketing the signifiers as the objects of discourse. A contemporaneous play, Vaclav Havel's *The Memorandum,* opens in much the same way with the Director reading a memo written in Ptydepe, a language neither he nor the audience understands:

> Ra ko hutu d dekotu ely trebomu emusohe, vdegar yd, stro reny er gryk kendy, alyv zvyde dezu, kvyndal fer tekynu sely. Degto yl tre entvester kyleg gh: orka epyl y bodur depty-depe emete. . . .
>
> (3)

Ptydepe has been scientifically created as a precise language, able to overcome the ambiguities of a natural language. As it turns out, though, Ptydepe is so difficult it cannot be learned or translated; at the end of the play, Chorukor, a new and equally unmanageable language, comes in to replace it. By privileging linguistic operations at the beginning and ending of the play, *The Memorandum* lodges itself in a semiotic universe, a linguistic circle in which the unreadability of language is brought to the foreground.

A metalinguistic event like Lawyer's opening speech thus places ***Tiny Alice*** in a similarly opaque, semiotic domain, the kind of "city of words" C. W. E. Bigsby sees in ***Virginia Woolf*** (267). The opening scenes of both Havel's and Albee's plays suggest a Saussurian arbitrariness in language, not only with respect to the referent but also within the sign itself. While not completely separable from content, since even in an incoherent discourse patterns can be detected, the signifiers in ***Tiny Alice*** tend to detach and drift along in chains more randomly fashioned than is usual, implying that the dramatic world constructed out of such materials will be highly arbitrary, more open to interpretative difficulties than most plays would allow.

Nevertheless, ***Tiny Alice*** does begin to assign some sort of meaning to Lawyer's "baby talk." It shows that his speech is not delivered to empty space but to a pair of birds, suggesting that this is the way to talk to birds, whether they can function as interpretants, at least in the world of ***Tiny Alice.*** The act of redirecting sense toward drifting signifiers reflects an aspect of the particular internal, linguistic system upon which ***Tiny Alice*** rests, making it one of those plays that embeds an unconventional method of textual generation within its own ontology. As in Beckett's *Not I,* the play acts on a misfiring in the process of signification, so that the signifiers at first do not produce a syntactically coherent structure in which a meaningful residue can collect. When the play does begin to produce coherence, the audience or reader retains a sense of unpredictability, a sense of random association underlying the entire structure.

Lawyer's gibberish, then, acts as an initiation into the play's discourse and dramatic world, a door one must go through in order to reach the play. The untranslatable language, meaningful only in its relation to the birds, eventually does become recognizable English. As Lawyer chatters to the birds, Cardinal enters and calls to him "Saint Francis?" (1). The text turns from the birds, which bear the generic name cardinal, to a man who bears the title and plays the role of a Cardinal; it turns from a man who bears the title and plays the role of a Lawyer to a man renamed St. Francis; it turns from the verbal patterns of nonsense to the verbal patterns of English. In other words, the course travelled from one "language" to the other consists of a carefully established mapping of metonymies, each of which is falling into an arrangement understandable by an English-speaking audience.

However, the nagging impression that ***Tiny Alice*** lacks a ground of referentiality or coherent discourse remains critical throughout the text. The play continues to refer back to Lawyer's opening lines, positioning reminders of its floating signifiers by inscribing references to birds: Julian is described as a fledgling and bird of prey/pray (41, 45), and a sonnet is described as a walking crow (168). Traces of gibberish reappear, most notably at the end of Act 1, Scene 1, when Lawyer actually returns to it:

> Do . . . do you . . . do you have much to say to one another, my dears? Do you? You find it comforting? Hmmmmmmm? Do you? Hmmmm? Do-do-do-do-do-do-do-do? Hmmmmmm? Do?
>
> (21)

Here, English begins to slide back into nonsense, reversing the original process of translation, working backwards along its mapping. As the "words" drift, the play undercuts the symbolic structure of the natural language, making it impossible to trust English as any more translatable, meaningful, or readable than Ptydepe.

The remapping of signifiers to other signifiers, or the reassigning of names to other names seen above, occurs often throughout the play, producing a series of displacements in which meaning and identity are indefinitely deferred. Like the Chief of Police and the General in Genet's *The Balcony,* Lawyer and Cardinal carry generic names because they are playing roles. And by the end of Act 1, Scene 1, they have been renamed several more times, Lawyer as St. Francis, Croesus's emissary, hyena, and Satan, and Cardinal as eminence, bastard, prince of the church, pig, and Buddy. Similar to Genet's mirror images, these violently incongruent names do not merely pose a modernist alienation of identity, but fragment and refract *the appearance* of identity. Identity is not realized as an unchanging core of existence, but as a trope, a metonymic association of differences disguised as a metaphorical necessity of resemblance among referents and between sign and referent.

Tiny Alice also plays with Butler's name, but in a slightly different way. In this case, rather than undergoing a process of contiguous renaming and refraction, "Butler" wavers within the status of the sign itself. Butler's name appears at first to pinpoint identity by linking cognomen with referent, as Julian Wasserman suggests, a joining of the real with the figurative (31). However, the surname "Butler," like all surnames today, is not linked by necessity to a role. Butler tells Julian that his name is "[a]ppropriate: Butler . . . butler. If my name were Carpenter, and I were a butler . . . or if I *were* a carpenter, and my name were Butler . . . it would not be so appropriate" (29). At the same time, though, even the appropriateness of the name is questionable, for Butler is a butler who abuses the role, standing in relation to the other characters as co-conspirator and ex-lover. Rather than playing through chains of metonymies as in the names of Lawyer and Cardinal, the name Butler retraces its own circular track. The signifier tries to grasp identity as the role both generates and rejects it. The metonymic structure of the text again draws attention to and undercuts the super-metaphorical disguise, yet mixes up the straightforward, so-called literal or real with the figural. Butler becomes a sign that recalls Paul de Man's rhetorical dilemma, the inability to tell whether a literal or figurative reading prevails (10). How can one determine the status of Butler who both is and is not a butler?

Even the play's name, ***Tiny Alice,*** becomes part of the linguistic problematic. The phrase "tiny Alice" is never mentioned in the play; however, there appear to be several characters who could attach themselves to it. One possibility is Miss Alice, who initially seems to be the main female character. Another possibility is the abstraction in the model, which Lawyer calls "only the mouse, the toy" (105) and which he implies is the mysterious Alice. However, the play ultimately defers the final distribution of the title to any single entity, refusing to locate identity in any construct and leaving the audience, as Wasserman notes, the task of assigning the name itself (35). Paolucci implies an association with *Alice in Wonderland* (65). Nevertheless, this task becomes even more arduous, for as the figure comes out of the model at the end of Act 3, Julian names and renames it "ALICE? . . . GOD? . . . God, Alice" (184). Which is it, and is it tiny Alice? Since the play's basis in language is one of deferred meaning and the refraction of identity into signs, the audience will have no more success in attaching the name "tiny Alice" to the figure in the model than Julian does, and it will have no more success in attaching the title to any one entity than the play does. Consequently, in encoding unnamability and the indeterminacy of identity into its structure, the play self-reflexively distorts its own status as a model in attempting to name itself ***Tiny Alice.*** This suggests that such distortion creates a loop in which the processes used by the play to name itself, by always falling short, generate refracted images of the text out to infinity.

Clearly, ***Tiny Alice*** presents a taxing semiotic structure, as much a linguistic riddle as Wasserman sees in ***The Zoo Story*** (33). In attempting to unravel the linguistic knot, critics have made insightful analyses of the language of ***Tiny Alice.*** Wasserman, for instance, uses speech act theory, viewing the language of Albee's plays as a meeting ground between the interior and exterior worlds of the speaker and listener (29). C. W. E. Bigsby notes that language is inadequate to command the real; to him, the theme of the play is "the need to penetrate symbols and to deal with the thing itself" (282).

Both of these interpretations suggest that ***Tiny Alice*** depicts the failure of language to communicate ideas, in its inability to bridge speaker and listener, subject and object. I would propose, however, that the problematic is much more fundamental, lying in the nature of the sign itself. In always deferring the signified, the signifier cannot exist as a mere conduit for meaning, thereby already compromising the ability of language to act as a medium between speaker and listener. The challenges of interpretation both within the play and for the audience occur not because language fails in its delivery of ideas, but because in the linguistic realm ideas are simply not fully attainable. Indeed, C.W.E. Bigsby's remarks invite the question of whether language can be penetrated at all, of whether we can deal with the "thing" as referent or as signified without the symbolic code. In fact, the play suggests that semiotic structures inhabit all aspects of its construction, that even the speakers and listeners tend to unfold as sign structures reverberating with textual problematics. I would agree with John Stark that the play presents reality as linguistic (165) and that the dichotomy of reality and illusion, seen by many critics as a major thematic concern, is actually a question of figural states within a semiotic structure.

In her study of ***A Delicate Balance,*** Patricia Fumerton does connect the issue of illusion and/or delusion with language. In this later play, the characters delimit and distort language, tending to move further away from any access to its meaning. In ***Tiny Alice*** Lawyer and Julian engender a similar situation, both characters having difficulty with tropologies. Because their statements help construct the dramatic world, they end up producing a day-to-day existence of contradictory and figural haziness. For instance, when Lawyer tries to describe Cardinal, he mixes and confuses figures:

> His Eminence . . . is a most . . . eminent man; and bold, very bold; behind—or, underneath—what would seem to be a solid rock of . . . pomposity, sham, peacocking, there is a . . . flows a secret river . . .
>
> (37)

To which Butler responds, "This is an endless metaphor." Lawyer continues to describe Cardinal as "a prince whose still waters . . ." run deep (finished by Butler), and then insists to Julian that he has learned "never to confuse the representative of a . . . thing with the thing itself." Butler responds, "though I wonder if you'd intended to get involved in *two* watery metaphors there: underground river, and still waters" (37-39). Although he appears to deliver metaphors, Lawyer's description is so internally contradictory, as Butler points out, that difference rather than resemblance tends to govern the process. For instance, in the description above the transience of behaviors like pomposity, shamming and peacocking displaces the solidity of a rock, turning the "endless metaphor" into an endless metonymy.

Further, because of Cardinal's role as representative of and substitute for the Catholic church, the text has rendered him as a synecdoche. Yet Cardinal is also a renaming of Lawyer's schoolmate "Buddy," which makes the process of contiguous renaming precede and surpass the substitutive function. In fact, Lawyer's knowledge of the pre-Cardinal metonymies is responsible for subverting the metaphorical arrangements. Lawyer cannot look at the Cardinal as synecdoche for the church without immediately processing a chain of deconstructive metonymies. The thing itself, the church, is beside the point, for Lawyer's difficulty rests in the status of the representative. In this way, he continuously confuses one figural state with another—the tropes of the church with the tropes of the man.

A similar indeterminacy within the status of language also haunts Julian's perspective; he cannot distinguish in a grammatical construction whether an event described should be taken as straightforwardly factual or as figural. For instance, there is a period in his life which is initially described as blank:

> LAWYER: . . . Such a mild life . . . save those six years in your thirties which are . . . blank . . . in our report on you.
>
> JULIAN (*A good covering laugh*): Oh, they were . . . mild, in their own way. Blank, but not black.
>
> LAWYER: Will you fill them for us? The blank years?
>
> JULIAN: . . . They were nothing.
>
> (32)

Nevertheless, Julian does have scenarios for this "blank" screen, which feature at times a realistic autobiography and at other times a metaphorical one. When Miss Alice asks him if he has ever had a sexual encounter with a woman, he doesn't know. He has the memory of an event occurring during these bracketed years, but he can't determine if it should be taken as a sexual act between himself and a woman or as a metaphorical act between himself and the Virgin Mary. Either way he looks at the problem, referentiality has been cut off, leaving him in the imagistic realm of revisionary memory.

This is one of the situations in the play that leads critics like Lawrence Kingsley, William Lucey, Anne Paolucci, Matthew Roudané, and Richard Coe to describe Julian's entrapment as an illusion/reality conflict. Keeping in mind the opaque semiotics of the play, illusion/reality would correspond to Paul de Man's figural/literal readings and figurative/grammatical patterns (8-9). Julian's problem approaches the status of rhetorical dilemma, for it becomes impossible to decide, especially in an already ungrounded discourse, which reading of the event is accurate. Julian recognizes that he is in danger of "piling delusion upon delusion" (63), displacing one figural reading with another. To make matters more complex, Miss Alice questions whether Julian really had a conversation with his doctor in which he was told the woman, rather than being pregnant, had cancer of the womb. The memory of a conversation can certainly be as subject to revision as the memory of an event and introduces the possibility of Julian's fictionalizing the event and perhaps the entire six "blank" years. This development places Julian's narrative into a fully textualized field and recesses fugural dynamics into an embedded construct. The unreadability of an event is thus allegorized as the unreadability of the text.

This sort of fictionalizing process occurs often in Albee's work. ***The Zoo Story,*** for instance, is processed out of the interaction among several embedded structures: Jerry's narrative of the dog is introduced as "THE STORY OF JERRY AND THE DOG!" (38), as if a title were being placed on a manuscript for submission to Peter the publisher (White 18); Jerry also weaves into the text the illusion of a sexual encounter between himself and the landlady, so that "she believes and relives," in the manner of Julian, "what never happened" (36); finally, Jerry tells the zoo story, a text that turns out to narrate or at least outline the events of ***The Zoo Story*** itself. While the technique is similar to the self-reflexive naming in ***Tiny Alice,*** since ***The Zoo Story*** does have the ability to entitle itself, the earlier play has a somewhat different effect. It forces a retrospective reinterpretation of the already read or seen rather than generating signs of itself. Nevertheless, both plays expose "reality" as textual and semiotic.

As in ***The Zoo Story, Fam and Yam*** forces an equally surprising retrospective re-reading. The innocent remarks by the Famous American Playwright are exposed at the end of the play as a text carefully fed by the Young American Playwright. The opinions produced by FAM become a text to be misinterpreted, fictionalized into another text that will claim to be an interview. Although it is deferred within the context of the play, the doctored text will be accepted as the truth. The play itself, as FAM comes to realize, is not a conversation but an exercise in the manipulation of writing and reading processes. Similarly, ***The Death of Bessie Smith*** handles its historical, title character as a fiction, suggesting that access to history is mediated by textual endeavors. Because Bessie Smith never appears in the play, her death is delivered as hearsay, a story narrated by Jack and thus regressed into a fictional domain. Albee turns her lack of presence and her death into a linguistic construct, much as he does the son of George and Martha, his most famous absent character.

While the fictional son in ***Who's Afraid of Virginia Woolf?*** is part of the verbal warfare used to generate the play, he is also part of the vast network of textual traces that permeate the structure with undecidability. With the arrival of the two-fold message of his death as an unseen character and as a transparent, fictional construct, as in ***The Zoo Story*** and ***Fam and Yam*** the play forces a retrospective re-reading of itself. Much of the play now begins to look like clusters of fictional material and poses the question, raised in ***Tiny Alice*** by Julian's delivery of the past, of what can be taken as factually accurate. Did Martha really have a stepmother? Did George really know a boy who killed his father and mother? Or is that story the content of George's first novel? Or is it, as Martha suggests in the story of his fight with her father, George's autobiography? Perhaps it is part of the fiction of their son, whom George kills off in the same way the boyhood friend (or George) killed the father. Within the construct of the play, the separation of illusion from reality, or illusion from illusion, is not an easy task, for the allegorical or metaphorical readings are thoroughly enmeshed with the literally straightforward. In fact, ***Virginia Woolf*** suggests that the attempt to draw a line between the two, as George does by killing the son, only reverberates unreadability back onto previous linguistic structures and forward on to those barely conceived. Certainly, the text implies that George and Martha's gamesmanship does not end with the final curtain.

All of these Albee plays are concerned with textual problematics, encoding issues of interpretation and ontological status into their very methods of operation. As in other absurdist works, the semiotic network itself becomes a topic of concern, implying that reality in these plays, whether we try to distinguish it as figurative or literal, is ultimately rhetorical. Although Wasserman finds in Albee's work a compromise between fact and truth (51), I would suggest that a compromise is never reached, for distinct oppositions are not identifiable within the plays. When both a child and a text are created out of words in ***Virginia Woolf,*** the only possible opposition apparent in the structure is that one fiction appears on stage while the other does not. In a similar way, the hazy, figural states of tropology, the fragmentations of identity and appearance, and the indeterminacy of textual status in ***Tiny Alice*** build a dramatic world replete with all the uncompromising instability of linguistic materials.

An important departure that ***Tiny Alice*** makes from the earlier Albee works, though, lies in its use of a non-linguistic structure in which to examine further sorts of semiotic and textual functions. As in Caryl Churchill's embedding of the jigsaw puzzle in *Traps,* ***Tiny Alice*** situates a textual trace in the three-dimensional site of the model. Because stage architecture, like dramatic discourse, works to create a dramatic world, sets and properties can become part of the metatextual examination, both generating and questioning the fictional construct. Rendering information about the play's larger environment, they usually act as synecdoches, in their limited numbers standing for a much larger context. Because they are also figural, the sets, particularly those in a play like ***Tiny Alice,*** can help foster an unreadable text.

Most critics of ***Tiny Alice*** have studied the model in terms of the connotative meanings it can produce, seeing it as a symbol of Julian's confusion (Paolucci 71), of his unconscious (Anderson 180), of the womb (Langdon 60), or as a shrine (Campbell 22) or microcosm (Roudané 96). As Lawyer points out, though, the model and the stage set have a critical relationship in their functional capacities, since one is a model of the other which in turn is a replica of the other (84). In acting as signs of each other, these two figures lock themselves into a revolving exchange of images, enacting the crisis in representation that occurs when semiotic forms find themselves only able to stand for other semiotic forms. For instance, the model and the replica cause a distortion in tropological status, creating, as in Butler's name and Julian's past, wavering figural states. The model both hides and duplicates the stage set, itself a replica of the model, and also situates the stage set within the larger, fuller architecture of the dramatic setting. The two introduce different kinds of synecdochic arrangements, because the part (stage set) replicates the whole (model) and the whole (model) stands in for the part (stage set). When Butler wonders if the model contains more models—"You don't suppose that within that tiny model in the model there, there is . . . another room like this, with yet a tinier model within it, and within . . ." (25)—the play also suggests that an infinite variety of sets (and settings) is possible, that the stage set and the model are only ostensive, replaceable versions that belong to an abstract class of possible sets. Furthermore, the figural wavering that goes on between the model and the replica now can be seen as extending into infinity, with the replica and the ever smaller models continuing to reproduce the two interchanging synecdoches. In fact, the problematic of figuration in ***Tiny Alice*** is taken beyond the text itself to be placed in the zone between written and performed material where the dramatic signs refer to an open, semiotic range of possible categories of referents (Eco, "Semiotics" 110), in this case possible sets and settings.

Tiny Alice achieves with the model, however, more than a way of considering its own stage set, for various characters indicate that the model may include other semiotic systems such as actors, which turns it into a replication of the dramatic world as a whole. For instance, the text suggests several times that the model contains more than furnishings:

> BUTLER: Is there anyone there? Are we there?
>
> JULIAN: . . . Uh . . . no. It seems to be quite . . . empty.
>
> BUTLER: . . . One feels one should see one's self . . . almost.
>
> (24)

Somewhat later, Lawyer, while teasing Miss Alice, also plants the suspicion that the model contains something: "Unless you mean all the little people running around inside here" (70). And of course, the model seems to hold the figure of Alice. Consequently, the model becomes more than simply a duplicate of the mansion: it becomes a quasi-reproduction of life in the household of the replica.

In this way, the model begins to stand for and point to the construction of the play world in performance and its relation to other worlds. The play world as a theatrical construct is hypothetical, an ostended possibility. Although self-referential by definition, it also relies upon "a pre-existing set of properties from the real world" (Eco, "Possible Worlds" 31). Nevertheless, the theatrical world is not imitative, for, as Keir Elam writes, "mimesis . . . is equivalent to definition through ostension" (112). The relation of the play world to the real is figurative; more precisely, it is metonymic since the two are parallel, contiguous structures. In dealing with their contiguity, drama theorists consider the two in the light of mathematical set theory, concluding that the play world is a subset of the real world and therefore accessible to the real world without being accessible from it. The two worlds are asymmetrical, since the real world always contains all of the theatrical items (properties, actors, etc.), while the theatrical world contains only a few items from the real world.

The model and the replica in ***Tiny Alice*** examine this situation. Encompassed by the play world of ***Tiny Alice,*** the model uses materials from that world and seems initially to be accessible to that world and not from it. For instance, when a fire starts in the model, it can only be extinguished by dousing the fire that also occurs in the mansion. Yet the model will also bend the rule of asymmetrical accessibility by suggesting that world-hopping can take place from model to replica. Julian's wedding apparently takes place in the model; puzzling over how strange it was for everyone to vanish immediately after the ceremony, he says that it was "as if I'd turned my back for a moment, and an hour elapsed, or a . . . dimension had . . ." (127). Contrary to theatrical logic, all of the characters in the wedding party return from the model to the mansion, and of course the implication at the end of the play is that the figure comes out of the model.

By showing a fictional rendition of the accessibility between the dimensions of duplicated real and play worlds, ***Tiny Alice*** can distort relationships without destroying itself as a play. In fact, the play is trying to stretch its frame outward to include the real world as part of the infinite series suggested by the model, making the audience uncomfortable with the threat of symmetrical accessibility. The real world becomes part of the play's vision. As an audience, we begin to experience the same kind of difficulty felt by Lawyer and Julian, the same kind of haziness among figural states. We sense the collapse of two metonymic structures, the real and play worlds, into each other.

The relations among the model, the replica, and the real world become more complex when taking into account the fact that the model also stands for one hypothetical play world within the abstract class of possible play worlds. As an absurdist *mise en abyme,* the model, in containing ever smaller versions of itself, becomes a schema for the traces of infinitely many, slightly distorted, play worlds. The traces of models within the model are therefore capable of supplanting each other as contiguous, hypothetical worlds. This pattern indicates that the play offers and becomes part of an infinite series of possible displacements for its own fictional construct, opening up a place of absence in its design which it tries to fill in with one version of the play world after another.

What the model ultimately ends up suggesting is a visual, three-dimensional site of unreadability, since the capacity to elicit an infinite number of possible play worlds rests on the capacity to elicit an infinite number of possible interpretations. In a slightly different way, the model examines the problematic raised in Pirandello's *Six Characters in Search of an Author,* in which the characters (as the written text) and the actors (as the performance text) argue over divergent interpretations of the same scene. As an embedded replication of the text, the model in ***Tiny Alice*** acts as a semiotic body, a non-linguistic sign structure which enacts a trace in the form of an infinite series and in the proliferation of signifiers as its own repeating architecture. As Michel Foucault appropriately writes:

> Interpretation finally [becomes] an infinite task. . . . There is nothing absolutely primary to interpret, because at bottom all is already interpretation, each sign is in itself not the thing which offers itself to interpretation, but the interpretation of other signs.
>
> (qtd. in Miller 3)

By encoding the distorting process of signs when they try to represent signs, the model thus illustrates both the basic unreadable quality of semiotic structures and the generative functions that leap into motion in the very attempt to interpret them.

Albee's use of the model as a sign structure also indicates his tendency to experiment with the intertextuality of semiotic systems. As Anne Paolucci notes, the model in ***Tiny Alice*** is "the most effective use to date of backdrop as dramatic script" (7), and as Julian Wasserman points out, Grandma's boxes in ***The American Dream*** can be taken as words (41). In fact, Albee continues the examination of semiosis and textuality we have been following in the model in ***Tiny Alice*** in later three-dimensional sites such as the box in ***Box*** and ***Quotations from Chairman Mao Tse-tung.***

The box in this piece forms a semiotic container for a play among texts. Interestingly, the stage directions state that the box is distorted (17), suggesting that the capacity for one sign structure to contain and act as the site for the generation of other sign structures impacts on the very shape of the text. Four texts are delivered within the box: the narrative of the Long-Winded Lady; the poem "Over the Hill to the Poor House" by the Old Woman, which continually repeats and loops back on itself; the quotations from Chairman Mao, which handle the historical personage as textually mediated in the manner of Bessie Smith; and the remarks of box itself, which come from outside the textual structure.

This last text is most interesting because, in forming a frame around the ***Quotations*** playlet, ***Box*** is in danger of too simplistically parodying the box-like structure of the fourth-wall play. However, by removing the voice from the box and having it come by recording or microphone from somewhere in the seats, the idea of theatrical presence is undercut. The semiotic systems of the play in performance are kept separate, so that the voice does not unite with the body of the box to produce phonocentrism. This separation also allows the voice to bleed out of its function as part of the container and to interrupt and become involved in the generation of texts within the box. Such an internal, allegorizing process tends to fold the texts into each other, dissolving the play's textual site into its own interior and producing a rhizomic design.

In fact, the swirl of texts seen in ***Box*** and ***Quotations*** is a later version of the play of signs and tropes appearing in the model in ***Tiny Alice.*** Enmeshed in a network of sign structures, the model also problematizes the idea of theatrical presence and undercuts the claims of a metaphysical center. As discussed above, Julian cannot positively identify or name the figure in the model since name and identity have been exposed as a series of metonymies and appearances. "God" and "Alice" are tropes in a process of *"différance"* which refuses to locate a center. Of course, this situation reverberates onto the act of reading, for the play provides only the mystery of reading for both Julian and the audience. And Albee seems to have fostered the impossibility of interpretation by offering two alternative explanations of the ending: "Either the abstraction personifies itself, is proved real, or the dying man, in the last necessary effort of self-delusion creates and believes in what he knows does not exist" ("Critics" 12).

Nevertheless, something does come out of the model which, as Leonard Casper itemizes, has been called an existentialist Nothingness, an Evil Deity, or a benevolent but devouring god (84). I would posit, however, that the only thing that can come out of a sign structure is another sign structure and that Julian, of course, cannot reach meaning because he can reach only another signifier. As in ***Box*** and ***Quotations,*** where the linguistic signs of the voice are already outside of the textual site, in ***Tiny Alice*** the semiotic sign of the figure is made to emerge from the model. The figure becomes the fabricated personification of a desire for presence, whether as existentialist or as Christian or as a gingerbread God with raisin eyes (104).

The metatextual space and the opaque semiotic network within it ultimately confront the reader or audience with the instability of interpretation and the fundamental insolubility of texts. In fact, the term "mystery play" has often been used, even by Albee himself, to attempt to define the play. However, rather than being comparable to the medieval morality play, ***Tiny Alice*** has more in common with postmodernist "detective" fiction, with novels like Thomas Pynchon's *The Crying of Lot 49.* Both works withhold important information from the reader or audience, throwing her into the roles of detective and literary critic, roles also played by Julian and Oedipa Maas. Forced to continually reassess language and action, the reader of ***Tiny Alice*** finds her own dilemma encoded into the very fabric of the text. The determination of a solution finally appears as an impossible task for those inside the play and for those outside. When it collapses distinctions between the reader's problematic and the character's, the play uncomfortably interferes with our attitudes toward reality. Even if it is a vast matrix of signs and codes, at least we like to think of the world as interpretable.

Works Cited

Albee, Edward. *Box and Quotations from Chairman Mao Tse-tung.* New York: Pocket Books, 1970.

———. "Critics Are Downgrading Audience's Taste And Have Obfuscated Simple *Tiny Alice.*" *The Dramatists Guild Quarterly* 2.1 (1965): 9-14.

———. *Fam and Yam. The Death of Bessie Smith.* New York: Signet Books, 1960.

———. "John Gielgud and Edward Albee Talk About the Theater." By R.S. Stewart. *The Atlantic Monthly* 215.4 (1965): 61-68.

———. *Tiny Alice.* New York: Pocket Books, 1966.

———. *Who's Afraid of Virginia Woolf?* New York: Pocket Books, 1964.

———. *The Zoo Story. Edward Albee: The Plays.* Vol. 1. New York: Coward, 1981.

Anderson, Mary. "Staging the Unconscious: Edward Albee's *Tiny Alice.*" *Renascence* 32 (1980): 178-92.

Baxandall, Lee. "The Theatre of Edward Albee." *Tulane Drama Review* 9.4 (1965): 19-40.

Bigsby, C. W. E. *A Critical Introduction to Twentieth-Century American Drama.* Cambridge: Cambridge UP, 1984.

Brustein, Robert. "Three Plays and a Protest." Rev. of *Tiny Alice,* by Edward Albee. *The New Republic* 23 Jan. 1965: 32-36.

Campbell, Mary E. "The Tempters in Albee's *Tiny Alice.*" *Modern Drama* 13 (1970): 22-33.

Casper, Leonard. "The Expense of Joy in the Persistence of Mystery." *Edward Albee: An Interview and Essays.* Ed. Julian N. Wasserman. Houston: U of St. Thomas P, 1983.

Coe, Richard M. "Beyond Absurdity: Albee's Awareness of Audience in *Tiny Alice.*" *Modern Drama* 18 (1975) 371-83.

DeMan, Paul. *Allegories of Reading.* New Haven: Yale UP, 1979.

Eco, Umberto. "Possible Worlds and Text Pragmatics: 'Un drame bien parisien.' " *Versus* 19/20 (1978): 5-72.

———. "Semiotics of Theatrical Performance." *The Drama Review* 21 (1977): 107-17.

Elam, Keir. *The Semiotics of Theatre and Drama.* London: Methuen, 1980.

Fumerton, M. Patricia. "Verbal Prisons: Language of *A Delicate Balance.*" *English Studies in Canada* 7 (1981): 201-11.

Havel, Vaclav. *The Memorandum.* Trans. Vera Blackwell. New York: Grove P, 1980.

Kingsley, Lawrence. "Reality and Illusion: Continuity of a Theme in Albee." *Educational Theatre Journal* 25 (1973): 71-79.

Langdon, Harry N. "Ritual Form: One Key to Albee's *Tiny Alice.*" *Theatre Annual* 35 (1980): 57-72.

Lucey, William F. "Albee's Tiny Alice: Truth and Appearance." *Renascence* 21 (1969): 76-80, 100.

Miller, J. Hillis. *The Linguistic Moment: From Wordsworth to Stevens.* Princeton: Princeton UP, 1985.

Oberg, Arthur K. "Edward Albee: His Language and Imagination." *Prairie Schooner* 40 (1966): 139-46.

Paolucci, Anne. *From Tension to Tonic: The Plays of Edward Albee.* Carbondale: Southern Illinois UP, 1972.

Roudané, Matthew C. *Understanding Edward Albee.* Columbia, South Carolina: U of South Carolina P, 1987.

Roth, Philip. "The Play that Dare Not Speak Its Name." Rev. of *Tiny Alice,* by Edward Albee. *New York Review of Books* 25 Feb. 1965: 4.

Stark, John. "Camping Out: *Tiny Alice* and Susan Sontag." *Critical Essays on Edward Albee.* Ed. Philip C. Kolin and J. Madison Davis. Boston: G. K. Hall, 1986.

Stavrou, C. N. "Albee in Wonderland." *Southwest Review* 60 (1975) 46-61.

Wasserman, Julian N. "'The Pitfalls of Drama': The Idea of Language in the Plays of Edward Albee." *Edward Albee: An Interview and Essays.* Ed. Julian N. Wasserman. Houston: U of St. Thomas, 1983.

White, Fred D. "Albee's Hunger Artist: *The Zoo Story* as a Parable of the Writer vs. Society." *Arizona Quarterly* 39 (1983): 15-22.

Wolfe, Peter. "The Social Theatre of Edward Albee." *Prairie Schooner* 39 (1965): 248-62.

FURTHER READING

Ballew, Leighton M. "Who's Afraid of *Tiny Alice*? "*The Georgia Review* XX, No. 3 (Fall 1966): 292-99.

Suggests that *Tiny Alice* "may take place entirely in the mind of the lay brother, Julian."

Campbell, Mary Elizabeth. "The Statement of Edward Albee's *Tiny Alice.* "*Papers on Language & Literature* IV, No. 1 (Winter 1968): 85-100.

Structural analysis that argues that *Tiny Alice* propounds the thesis that humanity's numerous scientific achievements "so potently free, ease, and expand his life that a man may tend, whether wittingly or no, to center his energies and hopes in these concerns, to such a degree that the spiritual aspects of his nature may dwindle away and his humanity be engulfed in materialism."

Clurman, Harold. A review of *Tiny Alice. The Nation* 200, No. 3 (18 January 1965): 65.

Negative evaluation that asserts: "The surface or fabric of *Tiny Alice* is specious."

Curry, Ryder Hector, and Michael Porte. "The Surprising Unconscious of Edward Albee."*Drama Survey* 7, Nos. 1-2 (Winter 1968-69): 59-68.

Maintains that *Tiny Alice* is "an exemplification of the workings of the collective unconscious," a "working out in dramatic form of [Carl Gustav] Jung."

Dukore, Bernard F. "Tiny Albee."*Drama Survey* 5, No. 1 (Spring 1966): 60-6.

Negative appraisal that finds *Tiny Alice* "preposterous" on the realistic level and confused on the symbolic level.

Hewes, Henry. "The *Tiny Alice* Caper." *Saturday Review* XLVIII, No. 5 (30 January 1965): 38-9, 65.

Surveys the critical disputes surrounding *Tiny Alice* and discusses the drama's meaning and significance with the play's author, director, and principal actors.

Lucey, William F. "Albee's *Tiny Alice*: Truth and Appearance." *Renascence* XXI, No. 2 (Winter 1969): 76-80, 110.

Allegorical reading of *Tiny Alice,* in which Julian searches for Truth, symbolized by Alice.

R. S. Stewart. "John Gielgud and Edward Albee Talk about the Theater." *The Atlantic Monthly*215, No. 4 (April 1965): 61-8.

Conversation between the author and principal actor of *Tiny Alice,* moderated by Stewart. Regarding the issue of what the play is about, Albee concedes, "I don't know yet, so I can't say."

Taubman, Howard. "Enigma That Runs Down." *The New York Times* (10 January 1965): II, 1.

Mixed review of *Tiny Alice.* Taubman contends: "In the final act *Tiny Alice* loses its richness of suggestion. The enigma remains, but the sense of mystery has been thinned."

Valgemae, Mardi. "Albee's Great God Alice." *Modern Drama* 10, No. 3 (December 1967): 267-73.

Explores the influence of Eugene O'Neill on the writing of *Tiny Alice.*

A Delicate Balance

INTRODUCTION

A Delicate Balance was first produced at the Martin Beck Theatre, New York, on 22 September 1966, in a staging directed by Alan Schneider. The play centers on Agnes and Tobias, a middle-aged suburban couple settled into an affluent but stultifying existence. The precarious balance of their accommodation to each other is upset by the arrival for extended stays of their daughter, Julia, who has left her third husband, and the couple's friends Harry and Edna, who are fleeing a vague but ominous dread of nothingness. The relationship of the domineering Agnes and the emasculated Tobias is further disrupted by the presence of Agnes's alcoholic sister, Claire, who attempts to seduce Tobias but is rebuffed. In the course of the play Agnes and Tobias come to an awareness of the emptiness of their life together, and both repudiate their habitual roles: Agnes refuses to be the decision-maker and Tobias rouses himself from his lethargy to take the decisive action of allowing Harry and Edna remain in the house, despite the objections of Julia, who views them as intruders. The second couple, however, decline to stay, realizing that the house offers them no refuge from their feelings of fear and alienation.

CRITICAL RECEPTION

Initial reaction to *A Delicate Balance* was decidedly mixed. Harold Clurman considered it a brilliant play that "dramatizes discomfort": in the world depicted in the drama "one's soul finds no resting place, no spiritual security." Robert Brustein, however, condemned it as "a very bad play . . . boring and trivial," while John Gassner pronounced it "neither a very good play nor a very bad one." When it was awarded the Pulitzer Prize, most regarded the decision as a belated attempt by the Pulitzer committee to atone for failing to give Albee the prize for *Who's Afraid of Virginia Woolf?*. Subsequent commentators have sought to identify the unnamed fear that suffuses the play by investigating the issues of isolation, alienation, and individual identity. John J. von Szeliski has called *A Delicate Balance* "a brilliant and highly significant play" in which the characters "suddenly realize . . . that their lives represent no real solace against the pressure of their mortality." M. Patricia Fumerton, in her examination of the play's language, has argued that in *A Delicate Balance* "language appears not as a medium for communication, but as a necessary protective device; it forms an impenetrable blockage, a thick layer of skin within which each individual may rest secure: isolated and lonely and—tragically—invulnerable."And Virginia I. Perry has asserted that *A Delicate Balance* underscores "the fragile nature of [one's] illusion of security by exploring the ill-defined boundaries which separate sanity from madness and by exposing just how delicate those boundaries can be."

PRODUCTION REVIEWS

Walter Kerr (review date 23 September 1966)

SOURCE: A review of *A Delicate Balance,* in *The New York Times,* 23 September 1966, p. 44.

[*The following negative review judges* A Delicate Balance *to be an empty play about hollowness and nameless dread.*]

T. S. Eliot once said, "I will show you fear in a handful of dust," and then he did it. In ***A Delicate Balance,*** Edward Albee talks about it and talks about it and talks about it, sometimes wittily, sometimes ruefully, sometimes truthfully. But showing might have done better.

A Delicate Balance is the sort of play that might be written if there were no theater. It exists outside itself, beside itself, aloof from itself, as detached from the hard floor of the Martin Beck, where it opened last night, as its alarmed characters are detached from themselves. The effect is deliberate—because it is precisely hollowness that is most on Mr. Albee's mind—and it is offered to us on an elegantly lacquered empty platter the moment the curtain goes up.

The curtain goes up on a setting that seems already to have floated away. There, in the background, are perfectly familiar bookshelves, probably solid chandeliers, all the potted palms of the world's onetime comfort. But everything that is solid is recessed, slipping off into shadow. Downstage, near us, is an amber void in which the characters live and have their non-being. Hume Cronyn clenches his fingers and stares in worry and near-exasperation at Jessica Tandy. Miss Tandy, silver-haired queen of all that is absent, smooths down the gray serenity of her utterly unwrinkled dress, and speaks quickly. She speculates, lightly at first, on the desirability of going mad.

Madness would be an acceptable enough escape for the people of the play because, in middle life and moving steadily toward less life, they are without occupation or preoccupation. What should they have on their minds, or in their house? Miss Tandy's sister is present, but present only to drink. A daughter is soon to come home, but only to take refuge from her latest detestable husband. Each adds negation to what is already lost. And there are friends on the threshold, shivering as the door is opened. The neighbors, Carmen Mathews and Henderson Forsythe, have dropped by because they have just had a fright. She was sitting doing her needlepoint, he brushing up his French, when something—or, rather, nothing—happened. Nothing at all happened. They just got scared. Perhaps friendship will be some sort of haven from anxiety, especially when the anxiety cannot be named or found hiding down the hall.

That Mr. Albee is prepared to do shadow-battle with a perfectly real phenomenon of our time is plain enough, and in the elusive feinting with the indefinable he has several successes. Mr. Cronyn, for instance, is given a first-act passage in which, at no one's request, he describes his desperately loving encounter with a cat. He had loved the cat and wanted the cat to love him. Insisted upon it, in fact. But cats and love cannot be insisted upon, and in the end there is clawing, slapping about, and coldly prearranged death.

Without warning, Mr. Cronyn seems to get his hands about the play's throat as he describes his fifth unsuccessful attempt to force a dearly loved pet to purr—there are echoes of ***The Zoo Story*** here, but they are good echoes—and the unbidden intensity that strains the muscles of his mouth until they seem ready to fray and snap is miraculous performing. Again, in the play's third and best act, the actor thrashes about the meaningless furniture in the early hours of the morning trying to find a good face to put on love and fidelity with the fire of a prophet whose message may be dragged by main force out of the heavens.

Miss Tandy's finest moment comes in a fierce assault on human withdrawal, on the evasive action each of us takes when he hears too much pain in the immediate neighborhood. Now the cool champagne-cocktail ice of her voice burns away and something nearer lava is served, neat. In and around these occasional yearnings to say what will never be said clearly enough, Rosemary Murphy scatters very dry alcoholic aphorisms, rather as though she were whipping the already exhausted contestants with a knotted towel of cheerful malice. Miss Murphy, at one time a green witch spilling orange juice on the rug, is a perfect vehicle for Mr. Albee's gratuitous, grinning barbs.

But in the end how *do* you get hold of hollowness, how do you flesh out what is drained of flesh and create suspense out of what isn't there? Harold Pinter has sometimes done it, and Harold Pinter is what comes to mind the moment the two terrified, baffled neighbors enter to lay claim to shelter in an upstairs room.

But Mr. Pinter does everything by suggestion, by playing on our own easily disturbed sensibilities. He never uses the word "fright," he simply frightens us. Mr. Albee, on the other hand, plays out his hand all too readily, revealing that there is so little in it. Miss Mathews and Mr. Forsythe keep telling us how rattled they are, and they do tremble—a bit too much, in fact. But we never inhabit their apprehensions, we only listen to them.

And, in an effort to find a stylized verbal technique that will convey the literally unspeakable, Mr. Albee has seemed to go directly back to the T. S. Eliot of, say, *Family Reunion,* and to use, much too abstractly and often too sonorously, the reiterations and the repeated rhythms of almost-but-not-quite poetry. The images seem to have hollows in them, like well-formed chocolate Easter bunnies that crack wide open at the very first bite. Words like "succor, comfort, warmth" recur as though they had no concrete referents, no tangible thread connecting them with days or nights or bodies or deeds, and when Mr. Cronyn announces that his daughter is having hysterics in a room above we come to expect the sort of reply we get: "That is a condition. I asked about an action." The play itself becomes a condition, standing still, though immaculately still.

Alan Schneider has staged it with infinite composure and considerable grace, William Ritman's setting is surely altogether right, and Marian Seldes, as the raven-haired Cassandra who is prey to hysterics, works hard at the passion of her utter distress. But it is an ungrounded distress, and Miss Seldes suffers most from having to flash so much anger over unseen, unknown wounds.

Henry Hewes (review date 8 October 1966)

SOURCE: "The Family that Stayed Separate," in *Saturday Review,* Vol. XLIX, No. 41, 8 October 1966, p. 90.

[*The essay below presents a mixed review of* A Delicate Balance, *stating that "if what we see is convincing and sophisticated, it is not steadily compelling."*]

Having more or less disposed of the university and the church in his last two plays, Edward Albee has now chosen to weave his intricate web around a more personal institution, American family life. ***A Delicate Balance*** commences at cocktail hour in the affluent suburban home of a sixtyish couple named Agnes and Tobias. All is cozy and comfortable, and even the presence of Agnes's alcoholic younger sister, Claire, fails seriously to disrupt their façcade of contentment. It is not smugness, but a contentment achieved through concern for what each thinks the other one wants. In doing this they have ceased to want anything themselves. They are not fools, however, and see the truth of their situation at the same time that they participate in its myth.

Two principal myths are examined in this play. The first is that people who are sufficiently happy together or enough in love to get married will forever remain happy and in love. Albee punctures this one early with the parable of Tobias and the cat. Here we see that a man who is unable to regain a love that has dissipated equates his inability with being judged—being betrayed—and reacts with hatred and viciousness. But married people often avoid such an outcome by pretending, by living up to a myth that they may privately recognize as untrue. Thus we resign ourselves and, as one character says, through "the gradual demise of intensity, the private preoccupations, the substitutions, we become allegorical. . . . The individuality we held so dearly sinks into crotchet; we see ourselves repeated by those we bring into it all, either by mirror or rejection. . . ."

The second myth is that best friends acquired through proximity and mutual activities can always depend upon each other's help no matter how great the sacrifice entailed. Albee suggests that if the latter myth can be shown to be absurd, so must the former also be.

To test the balance of "the regulated great gray life," Albee simply has Agnes's and Tobias's best friends, Harry and Edna, arrive unexpectedly at the door. They have experienced "the terror" (which, though never explained, is presumably that point at which awareness of the distance between myth and truth becomes unbearable), and demand to move in. Agnes recognizes that their terror could be contagious and calls upon Tobias to choose between letting them stay permanently or ordering them out. This eventually results in a remarkable mad eruption by Tobias in which his contradictory feelings are revealed. His position is at once hilariously ridiculous and touchingly pathetic. And though the play nominally ends on an anti-climatic note, we leave the theater feeling that we have seen a most important part of our way of life compassionately but accurately described.

We also feel, of course, that it has been challenged, though not as excoriatingly as we had anticipated. A remark by Claire that is almost a footnote is the play's strongest indictment. "We're not a communal nation, giving but not sharing, outgoing but not friendly. We submerge our truths and have our sunsets on untroubled waters. We live with our truths in the grassy bottom, and we examine all the interpretations of all the implications like we had a life for nothing else . . . We better develop gills."

The play is not easy to perform. In a way, Albee has tried to do in prose what T. S. Eliot did in verse in his later plays, and without the help of meter Albee's succession of paragraphed insights can seem talky. This is particularly true because of the lack of specific information that emerges from all the conversation. Fortunately, Albee sprinkles his script with his special humor—and theatricality—to keep us entertained when the plot does not.

Jessica Tandy plays the role of Agnes, "licensed wife," with so much composure that we tend to see her as an instrument of propriety. Hume Cronyn is excellent and versatile as Tobias, but he is so completely explicit that we sometimes miss the inner mystery and private grief, that might make him more protagonist and less demonstrator. Oddly enough, Henderson Forsythe and Carmen Mathews in the much smaller roles of Harry and Edna emerge with more human dimension. And most effective of all are Rosemary Murphy and Marian Seldes. As the alcoholic, outspoken Claire, Miss Murphy has the opportunity to speak nasty truths about everyone else and makes the mischievous most of it. Miss Seldes, as Julia, the daughter who keeps returning to the nursery dragging in broken marriages "like some Raggedy Ann doll by the foot," gives the fullest emotional performance of all. It is her rage and her frustration that most indict her elders' complaisance.

While Alan Schneider's direction is thorough, both it and William Ritman's large, handsome set make the people in this play seem remote. Perhaps this was the playwright's intention: for us to see ourselves from a distance in a space where elegant language seems natural and four-letter Anglo-Saxon words become seven-letter Latin ones.

If what we see is convincing and sophisticated, it is not steadily compelling. The audience keeps wanting to get closer to the characters. There is, for instance, the suggestion that Claire had been "upended" by Tobias one summer long ago, and that had he divorced Agnes to marry her things might have been better for everyone. Yet it is never explored. Obviously the playwright is concerned with the process of restoring delicate balances rather than what it takes to upset them.

However, steadily compelling plays are few these days, and, all things considered, ***A Delicate Balance*** will do. It will do because it manages to encompass a complex subject with such honesty and grace.

Robert Brustein (review date 8 October 1966)

SOURCE: "Albee Decorates an Old House," in *New Republic,* Vol. 155, No. 15, 8 October 1966, pp. 35-36.

[*The scathing review below condemns* A Delicate Balance *as "a very bad play . . . boring and trivial."*]

Edward Albee's recent work poses a number of problems for the reviewer, one of them being that it is virtually impossible to discuss it without falling into repetition. Looking over the anthology of pieces I have written about his annual procession of plays, I discover that I am continually returning to two related points: that his plays have no internal validity and that they are all heavily dependent upon the style of other dramatists. At the risk of boring the reader, I am forced to repeat these judgments about ***A Delicate Balance.*** The fourth in a series of disasters that Albee has been turning out since ***Who's Afraid of Virginia Woolf?,*** this work, like its predecessors, suffers from a borrowed style and a hollow center. It also suggests that Albee's talent for reproduction has begun to fail him until the labels on his lendings are all but exposed to public view. Reviewers have already noted the stamp of T. S. Eliot on ***A Delicate Balance*** (a name tag that was somewhat more subtly imprinted on ***Tiny Alice*** as well), and it is quite true that Albee, like Eliot before him, is now trying to invest the conventional drawing room comedy with metaphysical significance. But where Eliot was usually impelled by a religious vision, Albee seems to be stimulated by mere artifice, and the result is emptiness, emptiness, emptiness.

A Delicate Balance is, to my mind, a very bad play—not as bad as ***Malcolm,*** which had a certain special awfulness all its own—but boring and trivial nevertheless. It is also the most remote of Albee's plays—so far removed from human experience, in fact, that one wonders if Albee is not letting his servants do his living for him. Although the action is supposed to take place in suburban America—in the living room and conservatory of an upper middle-class family—the environment is more that of the English landed gentry as represented on the West End before the Osborne revolution. Leather-bound books sit on library shelves, elbowing copies of *Horizon;* brandy and anisette and martinis are constantly being decanted between, over, and under bits of dialogue; the help problem becomes an object of concern, as well as problems of friendship, marriage, sex, and the proper attitude to take towards pets; and characters discuss their relationships in a lapidary style as far from modern speech as the whistles of a dolphin.

The failure of the language, actually, is the most surprising failure of the play, especially since Albee's control of idiom has usually been his most confident feature. Here, on the other hand, banal analogies are forced to pass for wisdom: "Friendship is something like a marriage, is it not Tobias, for better or for worse?" The plot is signalled with all the subtlety of a railroad brakeman rerouting a train: "Julia is coming home. She is leaving Douglas which is no surprise to me." A relaxed idiom is continually sacrificed to clumsy grammatical accuracy: "You are a guest," observes one character, to which the other replies, "As you." If colloquialisms are spoken, they are invariably accompanied by self-conscious apologies: One character drinks "like the famous fish," while another observes, "You're copping out, as they say." Empty chatter is passed off as profound observation with the aid of irrelevant portentous subordinate clauses: "Time happens, I suppose, to people. Everything becomes too late finally." And the play ends with one of those vibrato rising sun lines familiar from at least a dozen such evenings: "Come now, we can begin the day."

It is clear that Albee has never heard such people talk, he has only read plays about them, and he has not retained enough from his reading to give his characters life. More surprisingly, he has not even borrowed creatively from his own work, for although a number of Albee's usual strategies are present in ***A Delicate Balance,*** they do not function with much cogency. One character, for example, tells of his difficulties with a cat that no longer loved him—a tale that recalls a similar tale about a dog in ***The Zoo Story***—but here the narrative is no more than a sentimental recollection. Similarly, a dead child figures in this work, as in so many Albee plays, but it has no organic relevance to the action and seems introduced only to reveal the sexual hangups of the protagonists and to fill up time.

Too much of the play, in fact, seems purely decorative: There simply isn't enough material here to make up a full evening. ***A Delicate Balance*** concerns a family of four—a passive husband, an imperious wife, an alcoholic sister-in-law, and a much divorced daughter—whose problems are exacerbated when they are visited by some married friends. This couple has just experienced a nameless terror in their home, and when they move in on the family for comfort and security, a delicate balance is upset, all the characters learning that terror is infectious, like the plague. This plot has a nice touch of mystery about it, but its main consequence is to move various sexually estranged couples into each other's rooms after various impassioned dialogues. What finally puzzles the will is how very little Albee now thinks can make up a play: A few confessions, a few revelations, a little spookiness, and an emotional third act speech.

Alan Schneider's production is stiff and pedestrian. One senses discomfort in the staging as well as in the performances: These are not roles that actors fill with pleasure. Rosemary Murphy has some vigor as the alcoholic sister-in-law, coming on like one of those sardonic (male) drunks that used to appear in the plays of Philip Barry, but like the other performers, she has a difficult time recovering the portentous rhythms of the play when she stumbles over a line. Hume Cronyn, usually one of our most dependable actors, is dry and uninteresting as the father; Jessica Tandy is delicate but high-pitched as the mother; and Marian Seldes as the daughter is vocally and physically angular. The director occasionally tries for an effect, as when he arranges four ladies with their coffee cups in the attitude of an Eliot chorus, but most of the time we are spared such tableaux and the stage is left as empty as the play. It is an emptiness that no amount of activity can fill. ***A Delicate Balance*** is an old house which an interior decorator has tried to furnish with reproductions and pieces bought at auction. But the house has never been lived in and the wind murmurs drily through its corridors.

Harold Clurman (review date 10 October 1966)

SOURCE: A review of *A Delicate Balance,* in *The Nation,* Vol. 203, No. 11, 10 October 1966, pp. 361-63.

[*The following favorable review maintains that* A Delicate Balance *is a brilliant play that conveys "the almost insuperable difficulty of loving one's neighbor, and the absolute necessity of behaving with love despite that difficulty."*]

If someone should tell you that Edward Albee's ***A Delicate Balance*** is a brilliant play (which it is), ask: "What is its theme?" If another declares that it is very well written (also true), insist on knowing exactly how. And if its staging is praised, try to discover in what regard.

One might discuss the play's accomplishment in the context of its craftsmanship: a slight plot suffices to sustain a long evening and to maintain suspense. In ***Who's Afraid of Virginia Woolf?*** this was achieved through the sparkling venom of the dialogue. The new play proceeds through a continuous enrichment of its theme. Its style crystallizes its meaning.

The play dramatizes discomfort. Its world is not absurd and it is not cruel; it is without comfort. Here one's soul finds no resting place, no spiritual security. The distress that plagues it is all the more acute for being encased in a glittering shell.

This private world which is Albee's, to a greater degree than most of us know or care to admit, is largely ours as well.

What produces this "plague"? We love and cannot bear one another. We need our fellow men desperately, yet cannot reconcile ourselves to their otherness. We yearn for closeness, yet a dismal distance separates us.

This is seldom apparent to us because we are not savages or hoodlums: we generally treat one another with courtesy. In ***A Delicate Balance*** we are, in contrast to ***The Zoo Story,*** among sophisticated circumstances. There is an unnatural elegance about the environment. The talk is colloquial enough to be thoroughly American and elaborate enough to approximate the speech of an 18th-century drawing-room play. This is deliberate. Albee wishes us to be at home and yet to remove us to a more abstract sphere. His people are familiar and somehow strangers. They are personae—masks. Ordinary words and phrases are transformed into a special language which we never hear spoken except on a stage. It removes us from the mundane; while it is peculiarly attractive it also disturbs and makes for a slight but persistent uneasiness. It hides its hurt and hate. It is not realism but perhaps high comedy. A jazzy decorum, usually euphonious, is the mark of an extreme tension.

The characters are well-to-do, though we never know how they earn their living. (The absence of a specific background passes unnoticed because the time of the play's action is compressed into thirty hours of a weekend.) A country club is mentioned; we are presumably in the sleek suburbia.

Middle-aged Agnes is the family's fulcrum: she keeps its balance by the force of propriety. Her husband, Tobias, is evasive, taciturn, suppressed: he is rarely allowed to finish a sentence. He is reasonable and invariably correct. Everything painful or messy, all emotional anarchy is firmly checked by Agnes.

Claire, Agnes' sister, is the dissonant but ineffectual voice of dissent. A resolute alcoholic, or more accurately, she asserts, a drunk, she understands everything but is incapable of decided action. She is a rebellious "outsider," herself in need of protection. She cannot even declare her desire for her brother-in-law.

Agnes and Tobias have had a son, who died. She wanted another child, but the shock of the boy's death has filled Tobias with terror at the idea of bringing new life into the world. As a result, his sex appetite is arrested. There is a daughter, Julia, who has been thrice married and divorced. On her return home we learn that she has left her husband.

Into this household where good manners barely clamp the lid on hysteria, come Harry and Edna, members of the country club. They have come to stay permanently. They have no other explanation for their intrusion except that they are *frightened.* Their fear is all the more scary for being without defined cause. They proclaim their right to take refuge in their best friends' home. Julia, who seeks solace in the bosom of her family—a cold bosom since there can be little warmth where so much is repressed—resents these friends who have pre-empted her room. She demands that her parents order Harry and Edna out.

The decision falls to Tobias because, as Agnes points out, by his very passivity Tobias has actually ruled the hearth. In the crucial confrontation of the play Tobias, through an anguished confession, finally takes a stand, the kind of moral decision that most of us seldom make. Though he has never really felt "one" with Harry, never really loved him and wishes he had never been troubled by Harry's sudden dependence on him, he pleads with Harry to stay. For they are *friends* and what does friendship mean unless it goes to the limit of giving all one has to give?

This scene might have been a trite bid for sympathy, in accordance with the Broadway stage code which demands that you must root for someone in every play. But the situation is saved from sentimentality when we hear Harry's admission that he would not have allowed Tobias to live with him if the case were reversed. Harry and Edna leave. Neither man is a good or a bad person. They are just folk. What Albee means to convey through them and the others is the almost insuperable difficulty of loving one's neighbor, and the absolute necessity of behaving with love despite that difficulty.

It would be beside the point at this juncture to compare Albee's play with those of foreign authors who treat adjacent themes. One must first of all recognize the American accent in Albee, his individuality. Nor will it profit us to resist him at present because his vision is not yet broad enough to give his subject greater scope. The play has social relevance, though in this vein insufficient social extension or precise dramatization. Like so many of his generation Albee is as yet too self-absorbed for the broader exertion. His present success lies in the very deft objectivation of his inner state. Our reservations should not mar our appreciation. The play is a further step in the author's progress: it is superior to the more sensational ***Virginia Woolf.***

The production is technically proficient. In most cases I am content to indicate as much and let it go at that because I am thoroughly aware how ungrateful an undertaking it is in our disorganized theatre to do full justice to a subtle play.

Able and sympathetic actors have been cast in all the parts, but several of them have been miscast. As performance, Hume Cronyn's is the best. He understands Tobias, he is relaxed and true; he has feeling. But since the play deals in *types*—notice that none of the characters is given a family name—something more is involved than the actor's personal merit.

Alan Schneider, the director, has realized that the play requires a certain reserve or coolness of statement. For this reason he has avoided insisting on seething emotion. Still, his method does not convey the play's quality. Tobias should not be rendered as a "little man" (I am not speaking of height) but as an outwardly imposing figure, a very "senator" of a man, a pillar of our business community in whom the springs of sensibility have begun to dry through disuse. The welling up of his being in the play's crisis would then become more stirring and, what is more important, exemplary. The "little man" of the play is Harry who as cast looks more like a Tobias.

Edna too should have a humbler look instead of the bearing of command Carmen Matthews assumes by her very presence. Thus when Edna claims her and her husband's right as friends she should not appear self-righteous but pathetically lost. Jessica Tandy, as handsome as a Gainsborough portrait, hews close to the director's "line" for Agnes, but this can only become dramatically moving through her almost heroic effort to control the surrounding as well as the inner havoc—the very thing which makes her suspect, in hope more than in dread, that she might some day go mad. This note is absent from Miss Tandy's playing. Her daughter Julia should give the impression of having been the pride of her "Vassar" class, a woman efficiently bright and smartly sexy whose clamorous outbreak should strike us as something entirely unpredictable. Marian Seldes looks as though she had always been as sensitive as a violin string. Rosemary Murphy is effective as the bibulous sister, but through the directorial unbalance she has been edged toward a complacent comedic comment. There is not sufficient torment beneath her sallies.

William Ritman's setting is just what the author has asked for but does not create the style or mood the play demands: a wan space in which amid the status-stamped appointments loneliness creeps under the door and pervades the proceedings like a fog. Such a setting need not appear obviously anti-realistic. Robert Edmond Jones, for example, knew how—through the disposition of properties, lights and colors—to make a setting speak a dramatic message without obstructing the audience's recognition of practical topography.

These critical remarks should not mitigate my readers' obligation to see the play at the Martin Beck. ***A Delicate Balance*** deserves our close attention. There will be very few new American plays this season to warrant the same.

John Gassner (review date December 1966)

SOURCE: "Broadway in Review," in *Educational Theatre Journal,* Vol. XVIII, No. 4, December 1966, pp. 450-52.

[*The review below contains a mixed assessment that judges* A Delicate Balance *"neither a very good play nor a very bad one," citing its "many diverse and incompletely realized elements" as contributing to its failure.*]

Undoubtedly Edward Albee's ***A Delicate Balance*** was intended to be the big opening of the 1966-67 season, and it was just that if controversy is any measure of importance. But is it? The controversy was inconsequential, since no particular issue was involved. Some reviewers considered it an extremely poor play while others went so far as to regard it as Albee's best work. Reviewers as far apart on basic matters as Walter Kerr, now ensconced in the seat of judgment at *The New York Times,* and Robert Brustein of the *New Republic* brought in a distinctly negative verdict, while the enthusiasts included such strange bedfellows as Richard Watts of the *New York Post* and Harold Clurman, who writes on plays in *The Nation* when not staging them on two continents. The public verdict unmistakably supported the "Ayes," and it was instantly evident that the investors in the show had made a good investment.

My own conclusion, if it matters to anyone, is that ***A Delicate Balance*** is neither a very good play nor a very bad one, an improvement certainly on the Albee plays that followed ***Who's Afraid of Virginia Woolf?*** that missed the mark in important respects and was not particularly distinguished when it seemed to hit it. In ***A Delicate Balance,*** Mr. Albee has returned to the world of domesticity which gave him his strongest full-length drama, and it is understandable that reviewers should have registered some relief at encountering a sympathetic approach to humanity in the work. He has exorcized the ghost of Strindberg without calling up the ghost of Pollyanna to take its place. In fact, some of the bad writing in the play retains memories of ***Virginia Woolf*** in the airing of the wife's grievances against her husband, and contains a startlingly tasteless reference to *coitus interruptus.* (One of the most deplorable habits our "advanced" playwrights have picked up from the surface Naturalism of modern drama is the fruitless resort to scatology in season or out.) The main trouble with Albee's "playmaking" in this work is in fact closely related to the interest and the potential strength of the play, which makes me wish he had worked longer on the play and that his director, Mr. Alan Schneider, had been more resistant to the author's theatrical guile and dramatic energy.

There is something, perhaps even a great deal, to be said for the domestic situation that the playwright uses to demonstrate how delicate is the balance that keeps a happiness in the home or a domestic relationship possible, and how easily it is upset by a variety of factors. In the present play, these include an element of accident in the antecedent death of a boy-child that ruined the sexual harmony of the husband and wife many years ago, its effect on the marital life of a much divorced daughter of the household as well as on the hysteria of the bleakly crisp middle-aged wife Agnes, impersonated by Jessica Tandy, and the arid passiveness of the husband Tobias, well, if depressingly, played by Hume Cronyn. It is unfortunate, however, that this theme remains muddily omnipresent in the play except in moments when the wife hurls reproaches at Tobias that seem both unwarranted by the objective realities of the play and *dramatically* irrelevant no matter how relevant they might be in a comparatively well executed novel based on this subject.

A second disruption factor is the presence of the wife's hard-drinking and defiant sister Claire. Rosemary Murphy plays her with a vivacity notably absent in the performances of Jessica Tandy and Hume Cronyn, and Claire's dialogue, a tissue of verbal provocations and cynical remarks in general, contains the best writing in the play. But it is virtually impossible to account for her presence in the drama as a disturbing force. Her presence seems arbitrary and is unconvincingly accounted for. Either she shouldn't be in the play or there should be a good reason for her being there. The wife's thin thread of insinuation that the husband had been unfaithful with Claire simply has no roots in either the present action or the present feelings of the characters that would reflect a past relationship.

A third disturbing factor is the much-married daughter who has just left her last husband. There is much talk on her part about the long-deceased sibling, which could account for something significant only in a painstakingly constructed novel. There is also perfervid talk by mother Agnes that Tobias has failed in his fatherly duty to send her back to her husbands containing an insinuation to the effect that he has always been glad to get her back after her various marriages. But this theme, too, seems arbitrary; it hangs like a Freudian spider's-web from the ceiling of the author's aspirations. The only things we can observe relevantly are that the young woman (in her thirties, I believe) simply loathes her mother and is hysterically averse to having two married house-guests occupy her bedroom when she shows up unexpectedly after her latest marital fiasco. Marian Seldes puts life, or at least drama, into the play with her playing of this daughter, Julia, so intolerable a creature that the audience was vastly relieved when the fine actress Carmen Mathews, playing the female house-guest, calmly slapped her face at one especially irritating point.

Next, I must consider the central situation of the intrusion of the neighboring couple, Harry and Edna, long-time friends of the suburban or, if you will, exurban Agnes and Tobias, who were suddenly overcome by indefinable fear while sitting quietly at home. They request succor from Agnes and Tobias and are politely allowed to occupy daughter Julia's bedroom until the latter raises such a row when she returns from her latest marital failure that it becomes necessary to tell the guests to leave. This duty devolves upon Tobias, or rather it is forced upon him by his wife. Haltingly he carries this out, being aided by Harry (effectively played by Henderson Forsythe) himself, who admits that he would have turned out Tobias from *his* home if the situation had been reversed. This scene, which is also the resolution of the play, accounts for some fifteen minutes of almost gripping and moderately penetrating drama that sums up much of the anguish of human aloneness. It is an anguish intensified in the case of Tobias, by the desire to respect friendship to the uttermost and the realization that he is at bottom neither capable of it nor really free to give it, even if he had it to give. If we do not want to betray a friendship, we do not really want to carry it very far. If we do, the others to whom we are commited by marital and parental relationships will force us to set narrow bourgeois limits to it. We will then have betrayed the one ideal we evidently cherished and thought we could afford, and the painful irony of it is that we were mistaken on both counts. We did not actually cherish it, of course, but merely took it for granted, in the spirit of easy neighborliness and country-club cordiality which costs us little and certainly causes no serious complications; that is, the relationship remains intact only as long as it costs us little and disturbs us less. Well prepared early in the play, actually *twice* prepared, this resolution of the play is reinforced rather than weakened by the fact that the friends' fears are never defined. Late in the play we sense, if we don't exactly know, that they were overcome by the pointlessness of their vaguely comfortable and socially acceptable lives and with the lovelessness of their middle-aged and middle-class marital status. It suddenly "hit" them both simultaneously, as it *should* have also overwhelmed Agnes and Toby, and would probably have done so if they had been left as alone as Harry and Edna were.

Nevertheless, even this central situation is ultimately frustrating, even on not very close inspection. It is "central" but insecurely so; that is, it has to share both the foreground and the background of the play with other, at best tenuously related, dramatic elements contributed by the daughter, the sister-in-law, and the central couple itself. And by the same token, the resolution of the play in the final confrontation between Tobias and Harry, good as it is as a dramatic scene *per se,* is not a resolution for a play that has so many diverse and incompletely realized elements. On the most obvious level, it resolves nothing about the daughter and the sister-in-law; and it is altogether vacuous as a resolution of the fuzzy failure of Agnes and Tobias as either separate individuals or as a married couple. And this leaves only one "delicate balance" to be accounted for, but on this subject the play does not contribute anything that is not obvious and banal.

I have proceeded in this methodical and humdrum fashion in order to explain as much as I can my uneasy reaction to ***A Delicate Balance.*** And I have played the schoolmaster, the egregiously commonplace schoolmaster, rather than the critic, because I believe that Edward Albee, his loyal associates, and his enthusiastic supporters need patient instruction much more than they need or deserve castigation in this instance. You may call my homiletics a lesson in "how not to write a play" when you are as talented as Edward Albee and could, with patience, write a much better one with virtually the same material and the same point of view.

If I refrain from discussing the staging it is because its defects are integral to the play. The direction is faithful, almost painfully so, to the script, and to the author's faults and defaults. I was not alone in the "second night" audience in finding Jessica Tandy much too high-pitched and irritatingly glittery, which is evidently the dramatic intention, and hard to understand in passages of great volubility. Still, the excess is in the author's lines through which he endeavored to convey a variety of tensions and uneasy pretentions on the part of the character. Presenting these would be tanta-

Hume Cronyn and Jessica Tandy in the premiere production of *A Delicate Balance.*

mount indeed to good characterization if the character of Agnes had any perceptible core rather than a posture, and if it did not try our patience more than it illuminated or, for that matter, defined the individual behind the brittle mask. Moreover, it is a mistake for a principal actress to try to define her role in a long play by irritating the audience, as in Miss Tandy's case, even with a display of energy and virtuosity. Just as it is a mistake for the author to overexpose his own virtuosity in speeches that may be abstrusely bright but have little human context! And, let me add, just as it has been a mistake for the designer of the setting, Mr. William Ritman, to turn out a stage set that is designed to suggest the emptiness of the occupants' lives without considering that an illusionistic setting should not fail to localize the action vividly and suggest a lived-in world for characters who are intended to be more than walking and talking symbols. A negative setting, no matter how metaphorically conceived, is visually vacuum, and it is difficult to find a vacuum interesting. Semi-abstractness in the designing and lighting of the environment, either abetted or condoned by the director, was quite unhelpful to the play, which was rather coreless and abstract to begin with so far as the characters are concerned.

John Simon (essay date 1966-67)

SOURCE: "Theatre Chronicle," in *The Hudson Review,* Vol. XIX, No. 4, Winter, 1966-67, pp. 627-36.

[*The following essay presents a harshly critical assessment of* A Delicate Balance, *judging the play confused, improbable, and dull.*]

Albee is progressing. ***Who's Afraid of Virginia Woolf?*** was about the emptiness that surrounds and threatens to swallow our relationships; ***Tiny Alice*** was about the void lurking behind our deepest beliefs; now, ***A Delicate Balance*** is about the nothingness, the bare nothingness of it all—it is a play about nothing. Nothing will come of nothing was not spoken of the theatre: *there* nothing has been known to yield glittering and even golden returns. *Heartbreak House,* for example, is a play more or less about nothing, and so are most of Beckett's plays. But Shaw fills his nothingness with incisive speculation, so that the mind, though working in a near-vacuum, begets its own thrilling parabolas; Beckett raises nothingness to fierce tragicomic, almost epic, heights. But the nothingness—perhaps more accurately *nothing-ness*—of Albee's play is petty, self-indulgent, stationary. Albee's nothing is as dull as anything.

Tobias and Agnes, a genteel, middle-aged couple, are the pillars of suburbia. They drink, vegetate, and speechify. With them lives Agnes's alcoholic younger sister, Claire, between whom and Tobias there may or may not be some hanky-panky. Claire and Agnes loathe each other, which allows Claire to pour out a steady stream of wisecracks floating out over the stream of liquor flowing down. The daughter of the house, Julia, aged 36, returns as her fourth marriage is breaking up; this phenomenon occurs every three years, and her parents keep her room ready to soothe the post-marital depression. This uneasy ménage could just barely be kept in a delicate balance if it weren't for the neighbors and best friends, Harry and Edna, who, sudden preys to a terrible but nameless fear, arrive unannounced and intending to stay, apparently, forever. They are given Julia's room, which causes that ungay divorcee to have hysterics and almost shoot the intruders. After much soul-searching and several storms in a martini glass, leading up to a frenzied tirade of Tobias's full of instant self-contradiction, Harry and Edna go home, after all, leaving the family quartet to play, in precarious equilibrium, sour-sweet music on one another's heartstrings.

The first thing to strike one about all this is its rank improbability. Why are any of these people here? Why should Agnes tolerate Claire's sniping, and why would Claire want this ungenial hostess, even with free drinks and the rather square host thrown in as an ice cube? Why should Julia rush home to recuperate, when she and her parents do not seem particularly in tune, and she is wealthy and big enough to undertake a hotel? Why should the neighbors wish to move in? Edna was at her knitting, Harry at his recorded French course, when the mysterious terror seized them. But what makes them think that they can move in with their friends indefinitely, or, rather, definitively? And why; when in that vacuous household, amid jangling cocktail glasses and nerves, there is plenty of room for the fear to move right in with them? Finally, the key problem makes no sense: should one put up one's neighbors, in the name of friendship, in perpetuity, or shouldn't one? No halfway sane people would arrive with such a request, and no halfway conceivable people would seriously entertain the notion of so entertaining them. Yet in Albee's play this is presented with a straight face, earnestly, though the idea belongs in absurdist farce, where, however, it would be handled with Ionescoan wit or Pinterish balefulness.

But, presumably, there is a deeper meaning: something, no doubt, like what is a marriage, a family, friendship, and how does one keep these relations going in the face of a world grown meaningless. Now, first of all, I am tired of this mythical "meaningless world" when the playwright fails to create or suggest any outer world (one isolated reference to income taxes might as well have been to Chinese calligraphy), and when he neglects to indicate what meaningfulness might have been before it got mislaid. This posturing play abounds in the cocktail-party profundities and family-reunion soundings that bloated up Eliot's drama, but at least Eliot was, however flatfootedly, after some sort of myth or metaphysic. Albee, too, must drop little hints: one can play with Claire's clairvoyance, with Julia as a latter-day Juliet, with Tobias and Agnes as Tobias and the Angel—but, as Elizabeth Hardwick notes, "a reading of the *Book of Tobit* did not produce any deepening allegory."

That may still leave Albee's language, which, according to a chorus of reviewers, is a marvel and a joy. Now, it is true that Albee is in love with language, which sets him above your average playwright who does not even realize that language exists, but, for all that, Albee's love affair is sadly one-sided. The language of ***Virginia Woolf,*** for example, often lapses into subliteracy: "He is breathing a little heavy; behaving a little manic," "A son who I have raised," "I have never robbed a hot-house without there is a light from heaven," the curious notion that *ibid* means something like "in the same way," which frequently recurs in the stage directions, e.g., "NICK (*very quietly*) . . . GEORGE (*ibid*)" etc. etc. In my review of ***Tiny Alice,*** I quoted a goodly number of similar lapses, and, mind you, always in the speech of supposedly cultivated persons. So again here, as in "You're not as young as either of us were," or in Claire's dogged distinction that she is not "an alcoholic" but "*a* alcoholic," which is supposed to be amusingly portentous, but manages to be merely nonsense, linguistically and otherwise.

But there is a much more profound insensitivity to language at work here, and the more painful since Albee (as he did in ***Tiny Alice***) has one of his characters apologize for his alleged articulateness. But Albee's "articulateness" is either self-conscious poeticism, "When the daylight comes, comes order with it," or long, syntactically overburdened sentences and paragraphs, or putative shockers like, "Your mummy got her pudenda scarred a couple of times before she met daddy," where "pudenda" is rather too recherché for Tobias, and "scarred" much too sadistic: it may be consistent with his character to be sardonic, but not to be beastly. Or, again, consider, "And if we were touching, ah, what a splendid cocoon that was!" How inept to use the weak word "touching" for sexual contact (as it is here used) and to match this up with "cocoon," which does not suggest two beings becoming one, but, on the contrary, one ego narcissistically shutting itself off. Or take this exchange: "You are not young, and you do not live at home.—Where do I live?—In the dark sadness, yes?" Is this supposed to be irony or lyricism? In either case, I say, the dark sadness, no. And even Albee's usually dependable bitchy wit fails him all too often here, as in "AGNES: Why don't you go to Kentucky or Tennessee and visit the distilleries? CLAIRE: Why don't you die?"

What, one wonders, was the real motive behind ***A Delicate Balance***? I, for one, still believe in Albee's perceptiveness and even in his talent (he did, after all, write ***The Zoo Story*** and ***Virginia Woolf***); why would he hurtle into such utter pointlessness? It occurs to me that at least since ***Virginia Woolf,*** Albee's plays and adaptations have been viewed by many as dealing overtly or covertly with homosexual matters; Albee may have resolved here to write a play reeking with heterosexuality. To be sure, the edges are fuzzy. The good friends Harry and Tobias spend a summer sleeping with the same girl, a practice about which psychoanalysis has a thing or two to tell. When an unprepossessing and gauche saleswoman tries to help Claire with a bathing suit and asks her what she could do for her, Claire replies with a nasty smirk fraught with *double entendre,* "Not very much, sweetheart," a piece of repartee appropriate only to an invert. And there is a whole sequence in which Agnes and Tobias figuratively (and sneeringly) reverse sexes and roles in their relationship with Julia. But all this is not at the heart of the play. At the heart of the play things are heterosexual and totally lifeless.

Under the circumstances, it is hard to evaluate the production. It would seem that Rosemary Murphy, as Claire, gives the best performance, but, then, she gets most of the good lines and few of the terrible ones; it would also seem that the others act passably, except for Marian Seldes whose Julia is unconvincing, and Carmen Mathews who makes Edna so smug and odious that no one, I should think, would let her cross his threshold. Alan Schneider's direction may be all that can be done for the play, and William Ritman's set has the proper look of an expensive, well-furnished cavern, to match the general hollowness. Liquors are by Renfield Importers, Ltd., and without them the play might be close to an act shorter.

CRITICAL COMMENTARY

Michael E. Rutenberg (essay date 1969)

SOURCE: *"A Delicate Balance,"* in *Edward Albee: Playwright in Protest,* DBS Publications, Inc., 1969, pp. 137-64.

[*In the essay below, Rutenberg maintains that* A Delicate Balance *is the "culmination" of the "mom and pop relationship," a recurring theme in Albee's work.*]

Notwithstanding the fact that Edward Albee received the Pulitzer Prize for ***A Delicate Balance,*** it still remains, aside from ***Tiny Alice,*** his most underrated play. Premiered on September 12, 1966, at the Martin Beck Theatre, its generally mild reception generated immediate controversy over Albee's continuing talent as a first-rate playwright. Martin Gottfried, reviewing for *Women's Wear Daily,* called the play "two hours of self-indulgence by a self-conscious and self-overrating writer."[1] Robert Brustein, now Dean of the revitalized Yale School of Drama, said the writing was "as far from modern speech as the whistles of a dolphin."[2] Conversely, John Chapman called it "a beautiful play—easily Albee's best and most mature."[3] And Harold Clurman considered it "superior to the more sensational ***Virginia Woolf.***"[4]

While the critics could not agree on the play's merits, they seemed to be in general agreement on its theme, which they stated in various ways as man's responsibility to man. Albee had hinted at the theme before the play's opening (he wasn't going to be misunderstood again) when he revealed that the new work was about "the nature of responsibility, that of family and friends—about responsibility as against selfishness, self-protectiveness, as against Christian responsibility."[5] In their reviews the critics simply paraphrased what Albee had said about the responsibilities of friendship since a major plot episode concerns the protagonists' best friends.

Norman Nadel claimed that the "delicate balance" was between "the right of privacy and the obligations of friendship."[6] *Vogue*'s reviewer echoed the other critics when he remarked that it is "when our friends make demands on us that we fail them."[7] Leonard Probst, reviewing for NBC-TV, said in his one minute critique that "the delicate balance is the balance between responsibility to friends (when they're in trouble) . . . and the conflict with our own reasonable desires."[8] John Gassner, in analyzing the play's structure, concluded that it was most concerned with saying "if we do not want to betray a friendship, we do not really want to carry it very far."[9] With this general agreement on its theme, the critics turned out an onslaught of reasons why the new play was not well written.

Norman Nadel, referring to the neighboring couple who decide out of a private fear to stay on indefinitely, commented that their personal problem split the play into two parts which "do not relate as they should."[10] John Gassner, writing for the *Educational Theatre Journal,* concluded that Albee had brought too many other elements into the play to simply resolve the friendship theme.[11] Perhaps the most outspoken criticism of the play's structure came from the *Village Voice.* Michael Smith wrote that the play's crisis had "not been resolved but uncreated . . . [because] . . . Harry and Edna, quite on their own, simply go away. . . . Balance has been restored not by the called for heroic leap, but by removal . . . this play is a cop-out."[12]

Each critic's evaluation was based on the premise that Albee had not carefully thought out the play's events as it related to the problem of friendship and its ensuing responsibilities. Professor Gassner, concentrating on what he considered Albee's intention, went so far as to say that certain major characters should not have been included in the play—specifically, that the alcoholic sister's appearance seemed somewhat arbitrary and the daughter's sudden homecoming uncalled for.[13] Walter Kerr complained that "there are no events—nothing follows necessarily from what has gone before, no two things fit, no present posture has a tangible past."[14] The critic for *Newsweek* summed up all the adverse criticism when he said there was a division between theme and procedure.[15]

But the play examines more levels of our existence than the need for truer friendship among men. Once properly understood, the play's events are perfectly sequential (though I am not categorically against a plotless play as we shall see in the chapter on ***Box-Mao-Box***), revealing an analysis of the modern scene that goes deeper than the reviews imply. One of the elements not discussed in any of the reviews is a continuation, and I believe culmination, of a major Albee theme.

From the very first Albee drama, through this play, two characters continually make their appearance: that domineering, man-eating, she-ogre of the American family—Mom—and her playmate, that weak-willed, spineless, castrated, avoider of arguments—Dad. Together these two have woven their way through every single play of Albee's with the exception of ***Tiny Alice***—although some critics have made an incorrect case for the existence of this sado-masochistic pair there also. Mom and Pop first showed up obliquely in ***The Zoo Story*** when Jerry began explaining his orphaned status to Peter. They next appeared as characters in both ***The Sandbox*** and ***The American Dream,*** its extention, playing out their roles of emasculator and emasculated, with Mom doing her part with such zest and relish that it made her male audience cringe with empathic pain. Even ***Bessie Smith,*** Albee's supposed civil rights play, got out of hand when his obsession with the battle of the sexes allowed the play's original theme to get away from him. It did, however, plant the seed of Daddy's fight for survival which came to fruition in the highly successful ***Virginia Woolf.*** The play's huge success is directly attributable to both the rich verbal texture and the fact that for the first time Albee gave Mom a formidable antagonist. This time Daddy would fight to the death before acquiescing to Mom's husband-destroying intentions.

Many critics have been quick to insist that Albee was really writing about his own foster parents and not about a typically American condition. A look into the many sociological texts on American life would negate that analysis. One such treatise, examining Dad's position in the American home, bluntly asserts that "in few societies is the role of the father more vestigial than in the United States."[16] This same text vividly points out that the success of such comics as *Blondie* (now seen on television) or its home-screen predecessors, *The Honeymooners* and *The Flintstones,* is that the American public is convinced that the American father is a blunderer and has given up authority, because with him at the head "the family would constantly risk disintegration and disaster."[17] One further example, this time analyzing Mom, should suffice as a preamble to the conflicts set forth in ***A Delicate Balance.*** The following condensed statement on Mom can be found in a standard sociology textbook sold in most college bookstores across the country:

> 'Mom' is the unquestioned authority in matters of mores and morals in her home. . . . She stands for the superior values of tradition, yet she herself does not want to become 'old.' In fact, she is mortally afraid of that status which in the past was the fruit of a rich life, namely, the status of the grandmother. . . . Mom—is not happy: she does not like herself; she is ridden by the anxiety that her life was a waste.[18]

A Delicate Balance is a continuation of the Mom and Pop relationship as they enter the age of retirement. Through a rather bizarre event, Albee has forced the famous couple to re-examine the sum total of their lives with conclusions startlingly similar to the ones reached by the above sociological analysis. Albee wrote this play on boat trips to Europe.[19] The relaxed slow pace of the ship's journey fit the needs of the playwright as he began to write his most introspective play. This particular style, not common to the American stage since it isn't filled with obvious physical action, was alien to many of the critics. Walter Kerr, in particular, reacted traditionally when he claimed that the play was "speculative rather than theatrical, an essay and an exercise when it might have been an experience."[20] In spite of Kerr's criticism, Albee went on to develop the introspective technique further until he completely broke from theatrical narrative in ***Box-Mao-Box.***

Mom and Pop begin ***A Delicate Balance*** in "the living room of a large and well-appointed suburban house." The couple, it will be remembered, started their careers as typically middle-class, later moved on to the university as intellectuals, and have now become well-to-do as they prepare for retirement. Placing Mom and Pop in the privileged class at the end of their lives is quite correct, because it is the symbolic end—the fitting reward for the dedicated American life. The American dream has come true; Mom and Pop have enough money now to isolate themselves from people and avoid any commitment to society. At one point in the play, Mom (Agnes) remarks, "I have reached an age, Tobias, when I wish we were always alone, you and I, without . . . hangers-on . . . or anyone." We find the two, self-isolated at the beginning of the play, as Agnes speaks to her husband, having quietly contemplated the possibility of going mad:

> AGNES: . . . that it is not beyond . . . happening; some gentle loosening of the moorings sending the balloon adrift.

There is a death wish in her thought of insanity. Not verbalized yet, it's subliminally in her very description of madness. A recent movie, *Charlie Bubbles,* commenting on our society today, used the same imagery to suggest the death or suicide of its hero. At the end of the film, Charlie, totally alienated from his society and unable to live alone, performs the ultimate retreat from life as he steps into a balloon and sails out of this world.

Death is not a new concern in Albee's writing. ***The Zoo Story*** states that only at the supreme moment of death is there any human contract. ***The Sandbox*** and ***The American Dream*** are noticeably concerned with the death and removal of grandma from the American home. The title of ***The Death of Bessie Smith*** speaks for itself. ***Virginia Woolf*** builds to the death of the imaginary child which symbolizes the demise of all illusions. Finally, ***Tiny Alice*** examines the death and subsequent martyrdom of a lay brother. This everpresent concern with death is continued in ***A Delicate Balance*** and is instrumental to the deepest meanings of the play.

Agnes is reassured by Tobias (Pop) that "there is no saner woman on earth," but unwilling to reciprocate her husband's support, she replies in her typically emasculating way that she "could never do it—go—adrift—for what would become of you?" Once again, as in all the past plays, Pop is reminded of his ineffectualness and total reliance on Mom. Presumably his life would disintegrate should Mom suddenly expire. Agnes continues her preoccupation with insanity, admitting now that thoughts of old age motivate her:

> AGNES: Yes; Agnes Sit-by-the-fire, her mouth full of ribbons, her mind aloft, adrift, nothing to do with the poor old thing but put her in a bin somewhere, sell the house, move to Tucson, say, and pine in the good sun, and live to be a hundred and four.

Ironically, in an earlier version of Mom, notably ***The Sandbox,*** she put her mother in a bin to die—which grandma promptly did. Agnes now wonders when it will be her turn to inherit the fate of our senior citizens. Tobias, too, is aware of his coming old age for he says a moment later, "I'm not as young as either of us once was." Agnes, still unnerved over her future, asks Tobias to tell her what he'd do if she really did go insane:

> TOBIAS: (*Shrugs*) Put you in a bin somewhere, sell the house and move to Tucson. Pine in the hot sun and live forever.
>
> AGNES: (*Ponders it*) Hmmmm, I bet you would.
>
> TOBIAS: (*Friendly*) Hurry, though.

Tobias is presumably joking, but under the friendly kidding is the same hatred that made George pull out a phony rifle in ***Virginia Woolf*** and shoot Martha. Agnes, somewhat taken aback by Tobias's admission that her senility and eventual death would not disturb him in the least, retaliates by assuring him that the perpetual blandness of her emotions would never lead to the psychological disintegration of insanity. She says, "I can't even raise my voice except in the most calamitous of events." Actually she makes the case for eventual psychosis even stronger by admitting that her personality doesn't allow her to respond normally to most events that circumscribe her life. She begins to consider various chemical ways to induce psychosis, and there is a hint that she would like to try LSD or its narcotic equivalent to induce the excitement needed to bring about a drastic change in her day-to-day boredom. She quickly gives up this idea of chemical madness when she realizes it isn't permanent:

> AGNES: Ah, but those are temporary; even addiction is a repeated temporary . . . stilling. I am concerned with peace . . . not mere relief.

Here, Agnes unconsciously wishes for death, the permanent peace, because it has begun now "to mean freedom from the acquired load and burden of the irrational."[21] Still unable to rid her mind of its chronological inheritance, she resumes describing the dreary picture of their remaining years:

> AGNES: You have hope, of growing even older than you are in the company of your steady wife, your alcoholic sister-in-law and occasional visits . . . from our melancholy Julia. (*A little sad*) That is what you have, my dear Tobias. Will it do?
>
> TOBIAS: (*A little sad, too, but warmth*) It will do.

Ted Hoffman, reviewing for New York radio station WINS, was completely correct when he realized that so much of ***A Delicate Balance*** "deals with the loneliness and corrosion of growing old."[22] This theme, introduced early in the play, propels the play's action and is directly related to its resolution.

This first section of the play ends as Claire, Agnes's alcoholic sister, enters and apologizes for her somewhat inebriated condition. She nevertheless accuses her sister of mistreating her because she is a drunk. Agnes defends herself in a way that Albee's heroine has never done, foreshadowing the change that will take place in her by the time the play ends:

> AGNES: . . . If I scold, it is because I wish I needn"t. If I am sharp, it is because I am neither less nor more than human. . . .

Only in this play does Mom apologize for her unpleasantness. This gnawing self-awareness later becomes a factor in her surprising decision to step down, at the end of the play, and relinquish her long-held role as head of the family. She leaves Claire and Tobias together in order to call her daughter Julia who is far enough away from her mother to effect a time differential of three hours. No sooner has Agnes left the living room than Claire asks Tobias why he doesn't kill Agnes. Tobias replies "Oh, no, I couldn't do that," intimating that he doesn't have the guts for an act of bloody passion.

Albee uses Claire periodically as a quasi-narrator, sardonically commenting on the action. I find this practice unnecessary and her peripheral position alienating and at odds with the otherwise tight entanglement of his characters. One illustration of this annoying practice should be sufficient. When, in the midst of family crises, father, mother, daughter, and audience became deeply involved with the situation at hand, Albee breaks this involvement and, using Claire, gets cute:

> CLAIRE: (*To* TOBIAS, *laughing*) Crisis sure brings out the best in us, don't it, Tobe? The family circle? Julia standing there . . . *asserting;* perpetual brat, and maybe ready

> to pull a Claire. *And* poor Claire! Not much help there either, is there? And lookit Agnes, talky Agnes, ruler of the roost, and Maitre d', *and* licensed wife—silent. All cozy, coffee, thinking of the menu for the week, *planning*. Poor Tobe.

Ostensibly, Claire's monologue is supposed to alienate the audience, in the Brechtian sense, by describing the moment while it's happening. Claire, in giving us information that is not necessary to the plot, serves no purpose other than to hold up the action while the viewer is jolted out of his empathy. Albee has used the aside as far back as ***The Sandbox,*** where Grandma talked to the audience and commented on the action. He used it again to less advantage in ***Everything in the Garden,*** but in these examples the aside was presentational in that the characters talked directly to the audience. It is clear now that Albee's periodic experiments with presentational speeches was a long-time predisposition, which eventually found its form in the later ***Box-Mao-Box.*** However, ***A Delicate Balance*** is structured representationally and periodic comments on the action from the sidelines does not work well in a post-Ibsen play.

Claire does serve another purpose, and it is here that her presence is effective. Claire tells the truth. She sees (clairvoyant) and tells it like it is. Perhaps this is why she drinks. She cannot cope with what she perceives and rather than kill herself or go insane, she drinks. When she isn't commenting sarcastically on the action, her propensity for the truth prods the characters on toward the play's resolution. The first truth emerges when Claire forces Tobias, now retired, to examine the genuineness and durability of his past business friendships.

> CLAIRE: . . . With your business friends, your indistinguishable if not necessarily similar friends . . . what did you have in common with them?
>
> TOBIAS: Well, uh . . . well, everything. (*Maybe slightly on the defensive, but more vague*) Our business; we all mixed well, were friends away from the office, too . . . clubs, our . . . an, an environment, I guess.
>
> CLAIRE: Unh-huh. But what did you have in common with them?

Claire asks the question twice more, but all Tobias can answer is "please, Claire." Claire's insistence serves two purposes: first, it reveals the relative superficiality of most friendships because Tobias cannot think of one thing he has had in common with his friends except proximity. An eminent sociologist came to the same conclusion when he noted that "Americans change both residence and job with the greatest of ease; and with each change of either, friends are changed, too."[23] Second, this brief revelation foreshadows and prepares the audience for the final tragic event concerning Tobias's closest friends.

Claire has made her point and is soon on to a new subject. She asks Tobias why he's switching from anisette to brandy. Tobias replies that the effects of anisette don't last as long. We realize that quiet, well-mannered Tobias looks to escape his surroundings by dulling his mind and memory for as long as possible. It is interesting to note that while Claire is said to be the alcoholic, Tobias drinks as often and as much as she does. Tobias is not off the hook though, because Claire will not let him forget. Reminding him of the time he was unfaithful to Agnes, she builds more evidence to dispel the image of tranquil, thoughtful Tobias, happily spending the final years of his life as the devoted, loving husband.

Claire then lies on the floor, arms outstretched in what Albee calls "a casual invitation." Tobias only moves away; he is not interested. Later we find out that he's not sexually interested in his wife either. Years of constant emasculation have debilitated his sex drive until he is now like George in ***Virginia Woolf***: impotent.

Impotency in Dad is a recurring theme in Albee's plays. We first hear of it in ***The American Dream*** (though Mommy and Daddy have no children in ***The Sandbox***) when Mommy refers to Daddy's impotency as a result of a recent operation. The theme again appears in ***Virginia Woolf*** if we consider the inability of George and Martha to have a child. Impotency suggests loss of manliness as well as depletion of physical strength—both characteristic of the American daddy, according to Albee. It also implies sterility or the inability to produce a new generation. We do not create anything new; we only perpetuate the old. At one point in the play Agnes corroborates this indictment. Talking about her only daughter she admits: "We see ourselves repeated by those we bring into it all. . . ." At another moment Claire makes the same observation when she says: "We can't have changes—throws the balance off."

Claire's remark also clarifies the title of the play, which is meant to mean the delicate balance of the *status quo,* whether it be in reference to an existing relationship within the family, a friendship outside, or the general state of affairs within the country or, for that matter, the world. Each and every relationship hangs in the balance of time, doggedly resistant to change. This difficulty of change within our lives is dramatically depicted as the play progresses, developing into the major theme of its denouement.

Unwilling to recognize Claire's open invitation to have sex with her, Tobias changes the subject, confessing that he can't remember the last time he saw his wife cry, "no matter what," indicating she is as dried up emotionally as he is sexually. Tobias asks Claire why Alcoholics Anonymous never helped her. She replies, in a rather descriptive monologue, that she could not accept a belief in God—the first tenet of the organization. Besides, she doesn't admit to being an alcoholic. Agnes re-enters and stuns Tobias with the news that their daughter, Julia, is coming home after the dissolution of her fourth marriage. Apparently everyone has been aware that the breakup was coming, except Tobias. He offers to talk to his son-in-law in an effort to save the marriage, which seems, from Agnes's reaction, to be a new role for her husband:

> AGNES: (*As if the opposite were expected from her*) I wish you would! If you had talked to Tom, or Charlie, yes! even Charlie, or . . . uh. . . .

CLAIRE: Phil?

AGNES: (*No recognition of* CLAIRE *helping her*) . . . Phil, it might have done some good. If you've decided to assert yourself, finally, too late, I imagine. . . .

This sudden turnabout for Tobias is structurally important because it represents the first manifestation of an inner crisis that will grow during the course of the play, finally forcing Tobias to act contrary to his nature, in a last-ditch attempt to hold together his fast disintegrating ego. Agnes's remark, "too late, I imagine," foreshadows the tragic failure of his attempt.

Claire breaks in and alters the mood temporarily by singing a little ditty about Julia's ex-husbands, which is Albee's way of reintroducing the death theme. This time it is to inform us of the death of four marriages, the stigma of which, Julia carries with her:

CLAIRE: (*A mocking sing-song*)

Philip loved to gamble.
Charlie loved the boys.
Tom went after women,
Douglas. . . .

It seems that Julia has a knack for picking marriage partners who must fail her. Unconsciously she doesn't want these marriages to work because she needs a reason to return home to the protection of her parents and to resume the old parent-child relationship. Whatever happened over the years, we can only know that Julia feels deprived of something in that relationship and keeps coming back to get it. Agnes reinforces Julia's neurosis by taking her back into the house and allowing her to resume the mother-daughter premarital kinship because it gives her the illusion she is still young enough to have an unmarried daughter.

Cued by Julia's homecoming, Tobias obliquely gives us the needed information about Julia's years at home. He does this by confessing to a rather pathetic and apparently unrelated incident in his past. It seems that for many years before his marriage to Agnes, he and a pet cat enjoyed a mutual affection. One day Tobias realized that his pet cat no longer liked him; it would not come to him when called, and retreated whenever he approached. The cat's unexplainable rejection made Tobias all the more anxious to win back his pet's love. Finally, after many overtures, in desperation and utter frustration, he shook the cat violently yelling, "Damn you, you like me; God damn it, you stop this! I haven't *done* anything to you." Frightened at the outburst, the cat bit him, and Tobias, in retaliation, viciously smacked it. Tobias describes the outcome:

TOBIAS: . . . She and I had lived together and been, well, you know, friends, and . . . there was no *reason.* And I hated her, well, I suppose because I was being accused of something, of . . . failing. But I hadn't been cruel by design; if I'd been neglectful well, my life was . . . I resented it. I resented having a . . . being judged. Being betrayed.

CLAIRE: What did you do?

TOBIAS: I had *lived* with her; I had done . . . *everything.* And . . . and if there was a, any responsibility I'd failed in . . . well . . . there was nothing I could do. And, and I was being accused

CLAIRE: Yes; what did you do?

TOBIAS: (*Defiance and self-loathing*) I had her killed.

Almost every critic referred to the "cat story." It is obviously Albee at his best. The critics likened it to the dog monologue in ***The Zoo Story,*** maintaining that the telling of it meant more than the unfortunate experience of one man and an animal. Henry Hewes thought it meant that Albee was trying to puncture the myth that "people who are sufficiently happy together and are enough in love to get married will forever remain in love."[4] Other reviewers thought the account was a lesson on friendship and tied the monologue to what they thought was the major point of the play. This is not at all the case. What Albee wanted, in having Tobias relate the tale, was to have the audience realize Tobias's sense of failure as a father. The thought is so unbearable that he is unable to confess it directly. The narrative implies that like the cat, Julia once loved and related to her father and that despite his attempt to provide a home for his daughter, she inexplicably withdrew from him until they now no longer communicate. The last thing Tobias says before he begins the cat story concerns his failure to relate to her. Filled with anxiety, he reneges on his earlier offer to talk to his daughter about reconsidering the dissolution of her marriage:

TOBIAS: (*Not rising from his chair, talks more or less to himself*) If I saw some point to it, I might—if I saw some reason, chance. If I thought I might . . . break through to her, and say, "Julia . . ." but then what would I say? "Julia . . ." then nothing.

Tobias blames himself for his failing relationship with his daughter and her resulting inability to develop a satisfactory and durable relationship with a man. The results of his ineffectualness are all around him. Guilt ridden because of his failure as husband and father, he privately yearns for change.

Unexpectedly, the scene is interrupted by the arrival of Harry and Edna, their closest friends. At first the call seems nothing more than the routine visit of lifetime friends, but after ignoring a question put to them four times, the family begins to sense that something is terribly wrong. Finally, after a little prodding from Claire, Harry and Edna tell their story:

HARRY: (*Looks at* EDNA) I . . . I don't know quite what happened then; we . . . we were . . . it was all very quiet, and we were all alone. (EDNA *begins to weep, quietly;* AGNES *notices, the others do not,* AGNES *does nothing*) . . . and then . . . nothing happened, but. . .

EDNA: (*Open weeping; loud*) WE GOT FRIGHTENED. (*Open sobbing; no one moves*)

HARRY: (*Quiet wonder, confusion*) We got scared.

EDNA: (*Through her sobbing*) WE WERE . . . FRIGHTENED.

HARRY: There was nothing . . . but we were scared.

AGNES: (*Comforts* EDNA, *who is in free sobbing anguish,* CLAIRE *lies slowly back on the floor*)

EDNA: We . . . were . . . terrified.

HARRY: We were scared. (*Silence;* AGNES *comforting* EDNA. HARRY *stock still. Quite innocent, almost childlike*) It was like being lost; very young again, with the dark, and lost. There was no . . . thing . . . to be . . . frightened of, but . . .

EDNA: (*Tears, quiet hysteria*) WE WERE FRIGHTENED . . . AND THERE WAS NOTHING. (*Silence in the room*)

Harry and Edna then ask if they may lie down in one of the bedrooms because they are too fearful to return home. Agnes admits them to Julia's room as Claire, in her clairvoyant role, predicts that something ominous is about to happen. Not until the next day, after Julia has come home, do Harry and Edna reveal just what it is they are up to. They have decided (without consulting Agnes or Tobias but in the name of friendship) to move into the house and live in Julia's bedroom; the thought of living alone another day is too terrifying for them. Julia hysterically screams that they have no right and demands that they leave. Harry and Edna refuse, and Julia looks to her parents to throw them out.

Much has been written about Harry and Edna and much has been suggested. In fact most of the adverse criticism has centered around who and what these people represent. Perhaps the most misguided interpretation of the intruders was that they are a questionable plot device to initiate conflict between Mom, Dad, and their daughter. The reviewer felt that the play concerned "the difficulty rich, emotionally immobilized parents faced with a daughter who at 36 is still an adolescent."[25] It is, of course, true that Agnes and Tobias are affluent and emotionally alien to the events in their lives, and that Julia is immature, but this situation is only a result and not the core of a much larger issue still to be resolved.

While most critics did not try to explain what it was the couple feared or why this fear had come about—even though the death imagery is quite clear in Harry's description of being "very young again, with the dark, and lost"—they did complain that the fear was not transferred to the audience. Walter Kerr, in an article printed after his review of the play, explained that Albee only talked about fear; he never showed it. He then went on to cite Harold Pinter as an example of a playwright who can frighten his audience without using the word fear.[26] Kerr, however, has missed the point concerning the frightened couple. It was not Albee's intention to put his audience into moral trepidation. All he wanted to do by introducing Harry and Edna was to exhibit two people traumatized by the sudden realization that death was not only a certainty, but close by. Psychologists would agree that fear of being lost in the dark is a symbolic death fear and that this "belief in one's death is an acquired and usually a late belief."[27] With the realization that most of their life is over (Edna specifically mentions it), it is natural that their thoughts should turn to wondering how much time there is left and whether they have wasted what time has already been given them. Relating the story of their sudden and inexplicable fright leads Harry to sum up his life with Edna:

HARRY: (*Subdued, almost apologetic*) Edna and I . . . there's so . . . much . . . over the dam, so many . . . disappointments, evasions, I guess, lies maybe . . . so much we remember we wanted, once . . . so little that we've settled for . . . we talk, sometimes, but mostly . . . no . . .

Harry looks into his memory and finds little, almost nothing, to comfort them in their mature years, underscoring the fact that both continually mention that "nothing" was there when they became frightened. Clurman described Harry and Edna's state very well when he wrote that there is "no past to sustain them or future to which they aspire. . . . It is as if they were survivors of some devastation of the moral order. . . . They hardly know to what universe or society they belong, the old having been so decimated that their memory apart from ache and disgust has become fragmentary, leaving them without sufficient energy to reconstruct anything new."[28] Clurman's vivid description points up rather clearly how completely alienated Harry and Edna are. They have no past, no forseeable future, and almost nothing in their present to hang on to except friendship with Agnes and Tobias. It is precisely this sense of "nothingness" that terrifies them. Erich Fromm recently wrote that "the alienated person . . . is lacking in a sense of self. This lack of self creates deep anxiety. The anxiety engendered by confronting him with the abyss of *nothingness,* [italics mine] is more terrifying than even the tortures of hell."[29] Fromm also mentions the way friendship are created in this country: "It is only another aspect of the alienated kind of interpersonal relationship that friendships are not formed on the basis of individual liking or attraction, but that they are determined by the location of one's own house or apartment in relation to the others."[30]

Harry and Edna, in the throes of personal anguish, try in the only way they know to refute their sense of nothingness, of alienation. They demand that Tobias and Agnes become more than superficial in their friendship to them. They try, in their demand for sanctuary, to refute the neutralness of the relationship by forcing it to take on more meaning than it has. Fromm again underscores Harry and Edna's feelings when he writes "there is not much love or hate to be found in human relationships of our day. There is, rather, a superficial friendliness and a more than superficial fairness, but behind that surface is distance and indifference."[31]

Albee's concern with modern man's sense of isolation and abandonment led him first to examine the possible truth of the Nietzschean "God is Dead" theory in ***Tiny Alice.*** Now, in ***A Delicate Balance*** he has dropped the metaphysical probings and returned to a more sociological explanation, which seems to assert that it is the death of friendship that produces these feelings of alienation. Evidence of this theme grows as it becomes clear that the weekend's episode has wrecked what superficial relationship the two couples had:

> EDNA: I'm going into town on Thursday, Agnes. Would you like to come? (*A longer pause than necessary,* CLAIRE *and* JULIA *look at* AGNES
>
> AGNES: (*Just a trifle awkward*) Well . . . no, I don't think so, Edna; I've . . . I've so much to do.
>
> EDNA: (*Cooler; sad*) Oh. Well . . . perhaps another week.
>
> AGNES: Oh, yes; we'll do it.

Edna tries pitifully to hold on to the severed friendship, but it's dead. The image of death, which has permeated this play from its first act until its conclusion, is reflected again in the final destruction of the forty-year friendship.

Perhaps the most devastating criticism of Harry and Edna concerned the diffusion of focus the interlopers caused. Evidently the strangeness of the couple's undisclosed fear and their apparent vulnerability to it, plus the outright daring of their demand to the right to disrupt another's privacy in the name of friendship, created a most impelling effect on the critics. Many felt that instead of remaining peripheral characters designed to upset the delicate balance of "the family armed truce,"[32] they took hold and pushed the protagonists right out of focus. Harry and Edna suddenly became the characters to write about, and the critics began tactfully suggesting that Albee rewrite his play because "those two people who are afraid of their own house are worth a play."[33] Norman Nadel was the most articulate in his analysis of the intruders:

> And this becomes the element of the play we want to know most about. We all have known the nameless fears, the terrors without shape or identity, that unexpectedly invade our lives. Yet only obliquely does Albee return to that theme. Fear is never even the tangible presence in the play that it should be. . . . The drama's insights impinge on this element of fear, without ever quite penetrating it. . . . And therein lies its weakness.[34]

Nadel's analysis presupposes that Albee was most concerned with writing a play that explored the nature of fear. If this were the case, there would be justification to his critique. Albee, however, uses fear as a by-product of other issues. As we have seen, he is most concerned with the ramifications of growing old in an alienated world. Agnes and Tobias should easily keep the audience's interest because their friends' demands have created enough of a turmoil within the household to jolt these two out of their emotional cocoons. The family crisis that takes place should be compelling enough to keep even Harry and Edna in their place as catalysts.

Tobias believes Harry and Edna are right when they say he must allow them to remain or admit that a forty-year friendship is meaningless and symbolic of his entire life. Yet Tobias is not used to making decisions; he has always deferred to Agnes. But this time Agnes will not accommodate him. Why she suddenly abandons her role as "ruler of the roost" is not at first clear. Perhaps she has finally seen a glimpse, a reflection, of her aliented life with Tobias as she watches her friends attempting to fill the "nothingness" in their lives. Edna does say to her, "Our lives are . . . the same." As she realizes that her marriage is much the same as her friends, it is conceivable that she will try to change it by forcing Tobias to assume a role he long ago abdicated. If she can get him to commit himself to accepting his traditional place as head of the household, this reaffirmation of the historical role might alter the present course of their lives and close the chasm that has isolated one from the other. She attempts the change:

> AGNES: (*Quiet, calm and almost smug*) We follow. We let our . . . men decide the moral issues.
>
> TOBIAS: (*Quite angry*) Never! You've never done that in your life!
>
> AGNES: Always, my darling. Whatever you decide . . . I'll make it work; I'll run it for you so you'll never know there's been a change in anything.

Tobias does not feel that it's necessary for him to make the decision. He tries again to resume the old relationship, maintaining it is Agnes's place to admit Harry and Edna. He asks her again to make the choice:

> TOBIAS: (*Quiet, rhetorical*) What are we going to do?
>
> AGNES: What did you decide?
>
> TOBIAS: (*Pause; they smile*) Nothing.
>
> AGNES: Well, you must. Your house is not in order, sir. It's full to bursting.
>
> TOBIAS: Yes. You've got to help me.
>
> AGNES: No. I don't *think* so.

Tobias is upset now; he wants an explanation for his wife's contrary behavior. Agnes tries to explain. In the ensuing dialogue her reasons for stepping down become clearer. We find out that she is convinced the marriage is a failure. Apparently she spent the night reviewing her life, for she approaches the subject by first telling Tobias that what she has to tell him stems from having "revisited our life, the years and years."

This is an important moment for Agnes and Tobias. In the early plays Mom was perfectly content to be king of the mountain. As a matter of fact she wouldn't have it any other way. She did all she could to insure her continued domination of the household—even if it meant the destruction of Dad's identity. In ***Virginia Woolf,*** Mom is still content to let everybody who'll listen know that Daddy is a "bog" incapable of accomplishing anything worthwhile. Only at the end does she submit to him at all, but we wonder if it occurs simply out of sheer exhaustion. This is an historic moment for Mom, because only in ***A Delicate Balance*** does she actively attempt to return the family unit to what it originally was—and only after a total re-examination of her history with Dad. It has taken Albee seven plays and two adaptations to allow Mom to come to the conclusion that her life with Dad is empty. Unfortunately, as we shall see, the decision to change has come too late for Mom. For the moment though, Agnes is unaware that her historic change of heart will be in vain. She again attempts the reversal of roles by a recapitulation of their lives, starting first with remembrances of Julia:

> AGNES: Each time that Julia comes, each clockwork time . . . do you send her back? Do you tell her, "Julia, go home to your husband, try again?" Do you? No, you let it . . . slip. It's your decision, sir.
>
> TOBIAS: It is not! I . . .
>
> AGNES: . . . and I must live with it, resign myself one marriage more, and wait, and hope that Julia's motherhood will come . . . one day, one marriage (*Tiny laugh*) I am almost too old to be a grandmother as I'd hoped . . . too young to be one. Oh, I had wanted that: the *youngest* older woman in the block, *Julia* is almost too old to have a child properly, *will* be if she ever does . . . if she marries again. *You* could have pushed her back . . . if you'd wanted to.

It is here that Agnes tries to show Tobias that the emptiness of their lives is symbolized in the discontinuance of the family line. She tries to explain that Tobias never wanted to see himself perpetuated in his grandchildren—that he is the one who all these years has chosen isolation and sterility as the symbols of their life together. Tobias's refusal to accept the blame forces Agnes to turn to a more brutal example of his wish to kill any chances of living on through a son. The death motif that hovers over this play emerges once again:

> AGNES: (*Remorseless*) When Teddy died? (*Pause*) We *could* have had another son; we could have tried. But . . . No . . . those months—or was it a year—?
>
> TOBIAS: No more of this!
>
> AGNES: . . . I think it was a year, when you spilled on my belly, sir? "Please? Please, Tobias?" No, you wouldn't even say it out: I don't want another child, another loss. "Please; Please, Tobias?" And guiding you, *trying* to hold you in?
>
> TOBIAS: (*Tortured*) Oh, Agnes! Please!
>
> AGNES: Don't leave me then, like that. Not again, Tobias. Please? I can take care of it; we *won't* have another child, but please don't . . . leave me like that. . . . Such . . . silent . . . sad, disgusted . . . love.

It is clear now that it was Tobias who first removed himself from the intimacies of marriage. Tobias may have felt he could not bring himself to risk another loss, but it may be more realistic to assume that his self-evaluation would not allow his seed to be continued into the next generation. Tobias on his own accord withdrew from the responsibilities of a father and husband, content to let Agnes take his place. Agnes pleads for him to return to her as she plays out her part in the evolution of the American family unit. One glimpse at a standard source book in sociology corroborates her predicament:

> American mothers stepped into the role of the grandfathers [sic] as the fathers abdicated their dominant place in the family, in the field of education, and in cultural life. The post-revolutionary descendants of the Founding Fathers forced their women to be mothers *and* fathers, while they continued to cultivate the role of freeborn sons.[35]

Unquestionably, it is the first time in an Albee play that the blame for whatever mess the American family is in, is placed with the father. Mom is not the usurper she was in the early plays; she has simply responded all these years out of a sense of duty, filling a position that has been vacated. Agnes even says to her husband, when she tries to define the woman's job in the home, that she "assumes whatever duties are demanded—if she is in love, or loves; and plans." And since she has always thought of herself as the "fulcrum" within the family, she will continuously adjust to wherever the new balance places her. Agnes continues her exposition, linking their present alienation to past sexual problems, implying that the isolation that now exists need not have occurred had he sought her help or at least confided in her:

> TOBIAS: (*Numb*) I didn't want you to have to . . . you know.
>
> AGNES: (*Laughs in spite of herself*) Oh, that was thoughtful of you! Like a pair of adolescents in a rented room, or in the family car. Doubtless you hated it as much as I.
>
> TOBIAS: Yes.
>
> AGNES: But wouldn't let me help you.
>
> TOBIAS: No.
>
> AGNES: Which is why you took to your own sweet room instead.
>
> TOBIAS: Yes.

It is interesting that while Agnes confesses to having "hated" sexual intercourse as much as he did, she earlier admitted to missing him when he left her bed: "I shall start missing you again—when you move from my room . . . if you do," she says. (They are temporarily together again because Tobias has given Julia his room while Harry and Edna remain in the house.) This seeming paradox is perhaps more widespread among "happily" married couples than might be expected. An internist, practicing in well-to-do suburbia, recently told me that the majority of his women patients, and to a lesser degree the men, ask him to write notes to their spouses requesting that for medical reasons they cease having intercourse. The reason given is that they are too tired to"accommodate" their mates. What doubly amazed me was that my friend felt this request was not symptomatic of any serious neurosis, but an understandable, rather normal request, not at all indicating these couples no longer love each other.

Agnes's talk of having been aware all these years of the mutual revulsion each felt about the sex act shames Tobias into asking just what she will do now that the truth is out. Determined, however, to abandon her place as dominator, she replies "Whatever you like, naturally."

Claire and Julia interrupt the colloquy but the topic continues. It is up to Tobias to make the final decision concerning Harry and Edna. Julia flatly states that she will leave the house permanently unless the invading couple are put out. Tobias, frustrated and in a rage, screams at his daughter that "HARRY AND EDNA ARE OUR FRIENDS." Julia, undaunted, equals him with "THEY ARE INTRUDERS." Tobias, very upset but still unable to commit himself to standing by his friends without his family's support, tries to make them realize that friendship based on any condition is empty. Agnes responds, warning him that Harry and Edna have brought with them a disease. The disease is terror and if Tobias allows them to stay, the family is in danger of infection. Nevertheless, it must be his decision alone. Finally seeing that Agnes will no longer fight his battles, Tobias summons his courage, and in the most stirring moment of his life, he jars himself loose of old and ingrained ways by telling Harry and Edna they may reside in his home for as long as they wish whether his family likes it or not.

It is too late, however. The tumult within the family, the momentous decision, were all for naught. Harry and Edna have changed their minds. They realize now it is impossible to alter forty years of pleasant indifference by force. Harry feebly tries to apologize for his and Edna's presumption:

> HARRY: . . . you're our best friends, but . . . I told Edna upstairs, I said Edna, what if they'd come to us? And she didn't say anything. And I said; Edna, if they'd come to us like this, and even though we don't have . . . Julia, and all that, I . . . Edna I wouldn't take them in. (*Brief silence*) I wouldn't take them in, Edna; they don't . . . have any right. And she said; yes, I know; they wouldn't have the right.

Tobias cannot accept Harry's realistic appraisal of their friendship and the vacuity it symbolizes; he is determined to take the interlopers in, in order to negate what both Harry and Agnes have intimated in their separate evaluations. In a three-page, orchestrated monologue, Tobias spills his guts out to Harry, first ordering him to stay, then begging him through tears of futility as he slowly realizes it is too late for any of them. A moment later Edna bleakly sums it all up:

> EDNA: (*Pause. Slight smile*) It's sad to come to the end of it, isn't it, nearly the end; so much more of it gone by . . . than left, and still not know—still not have learned . . . the boundaries what we may not do . . . not ask, for fear of looking in a mirror. We *shouldn't* have come.
>
> AGNES: (*A bit by rote*) Now, Edna . . .
>
> EDNA: For our own sake; our own . . . lack. It's sad to know you've gone through it all, or most of it, without . . . that the one body you've wrapped your arms around . . . the only skin you've ever known . . . is your own—and that it's dry . . . and not warm.

Harry and Edna, like George and Martha, are childless and isolated. Whereas George and Martha had to create an imaginary child to appease their loneliness and in the end had to kill it and the illusion it carried, Harry and Edna, in their attempt to bring solace to the same feeling of alienation, create an imaginary depth in a life-long friendship that doesn't exist. At the end, as in ***Virginia Woolf,*** the illusion must be destroyed.

In talking about ***A Delicate Balance,*** Albee has said that it "is about the fact that as time keeps happening options grow less. Freedom of choice vanishes. One is left with an illusion of choice."[36] The experience has been as crushing for Tobias and Agnes. They too must live the remaining years without illusion. But their reality is somewhat different from learning that their closest friendship was at best superficial; what they learn is that there comes a time in every life when hope of change no longer exists. What they have made of their lives must now stand because it is too late for undoing. Tobias cannot change his skin. Even his impassioned plea to Harry is an indication not of strength but continued weakness because of its uncontrollable hysterics. Tobias a long time ago chose passivity; he must now accept its outcome.

It is interesting to read Harold Clurman's analysis of Tobias, based on his belief that the play had only to do with that "insuperable difficulty of loving one's neighbor."[37] He feels that the character of Tobias should have been played not as a little man but rather as an "outwardly imposing figure, a very 'senator' of a man, a pillar of our business community in whom the springs of sensibility have begun to dry through disuse. The welling up of his being in the play's crisis would then become more stirring and, what is more important, exemplary."[38] What Clurman has neglected to see, however, is that Tobias does not succeed in his attempt at rescuing his life from the quicksand of indifference. What is exemplary is not his sudden feelings of remorse for a life of aloofness, but his realization that despite his willingness to change, the patterns of his past are forever stamped in the anguished memories of a wasted life and in the knowledge that choice ceases to exist as we approach the termination of our lives. Tobias was, and must remain always, small. This theme is summed up rather movingly by Agnes at the end of the play:

> AGNES: Time. (*Pause. They look at her*) Time happens, I suppose. (*Pause. They still look*) To people. Everything becomes . . . too late, finally. You know it's going on . . . up on the hill; you can see the dust, and hear the cries, and the steel . . . but you wait; and time happens. When you *do* go, sword, shield . . . finally . . . there's nothing there . . . save rust; bones; and the wind.

Despite the mixed reception ***A Delicate Balance*** received from the critics, on May 1, 1967, Albee was given the Pulitzer Prize. The next day he officially accepted the award, but remembering the controversy over the Pulitzer Advisory

Board's decisions to overrule John Gassner and John Mason Brown when they proposed that Albee be given the prize for ***Virginia Woolf,*** he warned that it "is in danger of losing its position of honor and could foreseeably, cease to be an honor at all."[39] The following day, speaking at a news conference, he reiterated his feelings, listing exactly why he accepted the award:

> I have decided to accept the award for three reasons: First, because if I were to refuse it out of hand, I wouldn't feel as free to criticize it as I do accepting it. Second, because I don't wish to embarrass the other recipients this year by seeming to suggest that they follow my lead. And finally, because while the Pulitzer Prize is an honor in decline, it is still an honor, a considerable one.[40]

Originally underrated by the majority of New York critics, yet heralded by the Pulitzer Committee as the best play of the year, ***A Delicate Balance*** has shown Edward Albee at his most sympathetic, his most gentle. There is more delicateness and maturity in this play than any of his other works, and it will prevail "not only [as] a brilliant and searching play but [as] a strangely beautiful one."[41]

Notes

[1]*Women's Wear Daily,* Sept. 23, 1966.

[2]*New Republic,* Oct. 8, 1966.

[3]*Daily News,* Sept. 23, 1966.

[4]*Nation,* Oct. 10, 1966.

[5]*New York Times,* Aug. 16, 1966.

[6]*Herald Tribune* (Paris) Sept. 23, 1966.

[7]*Vogue,* Nov. 1, 1966.

[8]NBC-TV News, 11:15 PM, Sept. 22, 1966.

[9]John Gassner, "Broadway in Review," *ETJ* (Dec., 1966) pp. 450-452.

[10]*Herald Tribune,* loc. cit.

[11]Gassner, *ETJ,* loc. cit.

[12]*Village Voice,* Sept. 29, 1966.

[13]Gassner, *ETJ,* loc. cit.

[14]*New York Times,* Oct. 2, 1966.

[15]*Newsweek,* Oct. 3, 1966.

[16]Geoffrey Gorer, *The American People: A Study in National Character* (New York: W. W. Norton & Co., Inc., 1964), p. 54.

[17]Ibid., p. 49.

[18]Erik H. Erikson, *Childhood and Society* (New York: W. W. Norton & Co., Inc., 1963), pp. 290-291.

[19]*New York Times,* Aug. 16, 1966.

[20]*New York Times,* Oct. 2, 1966.

[21]William Ernest Hocking, "Thoughts on Death and Life," in *Inquiry and Expression* ed. by Harold C. Martin and Richard M. Ohmann (New York: Holt, Rinehart and Winston, Inc., 1963), p. 582.

[22]WINS Radio, Aug. 23, 1966.

[23]Gorer, p. 131.

[24]*Saturday Review,* Oct. 8, 1966.

[25]*Toronto Daily Star,* Sept. 24, 1966.

[26]*New York Times,* Sept. 23, 1966.

[27]Hocking, p. 580.

[28]Harold Clurman, "Introduction," *The Playwrights Speak,* ed. Walter Wager (New York: Delacorte Press, 1967), pp. xx-xxi.

[29]Erich Fromm, *The Sane Society* (New York: Holt, Rinehart and Winston, Inc., 1962), p. 204.

[30]Ibid., p. 160.

[31]Ibid., p. 139.

[32]*New York Post,* Sept. 23, 1966.

[33]*Commonweal,* Oct. 14, 1966.

[34]*World Journal Tribune,* Oct. 2, 1966.

[35]Erikson, p. 295.

[36]*Newsweek,* May 29, 1966.

[37]*Nation,* loc. cit.

[38]Ibid.

[39]*New York Times,* May 2, 1967.

[40]*New York Times,* May 3, 1967.

[41]*New York Post,* Oct. 8, 1966.

John J. von Szeliski (essay date 1970)

SOURCE: "Albee: A Rare *Balance,*" in *Twentieth Century Literature: A Scholarly and Critical Journal,* Vol. 16, No. 2, April, 1970, pp. 123-30.

[*In this essay, the critic praises* A Delicate Balance *as "a brilliant and highly significant play." Von Szeliski goes on to call it "the best expression of the peculiar loneliness of our time which we have had in years."*]

It is several years now since the last substantial Edward Albee controversy—that is, the one centering on ***A Delicate Balance.*** This needs follow-up, I think, and it is time we had a wider perspective on what that play means in our theatre because it does deserve more attention on stage and in the journals. The subsequent annual offering, ***Everything in the Garden***—while more vital than Albee's previous ventures with adaptations—was not based on his own original material and thus is relatively less important as a sample of the playwright-thinker's true stature. And the next work, ***Box*** and ***Quotations from Chairman Mao Tse Tung,*** matches palely against the "new" Albee of the 1966 play. But the chief motive for new discussion is just that ***A Delicate Balance*** is Albee's best play—and that it ranks as a truly major drama. In this essay, I want to defend that ranking, and discuss the style and content of the play's meanings—which are the keys to its greatness.

The newspaper and periodical reviewers, it will be remembered, were quite widely split as to the merit of ***A Delicate Balance.*** As John Gassner pointed out in his own critique:

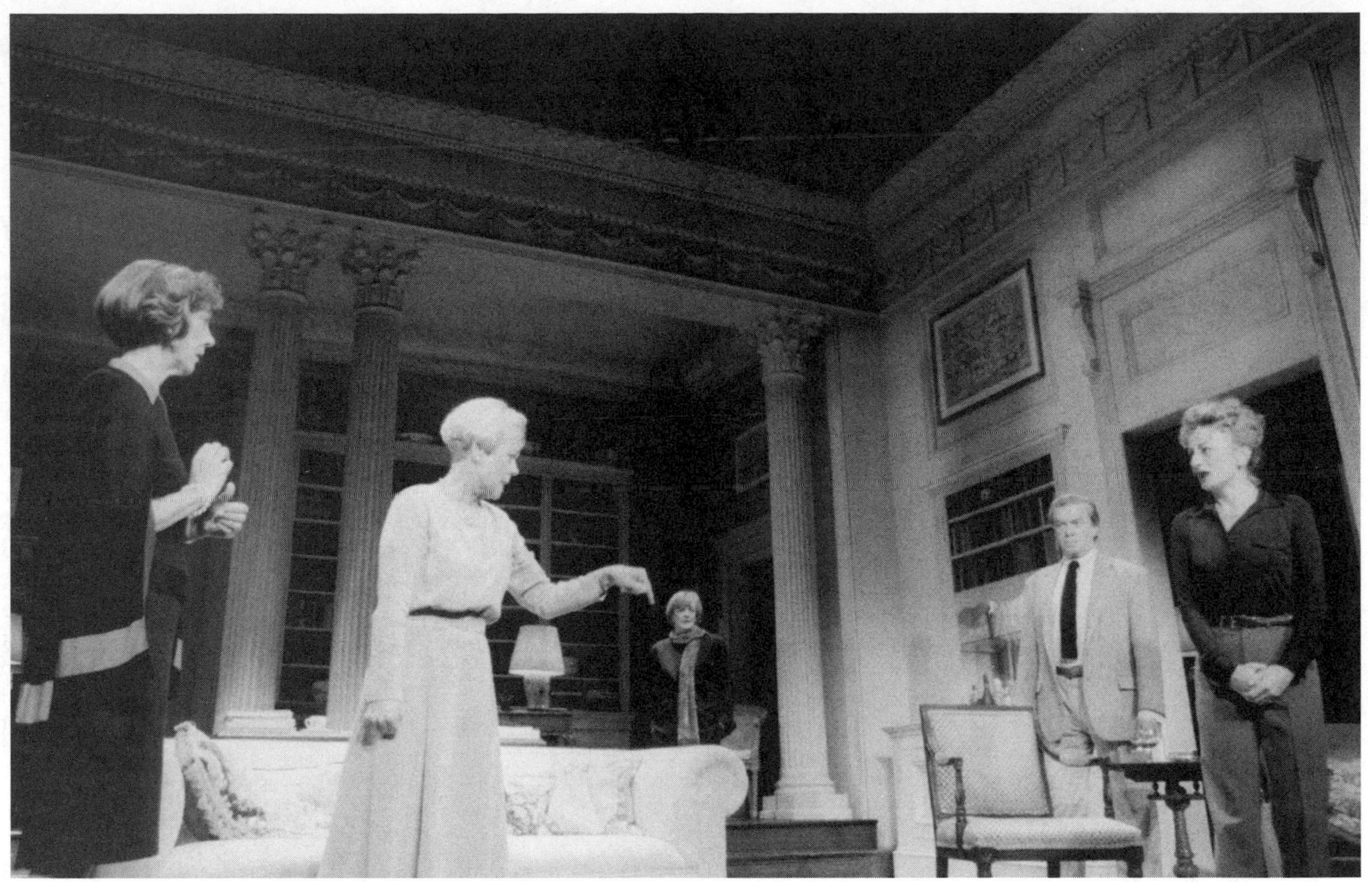

Eileen Atkins (Agnes), Annette Crosbie (Edna), Maggie Smith (Claire), James Laurenson (Harry), and Sian Thomas (Julia) in a production of *A Delicate Balance* at London's Theatre Royal, Haymarket, in 1997.

> Reviewers as far apart on basic matters as Walter Kerr . . . and Robert Brustein . . . brought in a distinctly negative verdict, while the enthusiasts included such strange bedfellows as Richard Watts . . . and Harold Clurman.[1]

Some of the negative response may have been conditioned by Albee's earlier failures or the irritating affectations of ***Malcolm, Tiny Alice,*** and other sub-par scripts. Brustein's review in *The New Republic* was without question the least responsible evaluation. He simply dismissed ***A Delicate Balance*** as "a very bad play" on the basis of totally personal prejudices and animosities and the alarmingly insensitive notion that it was "too far removed from human experience." The truth, of course, is that ***A Delicate Balance*** is painfully close to human experience in theme and comment—far more than in any of Brustein's indulgent paragons of "Third Theatre." Most of the other attacks on the play were similarly personal and resisted judging it on its own terms, the terms of the special world it tries to create. The flippancy of Wilfrid Sheed's review in *The Commonweal* also reflected the kind of suspicious bristling that stems from personal impatience with the seeming pretensions of Albee's situations and insights: making fun of the Harry and Edna subplot, for example, on the basis of its not being "believable." Again, conventional "belief" is hardly the point. The play, perhaps because it employs a difficult and unusual illusion, seems to invite these flawed criteria; the important observation, however, is that the reviewers' objections to the play were unusually unconvincing because they were not based on a more reasoned and objective analysis of how the play fails its intent, or how the intent is unsatisfactory. Significantly, the favorable verdicts were based on *the play,* not on an irrelevant personal attack on the playwright. Like ***Who's Afraid of Virginia Woolf?,*** the play's main strength is that it is the truth: perceptive, accurate, *real.* Unlike ***Who's Afraid,*** however, it is not dependent on theatricality and ups and downs of sensational excitement—and thus is willing to linger longer over naked thought which depends almost entirely on dialogue. This risk-taking is a major mark of the play's maturity. The promise in the dialogue of ***Tiny Alice*** is fulfilled in ***A Delicate Balance,*** and it represents one of the incredibly few major advances in the use of language in the contemporary theatre. The literate sounds really say something—a truly major contribution in such a theatrical era as we are now experiencing.

In suggesting weaknesses in the negative reviews and stating that ***A Delicate Balance*** is such a major triumph, I do not say that everyone can, or must, agree to such ranking. It is not a play about fully universal people or a very universal problem: it is not a play for *all* men. It is not a clear-cut winner, with a stature as easily and widely recognized as that of our consensus American classics—*Death of a Salesman* and *A Streetcar Named Desire.* It is not without problems for the spectator. For a while, at least, it can come across like some Priestley-esque didactic play (anyone remember *The Dragon's Mouth?*)—where people come and go in an arbitrarily forced French-scene system so that each character can conveniently expound his life credo, the credos then intermixing in the permutations and combinations afforded by the number of other principal mouthpieces. The strengths of the play, however, fully overshadow the relatively weak moments. One's reward for watching, listening, and entering-in includes several enormous insights into the unfortunate life-style of our age.

To support this, I want to discuss some specific characteristics and values of ***A Delicate Balance***—primarily in the areas of its level of illusion, style, characterization, theme, and meaning.

* * *

On what level are we meant to perceive the play? In many discussions of ***A Delicate Balance,*** this seems a major difficulty. Possibly those disliking the play do so because they do not pass beyond this point—perhaps through no fault of their own. A common problem seems to be inability to "believe" in the characters and what they do and want. At least two reviewers[2] mentioned the play's "surreal" quality, and yet spent all their critical verbiage on the problem of ordinary disbelief. The illusion *is* deceptive, and invites some latitude as to the levels of our belief. We might call it moderate surrealism, a hint of impressionism, perhaps a very dark comedy of manners. One thing we ought to be fairly absolutist about, however: it is wrong to relate to the play as absurdism, no matter how brief the given moment. Even semi-absurdism, by definition, posits a presentationalist rapport. Instead, ***A Delicate Balance*** is essentially a realistic play (even admitting overtones of surrealism, impressionism, or manners). Thus it is also representationalist—but with a difference.

Realism would have us get involved with the domestic frictions between Tobias and Agnes, the crisis of Tobias' "responsibility" for Harry and Edna, Claire's social dislocation, Julia's alienation, and the like—the whole thematic bag of specific suburbanites and "the truth" about fragmented, Identity-Crisis Living Today. ***A Delicate Balance*** does have the earmarks of the conventional realistic play: the detailed box set, the drawing-room schema conversations, rather conscious French-scene construction, and so forth. We *are* supposed to believe what these characters are saying and get involved with them essentially as real human beings; there are no stylistic clues to the contrary. But in the choice of pivotal action, and the selection and treatment of the dialogue, there are signs that the play is supra-real. It is the poetized reality of man *in extremis.* Tobias comes home with his newspaper under his arm like any other suburban executive, but we don't really know anything about his job, or how he earns enough to maintain this nice home, the unseen servants, and a position at "the club." Do we need to know? The fantastic precision and selection of language, though not absolutely impossible in reality, are also supra-real, as is the occasion of such speech (in the home Agnes makes, it is apparently customary to have unlimited time for talk hour after hour and day after day). Simple realism would tell us more about Harry and Edna, for instance, in order to avoid their excessive and risky mystery. Instead, there is discomfort—even laughter and embarrassment—with Harry's and Edna's arrival and the bald announcements:

> EDNA: WE GOT . . . FRIGHTENED. . . .
>
> EDNA: Can I go to bed now? Please?[3]

This is as it should be: no real details, no specific explanations, no logic. Again some reviewers and lobby critics found this hard to "accept"—or else insufficiently developed by Harry and Edna. Is such a moment, are such people, real? I think such questions largely irrelevant. This is not the psychologically motivated realism of a Stanley Kowalski or Willy Loman. Yes, Harry and Edna are more than usually manipulated by their playwright; but the unique image and dilemma they present makes for a brilliantly right pivotal action—makes the situation and forces the ideas of the play—whereas anything less or more "explicable" would not be right. Obviously this is a selected moment, but it is more than real, more than selective realism. Actually, what is *unreal* about the people and the action? There is nothing to put one's finger on except the sheer novelty of this outer limit social act; when pushed to a certain extreme, Harry and Edna *do* the thing that is really on their minds. This is the great catalytic metaphor of the whole play. Why *not* go to your friends and actually ask to be loved? Why *not* go to that "island off Paraguay," as Claire wistfully wishes? In your city-bred loneliness, at your next cocktail party, why *not* don a sandwich-board reading "LOVE ME, TALK TO ME? Why *not,* ultimately, say out loud what you have really thought many times all along: that we are all dying, that we don't know what to do about it, but that we vaguely sense we must come closer to each other to light the darkness of such a knowledge? I call this "supra-real" in more than the artistic sense: it is thus because what should be a perfectly human act—a real act—all too frustratingly cannot happen quite this way in our own reality.

Now let us look at the illusion level in another way—as suggested by Albee's characterization.

* * *

Characterization is another major indicator of the intended illusion, and here again we find something special and more than real. Harry and Tobias and the others are never *specific* and *whole* people like Willy Loman or Jimmy Porter. In a way, the characters of ***A Delicate Balance*** are monsters: they are extremes of their class (the upper-middles," what used to be the "power" class of our world)—over-educated, over-verbal, unmaliciously but helplessly selfish, guilty of too great an imbalance between thought and action. We can be quite sympathetic with their problems and how they evolved but, as with most of us middles and upper-middles, the fact remains that they *are* selfish in their protectiveness and hibernation in their separate worlds. Their sadness would not occur in a class other than the suburban sophisticates of the twentieth century, and Albee is saying something right here. Their drama occurs because they are the product of their class and era and such people collide in greatest anguish with one of the biggest terrors of this age. Affluent, industrious but really spiritually idle, arbitrary of personality, their intellects all too aware of the pessimistic facts of life—they end up playing avoidance games. For most of his life until now, Tobias (for example) has met the really personal questions with silence. His way out is detachment; after all, what can one do, what can one affirm? Faced with the finitude of your life, you must have your soporific or your "cover." This is the essential loneliness of the semi-intellectual semi-aristocrat—the sophisticate who cannot just simply *do,* or *act.* The avoidance games are the covers or the soporifics for this special but also representative family.

Like perhaps ninety per cent of the husbands of this world, Tobias plays the "Tune-Out." Claire calls him "predictable, stolid Tobias," and he has been satisfied to be that for its lack of commitment has meant security for him. Claire herself plays the "Put-On": games, laughter, sarcasm and satire, anything which will get people to take themselves (and her) less seriously and thus avoid confrontation. Honest as she sounds compared to the others, and as ready as she seems to really reveal herself, Claire is not about to face the real terror either. The alcoholic role-playing is both cover *and* soporific. When Agnes implies she need not decide the route for her family's journey out of confusion, Tobias yells: "You're copping out!" And it is true: Agnes plays "Cop-Out," which also is an effective method for avoiding confrontation. Her oververbal and ever-present perceptiveness about those under her wing has been a handy substitute for an ability to love or to enforce a decision based on love—and it has also been a wonderful sub-conscious weapon for domination. Julia expects a husband to do the work of consoling her—she is obviously unable to enjoy the world on her own—and is going through all the possibilities, automat-style, as fast as she can.

For all of them, their talk is their *hubris* and their doom—and the heart of their excellent and precise characterization by Albee. Agnes and Tobias (and no doubt *their* parents before them) have set up the highly verbal-semantic rules of their overall game for facing the days. They are fond of minutiae:

> TOBIAS: Succinct, but one of the rules of an aphorism . . .
>
> AGNES: An epigram, I thought.
>
> TOBIAS: An epigram is usually satiric, and you . . .

Such moments are suggestive of their lifelong moving away from personal contact and action. Even in crises, formal conversation rules apply. Talking about Julia, Tobias reports she is in hysterics, and Agnes says: "That is a condition; I inquired about an action." When Agnes says she will suffer the mantle of the drill sergeant to "keep this family in shape," she is really only speaking of the discipline of *talk.*

In all, these particular characters are the perfect people to reveal the terror and what Albee wants to say about it, and the terror in turn (when we find out what it is) only exists *as* a terror for this particular class of human beings. Simple and direct people, for example, could survive this in happiness. The old illustration of putting Othello in Hamlet's play is relevant: Othello would *act,* and there would be no play. Tobias and Agnes and their kind are verbal-mental or inept to the point where they cannot act (excepting the one desperate act of Harry and Edna), because they cannot indulge any simple little faiths and hopes in this age.

This display of appropriate characteristics leading to the desired crisis is nonetheless more demanding of the playwright. It is very hard to write a play this way—a play of all talk and little action. The talk thus has to connote the action of *ideas.* It does. While the talk does the characters little good, their relation to it increases our vision greatly. The audience is emotionally excited by the insights and images of seeing the characters in perspective against their thoughts and games. The play acts out the most telling form of going to the logical extreme on this question of love vs. the terror, of whether to let our Harrys and Ednas stay or not, and of what the terror is and how we avoid it.

Is the characterization symbolic? Yes, but not in the blatant way that ***Tiny Alice*** is symbolic. The people of ***A Delicate Balance*** represent totally real dilemmas and problems while being unspecific enough in background and surface detail to be representative more than naturalistically unique. The play also has symbolic actions and motifs, but not to the degree of real abstraction. Julia's room is a symbol, and the bar is a symbol—obvious security objects or associations with the comfort of ownerships and identities—but they are believably linked to real feelings on the part of the characters and they rightly reinforce the thematic ideas of the play.

Once the illusion has been accepted by the spectator, the play's seeming inaction begins to help rather than hinder. With no obvious action in which to participate, one is forced to enter into the thematic goals of the drama. And there one finds a great deal. I have said that "the truth" is a major pay-off in the play, but the theme does not deal in mere exposé truth, as in social-problem drama. It does not offer the trite and obvious revelation of truth about current psychological difficulty with living—that people do not relate to one another, that nothing means anything. Superficially, ***A Delicate Balance*** may say these things, but what is new in it, and a major contribution, is the treatment of this basically familiar notion. Yes, we can agree with Agnes' rueful humor about the "thirty million psychiatrists practicing in this land of ours" and the references to sexual identity crises, about Claire's need for something to occupy her mind (the purchase of the topless bathing suit in the hope of "a trip"), their *vins tristes,* and their fixation with drinking (which makes utter sense in their situation and on their budget). But the real meaning of the play is the metaphor of our continual loss, of having it be "too late" even as we are born:

> CLAIRE: Maybe Toby'll walk in one day, trailing travel folders, rip his tie off, announce he's fed up with the north, the east, the suburbs, the regulated great gray life, dwindling before him—poor Toby—and has bought him an island off Paraguay . . . and is taking us all to *that,* to hack through the whatever, build us an enormous lean-to, all of us. Take us away, to where it is always good and happy.
>
> JULIA: Would you, Dad?
>
> TOBIAS: It's . . . it's too late, or something.

The non-commital reply says much. They all know that *"that"* is what they need: an escape to the primal and away from the complicated sophistications of their mid-twentieth-century problems—but that it is too late, not just in time but in atrophied emotional capacity. They also know such hope is false to their true selves and their aptitude for simple, direct love and simple, direct pleasure-seeking. So it is one source of the terror. Agnes speaks of her fears about seeing her own life passing, about growing old—but it is not really age that produces the great sadness or the terror. It is, as she puts it, *"Le Temps Perdu."*

> AGNES: Time. Time happens, I suppose. To people. Everything becomes . . . too late, finally.

And elsewhere:

> CLAIRE: We're waiting, aren't we?
>
> TOBIAS: Hm?
>
> CLAIRE: Waiting. The room; the doctor's office; beautiful unconcern; intensive study of the dreadful curtains; absorption in *Field and Stream,* waiting for the Bi-op-see. (Looks from one to the other.) No? Don't know what I mean?

They do know, and it is their necessary selfishness that they must look to their own selves and resist such recognitions. The terror is now clear. These people suddenly realize, as might we, that they are at point X or Y or Z in this continuum of existence and that—even if they are assured of, say, thirty more years of life—any additional time cannot significantly affirm or accomplish much, or help them forget that their lives represent no real solace against the pressure of their mortality. Unfortunately, they are well enough off to have no great ambitions left. There is nothing major to work for—not better pay, a house on the hill, college for the kids, grandchildren, or any of the other Class Dreams. Somewhat reminiscent of John Updike in his short stories, Albee's theme is about time and dying and the burdens of mortality in the figurative and spiritual senses. This is why Harry and Edna "got scared." As Agnes says: "There is disease here and who in this family is immune?" No one really is. Tobias and Agnes offer themselves as mother and father, to keep the night lights burning which might push the shadows of fear into farther corners. Claire, while appearing "the strongest," needs the family unit and the home (a fine therapeutic punching-bag) which she cannot have on her own. Harry and Edna instinctively know there might be a hope of shelter in Tobias' and Agnes' "home"—and the incredible and potently dramatic thing is that they finally *act* (the only action of which they are capable) towards consummating the symbiosis. As Julia asks:

> JULIA: . . . Harry and Edna: what do they want?
>
> CLAIRE: Succor.
>
> JULIA: Pardon?
>
> CLAIRE: Comfort. Warmth. A special room with a night light, or the door ajar so you can look down the hall from the bed and see that Mommy's door is open. . . . It's the *room.*

The room and sleep (again, the need for soporifics) soothe and distract from what these people dare not dwell on. Harry and Edna spur the others' consciousness of their separate quests away from confrontation. The commandeering of the room and the other intolerable intimacy of serving themselves at Tobias' bar are the extreme intrusions which Julia (the only true child) cannot abide or will not share. But all of them, nonetheless, come "where the table has been laid." Through them we begin to admit or at least consider the truth about our own "time" and its passage. The more we become obsessed by it, or aware of it in our advancing knowledge of man's penchant for unhappiness (however wrong or "unfaithful" this might be), the more ironically we encourage the death of fellowship. Such preoccupation precludes accomplishment in human relationship. Maintaining this delicate balance between seeking the soporific or the cover versus admitting one's mortality is too much of a full-time job.

Does it help to admit the truth—that we are frightened, that we want the warmest and most secure part of this symbolic bomb shelter to ourselves, that we cannot relate because we are too fixated on our own depressions and losses? Or is it better to quietly maintain the soporifies, having made one's "adjustment?" (Where have the characters come with their exorcism? Agnes talks of sleeping to "let the demons out," then greeting the sunlight and its attendant "order" once again. We know her "order" is their "adjustment.") The big answer to the big question is left to the audience, but not as a mere convenient or titillating ending. Something of real substance has been said—in the right amount, in the most insightful metaphors—about the nature of the problem. The play itself achieves another kind of delicate balance as genuine content and thoughtful perspective compensate for colorful form. It ends on the right note of false balance, with Agnes' effortful "Come now; we can begin the day."

Robert Brustein didn't like this facile and pseudo-portentous coda—as it seemed to him. But it expresses precisely where the characters are left (in sad ambiguity) after they and we have really been somewhere—where there is little hope for them because of their major incapacities for faith and love, but where there could be hope for us out here. This might be so, at least, if we dealt with our emptiness through first understanding it.

The big (controversial) conclusion here, at any rate, is that ***A Delicate Balance*** is a brilliant and highly significant play. It is the best expression of the peculiar loneliness of our time which we have had in years, standing out in an age which desperately parades sensation and exhibition in the guise of "drama." This loneliness of grappling with "the terror," as I have already indicated, is not a problem in everyone's life style. Practically speaking, neither was Hamlet's. The fact remains that a genuine insight and a compelling poetic vision have been offered—and the play deserves to stand, to be studied, and to be confronted for a long time to come.

NOTES

[1]*Educational Theatre Journal,* (Dec. 1966), p. 450.

[2]Sheed in *The Commonweal* (Oct. 14, 1966) and Robert Graham Kemper in *Christian Century* (Nov. 23, 1966).

[3]All quotations from the play are from the Atheneum edition (New York, 1966).

E. G. Bierhaus, Jr. (essay date 1974)

SOURCE: "Strangers in a Room: *A Delicate Balance* Revisited," in *Modern Drama,* Vol. XVII, No. 2, June, 1974, pp. 199-206.

[*The following essay conducts a "political" reading of* A Delicate Balance, *which, the critic claims, focuses on "the rights of the individual or self."*]

W. H. Auden in *The Dyer's Hand* lists six functions of a critic, the fourth being: "Give a 'reading' of a work which increases my understanding of it."[1] In giving a new reading of Edward Albee's ***A Delicate Balance,*** I hope to increase the reader's understanding of this play by making him more aware of its ambiguities and by pointing out to him new associations within it. Although no one reading of ***A Delicate Balance,*** however careful, can reveal or distil or explain its full meaning simply because no work of art can ever finally be fully understood, a new reading does provide a new focus which changes the play's perspective.

My reading of ***A Delicate Balance*** is new because I do not think its primary focus is on the responsibilities of friendship. This is present but secondary. The primary focus is rather political, making the focus both a more moral and intellectual one. In friendship the emphasis is on the rights of the friend, in politics on the rights of the individual or self, in this case Tobias. To substantiate this reading, I shall examine three aspects of ***A Delicate Balance*** which to my mind require further attention: the significance of the characters' names, the surprising permutations of the characters, and finally the parable of Tobias and the cat.

I

Names have many resonances for Albee: biblical (Jerry and Peter in ***Zoo Story***), historical (George and Martha in ***Who's Afraid of Virginia Woolf?***), sexual (***Tiny Alice***).[2] "The Players" in ***A Delicate Balance*** are no exception. (Notice that we have players instead of a cast because this is to be a contest.) Agnes, lamb of God, is also a third century saint, a virgin martyr who was decapitated because her body refused to burn at the stake. Agnes, a transliteration of the Greek ἀγνός (pronounced hagnós), means "pure" and chaste." Tobias means "God is good." In *The Book of Tobit* Tobias cures his father's blindness with the help of the archangel Raphael, his guardian. Edna also appears in *The Book of Tobit* as Tobias' mother-in-law. Harry is the diminutive of Henry, a name which evolved from the Old German words for "house," or "home," and "ruler."

Julia is the feminine form of Julius. "The Romans supposed the name to be derived from Greek ιουλος'downy,' but there is no good evidence for this."[3] Downy means "feathery" or "fluffy," but it is also slang for "wide awake" or "knowing."[4] Claire of course means "to make clear" as Agnes observes: "Claire, who watches from the sidelines, has seen so very much, has seen us all so clearly, have you not, Claire. You were not named for nothing."[5] Lastly, there is Teddy. Teddy, the dead son of Agnes and Tobias, is the diminutive of Edward, an Old English compound meaning "rich," "happy," and "ward," "guardian," and of Theodore, Greek for "god's gift." Edward and Theodore are both saints; Edward is also a king and martyr.

The resonances are various and conflicting, though always pertinent and never deceptive. Agnes, more wolf than lamb (". . . I am grimly serious. Yes?"), far from saintly ("We do not attempt the impossible," and "I'm not a fool," both saintly imperatives), more sacrificing than sacrificed (to Claire: "If you are not an alcoholic, you are beyond forgiveness," and to Julia: "How dare you embarrass me and your father!" [notice the "me" first]), is neither pure nor chaste in either the physical or spiritual sense (Claire to Julia: "Your mommy got her pudenda scuffed a couple of times herself 'fore she met old Toby," and Agnes to Tobias: "We must always envy someone we should not, be jealous of those who have so much less. You and Claire make so much sense together, talk so well").

Although Agnes considers herself blessed in a qualified way (". . . it is simply that I am the one member of this . . . reasonably happy family blessed and burdened with the ability to view a situation objectively while I am in it," and "There are many things a woman does: she bears the children—if there *is* that blessing . . ., she also jokingly calls herself a "harridan," *e.g.*, a hag (" . . rid yourself of the harridan. Then you can run your mission and take out sainthood papers"). Ironically this last is addressed to Tobias, the only member of her family who is foolish enough to attempt the impossible.

Instead of having a blind father as in the apocrypha, this Tobias has a blind wife. Agnes is *not* the one member of her family who can view a situation objectively while in it. Claire does this much better: "Harry wants to tell you, Sis." If Agnes weren't so afraid of silence, Harry would have explained his presence sooner. Moreover Agnes' remark to Julia, ". . . nobody . . . *really* wants to talk about your latest . . . marital disorder . . ." is simply untrue. Claire does: "I have been trying, without very much success, to find out why Miss Julie here is come home." Agnes can't even see herself properly:

> AGNES: There was a stranger in my room last night.
>
> TOBIAS: Who?
>
> AGNES: You.
>
> TOBIAS: Ah.

It doesn't occur to Agnes, as Tobias' "Who?" suggests it does to him, that she herself is the stranger.

Even Harry and Edna are sufficiently self-aware to recognize that in a similar situation they would not grant sanctuary to Tobias and Agnes. Julia also questions her mother with new insight: "I must discover, sometime, who you think you are." Agnes' "icy" reply is significant: "You will learn . . . one day." We all learn by the end of the play: Agnes thinks of herself as guardian, but she is in fact mad. So she does "lose her head" because she refuses to be burned, one method of inoculation against the plague, the play's chief metaphor.

Although Tobias begins drinking anisette, he switches to brandy—Claire's drink. Brandy burns. It is brandy that Tobias later offers to Harry at the end of Act III, but he refuses: "No, oh, God, no." Harry has been burned enough for one week-end. Like Tobias, he was foolish enough to attempt the impossible and failed. That's why he leaves. Tobias has no place else to go. Although his house is not a home as Agnes uncomfortably reminds him: "Well, my darling, . . . you do not live at home," it is *his:* "I have built this house!" He is therefore free to exclaim to Harry: "I want your plague! . . . Bring it in!" But Agnes does not want it, and because she is nanny and drill sergeant (her drink is cognac: "It is suppose to be healthy") and *not* saint and martyr, Harry and Edna leave. Tobias remains to join Claire and Julia, "the walking wounded" (a deft description of sanity—and sainthood?), in another drink, while Agnes, the "steady wife," plans for them another day.

Harry and Edna return to their house where Harry can again be the ruler. The terror is still there, but they don't seem so overwhelmed by it. Their support of one another which at their entrance comes across as awkward and impersonal has mellowed. A tenderness has entered their relationship—EDNA: "I let him think I . . . wanted to make love"—which coupled with the quiet acceptance of their failure—EDNA: "We *shouldn't* have come . . . For our own sake; our own . . . lack"—lends a grace to their endurance which is not available to Tobias and Agnes who are locked in their separate worlds. Their lives may be the same, as Edna observes, but their responses are not. Harry and Edna at least have the vitality to feel, act, and see. Therefore the ramifications of their departure, which is final,

> EDNA: I'm going into town on Thursday, Agnes. Would you like to come?
>
> [*A longer pause than necessary,* CLAIRE *and* JULIA *look at* AGNES]
>
> AGNES: [*Just a trifle awkward*] Well . . . no, I don't think so, Edna; I've . . . I've so much to do . . .

is less severe for them than for Tobias because they have each other. Tobias is left with two resigned drinking companions and a house manager nattering away about millenniums.

Immunity to the plague is acquired through testing, which leaves one burned or isolated "unless we are saints" (Agnes' sarcastic alternative):

> CLAIRE: So one night . . . I'd had one martini—as a Test to see if I could—which, given my . . . stunning self-discipline, had become three;
>
> EDNA: We mustn't press our luck, must we: test.

The characters' immunity, Claire and Agnes excepted, exists in various stages: Tobias' is beginning; Harry and Edna's is advancing, though they resist it; Julia's is progressing nicely. Although she endured as a young girl a "two-year burn at suddenly having a brother" and subsequently has known four husbands (know in the biblical sense is sexual), Julia is still not sufficiently "wide awake" for the "great big world." She needs to return home to Tobias and Agnes.

Claire is the only character who believes her immunity to be complete: "I've had it. I'm still alive, I think." Without Claire who feels "a little bigger than life" and who is the real nexus of the household, we would have no way to identify the degree of Julia's immunity, or her ambivalence to it. Nor could we see by the end of the play that Agnes who is "neither less nor more than human" is also immune. For her inoculation is different from the others. They *resign* themselves to reality whereas Agnes *creates* her own—"I'm as young as the day I married you." They confront their demons in the daylight, but Agnes—"well, you know how little I vary"—quarantines hers in the unknown chambers of her heart. Thus the plague (and the play) becomes less mysterious when associations with the characters' names are permitted to illuminate it.

II

One of the consummate strengths of ***A Delicate Balance*** is its universality. It speaks not only to its time, but out of it. Every year is a plague year somewhere, and no one is immune. As Hamm remarks in *Endgame* (a play with which ***A Delicate Balance*** has close affinities): ". . . you're on earth, there's no cure for that!"[6] A major technique Albee employs to create this universality is characterization. This is partially achieved by the resonances, associations, and echoes the names of the characters have with life external to the play which fixes it in an historical—and literary—continuum. It is also partially achieved by the permutations of the characters themselves.

Just as Albee clues us in to the significance of names through Claire, so he clues us in to the significance of permutations by describing Harry and Edna as "very much like Agnes and Tobias." These internal resonances are as numerous and complex as the external ones. Furthermore, they determine the play's action and generate its vision, foci which are not coterminous.

When Claire declares to Tobias that "Love is not the problem. You love Agnes and Agnes loves Julia and Julia loves me and I love you. We all love each other; yes we do," she acknowledges that the boundaries of love in their household are set though circuitous. Trouble arises when these boundaries are challenged, *e.g.,* by Harry and Edna:

> TOBIAS: I almost went in *my* room . . . by habit . . . but then I realized that your room is my room because my room is Julia's because Julia's room is . . .

But while the boundaries are openly agreed upon by Agnes, Tobias, Claire, and Julia, they are constantly being unconsciously crossed: Claire, "like sister like sister"; Tobias, "My name is Claire"; Tobias calls Claire Agnes; Agnes becomes Julia's father, Tobias her mother; Claire calls Julia "daughter"; Harry becomes Tobias; Edna becomes Agnes. What this means is, as Claire points out, that like Tobias' friends they are all "indistinguishable if not necessarily similar. . . . " The share a common environment. "When one does nothing, one is threatened by the question is one nothing?"[7] It is a question which threatens them all.

It is in fact the terror. Tobias' despairing "Doesn't friendship grow to [love]?" is rhetorical for everyone except himself. Claire had already answered it: "We're not a communal nation . . . giving, but not sharing, outgoing, but not friendly." An earlier assessment by Claire had driven Tobias to examine his boundaries:

> TOBIAS: We'll do neither, I'd imagine. Take in; throw out.
>
> CLAIRE: Oh?
>
> TOBIAS: Well, yes, they're just . . . passing through.
>
> CLAIRE: As they have been . . . all these years.

A later claim by Edna pushes his examination further: "We are not . . . transients . . . like some." But they *are* transients. All of them. They each try the other's roles in an effort to belong, and although they meld perfectly (Julia talks like Claire, Tobias repeats Agnes, Harry mixes drinks like Tobias) they find that the new skin is just like their old one: "dry . . . and not warm." As Tobias eventually discovers, boundaries bind (blind?) more often than they enclose.

A Delicate Balance is neatly constructed. Agnes both opens and closes the play. Her opening speech is seemingly a descant on whether or not she will go mad, but upon closer examination we find that what really astonishes her most "is Claire." This of course italicizes Claire's enlightenment and establishes straight away the conflict between the two. It is the major conflict of the play with Tobias as the stake. Each wants to persuade him to embrace her vision of the world: Agnes, instinctively selfish, demands order; Claire, instinctively generous, accepts the absurd. Agnes wants "peace," Claire "merely relief." The appearance of Harry and Edna forces Tobias either to choose between these opposing visions or to adopt one of his own. He opts for the latter, and it becomes a last, desperate effort to inject meaning into his life ("God is good").[8]

Harry and Edna are thus pivotal because they upset the delicate balance of this trio. (The play is full of delicate balances: one exists between each of the characters, between appearance and reality, between the play and its reader or spectator.) But Harry and Edna are like Tobias and Agnes, Tobias is like Claire and Julia is like Agnes. Thus all the characters are pivotal, although each is "moving through his own jungle." "All happy families are alike," Claire tells Tobias, Agnes and Julia, quoting the opening of Tolstoy's *Anna Karenina.* And so are unhappy strangers.

III

As with Jerry's parable of the dog in ***Zoo Story,*** Tobias' parable of the cat is an analogue of the whole play. The parable contains eleven salient points: (1) the cat existed before Tobias met Agnes; (2) the cat was feminine; (3) she didn't like people; (4) but she was contented with Tobias; (5) one day he noticed that she no longer liked him; (6) he shook her; (7) she bit him; (8) he slapped her; (9) she judged him, accused him of failing; (10) he felt *betrayed;* (11) he had her killed.

Agnes is the obvious analogue to the cat: she is feminine, she replaces the cat in Tobias' affection, she does not like people ("You would not have a woman left about you—only Claire and Julia . . . not even people"), and she is contented with Tobias (". . . I have reached an age, Tobias, when I wish we were always alone, you and I, without . . . hangers-on . . . or anyone"). Tobias noticed that Agnes no longer liked him after the death of Teddy, "god's gift," Tobias' "ward" *and* "guardian" (his archangel?), whose death that hot, wet summer permanently altered the balance of all their lives. (AGNES: "Ah, the things I doubted then: that I was loved—that *I* loved, for that matter!") Tobias then "shook" Agnes by being unfaithful; she "bit" him by "trying to hold [him] in." He "slapped" her by sleeping alone. She then judged him, accused him of failing ("Did my husband . . . cheat on me?" and "*You* could have pushed her back . . . if you'd wanted to"). Since married to Agnes, Tobias has felt betrayed by Teddy's death, Agnes' failure as a mother, Claire's infidelity with Harry, Julia's failure as an adult, and finally by Harry's refusal to "stay."

The analogue seemingly breaks down with point eleven: Tobias does not kill Agnes. Nor does Anges kill Tobias. She does, however, see to it (Agnes is never blind to her own needs) that he is "put to sleep," her euphemism for killing, by injecting him with the plague, *e.g.,* by thwarting *his* vision which is to make Harry and Edna stay, by withholding her succor from him and them. And her injection, like the vet's, succeeds where his fails.

Albee carefully prepares us for this reversal in two ways. First he identifies Tobias with Claire (this identification began when Tobias switched to Claire's drink, brandy). Immediately before the parable, Agnes "decides Claire is not in the room," which is the reaction of the cat in the parable. During the parable Agnes again identifies herself with the cat when she wants to know if Tobias hurt her when he slapped her, while Claire identifies herself again with Tobias by asking what did he do, e.g., with the cat. Thus we intuitively feel that Tobias, like Claire, will succumb to Agnes' authoritarianism.

Second, Albee places the following exchange immediately after Tobias' "I had her *killed!*" which terminates the parable:

> AGNES: Well, what else could you have done? There was nothing to be done; there was no . . . meeting between you.
>
> TOBIAS: I might have tried longer . . . I might have worn a hair shirt, locked myself in the house with her, done penance.
>
> CLAIRE: You probably did the right *thing.* Distasteful alternative; the less . . . ugly choice.
>
> TOBIAS: Was it?
>
> [*A silence from them all*]
>
> AGNES: [*Noticing the window*] Was that a car in the drive?
>
> TOBIAS: "If we do not love someone . . . never have loved some one . . ."

Each of these speeches foreshadows the end of Act III: Agnes' ". . . what else could you have done?" is precisely her response to the departure of Harry and Edna, as is Tobias' "I might have tried longer." Claire's "distasteful alternative" is comforting and pragmatic, while Agnes' nervous remark about the "car in the drive" parallels her breaking the silence with her—and the play's—concluding speech. But it is Tobias' quiet "Was it?" that is the most revealing, for he is suggesting that "the less ugly choice" might have been his own death. This is reinforced by his quoting Agnes' "If we do not love someone . . . never have loved someone" which was originally her reply to Claire's "Or! Agnes; why don't you die?" The implication is that if one does not love someone, the generous "reflex" is to sacrifice oneself. This is what Tobias should have done with the cat; this is what he tried to do with Harry and Edna: "I DON'T WANT YOU HERE! I DON'T LOVE YOU! BUT BY GOD . . . YOU STAY!" The reversal is complete: Tobias is ultimately the cat as he is the saint. But because God is dead—"The bastard! He doesn't exist!," to quote Hamm once again—sainthood is dead as well. As Julia explains, she first thought of her father as a saint, then as a cipher, and finally as a "Nasty, violent, absolutely human man."

* * *

This is what we are left with at the end of ***A Delicate Balance***: three absolutely human beings—Tobias, Claire, Julia—seeking alcoholic "relief" from the disorder and "debris" of their stultifying existence, while the fourth member of their household, Agnes, speaking "To fill the silence," remarks upon "the wonder of daylight" before blithely welcoming the new day. The conflict is over. Agnes has won. The price? *Three* early morning drinkers and that "living room of a large and well-appointed suburban house" thoroughly infected with the plague.

Since 1966 when ***A Delicate Balance*** was first produced, the environment of America has become increasingly disordered and dirty. Mr. Nixon is a permutation of Mr. Johnson who was "very much like" Mr. Goldwater; Democrats become Republicans, Republicans Democrats: "everyone [is] moving through his own jungle." We are all "players," strangers in a room; our endings, like Agnes' (and like that unfinished sentence ending *Finnegans Wake* which continues on the first page of the book), are reminiscent of our beginnings, dependents seeking "relief." And this brings me back to W. H. Auden, whose sixth function of a critic is to "Throw light upon the relation of art to life. . . ."

NOTES

[1]W. H. Auden, *The Dyer's Hand,* New York, 1968, p. 8.

[2]Ruby Cohn, *Edward Albee,* Minneapolis, 1969, pp. 9, 25, 29.

[3]*The Oxford Dictionary of English Christian Names,* 2nd edition, London, 1950, p. 139. This dictionary is the main source for information about each name.

[4]*The Oxford English Dictionary,* ed. James A. H. Murray, Vol. III, London, 1897, p. 629.

[5]Quotations from *A Delicate Balance* are from the Pocket Book edition, New York, 1967.

[6]Quotations from Samuel Beckett's *Endgame* are from the Grove Press edition, New York, 1958.

[7]Paul Goodman, *Growing up Absurd,* New York, 1956, p. 41.

[8]For a different identification of the central conflict, see Cohn, pp. 38-39.

Anita Maria Stenz (essay date 1978)

SOURCE: *"A Delicate Balance,"* in *Edward Albee: The Poet of Loss,* Mouton Publishers, 1978, pp. 71-87.

[*The essay below examines* A Delicate Balance's *characters, "who, for all their symbolic resonances, are so disturbingly real in their ability to repel as well as arouse sympathy."*]

> Time happens, I suppose. To people. Everything becomes too late, finally. You know it's going on . . . up on the hill; and you can see the dust, and hear the cries, and the steel . . . but you wait; and time happens. When you *do* go, sword, shield . . . finally . . . there's nothing there . . . save rust; bones; and the wind.[1]

In ***A Delicate Balance,*** a drama about marriage and aging, there is little shouting and no breaking of bottles—just a modicum of hysterics. In fact, decorum and propriety are the rules of the game in this play which takes place during a fall weekend in the living room of a retired business man, Tobias, and of his wife, Agnes. The equilibrium of the household which includes Agnes' sister Claire is irrevocably shaken by the simultaneous invasion of daughter Julia in flight from her fourth marriage debacle and "best friends" Harry and Edna in quest of a solution to their first one. Albee further explores what George sadly describes to Nick in ***Who's Afraid of Virginia Woolf?*** as the "accommodation, malleability and adjustment" of life, and he investigates the proposition that the older people get the fewer choices they have when it comes to changing the pattern of their lives. Again, after confrontation and emotional crisis awareness grows. At the end of the play, the doors to six cages are left ajar.

After a busy and remunerative career in the city, Tobias has retired to the suburbs to enjoy the fruits of his success. He employs a gardener and several other servants and belongs to a country club where he plays golf. There is a conservatory with potted palms in his well-appointed home. His living room is adorned with crystal chandeliers and shelves filled with leather-bound books. He is "proud of his wines" and reads *Horizon* magazine. To all appearances Tobias is a man who has been an excellent provider. Agnes, who takes herself very seriously, is the model spouse. She has borne two children, "runs the house . . . makes sure there's food and not just anything, and decent linen; looks well; assumes whatever duties are demanded", and organizes her life around her husband's wishes. She finds herself, defines herself in the role of wife and mother. Feelings of unreality and abstraction were immediately suggested in the original New York production by a set in which everything solid was recessed and seemed to be slipping off into the shadows.[2] The false air of superiority and the superficial harmony between this husband and wife who practice concealment of emotion as if it were a virtue are in fact dangerously close to disruption at the moment the curtain rises. In the course of a weekend Tobias will be compelled to face the truth about himself as a husband, as a father and as a friend.

When the play begins the couple are getting ready to drink a cordial after their Friday evening meal but the atmosphere between them is anything but warm and cozy. In his review of the premier performance, Walter Kerr describes Tobias with his fingers clenched, an expression of worry and near exasperation on his face, and Agnes smoothing down "the grey serenity of her utterly unwrinkled dress, speaking quickly".[3] There has just been an ugly scene at dinner. Claire, the family dependent, came to the table unsteady, unintelligible and smelling of vodka one time too many. Sharp and scolding, "neither less nor more than human", Agnes let forth with what she later describes as "not brutality at all, but the souring side of love" and Claire has temporarily withdrawn to her room upstairs. Determinedly Agnes says to Tobias, "All the years we have put up with each other's wiles and crotchets have earned us each other's company". A little later, when the news that their thirty-six year old daughter Julia is about to return home from her fourth marriage has doubled her after-dinner pique, Agnes adds wearily, "I have reached an age Tobias, when I wish we were always alone, you and I, without . . . hangers-on . . . or anyone".

A recurring critical misunderstanding of the play and in particular of the character of Agnes is that this woman is literally threatened with insanity[4] and that she really wants to go mad.[5] On the contrary, as Tobias remarks, "There is no saner woman on earth". In her long-winded opening monologue Agnes tells Tobias precisely why she is angry:

> What I find most astonishing—aside from that belief of mine, which never ceases to surprise me by the very fact of its surprising lack of unpleasantness, the belief that I might very easily—as they say—lose my mind one day __________is Claire.

The perpetual presence—in or near the household—of the alcoholic sister, who is after all a parasite, a meddler, and a burden, has grated on the nerves of Agnes to the point where, as she contemplates the few remaining years of her married life, the situation is becoming mentally and physically unlivable. It is Claire's cumulative effect plus Tobias' reflex defence of everything she does which provokes her that night after dinner to indulge herself in a rambling reflection on the subject of "drifting-off". However, she also says, "Not that I suspect I am about to, or am even . . . nearby . . . for I'm not that sort". It is against Agnes' nature to be uninvolved with people, uncaring or detached. The woman is attracting attention to her unhappiness.

There is no evidence in the play to justify E.G. Bierhaus' accusation that Agnes is isolationist and selfish because she wants to be alone with her husband in their retirement.[6] There has been a deep and private sorrow between this man and woman, an emotional estrangement of many years. According to her lights Agnes has loved long and faithfully—

most of the time knowing she was being taken for granted. Her craving for an opportunity for Tobias and herself to find each other again before they die hardly earns her the epithet "domineering, man-eating, she-ogre of the American family".[7] Tobias has recently undergone serious internal surgery. Expecting to be alone soon, "abandoned by a heart attack or cancer", preparing for that, Agnes would like to round things out with her husband before it is all over. As their friend Harry puts it on Sunday morning, "There's . . . so much . . . over the dam, so many . . . disappointments, evasions, I guess, lies maybe . . . so much we remember we wanted once . . . so little that we've settled for". Agnes does not wish for anything as grand as an apotheosis but she would like to have peace in her home in her old age.

It is during the weekend when the action of the play takes place that the opportunity presents itself for Agnes and Tobias to get closer to each other. Although not altogether in privacy and solitude, they do make a start at breaking through "the demise of intensity, the private preoccupations, the substitutions" of the years between the beginning of it all and the end. The balance that was teetering on Friday night after the outburst at the dinner table and the news of Julia's fourth marriage disaster is severely jostled by bedtime when, near the end of Act One, Harry and Edna (who are very much like Agnes and Tobias) unexpectedly arrive. Refugees from their own loneliness and loss, they come looking for the warmth and the sense of belonging which they have failed to create between themselves in their marriage. The next evening, with Julia demanding her room, Claire providing provocative sideline commentary and their life-long friends emphatically invading the premises with piles of luggage, an explosion of suppressed emotional energy shatters the outward calm of the family. Agnes overcomes her natural reserve, her deference to Tobias' ambivalence, and states a preference. She finally compels him to acknowledge the truth about their marriage arrangement and to face the implications involved for all of them in their dilemma of the full house. By Sunday morning, after the pieces have fallen back into place, the patterns of these six lives have not been radically altered. It is too late for that. However, their emotional relationships are unequivocally improved. Humbled—all, they find that the way to a more affectionate and goodhumored harmony has been prepared for what remains of their lives together.

In ***A Delicate Balance*** the illusion that there is freedom of choice after a certain time is destroyed. As Albee puts it, "The point of the play (is) that we lose . . . we develop a kind of arthritis of the mind, of the morality, and change becomes impossible finally __________not whether we live up to our responsibilities of friendship".[8] On the whole, in spite of the tone of gentleness, compassion and warm—if often barbed—humor with which the author depicts the characters, critical response to them is hostile. For example, Anne Paolucci finds them "grasping and vicious, and even naive at the beginning", and says that "they all end up damned".[9] John Gassner feels that the play resolves nothing. "It is altogether vacuous, as a result of the fuzzy failure of Agnes and Tobias as either separate individuals or as a married couple."[10] Ronald Hayman's view is that "when Harry and Edna go, leaving the other four together, we have no clear picture of what has been changed by the incidents of the weekend".[11] Happily, in his discussion of this play C.W.E. Bigsby recognizes that, "Albee is concerned with locating the source of a limited but genuine hope" and that ***A Delicate Balance*** is another "calling for . . . a courageous determination to face the world as it is".[12] However, even Bigsby betrays the unwillingness of most of the critics to feel comfortable with characters who, for all their symbolic resonances, are so disturbingly real in their ability to repeal as well as to arouse sympathy.

In Albee's plays there are no heroes. His characters are never pleasant projections of wishful thinking. They do not present life as it should be or even could be but as it all too often is, whether people like to admit it or not. The seriousness under the jokes, the sadness and the wistfulness that permeate this play arise from the author's consciousness of the pitiful inability of so many people—for whatever good reasons—to respond adequately to all the demands of a lifetime, as well as from his painful awareness that sometimes people need to hurt each other in order to survive.

The mixed feelings of irritation and sympathy which Agnes arouses are very different from the emotional response which Martha provokes in ***Virginia Woolf.*** Martha, after all, does not take any interest in homemaking or in her husband and misses no opportunity to denigrate George and his work. Agnes is a very different woman. Having accepted the male role as primary she let her destiny be controlled by Tobias. Over the years, in her role as adjunct, she developed a formidable self-image. A lack of a sense of her own worth is not Agnes' problem. "I must discover sometime who you think you are", snaps Julia on Saturday evening after another unpleasant dinner. Icily, Agnes replies, "You will learn . . . one day".

Agnes married a man who provided well for her and the family. On that score she has no complaints: "It is a rolling, pleasant land . . . verdant, my darling, thank you." She has borne children, although there is some question in her mind whether she considers motherhood the normative experience which has defined the value of her life: "Blessing? Yes, I suppose, even with the sadness." Unlike Mommy and Martha, Agnes did not marry primarily for what the man would make her in the eyes of others; she joined her lot with Tobias for love—for better or for worse. In her capacity of wife and mother she competently took charge of her domain:

> When we keep something in shape we maintain its shape—whether we are proud of that shape, or not, is another matter—we keep *it* from falling apart. We do not attempt the impossible. We maintain. We hold.

As she approaches sixty Agnes' grief is that the shape she has struggled to hold together resounds with hollowness. She has, after all, not been alone for all the years. She has a partner who did very little to share in the arrangement beyond providing the home and the material goods for his wife to organize. Agnes' fault is not unlike the fault of George in ***Virginia Woolf***; she has been kind and understanding too long and let things go beyond what her judgement told her was good and right. It is she who says, "I am the one member of this . . . reasonably happy family blessed and burdened with the ability to view a situation objectively while I am in it ________ The double position of seeing not only facts but their implications . . . the longer view as well as the shorter". Yet, up to this weekend, her dedication to her life as adjunct and her devotion to her husband's will have unwittingly worked against the best interests of the whole family. When Tobias says, "You who make all the decisions, really rule the game", Agnes points out, "That is an illusion you have". She continues:

> The reins we hold! It's a team of twenty horses, and we sit there, and we watch the road and check the leather . . . if our man is so disposed. But there are things we do not do . . . we don't decide the route . . . We follow. We let our . . . men decide the moral issues.

At last she makes him see that directly or indirectly he himself helped to bring them all to the Friday night after-dinner-malaise, the state Jerry describes in ***The Zoo Story***: "We neither love nor hurt because we do not try to reach each other."

Something in the past was concealed between this husband and wife, something which Agnes allowed to be left unresolved and which still has a ruinous effect on the present. Like Jerry and like George, Agnes learns that "neither kindness nor cruelty by themselves, independent of each other, create any effect beyond themselves", that "the two combined, together, at the same time, are the teaching emotion". Much as Agnes makes Tobias face the truth about their lives together, she also has to admit that she herself waited too long to do something about it and that, in effect, she let Tobias make her unhappy and—up to this weekend—stood silently by while he reinforced his daughter's feeling of being unloved time and time again. The difficult and painful confrontation which Agnes forces on Tobias on Sunday morning at the beginning of Act Three is the crucial encounter which breaks the stalemate that began some thirty years before during the period of trial and loss of faith surrounding the death of their second child, Teddy. The unresolved events of that period concerned the four members of the extant family and complicated and compromised their relationships and affected their subsequent lives right up to the first evening of the play's action.

For Agnes it was an unreal time. When her small boy died, her husband gradually estranged himself from her "as if that had been the string". He deeply shook her self-confidence with an infidelity about which she learned something—but nothing specific. The sharp feeling of jealousy and resentment against her sister Claire finds one root of its intensity here, for not only is Agnes convinced that Claire knows about the episode in question—she suspects that her own sister betrayed her. In the prime of womanhood Agnes bent her will to the wishes of her husband. Without discussion or explanation, according to her sense of what it meant to be a wife, she accepted it when, after a year of "spilling (himself) on (her) belly", Tobias slept apart from her in another room. She remained "an honest woman" and found her refuge and defense against the emotional emptiness of her life by playing martinet—ordering, planning, organizing—assuring for Tobias a life that was the way he wanted it. Like a stubborn priestess Agnes presided over her family, preserving as best she could a delicate balance. A "stickler on points of manners, timing, tact—the graces", she has devoted her vital energy to externals—to form.

At one point Agnes says to Julia, "Men's problems are so easy; money and death". Tobias, a successful business man during the years when he spent all his time in the city, took refuge in being non-committal on the home front. He went to the country club a lot and played golf. However, what the death of his son meant to him is clearly expressed in his reaction to it. The emotional pain was so intolerable that he could not face the possibility of another child, another loss. Unable to cope with the ultimate implication of this double vulnerability, he terminated intimacy with his wife. Tobias is shy at home, not normally given to outbursts of temper or impulsive behavior, much less to easy talk about deeply personal matters. When Claire tries to tease him into recalling his single extramarital escapade "that dry and oh so wet July" after Teddy's death, he angrily mutters, "Common practice is hardly . . ." Ironically, during his retirement the one real emotional outlet—with the exception perhaps of gardening—for he no longer honestly enjoys golf, as Claire reminds him—the one area in which he lets his spirit soar and expand (as Claire also points out) is the safe, solitary pleasure of listening to the Romantic music of Bruckner.

When Agnes starts talking about *"le temps perdu"* on the morning after Tobias has slept in the same room with her for the first time in so many years because the inn is full, Albee is not talking about sexual revulsion in suburbia, as Michael E. Rutenberg would have it[13], but about the pitiful inability of people to respond adequately to all the demands of their lives and to the needs of those closest to them—especially in times of personal sorrow and self-absorption. "*Perdu* means lost, not merely . . . past . . . what a shame, what sadness", says Agnes:

> It was nice to have you there, though I remember, when it was a constancy, how easily I would fall asleep, pace my breathing to your breathing, and if we were touching! ah, what a splended cocoon that was.

There is no evidence that Agnes found sex disgusting. Rather than gossip about what a general practitioner he knows told him about the sex lives of the couples in his suburban practice, Mr. Rutenberg would have done better to inquire about the psychological implications of coitus interruptus for the woman. That is what Agnes is talking about when she says, "Such . . . silent . . . sad, disgusted . . . love". She also makes Tobias remember how she cried out to him, "Don't leave me then, like that. Not again, Tobias, please? I can take care of it; we *won't* have another child, but please don't . . . leave me like that". On Sunday morning in no uncertain terms Agnes points out to Tobias that he is racked with guilt, stupidly, and that she must suffer for it.

That John Gassner finds "the airing of the wife's grievances . . . tasteless"[14] is utterly irrelevant to the play. Sexuality in marriage, if it is not necessarily central, certainly is vital in the working out of the overall equilibrium in a relationship between partners. A source of pleasure and release that can be shared, it is also a means through which the loneliness of two separate people may be assuaged. That Tobias in his early thirties withdrew from his wife's bed and retired to another room and that Agnes put up with it is perhaps the most significant information there is about the two characters in the play. It is hardly fair to fault the author with the "deplorable habits of our 'advanced' playwrights" and to accuse him of a "fruitless resort to scatology", as Mr. Gassner does. Albee is depicting life. If in real life the springs of motivation usually remain obscure, the dramatist locates the moment between two people where the descent began. As Tobias puts it, "Once you drop . . . you can come back up part of the way . . . but never . . . really back again". In ***Who's Afraid of Virginia Woolf?*** Martha describes the boxing match, the way she impulsively and insensitively punched George in the chin, knocked him down and humiliated him in front of her father. "I hadn't meant it . . . honestly", she explains and then adds ruefully, "I think it's colored our whole life".

Agnes respected Tobias' wish to sleep apart not because she liked it but because she respected his wishes. *And* because of her own feelings of inadequacy at the time, her own agonizing uncertainty: "Ah, the things I doubted then: that I was loved—that I loved—I thought Tobias was unfaithful to me . . ." Because this breach between husband and wife was not dealt with candidly at the time it assumed the proportions of a skeleton in the closet. Not only did Agnes and Tobias' failure to confront their passions and feelings disrupt the development of their relationship. It had grave consequences on the emotional growth of their daughter, Julia, as well.

It is impossible to discuss the effect of the death of Teddy on Julia without examining Julia's relationship with her father. What is plain is that, emotionally inadequate, he failed to give his daughter the reassurance that she was still loved after the second child was born. Agnes recalls how "She felt unwanted, tricked". Perhaps the boy meant too much to him. There is an echo here of Peter's words in ***The Zoo Story***: "Naturally, every man wants a son." Tobias let Agnes down because of Teddy's death; clearly, he let Julia down at his birth. After her younger brother died the girl regularly appeared at the door with scraped knees, causing her mother to wonder whether she was just clumsy or if she was doing penance for feeling more relief than loss. In vain Julia tried to reassert herself in the central position of only child. The pattern of her failed marriages is a continuation of the succession of failures at different schools during her adolescence, an unbroken series of escapes from a kind of guilt which at the same time was a search for love. Agnes wonders whether Julia failed through hate or love, and we hear again the question that Jerry asks at the end of ***The Zoo Story***: "Was trying to feed the dog an act of love? And, perhaps was the dog's attempt to bite me *not* an act of love? If we can so misunderstand, well then, why have we invented the word love in the first place?"

The kind of men Julia married could not make up for what she missed from her father at home. Ironically, she strongly implies that all the choices weren't her own but that her well-meaning mother had a hand in them too. Agnes reflects on the various losses that come to a woman, as when her child becomes "an adult stranger instead of a growing one". She also says, "I am almost too old to be a grandmother as I'd hoped . . . too young to be one. Oh, I had wanted that: the *youngest* older woman in the block". On Sunday morning Agnes says to Tobias, "You have a problem with Julia". This is the other confrontation that should have taken place years before. Tobias never came to grips with being a father. Oversensitive to her husband's emotional problems, Agnes deferred to his wishes and to her misguided sense of love. Instead of listening to common sense and attempting to come to terms with the crucial issue—but perhaps also influenced by her eagerness to have a grandchild—she tried to stand by Julia herself in the girl's search for love by pushing her into one marriage after another. If the parents do not make an attempt to clear up their own difficulties first, there is little use helping a problem child. Julia is the product and the victim of the unresolved emotional conflict between her parents, and particularly of her father's problems.

Tobias tells Agnes and Claire a story about a cat he had put to sleep because it stopped responding to him the way he wanted it to. There is a pattern in Tobias' life. When he did not have things as he wanted them, he did not want them at all. As Agnes sarcastically puts it, "The theory being pat: that half a loaf is worse than none". When Julia went through her "angular adolescence" and he fell, as fathers are apt to do at this stage, from a marvel to a gray non-eminence in her eyes, Tobias stopped reaching out. He did not try to have contact with her anymore. Always, rather than risk loss or pain, Tobias retreated: "If I thought I might . . . break through to her and say, 'Julia . . . ' but then what would I say? 'Julia . . .' Then nothing." His story about his cat is a gloss on his relationship with his daughter:

> I hated her, well, I suppose because I was being accused of something, of . . . failing. But I had not been cruel, by design: If I'd been neglectful, well, my life was . . . I resented it. I resented having a . . . being judged. Being betrayed.

When she makes Tobias acknowledge his selfishness to her, Agnes also points out how every time Julia came back from a marriage he failed to assert himself as a father. He did not show any interest or active concern in the girl's problems but chose rather to remain uninvolved. In the crisis precipitated by Harry and Edna's invasion, Julia's desperate cry for recognition and acceptance helps to open an avenue of contact between father and daughter. As Agnes observes, "I do believe that's the first time she's called on her father in . . . since her childhood".

There is far more to Claire than the "stereotype wise drunk" C.W.E. Bigsby sees in her.[15] In that period of sadness and loss which had such an effect on the relationship between Agnes and Tobias, and on Julia, Claire was living out her—as Agnes phrases it—"emancipated womanhood" among the men in the neighborhood. When Claire asks Tobias what he has in common with his best friend Harry apart from the fact that they both "cheated" on their wives in the same summer with the same woman, she kindly and good-humoredly attempts to appease his lingering guilt. "And hardly a distinction", she says. "I believe she was upended that whole July ———— The distinction would have been to have not." She goes on and gratuitously offers a bit of gossip; Harry had the wanton two and a half times. A critical period in Claire's personal loss of faith certainly occurred during or shortly after the summer of promiscuity which she obliquely and glibly talks about to Tobias. With "all the promise . . . all the chance . . . wasted", the several men she found briefly, "none (her) own", Claire has degenerated into a parasite with a drinking problem. There is no evidence that she ever made a serious attempt to control her own destiny. However spicy, amusing and clear-seeing she may be, she is in fact a pitiful woman without much capacity for real life. When she asks Tobias to buy them an island and take them away "to where it is always good and happy", she is only half joking. To spite her older sister Claire did not let herself be "dumped out of the nest". In effect she remained an adolescent.

The love-hate relationship between the two sisters is central to an explanation of Claire's response to life. After the disastrous Friday evening meal she jokes with Tobias: "Unless you kill Agnes . . . how shall I ever know whether I want to live?" She is not being funny. Claire is a bitterly unhappy woman; the unsavory descriptions of her drunkenness speak for themselves. Vitally connected to her excuse for not living is Agnes. However, the open hostility between the two sisters started much earlier, before the alcoholism, before the death-bed promise to their father at the time when they were both still at home—before family feeling was violated by an oppressive sense of duty. Claire tells Julia, "Maw used to say, Claire girl ———— when you go out into the world, get dumped out of the nest, or pushed by your sister . . ." At this point Agnes' jealousy flashes full fire: "She kept you, allowed you . . . tolerated! Put up with your filth . . . Even in her teens, your Auntie Claire had her own very special ways, was very advanced." Ironically, we hear the echo of the pattern of jealousy between the older and the younger child in Agnes' reflection at the beginning of Act Two:

> The individuality we hold so dearly sinks into crotchet; we see ourselves repeated by those we bring into it all, either by mirror or reflection, honor or fault.

Between Claire's willful alcoholism and its disgusting and embarrassing consequences and her own very human doubts and feelings of sexual rivalry, it is no wonder that Agnes wishes that she and Tobias could be alone together. Her husband rises to Claire's defence every time there is an outspoken conflict between the two sisters, reopening the wound of uncertainty, the crack in the formidable structure Agnes balances around herself:

> We must always envy someone we should not, be jealous of those who have so much less. You and Claire make so much sense together, talk so well.

The family's connection with Harry and Edna is a long one. On Saturday night Claire mischievously reminds Harry of an incident in the greenhouse among the orange pots and the mulch during the critical "July". Agnes asks him point blank if Tobias was unfaithful to her that summer after Teddy died. Why have this couple come seeking refuge in the household of Agnes and Tobias? At home that Friday evening, too tired to go out to the club—he had been having his shortness of breath again—Harry decided to stay in and study his French and Edna was sitting in the room with him doing her needlepoint. She describes what happened: "It was all very quiet, and we were all alone . . . and the . . . nothing happened, but we got frightened . . . there was nothing . . . but we were very scared." Anne Paolucci considers the introduction of the Terror in this play "a rotten gimmick".[16] However, what it represents is crucial to an understanding of the author's overall intention. The terror which Harry and Edna drag with them into their friends' house is not something vague like "all the diversified horrors of life"[17] or, as C.A. Sykes would have it, something simple like "honesty".[18] Edna says precisely what it is on Sunday morning before she and Harry go home again. "It's sad to know you've gone through it all, or most of it, without . . . that the one body you've wrapped your arms around . . . the only skin you've ever known . . . is your own." The terror or "plague" as Agnes describes it is the failure of love and the fear of isolation. Behind the external form and finish of their lives, these two people are face to face with the emptiness of the world they have created around themselves in the course of their lives together. They know that Harry's heart attack is imminent and that death and separation are close. With only what they remember between them and nothing to look forward to—nothing left to hope for anymore—in an act of panic they try to break out. Under the motto of "best friends", in their death agony they clutch at their relationship with Agnes and Tobias.

From the moment Harry and Edna enter the house on Friday night new perspectives open for them. They start taking over. Harry looks the room up and down and jealously admires the leather-bound books. He lets Tobias help him with his luggage on Saturday night. Eventually he assumes the presiding role at the family bar. Almost the first thing Edna does when she enters the house is criticize Agnes' upholstery. Now that she is going to live there she will see to having it changed! Ironically, Edna reads the riot act to Julia for not having done the image of marriage much good, and she scolds Agnes and Claire for bickering with each other. "When an environment is not all that it might be", she says smugly, "we must be helpful when we can, my dear; that is the . . . responsibility, the double demand of friendship . . . is it not?"

Whatever the initial impulse was—perhaps the fulfillment of the first few years of their life together before Teddy's death—Agnes never lost sight of it. In spite of the extent to which she devoted her life to being a terribly necessary aspect of the lives of others, she never ceased to be a person in her own right. She still demands something for herself. To begin with Agnes knows that people cannot evade their own difficulties by trying to remedy those of others and, unlike Tobias, she has no sentimental feelings about abstractions like friendship. On Sunday morning she asks him five times, "What did you decide" about the invasion of Harry and Edna. With tact, patience and quiet deliberation she prompts her husband to reconsider his responsibilities to her and to Julia and to admit that if best friends should be something more than Harry and Edna are to them it is their poverty that they are not and too late now to do anything about it: "Blood binds us together when we've no more . . . deep affection for ourselves than others." Walter Kerr describes Agnes near the end of the play: "The cool champagne-cocktail ice of her voice burns away and something nearer lava is served neat."[19]

When Harry and Edna first arrive, Claire, the only one in the family who—when she is not numbed with alcohol—consciously lives with the terror, immediately understands what they want. "Warmth. A special room with a night light, or the door ajar so you can look down the hall from the bed and see that Mommy's door is open." Earlier Friday evening while teasing Tobias, she hints at something like this: "Now and then—you are suddenly frightened and you don't know why?" Tobias prevaricates. Agnes, however, admits that she knows the dangers that lurk around the edges of the shape that she so conscientiously strives to maintain. She understands the threat of "the plague"—the bleak sterility of life without hope, the despair of nothingness. She knows that her family is not stable enough to risk infection. On Sunday morning Harry and Edna depart of their own free will, having admitted to each other in the dark that, were the situation reversed, Agnes and Tobias would not have "rights" in their house either. They learn that people should not need to test each other too far for proof of love. Humbled and newly dependent upon one another they return to their own home to see things through to the end together. Shyly, Harry confides to Tobias:

> You know what I did last night? . . . I got out of bed and I . . . crawled in with Edna . . . she held me. She let me stay awhile, then I could see she wanted to, and I didn't . . . so I went back. But it was funny.

A little later, when the women are alone, Edna confides to them:

> Poor Harry: he's not a . . . callous man, for all his bluff. (*Relaxing a little, almost a contentment*) He . . . he came to my bed last night, got in with me, I . . . let him stay, and talk. I let him think I . . . wanted to make love; he . . . it pleases him I think—to know he would be wanted, if he . . .

During the emotional upset of that weekend Harry and Edna become re-acquainted. They speak about one another to their friends with consideration and new awareness. When they go back to their own house on Sunday morning it will not be as empty as it was when they left it on Friday night. They may talk more again. Touch more. Be a little less lonely.

As for Claire at the end of the play, she did say earlier that she was shopping for a bathing suit. Perhaps she will make Agnes happy and take a vacation while Julia is at home. Claire is in her fifties; she will not change much anymore. She has looked into the void and chosen not to commit suicide. And not to commit herself to anyone or anything else either. She seeks the cruel comfort of her older sister's household and the dubious consolation of alcohol. Monokini or two piece, with her attitude toward life there is small likelihood that she will "find a man". Claire will go on as she is, seeing everything, *doing* nothing. As Agnes observes, "(she) is the strongest of us all: the walking wounded often are the least susceptible". Claire will remain the embodiment of the aching of conscience and of the doubts and fears that are the companions of every life. She is the living representation of the disturbances and intrusions from the outside world which threaten the delicate balance of every marrige, of every relationship. Nevertheless, although not altogether unselfishly, for it is also in her own interest that Harry and Edna depart from the premises, with the "teaching emotion"—the proper mixture of kindness and cruelty—Claire is the one who pushes Julia to the edge of panic. She helps to provoke the hysterical outburst which has such a catalytic effect on the emotional lives of both families. Claire forces Julia to realize that at the age of thirty-six she is "a visitor as much as anyone now", that there is "a great big world __________ hotels, new cities". Even if she herself has turned her back on life and consciously chosen to remain a proud beggar, Claire knows in her heart that in order to cease to be a child each individual must detach himself from his parents.

Because of the events of the bizarre weekend, the most room for change has opened up in the life of Julia, the youngest of all of them. She feels herself reinstated in the family. This time when she asks for reassurance, Tobias is a father to her. In the clash between them on Saturday evening, as Tobias vents "the disgust of his declining years", he makes possible the beginning of a new meeting; the silence between father and daughter is broken. Julia is thrilled: "Sea monster, ram! Nasty, violent, absolutely human man!" Love by rejection and default becomes the love of mutual acceptance. "I'm sorry for having embarrassed you", she says when she comes down on Sunday morning. "Aren't you sorry for embarrassing me, too?" By the end of the play she is good humoredly bossing over the coffee cups. It is "Pop" this and "Julie" that. Perhaps she was "getting ready to pull a Claire" when she came home for the fourth time, but she does point out to her aunt, "I have left Doug. We are not divorced". Julia may go back to her husband and she may also—now that she has been given the background—be able to form a lasting relationship with a partner and as a mature woman start a family of her own.

The insight that Tobias gains on Sunday morning is shattering: "Have we meant, yes, but only if . . . if there's any condition, Agnes! Then it's . . . all been empty." In his head—and—heart confrontation with Harry he releases with "horror and exuberance" the emotions he has kept under control for so many years. In vain with his friend he tries to make up for his failures—his selfishness with his cat, with his wife, and with his daughter. However, as Albee says, "Tobias can no longer fill his life with the problem of making an important choice. He cries, 'Dilemma, come back!' But it is too late".[20] What is most important for Tobias is his recognition that, if things turned out the way they did, it was because of his own limitations. He does not blame Harry and Edna, or the others. He tries to be honest. Finally, he says to his family, "I'm sorry. I apologize".

At the very end when the four of them are alone together again among the empty glasses and the coffee cups (which a little earlier in a small but significant gesture, Tobias, who from his youth has been accustomed to have everything cleaned up for him, helps Julia to set aside), Agnes puts her arm around her husband. The question that she asked him on Friday night has answered itself: "You have hope, only, of growing older than you are in the company of your steady wife, your alcoholic sister-in-law and occasional visits . . . from our melancholy Julia. (*A little sad*) That is what you have, my dear Tobias. Will it do?" Tobias has seen that he has no further options. And he has survived the judgement of his three women without feeling betrayed. He knows that Agnes does not want him to leave her room again. It is too late to make up for the years they have wasted. Perhaps from now on, though, Tobias will trust himself to reach across to find his wife's hand in "the dark sadness".

Notes

[1]All quotations from this play are taken from Edward Albee, *A Delicate Balance* (New York: Pocket Books, Inc., 1967).

[2]The description of the set is taken from the following discussions of the original New York production of *A Delicate Balance:* Robert Brustein, "Albee Decorates an Old House," in *Edward Albee: Twentieth Century Views* ed. Maynard Mack, (Englewood Cliffs, N. J.: Prentice-Hall, Inc., 1975), p. 136, and Walter Kerr, *New York Times,* 23 Sept. 1966.

[3]Kerr, loc. cit.

[4]See Anne Paolucci, *From Tension to Tonic: The Plays of Edward Albee* (Carbondale: Southern Illinois University Press, 1972), p. 108.

[5]See C.W.E. Bigsby, *Albee* (Edinburgh: Oliver and Bogd, 1969), p. 99 and Michael E. Rutenberg, *Edward Albee: Playwright in Protest* (New York: DBS Publications, Inc., 1969), pp. 133-4.

[6]"Strangers in a Room: *A Delicate Balance* Revisited," *Modern Drama,* 17, No. 2 (June 1974), 201.

[7]Rutenberg, p. 130.

[8]Ibid., "Interview with Edward Albee, August 7, 1968," pp. 230-1.

[9]Paolucci, p. 107.

[10]"Broadway in Review," *Educational Theater Journal,* 18, No. 4 (Dec. 1966), 451.

[11]*Edward Albee,* p. 79.

[12]*Albee,* pp. 96-100.

[13]*Playwright in Protest,* p. 149.

[14]Gassner, "Broadway in Review," p. 450.

[15]*Albee,* p. 107.

[16]*From Tension to Tonic,* p. 106.

[17]Ibid., p. 110.

[18]"Albee's Beast Fables: *The Zoo Story* and *A Delicate Balance,*" *Educational Theater Journal,* 25, No. 4 (Dec. 1973), 435.

[19]Kerr, *New York Times,* loc. cit.

[20]*Life,* 28 Oct. 1966, p. 120.

M. Patricia Fumerton (essay date 1981)

SOURCE: "Verbal Prisons: The Language of Albee's *A Delicate Balance,*" in *English Studies in Canada,* Vol. VII, No. 2, Summer, 1981, pp. 201-11.

[*The following essay analyzes the separation of language from thought and meaning in* A Delicate Balance. *The critic asserts that by the end of the play, "language appears not as a medium for communication, but as a necessary protective device. . . ."*]

A Delicate Balance forms part of Edward Albee's continuing exploration into the potentialities and limitations of language, Surprisingly, however, no one has yet provided a detailed analysis of the play's language.[1] This work intends such a study. The characters of ***A Delicate Balance*** are conscious manipulators of their language: a frightened people who use language in an attempt to control or simply to survive fearful realities. They use the decorum of language to disguise anxieties, to balance between implications (as when Agnes habitually says "either . . . or" and "if . . . then"), and thus to evade truths and choices. At the same time, they sharpen their language of evasion into a precise instrument of persuasion—wielded by all, but most skillfully by the "fulcrum," Agnes. Yet in employing it to evade and coerce, the characters limit and distort their language, separating the "word" from its concrete and unconditional "meaning." Ironically—and tragically—they become trapped within the limits they themselves impose upon language.

The play opens with a conversation between Tobias and Agnes, a husband and wife who appear contented and very much in love. The mood is subdued, the characters are attentive, and the language, although formal, is cordial and pleasant. Agnes's opening speeches undulate like the rolling of hills, never descending into deep chasms nor climbing to mountainous peaks. She begins with an idea, glides into a parenthesis that becomes a digression (intermixed with questions to her husband), returns briefly to that idea—from which she again digresses—and finally completes this same thought three pages after it was originally introduced. Her sentences overlap, continually balancing and qualifying themselves:

> What I find most astonishing—aside from that belief of mine, which never ceases to surprise me by the very fact of its surprising lack of unpleasantness, the belief that I might very easily—as they say—lose my mind one day, not that I suspect I am about to, or am even . . . nearby. . . .
>
> (p. 13)[2]

Placid and lamb-like, Agnes appears well-suited to her name. And the further association, through her name, with Saint Agnes, a virgin martyr of the third century, evokes no striking sense of incongruity.[3]

As the play continues, however, it becomes apparent that Tobias and Agnes are not content and that even their love is to be questioned. Their language is a camouflaging tool that expertly conceals a depth of pain and fear. Rather than being an expression of love, the almost euphonious decorum permeating the play is a mark of heightened tension (as in the tea-pouring scene of Act III) or of extreme uneasiness (as in the exchange of names when Harry and Edna first arrive). Whenever uncomfortable or fearful, the characters turn to recognized formalities in order to distance what they fear and to conceal what they feel. Thus, when left alone in the living room in Act III, Harry and Tobias formally greet each other even though they have already been in this same room with the others for some time:

> HARRY: (*Watching them go; laughs ruefully*) Boy, look at 'em go. They got outa *here* quick enough. You'd think there was a . . . (*Trails off, sees* TOBIAS *is ill at ease; says, gently*) Morning, Tobias.
>
> TOBIAS: (*Grateful*) Morning, Harry.
>
> (pp. 158-59)

Ironically, Agnes, the "saint," is the most expert manipulator of this language of disguise. Her *very* correct, *very* polite, and *very* balanced language is deceptively open and articulate—it conceals, in fact, rather than reveals. When Agnes distinguishes between an hysterical condition and an hysterical action (in response to Tobias's declaration that Julia is in hysterics), she is actually using articulation as a defense. Similarly, when Agnes responds with the expression "either . . . or"—an expression frequently mocked by Claire—she articulates the alternatives, but never makes a choice: "She [Julia] will be down or she will not. She will stop, or she will . . . go on" (p. 116). Agnes is as noncommittal as Tobias and the others. By repeatedly using this expression, as well as "if . . . then"—expressions balancing like teeter-totters—Agnes focuses upon the implications and thus evades rather than faces the truths (which demand that one not only recognize, but actively choose between alternatives). Claire sees this clearly:

> We live with our truths in the grassy bottom, and we examine allll the interpretations of allll the implications like we had a life for nothing else, for God's sake.
>
> (pp. 100-01)

Claire's vision is indeed faithful to the meaning of her name:

> AGNES: (*An overly sweet smile*) Claire could tell us so much if she cared to, could you not, Claire. Claire, who watches from the sidelines, has seen so very much, has seen us all so clearly, have you not, Claire. You were not named for nothing.
>
> (p. 110)

Constantly striving to break the balance and expose truths, Claire threatens the equipoise Agnes so carefully maintains. Claire's sentences reach for peaks and descend into chasms. Stuffed with quick, short verbs, they build up and run headlong, rather than balance:

> Pretend you're very sick, Tobias, like you were with the stomach business, but pretend you feel your insides are all green, and stink, and mixed up, and your eyes hurt and you're half deaf and your brain keeps turning off, and you've got peripheral neuritis and you can hardly walk and you hate . . . and you notice—with a sort of detachment that amuses you, you think—that you're more like an animal every day . . . you snarl, and *grab* for things, and hide things and forget where you hid them like not-very-bright dogs, and you wash less, prefer to *be* washed, and once or twice you've actually soiled your bed and laid in it because you can't get up . . . pretend all that. No you don't like that, Tobias?
>
> (p. 32)

Like all potentially dangerous things, Claire must be controlled. With the mere mention of her name, before she even enters the room, Agnes's pleasantly rolling language becomes more forceful and oppressive. Her parenthetical comments (which had earlier acted digressively, dissipating her main idea) are now carefully laid one upon another in the building of her "mountain" of burdens. Note, in particular, the powerful accumulation of monosyllabic words in her first parenthesis:

> If I were to list the mountain of my burdens—if I had a thick pad and a month to spare—that bending my shoulders *most,* with the possible exception of Julia's trouble with marriage, would be your—it must be instinctive, I think, or *reflex,* that's more like it—your reflex defense of everything Claire. . . .
>
> (pp. 16-17)

Agnes describes herself most aptly as the "fulcrum" of the family. A fulcrum is not only a support or point of support on which a lever turns in raising or moving something, but also a means of exerting influence or pressure. As the sole support of her family, Agnes must exert pressure to maintain its shape. She does so through language. Exemplary of this is Agnes's technique of ending a question with "was it not?" or "have I not?" thus adding assertive force to an interrogative sentence:

> AGNES: (*Quietly; sadly*) Well, it was your decision, was it not?
>
> TOBIAS: (*Ibid.*) Yes.
>
> AGNES: And I have made the best of it. Have lived with it. Have I not?
>
> (pp. 144-45)

Harry and Edna are the only people Agnes cannot quite control. These two pose a far greater threat to Agnes than does Claire because they do not fall within Agnes's domain, the family circle. Indeed, the sudden arrival of Harry and Edna is seen as a hostile "invasion" (the verb "harry" means "to plunder"). Fearing for the safety of her stronghold, Agnes struggles to control these invaders—to grasp hold of them—by shifting her mode of address. Throughout the first half of the play, everyone, including Agnes, refers to them as "Harry and Edna." Midway, however, Agnes suddenly switches to "Edna and Harry" and she alone continues to address them in this way throughout the rest of the play:

> Would it seem . . . incomplete to you, my darling, were I to tell you Julia is upset that Har——Edna and Harry are here, that. . . .
>
> (p. 115)

But Harry and Edna remain ungovernable and, therefore, most threatening.

In all other cases, Agnes successfully exerts control through language. She is able to do so because language itself is presented as an authority. But it is only accepted as such if one has the "right" to speak authoritatively. Those who are not members of the family have no right at all—at least, not in the eyes of Julia and Agnes. Consequently, when Edna criticizes the way Agnes and Claire banter—"I wish you two would stop having at each other" (p. 117)—Agnes immediately questions her right to interfere: "Is that for you to say?" (p. 118).

In contrast with the above sequence is an exchange between two rightful members of the family, father and daughter:

> TOBIAS: (*Quiet anger and sorrow*) Your brother would not have grown up to be a fag.
>
> JULIA: (*Bitter smile*) Who is to say?
>
> TOBIAS: (*Hard look*) I!
>
> (p. 73)

Tobias, with verbal force, claims victory, and Julia silently accedes. However, the balance of power shifts at the beginning of Act III when, still dazed from his confrontation with Agnes, Tobias surrenders totally to what Julia says to him:

> JULIA: (*Setting the tray down*) There; now that's much better, isn't it?
>
> TOBIAS: (*In a fog*) Whatever you say, Julie.
>
> (p. 148)

In each of these dialogues one speaker emerges in control through the power of language alone. Of course, the right and ability to exercise this power rest foremost with Agnes. This is most evident when Agnes defines alcoholism:

> AGNES: (*Not looking at either of them*) If we change for the worse with drink, we are an alcoholic. It is as simple as that.
>
> CLAIRE: And who is to say!
>
> AGNES: I!
>
> (p. 38)

After an appeal to Tobias, which receives no response, Claire accepts the definition—she is what Agnes says she is: "Very well, then, Agnes, you win. I shall be an alcoholic" (p. 39). The very use of "if . . . then"—"If we change for the worse with drink, we are an alcoholic"—is authoritarian. This sentence structure leads one to focus upon the"then" clause while unquestioningly accepting or ignoring the "if" clause.

But because the family members have raised their language to an imperious position, even those who try to exert themselves through that language are actually controlled by it: captives of their own language, they think what they say rather than say what they think. Language is a ritual that has become separated from thought and, therefore, from real meaning. The characters are all extremely polite (they cordially address each other with "darling," "dear," "please," "thank you") but Tobias himself questions, as do we, whether this cordiality is only mechanical. Do they *really mean* "darling" and "thank you" or is this apparent sincerity, when actually analyzed, only conditional upon circumstances—like Agnes's "if . . . then?":

> When we talk to each other . . . what have we meant? Anything? When we touch, when we promise, and say . . . yes, or please . . . with our*selves?* . . . have we meant, yes, but only if . . . if there's any condition, Agnes! Then it's . . . all been empty.
>
> (p. 156)

The emptiness of this ritual is most apparent when one compares the long exchange of personal names, upon the first appearance of Harry and Edna, with the similar yet confused voicing of names at the end of the same Act:

> AGNES: (*Reaches doorway; turns to* TOBIAS; *a question that has no answer*) Tobias?
>
> HARRY: (*Rises, begins to follow* EDNA, *rather automaton-like*) Edna?
>
> TOBIAS: (*Confused*) Harry?
>
> (p. 57)

Each individual calls out helplessly, expecting no answer to alleviate his or her isolation.

Like the rules of etiquette, the rules of grammar must always be observed in ***A Delicate Balance.*** Claire deliberately breaks one of these grammatical laws by saying "a alcoholic" (p. 34) rather than "an," but Agnes is quick to catch any irregularity in her speech: "I dropped upstairs—well, *that* doesn't make very much sense, does it? I *happened* upstairs . . ." (p. 81). Here too, however, is an emptiness. The meaning which stands behind the order of language is missing:

> EDNA: Harry is helping Agnes and Tobias get our bags upstairs.
>
> JULIA: (*Slight schoolteacher tone*) Don't you mean Agnes and Tobias are helping Harry?
>
> EDNA: (*Tired*) If you like.
>
> (p. 101)

Individual words clank hollowly within this syntactical kettle-drum—as does the expression, "best friends" (p. 56), or Agnes's repeated use of "glad": "We're *glad* you're here; we're glad you came to surprise us!" (p. 51). The characters have command of their own language in the same way that Harry has mastered French:

> HARRY: . . . and I was reading my French; I've got it pretty good now—not the accent, but the . . . the words.
>
> (p. 54)

They know the lexicon and syntax of their language, but have lost, or forgotten, its meaning.

Several attempts are made to define or to redefine words in ***A Delicate Balance.*** When Agnes defines Claire as an alcoholic, she does so to gain control over her by labelling her. Edna similarly tries to manipulate the others by defining "friendship," yet she is also actually attempting to understand the meaning—or what the others mean—by the word:

> EDNA: (*To* JULIA) You must . . . what is the word? . . . coexist, my dear. (*To the others*) Must she not? (*Silence; calm*) Must she not. This is what you have meant by friendship . . . is it not?
>
> (p. 123)

But Edna's efforts are pathetically unsatisfactory. The language to which these people have reduced themselves is simply too limited for meaningful expression.

This is most evident when Harry and Edna try to explain their terror. Their language fails to provide an adequate description of this fear or of its cause: the characters can only repeat the adjectives, "frightened," "terrified," and "scared." The closest they come to identifying their fear is through a simile:

> HARRY: (*Quite innocent, almost childlike*) It was like being lost: very young again, with the dark, and lost.
>
> (p. 55)

Similarly, Julia, in her hysteria, is unable to express the full force of her pain and fear through language. In fact, the language actually disintegrates as she herself loses control: "Get them out of here, Daddy, getthemoutofheregetthemoutofheregetthemoutofheregetthemoutofhere . . ." (p. 119).

In their struggle to express themselves, individuals often distinguish between synonymous words:

> AGNES: (*More curious than anything*) Do you really want me dead, Claire?
>
> CLAIRE: Wish, yes. Want? I don't know; probably, though I might regret it if I had it.
>
> (p. 42)

They will even differentiate between identical words—as in Act III when Harry tries to explain his relationship with Edna to Tobias: "We don't . . . 'like.' Oh, sure we *like* . . ." (p. 163). In this same Act, Tobias screams that he does not "want" Harry and Edna to stay and yet he begs them to stay.

This word, "want," takes on special significance in ***A Delicate Balance.*** It denotes both a lack and a need of something:

> EDNA: . . . if all at once we . . . NEED . . . we come where we are wanted, where we know we are expected, not only where we want. . . .
>
> (p. 122)

When Edna and Harry come to the house, Julia repeatedly asks, "What do they want?" In Act II, Julia's horror-filled declaration, "THEY WANT!" (p. 106), is followed a few lines later by the pathetic cry, "I *want*!" (p. 107). But like the other characters, Julia does not know specifically what she lacks and needs:

> JULIA: I *want!*
>
> CLAIRE: (*Sad smile*) What do you want, Julia?
>
> JULIA: I . . .
>
> HARRY: Jesus.
>
> JULIA: I WANT . . . WHAT IS MINE!
>
> AGNES: (*Seemingly dispassionate; after a pause*) Well, then, my dear, you will have to decide what that is, will you not.
>
> (pp. 107-08)

"Want" lacks a definable object: it points to something beyond what each individual has, some unidentifiable thing that is missing from their lives:

> TOBIAS: (*Holding a glass out to* AGNES) Did you say you wanted?
>
> AGNES: (*Her eyes still on* CLAIRE) Yes, I did, thank you.
>
> (p. 82)

> HARRY: (*Subdued, almost apologetic*) Edna and I . . . there's . . . so much . . . over the dam, so many . . . disappointments, evasions, I guess, lies maybe . . . so much we remember we wanted, once . . . so little that we've . . . settled for. . . .
>
> (p. 163)

The word "want" exemplifies the casualties language suffers when warped into an instrument of disguise and control. Reduced to an evasive abstraction, "want" resonates with meaning yet is unable to communicate definite thoughts and feelings.

Dominated by this language, the characters themselves approach the undefinable and abstract. A distance separates them from the reader. Their talk is colloquial enough to be typically American, but elaborate enough to be found in a Restoration play like *The Way of the World.* Albee wishes us to be at home with these people and yet to remove them to a more abstract sphere. They are familiar, yet strangers, human and yet less vital than, for instance, George and Martha in ***Who's Afraid of Virginia Woolf?***:

> AGNES: Not even separation; that is taken care of, and in life: the gradual . . . demise of intensity, the private preoccupations, the substitutions. We become allegorical, my darling Tobias, as we grow older.
>
> (p. 90)

It is with the hope of arresting this process of substitution that Tobias reacts so violently against Agnes's evasively abstract use of language:

> TOBIAS: (*Frustration; anger*) I've not been . . . *wrestling* with some . . . abstract problem! These are *people!* Harry and Edna! These are our friends, God damn it!
>
> (pp. 155-56)

Ironically, these "invaders," Harry and Edna, unwittingly open up a path to salvation through self-revelation. Lifting the veil that has shielded but blinded his eyes, Tobias comes to see himself and Agnes in the figures of Harry and Edna. Indeed, Edna speaks in the same manner as Agnes (she uses the royal plural, "we," the affirmative interrogative, "didn't we?" and the expression, "if . . . then"), and Harry's speech mimics the vague language of Tobias (such as his repetitive use of "sure"). In one attempt at defining "friendship," Edna offers a simile that most closely "hits home": "Friendship is something like a marriage, *is* it not, Tobias? For better and for worse?" (p. 124). Tobias comes to see that the meaning of his relationships with his family is mirrored in the meaning of his friendship with Harry and Edna. Although Claire may also see this, she refuses to act. It is only Tobias—the vague, taciturn, and evasive Tobias—who accepts the revelation and makes a final bid for salvation. With open eyes Tobias makes his choice: he decides to go against what he wants—self-protection—for something he wants more—a true and meaningful relationship. Struck with the fear that love could only be error—

> CLAIRE: What else but love?
>
> TOBIAS: Error?
>
> (p. 47)

—he struggles to define such words as "best friends" and "right" in order to give them meanings that are not only meaningful, but concrete and unconditional:

> YOU'VE GOT THE RIGHT!
>
> THE RIGHT!
>
> DO YOU KNOW THE WORD?
>
> THE RIGHT!
>
> (*Soft*)
>
> You've put nearly forty years in it, baby; so have I, and if it's nothing, I don't give a damn, you've got the right to be here, you've earned it. . . .
>
> (p. 167)

Hoping to release himself and his family from their bonds, Tobias strives to reunite their divided language, to restore thought to language:

> I came down here and I sat, all night—hours—and I did something rather rare for this family: I *thought* about something. . . .
>
> (p. 152)

But when Tobias calls out to Harry, "DON'T WE LOVE EACH OTHER?" (p. 165)—a pathetic repetition of Agnes's emphatic "do we not?"—he is begging for an affirmative response to what he fears is untrue.[4]

Nevertheless, Tobias's "reaching out" is a saint-like gesture. As Agnes herself declares, "we quarantine, we ostracize—if we are not immune ourselves, or unless we are saints" (p. 156). The religious language in the play underscores this idea of sainthood. While such expressions as "for God's sake," "hell," and "Jesus" are commonplace expletives, they are selectively placed in ***A Delicate Balance.*** "For God's sake" is most conspicuous, occurring with unusual frequency throughout the play. Whenever upset, Tobias uses the adjective "goddamned." Here, in his hysterical speech to Harry, he pleads in the name of God:

> I DON'T WANT YOU HERE!
>
> YOU ASKED?!
>
> NO! I DON'T
>
> (*Loud*)
>
> BUT *BY CHRIST* YOU'RE GOING TO STAY HERE!
>
> . . . . .
>
> . . . you've got the
>
> right to be here, you've earned it
>
> (*Loud*)

AND *BY GOD* YOU'RE GOING TO

TAKE IT!

. . . . .

I DON'T WANT YOU HERE!

I DON'T LOVE YOU!

BUT *BY GOD* . . . YOU STAY!!

(pp. 166-67; my emphasis)

In fact, the name "Tobias" comes from the hebrew word *"tōbhīyah"* meaning "God is good." By extending hospitality to his neighbours (a connection with the Old Testament "Book of Tobias"), Tobias attempts to justify his name. But Tobias's offer is rejected and his name remains as split from his person as the language is split from meaning.

All of the characters in ***A Delicate Balance*** refuse to be saved—they dread upsetting the balance that so carefully hides and protects them from the naked truth. Each turns from salvation to the ritualistic language Agnes maintains. Indeed, the only religious expletives to be spoken after Tobias's scene with Harry—"good heavens" (p. 170) and "good Lord" (p. 171)—evoke a chilling sensation. For Agnes herself has become something of a substitute Lord. In fact, Agnes is a necessary factor in these people's lives: each individual—even Claire, the rebel—has fallen so low that the support Agnes offers, through language, has become both irresistible and indispensable.

The characters of ***A Delicate Balance*** momentarily waver between sanity and insanity, between revelation and self-deception. Drawn from their self-created—what Claire would call their "willfull"—illusions, they approach the truth, but quickly veer away from any openness, descending back into an even deeper mire of delusion. The language of the play follows a similar pattern: moving from a split between thought and language to a momentary union of words and meaning—the confrontation between Tobias and Agnes at the beginning of Act III, and Tobias' hysterical scene in the same Act—and outward again to a language even further divided from meaning and, therefore, to a language incapable of any real expression. By the end of ***A Delicate Balance,*** language appears not as a medium for communication, but as a necessary protective device; it forms an impenetrable blockage; a thick layer of skin within which each individual may rest secure: isolated and lonely and—tragically—invulnerable.

Notes

[1]The tendency, as with Albee's other plays, is to focus upon the psychology of characterization, theme, and symbolism. See, for example, C. W. E. Bigsby's "The Strategy of Madness: *A Delicate Balance,*" in *Albee* (Edinburgh: Oliver & Boyd Ltd., 1969); Robert M. Post's "Cognitive Dissonance in the Plays of Edward Albee," *Quarterly Journal of Speech,* 55 (1969), 54-60, and his "Fear Itself: Edward Albee's *A Delicate Balance,*" *College Language Association Journal,* 13 (1969), 163-71. A number of critics do include some attention to the play's language. E. G. Bierhaus Jr., in "Strangers in a Room: *A Delicate Balance* Revisited," *Modern Drama,* 17 (1974), 199-206, analyzes the significance of the character's names (pp. 199-202); Ronald Hayman, in *Edward Albee* (New York: Frederick Ungar Publishing Co., 1973), pp. 98-115, criticizes the play for its inactive and inflexible literary language; Terence Brown talks of the simultaneously literal and symbolic levels of the play's language in "Harmonia Discord and Stochastic Process," *Re: Arts & Letters,* 3, 2 (1970), 54-60. See also John J. von Szeliski's "Albee: A Rare Balance," *Twentieth Century Literature,* 16 (1970), 123-30; and Paul Witherington's most interesting study "Albee's Gothic: The Resonances of Cliché," *Comparative Drama,* 4 (1970), 151-65. None of these works, however, offers a close and thorough analysis of the language of the play.

[2]All quotations are from *A Delicate Balance* (New York: Pocket Books, 1968).

[3]For a fuller treatment of the etymology of the characters' names, see Bierhaus's study. My own comments on their names agree with Bierhaus. I add only the connection of "Harry" with the verb "to harry" (treated on p. 204).

[4]Hayman criticizes the flatness of Tobias's grand speech, declaring Albee's failure to express, through the speaker's language, a complexity of thought and feeling (pp. 112-13). Hayman is right that the little-varied style of the speech could never communicate the scope of expression demanded by Albee's notations. But this is the point, and no failure on Albee's part. The characters have so restricted their language and so warped it away from real meaning that, when actually called upon for full and accurate expression, the language inevitably fails to communicate.

Virginia I. Perry (essay date 1983)

SOURCE: "Disturbing Our Sense of Well-Being: The 'Univited' in *A Delicate Balance,*" in *Edward Albee: An Interview and Essays,* The University of St. Thomas, 1983, pp. 55-64.

[*In the essay below, Perry observes that* "A Delicate Balance *is intended to point out the fragile nature of [one's] illusion of security by exploring the ill-defined boundaries which separate sanity from madness and by exposing just how delicate those boundaries can be.*"]

In the first scene of the second act of ***A Delicate Balance,*** Agnes tells Julia about a recently published book: "It is a book to be read and disbelieved, for it disturbs our sense of well-being."[1] Ironically, Agnes' rather terse critical pronouncement might just as aptly be applied to the literary piece in which she herself appears, for by challenging and disturbing the "well-being" of critics and audience alike the play has continued to spark mixed critical response since it was first produced in September 1966. Terence Brown, after acknowledging this mixed reception, paradoxically states that "most of [Albee's] critics, including many of the severest, agree that the Pulitzer Prize-winning ***A Delicate Balance*** is probably his most mature play."[2] John J. von Szeliski goes even further, asserting that "***A Delicate Balance*** is Albee's best play—and that it ranks as a truly major drama."[3] One wonders, then, why this play has met with such unsympathetic criticism, ranging from a review in *The New Republic* where Brustein called the play "a very bad play" to a review in *The Commonweal* in which Wilfrid Sheed criticized the play for being unbelievable.[4] Perhaps it is precisely because the play *does* disturb one's sense of well-being that critics have judged it so harshly, not recognizing that ***A Delicate Balance*** is intended to point out the fragile nature of that illusion of security by exploring the ill-defined boundaries which separate sanity from madness and by exposing just how delicate those boundaries can be, even in a seemingly calm household like that of Agnes and Tobias.

From the beginning of the play, the subject of Agnes' conversation is incongruous not only with the well-ordered setting in which it takes place but also with Agnes' oddly detached attitude. In the living room of a well-appointed suburban house, most likely in Connecticut, one would expect a conversation about golf scores and the Dow Jones average rather than the wistful musings of Agnes on what it would be like to lose one's mind. She approaches the subject with ethereal high-mindedness, as if a descent into madness were nothing more than a graceful release. Her lyrical description of madness suggests floating upward, a spiritual transcendence: ". . . some gentle loosening of the moorings sending the balloon adrift—and I think that is the only outweighing thing: adrift: the . . . becoming a stranger in . . . the world, quite . . . involved, for I never see it as violent, only a drifting . . ." (p. 13).

Despite the fact that Agnes' casual consideration of the prospect of madness at first seems merely a bit of metaphoric whimsy in light of her apparent stability and affluence, one senses an undercurrent of apprehension in the fitful stops and starts, the sudden interjection of the concrete with the disconcerting reference to Agnes' sister Claire, and finally in the confused syntax. Moreover, the last line indicates that such thoughts are not the products of the moment but have been continually entertained many times before. As the play progresses, Agnes' reasons for her preoccupation with madness become more clear, particularly after she reveals her reaction to her son's death. In a rare moment of vulnerability, Agnes speaks of the existential doubts which brought her to the edge of insanity: "It was an unreal time: I thought Tobias was out of love with me—or rather, was tired of it, when Teddy died, as if that had been the string. . . . Ah, the things I doubted then, that I was loved—that *I* loved, for that matter!—that Teddy had ever lived at all—my mind, you see" (p. 109). The uncertainty and the loss of memory associated here with insanity are an echo of Albee's earlier play ***Tiny Alice*** in which Julian describes what he has called a nervous breakdown: "And when I was away from myself—never far enough, you know, to . . . blank, just to . . . fog over—when I was away from myself I could not sort out my imaginings from what was real."[5]

Significantly, for both Agnes and Julian, madness is portrayed as a confusing and painful loss of identity. For both, it is a frightful wrenching away from the known rather than the graceful slipping away of Agnes' first speech. After Miss Alice asks him, "Are you sure you're not describing what passes for sanity?" (p. 60), Julian gives a speech similar in stops and starts to the one Agnes gives; only Julian's doubts go even further: "But one night . . . now, there! You see? I said "one night," and I'm not sure, even now, whether or not this thing happened or, if it did not happen, it did or did not happen at noon, or in the morning, much less at night . . . yet I say night" (p. 61). Miss Alice neatly sums up the problem by asking, "Is the memory of something having happened the same as it having happened?" (p. 64). If such an important connection for the individual's sense of himself and the world as personal memory can so easily fail, then sanity may be more tenuous than one would like to believe. Julian no longer knows whether or not he can trust his own mind, just as Agnes after her son's death could no longer be sure if she loved or if Teddy had even lived. Thus, what seem to be the most basic facts of one's life can come into doubt with even a slight shift in the weight on the balancing board between sanity and madness.

Because Agnes has experienced this uncertainty, she is at the same time both intrigued and frightened by the prospect of madness. In the opening scene, she protects herself from what she fears by describing a descent into madness in ethereal terms. Induced madness is particularly appealing to Agnes because it substitutes control for uncertainty, predictability for spontaneity. By exploring the possibility of insanity in palatable terms, Agnes can feel as if she is gaining some measure of control over that which she fears most. However, despite her attempts to maintain order by redefining liabilities into assets and to prevent the unpredictable through the sheer power of the will, the "uninvited" comes—as if to stay. Despite Agnes' suggestion that she can control events by what she thinks—"And I promise you as well that I shall think good thoughts—healthy ones, positive—and to ward off madness, should it come by—uninvited" (p.21)—she soon discovers that mental well-being is not a function of the strength or weakness of an individual's will.

Agnes and Tobias, it seems, have been successful up to this point in avoiding the unexpected, largely by insisting on maintaining their control over themselves and their environment. For Agnes and Tobias, life has been a matter of stability and implementing one's will rather than of responding with emotion or flexibility. Nowhere is this more powerfully evident than in Agnes' eloquent speech to Julia: " 'To keep in shape.' Have you ever heard the expression? Most people misunderstand it, assume it means alteration, when it does not. Maintenance. When we keep something in shape, we maintain its shape—whether we are proud of that shape, or not, is another matter—we keep *it* from falling apart. We do not attempt the impossible. We maintain. We hold . . . I shall . . . keep this family in shape. I shall maintain it, hold it" (p. 88).

Tobias, also, with his motto of "We do what we can" (p. 19), believes in the power of the will to establish order. When that proves to be a failure as the play progresses, Tobias' distress at no longer being able to control events is manifested in his frantic demand that Harry remain: "I

DON'T WANT YOU HERE! YOU ASKED?! NO! I DON'T (*loud*) BUT BY CHRIST YOU'RE GOING TO STAY HERE! YOU'VE GOT THE RIGHT! THE RIGHT! DO YOU KNOW THE WORD? THE RIGHT! . . . AND BY GOD YOU'RE GOING TO TAKE IT! DO YOU HEAR ME?" (pp. 166-7). Hysterical, Tobias commands Harry to stay, but his orders are merely manifestations of the frustration Tobias feels in not being able to bring order through his commands.

In the course of the play, Tobias must confront the limits of his will along with the limits of friendship and love. Control is the antithesis of spontaneity and healthy love, a lesson that Tobias and Agnes can learn only when they are forced to surrender some of that control, which for both Agnes and Tobias is often manifested in language—especially in definitions. Critics have remarked that the language in this play is pretentious and self-conscious, overlooking the fact that such language intentionally calls attention to itself as a weapon against the "uninvited" and as a protection against the "dark side of reason" (p. 175). To have the proper words in a situation, like having the right glass for one's cognac, is to create stability and maintain order. As von Szeliski notes, "Even in crises, formal conversation rules apply. Talking about Julia, Tobias reports she is in hysterics and Agnes says, 'That is a condition; I inquired about an action.' When Agnes says she will suffer the mantle of the drill sergeant, she is really speaking of the discipline of *talk*."[6]

Conversation is, then, a means of control as well as protection. When Tobias suggests to Agnes that she should apologize to Claire, Agnes parries with a clever linguistic reversal: "Apologize! To her? To Claire? I have spent my adult life apologizing *for* her; I will not double my humiliation by apologizing *to* her" (p. 17). Tobias' response underscores the attention paid to words—"One does not apologize to those for whom one must?" (p. 17)—a retort delightful for its conciseness as well as for its demonstration that he too can play this verbal game. However, while Tobias displays his skill at this repartee, he, much more than Agnes, clearly understands the inherent limitations of language. In spite of his hope that he might help Julia by means of a "serious" talk, Tobias still doubts that such a talk will have any ameliorative effect on his daughter: "If I saw some point to it, I might—if I saw some reason, chance. If I thought, I might . . . break through to her, and say, 'Julia . . .' but then what would I say? 'Julia . . .' Then, nothing" (p. 42). Agnes replies, "If we do not love someone . . . never have loved them. . . ." But Tobias reveals a deeper understanding: "No; there can be silence, even having" (p. 42). Tobias understands the mysteries of the ineffable better than Agnes, but perhaps Agnes *needs* the weapon of language more than Tobias does. In Agnes' speech to Claire, she leaves no room for a response, her eloquence protecting her from whatever Claire might say to defend herself or accuse Agnes. In a *tour de force,* Agnes tells Claire:

> If you come to the dinner table unsteady, if when you try to say good evening and weren't the autumn colors lovely today you are nothing but vowels, and *if* one smells the vodka on you from across the room—and *don't* tell me again, *either* of you! that vodka leaves nothing on the breath: if you are expecting it, if you are sadly and wearily expecting it, it does . . . if these conditions exist . . . *persist* . . . if I should scold, it is because I wish I needn't. If I am sharp, it is because I am neither less nor more than human . . . I apologize for being articulate.
>
> (p. 23)

Her apology for being articulate could not be more sarcastic since it is her very ability to be articulate which allows her to have the last word; indeed, language is her most powerful weapon against what she perceives as the threatening alliance between Tobias and Claire. Verbal dexterity is Agnes' weapon against what she cannot understand, articulateness her mooring in the world.

In contrast to Agnes' remarkable eloquence, Harry's and Edna's description of what drove them out of their house is marked by confusion and struggle. They search for the words to express the fear so central to the play; that they cannot articulate the feeling of being lost and frightened in their own house is part of the terror. Unlike the fear felt by Agnes, the primal fear experienced by Harry and Edna is ill-defined, and, hence, it is a fear which cannot be controlled by language. Albee thus suggests that man's deepest fears are ineffable, unable to be assuaged by words. This realization, on the parts of the characters, creates an inconsolable sense of isolation, for as Robert Post points out, "Fear is a major fulcrum around which Albee's play is built. The fear is one which the characters realize but it is one which they are unable to define. It seems to be the kind of fear that all mankind has—fear which man realizes but which he cannot communicate to others or to himself."[7]

Agnes' attempt to order the world in such neat fashion is eclipsed by the chaos that arrives uninvited—"the disease". Agnes' eloquence is, after all, no weapon against the dread with which Harry and Edna confront her. Precisely because speech is her weapon, she is less armed against "the disease" when it arrives uninvited. In ***Lady From Dubuque,*** Sam is in a similar predicament. The wittiest and most articulate character at the beginning of the play, he is the most disturbed by the unexpected guests who come to help his wife through her very real disease. Sam takes longer to see these daemons as anything other than menacing characters, his intuitive sense having been blocked out by his reliance on language. In the face of disease—for Sam, his wife's cancer and for Agnes and Tobias, this mysterious "plague"—words cannot express, let alone dispel, fear. Sounding like children, Harry and Edna try to describe their primeval feeling: "We got . . . scared . . . We . . . were . . . terrified . . . we were scared. It was like being lost: very young again, with the dark, and lost. There was no . . . thing . . . to be frightened of, but . . . WE WERE FRIGHTENED . . . AND THERE WAS NOTHING" (p. 55). The pauses indicate how difficult it is for them to express what they have felt.

Critics have speculated about the source of Harry's and Edna's fear; C.W.E. Bigsby borrows from William James and Leo Tolstoy, saying they are faced with "an irremediable sense of precariousness" and an awareness of the "meaningless absurdity of life."[8] However, for critics to give a name to the fear is to make the same mistake as Agnes and Tobias, to limit with language. Moreover, Harry's and Edna's own words tell us what they are afraid of—"nothing, NOTHING." The nature of this "nothing" becomes crucial to the whole play, serving as it does as a backdrop to the attempts to maintain order. In effect, the "nothing" of which Harry and Edna are so frightened is a Nothing which nonetheless has substance; that is, the Abyss or the Void. Harry and Edna find themselves face to face with the pre-Logos nothingness—the emptiness before the order of language, before identity, before existence. That void is similar to what Agnes experiences when she doubted if Teddy ever existed. For a terrifying moment, Harry and Edna glimpse what the world would be without the meaning created by externally imposed patterns and structures. Because the emptiness which Harry and Edna feel comes from nothing in particular, their fear is even more startling than that of Agnes, whose doubts result from her son's death. Without a particular cause, the disease would seem to have no cure. Circumstance protects no more than does language. Albee deliberately disturbs the balance because, as von Szeliski says, Albee wants us "to deal with our emptiness through first understanding it."[9] Albee changes the patterns to reveal the Nothingness behind those patterns, exposing the connections and constructs which serve as moorings. Speaking for the playwright, Claire ridicules these patterns: ". . . the rules of the guestbook—be polite. We have our friends and guests for patterns, don't we?—known qualities. The drunks stay drunk; the Catholics go to Mass, the bounders bound. We can't have changes—throws the balance off" (p. 150).

Albee, of course, intends to throw his audience off balance, knowing that only through shifting the patterns can the patterns be revealed. At another point, Agnes says to Claire: "Those are the ground rules." Claire then turns to Tobias with a sad smile, "Tobias? Nothing? Are those the ground rules? Nothing? Too . . . settled? Too . . . dried up? Gone?" (p. 39). Although Claire is referring to Tobias' lack of intervention in the ground rules, Albee uses this conversation to refer to the situation he creates where such ground rules no longer apply, where "my room" becomes "our room" which is turn becomes "*the* room." Boundarics change, and limits reveal themselves to be mere functions of a particular situation Albee creates, not Platonic universals true for all cases and all times.

When Harry and Edna, on the basis of their friendship with Agnes and Tobias, move into Julia's room, they feel their relationship supercedes that of Julia who returns "home" after the failure of her fourth marriage. Julia is surprised to find herself "dispossessed." The confusion of the situation is indicated by the personal pronouns in Tobias' remark to Agnes: "I almost went into *my* room . . . by habit . . . by mistake, rather, but then I realized that your room is my room because my room is Julia's because Julia's is . . ." (p. 13). Because the ground rules have changed—friends taking precedence over family—possessive pronouns have virtually lost their meanings; the simple terms of ownership have been called into question. The questions of propriety so easily answered at the beginning of the play with the implied question of "What belongs where?"—the cognac in the glass—have been replaced by the more important but more difficult question of "Who belongs where?"

Claire and Julia discuss the new situation, and Julia says, "But that's my room," to which Claire replies, "It's . . . the *room.* Happens you were in it. You're a visitor as much as anyone, now." Julia, in turn, answers with a small whine, "But I *know* that room" (p. 99). One must ask, then, if knowledge is a necessary criterion of ownership, just as Alice demanded to know if the memory of an event was the same as its occurrence. Yct within the linguistic debate of ***A Delicate Balance,*** Julia, like Julian in ***Tiny Alice,*** seems to be fighting a losing battle. It is little wonder that her frustration becomes unbearable, upset as she is not only by being dispossessed but by losing her grasp on the criteria for possession. To Julia, the orderly world of her parents where logic reigned has become an incomprehensible game of chance. Her place has been usurped, and she does not know how or why this has happened. Edna grandly offers "her" room to Julia when Julia asks her mother for a room in which she can rest. The ground rules have changed with no explanation. Not only has Julia lost her room, but now the terms by which she had assumed it to be hers have been removed as well. In a very real sense, her identity is in question. Is it any wonder, then, that her frustrated response is a hysterical "I want . . . WHAT IS MINE!" (p. 108)? Agnes answers coolly, "Well, then, my dear, you will have to decide what that is, will you not?" (p. 108). The point here is not that such decisions can ultimately be made with any degree of certainty but, rather, that such decisions are necessary compromises made for the sake of one's mental well being in the face of the infinite.

The crisis of the room thus juxtaposes the rights of friends with the rights of family. Tobias wants to believe in the possibility of unconditional love in friendship and, therefore, wants to overlook Julia's claim to her room in favor of redefining the boundaries of friendship. Because he wants to offer unconditional friendship, out of both duty and his own needs rather than love, Tobias becomes obsessed with the right of Harry and Edna to stay. As Robert M. Post notes, "Even though in reality there is no deep bond between these 'friends,' Tobias insists that the fact that they are labelled as 'friends' gives them the right to live in his house."[10] It is Claire who earlier in the play says that love is not enough, but it is poor Tobias who has to learn what he can and cannot give.

Thus, if the play chronicles the rapid destruction of the sense of well-being among its central characters, it does so by making them aware of the limits or boundaries of human existence: limits of love, limits of language, limits to the control which one has over his own life, limits of self and self-expression. Within the course of the play, all learn that the boundaries of space and friendship and even family are neither fixed nor immutable and are but false stars by which they may only temporarily plot the course of their own lives, for the world of the play is an existential realm in which the accumulated patterns of a lifetime may be lost in an instant.

In the last act, Claire ironically muses, "Just think, Tobias, what would happen if the patterns changed, you wouldn't know where you stood, and the world would be full of strangers; that would never do" (p. 150). The supreme irony here is that Claire speaks as though such a change in patterns were a mere possibility, and a remote one at that, rather than the absolute certainty which such change has proven to be throughout the play. For all intents and purposes, the world is already full of strangers, strangers to each other, to those most intimate, even to themselves. Perhaps it is Edna who sees the truth most clearly: "It's sad to know you've gone through it all, or most of it, without . . . that the one body you've wrapped your arms around . . . the only skin you've ever known . . . is your own—and that it's dry . . . and not warm" (p. 169). The only limits which remain intact are those of human mortality, separation, and aloneness. The identification which the audience feels with the characters is not a matter of situation or experience, since those elements are the least realistic elements in the work. Rather, it is an identification based on a mutual feeling of uneasiness and a shared sense of personal vulnerability. Such is the discomfiting message with which the play confronts its audience and critics. A little later, Edna concludes: "finally . . . there's nothing there . . . save rust; bones; and the wind" (p. 169).

It is as a protection against this realization that mankind creates his daily patterns, and it is this very realization which demonstrates the brittleness of these fictions. At the end of the play, Agnes says, "They say we sleep to let the demons out—to let the mind go raving mad, our dreams and nightmares all our logic gone awry, the dark side of our reason. And when the daylight comes again . . . comes order with it" (p. 175). Theatre at its best can accomplish this exorcism by allowing us to participate in "the dark side of our reason" but at a comfortably safe distance. Albee has succeeded in showing us such demons that we may understand better the miracle of *not* becoming a stranger in a world where the foundation of our sense of well-being tends to be sand rather than rock. We can neither rely on the patterns as if they were etched in granite nor can we exist adrift, "strangers in the world, quite uninvolved." Edward Albee has explored this delicate balance in his play and, while disturbing our sense of well-being, has helped us to understand ourselves better.[11]

Notes

[1]Edward Albee, *A Delicate Balance* (New York: Atheneum Pocket Book edition, 1968), p. 65. All subsequent page references appear in the text.

[2]Terence Brown, "Harmonia Discord and Stochastic Process: Edward Albee's *A Delicate Balance,*" *re: arts and letters* 3, No. 2 (Spring 1970):54.

[3]John J. von Szeliski, "Albee: A Rare *Balance,*" *Twentieth Century Literature* 16, No. 2 (April 1970):127.

[4]For a survey of reprinted reviews of *A Delicate Balance,* see John Gassner, *Dramatic Soundings: Evaluations Culled from Thirty Years of Dramatic Criticism* (New York: Crown, 1968), pp. 604-7.

[5]Edward Albee, *Tiny Alice* (New York: Atheneum Pocket Book Edition, 1965), p. 60. All subsequent page references appear in the text.

[6]von Szeliski, "Albee," p. 123.

[7]Robert M. Post, "Fear Itself: Edward Albee's *A Delicate Balance,*" *C.L.A. Journal* 13, No. 1 (Sept. 1969):167.

[8]C. W. E. Bigsby, *Albee* (Edinburgh: Oliver & Boyd, 1969), p. 98.

[9]von Szeliski, "Albee," p. 130.

[10]Post, "Fear Itself," p. 167.

[11]I would like to thank Professor Sophia Morgan and Mrs. Aladeen Smith for their encouragement and help in the preparation of this essay.

FURTHER READING

Clurman, Harold. "Albee on Balance. "*The New York Times* (13 November 1966): II 1, 3.

Contends that in *A Delicate Balance* and other plays Albee demonstrates that "we are uneasy, without comfort, unhinged."

McCarten, John. "Six on a Seesaw. "*The New Yorker* XLII, No. 32 (1 October 1966): 121-22.

Review of *A Delicate Balance* that argues that the play is "lacking in cohesion, and the motivations of its characters [are] rather hard to follow."

Paolucci, Anne. "Albee and the Restructuring of the Modern Stage. "*Studies in American Drama, 1945-Present* 1 (1986): 3-23.

Analyzes Albee's innovative dramaturgy in *A Delicate Balance,* notably the "integration of language and musical effects--the arias, the large choral voices, the weaving of melodic strains "in the play.

Sheed, Wilfrid. "Liquor is Thicker. "*Commonweal* LXXXV, No. 2 (14 October 1966): 55-6.

Negative review that regards *A Delicate Balance* "no more than half a play, about a year's work from completion."

von Szeliski, John. "Between Optimism and Pessimism " In *Tragedy and Fear: Why Modern Tragic Drama Fails,* pp. 19-29. Chapel Hill: The University of North Carolina Press, 1971.

Includes a consideration of *A Delicate Balance,* calling it "an excellent philosophical image of our time precisely *because* it does not attempt the formula of tragedy."

Seascape

INTRODUCTION

Albee himself directed the initial production of *Seascape* on 26 January 1975, at the Sam S. Shubert Theatre in New York City. This work depicts an aging couple who are accosted on a beach by a pair of intelligent lizard-like creatures that have been driven from the sea by the processes of evolution. The four characters discuss topics of mutual understanding, including the purpose of existence, before concurring that human and alien creatures should aid and inspire one another to shape the conditions of life.

CRITICAL RECEPTION

Albee received his second Pulitzer Prize for *Seascape.* Although Walter Kerr found the play "predictable" and lacking dramatic energy and Stanley Kauffmann judged it "banal," many early reviewers commended its originality and—as several critics termed it—"exquisite" dialogue. Critical commentary on *Seascape* has focused on its analysis of existence, death, and the human spirit. Liam O. Purdom has viewed the play as a "treatise on human psychology," and Gerry McCarthy has seen it as a consideration of "the phenomenon we know as life and experience personally as existence." Lucinda P. Gabbard has read the play's "principal concern" as "the realization of the proximity of death," an awareness that Albee has gentled by means of the fairy tale form. Samuel J. Bernstein has argued that in *Seascape* Albee "has cast a broad, piercing light on the human condition" and revealed that love "is our only weapon against the void." Finally, Matthew C. Roudané has contended that in this play "Albee is not writing merely about the naturalistic evolution of the human species, but about growth patterns of humankind, about combining the visceral and the intellectual into a new whole which is the consciously aware person."

PRODUCTION REVIEWS

Clive Barnes (review date 27 January 1975)

SOURCE: "Albee's *Seascape* Is A Major Event," in *The New York Times,* 27 January 1975, p. 20.

[*The critic praises nearly every aspect of* Seascape *in the following review, especially its blending of the comic and the serious.*]

Hats off, and up in the air! A major dramatic event.

Edward Albee's play ***Seascape,*** which opened at the Shubert Theater last night, is fundamentally a play about life and resolution. It is that currently rare thing, a comedy rather than a farce, and it is a curiously compelling exploration into the basic tenets of life. It is asking in a light-hearted but heavy-minded fashion whether life is worth living. It decides that there is no alternative.

As Mr. Albee has matured as a playwright, his work has become leaner, sparer and simpler. He depends on strong theatrical strokes to attract the attention of the audience, but the tone of the writing is always thoughtful, even careful, even philosophic. As with any major artist he has his own distinct profile—an Albee play is recognizably an Albee play—but if he could usefully be linked with any of his contemporaries, they would be Samuel Beckett and Harold Pinter.

The story is simplicity itself. A middle-aged couple, with children departed and obviously of independent means, find themselves on a beach. They discuss, in the desultory fashion of old and friendly lovers, love, marriage and life. She paints, he snoozes. What has it all added up to? Eventually they are met by another middle-aged couple. The second couple happens to be lizards.

The lizards are deep-sea creatures at a very advanced stage of evolution who have decided to come up into the air. It is very nearly a foolish trick on the playwright's part. After all, anthropomorphic monsters from the nether depths, who wear scales but talk English in a stilted accent, should by all the rules of the game be childish. But plays have a happy way of not having rules.

What Mr. Albee has given us here is a play of great density, with many interesting emotional and intellectual reverberations. The trigger of the play's action is obvious enough—it is the old visitor from Mars examining human institutions and practices and comparing them with his own to the amusement and the amazement of the audience.

But the resonances go much deeper than could be offered by science-fiction pop-guns. Mr. Albee is suggesting that one of the purposes of an individual human existence is quite simply evolution—that we all play a part in this oddly questionable historic process. So that the purpose of life is life itself—it is a self-fulfilling destiny. We have to come out of the water and get onto the beach, we have to live and we have to die, simply because life is about life.

In a recent interview with Mel Gussow of The New York Times, Mr. Albee revealed that ***Seascape*** was a companion piece to his somber masterpiece about death some four years ago, ***All Over.*** This is an important fact for the audience to keep in mind. It is an optimistic play, a rose play rather than a black play, as Jean Anouilh would have said, but it is nevertheless serious and provocative. It is also funny, and the humor is all the funnier for having a point to it.

What marks out Mr. Albee as a comic writer is largely his compassion. Even in the bitchy dialogue of ***Who's Afraid of Virginia Woolf?*** there ran this deep concern for humanity—even his chilliest wit has a saving grace of warmth to it.

The tone of the beginning of the play irresistibly recalls—surely intentionally?—Beckett's *Happy Days.* There is the same discursive familiarity, the same apparent aimlessness, which is betrayed only by the occasional pellet of truth or the compellingly apt joke. With the arrival of the sea-creatures there is a sudden danger of triteness. There is a fear that after all we are just going to be told that "everyone is the same under the skin—black, white, yellow or lizard." But the danger passes as Mr. Albee, with that spare laconic language of his, probes deeper and deeper into the subterreanean seascape of our pasts, presents and futures.

This is the first play that Mr. Albee has directed, and he has done so with self-evident skill and ease. The directorial difficulty is obvious enough—to make the sea-creatures both strange enough to cast contrasting light upon our own humanity yet credible enough to speak English, and also to draw the humor out of the similarities between the two couples with subtlety rather than obviousness. This he achieves by virtually choreographing the sea-creatures (he is much helped by the splendid costumes of Fred Voelpel) and giving them a special diction rather than a special language or even a special accent. It works well, as does the handsome sand-duned set by James Tilton.

The actors have been carefully picked, coached and presented. Deborah Kerr (after far too long away from Broadway) starts beautifully and diffidently as a no-nonsense English matron, and then slowly slips off her pretenses and becomes a very warm woman. Barry Nelson (who, like Miss Kerr, and this is not truly a fair criticism, looks a little too young for the role) is a complete master of the off-hand. His accomplishment is so charming and unforced, and he works with Miss Kerr as if they had been married for years.

To my amazement I note from the playbill that this is Frank Langella's Broadway debut—he is among our most distinguished young actors, and Broadway should be ashamed of itself. It would be so easy to play a lizard as a sort of Demon King or Godzilla, but Mr. Langella plays him precisely as one of those animals you have always longed to communicate with but never had the language. His partner, Maureen Anderman, is also superbly lizard-like, but as humanly feminine as Mr. Langella is humanly masculine. A distinguished quartet both with and without scales.

See ***Seascape*** and you will get a good few hearty giggles, but also, if you listen attentively, a good few insights about the primeval ooze from which we all came, and the blind, inarticulative courage that keeps us all going.

Walter Kerr (review date 2 February 1975)

SOURCE: "Albee's Unwritten Part, McNally's Missing Joke," in *The New York Times,* 2 February 1975, p. 5.

[*The review that follows argues that* Seascape *lacks dynamic intensity.*]

It seems to me that the key to Edward Albee's interesting, sun-bleached but taffy-thin ***Seascape*** is the part he hasn't written for Barry Nelson. Mr. Nelson, lined, grumpy, a grandfatherly fiftyish, is spending a day on the dunes with his much more animated wife, Deborah Kerr.

Miss Kerr, as blonde as the blinding daylight that washes the stage almost clean of color, has no intention of wasting all she's been through: growing up, marriage, motherhood, worry. "What have we got left?" she'd like to know. And, since Mr. Nelson has so little to say, she answers her own question: "Ourselves—and some time." She wouldn't mind circling the globe exploring every beach that exists: she is the nearly spent life force still in motion.

But Mr. Nelson has gone under, relaxing inert on the sand, willing to offer only the bleakest dismissive phrases as antiphonal response to his wife's monologue ("Let it go," "We'll see"), extending himself just enough to suggest that "we've earned a little rest." "We've earned a little life!" she explodes, chatting on and on about how women really want divorces so that they can be 18 again, cupping her shoulders with her arms till she resembles a tight little Valentine as she prods him to remember sex.

She must even prod him to remember a passion he had as a boy, a curious one. He'd always been fond of sinking to the bottom of a pool or pond or shallow cove, measuring his exhalations to keep him from rising, weighting himself with stones if necessary. Life on the sea-floor has seemed native to him, the abundant flurry about him more hospitable than human society above. But when she urges him to go try it again—*now*—he can't be persuaded. It's no longer life, of any kind, he's looking for. "All caved in?" she asks him petulantly, acknowledging that her petulance swells inside her like a bee-sting. "All closed down?"

Yes. Then, as the first of the evening's two acts is about to terminate its wholly static relationship, two humanoid lizards in breast shells, Harlequin scales, and avocado ridges to mark their exterior spines, appear from the sea, thrown upward by an inevitable evolutionary advance. Mr. Albee reminds us that he can be a shrewd craftsman here: the lizards appear, seem to threaten, cause consternation before the curtain falls. But they do not speak. It is only when the curtain has gone up again, and we have had time to come to terms with an agreeable fantasy, that the creatures choose to communicate—in English, and in English jargon at that ("Now, listen here, Buddy" may be a bit much from a species in mutation, but on the whole the conceit works: the author has known precisely *when* to make it unsurprising).

What follows is sometimes amusing, more often elementary. The male lizard, superbly writhed by Frank Langella, is shocked that Miss Kerr should have breasts, like a whale; the comedy of his won't-take-no-for-an-answer curiosity is secured by Mr. Nelson's huffiness over his wife's too-eager "exhibitionism." But once it has been established that both couples copulate, the humor becomes biology-class predictable. Miss Kerr is astounded that Maureen Anderman, reptilian tail cosily coiled, should take pride in having produced 7,000 eggs but should have thereafter cared for none of them. Mr. Langella, wide eyes made wider by the white ovals of paint in which they are embedded, is even more astonished that Miss Kerr *should* have cared for her unimpressive three and cared for them a good 20 years each. We are perhaps less stunned than they, having listened to our own sixth-grade charges expatiate upon such matters interminably—if without recourse to Mr. Langella's interjected "Wows!"

The conversation advances to matters of "emotion," "separation," consciousness of death, none of which belong to an undersea vocabulary. When Mr. Nelson remarks that death will someday separate their visitors, Miss Anderman cries. The tears enrage Mr. Langella. Emotions are coming into play now, and the lizards do not find them attractive. The question we have known was coming comes: had the advancing species best go back down while there is still time?

It is at this point that the piece wants drama. We've had stillborn talk, kept alive with her customary expertise by Miss Kerr; we've had momentarily engaging surprise; we've played the kindergarten games that Darwin taught us. But there is at last an issue, a crisis, and it seems, as issue and crisis, very much related to Mr. Nelson's earlier urge to surrender. Why is that not now picked up, toward one end or another? Since the very problem so much *concerns* Mr. Nelson, why does he not engage himself, as devil's advocate, as newly enlightened human being, as something? His very boyhood games seem to make him a likely participant in the struggle—to advance or not to advance—and we wait for connections, for a door to be opened that will disclose whatever futures humans and lizards choose. But, with the key in his hand and a carefully built-up promise, Mr. Albee will not use it.

If Mr. Langella, turned even greener, senses that "It's rather dangerous up here," Mr. Nelson simply shrugs "Everywhere" and turns away, still counting himself out. It is Miss Kerr, pursuing precisely the same course she has from the beginning, who insists "You'll have to come back sooner or later, you don't have any choice," defending mutation simply because it's taken place. But if *she* has some effect on their so-tentative guests, neither she nor the new arrivals have any on the man in the case—or on the relation between man and wife—and the encounter comes out lopsided, lopsided and rather bland. We'd been expecting interaction all 'round, especially after what we've been told about Mr. Nelson. But the vital tangle is bypassed, and we must settle for a sometime charm.

James Tilton's dazzlingly lighted dunes beneath a faint swirl of clouds create a stunning stage picture—for once, the audience is honestly agape as it catches its first glimpse of the curving earth—and Mr. Albee has directed his own actors well, though directing Mr. Nelson has mainly, and necessarily, meant nothing more than finding him new recumbent postures. The writing is blessedly spare, free of the convoluted locutions that have sometimes grown like coral over the author's meanings. But he is sparing of more than language; an available dramatic energy is kept lying in wait.

Brendan Gill (review date 3 February 1975)

SOURCE: "Among the Dunes," in *The New Yorker,* Vol. L, No. 50, 3 February, 1975, pp. 75-77.

[*The following admiring review declares that "of all of Mr. Albee's plays,* Seascape *is the most exquisitely written."*]

Edward Albee's ***Seascape,*** at the Shubert, is a short, wryly witty, and sometimes touching play about discovery. Boldly and simply, it asserts that, at no matter what age and in no matter what time and place, acts of discovery remain to be undertaken. With luck, such acts will be found to have meaning; better still, there is the possibility that they will bear fruit. The plot is a charming toy: a well-to-do middle-aged couple, faced with the bleak certainty of the closing in and shutting down of their lives, have unexpectedly bestowed on them the boon of doubt; through a prodigious accident, they perceive that their lives may yet open out, may yet contain unlooked-for wonders. After many words of despair, the last word we hear spoken, in bright sunlight, under the bluest of blue skies, is a hesitant and yet hopeful "Begin!" And the word is spoken not by a member of the human race but by an enormous speckled lizard, exceptionally distinguished in bearing and utterance, who feels that he has much to learn. So, Mr. Albee hints, do the rest of us. But we must be quick; such willing creatures are not easily come by, even at the edge of our mother the sea.

Of all Mr. Albee's plays, ***Seascape*** is the most exquisitely written. He has calculated not only every immaculate line of dialogue but every word, every caesura; when the actors fall silent, we hold our breath and wait, as we wait at the reading of some superb long poem. Serving as his own director, Mr. Albee takes us as quickly as possible over the harsh terrain of the first of his two acts. The middle-aged couple, Nancy and Charlie, have just finished a pleasant summer picnic among the dunes. Nancy has brought along her paintbox and is essaying a sketch, which we have reason to guess will not be especially good. Charlie dozes. A Coast Guard plane goes over, very low: a recurrent nuisance. Nancy talks a lot—a trifle too much for the good of the play—and always with an undercurrent of well-bred nagging. Now she launches what amounts to a monologue, which Charlie listens to with reluctance, perhaps because he has heard it several times before. By Nancy's account, it appears that their lifelong good fortune threatens with age to become ill fortune. They have loved each other and have been almost mindlessly faithful to each other; they have raised three children, who are now producing children of their own. Soon enough, they will be dead, but before that necessary event they must seek whatever small adventures their minds and bodies are still capable of responding to. Charlie groans impatiently. There is such a thing as having had one's life; what more does she want? They begin to bicker, and it turns out that there is much that Nancy wants, and much that she requires of Charlie that he should want. At that moment, terrifyingly, two lizards appear at the top of the dunes; Nancy instructs Charlie to assume a posture of submission, straight out of Lorenz (Nancy is evidently a great reader), and the curtain descends.

In the second act, the lizards prove to be every bit as much a married couple as Nancy and Charlie. They are named Leslie and Sarah, and they have had seven thousand children. They speak admirable English, though their vocabularies are limited; experiencing love and fear, they are ignorant of the words "love" and "fear." The two couples warily test their intentions; Charlie grows impatient with Leslie and makes an insulting remark about brute beasts. He goes further—he makes Sarah cry. This is something she has never done; Leslie, in a fury, comes within an ace of killing Charlie. Then, dismayed by his misconduct, Leslie makes an apologetic retreat. Charlie is also, if only mildly, apologetic. Nancy sees that their encounter with Leslie and Sarah is the very adventure that she has been pleading with Charlie to seek. It is too good a chance to miss. Luckily, Leslie and Sarah agree with her; Leslie makes a gesture of friendship to Charlie and speaks one of the most thrilling of all words. Mr. Albee has sounded his magic flute and the harsh terrain of the first act has become a verdant pathway through Cloud-Cuckoo-Land.

Deborah Kerr and Barry Nelson play Nancy and Charlie, and Maureen Anderman and Frank Langella play Sarah and Leslie. Miss Kerr carries the heavy burden of exposition in the first act with exemplary grace and skill, and Mr. Langella dominates the second act with an unprecedented display of lizardly winsomeness. Is there a Tony award for Best Animal on Broadway? If so, Mr. Langella deserves it, and Miss Anderman deserves an award for Best Supporting Animal. The utterly convincing scenery—all sand, eelgrass, and glowing sky—is by James Tilton, and the ingenious costumes are by Fred Voelpel.

Stanley Kauffmann (review date 22 February 1975)

SOURCE: A review of *Seascape,* in *The New Republic,* Vol. 172, No. 8, 22 February 1975, p. 22.

[*In the following assessment, Kauffman dismisses* Seascape *as "banal" and "a trite anatomy of middle-class marriage and spiritual menopause."*]

In 1959 Edward Albee wrote a short one-act play called ***The Sandbox*** which takes place on a beach and has four (speaking) characters. It's a fantasy about the sterility of contemporary life and the relative authenticity of an older generation expressed in banality à la Ionesco. Now Albee has written a short two-act play, ***Seascape,*** which takes place on a sand dune overlooking an ocean and has four characters. This new play starts realistically, then becomes a fantasy. It, too, is about some sterilities of contemporary life. It, too, is expressed in banalities, but this time there is no reason to think that the diction is satirical.

When the curtain rises, a middle-aged couple, Nancy and Charlie, are sunning themselves. Almost the first line is Nancy's "Can't we stay here forever?" There, one thinks instinctively, is a hope for some banality-satire. But Charlie's reply, instead of being in a consciously banal pattern, takes that first line seriously. "You don't really mean it," he says sagely. Banality rolls in as the very medium of the piece, and we are off on a trite anatomy of middle-class marriage and spiritual menopause.

They are a typically typical couple: have made some money, have loved and liked one another through ups and downs, have loved and disliked their children, etc. One welcome change in Albee: as against his recent plays, he has here eschewed fake mandarinese. This dialogue is undistinguished, but at least it is decorated only with artificial broken sentences, not with artificial flowers. However he has clung to his pseudo-Chekhovian mode: a chief ingredient of this early section is reminiscence, in wistful voice, recalling one's silly but charming past self. Charlie in particular recalls how, as a child, he loved to sit as long as he could on the bottom of lakes and the ocean when he went swimming, worrying his parents but enjoying himself.

Then two human-size, lizard-like creatures, male and female, appear. Their sudden entry into this realistic play is pleasant: I felt that perhaps the long, basically familiar dialogue up to now was intended to lead somewhere. Anyway I found the lizard folk at least as credible as Charlie's knowing the author of *The Man Who Married a Dumb Wife,* which Nancy had asked him. (Anatole France.) The lizards speak English, and we soon learn that they live on the ocean bottom. Since it has been very carefully explained—planted, we can now say—that Charlie used to love to sit on the ocean bottom, it becomes apparent that these two creatures are meant to symbolize hidden aspects of Charlie and perhaps Nancy, who has also expressed interest in the ocean floor. (See the importance of water in Freud and Jung.) Presumably, at middle age, various buried elements in the earth couple have surfaced to be reckoned with.

This is hardly a startlingly original idea for a play, but it's not a bad one. The play itself *is* bad—because it is nothing more than its idea. The conversation before the lizards appear is only remastication of well-chewed play-film-TV cud. The conversation of the foursome is mostly sci-fi cuteness of a slightly refined take-me-to-your-leader kind, two alien societies sniffing at each other. It leads only to some sentimental affinities and some quarrels (meant to alter the tone briefly), with a final imposed determination of the lizards to learn and improve. In short the play never demonstrates in any degree a real necessity to exist. All it demonstrates is that Albee wants to exist, as a playwright. He cooked up an idea—worth maybe a half hour instead of a bloated hour and a half (including intermission)—and then forced some arbitrary trite points into it in order to justify using it. In character, in texture, in theme, ***Seascape*** is an echoingly hollow statement of bankruptcy.

I think it's fair to make an inference about Albee's career since ***Who's Afraid of Virginia Woolf?*** I think that he is caught in a modern trap. He wrote some good plays when he was young; thus by the conventions of our society, he is sentenced to be a playwright for the rest of his life, whether or not he has anything more, really, to write. This wasn't always so: Congreve, Wycherley, Vanbrugh, Sheridan all wrote some fine plays when they were young; then, for differing reasons, quit to do other things. Nowadays this doesn't seem possible if one has been successful early and then begins to run dry. (And it's not just an American phenomenon; see the work of John Osborne since *Inadmissible Evidence.*) I have no gifts of prophecy and wouldn't want them if offered; but Albee's work since ***Virginia Woolf*** (1962) seems so much more the product of compulsion to be a writer than to write, that there is no reason to hope for improvement. He's still relatively young and could do a lot of other things if he weren't shackled by fear of being thought a burned-out rocket. (For instance, as many of his comments show, he could be a perceptive critic.)

Albee himself directed ***Seascape*** with very mixed results. Deborah Kerr plays Nancy as if she were suspended in a noose of arch inflections and expressions. Barry Nelson, one of the last of the standard Broadway leading men—a player with a ready repertoire of "bits"—plays Charlie with modest technical competence. The she-lizard is Maureen Anderman who, completely covered with animal costume and grotesque make-up, still conveys sexuality with her voice and quivering thigh. The he-lizard is Frank Langella, who gives a good stylized performance. (If you saw the recent PBS telecast of the Williamstown production of *The Sea Gull,* you saw Langella play Trepleff, sensitively.) The lizard costumes by Fred Voelpel are excellent.

Henry Hewes (review date 8 March 1975)

SOURCE: "Albee Surfaces," in *Saturday Review,* Vol. 12, No. 12, 8 March, 1975, p. 40.

[*"Albee's random speculations delight the mind," Hewes asserts in the review below, adding that* Seascape *is ". . . written with an exquisite concern for the careful use of language."*]

Edward Albee has long been concerned with the ways things come to an end. And most of his plays suggest that the American way of life has had it. In 1971 he presented us with a despair-ridden drama of conversations around the bed of a dying man, called ***All Over,*** and it was hard to see where the brilliant pessimist could go from there.

Yet now, some four years later, he has surfaced again with a Broadway play (which he also directed) called ***Seascape.*** The title suggests both that the play takes place on a beach and that it deals with escape from or into the sea. Indeed it does. The entire first act is a conversation between Nancy, a middle-aged, affluent wife who urges her retired husband, Charlie, to take up again his childhood hobby of submerging himself in water and sitting there as long as he can. He declines and wants only to rest and do nothing. Nancy warns him that they are in danger of letting their minds go dim and slipping into a canasta-playing retirement, which she wittily labels "that purgatory *before* purgatory." In despair she asks, "But is this what we've come all this way for? Had the children? Spent all this time together? All the sharing? For nothing? To lie back down in the crib again? The same at the end as at the beginning? Sleep? Pacifier? Milk? Incomprehensible once more?" Samuel Beckett or the Edward Albee of ***All Over*** would have nodded a gloomy "Yes." But now Albee seems to be looking at Charlie and Nancy as representatives of an unsatisfactory civilization.

Albee seems to be suggesting that the real solution is for our civilization to recognize its failures and somehow to feed our experience into the evolution of a new and better species.

On a more comic level—and ***Seascape*** is a comedy—Albee can celebrate the wit and compassion with which this civilization deals with its dissatisfactions. For instance, Nancy tells Charlie that there was a time in their marriage when she felt that he had turned his back on her and she suspected it was another woman—"not prettier, even maybe a little plain, but unencumbered, or lonely, or lost." Charlie denies it, but Nancy reveals that her wise mother had once told her, "If he doesn't do it in the flesh, he'll think about it. One night in the dark if you listen hard enough, you'll hear him think the name of another woman, kiss *her,* touch *her* breasts as he has his hand and mouth on you. Then you'll know something about loneliness . . . you'll be halfway to compassion. . . ." "The other half?" Charlie asks, and Nancy replies, "Knowing how lonely he is." Charlie escapes from this heavy truth with a humorous confession that once while making love to her he had pretended that it was a previous time with her when it had been particularly good.

And so with wit and insight Albee dallies through the first half of his play, content merely to delineate these two drifting members of a growingly feckless species. Although there is a lack of dramatic urgency, Albee's random speculations delight the mind, for they are written with an exquisite concern for the careful use of language.

There is in this first act, however, an indication from Charlie that they are not up to facing the glaciers and the crags, which may mean that they no longer feel that they can cope with the trauma of vigorous living, or that the next Ice Age will destroy man, leaving the world to a new form of evolution, in which life will again try to emerge from the sea. Actually, of course, this process will take millions of years. But in the theater it can happen with the speed of imagination. Accordingly, the first act ends with the startling appearance of two sea creatures.

Fortunately for the playwright, these two lizard-like animals can speak English. They have ordinary names (Leslie and Sarah) and turn out to be more monogamous by instinct than their human counterparts are by religious and legal contract. Although they lack tools, art, and an awareness of their own mortality, they seem to have a passionate caring for each other that is more sensitive and more considerate than what most humans practice. There is much fun in Charlie and Nancy's trying to explain human customs to the animals, and Sarah and Leslie are particularly baffled to hear that we keep our offspring with us for 18 years. A serious crisis is created when Charlie cruelly makes Sarah aware that some day Leslie will die and leave her to live on without him. This is too much for them, and they decide to return to the sea. Charlie and Nancy tell them that they'll have to come back sooner or later, and they urge the creatures to stay and let them help them adapt to life on land. Leslie challenges them, saying, "All right. Begin."

This ending seems to say that the human race should use its retirement years to teach future civilizations how to acquire its virtues and avoid its mistakes. This positive thrust, and the compassion out of which it arises, allows ***Seascape*** to emerge as a benign comedy, without forcing the author into a renunciation of the scathing views he has expressed in his previous plays.

Albee has directed ***Seascape*** as if he understood the playwright's intent. Yet his unusual casting of the play has resulted in some slight incongruities. As Nancy, Deborah Kerr brings a proper British attitude to the role of an American housewife. And Barry Nelson's perennial boyishness seems at odds with Charlie's world-weariness. On the other hand, they both are excellent at keeping a comic tone in a play that is in great danger of slipping into a sober realism that its slight plot cannot support. But the outstanding performance is by Frank Langella as Leslie. Mr. Langella is wonderfully amusing in the moments when he expresses, with lizard-like movements, a startled bafflement at the strange human ideas he is hearing. And he is intensely moving when he becomes angry at Charlie's insensitivity. His response—"don't you talk to me about 'brute beast' "—pierces the separation between man and animal.

James Tilton's setting—some large-scale sand dunes—makes the actors seem smaller in contrast, an appropriate thing in comedy. Fred Voelpel's lizard costumes and facial make-up patterns are imaginative and beautiful, and they have just the right accent of absurdity. They enhance a unique comedy—one that gives us more to think about than any other of this season's new plays.

CRITICAL COMMENTARY

Lucina P. Gabbard (essay date 1978)

SOURCE: "Albee's *Seascape:* An Adult Fairy Tale," in *Modern Drama,* Vol. XXI, No. 3, September, 1978, pp. 307-17.

[*The essay below asserts that* Seascape *is a fairy tale that treats the problem of the acceptance of death, offering "a message of wisdom and comfort presented in a fanciful style that allows people to sip only as much as they thirst for."*]

Edward Albee's ***Seascape*** is obviously not a realistic play. When the two great lizards slide onto the stage, behaving like ordinary married human beings and speaking perfect English, realism is immediately dispelled. Encounters between human beings and talking animals are the stuff of fairy tales. Bruno Bettelheim, in *The Uses of Enchantment,* describes a fairy tale as a work of art which teaches about inner problems[1] through the language of symbols[2] and, therefore, communicates various depths of meaning to various levels of the personality at various times.[3] This is the method of ***Seascape.***

The play's principal concern is the realization of the proximity of death that comes with the passing of middle age. Albee depicts the adjustments that this realization entails, adjustments made difficult in the twentieth century by a tendency to deny mortality. Sigmund Freud spoke of this denial as an inner struggle between Eros and Thanatos which he viewed as the wellspring of all neuroses. Friedrich Nietzsche wrote about the need for a oneness that would embody the affirmation of death as well as life. More recently, Norman O. Brown has maintained that constructing "a human consciousness" capable of accepting death "is a task for the joint efforts of" psychoanalysis, philosophy, and art.[4] ***Seascape*** takes up this cause and earns importance because of it.

Symbols are the play's basic medium. Through symbolism the title announces that death is a part of the flux of life. A seascape is a view of the sea whose ever-moving waters are the meeting place between air and ground, heaven and earth, life and death. The waters of the sea are both the source and the goal of life. Returning to the sea is like returning to the birth waters of mother's womb; it is the symbolic equivalent of death.[5] The seascape is also vast: its final shore is beyond sight; its horizon is beyond reach. So is the flux of life; man is the product of continuous evolution—unstoppable in its insistent progress. The sea is also deep and dark; beneath its bright ripples are undercurrents, eddies, unseen life, and unplumbed depths. So is man's awareness merely the outer rim of an inner self that seethes with the buried life of the subconscious. Thus, the play intertwines three levels of meaning, ingeniously allowing each to add insight to the other. All three are condensed in the symbol of the lizards

Edward Albee

who come up from the sea. They concretize the evolution of mankind from water animals, the emergence of the individual embryo from its watery womb, and the return to consciousness of the repressed self.

All these levels of meaning can be communicated simultaneously when the fairy-tale events of the play are interpreted as an initiation rite. Joseph L. Henderson, in *Man and His Symbols,* explains the rites of passage and their associated symbols which, he says, can relate to the movement from any stage of life to any other—childhood to adolescence to maturity to old age to death. Moreover, the symbols of these rites are known to appear in the unconscious mind of man just as they did in ancient rituals.[6] One set of symbols that apply to this final stage of life, Henderson calls "symbols of transcendence" which concern "man's release from . . . any confining pattern of existence, as he moves toward a superior . . . stage" of his development. They provide for a union between the conscious and the unconscious contents of the mind.[7] The experience is usually presided over by a "feminine (i.e., anima) figure" who fosters a "spirit of compassion,"[8] and it occurs between middle age and old age when people are contemplating ways to spend their retirement—whether to travel or to stay home, to work or to play.[9] Often during this time the subject has dreams which incorporate a piece of wood, natural wood which represents primordial origins and, thus, links "contemporary existence to the distant origins of human life." Other subjects dream of being in a strange, lonely place "near a body of water." Such places are stops on a continuing journey which symbolizes the need for release.[10] The journey usually features an encounter with an animal that can live either on land or in the sea—a water pig, a lizard, a snake, or a fish. The amphibian quality of the animal is the universal symbol of transcendence. "These creatures, figuratively coming from the depths of the ancient Earth Mother, are symbolic denizens of the collective unconscious."[11] The full power of transcendence also incorporates symbols of flight. Thus, the "lower transcendence from the underworld snake-consciousness" passes "through the medium of earthly reality" and into the "superhuman or transpersonal reality" of winged flight.[12] In archaic patterns, the symbols of this final transcendence may havebeen winged horses or dragons or even wild birds. But Henderson says that today they can be jet planes or space rockets which also represent freedom from gravity. He notes that this final initiation begins in submission and moves through containment to further liberation. He warns, however, that the opportunity to experience these rites is not automatic; it must be understood and grasped. The individual who does "reconciles the conflicting elements of his personality" and strikes "a balance that makes him truly human, and truly master of himself."[13]

Other writers concur with Henderson and elaborate his statements. Joseph Campbell, in *Hero With A Thousand Faces,* calls this opportunity to be initiated "the call to adventure." He tells a fairy tale in which a frog heralds the call—to life, death, adventure, or self-realization. Regardless of the "stage or grade of life, the call rings up the curtain, always, on a mystery of transfiguration—a rite, or moment of spiritual passage, which, when complete, amounts to a dying and a birth."[14] Julius Heuscher, in his psychiatric approach to fairy tales, cites the story of the beautiful Czechoslovakian princess Zlatovlaska, who is won by a lowly cook, Yirik. This fairy tale introduces the "three realms of the physical world: earth, water, and air" which Yirik must befriend to gain his end, and it points out that death must be accepted as well as life if a true "spiritual awakening" is to occur, if a "wedding of the spirit or *animus* with the soul or *anima*" is to take place.[15] A third relevant comment comes from Carl Jung: "In myths and fairy tales, as in dreams, the psyche tells its own story, and the interplay of the archetype is revealed in its natural setting as 'formation, transformation/ the eternal Mind's eternal recreation.' "[16]

Familiarity with the archetype of initiation and the symbols of transcendence facilitates their recognition in the events of ***Seascape.*** Albee's play begins on a deserted sand dune in the bright sun.[17] The barrenness of the sand dune seems to suggest the absence of fertility at life's end. Traditionally, sand also represents time and life's journey. In this context, Albee's characters have travelled to the edge of the sands of time—the sea, home of the waters of life and death. The bright sunlight is associated with rebirth. According to J. E. Cirlot, the Moon becomes fragmented in its cycles, but the Sun can cross the heavens and descend without dissolving. "Hence, the death of the Sun necessarily implies the idea of resurrection and actually comes to be regarded as a death which is not a true death."[18]

Within this setting are Charlie and Nancy, whose names, perhaps by accident, identify them as representatives of the masculine and feminine spirits: the name *Charlie* implies manliness, strength and vigor; *Nancy,* a variation of Anne, suggests grace and mercy. The conversation of Charlie and Nancy tells of their presence in the retirement years. They speak of the long way they have come—the children, the sharing of much time, the prospects of settling in "old folks' cities" (p. 10). Nancy even verbalizes their awareness of approaching death. Twice she reminds Charlie that they "are not going to live forever" (p. 11). Their attitudes display a wish to stop their journey through time. Nancy wants to become a "seaside nomad" (p. 5), to "go around the world and never leave the beach" (p. 6). Charlie, on the other hand, wants to do "nothing" (p. 8); he feels he has earned "a little rest" (p. 10). Each in his own way, therefore, rejects continuing. She wants to treadmill it on the shores of life, and he wants to halt where he is. Their reluctance to continue is demonstrated symbolically as well. At the opening of the play, the deafening roar of a jet plane is heard passing overhead. Nancy complains of the noise, and Charlie declares that someday those jets will crash into the dunes. He fails to see "what good they do" (p. 3). If the planes are accepted as the symbols of winged transcendence, Nancy and Charlie's negative responses show their dread of this next higher plane of development. At the close of this scene, which sets up their present stage in life's journey, the jet planes fly over again. Charlie and Nancy repeat the same reactions and the same words, creating a refrain such as marks a stanza's end.

When conversation resumes, a new stanza presents another phase of their lives—their past. Charlie and Nancy review their progress through the earlier developmental stages. Charlie has always been slow to move forward into a new stage. When he was a little boy, his friends had wanted to soar on wings, like Icarus, but Charlie had wanted to be a fish and live under the sea (p. 13). His delight was to submerge himself and sit on the bottom. Until he was twelve or thirteen, he had enjoyed this symbolic regression to his beginnings in the womb. Finally, at seventeen he had begun his manhood and thereafter had been satisfied on earth's firm ground. Despite Nancy's entreaties that he recapture his youth by submerging again, Charlie refuses to retrench. He insists on remaining where he is. He had, however, had a seven-month decline before moving from maturity to middle age. Nancy was thirty when Charlie had had his "thing," his "melancholia" (p. 20). Then, as now, the deeper his inertia had gone, the more alive she had felt (p. 21). Finally, however, he had come back, but life had been quieter, more full of accommodations (p. 24). Now the time has come to progress from middle age to old age with its proximity to death. But Charlie wants to rest, to remain on familiar ground, to give in to inertia again. He fears "the crags" and "the glaciers" (p. 38). And the imagery of his words reveals his feelings about the next stage. He sees the future life as jagged and rough, like steep rocks rising above the surrounding rock mass. He sees the future life as cold and bleak, like a large mass of ice, rising where snow can accumulate faster than it melts. Like the jet plane, which Charlie figures will someday crash into the sandy earth, the glacier, when it does melt, slides down the mountain into the valley below. Charlie feels unequal to such a "scary" new life. He wants the comfort of "settling in"—where he is (pp. 38-39).

The backward look at Nancy's life reveals the differing role of woman. While he has accepted the traditionally active roles of manhood—wooer, sire, breadwinner, sturdy shoulder (pp. 29-30)—she has accepted the traditionally passive roles of womanhood. She has acquiesced to her husband's needs, accepted his way and place of life, reared their children, and waited out his inertia even at the height of her own sexuality. Nancy, therefore, feels she has earned "a little life" (p. 37). She is piqued by Charlie's use of the past tense with regard to her life. She compares her feelings about his phrase "You've *had* a good life" (p. 32) to his experience of being stung by a bee. He can still remember his swollen cheek and his half-closed eye (p. 33), and she can still remember all the ill-considered and near-impossible demands upon her ingenuity and her energy. Once he had called for "Mud!" and there was none; so he had insisted, "Well, *make* some." But she had felt helpless to make mud: she lacked a recipe, the right pan (pp. 32-33). She can remember staying neat and busy, not prying, during his "seven-month decline" (p. 21), wondering if he had found another girl, realizing their "rough and tumble in the sheets" was over, and considering a divorce as an entree into a more daring life (pp. 21-23). But she had passed through this difficult period by recognizing the mutuality of loneliness—even at the climax of love, *"Le petit mort"* (p. 24). Then he had come back, and she was "halfway there, halfway to compassion" (p. 24). Now they look back on the pyramid of children they have built together. She sees it as an individual, private effort—a precarious and difficult feat of engineering—which their children will now begin. He says, "It's all one" (pp. 14-15).

Each in his own way, then, has arrived at this new plateau—retirement age. Henderson says that those who have experienced adventure and change usually seek "a settled life" at this time, while those who have adhered to a pattern seek a "liberating change."[19] And he seems to be describing the contrast between Charlie and Nancy as they pause on the brink of a new transcendence.

The moment is appropriate, therefore, for the entrance of the lizards. Earlier Nancy had sensed their presence or spotted them in the distance during her recollections of Charlie's love of submerging (p. 14). Later they reenter her vision as she makes her final plea to him to descend into the sea again—bare (pp. 27-28). These references to excursions into the underworld make the lizards' ascent into the upper world somehow less astonishing, a foreshadowing in reverse. The lizards, thus linked to Charlie's past, appear now as heralds, callers to a new adventure. Joseph Campbell says that the herald is a "representative of the repressed fecundity" within man; this description is certainly fitting to the present aridity of the man who once behaved like a fish. Campbell also describes the herald as "dark, loathly, or terrifying."[20] and indeed the lizards do frighten Charlie. They arouse his deepest animal instincts, for he assumes a position on all fours. He also returns to his old habits and orders Nancy to get him a stick. Nancy reacts as though he had been stung by a bee again; she can see no sticks. Eventually, however, she does find him a thin, smallish one (p. 44). Perhaps this is the piece of wood symbolic of primordial origins. At any rate, she too takes to all fours as she crawls toward Charlie with the stick between her teeth (p. 44). Charlie's protective instincts are to the fore. When Leslie's throat-clearing assumes the character of a growl, "Charlie gathers Nancy to him," and he brandishes his stick in a pathetic attempt to "go down fighting" (p. 45). Nancy seems more fascinated than fearful. She is filled with wonder at the lizards' beauty (p. 45). But as Leslie threatens them by waving his own stout, four-foot stick, Charlie and Nancy remember to exchange, "I love you" (p. 46). They are prepared for crisis! Leslie and Sarah approach! Then the jet planes fly overhead again, frightening the lizards into a retreat toward the water. The refrain repeats its twofold function: symbolically it shows the creature-fear of unknown heights, and technically it marks the end of another stanza, so to speak.

The remainder of Act One gives Charlie and Nancy their moment to recover. Charlie intuitively recognizes that the lizards are the "glaciers and the crags" (p. 47). He even imagines he and Nancy are already dead—poisoned by Nancy's liver paste (p. 50). But when Leslie and Sarah approach again, Charlie and Nancy know by their fright that they are still alive. Nancy, with her feminine instinct, suggests they assume the animal posture of submission—on their backs, legs drawn up, hands curled like paws, "smiling broadly" (p. 51). Thus begins the rite of submission, the first step in answering the call, the prelude to the process of initiation.

The third stanza of Albee's poetic fairy tale is devoted to what Joseph Campbell has called the outgrowing of "old concepts and emotional patterns."[21] At this point, Leslie and Sarah, representing the unconscious selves and the evolutionary predecessors of Charlie and Nancy, provoke for their conscious, modern counterparts a new and instructive look at the familiar. Consequently, old behavior patterns give rise to new self-realizations. The submissive females turn out to be more adventuresome and less fearful than the supposedly aggressive males, for Nancy and Sarah prod their men into friendly contact. Charlie and Nancy are forced to recognize that they are members of a dangerous species who kill other living things and eat all but their own kind. Both the lizards and the human beings discover in their own responses that the different and the unknown cause fears which spur defensive hostility. Leslie brandishes his stick out of fright just as Charlie does. The lizards reveal themselves to be as bigoted against fish as men are against other races. In his own defense, Leslie asks what frightens Charlie, what makes him panic. Charlie answers the question for himself as well as Leslie: "Oh . . . deep space? Mortality? Nancy . . . not being with me? Great . . . green . . . creatures coming up from the sea." Leslie is able to sum it all up, "what we don't know" (p. 73). And his words occasion in the dramatic imagination a greater Consciousness beyond earthly comprehension.

In that spirit the lizards and the human beings consider the enormous differences that time has made between them. Man's simplest everyday customs, like shaking hands, are strange to the lizards, and Charlie and Nancy recall earlier forms of human greeting which are now strange to modern man. The lizards are puzzled by clothes, and Charlie and Nancy grope to explain them. Leslie and Sarah have never seen a woman's breasts. Nancy's willingness to show hers to both Sarah and Leslie causes Charlie to reassess his feelings of jealousy and of love for Nancy's body. The most startling revelation, however, is of the enormity of the changes wrought by evolution. Leslie and Sarah are not even mammals. Their reproductive patterns are entirely different. Sarah has laid perhaps seven thousand eggs, many of which floated away or were eaten (pp. 82-83). Bearing one child at a time and lovingly nurturing him for eighteen to twenty years take on the aspect of a wondrous gift. This insight leads to the discovery that Leslie and Sarah do not know the emotions of love and loss. To borrow Carl Jung's phrase, they have not yet "blundered into consciousness"; consequently, they "have a share" in both the "daemonically superhuman" and the "bestially subhuman."[22]

While contemplating their differences, the animals and the human beings exhibit some similarities also; these reinforce the notion that Leslie and Sarah are counterparts, in this instance more subhuman than superhuman, to Nancy and Charlie. Sarah, like Nancy, submits willingly to her mate's decisions (p. 100); like Nancy, Sarah is fascinated by new experiences (p. 103). Both males, on the other hand, feel inadequate at being unable to explain and understand, so they vent their feelings in anger at each other. Sarah is fascinated by the birds, but they activate Leslie's instinct to seek an escape route. Nancy is delighted to have been here "when Sarah saw it all" (p. 102), but Charlie, she chides, "has decided that the wonders do not occur; that what we have not known does not exist; that what we cannot fathom cannot be . . ." (p. 105). As a final similarity, both couples react negatively to the recurring sound of the jet planes overhead. Leslie and Sarah rush back over the dunes, and Charlie and Nancy repeat their refrain.

The last stanza brings the grasping of the opportunity offered by the initiation rites and the final understanding. It begins in Nancy's compassion for the lizards' fear of the jets: "Oh, Charlie; they're frightened. They're so frightened!" Charlie picks up her feelings: "They are" (p. 111); and both offer the comfort of explanations. Thus, they grasp their opportunity to consolidate the results of this encounter with the representatives of the unconscious, private and collective. The experiences which follow provide intuitive enlightenment to both the lizards and the human beings, and they also offer thematic statements to the student of Albee's play.

Overall the clear message is that individual human growth is analogous to the evolution of mankind. Authoritative testimony reinforces Albee's statement. Heuscher says a study of the "best known Grimms' tales" led repeatedly to the realization that "the growth of the individual is closely interrelated with the historical fate of the human race."[23] Charlie began in his mother's watery womb, and after his birth he liked to retire to its symbolic equivalent, but eventually he moved on to adolescence and then adulthood and middle age. Now he is ready for the final step of life on this intermediate stage of earth. In the same way, mankind began in the "primordial soup." There was a "heartbreaking second" when "the sugars and the acids and the ultraviolets" all came together, and creatures began "crawling around, and swimming and carrying on" down there (p. 118). In the eons that followed, they dropped tails and changed spots—they mutated (p. 123), until one day a "slimy creature poked his head out of the muck" and decided to stay up on land (p. 124). Thus, Charlie verbalizes one level of the symbolism of Leslie and Sarah. The implication is that Charlie and Nancy are the present product of the mutations that earlier Leslies and Sarahs have undergone. And now, as human beings, they must move on to the third level of life, symbolized by air.

Within this overall pattern are meaningful individual thematic statements. The first of these is that discontent is the springboard of growth. Henderson supports Albee's intuitive accuracy. He states that a "spirit of divine discontent . . . forces all free men to face some new discovery or to live their lives in a new way."[24] Charlie no longer wishes to submerge himself in the sea. He knows he could not find satisfaction now in this twelve-year-old's game: "it wasn't . . . finding out" (p. 115). Leslie and Sarah have come up from the sea because they no longer felt they *belonged* there (p. 116). The fish in the "glop" became dissatisfied and "sprouted things—tails, spots, fins, feathers" (p. 121).

Second, these developmental stages are gradual but inevitable. Creatures and men come to believe they have always been as they are. Leslie says he has "*always* had a *tail*" (p. 122). Sarah says that their discomfort under the sea was "a growing thing, nothing abrupt"; it was a "sense of having changed" (p. 116). Charlie calls it "flux" (p. 124). And it is ultimately unstoppable. Before each new transition, creatures, as well as men, have the urge to turn back. Leslie and Sarah epitomize this wish to retreat at the very end of the play. Leslie states sadly that he is ready to "go back down," and Sarah concurs (p. 132). But Nancy overrules them with her insistence that they will have to come back eventually. They have no choice, she says (p. 134). Charlie agrees, "You've got to *do* it—sooner or later" (p. 135). Heuscher also concludes that individually and culturally, "growth appears as a neverending process." He places this thought in an optimistic framework which parallels the bright future he says is always present in fairy tales. He explains that the adult person who knows the challenge of continuing development "finds himself wedded to the goddess of eternal youth."[25]

The play's third statement is the most meaningful: knowledge of one's own mortality is the key to being truly alive and human. Martin Grotjahn, in *The Voice of the Symbol,* confirms the importance of understanding finiteness. He explains that in old age man is given one last chance to understand himself and his world, and that chance "is created by the recognition that human life is terminable." Integrating the meaning of mortality and accepting it "without narcissistic delusion" accomplishes, he says, "the transition from maturation to wisdom."[26] Nancy sees this awareness as evidence of true progress in evolution; she thinks men are more interesting than animals because they "use tools, . . . make art" and know death (p. 125). Charlie, whose great fear is separation from Nancy in death, intuitively forces Sarah to face this same possibility. He asks her what she would do if she knew Leslie "was never coming back" (p. 129). Once they have absorbed Charlie's question, Leslie and Sarah have learned what emotion is. They know their love for each other; they know the fear of loss. Sarah says she would cry her eyes out if she lost Leslie. Leslie almost kills Charlie for making Sarah cry (p. 131). Both lizards wish to return to the sea where, in Charlie's parlance, the brute beasts are "free from it all" (p. 128). But the whole experience has deepened the human beings' compassion and the lizards' trust. The constructive feminine spirit of man, Nancy, points out the inevitability of growth, and her other half holds out his hand in their mutual offer of help. Leslie straightens as he accepts, "All right. Begin" (p. 135).

The full meaning of "Begin" is contained in the play's central analogy. Both couples are ready now to begin the death of the old life and the birth of the new. Leslie and Sarah will die as lizards to be reborn as men; by gaining consciousness they have moved their home from the underworld of the sea to the middle ground of earth. Charlie and Nancy will die as men and be reborn to a higher plane of existence symbolized by winged flight in the upper world of air. Albee's analogy spares him the necessity of prophesying the nature of this new plane of existence, but its prelude seems to be ego-integration. On another level, "Begin" suggests the start of total reconciliation of all conflicting elements of the self—the past with the present, the subconscious with the conscious, and even the animus with the anima. Charles and Nancy join hands with Leslie and Sarah to begin the attainment of oneness. Thus, through the language of symbols, Albee speaks his major theme—acceptance of death is transcendence.

Seascape offers a message of wisdom and comfort presented in a fanciful style that allows people to sip only as much as they thirst for. But Albee's intent is clear in his choice of form. Bettelheim has verbalized it: "If there is a central theme to the wide variety of fairy tales, it is that of rebirth to a higher plane."[27]

Notes

[1]Bruno Bettelheim, *The Uses of Enchantment* (New York, 1976), p. 5.

[2]*Ibid.*, p. 62.

[3]*Ibid.*, p. 12.

[4]Norman O. Brown, *Life Against Death* (Middletown, Conn., 1959), p. 108.

[5]J. E. Cirlot, *A Dictionary of Symbols,* trans., Jack Sage (New York, 1962), p. 268.

[6]Joseph L. Henderson, "Ancient Myths and Modern Man," in *Man and His Symbols,* ed. Carl G. Jung and M. L. von Franz (New York, 1968), p. 100.

[7]*Ibid.*, p. 146.

[8]*Ibid.*, p. 150.

[9]*Ibid.*, p. 151.

[10]*Ibid.*, p. 152.

[11]*Ibid.*, p. 153.

[12]*Ibid.*, p. 155.

[13]*Ibid.*, p. 156.

[14]Joseph Campbell, *Hero With A Thousand Faces* (Cleveland and New York, 1956), p. 51.

[15]Julius Heuscher, *A Psychiatric Study of Myths and Fairy Tales* (Springfield, Ill., 1974), p. 193.

[16]Carl G. Jung, *Four Archetypes,* trans. R.F.C. Hull (London, 1972), p. 95.

[17]Edward Albee, *Seascape* (New York, 1975), p. 3. (Subsequent references to this play will appear in the body of the text.)

[18]Cirlot, p. 303.

[19]Henderson, p. 151.

[20]Campbell, p. 53.

[21]*Ibid.*, p. 51.

[22]Jung, p. 108.

[23]Heuscher, p. 189.

[24]Henderson, p. 151.

[25]Heuscher, p. 189.

[26]Martin Grotjahn, *The Voice of the Symbol* (New York, 1973), p. 45.

[27]Bettelheim, p. 179.

Samuel J. Bernstein (essay date 1980)

SOURCE: "A Review of the Criticism," in *The Strands Entwined: A New Direction in American Drama,* Northeastern University Press, 1980, pp. 113-35.

[In the following essay, Bernstein offers a survey of the theatrical reviews of Seascape, *a critical analysis of the play, and a discussion of its place in twentieth-century American drama.]*

A Review of the Criticism

Mixed critical reaction has greeted Edward Albee's ***Seascape.*** Such critics as Clive Barnes, George Oppenheimer, Richard Watts, and Brendan Gill have written of their admiration for the work; others, including Walter Kerr, T. E. Kalem, Stanley Kauffmann, Jack Kroll, and Catharine Hughes, have been equally emphatic in deriding it. Harold Clurman, who scorns the hysteria of the love or hate reaction of his colleagues, has a generally favorable reaction to the play. Although he calls it a "little" play, his tone indicates that he is surely among that group of critics who might "find [the work] delightful."[1]

Mel Gussow, in a *New York Times* interview with Albee, reports that Albee began to think about ***Seascape*** in 1967, seven years before it was produced. It grew out of one of two companion pieces, at that time called *Life* and *Death.* *Death* ultimately became ***All Over,*** produced in 1971, and

Life became ***Seascape,*** to which Albee gave special attention for three years prior to its writing.

Gussow finds in ***Seascape,*** as in most of Albee's works, elements of both tragedy and comedy. During the interview, Albee credits Samuel Beckett with traits that may be credited to himself as well:

> Our best serious playwright, Samuel Beckett, is extremely funny. You've got to have a tragic sense of life to see the humor of the absurd.[2]

As the Gussow interview indicates, Albee was indeed quite serious in this dramatic effort. He allegedly has always been fascinated by the sea; in addition, he read extensively in anthropology and animal behavior in preparation for the writing. However, Albee does not see simple scientific knowledge as his substructure. Gussow calls it "still very much a play of the imagination." Albee states that it was the most difficult play he has ever written because he had no guidelines and because language and diction were particularly acute problems. He had to make the lizards seem believable and yet decidedly different from humans. As Albee states:

> They should be so real that in a sense we can smell them. They should be quite frightening. Seeing them for the first time, the audience should have that shock of recognition. After all, it's what we all were.[3]

However charming or witty the play might be, the Gussow interview indicates that Albee was attempting to confront weighty scientific and philosophical matters and to treat them in a fundamentally serious, though overtly whimsical, fashion.

It is precisely because of the seriousness of Albee's aim and posture that most of the criticism of the play has been leveled. In essence, a number of critics feel that ***Seascape*** is pretentious, dull, and pseudophilosophic; talky when it ought to have provided action; and abstract and distant when it ought to have conveyed intense feeling. Quite pointedly, T. E. Kalem of *Time* states that since ***Who's Afraid of Virginia Woolf,*** Albee's plays (including ***Seascape***) have been "flaccidly somnolent affairs." Claiming that Albee has "a very weak gift for plot construction," he scores the characterization and language, refers to the play's "thudding banalities," and calls the work "bland and innocuous, a two-hour sleeping pill of aimless chatter."[4] Similarly, Jack Kroll of *Newsweek* writes that Albee "seems drained of almost all vitality—theatrical, intellectual, artistic." Moveover, Kroll thinks that Albee has "committed the grisly error of becoming a 'sage.' "[5]

Catharine Hughes, who agrees with Kalem and Kroll that the play lacks "life," states:

> As a course in elementary Darwinism, ***Seascape*** just might have some value. As a play, it is pretentious, simplistic, verbose and banal.[6]

Essentially in agreement, Stanley Kauffmann calls it hollow, banal, and unrealized. He goes on to suggest that Albee give up playwriting, since he has allegedly produced nothing of worth since ***Virginia Woolf.***[7] In a more moderate but equally firm critique, Walter Kerr argues that the play fails principally because it is not dramatic. The play begins with a long conversational debate between the middle-aged couple, Charlie and Nancy. In retirement, Charlie wants only to rest, while Nancy wants wonder and excitement. The couple is joined by two sea creatures, with whom they compare notes on many facets of their lives. When the sea creatures decide—inevitably, Kerr contends—to return to the sea, we have a crisis, but Kerr believes that Albee fails to present this crisis effectively. Since Charlie had formerly wished to surrender to old age and death, Kerr asks, "Why does he not engage himself, as devil's advocate, as newly enlightened human being, as something?"[8]

While the questions of dramatic effectiveness, philosophical richness, construction, and vitality are surely points of disagreement among critics, nowhere is the debate so pointed and acrid as it is on the subject of Albee's language. For example, T. E. Kalem writes:

> Finally, he largely abandoned his strong suit, which was a flair for vituperatively explosive dialogue and bitchy humor. Instead, his characters have spoken for years now with intolerably stilted pomposity, as if they had wandered out of an unpublished work by some minor Victorian novelist.[9]

Similarly, Kroll censures Albee's "constipated language that moves in colonic spasms."[10] Catharine Hughes, another detractor, states that Albee's writing "is presumed (by the author) to be poetic and profound, resonant, when in reality it is devoid of life and artificial, the producer of inertia."[11]

Although such judgments on Albee's language are powerful, they are not universally held. For example, Walter Kerr comments:

> The writing is blessedly spare, free of the convoluted locutions that have sometimes grown like coral over [Albee's] meanings.[12]

Similarly, Brendan Gill writes in *The New Yorker*:

> Of all Mr. Albee's plays, ***Seascape*** is the most exquisitely written. He has calculated not only every immaculate line of dialogue but every word, every caesura; when the actors fall silent, we hold our breath and wait, as we wait at the reading of some superb long poem.[13]

Clive Barnes and Henry Hewes are affirmative in their overall assessment of the play. Because of its warmth and human compassion, Barnes calls ***Seascape*** a true comedy, "a major dramatic event," and further states: "What Mr. Albee has given us here is a play of great density, with many interesting emotional and intellectual reverberations."[14] Henry Hewes, agreeing that it is a comedy, praises Albee for his "wit," "insight," and "careful use of language." Although he believes that the first act lacks "dramatic urgency," Hewes concludes his critique by referring to ***Seascape*** as "a unique comedy—one that gives us more to think about than any other of this season's new plays."[15]

Harold Clurman seems to explain the differences in critical response to ***Seascape.*** He writes:

> It is his most relaxed play, a "philosophical" whimsy. You may find it delightful, or, if the nice notion on which it is based does not suit your temperament, you will consider it a drag.[16]

The term *philosophical whimsy* suggests the light tone, the wit, and the playful creativity of language, idea, and theatrical image that Albee attempted to employ. If one disregards this graceful blending of light manner and serious matter, the work surely seems pretentious, the metaphor insoluble, and the language heavy. Seen, however, from the vantage point that Clurman suggests, we are compelled to open our minds regarding ***Seascape,*** as Albee suggested in an interview with the editors of ***The New York Times***: "The most important thing you can ask from an audience is that it approach a new play with an open mind—without having predetermined the nature of the theatrical experience it will accept."[17]

While the detractors say little more of the play than that it is concerned with a troubled middle-aged couple and that it is concerned scientifically (or pseudoscientifically) with evolution, the play's supporters have attempted various interpretations, each more or less related to Albee's contention that the play is "a true-to-life story."[18] For example, Clive Barnes claims that the play confronts life itself—its history, processes, and current expression in the human condition-and optimistically reminds us about "the primeval ooze from which we all came, and the blind, inarticulative courage that keeps us all going."[19] Oblique but related is the interpretation of Henry Hewes:

> Albee seems to be suggesting that the real solution is for our civilization to recognize its failures and somehow to feed our experience into the evolution of a new and better species.[20]

Brendan Gill concludes:

> Boldly and simply, it asserts that, at no matter what age and in no matter what time and place, acts of discovery remain to be undertaken. With luck, such acts will be found to have meaning; better still, there is the possibility that they will bear fruit.[21]

Regardless of which critical opinion we adhere to, we would do well to ponder Clurman's judgment that ***Seascape*** "is a step in Albee's still green career, a step which, seen in a certain light, augurs well for the future."[22]

In addition to receiving the Pulitzer Prize for ***Seascape,*** Albee won the Elizabeth Hull-Kate Warriner Award, given by the Dramatists Guild Council, for the 1974-1975 season. This award "is given to a playwright whose work deals with a controversial subject involving political, religious or social mores."[23]

A Discussion

Edward Albee's ***Seascape,*** produced in 1975, won the Pulitzer Prize for that year. The tenth Albee play to be produced (the thirteenth if we include his adaptations), the work reassures us that Albee is still a powerful force in American theatre. Many critics have felt, throughout the course of Albee's career, that his most recent play would be his last. The notion that Albee had played himself out arose shortly after the production of ***Who's Afraid of Virginia Woolf?***; it was repeated for the next ten years and received new support in 1971 when ***All Over,*** which was concerned with death, seemed to state explicitly (in its title and symbolically throughout) that this would be the last Albee play. But Albee stunned critics and audiences again in 1975 with the production of ***Seascape.*** Hailed by Clive Barnes as "a major dramatic event," ***Seascape*** is of double significance. First, it reminds us that Albee is alive and well and writing superbly. More importantly, his winning a second Pulitzer Prize (he had won it in 1966 for ***A Delicate Balance***) affirmed his right to claim such a well-deserved honor, denied him for ***Virginia Woolf*** in 1962. (Because of the 1962 denial, John Mason Brown and John Gassner withdrew from the Pulitzer Prize Committee.)

Seascape is a two-act play concerned with a middle-aged couple, Nancy and Charlie. The setting is an isolated beach to which the couple has come for a vacation. The first act is largely a dialogue concerned with the couple's finding ways both to fill the emptiness and to combat the loneliness that have entered their lives. Basically, Nancy wants a life of excitement and new adventures, wandering from one secluded beach to another; Charlie wants simply to rest, to do absolutely nothing.

The first act begins with the deafening roar of a jet airplane passing overhead. This sound, which annoys and interrupts the couple's dialogue, is heard three times during the first act. It serves as a contrast to the quiet calm and pristine beauty of the sand dunes, and serves to remind us of the world outside the isolated beach. After the plane's initial roar passes, Nancy and Charlie debate whether to spend the remainder of their lives beachcombing and seeking adventure or to rest and let the years pass by uneventfully. Although the dialogue continues for a long time with no action, Albee keeps us absorbed in the conversation through his customary control of language. Although Nancy and Charlie speak of emptiness and inactivity, Albee's sense of verbal nuance, his ear for actual speech patterns, and his ability to heighten and intensify naturalistic speech endow the conversation with a wonderful energy. Moreover, we are drawn by the characters' situation (perhaps plight), the basic seriousness of their concerns, and the charming mixture of lightness and wit as a leaven to the sober communication.

The direct consideration of Nancy's beachcombing suggestion leads the couple to consider the meaning of life and the imminence of death. Nancy responds to Charlie's desire to rest by asking:

> But is this what we've . . . come all this way for? (*Some wonder and chiding*) Had the children? Spent all this time together? All the sharing? For nothing? To lie back down in the crib again? The same at the end as at the beginning? Sleep? Pacifier? Milk? Incomprehensible once more?
>
> (p. 9)[24]

This statement, coupled with Nancy's fervor in considering old age, retirement farms, and whether they will die together or alone, causes Charlie to agree smilingly to Nancy's proposition of a life of endless beachcombing; he does so principally in an effort to pacify Nancy and to rest. Just as they reach a state of relaxation, the jet plane again roars overhead. Almost ritually, Nancy repeats her initial line, which came after the plane first disturbed them: "Such noise they make!" (pp. 3, 13). The repetition is deceptive; the plane's droning actually serves as a kind of coda, leading the couple to a new area of discussion. Such a change might in fact happen quite naturally in any conversation after such a disturbance, and the purity and cleanness of the transition maintains the ritualistic quality that lies just beneath the naturalistic surface of Albee's play.

Although this new period of discussion concerns numerous subtopics, it focuses primarily upon Charlie's boyhood practice of diving underwater and staying submerged for long periods of time. Ever since Charlie was a little child, he wished to live under the sea, and so he often would let out all the air from his lungs, sink as far down as he could, and remain there as long as possible. He loved to watch the fish and see the variegated colors of the underwater world, and presumably he felt a sense of oneness with the sea, the place from which all living creatures originally came.

In contrast to Charlie's impulse toward sea life, Nancy reveals that she wanted to be only two things when she was young: a pony and a woman. As they banter about her having achieved her second aim, they move associatively—the play's method—to the marvel of having built a family ("a reversed *pyramid,* always in danger of toppling over when people don't behave themselves"—p. 15). The challenge, excitement, and wonder of having built a family and the continuity of life are matters to which the couple thrill in discussion. Albee indicates a true reverence for the beauty of togetherness and closeness, which the word *family* implies. There is truth and tenderness between this couple; there is also love. Albee reveals himself in this discussion and throughout the play as a man of much wisdom, warmth, and insight into life.

Again, Charlie returns to a description of his submergence—this time at a protected cove at a summer place when he was a teenager. He tells how he would enter naked and remain under for a very long time, becoming "part of the undulation and the silence" (p. 17). He remembers that it "was very good" (p. 17). Appreciating the richness of Charlie's experience, with its associations of youth, courage, sensuality, and deep communion with nature, Nancy, who from the play's start has been trying to reactivate Charlie's life impulses, encourages him to strip and submerge himself once more. When he hesitates, she encourages him by countering all of his objections, including the possibility that some other beachcombers would observe him. Nancy wants him to relive the experience both for himself and for her own vicarious excitement. Since this experience has many sexual associations and ramifications, her encouragement leads them to a discussion of sex and the loss of potency. Associatively again, they go on to discuss marital fidelity and sexual fantasy.

Nancy tells of how, during a period when Charlie was melancholic, she had thought of divorcing him. She had been a modest girl before her marriage, but by marrying and staying with only one man, she feels that she deprived herself of much sexual experience. She reveals that she has dreamed of former boyfriends with whom she missed her chance for sexual involvement. She has thought of liberation and of regaining her youth by starting again. Such thinking, she contends (presumably, Albee agrees), is the cause of many divorces. Nancy's own wavering came when she was thirty; she recalls an instance when she was quite pretty, pink, and literate; propped up beside Charlie in bed, she stared at the moles on his back while he, in a state of melancholia, lay there unresponsive and uninterested in her.

At that time, Nancy had wondered if Charlie had found another woman; knowing how various are the springs of attachment, she would not have really blamed him if he had had such a relationship. Her mother, she reveals, had said that if Charlie did leave and had then returned to her, he would have done so at a price, the price being some loss of spiritual fidelity. Her mother suggested that that would bring Nancy "halfway to compassion" (p. 24). When Charlie asks what would then establish *full* compassion, Nancy answers that the other half of the journey to compassion would have had to do with sensing his loneliness and male need for liberation. In any case, she divested herself of the divorce notion within a week.

While Charlie agrees with her that fantasy can play a significant part in sexual relations, he contends that he has been faithful to Nancy, both in mind and in spirit. They now feel quite close, and Nancy again encourages him to find his cove, to submerge, even to take her along if he wishes. She looks about and says that the other sunbathers have gone; he would not be observed. This renewed exhortation by Nancy is motivated by her sense that so much in life is fleeting, "so much goes" (p. 25). She mentions her eyesight specifically, and yet implies the more intangible commodities of youth and opportunity.

Then Nancy thinks she sees people farther up on the dunes. Since she cannot see them clearly, Charlie jests that she would be of little use if they went underwater together. She comments that she would depend on Charlie's protection; this notion causes them to compliment each other on the sharing they have enjoyed as lovers and as married people. Charlie, for example, had courted her as she wished, been a good husband, and provided a "sturdy shoulder and a comfortable life" (p. 30). This sense of having wrapped life up neatly makes Nancy bridle, and she petulantly insults Charlie, saying: "We'll wrap you in the flag when you're gone, and do taps" (p. 30). This remark hurts Charlie, and he says that he wants to go home.

A recollection of a past incident, however, diverts them. Nancy recalls the time that Charlie was stung by a bee and ordered her to make mud. She recalls how, after years of working from recipes, she could not figure out the recipe for mud. She explains that her petulance comes upon her like a bee sting, calling it involuntary behavior that momentarily closes off her impulse to kindness. Charlie accepts this explanation, and she goes on to state that what most often causes her petulance is his speaking as if their lives were over.

Charlie agrees with Nancy that all they really have is "ourselves and some time" (p. 37), and once more they express their opposed attitudes: Charlie wants to rest and Nancy wants to find excitement. Charlie contends that one must face reality, the reality of death. Nancy opts for not giving up, for seeking and scaling the "glaciers and the crags" (p. 38). Slowly the debate plays itself out and they speak of returning to the business of the day—writing postcards and gathering seashells.

At this moment the act (and the play) makes its most dramatic and sensational shift. As Charlie and Nancy speak, two huge sea lizards, Leslie and Sarah, come up on the dune and squat down on their tails. Rarely in any dramatic experience, American or foreign, has fantasy been so strikingly imposed on a naturalistic environment. Actually, the imposition is merited; the couple has just been speaking of reality and illusion, and the notion that life is dull and unexciting has been a major theme throughout. The appearance of Leslie and Sarah ends whatever it is that is dull.

To the appearance of these sea monsters, Charlie and Nancy have different reactions. Charlie is petrified, and demands (reminiscent of the bee-mud incident) that Nancy find a stick so that he can fight them. By contrast, Nancy, although somewhat frightened, is fascinated by the monsters. She brings a small twig to Charlie, while Leslie lifts a huge branch; the implied sexual play, particularly the contrast of male potency, is quite funny. Believing that they are both going to die after Charlie is defeated in battle by Leslie, Charlie and Nancy hastily declare their love for each other.

At that moment, the airplane roars overhead for the third time in the act, and Leslie and Sarah become frightened and run away. Symbolically, the flight of the sea creatures serves to remind us how frighteningly far our modern technology has taken us from nature. For Nancy and Charlie, of course, the flight is hardly symbolic.

Nancy is awestruck by the entire happening. Although she has been frightened by the lizards, her sense of wonder and her exhilaration are greater and more compelling than her fear. In contrast, Charlie is relieved at the disappearance of the lizards and theorizes that their appearance was only a dream; he further conjectures that he and Nancy are dead, that they have succumbed to food poisoning from eating spoiled liver paste. Nancy answers:

> We may be dead already, Charlie, but I think we're going to die again. Here they come!
>
> (p. 51)

With the reappearance of the monsters, both Nancy and Charlie are truly frightened. Upon Nancy's suggestion, they both assume postures of animal submission and take on fixed smiles. Thus ends Act I.

In this first act, which is largely conversational, a middle-aged couple moves from a discussion of humdrum ways to escape loneliness, dullness, and emptiness to a confrontation with sea lizards, a wonderful, frightening fantasy.

Act II begins where Act I ended, as though the play were one long, uninterrupted act. The act division is useful, however, for the opening of the second act provides almost as great a surprise as did the appearance of the monsters: the monsters talk! At least for the moment, we have entered a world of pure fantasy.

However, the sense of absolute fantasy lasts only a short time. That the fantastic creatures are capable of speech makes them less fearsome and more humanoid. Always aware at some level that the creatures are make-believe, we nevertheless become involved, in fact deeply involved, in the interaction between the two couples and in what is being discussed. During this act, in the midst of a consideration of differences and concomitant bigotry, Leslie, the male lizard, says:

> Being different is . . . interesting; there's nothing implicitly inferior or superior about it. *Great* difference, of course, produces natural caution; and if the differences are too extreme . . . well, then, reality tends to fade away.
>
> (p. 98)

Leslie's assertion is generally true. However, Albee has managed to maintain a keen sense of reality in us, despite the extreme differences between the lizards and the people, and between the world as depicted and the world of our quotidian existence. This is truly a remarkable achievement, not just a trick. The great chain of being (the human's direct link with the animal world) is a theme of the play, and Albee's powers of characterization, particularly his psychological insight and his great gifts of language, have enabled him to make a compelling portrayal of the monsters as early links in the chain. Through this linkage, Albee manages to bridge the gap between reality and unreality and to make our experience of each a means for a richer appreciation of the other.

More simply, just as Act I was essentially a dialogue between the two people, so Act II is a discussion between the two couples. As would be natural in a conversation, the pattern of couple-to-couple confrontation varies; each individual speaks to each other individual, and the partners sometimes address each other as a unit. The second act, like the first, is an extended conversation, interrupted periodically with a few instances of physical action.

The second act actually begins with an example of such action. Charlie and Nancy are still lying on their backs with feet in the air, the postures of submission they assumed at the end of Act I. Thus a comic bridge is extended from the first to the second act. After Leslie examines the humans, the couples speak apart. The lizards wonder what the humans are doing, and the humans then try to decide what to do in the face of this awful danger. On Nancy's urging, they decide to stay still and smile.

During this examination period we discover what is to be the keynote of the entire act. Leslie tells Sarah:

> Well . . . they don't look very . . . formidable—in the sense of prepossessing. Not young. They've got their teeth bared, but they don't look as though they're going to bite. Their hide is funny—feels soft.
>
> (p. 57)

He then declares that they smell "strange." This scrutiny of the humans as a different and strange species continues throughout the act. As this becomes more intense, it deeply affects Nancy and Charlie and, as the examination is applied to the lizards, it affects them as well. In this way, Albee can ask what it means to be human and whether it is worthwhile trying to survive, the questions that link Act II to Act I. The principal mode for this examination, set forth right away, is that of contrast. Two sets of beings from different worlds, or in some measure, two sets of humans from different cultures, meet and compare notes.

After their initial scrutiny, the monsters decide to approach the humans together; Charlie is frightened but Nancy is somewhat fascinated. Comically, Leslie and Sarah argue, like husband and wife, over whether she should approach with him. This speech, with its expression of fear of the unknown and its familiar husband-wife role relations, makes the monsters seem real and tends to link the couples. The lizards speak to the humans and the humans respond, despite Charlie's hesitancy. They all say "hello" and exchange pleasantries.

When both sets of creatures declare that they do not intend to eat the other, the way is paved for more facile and substantial interaction. This specific discussion of intention leads Charlie to comment more generally on the eating habits of humans; he tries to explain, for example, that "we don't eat our own kind" (p. 66), but he is somewhat frustrated in making clear his meaning. This pattern of humans trying to explain rather fundamental things to nonhumans will continue throughout the play and will have the effect of exposing and confronting much of what it means to be human. On the subject of cannibalism, Leslie agrees:

> Well, we don't eat our own kind, either. Most of us. Some.
>
> (p. 66).

Such remarks (here and elsewhere) indicate the closeness of the human species to the animal world and subtly imply the unpleasant deviations of some human beings from civilized behavior.

The human explanation moves from eating habits to an attempt to explain handshaking, which brings some funny moments. Nancy and Sarah seem to interact more smoothly than Charlie and Leslie; Charlie is driven nearly mad when he tries to explain to Leslie why humans differentiate between "arms" and "legs" while animals have merely "legs." Despite the conversational tensions, they all ultimately shake hands, and this ritual seems to bring the couples a step closer. We feel that the development of real friendship is possible.

From handshaking, they begin to consider what frightens them; this discussion is motivated by a desire to avoid panic and consequent belligerence if one of them should happen to become frightened. They all agree that they are frightened by the unknown. For example, Charlie answers:

> What frightens me? Oh . . . deep space? Mortality? Nancy . . . not being with me?
>
> (p. 73)

Then, on a lighter note, the humans try to explain what clothes are and why they wear them; Nancy defines the need as "to keep warm; to look pretty; to be decent" (p. 74). It is the attempt to explain *decency* (exposing the ridiculous puritanism of humans in the area of sex) that leads to a hilarious exploration—to Charlie's chagrin—of Nancy's breasts. Sarah's definitive analogy of Nancy's breasts to whale mammaries is both funny and serious; its funny side is the image of size with which Nancy's breasts are being associated. Its serious side is the linkage again of humans with other, supposedly lower, species.

When the couples begin to discuss pregnancy and birth, the apparently minor gap between animals and humans grows wider. While lizards lay eggs, humans do not. While lizards spawn hundreds of eggs at a time—Sarah estimates that she has laid seven thousand eggs—Nancy explains that humans give birth to one or two babies at a time. Sarah reveals that her eggs are carried for only a few weeks, while Nancy tells of the nine-month gestation period. Their subsequent discussion of child rearing also reveals radical differences. While Sarah's children merely float away, Nancy indicates that human children are kept at home for twenty years or so until they can care for themselves.

While this comparison has both its comic and educational facets, it actually leads into a rather serious area, one of vital concern to Albee in this play. In explaining "another reason" why humans keep their children with them, Nancy says "we *love* them" (p. 86). When the lizards inquire what *love* means, Nancy responds that it is "one of the *emotions*" (p. 87), which leads Sarah to ask for a definition of *emotions;* this definition is one of Charlie and Nancy's most difficult tasks. Although they cannot easily explain the emotions, especially love, it is Albee's notion that the human capacity for love and the range of emotional life are what separate humans from other animals. Later Charlie will make Sarah cry as he asks her to contemplate Leslie's ultimate departure through death. He will then explain that her reaction is an *emotional* response. It is Albee's notion that lower forms of life possess rudimentary emotional mechanisms, and that animals may not be as distant from us as we would wish to think.

Since this first attempt to explain the emotions fails, however, the couples discuss courtship and sex. This transition to lighter subject matter provides a relief and again emphasizes the similarity between humans and supposedly lower species. For example, when Sarah describes how males chased her and fought over her when she reached maturity, and when Leslie tells that he was attracted because she smelled good, we immediately recognize an analogy to the sensory components of human attraction and we realize how near we humans are to the world of the animals. This discussion of sex gets particularly funny when Nancy objects to Charlie's thinking Sarah may have had affairs.

Conversely, Charlie's assumption that human standards are inapplicable to the lizards nearly gets him into a fight with Leslie. He says that Leslie "has no grasp of conceptual matters, . . . hasn't heard of half the words in the English language, . . . lives on the bottom of the sea and has green scales" (p. 94). In fact, he suggests that Leslie is no more intelligent than a fish. This infuriates Leslie. Just as Charlie feels superior to Leslie, Leslie feels superior to fish; therefore, we perceive that both Charlie and Leslie are bigoted. But we also learn that Leslie is indeed capable of conceptualizing. It is he, in fact, who makes the observation that "*Great* difference . . . produces natural caution; and if the differences are too extreme . . . well, then, reality tends to fade away" (p. 98). In these lines, Albee once more lightly deflates human pride and pointedly reminds us of our link with the animal world.

Just at that moment, birds fly overhead and Nancy and Charlie try to explain what birds are. This discussion is intertwined with Sarah's description of how Leslie checks out conditions to make "sure a way is open for us . . ." (p. 99), and how he sets the parameters for their behavior. After Nancy says it is similar with humans, the discussion returns to birds, and Sarah likens their flying to the swimming of rays. Photography is also mentioned, but Charlie laughingly dismisses it as a topic, realizing it would be impossible to explain. They also laugh at how crazy everyone would think them were they to try to recount their interaction with the lizards.

This brings us back to Charlie's notion of the first act that they are dead, this time whimsically expressed by Nancy. She also returns to the first-act motif of Charlie's giving up versus her sense of wonder. She explains that Charlie thinks they must be dead because he is a realist and a pragmatist and has rejected all sense of wonder on this earth (wonder being a matter for which Albee has subtly and ambiguously argued by presenting two fantastic beasts as symbols of believable wonder).

Leslie jumps right in on this life-death/reality-illusion question, and both couples are drawn into the ultimately unanswerable question of the reality of existence. When Charlie mentions Descartes' proposition, "I think: therefore I am," the prospect of having to define *thinking* for Leslie overwhelms him. In fact, everything all at once seems to overwhelm him, and he starts to crumble, saying, "Death is a release, if you've lived all right, and *I* have" (p. 109). Nancy wins him back to the world of the living by inserting her tongue into his mouth and giving him a long, lovely, French kiss. She explains that Charlie is all right; it is just that he has gone through life and found it a bit overwhelming.

Once again, intensity is interrupted by the roar of a jet plane overhead, the fifth time in the play and the second in Act II. Once more Nancy says, "Such *noise* they make," and Charlie ritually answers, "They'll crash into the dunes one day" (p. 111). Meanwhile, Leslie and Sarah have again run off in fear. Noticing their fear, Nancy and Charlie seem keenly sympathetic. Perhaps Charlie's recent confrontation with his own vulnerability, brought about by the lizards' questions, makes him especially sensitive to their plight. After the roar dies down, the couples come together once more. Charlie explains that planes are machines and, to Leslie's dismay, reveals that humans even have machines that go underwater.

Such a reference leads Nancy to mention Charlie's boyhood habit of submerging himself. Charlie is reluctant to discuss it and angrily asks the creatures why they came up on earth. Under stress, they reveal that they had lost a sense of belonging, of being comfortable down there. Here Albee is showing how dissatisfaction is a cause of change and development and how thoroughly grounded our human experience is in the life of the sea. Charlie is heartbroken as he considers the transition from simple, beautiful sea life to so-called higher forms of being.

Charlie proceeds to explain that humans also came from the sea and this naturally leads to an explanation of the theory of evolution. Charlie finally tells them that the key point for him was when some creature "poked his head out of the muck" and decided to stay on earth; "he split apart and evolved and became tigers and gazelles and porcupines and Nancy here . . ." (p. 124). Charlie also points out that some creatures went under and "turned into porpoises and sharks, and manta rays, and whales . . . and you" (p. 124). Sarah asks if this development, this "progress," is constructive. Charlie is unable to respond, but Nancy assures everyone that it *is* constructive, "because I couldn't bear to think of it otherwise" (p. 125).

Nancy goes on to explain that she values tools, art, and an awareness of mortality, and the discussion deepens. Charlie points out, rather harshly, that these things "separate *us* from the brute beast" (p. 126). He explains that the brute beast is "not even aware it's *alive,* much less that it's going to die" (p. 127). Here Albee is suggesting that this awareness, this crucial element of being a human instead of an animal, is also a source of human pain and perhaps of human accomplishment. With an impulse that is at once jealous, vindictive, and loving, Charlie is struck with a need to make the lizards humanly aware of life, human emotions and death. He says:

> . . . I'm impatient for you. I want you to experience the whole thing! The full sweep! Maybe I envy you . . . down *there,* free from it all; down there with the beasts?
>
> (p. 128)

He tries to encourage Sarah toward an awareness of death, but in so doing, he makes her cry and he makes Leslie intensely angry. Sarah wails:

> I want to go back; I don't want to stay here anymore. (*Wailing*) I want to go *back*! (*Trying to break away*) I want to go *back*!
>
> (p. 129)

This is one of the most striking moments of the play, as Albee sets forth the liability of being human, the deep sense of death and isolation that the human condition imposes.

Nancy, who has grown very close to Sarah, tries to comfort her. Charlie is very sorry for having caused her deep sorrow. Wildly angry, Leslie tries to choke Charlie to death for making Sarah cry. When Leslie states that "she's never done anything like that" (p. 130), Albee drives home his point that to have emotion, to cry, to learn about death, is to begin to be human. Nancy and Sarah exhort Leslie to stop choking Charlie, and finally he does, declaring that he and Sarah ought to return to the sea. The beasts resist Nancy's attempts to make them stay and, when Leslie touchingly puts out his paw to "shake hands," Charlie takes it. Nancy, in a final attempt to persuade them to stay, explains that although they may leave, they (i.e., the lower species) will have to come back some day. Then, as the confused lizards hesitate on top of the dune, Nancy and Charlie make the only meaningful effort that creatures can make to each other in the face of the void. They offer to help the lizards in their struggle to exist on this earth. Leslie, after descending a step down the dune and crouching, stands up straight and speaks the final line of the play: "All right. Begin" (p. 135). This is a highly affirmative conclusion to an essentially affirmative play, for Albee is suggesting that it is worthwhile to live upon this earth despite its troubles, its mysteries, and the imminence of death.

In ***Seascape,*** Albee has cast a broad, piercing light on the human condition. He has suggested that the human is but a step away from the simpler, lower animals, and that the simpler life—the life of the sea—is in many ways more attractive than life on this earth. The peace and beauty and mindless integration of the individual with nature is not to be found here. However, in the more complex human world, we have developed much that is artistically beautiful and technologically precise; such products have been the fruit of the developed human mind. More importantly, we have developed two principal capacities that distinguish us from animals: the ability to love and the awareness of death. The two capacities are interrelated, for human awareness of mortality draws us closer to our fellow creatures. Love, then, is our only weapon against the void.

Charlie and Nancy are in the process of confronting the void when we first encounter them in Act I. Basically, he wants to give up and rest; she wants to live actively. While we feel that Nancy's inclination is better because it is more in tune with human energy and natural optimism, Albee's purpose is not to tell us how to live. What he does show us, particularly in Act II, is that we are very deeply a part of—and a development from—the lower orders of nature (perhaps not comparatively so low after all). Therefore, we ought not to feel arrogant and emptily proud of our elevated station in the ongoing evolutionary process; rather, our part in the process should make us aware of our link with nature and give us a feeling of belonging to the world. But this feeling is not enough; to be human is to be separate, and this separateness is frightening. To confront this isolation, Albee contends, we have only human love. He demonstrates this by showing the great closeness of Nancy and Charlie in their most difficult moments, and the associated closeness of the humans for the lizards, from whom they do not wish to part at the conclusion.

Despite the heaviness and seriousness of Albee's concern, it is the catholicity of his vision and technique that really distinguishes this play. Albee shows himself open and sensitive to all facets of the human condition: the serious, the funny, the physical, the metaphysical, the actual, and the illusionary. All of his devices deserve commendation: his wit; the purity of his style, so maginificent in its captivation and alteration of normal speech; and his lizard fantasy, through which he reveals the human reality. The lizards are a bold theatrical stroke. Their appearance has dramatic power, and they serve, as does the isolated beach setting, to objectify the human condition and to bring us to a fundamental consideration of that condition; quite clearly, this is Albee's primary purpose.

Seascape is not only a remarkable aesthetic achievement, but it is also a highly affirmative statement on the human condition. Albee, an American writer, seems to have employed the techniques of the European playwrights Pinter and Beckett, and transformed them so that he could make a highly personal statement, one almost antithetical to their own. He seems to be saying that human life is worth living and that it is desirable to climb the evolutionary ladder in order to experience love, art, and the complexities of human interaction. It is desirable even if that means a certain loss of freedom, natural beauty, and the security possessed by the creatures of the sea. Albee has never made so affirmative a statement in his career; it is significant that ***Seascape*** should follow ***All Over,*** which dealt so heavily with death. With ***Seascape,*** Albee has, as if in a Lazarus-like rebirth of mind and spirit, magnificently affirmed life.

Entwining of the Strands

Of the five plays treated in this study, ***Seascape*** has the least intense atmosphere and relies the most on dialogue to move its action along. Additionally, despite its crucial surrealistic dimension, it is second only to [Robert Anderson's] *Double Solitaire* in being the most realistic. Indeed, it is the confrontation of committed realism and outlandish surrealism, a primary Absurdist tool, that accounts for the play's considerable dramatic appeal and theatrical significance.

The play's realism lies in the human characters, whose speech, behavior, ethos, and situation clearly distinguish them as upper middle-class Americans. With their fortune made and their children grown, Charlie and Nancy are alone together on an extended vacation for the first time since they were married. They have come to a secluded beach—during the play they speak of seeing only a few other people farther down the beach—and we encounter them lolling and chatting in the afternoon sun, disturbed periodically by a passing airplane.

Since there is minimal action and much dialogue during most of the first act, the focus is firmly fixed on what Charlie and Nancy say to each other. Again, the conversation is essentially realistic, although the spareness of the dialogue, the couple's naturalistic objectification of life experience, and certain pronounced thematic strains indicate that their seemingly idle conversation is hardly the exercise in pure realism that it seems to be. Yet the overall manner and matter of the couple's conversation is decidedly realistic, and their relationship makes for easy identification. As is natural for a couple who have spent a life together, they talk about their mutual past and their hopes and plans for the future. In fact, much of their conversation during the first act focuses upon what plans, if any, they ought to make for their twilight years. Although Charlie seems to be content just to rest, Nancy wants a life of endless roaming and beachcombing—some excitement and vital involvements to insure and preserve their own vitality.

The couple speaks also of the family they have raised, of the pyramidal structure of that family, and of the children's probable astonishment at Nancy's notion of endless beachcombing. They speak also of Charlie's boyhood habit of enjoying submersion and of the present task of writing postcards even though it is boring. During all this conversation there is the verisimilitude of a familiar mutuality of concerns, believable dissatisfactions, easy camaraderie, interpersonal sensitivity, and serious and comic moments that characterize the behavior of a loving couple after long years of common struggle, common striving, and innumerable experiences deeply shared.

Among the most serious topics discussed by the couple, still ostensibly realistic in their manner, are the matters of aging and death. Both Charlie and Nancy are concerned with the passage of time and both indicate a desire to find tangible proof of the significance of the lives they have led. Clearly life is ongoing, but the determination of their particular imprint and/or raison d'être is frighteningly and amazingly elusive. In effect, their fear of old age and their effort to find an effective means to confront or elude it is the major motif of the first act. The couple finds no effective source of consolation, and the passage-of-time motif recurs like a refrain.

Although the talk of aging and death, with its concomitant objectification of life experience, falls within the realm of realistic dialogue, such discussion (and the fears it indicates and produces) creates tension and introduces strains of hopelessness and vulnerability. Such negativism is given further emphasis by the openness and vastness of the setting, the limitless and consequently frightening sea, surf, and sky. Such an environment serves to engender a cosmic loneliness in Charlie and Nancy, which gives their conversation a particular pungency. Moreover, the peace and quiet of the isolated beach is periodically violated by the roar of a passing airplane, which recurs throughout the play. This interruption not only is intrusive to Charlie and Nancy, but also seems to threaten them, if not all living creatures.

The motif of comfortable, passive escape versus active escape, the discussion of old age and death, the boundless setting, the spareness of the language, and the incursions by the airplane in themselves intensify the action until it reaches the very limits of realistic acceptability; what drives us clearly out of the domain of the purely realistic and into the nightmarish world of the Absurd is the surrealistic appearance, at the the end of Act I, of Leslie and Sarah, two great, green, humanoid sea lizards.

The theatrical shock at Act I's conclusion diminishes somewhat in Act II, when we learn that the lizards can communicate to the humans and do not intend harm. As the shock diminishes, the ensuing dialogue deepens our perception of realism versus surrealism; the conversation leads us to contemplate and explore the evolution of human life, the differences between human life and animal life, and, ultimately, the value amidst the pain of human life.

The essence of human life is subtly defined for us by Charlie and Nancy as they endeavor to explain various aspects of humanity to Leslie and Sarah. In a well-crafted, often comic series of comparisons and contrasts, Albee reveals both natural differences and ironic similarities between the two "species." Leslie and Sarah are husband and wife, and have a family, a history of biological attraction, a present mutual concern, a sense of pride, and a desire to learn and develop. The only real differences between the couples are in physical appearance; strength; the number of children each possesses; and the extent of technological, intellectual, and emotional development.

While the comparison produces much mirth and emphasizes and argues for a sense of wonder as one of the human being's greatest and most attractive capacities—the monsters become believable to us as well as to Charlie and Nancy—it also holds human life up to serious scrutiny. Furthermore, it produces a diminished sense of significance for Charlie and Nancy, inasmuch as they share so much with a lower species, and an even more trenchant sense that death and nothingness are a facet of both the human condition and the condition of all creatures. As with so many Absurdist plays, we do not know whether to laugh or cry as the amusing yet devastating interactional analysis between the couples proceeds.

Sarah, however, does know how to react; she begins to cry when Charlie explains to her what death is. This explanation and Sarah's raction to it constitute the play's climax, and it then moves swiftly towards its essentially, if ambivalently, affirmative denouement. When Sarah learns that death involves permanent loss of or separation from Leslie, the lizards hastily decide to return to the sea. But the humans (especially Nancy) convince them to stay. Nancy explains that evolution will send their species back anyway and that she and Charlie could, and would like to, help them make the evolutionary transition. Enticed by the logic of Nancy's assertion and the offer of assistance, the monsters decide to stay.

While this conclusion makes ***Seascape*** the most positive of all the plays discussed in this study, it is not entirely winsome. Just as Charlie and Nancy have had to confront the ineluctable contingency of their lives and the sense that humans are simply an ingredient in universal flux, so Leslie and Sarah agree, by staying, to enter into a condition that they already know to be dangerous. All four know that life is essentially an experiment that carries a high probability of pain, that ultimately ends in death, and that carries no certainty whatsoever as to the benefits of "progress," the entire evolutionary thrust.

In the first act, Albee leads us to contemplate what the human couple should do with their old age. At the end of that act and the beginning of Act II, he leads us to speculate what the monsters will do to the couple. Soon, however, the theatrical sensationalism of the monsters' appearance passes, and the monsters themselves become a vital ingredient in the dominant questions of the entire play (articulated only partially in Act I): what are the contours and what is the meaning of life itself?

Inasmuch as the couples share a closeness, there is vitalist (i.e., experiential, whether or not logically defensible) affirmation in the play; and the hope for a progressive development in nature is also affirmative. However, neither the camaraderie of the characters nor the possibilities of future development hold any real answers for any of the individuals. They are caught in time with death, and its concomitants of loss and separation, as their dominant individual and communal future prospects. Therefore, while ***Seascape*** is not as bleak in tone as the plays of Rabe, Guare, and Bullins, it does share their perception (as does the Absurdist theatre in general) that life requires human beings to face the void. Moreover, ***Seascape*** possesses many Absurdist features, including the fusion of comic and tragic elements, a certain circularity of plotline (tangentially Absurdist), and, of course, the dreamlike, intermittently nightmarish atmosphere that is highlighted by the stunning presence of Sarah and Leslie. Except for the monsters' behavior, the Absurdist elements of ***Seascape*** are more subtly intertwined than they are in the works of Rabe, Guare, or Bullins. In fact, the distortions inherent in many of Albee's Absurdist elements are recognizable only through objective analysis. Absorption of the monsters into a realistic framework at once enhances the realistic and surrealistic dimensions of the play. In ***Seascape,*** the models of realism and Absurdism appear like two hovering presences, essentially distinct yet capable of intertwining, disengaging, and intertwining once more. ***Seascape*** lacks a social protest dimension (except, perhaps, for a mild thrust at technology), and is clearly less realistic that Anderson's ***Double Solitaire,*** yet more realistic and, paradoxically, more fundamentally Absurdist than the works of Rabe, Guare, and Bullins.

Notes

[1]Harold Clurman, "Theatre," *The Nation,* 15 March 1975, p. 314.

[2]Mel Gussow, "Recalling Evolution of 'Seascape' Play, Albee Sees Tale Not of Lizard, but of Life," *The New York Times,* 21 January 1975, p. 40.

[3]Gussow, p. 40.

[4]T. E. Kalem, "Primordial Slime," *Time,* 10 February 1975, p. 57.

[5]Jack Kroll, "Leapin' Lizards," *Newsweek,* 10 February 1975, p. 75.

[6]Catharine Hughes, "Albee's *Seascape,*" *America,* 22 February 1975, p. 136.

[7]Stanley Kauffmann, "Seascape," *The New Republic,* 22 February 1975, p. 22.

[8]Walter Kerr, "Albee's Unwritten Part," *The New York Times,* 2 February 1975, II, p. 5.

[9]Kalem, p. 57.

[10]Kroll, p. 75.

[11]Hughes, pp. 136-137.

[12]Kerr, p. 5.

[13]Brendan Gill, "Among the Dunes," *The New Yorker,* 3 February 1975, p. 75.

[14]Clive Barnes, "Albee's *Seascape* Is a Major Event," *The New York Times,* 27 January 1975, p. 20.

[15]Henry Hewes, "Albee Surfaces." *Saturday Review,* 8 March 1975, p. 40.

[16]Clurman, p. 314.

[17]"Albee: 'I Write to Unclutter My Mind,' " *The New York Times,* 26 January 1975, II, pp. 1, 7.

[18]Gussow, p. 40.

[19]Barnes, p. 20.

[20]Hewes, p. 40.

[21]Gill, p. 75.

[22]Clurman, p. 314.

[23]"Marginalia: Albee Cited for 'Seascape,' " *The New York Times,* 25 December 1975, p. 27.

[24]Edward Albee, *Seascape* (New York: Atheneum, 1975). All pages cited are from this edition.

Liam O. Purdon (essay date 1983)

SOURCE: "The Limits of Reason: *Seascape* as Psychic Metaphor," in *Edward Albee: An Interview and Essays,* edited by Julian N. Wasserman, The University of St. Thomas, 1983, pp. 141-53.

[*In the essay below, Purdon asserts that it is ". . . in* Seascape *that Albee provides one of his clearest attempts to render his own understanding of the human psyche into extended and concrete metaphorical form."*]

One of the most notable aspects of Edward Albee's drama has been his recurrent interest in theatre as a means for the revelation of psychological process, for by his own admission Albee has, as a writer, been most interested in capturing the unconscious rhythms of his onstage characters rather than their superficial mannerisms. Clearly, with their extensive speeches directed to multiple audiences and their diminished physical action, many of Albee's plays have as their focus the motivation behind action rather than action itself. Thus one finds that with increasing regularity Albee's work seems to include both discussions of and metaphors for the cognitive process, so that within his works virtually no explanation for human consciousness—ranging from the brief discussion of the physio-electrical basis of knowledge in ***Listening*** to the use of the phrenological model as a prop in the psychological allegory, ***Tiny Alice***—is left unexplored. However, it is in ***Seascape*** that Albee provides one of his clearest attempts to render his own understanding of the human psyche into extended and concrete metaphorical form. While ***Tiny Alice,*** dubbed by its critics as "metafuzzical,"[1] works as an abstract treatise on human psychology, ***Seascape*** functions in the tradition of the medieval morality play with its more clearly defined figures serving as emblems for the distinct parts of the human consciousness.

In rendering his own version of human psychological makeup, Albee clearly borrows from but does not conspicuously adhere to the traditional psychic zones of Freudian tripartation, for the playwright does metaphorically dramatize the tension between the forces, or principles, which pull man between his desire for reality (order) and pleasure (chaos).[2] Indeed, the principal characters, Charlie and Nancy, call the audience's attention to what might be termed the American mid-life crisis: their children grown, Charlie feels that he has earned a little rest, while Nancy believes that they have earned a little life. Yet the conflict, if it may be called that, in the central characters' purposes takes on the proportions of crisis when, at the end of the first act, Charlie and Nancy encounter Albee's dramatically unique representation of the psychic energy of the unconscious: the saurian characters, Leslie and Sarah. As symbols of such psychic energy, the primordial lizard-creatures represent both the means and the opportunity for the central characters to act upon the conflicting desires which have been kept in balance until this moment of crisis. Thus, it is through the metaphorical confrontation between the dynamic principles for reality and pleasure with the unknown saurian creatures that Albee presents his allegory of the process of the regulation of that energy, a theme which comprises the didactic matter of the play.

As the play begins, Albee first introduces the audience to this metaphor of the psyche through the characters of Charlie and Nancy. They converse as might any couple on an outing to the seashore while the intrusive sound of a jet aircraft is heard overhead. But as their dialogue continues and transforms itself into an argument, the emphasis each places on his respective point of view illustrates the tension and perennial conflict between reason and desire. Each in turn becomes a spokesman for the reality and pleasure principles. Accordingly, Nancy, who believes they have "earned a little life,"[3] argues inconsistently but passionately for the pursuit of unreproved pleasure, especially in the leisure activity of beachcombing, while Charlie, who remains circumspect and noticeably inhibited, argues for moderation and the acceptance of the *status quo.*

The revelation of the pleasure principle through the character of Nancy in Act I is developed several ways, the most noticeable of which appears in Albee's parenthetical stage directions. From the moment the curtain rises, Nancy demonstrates the full spectrum of human emotion: one moment she laughs and is gay; the next, she is sad and testy. She is enthusiastic, then taunting, and an instant later disappointed; one moment she is cheerful and matter-of-fact; the next, bitter and begrudging. Furthermore, Albee puts the intensity of Nancy's passion and her emotional capriciousness in relief by comparing it to Charlie's stolid indifference. Even Nancy's seemingly insignificant movements on stage—her several returns to the paint box, for example—assume functional meaning, especially as they occur while Charlie remains lying in the supine position for nearly half of the first act.

In her mercurial changes of temperament and restive actions, Nancy is the embodiment of what Sigmund Freud describes as the primordial life-principle which knows "no organization and unified will, only an impulsion to obtain satisfaction."[4] Nancy is the very personification of inconsistent behavior bent on the fulfillment of appetitive desire. As such, she is the character with whom Albee associates the preparation of food. As the argument between Charlie and Nancy unfolds, it is Nancy and not Charlie who begins packing the lunch hamper. Later, as Charlie gropes for an explanation of the vision of the sea creatures and blames the whole experience on spoiled liver paste, Albee reveals that it was Nancy who had prepared the meal and chosen the fatal menu.

Yet Nancy embodies more than mere dietary appetite. In contrast to her husband, Nancy demonstrates an unrepressed appetite for the sensuous experience of nature. Arguing for a life spent by the seashore, she tells Charlie, "I love the water, and I love the air, and the sand and the dunes and the beach grass, and the sunshine on all of it and the white clouds way off, and the sunsets and the noise the shells make in the waves . . ." (p. 5). Such unabashed appreciation for the sensual naturally leads to the presentation of Nancy as a creature of sexual appetite as well. Recalling the vicissitudes of their earlier married life, Nancy, not Charlie, introduces, first, the subject of infidelity and, second, the subject of coital loneliness, a modification of the concept of La Petit Morte. While she reassures Charlie by confessing that she never succumbed to her passions and desires, Nancy does, nevertheless, reveal that earlier in her marriage she was obsessed with the idea of unrestrained sexuality for a short period of time:

> Yes, but the *mind.* And what bothered me was not what you might be doing . . . but that, all of a sudden, I had not. *Ever* . . . All at once I thought: it was over between us . . . and I thought back to before I married you, and the boys I would have done it with, if I had been that type, the firm-fleshed boys I would have taken in my arms had it occurred to me. And I began to think of them, Proust running on, pink and ribbons, looking at your back, and your back would turn and it would be Johnny Smythe or the Devlin boy, or one of the others, and he would smile, reach out a hand, undo my ribbons, draw me close, ease on. Oh, that was a troubling time.
>
> (p. 22)

Yet the speech reveals more about Nancy than the nature of her sexual fantasies. While it portrays her as a creature of what Freud termed "impulsion," it shows that those natural impulses have been kept in check by external and, perhaps to Nancy, alien forces; the societal concept of "that type." Moreover, Nancy's reference to Proust is especially significant here since, within the context of the passage, it introduces the Proustian concept of absence, one of the most revealing of the 19th century literary representations of the primordial life principle of the Freudian "impulsion to obtain satisfaction." This view of love as a "subjective creation of imagination which cannot thrive in the presence of its object" explains the essential motivation behind her ephemeral infidelity.[5]

Albee completes the development of the metaphoric representation of the pleasure principle in the character of Nancy by illustrating telling idiosyncrasies of her behavior and qualifying the nature of her relationship with Charlie. Nancy, for example, is conspicuously and frequently ebullient, especially as she returns to her painting and tries to persuade Charlie "to unfetter" himself and "see everything twice" (p. 10). While originating in a natural desire, this ebullience, owing to its frequency, illustrates the frenetic condition of the "impulsion to satisfaction." Further, her thinking—often muddled and, as she herself points out, contradictory—degenerates frequently into emotionalism, which further illustrates the disorganized condition of desire. Likewise, her repeated demonstrations of peevishness—to which she, again, admits guilt as she states to Charlie almost perfunctorily, "I was being petulant" (p. 31)—reveal a disunified will. And her subordinate relationship to Charlie, which she acknowledges several times, also contributes to the metaphor of the pleasure principle in that it intimates the dynamics of mental process. This subservient status takes on significant meaning and even explains much of Nancy's argument when she begins to tell Charlie how she nearly became unfaithful and states, "The deeper your inertia went, the more *I* felt alive" (p. 21). As reason loses control of desire, the impulsion to satisfaction assumes a stronger vitality. Hence, Charlie's direct response shortly thereafter to Nancy's taunting—"You're not cruel by nature; it's not your way" (p. 17)—functions in a severalfold manner: it enables Charlie to gain the advantage in the argument, provides a statement of her character, and introduces for the audience, on the one hand, an illustration of the dynamic process by which one force keeps the other in check, and, on the other, a significant non-judgmental account of the nature of unrestrained fulfillment of satisfaction. The primordial life function is neither good nor bad; it is just the manifestation of tremendous vitality. As Freud points out: "Naturally, the id knows no values, no good and evil, no morality."[6]

As Albee uses the character of Nancy to illustrate the pleasure principle, so he likewise uses Charlie to embody the corresponding reality principle and its role of restraining, or counter-balancing, the uncontrolled impulses of the former. Thus, while Nancy refers to Proust, Charlie is through his own allusion associated with Anatole France, a figure noted for his rationalistic, dispassionate approach to art.[7] While Nancy consistently reacts through the display of emotion, Charlie reacts through reason. Thus, Charlie's first reaction to the sight of Leslie and Sarah is to posit the "logical" explanation that he and Nancy have become victims of food poisoning, a logical if incorrect means of making the unknown and irrational fit neatly into the constructs of his own world. Thus, in Charlie one finds a man who finds it easier to yield up his own life, through the assumption of his own death, than to accept that which defies his own logic and experience. While Charlie first becomes distraught at the sight of the two reptilian creatures, he quickly gains control over his emotions, in contrast to Nancy, who is immediately attracted to the creatures precisely because they seem so alien and, hence, apart from ordinary, rational experience.

However, if Charlie and Nancy are so different in their initial responses to life in general and the sea-creatures in particular, it would be a mistake to conceive of their mid-life crisis as being analogous to that of the anonymous pair in ***Counting the Ways,*** whose lives are shown to have grown so separate and self-contained, for the point of conflict between Nancy and Charlie is the way in which their differently directed points of view act upon each other in order to create a workable psychological balance which allows them to function successfully in the world at large. Thus, Charlie and Nancy cannot ultimately be examined in isolation since both of their identities come from the continual tug-of-war between their conflicting desires, a conflict which results in their perpetual process of dynamic self-definition and their mutual dependency rather than separateness. One sees this self-defining tug-of-war in Nancy's attempt to convince Charlie to relive his boyhood experience of submerging himself in the ocean. Charlie points out to Nancy that as a child he enjoyed sensory delight and the condition of being submerged and contained in the water:

> I used to go way down; at our summer place; a protective cove. The breakers would come in with a storm, or a high wind, but not usually. I used to go way down, and try to stay. I remember before that, when I was tiny, I would go to the swimming pool, at the shallow end, let out my breath and sit on the bottom . . . and when I was older, we were by the sea. Twelve; yes, or thirteen.
>
> I used to lie on the warm boulders, strip off . . . learn about my body . . . And I would go into the water, take two stones, as large as I could manage, swim out a bit, tread, look up one final time at the sky . . . relax . . . begin to go down . . . just one more object come to the bottom, or living thing, part of the undulation and silence. It was very good.
>
> (p. 16)

Clearly, Charlie's description of this world of "undulation and silence" is one of a state of pre-consciousness, of the mind free and unrestricted by reason and, especially, social convention which restrains impulse. Nancy's prolonged insistence that Charlie attempt to re-enact what has become just a pleasant and remote memory is her attempt to convert Charlie into her own image by returning him to a type of prelapsarian state of consciousness. Significantly, Charlie's stern resistance to this letting go of the conscious world is rooted in his self-consciousness, his awareness of himself as an adult. As in the case of Nancy's early sexual urges, it is the category, or role, imposed from without which ultimately separates Charlie from the pleasures of his youth. For both Charlie and Nancy, then, the result of this verbal give and take concerning desire and restraint is a process of self-definition through assertion and defense of their own points of view as each tries to defend his own values while converting those of the other.[8]

Having established the tenuous balance between the two parts of the waking consciousness, Albee proceeds to examine and test that balance through the introduction of the two saurian creatures who have as their origin the hidden, subconscious world of "undulation and silence" described by Charlie much as the playwright does with Jerry's entrance into the well ordered, conventional world of Peter in ***The Zoo Story*** as well as in the unexpected appearance of Elizabeth in ***The Lady from Dubuque.*** If the appearance of the saurian creatures is intended as a litmus test of the central characters, the differences between Charlie and Nancy become apparent almost immediately. However, in order to understand these differences, it is important to recognize an important but subtle metamorphosis which occurs within the play. The first part of the play, the initial debate between Charlie and Nancy takes place in the realm of ordinary consciousness, the world of reason. It is a world in which Charlie, as a symbol of reason and convention, acts as indolent restraint on the more active pleasure principle. The interjection of reason into that world is symbolized by the intrusive sounds of jet aircraft into the naturalistic scenery of the first act. The jets, whose sounds are heard some four times within the first act, are representatives, *par excellence,* of controlling rationality—for they are non-natural machines created through reason in order to satisfy and, hence, channel the primordial, imaginative urge to fly.

With the appearance of Leslie and Sarah that world is transformed into a realm in which the laws no longer apply and where the non-rational is in control. In this made-over world, the jet airplanes, whose presence were so strongly and frequently felt in the first act, make only one brief appearance. The terror which they inspire in Leslie and Sarah as well as the discomfort they create for Nancy show just how alien such machines are to nature. Within this context even the "reasonable" Charlie doubts their worth—"They'll crash into the dunes one day; I don't know what good they do" (p. 111)—with the result that he repeatedly emphasizes their status as mere "machines" whose imitation of the flight of birds is as unsatisfactory and incomplete as he had earlier judged a parrot's unthinking mimicry of human speech to be. Thus the formerly lethargic Charlie becomes active and aggressive and has to be restrained by the previously restive Nancy. From the first appearance of the saurian creatures, Nancy has clearly been in control. She is the first to notice their approach. As she recalls her childhood desires, she sees Leslie and Sarah emerge from the water; as she and Charlie discuss the possibility of Charlie's submerging himself, she notices that the two visitors are lying prone on the beach; and as she almost cajoles Charlie into slipping into the water, she observes that she has lost track of Leslie and Sarah. Nancy is also the first to recognize the intrinsic beauty of the visitors, although, in keeping with the function of her characterization, she does not know why she finds them aesthetically pleasing. Thus, as Charlie recoils at the sight of Leslie and Sarah and assumes a defensive posture, Nancy almost dreamily responds to Charlie's commands, extolling Leslie's and Sarah's beauty, first, with "Charlie! They're magnificent!" (p. 44) and, later, with "Charlie, I think they're absolutely beautiful. What are they?" (p. 45).

Yet if Nancy is in her element, Charlie clearly is not. From the outset, the reason and restraint which he demonstrated in the first part of the play repeatedly fail him in his dealings with the saurian intruders. His rational explanation for the appearance of the creatures as a result of "bad liver paste" is painfully inadequate, even to the non-rational, intuitive Nancy. And with the movement into the non-rational world, the playwright's function becomes the demonstration of the failure of rationality in the face of the irrational. This is, of course, a familiar theme in many of Albee's works, such as ***A Delicate Balance*** and ***Tiny Alice,*** and is no doubt responsible for Albee's interest in and adaptation of Herman Melville's "Bartleby the Scrivener."[9] Thus, as reason breaks down, Albee proceeds to give the unconscious a conscious form just as, when the restraints of marriage weakened, Nancy found herself giving form to her fantasies of premarital encounters with young men. Yet what is unique about ***Seascape*** is that, while Leslie's and Sarah's appearance suggests promordiality, it is not their saurian physical natures but rather the lengthy and seemingly desultory conversations which they have with Charlie and Nancy that confirm their introduction as representations of psychic energy. On the one hand, these discussions reveal an absence of the laws of logic; on the other, they demonstrate a disregard for or ignorance of social convention, moral restraint, and cognitive awareness of the totality of being—in other words, the artificial restraints imposed from without upon the "impulsion to satisfaction." In this regard, Leslie and Sarah also provide a view of the source of aggression and desire, another principal aspect of libido.[10]

As the two couples encounter each other at the beginning of Act II, they reveal fear and a lack of trust. No sooner do they introduce themselves to each other than they begin a series of dialogues which, while intended to be informative, end in futility, without the exchange of any meaningful information. Significantly, the first of these dialogues concerns eating. Interestingly, it also introduces the correlative condition of the ignorance of social convention. Charlie points out to Leslie that he does not know Leslie's eating habits. He then adds that "It'd be perfectly normal to assume you . . . [that is, Leslie and Sarah] . . . ate whatever . . . you ran into . . . you know, whatever you ran into" (p. 65). Leslie's ingenious response—"No; I don't know" (p. 65)—reveals the weakness of Charlie's assumption. But the absurdity of the assumption is not exposed until Charlie, who is striving for a simple response to Leslie's initial inquiry regarding Nancy's and his disposition, states that he and Nancy do not eat "anything that talks; you know, English" (p. 66). Nancy at this turn in the dialogue points out that parrots do talk and that people eat parrots. This revelation not only emphasizes the illogic of Charlie's second generalization, which is reinforced by Leslie who asks, "What are you saying?" (p. 66) but also brings the dialogue to an abrupt halt, as Charlie attempts a restatement of his original assumption, saying "I'm trying to tell you . . . we don't eat our own kind" (p. 66). Charlie does not contradict himself, but his attempt to sustain his original assumption undermines itself and meaning vanishes.

Another exchange that brings to the fore the absence of logic appears shortly afterward as Nancy shows Sarah her breasts. As in the first case, this instance also provides another view of the ignorance of social convention on the parts of the saurian creatures. The passage in question begins with the discussion of the function of clothing, another artificial convention, but soon focuses on the subject of Nancy's breasts. While Nancy conducts herself in a straightforward manner and shows no shame in the hope of enlightening Leslie and Sarah who have never seen a mammalian breast, Charlie becomes irrational at the seeming breakdown of decorum. At first Charlie demonstrates a postlapsarian prudishness when he corrects Nancy, indicating that she should say "mammary" instead of "breast" (p. 75). Next, when Sarah ingenuously beckons Leslie to see Nancy's breasts, Charlie reveals possessiveness, stating that he does not want Leslie looking at Nancy's nakedness. But when Charlie is questioned by Nancy and Leslie as to the motivation for his possessiveness and Leslie states conditionally that he does not want to see Nancy's breasts, Charlie reverses his original attitude, defending and extolling the virtue and beauty of Nancy's anatomy: "They're not embarrassing; *or* sad! They're lovely! Some women . . . some women . . . Nancy's age, they're . . . some women . . . I *love* your breasts" (p. 77). While Charlie's about-face can certainly be viewed as a positive act of acceptance, it reveals the working of the emotional rather than the cognitive consciousness because it is predicated upon pride and follows a demonstration of repressive social behavior. It is no coincidence, then, that Albee includes in his stage directions for Charlie that he is "more flustered than angry" (p. 77). What Charlie achieves is what he needs to achieve; that he finally perceives beauty through the challenging of his possessive nature, however, demonstrates the absence of logic.

While several other instances of emotionalism and nonsequiturs appear in this act, the discussion of ontology provides the best example of the suspension of the laws of reason. In an effort to explain why they are dead, the absurdity of which cannot go unnoticed, Charlie tries to explain to Leslie that created reality is an illusion and that true existence comes about through thought. Instead of being logical, Charlie becomes flustered and angry, and the dialogue degenerates into an emotional bout which concludes ironically with Charlies losing control of himself, shouting the name of Descartes:

> LESLIE: Then I take it *we* don't *exist.*
>
> CHARLIE: *(Apologetic.)* Probably not; I'm sorry.
>
> LESLIE: *(To Nancy.)* That's quite a mind he's got there.
>
> NANCY: *(Grudgingly defending Charlie.)* Well . . . he thinks things through. (Very cheerful.) As for *me,* I couldn't care less; I'm having far too interesting a time.
>
> SARAH: *(Gets on all fours.)* Oh, I'm so glad!
>
> LESLIE: *(Comes three steps down L. ridge. Puzzled.)* I *think* I exist.
>
> CHARLIE: *(Shrugs.)* Well, that's all that matters; it's the same thing. . . .
>
> CHARLIE: What?
>
> LESLIE: What you *said.*
>
> CHARLIE: *(Barely in control.)* DESCARTES!! DESCARTES!! I THINK: THEREFORE I AM!! *(Pause.)* COGITO ERGO SUM! I THINK: THEREFORE I AM. . . .
>
> (p. 108)

Leslie's comment that Charlie has "quite a mind" adds a further touch of irony, but it is Charlie's final comment concerning death as a release that confirms that logic has indeed failed. That Charlie beckons death by describing the final moments of life shows that he prefers the dissolution of life or existence and, in turn, the absence of reason. While the sound of an airplane flying overhead ends the discussion, the actual termination of the exchange of ideas, then, occurs in Charlie's demonstration of emotion. Even with the invocation of Descartes, the laws of logic remain absent.

The final fight or disagreement which draws the play to a close might also be viewed as another instance of the suspension of the laws of logic. Charlie's attempt to make Sarah cry is certainly irrational; this persistent taunting is clearly cruel. But the fight also introduces another view of the unconscious; it reveals an account of aggression. As Charlie forces Sarah to admit that she would cry her heart out if Leslie ever left her, Leslie grabs Charlie by the throat and slowly strangles him. Leslie's act of aggression is a demonstration of brute force, but as Leslie himself implies shortly afterward in the line "Don't you talk to me about brute beast" (p. 132), Charlie's remorseless questioning illustrates a verbal manifestation of the same act. Leslie's implication also clarifies Charlie's previous statements concerning Leslie and Sarah. When Charlie begins the confrontation which nearly leads to his own strangulation, he exclaims that he does not understand his own feelings toward Leslie and Sarah: "I don't *know* what more I want. *(To Leslie and Sarah.)* I don't know what I want for *you.* I don't know what I feel toward you; it's either love or loathing. Take your pick" (p. 128). While Charlie's ambivalence represents a lack of conscious control, the fact that he does describe his feelings toward Leslie and Sarah as being either of love or loathing represents an acknowledgement of Leslie and Sarah as being either the source of aggression or of desire.

Several other minor instances of aggression also arise in the second act, such as Charlie's continued taunting of Leslie and Sarah, but the one that brings the question of the unconscious clearly to the fore, like the fight in the conclusion, occurs when Charlie questions Sarah's fidelity. Charlie gets Sarah to admit that she has not "coupled" with anyone but Leslie; however, Leslie, who, like Nancy, is confused by the line of questioning, asks Charlie to state precisely what "are you after" (p. 128). When Charlie cannot and evades making an attempt at a conceptual understanding of his own purpose, a fight nearly breaks out—Nancy's and Sarah's joint intercession notwithstanding. The conflict which arises, then, results partly from Charlie's effrontery but mostly from a breakdown in communication. Ironically, it is Charlie, not Leslie, who is incapable of maintaining symbolic logic, although he blames Leslie for his own ineffectuality when he condescendingly adds, "Especially to someone who has no grasp of conceptual matters, who hasn't heard of half the words in the English language, who lives on the bottom of the sea and has green scales!" (p. 94).

This representation of aggression resulting from the absence of conceptual ability introduces a third way in which Albee creates the metaphor of uncontrolled psychic energy. Throughout the second act, he calls attention to the need for and the absence of a cognitive awareness of the totality of being. The latter obviously appears in all of the instances of aggression and lack of logic that appear from the moment the second act begins. The former, on the other hand, appears twice: first, early in the act, as Charlie and Leslie enter into a discussion of anatomical differences and, second, as Nancy and Charlie later attempt to explain and define the concept of emotion for Leslie and Sarah. In the discussion of the anatomical differences, Leslie and Sarah learn the distinctions between toes and fingers, arms and legs. This knowledge then leads them to an understanding of the social convention of hand-shaking, which they perform enthusiastically. While the information allows Leslie and Sarah to experience something they have never known, the significance of the event lies in the fact that it represents the beginning of the fusion of the conscious, embodied by Nancy and Charlie, and the unconscious self, embodied by Leslie and Sarah. In the later discussions of emotion, the same thing happens but to a greater degree. As Nancy and Charlie explain the nature of emotion to Leslie and Sarah, not only do the two couples gradually overcome the differences that separate them, but each couple also gains its own emotional equilibrium. Charlie and Nancy work out the doubts that each has felt toward the other; Leslie and Sarah learn what love is. Furthermore, through the delineation of emotion and the attainment of the awareness of social convention, Nancy and Charlie discover the means by which to keep Leslie and Sarah from retreating to the sea. Thus, as Albee indicates in the conclusion, it is through the understanding of the physical that one begins to perceive the totality of his being, but it is through the examination of the emotions, difficult as it may be, that one attains the totality of being.

Seascape, then, is much more than a fantastic dramatic experience. Like many of Albee's other plays, it is a romance. It provides a view of order in the presentation of the metaphoric representations of the reality and pleasure principles and a dissolution of that order in the symbolic representation of psychic energy. Like all romances, it possesses an essentially comic structure and so offers a resolution to the dissolution. Symbolically, that resolution appears in the form of a handshake. But as the conclusion to the second act demonstrates, the means by which order is reestablished is through the maintaining of contact with and the understanding of the subconscious: hence, the function of Nancy's unremitting insistence in the closing moments of the play that Leslie and Sarah not leave. To attain consciousness, as Albee indicates, one must be willing to enter the seascape, or Charlie's "protected cove," where land and sea—consciousness and the unconscious—meet and learn to accept the meaning of the experience. In that sense, ***Seascape,*** with its face-to-face confrontation between its creatures of the land and the sea, is not the flawed tale of unanswered evolutionary questions often described by critics[11] but is, instead, an optimistic blueprint for the development of a higher consciousness, for in Albee's mind evolution is clearly a matter of consciousness rather than form.

Notes

[1]John Chapman, "Revival of *Tiny Alice:* Still a Metafuzzical Bore," *New York Daily News (NYDN),* 30 September 1969, contained in *New York Theatre Critic Reviews (NYTCR),* 1969, p. 256.

[2]For a brief discussion of these two principles, see Sigmund Freud, *A General Introduction to Psychoanalysis,* trans. by Joan Riveire (New York: Garden City, 1943), pp. 311-2.

[3]Edward Albee, *Seascape* (New York: Antheneum, 1975), p. 37. All future page references appear in the text.

[4]Sigmund Freud, *New Introductory Lectures on Psychoanalysis,* trans. by W. J. H. Sprott (New York: Norton, 1933), pp. 102ff.

[5]Geoffrey Brereton, *A Short History of French Literature* (Middlesex, England: Penguin, 1968), p. 243.

[6]Freud (Sprott), p. 105.

[7]Brereton, p. 232.

[8]In this, Charlie and Nancy are much like George and Martha of *Who's Afraid of Virginia Woolf?* Like Charlie and Leslie, George and Martha seem to embody dispassionate intellect and unrestrained sexuality locked in perpetual, self-defining battle. As becomes apparent at the end of the play, their verbal battles are not symptoms of the breaking apart of their marriage but, rather, the dynamic force which binds the two differently directed individuals together: hence, Martha's vigorous defense of George at the play's end. For a discussion of similarities between *Virginia Woolf* and *Seascape,* see Howard Kissel, "Seascape," *Women's Wear Daily,* 27 January 1975, reprinted in *NYTCR,* 1975, p. 370.

[9]Albee completed an unpublished libretto adaptation of Melville's short story in 1961.

[10]Freud (Sprott), pp. 140ff.

[11]See Edwin Wilson, "Disturbing Creatures of the Deep," *Wall Street Journal,* 28 January 1975, reprinted in *NYTCR,* 1975, p. 370. For the view that the play ends optimistically, see Henry Hewes, "Theatre," *Saturday Review,* 8 March 1975, p. 40, as well as Sam Coale, "The Visions of Edward Albee," *Providence Journal,* 28 December 1975. Reprinted in *Newsbank (Literature)* (Nov.-Dec., 1975), p. A3, and Clive Barnes, "Albee's *Seascape* is a Major Event," *New York Times,* 27 January 1975 reprinted in *NYTCR,* 1975, p. 368.

Gerry McCarthy (essay date 1987)

SOURCE: *"Seascape,"* in *Modern Dramatists: Edward Albee,* St. Martin's Press, 1987, pp. 115-28.

[*In the essay below, McCarthy asserts that in* Seascape, *"Albee escapes the particular social contexts within which he normally writes in order to consider in a fundamental way the phenomenon we know as life and experience personally as existence."*]

Long before the first performance of ***Seascape*** Albee teased his questioners over what it would contain. 'I'm moving from writing about people to writing about animals', he declared, and later described the play as a 'true to life story'. His audience could hardly have been prepared for the play they attended in January 1975. Many of the Albee ingredients are there. There is the married couple face to face with the problems of what is reality in their lives, and there is the intrusion of a second couple to create the quartet for which he writes so fluently.

When the setting is a holiday beach, and the atmosphere is one of love and seductive contentment, the scene seems strangely anodyne; but, when the crisis is provoked by two giant humanoid lizards crawling up from the primeval depths of the sea, then the result is something quite new. When he says that he is writing about animals Albee is teasing, but at the same time that is precisely what he is doing. Commentators who obstinately concentrate on the familial struggles in his plays ignore the fact that he writes in a wider context: a society, a way of life, even a species. ***Seascape*** is an important development in this process in that it treats the question of the future of the species.

It appears in the opening seconds of the play in a purely theatrical image that includes the seeds of much of what follows:

> *The curtain rises.* Nancy *and* Charlie *on a sand dune. Bright sun. They are dressed informally. There is a blanket and a picnic basket. Lunch is done;* Nancy *is finishing putting things away. There is a pause and then a jet plane is heard from stage right to stage left—growing, becoming deafeningly loud, diminishing.*
>
> Nancy: Such noise they make.
>
> Charlie: They'll crash into the dunes one day. I don't know what good they do.
>
> Nancy: (*looks toward the ocean; sighs*): Still . . . Oh, Charlie, it's so nice! Can't we stay here forever? Please!

There is the hint of apocalypse in Charlie's resentment of the noise and a yearning for a truer life in Nancy's delighted fascination with the seascape. (The same sort of combination of images is found in Elizabeth's dream of the holocaust in the final moments of ***The Lady from Dubuque.***) From time to time the sound of the plane returns to overshadow the events of the play, as they bring into perspective a view of life which Albee has not developed elsewhere on such a scale. There are suggestions of the dimensions to life as early as ***The Zoo Story,*** when Jerry explains that, to break out of isolation, *some* contact must be found:

> it's just that if you can't deal with people, you have to make a start somewhere, WITH ANIMALS.
>
> (*Much faster now and like a conspirator*) Don't you see? A person has to have some way of dealing with SOMETHING . . .

In ***Seascape*** Albee escapes the particular social contexts within which he normally writes in order to consider in a fundamental way the phenomenon we know as life and experience personally as existence.

The action of ***Seascape*** is elegantly simple. Nancy and Charlie are a warm, affectionate couple now entering their retirement. As they picnic by the seaside Nancy enthuses about the natural life around, and, wishing it were possible, innocently suggests that they should live always like this. Beside the sea. Always moving on in the sun.

> One great seashore after another; the pounding waves and quiet coves; white sand, and red and black, somewhere, I remember reading; palms, and pine trees, cliffs and reefs, and miles of jungle, sand dunes . . .
>
> CHARLIE: No.
>
> NANCY: . . . and all the people! Every language . . . every . . . race.

Charlie's refusal to consider Nancy's eccentric fancies is a contrast to the recollection she elicits from him that when he was a child he loved to escape down into the sea. Unlike his friends, who dreamed (significantly) of flight, he imagined himself 'a regular fish . . . fishlike arms and legs and everything, but able to go under'. As the couple reflect on their past life, including its moments of tension, a picture emerges of their fidelity and warm interdependence. The conflict appears now at the point where the children are grown—'nicely settled . . . to all appearances'—and the next generation has begun. Having done what they 'ought to do', they are at the point where they have new choices. As Nancy puts it, 'now we've got each other and some time, and all *you* want to do is become a vegetable'.

With the appearance of the two talking reptiles Sarah and Leslie, there is a more urgent confrontation. There is the threat of violence as the males face one another, but this gives way to the struggle they experience in explaining and, inevitably, evaluating what their lives are like. The climax of the play is produced as Charlie tries to explain how the four of them are part of a process of evolution. As he and Nancy attempt to explain the concept to their new friends, the images of life on land and in the sea are drawn together, and the truth emerges that what they are all involved in together is the progress of life. Charlie is moved, much to Nancy's wonder, from his inertia of the opening of the play to a demand that Sarah and Leslie accept emotion—which is expressed in the play as a feeling for the life in you. As the quartet weathers the storm of this new emotion, the sea creatures are persuaded to stay and adapt to the new life they have encountered and help the unfamiliar creatures they recognise as their fellows.

Very often there is a distinct reminiscence of ***All Over,*** suggesting an alternative presentation of similar material. In ***All Over*** the family appeared synonymous with sterility and failure. This is reversed in ***Seascape.*** Nancy plays with the engaging image of the pyramid of succeeding generations. They have succeeded but she knows the risks:

> everybody builds his own, starts fresh, starts up in the air, builds the base around him. Such levitation! Our own have started *theirs!* . . .
>
> . . . Or maybe it's the most . . . difficult, the most . . . breathtaking of all: the whole thing balanced on one point; a reversed *pyramid,* always in danger of toppling over when people don't behave themselves.

Nancy has lived her life looking forward. From the earliest days she wanted to be a woman: she wanted to grow up, unlike the Wife, who felt twelve years old when her husband came to her. There are two different values to the security the women see in their husbands: in ***All Over*** it is a security which involves an abdication in the face of life: in ***Seascape*** it is a progressive building, aware of the dangers but full of love and compassion.

The dangers are visible in the story of Charlie's seven months of depression, an episode which Albee invests with a particular richness of expression. At the heart of it is the idea of life as involving choice. The narration includes the choices that might have been: *if* Charlie had been unfaithful, *if* she had known other lovers; the consequences are worked out in the speech. Despite the fact that it all *was not,* Nancy learned and grew. 'The deeper your inertia went, the more *I* felt alive', says Nancy, and over the span of the narration the feeling for life is translated into the understanding present in a mature, even weatherbeaten, relationship. She recalls her mother's advice ('wise woman') and the stages of compassion: experiencing her own loneliness, and understanding *his.*

The picture is very much that of the Mistress in ***All Over*** and her compassion for her lover in, for instance, his loneliness on being separated from his family. Even the precision of language in the two characters is similar. Like the Mistress, Nancy insists on the importance of the tense of a verb: 'Am not *having?* Am not *having* a good life? . . . I know the language, and I know *you.* You're not careless with it, or didn't used to be.'

In ***Seascape*** Albee writes with energy about the potential there is in life, which largely he invests in the role of Nancy. Against this comes intermittent resistance in the character of Charlie. In much of the action of the first act there is a contest between Charlie's theme—'Well, we've earned a little rest'—and Nancy's determination to avoid the 'purgatory before the purgatory': 'I haven't come this long way . . . Nor have you! Not this long way to let loose. All the wisdom—by accident, some of it—all the wisdom and the . . . unfettering.'

Albee finds the everyday phrase and exploits its deeper meaning. Charlie is 'happy . . . doing . . . nothing'. He spells out his conviction and the dramatist anatomises it in a 'testy' exchange between the two. As Nancy 'busily' tidies up and Charlie refuses to move, she challenges the absurdity of giving up on life:

> We are not going to be around forever, Charlie, and you may *not* do nothing. If you don't want to do what I want to do—which doesn't matter—then we will do what *you* want to do, but we will not do nothing. We will do something.

There is a delightful comedy to this combination of the philosophical and the domestic, and it sets the tone for the play as a whole. In all his work Albee shows a fine inteligence, and the comic viewpoint is rarely far off. It is, however, rare to find the humour that there is in ***Seascape***: a fundamentally positive sense of life which, together with the compassion Albee always exhibits, makes ***Seascape*** an exceptional piece of work.

The comedy gathers momentum with the appearance of the sea creatures and so too does the density of thought which is worked into the play. Albee manages a sustained flow of questions about social and individual existence through the agency of his monsters. Initially Charlie refuses to believe what his eyes tell him. The answer to these 'wonders'—and in his direction of the original production Albee required that they really be quite frightening—is characteristically to choose to believe in death:

> We ate the liver paste and we died. That drowsy feeling . . . the sun . . . and the wine . . . none of it: all those night thoughts of what it would be like, the sudden scalding in the centre of the chest, or wasting away; milk in the eyes, voices from the other room; none of it. Chew your warm sandwich, wash it down, lie back, and let the poison have its way . . .

Nancy's reaction is to instruct Charlie to roll over like an animal and adopt a submission pose. Natural enough in the meeting of two sort of animals. Albee bridges his acts with this image of the lizards and the submitting humans, and it is a delightful piece of theatrical fun. Especially when the newcomers, who are reflections of the first couple, open the second act with a somewhat disdainful discussion of the panic they have provoked: 'Well . . . they don't look very formidable—in the sense of prepossessing. Not young. They've got their teeth bared, but they don't look as if they are going to bite. Their hide is funny—feels soft.'

What follows is a true comedy of manners. Charlie and Nancy have to negotiate every step of the way their exchanges with these imagined representatives of another line of evolution.

> SARAH: This is Leslie.
>
> NANCY (*extending her hand*): How do you do, Leslie?
>
> LESLIE (*regards her gesture*): What is that?
>
> NANCY: Oh; we . . . well, we shake hands . . . flippers, uh . . . Charlie?

Sarah is delighted to learn of the gesture, whereas Leslie, who adopts Charlie's brand of negative rationalism, is unconvinced and wishes to know why it is done. When Charlie, progressively more involved, explains the significance of the proffered right hand, Leslie is equally defensive in his manner:

> it used to be to prove nobody had a weapon, to prove they were friendly.
>
> LESLIE (*after a bit*): We're ambidextrous.
>
> CHARLIE (*rather miffed*): Well, that's *nice* for you. Very nice.

The essence of the comedy lies in the wonder that each couple presents for the other, and in the parallelism that Albee devises to show up inflexibility, particularly of the males' position. In the females there is a parallel sense of wonder but an eager curiosity about what the new encounter may contain. Clothing and 'decency', for example, are concepts the scaly newcomers require to be defined, and Albee's idea drives a neat wedge between the human couple. The effect is to make comedy out of social manners but also to suggest the gradual awakening of Charlie from his somnolent attitudes to his wife and his life in general. Nancy teaches by the direct method and invites Sarah to see her breasts. To Charlie's great dismay Sarah, full of wonder and excitement, calls her mate Leslie to see. When Charlie objects, Leslie adopts a suitable nonchalance:

> It's up to *you;* I mean, if they're something you *hide,* then may be they're embarrassing, or sad, and I shouldn't *want* to see them, and . . .
>
> CHARLIE (*more flustered than angry*): They're not embarrassing; or *sad;* They're lovely! Some women . . . some women Nancy's age, they're . . . some women . . .
>
> (*To* NANCY, *almost spontaneously bursting into tears*) I *love* your breasts.

With great skill Albee contrives a debate to combine the sharply differentiated reactions and characteristics in the four roles and a shifting discussion of various aspects of the new experience that the characters are called on to live. The subjects include marriage customs, flight and aerodynamics, child-bearing and rearing, and racialism. Albee establishes some hold over the form of the act by centring the conflicts in Charlie's progressive involvement. He makes one retreat into the negative rationalism he shares with Leslie when he staunchly reaffirms in the face of the facts that they are dead. Nancy explains

> I mean, we *have* to be dead, because Charlie has decided that the wonders do not occur; that what we have not known does not exist; that what we cannot fathom cannot be; that the miracles, if you will, are bedtime stories; he has taken the leap of faith, from agnostic to atheist; the world is flat; the sun and the planets revolve around it, and don't row out too far or you'll fall off.

This prompts a most elegantly ridiculous routine as Leslie the lizard engages Charlie in a discussion of the nature of existence and the theories of Descartes

> LESLIE: Then I take it *we* don't *exist.*
>
> CHARLIE (*apologetic*): Probably not; I'm sorry.
>
> LESLIE (*to* NANCY): That's quite a mind he's got there. (. . .)
>
> LESLIE (*to* CHARLIE): You mean it's all an illusion?
>
> CHARLIE: Could be.
>
> LESLIE: The whole thing? Existence?

CHARLIE: Um-hum!

LESLIE (*sitting down with* CHARLIE): I don't believe *that* at *all.*

Like meets like in the encounter and Leslie's dogged pursuit of the discussions runs into Charlie's hysterical rage as he has to explain Descartes's *Cogito.*

Charlie is reassured of the physical fact of his existence by a particularly lengthy and passionate embrace from Nancy, and this, together with the lizards' panic at another passing jet, brings him finally face to face with the 'wonders'. Albee gives the stage direction 'Awe' at this point.

The creatures can be seen as a threat but they are an aspect of the wonder of life. They are animals with whom Charlie shares life and with whom he can make a society. Albee consolidates the shift in the role with Nancy's proud revelation to her new companions that there was a time when Charlie escaped from the world 'up here' by diving down to the bottom of the sea—unlike his fellows who wished to take to the air and, implicitly, join the noise of the jets. Charlie is uneasy at the reminder of his childhood curiosity: 'It was just a game; it was enough for a twelve-year-old, maybe, but it wasn't . . . finding out, you know; it wasn't *real.*' Yet the arrival above water of Leslie and Sarah is the parallel to the childhood Charlie. They are looking for somewhere to belong, despite the former ease of their everyday existence.

As Charlie finally emerges from his inertia, he discovers again the wonder of life and its sense of purpose and development. In his lengthy discussion of evolution the boundary between sea and air becomes a focus: 'What do they call it . . . the primordial soup? the glop? the heartbreaking second when it all got together, the sugars and the acids and the ultra-violets and the next thing you knew there were tangerines and string quartets.' Charlie explains to them all that they are part of the same wonderful process of life: 'there was a time when we were all down there, crawling around, and swimming and carrying on—remember how we read about it, Nancy . . .

The sea-land exchange is crucial to Charlie's realisation that the four of them are united in all the implications of evolution from the 'aminos to the treble clef'.

> And do you know what happened once? Kind of the crowning moment of it all for me? It was when some . . . slimy creature poked its head out of the muck, looked around and decided to spend some time up here . . . came up into the air and decided to stay? And as time went on, he split apart and evolved and became tigers and gazelles and porcupines and Nancy here . . .
>
> LESLIE (*annoyed*): I don't believe a word of this!
>
> CHARLIE: Oh, you'd better, for he went back under, too; part of what he became didn't fancy it up on land, and went back down there, and turned into porpoises and sharks and manta rays, and whales . . . and you.

Charlie's vision includes them all as part of life and evolution. What is now vital is to know in what direction it is all going. Like the mirror couple they are, Leslie and Sarah react in opposite directions. Sarah asks if it is all for the better, Leslie tells her not to be 'taken in'. By the end of the play Albee has revolutionised the situation at the outset. Faced with a carbon copy of his own and Nancy's attitudes, Charlie crusades to convince the neophytes of the possibilities that lie before them: 'What are you going to tell me about? Slaughter and pointlessness? Come on *up* here. *Stay.*'

Albee doesn't sentimentalise the play at this late point; the role of Charlie is to remain sceptical, Nancy hopeful, but the alteration is into awareness and commitment. The man has been stung into life by the conflict with the inhabitants of the sea he loved as a child. His sense of wonder is once more awakened. The ultimate development of this is in terms of the tensions which the theatre can produce. Albee shifts the conflict to the plane of emotions. The translation is apt in ideological terms. The commitment to life can only be achieved by the recognition of the emotions which are proof of one's reaction to existence. Charlie provokes a final confrontation as he makes Sarah weep at the suggested loss of Leslie, and Leslie in his turn react violently in defence of his mate. Charlie's motives are stated clearly for the audience to understand:

> (*To* LESLIE *and* SARAH) I don't know what I want for *you.* I don't know what I feel toward you; it's either love or loathing. Take your pick; they're both emotions. And you're finding out about them, aren't you? About emotions? Well, I want you to know about *all* of it; I'm impatient for you, I want you to experience the whole thing! The full sweep!

As it stands, the play is concluded with the sea creatures coming to the arduous decision that they will stay on land when the painfulness of the experience they have been through seems too threatening. The final gestures of the play are touching but finally quite unsentimental as the quartet recognise in each other a necessary confrontation with life and the need to live. It is a choice that can be faced with, literally and figuratively, a helping hand. Hands and foot-paws are extended in the closing moments of the play. This conclusion contains the elements which resolve the questions and the experiences of the play, but nevertheless this work remains Albee's Unfinished Symphony. He has made it clear that there is a third act, which will complete the form of the play. As it stands, the play may seem slightly unbalanced, as the emphasis of discovery has shifted to the sea couple, and the ideas of wonder which are so joyously exposed in Nancy's speeches at the outset are overtaken by the development of relationships between the members of the oddly assorted quartet. This does work as a resolution of the action, for what is clearly and warmly felt by the audience is the primacy of life and genuine emotion in the play. However, one cannot help hoping that Albee will keep his promise to restore the final act, in which the positions are reserved and the human couple take up the theme of

Charlie's childhood dreams and descend beneath the waves to discover life as something totally new, strange and fabulous.

The decision to shorten the play and abandon the third act indicates in part Albee's desire to keep its effect fully under control. The final act would have depended upon a theatrical dissolve into the underwater scene, which would have been very demanding technically but also visually stunning. The spectacle of the lizards would have gone much further, with submarine encounters with sea creatures, including a fight with an octopus. (In this Leslie would have rescued Nancy but Sarah would have died in coming to Nancy's assistance.) The scenic effects in the unpublished third act show, like ***Tiny Alice,*** Albee's power of imagination, and it is revealing that he should have decided to cut the fantastic episide which was to conclude the play.

> At a certain moment part of the play took place at the bottom of the sea. This was not necessary, it was too fantastic, and it was very difficult to realise a changeable set. Finally it was becoming a play centred on set changes.[1]

Albee's distrust of the merely decorative style of theatre against which he has struggled so energetically is revealed in this decision, and it supports the impression given by the present text of a play, which aims at a high degree of internal relevance and organisation of ideas and events. The extrapolation of the action into the third-act adventure would have been a justifiable pleasure for Albee to give himself as a writer. However, he has left the play now as a balance of the actual and the imagined in which the future is left to the audience and its reflection. The play therefore ends with an invitation: 'All right. Let's begin!' It is the positive image of the negative supplied in ***All Over,*** the companion play. That concludes with the end of a life and the eclipse of the possibility of change: 'All Over'.

Note

[1]*New York Times,* 21 Jan 1975.

Matthew C. Roudané (essay date 1987)

SOURCE: "Death and Life: *Seascape,*" in *Understanding Edward Albee,* University of South Carolina Press, 1987, pp. 131-51.

[*The essay below examines Albee's "persistent concern with dramatizing what may occur if the human spirit withers." The critic further asserts that in* Seascape, *"Albee is not writing merely about the naturalistic evolution of the human species, but about growth patterns of humankind, about combining the visceral and the intellectual into a new whole which is the consciously aware person."*]

Albee's theater challenges those who, as the playwright has said, "turn off" to the complex business of living, who "don't stay fully awake" in relationships, who for various reasons choose not to immerse themselves in an "absolutely full, dangerous participation" in experience.[1] ***Seascape*** once again reflects those thematic concerns to which Albee continually gravitates. In ***Seascape*** he explores three interwoven forces: animal nature, as imaged by the sea lizards Sarah and Leslie; human nature, as reflected by Nancy and Charlie; and the kind of existentialist imperative forged by the curious intermixing of the animal world with the human world. The audience discovers Albee's response to the fact that so many people turn off. Originally titled *Life,* the play reconfirms Albee's ongoing battle to stage the various kinds of ethical problems with which his heroes struggle, whether they know it or not—or even care to know.[2]

The design of ***Seascape*** seems simple enough. Nancy and Charlie are vacationing at the beach, where they have finished a picnic. They are relaxing, reminiscing, figuring out what they will do with their lives now that their children are grown and their own years are numbered. They give voice to different selves and motivations, but during their encounter with the sea lizards their purposes ultimately unite, fixing on a shared consciousness concerning, to go back to Jerry's words in ***The Zoo Story,*** "the way people exist with animals, and the way animals exist with each other, and with people too."[3] Their new-tempered awareness, as seen throughout the Albee canon, objectifies Albee's central concern.

Charlie contends that they have "earned a little" rest from the hectic business of living.[4] Nancy, however, rejects this notion. In spite of their successful marriage Charlie and Nancy, currently on the threshold of beginning a new life—retirement—disagree on the way in which they will live out their remaining years. As in so many of his earlier plays Albee again joins opposites as a method of producing dramatic tension. Charlie is passive and inert, Nancy active and alive. Charlie elects withdrawal, while Nancy seeks engagement. He resists, she persists. She acts as a kind of benevolent instructor, he as the indifferent student. Charlie is tired of living, seems bereft of emotion, while Nancy is eager to investigate new terrain, willingly embracing change. Both clearly want to relax, but their interpretations of relaxation clash. Nancy craves to use their new free time by traveling along the world's shoreline as "seaside nomads" (5), exploring the wondrous sights of the earth. For Nancy life becomes meaningful when one *lives* it. She may have, in her older age, slight physical handicaps, but she does not suffer from the disabling psychological wounds that paralyze so many Albee protagonists. Albee shows her exuberance, enthusiasm, and spiritual vitality:

> I love the water, and I love the air, and the sand and the dunes and the beach grass, and the sunshine on all of it and the white clouds way off, and the sunsets and the noise that shells make in the waves and, oh, I love every bit of it, Charlie.
>
> (5)

The first act presents Nancy's optimistic stance toward living, as the tonal quality of her language suggests. Unlike the tonal quality of language in, say, ***Counting the Ways*** and ***Listening,*** which seems so tortured that the act of viewing or reading often becomes difficult, the language in ***Seascape*** emanates a lighthearted, humorous quality. Nancy voices this quality. For example, as her rapture with travel dreams continues, she exclaims to her lethargic husband, "My God, Charlie: See Everything Twice!" (10). Albee's thematic point centers on portraying a wife concerned with her husband, with loving attempts to revitalize his spirit.

Charlie resists. He has "to be pushed into everything" (7) because, as he informs Nancy, "I don't want to travel from beach to beach, cliff to sand dune, see the races, count the flies" (8). Retirement for Charlie means he can rest—and do nothing. He seems in many ways reminiscent of Peter in ***The Zoo Story,*** Daddy in ***The American Dream,*** Tobias in ***A Delicate Balance,*** and the Son in ***All Over,*** for Charlie also elects to withdraw from authentic engagement: "I'm happy . . . doing . . . nothing" (8). More than retiring from work, Albee suggests, Charlie is retiring from life itself, his spiritual laziness a willful surrendering of self-freedom.

Charlie defends his position. Claiming that Nancy's adventuresomeness would lead to "some . . . illusion" (38), he believes that "there's comfort in settling in" to doing nothing (39). After all, Charlie argues, "I *have* been a good husband to you" (31), and this is apparently true. He courted and loved Nancy, and fathered her children—just as she desired. By all accounts he has been faithful and forthright, the dependable provider and parent. From his point of view, Charlie has earned the right to do nothing. For him the choice to withdraw suggests that the whole affair of traveling, of being alive like Nancy, is too bothersome. If in functioning in a middle-class society, if in his efforts to uphold appearances, Charlie's vitality has diminished, it has clearly been his own conscious choice.

His attitude disturbs Nancy. They have not earned a little rest but, counters Nancy, "We've earned a little *life,* if you ask *me*" (37). She appears determined to begin anew, in qualitative terms, their life together. Nancy advocates what for the author is an important existentialist tenet when voicing her desire to experience life as fully as possible. Specifically she is aware of the finiteness of their existences: "We are *not* going to be around forever, Charlie, and you may *not* do nothing" (9). Nancy's zest for living, her impulse to respond, may remind the audience of Henry James's Lambert Strether, who, in *The Ambassadors,* confides to Bilham: "Live all you can; it's a mistake not to. It doesn't so much matter what you do in particular, so long as you have your life. If you haven't had that what *have* you had?"[5] Like Strether, Nancy feels her old age on a physical level but refuses to capitulate on a spiritual level; she too wishes to "live all you can." Because of her insight Nancy appears objectively open toward experience, and will try anything, as long as they "do *something*" (9). Her zest for living takes on a larger, more compelling dimension because her stance is not a product of philosophic intellection but emerges from the concreteness of her conviction to experience fully her surrounding. Even years ago when, just married, Charlie slipped into a period of psychological withdrawal from both Nancy and life itself (his "seven-month decline"), Nancy felt a driving impulse to live. As she said, "The deeper your inertia went, the more *I* felt alive" (21).

Albee dramatizes Nancy's passion for life throughout the play. This is comically as well as seriously presented when Nancy catches Charlie speaking of their relationship in the past tense. Nancy ardently believes that they are having "a good life," not that, as Charlie sometimes states, they have "had a good life" (34). For Nancy and Albee alike, it is more than semantic nitpicking. Rather, it points to a whole way of being. Charlie rationalizes, perhaps convincingly, that "it's a way of speaking!" but Nancy objects: "No! It's a way of thinking!" (35). Nancy exclaims that they now have "two things!" (36) left, namely, "ourselves and some time" (37). Aware of the significance and precariousness of these two precious elements—the self and time—Nancy squares her hopes on experiencing qualitatively the world external to her self. She appears innately opposed to the Tobias-like acquiescence that can neutralize the individual's impulse to live.

In the midst of their conversation during the waning moments of act 1 Nancy and Charlie encounter the two anthropomorphic, green-scaled sea lizards, Sarah and Leslie. At this point Albee begins accentuating Nancy's and Charlie's differing attitudes toward experience. He objectifies this difference by the couple's initial reaction to the sea lizards: Charlie panics, Nancy beckons. While he issues a call to arms—and brandishes a feeble stick—she gazes at the two creatures in awe, saying "They're magnificent!" (44). As the two imposing, curious sea lizards approach, Nancy takes peaceful command, assuming a submissive pose. Finally Charlie takes heed, holding his fright in check.

What follows, as in so many Albee plays, is the interacting of two distinct yet clearly related worlds—here represented by the human world and the animal world. The reader or viewer has witnessed this technique of joining two contrasting worlds before in the encounter of Peter and Jerry in ***The Zoo Story***; in the contrast of Grandma's earlier values versus the newer values of Mommy and Daddy in ***The Sandbox*** and ***The American Dream***; and in the meeting of the secular and the religious in ***Tiny Alice.*** In ***Seascape*** the yoking together of the human world and the sea lizard world provides a clear definition of Albee's thematic interest: that love and sharing and awareness are all necessary forces, forces to be integrated into one's inner reality if one is to live life honestly. But unlike some of Albee's earlier works, especially ***All Over, Seascape*** emphasizes the presence of love and sharing and awareness. In ***Seascape*** the bringing together of opposites—humans and sea lizards—does not produce illusions, deceit, or hatred. And it does not produce a Pyrrhic victory in which consciousness is gained, but with such terrible losses—alienation, suicide, murder, death—

that the value seems dubious. Rather, the joining of Nancy and Charlie's world with that of Sarah and Leslie generates understanding, education, sharing, and love, perhaps at the cost of merely two bruised male egos.

Act 2 embodies the education of the characters. It starts simply enough, with Leslie and Sarah asking a barrage of questions ranging from the banal to the profound. As Charlie's fear and Nancy's confusion wear away, as Leslie's skepticism and Sarah's apprehension subside, the characters establish communication. As the difficulty of the questions increases, Nancy and Charlie fumble with imprecise explanations regarding birth and children—as when Nancy notes that humans keep their offspring for eighteen or twenty years because, she tells the uncomprehending sea lizards, "we *love* them" (86). Pressed to explain what love signifies, Nancy replies, "Love is one of the emotions" (87), to which an impatient Leslie retorts, "Define your terms. Honestly, the imprecision! You're so thoughtless!" (87). The two humans struggle to elaborate and to educate their companions about human life, as their reliance on abstract concepts suggests. But abstractions do not adequately account for the richness and complexity of actual experience. A frustrated Charlie turns the tables on the sea lizards by asking them about their past. What follows ostensibly concerns the sea lizards' account of their courtship. Through their honest and humorous tale of courtship, however, Sarah and Leslie reveal very humanlike emotions: love, hate, anger, hurt, jealousy. Leslie fought to win Sarah's affection; and this show of commitment forever united them, as Sarah remembers: "And there he *was* . . . and there *I* was . . . and here we *are*" (90). The exchange emerges as a point of illumination. For now Charlie provides a graspable illustration of the emotions and the way in which they function. He succeeds in making the abstract concrete.

Of all their discussions, from prejudice and bigotry to aerodynamics and photography, one topic appears crucial to the play. Nancy and Charlie have been discussing tools, art, mortality, those qualities and things which separate man "from the brute beast" (126), and again the concept of emotions, particularly love, surfaces. Charlie, miffed at Leslie's presence but wanting to show him the concrete reality of love, turns to Sarah. He pointedly asks what she would do if she lost Leslie. Her response:

> I'd . . . cry; I'd . . . I'd cry! I'd . . . I'd cry my eyes out! Oh . . . Leslie!
>
> *Leslie* (*Trying to comfort Sarah*): It's all right, Sarah!
>
> *Sarah:* I want to go back; I don't want to stay here any more. (*Wailing*) I want to go *back!* (*Trying to break away*) I want to go *back!*
>
> (129)

Here is Sarah's sudden experience of terror, her sense of aloneness, her understanding of the possibility of profound loss. The precariousness of her life with Leslie suddenly made real, Sarah is, for the first time, experiencing an awakening. Sarah's dread brings forth Leslie's emotions, and in the only violent scene in the play he attacks Charlie, the instinctive response to terror:

> *Leslie:* You made her cry! (*Hit*)
>
> *Charlie:* STOP IT!
>
> *Leslie:* I ought to tear you apart!
>
> *Charlie:* Oh my God! (*Leslie begins to choke Charlie, standing behind Charlie, his arms around Charlie's throat. It has a look of slow, massive inevitability, not fight and panic*)
>
> (131)

While communicating (and fighting), the characters reveal one of Albee's basic concerns in ***Seascape,*** namely, the importance and process of evolution. For the playwright is clearly rendering what occurs, in part at least, when the species evolves into a higher form of life. "Like Arthur Miller's somewhat similar allegory, *The Creation of the World and Other Business,*" observes C. W. E. Bigsby, "***Seascape*** is best regarded as a consciously naïve attempt to trace human imperfection to its source by unwinding the process of history and myth."[6] Sarah explains that their evolutionary process was caused by a sense of alienation: "We had a sense of not belonging any more" (116). As with most complex growth patterns, Albee suggests, their evolution did not occur in an epiphanic moment but developed over a longer period of time, reflecting a gradual coming to consciousness. In Sarah's words, "It was a growing thing, nothing abrupt" (116). This is not to suggest, however, that ***Seascape*** celebrates a naturalistic evolution, that it is simply a Darwinian pierce dramatizing the advancement of the saurians. Rather, the impact of Sarah and Leslie's realization of their estrangement from their familiar environment radically altered their perceptions not only of place, but of themselves within their natural place. Although she finds it difficult to articulate, Sarah still persists in her efforts to define their "sense of not belonging," even over Leslie's objections:

> . . . all of a sudden, everything . . . down there . . . was terribly . . . interesting, I suppose; but what did it have to do with *us* any more?
>
> *Leslie:* Don't Sarah.
>
> *Sarah:* And it wasn't . . . comfortable any more. I mean, after all, you make your nest, and accept a whole . . . array . . . of things . . . and . . . we didn't feel we *belonged* there any more. And . . . what were we going to do?!
>
> (116)

Leslie and Sarah have experienced the divorce between man and his environment that Albert Camus described as the "feeling of absurdity."[7] They have been experientially forced to question the whole of their existence. Further, the passage illustrates Albee's deft interweaving of a serious subject within a lighthearted context. In spite of the humor permeating much of the play, the scene presents the characters as quite earnest because Albee stages the effects of alienation. But whereas in the earlier plays alienation typically begot more estrangement, even death, here it gives way to a sense of belonging, a sense of community. Even a stubborn Charlie begins lowering his defenses, becoming shy one moment, enthusiastic the next, all in an effort to understand the sea lizards' process of evolution.

The theme of evolution continues with Nancy and Charlie's explanations. Charlie, for example, reflects on the origins of humankind, linking the sea lizards' home with his own environment:

> What do they call it . . . the primordial soup? the glop? That heartbreaking second when it all got together, the sugars and the acids and the ultraviolets, and the next thing you knew there were tangerines and string quartets.
>
> (118)

Besides suggesting a mere biological interpretation of humankind's development, Charlie and Nancy also connect human evolution with the sea lizard's animal evolution:

> Listen to this—there was a time when we *all* were down there, crawling around, and swimming and carrying on—remember how we read about it, Nancy?
>
> (118)

The comments transcend a report of biological history, for they also operate on an archetypal level, unifying the animal world with the human world. As Charlie figuratively sums up to a skeptical Leslie and a fascinated Sarah, "It means that once upon a time you and I lived down there" (119). Nancy carries on the discussion, saying that the primitive creatures of long ago necessarily evolved to a higher plane of existence because "they were dissatisfied" (121) with their lives, just as Sarah and Leslie were not "comfortable" any more with theirs.

The reader, of course, sees the parallels between the worlds of the two couples. As Sarah voices her displeasure with their lizard life "down there" (117), so Nancy voices her dissatisfaction with their human life on land. As the women are open and enthusiastic, the men are closed, skeptical. Both couples throughout the drama are upset by the loud jets that fly over the dunes. The two couples come to recognize and appreciate the similarities between their worlds, and through their questioning and answering they learn about much more than the biological origins and evolution of the species. In Albee's presentation they also learn about the evolution of the spirit.

The evolution of the spirit draws the two couples intimately together. Nancy and Charlie, and Sarah and Leslie not only play counterpoint to each other but also mirror each other. Sarah's confession that they "considered the pros and the cons. Making do down there or trying something else" (117) directly mirrors Nancy's admission that her life with Charlie needs reevaluation too. If Leslie exemplifies brute bestiality, Charlie's actions at times reflect precisely such animalistic behavior. Like their sea lizard counterparts the humans must try "something else" if their lives are to avoid the potential stagnation inherent in "resting" too much. What this means, Albee implies, is that they should immerse themselves in the shape and energy of experience itself.

In ***A Delicate Balance,*** Claire mentions the value of developing gills as a way of adapting to and surviving life. But for Claire and most others in ***A Delicate Balance*** such evolutionary capability functions as a means of coping with a confusing, puckish reality. The subterfuges in ***A Delicate Balance*** are not present in ***Seascape.*** Here humankind's ability to evolve, to use "gills" when needed, becomes necessary if the individual is to grow. Charlie argues this very point when discussing the value of one's capacity to evolve:

> Mutate or perish. Let your tail drop off, change your spots, or maybe just your point of view. The dinosaurs knew a thing or two, but that was about it . . . great, enormous creatures, big as a diesel engine—(*To Leslie*) whatever that may be—leviathans! . . . with a brain the size of a lichee nut; couldn't cope, couldn't figure it all out; went down.
>
> (123)

Albee further develops the connectedness of the humans and sea lizards when Charlie describes his boyhood immersions in the sea. Nancy even asks if he developed a fishlike form: "Gills, too?" (13). In one passage in the play Charlie lapses into a pleasurable recollection:

> And I would go into the water, take two stones, as large as I could manage, swim out a bit, tread, look up one final time at the sky . . . relax . . . begin to go down. Oh, twenty feet, fifteen, soft landing without a sound, the white sand clouding up where your feet touch, and all around you ferns . . . and lichen. You can stay down there so long! You can build it up, and last . . . so long, enough for the sand to settle and the fish come back. And they do—come back—all sizes, some slowly, eyeing past; some streak, and you think for a moment they're larger than they are, sharks maybe, but they never are, and one stops being an intruder, finally—just one more object come to the bottom, or living thing, part of the undulation and the silence. It was very good.
>
> (16-17)

As Sarah and Leslie explore the solid earth, so Charlie, years ago, explored the sea. In both contexts sea creatures and humans are "eyeing past" each other. Thematically, Charlie's recollection of his submersion into the water directly correlates to the obvious archetypal patterns embodied in ***Seascape.***[8]

Returning to the sea, archetypalists tell us, is one way for man to reestablish a rapport with the natural cycle. It also symbolizes man's attempt to reestablish contact with his own psyche. Carl Jung wrote: "Water is no figure of speech, but a living symbol of the dark psyche."[9] Although as a boy Charlie could not intellectualize about his water experience, his account suggests that the immersion concretely placed him within his own dark psyche. In Charlie's account living on the surface was equated with "breakers" and "a storm, or a high wind"—chaotic forces which affected his external world. But "to go way down" to the cove's bottom, living underneath the surface, was equated with solitude and calming silence. Seeking adventure and a comforting refuge, Charlie established an intuitive, sympathetic correspondence with his self and the underworld. Jung discusses the influence of this kind of immersion:

> The unconscious is the psyche that reaches down from the daylight of mentality and morally lucid consciousness into the nervous system that for ages has been known as the "sympathetic." This . . . maintains the balance of life and, through the mysterious pathways of sympathetic excitation, not only gives us knowledge of the innermost life of other beings but also has an inner effect upon them.[10]

In his underwater experience Charlie was privy to just this form of unique "knowledge of the innermost life." Thus, on an archetypal level Charlie's submersion allowed him to be present to his inner self, his hidden self, as well as to the world external to himself—the ocean world. Charlie's archetypal water experience serves as a rite of passage, a form of initiation into a primordial setting that precedes any capacity to evolve. In Jung's words, "The descent into the depths always seems to precede the ascent."[11]

But where is Charlie's "ascent"? Apparently his psychic ascent came long after his physical surfacing. As a teen-ager he came in touch with his inner psyche (16), but integrating the meaning of this experience is only achieved a lifetime later. In his unique encounter on the dunes Charlie rekindles contact with the natural cycle and with his self. Leslie and Sarah, of course, represent that vital contact. They represent what Charlie and Nancy were "eons" ago (117). As Lucina P. Gabbard points out, Leslie and Sarah "concretize the evolution of mankind from water animals, the emergence of the individual embryo from its watery womb, and the return to consciousness of the repressed self."[12] Thus, the random encounter of the two couples on the dunes symbolically reveals the connectedness of animal nature and human nature, the biological as well as spiritual kinship which exists, at least in this play, between beast and human.

The intermingling of the animal and human world in ***Seascape,*** finally, precipitates an existentialist imperative which has become a familiar trademark of any Albee play: the need to communicate authentically with the other. Through mutual communication the characters of *Seascape* evolve into what Jung calls a "higher consciousness."[13] In a state of higher consciousness Nancy voices one of Albee's central concerns in the play, saying, "And I'm aware of my own mortality" (125). Passing middle age, Nancy feels the nearness of death. For Charlie the nearness of death remains, like his childhood experience, distant. Only when Leslie nearly strangles him do Nancy's attitudes become tangible to Charlie. Through their collective experience the characters begin to understand and live with, in Albee's words, "the cleansing consciousness of death."[14] That is, the characters gain an acute awareness of the proximity of extinction, of the finiteness of their existence, which in turn creates the possibility for living life fully, as Nancy advocates throughout.

In spite of the evolving spirits of the characters, the mythical uniting of brute beast with civilized person, Albee does not formulate a purely fairy-tale ending: there is no guarantee that their lives will be substantially changed. Sarah, for example, shyly voices her concern surrounding evolution: "Is it . . . is it for the better?" and Charlie can only reply honestly: "I don't *know*" (124). The tentativeness evident in Charlie's response, like George's "maybe" to Martha's questions at the close of ***Who's Afraid of Virginia Woolf?*** captures something of the precariousness of their newfound knowledge. But they discover that, with each other's compassion, they can help each other. As Leslie says in his play-closing line, "All right. Begin" (135).

If the couples learn anything during the play, Albee suggests that it involves the recognition of and the need for involvement, engagement, and love at a consciously aware level. Through their explanations of their respective roles on earth the couples come to view themselves in a larger context. If the sea lizards have much to learn about life "up here" (132), so, too, with the humans. Their struggle only highlights the archetypal circularity fusing the animal and human worlds. Nancy and Charlie realize that they are not "better" but are, perhaps, "more interesting" than animals (125); that they are but a more-developed link on the physical and spiritual evolutionary chain. Albee implies that through the sweep and play of evolutionary patterns humankind has transcended noble savagery and the instinctive response to nature, to become beings whose mentor increasingly is reason. Surely the power of reason, Albee would say, is useful, necessary; still, in ***Seascape*** the dominance of rational faculties poses a threat. The danger is that, with rationality triumphing over the instinctive, the primordial life-giving passions will dissipate, and, for Charlie at least, there will be no other source of vitality to replace them. Unless reason and the emotions exist in counterpoise, more will be lost in the wonders of evolution than gained. Albee implies that evolved humanity will cease to feel deeply, or, continuing to feel at all, the individual may care only for the wrong things. Perhaps this is why Albee has called ***Seascape*** "triste."[15]

Seascape, which opened on 26 January 1975 at the Sam S. Shubert Theatre, New York City, and which won Albee his second Pulitzer Prize, represents Albee's persistent concern with dramatizing what may occur if the human spirit withers. Here Albee is not writing merely about the naturalistic evolution of the human species, but about growth patterns of humankind, about combining the visceral and the intellectual into a new whole which is the consciously aware person.

Notes

[1]Matthew C. Roudané, "An Interview with Edward Albee," *Southern Humanities Review* 16 (1982): 41.

[2]Bigsby, 318.

[3]Edward Albee, *The Zoo Story* and *The American Dream* (New York: Signet, 1960) 39-40.

[4]Edward Albee, *Seascape* (New York: Atheneum, 1975) 10. Page references within the text are to this edition.

[5]Henry James, *The Ambassadors* (New York: Norton, 1964) 132.

[6]Bigsby 318.

[7]Albert Camus, *The Myth of Sisyphus and Other Essays* (New York: Vintage, 1955) 5.

[8]For elaboration of the archetypal patterns in *Seascape,* see Thomas P. Alder, "Albee's *Seascape:* Humanity at the Second Threshold, "*Renascence* 31 (1979): 107-14; Lucina P. Gabbard, "Albee's *Seascape:* An Adult Fairy Tale," *Modern Drama* 21 (1978): 307-17; and Kitty Harris Smither, "A Dream of Dragons: Albee as Star Thrower in *Seascape,*" *Edward Albee: Planned Wilderness,* ed. Patricia De La Fuente, (Edinburg, TX: Pan American University Press, 1980) 99-110.

[9]Carl G. Jung, "Archetypes of the Collective Unconscious," *Twentieth Century Criticism,* ed. William J. Handy and Max R. Westbrook (New York: Free Press, 1974) 215.

[10]Jung 217.

[11]Jung 216.

[12]Gabbard 308.

[13]Jung 230. For further discussion of the role of consciousness in the play see Liam O. Purdon, "The Limits of Reason: *Seascape* as Psychic Metaphor," *Edward Albee: An Interview and Essays,* ed. Julian N. Wasserman, Lee Lecture Series, University of St. Thomas, Houston, TX (Syracuse: Syracuse University Press, 1983) 141-53.

[14]Edward Albee, *The Plays* (New York: Coward, McCann, and Geoghegan, 1981) 1:10.

[15]Matthew C. Roudané, "Albee on Albee," *RE: Artes Liberales* 10 (1984): 4.

FURTHER READING

Clurman, Harold. A review of *Seascape. The Nation* 220, No. 10 (15 March 1975): 314.

Asserts that *Seascape* is "light and cheerful. It is above all benevolent and, perhaps for the first time with Albee, rather charming."

Gussow, Mel. Interview with Albee. *The New York Times* (21 January 1975): 40.

Conversation in which Albee discusses the genesis and development of *Seascape.* This play, he states, is "the most difficult I've ever written. . . . Since the two people in the play are experiencing things that people have not experienced before, I didn't have any guide lines. With the other two characters, it was a problem getting their tone exactly right."

Three Tall Women

INTRODUCTION

Three Tall Women premiered on 14 June 1991 at the English Theatre in Vienna, in a production directed by Albee. It debuted in America on 27 January 1994 at the Vineyard Theatre, New York. Douglas Aibel was the Artistic Director and Jon Nakagawa was the Managing director for this first U.S. staging. The play begins with a meeting between an elderly woman in her nineties known as A, her middle-aged caretaker B, and a young lawyer named C, who has come to help A settle her affairs. As the three women interact, each becomes aware of and impatient with the others' shortcomings. The first act ends as A suffers a stroke, and in subsequent scenes Albee departs from a strictly realistic plot, having all three characters appear as various manifestations of A at different times during her life. The play concerns stereotypes and familial ties, and is considered largely autobiographical; in his introduction to the published version of the play, Albee has stated that the character A was based on his mother, and the relationship between parent and playwright mirrors that of A and her homosexual son.

CRITICAL RECEPTION

Several reviewers have accorded *Three Tall Women* qualified approval, noting several shortcomings in the play; nevertheless, it has earned Albee his third Pulitzer Prize. Ben Brantley has found the play obvious but has admired its "affecting emotional core." Stefan Kanfer has labeled the play "elegant" but has judged it a decidedly "minor effort." Other critics, including John Simon, Robert Brustein, and John Lahr, have been enthusiastic in their appreciation of the drama. Lahr has called *Three Tall Women* "a wary act of reconciliation, whose pathos and poetry are a testament to the bond, however attenuated, between child and parent." A recurring theme in commentary on the play has been its relation to Albee's other works. Tim Appelo has noted several similarities between *Three Tall Women* and *Who's Afraid of Virginia Woolf?*. These two works, he has declared, "seem parallel, sister dramas reaching out to each other across the intervening wastes and oases of Albee's career." Marian Faux, too, has seen similarities between the two plays and has detected a characteristic concern with family conflict. William Hutchings, however, has observed affinities between *Three Tall Women* and works by Samuel Beckett, judging Albee's the lesser effort. August W. Staub has placed the play in a wider context, assessing it in terms of classical Greek views of life and art. He has concluded that *Three Tall Women* "is at once very ancient and completely contemporary, so contemporary, in fact, that it might well be called one of the great summation moments of 20th century theatre."

PRODUCTION REVIEWS

Ben Brantley (review date 14 February 1994)

SOURCE: "Edward Albee Conjures Up Three Ages of Women," in *The New York Times,* 14 February 1994, pp. C13, C16.

[*In the review below, Brantley expresses several reservations about* Three Tall Women, *but concedes that "there is an undeniably affecting emotional core and a shimmeringly black sense of humor" to the play.*]

The woman identified simply as A in Edward Albee's ***Three Tall Women,*** the startlingly personal work that is receiving its New York premiere at the Vineyard Theater, shares many of the linguistic and psychological traits common to characters in Mr. Albee's more abstract plays. She is given to questing reiteration of certain phrases that take on different shadings in the repetition; she shifts disjunctively between arrogant complacency and fearful disorientation; and her memory slides and stumbles like a neophyte skater. "I can't remember what I can't remember," she says.

But A is a woman whose speech patterns are not merely stylized representations of Mr. Albee's enduring obsessions with the elusiveness of personality and its self-deceptions. There is a purely naturalistic reason for her behavior. Played with virtuosic reversals of mood by the superb Myra Carter, A is a 92-year-old woman (or is it 91, as she insists?) who is on the threshold of death. And the way she talks is rooted in the very familiar struggle of the aged with encroaching senility.

Her presence reinforces what has always been implicit in the playwright's works: life must be defined by the inescapable proximity of death. As one character states, children should be made "aware they're dying from the moment they're born."

Three Tall Women, which is basically an anatomy of one life, is by no means an entirely, successful play. Cleanly directed by Lawrence Sacharow, it makes its points so blatantly and repeats them so often that one perversely longs for a bit more of the cryptic obliquity that is Mr. Albee's signature.

But it is often a truly moving work. Mr. Albee has admitted in interviews that it was directly inspired by his own adoptive mother, a domineering, Amazonian woman. And the details of A's life, including her ambitious marriage to a wealthy man and her warring relationship with her recalci-

Anastasia Hille (seated), Maggie Smith (center), and Frances de la Tour (right) in a 1994 staging of *Three Tall Women* at Wyndham's Theatre in London.

trant son, seem to tally with what we know of Mr. Albee's family history. He has described the writing of the play as "an exorcism." And one can see in A the roots of the controlling women who abound in the rest of his oeuvre.

The members of the play's speaking cast are indeed three tall women, whose roles, if not necessarily their functions, change in the play's two acts. (There is, very significantly, an additional wordless part, that of the prodigal son, played by Michael Rhodes, who arrives in the second act after his mother has a stroke.) Set in a bedroom (designed by James Noone) whose conventional but lavish appointments bespeak an insulating affluence, the play devotes its first half to dialogue among the aged A; B, her 52-year-old acerbic but empathetic caretaker (Marian Seldes); and C (Jordan Baker), a brashly confident 26-year-old from A's lawyer's office who has come to discuss finances.

Mr. Albee baldly sets these characters up as representatives of three ages of woman. C embodies all the intolerance and the conviction of immortality of youth, and is impatient with the old woman's meanderings. The caretaker, in turn, is impatient with C's impatience and given to sharp-tongued reminders that A represents C's future. (In this sense, she is a sort of stand-in for Mr. Albee, as playwright, not as son.) And throughout all this, A fades between past and present.

In the second act, a body with an oxygen mask, representing A, is found lying on the bed. The three actresses return, now as A at different phases in her life. Although this allows Mr. Albee to create a more complete and reflective biography of A, particularly involving her thorny relationship with her son, the symbolic triangle remains much the same, with the youngest woman shouting at the oldest, "I will not become you!"

There are some eloquently made statements in this act about the vantage points afforded by different ages, particularly on the subject of sexuality. Unfortunately, the revelations built around the reasons for A's son's leaving home have less than their intended dramatic impact. And one could do without such leaden touches as Ms. Seldes's choral repetition of the phrase "And so it goes."

All that said, there is an undeniably affecting emotional core and a shimmeringly black sense of humor, dazzlingly interpreted by the bold, inventive performances of Ms. Carter and Ms. Seldes. (Ms. Baker is unable to make much of the relatively thankless role of uncomprehending youth.)

In the first act, in particular, Ms. Carter is sublime. Alternately imperious, coquettish and infantilely mawkish, she captures the flame of exasperated willfulness that still burns in this woman, as she pursues her evanescent memories like a bloodhound.

Ms. Seldes is just as impressive, though in an utterly different, audaciously stylized way. As the caretaker in the first act, she has a sly, gremlin-like crouch and a delivery that slices the air. Like Mr. Albee himself, her character sees the grotesque universal joke in the old woman's situation. (The scene in which she pantomimes stealing the household silver, in response to suspicious questions from the old woman, is priceless.) In the second act, she trenchantly conveys the barbed, elegant worldliness of A at 52 as well as the swelling repository of anger behind it.

Ultimately, it appears that in working through autobiographical material, Mr. Albee has felt the need to be as carefully lucid and precise as possible. Though it seems unfair to accuse a playwright of excessive obviousness when he has so often been critically browbeaten for just the opposite, the play does suffer from didacticism and overstatement.

Nonetheless, ***Three Tall Women*** remains essential viewing for anyone interested in the forces that have shaped this influential writer. And the evening holds the considerable added benefit of two of the most riveting performances in town.

Stefan Kanfer (review date 14-28 February 1994)

SOURCE: "Time—and Again," in *The New Leader,* Vol. LXXVII, No. 2, 14-28 February 1994, pp. 22-3.

[*In the review below, Kanfer affords* Three Tall Women *qualified approval, considering it an "elegant minor effort."*]

Whatever happened to Edward Albee? *The* young playwright of the early '60s, he began his career with small but auspicious Off-Broadway efforts like ***The American Dream*** and ***The Sandbox,*** both about the sorrow and bitterness of old age. His first full-length work, ***Who's Afraid of Virginia Woolf?*** (1963), focused on ambition and self-deception, dazzled Broadway audiences, won critics' awards, and announced the arrival of a major talent. Albee went on to earn two Pulitzer prizes (for ***A Delicate Balance*** and ***Seascape***) and to write many original plays, plus adaptations of other people's writings (including Carson McCullers' ***The Ballad of the Sad Café,*** and Vladimir Nabokov's ***Lolita***).

His reward for all this industry has been a latter-day neglect. Too many of Albee's major works have failed on the main stem, and lesser plays have not prospered Off-Broadway. Who remembers ***The Lady from Dubuque, The Man Who Had Three Arms, Finding the Sun***? Although they are included in some anthologies of the American theater, an entire generation now regards the 65-year-old playwright as a supernova, a star that burned out long ago. The production of ***Three Tall Women*** at the Vineyard Theater may help to correct that impression—but just barely.

Here again is the once-famous amalgam of bitchiness and poignance. A rich and self-centered nonagenarian (Myra Carter) is failing rapidly. Known only as A, she is attended by B (Marian Seldes), a grim middle-aged factotum, and by

C (Jordan Baker), an attractive young lawyer who is there to straighten the old lady's tangled finances. Act I concerns A's infirmities and incontinence, as she rails against her weak bones and failing memory. B variously prods and pampers her, while C is the observer. Shocked and horrified at the trials of senescence, she wonders whether A is being mistreated or merely handled with the firmness she deserves.

For A is a collection of resentments and prejudices. Blacks are niggers. Jews are to be used but never trusted. Homosexuals, including her son ("He just packed up his attitude and left me"), are referred to contemptuously. Through the years, she suspected every servant of pilfering. Without any evidence, B is included in that disgraceful company.

Like her two listeners, A was a tall woman (although age has made her bones shrink a little). Her late husband was a small man with a glass eye and a lot of money. He is fondly recalled—but not as fondly as the horse trainer who seduced her and, of course, had to be fired after a month of furtive adultery. "I had a good deal," she explains. "I couldn't endanger my situation." A's testimony is more than C can bear. There is no way, she vows, that she will come to *this* sort of end. But she has spoken too soon and too late.

In Act II, as A lies on her deathbed, B and C are revealed as something far different from their first appearances. They are not individuals after all; they are, rather, the former selves of A, at the ages of 52 and 26. Time is annihilated, and the three tall women interact. The young one, C, is full of romantic expectations, whirling on a dance floor, speculating about a series of beaux, planning a vibrant and happy life. B is the older and wiser one, having compromised her dreams for decades of imprisoning security. A is a kind of Queen Lear, having outlived her friends and become estranged from her only child. When he returns, The Boy (Michael Rhodes) can simply sit wordlessly at her bedside, his body language pronouncing the elegy for the mother he can neither leave nor love.

Under Lawrence Sacharow's subtle direction, the trio of actresses find every possible nuance in the text. Baker moves easily from terror to radiance and back again; Seldes gives the play its *gravitas;* and Carter manages to be querulous and comic in the same short breath, dropping her voice an octave to confide a secret, then rising to an eerie cackle as she recalls her husband's indiscretions and her own sexual misadventures. James Noone's bedroom set is merely functional, but Muriel Stockdale's costumes amount to a fifth character, commenting on the passages of time and the alterations of personality.

If this were 1962, ***Three Tall Women*** would herald the arrival of a playwright as promising as David Ives. One could hardly wait to see his next production. But we have been through all that with Albee, and this elegant minor effort gives very little reason to cheer. After years of commercial and esthetic disappointments, Edward Albee is once again Off-Off-Broadway. Like so many of his characters through the decades, he is going out the way he came in.

John Simon (review date 28 February 1994)

SOURCE: "Trifurcating Mom," in *New York* Magazine, Vol. 27, No. 9, 28 February 1994, pp. 118-19.

[*In this review, Simon expresses pleasant surprise at the quality of* Three Tall Women. *If the device of three actors depicting different ages of the same character is a "gimmick," he declares, "it is an inspired one."*]

Few playwrights have had such a spectacular rise and fall as Edward Albee. The celebrated author of ***The Zoo Story*** and ***Who's Afraid of Virginia Woolf?*** turned into the execrated perpetrator of ***The Lady From Dubuque*** and ***The Man Who Had Three Arms,*** and landed somewhere between obloquy and oblivion. If someone had told me how good his ***Three Tall Women*** (1991) is, I wouldn't have believed him; I hardly believed my own eyes and ears.

The play is said to concern Albee's mother, but that is almost as irrelevant as that he was an adopted child who subsequently became estranged from his family. At most one could say that this allowed him both a special closeness to his protagonist and a certain distance, both of which he has turned to good advantage. In Act One, he views his nonagenarian heroine, A, from the outside, dispassionately. In Act Two, as she lies dying, he creates her passionately from the inside. From the outside, A is a bit of a pain both to B, her hired companion, and to C, the woman lawyer whom B has called in to straighten out A's finances. From the inside, Albee splits the woman into three selves—the young, the middle-aged, and the old (the actress playing C becoming the first of these; the one playing B, the second)—and brings them on in a three-way conversation to sort out the salient facts about her life and other lives intertwined with hers.

If this is a gimmick, it is an inspired one; the change of perspective is no more unsettling than reversing a reversible raincoat, and much more rewarding. Because B and C become different persons in the process, a double perspective operates for them, too: The tough, cynical C becomes the 26-year-old, naïve A, a woman sexually and existentially confused as marriage beckons; the hunched-over and subservient yet also saucy companion, B, becomes the fiftyish A, at the height of her rich woman's powers but also confronted with the setbacks a mediocre marriage and aging flesh are heir to. As for A, she is now no longer the dotty crone, a nuisance in her dotage, but the shrewd old lady with many a penetrating insight. And all this is played out against the background of . . . but no, I must leave room for surprise.

If you think I have revealed too much as is, I ask how else I could have conveyed the canniness and multivalence of Albee's construction. I do not share Albee's worldview—a kind of scurrilous bonhomie or amused contempt that sometimes parts to reveal better and worse things behind it—but no one can question its personal validity and dramatic efficacy. Especially noteworthy is the author's ability to keep the three women in Act Two both different and identical, the markedly diverse phases of the unmistakably same being. The three tall women of Act One become one tall woman in quirky triplicate, but in both acts, the tallness is not merely physical. Even senile or servile, stooped with age or inferior rank, these women retain proud vestiges of a shady, ambiguous grandeur.

What Albee has wrestled down here is his self-contradictory tendency toward attitudinizing hauteur and lowdown nastiness; to the extent that rudiments of both are still there, they have been polished and domesticated: There is no longer the freakish feel of a keyboard being played only at its two extremities. And he has been staunchly supported by his director and cast. Lawrence Sacharow moves his three women around as much as decently possible, avoiding both statically talking heads and arbitrary, gratuitous choreography. B's crouch in Act One may seem a bit B-movieish, but it works, and the use of the few but good props is telling.

As A, Myra Carter is A-1 in my book. She prattles on or zeroes in with equal command, and negotiates the terrain from Alzheimer's to zippiness with roguishly sportive ease, even when lightning U-turns are required. As B—indeed, as both Bs—Marian Seldes gives the performance of her lifetime: There is spice to her obsequiousness, bite to her throwaway lines, bemusement in her self-possession. As C—or the two Cs—Jordan Baker is not quite in the same league, but more or less holds her own. These three are not a crowd; they are a company.

Tim Appelo (review date 14 March 1994)

SOURCE: A review of *Three Tall Women,* in *The Nation,* Vol. 258, No. 10, 14 March 1994, pp. 355-56.

[*In the following admiring assessment, Appelo finds several parallels between* Three Tall Women *and* Who's Afraid of Virginia Woolf?]

Photos reveal Edward Albee to be stricken with the Dick Clark Syndrome: an inexplicable imperviousness to physical decay. Instead, time has taken its toll on his festering reputation.

But I'm thrilled to report that Albee the artist lives. The Vineyard Theater production of his 1991 play ***Three Tall Women,*** his first big New York premiere in over a decade, should help reverse his audience's exodus. No more the noisy young shockmeister pop star, now Albee plays unplugged, still singing, softly, his bitter old themes of domestic-*cum*-cosmic discord. Rod Stewart unplugged is a lazy disgrace, Clapton a drab craftsman, but Albee is more like Neil Young: chastened by age, sad where once he soared, yet still quavering on.

Three Tall Women is largely a portrait of Albee's late, very estranged adoptive mother at 92, though the character querulously insists she's 91. (In a 1966 *Paris Review* interview, Albee querulously insisted he was 37; the interviewer reminded him he'd be 38 when the piece was published.) James Noone's set neatly conveys the old woman's luxe past and funereal future: A central floral painting is flanked by floral wallpaper, floral prints, floral lace curtains, a bed with floral pillows and a blighted floral rug worn down to atoms.

So is the wraithlike heroine, but there's a death dance of semisenescent reminiscence left in the old gal yet. Myra Carter is, as the young people say, *awesome* in the role of A, the nonagenarian mom. Her phrasing of Albee's half-naturalistic, wholly calculated incipient-Alzheimer's talk is impeccable; her voice dwindles to an Edith Evans warble, ascends to a helium keening, erupts abruptly into lacerating sobs as required. Her moods, too, are musical—her memories lark and plunge. We're eager and grateful for each vivid bit of that past recaptured: her debutante milieu; her runty, randy groom; horseback riding; riding her horse's groom in the stables as she screams in sexual triumph. (Some of these memories are voiced by other actors, whom I'll introduce shortly.) ***Three Tall Women*** cops a bit of the puckish bleakness of Beckett (the sole dramatist Albee has claimed utterly to admire), and a bit of *Long Day's Journey Into Night,* but the grief and affection seem distant, glimpsed through the wrong end of a telescope. It's O'Neill without guilt, and with much less galumphing verbal rhythms. "Eventually he lets me talk about when he was a little boy," says A of her son's visits—Michael Rhodes plays the wordless role well enough—"but he never has an opinion on that; he doesn't seem to have an opinion on much of anything that has to do with us, with me." Creepily remote, Albee has predicted that he won't think much about his mom now that he's devoted a play to explicating her life. But I'll bet he didn't keep mum with Ma in real life: This is the guy of whom Richard Burton wrote, "A week with him would be a lifetime."

Old A is reproved by young C (Jordan Baker), a B-school type trying to get A's finances in order. The role is as thin as the pinstripes on C's suit, and Baker is way the hell the spindliest actor in the show. Twenty-six-year-old C is reproved by B (Marian Seldes), A's 52-year-old caretaker. As dazzling a talent as Carter, Seldes is earthy and spectral, not by turns but at once. Hunched like a sardonic question mark, she moderates the conflict between the old and young women, but she's openly on the old bat's side. She's like Mrs. Danvers on Prozac—still mean and weird, but detached, sourly entertained by life as if watching it from beyond, a well-adjusted shade. Her sly arched-brow amusement reminds me of Ian McKellen; her marvelously odd hand gestures remind me of Thai opera, except that I can't comprehend Thai opera, while her gestures clearly underline the dialogue. Many lovely ensemble moments seem centered on her hands, as if she were conducting. (Though Lawrence Sacharow's direction must have been superb, Ingmar Bergman was probably right to say that Albee's best plays can do without a director, just as chamber music doesn't require a dictatorial baton. The man is a composer, just as he wanted to be at age 11.)

Albee has this little problem as a dramatist: He abhors plots. But just as one realizes, with mounting irritation, that A's colorful fragmented vignettes will never cohere into a single structured picture—nobody cracks Albee's mosaic code—the author saves the play with a big switch in the second act. The three actresses fuse into one contrapuntally evoked character, A through the ages. It's played wonderfully (even Baker gets better), like a close basketball game going down to the wire. While the finale is a characteristic letdown (Albee favors inconclusive conclusions), by then the play has wandered around A's life long enough to give us a satisfying sense of her.

Mysteriously, we get very little sense of her relationship with her son, just a sketchy recounted encounter or two. I wanted more on this relationship, and fewer of the life lessons the play overbearingly urges upon us: "It's downhill from 16 on for all of us . . . stroke, cancer . . . walking off a curb into a 60-mile-an-hour wall . . . slit your throat. . . . All that blood on the Chinese rug. My, my." You can get deeper philosophical insights from Dionne Warwick's Psychic Friends Network. Yet even when Albee says something stupid, he says it in cadences of great and practiced beauty. The wisdom that eludes him in platitudes ("[Women] cheat because we're lonely; men cheat because they're men") he expresses better in drama: the anecdote of the pricey bracelet A's fellatio-craving husband proffers upon his angry penis is funny and scary, a lightning glimpse of a nightmare marriage.

I freely admit that much of the value of ***Three Tall Women*** is the light it sheds on Albee's life and other work. He has described ***TTW*** as an "exorcism." The original title of ***Who's Afraid of Virginia Woolf?*** was *The Exorcism,* which was retained as the title of the third act, and ***TTW*** makes me wonder whether critics haven't been misinterpreting his masterpiece all these years, focusing on George and Martha as archetypal man and wife (or, in a popular interpretation that infuriates Albee, as a gay couple in hetero drag. I don't see what difference it makes, nor why Albee sternly forbids all-male productions of the show). What gets exorcised—killed off—in ***Woolf*** is the imaginary kid. In ***TTW,*** the kid kills off the memory of his mom. What if George and Martha are "really" Edward and his everbickering mother, who needled him cruelly about his adoption and never forgave his desertion? In any case, the heroine A of ***TTW*** is a kind of combination of the Liz Taylor and Sandy Dennis characters in ***Woolf***: alternately a snarly and simpering, sickly fake mother, yet admirably defiant of the unmitigated insult of old age. From the first-act debate about a classic actress (Bette Davis in the case of ***Woolf,*** Norma Shearer in ***TTW***) to the last act's rather heavy-handed stripping away of bourgeois illusions (who has them anymore?), the plays seem parallel, sister dramas reaching out to each other across the intervening wastes and oases of Albee's career.

Why is such a self-conscious iconoclast so annoyingly moralistic? Albee is the third-generation namesake of a top vaudeville impresario who got started with a revolting attraction: a twenty-four-ounce preemie advertised as "small enough to fit in a milk bottle." The child's name was Baby Alice. Does this have something to do with his reviled abstract play ***Tiny Alice***? Edward Albee I ran a theatrical enterprise so bluenosed it blacklisted the actors it ruthlessly enslaved if they so much as uttered the words "son of a gun" on any of its nationwide stages. Having authored five "son of a bitch's" in ***Woolf*** alone, Edward Albee III was the Tom Paine of the dirty-speech movement in American theater, though he was more besides. Maybe there's an in-joke in his ***Alice,*** and a secret triumph in its commercial oblivion: the horribly lowest-common-denominator entertainment answered by a work of arrogant mandarin incomprehensibility, spurned by the ignorant masses.

With the entirely intelligible ***Three Tall Women,*** Albee is evidently mature enough not to crave our hatred. Maybe he doesn't even hate his mother anymore. What's more, he's back in tune with his times. In the three tall women's last-ditch attempt to define the nature of happiness, Seldes's B muses that her position at 52 is ideal: "Enough shit gone through to have a sense of the shit that's ahead, but way past sitting and *playing* in it. This *has* to be the happiest time." Shit happens—in a day when the nation's leading dramatic characters are Beavis and Butthead, what moral could be more modish than that?

Robert Brustein (review date 4 April 1994)

SOURCE: "The Rehabilitation of Edward Albee," in *The New Republic,* Vol. 210, No. 14, 4 April 1994, pp. 26-8.

[*In the following, Brustein offers a laudatory review of* Three Tall Women. *"Most of us have encountered horrible old women like A," he notes; "It is Albee's personal and professional triumph to have made such a woman fully human."*]

A number of years ago, while praising Edward Albee's much reviled stage adaptation of ***Lolita,*** I commented on the startling reverses in the fortunes of this once lionized American dramatist: "The crunching noises the press pack makes while savaging his recent plays are in startling contrast to the slavering sounds they once made in licking his earlier ones. . . . If each man kills the thing he loves, then each critic kills the thing he hypes . . . brutalizing the very celebrity he has created."

I was generalizing not only from Albee's career, but from that of Miller, Williams and Inge, for although I had often depreciated works by these playwrights myself, it struck me as unseemly that mainstream reviewers were displaying such fickleness toward their favorite Broadway icons. This may sound territorial, but it's not. Readers expect more intellectual critics to express dissent about an overinflated dramatic work, but it is an entirely different matter when those with the power to close a show become so savage and dismissive in their judgments. If it is a function of the weekly critic to try to correct taste, it is the function of the daily critic to guide theatergoers, not to trash careers or demolish reputations.

Fortunately, Albee's stubborn streak has kept him writing in the face of continual disappointment, a persistence he shares with a number of other artists battered by the New York press (Arthur Miller, David Rabe, Arthur Kopit, Christopher Durang, Philip Glass, etc.). I call this fortunate because Albee has a vein of genuine talent buried in the fool's gold, and there was always a hope, provided he was not discouraged from playwriting, that this would appear again in a work of some consequence. That work has now arrived in ***Three Tall Women*** (Vineyard Theater), and I am happy to join his other former detractors in saluting Albee's accomplishment.

Three Tall Women is a mature piece of writing, clearly autobiographical, in which Albee seems to be coming to terms not only with a socialite foster parent he once satirized in past plays, but with his own advancing age. Three women are discovered in a sumptuously appointed bedroom decorated with Louis Quatorze furniture, a rare carpet and a parquet floor. They are called A, B and C, which suggests a Beckett influence, though on the surface the play appears to be a drawing-room comedy in the style of A. R. Gurney. The oldest of the women (known as A) is an imperious, rich invalid who appears hobbling on a cane, her left arm in a sling. She is attended by a middle-aged companion (B), who is an angular woman with a caustic tongue and a humped back, and a young, politically correct lawyer (C), who has come to discuss A's business affairs.

The first of the two acts examines some scratchy transactions among this symbiotic trio, consisting of A's recollections (clearly not in tranquility) and the shocked reactions of her companions. A has turned sour and abrupt in old age, and there are traces of Albee's celebrated talent for invective in her rage against life. Her spine has collapsed, she has broken her arm in a fall and now the bone has disintegrated around the pins. Likely to wet herself when she rises from a chair ("A sort of greeting to the day—the cortex out of sync with the sphincter"), she is inordinately preoccupied with the aging process—"downhill from 16 on for all of us." She even wants to indoctrinate children with the awareness that they're dying from the moment they're born, and that anyone who thinks she's healthy, as C does, had better just wait.

In short, A is an entirely vicious old wretch, with a volatile tongue and a narrow mind, but it is a tribute to the writing and the acting that she gradually wins our affections. Although prejudiced against "kikes," "niggers," "wops" and "fairies" (among them her own son), she is a model of vitality and directness when compared with the humor-impaired liberal C, who protests her intolerance. A remembers a past of supreme emptiness, of horse shows, dances and loveless affairs, and she remembers the time her husband advanced upon her with a bracelet dangling from his erect penis ("I can't do that," she said, "and his peepee got soft, and the bracelet fell into my lap"). That arid marriage, and the son who brings her chocolates but doesn't love her ("He loves his boys"), represent memories that can bring A to tears. They also bring her to a stroke at the end of the first act, as she freezes in midsentence describing her deepest family secrets.

The second act begins with A lying in bed under an oxygen mask. By this time B has been transformed from a sardonic, hunchbacked factotum, slouching toward Bethlehem like Igor or Richard III, into a stately matron in pearls, while C has become an elegant debutante in pink chiffon. Before long they are surprisingly joined by A, newly rejuvenated (the figure in the bed is a dummy), and the play shifts gears into a story of one woman at three different moments in time (A at 90, B at 52 and C at 26). Just as B has shed her hump and C her primness, A has lost her feebleness. All three share the same history, the same child, the same sexual experiences, but A and B are united against C in their hatred of illusions. They warn C that her future will be one of deception and infidelity: "Men cheat a lot. We cheat less, but we cheat because we're lonely. Men cheat because they're men."

The prodigal child, now a young man carrying flowers, returns to sit by the bedside of his dying mother ("his dry lips on my dry cheeks"), silent and forlorn. None of the women will forgive him, nor will they forgive each other. A dislikes C and C refuses to become A, while B bursts out bitterly against "parents, teachers, all of you, you lie, you never tell us things change." The inevitability of change is responsible for the obscenities of sickness, pain, old age and death, but A, having accepted her fate, affirms that "the happiest moment is coming to the end of it." Taking a deep breath, she allows the action and her life to stop.

Beckett was the first dramatist to condense the past and present lives of a character into a single dramatic action, and *Krapp's Last Tape* is a play to which ***Three Tall Women*** owes a deep spiritual debt. (It was also the companion piece to Albee's first New York production, ***The Zoo Story,*** in 1960.) Beckett compressed youth and age through the device of a tape recorder, Albee uses doppelgängers; but both plays evoke the same kind of existential poignance. Lawrence Sacharow's direction reinforces this mood, shaping performances of considerable grace.

Myra Carter as the aged A combines the classic calm of Gladys Cooper with the snappish temper of Bette Davis. She can move from meanness to winsomeness and back again in nothing flat. (When C, coolly played by Jordan Baker, accidentally hurts A's shoulder, Carter throws her a look of such ferocity I expected the younger actress to shatter.) Marian Seldes, angular and inscrutable as B, her hands thrust deeply into her cardigan, plays the part as if she is continually tasting something bitter, screaming "Bad Girl!" when A breaks a glass in the sink. Most of us have encountered horrible old women like A, fuming over their pain and helplessness. It is Albee's personal and professional triumph to have made such a woman fully human. His late career is beginning to resemble O'Neill's, another dramatist who wrote his greatest plays after having been rejected and abandoned by the culture. Happily, unlike O'Neill, he may not have to wait for death to rehabilitate him.

John Lahr (review date 16 May 1994)

SOURCE: "Sons and Mothers," in *The New Yorker,* Vol. LXX, No. 13, 16 May 1994, pp. 102-05.

[*In the highly favorable review below, Lahr declares* Three Tall Women *"a wary act of reconciliation, whose pathos and poetry are a testament to the bond, however attenuated, between child and parent."*]

For one terrible moment at the beginning of ***Three Tall Women,*** the pretension that has sunk so many of Edward Albee's theatrical vehicles in his middle years looms menacingly on the horizon. "It's downhill from sixteen on," says one of the women, a middle-aged character called B, who takes care of a rich, imperious, senile old bird called A and is herself a connoisseur of collapse. She goes on, "I'd like to see children learn it—have a six-year-old say 'I'm dying' and know what it means." But then, as we and the old lady settle into the demented fog of her remembering and forgetting, it becomes apparent that Albee has found his way back to the sour and passionate straight talking of his early, best plays.

The last great gift a parent gives to a child is his or her own death, and the energy underneath ***Three Tall Women*** is the exhilaration of a writer calling it quits with the past—specifically, the rueful standoff between Albee and his mother, the late Frances Cotter Albee, who adopted him only to kick him out of the family home, at eighteen, for his homosexual shenanigans and later to cut him out of her sizable will. The play has earned Albee, who is sixty-six, his third (and most deserved) Pulitzer Prize, but the writer's real victory is a psychological one—honoring the ambiguity of "the long unpleasant life she led" while keeping her memory vividly alive. Far from being an act of revenge or special pleading, the play is a wary act of reconciliation, whose pathos and poetry are a testament to the bond, however attenuated, between child and parent. ***Three Tall Women*** bears witness to the son's sad wish to be loved, but with this liberating difference: the child is now finally in control of the parent's destiny, instead of the parent's being in control of the child's. Here, in a set whose Empire furniture, mahogany parquet, flocked blue bedroom wallpaper, and resplendent silver tea service emphasize the iconography of privilege, and not the clutter of decline, sits the ninety-two-year-old A, a fragile, white-haired replica of Albee's mother. A is a spoiled, petulant, demanding, bigoted, manipulative old bat. "*I'll* fix him" she says of her absent son, her quicksilver emotions veering suddenly from tears to a hatred that includes B and a twenty-something female lawyer, C. "I'll fix *all* of 'em. They all think they can treat me like this. You all think you can get away with anything." A's transparent impotence makes the once horrible hectoring now merely laughable. But she is still a potent amalgam of dyspepsia and decrepitude. A former beauty (Albee's mother was briefly a model), A was protected first by the fortune of a face and then by a fortune. Her narcissism and her isolation are spectacular. "You take people as friends and you spend time at it, you put effort in, and it doesn't matter if you don't like them anymore—who likes anybody anymore?—you've put in all that time, and what right do they have to . . . to . . ." she says, her thoughts, like her life, evaporating disconcertingly before her eyes.

Act I paints the landscape of A's old age—the humiliations of incontinence, memory loss, confusion, and regret—and is dominated by the huge, heroic performance of Myra Carter. Ms. Carter, who is sixty-four and is new to me, gives one of the finest performances I've ever seen on the New York stage—an enormous feat of memory, energy, and observation. "I've shrunk!" she says, overwhelmed by the confusions, real and imagined, that beset her. "I'm not tall! I used to be so tall! Why have I shrunk?" Carter hits every vowel and consonant of Albee's words, filling each one with lucid thought and wonderful music. She growls, squawks, cackles, whimpers, rages through the torrent of emotion and memory that's called out of her by the two interlocutors. A's life turns out to have been a series of punishing losses: a sister who became a drunk; a mother who, when she moved into her daughter's home, became an enemy; a son who became a stranger; a husband who became first a philanderer and then a victim of cancer. Carter's face is still beautiful, and it lights up intermittently with childlike delight, even sweetness, which reminds us of the charm that A's former good looks exerted on the world, and mitigates the emptiness of the frivolous life she describes. "I was . . . well, I was naked; I didn't have a stitch, except I had on all my jewelry. I hadn't taken off my jewelry," A says, giggling, about a crucial episode of her early marriage, when "his peepee was all hard, and . . . and hanging on it was a new bracelet." Her husband wants a sexual favor that the well-mannered A can't and won't perform. She continues, "Well, it started to go soft, and the bracelet slid off, and it fell into my lap. I was naked; deep into my lap. 'Keep it,' he said and he turned and he walked out of my dressing room." She weeps at the memory, which sounds the first note of her husband's emotional retreat.

The ballast to A's dementia is provided by B, the droll and delightful Marian Seldes, who moves like a slow loris around the stage, her shoulders hunched as if lumbered with the weight of both her own and A's boredom with old age. "And so it goes" is her recurring catchphrase, which announces the giddy zone of resignation and detachment that she inhabits. "In the morning, when she wakes up she wets—a kind of greeting to the day, I suppose," she tells C, translating her irritation into little dollops of snideness to make it bearable. "The sphincter and the cortex not in synch.

Never during the *night,* but *as* she wakes." B exists to register the old woman's existential anguish; and the inflexible C is there to broadcast moral horror. Albee is less successful with C, who is meant to be callow but—in the first act, at least—is just a poorly written prig. A lawyer sorting out A's unpaid bills, C (played by Jordan Baker) behaves more like an intemperate and insensitive teen-ager than like an employee. A, who is full of antique phrases like "Don't you get fresh," is also full of the ancient bigotries of her class. These draw implausible reactions from C. A's recollection of Irving Thalberg as "a real smart little Jew" prompts C's dopey outrage: "I'm a democrat." And, later, when A talks about "colored help" knowing their place ("none of those uppity niggers, the city ones"), C explodes in dismay, "Oh, Jesus Christ!" Her tone soon becomes predictable, and the character loses a purchase on the audience's imagination, which is focussed on A and on what she sees, at the end of Act I, as her inheritance of hate. "I think they all hated me, because I was strong, because I *had* to be," A says, rationalizing her self-involvement. "Sis hated me; Ma hated me; all those others, *they* hated me." She goes strangely silent after the speech. And Albee brings the curtain down with B and C realizing that their employer has had a stroke.

In Act II, by an ingenious coup de théâtre, ***Three Tall Women*** expands from a parental cameo to a vista of decline. At curtain rise, A is still collapsed in bed but now has an oxygen mask over her face. B and C seem to have dressed up for their bedside vigil in period high fashion—B in pearls and an elegant gray frock with a full, pleated fifties skirt, and C in a layered ankle-length cream chiffon dress that evokes the twenties. Then, as B and C bicker about death, and the conversation drifts to the absence of a living will and why A didn't write one, A herself, in an elegant lavender dress, walks in from the wings. "I was going to but then I forgot, or it slipped my mind, or something," she says. The moment is electrifying. The body in the bed turns out to be a mannequin. In this theatrical filip, Albee goes from a familiar external reality to a bold interior one. B and C are now projections of A, who speaks rationally for the duration of the play, responding from different stages of her life. Albee's wonderful invention allows him both to incarnate A's narcissism and to lift the play from characterization to meditation. What we get is a kind of Cubist stage picture, where the characters are fragments of a single self. The device is at its most eloquent when the son appears, in preppy clothes and clasping freesias, to sit by his comatose mother in a dumb show of devotion. The characters circle him:

> C (*Wonder*): I have children?
>
> B (*None too pleasant*): We have one; we have a boy.
>
> A (*Same*): Yes, we do. I have a son.
>
> B (*Seeing him, sneering*): Well, fancy seeing you again. (*Sudden, and enraged, into his face*) Get out of my house!

In this terrifying and terrible moment, the son doesn't react. In fact, he never speaks. B, the voice the son heard when he was growing up, berates him as "filthy," but A, from the distance of her dotage, begs for tolerance. "He came back; he never loved me, he never loved us, but he came back. Let him alone," she says, adding later, "Twenty-plus years? That's a long enough sulk—on both sides." Lawrence Sacharow, the director, stages these lines impeccably and with awful authenticity. The boy's muteness is a metaphor for the inconsolable gap between parent and child. It's also another of Albee's brilliant dramatic maneuvers: the child is forever outside the narcissistic parental embrace—seen but not heard.

The son's leave-taking ("He packed up his attitudes and he *left,*" B says) is just one of a litany of losses that A and her former selves pick over in this fugue of hope and hurt. Inevitably, the play becomes a dance of A's defensiveness, as her psyche struggles to idealize itself. "I . . . will . . . not . . . become . . . you. I will *not.* I . . . I deny *you,*" C says to A, who, in turn, is unrepentant and rejects their versions of life: "I'm *here,* and I deny you *all;* I deny every *one* of you." In this landscape of loneliness and heartache, C, at the finale, asks about the happy times. "I *know* my best times—what is it? happiest?—haven't happened yet. They're to *come,*" she says. "Aren't they? Please?" B can't agree, preferring her own middle age: "It's the only time you get a three-hundred-and-sixty-degree view—see in all directions. Wow! What a view!" But A has the final say, which is pitched, sardonically, like the happy ending of a Restoration play, with the characters joining hands to face the audience. With B and C on either side of her, A speaks her notion of the happiest moment in life. "When we stop. When we can stop," she says, and, as they together breathe and exhale for the last time, the lights fade to black. At the beginning of this gorgeous final speech, A catches herself lying about her age—a sweet vanity that Albee pays off with a joke. "Give a girl a break," she says to B. And that, finally, is what Albee's ***Three Tall Women*** does for his mother. The mute young man in the play can now, in his own middle age, give her the gift of his words, and make something beautiful and enduring about both her privilege and her neglect.

Richard Hornby (review date Autumn 1994)

SOURCE: A review of *Three Tall Women,* in *The Hudson Review,* Vol. XLVII, No. 3, Autumn 1994, pp. 434-35.

[*In the mixed review below, Hornby judges* Three Tall Women *overwritten and "sluggish," but a "fairly good play" nonetheless.*]

Edward Albee's latest play, ***Three Tall Women,*** won the Pulitzer and three other major prizes, plus the hearts and minds of almost every critic in New York except me. It is, in fact, a fairly good play, but suffers from the excessive narrative that, although beautifully written, makes so much of Albee's late work sluggish. The central figure is a wealthy, nameless widow aged ninety-two, incontinent and

A 1994 English production of *Three Tall Women* featuring (left to right) Anastasia Hille, Frances de la Tour, and Maggie Smith.

senile, with a painful broken arm that will not heal. In contrast to her decrepit condition, her surroundings are lavish—in the Promenade Theatre production, the setting, designed by James Noone, was a gorgeous, French-style bedroom, with patterned blue silk wallpaper, parquet floors, and an Oriental carpet.

The old woman, identified in the program only as "A," is attended by a paid companion, a restless grumbler identified as "B," played by Marian Seldes as bony, angular, and twisted, with an evil grin on her face, a nightmarish, Strindbergian figure. "C," a young woman lawyer, has arrived to try to take charge of A's financial affairs; unsigned checks and unpaid bills have piled up. The old woman babbles of her youth; the companion smiles and complains; the lawyer makes snide comments.

After an hour of these three decidedly unpleasant tall women, I was ready to leave, but Albee was setting us up. At the end of Act 1, the old woman has a stroke; Act 2 consists of her fantasies as she is dying. She imagines herself as holding a conversation among herself as a young woman in her twenties, a middle-aged matron in her fifties, and as her ancient, dying self. The two younger women are played, in her dream, by C and B, respectively. Reexamining her life through the wrong end of the telescope gives it a pattern, a meaning, though it is in fact a story of betrayal, alienation, and physical suffering. Her husband, whom she married for money, turned out to be a philanderer; she had an affair with a stableman in revenge, and then got the man fired. The husband died a lingering death from prostate cancer (reiterating the theme of gross physicality in the midst of affluence). Her son became completely alienated from her. The arguments in Act 2 are on a different plane from the bickering in Act 1: What is the best age of life? What is the happiest moment? What does it all mean? The emotional coldness that has characterized her personality is finally transfigured, into art.

Myra Carter was superb as the ninety-two-year-old, a large and demanding role that would tax even a young person. Jordan Baker was convincing as the lawyer, but was hampered by a shrill voice and muscular tension around her mouth. Marian Seldes, as mentioned, gave a potent performance as the twisted companion, made all the more impressive by her transformation into an elegant matron in a fifties Dior dress in Act 2. The costumes, by Muriel Stockdale, were quietly impressive, while Lawrence Sacharow's direction was brisk and polished.

Marian Faux (review date December 1994)

SOURCE: A review of *Three Tall Women,* in *Theatre Journal,* Vol. 46, No. 4, December 1994, pp. 541-43.

[*In this evaluation of* Three Tall Women, *Faux observes that "the family—his family—has always been [Albee's] great subject, but rarely has he managed to write about it with so little personal rancor."*]

Edward Albee's third Pulitzer prize-winning play ***Three Tall Women*** is a meditation on a woman's life and mortality cleverly viewed from three different stages (no pun intended) of life: youth, middle age, and old age. In the first act, a woman known only as "A," played splendidly by English actress Myra Carter, who originated the role at Vienna's English Theatre in June 1991 (see *Theatre Journal,* 44: 251-52), is a stately and very rich powerhouse trying to come to terms with her diminished powers—physical, mental, and emotional.

As is usual in Albee plays, what is clear is also often contradictory. A's character being no exception, she was born to a lower-middle class family, to parents who may, or may not, have been overly strict, or overly permissive. In any event, they send her to live in New York City. Her mission: To marry rich. Because A has no fortune of her own, her choices are limited, and she ends up marrying a rich, short, one-eyed man whose wit and fortune are real enough but whose social cachet is obviously yet to be determined by her. By her own account, A does her job admirably, and she and her husband end up an American version of horsey country gentry.

A is attended by a crone named B, "crone" being the only word to describe Marian Seldes' first-act performance as A's solicitous (but perhaps malicious), mostly kind (but perhaps cruel) caretaker.

Also present when the play opens is a beautiful young lawyer—C—who has come to visit in order to lecture A on her financial affairs. (She's played by Jordan Baker.) With her beauty and youth, C is incapable of either sympathy or empathy, unable to imagine that she could ever turn into a peevish, impotent old woman. She's impatient at having to listen to the reminiscences of A, even though A was once a great beauty like herself.

Act 1 ends abruptly when A suffers a stroke in mid-sentence. In a wonderful kind of reversal of fates that can only happen in the theatre, in act 2 C does become A—at a slightly insipid and narcissistic twenty-six years of age. The only surprise from her is her determination to have a little fun before she settles down to a marriage that she openly acknowledges will be more about business than love. Carter's character becomes herself about twenty years earlier, still spritely and full of a kind of wisdom that had abandoned her in act 1. Most miraculously, B is transformed into A in sumptuous middle age, a woman truly in her prime. The women spar with one another to show what really happened, or should have happened, in their lives.

If a middle-aged A had the best perspective, an elderly A is the most contemplative, the most capable of parsing out what exactly it was that she accomplished—or failed to accomplish. She no longer cares about the luxurious surroundings she's spent her entire life struggling to obtain, and in fact is no longer sure the struggle was worth it: "It's all glitter," she observes. But her young self disagrees: "No, it's tangible proof we're valued."

This is a highly personal play. In countless interviews, Albee has said he wrote it as a kind of exorcism of his adoptive mother, who, he claims, never learned to like, let alone love him. If so, he appears to have come to terms with their relationship, including how she lived her life, and even manages to be quite generous toward her—and by extension, to other women like her. While making the point that this is a world where all women are kept in one way or another, he still manages to see what it took for her to survive. "They all hated me because I was strong," A recalls. "Strong and tall."

Albee is especially empathic to the middle-aged A. In our ageist society, where a woman's power is widely viewed as declining in direct proportion to her age (and diminishing beauty), he introduces a novel idea, namely, that age fifty can be as satisfying to a woman as to a man. Age fifty really was the best time, an elegantly mid-life Marian Seldes pronounces, the only time when "you're really happy," when you "get a 360-degree view" of your life.

James Noone has designed a set that is appropriately Park Avenue WASP—heavy draperies; a small French chair; a large, well-dressed bed; lush fabrics; and small pillows laden with fringe and braid. It all implies a sort of order than cannot be invaded by the outside world—although in this play, it is indeed order, of a most personal sort, that is crumbling before our eyes. At various times, both C and B (the latter playing a middle-aged A) smooth the fringe on the same pillow. To the elderly A, though, the pillow no longer symbolizes anything. Order in her life now boils down to her daily struggle against the ravages of a weak bladder.

For a playwright who has built a career around challenging audiences with his minimalism and obscurantism, it's ironic that Albee's two most successful plays, ***Who's Afraid of Virginia Wolf*** and ***Three Tall Women,*** are his most accessible and also his most traditional, more so in their staging but also in their language and ideas. Can it be that his adoptive mother's death has freed him to confront his demons more directly than he has done in past plays? Like Tennessee Williams, the family—his family—has always been his great subject, but rarely has he managed to write about it with so little personal rancor.

CRITICAL COMMENTARY

William Hutchings (essay date 1995)

SOURCE: A review of *Three Tall Women,* in *World Literature Today,* Vol. 69, No. 4, Autumn 1995, pp. 799-800.

[*In the following evaluation of the published version of* Three Tall Women, *Hutchings observes numerous similarities between the play and works by Samuel Beckett. Albee's drama, the critic complains, "domesticates the dramatic territories that Beckett so relentlessly, evocatively, and innovatively explored. They have now been made accessible and—in every sense—plain."*]

Identified only as B and C, two of the three tall women of Edward Albee's Pulitzer Prize-winning drama are engaged in a deathwatch for the third, the ninety-two-year-old, bedridden, bitingly sarcastic A. B, according to Albee's production notes, "looks rather as A would have at 52," while C "looks rather as B would have at 26." In the first act the three are distinctly separate characters, generationally different but sometimes overcoming their mutual incomprehensions. The second act, however, perpetrates an intriguing, Pirandello-like change: the three generations represented on stage are no longer three separate people in the room at one time but *one* person at three separate ages in her life. As in the first act, though from an entirely different and newly subjective perspective, the women's interactions and mutual interrogations mingle past and present, youth and age, memory and desire.

Albee's three-page introduction provides particularly candid insights into his personal animus—in both senses of that word. The character of A is based on

> . . . my adoptive mother, whom I knew from infancy . . . until her death over sixty years later. . . . We had managed to make each other very unhappy over the years. . . . It is true I did not like her much, could not abide her prejudices, her loathings, her paranoias, but I did admire her pride, her sense of self. As she moved toward ninety, began failing both physically and mentally, I was touched by the survivor, the figure clinging to the wreckage only partly of her own making, refusing to go under.

Nevertheless, he insists, the play is neither a "revenge play" nor a search for "self-catharsis."

With its relatively static dramatic form, its thanatopsic subject matter, and some of its specific imagery, ***Three Tall Women*** has strong affinities with a number of Samuel Beckett's shorter plays. The second act's poignant juxtaposition of past and present selves resembles *Krapp's Last Tape,* though Albee depicts them as physical presences on stage rather than as a technologically evoked absence—and each can interrogate the others. The voices of Beckett's *That Time* are similarly identified as A, B, and C and are all the single character's own, coming from three distinct points in the darkness; the presence of the women for the deathwatch also suggests, in varying ways, *Footfalls, Rockaby,* and *Come and Go.* After much weeping (which Beckett's characters never do) and after talk of "going on" (that most familiar Beckettian refrain), A, dying, attains "the point where you *can* think about yourself in the third person without being crazy"—as in Beckett's *Not I.* In the final speech of Albee's play, A concludes that life's "happiest moment" is "coming to the end of it [her own existence]"—attaining (perhaps) the oblivion for which, futilely, many of Beckett's characters yearn.

Michael Learned in a scene from a 1996 Los Angeles presentation of *Three Tall Women.*

With its realistic set of "a 'wealthy' bedroom" rather than the ominous darkness of the Beckettian void, with characters of a specific and privileged social class, ***Three Tall Women*** domesticates the dramatic territories that Beckett so relentlessly, evocatively, and innovatively explored. They have now been made accessible and—in every sense—plain.

August W. Staub (essay date 1997)

SOURCE: "Public and Private Thought: The Enthymeme of Death in Albee's *Three Tall Women,*" in *Journal of Dramatic Theory and Criticism,* Vol. XII, No. 1, Fall 1997, pp. 149-58.

[*In the essay below, Staub examines Albee's dilemma in presenting the act of dying in* Three Tall Women. *"Stated simply," he observes, "Albee's problem . . . is how, in a completely public art such as theatre, can the single most intimate and private act of an individual's life be presented for public consideration?"*]

The issue of the public and the private is especially poignant in our culture because, even as we contemporaries are defined by our privacies, we are driven by our politics to find means of presenting those privacies in public. Twentieth-century culture displays a history of seeking boundary crossings between the signifier and the signified, between the sign shared by the public and the event in its privacy. Jacques Lacan argues in "The Agency of the Letter in the Unconscious" that metaphor is the agent that crosses the bar which divides the signified from the signifier (515).

The intense sentimentalism of Lacan's observation appeals to those of us in the arts, for we see it as a triumph of poetry over science. But the burden of this paper is to differ with Lacan and to argue that both science and poetry speak in the same manner in our culture and that manner is by way of public, not private, thought. In this regard, I am most interested in the function of theatre as an ideal medium for *public thought.*[1]

I do not mean by public thought a formal system of logic, but rather a mental process shared by a given civic order. This mental process was called the *enthymeme* by Aristotle some 2,500 years ago. I want to explore the enthymeme as it operated in ancient Greek culture, and as it operates today, especially in the theatre and especially in contemporary treatments of death and dying such as Edward Albee's ***Three Tall Women.***

In the *Poetics,* Aristotle lists *dianoia* as one of the six elements of structure. The term may perhaps be translated as "thought," but Aristotle gives no definition. Instead he refers us to his work on rhetoric, to which he says the issue of thought properly belongs (*Poetics,* XIX, 2). In the *Rhetoric,* Aristotle makes clear immediately that rhetoric is a type of thinking the counterpart of dialectic (Book I, 1) but it is not concerned with what seems logical to an individual but what seems logical to a given class (Book I, 2). That is, rhetoric is concerned with public thinking, *phronesis,* or the practical thought processes common to a given civic order. As such, rhetoric is characterized by the *enthymeme,* a thought process used by the group, as opposed to formal logic or the syllogism (Staub, "Rhetoric and Poetic" 5).

Because Aristotle gives no further definition, the traditional assumption has been that the *enthymeme* is some sort of faulty syllogism, but of late new rhetoricians have taken issue with such an assumption.[2] As Eugene Garver declares in his recent and illuminating study of *Rhetoric,* we cannot define the *enthymeme* as a syllogism with defective or probable premises or with a missing premise (Garver 150). The *enthymeme* is not poor or secondary logic but, as Garver observes, the process of thought employed by a civic intelligence.

Since the whole thrust of classical Greek culture was the perfection of civic life, it is not surprising that Aristotle felt no compulsion to defend the value of the *enthymeme* or to engage in lengthy definition. Of its nature he says only that it must not employ long chains of reasoning or it will lose clarity nor should it include every link else it fall into prolixity (*Rhetoric,* Book II, 22).

But there is considerably more to the *enthymeme* than brevity. To understand its complexity, we must see the *enthymeme* as suasion in action, and to do that we must go to the only complete surviving examples of public life in ancient Greece: the *dramenon* of the city-wide festivals, frequently cited by Aristotle himself. Unquestionably, in Greek theatre the method was to present public figures (Kings, Queens, Potentates, Gods) thinking and acting publicly to encourage a public thought process in the spectators. Greek plays are clearly events of the civic assembly, organized around a chorus which represents the civic order of the play, and presented at public festivals before spectators who are only too aware of each other's presence in a sunlit and open seeing place. Indeed, the very seeing-place itself is crucial to all Greek thinking, for as Charles Segal and others point out: "The Greeks are a race of spectators." To see a thing is to understand that thing. "The Greek word *theoria* implies the same identification of knowledge with vision as that expressed in the common verb to know, *oida,* taken from the root *vid*—to see (*The Greeks* 193).

Moreover, the dramas were the first public events in which myth was used enthymemeically, as a rational device for a public assemblage. Of course, the epic preceded the drama and the *rhapsode* was also presenting myth in a public assemblage. But the art of the *rhapsode* is one based on example, a string of examples, not upon an *enthymeme.* Indeed, Aristotle clearly differentiates in the *Rhetoric* between the *enthymeme* and the example (Book II, 19-20). The essential difference lies in the dynamics of the thought process. The *enthymeme,* particularly in drama, entails twisting ideas together in a non-linear action; reasoning from example, as in the epic, requires a linear procedure and thus a longer chain of reasoning, the very thing Aristotle cautions against in rhetorical argument. Indeed, the Greeks recognized the difference between linear thought—*logos*—and the more supple and more active and twisted practical thought—*metis* (Detienne and Vernant, *Cunning Intelligence in Greek Culture and Society*), a difference which today might be drawn between binary choices and a more fluid quantum suasion.

The maker of a *dramenon* was a transition agent. On the one hand, he was a *logo-graphien:* a writer of stories engaged in the structuring of narratives, but unlike the epic maker, his narratives were for the sighted and therefore immediately-knowing group. Dramas are for spectators not audiences, and as a consequence they are enthymemic and mythic. As with any myth, they are to be grasped as a thing-in-action which serves as a singular proof of its own validity because it is *seen* to be. Indeed, as Aristotle points out, it is the *mythos* that is the soul of the *dramenon* just as the *enthymeme* is the soul of rhetoric. It is my contention that the two are the same and that the mythos of drama may be called the dramatic *enthymeme.*

What is the nature of the dramatic mythos that makes it identical with the rhetorical *enthymeme?* Like the rhetorical *enthymeme,* dramatic *mythos* begins close to the point of suasion so that its action will not be obscure and, like the rhetorical *enthymeme,* it does not fill in all the links so that it may be brief. But most important of all, the dramatic *enthymeme* is always a *trope,* in the true Greek sense of the word as a full turn about.[3] That is, the dramatic *enthymeme* always presents two or more actions turned-in upon themselves. This turning-in is the *stasis* (Aristotle also uses the term *peripetia* or turn around). The most common meaning for the term *stasis* is civil war, and like war the dramatic *stasis* is not a fixed point, as it will become in Roman thought, but a collection of agonistic energies (*dynamos*), a dynamic event which holds in tension the actions of the *prostasis* and that of the *exstasis* (ecstasy) so that the entire movement may be seen altogether, just as we currently perceive the universe in quantum terms. That is why it is appropriate to call the dramatic *enthymeme* a *trope*—a turning-upon or twisting about. All mythoi in drama are so constructed.

Agamemnon's sacrifice of his daughter is finally twisted together with his own sacrifice by Clytemnestra. Indeed, the very *peripetia* which entwines the two killings is a public and entirely visual event—Agamemnon's removing of some sort of foot gear and his treading barefoot on some sort of sacred carpet. It was a very public spectacle of great potency to be grasped by the civic intelligence of the assembled Greek spectators. We sense that some powerful energy is at work, but it is no longer convincing to us. It is not our *enthymeme,* but theirs.

"In the twining or braiding together of the existing assumptions of a given cultural group the suasion of the *enthymeme* occurs" (Staub 8). On the simplest metaphorical or metonymic level we can see the *enthymeme* at work in such a phrase as "Richard the Lionhearted," an *enthymeme* in which we literally argue that a particular English king was brave because we, as a group, have twisted together his name, the part of his body considered to be the source of such emotions, and the image of a lion. This is a brief but extremely complex *trope* which calls for considerable mental agility.

But a culture which knew not lions would draw no conclusion from the joining of Richard's heart with a lion. That group could not nor should not be considered unintelligent because they were not affected by a particular *trope.* On the other hand, we should be cautious in assuming that *tropes* are faulty or simplistic thought. They may well be classified as the highest order of thought, even though they depend upon a civic and not a singular intelligence.

Indeed, it is precisely because troping, the fundamental *enthymeme,* is so complex and agile, exactly because it involves the apprehension and joining of energy and motion in its very structure, that it must grow out of a *public* and *civic* intelligence. Consider the complicated web of entwined events which make up the stunning and disturbing *enthymeme* known as *Oedipus Tyrannus.* First, there is the act of abandoning the infant to prevent his murdering his father, enfolded with the action of the grown son fleeing his home to escape his murdering his father, twisted with the action of his inadvertently killing his father, entwined with his unwittingly marrying his mother and having children by her, children who are his own brothers and sisters. This whole *trope* is enmeshed within itself even as the narrative of the *dramenon* begins so that it is an active helix turning endlessly upon itself, imploding throughout the short play. Indeed, the most significant event of the *dramenon* proper is the *stasis* or civil war between Oedipus and Jocasta in which she realizes that public shame is inevitable and commits suicide. Following his vision of his dead mother, Oedipus explodes the *stasis* into a public ecstasy of sorrow. The final suasive twist by which the whole *trope* is displayed is Oedipus' embracing of his own siblings as his children. The poet's intent is that the spectators are persuaded to pity and terror, because they see the final explosion of the complicated *trope* which they knew from their cultural assumptions could not forever implode. This logic of implosion-explosion, of tension and release, is the logic of the *trope.* Moreover, tropic logic consists in equal parts of past—and therefore—proven events entwined with present actions forming a single complex presented in a see-able whole movement.

The great achievement of the Greek dramatic poets, what raises them above the epic poet in the estimation of Aristotle, is the fashioning of the dramatic *trope*—the twisting together of images in an implosion-explosion turn-about—which is the very essence of public thought. That creation depends in great part on the facility of sight and therefore is especially the province of theatre—the art of the seeing place.

The Greek achievement was to last for centuries, even to our present time. Among the more telling of modern variations on the dramatic *trope* are found in the sciences: the Special Theory of Relativity and Quantum Mechanics. As John Casti in his delightful little study, *Paradigms Lost,* points out, Einstein introduced the idea that there is no such thing as an objective, observer-independent event (418), that is, one to be understood as linear. In short, the Special Theory of Relativity argued that understanding the universe was an enthymemic act, and moreover, since time and space were braided together in a single *trope,* that the *enthymeme* was a dramatic one.

Quantum Mechanics goes one step further in offering all of reality as an interchangeable braid: an *enthymeme* in which we may untangle the braid—to see it as wave or particle—as we wish, depending upon our way of seeing. Indeed, in John Cramer's special concept of Transactional Interpretation, the very act of observing is a complex dramatic trope in which the light of the past as it comes to us from a very distant star reaching into the present is "met half-way" as it were, by the agonistic light emanating from our eyes reaching back into the past (Casti 465). Thus we not only see the past, but at a certain point-of-turn-around, we see into the past just as the past sees into us. In an extraordinary way, Cramer's transactional interpretation restates the ancient Greek view of vision in which the rays sent forth by an object combine with the rays sent forth from the observer's eyes so that an image is constructed between the two. Talk about a quantum universe!

I bring this long argument now to an especially contemporary moment in the theatre: Edward Albee's 1994 Pulitzer Prize winning play, ***Three Tall Women.*** Here is a work centered on the event of one woman's death. In its structure, it is at once very ancient and completely contemporary, so contemporary, in fact that it might well be called one of the great summation moments of 20th century theatre. ***Three Tall Women*** could not have been written before the theatre had been won for the *enthymeme* known as Realism, nor before the breakthrough of the Expressionists into the inner vision of the consciousness, what Carol Mavor calls "the *gaze* of the invisible, a sensate gaze from inside the body" (82). Nor could ***Three Tall Women*** have been written before Einstein's concepts of relativity, nor before Quantum Mechanics, nor before the fluidity of cinema, nor even before the outrageous manipulation of time in the theatre by such postmoderns as Caryl Churchill.

This is not to argue that ***Three Tall Women*** is not a completely original work. It is indeed, but it is a work of the theatre of its times and a work of a seeing and public art. ***Three Tall Women*** is also an ancient work, for it clearly invokes one of humanity's oldest myths, that of the triple goddess in her trinity of girl, nymph and hag. In its ancient guise, ***Three Tall Women*** makes it clear that it intends to be an *enthymeme* not a syllogism, for its subject matter can only be understood enthymemically.

Stated simply, Albee's problem in ***Three Tall Women*** is how, in a completely public art such as theatre, can the single most intimate and private act of an individual's life be presented for public consideration? His solution is embedded in the late 20th century. He chooses, without apology or explanation, the contemporary *enthymemes* of science. In the first act of Albee's drama, we meet three women: one ancient, rich and garrulous; a second, her middle-aged nurse-companion; a third, a comely young lawyer come to advise on financial matters. The three women, gathered in the old woman's boudoir, are presented "realistically," as in a Chekhov play, a Newtonian universe, a recognized syllogism. The burden of the first act is the old woman's reminiscences and confessions, interspersed with her bouts with various incontinencies, and the growing antagonisms of the younger women in dealing with her frailties. The act ends with the old woman suffering a seizure, the logical conclusion of the syllogism.

In Act Two we return to the boudoir to find the old woman in bed, face covered with an oxygen mask, tubes running from her body to life support machines: the standard external medical image of dying in our times. The two younger women enter and begin a conversation which seems somehow less real than in Act One. Their dress is more formal, their movements more dance-like. Presently, the old woman, beautifully gowned, joins them, and we realize that we are not dealing with three women but one, that the stricken woman in bed and the three women are actually the many in the one twisted together in a single event: death. We realize this because we see it as a whole in action before us.

The three women begin a *pas de troi* of words and movement that is literally a dance of death in which *all time* is held together by the woman's several agonistic forces. The past now projects itself into the present; the present reaches back to meet the past. The old woman speaks of an ugly death; the young woman cries out, "Stop it!" "Grow up," says the old woman, as if to a naughty child. "She will," smiles the middle aged woman indulgently. "She does," she adds knowingly (Albee 34). With this interchange the audience is moved subtly from the Newtonian universe to the Einsteinian. What follows are a series of Cramer transactional interpretations. The young woman tells the other two to "Stay out of my life," and even pleads with the audience, "Don't listen to them. They don't *know* me" (35). This remark elicits sarcastic responses from the other two. The young woman, simply identified as C in the play, goes on to describe a sexual encounter and summarizes by saying, ". . . I'm a good girl. The boy who took me was a good boy." The middle-aged woman known as B replies, "Oh, yes. He was." A, the old woman, says, "Yes? He was?"

> B. You remember
>
> A. (*Laughs*) Well, it was a while ago.
>
> B. But you do remember?
>
> A. Oh, yes, I remember him. He was . . .
>
> B. . . . Sweet and handsome; no, not handsome: beautiful. He was beautiful.
>
> A. (*To B*) He was; yes.
>
> B. (*To A and herself*) Yes.
>
> (36)

Here is a Quantum Universe in which the audience may still measure as they wish: wave or particle. The above conversation can be understood as two actual older women filling in the pastel memories of a young friend. But the conversation also sets the measuring devices of the remainder of the play in which each of the women reach back and forth across time to transactually interpret the same memories. Take the following exchange as recalls of a night of love:

> C. I'm not that kind of girl . . . Yes you are, he said; *you're* that kind of girl.
>
> B. And I was, and my God, it was wonderful.
>
> A. It hurt! (*Afterthought to B*) Didn't it?
>
> B. (*Admonishing*) Oh, . . . well, a little.
>
> C. You're that kind of girl and I guess I was.
>
> (37)

We are, by now, pitched headlong by Albee into the most suasive *enthymeme* of our science oriented culture. The audience is persuaded to enter the private moment of death and to think about that most private moment publicly in the prevailing fashion of the civic order of the late 20th century. Nor is it my experience that there is the least hesitation on the part of the audience. When I saw the play in New York, the attendees were seized with delight at the prospect of being able to think together with the dying character about the moment of death. This phenomenon was brought on, I am convinced by Albee's ability to turn the audience into spectators, so that they could *see* his very point before them.

During Act One, there was in the theatre the formal reserve that audiences of Realistic plays have towards the characters. They listened to the familiar *enthymemes* of late 19th-century Realism. But when Albee turns the full dramatic *trope* by using the old woman's seizure to convert the agony of the three women into the civil war (*stasis*) of a single woman, the spectators are energized and ready to see and think creatively. Now a private death is made public, becomes *their* thinking about death. And when the old woman sheds herself of life, the spectators, in catharsis, share in that shedding.

Albee's achievement is to bring to us a contemporary *enthymeme* fashioned about what Lewis Carroll calls the after-time (*Alice in Wonderland* 164), that time of "remembering remembering" (Albee 53) after childhood or after life is lived to its fullest. And like Carroll, Albee does it as simply and as profoundly as A-B-C. Indeed throughout Act Two, these three aspects of the Albee female share the past among them as if they were serving a gourmet meal with all the complex seasonings of life. We see them perform a medieval dance of death, but also hear them in an ancient Greek *symposium*. They share lost loves and found loves, lost parents and even a lost son. And we all think their thoughts as participants in the dying process. Near the end of the dance, the following exchange seems to pull the argument tightly together.

> B. Does that tell you a little something about change? Does that tell you what you want to know?
>
> C. (*Pause; softly*) Yes. Thank you. (*Silence*)
>
> A. (*Curious*) You want some more?
>
> C. No, thank you.
>
> B. I shouldn't think so.
>
> A. Yes, you do. You want some more.
>
> C. (*Trying to be polite*) I said, no, thank you.
>
> A. That doesn't cut any ice around here. (*Points to B*) How you got to her is one thing; how you got to me is another. How do you put it . . . that thing there. (*Points to "A"*)
>
> (47)

Phillipe Aries paraphrases St. Ignatius in pointing out that one conclusion is that death is no more than the means of living well (301). Albee's dying woman rephrases Ignatius for our times when she finally realizes that death is the release of all the inner vision, all the antagonism of being an individual. Death is when we contemporary, highly subjective creatures come "to the point where you can think about yourself in the third person without being crazy" (54). With this realization, we turn-about once more, end the civil war of dying, and return to the logic of the first act. As A says: "That's the happiest moment. When it's all done. When we stop. When we can stop." (55). The three women join hands. The *agon* is ended. We see the solitary dead woman in her bed, but we also see the triple woman as a cohesive whole, a logical unit. The enthymeme is over. Persuasion is apparent. Catharsis is won.

Notes

[1]I discuss the issue of public thought in great detail in "Rhetoric and Poetic: The *Enthymeme* and the Invention of Troping in Ancient Greek Drama," *Theatre Symposium* (Tuscalusca, Alabama: U of Alabama P, 1997).

[2]Led by the work of Kenneth Burke (*A Rhetoric of Motives,* 1958), the new rhetoric movement has done much to reclaim the importance of rhetoric as something deeper than mere decorative language. Some recent basic works of the new rhetoricians include E. L. Bowie's *The Importance of Sophists* (New Haven: Yale UP, 1982); B. Vicker's *Defense of Rhetoric* (Oxford: Oxford UP, 1988); J. Fernandez's *Persuasions and Performances* (Bloomington, Illinois: U of Illinois P, 1986); and *The Social Uses of Metaphor: Essays in the Anthropology of Rhetoric,* ed. J. C. Crocker and J. D. Sapir (Philadelphia, Pennsylvania: 1977).

[3]We tend to take the Roman and Renaissance rhetoricians' definition of *trope* as any figure of speech. The Greek word *trope* meant a sudden and highly contested turn-about, as when one side in battle suddenly turns and flees. The weapons and other items of value discarded by the defeated and fleeing army thus become trophies. Drama as a *stasis* (civil war), an *agon* (struggle) would, by its very nature, be structured tropically. And the chorus, the most public element of the *dramemnon,* would dance the double *trope* of *strophe* (a step against one's motion) and *antistrophe* (another turn-about step against the *strophe*).

Works Cited

Albee, Edward. *Three Tall Women.* New York: Dramatists Play Service, 1994.

———. *Three Tall Women*. Produced at the Promenade Theatre, New York, 1994-96. Directed by Lawrence Sacharow, featuring Myra Carter as A, Marian Seldes as B, Jordon Baker as C, and Michael Rhodes as The Boy.

Aries, Phillipe. *The Hour of Our Death*. New York: Alfred A. Knopf, 1981.

Aristotle. *The Art of Poetry*. Trans. Philip Wheelwright. New York: Odyssey Press, Inc., 1951.

———. *The Rhetoric*. Trans. Lane Cooper. New York: D. Appleton-Century Company, Inc., 1921.

Carroll, Lewis. *Alice's Adventures in Wonderland*. New York: Meridian, 1964.

Casti, John L. *Paradigms Lost*. New York: Avon Books, 1989.

Detienne, Marcel and Jean-Pierre Vernant. *Cunning Intelligence in Greek Society and Culture*. Trans. Janet Lloyd. Chicago: U of Chicago P, 1991.

Garver, Eugene. *Aristotle's Rhetoric: An Art of Character*. Chicago: U of Chicago P, 1994.

Lacan, Jacques. *Ecrits*. Paris: Seuil, 1966.

Mavor, Carol. *Pleasures Taken: Performances of Sexuality and Loss in Victorian Photographs*. Raleigh, NC: Duke UP, 1995.

Staub, August. "Rhetoric and Poetic: The Enthymeme and the Invention of Troping in Ancient Greek Drama," *Theatre Symposium*. Tuscalusa, AL: U of Alabama P, 1997.

Vernant, Jean Pierre, ed. *The Greeks*. Trans. Charles Lamber and Teresa Lavender Fagan. Chicago: U of Chicago P, 1995.

FURTHER READING

Henry, William A., III. "Albee is Back." *Time* 143, No. 8 (21 February 1994): 64.

Highly favorable review that calls *Three Tall Women* "a spellbinder."

King, Robert L. "Eastern Regionals." *The North American Review* 281, No. 2 (March-April 1996): 44-8.

Includes a review of a production of *Three Tall Women* at StageWest. King contends that the play is "basically a-social; the character relationships are not human ones. Its metaphysics are a-moral, self-centered existentialism."

Kroll, Jack. "Trinity of Women." *Newsweek* CXXIII, No. 8 (21 February 1994): 62.

Review that considers *Three Tall Women* one of Albee's best works.

Luere, Jeane. A review of *Three Tall Women. Theatre Journal* 44, No. 2 (May 1992): 251-52.

Assessment of the production of *Three Tall Women* at the English Theatre in Vienna, observing that in this work "Albee moves from his demons toward joy, surcease, and death."

Richards, David. "Critical Winds Shift for Albee, a Master of the Steady Course." *The New York Times* (13 April 1994): C 15, 19.

Article that incorporates comments by Albee on winning the Pulitzer Prize for *Three Tall Women* and the autobiographical basis of the play.

How to Use This Index

The main references

Calvino, Italo
1923-1985 .... **CLC 5, 8, 11, 22, 33, 39, 73; SSC 3**

list all author entries in the following Gale Literary Criticism series:

BLC = *Black Literature Criticism*
CLC = *Contemporary Literary Criticism*
CLR = *Children's Literature Review*
CMLC = *Classical and Medieval Literature Criticism*
DA = *DISCovering Authors*
DAB = *DISCovering Authors: British*
DAC = *DISCovering Authors: Canadian*
DAM = *DISCovering Authors: Modules*
DRAM: *Dramatists Module;* ***MST:*** *Most-Studied Authors Module;*
MULT: *Multicultural Authors Module;* ***NOV:*** *Novelists Module;*
POET: *Poets Module;* ***POP:*** *Popular Fiction and Genre Authors Module*
DC = *Drama Criticism*
HLC = *Hispanic Literature Criticism*
LC = *Literature Criticism from 1400 to 1800*
NCLC = *Nineteenth-Century Literature Criticism*
PC = *Poetry Criticism*
SSC = *Short Story Criticism*
TCLC = *Twentieth-Century Literary Criticism*
WLC = *World Literature Criticism, 1500 to the Present*

The cross-references

See also CANR 23; CA 85-88;
obituary CA116

list all author entries in the following Gale biographical and literary sources:

AAYA = *Authors & Artists for Young Adults*
AITN = *Authors in the News*
BEST = *Bestsellers*
BW = *Black Writers*
CA = *Contemporary Authors*
CAAS = *Contemporary Authors Autobiography Series*
CABS = *Contemporary Authors Bibliographical Series*
CANR = *Contemporary Authors New Revision Series*
CAP = *Contemporary Authors Permanent Series*
CDALB = *Concise Dictionary of American Literary Biography*
CDBLB = *Concise Dictionary of British Literary Biography*
DLB = *Dictionary of Literary Biography*
DLBD = *Dictionary of Literary Biography Documentary Series*
DLBY = *Dictionary of Literary Biography Yearbook*
HW = *Hispanic Writers*
JRDA = *Junior DISCovering Authors*
MAICYA = *Major Authors and Illustrators for Children and Young Adults*
MTCW = *Major 20th-Century Writers*
NNAL = *Native North American Literature*
SAAS = *Something about the Author Autobiography Series*
SATA = *Something about the Author*
YABC = *Yesterday's Authors of Books for Children*

Literary Criticism Series Cumulative Author Index

Aksenov, Vassily
See Aksyonov, Vassily (Pavlovich)

Akst, Daniel 1956-.................**CLC 109**
See CA 161

Aksyonov, Vassily (Pavlovich) 1932-.....**CLC 22, 37, 101**
See CA 53-56; CANR 12, 48, 77

Akutagawa, Ryunosuke 1892-1927.....**TCLC 16**
See CA 117; 154

Alain 1868-1951..................**TCLC 41**
See CA 163

Alain-Fournier....................**TCLC 6**
See Fournier, Henri Alban

Alarcon, Pedro Antonio de 1833-1891....................**NCLC 1**

Alas (y Urena), Leopoldo (Enrique Garcia) 1852-1901...................**TCLC 29**
See CA 113; 131; HW 1

Albee, Edward (Franklin III) 1928-......**CLC 1, 2, 3, 5, 9, 11, 13, 25, 53, 86, 113; DA; DAB; DAC; DAM DRAM, MST; DC 11; WLC**
See AITN 1; CA 5-8R; CABS 3; CANR 8, 54, 74; CDALB 1941-1968; DLB 7; INT CANR-8; MTCW 1, 2

Alberti, Rafael 1902-................ **CLC 7**
See CA 85-88; DLB 108; HW 2

Albert the Great 1200(?)-1280......**CMLC 16**
See DLB 115

Alcala-Galiano, Juan Valera y
See Valera y Alcala-Galiano, Juan

Alcott, Amos Bronson 1799-1888.....**NCLC 1**
See DLB 1

Alcott, Louisa May 1832-1888.......**NCLC 6, 58; DA; DAB; DAC; DAM MST, NOV; SSC 27; WLC**
See AAYA 20; CDALB 1865-1917; CLR 1, 38; DLB 1, 42, 79; DLBD 14; JRDA; MAICYA; SATA 100; YABC 1

Aldanov, M. A.
See Aldanov, Mark (Alexandrovich)

Aldanov, Mark (Alexandrovich) 1886(?)-1957.................**TCLC 23**
See CA 118

Aldington, Richard 1892-1962........**CLC 49**
See CA 85-88; CANR 45; DLB 20, 36, 100, 149

Aldiss, Brian W(ilson) 1925-.......**CLC 5, 14, 40; DAM NOV**
See CA 5-8R; CAAS 2; CANR 5, 28, 64; DLB 14; MTCW 1, 2; SATA 34

Alegria, Claribel 1924-........**CLC 75; DAM MULT; PC 26**
See CA 131; CAAS 15; CANR 66; DLB 145; HW 1; MTCW 1

Alegria, Fernando 1918-............ **CLC 57**
See CA 9-12R; CANR 5, 32, 72; HW 1, 2

Aleichem, Sholom....... **TCLC 1, 35; SSC 33**
See Rabinovitch, Sholem

Alepoudelis, Odysseus
See Elytis, Odysseus

Aleshkovsky, Joseph 1929-
See Aleshkovsky, Yuz

Aleshkovsky, Yuz.................. **CLC 44**
See Aleshkovsky, Joseph

Alexander, Lloyd (Chudley) 1924-.......**CLC 35**
See AAYA 1, 27; CA 1-4R; CANR 1, 24, 38, 55; CLR 1, 5, 48; DLB 52; JRDA; MAICYA; MTCW 1; SAAS 19; SATA 3, 49, 81

Alexander, Samuel 1859-1938.......**TCLC 77**

Alexie, Sherman (Joseph, Jr.) 1966-..... **CLC 96; DAM MULT**
See AAYA 28; CA 138; CANR 65; DLB 175, 206; MTCW 1; NNAL

Alfau, Felipe 1902-................. **CLC 66**
See CA 137

Alger, Horatio, Jr. 1832-1899........**NCLC 8**
See DLB 42; SATA 16

Algren, Nelson 1909-1981......**CLC 4, 10, 33; SSC 33**
See CA 13-16R; 103; CANR 20, 61; CDALB 1941-1968; DLB 9; DLBY 81, 82; MTCW 1, 2

Ali, Ahmed 1910-.................. **CLC 69**
See CA 25-28R; CANR 15, 34

Alighieri, Dante
See Dante

Allan, John B.
See Westlake, Donald E(dwin)

Allan, Sidney
See Hartmann, Sadakichi

Allan, Sydney
See Hartmann, Sadakichi

Allen, Edward 1948-................**CLC 59**

Allen, Fred 1894-1956............. **TCLC 87**

Allen, Paula Gunn 1939-...... **CLC 84; DAM MULT**
See CA 112; 143; CANR 63; DLB 175; MTCW 1; NNAL

Allen, Roland
See Ayckbourn, Alan

Allen, Sarah A.
See Hopkins, Pauline Elizabeth

Allen, Sidney H.
See Hartmann, Sadakichi

Allen, Woody 1935-........**CLC 16, 52; DAM POP**
See AAYA 10; CA 33-36R; CANR 27, 38, 63; DLB 44; MTCW 1

Allende, Isabel 1942-.........**CLC 39, 57, 97; DAM MULT, NOV; HLC; WLCS**
See AAYA 18; CA 125; 130; CANR 51, 74; DLB 145; HW 1, 2; INT 130; MTCW 1, 2

Alleyn, Ellen
See Rossetti, Christina (Georgina)

Allingham, Margery (Louise) 1904-1966.................... **CLC 19**
See CA 5-8R; 25-28R; CANR 4, 58; DLB 77; MTCW 1, 2

Allingham, William 1824-1889......**NCLC 25**
See DLB 35

Allison, Dorothy E. 1949-............**CLC 78**
See CA 140; CANR 66; MTCW 1

Allston, Washington 1779-1843...... **NCLC 2**
See DLB 1

Almedingen, E. M.................. **CLC 12**
See Almedingen, Martha Edith von

Almedingen, Martha Edith von 1898-1971
See Almedingen, E. M.

Almodovar, Pedro 1949(?)-........ **CLC 114; HLCS 1**
See CA 133; CANR 72; HW 2

Almqvist, Carl Jonas Love 1793-1866...................**NCLC 42**

Alonso, Damaso 1898-1990.......... **CLC 14**
See CA 110; 131; 130; CANR 72; DLB 108; HW 1, 2

Alov
See Gogol, Nikolai (Vasilyevich)

Alta 1942-........................ **CLC 19**
See CA 57-60

Alter, Robert B(ernard) 1935-........**CLC 34**
See CA 49-52; CANR 1, 47

Alther, Lisa 1944-................**CLC 7, 41**
See CA 65-68; CAAS 30; CANR 12, 30, 51; MTCW 1

Althusser, L.
See Althusser, Louis

Althusser, Louis 1918-1990......... **CLC 106**
See CA 131; 132

Altman, Robert 1925-...........**CLC 16, 116**
See CA 73-76; CANR 43

Alvarez, A(lfred) 1929-............**CLC 5, 13**
See CA 1-4R; CANR 3, 33, 63; DLB 14, 40

Alvarez, Alejandro Rodriguez 1903-1965
See Casona, Alejandro

Alvarez, Julia 1950-........ **CLC 93; HLCS 1**
See AAYA 25; CA 147; CANR 69; MTCW 1

Alvaro, Corrado 1896-1956.........**TCLC 60**
See CA 163

Amado, Jorge 1912-........ **CLC 13, 40, 106; DAM MULT, NOV; HLC**
See CA 77-80; CANR 35, 74; DLB 113; HW 2; MTCW 1, 2

Ambler, Eric 1909-1998..........**CLC 4, 6, 9**
See CA 9-12R; 171; CANR 7, 38, 74; DLB 77; MTCW 1, 2

Amichai, Yehuda 1924-........**CLC 9, 22, 57, 116**
See CA 85-88; CANR 46, 60; MTCW 1

Amichai, Yehudah
See Amichai, Yehuda

Amiel, Henri Frederic 1821-1881.....**NCLC 4**

Amis, Kingsley (William) 1922-1995..... **CLC 1, 2, 3, 5, 8, 13, 40, 44; DA; DAB; DAC; DAM MST, NOV**
See AITN 2; CA 9-12R; 150; CANR 8, 28, 54; CDBLB 1945-1960; DLB 15, 27, 100, 139; DLBY 96; INT CANR-8; MTCW 1, 2

Amis, Martin (Louis) 1949-..... **CLC 4, 9, 38, 62, 101**
See BEST 90:3; CA 65-68; CANR 8, 27, 54, 73; DLB 14, 194; INT CANR-27; MTCW 1

Ammons, A(rchie) R(andolph) 1926-. . . . . **CLC 2, 3, 5, 8, 9, 25, 57, 108; DAM POET; PC 16**
See AITN 1; CA 9-12R; CANR 6, 36, 51, 73; DLB 5, 165; MTCW 1, 2

Amo, Tauraatua i
See Adams, Henry (Brooks)

Amory, Thomas 1691(?)-1788. . . . . **LC 48**

Anand, Mulk Raj 1905-. . . . . **CLC 23, 93; DAM NOV**
See CA 65-68; CANR 32, 64; MTCW 1, 2

Anatol
See Schnitzler, Arthur

Anaximander c. 610B.C.-c. 546B.C.. **CMLC 22**

Anaya, Rudolfo A(lfonso) 1937-. . . . . . **CLC 23; DAM MULT, NOV; HLC**
See AAYA 20; CA 45-48; CAAS 4; CANR 1, 32, 51, DLB 82, 206; HW 1; MTCW 1, 2

Andersen, Hans Christian 1805-1875. . . . . **NCLC 7; DA; DAB; DAC; DAM MST, POP; SSC 6; WLC**
See CLR 6; MAICYA; SATA 100; YABC 1

Anderson, C. Farley
See Mencken, H(enry) L(ouis); Nathan, George Jean

Anderson, Jessica (Margaret) Queale 1916-. . . . . **CLC 37**
See CA 9-12R; CANR 4, 62

Anderson, Jon (Victor) 1940-. . . . . **CLC 9; DAM POET**
See CA 25-28R; CANR 20

Anderson, Lindsay (Gordon) 1923-1994. **CLC 20**
See CA 125; 128; 146; CANR 77

Anderson, Maxwell 1888-1959. . . . . . **TCLC 2; DAM DRAM**
See CA 105; 152; DLB 7; MTCW 2

Anderson, Poul (William) 1926-. . . . . . **CLC 15**
See AAYA 5; CA 1-4R; CAAS 2; CANR 2, 15, 34, 64; CLR 58; DLB 8; INT CANR-15; MTCW 1, 2; SATA 90; SATA-Brief 39; SATA-Essay 106

Anderson, Robert (Woodruff) 1917-. . . . . **CLC 23; DAM DRAM**
See AITN 1; CA 21-24R; CANR 32; DLB 7

Anderson, Sherwood 1876-1941. . . . . **TCLC 1, 10, 24; DA; DAB; DAC; DAM MST, NOV; SSC 1; WLC**
See AAYA 30; CA 104; 121; CANR 61; CDALB 1917-1929; DLB 4, 9, 86; DLBD 1; MTCW 1, 2

Andier, Pierre
See Desnos, Robert

Andouard
See Giraudoux, (Hippolyte) Jean

Andrade, Carlos Drummond de. . . . . . **CLC 18**
See Drummond de Andrade, Carlos

Andrade, Mario de 1893-1945. . . . . . **TCLC 43**

Andreae, Johann V(alentin) 1586-1654. . . . .**LC 32**
See DLB 164

Andreas-Salome, Lou 1861-1937. . . . . . . **TCLC 56**
See DLB 66

Andress, Lesley
See Sanders, Lawrence

Andrewes, Lancelot 1555-1626. . . . .**LC 5**
See DLB 151, 172

Andrews, Cicily Fairfield
See West, Rebecca

Andrews, Elton V.
See Pohl, Frederik

Andreyev, Leonid (Nikolaevich) 1871-1919. . . . .**TCLC 3**
See CA 104

Andric, Ivo 1892-1975. . . . . **CLC 8**
See CA 81-84; 57-60; CANR 43, 60; DLB 147; MTCW 1

Androvar
See Prado (Calvo), Pedro

Angelique, Pierre
See Bataille, Georges

Angell, Roger 1920-. . . . . **CLC 26**
See CA 57-60; CANR 13, 44, 70; DLB 171, 185

Angelou, Maya 1928-. . . . . **CLC 12, 35, 64, 77; BLC 1; DA; DAB; DAC; DAM MST, MULT, POET, POP; WLCS**
See AAYA 7, 20; BW 2, 3; CA 65-68; CANR 19, 42, 65; CDALBS; CLR 53; DLB 38; MTCW 1, 2; SATA 49

Anna Comnena 1083-1153. . . . . **CMLC 25**

Annensky, Innokenty (Fyodorovich) 1856-1909. . . . . **TCLC 14**
See CA 110; 155

Annunzio, Gabriele d'
See D'Annunzio, Gabriele

Anodos
See Coleridge, Mary E(lizabeth)

Anon, Charles Robert
See Pessoa, Fernando (Antonio Nogueira)

Anouilh, Jean (Marie Lucien Pierre) 1910-1987. . . . . . . **CLC 1, 3, 8, 13, 40, 50; DAM DRAM; DC 8**
See CA 17-20R; 123; CANR 32; MTCW 1, 2

Anthony, Florence
See Ai

Anthony, John
See Ciardi, John (Anthony)

Anthony, Peter
See Shaffer, Anthony (Joshua); Shaffer, Peter (Levin)

Anthony, Piers 1934-. . . . . **CLC 35; DAM POP**
See AAYA 11; CA 21-24R; CANR 28, 56, 73; DLB 8; MTCW 1, 2; SAAS 22; SATA 84

Anthony, Susan B(rownell) 1916-1991. . . . . **TCLC 84**
See CA 89-92; 134

Antoine, Marc
See Proust, (Valentin-Louis-George-Eugene-) Marcel

Antoninus, Brother
See Everson, William (Oliver)

Antonioni, Michelangelo 1912-. . . . . . . **CLC 20**
See CA 73-76; CANR 45, 77

Antschel, Paul 1920-1970
See Celan, Paul

Anwar, Chairil 1922-1949. . . . . **TCLC 22**
See CA 121

Apess, William 1798-1839(?). . . . . . . **NCLC 73; DAM MULT**
See DLB 175; NNAL

Apollinaire, Guillaume 1880-1918. . . . . .**TCLC 3, 8, 51; DAM POET; PC 7**
See Kostrowitzki, Wilhelm Apollinaris de

Appelfeld, Aharon 1932-. . . . . **CLC 23, 47**
See CA 112; 133

Apple, Max (Isaac) 1941-. . . . . **CLC 9, 33**
See CA 81-84; CANR 19, 54; DLB 130

Appleman, Philip (Dean) 1926-. . . . . . . **CLC 51**
See CA 13-16R; CAAS 18; CANR 6, 29, 56

Appleton, Lawrence
See Lovecraft, H(oward) P(hillips)

Apteryx
See Eliot, T(homas) S(tearns)

Apuleius, (Lucius Madaurensis) 125(?)-175(?). . . . .**CMLC 1**
See DLB 211

Aquin, Hubert 1929-1977. . . . .**CLC 15**
See CA 105; DLB 53

Aquinas, Thomas 1224(?)-1274. . . . . **CMLC 33**
See DLB 115

Aragon, Louis 1897-1982. . . . . **CLC 3, 22; DAM NOV, POET**
See CA 69-72; 108; CANR 28, 71; DLB 72; MTCW 1, 2

Arany, Janos 1817-1882. . . . . **NCLC 34**

Aranyos, Kakay
See Mikszath, Kalman

Arbuthnot, John 1667-1735. . . . . **LC 1**
See DLB 101

Archer, Herbert Winslow
See Mencken, H(enry) L(ouis)

Archer, Jeffrey (Howard) 1940-. . . . . .**CLC 28; DAM POP**
See AAYA 16; BEST 89:3; CA 77-80; CANR 22, 52; INT CANR-22

Archer, Jules 1915-. . . . .**CLC 12**
See CA 9-12R; CANR 6, 69; SAAS 5; SATA 4, 85

Archer, Lee
See Ellison, Harlan (Jay)

Arden, John 1930-. . . . . . .**CLC 6, 13, 15; DAM DRAM**
See CA 13-16R; CAAS 4; CANR 31, 65, 67; DLB 13; MTCW 1

Arenas, Reinaldo 1943-1990. . . . .**CLC 41; DAM MULT; HLC**
See CA 124; 128; 133; CANR 73; DLB 145; HW 1; MTCW 1

Arendt, Hannah 1906-1975. . . . . . . **CLC 66, 98**
See CA 17-20R; 61-64; CANR 26, 60; MTCW 1, 2

Axton, David
See Koontz, Dean R(ay)

Ayckbourn, Alan 1939-...... **CLC 5, 8, 18, 33, 74; DAB; DAM DRAM**
See CA 21-24R; CANR 31, 59; DLB 13; MTCW 1, 2

Aydy, Catherine
See Tennant, Emma (Christina)

Ayme, Marcel (Andre) 1902-1967..... **CLC 11**
See CA 89-92; CANR 67; CLR 25; DLB 72; SATA 91

Ayrton, Michael 1921-1975........... **CLC 7**
See CA 5-8R; 61-64; CANR 9, 21

Azorin........................... **CLC 11**
See Martinez Ruiz, Jose

Azuela, Mariano 1873-1952......... **TCLC 3; DAM MULT; HLC**
See CA 104; 131; HW 1, 2; MTCW 1, 2

Baastad, Babbis Friis
See Friis-Baastad, Babbis Ellinor

Bab
See Gilbert, W(illiam) S(chwenck)

Babbis, Eleanor
See Friis-Baastad, Babbis Ellinor

Babel, Isaac
See Babel, Isaak (Emmanuilovich)

Babel, Isaak (Emmanuilovich)
1894-1941(?)....... **TCLC 2, 13; SSC 16**
See CA 104; 155; MTCW 1

Babits, Mihaly 1883-1941.......... **TCLC 14**
See CA 114

Babur 1483-1530.................... **LC 18**

Bacchelli, Riccardo 1891-1985........ **CLC 19**
See CA 29-32R; 117

Bach, Richard (David) 1936-........ **CLC 14; DAM NOV, POP**
See AITN 1; BEST 89:2; CA 9-12R; CANR 18; MTCW 1; SATA 13

Bachman, Richard
See King, Stephen (Edwin)

Bachmann, Ingeborg 1926-1973...... **CLC 69**
See CA 93-96; 45-48; CANR 69; DLB 85

Bacon, Francis 1561-1626.......... **LC 18, 32**
See CDBLB Before 1660; DLB 151

Bacon, Roger 1214(?)-1292........ **CMLC 14**
See DLB 115

Bacovia, George.................. **TCLC 24**
See Vasiliu, Gheorghe

Badanes, Jerome 1937-.............. **CLC 59**

Bagehot, Walter 1826-1877......... **NCLC 10**
See DLB 55

Bagnold, Enid 1889-1981...... **CLC 25; DAM DRAM**
See CA 5-8R; 103; CANR 5, 40; DLB 13, 160, 191; MAICYA; SATA 1, 25

Bagritsky, Eduard 1895-1934....... **TCLC 60**

Bagrjana, Elisaveta
See Belcheva, Elisaveta

Bagryana, Elisaveta................ **CLC 10**
See Belcheva, Elisaveta

Bailey, Paul 1937-.................. **CLC 45**
See CA 21-24R; CANR 16, 62; DLB 14

Baillie, Joanna 1762-1851.......... **NCLC 71**
See DLB 93

Bainbridge, Beryl (Margaret) 1933-..... **CLC 4, 5, 8, 10, 14, 18, 22, 62; DAM NOV**
See CA 21-24R; CANR 24, 55, 75; DLB 14; MTCW 1, 2

Baker, Elliott 1922-.................. **CLC 8**
See CA 45-48; CANR 2, 63

Baker, Jean H.................. **TCLC 3, 10**
See Russell, George William

Baker, Nicholson 1957-........ **CLC 61; DAM POP**
See CA 135; CANR 63

Baker, Ray Stannard 1870-1946..... **TCLC 47**
See CA 118

Baker, Russell (Wayne) 1925-........ **CLC 31**
See BEST 89:4; CA 57-60; CANR 11, 41, 59; MTCW 1, 2

Bakhtin, M.
See Bakhtin, Mikhail Mikhailovich

Bakhtin, M. M.
See Bakhtin, Mikhail Mikhailovich

Bakhtin, Mikhail
See Bakhtin, Mikhail Mikhailovich

Bakhtin, Mikhail Mikhailovich
1895-1975.................... **CLC 83**
See CA 128; 113

Bakshi, Ralph 1938(?)-............. **CLC 26**
See CA 112; 138

Bakunin, Mikhail (Alexandrovich)
1814-1876................ **NCLC 25, 58**

Baldwin, James (Arthur) 1924-1987..... **CLC 1, 2, 3, 4, 5, 8, 13, 15, 17, 42, 50, 67, 90; BLC 1; DA; DAB; DAC; DAM MST, MULT, NOV, POP; DC 1; SSC 10, 33; WLC**
See AAYA 4; BW 1; CA 1-4R; 124; CABS 1; CANR 3, 24; CDALB 1941-1968; DLB 2, 7, 33; DLBY 87; MTCW 1, 2; SATA 9; SATA-Obit 54

Ballard, J(ames) G(raham) 1930-..... **CLC 3, 6, 14, 36; DAM NOV, POP; SSC 1**
See AAYA 3; CA 5-8R; CANR 15, 39, 65; DLB 14, 207; MTCW 1, 2; SATA 93

Balmont, Konstantin (Dmitriyevich)
1867-1943................... **TCLC 11**
See CA 109; 155

Baltausis, Vincas
See Mikszath, Kalman

Balzac, Honore de 1799-1850..... **NCLC 5, 35, 53; DA; DAB; DAC; DAM MST, NOV; SSC 5; WLC**
See DLB 119

Bambara, Toni Cade 1939-1995...... **CLC 19, 88; BLC 1; DA; DAC; DAM MST, MULT; SSC 35; WLCS**
See AAYA 5; BW 2, 3; CA 29-32R; 150; CANR 24, 49; CDALBS; DLB 38; MTCW 1, 2

Bamdad, A.
See Shamlu, Ahmad

Banat, D. R.
See Bradbury, Ray (Douglas)

Bancroft, Laura
See Baum, L(yman) Frank

Banim, John 1798-1842............ **NCLC 13**
See DLB 116, 158, 159

Banim, Michael 1796-1874......... **NCLC 13**
See DLB 158, 159

Banjo, The
See Paterson, A(ndrew) B(arton)

Banks, Iain
See Banks, Iain M(enzies)

Banks, Iain M(enzies) 1954-.......... **CLC 34**
See CA 123; 128; CANR 61; DLB 194; INT 128

Banks, Lynne Reid................. **CLC 23**
See Reid Banks, Lynne

Banks, Russell 1940-............. **CLC 37, 72**
See CA 65-68; CAAS 15; CANR 19, 52, 73; DLB 130

Banville, John 1945-............ **CLC 46, 118**
See CA 117; 128; DLB 14; INT 128

Banville, Theodore (Faullain) de
1832-1891.................... **NCLC 9**

Baraka, Amiri 1934-....... **CLC 1, 2, 3, 5, 10, 14, 33, 115; BLC 1; DA; DAC; DAM MST, MULT, POET, POP; DC 6; PC 4; WLCS**
See Jones, LeRoi

Barbauld, Anna Laetitia
1743-1825................... **NCLC 50**
See DLB 107, 109, 142, 158

Barbellion, W. N. P................ **TCLC 24**
See Cummings, Bruce F(rederick)

Barbera, Jack (Vincent) 1945-........ **CLC 44**
See CA 110; CANR 45

Barbey d'Aurevilly, Jules Amedee
1808-1889............ **NCLC 1; SSC 17**
See DLB 119

Barbour, John c. 1316-1395........ **CMLC 33**
See DLB 146

Barbusse, Henri 1873-1935.......... **TCLC 5**
See CA 105; 154; DLB 65

Barclay, Bill
See Moorcock, Michael (John)

Barclay, William Ewert
See Moorcock, Michael (John)

Barea, Arturo 1897-1957........... **TCLC 14**
See CA 111

Barfoot, Joan 1946-................ **CLC 18**
See CA 105

Barham, Richard Harris
1788-1845................... **NCLC 77**
See DLB 159

Baring, Maurice 1874-1945.......... **TCLC 8**
See CA 105; 168; DLB 34

Baring-Gould, Sabine 1834-1924....... **TCLC 88**
See DLB 156, 190

Barker, Clive 1952-...... **CLC 52; DAM POP**
See AAYA 10; BEST 90:3; CA 121; 129; CANR 71; INT 129; MTCW 1, 2

Barker, George Granville 1913-1991. . . . . **CLC 8, 48; DAM POET**
See CA 9-12R; 135; CANR 7, 38; DLB 20; MTCW 1

Barker, Harley Granville
See Granville-Barker, Harley

Barker, Howard 1946-. . . . . **CLC 37**
See CA 102; DLB 13

Barker, Jane 1652-1732. . . . . **LC 42**

Barker, Pat(ricia) 1943-. . . . . **CLC 32, 94**
See CA 117; 122; CANR 50; INT 122

Barlach, Ernst 1870-1938. . . . . **TCLC 84**
See DLB 56, 118

Barlow, Joel 1754-1812. . . . . **NCLC 23**
See DLB 37

Barnard, Mary (Ethel) 1909-. . . . . **CLC 48**
See CA 21-22; CAP 2

Barnes, Djuna 1892-1982. . . . . **CLC 3, 4, 8, 11, 29; SSC 3**
See CA 9-12R; 107; CANR 16, 55; DLB 4, 9, 45; MTCW 1, 2

Barnes, Julian (Patrick) 1946-. . . . . . . **CLC 42; DAB**
See CA 102; CANR 19, 54; DLB 194; DLBY 93; MTCW 1

Barnes, Peter 1931-. . . . . **CLC 5, 56**
See CA 65-68; CAAS 12; CANR 33, 34, 64; DLB 13; MTCW 1

Barnes, William 1801-1886. . . . . **NCLC 75**
See DLB 32

Baroja (y Nessi), Pio 1872-1956. . . . . . **TCLC 8; HLC**
See CA 104

Baron, David
See Pinter, Harold

Baron Corvo
See Rolfe, Frederick (William Serafino Austin Lewis Mary)

Barondess, Sue K(aufman) 1926-1977. . . . . **CLC 8**
See Kaufman, Sue

Baron de Teive
See Pessoa, Fernando (Antonio Nogueira)

Baroness Von S.
See Zangwill, Israel

Barres, (Auguste-) Maurice 1862-1923. . . . . **TCLC 47**
See CA 164; DLB 123

Barreto, Afonso Henrique de Lima
See Lima Barreto, Afonso Henrique de

Barrett, (Roger) Syd 1946-. . . . . **CLC 35**

Barrett, William (Christopher) 1913-1992. **CLC 27**
See CA 13-16R; 139; CANR 11, 67; INT CANR-11

Barrie, J(ames) M(atthew) 1860-1937. . . . . **TCLC 2; DAB; DAM DRAM**
See CA 104; 136; CANR 77; CDBLB 1890-1914; CLR 16; DLB 10, 141, 156; MAICYA; MTCW 1; SATA 100; YABC 1

Barrington, Michael
See Moorcock, Michael (John)

Barrol, Grady
See Bograd, Larry

Barry, Mike
See Malzberg, Barry N(athaniel)

Barry, Philip 1896-1949. . . . . **TCLC 11**
See CA 109; DLB 7

Bart, Andre Schwarz
See Schwarz-Bart, Andre

Barth, John (Simmons) 1930-. . . . . **CLC 1, 2, 3, 5, 7, 9, 10, 14, 27, 51, 89; DAM NOV; SSC 10**
See AITN 1, 2; CA 1-4R; CABS 1; CANR 5, 23, 49, 64; DLB 2; MTCW 1

Barthelme, Donald 1931-1989. . . . . . **CLC 1, 2, 3, 5, 6, 8, 13, 23, 46, 59, 115; DAM NOV; SSC 2**
See CA 21-24R; 129; CANR 20, 58; DLB 2; DLBY 80, 89; MTCW 1, 2; SATA 7; SATA-Obit 62

Barthelme, Frederick 1943-. . . . . . **CLC 36, 117**
See CA 114; 122; CANR 77; DLBY 85; INT 122

Barthes, Roland (Gerard) 1915-1980. . . . . **CLC 24, 83**
See CA 130; 97-100; CANR 66; MTCW 1, 2

Barzun, Jacques (Martin) 1907-. . . . . . **CLC 51**
See CA 61-64; CANR 22

Bashevis, Isaac
See Singer, Isaac Bashevis

Bashkirtseff, Marie 1859-1884. . . . . . **NCLC 27**

Basho
See Matsuo Basho

Bass, Kingsley B., Jr.
See Bullins, Ed

Bass, Rick 1958-. . . . . **CLC 79**
See CA 126; CANR 53; DLB 212

Bassani, Giorgio 1916-. . . . . **CLC 9**
See CA 65-68; CANR 33; DLB 128, 177; MTCW 1

Bastos, Augusto (Antonio) Roa
See Roa Bastos, Augusto (Antonio)

Bataille, Georges 1897-1962. . . . . **CLC 29**
See CA 101; 89-92

Bates, H(erbert) E(rnest) 1905-1974. . . . . **CLC 46; DAB; DAM POP; SSC 10**
See CA 93-96; 45-48; CANR 34; DLB 162, 191; MTCW 1, 2

Bauchart
See Camus, Albert

Baudelaire, Charles 1821-1867. . . . . . **NCLC 6, 29, 55; DA; DAB; DAC; DAM MST, POET; PC 1; SSC 18; WLC**

Baudrillard, Jean 1929-. . . . . **CLC 60**

Baum, L(yman) Frank 1856-1919. . . . . . **TCLC 7**
See CA 108; 133; CLR 15; DLB 22; JRDA; MAICYA; MTCW 1, 2; SATA 18, 100

Baum, Louis F.
See Baum, L(yman) Frank

Baumbach, Jonathan 1933-. . . . . **CLC 6, 23**
See CA 13-16R; CAAS 5; CANR 12, 66; DLBY 80; INT CANR-12; MTCW 1

Bausch, Richard (Carl) 1945-. . . . . **CLC 51**
See CA 101; CAAS 14; CANR 43, 61; DLB 130

Baxter, Charles (Morley) 1947-. . . . . . **CLC 45, 78; DAM POP**
See CA 57-60; CANR 40, 64; DLB 130; MTCW 2

Baxter, George Owen
See Faust, Frederick (Schiller)

Baxter, James K(eir) 1926-1972. . . . . . **CLC 14**
See CA 77-80

Baxter, John
See Hunt, E(verette) Howard, (Jr.)

Bayer, Sylvia
See Glassco, John

Baynton, Barbara 1857-1929. . . . . . . **TCLC 57**

Beagle, Peter S(oyer) 1939-. . . . . . . **CLC 7, 104**
See CA 9-12R; CANR 4, 51, 73; DLBY 80; INT CANR-4; MTCW 1; SATA 60

Bean, Normal
See Burroughs, Edgar Rice

Beard, Charles A(ustin) 1874-1948. . . . . **TCLC 15**
See CA 115; DLB 17; SATA 18

Beardsley, Aubrey 1872-1898. . . . . **NCLC 6**

Beattie, Ann 1947-. . . . . . **CLC 8, 13, 18, 40, 63; DAM NOV, POP; SSC 11**
See BEST 90:2; CA 81-84; CANR 53, 73; DLBY 82; MTCW 1, 2

Beattie, James 1735-1803. . . . . **NCLC 25**
See DLB 109

Beauchamp, Kathleen Mansfield 1888-1923
See Mansfield, Katherine

Beaumarchais, Pierre-Augustin Caron de 1732-1799. . . . . **DC 4**
See DAM DRAM

Beaumont, Francis 1584(?)-1616. . . . . . **LC 33; DC 6**
See CDBLB Before 1660; DLB 58, 121

Beauvoir, Simone (Lucie Ernestine Marie Bertrand) de 1908-1986. . . . . **CLC 1, 2, 4, 8, 14, 31, 44, 50, 71; DA; DAB; DAC; DAM MST, NOV; SSC 35; WLC**
See CA 9-12R; 118; CANR 28, 61; DLB 72; DLBY 86; MTCW 1, 2

Becker, Carl (Lotus) 1873-1945. . . . . **TCLC 63**
See CA 157; DLB 17

Becker, Jurek 1937-1997. . . . . **CLC 7, 19**
See CA 85-88; 157; CANR 60; DLB 75

Becker, Walter 1950-. . . . . **CLC 26**

Beckett, Samuel (Barclay) 1906-1989. . . . . **CLC 1, 2, 3, 4, 6, 9, 10, 11, 14, 18, 29, 57, 59, 83; DA; DAB; DAC; DAM DRAM, MST, NOV; SSC 16; WLC**
See CA 5-8R; 130; CANR 33, 61; CDBLB 1945-1960; DLB 13, 15; DLBY 90; MTCW 1, 2

Beckford, William 1760-1844. . . . . . . **NCLC 16**
See DLB 39

Beckman, Gunnel 1910-. . . . . **CLC 26**
See CA 33-36R; CANR 15; CLR 25; MAICYA; SAAS 9; SATA 6

Becque, Henri 1837-1899........... **NCLC 3**
See DLB 192

Beddoes, Thomas Lovell 1803-1849.................... **NCLC 3**
See DLB 96

Bede c. 673-735.................. **CMLC 20**
See DLB 146

Bedford, Donald F.
See Fearing, Kenneth (Flexner)

Beecher, Catharine Esther 1800-1878................... **NCLC 30**
See DLB 1

Beecher, John 1904-1980............. **CLC 6**
See AITN 1; CA 5-8R; 105; CANR 8

Beer, Johann 1655-1700............... **LC 5**
See DLB 168

Beer, Patricia 1924-................ **CLC 58**
See CA 61-64; CANR 13, 46; DLB 40

Beerbohm, Max
See Beerbohm, (Henry) Max(imilian)

Beerbohm, (Henry) Max(imilian) 1872-1956................. **TCLC 1, 24**
See CA 104; 154; CANR 79; DLB 34, 100

Beer-Hofmann, Richard 1866-1945..... **TCLC 60**
See CA 160; DLB 81

Begiebing, Robert J(ohn) 1946-....... **CLC 70**
See CA 122; CANR 40

Behan, Brendan 1923-1964...... **CLC 1, 8, 11, 15, 79; DAM DRAM**
See CA 73-76; CANR 33; CDBLB 1945-1960; DLB 13; MTCW 1, 2

Behn, Aphra 1640(?)-1689....... **LC 1, 30, 42; DA; DAB; DAC; DAM DRAM, MST, NOV, POET; DC 4; PC 13; WLC**
See DLB 39, 80, 131

Behrman, S(amuel) N(athaniel) 1893-1973..................... **CLC 40**
See CA 13-16; 45-48; CAP 1; DLB 7, 44

Belasco, David 1853-1931........... **TCLC 3**
See CA 104; 168; DLB 7

Belcheva, Elisaveta 1893-............ **CLC 10**
See Bagryana, Elisaveta

Beldone, Phil "Cheech"
See Ellison, Harlan (Jay)

Beleno
See Azuela, Mariano

Belinski, Vissarion Grigoryevich 1811-1848.................... **NCLC 5**
See DLB 198

Belitt, Ben 1911-................... **CLC 22**
See CA 13-16R; CAAS 4; CANR 7, 77; DLB 5

Bell, Gertrude (Margaret Lowthian) 1868-1926................... **TCLC 67**
See CA 167; DLB 174

Bell, J. Freeman
See Zangwill, Israel

Bell, James Madison 1826-1902..... **TCLC 43; BLC 1; DAM MULT**
See BW 1; CA 122; 124; DLB 50

Bell, Madison Smartt 1957-...... **CLC 41, 102**
See CA 111; CANR 28, 54, 73; MTCW 1

Bell, Marvin (Hartley) 1937-...... **CLC 8, 31; DAM POET**
See CA 21-24R; CAAS 14; CANR 59; DLB 5; MTCW 1

Bell, W. L. D.
See Mencken, H(enry) L(ouis)

Bellamy, Atwood C.
See Mencken, H(enry) L(ouis)

Bellamy, Edward 1850-1898......... **NCLC 4**
See DLB 12

Bellin, Edward J.
See Kuttner, Henry

Belloc, (Joseph) Hilaire (Pierre Sebastien Rene Swanton) 1870-1953........ **TCLC 7, 18; DAM POET; PC 24**
See CA 106; 152; DLB 19, 100, 141, 174; MTCW 1; YABC 1

Belloc, Joseph Peter Rene Hilaire
See Belloc, (Joseph) Hilaire (Pierre Sebastien Rene Swanton)

Belloc, Joseph Pierre Hilaire
See Belloc, (Joseph) Hilaire (Pierre Sebastien Rene Swanton)

Belloc, M. A.
See Lowndes, Marie Adelaide (Belloc)

Bellow, Saul 1915-....... **CLC 1, 2, 3, 6, 8, 10, 13, 15, 25, 33, 34, 63, 79; DA; DAB; DAC; DAM MST, NOV, POP; SSC 14; WLC**
See AITN 2; BEST 89:3; CA 5-8R; CABS 1; CANR 29, 53; CDALB 1941-1968; DLB 2, 28; DLBD 3; DLBY 82; MTCW 1, 2

Belser, Reimond Karel Maria de 1929-
See Ruyslinck, Ward

Bely, Andrey............... **TCLC 7; PC 11**
See Bugayev, Boris Nikolayevich

Belyi, Andrei
See Bugayev, Boris Nikolayevich

Benary, Margot
See Benary-Isbert, Margot

Benary-Isbert, Margot 1889-1979..... **CLC 12**
See CA 5-8R; 89-92; CANR 4, 72; CLR 12; MAICYA; SATA 2; SATA-Obit 21

Benavente (y Martinez), Jacinto 1866-1954....... **TCLC 3; DAM DRAM, MULT; HLCS 1**
See CA 106; 131; HW 1, 2; MTCW 1, 2

Benchley, Peter (Bradford) 1940-..... **CLC 4, 8; DAM NOV, POP**
See AAYA 14; AITN 2; CA 17-20R; CANR 12, 35, 66; MTCW 1, 2; SATA 3, 89

Benchley, Robert (Charles) 1889-1945................. **TCLC 1, 55**
See CA 105; 153; DLB 11

Benda, Julien 1867-1956........... **TCLC 60**
See CA 120; 154

Benedict, Ruth (Fulton) 1887-1948..... **TCLC 60**
See CA 158

Benedict, Saint c. 480-c. 547........ **CMLC 29**

Benedikt, Michael 1935-........... **CLC 4, 14**
See CA 13-16R; CANR 7; DLB 5

Benet, Juan 1927-.................. **CLC 28**
See CA 143

Benet, Stephen Vincent 1898-1943..... **TCLC 7; DAM POET; SSC 10**
See CA 104; 152; DLB 4, 48, 102; DLBY 97; MTCW 1; YABC 1

Benet, William Rose 1886-1950..... **TCLC 28; DAM POET**
See CA 118; 152; DLB 45

Benford, Gregory (Albert) 1941-...... **CLC 52**
See CA 69-72, 175; CAAE 175; CAAS 27; CANR 12, 24, 49; DLBY 82

Bengtsson, Frans (Gunnar) 1894-1954................... **TCLC 48**
See CA 170

Benjamin, David
See Slavitt, David R(ytman)

Benjamin, Lois
See Gould, Lois

Benjamin, Walter 1892-1940....... **TCLC 39**
See CA 164

Benn, Gottfried 1886-1956.......... **TCLC 3**
See CA 106; 153; DLB 56

Bennett, Alan 1934-....... **CLC 45, 77; DAB; DAM MST**
See CA 103; CANR 35, 55; MTCW 1, 2

Bennett, (Enoch) Arnold 1867-1931................. **TCLC 5, 20**
See CA 106; 155; CDBLB 1890-1914; DLB 10, 34, 98, 135; MTCW 2

Bennett, Elizabeth
See Mitchell, Margaret (Munnerlyn)

Bennett, George Harold 1930-
See Bennett, Hal

Bennett, Hal........................ **CLC 5**
See Bennett, George Harold

Bennett, Jay 1912-................ **CLC 35**
See AAYA 10; CA 69-72; CANR 11, 42, 79; JRDA; SAAS 4; SATA 41, 87; SATA-Brief 27

Bennett, Louise (Simone) 1919-...... **CLC 28; BLC 1; DAM MULT**
See BW 2, 3; CA 151; DLB 117

Benson, E(dward) F(rederic) 1867-1940................... **TCLC 27**
See CA 114; 157; DLB 135, 153

Benson, Jackson J. 1930-............ **CLC 34**
See CA 25-28R; DLB 111

Benson, Sally 1900-1972............. **CLC 17**
See CA 19-20; 37-40R; CAP 1; SATA 1, 35; SATA-Obit 27

Benson, Stella 1892-1933........... **TCLC 17**
See CA 117; 155; DLB 36, 162

Bentham, Jeremy 1748-1832........ **NCLC 38**
See DLB 107, 158

Bentley, E(dmund) C(lerihew) 1875-1956................... **TCLC 12**
See CA 108; DLB 70

Bentley, Eric (Russell) 1916-......... **CLC 24**
See CA 5-8R; CANR 6, 67; INT CANR-6

Black Hobart
See Sanders, (James) Ed(ward)

Blacklin, Malcolm
See Chambers, Aidan

Blackmore, R(ichard) D(oddridge) 1825-1900. . . . . **TCLC 27**
See CA 120; DLB 18

Blackmur, R(ichard) P(almer) 1904-1965. . . . . **CLC 2, 24**
See CA 11-12; 25-28R; CANR 71; CAP 1; DLB 63

Black Tarantula
See Acker, Kathy

Blackwood, Algernon (Henry) 1869-1951. . . . . **TCLC 5**
See CA 105; 150; DLB 153, 156, 178

Blackwood, Caroline 1931-1996. . . . . **CLC 6, 9, 100**
See CA 85-88; 151; CANR 32, 61, 65; DLB 14, 207; MTCW 1

Blade, Alexander
See Hamilton, Edmond; Silverberg, Robert

Blaga, Lucian 1895-1961. . . . . **CLC 75**
See CA 157

Blair, Eric (Arthur) 1903-1950
See Orwell, George

Blair, Hugh 1718-1800. . . . . **NCLC 75**

Blais, Marie-Claire 1939-. . . . . **CLC 2, 4, 6, 13, 22; DAC; DAM MST**
See CA 21-24R; CAAS 4; CANR 38, 75; DLB 53; MTCW 1, 2

Blaise, Clark 1940-. . . . . **CLC 29**
See AITN 2; CA 53-56; CAAS 3; CANR 5, 66; DLB 53

Blake, Fairley
See De Voto, Bernard (Augustine)

Blake, Nicholas
See Day Lewis, C(ecil)

Blake, William 1757-1827. . . . . . **NCLC 13, 37, 57; DA; DAB; DAC; DAM MST, POET; PC 12; WLC**
See CDBLB 1789-1832; CLR 52; DLB 93, 163; MAICYA; SATA 30

Blasco Ibanez, Vicente 1867-1928. . . . . . **TCLC 12; DAM NOV**
See CA 110; 131; HW 1, 2; MTCW 1

Blatty, William Peter 1928-. . . . . **CLC 2; DAM POP**
See CA 5-8R; CANR 9

Bleeck, Oliver
See Thomas, Ross (Elmore)

Blessing, Lee 1949-. . . . . **CLC 54**

Blish, James (Benjamin) 1921-1975. . . . . . **CLC 14**
See CA 1-4R; 57-60; CANR 3; DLB 8; MTCW 1; SATA 66

Bliss, Reginald
See Wells, H(erbert) G(eorge)

Blixen, Karen (Christentze Dinesen) 1885-1962
See Dinesen, Isak

Bloch, Robert (Albert) 1917-1994. . . . . **CLC 33**
See AAYA 29; CA 5-8R; 146; CAAS 20; CANR 5, 78; DLB 44; INT CANR-5; MTCW 1; SATA 12; SATA-Obit 82

Blok, Alexander (Alexandrovich) 1880-1921. . . . . **TCLC 5; PC 21**
See CA 104

Blom, Jan
See Breytenbach, Breyten

Bloom, Harold 1930-. . . . . **CLC 24, 103**
See CA 13-16R; CANR 39, 75; DLB 67; MTCW 1

Bloomfield, Aurelius
See Bourne, Randolph S(illiman)

Blount, Roy (Alton), Jr. 1941-. . . . . **CLC 38**
See CA 53-56; CANR 10, 28, 61; INT CANR-28; MTCW 1, 2

Bloy, Leon 1846-1917. . . . . **TCLC 22**
See CA 121; DLB 123

Blume, Judy (Sussman) 1938-. . . . . . . **CLC 12, 30; DAM NOV, POP**
See AAYA 3, 26; CA 29-32R; CANR 13, 37, 66; CLR 2, 15; DLB 52; JRDA; MAICYA; MTCW 1, 2; SATA 2, 31, 79

Blunden, Edmund (Charles) 1896-1974. . . . . **CLC 2, 56**
See CA 17-18; 45-48; CANR 54; CAP 2; DLB 20, 100, 155; MTCW 1

Bly, Robert (Elwood) 1926-. . . . . . **CLC 1, 2, 5, 10, 15, 38; DAM POET**
See CA 5-8R; CANR 41, 73; DLB 5; MTCW 1, 2

Boas, Franz 1858-1942. . . . . **TCLC 56**
See CA 115

Bobette
See Simenon, Georges (Jacques Christian)

Boccaccio, Giovanni 1313-1375. . . . . . . **CMLC 13; SSC 10**

Bochco, Steven 1943-. . . . . **CLC 35**
See AAYA 11; CA 124; 138

Bodel, Jean 1167(?)-1210. . . . . **CMLC 28**

Bodenheim, Maxwell 1892-1954. . . . . **TCLC 44**
See CA 110; DLB 9, 45

Bodker, Cecil 1927-. . . . . **CLC 21**
See CA 73-76; CANR 13, 44; CLR 23; MAICYA; SATA 14

Boell, Heinrich (Theodor) 1917-1985. . . . . **CLC 2, 3, 6, 9, 11, 15, 27, 32, 72; DA; DAB; DAC; DAM MST, NOV; SSC 23; WLC**
See CA 21-24R; 116; CANR 24; DLB 69; DLBY 85; MTCW 1, 2

Boerne, Alfred
See Doeblin, Alfred

Boethius 480(?)-524(?). . . . . **CMLC 15**
See DLB 115

Bogan, Louise 1897-1970. . . . . . **CLC 4, 39, 46, 93; DAM POET; PC 12**
See CA 73-76; 25-28R; CANR 33; DLB 45, 169; MTCW 1, 2

Bogarde, Dirk. . . . . **CLC 19**
See Van Den Bogarde, Derek Jules Gaspard Ulric Niven

Bogosian, Eric 1953-. . . . . **CLC 45**
See CA 138

Bograd, Larry 1953-. . . . . **CLC 35**
See CA 93-96; CANR 57; SAAS 21; SATA 33, 89

Boiardo, Matteo Maria 1441-1494. . . . . . . **LC 6**

Boileau-Despreaux, Nicolas 1636-1711. . . . . **LC 3**

Bojer, Johan 1872-1959. . . . . **TCLC 64**

Boland, Eavan (Aisling) 1944-. . . . . . . **CLC 40, 67, 113; DAM POET**
See CA 143; CANR 61; DLB 40; MTCW 2

Boll, Heinrich
See Boell, Heinrich (Theodor)

Bolt, Lee
See Faust, Frederick (Schiller)

Bolt, Robert (Oxton) 1924-1995. . . . . . **CLC 14; DAM DRAM**
See CA 17-20R; 147; CANR 35, 67; DLB 13; MTCW 1

Bombet, Louis-Alexandre-Cesar
See Stendhal

Bomkauf
See Kaufman, Bob (Garnell)

Bonaventura. . . . . **NCLC 35**
See DLB 90

Bond, Edward 1934-. . . . . **CLC 4, 6, 13, 23; DAM DRAM**
See CA 25-28R; CANR 38, 67; DLB 13; MTCW 1

Bonham, Frank 1914-1989. . . . . **CLC 12**
See AAYA 1; CA 9-12R; CANR 4, 36; JRDA; MAICYA; SAAS 3; SATA 1, 49; SATA-Obit 62

Bonnefoy, Yves 1923-. . . . . **CLC 9, 15, 58; DAM MST, POET**
See CA 85-88; CANR 33, 75; MTCW 1, 2

Bontemps, Arna(ud Wendell) 1902-1973. . . . . **CLC 1, 18; BLC 1; DAM MULT, NOV, POET**
See BW 1; CA 1-4R; 41-44R; CANR 4, 35; CLR 6; DLB 48, 51; JRDA; MAICYA; MTCW 1, 2; SATA 2, 44; SATA-Obit 24

Booth, Martin 1944-. . . . . **CLC 13**
See CA 93-96; CAAS 2

Booth, Philip 1925-. . . . . **CLC 23**
See CA 5-8R; CANR 5; DLBY 82

Booth, Wayne C(layson) 1921-. . . . . . . **CLC 24**
See CA 1-4R; CAAS 5; CANR 3, 43; DLB 67

Borchert, Wolfgang 1921-1947. . . . . . . **TCLC 5**
See CA 104; DLB 69, 124

Borel, Petrus 1809-1859. . . . . **NCLC 41**

Borges, Jorge Luis 1899-1986. . . . . **CLC 1, 2, 3, 4, 6, 8, 9, 10, 13, 19, 44, 48, 83; DA; DAB; DAC; DAM MST, MULT; HLC; PC 22; SSC 4; WLC**
See AAYA 26; CA 21-24R; CANR 19, 33, 75; DLB 113; DLBY 86; HW 1, 2; MTCW 1, 2

Borowski, Tadeusz 1922-1951. . . . . **TCLC 9**
See CA 106; 154

Borrow, George (Henry) 1803-1881. . . . . **NCLC 9**
See DLB 21, 55, 166

Brunner, John (Kilian Houston) 1934-1995........**CLC 8, 10; DAM POP**
See CA 1-4R; 149; CAAS 8; CANR 2, 37; MTCW 1, 2

Bruno, Giordano 1548-1600...........**LC 27**

Brutus, Dennis 1924-........**CLC 43; BLC 1; DAM MULT, POET; PC 24**
See BW 2, 3; CA 49-52; CAAS 14; CANR 2, 27, 42; DLB 117

Bryan, C(ourtlandt) D(ixon) B(arnes) 1936-........................**CLC 29**
See CA 73-76; CANR 13, 68; DLB 185; INT CANR-13

Bryan, Michael
See Moore, Brian

Bryant, William Cullen 1794-1878.....**NCLC 6, 46; DA; DAB; DAC; DAM MST, POET; PC 20**
See CDALB 1640-1865; DLB 3, 43, 59, 189

Bryusov, Valery Yakovlevich 1873-1924...................**TCLC 10**
See CA 107; 155

Buchan, John 1875-1940.....**TCLC 41; DAB; DAM POP**
See CA 108; 145; DLB 34, 70, 156; MTCW 1; YABC 2

Buchanan, George 1506-1582...........**LC 4**
See DLB 152

Buchheim, Lothar-Guenther 1918-.....**CLC 6**
See CA 85-88

Buchner, (Karl) Georg 1813-1837......**NCLC 26**

Buchwald, Art(hur) 1925-...........**CLC 33**
See AITN 1; CA 5-8R; CANR 21, 67; MTCW 1, 2; SATA 10

Buck, Pearl S(ydenstricker) 1892-1973.....**CLC 7, 11, 18; DA; DAB; DAC; DAM MST, NOV**
See AITN 1; CA 1-4R; 41-44R; CANR 1, 34; CDALBS; DLB 9, 102; MTCW 1, 2; SATA 1, 25

Buckler, Ernest 1908-1984.....**CLC 13; DAC; DAM MST**
See CA 11-12; 114; CAP 1; DLB 68; SATA 47

Buckley, Vincent (Thomas) 1925-1988....................**CLC 57**
See CA 101

Buckley, William F(rank), Jr. 1925-.....**CLC 7, 18, 37; DAM POP**
See AITN 1; CA 1-4R; CANR 1, 24, 53; DLB 137; DLBY 80; INT CANR-24; MTCW 1, 2

Buechner, (Carl) Frederick 1926-.....**CLC 2, 4, 6, 9; DAM NOV**
See CA 13-16R; CANR 11, 39, 64; DLBY 80; INT CANR-11; MTCW 1, 2

Buell, John (Edward) 1927-..........**CLC 10**
See CA 1-4R; CANR 71; DLB 53

Buero Vallejo, Antonio 1916-.....**CLC 15, 46**
See CA 106; CANR 24, 49, 75; HW 1; MTCW 1, 2

Bufalino, Gesualdo 1920(?)-..........**CLC 74**
See DLB 196

Bugayev, Boris Nikolayevich 1880-1934.............**TCLC 7; PC 11**
See Bely, Andrey

Bukowski, Charles 1920-1994.....**CLC 2, 5, 9, 41, 82, 108; DAM NOV, POET; PC 18**
See CA 17-20R; 144; CANR 40, 62; DLB 5, 130, 169; MTCW 1, 2

Bulgakov, Mikhail (Afanas'evich) 1891-1940...........**TCLC 2, 16; DAM DRAM, NOV; SSC 18**
See CA 105; 152

Bulgya, Alexander Alexandrovich 1901-1956...................**TCLC 53**
See Fadeyev, Alexander

Bullins, Ed 1935-........**CLC 1, 5, 7; BLC 1; DAM DRAM, MULT; DC 6**
See BW 2, 3; CA 49-52; CAAS 16; CANR 24, 46, 73; DLB 7, 38; MTCW 1, 2

Bulwer-Lytton, Edward (George Earle Lytton) 1803-1873..........**NCLC 1, 45**
See DLB 21

Bunin, Ivan Alexeyevich 1870-1953.............**TCLC 6; SSC 5**
See CA 104

Bunting, Basil 1900-1985.....**CLC 10, 39, 47; DAM POET**
See CA 53-56; 115; CANR 7; DLB 20

Bunuel, Luis 1900-1983..........**CLC 16, 80; DAM MULT; HLC**
See CA 101; 110; CANR 32, 77; HW 1

Bunyan, John 1628-1688.....**LC 4; DA; DAB; DAC; DAM MST; WLC**
See CDBLB 1660-1789; DLB 39

Burckhardt, Jacob (Christoph) 1818-1897..................**NCLC 49**

Burford, Eleanor
See Hibbert, Eleanor Alice Burford

Burgess, Anthony.....**CLC 1, 2, 4, 5, 8, 10, 13, 15, 22, 40, 62, 81, 94; DAB**
See Wilson, John (Anthony) Burgess

Burke, Edmund 1729(?)-1797.......**LC 7, 36; DA; DAB; DAC; DAM MST; WLC**
See DLB 104

Burke, Kenneth (Duva) 1897-1993.....**CLC 2, 24**
See CA 5-8R; 143; CANR 39, 74; DLB 45, 63; MTCW 1, 2

Burke, Leda
See Garnett, David

Burke, Ralph
See Silverberg, Robert

Burke, Thomas 1886-1945..........**TCLC 63**
See CA 113; 155; DLB 197

Burney, Fanny 1752-1840.......**NCLC 12, 54**
See DLB 39

Burns, Robert 1759-1796........**LC 3, 29, 40; DA; DAB; DAC; DAM MST, POET; PC 6; WLC**
See CDBLB 1789-1832; DLB 109

Burns, Tex
See L'Amour, Louis (Dearborn)

Burnshaw, Stanley 1906-.......**CLC 3, 13, 44**
See CA 9-12R; DLB 48; DLBY 97

Burr, Anne 1937-...................**CLC 6**
See CA 25-28R

Burroughs, Edgar Rice 1875-1950.....**TCLC 2, 32; DAM NOV**
See AAYA 11; CA 104; 132; DLB 8; MTCW 1, 2; SATA 41

Burroughs, William S(eward) 1914-1997.....**CLC 1, 2, 5, 15, 22, 42, 75, 109; DA; DAB; DAC; DAM MST, NOV, POP; WLC**
See AITN 2; CA 9-12R; 160; CANR 20, 52; DLB 2, 8, 16, 152; DLBY 81, 97; MTCW 1, 2

Burton, SirRichard F(rancis) 1821-1890...................**NCLC 42**
See DLB 55, 166, 184

Busch, Frederick 1941-.....**CLC 7, 10, 18, 47**
See CA 33-36R; CAAS 1; CANR 45, 73; DLB 6

Bush, Ronald 1946-.................**CLC 34**
See CA 136

Bustos, F(rancisco)
See Borges, Jorge Luis

Bustos Domecq, H(onorio)
See Bioy Casares, Adolfo; Borges, Jorge Luis

Butler, Octavia E(stelle) 1947-.......**CLC 38; BLCS; DAM MULT, POP**
See AAYA 18; BW 2, 3; CA 73-76; CANR 12, 24, 38, 73; DLB 33; MTCW 1, 2; SATA 84

Butler, Robert Olen (Jr.) 1945-......**CLC 81; DAM POP**
See CA 112; CANR 66; DLB 173; INT 112; MTCW 1

Butler, Samuel 1612-1680..........**LC 16, 43**
See DLB 101, 126

Butler, Samuel 1835-1902.......**TCLC 1, 33; DA; DAB; DAC; DAM MST, NOV; WLC**
See CA 143; CDBLB 1890-1914; DLB 18, 57, 174

Butler, Walter C.
See Faust, Frederick (Schiller)

Butor, Michel (Marie Francois) 1926-...............**CLC 1, 3, 8, 11, 15**
See CA 9-12R; CANR 33, 66; DLB 83; MTCW 1, 2

Butts, Mary 1892(?)-1937..........**TCLC 77**
See CA 148

Buzo, Alexander (John) 1944-........**CLC 61**
See CA 97-100; CANR 17, 39, 69

Buzzati, Dino 1906-1972.............**CLC 36**
See CA 160; 33-36R; DLB 177

Byars, Betsy (Cromer) 1928-.........**CLC 35**
See AAYA 19; CA 33-36R; CANR 18, 36, 57; CLR 1, 16; DLB 52; INT CANR-18; JRDA; MAICYA; MTCW 1; SAAS 1; SATA 4, 46, 80; SATA-Essay 108

Byatt, A(ntonia) S(usan Drabble) 1936-.....**CLC 19, 65; DAM NOV, POP**
See CA 13-16R; CANR 13, 33, 50, 75; DLB 14, 194; MTCW 1, 2

Byrne, David 1952-.................**CLC 26**
See CA 127

Carlyle, Thomas 1795-1881........**NCLC 70; DA; DAB; DAC; DAM MST**
See CDBLB 1789-1832; DLB 55; 144

Carman, (William) Bliss 1861-1929..............**TCLC 7; DAC**
See CA 104; 152; DLB 92

Carnegie, Dale 1888-1955..........**TCLC 53**

Carossa, Hans 1878-1956..........**TCLC 48**
See CA 170; DLB 66

Carpenter, Don(ald Richard) 1931-1995....................**CLC 41**
See CA 45-48; 149; CANR 1, 71

Carpenter, Edward 1844-1929......**TCLC 88**
See CA 163

Carpentier (y Valmont), Alejo 1904-1980.....**CLC 8, 11, 38, 110; DAM MULT; HLC; SSC 35**
See CA 65-68; 97-100; CANR 11, 70; DLB 113; HW 1, 2

Carr, Caleb 1955(?)-................**CLC 86**
See CA 147; CANR 73

Carr, Emily 1871-1945............**TCLC 32**
See CA 159; DLB 68

Carr, John Dickson 1906-1977........**CLC 3**
See Fairbairn, Roger

Carr, Philippa
See Hibbert, Eleanor Alice Burford

Carr, Virginia Spencer 1929-........**CLC 34**
See CA 61-64; DLB 111

Carrere, Emmanuel 1957-...........**CLC 89**

Carrier, Roch 1937-.......**CLC 13, 78; DAC; DAM MST**
See CA 130; CANR 61; DLB 53; SATA 105

Carroll, James P. 1943(?)-...........**CLC 38**
See CA 81-84; CANR 73; MTCW 1

Carroll, Jim 1951-..................**CLC 35**
See AAYA 17; CA 45-48; CANR 42

Carroll, Lewis.....**NCLC 2, 53; PC 18; WLC**
See Dodgson, Charles Lutwidge

Carroll, Paul Vincent 1900-1968......**CLC 10**
See CA 9-12R; 25-28R; DLB 10

Carruth, Hayden 1921-......**CLC 4, 7, 10, 18, 84; PC 10**
See CA 9-12R; CANR 4, 38, 59; DLB 5, 165; INT CANR-4; MTCW 1, 2; SATA 47

Carson, Rachel Louise 1907-1964.......**CLC 71; DAM POP**
See CA 77-80; CANR 35; MTCW 1, 2; SATA 23

Carter, Angela (Olive) 1940-1992.....**CLC 5, 41, 76; SSC 13**
See CA 53-56; 136; CANR 12, 36, 61; DLB 14, 207; MTCW 1, 2; SATA 66; SATA-Obit 70

Carter, Nick
See Smith, Martin Cruz

Carver, Raymond 1938-1988.....**CLC 22, 36, 53, 55; DAM NOV; SSC 8**
See CA 33-36R; 126; CANR 17, 34, 61; DLB 130; DLBY 84, 88; MTCW 1, 2

Cary, Elizabeth, Lady Falkland 1585-1639......................**LC 30**

Cary, (Arthur) Joyce (Lunel) 1888-1957................**TCLC 1, 29**
See CA 104; 164; CDBLB 1914-1945; DLB 15, 100; MTCW 2

Casanova de Seingalt, Giovanni Jacopo 1725-1798.....................**LC 13**

Casares, Adolfo Bioy
See Bioy Casares, Adolfo

Casely-Hayford, J(oseph) E(phraim) 1866-1930......**TCLC 24; BLC 1; DAM MULT**
See BW 2; CA 123; 152

Casey, John (Dudley) 1939-..........**CLC 59**
See BEST 90:2; CA 69-72; CANR 23

Casey, Michael 1947-................**CLC 2**
See CA 65-68; DLB 5

Casey, Patrick
See Thurman, Wallace (Henry)

Casey, Warren (Peter) 1935-1988.....**CLC 12**
See CA 101; 127; INT 101

Casona, Alejandro.................**CLC 49**
See Alvarez, Alejandro Rodriguez

Cassavetes, John 1929-1989..........**CLC 20**
See CA 85-88; 127

Cassian, Nina 1924-..................**PC 17**

Cassill, R(onald) V(erlin) 1919-.....**CLC 4, 23**
See CA 9-12R; CAAS 1; CANR 7, 45; DLB 6

Cassirer, Ernst 1874-1945..........**TCLC 61**
See CA 157

Cassity, (Allen) Turner 1929-......**CLC 6, 42**
See CA 17-20R; CAAS 8; CANR 11; DLB 105

Castaneda, Carlos (Cesar Aranha) 1931(?)-1998.............**CLC 12, 119**
See CA 25-28R; CANR 32, 66; HW 1; MTCW 1

Castedo, Elena 1937-...............**CLC 65**
See CA 132

Castedo-Ellerman, Elena
See Castedo, Elena

Castellanos, Rosario 1925-1974......**CLC 66; DAM MULT; HLC**
See CA 131; 53-56; CANR 58; DLB 113; HW 1; MTCW 1

Castelvetro, Lodovico 1505-1571.......**LC 12**

Castiglione, Baldassare 1478-1529......**LC 12**

Castle, Robert
See Hamilton, Edmond

Castro, Guillen de 1569-1631..........**LC 19**

Castro, Rosalia de 1837-1885........**NCLC 3, 78; DAM MULT**

Cather, Willa
See Cather, Willa Sibert

Cather, Willa Sibert 1873-1947......**TCLC 1, 11, 31; DA; DAB; DAC; DAM MST, NOV; SSC 2; WLC**
See AAYA 24; CA 104; 128; CDALB 1865-1917; DLB 9, 54, 78; DLBD 1; MTCW 1, 2; SATA 30

Catherine, Saint 1347-1380........**CMLC 27**

Cato, Marcus Porcius 234B.C.-149B.C..............**CMLC 21**
See DLB 211

Catton, (Charles) Bruce 1899-1978......**CLC 35**
See AITN 1; CA 5-8R; 81-84; CANR 7, 74; DLB 17; SATA 2; SATA-Obit 24

Catullus c. 84B.C.-c. 54B.C.........**CMLC 18**
See DLB 211

Cauldwell, Frank
See King, Francis (Henry)

Caunitz, William J. 1933-1996.......**CLC 34**
See BEST 89:3; CA 125; 130; 152; CANR 73; INT 130

Causley, Charles (Stanley) 1917-.......**CLC 7**
See CA 9-12R; CANR 5, 35; CLR 30; DLB 27; MTCW 1; SATA 3, 66

Caute, (John) David 1936-.....**CLC 29; DAM NOV**
See CA 1-4R; CAAS 4; CANR 1, 33, 64; DLB 14

Cavafy, C(onstantine) P(eter) 1863-1933......**TCLC 2, 7; DAM POET**
See Kavafis, Konstantinos Petrou

Cavallo, Evelyn
See Spark, Muriel (Sarah)

Cavanna, Betty....................**CLC 12**
See Harrison, Elizabeth Cavanna

Cavendish, Margaret Lucas 1623-1673.......................**LC 30**
See DLB 131

Caxton, William 1421(?)-1491(?).......**LC 17**
See DLB 170

Cayer, D. M.
See Duffy, Maureen

Cayrol, Jean 1911-.................**CLC 11**
See CA 89-92; DLB 83

Cela, Camilo Jose 1916-.......**CLC 4, 13, 59; DAM MULT; HLC**
See BEST 90:2; CA 21-24R; CAAS 10; CANR 21, 32, 76; DLBY 89; HW 1; MTCW 1, 2

Celan, Paul........**CLC 10, 19, 53, 82; PC 10**
See Antschel, Paul

Celine, Louis-Ferdinand.....**CLC 1, 3, 4, 7, 9, 15, 47**
See Destouches, Louis-Ferdinand

Cellini, Benvenuto 1500-1571...........**LC 7**

Cendrars, Blaise 1887-1961......**CLC 18, 106**
See Sauser-Hall, Frederic

Cernuda (y Bidon), Luis 1902-1963......**CLC 54; DAM POET**
See CA 131; 89-92; DLB 134; HW 1

Cervantes (Saavedra), Miguel de 1547-1616.........**LC 6, 23; DA; DAB; DAC; DAM MST, NOV; SSC 12; WLC**

Cesaire, Aime (Fernand) 1913-......**CLC 19, 32, 112; BLC 1; DAM MULT, POET; PC 25**
See BW 2, 3; CA 65-68; CANR 24, 43; MTCW 1, 2

Cohen, Leonard (Norman) 1934-...... **CLC 3, 38; DAC; DAM MST**
See CA 21-24R; CANR 14, 69; DLB 53; MTCW 1

Cohen, Matt 1942-............ **CLC 19; DAC**
See CA 61-64; CAAS 18; CANR 40; DLB 53

Cohen-Solal, Annie 19(?)-........... **CLC 50**

Colegate, Isabel 1931-............... **CLC 36**
See CA 17-20R; CANR 8, 22, 74; DLB 14; INT CANR-22; MTCW 1

Coleman, Emmett
See Reed, Ishmael

Coleridge, M. E.
See Coleridge, Mary E(lizabeth)

Coleridge, Mary E(lizabeth)
1861-1907................... **TCLC 73**
See CA 116; 166; DLB 19, 98

Coleridge, Samuel Taylor
1772-1834....... **NCLC 9, 54; DA; DAB; DAC; DAM MST, POET; PC 11; WLC**
See CDBLB 1789-1832; DLB 93, 107

Coleridge, Sara 1802-1852......... **NCLC 31**
See DLB 199

Coles, Don 1928-................... **CLC 46**
See CA 115; CANR 38

Coles, Robert (Martin) 1929-........ **CLC 108**
See CA 45-48; CANR 3, 32, 66, 70; INT CANR-32; SATA 23

Colette, (Sidonie-Gabrielle)
1873-1954......... **TCLC 1, 5, 16; DAM NOV; SSC 10**
See CA 104; 131; DLB 65; MTCW 1, 2

Collett, (Jacobine) Camilla (Wergeland)
1813-1895................... **NCLC 22**

Collier, Christopher 1930-........... **CLC 30**
See AAYA 13; CA 33-36R; CANR 13, 33; JRDA; MAICYA; SATA 16, 70

Collier, James L(incoln) 1928-....... **CLC 30; DAM POP**
See AAYA 13; CA 9-12R; CANR 4, 33, 60; CLR 3; JRDA; MAICYA; SAAS 21; SATA 8, 70

Collier, Jeremy 1650-1726............. **LC 6**

Collier, John 1901-1980.............. **SSC 19**
See CA 65-68; 97-100; CANR 10; DLB 77

Collingwood, R(obin) G(eorge)
1889(?)-1943................. **TCLC 67**
See CA 117; 155

Collins, Hunt
See Hunter, Evan

Collins, Linda 1931-................ **CLC 44**
See CA 125

Collins, (William) Wilkie
1824-1889................. **NCLC 1, 18**
See CDBLB 1832-1890; DLB 18, 70, 159

Collins, William 1721-1759......... **LC 4, 40; DAM POET**
See DLB 109

Collodi, Carlo 1826-1890........... **NCLC 54**
See Lorenzini, Carlo

Colman, George 1732-1794
See Glassco, John

Colt, Winchester Remington
See Hubbard, L(afayette) Ron(ald)

Colter, Cyrus 1910-................ **CLC 58**
See BW 1; CA 65-68; CANR 10, 66; DLB 33

Colton, James
See Hansen, Joseph

Colum, Padraic 1881-1972........... **CLC 28**
See CA 73-76; 33-36R; CANR 35; CLR 36; MAICYA; MTCW 1; SATA 15

Colvin, James
See Moorcock, Michael (John)

Colwin, Laurie (E.) 1944-1992..... **CLC 5, 13, 23, 84**
See CA 89-92; 139; CANR 20, 46; DLBY 80; MTCW 1

Comfort, Alex(ander) 1920-..... **CLC 7; DAM POP**
See CA 1-4R; CANR 1, 45; MTCW 1

Comfort, Montgomery
See Campbell, (John) Ramsey

Compton-Burnett, I(vy)
1884(?)-1969....... **CLC 1, 3, 10, 15, 34; DAM NOV**
See CA 1-4R; 25-28R; CANR 4; DLB 36; MTCW 1

Comstock, Anthony 1844-1915...... **TCLC 13**
See CA 110; 169

Comte, Auguste 1798-1857......... **NCLC 54**

Conan Doyle, Arthur
See Doyle, Arthur Conan

Conde, Maryse 1937-..... **CLC 52, 92; BLCS; DAM MULT**
See Boucolon, Maryse

Condillac, Etienne Bonnot de
1714-1780...................... **LC 26**

Condon, Richard (Thomas)
1915-1996...... **CLC 4, 6, 8, 10, 45, 100; DAM NOV**
See BEST 90:3; CA 1-4R; 151; CAAS 1; CANR 2, 23; INT CANR-23; MTCW 1, 2

Confucius 551B.C.-479B.C.......... **CMLC 19; DA; DAB; DAC; DAM MST; WLCS**

Congreve, William 1670-1729....... **LC 5, 21; DA; DAB; DAC; DAM DRAM, MST, POET; DC 2; WLC**
See CDBLB 1660-1789; DLB 39, 84

Connell, Evan S(helby), Jr. 1924-...... **CLC 4, 6, 45; DAM NOV**
See AAYA 7; CA 1-4R; CAAS 2; CANR 2, 39, 76; DLB 2; DLBY 81; MTCW 1, 2

Connelly, Marc(us Cook) 1890-1980..... **CLC 7**
See CA 85-88; 102; CANR 30; DLB 7; DLBY 80; SATA-Obit 25

Connor, Ralph................... **TCLC 31**
See Gordon, Charles William

Conrad, Joseph 1857-1924..... **TCLC 1, 6, 13, 25, 43, 57; DA; DAB; DAC; DAM MST, NOV; SSC 9; WLC**
See AAYA 26; CA 104; 131; CANR 60; CDBLB 1890-1914; DLB 10, 34, 98, 156; MTCW 1, 2; SATA 27

Conrad, Robert Arnold
See Hart, Moss

Conroy, Pat
See Conroy, (Donald) Pat(rick)

Conroy, (Donald) Pat(rick) 1945-....... **CLC 30, 74; DAM NOV, POP**
See Conroy, Pat

Constant (de Rebecque), (Henri) Benjamin
1767-1830.................... **NCLC 6**
See DLB 119

Conybeare, Charles Augustus
See Eliot, T(homas) S(tearns)

Cook, Michael 1933-................ **CLC 58**
See CA 93-96; CANR 68; DLB 53

Cook, Robin 1940-....... **CLC 14; DAM POP**
See BEST 90:2; CA 108; 111; CANR 41; INT 111

Cook, Roy
See Silverberg, Robert

Cooke, Elizabeth 1948-.............. **CLC 55**
See CA 129

Cooke, John Esten 1830-1886........ **NCLC 5**
See DLB 3

Cooke, John Estes
See Baum, L(yman) Frank

Cooke, M. E.
See Creasey, John

Cooke, Margaret
See Creasey, John

Cook-Lynn, Elizabeth 1930-......... **CLC 93; DAM MULT**
See CA 133; DLB 175; NNAL

Cooney, Ray...................... **CLC 62**

Cooper, Douglas 1960-.............. **CLC 86**

Cooper, Henry St. John
See Creasey, John

Cooper, J(oan) California (?)-....... **CLC 56; DAM MULT**
See AAYA 12; BW 1; CA 125; CANR 55; DLB 212

Cooper, James Fenimore
1789-1851.............. **NCLC 1, 27, 54**
See AAYA 22; CDALB 1640-1865; DLB 3; SATA 19

Coover, Robert (Lowell) 1932-...... **CLC 3, 7, 15, 32, 46, 87; DAM NOV; SSC 15**
See CA 45-48; CANR 3, 37, 58; DLB 2; DLBY 81; MTCW 1, 2

Copeland, Stewart (Armstrong)
1952-........................ **CLC 26**

Copernicus, Nicolaus 1473-1543....... **LC 45**

Coppard, A(lfred) E(dgar)
1878-1957............ **TCLC 5; SSC 21**
See CA 114; 167; DLB 162; YABC 1

Coppee, Francois 1842-1908........ **TCLC 25**
See CA 170

Coppola, Francis Ford 1939-......... **CLC 16**
See CA 77-80; CANR 40, 78; DLB 44

Corbiere, Tristan 1845-1875........ **NCLC 43**

Corcoran, Barbara 1911-............ **CLC 17**
See AAYA 14; CA 21-24R; CAAS 2; CANR 11, 28, 48; CLR 50; DLB 52; JRDA; SAAS 20; SATA 3, 77

Author Index

Crothers, Rachel 1878(?)-1958...... **TCLC 19**
See CA 113; DLB 7

Croves, Hal
See Traven, B.

Crow Dog, Mary (Ellen) (?)-......... **CLC 93**
See Brave Bird, Mary

Crowfield, Christopher
See Stowe, Harriet (Elizabeth) Beecher

Crowley, Aleister.................. **TCLC 7**
See Crowley, Edward Alexander

Crowley, Edward Alexander 1875-1947
See Crowley, Aleister

Crowley, John 1942-................**CLC 57**
See CA 61-64; CANR 43; DLBY 82; SATA 65

Crud
See Crumb, R(obert)

Crumarums
See Crumb, R(obert)

Crumb, R(obert) 1943-..............**CLC 17**
See CA 106

Crumbum
See Crumb, R(obert)

Crumski
See Crumb, R(obert)

Crum the Bum
See Crumb, R(obert)

Crunk
See Crumb, R(obert)

Crustt
See Crumb, R(obert)

Cryer, Gretchen (Kiger) 1935-....... **CLC 21**
See CA 114; 123

Csath, Geza 1887-1919............ **TCLC 13**
See CA 111

Cudlip, David 1933-................ **CLC 34**

Cullen, Countee 1903-1946...... **TCLC 4, 37; BLC 1; DA; DAC; DAM MST, MULT, POET; PC 20; WLCS**
See BW 1; CA 108; 124; CDALB 1917-1929; DLB 4, 48, 51; MTCW 1, 2; SATA 18

Cum, R.
See Crumb, R(obert)

Cummings, Bruce F(rederick) 1889-1919
See Barbellion, W. N. P.

Cummings, E(dward) E(stlin) 1894-1962....... **CLC 1, 3, 8, 12, 15, 68; DA; DAB; DAC; DAM MST, POET; PC 5; WLC**
See CA 73-76; CANR 31; CDALB 1929-1941; DLB 4, 48; MTCW 1, 2

Cunha, Euclides (Rodrigues Pimenta) da 1866-1909..................**TCLC 24**
See CA 123

Cunningham, E. V.
See Fast, Howard (Melvin)

Cunningham, J(ames) V(incent) 1911-1985.................. **CLC 3, 31**
See CA 1-4R; 115; CANR 1, 72; DLB 5

Cunningham, Julia (Woolfolk) 1916-....................... **CLC 12**
See CA 9-12R; CANR 4, 19, 36; JRDA; MAICYA; SAAS 2; SATA 1, 26

Cunningham, Michael 1952-......... **CLC 34**
See CA 136

Cunninghame Graham, R(obert) B(ontine) 1852-1936...................**TCLC 19**
See Graham, R(obert) B(ontine) Cunninghame

Currie, Ellen 19(?)-.................**CLC 44**

Curtin, Philip
See Lowndes, Marie Adelaide (Belloc)

Curtis, Price
See Ellison, Harlan (Jay)

Cutrate, Joe
See Spiegelman, Art

Cynewulf c. 770-c. 840............ **CMLC 23**

Czaczkes, Shmuel Yosef
See Agnon, S(hmuel) Y(osef Halevi)

Dabrowska, Maria (Szumska) 1889-1965.................... **CLC 15**
See CA 106

Dabydeen, David 1955-............. **CLC 34**
See BW 1; CA 125; CANR 56

Dacey, Philip 1939-.................**CLC 51**
See CA 37-40R; CAAS 17; CANR 14, 32, 64; DLB 105

Dagerman, Stig (Halvard) 1923-1954...................**TCLC 17**
See CA 117; 155

Dahl, Roald 1916-1990...... **CLC 1, 6, 18, 79; DAB; DAC; DAM MST, NOV, POP**
See AAYA 15; CA 1-4R; 133; CANR 6, 32, 37, 62; CLR 1, 7, 41; DLB 139; JRDA; MAICYA; MTCW 1, 2; SATA 1, 26, 73; SATA-Obit 65

Dahlberg, Edward 1900-1977.......**CLC 1, 7, 14**
See CA 9-12R; 69-72; CANR 31, 62; DLB 48; MTCW 1

Daitch, Susan 1954-............... **CLC 103**
See CA 161

Dale, Colin...................... **TCLC 18**
See Lawrence, T(homas) E(dward)

Dale, George E.
See Asimov, Isaac

Daly, Elizabeth 1878-1967........... **CLC 52**
See CA 23-24; 25-28R; CANR 60; CAP 2

Daly, Maureen 1921-............... **CLC 17**
See AAYA 5; CANR 37; JRDA; MAICYA; SAAS 1; SATA 2

Damas, Leon-Gontran 1912-1978..... **CLC 84**
See BW 1; CA 125; 73-76

Dana, Richard Henry Sr. 1787-1879..................**NCLC 53**

Daniel, Samuel 1562(?)-1619.......... **LC 24**
See DLB 62

Daniels, Brett
See Adler, Renata

Dannay, Frederic 1905-1982........ **CLC 11; DAM POP**
See Queen, Ellery

D Annunzio, Gabriele 1863-1938.....**TCLC 6, 40**
See CA 104; 155

Danois, N. le
See Gourmont, Remy (-Marie-Charles) de

Dante 1265-1321..... **CMLC 3, 18; DA; DAB; DAC; DAM MST, POET; PC 21; WLCS**

d'Antibes, Germain
See Simenon, Georges (Jacques Christian)

Danticat, Edwidge 1969-............ **CLC 94**
See AAYA 29; CA 152; CANR 73; MTCW 1

Danvers, Dennis 1947-.............. **CLC 70**

Danziger, Paula 1944-.............. **CLC 21**
See AAYA 4; CA 112; 115; CANR 37; CLR 20; JRDA; MAICYA; SATA 36, 63, 102; SATA-Brief 30

Da Ponte, Lorenzo 1749-1838.......**NCLC 50**

Dario, Ruben 1867-1916...... **TCLC 4; DAM MULT; HLC; PC 15**
See CA 131; HW 1, 2; MTCW 1, 2

Darley, George 1795-1846...........**NCLC 2**
See DLB 96

Darrow, Clarence (Seward) 1857-1938...................**TCLC 81**
See CA 164

Darwin, Charles 1809-1882.........**NCLC 57**
See DLB 57, 166

Daryush, Elizabeth 1887-1977......**CLC 6, 19**
See CA 49-52; CANR 3; DLB 20

Dasgupta, Surendranath 1887-1952...................**TCLC 81**
See CA 157

Dashwood, Edmee Elizabeth Monica de la Pasture 1890-1943
See Delafield, E. M.

Daudet, (Louis Marie) Alphonse 1840-1897....................**NCLC 1**
See DLB 123

Daumal, Rene 1908-1944...........**TCLC 14**
See CA 114

Davenant, William 1606-1668......... **LC 13**
See DLB 58, 126

Davenport, Guy (Mattison, Jr.) 1927-............**CLC 6, 14, 38; SSC 16**
See CA 33-36R; CANR 23, 73; DLB 130

Davidson, Avram (James) 1923-1993
See Queen, Ellery

Davidson, Donald (Grady) 1893-1968............... **CLC 2, 13, 19**
See CA 5-8R; 25-28R; CANR 4; DLB 45

Davidson, Hugh
See Hamilton, Edmond

Davidson, John 1857-1909..........**TCLC 24**
See CA 118; DLB 19

Davidson, Sara 1943-................ **CLC 9**
See CA 81-84; CANR 44, 68; DLB 185

Davie, Donald (Alfred) 1922-1995..... **CLC 5, 8, 10, 31**
See CA 1-4R; 149; CAAS 3; CANR 1, 44; DLB 27; MTCW 1

Deren, Maya 1917-1961. . . . . **CLC 16, 102**
See Deren, Eleanora

Derleth, August (William) 1909-1971. **CLC 31**
See CA 1-4R; 29-32R; CANR 4; DLB 9; DLBD 17; SATA 5

Der Nister 1884-1950. . . . . **TCLC 56**

de Routisie, Albert
See Aragon, Louis

Derrida, Jacques 1930-. . . . . **CLC 24, 87**
See CA 124; 127; CANR 76; MTCW 1

Derry Down Derry
See Lear, Edward

Dersonnes, Jacques
See Simenon, Georges (Jacques Christian)

Desai, Anita 1937-. . . . . . **CLC 19, 37, 97; DAB; DAM NOV**
See CA 81-84; CANR 33, 53; MTCW 1, 2; SATA 63

Desai, Kiran 1971-. . . . . **CLC 119**
See CA 171

de Saint-Luc, Jean
See Glassco, John

de Saint Roman, Arnaud
See Aragon, Louis

Descartes, Rene 1596-1650. . . . . **LC 20, 35**

De Sica, Vittorio 1901(?)-1974. . . . . **CLC 20**
See CA 117

Desnos, Robert 1900-1945. . . . . **TCLC 22**
See CA 121; 151

Destouches, Louis-Ferdinand 1894-1961. . . . . **CLC 9, 15**
See Celine, Louis-Ferdinand

de Tolignac, Gaston
See Griffith, D(avid Lewelyn) W(ark)

Deutsch, Babette 1895-1982. . . . . **CLC 18**
See CA 1-4R; 108; CANR 4, 79; DLB 45; SATA 1; SATA-Obit 33

Devenant, William 1606-1649. . . . . **LC 13**

Devkota, Laxmiprasad 1909-1959. . . . . . **TCLC 23**
See CA 123

De Voto, Bernard (Augustine) 1897-1955. . . . . **TCLC 29**
See CA 113; 160; DLB 9

De Vries, Peter 1910-1993. . . . . . **CLC 1, 2, 3, 7, 10, 28, 46; DAM NOV**
See CA 17-20R; 142; CANR 41; DLB 6; DLBY 82; MTCW 1, 2

Dexter, John
See Bradley, Marion Zimmer

Dexter, Martin
See Faust, Frederick (Schiller)

Dexter, Pete 1943-. . . . . **CLC 34, 55; DAM POP**
See BEST 89:2; CA 127; 131; INT 131; MTCW 1

Diamano, Silmang
See Senghor, Leopold Sedar

Diamond, Neil 1941-. . . . . **CLC 30**
See CA 108

Diaz del Castillo, Bernal 1496-1584. . . . . . . **LC 31; HLCS 1**

di Bassetto, Corno
See Shaw, George Bernard

Dick, Philip K(indred) 1928-1982. . . . . . . **CLC 10, 30, 72; DAM NOV, POP**
See AAYA 24; CA 49-52; 106; CANR 2, 16; DLB 8; MTCW 1, 2

Dickens, Charles (John Huffam) 1812-1870. . . . . **NCLC 3, 8, 18, 26, 37, 50; DA; DAB; DAC; DAM MST, NOV; SSC 17; WLC**
See AAYA 23; CDBLB 1832-1890; DLB 21, 55, 70, 159, 166; JRDA; MAICYA; SATA 15

Dickey, James (Lafayette) 1923-1997. . . . . . **CLC 1, 2, 4, 7, 10, 15, 47, 109; DAM NOV, POET, POP**
See AITN 1, 2; CA 9-12R; 156; CABS 2, CANR 10, 48, 61; CDALB 1968-1988; DLB 5, 193; DLBD 7; DLBY 82, 93, 96, 97, 98; INT CANR-10; MTCW 1, 2

Dickey, William 1928-1994. . . . . **CLC 3, 28**
See CA 9-12R; 145; CANR 24, 79; DLB 5

Dickinson, Charles 1951-. . . . . **CLC 49**
See CA 128

Dickinson, Emily (Elizabeth) 1830-1886. . . . . . **NCLC 21, 77; DA; DAB; DAC; DAM MST, POET; PC 1; WLC**
See AAYA 22; CDALB 1865-1917; DLB 1; SATA 29

Dickinson, Peter (Malcolm) 1927-. . . . . . . **CLC 12, 35**
See AAYA 9; CA 41-44R; CANR 31, 58; CLR 29; DLB 87, 161; JRDA; MAICYA; SATA 5, 62, 95

Dickson, Carr
See Carr, John Dickson

Dickson, Carter
See Carr, John Dickson

Diderot, Denis 1713-1784. . . . . **LC 26**

Didion, Joan 1934-. . . . . **CLC 1, 3, 8, 14, 32; DAM NOV**
See AITN 1; CA 5-8R; CANR 14, 52, 76; CDALB 1968-1988; DLB 2, 173, 185; DLBY 81, 86; MTCW 1, 2

Dietrich, Robert
See Hunt, E(verette) Howard, (Jr.)

Difusa, Pati
See Almodovar, Pedro

Dillard, Annie 1945-. . . . . **CLC 9, 60, 115; DAM NOV**
See AAYA 6; CA 49-52; CANR 3, 43, 62; DLBY 80; MTCW 1, 2; SATA 10

Dillard, R(ichard) H(enry) W(ilde) 1937-. . . . . **CLC 5**
See CA 21-24R; CAAS 7; CANR 10; DLB 5

Dillon, Eilis 1920-1994. . . . . **CLC 17**
See CA 9-12R; 147; CAAS 3; CANR 4, 38, 78; CLR 26; MAICYA; SATA 2, 74; SATA-Essay 105; SATA-Obit 83

Dimont, Penelope
See Mortimer, Penelope (Ruth)

Dinesen, Isak. . . . . **CLC 10, 29, 95; SSC 7**
See Blixen, Karen (Christentze Dinesen)

Ding Ling. . . . . **CLC 68**
See Chiang, Pin-chin

Diphusa, Patty
See Almodovar, Pedro

Disch, Thomas M(ichael) 1940-. . . . . **CLC 7, 36**
See AAYA 17; CA 21-24R; CAAS 4; CANR 17, 36, 54; CLR 18; DLB 8; MAICYA; MTCW 1, 2; SAAS 15; SATA 92

Disch, Tom
See Disch, Thomas M(ichael)

d'Isly, Georges
See Simenon, Georges (Jacques Christian)

Disraeli, Benjamin 1804-1881. . . . . **NCLC 2, 39**
See DLB 21, 55

Ditcum, Steve
See Crumb, R(obert)

Dixon, Paige
See Corcoran, Barbara

Dixon, Stephen 1936-. . . . . **CLC 52; SSC 16**
See CA 89-92; CANR 17, 40, 54; DLB 130

Doak, Annie
See Dillard, Annie

Dobell, Sydney Thompson 1824-1874. . . . . **NCLC 43**
See DLB 32

Doblin, Alfred. **TCLC 13**
See Doeblin, Alfred

Dobrolyubov, Nikolai Alexandrovich 1836-1861. **NCLC 5**

Dobson, Austin 1840-1921. . . . . **TCLC 79**
See DLB 35; 144

Dobyns, Stephen 1941-. . . . . **CLC 37**
See CA 45-48; CANR 2, 18

Doctorow, E(dgar) L(aurence) 1931-. . . . . **CLC 6, 11, 15, 18, 37, 44, 65, 113; DAM NOV, POP**
See AAYA 22; AITN 2; BEST 89:3; CA 45-48; CANR 2, 33, 51, 76; CDALB 1968-1988; DLB 2, 28, 173; DLBY 80; MTCW 1, 2

Dodgson, Charles Lutwidge 1832-1898
See Carroll, Lewis

Dodson, Owen (Vincent) 1914-1983. . . . . . **CLC 79; BLC 1; DAM MULT**
See BW 1; CA 65-68; 110; CANR 24; DLB 76

Doeblin, Alfred 1878-1957. . . . . **TCLC 13**
See Doblin, Alfred

Doerr, Harriet 1910-. . . . . **CLC 34**
See CA 117; 122; CANR 47; INT 122

Domecq, H(onorio) Bustos
See Bioy Casares, Adolfo; Borges, Jorge Luis

Domini, Rey
See Lorde, Audre (Geraldine)

Dominique
See Proust, (Valentin-Louis-George-Eugene-) Marcel

Don, A
See Stephen, SirLeslie

Donaldson, Stephen R. 1947-. . . . . **CLC 46; DAM POP**
See CA 89-92; CANR 13, 55; INT CANR-13

Endo, Shusaku 1923-1996...... **CLC 7, 14, 19, 54, 99; DAM NOV**
See CA 29-32R; 153; CANR 21, 54; DLB 182; MTCW 1, 2

Engel, Marian 1933-1985............ **CLC 36**
See CA 25-28R; CANR 12; DLB 53; INT CANR-12

Engelhardt, Frederick
See Hubbard, L(afayette) Ron(ald)

Enright, D(ennis) J(oseph) 1920-...... **CLC 4, 8, 31**
See CA 1-4R; CANR 1, 42; DLB 27; SATA 25

Enzensberger, Hans Magnus 1929-...... **CLC 43**
See CA 116; 119

Ephron, Nora 1941-............. **CLC 17, 31**
See AITN 2; CA 65-68; CANR 12, 39

Epicurus 341B.C.-270B.C......... **CMLC 21**
See DLB 176

Epsilon
See Betjeman, John

Epstein, Daniel Mark 1948-........... **CLC 7**
See CA 49-52; CANR 2, 53

Epstein, Jacob 1956-................ **CLC 19**
See CA 114

Epstein, Jean 1897-1953........... **TCLC 92**

Epstein, Joseph 1937-............... **CLC 39**
See CA 112; 119; CANR 50, 65

Epstein, Leslie 1938-................ **CLC 27**
See CA 73-76; CAAS 12; CANR 23, 69

Equiano, Olaudah 1745(?)-1797....... **LC 16; BLC 2; DAM MULT**
See DLB 37, 50

ER............................ **TCLC 33**
See CA 160; DLB 85

Erasmus, Desiderius 1469(?)-1536...... **LC 16**

Erdman, Paul E(mil) 1932-.......... **CLC 25**
See AITN 1; CA 61-64; CANR 13, 43

Erdrich, Louise 1954-....... **CLC 39, 54, 120; DAM MULT, NOV, POP**
See AAYA 10; BEST 89:1; CA 114; CANR 41, 62; CDALBS; DLB 152, 175, 206; MTCW 1; NNAL; SATA 94

Erenburg, Ilya (Grigoryevich)
See Ehrenburg, Ilya (Grigoryevich)

Erickson, Stephen Michael 1950-
See Erickson, Steve

Erickson, Steve 1950-............... **CLC 64**
See Erickson, Stephen Michael

Ericson, Walter
See Fast, Howard (Melvin)

Eriksson, Buntel
See Bergman, (Ernst) Ingmar

Ernaux, Annie 1940-................ **CLC 88**
See CA 147

Erskine, John 1879-1951........... **TCLC 84**
See CA 112; 159; DLB 9, 102

Eschenbach, Wolfram von
See Wolfram von Eschenbach

Eseki, Bruno
See Mphahlele, Ezekiel

Esenin, Sergei (Alexandrovich) 1895-1925.................... **TCLC 4**
See CA 104

Eshleman, Clayton 1935-............. **CLC 7**
See CA 33-36R; CAAS 6; DLB 5

Espriella, Don Manuel Alvarez
See Southey, Robert

Espriu, Salvador 1913-1985........... **CLC 9**
See CA 154; 115; DLB 134

Espronceda, Jose de 1808-1842..... **NCLC 39**

Esse, James
See Stephens, James

Esterbrook, Tom
See Hubbard, L(afayette) Ron(ald)

Estleman, Loren D. 1952-...... **CLC 48; DAM NOV, POP**
See AAYA 27; CA 85-88; CANR 27, 74; INT CANR-27; MTCW 1, 2

Euclid 306B.C.-283B.C............ **CMLC 25**

Eugenides, Jeffrey 1960(?)-.......... **CLC 81**
See CA 144

Euripides c. 485B.C.-406B.C...... **CMLC 23; DA; DAB; DAC; DAM DRAM, MST; DC 4; WLCS**
See DLB 176

Evan, Evin
See Faust, Frederick (Schiller)

Evans, Caradoc 1878-1945......... **TCLC 85**

Evans, Evan
See Faust, Frederick (Schiller)

Evans, Marian
See Eliot, George

Evans, Mary Ann
See Eliot, George

Evarts, Esther
See Benson, Sally

Everett, Percival L. 1956-........... **CLC 57**
See BW 2; CA 129

Everson, R(onald) G(ilmour) 1903-...... **CLC 27**
See CA 17-20R; DLB 88

Everson, William (Oliver) 1912-1994................ **CLC 1, 5, 14**
See CA 9-12R; 145; CANR 20; DLB 212; MTCW 1

Evtushenko, Evgenii Aleksandrovich
See Yevtushenko, Yevgeny (Alexandrovich)

Ewart, Gavin (Buchanan) 1916-1995..... **CLC 13, 46**
See CA 89-92; 150; CANR 17, 46; DLB 40; MTCW 1

Ewers, Hanns Heinz 1871-1943..... **TCLC 12**
See CA 109; 149

Ewing, Frederick R.
See Sturgeon, Theodore (Hamilton)

Exley, Frederick (Earl) 1929-1992..... **CLC 6, 11**
See AITN 2; CA 81-84; 138; DLB 143; DLBY 81

Eynhardt, Guillermo
See Quiroga, Horacio (Sylvestre)

Ezekiel, Nissim 1924-............... **CLC 61**
See CA 61-64

Ezekiel, Tish O'Dowd 1943-......... **CLC 34**
See CA 129

Fadeyev, A.
See Bulgya, Alexander Alexandrovich

Fadeyev, Alexander............... **TCLC 53**
See Bulgya, Alexander Alexandrovich

Fagen, Donald 1948-................ **CLC 26**

Fainzilberg, Ilya Arnoldovich 1897-1937
See Ilf, Ilya

Fair, Ronald L. 1932-............... **CLC 18**
See BW 1; CA 69-72; CANR 25; DLB 33

Fairbairn, Roger
See Carr, John Dickson

Fairbairns, Zoe (Ann) 1948-......... **CLC 32**
See CA 103; CANR 21

Falco, Gian
See Papini, Giovanni

Falconer, James
See Kirkup, James

Falconer, Kenneth
See Kornbluth, C(yril) M.

Falkland, Samuel
See Heijermans, Herman

Fallaci, Oriana 1930-........... **CLC 11, 110**
See CA 77-80; CANR 15, 58; MTCW 1

Faludy, George 1913-............... **CLC 42**
See CA 21-24R

Faludy, Gyoergy
See Faludy, George

Fanon, Frantz 1925-1961....... **CLC 74; BLC 2; DAM MULT**
See BW 1; CA 116; 89-92

Fanshawe, Ann 1625-1680............ **LC 11**

Fante, John (Thomas) 1911-1983..... **CLC 60**
See CA 69-72; 109; CANR 23; DLB 130; DLBY 83

Farah, Nuruddin 1945-...... **CLC 53; BLC 2; DAM MULT**
See BW 2, 3; CA 106; DLB 125

Fargue, Leon-Paul 1876(?)-1947..... **TCLC 11**
See CA 109

Farigoule, Louis
See Romains, Jules

Farina, Richard 1936(?)-1966......... **CLC 9**
See CA 81-84; 25-28R

Farley, Walter (Lorimer) 1915-1989..... **CLC 17**
See CA 17-20R; CANR 8, 29; DLB 22; JRDA; MAICYA; SATA 2, 43

Farmer, Philip Jose 1918-......... **CLC 1, 19**
See AAYA 28; CA 1-4R; CANR 4, 35; DLB 8; MTCW 1; SATA 93

Farquhar, George 1677-1707......... **LC 21; DAM DRAM**
See DLB 84

Farrell, J(ames) G(ordon) 1935-1979..................... **CLC 6**
See CA 73-76; 89-92; CANR 36; DLB 14; MTCW 1

Author Index

Farrell, James T(homas) 1904-1979. . . . . .**CLC 1, 4, 8, 11, 66; SSC 28**
See CA 5-8R; 89-92; CANR 9, 61; DLB 4, 9, 86; DLBD 2; MTCW 1, 2

Farren, Richard J.
See Betjeman, John

Farren, Richard M.
See Betjeman, John

Fassbinder, Rainer Werner 1946-1982. **CLC 20**
See CA 93-96; 106; CANR 31

Fast, Howard (Melvin) 1914-. . . . . **CLC 23; DAM NOV**
See AAYA 16; CA 1-4R; CAAS 18; CANR 1, 33, 54, 75; DLB 9; INT CANR-33; MTCW 1; SATA 7; SATA-Essay 107

Faulcon, Robert
See Holdstock, Robert P.

Faulkner, William (Cuthbert) 1897-1962. . . . . . .**CLC 1, 3, 6, 8, 9, 11, 14, 18, 28, 52, 68; DA; DAB; DAC; DAM MST, NOV; SSC 1, 35; WLC**
See AAYA 7; CA 81-84; CANR 33; CDALB 1929-1941; DLB 9, 11, 44, 102; DLBD 2; DLBY 86, 97; MTCW 1, 2

Fauset, Jessie Redmon 1884(?)-1961. . . . . **CLC 19, 54; BLC 2; DAM MULT**
See BW 1; CA 109; DLB 51

Faust, Frederick (Schiller) 1892-1944(?). . . . . . **TCLC 49; DAM POP**
See CA 108; 152

Faust, Irvin 1924-. . . . .**CLC 8**
See CA 33-36R; CANR 28, 67; DLB 2, 28; DLBY 80

Fawkes, Guy
See Benchley, Robert (Charles)

Fearing, Kenneth (Flexner) 1902-1961. . . . . **CLC 51**
See CA 93-96; CANR 59; DLB 9

Fecamps, Elise
See Creasey, John

Federman, Raymond 1928-. . . . . **CLC 6, 47**
See CA 17-20R; CAAS 8; CANR 10, 43; DLBY 80

Federspiel, J(uerg) F. 1931-. . . . .**CLC 42**
See CA 146

Feiffer, Jules (Ralph) 1929-. . . . . **CLC 2, 8, 64; DAM DRAM**
See AAYA 3; CA 17-20R; CANR 30, 59; DLB 7, 44; INT CANR-30; MTCW 1; SATA 8, 61

Feige, Hermann Albert Otto Maximilian
See Traven, B.

Feinberg, David B. 1956-1994. . . . . **CLC 59**
See CA 135; 147

Feinstein, Elaine 1930-. . . . .**CLC 36**
See CA 69-72; CAAS 1; CANR 31, 68; DLB 14, 40; MTCW 1

Feldman, Irving (Mordecai) 1928-. . . . . **CLC 7**
See CA 1-4R; CANR 1; DLB 169

Felix-Tchicaya, Gerald
See Tchicaya, Gerald Felix

Fellini, Federico 1920-1993. . . . . . . **CLC 16, 85**
See CA 65-68; 143; CANR 33

Felsen, Henry Gregor 1916-. . . . .**CLC 17**
See CA 1-4R; CANR 1; SAAS 2; SATA 1

Fenno, Jack
See Calisher, Hortense

Fenollosa, Ernest (Francisco) 1853-1908. . . . .**TCLC 91**

Fenton, James Martin 1949-. . . . . **CLC 32**
See CA 102; DLB 40

Ferber, Edna 1887-1968. . . . .**CLC 18, 93**
See AITN 1; CA 5-8R; 25-28R; CANR 68; DLB 9, 28, 86; MTCW 1, 2; SATA 7

Ferguson, Helen
See Kavan, Anna

Ferguson, Samuel 1810-1886. . . . . . . **NCLC 33**
See DLB 32

Fergusson, Robert 1750-1774. . . . .**LC 29**
See DLB 109

Ferling, Lawrence
See Ferlinghetti, Lawrence (Monsanto)

Ferlinghetti, Lawrence (Monsanto) 1919(?)-. . . . . **CLC 2, 6, 10, 27, 111; DAM POET; PC 1**
See CA 5-8R; CANR 3, 41, 73; CDALB 1941-1968; DLB 5, 16; MTCW 1, 2

Fernandez, Vicente Garcia Huidobro
See Huidobro Fernandez, Vicente Garcia

Ferrer, Gabriel (Francisco Victor) Miro
See Miro (Ferrer), Gabriel (Francisco Victor)

Ferrier, Susan (Edmonstone) 1782-1854. . . . .**NCLC 8**
See DLB 116

Ferrigno, Robert 1948(?)-. . . . . **CLC 65**
See CA 140

Ferron, Jacques 1921-1985. . . . . **CLC 94; DAC**
See CA 117; 129; DLB 60

Feuchtwanger, Lion 1884-1958. . . . . . .**TCLC 3**
See CA 104; DLB 66

Feuillet, Octave 1821-1890. . . . . **NCLC 45**
See DLB 192

Feydeau, Georges (Leon Jules Marie) 1862-1921. . . . . . **TCLC 22; DAM DRAM**
See CA 113; 152; DLB 192

Fichte, Johann Gottlieb 1762-1814. . . . . **NCLC 62**
See DLB 90

Ficino, Marsilio 1433-1499. . . . . **LC 12**

Fiedeler, Hans
See Doeblin, Alfred

Fiedler, Leslie A(aron) 1917-. . . . . . **CLC 4, 13, 24**
See CA 9-12R; CANR 7, 63; DLB 28, 67; MTCW 1, 2

Field, Andrew 1938-. . . . . **CLC 44**
See CA 97-100; CANR 25

Field, Eugene 1850-1895. . . . .**NCLC 3**
See DLB 23, 42, 140; DLBD 13; MAICYA; SATA 16

Field, Gans T.
See Wellman, Manly Wade

Field, Michael 1915-1971. . . . .**TCLC 43**
See CA 29-32R

Field, Peter
See Hobson, Laura Z(ametkin)

Fielding, Henry 1707-1754. . . . . **LC 1, 46; DA; DAB; DAC; DAM DRAM, MST, NOV; WLC**
See CDBLB 1660-1789; DLB 39, 84, 101

Fielding, Sarah 1710-1768. . . . . **LC 1, 44**
See DLB 39

Fields, W. C. 1880-1946. . . . .**TCLC 80**
See DLB 44

Fierstein, Harvey (Forbes) 1954-. . . . . **CLC 33; DAM DRAM, POP**
See CA 123; 129

Figes, Eva 1932-. . . . . **CLC 31**
See CA 53-56; CANR 4, 44; DLB 14

Finch, Anne 1661-1720. . . . .**LC 3; PC 21**
See DLB 95

Finch, Robert (Duer Claydon) 1900-. . . . . **CLC 18**
See CA 57-60; CANR 9, 24, 49; DLB 88

Findley, Timothy 1930-. . . . .**CLC 27, 102; DAC; DAM MST**
See CA 25-28R; CANR 12, 42, 69; DLB 53

Fink, William
See Mencken, H(enry) L(ouis)

Firbank, Louis 1942-
See Reed, Lou

Firbank, (Arthur Annesley) Ronald 1886-1926. . . . .**TCLC 1**
See CA 104; DLB 36

Fisher, Dorothy (Frances) Canfield 1879-1958. . . . .**TCLC 87**
See CA 114; 136; CANR 80; DLB 9, 102; MAICYA; YABC 1

Fisher, M(ary) F(rances) K(ennedy) 1908-1992. . . . . **CLC 76, 87**
See CA 77-80; 138; CANR 44; MTCW 1

Fisher, Roy 1930-. . . . . **CLC 25**
See CA 81-84; CAAS 10; CANR 16; DLB 40

Fisher, Rudolph 1897-1934. . . . . **TCLC 11; BLC 2; DAM MULT; SSC 25**
See BW 1, 3; CA 107; 124; CANR 80; DLB 51, 102

Fisher, Vardis (Alvero) 1895-1968. . . . . **CLC 7**
See CA 5-8R; 25-28R; CANR 68; DLB 9, 206

Fiske, Tarleton
See Bloch, Robert (Albert)

Fitch, Clarke
See Sinclair, Upton (Beall)

Fitch, John IV
See Cormier, Robert (Edmund)

Fitzgerald, Captain Hugh
See Baum, L(yman) Frank

FitzGerald, Edward 1809-1883. . . . . . **NCLC 9**
See DLB 32

Fitzgerald, F(rancis) Scott (Key) 1896-1940. . . . . . . **TCLC 1, 6, 14, 28, 55; DA; DAB; DAC; DAM MST, NOV; SSC 6, 31; WLC**
See AAYA 24; AITN 1; CA 110; 123; CDALB 1917-1929; DLB 4, 9, 86; DLBD 1, 15, 16; DLBY 81, 96; MTCW 1, 2

Fitzgerald, Penelope 1916-.....**CLC 19, 51, 61**
See CA 85-88; CAAS 10; CANR 56; DLB 14, 194; MTCW 2

Fitzgerald, Robert (Stuart) 1910-1985....................**CLC 39**
See CA 1-4R; 114; CANR 1; DLBY 80

FitzGerald, Robert D(avid) 1902-1987....................**CLC 19**
See CA 17-20R

Fitzgerald, Zelda (Sayre) 1900-1948...................**TCLC 52**
See CA 117; 126; DLBY 84

Flanagan, Thomas (James Bonner) 1923-.....................**CLC 25, 52**
See CA 108; CANR 55; DLBY 80; INT 108; MTCW 1

Flaubert, Gustave 1821-1880.....**NCLC 2, 10, 19, 62, 66; DA; DAB; DAC; DAM MST, NOV; SSC 11; WLC**
See DLB 119

Flecker, Herman Elroy
See Flecker, (Herman) James Elroy

Flecker, (Herman) James Elroy 1884-1915...................**TCLC 43**
See CA 109; 150; DLB 10, 19

Fleming, Ian (Lancaster) 1908-1964..... **CLC 3, 30; DAM POP**
See AAYA 26; CA 5-8R; CANR 59; CDBLB 1945-1960; DLB 87, 201; MTCW 1, 2; SATA 9

Fleming, Thomas (James) 1927-...... **CLC 37**
See CA 5-8R; CANR 10; INT CANR-10; SATA 8

Fletcher, John 1579-1625........**LC 33; DC 6**
See CDBLB Before 1660; DLB 58

Fletcher, John Gould 1886-1950.....**TCLC 35**
See CA 107; 167; DLB 4, 45

Fleur, Paul
See Pohl, Frederik

Flooglebuckle, Al
See Spiegelman, Art

Flying Officer X
See Bates, H(erbert) E(rnest)

Fo, Dario 1926-.......... **CLC 32, 109; DAM DRAM; DC 10**
See CA 116; 128; CANR 68; DLBY 97; MTCW 1, 2

Fogarty, Jonathan Titulescu Esq.
See Farrell, James T(homas)

Folke, Will
See Bloch, Robert (Albert)

Follett, Ken(neth Martin) 1949-......**CLC 18; DAM NOV, POP**
See AAYA 6; BEST 89:4; CA 81-84; CANR 13, 33, 54; DLB 87; DLBY 81; INT CANR-33; MTCW 1

Fontane, Theodor 1819-1898....... **NCLC 26**
See DLB 129

Foote, Horton 1916-....... **CLC 51, 91; DAM DRAM**
See CA 73-76; CANR 34, 51; DLB 26; INT CANR-34

Foote, Shelby 1916-..... **CLC 75; DAM NOV, POP**
See CA 5-8R; CANR 3, 45, 74; DLB 2, 17; MTCW 2

Forbes, Esther 1891-1967............**CLC 12**
See AAYA 17; CA 13-14; 25-28R; CAP 1; CLR 27; DLB 22; JRDA; MAICYA; SATA 2, 100

Forche, Carolyn (Louise) 1950-...... **CLC 25, 83, 86; DAM POET; PC 10**
See CA 109; 117; CANR 50, 74; DLB 5, 193; INT 117; MTCW 1

Ford, Elbur
See Hibbert, Eleanor Alice Burford

Ford, Ford Madox 1873-1939....... **TCLC 1, 15, 39, 57; DAM NOV**
See CA 104; 132; CANR 74; CDBLB 1914-1945; DLB 162; MTCW 1, 2

Ford, Henry 1863-1947............ **TCLC 73**
See CA 115; 148

Ford, John 1586-(?)...................**DC 8**
See CDBLB Before 1660; DAM DRAM; DLB 58

Ford, John 1895-1973...............**CLC 16**
See CA 45-48

Ford, Richard 1944-.............**CLC 46, 99**
See CA 69-72; CANR 11, 47; MTCW 1

Ford, Webster
See Masters, Edgar Lee

Foreman, Richard 1937-............ **CLC 50**
See CA 65-68; CANR 32, 63

Forester, C(ecil) S(cott) 1899-1966.......**CLC 35**
See CA 73-76; 25-28R; DLB 191; SATA 13

Forez
See Mauriac, Francois (Charles)

Forman, James Douglas 1932-........**CLC 21**
See AAYA 17; CA 9-12R; CANR 4, 19, 42; JRDA; MAICYA; SATA 8, 70

Fornes, Maria Irene 1930-....... **CLC 39, 61; DC 10; HLCS 1**
See CA 25-28R; CANR 28; DLB 7; HW 1, 2; INT CANR-28; MTCW 1

Forrest, Leon (Richard) 1937-1997...... **CLC 4; BLCS**
See BW 2; CA 89-92; 162; CAAS 7; CANR 25, 52; DLB 33

Forster, E(dward) M(organ) 1879-1970.......**CLC 1, 2, 3, 4, 9, 10, 13, 15, 22, 45, 77; DA; DAB; DAC; DAM MST, NOV; SSC 27; WLC**
See AAYA 2; CA 13-14; 25-28R; CANR 45; CAP 1; CDBLB 1914-1945; DLB 34, 98, 162, 178, 195; DLBD 10; MTCW 1, 2; SATA 57

Forster, John 1812-1876........... **NCLC 11**
See DLB 144, 184

Forsyth, Frederick 1938-....... **CLC 2, 5, 36; DAM NOV, POP**
See BEST 89:4; CA 85-88; CANR 38, 62; DLB 87; MTCW 1, 2

Forten, Charlotte L......... **TCLC 16; BLC 2**
See Grimke, Charlotte L(ottie) Forten

Foscolo, Ugo 1778-1827.............**NCLC 8**

Fosse, Bob........................ **CLC 20**
See Fosse, Robert Louis

Fosse, Robert Louis 1927-1987
See Fosse, Bob

Foster, Stephen Collins 1826-1864..... **NCLC 26**

Foucault, Michel 1926-1984...... **CLC 31, 34, 69**
See CA 105; 113; CANR 34; MTCW 1, 2

Fouque, Friedrich (Heinrich Karl) de la Motte 1777-1843...................**NCLC 2**
See DLB 90

Fourier, Charles 1772-1837........ **NCLC 51**

Fournier, Henri Alban 1886-1914
See Alain-Fournier

Fournier, Pierre 1916-.............. **CLC 11**
See Gascar, Pierre

Fowles, John (Philip) 1926-.....**CLC 1, 2, 3, 4, 6, 9, 10, 15, 33, 87; DAB; DAC; DAM MST; SSC 33**
See CA 5-8R; CANR 25, 71; CDBLB 1960 to Present; DLB 14, 139, 207; MTCW 1, 2; SATA 22

Fox, Paula 1923-.................. **CLC 2, 8**
See AAYA 3; CA 73-76; CANR 20, 36, 62; CLR 1, 44; DLB 52; JRDA; MAICYA; MTCW 1; SATA 17, 60

Fox, William Price (Jr.) 1926-........**CLC 22**
See CA 17-20R; CAAS 19; CANR 11; DLB 2; DLBY 81

Foxe, John 1516(?)-1587.............. **LC 14**
See DLB 132

Frame, Janet 1924-....... **CLC 2, 3, 6, 22, 66, 96; SSC 29**
See Clutha, Janet Paterson Frame

France, Anatole................... **TCLC 9**
See Thibault, Jacques Anatole Francois

Francis, Claude 19(?)-.............. **CLC 50**

Francis, Dick 1920-....... **CLC 2, 22, 42, 102; DAM POP**
See AAYA 5, 21; BEST 89:3; CA 5-8R; CANR 9, 42, 68; CDBLB 1960 to Present; DLB 87; INT CANR-9; MTCW 1, 2

Francis, Robert (Churchill) 1901-1987..................... **CLC 15**
See CA 1-4R; 123; CANR 1

Frank, Anne(lies Marie) 1929-1945.....**TCLC 17; DA; DAB; DAC; DAM MST; WLC**
See AAYA 12; CA 113; 133; CANR 68; MTCW 1, 2; SATA 87; SATA-Brief 42

Frank, Bruno 1887-1945........... **TCLC 81**
See DLB 118

Frank, Elizabeth 1945-..............**CLC 39**
See CA 121; 126; CANR 78; INT 126

Frankl, Viktor E(mil) 1905-1997......**CLC 93**
See CA 65-68; 161

Franklin, Benjamin
See Hasek, Jaroslav (Matej Frantisek)

Franklin, Benjamin 1706-1790........ **LC 25; DA; DAB; DAC; DAM MST; WLCS**
See CDALB 1640-1865; DLB 24, 43, 73

Franklin, (Stella Maria Sarah) Miles (Lampe) 1879-1954. **TCLC 7**
See CA 104; 164

Fraser, (Lady) Antonia (Pakenham) 1932-. **CLC 32, 107**
See CA 85-88; CANR 44, 65; MTCW 1, 2; SATA-Brief 32

Fraser, George MacDonald 1925-. . . . . . **CLC 7**
See CA 45-48; CANR 2, 48, 74; MTCW 1

Fraser, Sylvia 1935-. . . . . **CLC 64**
See CA 45-48; CANR 1, 16, 60

Frayn, Michael 1933-. . . . . . . **CLC 3, 7, 31, 47; DAM DRAM, NOV**
See CA 5-8R; CANR 30, 69; DLB 13, 14, 194; MTCW 1, 2

Fraze, Candida (Merrill) 1945-. . . . . . . **CLC 50**
See CA 126

Frazer, J(ames) G(eorge) 1854-1941. . . . . **TCLC 32**
See CA 118

Frazer, Robert Caine
See Creasey, John

Frazer, Sir James George
See Frazer, J(ames) G(eorge)

Frazier, Charles 1950-. . . . . **CLC 109**
See CA 161

Frazier, Ian 1951-. . . . . **CLC 46**
See CA 130; CANR 54

Frederic, Harold 1856-1898. . . . . **NCLC 10**
See DLB 12, 23; DLBD 13

Frederick, John
See Faust, Frederick (Schiller)

Frederick the Great 1712-1786. . . . . **LC 14**

Fredro, Aleksander 1793-1876. . . . . . . **NCLC 8**

Freeling, Nicolas 1927-. . . . . **CLC 38**
See CA 49-52; CAAS 12; CANR 1, 17, 50; DLB 87

Freeman, Douglas Southall 1886-1953. . . . . **TCLC 11**
See CA 109; DLB 17; DLBD 17

Freeman, Judith 1946-. . . . . **CLC 55**
See CA 148

Freeman, Mary Eleanor Wilkins 1852-1930. . . . . **TCLC 9; SSC 1**
See CA 106; DLB 12, 78

Freeman, R(ichard) Austin 1862-1943. . . . . **TCLC 21**
See CA 113; DLB 70

French, Albert 1943-. . . . . **CLC 86**
See BW 3; CA 167

French, Marilyn 1929-. . . . . . . **CLC 10, 18, 60; DAM DRAM, NOV, POP**
See CA 69-72; CANR 3, 31; INT CANR-31; MTCW 1, 2

French, Paul
See Asimov, Isaac

Freneau, Philip Morin 1752-1832. . . . . **NCLC 1**
See DLB 37, 43

Freud, Sigmund 1856-1939. . . . . **TCLC 52**
See CA 115; 133; CANR 69; MTCW 1, 2

Friedan, Betty (Naomi) 1921-. . . . . **CLC 74**
See CA 65-68; CANR 18, 45, 74; MTCW 1, 2

Friedlander, Saul 1932-. . . . . **CLC 90**
See CA 117; 130; CANR 72

Friedman, B(ernard) H(arper) 1926-. . . . . **CLC 7**
See CA 1-4R; CANR 3, 48

Friedman, Bruce Jay 1930-. . . . . . **CLC 3, 5, 56**
See CA 9-12R; CANR 25, 52; DLB 2, 28; INT CANR-25

Friel, Brian 1929-. . . . . **CLC 5, 42, 59, 115; DC 8**
See CA 21-24R; CANR 33, 69; DLB 13; MTCW 1

Friis-Baastad, Babbis Ellinor 1921-1970. **CLC 12**
See CA 17-20R; 134; SATA 7

Frisch, Max (Rudolf) 1911-1991. . . . . **CLC 3, 9, 14, 18, 32, 44; DAM DRAM, NOV**
See CA 85-88; 134; CANR 32, 74; DLB 69, 124; MTCW 1, 2

Fromentin, Eugene (Samuel Auguste) 1820-1876. . . . . **NCLC 10**
See DLB 123

Frost, Frederick
See Faust, Frederick (Schiller)

Frost, Robert (Lee) 1874-1963. . . . . . **CLC 1, 3, 4, 9, 10, 13, 15, 26, 34, 44; DA; DAB; DAC; DAM MST, POET; PC 1; WLC**
See AAYA 21; CA 89-92; CANR 33; CDALB 1917-1929; DLB 54; DLBD 7; MTCW 1, 2; SATA 14

Froude, James Anthony 1818-1894. . . . . **NCLC 43**
See DLB 18, 57, 144

Froy, Herald
See Waterhouse, Keith (Spencer)

Fry, Christopher 1907-. . . . . **CLC 2, 10, 14; DAM DRAM**
See CA 17-20R; CAAS 23; CANR 9, 30, 74; DLB 13; MTCW 1, 2; SATA 66

Frye, (Herman) Northrop 1912-1991. . . . . **CLC 24, 70**
See CA 5-8R; 133; CANR 8, 37; DLB 67, 68; MTCW 1, 2

Fuchs, Daniel 1909-1993. . . . . **CLC 8, 22**
See CA 81-84; 142; CAAS 5; CANR 40; DLB 9, 26, 28; DLBY 93

Fuchs, Daniel 1934-. . . . . **CLC 34**
See CA 37-40R; CANR 14, 48

Fuentes, Carlos 1928-. . . . . . . **CLC 3, 8, 10, 13, 22, 41, 60, 113; DA; DAB; DAC; DAM MST, MULT, NOV; HLC; SSC 24; WLC**
See AAYA 4; AITN 2; CA 69-72; CANR 10, 32, 68; DLB 113; HW 1, 2; MTCW 1, 2

Fuentes, Gregorio Lopez y
See Lopez y Fuentes, Gregorio

Fugard, (Harold) Athol 1932-. . . . . . . **CLC 5, 9, 14, 25, 40, 80; DAM DRAM; DC 3**
See AAYA 17; CA 85-88; CANR 32, 54; MTCW 1

Fugard, Sheila 1932-. . . . . **CLC 48**
See CA 125

Fuller, Charles (H., Jr.) 1939-. . . . . . . **CLC 25; BLC 2; DAM DRAM, MULT; DC 1**
See BW 2; CA 108; 112; DLB 38; INT 112; MTCW 1

Fuller, John (Leopold) 1937-. . . . . **CLC 62**
See CA 21-24R; CANR 9, 44; DLB 40

Fuller, Margaret. . . . . **NCLC 5, 50**
See Ossoli, Sarah Margaret (Fuller marchesa d')

Fuller, Roy (Broadbent) 1912-1991. . . . . . **CLC 4, 28**
See CA 5-8R; 135; CAAS 10; CANR 53; DLB 15, 20; SATA 87

Fulton, Alice 1952-. . . . . **CLC 52**
See CA 116; CANR 57; DLB 193

Furphy, Joseph 1843-1912. . . . . **TCLC 25**
See CA 163

Fussell, Paul 1924-. . . . . **CLC 74**
See BEST 90:1; CA 17-20R; CANR 8, 21, 35, 69; INT CANR-21; MTCW 1, 2

Futabatei, Shimei 1864-1909. . . . . **TCLC 44**
See CA 162; DLB 180

Futrelle, Jacques 1875-1912. . . . . **TCLC 19**
See CA 113; 155

Gaboriau, Emile 1835-1873. . . . . **NCLC 14**

Gadda, Carlo Emilio 1893-1973. . . . . . **CLC 11**
See CA 89-92; DLB 177

Gaddis, William 1922-1998. . . . . **CLC 1, 3, 6, 8, 10, 19, 43, 86**
See CA 17-20R; 172; CANR 21, 48; DLB 2; MTCW 1, 2

Gage, Walter
See Inge, William (Motter)

Gaines, Ernest J(ames) 1933-. . . . . . **CLC 3, 11, 18, 86; BLC 2; DAM MULT**
See AAYA 18; AITN 1; BW 2, 3; CA 9-12R; CANR 6, 24, 42, 75; CDALB 1968-1988; DLB 2, 33, 152; DLBY 80; MTCW 1, 2; SATA 86

Gaitskill, Mary 1954-. . . . . **CLC 69**
See CA 128; CANR 61

Galdos, Benito Perez
See Perez Galdos, Benito

Gale, Zona 1874-1938. . . . . **TCLC 7; DAM DRAM**
See CA 105; 153; DLB 9, 78

Galeano, Eduardo (Hughes) 1940-. . . . . . . **CLC 72; HLCS 1**
See CA 29-32R; CANR 13, 32; HW 1

Galiano, Juan Valera y Alcala
See Valera y Alcala-Galiano, Juan

Galilei, Galileo 1546-1642. . . . . **LC 45**

Gallagher, Tess 1943-. . . . . . **CLC 18, 63; DAM POET; PC 9**
See CA 106; DLB 212

Gallant, Mavis 1922-. . . . . **CLC 7, 18, 38; DAC; DAM MST; SSC 5**
See CA 69-72; CANR 29, 69; DLB 53; MTCW 1, 2

Gallant, Roy A(rthur) 1924-. . . . . **CLC 17**
See CA 5-8R; CANR 4, 29, 54; CLR 30; MAICYA; SATA 4, 68

Gallico, Paul (William) 1897-1976. . . . . **CLC 2**
See AITN 1; CA 5-8R; 69-72; CANR 23; DLB 9, 171; MAICYA; SATA 13

Gallo, Max Louis 1932-. . . . . **CLC 95**
See CA 85-88

Gallois, Lucien
See Desnos, Robert

Gallup, Ralph
See Whitemore, Hugh (John)

Galsworthy, John 1867-1933. . . . . **TCLC 1, 45; DA; DAB; DAC; DAM DRAM, MST, NOV; SSC 22; WLC**
See CA 104; 141; CANR 75; CDBLB 1890-1914; DLB 10, 34, 98, 162; DLBD 16; MTCW 1

Galt, John 1779-1839. . . . .**NCLC 1**
See DLB 99, 116, 159

Galvin, James 1951-. . . . . **CLC 38**
See CA 108; CANR 26

Gamboa, Federico 1864-1939. . . . . . . **TCLC 36**
See CA 167; HW 2

Gandhi, M. K.
See Gandhi, Mohandas Karamchand

Gandhi, Mahatma
See Gandhi, Mohandas Karamchand

Gandhi, Mohandas Karamchand
1869-1948. . . . . . **TCLC 59; DAM MULT**
See CA 121; 132; MTCW 1, 2

Gann, Ernest Kellogg 1910-1991. . . . . .**CLC 23**
See AITN 1; CA 1-4R; 136; CANR 1

Garcia, Cristina 1958-. . . . . **CLC 76**
See CA 141; CANR 73; HW 2

Garcia Lorca, Federico 1898-1936. . . . . **TCLC 1, 7, 49; DA; DAB; DAC; DAM DRAM, MST, MULT, POET; DC 2; HLC; PC 3; WLC**
See CA 104; 131; DLB 108; HW 1, 2; MTCW 1, 2

Garcia Marquez, Gabriel (Jose)
1928-. . . . . .**CLC 2, 3, 8, 10, 15, 27, 47, 55, 68; DA; DAB; DAC; DAM MST, MULT, NOV, POP; HLC; SSC 8; WLC**
See AAYA 3; BEST 89:1, 90:4; CA 33-36R; CANR 10, 28, 50, 75; DLB 113; HW 1, 2; MTCW 1, 2

Gard, Janice
See Latham, Jean Lee

Gard, Roger Martin du
See Martin du Gard, Roger

Gardam, Jane 1928-. . . . . **CLC 43**
See CA 49-52; CANR 2, 18, 33, 54; CLR 12; DLB 14, 161; MAICYA; MTCW 1; SAAS 9; SATA 39, 76; SATA-Brief 28

Gardner, Herb(ert) 1934-. . . . . **CLC 44**
See CA 149

Gardner, John (Champlin), Jr.
1933-1982. . . . . . .**CLC 2, 3, 5, 7, 8, 10, 18, 28, 34; DAM NOV, POP; SSC 7**
See AITN 1; CA 65-68; 107; CANR 33, 73; CDALBS; DLB 2; DLBY 82; MTCW 1; SATA 40; SATA-Obit 31

Gardner, John (Edmund) 1926-. . . . . .**CLC 30; DAM POP**
See CA 103; CANR 15, 69; MTCW 1

Gardner, Miriam
See Bradley, Marion Zimmer

Gardner, Noel
See Kuttner, Henry

Gardons, S. S.
See Snodgrass, W(illiam) D(e Witt)

Garfield, Leon 1921-1996. . . . .**CLC 12**
See AAYA 8; CA 17-20R; 152; CANR 38, 41, 78; CLR 21; DLB 161; JRDA; MAICYA; SATA 1, 32, 76; SATA-Obit 90

Garland, (Hannibal) Hamlin
1860-1940. . . . . **TCLC 3; SSC 18**
See CA 104; DLB 12, 71, 78, 186

Garneau, (Hector de) Saint-Denys
1912-1943. . . . .**TCLC 13**
See CA 111; DLB 88

Garner, Alan 1934-. . . . . **CLC 17; DAB; DAM POP**
See AAYA 18; CA 73-76; CANR 15, 64; CLR 20; DLB 161; MAICYA; MTCW 1, 2; SATA 18, 69; SATA-Essay 108

Garner, Hugh 1913-1979. . . . . **CLC 13**
See CA 69-72; CANR 31; DLB 68

Garnett, David 1892-1981. . . . . **CLC 3**
See CA 5-8R; 103; CANR 17, 79; DLB 34; MTCW 2

Garos, Stephanie
See Katz, Steve

Garrett, George (Palmer) 1929-. . . . . . .**CLC 3, 11, 51; SSC 30**
See CA 1-4R; CAAS 5; CANR 1, 42, 67; DLB 2, 5, 130, 152; DLBY 83

Garrick, David 1717-1779. . . . . . .**LC 15; DAM DRAM**
See DLB 84

Garrigue, Jean 1914-1972. . . . . **CLC 2, 8**
See CA 5-8R; 37-40R; CANR 20

Garrison, Frederick
See Sinclair, Upton (Beall)

Garth, Will
See Hamilton, Edmond; Kuttner, Henry

Garvey, Marcus (Moziah, Jr.)
1887-1940. . . . . . **TCLC 41; BLC 2; DAM MULT**
See BW 1; CA 120; 124; CANR 79

Gary, Romain. . . . . **CLC 25**
See Kacew, Romain

Gascar, Pierre. . . . .**CLC 11**
See Fournier, Pierre

Gascoyne, David (Emery) 1916-. . . . . . **CLC 45**
See CA 65-68; CANR 10, 28, 54; DLB 20; MTCW 1

Gaskell, Elizabeth Cleghorn
1810-1865. . . . . . . **NCLC 70; DAB; DAM MST; SSC 25**
See CDBLB 1832-1890; DLB 21, 144, 159

Gass, William H(oward) 1924-. . . . . .**CLC 1, 2, 8, 11, 15, 39; SSC 12**
See CA 17-20R; CANR 30, 71; DLB 2; MTCW 1, 2

Gasset, Jose Ortega y
See Ortega y Gasset, Jose

Gates, Henry Louis, Jr. 1950-. . . . . . . **CLC 65; BLCS; DAM MULT**
See BW 2, 3; CA 109; CANR 25, 53, 75; DLB 67; MTCW 1

Gautier, Theophile 1811-1872. . . . . . .**NCLC 1, 59; DAM POET; PC 18; SSC 20**
See DLB 119

Gawsworth, John
See Bates, H(erbert) E(rnest)

Gay, John 1685-1732. . . . .**LC 49; DAM DRAM**
See DLB 84, 95

Gay, Oliver
See Gogarty, Oliver St. John

Gaye, Marvin (Penze) 1939-1984. . . . . **CLC 26**
See CA 112

Gebler, Carlo (Ernest) 1954-. . . . .**CLC 39**
See CA 119; 133

Gee, Maggie (Mary) 1948-. . . . .**CLC 57**
See CA 130; DLB 207

Gee, Maurice (Gough) 1931-. . . . .**CLC 29**
See CA 97-100; CANR 67; CLR 56; SATA 46, 101

Gelbart, Larry (Simon) 1923-. . . . . **CLC 21, 61**
See CA 73-76; CANR 45

Gelber, Jack 1932-. . . . . **CLC 1, 6, 14, 79**
See CA 1-4R; CANR 2; DLB 7

Gellhorn, Martha (Ellis) 1908-1998. . . . . .**CLC 14, 60**
See CA 77-80; 164; CANR 44; DLBY 82, 98

Genet, Jean 1910-1986. . . . .**CLC 1, 2, 5, 10, 14, 44, 46; DAM DRAM**
See CA 13-16R; CANR 18; DLB 72; DLBY 86; MTCW 1, 2

Gent, Peter 1942-. . . . . **CLC 29**
See AITN 1; CA 89-92; DLBY 82

Gentlewoman in New England, A
See Bradstreet, Anne

Gentlewoman in Those Parts, A
See Bradstreet, Anne

George, Jean Craighead 1919-. . . . . . . **CLC 35**
See AAYA 8; CA 5-8R; CANR 25; CLR 1; DLB 52; JRDA; MAICYA; SATA 2, 68

George, Stefan (Anton) 1868-1933. . . . . **TCLC 2, 14**
See CA 104

Georges, Georges Martin
See Simenon, Georges (Jacques Christian)

Gerhardi, William Alexander
See Gerhardie, William Alexander

Gerhardie, William Alexander
1895-1977. . . . . **CLC 5**
See CA 25-28R; 73-76; CANR 18; DLB 36

Gerstler, Amy 1956-. . . . .**CLC 70**
See CA 146

Gertler, T.. . . . . **CLC 34**
See CA 116; 121; INT 121

Ghalib. . . . .**NCLC 39, 78**
See Ghalib, Hsadullah Khan

Ghalib, Hsadullah Khan 1797-1869
See Ghalib

Gheldrode, Michel de 1898-1962. . . . . **CLC 6, 11; DAM DRAM**
See CA 85-88; CANR 40, 77

Ghiselin, Brewster 1903-. . . . . **CLC 23**
See CA 13-16R; CAAS 10; CANR 13

Ghose, Aurabinda 1872-1950. . . . . . . **TCLC 63**
See CA 163

Ghose, Zulfikar 1935-. . . . .**CLC 42**
See CA 65-68; CANR 67

Ghosh, Amitav 1956-. . . . . **CLC 44**
See CA 147; CANR 80

Giacosa, Giuseppe 1847-1906. . . . . **TCLC 7**
See CA 104

Gibb, Lee
See Waterhouse, Keith (Spencer)

Gibbon, Lewis Grassic. . . . .**TCLC 4**
See Mitchell, James Leslie

Gibbons, Kaye 1960-. . . . . . .**CLC 50, 88; DAM POP**
See CA 151; CANR 75; MTCW 1

Gibran, Kahlil 1883-1931. . . . .**TCLC 1, 9; DAM POET, POP; PC 9**
See CA 104; 150; MTCW 2

Gibran, Khalil
See Gibran, Kahlil

Gibson, William 1914-. . . . . **CLC 23; DA; DAB; DAC; DAM DRAM, MST**
See CA 9-12R; CANR 9, 42, 75; DLB 7; MTCW 1; SATA 66

Gibson, William (Ford) 1948-. . . . .**CLC 39, 63; DAM POP**
See AAYA 12; CA 126; 133; CANR 52; MTCW 1

Gide, Andre (Paul Guillaume) 1869-1951. . . . . **TCLC 5, 12, 36; DA; DAB; DAC; DAM MST, NOV; SSC 13; WLC**
See CA 104; 124; DLB 65; MTCW 1, 2

Gifford, Barry (Colby) 1946-. . . . . **CLC 34**
See CA 65-68; CANR 9, 30, 40

Gilbert, Frank
See De Voto, Bernard (Augustine)

Gilbert, W(illiam) S(chwenck) 1836-1911. . . . . . .**TCLC 3; DAM DRAM, POET**
See CA 104; 173; SATA 36

Gilbreth, Frank B., Jr. 1911-. . . . .**CLC 17**
See CA 9-12R; SATA 2

Gilchrist, Ellen 1935-. . . . . . **CLC 34, 48; DAM POP; SSC 14**
See CA 113; 116; CANR 41, 61; DLB 130; MTCW 1, 2

Giles, Molly 1942-. . . . .**CLC 39**
See CA 126

Gill, Eric 1882-1940. . . . . **TCLC 85**

Gill, Patrick
See Creasey, John

Gilliam, Terry (Vance) 1940-. . . . .**CLC 21**
See Monty Python

Gillian, Jerry
See Gilliam, Terry (Vance)

Gilliatt, Penelope (Ann Douglass) 1932-1993. . . . . **CLC 2, 10, 13, 53**
See AITN 2; CA 13-16R; 141; CANR 49; DLB 14

Gilman, Charlotte (Anna) Perkins (Stetson) 1860-1935. . . . . **TCLC 9, 37; SSC 13**
See CA 106; 150; MTCW 1

Gilmour, David 1949-. . . . .**CLC 35**
See CA 138, 147

Gilpin, William 1724-1804. . . . . **NCLC 30**

Gilray, J. D.
See Mencken, H(enry) L(ouis)

Gilroy, Frank D(aniel) 1925-. . . . .**CLC 2**
See CA 81-84; CANR 32, 64; DLB 7

Gilstrap, John 1957(?)-. . . . .**CLC 99**
See CA 160

Ginsberg, Allen 1926-1997. . . . . **CLC 1, 2, 3, 4, 6, 13, 36, 69, 109; DA; DAB; DAC; DAM MST, POET; PC 4; WLC**
See AITN 1; CA 1-4R; 157; CANR 2, 41, 63; CDALB 1941-1968; DLB 5, 16, 169; MTCW 1, 2

Ginzburg, Natalia 1916-1991. . . . . . **CLC 5, 11, 54, 70**
See CA 85-88; 135; CANR 33; DLB 177; MTCW 1, 2

Giono, Jean 1895-1970. . . . .**CLC 4, 11**
See CA 45-48; 29-32R; CANR 2, 35; DLB 72; MTCW 1

Giovanni, Nikki 1943-. . . . . . . **CLC 2, 4, 19, 64, 117; BLC 2; DA; DAB; DAC; DAM MST, MULT, POET; PC 19; WLCS**
See AAYA 22; AITN 1; BW 2, 3; CA 29-32R; CAAS 6; CANR 18, 41, 60; CDALBS; CLR 6; DLB 5, 41; INT CANR-18; MAICYA; MTCW 1, 2; SATA 24, 107

Giovene, Andrea 1904-. . . . .**CLC 7**
See CA 85-88

Gippius, Zinaida (Nikolayevna) 1869-1945
See Hippius, Zinaida

Giraudoux, (Hippolyte) Jean 1882-1944. . . . . **TCLC 2, 7; DAM DRAM**
See CA 104; DLB 65

Gironella, Jose Maria 1917-. . . . .**CLC 11**
See CA 101

Gissing, George (Robert) 1857-1903. . . . .**TCLC 3, 24, 47**
See CA 105; 167; DLB 18, 135, 184

Giurlani, Aldo
See Palazzeschi, Aldo

Gladkov, Fyodor (Vasilyevich) 1883-1958. . . . .**TCLC 27**
See CA 170

Glanville, Brian (Lester) 1931-. . . . . **CLC 6**
See CA 5-8R; CAAS 9; CANR 3, 70; DLB 15, 139; SATA 42

Glasgow, Ellen (Anderson Gholson) 1873-1945. . . . . **TCLC 2, 7; SSC 34**
See CA 104; 164; DLB 9, 12; MTCW 2

Glaspell, Susan 1882(?)-1948. . . . . . .**TCLC 55; DC 10**
See CA 110; 154; DLB 7, 9, 78; YABC 2

Glassco, John 1909-1981. . . . . **CLC 9**
See CA 13-16R; 102; CANR 15; DLB 68

Glasscock, Amnesia
See Steinbeck, John (Ernst)

Glasser, Ronald J. 1940(?)-. . . . . **CLC 37**

Glassman, Joyce
See Johnson, Joyce

Glendinning, Victoria 1937-. . . . . **CLC 50**
See CA 120; 127; CANR 59; DLB 155

Glissant, Edouard 1928-. . . . . **CLC 10, 68; DAM MULT**
See CA 153

Gloag, Julian 1930-. . . . .**CLC 40**
See AITN 1; CA 65-68; CANR 10, 70

Glowacki, Aleksander
See Prus, Boleslaw

Gluck, Louise (Elisabeth) 1943-. . . . . . . **CLC 7, 22, 44, 81; DAM POET; PC 16**
See CA 33-36R; CANR 40, 69; DLB 5; MTCW 2

Glyn, Elinor 1864-1943. . . . . **TCLC 72**
See DLB 153

Gobineau, Joseph Arthur (Comte) de 1816-1882. . . . .**NCLC 17**
See DLB 123

Godard, Jean-Luc 1930-. . . . . **CLC 20**
See CA 93-96

Godden, (Margaret) Rumer 1907-1998. **CLC 53**
See AAYA 6; CA 5-8R; 172; CANR 4, 27, 36, 55, 80; CLR 20; DLB 161; MAICYA; SAAS 12; SATA 3, 36; SATA-Obit 109

Godoy Alcayaga, Lucila 1889-1957
See Mistral, Gabriela

Godwin, Gail (Kathleen) 1937-. . . . . .**CLC 5, 8, 22, 31, 69; DAM POP**
See CA 29-32R; CANR 15, 43, 69; DLB 6; INT CANR-15; MTCW 1, 2

Godwin, William 1756-1836. . . . . **NCLC 14**
See CDBLB 1789-1832; DLB 39, 104, 142, 158, 163

Goebbels, Josef
See Goebbels, (Paul) Joseph

Goebbels, (Paul) Joseph 1897-1945. . . . . **TCLC 68**
See CA 115; 148

Goebbels, Joseph Paul
See Goebbels, (Paul) Joseph

Goethe, Johann Wolfgang von 1749-1832. . . . . **NCLC 4, 22, 34; DA; DAB; DAC; DAM DRAM, MST, POET; PC 5; WLC**
See DLB 94

Gogarty, Oliver St. John 1878-1957. . . . . **TCLC 15**
See CA 109; 150; DLB 15, 19

Gogol, Nikolai (Vasilyevich) 1809-1852. . . . . **NCLC 5, 15, 31; DA; DAB; DAC; DAM DRAM, MST; DC 1; SSC 4, 29; WLC**
See DLB 198

Goines, Donald 1937(?)-1974. . . . . **CLC 80; BLC 2; DAM MULT, POP**
See AITN 1; BW 1, 3; CA 124; 114; DLB 33

Graves, Valerie
See Bradley, Marion Zimmer

Gray, Alasdair (James) 1934- . . . . **CLC 41**
See CA 126; CANR 47, 69; DLB 194; INT 126; MTCW 1, 2

Gray, Amlin 1946- . . . . **CLC 29**
See CA 138

Gray, Francine du Plessix 1930- . . . . . **CLC 22; DAM NOV**
See BEST 90:3; CA 61-64; CAAS 2; CANR 11, 33, 75; INT CANR-11; MTCW 1, 2

Gray, John (Henry) 1866-1934 . . . . . . **TCLC 19**
See CA 119; 162

Gray, Simon (James Holliday) 1936- . . . . . **CLC 9, 14, 36**
See AITN 1; CA 21-24R; CAAS 3; CANR 32, 69; DLB 13; MTCW 1

Gray, Spalding 1941- . . . . . **CLC 49, 112; DAM POP; DC 7**
See CA 128; CANR 74; MTCW 2

Gray, Thomas 1716-1771 . . . . **LC 4, 40; DA; DAB; DAC; DAM MST; PC 2; WLC**
See CDBLB 1660-1789; DLB 109

Grayson, David
See Baker, Ray Stannard

Grayson, Richard (A.) 1951- . . . . **CLC 38**
See CA 85-88; CANR 14, 31, 57

Greeley, Andrew M(oran) 1928- . . . . . **CLC 28; DAM POP**
See CA 5-8R; CAAS 7; CANR 7, 43, 69; MTCW 1, 2

Green, Anna Katharine 1846-1935 . . . . . **TCLC 63**
See CA 112; 159; DLB 202

Green, Brian
See Card, Orson Scott

Green, Hannah
See Greenberg, Joanne (Goldenberg)

Green, Hannah 1927(?)-1996 . . . . **CLC 3**
See CA 73-76; CANR 59

Green, Henry 1905-1973 . . . . **CLC 2, 13, 97**
See Yorke, Henry Vincent

Green, Julian (Hartridge) 1900-1998
See Green, Julien

Green, Julien . . . . **CLC 3, 11, 77**
See Green, Julian (Hartridge)

Green, Paul (Eliot) 1894-1981 . . . . **CLC 25; DAM DRAM**
See AITN 1; CA 5-8R; 103; CANR 3; DLB 7, 9; DLBY 81

Greenberg, Ivan 1908-1973
See Rahv, Philip

Greenberg, Joanne (Goldenberg) 1932- . . . . **CLC 7, 30**
See AAYA 12; CA 5-8R; CANR 14, 32, 69; SATA 25

Greenberg, Richard 1959(?)- . . . . **CLC 57**
See CA 138

Greene, Bette 1934- . . . . **CLC 30**
See AAYA 7; CA 53-56; CANR 4; CLR 2; JRDA; MAICYA; SAAS 16; SATA 8, 102

Greene, Gael . . . . **CLC 8**
See CA 13-16R; CANR 10

Greene, Graham (Henry) 1904-1991 . . . . . **CLC 1, 3, 6, 9, 14, 18, 27, 37, 70, 72; DA; DAB; DAC; DAM MST, NOV; SSC 29; WLC**
See AITN 2; CA 13-16R; 133; CANR 35, 61; CDBLB 1945-1960; DLB 13, 15, 77, 100, 162, 201, 204; DLBY 91; MTCW 1, 2; SATA 20

Greene, Robert 1558-1592 . . . . **LC 41**
See DLB 62, 167

Greer, Richard
See Silverberg, Robert

Gregor, Arthur 1923- . . . . **CLC 9**
See CA 25-28R; CAAS 10; CANR 11; SATA 36

Gregor, Lee
See Pohl, Frederik

Gregory, Isabella Augusta (Persse) 1852-1932 . . . . **TCLC 1**
See CA 104; DLB 10

Gregory, J. Dennis
See Williams, John A(lfred)

Grendon, Stephen
See Derleth, August (William)

Grenville, Kate 1950- . . . . **CLC 61**
See CA 118; CANR 53

Grenville, Pelham
See Wodehouse, P(elham) G(renville)

Greve, Felix Paul (Berthold Friedrich) 1879-1948
See Grove, Frederick Philip

Grey, Zane 1872-1939 . . . . **TCLC 6; DAM POP**
See CA 104; 132; DLB 212; MTCW 1, 2

Grieg, (Johan) Nordahl (Brun) 1902-1943 . . . . **TCLC 10**
See CA 107

Grieve, C(hristopher) M(urray) 1892-1978 . . . . . **CLC 11, 19; DAM POET**
See MacDiarmid, Hugh; Pteleon

Griffin, Gerald 1803-1840 . . . . **NCLC 7**
See DLB 159

Griffin, John Howard 1920-1980 . . . . . . **CLC 68**
See AITN 1; CA 1-4R; 101; CANR 2

Griffin, Peter 1942- . . . . **CLC 39**
See CA 136

Griffith, D(avid Lewelyn) W(ark) 1875(?)-1948 . . . . **TCLC 68**
See CA 119; 150; CANR 80

Griffith, Lawrence
See Griffith, D(avid Lewelyn) W(ark)

Griffiths, Trevor 1935- . . . . **CLC 13, 52**
See CA 97-100; CANR 45; DLB 13

Griggs, Sutton Elbert 1872-1930(?) . . . . . **TCLC 77**
See CA 123; DLB 50

Grigson, Geoffrey (Edward Harvey) 1905-1985 . . . . **CLC 7, 39**
See CA 25-28R; 118; CANR 20, 33; DLB 27; MTCW 1, 2

Grillparzer, Franz 1791-1872 . . . . **NCLC 1**
See DLB 133

Grimble, Reverend Charles James
See Eliot, T(homas) S(tearns)

Grimke, Charlotte L(ottie) Forten 1837(?)-1914
See Forten, Charlotte L.

Grimm, Jacob Ludwig Karl 1785-1863 . . . . **NCLC 3, 77**
See DLB 90; MAICYA; SATA 22

Grimm, Wilhelm Karl 1786-1859 . . . . . . **NCLC 3, 77**
See DLB 90; MAICYA; SATA 22

Grimmelshausen, Johann Jakob Christoffel von 1621-1676 . . . . **LC 6**
See DLB 168

Grindel, Eugene 1895-1952
See Eluard, Paul

Grisham, John 1955- . . . . . **CLC 84; DAM POP**
See AAYA 14; CA 138; CANR 47, 69; MTCW 2

Grossman, David 1954- . . . . **CLC 67**
See CA 138

Grossman, Vasily (Semenovich) 1905-1964 . . . . **CLC 41**
See CA 124; 130; MTCW 1

Grove, Frederick Philip . . . . **TCLC 4**
See Greve, Felix Paul (Berthold Friedrich)

Grubb
See Crumb, R(obert)

Grumbach, Doris (Isaac) 1918- . . . . . . **CLC 13, 22, 64**
See CA 5-8R; CAAS 2; CANR 9, 42, 70; INT CANR-9; MTCW 2

Grundtvig, Nicolai Frederik Severin 1783-1872 . . . . **NCLC 1**

Grunge
See Crumb, R(obert)

Grunwald, Lisa 1959- . . . . **CLC 44**
See CA 120

Guare, John 1938- . . . . **CLC 8, 14, 29, 67; DAM DRAM**
See CA 73-76; CANR 21, 69; DLB 7; MTCW 1, 2

Gudjonsson, Halldor Kiljan 1902-1998
See Laxness, Halldor

Guenter, Erich
See Eich, Guenter

Guest, Barbara 1920- . . . . **CLC 34**
See CA 25-28R; CANR 11, 44; DLB 5, 193

Guest, Judith (Ann) 1936- . . . . **CLC 8, 30; DAM NOV, POP**
See AAYA 7; CA 77-80; CANR 15, 75; INT CANR-15; MTCW 1, 2

Guevara, Che . . . . **CLC 87; HLC**
See Guevara (Serna), Ernesto

Guevara (Serna), Ernesto 1928-1967
See Guevara, Che

Guicciardini, Francesco 1483-1540 . . . . . **LC 49**

Guild, Nicholas M. 1944- . . . . **CLC 33**
See CA 93-96

Guillemin, Jacques
See Sartre, Jean-Paul

Guillen, Jorge 1893-1984 . . . . . . **CLC 11; DAM MULT, POET; HLCS 1**
See CA 89-92; 112; DLB 108; HW 1

Author Index

Herbert, Frank (Patrick) 1920-1986. . . . . **CLC 12, 23, 35, 44, 85; DAM POP**
See AAYA 21; CA 53-56; 118; CANR 5, 43; CDALBS; DLB 8; INT CANR-5; MTCW 1, 2; SATA 9, 37; SATA-Obit 47

Herbert, George 1593-1633. . . . . **LC 24; DAB; DAM POET; PC 4**
See CDBLB Before 1660; DLB 126

Herbert, Zbigniew 1924-1998. . . . . .**CLC 9, 43; DAM POET**
See CA 89-92; 169; CANR 36, 74; MTCW 1

Herbst, Josephine (Frey) 1897-1969. . . . . **CLC 34**
See CA 5-8R; 25-28R; DLB 9

Hergesheimer, Joseph 1880-1954. . . . . . **TCLC 11**
See CA 109; DLB 102, 9

Herlihy, James Leo 1927-1993. . . . .**CLC 6**
See CA 1-4R; 143; CANR 2

Hermogenes fl. c. 175-. . . . .**CMLC 6**

Hernandez, Jose 1834-1886. . . . .**NCLC 17**

Herodotus c. 484B.C.-429B.C.. . . . . . **CMLC 17**
See DLB 176

Herrick, Robert 1591-1674. . . . . . . **LC 13; DA; DAB; DAC; DAM MST, POP; PC 9**
See DLB 126

Herring, Guilles
See Somerville, Edith

Herriot, James 1916-1995. . . . . **CLC 12; DAM POP**
See Wight, James Alfred

Herrmann, Dorothy 1941-. . . . . **CLC 44**
See CA 107

Herrmann, Taffy
See Herrmann, Dorothy

Hersey, John (Richard) 1914-1993. . . . .**CLC 1, 2, 7, 9, 40, 81, 97; DAM POP**
See AAYA 29; CA 17-20R; 140; CANR 33; CDALBS; DLB 6, 185; MTCW 1, 2; SATA 25; SATA-Obit 76

Herzen, Aleksandr Ivanovich 1812-1870. . . . .**NCLC 10, 61**

Herzl, Theodor 1860-1904. . . . .**TCLC 36**
See CA 168

Herzog, Werner 1942-. . . . . **CLC 16**
See CA 89-92

Hesiod c. 8th cent. B.C.-. . . . . **CMLC 5**
See DLB 176

Hesse, Hermann 1877-1962. . . . .**CLC 1, 2, 3, 6, 11, 17, 25, 69; DA; DAB; DAC; DAM MST, NOV; SSC 9; WLC**
See CA 17-18; CAP 2; DLB 66; MTCW 1, 2; SATA 50

Hewes, Cady
See De Voto, Bernard (Augustine)

Heyen, William 1940-. . . . .**CLC 13, 18**
See CA 33-36R; CAAS 9; DLB 5

Heyerdahl, Thor 1914-. . . . .**CLC 26**
See CA 5-8R; CANR 5, 22, 66, 73; MTCW 1, 2; SATA 2, 52

Heym, Georg (Theodor Franz Arthur) 1887-1912. . . . .**TCLC 9**
See CA 106

Heym, Stefan 1913-. . . . .**CLC 41**
See CA 9-12R; CANR 4; DLB 69

Heyse, Paul (Johann Ludwig von) 1830-1914. . . . .**TCLC 8**
See CA 104; DLB 129

Heyward, (Edwin) DuBose 1885-1940. . . . .**TCLC 59**
See CA 108; 157; DLB 7, 9, 45; SATA 21

Hibbert, Eleanor Alice Burford 1906-1993. . . . .**CLC 7; DAM POP**
See BEST 90:4; CA 17-20R; 140; CANR 9, 28, 59; MTCW 2; SATA 2; SATA-Obit 74

Hichens, Robert (Smythe) 1864-1950. . . . .**TCLC 64**
See CA 162; DLB 153

Higgins, George V(incent) 1939-. . . . . . **CLC 4, 7, 10, 18**
See CA 77-80; CAAS 5; CANR 17, 51; DLB 2; DLBY 81, 98; INT CANR-17; MTCW 1

Higginson, Thomas Wentworth 1823-1911. . . . .**TCLC 36**
See CA 162; DLB 1, 64

Highet, Helen
See MacInnes, Helen (Clark)

Highsmith, (Mary) Patricia 1921-1995. . . . . **CLC 2, 4, 14, 42, 102; DAM NOV, POP**
See CA 1-4R; 147; CANR 1, 20, 48, 62; MTCW 1, 2

Highwater, Jamake (Mamake) 1942(?)-. . . . .**CLC 12**
See AAYA 7; CA 65-68; CAAS 7; CANR 10, 34; CLR 17; DLB 52; DLBY 85; JRDA; MAICYA; SATA 32, 69; SATA-Brief 30

Highway, Tomson 1951-. . . . . . **CLC 92; DAC; DAM MULT**
See CA 151; CANR 75; MTCW 2; NNAL

Higuchi, Ichiyo 1872-1896. . . . .**NCLC 49**

Hijuelos, Oscar 1951-. . . . . **CLC 65; DAM MULT, POP; HLC**
See AAYA 25; BEST 90:1; CA 123; CANR 50, 75; DLB 145; HW 1, 2; MTCW 2

Hikmet, Nazim 1902(?)-1963. . . . . **CLC 40**
See CA 141; 93-96

Hildegard von Bingen 1098-1179. . . . . . **CMLC 20**
See DLB 148

Hildesheimer, Wolfgang 1916-1991. . . . . . **CLC 49**
See CA 101; 135; DLB 69, 124

Hill, Geoffrey (William) 1932-. . . . . . **CLC 5, 8, 18, 45; DAM POET**
See CA 81-84; CANR 21; CDBLB 1960 to Present; DLB 40; MTCW 1

Hill, George Roy 1921-. . . . .**CLC 26**
See CA 110; 122

Hill, John
See Koontz, Dean R(ay)

Hill, Susan (Elizabeth) 1942-. . . . . **CLC 4, 113; DAB; DAM MST, NOV**
See CA 33-36R; CANR 29, 69; DLB 14, 139; MTCW 1

Hillerman, Tony 1925-. . . . . **CLC 62; DAM POP**
See AAYA 6; BEST 89:1; CA 29-32R; CANR 21, 42, 65; DLB 206; SATA 6

Hillesum, Etty 1914-1943. . . . . **TCLC 49**
See CA 137

Hilliard, Noel (Harvey) 1929-. . . . . **CLC 15**
See CA 9-12R; CANR 7, 69

Hillis, Rick 1956-. . . . .**CLC 66**
See CA 134

Hilton, James 1900-1954. . . . . **TCLC 21**
See CA 108; 169; DLB 34, 77; SATA 34

Himes, Chester (Bomar) 1909-1984. . . . . .**CLC 2, 4, 7, 18, 58, 108; BLC 2; DAM MULT**
See BW 2; CA 25-28R; 114; CANR 22; DLB 2, 76, 143; MTCW 1, 2

Hinde, Thomas. . . . . **CLC 6, 11**
See Chitty, Thomas Willes

Hindin, Nathan
See Bloch, Robert (Albert)

Hine, (William) Daryl 1936-. . . . . **CLC 15**
See CA 1-4R; CAAS 15; CANR 1, 20; DLB 60

Hinkson, Katharine Tynan
See Tynan, Katharine

Hinton, S(usan) E(loise) 1950-. . . . . . . **CLC 30, 111; DA; DAB; DAC; DAM MST, NOV**
See AAYA 2; CA 81-84; CANR 32, 62; CDALBS; CLR 3, 23; JRDA; MAICYA; MTCW 1, 2; SATA 19, 58

Hippius, Zinaida. . . . . **TCLC 9**
See Gippius, Zinaida (Nikolayevna)

Hiraoka, Kimitake 1925-1970
See Mishima, Yukio

Hirsch, E(ric) D(onald), Jr. 1928-. . . . . **CLC 79**
See CA 25-28R; CANR 27, 51; DLB 67; INT CANR-27; MTCW 1

Hirsch, Edward 1950-. . . . . **CLC 31, 50**
See CA 104; CANR 20, 42; DLB 120

Hitchcock, Alfred (Joseph) 1899-1980. **CLC 16**
See AAYA 22; CA 159; 97-100; SATA 27; SATA-Obit 24

Hitler, Adolf 1889-1945. . . . . **TCLC 53**
See CA 117; 147

Hoagland, Edward 1932-. . . . . **CLC 28**
See CA 1-4R; CANR 2, 31, 57; DLB 6; SATA 51

Hoban, Russell (Conwell) 1925-. . . . . . . **CLC 7, 25; DAM NOV**
See CA 5-8R; CANR 23, 37, 66; CLR 3; DLB 52; MAICYA; MTCW 1, 2; SATA 1, 40, 78

Hobbes, Thomas 1588-1679. . . . . **LC 36**
See DLB 151

Hobbs, Perry
See Blackmur, R(ichard) P(almer)

Hobson, Laura Z(ametkin) 1900-1986. . . . . **CLC 7, 25**
See CA 17-20R; 118; CANR 55; DLB 28; SATA 52

Hochhuth, Rolf 1931-......... **CLC 4, 11, 18; DAM DRAM**
See CA 5-8R; CANR 33, 75; DLB 124; MTCW 1, 2

Hochman, Sandra 1936-............**CLC 3, 8**
See CA 5-8R; DLB 5

Hochwaelder, Fritz 1911-1986....... **CLC 36; DAM DRAM**
See CA 29-32R; 120; CANR 42; MTCW 1

Hochwalder, Fritz
See Hochwaelder, Fritz

Hocking, Mary (Eunice) 1921-....... **CLC 13**
See CA 101; CANR 18, 40

Hodgins, Jack 1938-................ **CLC 23**
See CA 93-96; DLB 60

Hodgson, William Hope 1877(?)-1918................**TCLC 13**
See CA 111; 164; DLB 70, 153, 156, 178; MTCW 2

Hoeg, Peter 1957-.................. **CLC 95**
See CA 151; CANR 75; MTCW 2

Hoffman, Alice 1952-......... **CLC 51; DAM NOV**
See CA 77-80; CANR 34, 66; MTCW 1, 2

Hoffman, Daniel (Gerard) 1923-...... **CLC 6, 13, 23**
See CA 1-4R; CANR 4; DLB 5

Hoffman, Stanley 1944-.............. **CLC 5**
See CA 77-80

Hoffman, William M(oses) 1939-......**CLC 40**
See CA 57-60; CANR 11, 71

Hoffmann, E(rnst) T(heodor) A(madeus) 1776-1822............ **NCLC 2; SSC 13**
See DLB 90; SATA 27

Hofmann, Gert 1931-............... **CLC 54**
See CA 128

Hofmannsthal, Hugo von 1874-1929..... **TCLC 11; DAM DRAM; DC 4**
See CA 106; 153; DLB 81, 118

Hogan, Linda 1947-.......... **CLC 73; DAM MULT**
See CA 120; CANR 45, 73; DLB 175; NNAL

Hogarth, Charles
See Creasey, John

Hogarth, Emmett
See Polonsky, Abraham (Lincoln)

Hogg, James 1770-1835.............**NCLC 4**
See DLB 93, 116, 159

Holbach, Paul Henri Thiry Baron 1723-1789......................**LC 14**

Holberg, Ludvig 1684-1754............ **LC 6**

Holden, Ursula 1921-............... **CLC 18**
See CA 101; CAAS 8; CANR 22

Holderlin, (Johann Christian) Friedrich 1770-1843............. **NCLC 16; PC 4**

Holdstock, Robert
See Holdstock, Robert P.

Holdstock, Robert P. 1948-.......... **CLC 39**
See CA 131

Holland, Isabelle 1920-..............**CLC 21**
See AAYA 11; CA 21-24R; CANR 10, 25, 47; CLR 57; JRDA; MAICYA; SATA 8, 70; SATA-Essay 103

Holland, Marcus
See Caldwell, (Janet Miriam) Taylor (Holland)

Hollander, John 1929-........ **CLC 2, 5, 8, 14**
See CA 1-4R; CANR 1, 52; DLB 5; SATA 13

Hollander, Paul
See Silverberg, Robert

Holleran, Andrew 1943(?)-.......... **CLC 38**
See CA 144

Hollinghurst, Alan 1954-......... **CLC 55, 91**
See CA 114; DLB 207

Hollis, Jim
See Summers, Hollis (Spurgeon, Jr.)

Holly, Buddy 1936-1959........... **TCLC 65**

Holmes, Gordon
See Shiel, M(atthew) P(hipps)

Holmes, John
See Souster, (Holmes) Raymond

Holmes, John Clellon 1926-1988......**CLC 56**
See CA 9-12R; 125; CANR 4; DLB 16

Holmes, Oliver Wendell, Jr. 1841-1935...................**TCLC 77**
See CA 114

Holmes, Oliver Wendell 1809-1894.....**NCLC 14**
See CDALB 1640-1865; DLB 1, 189; SATA 34

Holmes, Raymond
See Souster, (Holmes) Raymond

Holt, Victoria
See Hibbert, Eleanor Alice Burford

Holub, Miroslav 1923-1998........... **CLC 4**
See CA 21-24R; 169; CANR 10

Homer c. 8th cent. B.C.-.....**CMLC 1, 16; DA; DAB; DAC; DAM MST, POET; PC 23; WLCS**
See DLB 176

Hongo, Garrett Kaoru 1951-.......... **PC 23**
See CA 133; CAAS 22; DLB 120

Honig, Edwin 1919-................ **CLC 33**
See CA 5-8R; CAAS 8; CANR 4, 45; DLB 5

Hood, Hugh (John Blagdon) 1928-.......**CLC 15, 28**
See CA 49-52; CAAS 17; CANR 1, 33; DLB 53

Hood, Thomas 1799-1845.......... **NCLC 16**
See DLB 96

Hooker, (Peter) Jeremy 1941-........ **CLC 43**
See CA 77-80; CANR 22; DLB 40

hooks, bell..................**CLC 94; BLCS**
See Watkins, Gloria

Hope, A(lec) D(erwent) 1907-...... **CLC 3, 51**
See CA 21-24R; CANR 33, 74; MTCW 1, 2

Hope, Anthony 1863-1933..........**TCLC 83**
See CA 157; DLB 153, 156

Hope, Brian
See Creasey, John

Hope, Christopher (David Tully) 1944-........................ **CLC 52**
See CA 106; CANR 47; SATA 62

Hopkins, Gerard Manley 1844-1889.........**NCLC 17; DA; DAB; DAC; DAM MST, POET; PC 15; WLC**
See CDBLB 1890-1914; DLB 35, 57

Hopkins, John (Richard) 1931-1998..... **CLC 4**
See CA 85-88; 169

Hopkins, Pauline Elizabeth 1859-1930...... **TCLC 28; BLC 2; DAM MULT**
See BW 2, 3; CA 141; DLB 50

Hopkinson, Francis 1737-1791.........**LC 25**
See DLB 31

Hopley-Woolrich, Cornell George 1903-1968
See Woolrich, Cornell

Horatio
See Proust, (Valentin-Louis-George-Eugene-) Marcel

Horgan, Paul (George Vincent O'Shaughnessy) 1903-1995...... **CLC 9, 53; DAM NOV**
See CA 13-16R; 147; CANR 9, 35; DLB 212; DLBY 85; INT CANR-9; MTCW 1, 2; SATA 13; SATA-Obit 84

Horn, Peter
See Kuttner, Henry

Hornem, Horace Esq.
See Byron, George Gordon (Noel)

Horney, Karen (Clementine Theodore Danielsen) 1885-1952......... **TCLC 71**
See CA 114; 165

Hornung, E(rnest) W(illiam) 1866-1921...................**TCLC 59**
See CA 108; 160; DLB 70

Horovitz, Israel (Arthur) 1939-...... **CLC 56; DAM DRAM**
See CA 33-36R; CANR 46, 59; DLB 7

Horvath, Odon von
See Horvath, Oedoen von

Horvath, Oedoen von 1901-1938....... **TCLC 45**
See Horvath, Odon von

Horwitz, Julius 1920-1986........... **CLC 14**
See CA 9-12R; 119; CANR 12

Hospital, Janette Turner 1942-....... **CLC 42**
See CA 108; CANR 48

Hostos, E. M. de
See Hostos (y Bonilla), Eugenio Maria de

Hostos, Eugenio M. de
See Hostos (y Bonilla), Eugenio Maria de

Hostos, Eugenio Maria
See Hostos (y Bonilla), Eugenio Maria de

Hostos (y Bonilla), Eugenio Maria de 1839-1903...................**TCLC 24**
See CA 123; 131; HW 1

Houdini
See Lovecraft, H(oward) P(hillips)

Hougan, Carolyn 1943-............. **CLC 34**
See CA 139

Household, Geoffrey (Edward West) 1900-1988. . . . . **CLC 11**
See CA 77-80; 126; CANR 58; DLB 87; SATA 14; SATA-Obit 59

Housman, A(lfred) E(dward) 1859-1936. . . . . . . **TCLC 1, 10; DA; DAB; DAC; DAM MST, POET; PC 2; WLCS**
See CA 104; 125; DLB 19; MTCW 1, 2

Housman, Laurence 1865-1959. . . . . . **TCLC 7**
See CA 106; 155; DLB 10; SATA 25

Howard, Elizabeth Jane 1923-. . . . . . **CLC 7, 29**
See CA 5-8R; CANR 8, 62

Howard, Maureen 1930-. . . . . . . **CLC 5, 14, 46**
See CA 53-56; CANR 31, 75; DLBY 83; INT CANR-31; MTCW 1, 2

Howard, Richard 1929-. . . . . **CLC 7, 10, 47**
See AITN 1; CA 85-88; CANR 25, 80; DLB 5; INT CANR-25

Howard, Robert E(rvin) 1906-1936. . . . . **TCLC 8**
See CA 105; 157

Howard, Warren F.
See Pohl, Frederik

Howe, Fanny (Quincy) 1940-. . . . . **CLC 47**
See CA 117; CAAS 27; CANR 70; SATA-Brief 52

Howe, Irving 1920-1993. . . . . **CLC 85**
See CA 9-12R; 141; CANR 21, 50; DLB 67; MTCW 1, 2

Howe, Julia Ward 1819-1910. . . . . . . **TCLC 21**
See CA 117; DLB 1, 189

Howe, Susan 1937-. . . . . **CLC 72**
See CA 160; DLB 120

Howe, Tina 1937-. . . . . **CLC 48**
See CA 109

Howell, James 1594(?)-1666. . . . . **LC 13**
See DLB 151

Howells, W. D.
See Howells, William Dean

Howells, William D.
See Howells, William Dean

Howells, William Dean 1837-1920. . . . . . **TCLC 7, 17, 41**
See CA 104; 134; CDALB 1865-1917; DLB 12, 64, 74, 79, 189; MTCW 2

Howes, Barbara 1914-1996. . . . . **CLC 15**
See CA 9-12R; 151; CAAS 3; CANR 53; SATA 5

Hrabal, Bohumil 1914-1997. . . . . . . **CLC 13, 67**
See CA 106; 156; CAAS 12; CANR 57

Hroswitha of Gandersheim c. 935-c. 1002. . . . . **CMLC 29**
See DLB 148

Hsun, Lu
See Lu Hsun

Hubbard, L(afayette) Ron(ald) 1911-1986. . . . . **CLC 43; DAM POP**
See CA 77-80; 118; CANR 52; MTCW 2

Huch, Ricarda (Octavia) 1864-1947. . . . . **TCLC 13**
See CA 111; DLB 66

Huddle, David 1942-. . . . . **CLC 49**
See CA 57-60; CAAS 20; DLB 130

Hudson, Jeffrey
See Crichton, (John) Michael

Hudson, W(illiam) H(enry) 1841-1922. . . . . **TCLC 29**
See CA 115; DLB 98, 153, 174; SATA 35

Hueffer, Ford Madox
See Ford, Ford Madox

Hughart, Barry 1934-. . . . . **CLC 39**
See CA 137

Hughes, Colin
See Creasey, John

Hughes, David (John) 1930-. . . . . **CLC 48**
See CA 116; 129; DLB 14

Hughes, Edward James
See Hughes, Ted

Hughes, (James) Langston 1902-1967. . . . . . . **CLC 1, 5, 10, 15, 35, 44, 108; BLC 2; DA; DAB; DAC; DAM DRAM, MST, MULT, POET; DC 3; PC 1; SSC 6; WLC**
See AAYA 12; BW 1, 3; CA 1-4R; 25-28R; CANR 1, 34; CDALB 1929-1941; CLR 17; DLB 4, 7, 48, 51, 86; JRDA; MAICYA; MTCW 1, 2; SATA 4, 33

Hughes, Richard (Arthur Warren) 1900-1976. . . . . . . **CLC 1, 11; DAM NOV**
See CA 5-8R; 65-68; CANR 4; DLB 15, 161; MTCW 1; SATA 8; SATA-Obit 25

Hughes, Ted 1930-1998. . . . . . . **CLC 2, 4, 9, 14, 37, 119; DAB; DAC; PC 7**
See Hughes, Edward James

Hugo, Richard F(ranklin) 1923-1982. . . . . **CLC 6, 18, 32; DAM POET**
See CA 49-52; 108; CANR 3; DLB 5, 206

Hugo, Victor (Marie) 1802-1885. . . . . **NCLC 3, 10, 21; DA; DAB; DAC; DAM DRAM, MST, NOV, POET; PC 17; WLC**
See AAYA 28; DLB 119, 192; SATA 47

Huidobro, Vicente
See Huidobro Fernandez, Vicente Garcia

Huidobro Fernandez, Vicente Garcia 1893-1948. . . . . **TCLC 31**
See CA 131; HW 1

Hulme, Keri 1947-. . . . . **CLC 39**
See CA 125; CANR 69; INT 125

Hulme, T(homas) E(rnest) 1883-1917. . . . . **TCLC 21**
See CA 117; DLB 19

Hume, David 1711-1776. . . . . **LC 7**
See DLB 104

Humphrey, William 1924-1997. . . . . . . **CLC 45**
See CA 77-80; 160; CANR 68; DLB 212

Humphreys, Emyr Owen 1919-. . . . . . . **CLC 47**
See CA 5-8R; CANR 3, 24; DLB 15

Humphreys, Josephine 1945-. . . . . . **CLC 34, 57**
See CA 121; 127; INT 127

Huneker, James Gibbons 1857-1921. . . . . **TCLC 65**
See DLB 71

Hungerford, Pixie
See Brinsmead, H(esba) F(ay)

Hunt, E(verette) Howard, (Jr.) 1918-. . . . . **CLC 3**
See AITN 1; CA 45-48; CANR 2, 47

Hunt, Kyle
See Creasey, John

Hunt, (James Henry) Leigh 1784-1859. . . . . **NCLC 1, 70; DAM POET**
See DLB 96, 110, 144

Hunt, Marsha 1946-. . . . . **CLC 70**
See BW 2, 3; CA 143; CANR 79

Hunt, Violet 1866(?)-1942. . . . . **TCLC 53**
See DLB 162, 197

Hunter, E. Waldo
See Sturgeon, Theodore (Hamilton)

Hunter, Evan 1926-. . . . . **CLC 11, 31; DAM POP**
See CA 5-8R; CANR 5, 38, 62; DLBY 82; INT CANR-5; MTCW 1; SATA 25

Hunter, Kristin (Eggleston) 1931-. . . . . **CLC 35**
See AITN 1; BW 1; CA 13-16R; CANR 13; CLR 3; DLB 33; INT CANR-13; MAICYA; SAAS 10; SATA 12

Hunter, Mollie 1922-. . . . . **CLC 21**
See McIlwraith, Maureen Mollie Hunter

Hunter, Robert (?)-1734. . . . . **LC 7**

Hurston, Zora Neale 1903-1960. . . . . . . **CLC 7, 30, 61; BLC 2; DA; DAC; DAM MST, MULT, NOV; SSC 4; WLCS**
See AAYA 15; BW 1, 3; CA 85-88; CANR 61; CDALBS; DLB 51, 86; MTCW 1, 2

Huston, John (Marcellus) 1906-1987. . . . . **CLC 20**
See CA 73-76; 123; CANR 34; DLB 26

Hustvedt, Siri 1955-. . . . . **CLC 76**
See CA 137

Hutten, Ulrich von 1488-1523. . . . . **LC 16**
See DLB 179

Huxley, Aldous (Leonard) 1894-1963. . . . . . . **CLC 1, 3, 4, 5, 8, 11, 18, 35, 79; DA; DAB; DAC; DAM MST, NOV; WLC**
See AAYA 11; CA 85-88; CANR 44; CDBLB 1914-1945; DLB 36, 100, 162, 195; MTCW 1, 2; SATA 63

Huxley, T(homas) H(enry) 1825-1895. . . . . **NCLC 67**
See DLB 57

Huysmans, Joris-Karl 1848-1907. . . . . . **TCLC 7, 69**
See CA 104; 165; DLB 123

Hwang, David Henry 1957-. . . . . **CLC 55; DAM DRAM; DC 4**
See CA 127; 132; CANR 76; DLB 212; INT 132; MTCW 2

Hyde, Anthony 1946-. . . . . **CLC 42**
See CA 136

Hyde, Margaret O(ldroyd) 1917-. . . . . **CLC 21**
See CA 1-4R; CANR 1, 36; CLR 23; JRDA; MAICYA; SAAS 8; SATA 1, 42, 76

Hynes, James 1956(?)-. . . . . **CLC 65**
See CA 164

Ian, Janis 1951-. **CLC 21**
See CA 105

James I 1394-1437. . . . . **LC 20**

Jameson, Anna 1794-1860. . . . .**NCLC 43**
See DLB 99, 166

Jami, Nur al-Din 'Abd al-Rahman 1414-1492. . . . .**LC 9**

Jammes, Francis 1868-1938. . . . . **TCLC 75**

Jandl, Ernst 1925-. . . . .**CLC 34**

Janowitz, Tama 1957-. . . . .**CLC 43; DAM POP**
See CA 106; CANR 52

Japrisot, Sebastien 1931-. . . . . **CLC 90**

Jarrell, Randall 1914-1965. . . . . **CLC 1, 2, 6, 9, 13, 49; DAM POET**
See CA 5-8R; 25-28R; CABS 2; CANR 6, 34; CDALB 1941-1968; CLR 6; DLB 48, 52; MAICYA; MTCW 1, 2; SATA 7

Jarry, Alfred 1873-1907. . . . .**TCLC 2, 14; DAM DRAM; SSC 20**
See CA 104; 153; DLB 192

Jarvis, E. K.
See Bloch, Robert (Albert); Ellison, Harlan (Jay); Silverberg, Robert

Jeake, Samuel, Jr.
See Aiken, Conrad (Potter)

Jean Paul 1763-1825. . . . . **NCLC 7**

Jefferies, (John) Richard 1848-1887. . . . .**NCLC 47**
See DLB 98, 141; SATA 16

Jeffers, (John) Robinson 1887-1962. . . . . .**CLC 2, 3, 11, 15, 54; DA; DAC; DAM MST, POET; PC 17; WLC**
See CA 85-88; CANR 35; CDALB 1917-1929; DLB 45, 212; MTCW 1, 2

Jefferson, Janet
See Mencken, H(enry) L(ouis)

Jefferson, Thomas 1743-1826. . . . . . . **NCLC 11**
See CDALB 1640-1865; DLB 31

Jeffrey, Francis 1773-1850. . . . . **NCLC 33**
See DLB 107

Jelakowitch, Ivan
See Heijermans, Herman

Jellicoe, (Patricia) Ann 1927-. . . . .**CLC 27**
See CA 85-88; DLB 13

Jen, Gish. . . . . **CLC 70**
See Jen, Lillian

Jen, Lillian 1956(?)-
See Jen, Gish

Jenkins, (John) Robin 1912-. . . . . **CLC 52**
See CA 1-4R; CANR 1; DLB 14

Jennings, Elizabeth (Joan) 1926-. . . . . . **CLC 5, 14**
See CA 61-64; CAAS 5; CANR 8, 39, 66; DLB 27; MTCW 1; SATA 66

Jennings, Waylon 1937-. . . . .**CLC 21**

Jensen, Johannes V. 1873-1950. . . . . .**TCLC 41**
See CA 170

Jensen, Laura (Linnea) 1948-. . . . . **CLC 37**
See CA 103

Jerome, Jerome K(lapka) 1859-1927. . . . .**TCLC 23**
See CA 119; DLB 10, 34, 135

Jerrold, Douglas William 1803-1857. . . . .**NCLC 2**
See DLB 158, 159

Jewett, (Theodora) Sarah Orne 1849-1909. . . . . **TCLC 1, 22; SSC 6**
See CA 108; 127; CANR 71; DLB 12, 74; SATA 15

Jewsbury, Geraldine (Endsor) 1812-1880. . . . .**NCLC 22**
See DLB 21

Jhabvala, Ruth Prawer 1927-. . . . . . .**CLC 4, 8, 29, 94; DAB; DAM NOV**
See CA 1-4R; CANR 2, 29, 51, 74; DLB 139, 194; INT CANR-29; MTCW 1, 2

Jibran, Kahlil
See Gibran, Kahlil

Jibran, Khalil
See Gibran, Kahlil

Jiles, Paulette 1943-. . . . . **CLC 13, 58**
See CA 101; CANR 70

Jimenez (Mantecon), Juan Ramon 1881-1958. . . . . . .**TCLC 4; DAM MULT, POET; HLC; PC 7**
See CA 104; 131; CANR 74; DLB 134; HW 1; MTCW 1, 2

Jimenez, Ramon
See Jimenez (Mantecon), Juan Ramon

Jimenez Mantecon, Juan
See Jimenez (Mantecon), Juan Ramon

Jin, Ha 1956-. . . . .**CLC 109**
See CA 152

Joel, Billy. . . . .**CLC 26**
See Joel, William Martin

Joel, William Martin 1949-
See Joel, Billy

John, Saint 7th cent. -. . . . . **CMLC 27**

John of the Cross, St. 1542-1591. . . . . . . **LC 18**

Johnson, B(ryan) S(tanley William) 1933-1973. . . . . **CLC 6, 9**
See CA 9-12R; 53-56; CANR 9; DLB 14, 40

Johnson, Benj. F. of Boo
See Riley, James Whitcomb

Johnson, Benjamin F. of Boo
See Riley, James Whitcomb

Johnson, Charles (Richard) 1948-. . . . . **CLC 7, 51, 65; BLC 2; DAM MULT**
See BW 2, 3; CA 116; CAAS 18; CANR 42, 66; DLB 33; MTCW 2

Johnson, Denis 1949-. . . . . **CLC 52**
See CA 117; 121; CANR 71; DLB 120

Johnson, Diane 1934-. . . . . **CLC 5, 13, 48**
See CA 41-44R; CANR 17, 40, 62; DLBY 80; INT CANR-17; MTCW 1

Johnson, Eyvind (Olof Verner) 1900-1976. **CLC 14**
See CA 73-76; 69-72; CANR 34

Johnson, J. R.
See James, C(yril) L(ionel) R(obert)

Johnson, James Weldon 1871-1938. . . . .**TCLC 3, 19; BLC 2; DAM MULT, POET; PC 24**
See BW 1, 3; CA 104; 125; CDALB 1917-1929; CLR 32; DLB 51; MTCW 1, 2; SATA 31

Johnson, Joyce 1935-. . . . . **CLC 58**
See CA 125; 129

Johnson, Judith (Emlyn) 1936-. . . . . **CLC 7, 15**
See CA 25-28R, 153; CANR 34

Johnson, Lionel (Pigot) 1867-1902. . . . . **TCLC 19**
See CA 117; DLB 19

Johnson, Marguerite (Annie)
See Angelou, Maya

Johnson, Mel
See Malzberg, Barry N(athaniel)

Johnson, Pamela Hansford 1912-1981. . . . . **CLC 1, 7, 27**
See CA 1-4R; 104; CANR 2, 28; DLB 15; MTCW 1, 2

Johnson, Robert 1911(?)-1938. . . . . . **TCLC 69**
See BW 3; CA 174

Johnson, Samuel 1709-1784. . . . . . **LC 15; DA; DAB; DAC; DAM MST; WLC**
See CDBLB 1660-1789; DLB 39, 95, 104, 142

Johnson, Uwe 1934-1984. . . . . . .**CLC 5, 10, 15, 40**
See CA 1-4R; 112; CANR 1, 39; DLB 75; MTCW 1

Johnston, George (Benson) 1913-. . . . . **CLC 51**
See CA 1-4R; CANR 5, 20; DLB 88

Johnston, Jennifer 1930-. . . . . **CLC 7**
See CA 85-88; DLB 14

Jolley, (Monica) Elizabeth 1923-. . . . . **CLC 46; SSC 19**
See CA 127; CAAS 13; CANR 59

Jones, Arthur Llewellyn 1863-1947
See Machen, Arthur

Jones, D(ouglas) G(ordon) 1929-. . . . . .**CLC 10**
See CA 29-32R; CANR 13; DLB 53

Jones, David (Michael) 1895-1974. . . . . **CLC 2, 4, 7, 13, 42**
See CA 9-12R; 53-56; CANR 28; CDBLB 1945-1960; DLB 20, 100; MTCW 1

Jones, David Robert 1947-
See Bowie, David

Jones, Diana Wynne 1934-. . . . .**CLC 26**
See AAYA 12; CA 49-52; CANR 4, 26, 56; CLR 23; DLB 161; JRDA; MAICYA; SAAS 7; SATA 9, 70, 108

Jones, Edward P. 1950-. . . . . **CLC 76**
See BW 2, 3; CA 142; CANR 79

Jones, Gayl 1949-. . . . .**CLC 6, 9; BLC 2; DAM MULT**
See BW 2, 3; CA 77-80; CANR 27, 66; DLB 33; MTCW 1, 2

Jones, James 1921-1977. . . . . . **CLC 1, 3, 10, 39**
See AITN 1, 2; CA 1-4R; 69-72; CANR 6; DLB 2, 143; DLBD 17; DLBY 98; MTCW 1

Jones, John J.
See Lovecraft, H(oward) P(hillips)

Jones, LeRoi. . . . . **CLC 1, 2, 3, 5, 10, 14**
See Baraka, Amiri

Jones, Louis B. 1953-. . . . . **CLC 65**
See CA 141; CANR 73

Landor, Walter Savage 1775-1864. . . . . **NCLC 14**
See DLB 93, 107

Landwirth, Heinz 1927-
See Lind, Jakov

Lane, Patrick 1939-. . . . .**CLC 25; DAM POET**
See CA 97-100; CANR 54; DLB 53; INT 97-100

Lang, Andrew 1844-1912. . . . . **TCLC 16**
See CA 114; 137; DLB 98, 141, 184; MAICYA; SATA 16

Lang, Fritz 1890-1976. . . . . **CLC 20, 103**
See CA 77-80; 69-72; CANR 30

Lange, John
See Crichton, (John) Michael

Langer, Elinor 1939-. . . . . **CLC 34**
See CA 121

Langland, William 1330(?)-1400(?). . . . .**LC 19; DA; DAB; DAC; DAM MST, POET**
See DLB 146

Langstaff, Launcelot
See Irving, Washington

Lanier, Sidney 1842-1881. . . . . **NCLC 6; DAM POET**
See DLB 64; DLBD 13; MAICYA; SATA 18

Lanyer, Aemilia 1569-1645. . . . .**LC 10, 30**
See DLB 121

Lao-Tzu
See Lao Tzu

Lao Tzu fl. 6th cent. B.C.-. . . . .**CMLC 7**

Lapine, James (Elliot) 1949-. . . . . **CLC 39**
See CA 123; 130; CANR 54; INT 130

Larbaud, Valery (Nicolas)
1881-1957. . . . .**TCLC 9**
See CA 106; 152

Lardner, Ring
See Lardner, Ring(gold) W(ilmer)

Lardner, Ring W., Jr.
See Lardner, Ring(gold) W(ilmer)

Lardner, Ring(gold) W(ilmer)
1885-1933. . . . . **TCLC 2, 14; SSC 32**
See CA 104; 131; CDALB 1917-1929; DLB 11, 25, 86; DLBD 16; MTCW 1, 2

Laredo, Betty
See Codrescu, Andrei

Larkin, Maia
See Wojciechowska, Maia (Teresa)

Larkin, Philip (Arthur) 1922-1985. . . . .**CLC 3, 5, 8, 9, 13, 18, 33, 39, 64; DAB; DAM MST, POET; PC 21**
See CA 5-8R; 117; CANR 24, 62; CDBLB 1960 to Present; DLB 27; MTCW 1, 2

Larra (y Sanchez de Castro), Mariano Jose de
1809-1837. . . . .**NCLC 17**

Larsen, Eric 1941-. . . . . **CLC 55**
See CA 132

Larsen, Nella 1891-1964. . . . . **CLC 37; BLC 2; DAM MULT**
See BW 1; CA 125; DLB 51

Larson, Charles R(aymond) 1938-. . . . . . .**CLC 31**
See CA 53-56; CANR 4

Larson, Jonathan 1961-1996. . . . . **CLC 99**
See AAYA 28; CA 156

Las Casas, Bartolome de 1474-1566. . . . . . . **LC 31**

Lasch, Christopher 1932-1994. . . . . . .**CLC 102**
See CA 73-76; 144; CANR 25; MTCW 1, 2

Lasker-Schueler, Else 1869-1945. . . . . . .**TCLC 57**
See DLB 66, 124

Laski, Harold 1893-1950. . . . . **TCLC 79**

Latham, Jean Lee 1902-1995. . . . .**CLC 12**
See AITN 1; CA 5-8R; CANR 7; CLR 50; MAICYA; SATA 2, 68

Latham, Mavis
See Clark, Mavis Thorpe

Lathen, Emma. . . . .**CLC 2**
See Hennissart, Martha; Latsis, Mary J(ane)

Lathrop, Francis
See Leiber, Fritz (Reuter, Jr.)

Latsis, Mary J(ane) 1927(?)-1997
See Lathen, Emma

Lattimore, Richmond (Alexander)
1906-1984. **CLC 3**
See CA 1-4R; 112; CANR 1

Laughlin, James 1914-1997. . . . . **CLC 49**
See CA 21-24R; 162; CAAS 22; CANR 9, 47; DLB 48; DLBY 96, 97

Laurence, (Jean) Margaret (Wemyss)
1926-1987. . . . . **CLC 3, 6, 13, 50, 62; DAC; DAM MST; SSC 7**
See CA 5-8R; 121; CANR 33; DLB 53; MTCW 1, 2; SATA-Obit 50

Laurent, Antoine 1952-. . . . . **CLC 50**

Lauscher, Hermann
See Hesse, Hermann

Lautreamont, Comte de 1846-1870. . . . .**NCLC 12; SSC 14**

Laverty, Donald
See Blish, James (Benjamin)

Lavin, Mary 1912-1996. . . . .**CLC 4, 18, 99; SSC 4**
See CA 9-12R; 151; CANR 33; DLB 15; MTCW 1

Lavond, Paul Dennis
See Kornbluth, C(yril) M.; Pohl, Frederik

Lawler, Raymond Evenor 1922-. . . . . . **CLC 58**
See CA 103

Lawrence, D(avid) H(erbert Richards)
1885-1930. . . . . **TCLC 2, 9, 16, 33, 48, 61, 93; DA; DAB; DAC; DAM MST, NOV, POET; SSC 4, 19; WLC**
See CA 104; 121; CDBLB 1914-1945; DLB 10, 19, 36, 98, 162, 195; MTCW 1, 2

Lawrence, T(homas) E(dward)
1888-1935. . . . . **TCLC 18**
See Dale, Colin

Lawrence of Arabia
See Lawrence, T(homas) E(dward)

Lawson, Henry (Archibald Hertzberg)
1867-1922. . . . . **TCLC 27; SSC 18**
See CA 120

Lawton, Dennis
See Faust, Frederick (Schiller)

Laxness, Halldor. . . . .**CLC 25**
See Gudjonsson, Halldor Kiljan

Layamon fl. c. 1200-. . . . . **CMLC 10**
See DLB 146

Laye, Camara 1928-1980. . . . .**CLC 4, 38; BLC 2; DAM MULT**
See BW 1; CA 85-88; 97-100; CANR 25; MTCW 1, 2

Layton, Irving (Peter) 1912-. . . . . . .**CLC 2, 15; DAC; DAM MST, POET**
See CA 1-4R; CANR 2, 33, 43, 66; DLB 88; MTCW 1, 2

Lazarus, Emma 1849-1887. . . . . **NCLC 8**

Lazarus, Felix
See Cable, George Washington

Lazarus, Henry
See Slavitt, David R(ytman)

Lea, Joan
See Neufeld, John (Arthur)

Leacock, Stephen (Butler)
1869-1944. . . . . **TCLC 2; DAC; DAM MST**
See CA 104; 141; CANR 80; DLB 92; MTCW 2

Lear, Edward 1812-1888. . . . .**NCLC 3**
See CLR 1; DLB 32, 163, 166; MAICYA; SATA 18, 100

Lear, Norman (Milton) 1922-. . . . . **CLC 12**
See CA 73-76

Leautaud, Paul 1872-1956. . . . .**TCLC 83**
See DLB 65

Leavis, F(rank) R(aymond)
1895-1978. **CLC 24**
See CA 21-24R; 77-80; CANR 44; MTCW 1, 2

Leavitt, David 1961-. . . . . **CLC 34; DAM POP**
See CA 116; 122; CANR 50, 62; DLB 130; INT 122; MTCW 2

Leblanc, Maurice (Marie Emile)
1864-1941. . . . .**TCLC 49**
See CA 110

Lebowitz, Fran(ces Ann) 1951(?)-. . . . . . . **CLC 11, 36**
See CA 81-84; CANR 14, 60, 70; INT CANR-14; MTCW 1

Lebrecht, Peter
See Tieck, (Johann) Ludwig

le Carre, John. . . . . **CLC 3, 5, 9, 15, 28**
See Cornwell, David (John Moore)

Le Clezio, J(ean) M(arie) G(ustave)
1940-. . . . . **CLC 31**
See CA 116; 128; DLB 83

Leconte de Lisle, Charles-Marie-Rene
1818-1894. . . . .**NCLC 29**

Le Coq, Monsieur
See Simenon, Georges (Jacques Christian)

Leduc, Violette 1907-1972. . . . . **CLC 22**
See CA 13-14; 33-36R; CANR 69; CAP 1

Ledwidge, Francis 1887(?)-1917. . . . .**TCLC 23**
See CA 123; DLB 20

Lee, Andrea 1953-. . . . . **CLC 36; BLC 2; DAM MULT**
See BW 1, 3; CA 125

Malamud, Bernard 1914-1986...... **CLC 1, 2, 3, 5, 8, 9, 11, 18, 27, 44, 78, 85; DA; DAB; DAC; DAM MST, NOV, POP; SSC 15; WLC**
See AAYA 16; CA 5-8R; 118; CABS 1; CANR 28, 62; CDALB 1941-1968; DLB 2, 28, 152; DLBY 80, 86; MTCW 1, 2

Malan, Herman
See Bosman, Herman Charles; Bosman, Herman Charles

Malaparte, Curzio 1898-1957....... **TCLC 52**

Malcolm, Dan
See Silverberg, Robert

Malcolm X...... **CLC 82, 117; BLC 2; WLCS**
See Little, Malcolm

Malherbe, Francois de 1555-1628....... **LC 5**

Mallarme, Stephane 1842-1898...... **NCLC 4, 41; DAM POET; PC 4**

Mallet-Joris, Francoise 1930-........ **CLC 11**
See CA 65-68; CANR 17; DLB 83

Malley, Ern
See McAuley, James Phillip

Mallowan, Agatha Christie
See Christie, Agatha (Mary Clarissa)

Maloff, Saul 1922-.................... **CLC 5**
See CA 33-36R

Malone, Louis
See MacNeice, (Frederick) Louis

Malone, Michael (Christopher) 1942-........................ **CLC 43**
See CA 77-80; CANR 14, 32, 57

Malory, (Sir) Thomas 1410(?)-1471(?)..... **LC 11; DA; DAB; DAC; DAM MST; WLCS**
See CDBLB Before 1660; DLB 146; SATA 59; SATA-Brief 33

Malouf, (George Joseph) David 1934-..................... **CLC 28, 86**
See CA 124; CANR 50, 76; MTCW 2

Malraux, (Georges-)Andre 1901-1976....... **CLC 1, 4, 9, 13, 15, 57; DAM NOV**
See CA 21-22; 69-72; CANR 34, 58; CAP 2; DLB 72; MTCW 1, 2

Malzberg, Barry N(athaniel) 1939-..... **CLC 7**
See CA 61-64; CAAS 4; CANR 16; DLB 8

Mamet, David (Alan) 1947-....... **CLC 9, 15, 34, 46, 91; DAM DRAM; DC 4**
See AAYA 3; CA 81-84; CABS 3; CANR 15, 41, 67, 72; DLB 7; MTCW 1, 2

Mamoulian, Rouben (Zachary) 1897-1987.................... **CLC 16**
See CA 25-28R; 124

Mandelstam, Osip (Emilievich) 1891(?)-1938(?)....... **TCLC 2, 6; PC 14**
See CA 104; 150; MTCW 2

Mander, (Mary) Jane 1877-1949....... **TCLC 31**
See CA 162

Mandeville, John fl. 1350-.......... **CMLC 19**
See DLB 146

Mandiargues, Andre Pieyre de....... **CLC 41**
See Pieyre de Mandiargues, Andre

Mandrake, Ethel Belle
See Thurman, Wallace (Henry)

Mangan, James Clarence 1803-1849................... **NCLC 27**

Maniere, J.-E.
See Giraudoux, (Hippolyte) Jean

Mankiewicz, Herman (Jacob) 1897-1953................... **TCLC 85**
See CA 120; 169; DLB 26

Manley, (Mary) Delariviere 1672(?)-1724................. **LC 1, 42**
See DLB 39, 80

Mann, Abel
See Creasey, John

Mann, Emily 1952-................... **DC 7**
See CA 130; CANR 55

Mann, (Luiz) Heinrich 1871-1950...... **TCLC 9**
See CA 106; 164; DLB 66, 118

Mann, (Paul) Thomas 1875-1955..... **TCLC 2, 8, 14, 21, 35, 44, 60; DA; DAB; DAC; DAM MST, NOV; SSC 5; WLC**
See CA 104; 128; DLB 66; MTCW 1, 2

Mannheim, Karl 1893-1947........ **TCLC 65**

Manning, David
See Faust, Frederick (Schiller)

Manning, Frederic 1887(?)-1935....... **TCLC 25**
See CA 124

Manning, Olivia 1915-1980........ **CLC 5, 19**
See CA 5-8R; 101; CANR 29; MTCW 1

Mano, D. Keith 1942-............. **CLC 2, 10**
See CA 25-28R; CAAS 6; CANR 26, 57; DLB 6

Mansfield, Katherine......... **TCLC 2, 8, 39; DAB; SSC 9, 23; WLC**
See Beauchamp, Kathleen Mansfield

Manso, Peter 1940-................. **CLC 39**
See CA 29-32R; CANR 44

Mantecon, Juan Jimenez
See Jimenez (Mantecon), Juan Ramon

Manton, Peter
See Creasey, John

Man Without a Spleen, A
See Chekhov, Anton (Pavlovich)

Manzoni, Alessandro 1785-1873..... **NCLC 29**

Map, Walter 1140-1209........... **CMLC 32**

Mapu, Abraham (ben Jekutiel) 1808-1867................... **NCLC 18**

Mara, Sally
See Queneau, Raymond

Marat, Jean Paul 1743-1793........... **LC 10**

Marcel, Gabriel Honore 1889-1973...... **CLC 15**
See CA 102; 45-48; MTCW 1, 2

Marchbanks, Samuel
See Davies, (William) Robertson

Marchi, Giacomo
See Bassani, Giorgio

Margulies, Donald................. **CLC 76**

Marie de France c. 12th cent. -...... **CMLC 8; PC 22**
See DLB 208

Marie de l'Incarnation 1599-1672...... **LC 10**

Marier, Captain Victor
See Griffith, D(avid Lewelyn) W(ark)

Mariner, Scott
See Pohl, Frederik

Marinetti, Filippo Tommaso 1876-1944................... **TCLC 10**
See CA 107; DLB 114

Marivaux, Pierre Carlet de Chamblain de 1688-1763................. **LC 4; DC 7**

Markandaya, Kamala............ **CLC 8, 38**
See Taylor, Kamala (Purnaiya)

Markfield, Wallace 1926-............. **CLC 8**
See CA 69-72; CAAS 3; DLB 2, 28

Markham, Edwin 1852-1940........ **TCLC 47**
See CA 160; DLB 54, 186

Markham, Robert
See Amis, Kingsley (William)

Marks, J
See Highwater, Jamake (Mamake)

Marks-Highwater, J
See Highwater, Jamake (Mamake)

Markson, David M(errill) 1927-...... **CLC 67**
See CA 49-52; CANR 1

Marley, Bob....................... **CLC 17**
See Marley, Robert Nesta

Marley, Robert Nesta 1945-1981
See Marley, Bob

Marlowe, Christopher 1564-1593...... **LC 22, 47; DA; DAB; DAC; DAM DRAM, MST; DC 1; WLC**
See CDBLB Before 1660; DLB 62

Marlowe, Stephen 1928-
See Queen, Ellery

Marmontel, Jean-Francois 1723-1799..... **LC 2**

Marquand, John P(hillips) 1893-1960.................. **CLC 2, 10**
See CA 85-88; CANR 73; DLB 9, 102; MTCW 2

Marques, Rene 1919-1979..... **CLC 96; DAM MULT; HLC**
See CA 97-100; 85-88; CANR 78; DLB 113; HW 1, 2

Marquez, Gabriel (Jose) Garcia
See Garcia Marquez, Gabriel (Jose)

Marquis, Don(ald Robert Perry) 1878-1937.................... **TCLC 7**
See CA 104; 166; DLB 11, 25

Marric, J. J.
See Creasey, John

Marryat, Frederick 1792-1848....... **NCLC 3**
See DLB 21, 163

Marsden, James
See Creasey, John

Marsh, (Edith) Ngaio 1899-1982...... **CLC 7, 53; DAM POP**
See CA 9-12R; CANR 6, 58; DLB 77; MTCW 1, 2

Marshall, Garry 1934-.............. **CLC 17**
See AAYA 3; CA 111; SATA 60

Marshall, Paule 1929-...... **CLC 27, 72; BLC 3; DAM MULT; SSC 3**
See BW 2, 3; CA 77-80; CANR 25, 73; DLB 157; MTCW 1, 2

Marshallik
See Zangwill, Israel

Marsten, Richard
See Hunter, Evan

Marston, John 1576-1634....... **LC 33; DAM DRAM**
See DLB 58, 172

Martha, Henry
See Harris, Mark

Marti (y Perez), Jose (Julian) 1853-1895......**NCLC 63; DAM MULT; HLC**
See HW 2

Martial c. 40-c. 104.................. **PC 10**
See DLB 211

Martin, Ken
See Hubbard, L(afayette) Ron(ald)

Martin, Richard
See Creasey, John

Martin, Steve 1945-................ **CLC 30**
See CA 97-100; CANR 30; MTCW 1

Martin, Valerie 1948-...............**CLC 89**
See BEST 90:2; CA 85-88; CANR 49

Martin, Violet Florence 1862-1915..... **TCLC 51**

Martin, Webber
See Silverberg, Robert

Martindale, Patrick Victor
See White, Patrick (Victor Martindale)

Martin du Gard, Roger 1881-1958..... **TCLC 24**
See CA 118; DLB 65

Martineau, Harriet 1802-1876...... **NCLC 26**
See DLB 21, 55, 159, 163, 166, 190; YABC 2

Martines, Julia
See O'Faolain, Julia

Martinez, Enrique Gonzalez
See Gonzalez Martinez, Enrique

Martinez, Jacinto Benavente y
See Benavente (y Martinez), Jacinto

Martinez Ruiz, Jose 1873-1967
See Azorin; Ruiz, Jose Martinez

Martinez Sierra, Gregorio 1881-1947...................**TCLC 6**
See CA 115

Martinez Sierra, Maria (de la O'LeJarraga) 1874-1974...................**TCLC 6**
See CA 115

Martinsen, Martin
See Follett, Ken(neth Martin)

Martinson, Harry (Edmund) 1904-1978.................... **CLC 14**
See CA 77-80; CANR 34

Marut, Ret
See Traven, B.

Marut, Robert
See Traven, B.

Marvell, Andrew 1621-1678........ **LC 4, 43; DA; DAB; DAC; DAM MST, POET; PC 10; WLC**
See CDBLB 1660-1789; DLB 131

Marx, Karl (Heinrich) 1818-1883...... **NCLC 17**
See DLB 129

Masaoka Shiki................... **TCLC 18**
See Masaoka Tsunenori

Masaoka Tsunenori 1867-1902
See Masaoka Shiki

Masefield, John (Edward) 1878-1967..... **CLC 11, 47; DAM POET**
See CA 19-20; 25-28R; CANR 33; CAP 2; CDBLB 1890-1914; DLB 10, 19, 153, 160; MTCW 1, 2; SATA 19

Maso, Carole 19(?)-................ **CLC 44**
See CA 170

Mason, Bobbie Ann 1940-.....**CLC 28, 43, 82; SSC 4**
See AAYA 5; CA 53-56; CANR 11, 31, 58; CDALBS; DLB 173; DLBY 87; INT CANR-31; MTCW 1, 2

Mason, Ernst
See Pohl, Frederik

Mason, Lee W.
See Malzberg, Barry N(athaniel)

Mason, Nick 1945-................. **CLC 35**

Mason, Tally
See Derleth, August (William)

Mass, William
See Gibson, William

Master Lao
See Lao Tzu

Masters, Edgar Lee 1868-1950...... **TCLC 2, 25; DA; DAC; DAM MST, POET; PC 1; WLCS**
See CA 104; 133; CDALB 1865-1917; DLB 54; MTCW 1, 2

Masters, Hilary 1928-...............**CLC 48**
See CA 25-28R; CANR 13, 47

Mastrosimone, William 19(?)-........**CLC 36**

Mathe, Albert
See Camus, Albert

Mather, Cotton 1663-1728............ **LC 38**
See CDALB 1640-1865; DLB 24, 30, 140

Mather, Increase 1639-1723...........**LC 38**
See DLB 24

Matheson, Richard Burton 1926-..... **CLC 37**
See CA 97-100; DLB 8, 44; INT 97-100

Mathews, Harry 1930-............ **CLC 6, 52**
See CA 21-24R; CAAS 6; CANR 18, 40

Mathews, John Joseph 1894-1979....... **CLC 84; DAM MULT**
See CA 19-20; 142; CANR 45; CAP 2; DLB 175; NNAL

Mathias, Roland (Glyn) 1915-........**CLC 45**
See CA 97-100; CANR 19, 41; DLB 27

Matsuo Basho 1644-1694...............**PC 3**
See DAM POET

Mattheson, Rodney
See Creasey, John

Matthews, Greg 1949-.............. **CLC 45**
See CA 135

Matthews, William (Procter, III) 1942-1997.................... **CLC 40**
See CA 29-32R; 162; CAAS 18; CANR 12, 57; DLB 5

Matthias, John (Edward) 1941-........**CLC 9**
See CA 33-36R; CANR 56

Matthiessen, Peter 1927-.....**CLC 5, 7, 11, 32, 64; DAM NOV**
See AAYA 6; BEST 90:4; CA 9-12R; CANR 21, 50, 73; DLB 6, 173; MTCW 1, 2; SATA 27

Maturin, Charles Robert 1780(?)-1824................. **NCLC 6**
See DLB 178

Matute (Ausejo), Ana Maria 1925-...... **CLC 11**
See CA 89-92; MTCW 1

Maugham, W. S.
See Maugham, W(illiam) Somerset

Maugham, W(illiam) Somerset 1874-1965........ **CLC 1, 11, 15, 67, 93; DA; DAB; DAC; DAM DRAM, MST, NOV; SSC 8; WLC**
See CA 5-8R; 25-28R; CANR 40; CDBLB 1914-1945; DLB 10, 36, 77, 100, 162, 195; MTCW 1, 2; SATA 54

Maugham, William Somerset
See Maugham, W(illiam) Somerset

Maupassant, (Henri Rene Albert) Guy de 1850-1893.......**NCLC 1, 42; DA; DAB; DAC; DAM MST; SSC 1; WLC**
See DLB 123

Maupin, Armistead 1944-..... **CLC 95; DAM POP**
See CA 125; 130; CANR 58; INT 130; MTCW 2

Maurhut, Richard
See Traven, B.

Mauriac, Claude 1914-1996...........**CLC 9**
See CA 89-92; 152; DLB 83

Mauriac, Francois (Charles) 1885-1970.........**CLC 4, 9, 56; SSC 24**
See CA 25-28; CAP 2; DLB 65; MTCW 1, 2

Mavor, Osborne Henry 1888-1951
See Bridie, James

Maxwell, William (Keepers, Jr.) 1908-........................ **CLC 19**
See CA 93-96; CANR 54; DLBY 80; INT 93-96

May, Elaine 1932-..................**CLC 16**
See CA 124; 142; DLB 44

Mayakovski, Vladimir (Vladimirovich) 1893-1930.................**TCLC 4, 18**
See CA 104; 158; MTCW 2

Mayhew, Henry 1812-1887.........**NCLC 31**
See DLB 18, 55, 190

Medoff, Mark (Howard) 1940- . . . . . **CLC 6, 23; DAM DRAM**
See AITN 1; CA 53-56; CANR 5; DLB 7; INT CANR-5

Medvedev, P. N.
See Bakhtin, Mikhail Mikhailovich

Meged, Aharon
See Megged, Aharon

Meged, Aron
See Megged, Aharon

Megged, Aharon 1920- . . . . **CLC 9**
See CA 49-52; CAAS 13; CANR 1

Mehta, Ved (Parkash) 1934- . . . . **CLC 37**
See CA 1-4R; CANR 2, 23, 69; MTCW 1

Melanter
See Blackmore, R(ichard) D(oddridge)

Melies, Georges 1861-1938 . . . . **TCLC 81**

Melikow, Loris
See Hofmannsthal, Hugo von

Melmoth, Sebastian
See Wilde, Oscar

Meltzer, Milton 1915- . . . . **CLC 26**
See AAYA 8; CA 13-16R; CANR 38; CLR 13; DLB 61; JRDA; MAICYA; SAAS 1; SATA 1, 50, 80

Melville, Herman 1819-1891 . . . . . **NCLC 3, 12, 29, 45, 49; DA; DAB; DAC; DAM MST, NOV; SSC 1, 17; WLC**
See AAYA 25; CDALB 1640-1865; DLB 3, 74; SATA 59

Menander c. 342B.C.-c. 292B.C. . . . . . **CMLC 9; DAM DRAM; DC 3**
See DLB 176

Mencken, H(enry) L(ouis) 1880-1956 . . . . **TCLC 13**
See CA 105; 125; CDALB 1917-1929; DLB 11, 29, 63, 137; MTCW 1, 2

Mendelsohn, Jane 1965(?)- . . . . **CLC 99**
See CA 154

Mercer, David 1928-1980 . . . . **CLC 5; DAM DRAM**
See CA 9-12R; 102; CANR 23; DLB 13; MTCW 1

Merchant, Paul
See Ellison, Harlan (Jay)

Meredith, George 1828-1909 . . . . **TCLC 17, 43; DAM POET**
See CA 117; 153; CANR 80; CDBLB 1832-1890; DLB 18, 35, 57, 159

Meredith, William (Morris) 1919- . . . . . **CLC 4, 13, 22, 55; DAM POET**
See CA 9-12R; CAAS 14; CANR 6, 40; DLB 5

Merezhkovsky, Dmitry Sergeyevich 1865-1941 . . . . **TCLC 29**
See CA 169

Merimee, Prosper 1803-1870 . . . . . **NCLC 6, 65; SSC 7**
See DLB 119, 192

Merkin, Daphne 1954- . . . . **CLC 44**
See CA 123

Merlin, Arthur
See Blish, James (Benjamin)

Merrill, James (Ingram) 1926-1995 . . . . . . **CLC 2, 3, 6, 8, 13, 18, 34, 91; DAM POET**
See CA 13-16R; 147; CANR 10, 49, 63; DLB 5, 165; DLBY 85; INT CANR-10; MTCW 1, 2

Merriman, Alex
See Silverberg, Robert

Merriman, Brian 1747-1805 . . . . **NCLC 70**

Merritt, E. B.
See Waddington, Miriam

Merton, Thomas 1915-1968 . . . . . **CLC 1, 3, 11, 34, 83; PC 10**
See CA 5-8R; 25-28R; CANR 22, 53; DLB 48; DLBY 81; MTCW 1, 2

Merwin, W(illiam) S(tanley) 1927- . . . . . . **CLC 1, 2, 3, 5, 8, 13, 18, 45, 88; DAM POET**
See CA 13-16R; CANR 15, 51; DLB 5, 169; INT CANR-15; MTCW 1, 2

Metcalf, John 1938- . . . . **CLC 37**
See CA 113; DLB 60

Metcalf, Suzanne
See Baum, L(yman) Frank

Mew, Charlotte (Mary) 1870-1928 . . . . . **TCLC 8**
See CA 105; DLB 19, 135

Mewshaw, Michael 1943- . . . . **CLC 9**
See CA 53-56; CANR 7, 47; DLBY 80

Meyer, June
See Jordan, June

Meyer, Lynn
See Slavitt, David R(ytman)

Meyer-Meyrink, Gustav 1868-1932
See Meyrink, Gustav

Meyers, Jeffrey 1939- . . . . **CLC 39**
See CA 73-76; CANR 54; DLB 111

Meynell, Alice (Christina Gertrude Thompson) 1847-1922 . . . . **TCLC 6**
See CA 104; DLB 19, 98

Meyrink, Gustav . . . . **TCLC 21**
See Meyer-Meyrink, Gustav

Michaels, Leonard 1933- . . . . . **CLC 6, 25; SSC 16**
See CA 61-64; CANR 21, 62; DLB 130; MTCW 1

Michaux, Henri 1899-1984 . . . . **CLC 8, 19**
See CA 85-88; 114

Micheaux, Oscar (Devereaux) 1884-1951 . . . . **TCLC 76**
See BW 3; CA 174; DLB 50

Michelangelo 1475-1564 . . . . **LC 12**

Michelet, Jules 1798-1874 . . . . **NCLC 31**

Michels, Robert 1876-1936 . . . . **TCLC 88**

Michener, James A(lbert) 1907(?)-1997 . . . . **CLC 1, 5, 11, 29, 60, 109; DAM NOV, POP**
See AAYA 27; AITN 1; BEST 90:1; CA 5-8R; 161; CANR 21, 45, 68; DLB 6; MTCW 1, 2

Mickiewicz, Adam 1798-1855 . . . . **NCLC 3**

Middleton, Christopher 1926- . . . . **CLC 13**
See CA 13-16R; CANR 29, 54; DLB 40

Middleton, Richard (Barham) 1882-1911 . . . . **TCLC 56**
See DLB 156

Middleton, Stanley 1919- . . . . **CLC 7, 38**
See CA 25-28R; CAAS 23; CANR 21, 46; DLB 14

Middleton, Thomas 1580-1627 . . . . **LC 33; DAM DRAM, MST; DC 5**
See DLB 58

Migueis, Jose Rodrigues 1901- . . . . **CLC 10**

Mikszath, Kalman 1847-1910 . . . . **TCLC 31**
See CA 170

Miles, Jack . . . . **CLC 100**

Miles, Josephine (Louise) 1911-1985 . . . . . **CLC 1, 2, 14, 34, 39; DAM POET**
See CA 1-4R; 116; CANR 2, 55; DLB 48

Militant
See Sandburg, Carl (August)

Mill, John Stuart 1806-1873 . . . . . **NCLC 11, 58**
See CDBLB 1832-1890; DLB 55, 190

Millar, Kenneth 1915-1983 . . . . **CLC 14; DAM POP**
See Macdonald, Ross

Millay, E. Vincent
See Millay, Edna St. Vincent

Millay, Edna St. Vincent 1892-1950 . . . . **TCLC 4, 49; DA; DAB; DAC; DAM MST, POET; PC 6; WLCS**
See CA 104; 130; CDALB 1917-1929; DLB 45; MTCW 1, 2

Miller, Arthur 1915- . . . . . . **CLC 1, 2, 6, 10, 15, 26, 47, 78; DA; DAB; DAC; DAM DRAM, MST; DC 1; WLC**
See AAYA 15; AITN 1; CA 1-4R; CABS 3; CANR 2, 30, 54, 76; CDALB 1941-1968; DLB 7; MTCW 1, 2

Miller, Henry (Valentine) 1891-1980 . . . . . **CLC 1, 2, 4, 9, 14, 43, 84; DA; DAB; DAC; DAM MST, NOV; WLC**
See CA 9-12R; 97-100; CANR 33, 64; CDALB 1929-1941; DLB 4, 9; DLBY 80; MTCW 1, 2

Miller, Jason 1939(?)- . . . . **CLC 2**
See AITN 1; CA 73-76; DLB 7

Miller, Sue 1943- . . . . **CLC 44; DAM POP**
See BEST 90:3; CA 139; CANR 59; DLB 143

Miller, Walter M(ichael, Jr.) 1923- . . . . . . **CLC 4, 30**
See CA 85-88; DLB 8

Millett, Kate 1934- . . . . **CLC 67**
See AITN 1; CA 73-76; CANR 32, 53, 76; MTCW 1, 2

Millhauser, Steven (Lewis) 1943- . . . . . **CLC 21, 54, 109**
See CA 110; 111; CANR 63; DLB 2; INT 111; MTCW 2

Millin, Sarah Gertrude 1889-1968 . . . . **CLC 49**
See CA 102; 93-96

Milne, A(lan) A(lexander) 1882-1956 . . . . . **TCLC 6, 88; DAB; DAC; DAM MST**
See CA 104; 133; CLR 1, 26; DLB 10, 77, 100, 160; MAICYA; MTCW 1, 2; SATA 100; YABC 1

Milner, Ron(ald) 1938- . . . . . . **CLC 56; BLC 3; DAM MULT**
See AITN 1; BW 1; CA 73-76; CANR 24; DLB 38; MTCW 1

Milnes, Richard Monckton 1809-1885. . . . .**NCLC 61**
See DLB 32, 184

Milosz, Czeslaw 1911- . . . . . . **CLC 5, 11, 22, 31, 56, 82; DAM MST, POET; PC 8; WLCS**
See CA 81-84; CANR 23, 51; MTCW 1, 2

Milton, John 1608-1674. . . . . **LC 9, 43; DA; DAB; DAC; DAM MST, POET; PC 19; WLC**
See CDBLB 1660-1789; DLB 131, 151

Min, Anchee 1957- . . . . **CLC 86**
See CA 146

Minehaha, Cornelius
See Wedekind, (Benjamin) Frank(lin)

Miner, Valerie 1947- . . . . **CLC 40**
See CA 97-100; CANR 59

Minimo, Duca
See D'Annunzio, Gabriele

Minot, Susan 1956- . . . . **CLC 44**
See CA 134

Minus, Ed 1938- . . . . **CLC 39**

Miranda, Javier
See Bioy Casares, Adolfo

Mirbeau, Octave 1848-1917. . . . . **TCLC 55**
See DLB 123, 192

Miro (Ferrer), Gabriel (Francisco Victor) 1879-1930. **TCLC 5**
See CA 104

Mishima, Yukio 1925-1970. . . . . **CLC 2, 4, 6, 9, 27; DC 1; SSC 4**
See Hiraoka, Kimitake

Mistral, Frederic 1830-1914. . . . . **TCLC 51**
See CA 122

Mistral, Gabriela. . . . . **TCLC 2; HLC**
See Godoy Alcayaga, Lucila

Mistry, Rohinton 1952- . . . . **CLC 71; DAC**
See CA 141

Mitchell, Clyde
See Ellison, Harlan (Jay); Silverberg, Robert

Mitchell, James Leslie 1901-1935
See Gibbon, Lewis Grassic

Mitchell, Joni 1943- . . . . **CLC 12**
See CA 112

Mitchell, Joseph (Quincy) 1908-1996. . . . . **CLC 98**
See CA 77-80; 152; CANR 69; DLB 185; DLBY 96

Mitchell, Margaret (Munnerlyn) 1900-1949. . . . . . . **TCLC 11; DAM NOV, POP**
See AAYA 23; CA 109; 125; CANR 55; CDALBS; DLB 9; MTCW 1, 2

Mitchell, Peggy
See Mitchell, Margaret (Munnerlyn)

Mitchell, S(ilas) Weir 1829-1914. . . . . **TCLC 36**
See CA 165; DLB 202

Mitchell, W(illiam) O(rmond) 1914-1998. . . . . **CLC 25; DAC; DAM MST**
See CA 77-80; 165; CANR 15, 43; DLB 88

Mitchell, William 1879-1936. . . . . **TCLC 81**

Mitford, Mary Russell 1787-1855. . . . . **NCLC 4**
See DLB 110, 116

Mitford, Nancy 1904-1973. . . . . **CLC 44**
See CA 9-12R; DLB 191

Miyamoto, (Chujo) Yuriko 1899-1951. . . . . **TCLC 37**
See CA 170, 174; DLB 180

Miyazawa, Kenji 1896-1933. . . . . **TCLC 76**
See CA 157

Mizoguchi, Kenji 1898-1956. . . . . **TCLC 72**
See CA 167

Mo, Timothy (Peter) 1950(?)- . . . . **CLC 46**
See CA 117; DLB 194; MTCW 1

Modarressi, Taghi (M.) 1931- . . . . **CLC 44**
See CA 121; 134; INT 134

Modiano, Patrick (Jean) 1945- . . . . **CLC 18**
See CA 85-88; CANR 17, 40; DLB 83

Moerck, Paal
See Roelvaag, O(le) E(dvart)

Mofolo, Thomas (Mokopu) 1875(?)-1948. . . . . **TCLC 22; BLC 3; DAM MULT**
See CA 121; 153; MTCW 2

Mohr, Nicholasa 1938- . . . . **CLC 12; DAM MULT; HLC**
See AAYA 8; CA 49-52; CANR 1, 32, 64; CLR 22; DLB 145; HW 1, 2; JRDA; SAAS 8; SATA 8, 97

Mojtabai, A(nn) G(race) 1938- . . . . . . **CLC 5, 9, 15, 29**
See CA 85-88

Moliere 1622-1673. . . . . . **LC 10, 28; DA; DAB; DAC; DAM DRAM, MST; WLC**

Molin, Charles
See Mayne, William (James Carter)

Molnar, Ferenc 1878-1952. . . . . **TCLC 20; DAM DRAM**
See CA 109; 153

Momaday, N(avarre) Scott 1934- . . . . . . **CLC 2, 19, 85, 95; DA; DAB; DAC; DAM MST, MULT, NOV, POP; PC 25; WLCS**
See AAYA 11; CA 25-28R; CANR 14, 34, 68; CDALBS; DLB 143, 175; INT CANR-14; MTCW 1, 2; NNAL; SATA 48; SATA-Brief 30

Monette, Paul 1945-1995. . . . . **CLC 82**
See CA 139; 147

Monroe, Harriet 1860-1936. . . . . **TCLC 12**
See CA 109; DLB 54, 91

Monroe, Lyle
See Heinlein, Robert A(nson)

Montagu, Elizabeth 1720-1800. . . . . . . **NCLC 7**

Montagu, Mary (Pierrepont) Wortley 1689-1762. . . . . **LC 9; PC 16**
See DLB 95, 101

Montagu, W. H.
See Coleridge, Samuel Taylor

Montague, John (Patrick) 1929- . . . . . . **CLC 13, 46**
See CA 9-12R; CANR 9, 69; DLB 40; MTCW 1

Montaigne, Michel (Eyquem) de 1533-1592. . . . . . . **LC 8; DA; DAB; DAC; DAM MST; WLC**

Montale, Eugenio 1896-1981. . . . . **CLC 7, 9, 18; PC 13**
See CA 17-20R; 104; CANR 30; DLB 114; MTCW 1

Montesquieu, Charles-Louis de Secondat 1689-1755. . . . . **LC 7**

Montgomery, (Robert) Bruce 1921-1978
See Crispin, Edmund

Montgomery, L(ucy) M(aud) 1874-1942. . . . . . . **TCLC 51; DAC; DAM MST**
See AAYA 12; CA 108; 137; CLR 8; DLB 92; DLBD 14; JRDA; MAICYA; MTCW 2; SATA 100; YABC 1

Montgomery, Marion H., Jr. 1925- . . . . . **CLC 7**
See AITN 1; CA 1-4R; CANR 3, 48; DLB 6

Montgomery, Max
See Davenport, Guy (Mattison, Jr.)

Montherlant, Henry (Milon) de 1896-1972. . . . . **CLC 8, 19; DAM DRAM**
See CA 85-88; 37-40R; DLB 72; MTCW 1

Monty Python
See Chapman, Graham; Cleese, John (Marwood); Gilliam, Terry (Vance); Idle, Eric; Jones, Terence Graham Parry; Palin, Michael (Edward)

Moodie, Susanna (Strickland) 1803-1885. . . . . **NCLC 14**
See DLB 99

Mooney, Edward 1951-
See Mooney, Ted

Mooney, Ted. . . . . **CLC 25**
See Mooney, Edward

Moorcock, Michael (John) 1939- . . . . . . **CLC 5, 27, 58**
See Bradbury, Edward P.

Moore, Brian 1921-1999. . . . . **CLC 1, 3, 5, 7, 8, 19, 32, 90; DAB; DAC; DAM MST**
See CA 1-4R; 174; CANR 1, 25, 42, 63; MTCW 1, 2

Moore, Edward
See Muir, Edwin

Moore, G. E. 1873-1958. . . . . **TCLC 89**

Moore, George Augustus 1852-1933. . . . . **TCLC 7; SSC 19**
See CA 104; DLB 10, 18, 57, 135

Moore, Lorrie. . . . . **CLC 39, 45, 68**
See Moore, Marie Lorena

Moore, Marianne (Craig) 1887-1972. . . . . **CLC 1, 2, 4, 8, 10, 13, 19, 47; DA; DAB; DAC; DAM MST, POET; PC 4; WLCS**
See CA 1-4R; 33-36R; CANR 3, 61; CDALB 1929-1941; DLB 45; DLBD 7; MTCW 1, 2; SATA 20

Moore, Marie Lorena 1957-
See Moore, Lorrie

Moore, Thomas 1779-1852. . . . . **NCLC 6**
See DLB 96, 144

Morand, Paul 1888-1976. . . . . **CLC 41; SSC 22**
See CA 69-72; DLB 65

Morante, Elsa 1918-1985. . . . . **CLC 8, 47**
See CA 85-88; 117; CANR 35; DLB 177; MTCW 1, 2

Moravia, Alberto 1907-1990. . . . . **CLC 2, 7, 11, 27, 46; SSC 26**
See Pincherle, Alberto

More, Hannah 1745-1833. . . . . **NCLC 27**
See DLB 107, 109, 116, 158

More, Henry 1614-1687. . . . . **LC 9**
See DLB 126

More, Sir Thomas 1478-1535. . . . . . . **LC 10, 32**

Moreas, Jean. . . . . **TCLC 18**
See Papadiamantopoulos, Johannes

Morgan, Berry 1919-. . . . . **CLC 6**
See CA 49-52; DLB 6

Morgan, Claire
See Highsmith, (Mary) Patricia

Morgan, Edwin (George) 1920-. . . . . . . **CLC 31**
See CA 5-8R; CANR 3, 43; DLB 27

Morgan, (George) Frederick 1922-. . . . . . **CLC 23**
See CA 17-20R; CANR 21

Morgan, Harriet
See Mencken, H(enry) L(ouis)

Morgan, Jane
See Cooper, James Fenimore

Morgan, Janet 1945-. . . . . **CLC 39**
See CA 65-68

Morgan, Lady 1776(?)-1859. . . . . **NCLC 29**
See DLB 116, 158

Morgan, Robin (Evonne) 1941-. . . . . **CLC 2**
See CA 69-72; CANR 29, 68; MTCW 1; SATA 80

Morgan, Scott
See Kuttner, Henry

Morgan, Seth 1949(?)-1990. . . . . **CLC 65**
See CA 132

Morgenstern, Christian 1871-1914. . . . . **TCLC 8**
See CA 105

Morgenstern, S.
See Goldman, William (W.)

Moricz, Zsigmond 1879-1942. . . . . . . **TCLC 33**
See CA 165

Morike, Eduard (Friedrich) 1804-1875. . . . . **NCLC 10**
See DLB 133

Moritz, Karl Philipp 1756-1793. . . . . **LC 2**
See DLB 94

Morland, Peter Henry
See Faust, Frederick (Schiller)

Morley, Christopher (Darlington) 1890-1957. . . . . **TCLC 87**
See CA 112; DLB 9

Morren, Theophil
See Hofmannsthal, Hugo von

Morris, Bill 1952-. . . . . **CLC 76**

Morris, Julian
See West, Morris L(anglo)

Morris, Steveland Judkins 1950(?)-
See Wonder, Stevie

Morris, William 1834-1896. . . . . **NCLC 4**
See CDBLB 1832-1890; DLB 18, 35, 57, 156, 178, 184

Morris, Wright 1910-1998. . . . . . . **CLC 1, 3, 7, 18, 37**
See CA 9-12R; 167; CANR 21; DLB 2, 206; DLBY 81; MTCW 1, 2

Morrison, Arthur 1863-1945. . . . . **TCLC 72**
See CA 120; 157; DLB 70, 135, 197

Morrison, Chloe Anthony Wofford
See Morrison, Toni

Morrison, James Douglas 1943-1971
See Morrison, Jim

Morrison, Jim. . . . . **CLC 17**
See Morrison, James Douglas

Morrison, Toni 1931-. . . . . . . **CLC 4, 10, 22, 55, 81, 87; BLC 3; DA; DAB; DAC; DAM MST, MULT, NOV, POP**
See AAYA 1, 22; BW 2, 3; CA 29-32R; CANR 27, 42, 67; CDALB 1968-1988; DLB 6, 33, 143; DLBY 81; MTCW 1, 2; SATA 57

Morrison, Van 1945-. . . . . **CLC 21**
See CA 116; 168

Morrissy, Mary 1958-. . . . . **CLC 99**

Mortimer, John (Clifford) 1923-. . . . . **CLC 28, 43; DAM DRAM, POP**
See CA 13-16R; CANR 21, 69; CDBLB 1960 to Present; DLB 13; INT CANR-21; MTCW 1, 2

Mortimer, Penelope (Ruth) 1918-. . . . . . **CLC 5**
See CA 57-60; CANR 45

Morton, Anthony
See Creasey, John

Mosca, Gaetano 1858-1941. . . . . **TCLC 75**

Mosher, Howard Frank 1943-. . . . . **CLC 62**
See CA 139; CANR 65

Mosley, Nicholas 1923-. . . . . **CLC 43, 70**
See CA 69-72; CANR 41, 60; DLB 14, 207

Mosley, Walter 1952-. . . . . **CLC 97; BLCS; DAM MULT, POP**
See AAYA 17; BW 2; CA 142; CANR 57; MTCW 2

Moss, Howard 1922-1987. . . . . . **CLC 7, 14, 45, 50; DAM POET**
See CA 1-4R; 123; CANR 1, 44; DLB 5

Mossgiel, Rab
See Burns, Robert

Motion, Andrew (Peter) 1952-. . . . . **CLC 47**
See CA 146; DLB 40

Motley, Willard (Francis) 1909-1965. . . . . **CLC 18**
See BW 1; CA 117; 106; DLB 76, 143

Motoori, Norinaga 1730-1801. . . . . . . **NCLC 45**

Mott, Michael (Charles Alston) 1930-. . . . . **CLC 15, 34**
See CA 5-8R; CAAS 7; CANR 7, 29

Mountain Wolf Woman 1884-1960. . . . . . **CLC 92**
See CA 144; NNAL

Moure, Erin 1955-. . . . . **CLC 88**
See CA 113; DLB 60

Mowat, Farley (McGill) 1921-. . . . . . . **CLC 26; DAC; DAM MST**
See AAYA 1; CA 1-4R; CANR 4, 24, 42, 68; CLR 20; DLB 68; INT CANR-24; JRDA; MAICYA; MTCW 1, 2; SATA 3, 55

Mowatt, Anna Cora 1819-1870. . . . . . **NCLC 74**

Moyers, Bill 1934-. . . . . **CLC 74**
See AITN 2; CA 61-64; CANR 31, 52

Mphahlele, Es'kia
See Mphahlele, Ezekiel

Mphahlele, Ezekiel 1919-. . . . . . . **CLC 25; BLC 3; DAM MULT**
See Mphahlele, Es'kia

Mqhayi, S(amuel) E(dward) K(rune Loliwe) 1875-1945. . . . . . **TCLC 25; BLC 3; DAM MULT**
See CA 153

Mrozek, Slawomir 1930-. . . . . **CLC 3, 13**
See CA 13-16R; CAAS 10; CANR 29; MTCW 1

Mrs. Belloc-Lowndes
See Lowndes, Marie Adelaide (Belloc)

Mtwa, Percy (?)-. . . . . **CLC 47**

Mueller, Lisel 1924-. . . . . **CLC 13, 51**
See CA 93-96; DLB 105

Muir, Edwin 1887-1959. . . . . **TCLC 2, 87**
See CA 104; DLB 20, 100, 191

Muir, John 1838-1914. . . . . **TCLC 28**
See CA 165; DLB 186

Mujica Lainez, Manuel 1910-1984. . . . . . . **CLC 31**
See Lainez, Manuel Mujica

Mukherjee, Bharati 1940-. . . . . . **CLC 53, 115; DAM NOV**
See BEST 89:2; CA 107; CANR 45, 72; DLB 60; MTCW 1, 2

Muldoon, Paul 1951-. . . . . . . **CLC 32, 72; DAM POET**
See CA 113; 129; CANR 52; DLB 40; INT 129

Mulisch, Harry 1927-. . . . . **CLC 42**
See CA 9-12R; CANR 6, 26, 56

Mull, Martin 1943-. . . . . **CLC 17**
See CA 105

Muller, Wilhelm. . . . . **NCLC 73**

Mulock, Dinah Maria
See Craik, Dinah Maria (Mulock)

Munford, Robert 1737(?)-1783. . . . . **LC 5**
See DLB 31

Mungo, Raymond 1946-. . . . . **CLC 72**
See CA 49-52; CANR 2

Munro, Alice 1931-. . . . . **CLC 6, 10, 19, 50, 95; DAC; DAM MST, NOV; SSC 3; WLCS**
See AITN 2; CA 33-36R; CANR 33, 53, 75; DLB 53; MTCW 1, 2; SATA 29

Munro, H(ector) H(ugh) 1870-1916
See Saki

Pa Chin. . . . . **CLC 18**
See Li Fei-kan

Pack, Robert 1929-. . . . . **CLC 13**
See CA 1-4R; CANR 3, 44; DLB 5

Padgett, Lewis
See Kuttner, Henry

Padilla (Lorenzo), Heberto 1932-. . . . . **CLC 38**
See AITN 1; CA 123; 131; HW 1

Page, Jimmy 1944-. . . . . **CLC 12**

Page, Louise 1955-. . . . . **CLC 40**
See CA 140; CANR 76

Page, P(atricia) K(athleen) 1916-. . . . . . **CLC 7, 18; DAC; DAM MST; PC 12**
See CA 53-56; CANR 4, 22, 65; DLB 68; MTCW 1

Page, Thomas Nelson 1853-1922. . . . . . **SSC 23**
See CA 118; DLB 12, 78; DLBD 13

Pagels, Elaine Hiesey 1943-. . . . . **CLC 104**
See CA 45-48; CANR 2, 24, 51

Paget, Violet 1856-1935
See Lee, Vernon

Paget-Lowe, Henry
See Lovecraft, H(oward) P(hillips)

Paglia, Camille (Anna) 1947-. . . . . **CLC 68**
See CA 140; CANR 72; MTCW 2

Paige, Richard
See Koontz, Dean R(ay)

Paine, Thomas 1737-1809. . . . . **NCLC 62**
See CDALB 1640-1865; DLB 31, 43, 73, 158

Pakenham, Antonia
See Fraser, (Lady) Antonia (Pakenham)

Palamas, Kostes 1859-1943. . . . . **TCLC 5**
See CA 105

Palazzeschi, Aldo 1885-1974. . . . . **CLC 11**
See CA 89-92; 53-56; DLB 114

Paley, Grace 1922-. . . . . . . **CLC 4, 6, 37; DAM POP; SSC 8**
See CA 25-28R; CANR 13, 46, 74; DLB 28; INT CANR-13; MTCW 1, 2

Palin, Michael (Edward) 1943-. . . . . . . **CLC 21**
See Monty Python

Palliser, Charles 1947-. . . . . **CLC 65**
See CA 136; CANR 76

Palma, Ricardo 1833-1919. . . . . **TCLC 29**
See CA 168

Pancake, Breece Dexter 1952-1979
See Pancake, Breece D'J

Pancake, Breece D'J. . . . . **CLC 29**
See Pancake, Breece Dexter

Panko, Rudy
See Gogol, Nikolai (Vasilyevich)

Papadiamantis, Alexandros 1851-1911. . . . . **TCLC 29**
See CA 168

Papadiamantopoulos, Johannes 1856-1910
See Moreas, Jean

Papini, Giovanni 1881-1956. . . . . **TCLC 22**
See CA 121

Paracelsus 1493-1541. . . . . **LC 14**
See DLB 179

Parasol, Peter
See Stevens, Wallace

Pardo Bazan, Emilia 1851-1921. . . . . . . **SSC 30**

Pareto, Vilfredo 1848-1923. . . . . **TCLC 69**
See CA 175

Parfenie, Maria
See Codrescu, Andrei

Parini, Jay (Lee) 1948-. . . . . **CLC 54**
See CA 97-100; CAAS 16; CANR 32

Park, Jordan
See Kornbluth, C(yril) M.; Pohl, Frederik

Park, Robert E(zra) 1864-1944. . . . . . **TCLC 73**
See CA 122; 165

Parker, Bert
See Ellison, Harlan (Jay)

Parker, Dorothy (Rothschild) 1893-1967. . . . . **CLC 15, 68; DAM POET; SSC 2**
See CA 19-20; 25-28R; CAP 2; DLB 11, 45, 86; MTCW 1, 2

Parker, Robert B(rown) 1932-. . . . . . . **CLC 27; DAM NOV, POP**
See AAYA 28; BEST 89:4; CA 49-52; CANR 1, 26, 52; INT CANR-26; MTCW 1

Parkin, Frank 1940-. . . . . **CLC 43**
See CA 147

Parkman, Francis, Jr. 1823-1893. . . . . . **NCLC 12**
See DLB 1, 30, 186

Parks, Gordon (Alexander Buchanan) 1912-. . . . . **CLC 1, 16; BLC 3; DAM MULT**
See AITN 2; BW 2, 3; CA 41-44R; CANR 26, 66; DLB 33; MTCW 2; SATA 8, 108

Parmenides c. 515B.C.-c. 450B.C.. . . . . . **CMLC 22**
See DLB 176

Parnell, Thomas 1679-1718. . . . . **LC 3**
See DLB 94

Parra, Nicanor 1914-. . . . . . **CLC 2, 102; DAM MULT; HLC**
See CA 85-88; CANR 32; HW 1; MTCW 1

Parrish, Mary Frances
See Fisher, M(ary) F(rances) K(ennedy)

Parson
See Coleridge, Samuel Taylor

Parson Lot
See Kingsley, Charles

Partridge, Anthony
See Oppenheim, E(dward) Phillips

Pascal, Blaise 1623-1662. . . . . **LC 35**

Pascoli, Giovanni 1855-1912. . . . . **TCLC 45**
See CA 170

Pasolini, Pier Paolo 1922-1975. . . . . . . **CLC 20, 37, 106; PC 17**
See CA 93-96; 61-64; CANR 63; DLB 128, 177; MTCW 1

Pasquini
See Silone, Ignazio

Pastan, Linda (Olenik) 1932-. . . . . **CLC 27; DAM POET**
See CA 61-64; CANR 18, 40, 61; DLB 5

Pasternak, Boris (Leonidovich) 1890-1960. . . . . . . **CLC 7, 10, 18, 63; DA; DAB; DAC; DAM MST, NOV, POET; PC 6; SSC 31; WLC**
See CA 127; 116; MTCW 1, 2

Patchen, Kenneth 1911-1972. . . . . . . **CLC 1, 2, 18; DAM POET**
See CA 1-4R; 33-36R; CANR 3, 35; DLB 16, 48; MTCW 1

Pater, Walter (Horatio) 1839-1894. . . . . **NCLC 7**
See CDBLB 1832-1890; DLB 57, 156

Paterson, A(ndrew) B(arton) 1864-1941. . . . . **TCLC 32**
See CA 155; SATA 97

Paterson, Katherine (Womeldorf) 1932-. . . . . **CLC 12, 30**
See AAYA 1; CA 21-24R; CANR 28, 59; CLR 7, 50; DLB 52; JRDA; MAICYA; MTCW 1; SATA 13, 53, 92

Patmore, Coventry Kersey Dighton 1823-1896. **NCLC 9**
See DLB 35, 98

Paton, Alan (Stewart) 1903-1988. . . . . . **CLC 4, 10, 25, 55, 106; DA; DAB; DAC; DAM MST, NOV; WLC**
See AAYA 26; CA 13-16; 125; CANR 22; CAP 1; DLBD 17; MTCW 1, 2; SATA 11; SATA-Obit 56

Paton Walsh, Gillian 1937-
See Walsh, Jill Paton

Patton, George S. 1885-1945. . . . . **TCLC 79**

Paulding, James Kirke 1778-1860. . . . . . **NCLC 2**
See DLB 3, 59, 74

Paulin, Thomas Neilson 1949-
See Paulin, Tom

Paulin, Tom. . . . . **CLC 37**
See Paulin, Thomas Neilson

Paustovsky, Konstantin (Georgievich) 1892-1968. **CLC 40**
See CA 93-96; 25-28R

Pavese, Cesare 1908-1950. . . . . . . **TCLC 3; PC 13; SSC 19**
See CA 104; 169; DLB 128, 177

Pavic, Milorad 1929-. . . . . **CLC 60**
Scc CA 136; DLB 181

Pavlov, Ivan Petrovich 1849-1936. . . . . . **TCLC 91**
See CA 118

Payne, Alan
See Jakes, John (William)

Paz, Gil
See Lugones, Leopoldo

Paz, Octavio 1914-1998. . . . . . . **CLC 3, 4, 6, 10, 19, 51, 65, 119; DA; DAB; DAC; DAM MST, MULT, POET; HLC; PC 1; WLC**
See CA 73-76; 165; CANR 32, 65; DLBY 90, 98; HW 1, 2; MTCW 1, 2

p'Bitek, Okot 1931-1982. . . . . **CLC 96; BLC 3; DAM MULT**
See BW 2, 3; CA 124; 107; DLB 125; MTCW 1, 2

Peacock, Molly 1947-............... **CLC 60**
See CA 103; CAAS 21; CANR 52; DLB 120

Peacock, Thomas Love 1785-1866......**NCLC 22**
See DLB 96, 116

Peake, Mervyn 1911-1968......... **CLC 7, 54**
See CA 5-8R; 25-28R; CANR 3; DLB 15, 160; MTCW 1; SATA 23

Pearce, Philippa.................. **CLC 21**
See Christie, (Ann) Philippa

Pearl, Eric
See Elman, Richard (Martin)

Pearson, T(homas) R(eid) 1956-...... **CLC 39**
See CA 120; 130; INT 130

Peck, Dale 1967-.................. **CLC 81**
See CA 146; CANR 72

Peck, John 1941-....................**CLC 3**
See CA 49-52; CANR 3

Peck, Richard (Wayne) 1934-........ **CLC 21**
See AAYA 1, 24; CA 85-88; CANR 19, 38; CLR 15; INT CANR-19; JRDA; MAICYA; SAAS 2; SATA 18, 55, 97

Peck, Robert Newton 1928-..... **CLC 17; DA; DAC; DAM MST**
See AAYA 3; CA 81-84; CANR 31, 63; CLR 45; JRDA; MAICYA; SAAS 1; SATA 21, 62; SATA-Essay 108

Peckinpah, (David) Sam(uel) 1925-1984.................... **CLC 20**
See CA 109; 114

Pedersen, Knut 1859-1952
See Hamsun, Knut

Peeslake, Gaffer
See Durrell, Lawrence (George)

Peguy, Charles Pierre 1873-1914.......**TCLC 10**
See CA 107

Peirce, Charles Sanders 1839-1914..... **TCLC 81**

Pena, Ramon del Valle y
See Valle-Inclan, Ramon (Maria) del

Pendennis, Arthur Esquir
See Thackeray, William Makepeace

Penn, William 1644-1718............. **LC 25**
See DLB 24

PEPECE
See Prado (Calvo), Pedro

Pepys, Samuel 1633-1703.........**LC 11; DA; DAB; DAC; DAM MST; WLC**
See CDBLB 1660-1789; DLB 101

Percy, Walker 1916-1990...... **CLC 2, 3, 6, 8, 14, 18, 47, 65; DAM NOV, POP**
See CA 1-4R; 131; CANR 1, 23, 64; DLB 2; DLBY 80, 90; MTCW 1, 2

Percy, William Alexander 1885-1942...................**TCLC 84**
See CA 163; MTCW 2

Perec, Georges 1936-1982....... **CLC 56, 116**
See CA 141; DLB 83

Pereda (y Sanchez de Porrua), Jose Maria de 1833-1906...................**TCLC 16**
See CA 117

Pereda y Porrua, Jose Maria de
See Pereda (y Sanchez de Porrua), Jose Maria de

Peregoy, George Weems
See Mencken, H(enry) L(ouis)

Perelman, S(idney) J(oseph) 1904-1979........**CLC 3, 5, 9, 15, 23, 44, 49; DAM DRAM; SSC 32**
See AITN 1, 2; CA 73-76; 89-92; CANR 18; DLB 11, 44; MTCW 1, 2

Peret, Benjamin 1899-1959......... **TCLC 20**
See CA 117

Peretz, Isaac Loeb 1851(?)-1915....... **TCLC 16; SSC 26**
See CA 109

Peretz, Yitzkhok Leibush
See Peretz, Isaac Loeb

Perez Galdos, Benito 1843-1920....... **TCLC 27; HLCS 1**
See CA 125; 153; HW 1

Perrault, Charles 1628-1703............**LC 2**
See MAICYA; SATA 25

Perry, Brighton
See Sherwood, Robert E(mmet)

Perse, St.-John
See Leger, (Marie-Rene Auguste) Alexis Saint-Leger

Perutz, Leo(pold) 1882-1957........ **TCLC 60**
See CA 147; DLB 81

Peseenz, Tulio F.
See Lopez y Fuentes, Gregorio

Pesetsky, Bette 1932-............... **CLC 28**
See CA 133; DLB 130

Peshkov, Alexei Maximovich 1868-1936
See Gorky, Maxim

Pessoa, Fernando (Antonio Nogueira) 1888-1935......**TCLC 27; DAM MULT; HLC; PC 20**
See CA 125

Peterkin, Julia Mood 1880-1961...... **CLC 31**
See CA 102; DLB 9

Peters, Joan K(aren) 1945-.......... **CLC 39**
See CA 158

Peters, Robert L(ouis) 1924-.......... **CLC 7**
See CA 13-16R; CAAS 8; DLB 105

Petofi, Sandor 1823-1849...........**NCLC 21**

Petrakis, Harry Mark 1923-.......... **CLC 3**
See CA 9-12R; CANR 4, 30

Petrarch 1304-1374.........**CMLC 20; DAM POET; PC 8**

Petrov, Evgeny.................. **TCLC 21**
See Kataev, Evgeny Petrovich

Petry, Ann (Lane) 1908-1997.....**CLC 1, 7, 18**
See BW 1, 3; CA 5-8R; 157; CAAS 6; CANR 4, 46; CLR 12; DLB 76; JRDA; MAICYA; MTCW 1; SATA 5; SATA-Obit 94

Petursson, Halligrimur 1614-1674.......**LC 8**

Peychinovich
See Vazov, Ivan (Minchov)

Phaedrus c. 18B.C.-c. 50...........**CMLC 25**
See DLB 211

Philips, Katherine 1632-1664.......... **LC 30**
See DLB 131

Philipson, Morris H. 1926-...........**CLC 53**
See CA 1-4R; CANR 4

Phillips, Caryl 1958-.........**CLC 96; BLCS; DAM MULT**
See BW 2; CA 141; CANR 63; DLB 157; MTCW 2

Phillips, David Graham 1867-1911..... **TCLC 44**
See CA 108; DLB 9, 12

Phillips, Jack
See Sandburg, Carl (August)

Phillips, Jayne Anne 1952-....... **CLC 15, 33; SSC 16**
See CA 101; CANR 24, 50; DLBY 80; INT CANR-24; MTCW 1, 2

Phillips, Richard
See Dick, Philip K(indred)

Phillips, Robert (Schaeffer) 1938-..... **CLC 28**
See CA 17-20R; CAAS 13; CANR 8; DLB 105

Phillips, Ward
See Lovecraft, H(oward) P(hillips)

Piccolo, Lucio 1901-1969............ **CLC 13**
See CA 97-100; DLB 114

Pickthall, Marjorie L(owry) C(hristie) 1883-1922...................**TCLC 21**
See CA 107; DLB 92

Pico della Mirandola, Giovanni 1463-1494......................**LC 15**

Piercy, Marge 1936-......**CLC 3, 6, 14, 18, 27, 62**
See CA 21-24R; CAAS 1; CANR 13, 43, 66; DLB 120; MTCW 1, 2

Piers, Robert
See Anthony, Piers

Pieyre de Mandiargues, Andre 1909-1991
See Mandiargues, Andre Pieyre de

Pilnyak, Boris.................... **TCLC 23**
See Vogau, Boris Andreyevich

Pincherle, Alberto 1907-1990.....**CLC 11, 18; DAM NOV**
See Moravia, Alberto

Pinckney, Darryl 1953-............. **CLC 76**
See BW 2, 3; CA 143; CANR 79

Pindar 518B.C.-446B.C......**CMLC 12; PC 19**
See DLB 176

Pineda, Cecile 1942-................ **CLC 39**
See CA 118

Pinero, Arthur Wing 1855-1934....... **TCLC 32; DAM DRAM**
See CA 110; 153; DLB 10

Pinero, Miguel (Antonio Gomez) 1946-1988................. **CLC 4, 55**
See CA 61-64; 125; CANR 29; HW 1

Pinget, Robert 1919-1997.......**CLC 7, 13, 37**
See CA 85-88; 160; DLB 83

Pink Floyd
See Barrett, (Roger) Syd; Gilmour, David; Mason, Nick; Waters, Roger; Wright, Rick

Powell, Padgett 1952-. . . . . **CLC 34**
See CA 126; CANR 63

Power, Susan 1961-. . . . .**CLC 91**

Powers, J(ames) F(arl) 1917-. . . . . **CLC 1, 4, 8, 57; SSC 4**
See CA 1-4R; CANR 2, 61; DLB 130; MTCW 1

Powers, John J(ames) 1945-
See Powers, John R.

Powers, John R.. . . . . **CLC 66**
See Powers, John J(ames)

Powers, Richard (S.) 1957-. . . . . **CLC 93**
See CA 148; CANR 80

Pownall, David 1938-. . . . . **CLC 10**
See CA 89-92; CAAS 18; CANR 49; DLB 14

Powys, John Cowper 1872-1963. . . . .**CLC 7, 9, 15, 46**
See CA 85-88; DLB 15; MTCW 1, 2

Powys, T(heodore) F(rancis) 1875-1953. . . . .**TCLC 9**
See CA 106; DLB 36, 162

Prado (Calvo), Pedro 1886-1952. . . . .**TCLC 75**
See CA 131; HW 1

Prager, Emily 1952-. . . . . **CLC 56**

Pratt, E(dwin) J(ohn) 1883(?)-1964. . . . . . **CLC 19; DAC; DAM POET**
See CA 141; 93-96; CANR 77; DLB 92

Premchand. . . . . **TCLC 21**
See Srivastava, Dhanpat Rai

Preussler, Otfried 1923-. . . . .**CLC 17**
See CA 77-80; SATA 24

Prevert, Jacques (Henri Marie) 1900-1977. . . . . **CLC 15**
See CA 77-80; 69-72; CANR 29, 61; MTCW 1; SATA-Obit 30

Prevost, Abbe (Antoine Francois) 1697-1763. . . . .**LC 1**

Price, (Edward) Reynolds 1933-. . . . .**CLC 3, 6, 13, 43, 50, 63; DAM NOV; SSC 22**
See CA 1-4R; CANR 1, 37, 57; DLB 2; INT CANR-37

Price, Richard 1949-. . . . .**CLC 6, 12**
See CA 49-52; CANR 3; DLBY 81

Prichard, Katharine Susannah 1883-1969. **CLC 46**
See CA 11-12; CANR 33; CAP 1; MTCW 1; SATA 66

Priestley, J(ohn) B(oynton) 1894-1984. . . . . **CLC 2, 5, 9, 34; DAM DRAM, NOV**
See CA 9-12R; 113; CANR 33; CDBLB 1914-1945; DLB 10, 34, 77, 100, 139; DLBY 84; MTCW 1, 2

Prince 1958(?)-. **CLC 35**

Prince, F(rank) T(empleton) 1912-. . . . . . **CLC 22**
See CA 101; CANR 43, 79; DLB 20

Prince Kropotkin
See Kropotkin, Peter (Aleksieevich)

Prior, Matthew 1664-1721. . . . . **LC 4**
See DLB 95

Prishvin, Mikhail 1873-1954. . . . . **TCLC 75**

Pritchard, William H(arrison) 1932-. . . . . **CLC 34**
See CA 65-68; CANR 23; DLB 111

Pritchett, V(ictor) S(awdon) 1900-1997. . . . . . **CLC 5, 13, 15, 41; DAM NOV; SSC 14**
See CA 61-64; 157; CANR 31, 63; DLB 15, 139; MTCW 1, 2

Private 19022
See Manning, Frederic

Probst, Mark 1925-. . . . .**CLC 59**
See CA 130

Prokosch, Frederic 1908-1989. . . . . . **CLC 4, 48**
See CA 73-76; 128; DLB 48; MTCW 2

Propertius, Sextus c. 50B.C.-c. 16B.C.. . . . . **CMLC 32**
See DLB 211

Prophet, The
See Dreiser, Theodore (Herman Albert)

Prose, Francine 1947-. . . . .**CLC 45**
See CA 109; 112; CANR 46; SATA 101

Proudhon
See Cunha, Euclides (Rodrigues Pimenta) da

Proulx, Annie
See Proulx, E(dna) Annie

Proulx, E(dna) Annie 1935-. . . . . **CLC 81; DAM POP**
See CA 145; CANR 65; MTCW 2

Proust, (Valentin-Louis-George-Eugene-) Marcel 1871-1922. . . . . . .**TCLC 7, 13, 33; DA; DAB; DAC; DAM MST, NOV; WLC**
See CA 104; 120; DLB 65; MTCW 1, 2

Prowler, Harley
See Masters, Edgar Lee

Prus, Boleslaw 1845-1912. . . . . **TCLC 48**

Pryor, Richard (Franklin Lenox Thomas) 1940-. . . . . **CLC 26**
See CA 122; 152

Przybyszewski, Stanislaw 1868-1927. . . . .**TCLC 36**
See CA 160; DLB 66

Pteleon
See Grieve, C(hristopher) M(urray)

Puckett, Lute
See Masters, Edgar Lee

Puig, Manuel 1932-1990. . . . . **CLC 3, 5, 10, 28, 65; DAM MULT; HLC**
See CA 45-48; CANR 2, 32, 63; DLB 113; HW 1, 2; MTCW 1, 2

Pulitzer, Joseph 1847-1911. . . . . **TCLC 76**
See CA 114; DLB 23

Purdy, A(lfred) W(ellington) 1918-. . . . . . **CLC 3, 6, 14, 50; DAC; DAM MST, POET**
See CA 81-84; CAAS 17; CANR 42, 66; DLB 88

Purdy, James (Amos) 1923-. . . . . **CLC 2, 4, 10, 28, 52**
See CA 33-36R; CAAS 1; CANR 19, 51; DLB 2; INT CANR-19; MTCW 1

Pure, Simon
See Swinnerton, Frank Arthur

Pushkin, Alexander (Sergeyevich) 1799-1837. . . . . . .**NCLC 3, 27; DA; DAB; DAC; DAM DRAM, MST, POET; PC 10; SSC 27; WLC**
See DLB 205; SATA 61

P'u Sung-ling 1640-1715. . . . . . .**LC 49; SSC 31**

Putnam, Arthur Lee
See Alger, Horatio, Jr.

Puzo, Mario 1920-1999. . . . . . . **CLC 1, 2, 6, 36, 107; DAM NOV, POP**
See CA 65-68; CANR 4, 42, 65; DLB 6; MTCW 1, 2

Pygge, Edward
See Barnes, Julian (Patrick)

Pyle, Ernest Taylor 1900-1945
See Pyle, Ernie

Pyle, Ernie 1900-1945. . . . . **TCLC 75**
See Pyle, Ernest Taylor

Pyle, Howard 1853-1911. . . . . **TCLC 81**
See CA 109; 137; CLR 22; DLB 42, 188; DLBD 13; MAICYA; SATA 16, 100

Pym, Barbara (Mary Crampton) 1913-1980. . . . . **CLC 13, 19, 37, 111**
See CA 13-14; 97-100; CANR 13, 34; CAP 1; DLB 14, 207; DLBY 87; MTCW 1, 2

Pynchon, Thomas (Ruggles, Jr.) 1937-. . . . . . .**CLC 2, 3, 6, 9, 11, 18, 33, 62, 72; DA; DAB; DAC; DAM MST, NOV, POP; SSC 14; WLC**
See BEST 90:2; CA 17-20R; CANR 22, 46, 73; DLB 2, 173; MTCW 1, 2

Pythagoras c. 570B.C.-c. 500B.C.. . . . . . . **CMLC 22**
See DLB 176

Q
See Quiller-Couch, SirArthur (Thomas)

Qian Zhongshu
See Ch'ien Chung-shu

Qroll
See Dagerman, Stig (Halvard)

Quarrington, Paul (Lewis) 1953-. . . . . .**CLC 65**
See CA 129; CANR 62

Quasimodo, Salvatore 1901-1968. . . . . **CLC 10**
See CA 13-16; 25-28R; CAP 1; DLB 114; MTCW 1

Quay, Stephen 1947-. . . . .**CLC 95**

Quay, Timothy 1947-. . . . . **CLC 95**

Queen, Ellery. . . . .**CLC 3, 11**
See Dannay, Frederic; Davidson, Avram (James); Lee, Manfred B(ennington); Marlowe, Stephen; Sturgeon, Theodore (Hamilton); Vance, John Holbrook

Queen, Ellery, Jr.
See Dannay, Frederic; Lee, Manfred B(ennington)

Queneau, Raymond 1903-1976. . . . . .**CLC 2, 5, 10, 42**
See CA 77-80; 69-72; CANR 32; DLB 72; MTCW 1, 2

Quevedo, Francisco de 1580-1645. . . . . . **LC 23**

Quiller-Couch, SirArthur (Thomas) 1863-1944. . . . .**TCLC 53**
See CA 118; 166; DLB 135, 153, 190

Quin, Ann (Marie) 1936-1973 . . . . **CLC 6**
See CA 9-12R; 45-48; DLB 14

Quinn, Martin
See Smith, Martin Cruz

Quinn, Peter 1947- . . . . **CLC 91**

Quinn, Simon
See Smith, Martin Cruz

Quiroga, Horacio (Sylvestre) 1878-1937 . . . . . . **TCLC 20; DAM MULT; HLC**
See CA 117; 131; HW 1; MTCW 1

Quoirez, Francoise 1935- . . . . **CLC 9**
See Sagan, Francoise

Raabe, Wilhelm (Karl) 1831-1910 . . . . . . **TCLC 45**
See CA 167; DLB 129

Rabe, David (William) 1940- . . . . **CLC 4, 8, 33; DAM DRAM**
See CA 85-88; CABS 3; CANR 59; DLB 7

Rabelais, Francois 1483-1553 . . . . . . **LC 5; DA; DAB; DAC; DAM MST; WLC**

Rabinovitch, Sholem 1859-1916
See Aleichem, Sholom

Rabinyan, Dorit 1972- . . . . **CLC 119**
See CA 170

Rachilde 1860-1953 . . . . **TCLC 67**
See DLB 123, 192

Racine, Jean 1639-1699 . . . . **LC 28; DAB; DAM MST**

Radcliffe, Ann (Ward) 1764-1823 . . . . . . **NCLC 6, 55**
See DLB 39, 178

Radiguet, Raymond 1903-1923 . . . . . . **TCLC 29**
See CA 162; DLB 65

Radnoti, Miklos 1909-1944 . . . . **TCLC 16**
See CA 118

Rado, James 1939- . . . . **CLC 17**
See CA 105

Radvanyi, Netty 1900-1983
See Seghers, Anna

Rae, Ben
See Griffiths, Trevor

Raeburn, John (Hay) 1941- . . . . **CLC 34**
See CA 57-60

Ragni, Gerome 1942-1991 . . . . **CLC 17**
See CA 105; 134

Rahv, Philip 1908-1973 . . . . **CLC 24**
See Greenberg, Ivan

Raimund, Ferdinand Jakob 1790-1836 . . . . **NCLC 69**
See DLB 90

Raine, Craig 1944- . . . . **CLC 32, 103**
See CA 108; CANR 29, 51; DLB 40

Raine, Kathleen (Jessie) 1908- . . . . . . **CLC 7, 45**
See CA 85-88; CANR 46; DLB 20; MTCW 1

Rainis, Janis 1865-1929 . . . . **TCLC 29**
See CA 170

Rakosi, Carl 1903- . . . . **CLC 47**
See Rawley, Callman

Raleigh, Richard
See Lovecraft, H(oward) P(hillips)

Raleigh, Sir Walter 1554(?)-1618 . . . . . . **LC 31, 39**
See CDBLB Before 1660; DLB 172

Rallentando, H. P.
See Sayers, Dorothy L(eigh)

Ramal, Walter
See de la Mare, Walter (John)

Ramana Maharshi 1879-1950 . . . . **TCLC 84**

Ramoacn y Cajal, Santiago 1852-1934 . . . . **TCLC 93**

Ramon, Juan
See Jimenez (Mantecon), Juan Ramon

Ramos, Graciliano 1892-1953 . . . . **TCLC 32**
See CA 167; HW 2

Rampersad, Arnold 1941- . . . . **CLC 44**
See BW 2, 3; CA 127; 133; DLB 111; INT 133

Rampling, Anne
See Rice, Anne

Ramsay, Allan 1684(?)-1758 . . . . **LC 29**
See DLB 95

Ramuz, Charles-Ferdinand 1878-1947 . . . . **TCLC 33**
See CA 165

Rand, Ayn 1905-1982 . . . . . . **CLC 3, 30, 44, 79; DA; DAC; DAM MST, NOV, POP; WLC**
See AAYA 10; CA 13-16R; 105; CANR 27, 73; CDALBS; MTCW 1, 2

Randall, Dudley (Felker) 1914- . . . . **CLC 1; BLC 3; DAM MULT**
See BW 1, 3; CA 25-28R; CANR 23; DLB 41

Randall, Robert
See Silverberg, Robert

Ranger, Ken
See Creasey, John

Ransom, John Crowe 1888-1974 . . . . . . **CLC 2, 4, 5, 11, 24; DAM POET**
See CA 5-8R; 49-52; CANR 6, 34; CDALBS; DLB 45, 63; MTCW 1, 2

Rao, Raja 1909- . . . . . . **CLC 25, 56; DAM NOV**
See CA 73-76; CANR 51; MTCW 1, 2

Raphael, Frederic (Michael) 1931- . . . . . . **CLC 2, 14**
See CA 1-4R; CANR 1; DLB 14

Ratcliffe, James P.
See Mencken, H(enry) L(ouis)

Rathbone, Julian 1935- . . . . **CLC 41**
See CA 101; CANR 34, 73

Rattigan, Terence (Mervyn) 1911-1977 . . . . **CLC 7; DAM DRAM**
See CA 85-88; 73-76; CDBLB 1945-1960; DLB 13; MTCW 1, 2

Ratushinskaya, Irina 1954- . . . . **CLC 54**
See CA 129; CANR 68

Raven, Simon (Arthur Noel) 1927- . . . . . . **CLC 14**
See CA 81-84

Ravenna, Michael
See Welty, Eudora

Rawley, Callman 1903-
See Rakosi, Carl

Rawlings, Marjorie Kinnan 1896-1953 . . . . **TCLC 4**
See AAYA 20; CA 104; 137; CANR 74; DLB 9, 22, 102; DLBD 17; JRDA; MAICYA; MTCW 2; SATA 100; YABC 1

Ray, Satyajit 1921-1992 . . . . **CLC 16, 76; DAM MULT**
See CA 114; 137

Read, Herbert Edward 1893-1968 . . . . . **CLC 4**
See CA 85-88; 25-28R; DLB 20, 149

Read, Piers Paul 1941- . . . . **CLC 4, 10, 25**
See CA 21-24R; CANR 38; DLB 14; SATA 21

Reade, Charles 1814-1884 . . . . **NCLC 2, 74**
See DLB 21

Reade, Hamish
See Gray, Simon (James Holliday)

Reading, Peter 1946- . . . . **CLC 47**
See CA 103; CANR 46; DLB 40

Reaney, James 1926- . . . . **CLC 13; DAC; DAM MST**
See CA 41-44R; CAAS 15; CANR 42; DLB 68; SATA 43

Rebreanu, Liviu 1885-1944 . . . . **TCLC 28**
See CA 165

Rechy, John (Francisco) 1934- . . . . . . **CLC 1, 7, 14, 18, 107; DAM MULT; HLC**
See CA 5-8R; CAAS 4; CANR 6, 32, 64; DLB 122; DLBY 82; HW 1, 2; INT CANR-6

Redcam, Tom 1870-1933 . . . . **TCLC 25**

Reddin, Keith . . . . **CLC 67**

Redgrove, Peter (William) 1932- . . . . . . **CLC 6, 41**
See CA 1-4R; CANR 3, 39, 77; DLB 40

Redmon, Anne . . . . **CLC 22**
See Nightingale, Anne Redmon

Reed, Eliot
See Ambler, Eric

Reed, Ishmael 1938- . . . . . **CLC 2, 3, 5, 6, 13, 32, 60; BLC 3; DAM MULT**
See BW 2, 3; CA 21-24R; CANR 25, 48, 74; DLB 2, 5, 33, 169; DLBD 8; MTCW 1, 2

Reed, John (Silas) 1887-1920 . . . . **TCLC 9**
See CA 106

Reed, Lou . . . . **CLC 21**
See Firbank, Louis

Reeve, Clara 1729-1807 . . . . **NCLC 19**
See DLB 39

Reich, Wilhelm 1897-1957 . . . . **TCLC 57**

Reid, Christopher (John) 1949- . . . . **CLC 33**
See CA 140; DLB 40

Reid, Desmond
See Moorcock, Michael (John)

Reid Banks, Lynne 1929-
See Banks, Lynne Reid

Reilly, William K.
See Creasey, John

Reiner, Max
See Caldwell, (Janet Miriam) Taylor (Holland)

Reis, Ricardo
See Pessoa, Fernando (Antonio Nogueira)

Rossetti, Dante Gabriel 1828-1882..... **NCLC 4, 77; DA; DAB; DAC; DAM MST, POET; WLC**
See CDBLB 1832-1890; DLB 35

Rossner, Judith (Perelman) 1935-..... **CLC 6, 9, 29**
See AITN 2; BEST 90:3; CA 17-20R; CANR 18, 51, 73; DLB 6; INT CANR-18; MTCW 1, 2

Rostand, Edmond (Eugene Alexis) 1868-1918.......**TCLC 6, 37; DA; DAB; DAC; DAM DRAM, MST; DC 10**
See CA 104; 126; DLB 192; MTCW 1

Roth, Henry 1906-1995..... **CLC 2, 6, 11, 104**
See CA 11-12; 149; CANR 38, 63; CAP 1; DLB 28; MTCW 1, 2

Roth, Philip (Milton) 1933-.....**CLC 1, 2, 3, 4, 6, 9, 15, 22, 31, 47, 66, 86, 119; DA; DAB; DAC; DAM MST, NOV, POP; SSC 26; WLC**
See BEST 90:3; CA 1-4R; CANR 1, 22, 36, 55; CDALB 1968-1988; DLB 2, 28, 173; DLBY 82; MTCW 1, 2

Rothenberg, Jerome 1931-.........**CLC 6, 57**
See CA 45-48; CANR 1; DLB 5, 193

Roumain, Jacques (Jean Baptiste) 1907-1944...... **TCLC 19; BLC 3; DAM MULT**
See BW 1; CA 117; 125

Rourke, Constance (Mayfield) 1885-1941................... **TCLC 12**
See CA 107; YABC 1

Rousseau, Jean-Baptiste 1671-1741......**LC 9**

Rousseau, Jean-Jacques 1712-1778.....**LC 14, 36; DA; DAB; DAC; DAM MST; WLC**

Roussel, Raymond 1877-1933....... **TCLC 20**
See CA 117

Rovit, Earl (Herbert) 1927-........... **CLC 7**
See CA 5-8R; CANR 12

Rowe, Elizabeth Singer 1674-1737......**LC 44**
See DLB 39, 95

Rowe, Nicholas 1674-1718............. **LC 8**
See DLB 84

Rowley, Ames Dorrance
See Lovecraft, H(oward) P(hillips)

Rowson, Susanna Haswell 1762(?)-1824.............. **NCLC 5, 69**
See DLB 37, 200

Roy, Arundhati 1960(?)-........... **CLC 109**
See CA 163; DLBY 97

Roy, Gabrielle 1909-1983........ **CLC 10, 14; DAB; DAC; DAM MST**
See CA 53-56; 110; CANR 5, 61; DLB 68; MTCW 1; SATA 104

Royko, Mike 1932-1997............ **CLC 109**
See CA 89-92; 157; CANR 26

Rozewicz, Tadeusz 1921-......... **CLC 9, 23; DAM POET**
See CA 108; CANR 36, 66; MTCW 1, 2

Ruark, Gibbons 1941-............... **CLC 3**
See CA 33-36R; CAAS 23; CANR 14, 31, 57; DLB 120

Rubens, Bernice (Ruth) 1923-..... **CLC 19, 31**
See CA 25-28R; CANR 33, 65; DLB 14, 207; MTCW 1

Rubin, Harold
See Robbins, Harold

Rudkin, (James) David 1936-........ **CLC 14**
See CA 89-92; DLB 13

Rudnik, Raphael 1933-...............**CLC 7**
See CA 29-32R

Ruffian, M.
See Hasek, Jaroslav (Matej Frantisek)

Ruiz, Jose Martinez................ **CLC 11**
See Martinez Ruiz, Jose

Rukeyser, Muriel 1913-1980.......**CLC 6, 10, 15, 27; DAM POET; PC 12**
See CA 5-8R; 93-96; CANR 26, 60; DLB 48; MTCW 1, 2; SATA-Obit 22

Rule, Jane (Vance) 1931-............ **CLC 27**
See CA 25-28R; CAAS 18; CANR 12; DLB 60

Rulfo, Juan 1918-1986...... **CLC 8, 80; DAM MULT; HLC; SSC 25**
See CA 85-88; 118; CANR 26; DLB 113; HW 1, 2; MTCW 1, 2

Rumi, Jalal al-Din 1297-1373.......**CMLC 20**

Runeberg, Johan 1804-1877........ **NCLC 41**

Runyon, (Alfred) Damon 1884(?)-1946.................**TCLC 10**
See CA 107; 165; DLB 11, 86, 171; MTCW 2

Rush, Norman 1933-................**CLC 44**
See CA 121; 126; INT 126

Rushdie, (Ahmed) Salman 1947-..... **CLC 23, 31, 55, 100; DAB; DAC; DAM MST, NOV, POP; WLCS**
See BEST 89:3; CA 108; 111; CANR 33, 56; DLB 194; INT 111; MTCW 1, 2

Rushforth, Peter (Scott) 1945-........**CLC 19**
See CA 101

Ruskin, John 1819-1900........... **TCLC 63**
See CA 114; 129; CDBLB 1832-1890; DLB 55, 163, 190; SATA 24

Russ, Joanna 1937-.................**CLC 15**
See CANR 11, 31, 65; DLB 8; MTCW 1

Russell, George William 1867-1935
See Baker, Jean H.

Russell, (Henry) Ken(neth Alfred) 1927-........................ **CLC 16**
See CA 105

Russell, William Martin 1947-........**CLC 60**
See CA 164

Rutherford, Mark................ **TCLC 25**
See White, William Hale

Ruyslinck, Ward 1929-..............**CLC 14**
See Belser, Reimond Karel Maria de

Ryan, Cornelius (John) 1920-1974..... **CLC 7**
See CA 69-72; 53-56; CANR 38

Ryan, Michael 1946-................**CLC 65**
See CA 49-52; DLBY 82

Ryan, Tim
See Dent, Lester

Rybakov, Anatoli (Naumovich) 1911-1998................. **CLC 23, 53**
See CA 126; 135; 172; SATA 79; SATA-Obit 108

Ryder, Jonathan
See Ludlum, Robert

Ryga, George 1932-1987...... **CLC 14; DAC; DAM MST**
See CA 101; 124; CANR 43; DLB 60

S. H.
See Hartmann, Sadakichi

S. S.
See Sassoon, Siegfried (Lorraine)

Saba, Umberto 1883-1957.......... **TCLC 33**
See CA 144; CANR 79; DLB 114

Sabatini, Rafael 1875-1950......... **TCLC 47**
See CA 162

Sabato, Ernesto (R.) 1911-....... **CLC 10, 23; DAM MULT; HLC**
See CA 97-100; CANR 32, 65; DLB 145; HW 1, 2; MTCW 1, 2

Sa-Carniero, Mario de 1890-1916...... **TCLC 83**

Sacastru, Martin
See Bioy Casares, Adolfo

Sacher-Masoch, Leopold von 1836(?)-1895................ **NCLC 31**

Sachs, Marilyn (Stickle) 1927-........**CLC 35**
See AAYA 2; CA 17-20R; CANR 13, 47; CLR 2; JRDA; MAICYA; SAAS 2; SATA 3, 68

Sachs, Nelly 1891-1970...........**CLC 14, 98**
See CA 17-18; 25-28R; CAP 2; MTCW 2

Sackler, Howard (Oliver) 1929-1982..... **CLC 14**
See CA 61-64; 108; CANR 30; DLB 7

Sacks, Oliver (Wolf) 1933-...........**CLC 67**
See CA 53-56; CANR 28, 50, 76; INT CANR-28; MTCW 1, 2

Sadakichi
See Hartmann, Sadakichi

Sade, Donatien Alphonse Francois, Comte de 1740-1814....................**NCLC 47**

Sadoff, Ira 1945-.................... **CLC 9**
See CA 53-56; CANR 5, 21; DLB 120

Saetone
See Camus, Albert

Safire, William 1929-............... **CLC 10**
See CA 17-20R; CANR 31, 54

Sagan, Carl (Edward) 1934-1996..... **CLC 30, 112**
See AAYA 2; CA 25-28R; 155; CANR 11, 36, 74; MTCW 1, 2; SATA 58; SATA-Obit 94

Sagan, Francoise..........**CLC 3, 6, 9, 17, 36**
See Quoirez, Francoise

Sahgal, Nayantara (Pandit) 1927-.....**CLC 41**
See CA 9-12R; CANR 11

Saint, H(arry) F. 1941-..............**CLC 50**
See CA 127

St. Aubin de Teran, Lisa 1953-
See Teran, Lisa St. Aubin de

Singer, Isaac
See Singer, Isaac Bashevis

Singer, Isaac Bashevis 1904-1991...... **CLC 1, 3, 6, 9, 11, 15, 23, 38, 69, 111; DA; DAB; DAC; DAM MST, NOV; SSC 3; WLC**
See AITN 1, 2; CA 1-4R; 134; CANR 1, 39; CDALB 1941-1968; CLR 1; DLB 6, 28, 52; DLBY 91; JRDA; MAICYA; MTCW 1, 2; SATA 3, 27; SATA-Obit 68

Singer, Israel Joshua 1893-1944..... **TCLC 33**
See CA 169

Singh, Khushwant 1915-............ **CLC 11**
See CA 9-12R; CAAS 9; CANR 6

Singleton, Ann
See Benedict, Ruth (Fulton)

Sinjohn, John
See Galsworthy, John

Sinyavsky, Andrei (Donatevich) 1925-1997..................... **CLC 8**
See CA 85-88; 159

Sirin, V.
See Nabokov, Vladimir (Vladimirovich)

Sissman, L(ouis) E(dward) 1928-1976.................. **CLC 9, 18**
See CA 21-24R; 65-68; CANR 13; DLB 5

Sisson, C(harles) H(ubert) 1914-....... **CLC 8**
See CA 1-4R; CAAS 3; CANR 3, 48; DLB 27

Sitwell, Dame Edith 1887-1964...... **CLC 2, 9, 67; DAM POET; PC 3**
See CA 9-12R; CANR 35; CDBLB 1945-1960; DLB 20; MTCW 1, 2

Siwaarmill, H. P.
See Sharp, William

Sjoewall, Maj 1935-................. **CLC 7**
See CA 65-68; CANR 73

Sjowall, Maj
See Sjoewall, Maj

Skelton, John 1463-1529.............. **PC 25**

Skelton, Robin 1925-1997........... **CLC 13**
See AITN 2; CA 5-8R; 160; CAAS 5; CANR 28; DLB 27, 53

Skolimowski, Jerzy 1938-............ **CLC 20**
See CA 128

Skram, Amalie (Bertha) 1847-1905..... **TCLC 25**
See CA 165

Skvorecky, Josef (Vaclav) 1924-...... **CLC 15, 39, 69; DAC; DAM NOV**
See CA 61-64; CAAS 1; CANR 10, 34, 63; MTCW 1, 2

Slade, Bernard................. **CLC 11, 46**
See Newbound, Bernard Slade

Slaughter, Carolyn 1946-............ **CLC 56**
See CA 85-88

Slaughter, Frank G(ill) 1908-........ **CLC 29**
See AITN 2; CA 5-8R; CANR 5; INT CANR-5

Slavitt, David R(ytman) 1935-...... **CLC 5, 14**
See CA 21-24R; CAAS 3; CANR 41; DLB 5, 6

Slesinger, Tess 1905-1945.......... **TCLC 10**
See CA 107; DLB 102

Slessor, Kenneth 1901-1971.......... **CLC 14**
See CA 102; 89-92

Slowacki, Juliusz 1809-1849........ **NCLC 15**

Smart, Christopher 1722-1771......... **LC 3; DAM POET; PC 13**
See DLB 109

Smart, Elizabeth 1913-1986.......... **CLC 54**
See CA 81-84; 118; DLB 88

Smiley, Jane (Graves) 1949-...... **CLC 53, 76; DAM POP**
See CA 104; CANR 30, 50, 74; INT CANR-30

Smith, A(rthur) J(ames) M(arshall) 1902-1980............... **CLC 15; DAC**
See CA 1-4R; 102; CANR 4; DLB 88

Smith, Adam 1723-1790.............. **LC 36**
See DLB 104

Smith, Alexander 1829-1867........ **NCLC 59**
See DLB 32, 55

Smith, Anna Deavere 1950-.......... **CLC 86**
See CA 133

Smith, Betty (Wehner) 1896-1972..... **CLC 19**
See CA 5-8R; 33-36R; DLBY 82; SATA 6

Smith, Charlotte (Turner) 1749-1806................... **NCLC 23**
See DLB 39, 109

Smith, Clark Ashton 1893-1961...... **CLC 43**
See CA 143; MTCW 2

Smith, Dave.................... **CLC 22, 42**
See Smith, David (Jeddie)

Smith, David (Jeddie) 1942-
See Smith, Dave

Smith, Florence Margaret 1902-1971
See Smith, Stevie

Smith, Iain Crichton 1928-1998...... **CLC 64**
See CA 21-24R; 171; DLB 40, 139

Smith, John 1580(?)-1631.............. **LC 9**
See DLB 24, 30

Smith, Johnston
See Crane, Stephen (Townley)

Smith, Joseph, Jr. 1805-1844....... **NCLC 53**

Smith, Lee 1944-................ **CLC 25, 73**
See CA 114; 119; CANR 46; DLB 143; DLBY 83; INT 119

Smith, Martin
See Smith, Martin Cruz

Smith, Martin Cruz 1942-..... **CLC 25; DAM MULT, POP**
See BEST 89:4; CA 85-88; CANR 6, 23, 43, 65; INT CANR-23; MTCW 2; NNAL

Smith, Mary-Ann Tirone 1944-....... **CLC 39**
See CA 118; 136

Smith, Patti 1946-.................. **CLC 12**
See CA 93-96; CANR 63

Smith, Pauline (Urmson) 1882-1959................... **TCLC 25**

Smith, Rosamond
See Oates, Joyce Carol

Smith, Sheila Kaye
See Kaye-Smith, Sheila

Smith, Stevie........ **CLC 3, 8, 25, 44; PC 12**
See Smith, Florence Margaret

Smith, Wilbur (Addison) 1933-....... **CLC 33**
See CA 13-16R; CANR 7, 46, 66; MTCW 1, 2

Smith, William Jay 1918-............. **CLC 6**
See CA 5-8R; CANR 44; DLB 5; MAICYA; SAAS 22; SATA 2, 68

Smith, Woodrow Wilson
See Kuttner, Henry

Smolenskin, Peretz 1842-1885...... **NCLC 30**

Smollett, Tobias (George) 1721-1771...... **LC 2, 46**
See CDBLB 1660-1789; DLB 39, 104

Snodgrass, W(illiam) D(e Witt) 1926-........ **CLC 2, 6, 10, 18, 68; DAM POET**
See CA 1-4R; CANR 6, 36, 65; DLB 5; MTCW 1, 2

Snow, C(harles) P(ercy) 1905-1980...... **CLC 1, 4, 6, 9, 13, 19; DAM NOV**
See CA 5-8R; 101; CANR 28; CDBLB 1945-1960; DLB 15, 77; DLBD 17; MTCW 1, 2

Snow, Frances Compton
See Adams, Henry (Brooks)

Snyder, Gary (Sherman) 1930-..... **CLC 1, 2, 5, 9, 32, 120; DAM POET; PC 21**
See CA 17-20R; CANR 30, 60; DLB 5, 16, 165, 212; MTCW 2

Snyder, Zilpha Keatley 1927-........ **CLC 17**
See AAYA 15; CA 9-12R; CANR 38; CLR 31; JRDA; MAICYA; SAAS 2; SATA 1, 28, 75

Soares, Bernardo
See Pessoa, Fernando (Antonio Nogueira)

Sobh, A.
See Shamlu, Ahmad

Sobol, Joshua...................... **CLC 60**

Socrates 469B.C.-399B.C.......... **CMLC 27**

Soderberg, Hjalmar 1869-1941...... **TCLC 39**

Sodergran, Edith (Irene)
See Soedergran, Edith (Irene)

Soedergran, Edith (Irene) 1892-1923................... **TCLC 31**

Softly, Edgar
See Lovecraft, H(oward) P(hillips)

Softly, Edward
See Lovecraft, H(oward) P(hillips)

Sokolov, Raymond 1941-............. **CLC 7**
See CA 85-88

Solo, Jay
See Ellison, Harlan (Jay)

Sologub, Fyodor................... **TCLC 9**
See Teternikov, Fyodor Kuzmich

Solomons, Ikey Esquir
See Thackeray, William Makepeace

Solomos, Dionysios 1798-1857...... **NCLC 15**

Solwoska, Mara
See French, Marilyn

Solzhenitsyn, Aleksandr I(sayevich) 1918-..... **CLC 1, 2, 4, 7, 9, 10, 18, 26, 34, 78; DA; DAB; DAC; DAM MST, NOV; SSC 32; WLC**
See AITN 1; CA 69-72; CANR 40, 65; MTCW 1, 2

Somers, Jane
See Lessing, Doris (May)

Somerville, Edith 1858-1949........ **TCLC 51**
See DLB 135

Somerville & Ross
See Martin, Violet Florence; Somerville, Edith

Sommer, Scott 1951-................ **CLC 25**
See CA 106

Sondheim, Stephen (Joshua) 1930-...... **CLC 30, 39; DAM DRAM**
See AAYA 11; CA 103; CANR 47, 68

Song, Cathy 1955-................... **PC 21**
See CA 154; DLB 169

Sontag, Susan 1933-...... **CLC 1, 2, 10, 13, 31, 105; DAM POP**
See CA 17-20R; CANR 25, 51, 74; DLB 2, 67; MTCW 1, 2

Sophocles 496(?)B.C.-406(?)B.C........ **CMLC 2; DA; DAB; DAC; DAM DRAM, MST; DC 1; WLCS**
See DLB 176

Sordello 1189-1269............... **CMLC 15**

Sorel, Georges 1847-1922.......... **TCLC 91**
See CA 118

Sorel, Julia
See Drexler, Rosalyn

Sorrentino, Gilbert 1929-....... **CLC 3, 7, 14, 22, 40**
See CA 77-80; CANR 14, 33; DLB 5, 173; DLBY 80; INT CANR-14

Soto, Gary 1952-.......... **CLC 32, 80; DAM MULT; HLC**
See AAYA 10; CA 119; 125; CANR 50, 74; CLR 38; DLB 82; HW 1, 2; INT 125; JRDA; MTCW 2; SATA 80

Soupault, Philippe 1897-1990........ **CLC 68**
See CA 116; 147; 131

Souster, (Holmes) Raymond 1921-..... **CLC 5, 14; DAC; DAM POET**
See CA 13-16R; CAAS 14; CANR 13, 29, 53; DLB 88; SATA 63

Southern, Terry 1924(?)-1995......... **CLC 7**
See CA 1-4R; 150; CANR 1, 55; DLB 2

Southey, Robert 1774-1843.......... **NCLC 8**
See DLB 93, 107, 142; SATA 54

Southworth, Emma Dorothy Eliza Nevitte
1819-1899.................. **NCLC 26**

Souza, Ernest
See Scott, Evelyn

Soyinka, Wole 1934-..... **CLC 3, 5, 14, 36, 44; BLC 3; DA; DAB; DAC; DAM DRAM, MST, MULT; DC 2; WLC**
See BW 2, 3; CA 13-16R; CANR 27, 39; DLB 125; MTCW 1, 2

Spackman, W(illiam) M(ode)
1905-1990.................... **CLC 46**
See CA 81-84; 132

Spacks, Barry (Bernard) 1931-....... **CLC 14**
See CA 154; CANR 33; DLB 105

Spanidou, Irini 1946-............... **CLC 44**

Spark, Muriel (Sarah) 1918-...... **CLC 2, 3, 5, 8, 13, 18, 40, 94; DAB; DAC; DAM MST, NOV; SSC 10**
See CA 5-8R; CANR 12, 36, 76; CDBLB 1945-1960; DLB 15, 139; INT CANR-12; MTCW 1, 2

Spaulding, Douglas
See Bradbury, Ray (Douglas)

Spaulding, Leonard
See Bradbury, Ray (Douglas)

Spence, J. A. D.
See Eliot, T(homas) S(tearns)

Spencer, Elizabeth 1921-............ **CLC 22**
See CA 13-16R; CANR 32, 65; DLB 6; MTCW 1; SATA 14

Spencer, Leonard G.
See Silverberg, Robert

Spencer, Scott 1945-................ **CLC 30**
See CA 113; CANR 51; DLBY 86

Spender, Stephen (Harold)
1909-1995....... **CLC 1, 2, 5, 10, 41, 91; DAM POET**
See CA 9-12R; 149; CANR 31, 54; CDBLB 1945-1960; DLB 20; MTCW 1, 2

Spengler, Oswald (Arnold Gottfried)
1880-1936.................. **TCLC 25**
See CA 118

Spenser, Edmund 1552(?)-1599..... **LC 5, 39; DA; DAB; DAC; DAM MST, POET; PC 8; WLC**
See CDBLB Before 1660; DLB 167

Spicer, Jack 1925-1965........ **CLC 8, 18, 72; DAM POET**
See CA 85-88; DLB 5, 16, 193

Spiegelman, Art 1948-.............. **CLC 76**
See AAYA 10; CA 125; CANR 41, 55, 74; MTCW 2; SATA 109

Spielberg, Peter 1929-............... **CLC 6**
See CA 5-8R; CANR 4, 48; DLBY 81

Spielberg, Steven 1947-............. **CLC 20**
See AAYA 8, 24; CA 77-80; CANR 32; SATA 32

Spillane, Frank Morrison 1918-
See Spillane, Mickey

Spillane, Mickey................. **CLC 3, 13**
See Spillane, Frank Morrison

Spinoza, Benedictus de 1632-1677....... **LC 9**

Spinrad, Norman (Richard) 1940-....... **CLC 46**
See CA 37-40R; CAAS 19; CANR 20; DLB 8; INT CANR-20

Spitteler, Carl (Friedrich Georg)
1845-1924.................. **TCLC 12**
See CA 109; DLB 129

Spivack, Kathleen (Romola Drucker)
1938-......................... **CLC 6**
See CA 49-52

Spoto, Donald 1941-................ **CLC 39**
See CA 65-68; CANR 11, 57

Springsteen, Bruce (F.) 1949-........ **CLC 17**
See CA 111

Spurling, Hilary 1940-.............. **CLC 34**
See CA 104; CANR 25, 52

Spyker, John Howland
See Elman, Richard (Martin)

Squires, (James) Radcliffe
1917-1993.................... **CLC 51**
See CA 1-4R; 140; CANR 6, 21

Srivastava, Dhanpat Rai 1880(?)-1936
See Premchand

Stacy, Donald
See Pohl, Frederik

Stael, Germaine de 1766-1817
See Stael-Holstein, Anne Louise Germaine Necker Baronn

Stael-Holstein, Anne Louise Germaine Necker Baronn 1766-1817............. **NCLC 3**
See Stael, Germaine de

Stafford, Jean 1915-1979........ **CLC 4, 7, 19, 68; SSC 26**
See CA 1-4R; 85-88; CANR 3, 65; DLB 2, 173; MTCW 1, 2; SATA-Obit 22

Stafford, William (Edgar) 1914-1993..... **CLC 4, 7, 29; DAM POET**
See CA 5-8R; 142; CAAS 3; CANR 5, 22; DLB 5, 206; INT CANR-22

Stagnelius, Eric Johan 1793-1823...... **NCLC 61**

Staines, Trevor
See Brunner, John (Kilian Houston)

Stairs, Gordon
See Austin, Mary (Hunter)

Stalin, Joseph 1879-1953........... **TCLC 92**

Stannard, Martin 1947-............. **CLC 44**
See CA 142; DLB 155

Stanton, Elizabeth Cady
1815-1902................... **TCLC 73**
See CA 171; DLB 79

Stanton, Maura 1946-................ **CLC 9**
See CA 89-92; CANR 15; DLB 120

Stanton, Schuyler
See Baum, L(yman) Frank

Stapledon, (William) Olaf
1886-1950................... **TCLC 22**
See CA 111; 162; DLB 15

Starbuck, George (Edwin)
1931-1996........ **CLC 53; DAM POET**
See CA 21-24R; 153; CANR 23

Stark, Richard
See Westlake, Donald E(dwin)

Staunton, Schuyler
See Baum, L(yman) Frank

Stead, Christina (Ellen) 1902-1983...... **CLC 2, 5, 8, 32, 80**
See CA 13-16R; 109; CANR 33, 40; MTCW 1, 2

Stead, William Thomas 1849-1912..... **TCLC 48**
See CA 167

Steele, Richard 1672-1729............. **LC 18**
See CDBLB 1660-1789; DLB 84, 101

Steele, Timothy (Reid) 1948-......... **CLC 45**
See CA 93-96; CANR 16, 50; DLB 120

Steffens, (Joseph) Lincoln
1866-1936................... **TCLC 20**
See CA 117

Stegner, Wallace (Earle) 1909-1993...... **CLC 9, 49, 81; DAM NOV; SSC 27**
See AITN 1; BEST 90:3; CA 1-4R; 141; CAAS 9; CANR 1, 21, 46; DLB 9, 206; DLBY 93; MTCW 1, 2

Stein, Gertrude 1874-1946..... **TCLC 1, 6, 28, 48; DA; DAB; DAC; DAM MST, NOV, POET; PC 18; WLC**
See CA 104; 132; CDALB 1917-1929; DLB 4, 54, 86; DLBD 15; MTCW 1, 2

Steinbeck, John (Ernst) 1902-1968...... **CLC 1, 5, 9, 13, 21, 34, 45, 75; DA; DAB; DAC; DAM DRAM, MST, NOV; SSC 11; WLC**
See AAYA 12; CA 1-4R; 25-28R; CANR 1, 35; CDALB 1929-1941; DLB 7, 9, 212; DLBD 2; MTCW 1, 2; SATA 9

Steinem, Gloria 1934-............... **CLC 63**
See CA 53-56; CANR 28, 51; MTCW 1, 2

Steiner, George 1929-......... **CLC 24; DAM NOV**
See CA 73-76; CANR 31, 67; DLB 67; MTCW 1, 2; SATA 62

Steiner, K. Leslie
See Delany, Samuel R(ay, Jr.)

Steiner, Rudolf 1861-1925.......... **TCLC 13**
See CA 107

Stendhal 1783-1842....... **NCLC 23, 46; DA; DAB; DAC; DAM MST, NOV; SSC 27; WLC**
See DLB 119

Stephen, Adeline Virginia
See Woolf, (Adeline) Virginia

Stephen, SirLeslie 1832-1904....... **TCLC 23**
See CA 123; DLB 57, 144, 190

Stephen, Sir Leslie
See Stephen, SirLeslie

Stephen, Virginia
See Woolf, (Adeline) Virginia

Stephens, James 1882(?)-1950........ **TCLC 4**
See CA 104; DLB 19, 153, 162

Stephens, Reed
See Donaldson, Stephen R.

Steptoe, Lydia
See Barnes, Djuna

Sterchi, Beat 1949-................. **CLC 65**

Sterling, Brett
See Bradbury, Ray (Douglas); Hamilton, Edmond

Sterling, Bruce 1954-............... **CLC 72**
See CA 119; CANR 44

Sterling, George 1869-1926......... **TCLC 20**
See CA 117; 165; DLB 54

Stern, Gerald 1925-............ **CLC 40, 100**
See CA 81-84; CANR 28; DLB 105

Stern, Richard (Gustave) 1928-..... **CLC 4, 39**
See CA 1-4R; CANR 1, 25, 52; DLBY 87; INT CANR-25

Sternberg, Josef von 1894-1969....... **CLC 20**
See CA 81-84

Sterne, Laurence 1713-1768........ **LC 2, 48; DA; DAB; DAC; DAM MST, NOV; WLC**
See CDBLB 1660-1789; DLB 39

Sternheim, (William Adolf) Carl 1878-1942.................... **TCLC 8**
See CA 105; DLB 56, 118

Stevens, Mark 1951-................ **CLC 34**
See CA 122

Stevens, Wallace 1879-1955...... **TCLC 3, 12, 45; DA; DAB; DAC; DAM MST, POET; PC 6; WLC**
See CA 104; 124; CDALB 1929-1941; DLB 54; MTCW 1, 2

Stevenson, Anne (Katharine) 1933-...... **CLC 7, 33**
See CA 17-20R; CAAS 9; CANR 9, 33; DLB 40; MTCW 1

Stevenson, Robert Louis (Balfour) 1850-1894......... **NCLC 5, 14, 63; DA; DAB; DAC; DAM MST, NOV; SSC 11; WLC**
See AAYA 24; CDBLB 1890-1914; CLR 10, 11; DLB 18, 57, 141, 156, 174; DLBD 13; JRDA; MAICYA; SATA 100; YABC 2

Stewart, J(ohn) I(nnes) M(ackintosh) 1906-1994............... **CLC 7, 14, 32**
See CA 85-88; 147; CAAS 3; CANR 47; MTCW 1, 2

Stewart, Mary (Florence Elinor) 1916-............. **CLC 7, 35, 117; DAB**
See AAYA 29; CA 1-4R; CANR 1, 59; SATA 12

Stewart, Mary Rainbow
See Stewart, Mary (Florence Elinor)

Stifle, June
See Campbell, Maria

Stifter, Adalbert 1805-1868........ **NCLC 41; SSC 28**
See DLB 133

Still, James 1906-.................. **CLC 49**
See CA 65-68; CAAS 17; CANR 10, 26; DLB 9; SATA 29

Sting 1951-
See Sumner, Gordon Matthew

Stirling, Arthur
See Sinclair, Upton (Beall)

Stitt, Milan 1941-.................. **CLC 29**
See CA 69-72

Stockton, Francis Richard 1834-1902
See Stockton, Frank R.

Stockton, Frank R................. **TCLC 47**
See Stockton, Francis Richard

Stoddard, Charles
See Kuttner, Henry

Stoker, Abraham 1847-1912
See Stoker, Bram

Stoker, Bram 1847-1912...... **TCLC 8; DAB; WLC**
See Stoker, Abraham

Stolz, Mary (Slattery) 1920-.......... **CLC 12**
See AAYA 8; AITN 1; CA 5-8R; CANR 13, 41; JRDA; MAICYA; SAAS 3; SATA 10, 71

Stone, Irving 1903-1989........ **CLC 7; DAM POP**
See AITN 1; CA 1-4R; 129; CAAS 3; CANR 1, 23; INT CANR-23; MTCW 1, 2; SATA 3; SATA-Obit 64

Stone, Oliver (William) 1946-........ **CLC 73**
See AAYA 15; CA 110; CANR 55

Stone, Robert (Anthony) 1937-..... **CLC 5, 23, 42**
See CA 85-88; CANR 23, 66; DLB 152; INT CANR-23; MTCW 1

Stone, Zachary
See Follett, Ken(neth Martin)

Stoppard, Tom 1937-..... **CLC 1, 3, 4, 5, 8, 15, 29, 34, 63, 91; DA; DAB; DAC; DAM DRAM, MST; DC 6; WLC**
See CA 81-84; CANR 39, 67; CDBLB 1960 to Present; DLB 13; DLBY 85; MTCW 1, 2

Storey, David (Malcolm) 1933-...... **CLC 2, 4, 5, 8; DAM DRAM**
See CA 81-84; CANR 36; DLB 13, 14, 207; MTCW 1

Storm, Hyemeyohsts 1935-...... **CLC 3; DAM MULT**
See CA 81-84; CANR 45; NNAL

Storm, Theodor 1817-1888........... **SSC 27**

Storm, (Hans) Theodor (Woldsen) 1817-1888............ **NCLC 1; SSC 27**
See DLB 129

Storni, Alfonsina 1892-1938......... **TCLC 5; DAM MULT; HLC**
See CA 104; 131; HW 1

Stoughton, William 1631-1701......... **LC 38**
See DLB 24

Stout, Rex (Todhunter) 1886-1975..... **CLC 3**
See AITN 2; CA 61-64; CANR 71

Stow, (Julian) Randolph 1935-....... **CLC 23, 48**
See CA 13-16R; CANR 33; MTCW 1

Stowe, Harriet (Elizabeth) Beecher 1811-1896....... **NCLC 3, 50; DA; DAB; DAC; DAM MST, NOV; WLC**
See CDALB 1865-1917; DLB 1, 12, 42, 74, 189; JRDA; MAICYA; YABC 1

Strachey, (Giles) Lytton 1880-1932..... **TCLC 12**
See CA 110; DLB 149; DLBD 10; MTCW 2

Strand, Mark 1934-........ **CLC 6, 18, 41, 71; DAM POET**
See CA 21-24R; CANR 40, 65; DLB 5; SATA 41

Straub, Peter (Francis) 1943-........ **CLC 28, 107; DAM POP**
See BEST 89:1; CA 85-88; CANR 28, 65; DLBY 84; MTCW 1, 2

Strauss, Botho 1944-................ **CLC 22**
See CA 157; DLB 124

Streatfeild, (Mary) Noel 1895(?)-1986.................. **CLC 21**
See CA 81-84; 120; CANR 31; CLR 17; DLB 160; MAICYA; SATA 20; SATA-Obit 48

Stribling, T(homas) S(igismund) 1881-1965.................... **CLC 23**
See CA 107; DLB 9

Strindberg, (Johan) August 1849-1912....... **TCLC 1, 8, 21, 47; DA; DAB; DAC; DAM DRAM, MST; WLC**
See CA 104; 135; MTCW 2

Stringer, Arthur 1874-1950......... **TCLC 37**
See CA 161; DLB 92

Tarassoff, Lev
See Troyat, Henri

Tarbell, Ida M(inerva) 1857-1944...... **TCLC 40**
See CA 122; DLB 47

Tarkington, (Newton) Booth 1869-1946.................... **TCLC 9**
See CA 110; 143; DLB 9, 102; MTCW 2; SATA 17

Tarkovsky, Andrei (Arsenyevich) 1932-1986.................... **CLC 75**
See CA 127

Tartt, Donna 1964(?)-............... **CLC 76**
See CA 142

Tasso, Torquato 1544-1595............. **LC 5**

Tate, (John Orley) Allen 1899-1979...... **CLC 2, 4, 6, 9, 11, 14, 24**
See CA 5-8R; 85-88; CANR 32; DLB 4, 45, 63; DLBD 17; MTCW 1, 2

Tate, Ellalice
See Hibbert, Eleanor Alice Burford

Tate, James (Vincent) 1943-..... **CLC 2, 6, 25**
See CA 21-24R; CANR 29, 57; DLB 5, 169

Tavel, Ronald 1940-.................. **CLC 6**
See CA 21-24R; CANR 33

Taylor, C(ecil) P(hilip) 1929-1981..... **CLC 27**
See CA 25-28R; 105; CANR 47

Taylor, Edward 1642(?)-1729..... **LC 11; DA; DAB; DAC; DAM MST, POET**
See DLB 24

Taylor, Eleanor Ross 1920-........... **CLC 5**
See CA 81-84; CANR 70

Taylor, Elizabeth 1912-1975..... **CLC 2, 4, 29**
See CA 13-16R; CANR 9, 70; DLB 139; MTCW 1; SATA 13

Taylor, Frederick Winslow 1856-1915................... **TCLC 76**

Taylor, Henry (Splawn) 1942-........ **CLC 44**
See CA 33-36R; CAAS 7; CANR 31; DLB 5

Taylor, Kamala (Purnaiya) 1924-
See Markandaya, Kamala

Taylor, Mildred D.................. **CLC 21**
See AAYA 10; BW 1; CA 85-88; CANR 25; CLR 9, 59; DLB 52; JRDA; MAICYA; SAAS 5; SATA 15, 70

Taylor, Peter (Hillsman) 1917-1994...... **CLC 1, 4, 18, 37, 44, 50, 71; SSC 10**
See CA 13-16R; 147; CANR 9, 50; DLBY 81, 94; INT CANR-9; MTCW 1, 2

Taylor, Robert Lewis 1912-1998...... **CLC 14**
See CA 1-4R; 170; CANR 3, 64; SATA 10

Tchekhov, Anton
See Chekhov, Anton (Pavlovich)

Tchicaya, Gerald Felix 1931-1988....... **CLC 101**
See CA 129; 125

Tchicaya U Tam'si
See Tchicaya, Gerald Felix

Teasdale, Sara 1884-1933........... **TCLC 4**
See CA 104; 163; DLB 45; SATA 32

Tegner, Esaias 1782-1846........... **NCLC 2**

Teilhard de Chardin, (Marie Joseph) Pierre 1881-1955.................... **TCLC 9**
See CA 105

Temple, Ann
See Mortimer, Penelope (Ruth)

Tennant, Emma (Christina) 1937-....... **CLC 13, 52**
See CA 65-68; CAAS 9; CANR 10, 38, 59; DLB 14

Tenneshaw, S. M.
See Silverberg, Robert

Tennyson, Alfred 1809-1892....... **NCLC 30, 65; DA; DAB; DAC; DAM MST, POET; PC 6; WLC**
See CDBLB 1832-1890; DLB 32

Teran, Lisa St. Aubin de............ **CLC 36**
See St. Aubin de Teran, Lisa

Terence c. 184B.C.-c. 159B.C..... **CMLC 14; DC 7**
See DLB 211

Teresa de Jesus, St. 1515-1582......... **LC 18**

Terkel, Louis 1912-
See Terkel, Studs

Terkel, Studs...................... **CLC 38**
See Terkel, Louis

Terry, C. V.
See Slaughter, Frank G(ill)

Terry, Megan 1932-................ **CLC 19**
See CA 77-80; CABS 3; CANR 43; DLB 7

Tertullian c. 155-c. 245............ **CMLC 29**

Tertz, Abram
See Sinyavsky, Andrei (Donatevich)

Tesich, Steve 1943(?)-1996........ **CLC 40, 69**
See CA 105; 152; DLBY 83

Tesla, Nikola 1856-1943............ **TCLC 88**

Teternikov, Fyodor Kuzmich 1863-1927
See Sologub, Fyodor

Tevis, Walter 1928-1984............. **CLC 42**
See CA 113

Tey, Josephine................... **TCLC 14**
See Mackintosh, Elizabeth

Thackeray, William Makepeace 1811-1863...... **NCLC 5, 14, 22, 43; DA; DAB; DAC; DAM MST, NOV; WLC**
See CDBLB 1832-1890; DLB 21, 55, 159, 163; SATA 23

Thakura, Ravindranatha
See Tagore, Rabindranath

Tharoor, Shashi 1956-.............. **CLC 70**
See CA 141

Thelwell, Michael Miles 1939-........ **CLC 22**
See BW 2; CA 101

Theobald, Lewis, Jr.
See Lovecraft, H(oward) P(hillips)

Theodorescu, Ion N. 1880-1967
See Arghezi, Tudor

Theriault, Yves 1915-1983..... **CLC 79; DAC; DAM MST**
See CA 102; DLB 88

Theroux, Alexander (Louis) 1939-..... **CLC 2, 25**
See CA 85-88; CANR 20, 63

Theroux, Paul (Edward) 1941-...... **CLC 5, 8, 11, 15, 28, 46; DAM POP**
See AAYA 28; BEST 89:4; CA 33-36R; CANR 20, 45, 74; CDALBS; DLB 2; MTCW 1, 2; SATA 44, 109

Thesen, Sharon 1946-................ **CLC 56**
See CA 163

Thevenin, Denis
See Duhamel, Georges

Thibault, Jacques Anatole Francois 1844-1924
See France, Anatole

Thiele, Colin (Milton) 1920-.......... **CLC 17**
See CA 29-32R; CANR 12, 28, 53; CLR 27; MAICYA; SAAS 2; SATA 14, 72

Thomas, Audrey (Callahan) 1935-..... **CLC 7, 13, 37, 107; SSC 20**
See AITN 2; CA 21-24R; CAAS 19; CANR 36, 58; DLB 60; MTCW 1

Thomas, D(onald) M(ichael) 1935-...... **CLC 13, 22, 31**
See CA 61-64; CAAS 11; CANR 17, 45, 75; CDBLB 1960 to Present; DLB 40, 207; INT CANR-17; MTCW 1, 2

Thomas, Dylan (Marlais) 1914-1953..... **TCLC 1, 8, 45; DA; DAB; DAC; DAM DRAM, MST, POET; PC 2; SSC 3; WLC**
See CA 104; 120; CANR 65; CDBLB 1945-1960; DLB 13, 20, 139; MTCW 1, 2; SATA 60

Thomas, (Philip) Edward 1878-1917....... **TCLC 10; DAM POET**
See CA 106; 153; DLB 98

Thomas, Joyce Carol 1938-.......... **CLC 35**
See AAYA 12; BW 2, 3; CA 113; 116; CANR 48; CLR 19; DLB 33; INT 116; JRDA; MAICYA; MTCW 1, 2; SAAS 7; SATA 40, 78

Thomas, Lewis 1913-1993........... **CLC 35**
See CA 85-88; 143; CANR 38, 60; MTCW 1, 2

Thomas, M. Carey 1857-1935....... **TCLC 89**

Thomas, Paul
See Mann, (Paul) Thomas

Thomas, Piri 1928-......... **CLC 17; HLCS 1**
See CA 73-76; HW 1

Thomas, R(onald) S(tuart) 1913-...... **CLC 6, 13, 48; DAB; DAM POET**
See CA 89-92; CAAS 4; CANR 30; CDBLB 1960 to Present; DLB 27; MTCW 1

Thomas, Ross (Elmore) 1926-1995....... **CLC 39**
See CA 33-36R; 150; CANR 22, 63

Thompson, Francis Clegg
See Mencken, H(enry) L(ouis)

Thompson, Francis Joseph 1859-1907.................... **TCLC 4**
See CA 104; CDBLB 1890-1914; DLB 19

Thompson, Hunter S(tockton) 1939-..... **CLC 9, 17, 40, 104; DAM POP**
See BEST 89:1; CA 17-20R; CANR 23, 46, 74, 77; DLB 185; MTCW 1, 2

Thompson, James Myers
See Thompson, Jim (Myers)

Thompson, Jim (Myers) 1906-1977(?) . . . . **CLC 69**
See CA 140

Thompson, Judith . . . . **CLC 39**

Thomson, James 1700-1748 . . . . **LC 16, 29, 40; DAM POET**
See DLB 95

Thomson, James 1834-1882 . . . . **NCLC 18; DAM POET**
See DLB 35

Thoreau, Henry David 1817-1862 . . . . **NCLC 7, 21, 61; DA; DAB; DAC; DAM MST; WLC**
See CDALB 1640-1865; DLB 1

Thornton, Hall
See Silverberg, Robert

Thucydides c. 455B.C.-399B.C. . . . . **CMLC 17**
See DLB 176

Thurber, James (Grover) 1894-1961 . . . . **CLC 5, 11, 25; DA; DAB; DAC; DAM DRAM, MST, NOV; SSC 1**
See CA 73-76; CANR 17, 39; CDALB 1929-1941; DLB 4, 11, 22, 102; MAICYA; MTCW 1, 2; SATA 13

Thurman, Wallace (Henry) 1902-1934 . . . . **TCLC 6; BLC 3; DAM MULT**
See BW 1, 3; CA 104; 124; DLB 51

Ticheburn, Cheviot
See Ainsworth, William Harrison

Tieck, (Johann) Ludwig 1773-1853 . . . . **NCLC 5, 46; SSC 31**
See DLB 90

Tiger, Derry
See Ellison, Harlan (Jay)

Tilghman, Christopher 1948(?)- . . . . **CLC 65**
See CA 159

Tillinghast, Richard (Williford) 1940- . . . . **CLC 29**
See CA 29-32R; CAAS 23; CANR 26, 51

Timrod, Henry 1828-1867 . . . . **NCLC 25**
See DLB 3

Tindall, Gillian (Elizabeth) 1938- . . . . **CLC 7**
See CA 21-24R; CANR 11, 65

Tiptree, James, Jr. . . . . **CLC 48, 50**
See Sheldon, Alice Hastings Bradley

Titmarsh, Michael Angelo
See Thackeray, William Makepeace

Tocqueville, Alexis (Charles Henri Maurice Clerel, Comte) de 1805-1859 . . . . **NCLC 7, 63**

Tolkien, J(ohn) R(onald) R(euel) 1892-1973 . . . . **CLC 1, 2, 3, 8, 12, 38; DA; DAB; DAC; DAM MST, NOV, POP; WLC**
See AAYA 10; AITN 1; CA 17-18; 45-48; CANR 36; CAP 2; CDBLB 1914-1945; CLR 56; DLB 15, 160; JRDA; MAICYA; MTCW 1, 2; SATA 2, 32, 100; SATA-Obit 24

Toller, Ernst 1893-1939 . . . . **TCLC 10**
See CA 107; DLB 124

Tolson, M. B.
See Tolson, Melvin B(eaunorus)

Tolson, Melvin B(eaunorus) 1898(?)-1966 . . . . **CLC 36, 105; BLC 3; DAM MULT, POET**
See BW 1, 3; CA 124; 89-92; CANR 80; DLB 48, 76

Tolstoi, Aleksei Nikolaevich
See Tolstoy, Alexey Nikolaevich

Tolstoy, Alexey Nikolaevich 1882-1945 . . . . **TCLC 18**
See CA 107; 158

Tolstoy, Count Leo
See Tolstoy, Leo (Nikolaevich)

Tolstoy, Leo (Nikolaevich) 1828-1910 . . . . **TCLC 4, 11, 17, 28, 44, 79; DA; DAB; DAC; DAM MST, NOV; SSC 9, 30; WLC**
See CA 104; 123; SATA 26

Tomasi di Lampedusa, Giuseppe 1896-1957
See Lampedusa, Giuseppe (Tomasi) di

Tomlin, Lily . . . . **CLC 17**
See Tomlin, Mary Jean

Tomlin, Mary Jean 1939(?)-
See Tomlin, Lily

Tomlinson, (Alfred) Charles 1927- . . . . **CLC 2, 4, 6, 13, 45; DAM POET; PC 17**
See CA 5-8R; CANR 33; DLB 40

Tomlinson, H(enry) M(ajor) 1873-1958 . . . . **TCLC 71**
See CA 118; 161; DLB 36, 100, 195

Tonson, Jacob
See Bennett, (Enoch) Arnold

Toole, John Kennedy 1937-1969 . . . . **CLC 19, 64**
See CA 104; DLBY 81; MTCW 2

Toomer, Jean 1894-1967 . . . . **CLC 1, 4, 13, 22; BLC 3; DAM MULT; PC 7; SSC 1; WLCS**
See BW 1; CA 85-88; CDALB 1917-1929; DLB 45, 51; MTCW 1, 2

Torley, Luke
See Blish, James (Benjamin)

Tornimparte, Alessandra
See Ginzburg, Natalia

Torre, Raoul della
See Mencken, H(enry) L(ouis)

Torrey, E(dwin) Fuller 1937- . . . . **CLC 34**
See CA 119; CANR 71

Torsvan, Ben Traven
See Traven, B.

Torsvan, Benno Traven
See Traven, B.

Torsvan, Berick Traven
See Traven, B.

Torsvan, Berwick Traven
See Traven, B.

Torsvan, Bruno Traven
See Traven, B.

Torsvan, Traven
See Traven, B.

Tournier, Michel (Edouard) 1924- . . . . **CLC 6, 23, 36, 95**
See CA 49-52; CANR 3, 36, 74; DLB 83; MTCW 1, 2; SATA 23

Tournimparte, Alessandra
See Ginzburg, Natalia

Towers, Ivar
See Kornbluth, C(yril) M.

Towne, Robert (Burton) 1936(?)- . . . . **CLC 87**
See CA 108; DLB 44

Townsend, Sue . . . . **CLC 61**
See Townsend, Susan Elaine

Townsend, Susan Elaine 1946-
See Townsend, Sue

Townshend, Peter (Dennis Blandford) 1945- . . . . **CLC 17, 42**
See CA 107

Tozzi, Federigo 1883-1920 . . . . **TCLC 31**
See CA 160

Traill, Catharine Parr 1802-1899 . . . . **NCLC 31**
See DLB 99

Trakl, Georg 1887-1914 . . . . **TCLC 5; PC 20**
See CA 104; 165; MTCW 2

Transtroemer, Tomas (Goesta) 1931- . . . . **CLC 52, 65; DAM POET**
See CA 117; 129; CAAS 17

Transtromer, Tomas Gosta
See Transtroemer, Tomas (Goesta)

Traven, B. (?)-1969 . . . . **CLC 8, 11**
See CA 19-20; 25-28R; CAP 2; DLB 9, 56; MTCW 1

Treitel, Jonathan 1959- . . . . **CLC 70**

Tremain, Rose 1943- . . . . **CLC 42**
See CA 97-100; CANR 44; DLB 14

Tremblay, Michel 1942- . . . . **CLC 29, 102; DAC; DAM MST**
See CA 116; 128; DLB 60; MTCW 1, 2

Trevanian . . . . **CLC 29**
See Whitaker, Rod(ney)

Trevor, Glen
See Hilton, James

Trevor, William 1928- . . . . **CLC 7, 9, 14, 25, 71, 116; SSC 21**
See Cox, William Trevor

Trifonov, Yuri (Valentinovich) 1925-1981 . . . . **CLC 45**
See CA 126; 103; MTCW 1

Trilling, Lionel 1905-1975 . . . . **CLC 9, 11, 24**
See CA 9-12R; 61-64; CANR 10; DLB 28, 63; INT CANR-10; MTCW 1, 2

Trimball, W. H.
See Mencken, H(enry) L(ouis)

Tristan
See Gomez de la Serna, Ramon

Tristram
See Housman, A(lfred) E(dward)

Trogdon, William (Lewis) 1939-
See Heat-Moon, William Least

Voltaire 1694-1778........ **LC 14; DA; DAB; DAC; DAM DRAM, MST; SSC 12; WLC**

von Aschendrof, BaronIgnatz
See Ford, Ford Madox

von Daeniken, Erich 1935-...........**CLC 30**
See AITN 1; CA 37-40R; CANR 17, 44

von Daniken, Erich
See von Daeniken, Erich

von Heidenstam, (Carl Gustaf) Verner
See Heidenstam, (Carl Gustaf) Verner von

von Heyse, Paul (Johann Ludwig)
See Heyse, Paul (Johann Ludwig von)

von Hofmannsthal, Hugo
See Hofmannsthal, Hugo von

von Horvath, Odon
See Horvath, Oedoen von

von Horvath, Oedoen
See Horvath, Oedoen von

von Liliencron, (Friedrich Adolf Axel) Detlev
See Liliencron, (Friedrich Adolf Axel) Detlev von

Vonnegut, Kurt, Jr. 1922-......**CLC 1, 2, 3, 4, 5, 8, 12, 22, 40, 60, 111; DA; DAB; DAC; DAM MST, NOV, POP; SSC 8; WLC**
See AAYA 6; AITN 1; BEST 90:4; CA 1-4R; CANR 1, 25, 49, 75; CDALB 1968-1988; DLB 2, 8, 152; DLBD 3; DLBY 80; MTCW 1, 2

Von Rachen, Kurt
See Hubbard, L(afayette) Ron(ald)

von Rezzori (d'Arezzo), Gregor
See Rezzori (d'Arezzo), Gregor von

von Sternberg, Josef
See Sternberg, Josef von

Vorster, Gordon 1924-..............**CLC 34**
See CA 133

Vosce, Trudie
See Ozick, Cynthia

Voznesensky, Andrei (Andreievich) 1933-....... **CLC 1, 15, 57; DAM POET**
See CA 89-92; CANR 37; MTCW 1

Waddington, Miriam 1917-..........**CLC 28**
See CA 21-24R; CANR 12, 30; DLB 68

Wagman, Fredrica 1937-.............**CLC 7**
See CA 97-100; INT 97-100

Wagner, Linda W.
See Wagner-Martin, Linda (C.)

Wagner, Linda Welshimer
See Wagner-Martin, Linda (C.)

Wagner, Richard 1813-1883.........**NCLC 9**
See DLB 129

Wagner-Martin, Linda (C.) 1936-.....**CLC 50**
See CA 159

Wagoner, David (Russell) 1926-.....**CLC 3, 5, 15**
See CA 1-4R; CAAS 3; CANR 2, 71; DLB 5; SATA 14

Wah, Fred(erick James) 1939-....... **CLC 44**
See CA 107; 141; DLB 60

Wahloo, Per 1926-1975.............. **CLC 7**
See CA 61-64; CANR 73

Wahloo, Peter
See Wahloo, Per

Wain, John (Barrington) 1925-1994..... **CLC 2, 11, 15, 46**
See CA 5-8R; 145; CAAS 4; CANR 23, 54; CDBLB 1960 to Present; DLB 15, 27, 139, 155; MTCW 1, 2

Wajda, Andrzej 1926-............. **CLC 16**
See CA 102

Wakefield, Dan 1932-................**CLC 7**
See CA 21-24R; CAAS 7

Wakoski, Diane 1937-...... **CLC 2, 4, 7, 9, 11, 40; DAM POET; PC 15**
See CA 13-16R; CAAS 1; CANR 9, 60; DLB 5; INT CANR-9; MTCW 2

Wakoski-Sherbell, Diane
See Wakoski, Diane

Walcott, Derek (Alton) 1930-..... **CLC 2, 4, 9, 14, 25, 42, 67, 76; BLC 3; DAB; DAC; DAM MST, MULT, POET; DC 7**
See BW 2; CA 89-92; CANR 26, 47, 75, 80; DLB 117; DLBY 81; MTCW 1, 2

Waldman, Anne (Lesley) 1945-........**CLC 7**
See CA 37-40R; CAAS 17; CANR 34, 69; DLB 16

Waldo, E. Hunter
See Sturgeon, Theodore (Hamilton)

Waldo, Edward Hamilton
See Sturgeon, Theodore (Hamilton)

Walker, Alice (Malsenior) 1944-...... **CLC 5, 6, 9, 19, 27, 46, 58, 103; BLC 3; DA; DAB; DAC; DAM MST, MULT, NOV, POET, POP; SSC 5; WLCS**
See AAYA 3; BEST 89:4; BW 2, 3; CA 37-40R; CANR 9, 27, 49, 66; CDALB 1968-1988; DLB 6, 33, 143; INT CANR-27; MTCW 1, 2; SATA 31

Walker, David Harry 1911-1992......**CLC 14**
See CA 1-4R; 137; CANR 1; SATA 8; SATA-Obit 71

Walker, Edward Joseph 1934-
See Walker, Ted

Walker, George F. 1947-.........**CLC 44, 61; DAB; DAC; DAM MST**
See CA 103; CANR 21, 43, 59; DLB 60

Walker, Joseph A. 1935-...... **CLC 19; DAM DRAM, MST**
See BW 1, 3; CA 89-92; CANR 26; DLB 38

Walker, Margaret (Abigail) 1915-1998........ **CLC 1, 6; BLC; DAM MULT; PC 20**
See BW 2, 3; CA 73-76; 172; CANR 26, 54, 76; DLB 76, 152; MTCW 1, 2

Walker, Ted.......................**CLC 13**
See Walker, Edward Joseph

Wallace, David Foster 1962-..... **CLC 50, 114**
See CA 132; CANR 59; MTCW 2

Wallace, Dexter
See Masters, Edgar Lee

Wallace, (Richard Horatio) Edgar 1875-1932...................**TCLC 57**
See CA 115; DLB 70

Wallace, Irving 1916-1990........ **CLC 7, 13; DAM NOV, POP**
See AITN 1; CA 1-4R; 132; CAAS 1; CANR 1, 27; INT CANR-27; MTCW 1, 2

Wallant, Edward Lewis 1926-1962...... **CLC 5, 10**
See CA 1-4R; CANR 22; DLB 2, 28, 143; MTCW 1, 2

Wallas, Graham 1858-1932.........**TCLC 91**

Walley, Byron
See Card, Orson Scott

Walpole, Horace 1717-1797........... **LC 49**
See DLB 39, 104

Walpole, Hugh (Seymour) 1884-1941....................**TCLC 5**
See CA 104; 165; DLB 34; MTCW 2

Walser, Martin 1927-...............**CLC 27**
See CA 57-60; CANR 8, 46; DLB 75, 124

Walser, Robert 1878-1956..... **TCLC 18; SSC 20**
See CA 118; 165; DLB 66

Walsh, Jill Paton..................**CLC 35**
See Paton Walsh, Gillian

Walter, Villiam Christian
See Andersen, Hans Christian

Wambaugh, Joseph (Aloysius, Jr.) 1937-...... **CLC 3, 18; DAM NOV, POP**
See AITN 1; BEST 89:3; CA 33-36R; CANR 42, 65; DLB 6; DLBY 83; MTCW 1, 2

Wang Wei 699(?)-761(?).............. **PC 18**

Ward, Arthur Henry Sarsfield 1883-1959
See Rohmer, Sax

Ward, Douglas Turner 1930-.........**CLC 19**
See BW 1; CA 81-84; CANR 27; DLB 7, 38

Ward, Mary Augusta
See Ward, Mrs. Humphry

Ward, Mrs. Humphry 1851-1920...... **TCLC 55**
See DLB 18

Ward, Peter
See Faust, Frederick (Schiller)

Warhol, Andy 1928(?)-1987..........**CLC 20**
See AAYA 12; BEST 89:4; CA 89-92; 121; CANR 34

Warner, Francis (Robert le Plastrier) 1937-........................ **CLC 14**
See CA 53-56; CANR 11

Warner, Marina 1946-.............. **CLC 59**
See CA 65-68; CANR 21, 55; DLB 194

Warner, Rex (Ernest) 1905-1986......**CLC 45**
See CA 89-92; 119; DLB 15

Warner, Susan (Bogert) 1819-1885.....**NCLC 31**
See DLB 3, 42

Warner, Sylvia (Constance) Ashton
See Ashton-Warner, Sylvia (Constance)

Warner, Sylvia Townsend 1893-1978...........**CLC 7, 19; SSC 23**
See CA 61-64; 77-80; CANR 16, 60; DLB 34, 139; MTCW 1, 2

Warren, Mercy Otis 1728-1814..... **NCLC 13**
See DLB 31, 200

Author Index

Wertmueller, Lina 1928-. . . . . **CLC 16**
See CA 97-100; CANR 39, 78

Wescott, Glenway 1901-1987. . . . . **CLC 13; SSC 35**
See CA 13-16R; 121; CANR 23, 70; DLB 4, 9, 102

Wesker, Arnold 1932-. . . . . **CLC 3, 5, 42; DAB; DAM DRAM**
See CA 1-4R; CAAS 7; CANR 1, 33; CDBLB 1960 to Present; DLB 13; MTCW 1

Wesley, Richard (Errol) 1945-. . . . . **CLC 7**
See BW 1; CA 57-60; CANR 27; DLB 38

Wessel, Johan Herman 1742-1785. . . . . . . **LC 7**

West, Anthony (Panther) 1914-1987. . . . . **CLC 50**
See CA 45-48; 124; CANR 3, 19; DLB 15

West, C. P.
See Wodehouse, P(elham) G(renville)

West, (Mary) Jessamyn 1902-1984. . . . . . **CLC 7, 17**
See CA 9-12R; 112; CANR 27; DLB 6; DLBY 84; MTCW 1, 2; SATA-Obit 37

West, Morris L(anglo) 1916-. . . . . . . **CLC 6, 33**
See CA 5-8R; CANR 24, 49, 64; MTCW 1, 2

West, Nathanael 1903-1940. . . . . . **TCLC 1, 14, 44; SSC 16**
See CA 104; 125; CDALB 1929-1941; DLB 4, 9, 28; MTCW 1, 2

West, Owen
See Koontz, Dean R(ay)

West, Paul 1930-. . . . . **CLC 7, 14, 96**
See CA 13-16R; CAAS 7; CANR 22, 53, 76; DLB 14; INT CANR-22; MTCW 2

West, Rebecca 1892-1983. . . . . **CLC 7, 9, 31, 50**
See CA 5-8R; 109; CANR 19; DLB 36; DLBY 83; MTCW 1, 2

Westall, Robert (Atkinson) 1929-1993. **CLC 17**
See AAYA 12; CA 69-72; 141; CANR 18, 68; CLR 13; JRDA; MAICYA; SAAS 2; SATA 23, 69; SATA-Obit 75

Westermarck, Edward 1862-1939. . . . . . **TCLC 87**

Westlake, Donald E(dwin) 1933-. . . . . . **CLC 7, 33; DAM POP**
See CA 17-20R; CAAS 13; CANR 16, 44, 65; INT CANR-16; MTCW 2

Westmacott, Mary
See Christie, Agatha (Mary Clarissa)

Weston, Allen
See Norton, Andre

Wetcheek, J. L.
See Feuchtwanger, Lion

Wetering, Janwillem van de
See van de Wetering, Janwillem

Wetherald, Agnes Ethelwyn 1857-1940. . . . . **TCLC 81**
See DLB 99

Wetherell, Elizabeth
See Warner, Susan (Bogert)

Whale, James 1889-1957. . . . . **TCLC 63**

Whalen, Philip 1923-. . . . . **CLC 6, 29**
See CA 9-12R; CANR 5, 39; DLB 16

Wharton, Edith (Newbold Jones) 1862-1937. . . . . . . **TCLC 3, 9, 27, 53; DA; DAB; DAC; DAM MST, NOV; SSC 6; WLC**
See AAYA 25; CA 104; 132; CDALB 1865-1917; DLB 4, 9, 12, 78, 189; DLBD 13; MTCW 1, 2

Wharton, James
See Mencken, H(enry) L(ouis)

Wharton, William (a pseudonym). . . . . . . **CLC 18, 37**
See CA 93-96; DLBY 80; INT 93-96

Wheatley (Peters), Phillis 1754(?)-1784. . . . . . **LC 3, 50; BLC 3; DA; DAC; DAM MST, MULT, POET; PC 3; WLC**
See CDALB 1640-1865; DLB 31, 50

Wheelock, John Hall 1886-1978. . . . . . **CLC 14**
See CA 13-16R; 77-80; CANR 14; DLB 45

White, E(lwyn) B(rooks) 1899-1985. . . . . . **CLC 10, 34, 39; DAM POP**
See AITN 2; CA 13-16R; 116; CANR 16, 37; CDALBS; CLR 1, 21; DLB 11, 22; MAICYA; MTCW 1, 2; SATA 2, 29, 100; SATA-Obit 44

White, Edmund (Valentine III) 1940-. . . . . **CLC 27, 110; DAM POP**
See AAYA 7; CA 45-48; CANR 3, 19, 36, 62; MTCW 1, 2

White, Patrick (Victor Martindale) 1912-1990. . . . . . . **CLC 3, 4, 5, 7, 9, 18, 65, 69**
See CA 81-84; 132; CANR 43; MTCW 1

White, Phyllis Dorothy James 1920-
See James, P. D.

White, T(erence) H(anbury) 1906-1964. **CLC 30**
See AAYA 22; CA 73-76; CANR 37; DLB 160; JRDA; MAICYA; SATA 12

White, Terence de Vere 1912-1994. . . . . . **CLC 49**
See CA 49-52; 145; CANR 3

White, Walter
See White, Walter F(rancis)

White, Walter F(rancis) 1893-1955. . . . . **TCLC 15**
See White, Walter

White, William Hale 1831-1913
See Rutherford, Mark

Whitehead, E(dward) A(nthony) 1933-. . . . . **CLC 5**
See CA 65-68; CANR 58

Whitemore, Hugh (John) 1936-. . . . . . . **CLC 37**
See CA 132; CANR 77; INT 132

Whitman, Sarah Helen (Power) 1803-1878. . . . . **NCLC 19**
See DLB 1

Whitman, Walt(er) 1819-1892. . . . . . . **NCLC 4, 31; DA; DAB; DAC; DAM MST, POET; PC 3; WLC**
See CDALB 1640-1865; DLB 3, 64; SATA 20

Whitney, Phyllis A(yame) 1903-. . . . . . **CLC 42; DAM POP**
See AITN 2; BEST 90:3; CA 1-4R; CANR 3, 25, 38, 60; CLR 59; JRDA; MAICYA; MTCW 2; SATA 1, 30

Whittemore, (Edward) Reed (Jr.) 1919-. . . . . **CLC 4**
See CA 9-12R; CAAS 8; CANR 4; DLB 5

Whittier, John Greenleaf 1807-1892. . . . . **NCLC 8, 59**
See DLB 1

Whittlebot, Hernia
See Coward, Noel (Peirce)

Wicker, Thomas Grey 1926-
See Wicker, Tom

Wicker, Tom. . . . . **CLC 7**
See Wicker, Thomas Grey

Wideman, John Edgar 1941-. . . . . . **CLC 5, 34, 36, 67; BLC 3; DAM MULT**
See BW 2, 3; CA 85-88; CANR 14, 42, 67; DLB 33, 143; MTCW 2

Wiebe, Rudy (Henry) 1934-. . . . . . . **CLC 6, 11, 14; DAC; DAM MST**
See CA 37-40R; CANR 42, 67; DLB 60

Wieland, Christoph Martin 1733-1813. . . . . **NCLC 17**
See DLB 97

Wiene, Robert 1881-1938. . . . . **TCLC 56**

Wieners, John 1934-. . . . . **CLC 7**
See CA 13-16R; DLB 16

Wiesel, Elie(zer) 1928-. . . . . . **CLC 3, 5, 11, 37; DA; DAB; DAC; DAM MST, NOV; WLCS**
See AAYA 7; AITN 1; CA 5-8R; CAAS 4; CANR 8, 40, 65; CDALBS; DLB 83; DLBY 87; INT CANR-8; MTCW 1, 2; SATA 56

Wiggins, Marianne 1947-. . . . . **CLC 57**
See BEST 89:3; CA 130; CANR 60

Wight, James Alfred 1916-1995
See Herriot, James

Wilbur, Richard (Purdy) 1921-. . . . . **CLC 3, 6, 9, 14, 53, 110; DA; DAB; DAC; DAM MST, POET**
See CA 1-4R; CABS 2; CANR 2, 29, 76; CDALBS; DLB 5, 169; INT CANR-29; MTCW 1, 2; SATA 9, 108

Wild, Peter 1940-. . . . . **CLC 14**
See CA 37-40R; DLB 5

Wilde, Oscar 1854(?)-1900. . . . . **TCLC 1, 8, 23, 41; DA; DAB; DAC; DAM DRAM, MST, NOV; SSC 11; WLC**
See CA 104; 119; CDBLB 1890-1914; DLB 10, 19, 34, 57, 141, 156, 190; SATA 24

Wilder, Billy. . . . . **CLC 20**
See Wilder, Samuel

Wilder, Samuel 1906-
See Wilder, Billy

Wilder, Thornton (Niven) 1897-1975. . . . . **CLC 1, 5, 6, 10, 15, 35, 82; DA; DAB; DAC; DAM DRAM, MST, NOV; DC 1; WLC**
See AAYA 29; AITN 2; CA 13-16R; 61-64; CANR 40; CDALBS; DLB 4, 7, 9; DLBY 97; MTCW 1, 2

Drama Criticism Cumulative Nationality Index

Drama Criticism
Cumulative Title Index

Title Index

Title Index

Title Index

Title Index

Title Index

ISBN 0-7876-3139-6